Reference Works
in British and American
Literature

Reference Sources in the Humanities

James Rettig, Series Editor

Reference Works
in British and American
Literature

Second Edition

James K. Bracken

1998
Libraries Unlimited, Inc.
Englewood, Colorado

Libraries Unlimited, Inc.
P.O. Box 6633
Englewood, CO 80155-6633
1-800-237-6124
www.lu.com

Production Editor: Kevin W. Perizzolo
Copy Editor: Thea deHart
Subject Indexer: Christine J. Smith
Interior Design and Layout: Judy Gay Matthews

Library of Congress Cataloging-in-Publication Data

Bracken, James K., 1952-
  Reference works in British and American literature / by James K.
Bracken. -- 2nd ed.
    xlv, 726p.   17x25 cm.
    Includes bibliographical references and index.
    ISBN 1-56308-518-6
    1. Reference books--English literature--Bibliography. 2. Reference
books--American literature--Bibliography. 3. English literature--
History and criticism--Bibliography. 4. American literature--
History and criticism--Bibliography. I. Title. II. Series.
Z2011.B74   1998
[PR83]
016.8209--dc21   98-5231
                                                                 CIP

To Cory

Contents

Acknowledgments

Dr. William J. Studer and Ohio State UniversityLibraries' Advisory Committee on Research provided me with a special research leave and funds to work on this project. To members of Ohio State University Libraries' Main Library's Circulation and Interlibrary Loan departments, thank you for obtaining via your counterparts in the OhioLink libraries and innumerable libraries across the country the many items that were not locally available.

Colleagues in Ohio State University Libraries' Main Library—Patricia McCandless, Robert Lynch, David Lincove, Jean Ives, Linda Krikos, Virginia Reynolds, and Martha Alt—deserve particular thanks. Most especially, my colleague in the English, Theater, and Communication Reading Room, Akua Bandele, dutifully and persistently moved books and journals, new and old alike, through processing, across my desk, and into the ETC collection. Both University Libraries and this book are better by Akua's efforts.

Introduction

Reference Works in British and American Literature, a revision and expansion of *Reference Works in British and American Literature: Volume I, English and American Literature* (Englewood, CO: Libraries Unlimited, 1990) and *Reference Works in British and American Literature: Volume II, English and American Writers* (Englewood, CO: Libraries Unlimited, 1991), attempts to describe just a portion of the presently available reference resources in British and American literature, namely, resources devoted to individual writers. The "Introduction" of the first edition's second volume imagines an idealized landscape of literary reference works for individual writers: where "every author would be the subject of (1) a definitive primary bibliography describing writings and other works by the author; (2) a comprehensive secondary bibliography describing writings about the author; (3) a factually based and critically authoritative dictionary, encyclopedia, handbook, or some other compendia that gives significant details about an author's life and works; (4) a comprehensive concordance to the author's writings based on his or her standard editions; and (5) a current journal that publishes critical scholarly studies of the author (including checklists of primary and secondary materials intended to update the primary and secondary bibliographies), reviews of works about the author, and other miscellaneous information of interest to scholars devoted to the study of that particular author" (p. xxiii). Today we might consider adding, as a sixth kind of reference resource, the Internet or World Wide Web (WWW) site and other electronic products that would cumulate, supplement, enhance, or even supersede some or all of the kinds of bibliographic, lexical, and factual information provided for a writer in traditional printed resources.

Despite the increasing availability of resources in electronic formats, the principal, but not exclusive, focus of *Reference Works in British and American Literature* is separately published printed reference resources for individual British and American writers. To define British and American writers, this guide has relied on Margaret Drabble's *Oxford Companion to English Literature* and James D. Hart's *Oxford Companion to American Literature*. These two standard resources determine spellings of writers' names and pseudonyms and the titles of works; dates for writers and works; and, more significantly, the alphabetization, form, and order of the entries. It is hoped that some ultimate version of this guide might serve as a reference supplement to these companions.

Coverage of *Reference Works in British and American Literature* represents all writers listed in several standard literary bibliographies, including Jacob Blanck's *Bibliography of American Literature* (recently made all the more useful by the completion of Michael Winship's *Epitome* and *Selective*

Index), *First Printings of American Authors*, and *Index of English Literary Manuscripts*; all writers with major entries in the *New Cambridge Bibliography of English Literature*; and, more selectively, many writers listed in Facts on File's recent *Bibliography of American Fiction to 1865*; *Bibliography of American Fiction, 1865-1918*; and *Bibliography of American Fiction, 1919-1988*. I have also attempted to identify resources for selected writers of more recent reputations who are unlisted in the Oxford companions.

Among the described reference resources for individual writers are bibliographies (including exhibition, book dealer's, and library catalogs); dictionaries, encyclopedias, and handbooks (ranging from chronologies and gazetteers to companions and prefaces); indexes and concordances (including topical indexes and collections of quotations, proverbs, symbolic language, and critical terminology); and currently published, or recently ceased, periodicals (ranging from yearbooks to newsletters, but excluding monographic series). Coverage of resources is always selective, aiming to indicate the most important and useful resources. Indeed, every effort was made to identify any printed separately published resource of reference usefulness for an individual writer. A few resources that I was not able to access are identified as "unseen."

Difficulties in classifying resources, however, were not always easily or consistently resolved: Distinctions blurred with the present vogue of titling resources as sourcebooks, casebooks, files, and the like. Likewise, coverage emphasizes recent, mostly English-language publications, although I do not hesitate to describe many long out-of-print and rather hard-to-locate titles, numerous non-English language imprints, and even some dissertations and master's theses when these are of reference value. Exclusions and exceptions are myriad. For example, I exclude references to individual volumes in several recent series of reference-like resources despite their undeniable reference usefulness. Among these are volumes in the Modern Language Association of America's "Approaches to Teaching Masterpieces of World Literature" and Methuen's "Writer-Files." On the other hand, although I note and often describe many volumes in Cambridge University Press's Companion series, only a few volumes contain information of reference usefulness: Most volumes are collections of original critical studies aimed at advanced scholars and only nominally reference resources.

Annotations are both descriptive, noting specific features, and evaluative whenever possible, with cross-references to other entries. Most annotations cite or acknowledge superseded, comparable, and other related resources. In particular, descriptions of bibliographies indicate scope and extent of coverage, with those for primary bibliographies distinguishing full bibliographic information (title page transcriptions, collations, physical descriptions, contents, publication histories, etc.) from brief bibliographic information (imprint data). Entries for concordances, indexes, collections of quotations, and similarly textually based resources identify the source editions as fully as possible. Descriptions of journals note specific regular and incidental features of reference usefulness, such as inclusion of book reviews, bibliographies, and articles detailing library collections. Information regarding a journal's indexing is selective. For the most up-to-date editorial and other information for journals, including E-mail addresses, researchers should consult the biennial *MLA Directory of Periodicals* (New York: Modern Language Association of America, 1979-).

In preparing *Reference Works in British and American Literature*, I attempted a thorough review of reference resources available through 1996 and a portion of 1997. This guide does not claim to offer a census of reference resources either collectively or for any individual writer. For a more complete listing of bibliographies for individual British writers, researchers should consult volumes of Trevor Howard Howard-Hill's *Index to British Literary Bibliography* (New York: Oxford University Press, 1969- ; 2d ed., 1987-). For bibliographies of American writers, see Charles H. Nilon's badly dated *Bibliography of Bibliographies in American Literature* (New York: Bowker, 1970) and Patricia P. Havlice's equally badly dated *Index to American Author Bibliographies* (Metuchen, NJ: Scarecrow Press, 1971). William A. Wortman's *A Guide to Serial Bibliographies for Modern Literatures* is particularly useful for serial bibliographies. For descriptions of current (as of 1979) and historical journals for a wide selection of writers, see Margaret C. Patterson's *Author Newsletters and Journals*. This edition of *Reference Works in British and American Literature* describes more than 1,500 specific reference works for individual writers.

At the same time, in that resources for individual writers constitute just a portion of literature's reference resources and (as indicated in the first edition) often those resources are either confusingly abundant or simply nonexistent, to serve as a guide for a wide range of British and American writers *Reference Works in British and American Literature* identifies coverage of many individual writers in selected major collective or composite literary reference resources. As noted, the present guide references entries for all writers listed in Blanck's *Bibliography of American Literature, First Printings of American Authors, Index of English Literary Manuscripts* and major writers listed in *New Cambridge Bibliography of English Literature*. In addition to volumes in the Facts on File Bibliography of American Fiction series, entries also reference a significant number of separately- and serially-published composite bibliographies, research guides, and annual reviews and indexes. Although some overlap of the coverage of Alan R. Weiner and Spencer Means' *Literary Criticism Index*, 2d ed. (Metuchen, NJ: Scarecrow Press, 1994) was unavoidable, *Reference Works in British and American Literature* in no way attempts to replicate the analytics for all of the approximately 150 important resources provided in Weiner and Means' excellent index, such as Warren S. Walker's *Twentieth-Century Short Story Explication* (Hamden, CT: Shoe String Press, 1977-) series and many volumes in Gale's "Gale Information Guide Library" and Appleton/AHM's "Goldentree Bibliographies in Language and Literature." Moreover, whereas Weiner and Means' coverage emphasizes criticism, *Reference Works in British and American Literature* somewhat consciously and equally emphasizes primary bibliography. It is noteworthy that neither the first nor second edition of Weiner and Means' *Literary Criticism Index* analyzes important compilations such as Blanck's

Bibliography of American Literature, First Printings of American Authors, or the *New Cambridge Bibliography of English Literature;* other significant standard listings of primary (and secondary) materials, such as Stanley B. Greenfield and Fred C. Robinson's *A Bibliography of Publications on Old English Literature to the End of 1972,* volumes of J. B. Severs and A. E. Hartung's *A Manual of Writings in Middle English, 1050-1500,* Theodore G. Ehrsam's *Bibliographies of Twelve Victorian Authors,* Daniel A. Wells' *The Literary Index to American Magazines, 1815-1865,* and *The Literary Index to American Magazines, 1850-1900;* or the many literature review volumes published by the Modern Language Association of America, such as Lionel Stevenson's *Victorian Fiction: A Guide to Research* and Joel Myerson's *The Transcendentalists: A Review of Research and Criticism.* This edition of *Reference Works in British and American Literature* attempts to remedy this. The significant coverage of individual writers and works in these and other standard composite and collective literary reference resources falls within the scope of *Reference Works in British and American Literature*: I have referenced resources of this kind whenever their coverage is noteworthy. Whereas the two-volume first edition contained entries for about 600 individual writers, the present guide identifies resources for more than 1,500 writers.

The penultimate updating resources for identifying materials related to British and American writers remain the Modern Language Association of America's *MLA International Bibliography* and Modern Humanities Research Association's *Annual Bibliography of English Language and Literature,* followed closely, on the one hand, by such annual scholarly period bibliographies as the *Romantic Movement* (New York: Garland, 1980-) and *Eighteenth Century: A Current Bibliography* (Philadelphia, PA: American Society for Eighteenth-Century Studies, 1978-) and, on the other, by more generalized humanities indexes, such as *American Humanities Index, Arts and Humanities Citation Index,* and *Humanities Index.* For a thorough review of general resources for British and American literature, researchers should consult James L. Harner's *Literary Research Guide: A Guide to Reference Sources for the Study of Literatures in English and Related Topics,* 2d ed. (New York: Modern Language Association of America, 1993). (A 3d edition of Harner's guide is scheduled for publication in 1998.) Photocopying (or scanning in) or printing off (or downloading to disk/uploading to E-mail) listings from either the printed or electronic versions of the *MLA, MHRA,* or many other resources can provide "instant" bibliographies for many more individual writers than any edition of a guide like this will ever be able to contain. Similarly, access to the electronic versions of such resources as *Encyclopaedia Britannica,* the *Oxford English Dictionary,* or the several Chadwyck-Healey full-text databases makes it possible to create customized arrays of reference works for particular writers.

Yet despite the momentarily increasing abundance of electronic stand-alone and networked resources for individual writers and works, the attractiveness of adjustable and interactive presentations, and the fundamental usefulness of their textual data, few electronic resources presently afford the bibliographical detail and historical depth of printed reference resources. Compare a modern OCLC or RLIN cataloging record with a full bibliographic description in any of the volumes in the "Pittsburgh Series in Bibliography" or "Soho Bibliographies" to assess the differences. Something similar might be said regarding the authority of the lexical data for a Shakespeare sonnet, for example, available in Chadwyck-Healey's *English Poetry Database* versus in Marvin Spevack's *A Complete and Systematic Concordance to the Works of Shakespeare* (entry 1194). An index is only as valid as the text upon which it is based.

Perhaps even more significantly, however, only a few electronic resources, namely those that stand alone (just like printed resources), can guarantee that they will be locatable tomorrow. That writers' works will ultimately merge with criticism and other supporting materials in a virtual electronic literary database or site, thereby short-circuiting the need for reference resources (and librarians), may become reality, but even Sven Birkerts in *The Gutenberg Elegies: The Fate of Reading in an Electronic Age* (Boston: Faber and Faber, 1994, p. 121), allows 50 years for the "historical moment" of this transition. In the meantime, among the several relatively stable Internet resources that identify numerous, but certainly not yet innumerable, WWW sites for individual writers are:

Willett, Perry. 1995. *WWW Resources for English and American Literature.* The Trustees of Indiana University. Available: http://www.indiana.edu/~libsalc/pwillett/english-www.html. (11 November 1997).
>> Voice: 812-855-1891
>> E-mail: PWILLETT@indiana.edu

Liu, Alan. Undated. *The Voice of the Shuttle: English Literature Main Page.* No copyright. Available: http://humanitas.ucsb.edu/ shuttle/english.html. (11 November 1997).
>> Fax: 805-893-4622.
>> E-mail: ayliu@humanitas.ucsb.edu

Lynch, Jack. Undated. *Literary Resources on the Net.* No copyright. Available: http://www.english.upenn.edu/~jlynch/Lit/. (11 November 1997).
>> E-mail: jlynch@english.upenn.edu

Sauer, Geoffrey. 1990. *The English Server.* No copyright. Available: http://english-www.hss.cmu.edu/. (11 November 1997).
>> E-mail: Geoffrey Sauer aster@eng.hss.cmu.edu

No author. Undated. *Literature Resources.* No copyright. Available: http://nimrod.mit.edu/depts/humanities/lit/ top.html. (11 November 1997).

Additionally, OCLC's *NetFirst* database, available via OCLC's FirstSearch and updated weekly, gives bibliographical descriptions for both Internet-accessible and other electronic resources. Researchers should also consult *Gale Directory of Databases* (Detroit, MI: Gale, 1993-), offering semiannually updated coverage of online, CD-ROM, diskette, magnetic tape, handheld, and batch-access electronic resources.

At the opposite extreme, of course, are the many printed resources for which I have discovered references but have been unable to locate or physically obtain; and certainly exceeding these are the many worthy reference works for individual writers that I have simply missed. I apologize for all errors and omissions. I welcome both desiderata as well as corrections or suggestions regarding this work's shortcomings.

JAMES K. BRACKEN
Associate Professor
University Libraries
Ohio State University
224 Main Library
1858 Neil Avenue Mall
Columbus, OH 43210-1286
Voice: 614-292-2786 — Fax: 614-292-7859 — E-mail: bracken.1@osu.edu

Frequently Cited Works and Acronyms

Abstracts of English Studies. Calgary: University of Alberta, 1958- . 4/yr. ISSN 0001-3560. *AES*

American Humanities Index. Troy, NY: Whitston, 1975- . 4/yr. ISSN 0361-0144. *AHI*

American Literary Scholarship. Durham, NC: Duke University Press, 1965- . Annual. ISSN 0065-9142. *ALS*

Annual Bibliography of English Language and Literature. London: Modern Humanities Research Association, 1921- . Annual. ISSN 0066-3786. *MHRA*

Arts and Humanities Citation Index. Philadelphia, PA: ISI, 1977- . 3/yr. ISSN 0162-8445. *A&HCI*

Bain, Robert, and Joseph M. Flora. **Contemporary Poets, Dramatists, Essayists, and Novelists of the South: A Bio-Bibliographical Sourcebook**. Westport, CT: Greenwood, 1994. 642p. LC 93-43750. ISBN 0-313-28765-1.

Bain, Robert, and Joseph M. Flora, eds. **Fifty Southern Writers Before 1900: A Bio-Bibliographical Sourcebook**. Westport, CT: Greenwood Press, 1987. 601p. LC 86-31832. ISBN 0-3132-24518-5.

Bibliography of American Fiction Through 1865. Ed. Kent P. Ljungquist. New York: Facts on File, 1994. 326p. LC 94-26621. ISBN 0-8160-2115-5.

Bibliography of American Fiction, 1866-1918. Ed. James Nagel, Gwen L. Nagel, and Judith S. Baughman. New York: Facts on File, 1993. 412p. LC 92-32466. ISBN 0-8160-2116-3.

Bibliography of American Fiction, 1919-1988. Ed. Matthew J. Bruccoli and Judith S. Baughman. New York: Facts on File, 1991. 2 vols. LC 90-28140. ISBN (vol. 1) 0-8160-2117-1; (vol. 2) 0-8160-2118-X.

Blanck, Jacob Nathaniel, ed. **Bibliography of American Literature**. New Haven, CT: Yale University Press, 1955-91. 9 vols. LC 54-5283.
Completed by:

Winship, Michael, Philip B. Eppard, and Rachel J. Howarth. **Bibliography of American Literature: A Selective Index.** Golden, CO: North American Press, 1995. 345p. LC 94-37184. ISBN 1-555-91951-0.

Winship, Michael, Philip B. Eppard, and Rachel J. Howarth. **Epitome of Bibliography of American Literature.** Golden, CO: North American Press, 1995. 325p. LC 94-36955. ISBN 1-555-91950-2.

Bruccoli, Matthew J., series ed. **First Printings of American Authors: Contributions Toward Descriptive Checklists.** Detroit, MI: Gale, 1977-87. 5 vols. LC 74-11756. ISBN 0-8103-0933-5.

Bryer, Jackson R., ed. **Sixteen Modern American Authors: A Survey of Research and Criticism.** 3d ed. Durham, NC: Duke University Press, 1974. 673p. LC 72-97454. ISBN 0-8223-0297-7.

Bryer, Jackson R. **Sixteen Modern American Authors: Volume 2: A Survey of Research and Criticism Since 1972.** Durham, NC: Duke University Press, 1990. 810p. LC 89-11789. ISBN 0-8223-0976-9.

Caie, Graham D. **Bibliography of Junius XI Manuscript: With Appendix on Caedmon's Hymn.** Copenhagen: Faculty of Humanities, University of Copenhagen, 1979. 76p. (Anglica et Americana, no. 6). OCLC 8052660.

Contemporary Authors: Bibliographical Series. Detroit, MI: Gale, 1986-89. 3 vols. ISSN 0887-3070.

DeLaura, David J., ed. **Victorian Prose: A Guide to Research.** New York: Modern Language Association of American, 1973. 560p. LC 73-80586. ISBN 0-8735-2250-8.

Demastes, William W. **American Playwrights, 1880-1945: A Research and Production Sourcebook.** Westport, CT: Greenwood, 1995. 494p. LC 94-13690. ISBN 0-313-28638-8.

Demastes, William W., and Katherine E. Kelly. **British Playwrights, 1880-1956: A Research and Production Sourcebook.** Westport, CT: Greenwood, 1995. 457p. LC 95-53105. ISBN 0-313-28758-9.

Duke, Maurice, Jackson R. Bryer, and M. Thomas Inge, eds. **American Women Writers: Bibliographical Essays.** Westport, CT: Greenwood Press, 1983. 434p. LC 82-6156. ISBN 0-313-22116-2.

Dyson, A. E., ed. **The English Novel: Select Bibliographical Guides.** London: Oxford University Press, 1974. 372p. LC 74-17053. ISBN 0-19-871033-X.

Dyson, A. E., ed. **English Poetry: Select Bibliographical Guides**. London: Oxford University Press, 1971. 375p. LC 72-179303.

Edwards, A. S. G., ed. **Middle English Prose: A Critical Guide to Major Authors and Genres**. New Brunswick, NJ: Rutgers University Press, 1984. 452p. LC 83-2914. ISBN 0-8135-1001-5.

Ehrsam, Theodore G. **Bibliographies of Twelve Victorian Authors**. 1936; reprint New York: Octagon, 1968. 362p. LC 68-16773.

Elizabethan Bibliographies. Eds. Samuel A. Tannenbaum and Dorothy R. Tannenbaum. 1937-50; reprint Port Washington, NY: Kennikat Press, 1967. 10 vols. LC 67-19738.
Includes the following:

Vol. 1: **Roger Ascham, Beaumont and Fletcher, Nicholas Breton, George Chapman**.

Vol. 2: **Samuel Daniel, Thomas Dekker, Michael Drayton, John Ford, George Gascoigne**.

Vol. 3: **Robert Greene, George Herbert, Robert Herrick, John Heywood, Thomas Heywood**.

Vol. 4: **Ben Jonson, Thomas Kyd, Thomas Lodge**.

Vol. 5: **John Lyly, Thomas Middleton, Christopher Marlowe, John Marston**.

Vol. 6: **Philip Massinger, Michel de Montaigne, Anthony Mundy, Thomas Nashe, George Peele, Thomas Randolph**.

Vol. 7: **William Shakespeare: King Lear, Macbeth**.

Vol. 8: **William Shakespeare: Merchant of Venice, Othello**.

Vol. 9: **William Shakespeare: Romeo and Juliet, Sonnets, Troilus and Cressida, James Shirley, Sir Philip Sidney**.

Vol. 10: **Marie Stuart, Cyril Tourneur, John Webster**.

Elizabethan Bibliographies Supplements. Eds. Charles A. Pennel and William P. Williams. London: Nether Press, 1967-71. LC 72-365796. Vols. 13-14 and 16 were not published.

No. 1: **Thomas Middleton, 1939-1965; John Webster, 1940-1965**. Ed. Dennis Donovan. London: Nether Press, 1967. 61p. LC 75-365995.

No. 2: **Thomas Dekker, 1945-1965; Thomas Heywood, 1938-1965; Cyril Tourneur, 1945-1965**. Ed. Dennis Donovan. London: Nether Press, 1967. 56p. LC 79-365795.

No. 3: **Robert Herrick, 1949-1965; Ben Jonson, 1947-1965; Thomas Randolph, 1949-1965**. Ed. George Robert Guffey. London: Nether Press, 1968. 53p. LC 74-423097.

No. 4: **George Chapman, 1937-1965; John Marston, 1939-1965**. Ed. Charles A. Pennel and William P. Williams. London: Nether Press, 1968. 48p. OCLC 1426708.

No. 5: **Robert Greene, 1945-1965; Thomas Lodge, 1939-1965; John Lyly, 1941-1965; Thomas Nashe, 1941-1965; George Peele, 1939-1965**. Ed. Robert C. Johnson. London: Nether Press, 1968. 69p. LC 70-365766.

No. 6: **Christopher Marlowe, 1946-1965**. Ed. Robert C. Johnson. London: Nether Press, 1967. 45p. LC 73-365764.

No. 7: **Samuel Daniel, 1942-1965; Michael Drayton, 1941-1965; Sir Philip Sidney, 1941-1965**. Ed. George Robert Guffey. London: Nether Press, 1967. 52p. OCLC 403427.

No. 8: **Francis Beaumont—John Fletcher—Philip Massinger, 1937-1965; John Ford, 1940-1965; James Shirley, 1945-1965**. Ed. Charles A. Pennel and William P. Williams. London: Nether Press, 1968. 52p. LC 76-382498.

No. 9: **Roger Ascham, 1946-1966; George Gascoigne, 1941-1966; John Heywood, 1944-1966; Thomas Kyd, 1940-1966; Anthony Munday, 1941-1966**. Ed. Robert Carl Johnson. London: Nether Press, 1968. 51p. LC 75-379956.

No. 10: **Sir Thomas Browne, 1924-1966; Robert Burton, 1924-1966**. Ed. Dennis G. Donovan. London: Nether Press, 1968. 50p. LC 77-373982.

No. 11: **Traherne and the Seventeenth-Century English Platonists, 1900-1966**. Ed. George Robert Guffey. London: Nether Press, 1969. 110p. LC 75-556477.
[Covers Ralph Cudworth, Nathaniel Culverwel, Henry More, John Norris, George Rust, John Smith, Peter Sterry, Thomas Traherne, Benjamin Whichcote, and John Worthington.]

No. 12: **Andrew Marvell, 1926-1967**. Ed. Dennis G. Donovan. London: Nether Press, 1969. 50p. OCLC 401151.

No. 15: **Francis Bacon, 1926-1966**. Ed. J. Kemp Houck. London: Nether Press, 1968. 72p. OCLC 179920.

No. 17: **Sir Walter Ralegh, 1900-1968**. Ed. Humphrey Tonkin. London: Nether Press, 1971. 79p. OCLC 594801.

No. 18: **John Evelyn, 1920-1968; Samuel Pepys, 1933-1968**. Ed. Dennis G. Donovan. London: Nether Press, 1970. 64p. LC 71-022857.

Emerson, Everett. **Major Writers of Early American Literature**. Madison, WI: University of Wisconsin Press, 1972. 301p. OCLC 554604.

Erisman, Fred, and Richard W. Etulain, eds. **Fifty Western Writers: A Bio-Bibliographical Sourcebook**. Westport, CT: Greenwood Press, 1982. 562p. LC 81-13462. ISBN 0-313-22167-7.

Faverty, Frederic Everett, ed. **The Victorian Poets: A Guide to Research**. 2d ed. Cambridge, MA: Harvard University Press, 1968. 433p. LC 68-15636.

Finneran, Richard J., ed. **Anglo-Irish Literature: A Review of Research**. New York: Modern Language Association of America, 1976. 596p. LC 74-31959. ISBN 0-87352-252-4.

Finneran, Richard J., ed. **Recent Research on Anglo-Irish Writers**. New York: Modern Language Association of America, 1983. 361p. LC 82-12575. ISBN 0-8735-2259-1.

Fisher, John H., ed. **The Medieval Literature of Western Europe: A Review of Research, Mainly 1930-1960**. New York: Modern Language Association of America, 1966. 432p. LC 66-22346.

Flora, Joseph M., and Robert Bain, eds. **Fifty Southern Writers After 1900: A Bio-Bibliographical Sourcebook**. Westport, CT: Greenwood Press, 1987. 628p. LC 86-19460. ISBN 0-313-24519-3.

Ford, George H., ed. **Victorian Fiction: A Second Guide to Research**. New York: Modern Language Association of America, 1978. 401p. LC 77-083468. ISBN 0-87352-254-0.

Greenfield, Stanley B., and Fred C. Robinson. **A Bibliography of Publications on Old English Literature to the End of 1972**. Toronto, Ont.: University of Toronto Press, 1980. 436p. LC 78-4989. ISBN 0-8020-2292-8.

Harbert, Earl N., and Robert A. Rees, eds. **Fifteen American Authors Before 1900: Bibliographical Essays on Research and Criticism**.

Revised ed. Madison, WI: University of Wisconsin Press, 1984. 531p. LC 83-40263. ISBN 0-299-09590-8.

Houtchens, Carolyn Washburn, and Lawrence Huston Houtchens, eds. **The English Romantic Poets and Essayists: A Review of Research and Criticism**. Revised ed. New York: New York University Press, 1966. 395p. LC 66-12599.

Humanities Index. New York: H. W. Wilson, 1974- . 4/yr. ISSN 0095-5981. *HI*

Index of English Literary Manuscripts. General eds. P. J. Croft, Theodore Hofmann, and John Horden. London: Mansell; New York: R. R. Bowker, 1980- . ISBN 0-8352-1216-5 (5 vol. set).

Volume 1: 1450-1625, Part I: Andrewes-Donne; Part 2: Douglas-Wyatt. Ed. Peter Beal. London: Mansell; New York: R. R. Bowker, 1980. 2 vols.

Volume II: 1625-1700, Part I: Behn-King; Part 2, Lee-Wycherley. Ed. Peter Beal. London and New York: Mansell, 1987-93. 2 vols.

Volume III: 1700-1800, Part I: Addison-Fielding; Part 2: John Gay-Ambrose Philips, with a First-Line Index to Parts 1 and 2; Alexander Pope-Sir Richard Steele, with a First-Line Index to Parts 1-3. Ed. Margaret M. Smith (and Alexander Lindsay). London and New York: Mansell, 1986-. 3 vols. to date.

Volume IV: 1800-1900, Part I: Arnold-Gissing; Part 2: Hardy-Lamb. Ed. Barbara Rosenbaum (and Pamela White). London and New York: Mansell, 1982-. 2 vols. to date.

Inge, Thomas M., Maurice Duke, and Jackson R. Bryer, eds. **Black American Writers: Bibliographical Essays. Volume 1: The Beginnings Through the Harlem Renaissance and Langston Hughes; Volume 2: Richard Wright, Ralph Ellison, James Baldwin, and Amiri Baraka**. New York: St. Martin's Press, 1978. LC 77-85987. ISBN (vol. 1) 0-312-08260-6; (vol. 2) 0-312-08295-9.

Jordan, Frank. **The English Romantic Poets: A Review of Research and Criticism**. 4th ed., revised. New York: Modern Language Association of America, 1985. 765p. (Reviews of Research). LC 85-7216. ISBN 0-8735-2262-1.

King, Kimball. **Ten Modern Irish Playwrights: A Comprehensive Annotated Bibliography**. New York: Garland, 1979. 111p. (Garland Reference Library of the Humanities, vol. 153). LC 78-68289. ISBN 0-8240-9789-0.

King, Kimball. **Ten Modern American Playwrights: An Annotated Bibliography**. New York: Garland, 1982. 251p. (Garland Reference Library of the Humanities, vol. 234). LC 80-8498. ISBN 0-8240-9489-1.

King, Kimball. **Twenty Modern British Playwrights: A Bibliography, 1956 to 1976**. New York: Garland, 1977. 289p. (Garland Reference Library of the Humanities, vol. 96). LC 77-83353. ISBN 0-8240-9853-6.

Lidman, Mark J. **Studies in Jacobean Drama, 1973-1984: An Annotated Bibliography**. New York: Garland, 1986. 278p. (Garland Reference Library of the Humanities, vol. 597). LC 85-45146. ISBN 0-8240-8725-9.

Logan, Terence P., and Denzell S. Smith, eds. **Recent Studies in English Renaissance Drama**. Lincoln, NE: University of Nebraska Press, 1973-78. 4 vols.
The set includes:

The Predecessors of Shakespeare: A Survey and Bibliography of Recent Studies in English Renaissance Drama. Lincoln, NE: University of Nebraska Press, 1973. 348p. LC 72-75344. ISBN 0-8032-0775-1.

The Popular School: A Survey and Bibliography of Recent Studies in English Renaissance Drama. Lincoln, NE: University of Nebraska Press, 1975. 299p. LC 74-81364. ISBN 0-8032-0844-8.

The New Intellectuals: A Survey and Bibliography of Recent Studies in English Renaissance Drama. Lincoln, NE: University of Nebraska Press, 1977. 370p. LC 75-38051. ISBN 0-8032-0859-6.

The Later Jacobean and Caroline Dramatists: A Survey and Bibliography of Recent Studies in English Renaissance Drama. Lincoln, NE: University of Nebraska Press, 1978. 279p. LC 77-25265. ISBN 0-8032-2850-3.

McCaffery, Larry, ed. **Postmodern Fiction: A Bio-Bibliographical Guide**. Westport, CT: Greenwood Press, 1986. 604p. (Movements in the Arts, no. 2). LC 85-17723. ISBN 0-313-24170-8.

McCarron, William, and Robert Shenk. **Lesser Metaphysical Poets: A Bibliography, 1961-1980**. San Antonio, TX: Trinity University Press, 1983. 51p. (Checklists in the Humanities and Education, no. 7). LC 83-448. ISBN 0-911536-99-X.

McNutt, Dan J. **The Eighteenth-Century Gothic Novel: An Annotated Bibliography of Criticism and Selected Texts**. New York: Garland, 1975. 330p. (Garland Reference Library of the Humanities, vol. 4). LC 74-22490. ISBN 0-8240-1058-2.

Middle English Dictionary. Ed. Hans Kurath; associate ed. Sherman M. Kuhn. Ann Arbor, MI: University of Michigan Press, 1952- . LC 53-62158. *MED*

MLA International Bibliography of Books and Articles on the Modern Languages and Literatures. New York: Modern Language Association of America, 1921- . Annual. ISSN 0024-8215. *MLA*

Munton, Alan, and Alan Young. **Seven Writers of the English Left: A Bibliography of Literature and Politics, 1916-1980**. New York: Garland, 1981. 365p. (Garland Reference Library of the Humanities, vol. 162). LC 78-68261. ISBN 0-8240-9777-7.

Myerson, Joel, ed. **The Transcendentalists: A Review of Research and Criticism**. New York: Modern Language Association of America, 1984. 534p. (The Modern Language Association of America Reviews of Research). LC 83-19442. ISBN 0-87352-260-5.

The **New Cambridge Bibliography of English Literature**. Cambridge: Cambridge University Press, 1969-77. 5 vols. ISBN 0-521-34378-X. *NCBEL*

The separately published volumes that constitute *NCBEL* include:

Vol 1: **600-1660**. Ed. George Watson. Cambridge: Cambridge University Press, 1974. 2,491p. LC 73-82455. ISBN 0-521-2004-0.

Vol. 2: **1660-1800**. Ed. George Watson. Cambridge: Cambridge University Press, 1971. 2,092p. LC 69-10199. ISBN 0-521-07934-9.

Vol. 3: **1800-1900**. Ed. George Watson. Cambridge: Cambridge University Press, 1969. 1,956p. LC 69-10199. ISBN 0-521-07255-7.

Vol. 4: **1900-1950**. Ed. Ian R. Willison. Cambridge: Cambridge University Press, 1972. 1,414p. LC 69-10199. ISBN 0-521-08535-7.

Vol. 5: **Index** Ed. J. D. Pickles. Cambridge: Cambridge University Press, 1977. 542p. LC 69-10199. ISBN 0-521-21310-x.

Oxford Companion to American Literature. Ed. James D. Hart, with revisions and additions by Phillip W. Leininger. 6th ed. New York: Oxford University Press, 1995. 779p. LC 94-45727. ISBN 0-1950-6548-4.

Oxford Companion to English Literature. Ed. Margaret Drabble. Revised ed. New York: Oxford University Press, 1995. 1,171p. LC 95-11322. ISBN 0-1986-6221-1.

Oxford English Dictionary. Eds. J. A. Simpson and E. S. C. Weiner. 2d ed. Oxford: Clarendon Press ; New York: Oxford University Press, 1989. 20 vols. LC 88-5330. ISBN 0-1986-1186-2. *OED*.

Patterson, Margaret C. **Author Newsletters and Journals: An International Annotated Bibliography of Serial Publications Concerned with the Life and Works of Individual Authors**. Detroit, MI: Gale Research, 1979. 497p. (Gale Information Guide Library: American Literature, English Literature, and World Literatures in English Information Guide Series, vol. 19; Gale Information Guide Library). LC 79-63742. ISBN 0-8103-1432-0.

Perry, Margaret. **The Harlem Renaissance: An Annotated Bibliography and Commentary**. New York: Garland, 1982. 272p. (Critical Studies on Black Life and Culture, vol. 2; Garland Reference Library of the Humanities, vol. 278). LC 80-9048. ISBN-0-8240-9320-8.

Robbins, J. Albert. **American Literary Manuscripts: A Checklist of Holdings in Academic, Historical, and Public Libraries, Museums, and Authors' Homes in the United States**. 2d ed. Athens: University of Georgia Press, 1977. 387p. LC 76-49156. ISBN 0-8203-0412-3.

Schrank, Bernice, and William W. Demastes. **Irish Playwrights, 1880-1995: A Research and Production Sourcebook**. Westport, CT: Greenwood, 1997. 454p. LC 95-48349. ISBN 0-313-28805-4.

Severs, J. B. (vols. 1-2), and A. E. Hartung (vols. 3-), general eds. **A Manual of the Writings in Middle English, 1050-1500**. New Haven, CT: Connecticut Academy of Arts and Sciences, 1967- . Irregular. LC 67-7687.

Fascicle 1: **I. Romances**. Ed. Mortimer J. Donovan, Charles W. Dunn, Lillian Herlands Hornstein, R. M. Lumiansky, Helaine Newstead, and H. M. Smyser. New Haven, CT: Connecticut Academy of Arts and Sciences, 1967. pp. 338.

Vol. 2: **II. The Pearl Poet**. Ed. Marie P. Hamilton; **III. Wyclif and His Followers**. Ed. Ernest W. Talbert and S. Harrison Thomson; **IV. Translations and Paraphrases of the Bible, and Commentaries**. Ed. Laurence Muir; **V. Saint's Legends**. Ed. Charlotte D'Evelyn and Frances A. Foster; **VI. Instructions for Religious**. Ed. Charlotte D'Evelyn. New Haven, CT: Connecticut Academy of Arts and Sciences, 1970. pp. 668.

Vol. 3: **VII. Dialogues, Debates, and Catechisms**. Ed. Francis Lee Utley; **VIII. Thomas Hoccleve**. Ed. William Matthews; **IX. Malory and Caxton**. Ed. Robert H. Wilson. New Haven, CT: Connecticut Academy of Arts and Sciences, 1972. pp. 960.

Vol. 4: **X. Middle Scots Writers**. Ed. Florence H. Ridley; **XI. The Chaucerian Apocrypha**. Ed. Rossell Hope Robbins. New Haven, CT: Connecticut Academy of Arts and Sciences, 1973. pp. 1,313.

Vol. 5: **XII. Dramatic Pieces**. Ed. Anna J. Mill, Sheila Lindenbaum, Francis Lee Utley, and Barry Ward; **XIII. Poems Dealing with Contemporary Conditions**. Ed. Rossell Hope Robbins. New Haven, CT: Connecticut Academy of Arts and Sciences, 1975. pp. 1,742.

Vol. 6: **XIV. Carols**. Ed. Richard Leighton Greene; **XV. Ballads**. Ed. David C. Fowler; **XVI. John Lydgate**. Ed. Alain Renoir and C. David Benson. New Haven, CT: Connecticut Academy of Arts and Sciences, 1980. pp. 2,194.

Vol. 7: **XVII. John Gower**. Ed. John H. Fisher, R. Wayne Hamm, Peter G. Beidler, and Robert F. Yeager; **XVIII. Piers Plowman**. Ed. Anne Middleton; **XIX. Travel and Geographical Writing**. Ed. Christian K. Zacher; **XX. Works of Religious and Philosophical Instruction**. Ed. Robert R. Raymo. New Haven, CT: Connecticut Academy of Arts and Sciences, 1986. pp. 2,595.

Vol. 8: **XII [XXI] Chronicles and Other Historical Writings**. Ed. Edward Donald Kennedy. Hamden CT: Archon Books for the Connecticut Academy of Arts and Sciences, 1989. pp. 2,956.

Vol. 9: **XXII. Proverbs, Precepts, and Monitory Pieces**. Ed. Cameron Louis. **XXIII. English Mystical Writings**. Ed. Valerie M. Lagorio, Michael G. Sargent, and Ritamary Bradley. **XXIV. Tales**. Ed. Thomas D. Cooke, Peter Whiteford, and Nancy Mohr McKinley. New Haven, CT: Connecticut Academy of Arts and Sciences, 1993. pp. 3,592.

Shapiro, Ann R. **Jewish American Women Writers: A Bio-Bibliographical and Critical Sourcebook**. Westport, CT: Greenwood, 1994. 557p. ISBN 0-313-28437-7. LC 93-40618.

Shields, Ellen F. **Contemporary English Poetry: An Annotated Bibliography of Criticism to 1980**. New York: Garland, 1984. 238p. (Garland Reference Library of the Humanities, vol. 460). LC 83-49082. ISBN 0-8240-9016-0.

A Short-Title Catalogue of Books Printed in England, Scotland, & Ireland and of English Books Printed Abroad, 1475-1640. Ed. Katharine F. Pantzer, W. A. Jackson, and F. S. Ferguson. 2d ed., revised and enlarged. 3 vols. London: The Bibliographical Society, 1976-91. LC 76-374523. *STC.*

Spector, Robert Donald. **The English Gothic: A Bibliographic Guide to Writers from Horace Walpole to Mary Shelley.** Westport, CT: Greenwood Press, 1984. 269p. LC 83-1443. ISBN 0-313-22536-2.

Stanton, Robert J. **A Bibliography of Modern British Novelists.** Troy, NY: Whitston, 1978. 2 vols. LC 76-21471. ISBN 0-87875-115-7.

Stevenson, Lionel, ed. **Victorian Fiction: A Guide to Research.** 1964; Reprint, New York: Modern Language Association of America, 1980. 440p. LC 64-21246. ISBN 0-8352-258-3.

Wells, Daniel A. **The Literary Index to American Magazines, 1815-1865.** Metuchen, NJ: Scarecrow, 1980. 218p. LC 79-24022. ISBN 0-8108-1272-X.

Wells, Daniel A. **The Literary Index to American Magazines, 1850-1900.** Westport, CT: Greenwood, 1996. 441p. (Bibliographies and Indexes in American Literature, no. 22). LC 96-26447. ISBN 0-313-29840-8.

Wells, Stanley, ed. **English Drama (Excluding Shakespeare): Select Bibliographical Guides.** London; New York: Oxford University Press, 1975. 320p. ISBN 0-19-871034-8.

Wing, Donald, ed. **Short-Title Catalogue of Books Printed in England, Scotland, Ireland, Wales, and British America, and of English Books Printed in Other Countries, 1641-1700.** 2d ed., revised and enlarged. New York: Index Committee of the Modern Language Association of America, 1972-88. 3 vols. LC 70-185211. *Wing*

Woodress, James, ed. **Eight American Authors: A Review of Research and Criticism.** Revised ed. New York: Norton, 1971. 392p. LC 73-160485.

Wortman, William A. **A Guide to Serial Bibliographies for Modern Literatures.** 2d ed. New York: Modern Language Association of America, 1995. 333p. LC 95-33134. ISBN 0-8735-2965-0.

Year's Work in English Studies. London: English Association, 1921- . Annual. ISSN 0084-4144. *YWES*

Writers and Works

Lascelles Abercrombie, 1881-1938
Bibliographies
1. Cooper, Jeffrey. **A Bibliography and Notes on the Works of Lascelles Abercrombie**. Hamden, CT: Archon, 1969. 166p. LC 75-4644. ISBN 0-208-00719-9.

Full bibliographic descriptions of Abercrombie's works chronologically arranged in sections for principal books; contributions to books; and contributions to periodicals and newspapers, with appendixes for broadcasts made by Abercrombie and a chronological table of all entries. Entries for issues of first editions give title-page transcriptions, physical descriptions and collations, contents, and brief information on publication histories. Identifies about 400 periodical first appearances. Index of names and titles. Also for a bibliography of works by and about Abercrombie, see *NCBEL*, IV, pp. 995-97.

Louis Adamic, 1899-1951
Bibliographies
2. Christian, Henry A. **Louis Adamic: A Checklist**. Kent, OH: Kent State University Press, 1971. 164p. (The Serif Series: Bibliographies and Checklists, no. 20). LC 76-634011. ISBN 0-87338-115-7.

Christian offers an unannotated listing of writings by and about Adamic, including more than 600 entries for primary works (periodical articles, books and pamphlets, and forewords and other minor contributions) as well as special collections of Adamic's autographs, typescripts, and other materials in libraries at Princeton University and in Llubjana, Yugoslavia (pp. 83-92). In addition, Christian lists about 500 entries for biographical and critical works about Adamic. Primary materials indexed by titles. Index of critics and editors for secondary works. Adamic's manuscripts are listed in Robbins' *American Literary Manuscripts*, pp. 1-2.

Andy Adams, 1859-1935
Bibliographies
For works by Adams, see *First Printings of American Authors*, vol. 4, pp. 3-5. Adams' manuscripts are listed in Robbins' *American Literary Manuscripts*, p. 2. See *Bibliography of American Fiction, 1866-1918*, pp. 33-34, for Christine M. Bernsen's checklist of works by and about Adams. Don Graham surveys works by and about Adams in Erisman and Etulain's *Fifty Western Writers*, pp. 13-20.

Henry (Brooks) Adams, 1838-1918
Bibliographies
3. Harbert, Earl N. **Henry Adams: A Reference Guide**. Boston: G. K. Hall, 1978. 96p. (Reference Publications in Literature). LC 77-13492. ISBN 0-8161-7975-1.

Chronologically arranges annotated entries for about 500 studies of Adams published from 1879 through 1975. Identifies substantial numbers of anonymous reviews, but excludes unpublished dissertations and passing references. Critically evaluative annotations indicate significant studies. A comprehensive index provides limited topical access, with subheadings for bibliographies and biographies under Adams' name. Harbert previously surveyed Adams' texts and criticism in Harbert and Rees' *Fifteen American Authors Before 1900*, pp. 3-54. Also for works by Adams, see *Bibliography of American Literature*, vol. 1, pp. 1-11. Wells' *The Literary Index to American Magazines*, 1850-1900, pp. 2-3, identifies Adams' contributions to selected periodicals. Adams' manuscripts are listed in Robbins' *American Literary Manuscripts*, p. 3.

John Turvill Adams, 1805-1882
Bibliographies

> For works by Adams, see *First Printings of American Authors*, vol. 4, p. 7.

Leonie Adams (Fuller), 1899-1988
Bibliographies

> For works by Adams, see *First Printings of American Authors*, vol. 4, pp. 9-10. Adams' manuscripts are listed in Robbins' *American Literary Manuscripts*, p. 5.

Oscar Fay Adams, 1855-1919
Bibliographies

> For works by Adams, see *Bibliography of American Literature*, vol. 1, pp. 12-19.

Samuel Hopkins Adams, 1871-1958
Bibliographies

> See *Bibliography of American Fiction, 1866-1918*, pp. 34-35, for Philip B. Eppard's checklist of works by and about Adams. Adams' manuscripts are listed in Robbins' *American Literary Manuscripts*, p. 5.

Joseph Addison, 1672-1719
Bibliographies

> 4.   Evans, James E., and John N. Wall, Jr. **A Guide to Prose Fiction in the Tatler and the Spectator**. New York: Garland, 1977. 396p. (Garland Reference Library of the Humanities, vol. 71). LC 76-24751. ISBN 0-8240-9926-5.
>
> Evans and Wall give an issue-by-issue account of broadly defined pieces of prose fiction in *The Tatler* and *The Spectator*, with extensive descriptive summaries that attempt to classify each piece by narrative form (character, dream vision, eyewitness account, and the like). Indexes for forms and selected subjects (the church, country life, and politics, among others) cross-reference the descriptions. Includes unindexed, selected annotated list of about 100 studies of prose fiction in *The Tatler* and *The Spectator*. Also still useful for research on *The Spectator*, William Wheeler's *A Concordance to "The Spectator"* (London: Routledge, n.d.) offers a name and topic index with pages, columns, and paragraphs keyed to Henry Morley's *The Spectator: A New Edition Reproducing the Original Text* (London: Routledge, 1888).

> 5.   Knight, Charles A. **Joseph Addison and Richard Steele: A Reference Guide, 1730-1991**. New York: G. K. Hall, 1994. 561p. (Reference Guide to Literature). LC 94-21458. ISBN 0-8161-8980-3.
>
> Following separate listings of the works of Addison and Steele, Knight chronologically arranges annotated entries for about 2,500 studies of Addison and Steele from 1930 through 1991. Comprehensive but not exhaustive coverage includes contemporary notices (with references to reprintings), early and modern editions, substantial entries in literary histories and reference works, dissertations, and non-English-language criticisms. Although annotations are "impartial" (p. x) and informative, Knight's introduction identifies major critical works. Separate indexes of authors and subjects, with detailed and elaborate topical headings, offer exemplary access. Knight notes several preliminary descriptive bibliographies of the works of Addison and Steele. No complete primary bibliography now exists for either. Also for a works by and about Addison, see Donald F. Bond's bibliography in *NCBEL*, II, pp. 1098-112. Addison's manuscripts are described in *Index of English Literary Manuscripts*, III, pt. 1:3-12.

Journals

> "Recent Articles" in *The Scriblerian and the Kit Cats* (entry 1084) also regularly includes a selection of reviews of studies on Addison and Steele.

George Ade, 1866-1944
Bibliographies
6.   Russo, Dorothy Ritter. **A Bibliography of George Ade, 1866-1944**. Indianapolis, IN: Indiana Historical Society, 1947. 314p. LC 48-6799.

Russo describes Ade's primary works, including separate listings for first editions of books and ephemeral publications (pamphlets, sheet music, broadsides, and the like); contributions to books, magazines, and newspapers: and reprints of Ade's works. Descriptive entries give title-page transcriptions; details on collations, contents, illustrations, and bindings; and notes on printing and publishing histories. In addition, Russo lists selected works about Ade. Also for works by Ade, see *First Printings of American Authors*, vol. 2, pp. 1-12. Ade's manuscripts are listed in Robbins' *American Literary Manuscripts*, p. 6. See *Bibliography of American Fiction, 1866-1918*, pp. 36-38, for Patricia R. New's checklist of works by and about Ade.

Aelfric, c. 955-c. 1010
Bibliographies
7.   Reinsma, Luke M. **Aelfric: An Annotated Bibliography**. New York: Garland, 1987. 306p. (Garland Reference Library of the Humanities, vol. 617). LC 85-45125. ISBN 0-8240-8665-1.

Aimed at advanced scholars and upper-division students, Reinsma offers some 882 annotated entries for editions of works by Aelfric and critical studies about Aelfric from William of Malmesbury through 1982. Comprehensive international coverage includes dissertations and non-English-language criticism but excludes book reviews. Chronologically arranged in nine sections for bibliographies; scholarship through 1800 (with references to such standard bibliographies as *STC* and *Wing*); general studies and biographies; histories and surveys; manuscripts, editions, and anthologies; linguistic and stylistic studies (the most useful and extensive sections, each with about 150 entries); and editions and studies of individual works. The manuscripts section, with about 150 entries, offers detailed descriptions of collections. Although largely descriptive, Reinsma's annotations give advice about standard works. Separate indexes for critics, manuscripts, and primary works, unfortunately, lack subdivisions for bibliography, biography, imagery, and similar topics. Reinsma's bibliography supersedes Malcolm R. Godden's classified listing for Aelfric in Caroline Louisa White's *Aelfric: A New Study of His Life and Writings* (1898; reprint Hamden, CT: Archon Books, 1974). In addition, by identifying scholarship on Aelfric's Latin works, Reinsma's guide complements the listings for Aelfric in Greenfield and Robinson's *A Bibliography of Publications on Old English Literature to the End of 1972*, pp. 295-308. Works by and about Aelfric are also listed in *NCBEL*, I, pp. 317-21. These listings can be updated by consulting issues of *Old English Newsletter* (Binghamton, NY: State University of New York at Binghamton, 1968-). Manuscripts related to Aelfric are described in Neil R. Ker's *Catalogue of Manuscripts Containing Anglo-Saxon* (Oxford: Clarendon Press, 1957).

James Agee, 1909-1955
Bibliographies
For works by Agee, see *First Printings of American Authors*, vol. 1, pp. 1-2. Agee's manuscripts are listed in Robbins' *American Literary Manuscripts*, p. 7. See Huse's *John Hersey and James Agee* (entry 665) for works about Agee from 1940 through 1977; and Robert E. Burkholder's checklist of works by and about Agee in *Bibliography of American Fiction, 1919-1988*, pp. 47-50. Research on Agee is reviewed by Richard R. Schramm in Flora and Bain's *Fifty Southern Writers After 1900*, pp. 9-20.

Conrad (Potter) Aiken, 1889-1973
Bibliographies

8.   Bonnell, F. W., and F. C. Bonnell. **Conrad Aiken: A Bibliography (1902-1978)**. San Marino, CA: Huntington Library, 1982. 291p. LC 82-9241. ISBN 0-87328-118-7.

The most comprehensive bibliography of Aiken's primary materials now available. Separate chronologically arranged sections include descriptive entries for Aiken's 64 books and pamphlets (giving title-page transcriptions; descriptions of collations, contents, and bindings; and printing and publishing histories); 93 contributions to books; 761 contributions to periodicals and newspapers; translations of books and essays in 15 languages; and miscellaneous publications, ranging from recordings, radio and television broadcasts, film adaptations, musical settings, and books announced but not published to broadsides and Christmas cards. Also for works by Aiken, see *First Printings of American Authors*, vol. 4, pp. 11-25. Aiken's manuscripts are listed in Robbins' *American Literary Manuscripts*, p. 7.

9.   Harris, Catherine Kirk. **Conrad Aiken: Critical Recognition, 1914-1981: A Bibliographic Guide**. New York: Garland, 1983. 324p. (Garland Reference Library of the Humanities, vol. 391). LC 82-49032. ISBN 0-8240-9187-6.

Harris' comprehensive secondary bibliography contains separate, selectively annotated listings of Aiken's books, with citations for their reviews, and listings of works about Aiken, including critical and biographical articles; books and parts of books; and unpublished studies (dissertations and theses, conference papers, and other academic writings). Includes chronologies of "Books Written or Edited" by Aiken and of Aiken's literary awards. Provides nominal indexing for critics, primary titles, periodical titles, and institutions sponsoring Aiken research. No subject indexing. Supersedes Harris' "Conrad Aiken: Critical Reception, 1914-1976," *Bulletin of Bibliography* 34 (1977): 29-34, 137-40.

William Harrison Ainsworth, 1805-1882
Bibliographies

10.   Locke, Harold. **A Bibliographical Catalogue of the Published Novels and Ballads of William Harrison Ainsworth**. London: Elkin Mathews, 1925. 68p. LC 26-13965.

Aimed at collectors, offering chronologically arranged title-page transcriptions and brief physical descriptions, with particular attention to bibliographical points and valuation (as of 1925) for the "principal English issues of the novels and ballads" (p. [3]). Brief title index. Reviews of Ainsworth's works in selected periodicals are identified in Wells' *The Literary Index to American Magazines, 1815-1865*, p. 1. Also for a bibliography of works by and about Ainsworth, see *NCBEL*, III, pp. 911-14.

Mark Akenside, 1721-1770
Bibliographies

See Williams' *Seven XVIIIth Century Bibliographies* (entry 35), pp. [73]-97, for bibliographic descriptions of Akenside's separate publications; and *NCBEL*, II, pp. 637-38, for works by and about Akenside. Akenside's manuscripts are described in *Index of English Literary Manuscripts*, III, pt. 1:13-16. Robin C. Dix and John Lancaster's *The Poetical Manuscripts of Mark Akenside in the Ralph M. Williams Collection, Amherst College Library: Reproduced in Facsimile* (Amherst, MA: Amherst College Press, 1988) reproduces holdings that "were originally mounted in Dyson's own copy of the 1772 *Poems*, and together they form the largest single collection of his poetic manuscripts" (Introduction).

Edward (Franklin) Albee, 1928-
Bibliographies

11.   Giantvalley, Scott. **Edward Albee: A Reference Guide**. Boston: G. K. Hall, 1987. 459p. (A Reference Guide to Literature). LC 87-25047. ISBN 0-8161-8783-5.

An initial section contains 88 entries for Albee's plays (published and unpublished through 1987), nondramatic prose, poetry, and juvenilia. The bulk of the work, however, consists of 2,800 chronologically arranged, nonevaluative annotated entries from 1959 though 1987 for writings about Albee, including books, articles, reviews in journals and newspapers (such as *Variety* and the *New York Times*), and dissertations and theses. Cumulative index of critics, primary and periodical titles, and subjects complicates access by referencing individual plays and specific topics under Albee's name: Studies of Albee's views on direction, for example, are cited under "Albee—Directing—Albee on." Subentries under *Albee* extend for 17 pages. Giantvalley's bibliography complements Tyce's *Edward Albee* (entry 12). Anne Paolucci and Henry Paolucci review research on Albee in *Contemporary Authors: Bibliographical Series: Volume 3: American Dramatists*, pp. 3-47.

12. Tyce, Richard. **Edward Albee: A Bibliography**. Metuchen, NJ: Scarecrow Press, 1986. 212p. (Scarecrow Author Bibliographies, no. 76). LC 86-25969. ISBN 0-8108-1915-5.

Unannotated listing of 2,711 entries for works by and about Albee published through 1984 arranged in sections that contain a chronology of performances of Albee's plays; bibliographies of their published texts and of Albee's "early" and more recent writings; and bibliographies of general critical studies, theses and dissertations and studies and reviews of Albee's individual works. Information recorded for initial productions is specific, identifying both performance dates and theaters to supplement data for Albee's published plays found in Giantvalley's bibliography (entry 11). Likewise, Tyce records a list of 85 primary works that complements Giantvalley's list of Albee's publications. A critic-title index is provided but no subject indexing. Both Tyce's and Giantvalley's bibliographies supersede Richard Amacher and Margaret F. Rule's *Edward Albee at Home and Abroad* (New York: AMS Press, 1973), which covered works by and about Albee from 1958 to 1968; Charles Lee Green's *Edward Albee: An Annotated Bibliography, 1968-1977* (New York: AMS Press, 1980), which provided 579 entries for works by and about Albee from the period 1968 to 1977; and listings for Albee in King's *Ten Modern American Playwrights*, pp. 1-108. It should be noted, however, that Green's guide lists special collections of Albee materials. Also for works by Albee, see *First Printings of American Authors*, vol. 3, pp. 1-9. Albee's manuscripts are listed in Robbins' *American Literary Manuscripts*, p. 8.

(Amos) Bronson Alcott, 1799-1888
Bibliographies

For works by Alcott, see *Bibliography of American Literature*, vol. 1, pp. 20-26. Alcott's contributions to selected periodicals and reviews of Alcott's works are identified in Wells' *The Literary Index to American Magazines, 1815-1865*, p. 1; and *The Literary Index to American Magazines, 1850-1900*, p. 4. Alcott's manuscripts are listed in Robbins' *American Literary Manuscripts*, p. 8. See the review of research on Alcott by Frederick C. Dahlstrand in Myerson's *The Transcendentalists*, pp. 87-96. Kenneth Walter Cameron's *Transcendental Curriculum, or, Bronson Alcott's Library: The Inventory of 1858-1860 with Addenda to 1888, Including the Library at Fruitlands (1842-1843), to Which Is Added a Sheaf of Ungathered Alcott Letters* (Hartford, CT: Transcendental Books, 1984) offers a "consolidated inventory of the volumes known to have been under his control either at Boston, Concord or Fruitlands" (Introduction).

Louisa May Alcott, 1832-1888
Bibliographies

13. Gulliver, Lucile. **Louisa May Alcott: A Bibliography**. Boston: Little, Brown, 1932. 71p. LC 32-34822.

The standard descriptive bibliography of Alcott's works, Gulliver's guide gives brief bibliographic information and notes on contents for first and subsequent editions of Alcott's writings, including separate reprintings of works previously published in periodicals, and a list of international editions. Also appends annotated entries for 20 biographical works about Alcott. Available in a reprinted edition (New York: B. Franklin, 1973). Additional information on Alcott's primary bibliography is provided in Blanck's *Bibliography of American Literature*, vol. 1, pp. 27-45, as well as in Leona Rostenberg's "Some Anonymous and Pseudonymous Thrillers of Louisa May Alcott," *PBSA* 37 (1943): 131-40; and Madeleine B. Stern's "Louisa May Alcott's Contributions to Periodicals, 1868-1888," *More Books* 18 (1943): 411-20. Judith C. Ullom's exhibition catalog, *Louisa May Alcott: A Centennial for Little Women* (Washington, DC: Library of Congress, 1969), describes early editions of Alcott's works. Alcott's manuscripts are listed in Robbins' *American Literary Manuscripts*, p. 8.

14. Payne, Alma J. **Louisa May Alcott: A Reference Guide**. Boston: G. K. Hall, 1980. 87p. (A Reference Publication in Literature). LC 79-23374. ISBN 0-8161-8032-6.

Payne's guide contains an introductory survey of Alcott's literary career and critical reputation; a checklist of her books, short fiction, and nonfiction writings; and a chronologically arranged listing of about 400 works about Alcott published from 1854 to 1979. Secondary coverage is especially comprehensive, identifying books, journal and newspaper articles, anonymous reviews, dissertations, and ERIC documents, with descriptive annotations. Index headings for broad topics (bibliography and biography) offer limited subject access. See *Bibliography of American Fiction 1866-1918*, pp. 38-41, for Joel Myerson's checklist of works by and about Alcott.

Richard (Edward Godfree) Aldington, 1892-1962
Bibliographies

15. Kershaw, Alister. **A Bibliography of the Works of Richard Aldington from 1915 to 1948**. Burlingame, CA: William P. Wreden, 1950. 57p. LC 50-13142.

Supplies title-page transcriptions, brief physical descriptions (page size in inches and number of pages), and brief notes on publication histories in 231 entries in sections for poetry, essays, novels, short stories, biography and autobiography, books edited by Aldington or with contributions by him, translations, and a dramatic adaptation of a story by Aldington, with a list of works by Aldington "at present in preparation" (p. 56). Includes an introduction by Aldington. Intended for collectors. Also for a bibliography of works by and about Aldington, see *NCBEL*, IV, pp. 511-14.

Thomas Bailey Aldrich, 1836-1907
Bibliographies

For separately published works by Aldrich, see *Bibliography of American Literature*, vol. 1, pp. 46-77. Blanck's coverage surpasses in detail that of Frederic Fairchild Sherman's *A Check List of First Editions of Thomas Bailey Aldrich* (New York: Privately Printed, 1921), a chronologically arranged checklist of first editions of 65 separately published books and pamphlets (including limited editions) and collected works, with brief data on contents and bindings. Aldrich's contributions to selected periodicals and reviews of Aldrich's works are identified in Wells' *The Literary Index to American Magazines, 1815-1865*, pp. 1-2; and *The Literary Index to American Magazines, 1850-1900*, pp. 6-7. Aldrich's manuscripts are listed in Robbins' *American Literary Manuscripts*, pp. 9-10. See *Bibliography of American Fiction, 1866-1918*, pp. 42-43, for Catherine Schultz's checklist of works by and about Aldrich.

Lloyd Alexander, 1924-
Bibliographies

16. Jacobs, James S., and Michael O. Tunnell. **Lloyd Alexander: A Bio-Bibliography**. New York: Greenwood Press, 1991. 145p. (Bio-Bibliographies in American Literature, no. 1). LC 90-24515. ISBN 0-313-26586-0.

Covers works by and about Alexander. The first part gives brief bibliographic information and summaries of contents for first and subsequent editions and translations of Alexander's works in sections for books, short fiction, other writings (reviews, interviews, etc.), illustrations by Alexander, and unpublished speeches and writings. The second part describes works about Alexander, supplying annotated entries in sections for four books, seven dissertations, 53 articles and chapters, 419 book reviews (sublisted by book title), translated comments, audiovisual sources related to Alexander, and miscellaneous references (largely entries in reference works). An extensive biographical introduction emphasizes Alexander's development as a writer. Includes chronology and list of awards. Index of names, titles, and selected topics. Jacobs and Tunnell's guide supersedes coverage of works by and about Alexander in Zahorski and Boyer's *Lloyd Alexander, Evangeline Walton Ensley, Kenneth Morris: A Primary and Secondary Bibliography* (entry 469).

Dictionaries, Encyclopedias, and Handbooks
17. Tunnell, Michael O. **The Prydain Companion: A Reference Guide to Lloyd Alexander's Prydain Chronicles**. New York: Greenwood Press, 1989. 257p. LC 88-7705. ISBN 0-313-26585-2.

Dictionary of names and terms for persons, places, and things in Alexander's Prydain series, including animals, castles, characters, emblems, magic objects, weapons, and the like, with book and page references. Based on New York: Holt, Rinehart, and Winston "hard cover editions" (p. xvi) and other sources listed in "References" (p. [255]-57). Category index of entry headings.

Alfred (the Great), 848-899
Bibliographies
Greenfield and Robinson's *A Bibliography of Publications on Old English Literature to the End of 1972*, pp. 309-28, lists editions, translations, and studies of Alfred, with citations for reviews. Also for a bibliography of works by and about Alfred, see *NCBEL*, I, pp. 313-15.

Horatio Alger, Jr., 1832-1899
Bibliographies
18. Bennett, Bob. **Horatio Alger, Jr.: A Comprehensive Bibliography**. Mt. Pleasant, MI: Flying Eagle Publishing, 1980. 200p. LC 81-105956.

Mainly intended to help collectors of Alger materials distinguish first editions from reprints and other variants, Bennett gives a list of each known title and subtitle variation and descriptions of Alger's books, with full bibliographical details for title pages, collations, bindings, and other significant and identifying "points," as well as descriptive entries for his serialized stories. Includes lists of Alger's works by publishers of hard- and paper-covered editions in addition to sources of short stories, articles, and poetry. Ralph D. Gardner's *Road to Success: The Bibliography of the Works of Horatio Alger* (1964; revised ed., Mendota, IL: Wayside Press, 1971) and Frank Gruber's *Horatio Alger, Jr.: A Biography and Bibliography* (West Los Angeles, CA: Grover Jones Press, 1961), similarly aimed at Alger collectors, emphasize bibliographic points. Also for works by Alger, see *First Printings of American Authors*, vol. 5, pp. 3-25. Alger's manuscripts are listed in Robbins' *American Literary Manuscripts*, p. 10.

19. Scharnhorst, Gary, and Jack Bales. **Horatio Alger, Jr.: An Annotated Bibliography of Comment and Criticism**. Metuchen, NJ: Scarecrow Press, 1981. 179p. (Scarecrow Author Bibliographies, no. 54). LC 80-25960. ISBN 0-8108-1387-4.

Following an extensive introductory "biobibliographical essay" locating Alger's manuscripts and other materials in American libraries, Scharnhorst and Bales give separate listings for about 700 reviews of Alger's books, biographies, bibliographies, "literary analyses" from 1928 through 1979, introductions to reprints of

Alger's works, articles and essays in popular and "hobbyist" periodicals and newspapers, non-English-language commentaries, dissertations and theses, and other miscellaneous writings on Alger, with descriptive annotations. See also *Bibliography of American Fiction, 1866-1918*, pp. 44-48, for Scharnhorst's checklist of works by and about Alger.

Journals
20. **Newsboy**. Mundelein, IL: Horatio Alger Society, 1962-. 6/yr. ISSN 0028-9396.
Sponsored by the Horatio Alger Society, issues publish two to four brief articles, notes, and reviews of new publications about Alger's life and works. The dominant theme of critical studies is the adolescent male in American culture. Contributions have discussed racial stereotypes in Alger's works and his attitudes toward Unitarianism, the American union movement, and the treatment of factory workers. Studies of sources are also typical, such as "Whence Came the Name Rover?: Speculations from the Correspondence," which traces the source of the name of the "Rover Boys"; and "Alger's Source for *The Boy Guide of Rich Mountain: A Story of West Virginia*." A significant number of publishing histories have appeared, with descriptions of publishers' records, previously unreported Alger materials, textual variants, and editions. *Newsboy* is indexed in *MLA*.

Nelson Algren, 1909-1981
Bibliographies
21. Bruccoli, Matthew J., and Judith Baughman. **Nelson Algren: A Descriptive Bibliography**. Pittsburgh, PA: University of Pittsburgh Press, 1985. 185p. (Pittsburgh Series in Bibliography). LC 85-1180. ISBN 0-8229-3517-1.
The standard bibliography of Algren's works, Bruccoli and Baughman's guide gives full bibliographic descriptions (facsimiles of title pages; collations and paginations; contents; and data for typography, paper, bindings, and dust jackets; notes on printing and publishing; and copy locations) for all editions and variant printings of books and pamphlets in English by Algren. Also includes separate listings of Algren's contributions to books and serials, Algren's reviews, and other writings by Algren, with a list of six works about Algren. Bruccoli and Baughman's guide supersedes Kenneth G. McCollum's *Nelson Algren: A Checklist* (Detroit, MI: Gale, 1973). Also for works by Algren, see *First Printings of American Authors*, vol. 1, pp. 3-5. Algren's manuscripts are listed in Robbins' *American Literary Manuscripts*, p. 10. See *Bibliography of American Fiction, 1919-1988*, pp. 50-51, for J. M. Brook's checklist of works by and about Algren.

Elizabeth Akers Allen, 1832-1911
Bibliographies
For works by Allen, see *Bibliography of American Literature*, vol. 1, pp. 78-87. Allen's contributions to and reviews of Allen's works in selected periodicals are identified in Wells' *The Literary Index to American Magazines, 1850-1900*, pp. 8-9. Allen's manuscripts are listed in Robbins' *American Literary Manuscripts*, p. 10.

(William) Hervey Allen, 1889-1949
Bibliographies
See *Bibliography of American Fiction, 1919-1988*, p. 52, for a checklist of works by and about Allen. Allen's manuscripts are listed in Robbins' *American Literary Manuscripts*, p. 10.

James Lane Allen, 1849-1925
Bibliographies
For works by Allen, see *Bibliography of American Literature*, vol. 1, pp. 88-95. Allen's contributions to and reviews of Allen's works in selected periodicals are identified in Wells' *The Literary Index to American Magazines, 1850-1900*, p. 9. Allen's manuscripts are listed in Robbins' *American Literary*

Manuscripts, p. 11. See *Bibliography of American Fiction, 1866-1918*, pp. 49-50, for Eric Damon Larison's checklist of works by and about Allen.

Paul Allen, 1775-1826
Bibliographies
> For works by Allen, see *First Printings of American Authors*, vol. 4, pp. 27-29. Allen's manuscripts are listed in Robbins' *American Literary Manuscripts*, p. 11.

William Allingham, 1824-1889
Bibliographies
> For a bibliography of works by and about Allingham, see *NCBEL*, III, pp. 502-503. Research on Allingham is reviewed by James F. Kilroy in Finneran's *Anglo-Irish Literature*, pp. 45-46.

Washington Allston, 1779-1843
Bibliographies
> For works by Allston, see *Bibliography of American Literature*, vol. 1, pp. 96-102. Allston's contributions to and reviews of Allston's works in selected periodicals are identified in Wells' *The Literary Index to American Magazines, 1815-1865*, p. 2; and *The Literary Index to American Magazines, 1850-1900*, p. 9. Allston's manuscripts are listed in Robbins' *American Literary Manuscripts*, p. 12.

Richard Alsop, 1761-1815
Bibliographies
> For works by Alsop, see *First Printings of American Authors*, vol. 1, pp. 7-8. Alsop's manuscripts are listed in Robbins' *American Literary Manuscripts*, p. 12.

Sir Kingsley Amis, 1922-
Bibliographies
> 22.   Gohn, Jack Benoit. **Kingsley Amis: A Checklist**. Kent, OH: Kent State University Press, 1976. 230p. (Serif Series: Bibliographies and Checklists, no. 34). LC 75-44709. ISBN 0-87338-182-3.
>
> Although attempting to provide a descriptive listing of Amis' primary bibliography, Gohn's work is in no way comprehensive. Coverage includes Amis' writings from 1953 through 1975 (excluding juvenilia and early contributions to magazines), with separate listings for unpublished and published works by Amis and for works about him. Unpublished works include six letters; eight radio and television scripts, transcripts, or recordings (of interviews and the like); and manuscripts and typescripts of published works. Among the published works are Amis' books and pamphlets, short stories, and short nonfiction writings (largely reviews), with references to replies and responses. With 432 entries, this latter section is most extensive. The listings for books, with 41 entries, is at best a checklist, noting translations into other languages and subsequent serializations but offering little bibliographic detail. Fourteen entries for short stories note reprintings. The section for secondary materials offers separate listings of unannotated entries for 190 critical, biographical, and bibliographical works; and for 588 reviews. Gohn employs a system of pluses, minuses, checks, and question marks to indicate each review's content and offer critical guidance. Significant bibliographical spadework remains to be done to provide a comprehensive listing of Amis' primary works. Additionally, Stanton's *A Bibliography of Modern British Novelists*, pp. 53-133, 1,073-80, contains classified unannotated entries giving brief bibliographic data for 267 works by Amis and for 575 works about him (especially reviews), with an addendum. Also for a bibliography of works by and about Amis, see *NCBEL*, IV, p. 1,397.

> 23.   Salwak, Dale. **Kingsley Amis: A Reference Guide**. Boston: G. K. Hall, 1978. 169p. (Reference Publication in Literature). LC 78-4244. ISBN 0-8161-8062-8.

While Salwak's comprehensive bibliography of works about Amis partially supersedes the coverage of Gohn's checklist (entry 22), the bibliography is now badly in need of updating. Salwak attempts to cover criticism of Amis from 1951 through 1977, chronologically arranging about 1,000 entries within subsections for books and dissertations (the earliest book-length study appeared in 1965) and for articles and reviews. Entries cite English-language reviews of Amis' publications. Although many reviews were published anonymously, others by the likes of Edmund Wilson and W. S. Merwin suggest possible avenues for research. Although descriptive, annotations are much more informative than those provided by Gohn. Index of primary titles and critics; no subject access.

A(rchie) R(andolph) Ammons, 1926-
Bibliographies

24. Wright, Stuart. **A. R. Ammons: A Bibliography, 1954-1979.** Winston-Salem, NC: Wake Forest University Press, 1980. 179p. LC 86-672206.

A descriptive bibliography following the model of those in the Pittsburgh Series in Bibliography, Wright' guide gives separate listings for Ammons' books, pamphlets, and broadsides; contributions to books; contributions of poetry and prose to periodicals; interviews and published comments; and other miscellaneous publications. Entries give full bibliographic descriptions, with title-page transcriptions; pagination and collations; contents; details on typography, paper, dust jackets, and bindings; notes on publication histories; and copy locations. Indexed by primary titles, periodical titles, and personal names. Also for works by Ammons, see *First Printings of American Authors*, vol. 1, pp. 9-10. Research on Ammons is reviewed by William Harmon in Flora and Bain's *Fifty Southern Writers After 1900*, pp. 21-32; and supplemented in Bain and Flora's *Contemporary Poets, Dramatists, Essayists, and Novelists of the South*, pp. 563-64.

Ancrene Wisse, c. 1230
Bibliographies

Charlotte D'Evelyn offers a comprehensive guide to primary materials of the *Ancrene Wisse* with a bibliography of editions and criticism in Severs and Hartung's *A Manual of the Writings in Middle English*, vol. II, pp. 458-60, 650-54. Roger Dahood reviews research on the Middle English poem in "*Ancrene Wisse*, the Katherine Group, and the *Wohunge* Group," in Edwards' *Middle English Prose*, pp. 1-34.

Indexes and Concordances

25. Potts, Jennifer, Lorna Stevenson, and Jocelyn Wogan-Browne, eds. **Concordance to Ancrene Wisse: MS Corpus Christi College, Cambridge 402.** Woodbridge, Suffolk: D. S. Brewer, 1993. 1,249p. LC 93-27291. ISBN 0-85991-395-3.

Based on a single text: MS Corpus Christi College, Cambridge 402. Contains lists of vernacular, Latin, Greek, and Hebrew forms and names, frequency indexes, and reverse vocabulary.

Fredrick Irving Anderson, 1877-1947
Bibliographies

26. Fisher, Benjamin Franklin, IV. **Fredrick Irving Anderson, 1877-1947: A Bio-Bibliography.** San Bernardino, CA: Borgo Press, 1988. 43p. (Brownstone Chapbook Series, vol. 4). LC 88-34112. ISBN 0-8905-6403-3.

Fisher gives brief bibliographic information (with summaries) for Anderson's nonfiction and semifiction books and short fiction (82 entries) and lists 87 reviews and criticisms of Anderson's works. The volume lacks an index.

Maxwell Anderson, 1888-1959
Bibliographies

27. Horn, Barbara Lee. **Maxwell Anderson: A Research and Production Source-book**. Westport, CT: Greenwood Press, 1996. 193p. (Modern Dramatists Research and Production Sourcebooks, no. 100). LC 96-1200. ISBN 0-31329-070-9.

As much a handbook for Anderson's life and works as a primary and secondary bibliography. Horn offers an overview of Anderson's life with a chronology; synopses of his stage, radio, and television plays, stage histories, and critical overviews; a brief, classified primary bibliography covering plays, theater criticism, contributions to books and periodicals, and archives; and chronologically arranged sections of briefly annotated entries for works about Anderson, including 475 reviews and 214 books, articles, and chapters published from 1923 through 1994. Play synopses and critical overviews cross-reference entries in sections for reviews and criticisms. Index of critics and scholars with a general index offering selected subject access. Horn's coverage of American productions is complemented by Ron Engle's *Maxwell Anderson on the European Stage 1929-1992: A Production History and Annotated Bibliography of Source Materials in Foreign Translation* (Monroe, NY: Library Research Associates, 1996), which gives production and cast information for performances in Western and Eastern Europe (including the former Soviet republics) and Israel, lists of translated editions, and annotated entries for publication and performance reviews and criticism in all languages. Horn also identifies works by and about Anderson in Demastes' *American Playwrights, 1880-1945*, pp. 14-28.

28. Shivers, Alfred S. **Maxwell Anderson: An Annotated Bibliography of Primary and Secondary Works**. Metuchen, NJ: Scarecrow Press, 1985. 287p. (Scarecrow Author Bibliographies, no. 72). LC 85-14227. ISBN 0-8108-1833-7.

Covers works by and about Anderson. The section for "Primary Works" gives brief bibliographic information and contents for Anderson's published and unpublished plays, poetry, short fiction, novels, and miscellaneous prose writings (including letters). Identifies and locates surviving manuscripts of complete plays (pp. 31-44). A comprehensive, selectively annotated listing of Anderson criticism covers books, articles, reviews, dissertations, theses, transcripts of interviews, and other materials about Anderson. Shivers' bibliography is more comprehensive than William Klink's *Maxwell Anderson and S. N. Behrman* (Boston: G. K. Hall, 1977), which lists materials about Anderson published through 1979. Horn's *Maxwell Anderson: A Research and Production Sourcebook* (entry 27) updates coverage of reviews and criticisms through 1994. No existing guide gives full bibliographic descriptions of Anderson's primary works. Martha Cox's *Maxwell Anderson Bibliography* (Charlottesville, VA: Bibliographical Society of the University of Virginia, 1958) gives brief information for the plays and Anderson's other works as well as criticism and reviews of Anderson's works. Also for works by Anderson, see *First Printings of American Authors*, vol. 1, pp. 11-14. Additionally, descriptions of Anderson's primary materials in the Humanities Research Center's Maxwell Anderson Collection (the largest collection of Anderson's literary manuscripts, correspondence, diaries, and biographical materials) is described in Laurence G. Avery's *A Catalogue of the Maxwell Anderson Collection at the University of Texas* (Austin, TX: University of Texas, Humanities Research Center, 1968). Anderson's manuscripts are also listed in Robbins' *American Literary Manuscripts*, p. 13.

Poul Anderson, 1926-
Bibliographies

29. Benson, Gordon, Jr., and Phil Stephensen-Payne. **Poul Anderson, Myth-Master and Wonder-Weaver: A Working Bibliography**. 5th revised ed. San Bernardino, CA: Borgo Press, 1990. 123p. (Galactic Central Bibliographies for the Avid Reader, vol. 1). LC 90-1934. ISBN 0-8095-4700-7.

An awkwardly arranged guide to works by and about Anderson that largely amounts to cross-referenced checklists in sections for stories, books, series, poems and songs, poem and song collections (an empty section), articles, miscellaneous works (forewords and reviews, mostly), nonfiction books, edited books, media presentations, seventy articles about Anderson, about 300 reviews of Anderson's works, three books about Anderson, apocrypha and forthcoming titles, related works by other authors, and textual variations (another empty section). Benson and Stephensen-Payne give little bibliographic data for primary works and annotate neither criticism nor reviews nor do they cover non-English-language criticism. A chronological listing of fiction serves as an index. Anderson deserves a better bibliography. See *Bibliography of American Fiction, 1919-1988*, pp. 53-55, for Lorraine A. Jean's checklist of works by and about Anderson.

Sherwood Anderson, 1876-1941
Bibliographies
30. Sheehy, Eugene P., and Kenneth A. Lohf. **Sherwood Anderson: A Bibliography**. Los Gatos, CA: Talisman Press, 1960. 125p. LC 60-53225.

The major comprehensive descriptive bibliography of Anderson's works, with sections for Anderson's separate publications, essays and stories, introductions and forewords, published letters, dramatizations, contributions to periodicals, edited journals, and "Smyth County News Contributions." Also lists about 1,000 works on Anderson (criticisms, poems, parodies, and reviews). Available in reprinted edition (Millwood, NY: Kraus Reprint, 1973). Supplemental descriptions of Anderson's primary works are presented in G. Thomas Tanselle's "Additional Reviews of Sherwood Anderson's Work," *PBSA* 56 (1962): 358-65; and "Addenda to Sheehy and Lohf's *Sherwood Anderson*: Copyright Information and Later Printings," in Hilbert H. Campbell and Charles E. Modlin's *Sherwood Anderson* (Troy, NY: Whitston, 1976), pp. 145-50. Also for works by Anderson, see *First Printings of American Authors*, vol. 2, pp. 13-20. Anderson's manuscripts are listed in Robbins' *American Literary Manuscripts*, p. 13. A useful essay by Walter B. Rideout in Bryer's *Sixteen Modern American Authors*, pp. 3-28; and Rideout's supplement in Bryer's *Sixteen Modern American Authors: Volume 2: A Survey of Research and Criticism Since 1972*, pp. 1-41, review Anderson's texts and criticism.

31. White, Ray Lewis. **Sherwood Anderson: A Reference Guide**. Boston: G. K. Hall, 1977. 430p. (Reference Guides in Literature). LC 76-46388. ISBN 0-8161-7818-6.

White's guide is regarded as the best secondary bibliography for Anderson, chronologically arranging descriptively annotated entries for 2,550 works about Anderson. International coverage includes articles in newspapers, dissertations, and non-English-language studies. White's bibliography supersedes his previous *Merrill Checklist of Sherwood Anderson* (Columbus, OH: Merrill, 1969); and Douglas G. Rogers' *Sherwood Anderson: A Selective, Annotated Bibliography* (Metuchen, NJ: Scarecrow Press, 1976), which describes about 500 works about Anderson and the major collection of Anderson materials in the Newberry Library (p. 44). See *Bibliography of American Fiction, 1866-1918*, pp. 50-54, for White's more recent checklist of works by and about Anderson.

Dictionaries, Encyclopedias, and Handbooks
32. Small, Judy Jo. **A Reader's Guide to the Short Stories of Sherwood Anderson**. New York: G. K. Hall, 1994. 446p. (Reference Publication in Literature). LC 93-7883. ISBN 0-8161-8968-4.

"Compendium of historical and critical information" for 61 collected and uncollected short stories, providing critical surveys, publication histories, and original interpretations. Discussions of each story conclude with selected bibliographies. Includes an index of Anderson's works and a general index of proper names and selected subjects. Useful for updating critical coverage of short fiction in White's *Sherwood Anderson* (entry 31).

Journals
33. **The Winesburg Eagle: "The Official Publication of the Sherwood Anderson Society."** Blacksburg, VA: Sherwood Anderson Society, 1975- . 2/yr. ISSN 0147-3166.

Sponsored by the Sherwood Anderson Society, *The Winesburg Eagle* largely includes reprinted memoirs and reminiscences (with photographs) related to Anderson, his family, and his circle. Among the recently published two to four biographical and critical studies per issue are Ray Lewis White's "Anderson's Will and Estate," 21 (Summer 1996): 3-5, which transcribes Anderson's will and other probate documents; and Walter B. Rideout's "Dark Laughter Revisited," 20 (Winter 1995): 1-4, originally presented at the 1991 Sherwood Anderson Conference. In addition to information about upcoming conferences, brief announcements, and reviews of new publications, the journal annually publishes "A Sherwood Anderson Checklist," now compiled by Margaret Kulis, which identifies editions and critical books, articles, and dissertations about Anderson. *Winesburg Eagle* is indexed in *MHRA* and *MLA*.

Patterson's *Author Newsletters and Journals*, pp. 2-3, describes other previously published journals for Anderson.

Andreas, late 9th century
Bibliographies
Greenfield and Robinson's *A Bibliography of Publications on Old English Literature to the End of 1972*, pp. 112-16, lists editions, translations, and studies of *Andreas*, with citations for reviews.

Lancelot Andrewes, 1555-1626
Bibliographies
For a bibliography of works by and about Andrewes, see *NCBEL*, I, pp. 1,918-22. Andrewes' manuscripts are described in *Index of English Literary Manuscripts*, I, pt. 1:3-11, 565.

Anglo-Saxon Chronicle, c. 1154
Bibliographies
Greenfield and Robinson's *A Bibliography of Publications on Old English Literature to the End of 1972*, pp. 346-53, lists editions, translations, and studies of the *Anglo-Saxon Chronicle*, with citations for reviews.

F. Anstey (Thomas Anstey Guthrie), 1865-1934
Bibliographies
34. John Turner, Martin. **A Bibliography of the Works of F. Anstey [Thomas Anstey Guthrie].** London: Privately printed, 1931. 44p. LC 33-2489.

Title-page transcriptions, collations and paginations, binding descriptions, and contents (with information for first appearances) for Anstey's "Editiones Principes, Etc." (33 book-length works and variants), adaptations, contributions to books, and contributions to periodicals other than *Punch*. Also for a bibliography of works by and about Anstey, see *NCBEL*, III, pp. 1,034, 1,097.

Mary Antin (Grabau), 1881-1949
Bibliographies
For works by Antin, see *First Printings of American Authors*, vol. 5, pp. 27-28. Antin's manuscripts are listed in Robbins' *American Literary Manuscripts*, p. 14. Kirsten Wasson reviews works by and about Antin in Shapiro's *Jewish American Women Writers*, pp. 15-21.

John Arbuthnot, 1667-1735
Bibliographies

For a bibliography of works by and about Arbuthnot, see *NCBEL*, II, pp. 1,050-54. Arbuthnot's manuscripts are described in *Index of English Literary Manuscripts*, pt. 1:17-20. Patricia Koster facsimiles the sale catalog of Arbuthnot's library in *Arbuthnotiana: The Story of the St. Alb-n's Ghost (1712); A Catalogue of Dr. Arbuthnot's Library (1779)*, Augustan Reprint Society Publication, no. 154 (Los Angeles: William Andrews Clark Memorial Library, University of California, 1972), with an introduction that points out that much can be discovered about Arbuthnot's "intellectual method" (p. vii) by examining the books that he owned.

John Arden, 1930-
Bibliographies

King's *Twenty Modern British Playwrights*, pp. 1-26, lists works by Arden and describes works about him.

John Armstrong, 1709-1779
Bibliographies

35. Williams, Iolo Aneurin. **Seven XVIIIth Century Bibliographies**. London: Dulau, 1924. 244p. LC 24-8573.

Williams gives full bibliographic descriptions (title-page transcriptions, physical descriptions, and publishing histories) for the first editions of the works of John Armstrong (pp. [15]-38), William Shenstone, Mark Akenside, William Collins, Oliver Goldsmith, Charles Churchill, and Richard Brinsley Sheridan. Contributions to books and periodicals are not covered. Indexed. Also for a bibliography of works by and about Armstrong, see *NCBEL*, II, pp. 534-35.

Martin Donisthorpe Armstrong, 1882-1974
Bibliographies

For a bibliography of works by and about Armstrong, see *NCBEL*, IV, p. 796.

Matthew Arnold, 1822-1888
Bibliographies

36. Davis, Arthur Kyle, Jr. **Matthew Arnold's Letters: A Descriptive Checklist**. Charlottesville, VA: University Press of Virginia, 1968. 429p. LC 68-14092.

Part 1 chronologically gives detailed descriptions of Arnold's letters from 1832 to 1888, indicating locations of manuscripts as well as printed and microform editions and reproductions of the letters. Part 2 arranges the letters by correspondents. Appendixes serve as indexes, identifying correspondents of multiple letters and libraries and collections owning manuscripts. A third appendix lists bibliographic sources cited in the descriptions. Davis' guide supplements Smart's descriptive bibliography (entry 38).

37. Machann, Clinton. **The Essential Matthew Arnold: An Annotated Bibliography of Major Modern Studies**. New York: G. K. Hall, 1993. 177p. (A Reference Publication in Literature). LC 92-36565. ISBN 0-8161-9087-9.

Arranges descriptive entries for 796 major studies of Arnold published since 1900 in specific topical sections for bibliographies, concordances, and biographical studies; editions; letters; biographies; general studies; sources and formative influences; critical reception, reputation, and influence; poetry (general studies, early poems, poems of 1852, and later poems); prose (general studies, educational writings, literary theory and criticism, religious criticism, and social and political criticism); and special topics related to Arnold, including America, Celtic studies, the classics, his contemporaries, the Continent, gender, history, Romanticism, and science. Except for two dissertations and one French-language book, Machann limits coverage to English-language scholarly books, chapters, and periodical articles. The length of descriptive annotations generally indicates a critical work's importance. Comments on bibliographies and editions are more particularly evaluative. Machann clearly identifies bibliographies that update and correct Smart's standard bibliography (entry 38). Annotations sometimes give bibliographic citations for criticism not otherwise listed in the guide. A comprehensive author, primary title, and subject index (with headings for "language," "style," and "culture") provides excellent access. Machann's guide updates Tollers' *A Bibliography of Matthew Arnold* (entry 39) for major recent criticisms. Research on Arnold is reviewed in essays by Frederic E. Faverty in Faverty's *The Victorian Poets*, pp. 163-226; David J. DeLaura in DeLaura's *Victorian Prose*, pp. 249-320; and James Bertram in Dyson's *English Poetry*, pp. 316-33.

38. Smart, Thomas Burnett. **The Bibliography of Matthew Arnold.** London: J. Davy and Sons, 1892. 90p. LC 9-25005.
　　　The standard although dated guide to Arnold's primary works, Smart's bibliography gives full descriptions of Arnold's prose, verse, and miscellaneous writings, presenting title-page transcriptions, physical details, and information on printing and publishing histories. Available in a reprinted edition (New York: B. Franklin, 1968). In addition to Davis' *Matthew Arnold's Letters* (entry 36), Smart's guide is supplemented by numerous articles—identified in Machann's *The Essential Matthew Arnold* (entry 37)—such as Marion Mainwaring's "Notes Toward a Matthew Arnold Bibliography," *Modern Philology* 49 (1952): 189-94. Tollers' bibliography (entry 39) records some additional items. Also for a bibliography of works by and about Arnold, see *NCBEL*, III, pp. 465-83. Arnold's manuscripts are described in *Index of English Literary Manuscripts*, IV, pt. 1:3-19, 825.

39. Tollers, Vincent L. **A Bibliography of Matthew Arnold, 1932-1970.** University Park, PA: Pennsylvania State University Press, 1974. 172p. LC 70-38635. ISBN 0-271-01113-0.
　　　Largely valuable for criticism not cited in Machann's *The Essential Matthew Arnold* (entry 37), Tollers' bibliography offers about 1,800 unannotated entries in topical sections for editions; general studies; studies of Arnold and the classics, education, religion, and science, among other subjects; and studies of individual works. Entries include references to reviews. In turn, Tollers' guide supplements earlier coverage of Arnold in Ehrsam's *Bibliographies of Twelve Victorian Authors*, pp. [13]-45, which cites international comments, criticism, and reviews for Arnold through the early twentieth century.

Indexes and Concordances
40. Parrish, Stephen Maxfield. **A Concordance to the Poems of Matthew Arnold.** Ithaca, NY: Cornell University Press, 1959. 965p. (The Cornell Concordances). LC 59-4899.
　　　The first published volume in Cornell's important series of concordances. Parrish concords the text of C. B. Tinker and H. F. Lowry's edition of *The Poetical Works of Matthew Arnold* (New York: Oxford University Press, 1950) and variants from other editions. The volume includes frequency lists.

Journals
41. **Nineteenth-Century Prose.** Niwot, CO: University Press of Colorado, 1989-. 2/yr. ISSN 0160-4848.
　　　With vol. 16 (1988/89), *Nineteenth-Century Prose* continues the *Arnold Newsletter* (1973-1975) and *The Arnoldian: A Review of Mid-Victorian Culture* (1975-1988). Issues feature one to six articles and notes focusing on Arnold, other literary figures, such as Leigh Hunt, Walter Pater, James Frazer, Alfred Tennyson, and Thomas Carlyle, and Victorian literature in general. *Nineteenth-Century Prose* also publishes book reviews. Studies of authorship, sources, and biography predominated

in *The Arnoldian*, with the third issue including an annual bibliographic essay. Both *Nineteenth-Century Prose* and *The Arnoldian* are indexed in *MLA*.

Patterson's *Author Newsletters and Journals*, p. 5, describes other previously published journals for Arnold.

Harriette (Simpson) Arnow, 1908-1986
Bibliographies

For works by Arnow, see *First Printings of American Authors*, vol. 2, pp. 21-22. Arnow's manuscripts are listed in Robbins' *American Literary Manuscripts*, p. 15.

T(imothy) S(hay) Arthur, 1809-1885
Bibliographies

See *Bibliography of American Fiction Through 1865*, pp. 43-48, for a checklist of works by and about Arthur. Arthur's contributions to and reviews of Arthur's works in selected periodicals are identified in Wells' *The Literary Index to American Magazines, 1815-1865*, pp. 5-6; and *The Literary Index to American Magazines, 1850-1900*, p. 18. Arthur's manuscripts are listed in Robbins' *American Literary Manuscripts*, p. 15.

Nathan Asch, 1902-1964
Bibliographies

See *Bibliography of American Fiction, 1919-1988*, p. 56, for a checklist of works by and about Asch.

Sholem Asch, 1880-1957
Bibliographies

See *Bibliography of American Fiction, 1919-1988*, pp. 57-58, for a checklist of works by and about Asch. Asch's manuscripts are listed in Robbins' *American Literary Manuscripts*, p. 15.

Roger Ascham, 1515/16-1568
Bibliographies

Modern editions and critical studies of Ascham are identified in the Tannenbaums' *Elizabethan Bibliographies*, vol. 1; and *Elizabethan Bibliographies Supplements*, no. 9. Dees' *Sir Thomas Elyot and Roger Ascham* (entry 458) describes comments and criticism on Ascham from 1576 to 1981. Also for a bibliography of works by and about Ascham, see *NCBEL*, I, pp. 1,822-23. Ascham's manuscripts are described in *Index of English Literary Manuscripts*, I, pt. 1:13-15.

John (Lawrence) Ashbery, 1927-
Bibliographies

42.   Kermani, David K. **John Ashbery: A Comprehensive Bibliography, Including His Art Criticism, and with Selected Notes from Unpublished Materials**. New York: Garland, 1976. 244p. (Garland Reference Library of the Humanities, vol. 14). LC 75-5138. ISBN 0-8240-9997-4.

Kermani gives full bibliographic descriptions of Ashbery's primary works in sections for books, pamphlets, broadsides, and translations by Ashbery; contributions to books; contributions to periodicals and newspapers; books, periodicals, and series edited or including selections by Ashbery; art books, exhibition catalogs, and announcements; Ashbery's art criticism (some 478 entries) in newspapers and journals; translations of Ashbery's works (arranged by works); and miscellaneous materials, such as interviews, biographical statements, and tape and video recordings; artworks, musical settings, performances by Ashbery in plays, artworks with Ashbery as the subject, and other materials. Entries give title-page transcriptions, physical descriptions, and brief publishing histories. Also for works by Ashbery, see *First Printings of American Authors*, vol. 1, pp. 15-19.

Isaac Asimov, 1920-1992

Bibliographies

43.   Green, Scott E. **Isaac Asimov: An Annotated Bibliography of the Asimov Collection at Boston University**. Westport, CT: Greenwood Press, 1995. 146p. (Bibliographies and Indexes in Science Fiction, Fantasy, and Horror, no. 6). LC 95-22752. ISBN 0-313-28896-8.

"Covers Asimov's personal book collection which is located with his papers in the Special Collections Department at Mugar Library of Boston University," including titles by Asimov and books by others that Asimov possessed (p. [xi]). Although not a definitive primary bibliography, by assembling descriptions of Asimov's writings to supplement Miller's checklist (entry 44) Green's guide amounts to a solid foundation for more thorough and systematic assessment of Asimov's canon. Offers brief bibliographic information and other notes for nearly 400 editions of Asimov's different works in sections for novels, short-story collections edited by others, anthologies edited or coedited by Asimov, nonfiction (including essay collections), and poetry. Separate sections cover works by others (novels, anthologies, nonfiction, and poetry), periodicals, and miscellaneous works in Asimov's library. Annotations indicate a work's format and contents, the numbers of copies of particular editions and translations in the Boston collection, and physical descriptions. Title and general indexes.

44.   Miller, Marjorie M. **Isaac Asimov: A Checklist of Works Published in the United States, March 1939-May 1972**. Kent, OH: Kent State University Press, 1972. 98p. (Serif Series: Bibliographies and Checklists, no. 25). LC 72-76948. ISBN 0-87338-126-2.

Miller chronologically lists brief bibliographic information for works by Asimov, integrating descriptions of separate publications and contributions to books and periodicals. Coverage is limited to American publications and British and Canadian editions. In addition, Miller describes some 30 works about Asimov. A succession of checklists updates Miller's guide, including Asimov's "My Second Hundred Books," in *Opus 200* (Boston: Houghton Mifflin, 1979), pp. 325-29; and "My Third Hundred Books," in *Opus 300* (Boston: Houghton Mifflin, 1984), pp. 373-77. Asimov's manuscripts are listed in Robbins' *American Literary Manuscripts*, p. 15. See *Bibliography of American Fiction, 1919-1988*, pp. 59-68, for Stephen H. Goldman's checklist of works by and about Asimov.

Journals

See Patterson's *Author Newsletters and Journals*, p. 357, for previously published journals for Asimov.

Gertrude (Franklin) Atherton, 1857-1948

Bibliographies

See *Bibliography of American Fiction, 1866-1918*, pp. 55-57, for Charlotte S. McClure's checklist of works by and about Atherton. Atherton's manuscripts are listed in Robbins' *American Literary Manuscripts*, p. 15.

William Attaway, 1911-1986

Bibliographies

For works by Attaway, see *First Printings of American Authors*, vol. 2, p. 23. Attaway's manuscripts are listed in Robbins' *American Literary Manuscripts*, p. 15.

Margaret Atwood, 1939-

Bibliographies

45.   Horne, Alan J. **Margaret Atwood: An Annotated Bibliography**. Downsview, ON: ECW Press, 1979-1980. 2 vols. OCLC 8830266.

Covers works (vol. 1: Prose and vol. 2: Poetry) by and about Atwood. The first part of each volume includes brief bibliographic information for first and subsequent editions and translations of Atwood's books; lists of manuscripts; and descriptions of contributions to periodicals, books, and anthologies (short stories, articles, book reviews, published graphic work, and other works). The second part of each volume covers works about Atwood, with annotated entries in sections for critical studies and book reviews. Horne updates both volumes in "Margaret Atwood: A Checklist of Writings by and About Margaret Atwood," in Arnold E. Davidson and Cathy N. Davidson's *The Art of Margaret Atwood: Essays in Criticism* (Toronto: Anansi, 1981), pp. 243-85. Horne's critical coverage is superseded by McCombs and Palmer's *Margaret Atwood* (entry 46).

46.   McCombs, Judith, and Carole L. Palmer. **Margaret Atwood: A Reference Guide**. Boston: G. K. Hall, 1991. 735p. (Reference Guide to Literature). LC 91-11385. ISBN 0-8161-8940-4.

Following a preliminary chronological checklist of Atwood's writings, McCombs and Palmer chronologically arrange descriptively annotated entries for approximately 1,800 works about Atwood published from 1962 through 1988. Comprehensive international coverage includes parts of books, reviews, newspaper articles, dissertations, and non-English-language criticism. An introductory chapter surveys reception and criticism of each work. Separate author and subject indexes, the latter giving detailed topical access.

Journals
47.   **Newsletter of the Margaret Atwood Society**. Oxford, OH: Miami University, 1984- . 2/yr. ISSN 1081-9622.

Since 1986 the journal has included an annual "Current Atwood Checklist," listing works by Atwood as well as criticisms, reviews, and dissertations.

Louis (Stanton) Auchincloss, 1917-
Bibliographies
48.   Bryer, Jackson R. **Louis Auchincloss and His Critics: A Bibliographical Record**. Boston: G. K. Hall, 1977. 261p. (Reference Guides in Literature). LC 76-25421. ISBN 0-8161-7965-4.

"A bibliography is like the Day of Judgment," remarks Auchincloss in the Preface (p. ix). In the case of Bryer's checklist of works by and about Auchincloss, the date is postponed: Bryer's bibliography is at best a preliminary checklist of primary and secondary materials, with sections covering first American and English editions of Auchincloss' books (211 entries), with references to subsequent hardcover English-language editions and translations into other languages; contributions to books; and contributions to periodicals and newspapers (subarranged for fiction, essays, theater reviews, book reviews, and miscellaneous writings, such as letters to the editor). Bibliographic descriptions of separate publications typically note contents but lack collations. Separate listings identify critical works, including briefly annotated entries for seven books and 103 articles and for reviews of Auchincloss' works. Cumulative critic and subject index affords good access, containing headings for Auchincloss' works as well as for the names of other writers, such as Edith Wharton and Nathaniel Hawthorne. Also for works by Auchincloss, see *First Printings of American Authors*, vol. 1, pp. 21-24. Auchincloss' manuscripts are listed in Robbins' *American Literary Manuscripts*, pp. 15-16. See *Bibliography of American Fiction, 1919-1988*, pp. 69-70, for Bryer's recent checklist of works by and about Auchincloss.

W(ystan) H(ugh) Auden, 1907-1973
Bibliographies
49.   Bloomfield, B. C., and Edward Mendelson. **W. H. Auden: A Bibliography, 1924-1969**. 2d ed. Charlottesville, VA: Published for the Bibliographical Society of

the University of Virginia by the University Press of Virginia, 1972. 420p. LC 71-772060. ISBN 0-8139-0395-5.

First published in 1964, Bloomfield and Mendelson's 2nd edition is the definitive listing of Auden's primary bibliography and an exemplary descriptive bibliography. Its comprehensiveness is most impressive, including entries for British and American first editions and variants for 64 books and pamphlets; 115 works edited, translated, or otherwise contributed by Auden; and about 800 contributions to periodicals as well as miscellaneous contributions to theater programs, record sleeves, and the like. Other listings describe interviews; published letters; manuscripts, unpublished and unfinished works located in the University of Texas' Harry Ransom Humanities Research Center and in other collections (pp. 243-51); filmed, radio broadcast, televised, and otherwise recorded versions or productions of Auden's writings; anthologies; musical settings of Auden's poetry; and translations. Descriptions give title-page transcriptions; collations; contents; notes on bindings, paper, printing and publishing histories; and citations for reviews. Also appends a selectively annotated bibliography of critical studies of Auden. Comprehensive index of critics, editors, and primary works concludes the volume. This guide replaces Bloomfield's previous *W. H. Auden: A Bibliography: The Early Years Through 1955* (Charlottesville, VA: University Press of Virginia, 1964) and supersedes Edward Callan's *An Annotated Check List of the Works of W. H. Auden* (Denver, CO: Swallow Press, 1958), and its update, "W. H. Auden: Annotated Checklist II," *Twentieth Century Literature* 16 (January 1970): 27-56. Also significant is Robert A. Wilson's *Auden's Library* (New York: Bob Wilson and the Phoenix Book Shop, 1975). Auden's manuscripts are listed in Robbins' *American Literary Manuscripts*, p. 17. Also for a bibliography of works by and about Auden, see *NCBEL*, IV, pp. 207-20. Jane Seay Haspel surveys and identifies works by and about Auden in Demastes and Kelly's *British Playwrights, 1880-1956*, pp. [15]-24.

50. Gingerich, Martin E. **W. H. Auden: A Reference Guide**. Boston: G. K. Hall, 1977. 145p. (Reference Guides in Literature). LC 77-465. ISBN 0-8161-7889-5.

Including annotated entries for books, articles, dissertations, and reviews in a chronological arrangement from 1931 to 1976, Gingerich provides a useful, selective guide to critical materials about Auden. Gingerich omits criticism published in *The Explicator* and non-English-language studies. Although largely descriptive, annotations also indicate major and standard works. A cumulative index of primary and secondary titles, critics, and subjects, with broad headings (for bibliographies, biographies, and the like), completes the volume. Gingerich's bibliography complements but does not supersede the listings for secondary materials in Bloomfield and Mendelson's definitive Auden bibliography (entry 49).

Dictionaries, Encyclopedias, and Handbooks

51. Fuller, John. **A Reader's Guide to W. H. Auden**. New York: Farrar, Straus & Giroux, 1970. 288p. LC 75-105621.

Fuller offers introductory commentaries on Auden's poetry and plays. References cite the texts of *Collected Shorter Poems* (London: Faber, 1966) and *Collected Longer Poems* (London: Faber, 1968).

Indexes and Concordances

52. Dowling, Dean Edward. **A Concordance to the Poetry of W. H. Auden**. Ph.D. dissertation, New York: Columbia University, 1972. 4 vols. OCLC 8770804.

Concords the texts of *About the House* (London: Faber, 1966), *Academic Graffiti* (London: Faber, 1971), *City Without Walls* (London: Faber, 1969), *Collected Longer Poems* (London: Faber, 1968), *Collected Shorter Poems* (London: Faber, 1966), *Epistle to a Godson* (London: Faber, 1972), and *Homage to Clio* (London: Faber, 1960).

John James Audubon, 1785-1851
Bibliographies

For works by Audubon, see *First Printings of American Authors*, vol. 1, pp. 25-26. Audubon's contributions to selected periodicals and reviews of Audubon's works are identified in Wells' *The Literary Index to American Magazines, 1815-1865*, p. 6; and *The Literary Index to American Magazines, 1850-1900*, p. 19. Audubon's manuscripts are listed in Robbins' *American Literary Manuscripts*, p. 16.

Jane Austen, 1775-1817
Bibliographies

53.　Gilson, David. **A Bibliography of Jane Austen**. New York: Oxford University Press, 1982. 877p. (Soho Bibliographies, vol. 21). LC 82-219960. ISBN 0-19-818173-6.

This is the standard descriptive bibliography of writings by Austen. Originally intended as a revision of Sir Geoffrey Keynes' classic bibliography of Austen's writings, *Jane Austen: A Bibliography* (London: Nonesuch Press, 1929; reprint, New York: B. Franklin, 1968), Gilson's guide gives full bibliographic descriptions of Austen's works in sections for first editions, first American editions, translations, editions published by Richard Bentley, later editions and selections, minor works, letters, dramatizations, and continuations and completions. Entries for books give facsimiles of title pages, collations and detailed physical descriptions, publishing histories, records of sales, and locations of copies examined. Also lists books owned by Austen and miscellaneous works (verses addressed to Austen, imaginary conversations with her, and recorded readings of her works). A section for secondary works chronologically arranges selectively annotated entries for 1,814 critical and biographical studies of Austen from 1813 through 1978. The comprehensive index gives thorough topical access by names, titles, and subjects. Gilson's bibliography has been reprinted with corrections (Oxford: Clarendon Press, 1985). Superseded by Gilson's guide, R. W. Chapman's brief *Jane Austen: A Critical Bibliography* (Oxford: Clarendon Press, 1953; 2d ed., Oxford: Clarendon Press, 1969) essentially distills data from Keynes' bibliography for selected Austen works. Austen's manuscripts are described in *Index of English Literary Manuscripts*, IV, pt. 1:21-31. More specifically, Charles Ryskamp's *Jane Austen: Letters & Manuscripts in the Pierpont Morgan Library* (New York: Pierpont Morgan Library, 1975) provides descriptions of the largest collection of Austen's manuscripts, including literary manuscripts of major and minor works and letters. John Barr and Hilton Kelliher's *Jane Austen, 1775-1817: Catalogue of an Exhibition Held in the King's Library, British Library Reference Division, 9 December 1975 to 29 February 1976* (London: British Museum Publications for the British Library, 1975) also offers useful descriptions of manuscripts. Recently published facsimiles of Austen manuscripts include R. W. Chapman's *The Manuscript Chapters of Persuasion* (London: Athlone Press, 1985); A. Walton Litz's *Jane Austen's Lady Susan* (New York: Garland, 1989); Jo Modert's *Jane Austen's Manuscript Letters in Facsimile: Reproductions of Every Known Extant Letter, Fragment, and Autograph Copy, with an Annotated List of All Known Letters* (Carbondale, IL: Southern Illinois University, 1990); and Teran Lee Sacco's *A Transcription and Analysis of Jane Austen's Last Work, Sanditon* (Lewiston: E. Mellen Press, 1995). Also useful is Laurie Kaplan's *A Guide to the Jane Austen Collection of the Julia Rogers Library, Goucher College* (Baltimore, MD: Goucher College Library, 1993).

54.　Roth, Barry, and Joel Weinsheimer. **An Annotated Bibliography of Jane Austen Studies, 1952-1972**. Charlottesville, VA: Published for the Bibliographical Society of the University of Virginia by the University Press of Virginia, 1973. 272p. LC 73-86212. ISBN 0-8139-0544-3.

Updated by:

54.1. Roth, Barry. **An Annotated Bibliography of Jane Austen Studies, 1973-83.** Charlottesville, VA: Published for the Bibliographical Society of the University of Virginia by the University Press of Virginia, 1985. 359p. LC 84-20814. ISBN 0-8139-1054-4.

54.2. Roth, Barry. **An Annotated Bibliography of Jane Austen Studies, 1984-94.** Athens, OH: Ohio University Press, 1996. 438p. LC 96-17026. ISBN 0-8214-1167-5.

With the publication of the supplement for studies of Austen through 1994, the bibliographies of Roth and Weinsheimer become the most comprehensive guides to criticism of Austen. Roth and Weinsheimer's 1973 volume describes 794 studies of Austen. Roth's 1985 volume includes more than 1,060 additional studies, updating coverage of secondary works in Gilson's bibliography (entry 53). The 1996 volume offers 1,327 entries. Coverage of all three volumes includes books, chapters and parts of books, articles, reviews, dissertations, non-English-language studies, and other "significant mentions" (1996 ed., p. [ix]). Thorough descriptive annotations cite reprintings and reviews. Major studies are systematically analyzed at length. Separate indexes of critics, Austen titles, and detailed subjects offer excellent access in all volumes. Also for a bibliography of works by and about Austen, see *NCBEL*, III, pp. 692-700. B. C. Southam's essay in Dyson's *The English Novel*, pp. 145-63, reviews scholarship on Austen.

Dictionaries, Encyclopedias, and Handbooks
55. Grey, J. David, A. Walton Litz, Brian Southam, and H. Abigail Bok. **The Jane Austen Companion with a Dictionary of Jane Austen's Life and Works.** New York: Macmillan, 1986. 511p. LC 85-18314. ISBN 0-02-545540-0.

Providing a tremendous starting point for all aspects of research on Austen, the companion includes 64 essays by prominent Austen scholars (such as Norman Page, Janet Todd, and David Gilson) who survey subjects ranging from gardens to medicine to servants; summarize the plots of Austen's works; critically comment on events and topics (her reading and family) and scholarship related to Austen's life; and review her critical reputation. In addition, the guide describes Austen's family tree and includes a dictionary of Austen's life and works, identifying characters, places, and allusions. Substantial bibliographic references accompany the essays. Other useful companions to Austen works and studies are Michael Hardwick's *The Osprey Guide to Jane Austen* (Reading, England: Osprey Publishing, 1973); and F. G. Pinion's *Jane Austen Companion: A Critical Survey and Reference Book* (London: Macmillan, 1973).

56. Halperin, John, and Janet Kunert. **Plots and Characters in the Fiction of Jane Austen, the Brontes, and George Eliot.** Hamden, CT: Archon Books, 1976. 282p. (Plots and Characters Series). LC 76-14451. ISBN 0-208-01460-8.

Arranges the plot summaries alphabetically by titles, with lists of characters, of the novels of Jane Austen, George Eliot, and Ann, Elizabeth, and Charlotte Bronte. An index cumulates and locates all characters. Glenda Leeming's *Who's Who in Jane Austen and the Brontes* (New York: Taplinger, 1974) affords additional assistance in identifying Austen's characters. G. L. Apperson's *A Jane Austen Dictionary* (1932; reprint New York: Haskell House, 1968) briefly identifies Austen's works, characters, place names, and other allusions.

Indexes and Concordances
57. DeRose, Peter, and S. W. McGuire. **A Concordance to the Works of Jane Austen.** New York: Garland, 1982. 3 vols. (Garland Reference Library of the Humanities, vol. 357). LC 82-48283. ISBN 0-8240-9245-7.

DeRose and McGuire concord the texts of *Northanger Abbey, Sense and Sensibility, Pride and Prejudice, Emma, Mansfield Park*, and *Persuasion*, as well as the fragments *Lady Susan, The Watsons*, and *Sanditon*, included in R. W. Chapman's edition of *The Novels of Jane Austen*, 3d ed. (London: Oxford University Press, 1932-34) and volume VI of *Minor Works* (London: Oxford University Press, 1954). Appends alphabetical lists of headwords, with frequency counts, stop words, and other words omitted from the concordance. Maggie McKernan's *The Sayings of Jane Austen* (London: Duckworth, 1993) and Cathryn Michon and Pamela Norris' *Jane Austen's Little Advice Book* (New York: HarperCollins Publishers, 1996) both topically arrange (under subjects such as love, marriage, and reading) selected quotations from Jane Austen's works, with McKernan's dictionary citing work, chapter, and line.

Journals

58. **JASNA News**. Villanova, PA: Jane Austen Society of North America, 1985-94. 2/yr. ISSN 0892-8665.

Complementing the scholarly *Persuasions* (entry 59), *JASNA News* featured social information of interest to society members, including announcements of upcoming conferences, calls for papers, queries relevant to research in progress, descriptions of new publications, reviews of current stage and media adaptations of Austen's works, news from regional groups, letters to the editor, and the like. Occasional articles highlighted new discoveries about Austen. *JASNA News* was indexed in *MHRA*.

59. **Persuasions**. Tucson, AZ: Jane Austen Society of North America, 1979- . Annual. ISSN 0821-0314.

Sponsored by the Jane Austen Society of North America and published annually on 16 December, Austen's birthday, *Persuasions* features brief critical articles on all aspects of Austen's life and works. Wicked mothers and madness in Austen's works are typical topics of the six to 12 studies. Occasional bibliographic features include Patricia Latkin's "Looking for Jane in All the Wrong Places: Collecting Books in Gilson's Category J," 15 (1993): 63-68, which updates coverage of modern adaptations in Gilson's *A Bibliography of Jane Austen* (entry 53). Since 15 (1993), Latkin, with Barry Roth in 1995, contribute an annual bibliography, "Jane Austen Works and Studies," which complements Roth's *An Annotated Bibliography of Jane Austen Studies, 1984-94* (entry 54.2). Extensive selections of conference papers (as many as a dozen), information on upcoming conferences, and announcements of research competitions sponsored by the society predominate in most issues. A regular department intended to entertain offers quizzes on Austen's works. *Persuasions* is indexed in *MLA*.

Patterson's *Author Newsletters and Journals*, p. 9, describes other previously published journals for Austen.

Jane Goodwin Austin, 1831-1894
Bibliographies

For works by Austin, see *Bibliography of American Literature*, vol. 1, pp. 103-109. Austin's contributions to and reviews of Austin's works in selected periodicals are identified in Wells' *The Literary Index to American Magazines, 1850-1900*, pp. 20-21. Austin's manuscripts are listed in Robbins' *American Literary Manuscripts*, pp. 16-17. See *Bibliography of American Fiction, 1866-1918*, pp. 57-58, for Jane Atteridge Rose's checklist of works by and about Austin.

Mary (Hunter) Austin, 1868-1934
Bibliographies

60. Gaer, Joseph. **Mary Austin: Bibliography and Biographical Data**. [s. l.: s. n., 1934]. 43 leaves. (California Literary Research: Monograph, no. 2). LC 35-27522.

Gives brief bibliographic information for Austin's works in sections for fiction; plays; poetry; history and travel; sociology and religion; and essays, stories, articles, and poems. Entries identify contents and note reprints. Also lists 14 criticisms of Austin (pp. 33-34). Austin's manuscripts are listed in Robbins'

American Literary Manuscripts, p. 17. See *Bibliography of American Fiction, 1866-1918*, pp. 58-60, for Emily Schiller's checklist of works by and about Austin. T. M. Pearce surveys works by and about Austin in Erisman and Etulain's *Fifty Western Writers*, pp. 21-31.

William Austin, 1778-1841
Bibliographies
> See *Bibliography of American Fiction Through 1865*, p. 49, for a checklist of works by and about Austin. Austin's manuscripts are listed in Robbins' *American Literary Manuscripts*, p. 17.

Alan Ayckbourn, 1939-
Bibliographies
> King's *Twenty Modern British Playwrights*, pp. 27-29, lists works by Ayckbourn and describes works about him.

Irving Bacheller, 1859-1950
Bibliographies
> 61. Hanna, Alfred Jackson. **A Bibliography of the Writings of Irving Bacheller.** Winter Park, FL: Rollins College, 1939. 48p. LC 40-2901.
> Following a brief chronology of Bacheller's life and career, Hanna chronologically arranges entries for Bacheller's collected works; edited and autobiographical works; novels; poems and verses; and essays and miscellaneous contributed articles published from 1880 through 1938. Entries give brief bibliographic data for first editions and subsequent reprintings and serializations, with notes on contents and edition sizes and citations for notices and reviews. Hanna's guide also appeared in *Rollins College Bulletin*, vol. 35, no. 1 (September 1939). Bacheller's manuscripts are listed in Robbins' *American Literary Manuscripts*, p. 17. See *Bibliography of American Fiction, 1866-1918*, pp. 61-62, for Shonda Skillern's checklist of works by and about Bacheller.

Delia Salter Bacon, 1811-1859
Bibliographies
> For works by Bacon, see *Bibliography of American Literature*, vol. 1, pp. 110-12. Bacon's manuscripts are listed in Robbins' *American Literary Manuscripts*, p. 18.

Francis Bacon, 1561-1626
Bibliographies
> 62. Gibson, R. W. **Francis Bacon: A Bibliography of His Works and of Baconiana to the Year 1750.** Oxford: Scrivener Press, 1950. 369p. LC 51-913.
> The standard listing of Bacon's published writings, Gibson gives full bibliographic descriptions for editions of Bacon's works (from 1597), including facsimiles of title pages, collations, and notes on printing and publishing histories as well as for Baconiana (about 400 entries for quotations and selections from his works published in works of others, allusions to Bacon, works dedicated to Bacon, works ascribed to Bacon, portraits of Bacon, and the like). Indexes for libraries, printers and publishers, and a general index provide access. Gibson's guide is supplemented by:

> 62.1. **Francis Bacon: A Bibliography of His Works and Baconiana to the Year 1750: Supplement.** Pasadena, CA: Francis Bacon Foundation, 1959. 20p. OCLC 3740002.
> S. E. Sprott's *A Short-Title Catalogue of the Dalhousie Bacon Collection* (Halifax, Nova Scotia: Dalhousie University Press, 1978) describes the collection that Gibson used as the basis of his bibliography. Other major collections

of Bacon materials are located at Harvard University and the University of Texas' Harry Ransom Humanities Research Center. Also for a bibliography of works by and about Bacon, see *NCBEL*, I, pp. 2,324-25. Bacon's manuscripts are described in *Index of English Literary Manuscripts*, I, pt. 1:17-52, 565. Modern editions and critical materials about Bacon are identified in J. Kemp Houck *Elizabethan Bibliographies Supplements*, no. 15; as well as in William A. Sessions' "Recent Studies in Francis Bacon," *English Literary Renaissance* 17 (Autumn 1987): 351-71.

Indexes and Concordances

63.   Davies, David W., and Elizabeth S. Wrigley. **A Concordance to the Essays of Francis Bacon**. Detroit, MI: Gale, 1973. 392p. LC 73-8947.
  Based on the text of J. Spedding, R. L. Ellis, and D. D. Heath's edition of *The Works of Francis Bacon* (London: Longman, 1857-74) and includes alphabetical and frequency lists.

Journals

  See Patterson's *Author Newsletters and Journals*, pp. 10-11, for previously published journals for Bacon.

George William Bagby, 1828-1883
Bibliographies

  For works by Bagby, see *Bibliography of American Literature*, vol. 1, pp. 113-15. Harold Woodell surveys works by and about Bagby in Bain and Flora's *Fifty Southern Writers Before 1900*, pp. 20-28.

Walter Bagehot, 1826-1877
Bibliographies

  For a bibliography of works by and about Bagehot, see *NCBEL*, III, pp. 1,368-70. Wendell V. Harris reviews research on Bagehot in DeLaura's *Victorian Prose*, pp. 440-42.

Alexander Bain, 1818-1903
Bibliographies

  For a bibliography of works by and about Bain, see *NCBEL*, III, pp. 1,514-16.

Dorothy Baker, 1907-1968
Bibliographies

  For works by Baker, see *First Printings of American Authors*, vol. 2, p. 25. Baker's manuscripts are listed in Robbins' *American Literary Manuscripts*, p. 18.

Elliott Baker, 1922-
Bibliographies

  For works by Baker, see *First Printings of American Authors*, vol. 1, p. 27.

James Baldwin, 1924-1987
Bibliographies

64.   Standley, Fred L., and Nancy V. Standley. **James Baldwin: A Reference Guide**. Boston: G. K. Hall, 1980. 310p. (Reference Publication in Literature). LC 79-19992. ISBN 0-8161-7844-5.
  Covers works by and about Baldwin. Includes a checklist of Baldwin's primary works (novels, dramas, essays, short stories, dialogues, scenarios, reviews, letters, excerpts of stories, interviews, recordings, and films) and chronologically arranged, annotated entries for about 1,300 secondary books, periodical and newspaper articles and reviews, dissertations, and non-English-language studies published from 1946 through 1978. Although largely descriptive, annotations describe important works in detail. Index headings for a full range of topics

("aesthetics," "black experience," "homosexuality," "manuscripts," "plot and struc-
ture," among others), Baldwin's works, and names in annotations offer good access.
For works by Baldwin, see *First Printings of American Authors*, vol. 5, pp. 29-33.
Baldwin's manuscripts are listed in Robbins' *American Literary Manuscripts*, p. 19. See
Bibliography of American Fiction, 1919-1988, pp. 71-75, for Fred L. Standley's checklist
of works by and about Baldwin. Research on Baldwin is reviewed by Daryl Dance in
Inge, Duke, and Bryer's *Black American Writers*, vol. 2, pp. 73-120; and by James F.
Smith in *Contemporary Authors: Bibliographical Series: Volume 1: American Novelists*,
pp. 3-41.

Joseph Glover Baldwin, 1815-1864
Bibliographies
        For works by Baldwin, see *Bibliography of American Literature*, vol. 1, pp.
116-17. Baldwin's contributions to selected periodicals and reviews of Baldwin's
works are identified in Wells' *The Literary Index to American Magazines, 1815-1865*,
p. 7; and *The Literary Index to American Magazines, 1850-1900*, p. 21. Baldwin's
manuscripts are listed in Robbins' *American Literary Manuscripts*, p. 19. *Bibliography of American Fiction Through 1865*, pp. 50-51, gives a checklist of works by and
about Baldwin. Merritt W. Moseley Jr. surveys works by and about Baldwin in
Bain and Flora's *Fifty Southern Writers Before 1900*, pp. 29-37.

John Bale, 1495-1563
Bibliographies
        For a bibliography of works by and about Bale, see *NCBEL*, I, pp. 1,403-405.
Bale's manuscripts are described in *Index of English Literary Manuscripts*, I, pt.
1:53-61.

Ballads, Middle English
Bibliographies
        David C. Fowler offers a comprehensive guide to primary materials for
Middle English ballads with a bibliography of editions and criticism in Severs and
Hartung's *A Manual of Writings in Middle English*, vol. XV, pp. 1753-1808, 2019-70.
NCBEL, 1, pp. 711-20, also lists editions and studies.

R(obert) M(ichael) Ballantyne, 1825-1894
Bibliographies
        65.   Quayle, Eric. **R. M. Ballantyne: A Bibliography of First Editions**. London:
Dawsons, 1968. 128p. LC 68-111673. ISBN 0-7129-0220-1.
        Thorough, but not full, bibliographic descriptions of Ballantyne's works are
chronologically arranged in sections for his 92 books; "Ballantyne's Miscellany,"
a numbered series; selected contributions to periodicals; and manuscripts. Entries
for books give title-page transcriptions, collations, descriptions of bindings, and
details about variants but do not offer information about contents, publication
histories, or copy locations. Index of names and titles. Also for a bibliography of
works by and about Ballantyne, see *NCBEL*, III, pp. 1,092-93.

J(ames) G(raham) Ballard, 1930-
Bibliographies
        66.   Pringle, David. **J. G. Ballard: A Primary and Secondary Bibliography**.
Boston: G. K. Hall, 1984. 156p. (Masters of Science Fiction and Fantasy). LC
83-18528. ISBN 0-8161-8603-0.
        A transcription of an interview with Ballard precedes brief bibliographic
information for Ballard's fiction in books, collections, and journals from 1951
through 1982 (some 150 entries, with summaries of contents); miscellaneous prose
and poetry; and nonfiction (reviews, articles, and interviews). In addition, Pringle
briefly describes some 167 works about Ballard from 1956 through 1982. An

appendix lists non-English-language editions of Ballard's works. See Stephen W. Pott's summary biography, critical assessment of major works, and selected primary and secondary bibliography for Ballard in McCaffery's *Postmodern Fiction: A Bio-Bibliographical Guide*, pp. 255-57.

George Bancroft, 1800-1891
Bibliographies

For works by Bancroft, see *Bibliography of American Literature*, vol. 1, pp. 118-38. Bancroft's contributions to and reviews of Bancroft's works in selected periodicals are identified in Wells' *The Literary Index to American Magazines, 1815-1865*, pp. 7-8; and *The Literary Index to American Magazines, 1850-1900*, p. 24. Bancroft's manuscripts are listed in Robbins' *American Literary Manuscripts*, pp. 19-20.

John Kendrick Bangs, 1862-1922
Bibliographies

For works by Bangs, see *Bibliography of American Literature*, vol. 1, pp. 139-61. Bangs' contributions to and reviews of Bangs' works in selected periodicals are identified in Wells' *The Literary Index to American Magazines, 1850-1900*, pp. 24-25. Bangs' manuscripts are listed in Robbins' *American Literary Manuscripts*, pp. 20-21. See *Bibliography of American Fiction, 1866-1918*, pp. 62-64, for Arthur J. Leo's checklist of works by and about Bangs.

Benjamin Banneker, 1731-1806
Bibliographies

Banneker's manuscripts are listed in Robbins' *American Literary Manuscripts*, p. 21. See the review of research by Jerome Klinkowitz in Inge, Duke, and Bryer's *Black American Writers*, vol. I, pp. 1-20.

Anna Laetitia (Aikin) Barbauld, 1743-1824
Bibliographies

For a bibliography of works by and about Barbauld, see *NCBEL*, II, pp. 639-40.

Alexander Barclay, 1475?-1552
Bibliographies

For a bibliography of works by and about Barclay, see *NCBEL*, I, pp. 1,019-20. Barclay's manuscripts are described in *Index of English Literary Manuscripts*, I, pt. 1:63-64.

James Nelson Barker, 1784-1858
Bibliographies

For works by Barker, see *Bibliography of American Literature*, vol. 1, pp. 162-68. Barker's manuscripts are listed in Robbins' *American Literary Manuscripts*, p. 21.

Joel Barlow, 1754-1812
Bibliographies

For works by Barlow, see *Bibliography of American Literature*, vol. 1, pp. 169-84. Barlow's contributions to and reviews of Barlow's works in selected periodicals are identified in Wells' *The Literary Index to American Magazines, 1815-1865*, p. 8; and *The Literary Index to American Magazines, 1850-1900*, pp. 25-26. Barlow's manuscripts are listed in Robbins' *American Literary Manuscripts*, p. 21.

Djuna (Chappell) Barnes, 1892-1982
Bibliographies

67. Messerli, Douglas. **Djuna Barnes: A Bibliography**. New York: David Lewis, 1976. 131p. LC 75-43407.

Covers works by and about Barnes. Messerli gives full bibliographic descriptions for Barnes' primary works, providing some 286 entries for books; contributions to books; and contributed poetry, fiction, drama, and nonfiction to journals and newspapers. Entries present title-page transcriptions (with selected facsimiles), physical descriptions, contents, printing histories, and references to subsequent editions and printings. Messerli also supplies briefly descriptive entries for about 650 books, articles, book reviews (arranged by works), production reviews, non-English-language criticisms (including reviews), and Master's theses and dissertations about Barnes. Also for works by Barnes, see *First Printings of American Authors*, vol. 1, pp. 29-30. Barnes' manuscripts are listed in Robbins' *American Literary Manuscripts*, p. 22. See *Bibliography of American Fiction 1919-1988*, pp. 75-77, for James B. Scott's checklist of works by and about Barnes. Research on Barnes is reviewed by Barbara J. Griffin in Duke, Bryer, and Inge's *American Women Writers*, pp. 135-66.

Peter Barnes, 1931-
Bibliographies

King's *Twenty Modern British Playwrights*, pp. 31-33, lists works by Barnes and describes works about him.

William Barnes, 1801-1886
Bibliographies

For a bibliography of works by and about Barnes, see *NCBEL*, III, pp. 505-507.

Richard Barnfield, 1574-1627
Bibliographies

For a bibliography of works by and about Barnfield, see *NCBEL*, I, pp. 1085-86. Barnfield's manuscripts are described in *Index of English Literary Manuscripts*, I, pt. 1:65-66, 565.

Sir J(ames) M(atthew) Barrie, 1860-1937
Bibliographies

68. Cutler, B. D. **Sir James M. Barrie: A Bibliography, with Full Collations of the American Unauthorized Editions.** New York: Greenberg, 1931. 242p. LC 31-10629.

Regarded as the standard bibliography of Barrie's works, Cutler gives full bibliographic descriptions in chronologically arranged sections for first English and American editions and variants; collected editions; and prefaces and introductions by Barrie, with a list of books about Barrie. Entries for 94 books published from 1888 to 1930 supply title-page transcriptions, collations, binding and other physical descriptions, information about previous appearances and variants, and notes on publication history. A final chapter offers data on prices of editions. Name and title index. Available in a reprinted edition (New York: Burt Franklin, 1968). Although providing less bibliographic detail for editions, Herbert Garland's *A Bibliography of the Writings of Sir James Matthew Barrie, Bart., O.M.* (London: The Bookman's Journal, 1928) supplements Cutler with a listing of Barrie's contributions to periodicals.

69. Markgraf, Carl. **J. M. Barrie: An Annotated Secondary Bibliography.** Greensboro, NC: ELT Press, 1989. 439p. (1880-1920 British Authors series, no. 4). LC 89-84405. ISBN 0-944318-03-7.

Intends "to cite all published references to the life and works of Barrie"—without being "so foolish as to guarantee it"—and "to annotate those references so as to indicate their content" (p. xv). Annotated entries for 5,550 works about Barrie in sections for general criticism and biography and criticism of individual works, arranged alphabetically by work. Covers books, chapters, scholarly articles, features in newspapers, book and performance reviews, and some non-English-language criticism. Annotations are descriptive. Also includes a checklist of Barrie's writings, and stage productions and media adaptations of his works. Indexes of Barrie's works, secondary titles, and names. For a bibliography of works by and about Barrie, see *NCBEL*, III, pp. 1,188-92. Valerie C. Rudolph surveys and identifies works by and about Barrie in Demastes and Kelly's *British Playwrights, 1880-1956*, pp. [25]-36.

John (Simmons) Barth, 1930-

Bibliographies

70. Weixlmann, Joseph. **John Barth: A Descriptive Primary and Annotated Secondary Bibliography, Including a Descriptive Catalog of Manuscript Holdings in United States Libraries**. New York: Garland, 1976. 214p. (Reference Library of the Humanities, vol. 25). LC 76-24076. ISBN 0-8240-9987-7.

The most authoritative and comprehensive descriptive bibliography of Barth's writings to date, Weixlmann gives detailed entries for Barth's novels, contributions to books, contributed fiction and nonfiction to journals and newspapers, and reprinted editions of works, as well as interviews and recordings. Entries contain title-page transcriptions, collations, notes on publishing history, and references to translations. Additionally, Weixlmann locates Barth's manuscripts in collections of the Library of Congress and of Penn State, Johns Hopkins, and Washington universities (pp. 41-63). Concluding sections include annotated entries for 112 biographical and 342 critical studies, 216 reviews (unannotated), and other secondary works, including bibliographies. A separate subject index offers headings for such topics as "black humor," "Pocohontas," and "science fiction." Weixlmann's bibliography is preferable to Richard Allan Vine's *John Barth: An Annotated Bibliography* (Metuchen, NJ: Scarecrow Press, 1977), which includes 377 entries for writings by and about Barth; and also the coverage of Barth in Thomas P. Walsh and Cameron Northouse's *John Barth, Jerzy Kosinski, and Thomas Pynchon* (entry 796), which lists works by and about Barth through 1973. Also for works by Barth, see *First Printings of American Authors*, vol. 2, pp. 27-28. Barth's manuscripts are listed in Robbins' *American Literary Manuscripts*, p. 23. See *Bibliography of American Fiction, 1919-1988*, pp. 77-81, for Weixlmann's recent checklist of works by and about Barth. Research on Barth is reviewed by Weixlmann in *Contemporary Authors: Bibliographical Series: Volume 1: American Novelists*, pp. 43-81; and Charles B. Harris in Flora and Bain's *Fifty Southern Writers After 1900*, pp. 33-42.

Donald Barthelme, 1931-1989

Bibliographies

71. Klinkowitz, Jerome, Asa Pieratt, and Robert Murray Davis. **Donald Barthelme: A Comprehensive and Annotated Secondary Checklist**. Hamden, CT: Archon Books, 1977. 128p. LC 77-12966. ISBN 0-208-01712-7.

More a primary than secondary bibliography. Provides entries for Barthelme's books, short fiction, essays, dramatic adaptations, and early writings from 1948 through 1956 (some 430 entries) as well as interviews with him and recordings of his works. Entries include title-page transcriptions, collations, physical descriptions, contents, and brief publishing histories. Separate lists of about 150 works about Barthelme (bibliographies, critical studies, and reviews). Also for works by Barthelme, see *First Printings of American Authors*, vol. 2, pp. 29-30. Maurice Couturier offers a summary biography, critical assessment of major works, and selected primary and secondary bibliography for Barthelme in McCaffery's *Postmodern Fiction: A Bio-Bibliographical Guide*, pp. 260-63.

Cyrus Augustus Bartol, 1813-1900

Bibliographies

Bartol's contributions to and reviews of Bartol's works in selected periodicals are identified in Wells' *The Literary Index to American Magazines, 1850-1900*, p. 28. William G. Heath reviews research on Bartol in Myerson's *The Transcendentalists*, pp. 97-99.

John Bartram, 1699-1777

Bibliographies

72. Cutting, Rose Marie. **John and William Bartram, William Byrd II, and St. John de Crevecoeur: A Reference Guide**. Boston: G. K. Hall, 1976. 174p. (Reference Guides in Literature, no. 12). LC 76-2501. ISBN 0-8161-1176-6.

Comprehensive coverage of works about these writers, identifying early notices as well as books, articles, dissertations, entries in reference works, and other passing references through 1974. Coverage for John Bartram extends from 1715; for William Bartram, from 1792; for Byrd, from 1817; and for Crevecoeur, from 1782, comprising about 150 items for each writer. Annotations are descriptive. A single index includes broad topical headings (for bibliographies, biographies, and the like) under each writer's name. Bartram's manuscripts are listed in Robbins' *American Literary Manuscripts*, p. 23.

William Bartram, 1739-1823

Bibliographies

For works by Bartram, see *First Printings of American Authors*, vol. 4, p. 31; and *NCBEL*, II, pp. 1,464, 1,473. Bartram's manuscripts are listed in Robbins' *American Literary Manuscripts*, p. 23. See Cutting's *John and William Bartram, William Byrd II, and St. John de Crevecoeur: A Reference Guide* (entry 72) for works about Bartram from 1792 to 1974.

(Joseph) Hamilton Basso, 1904-1964

Bibliographies

For works by Basso, see *First Printings of American Authors*, vol. 2, pp. 31-32. Basso's manuscripts are listed in Robbins' *American Literary Manuscripts*, p. 24. Joseph R. Millichap surveys works by and about Basso in Flora and Bain's *Fifty Southern Writers After 1900*, pp. 43-52.

H(erbert) E(rnest) Bates, 1905-1974

Bibliographies

73. Eads, Peter. **H. E. Bates: A Bibliographical Study**. Winchester: St. Paul's Bibliographies, 1990. 224p. (St. Paul's Bibliographies; St. Paul's 20th Century Writers series, no. 6). LC 89-43504. ISBN 0-906795-76-1.

Eads presents detailed descriptions of British and American first editions of Bates' books, plays, and pamphlets (126 entries); short stories and novellas; essays, articles, commentaries (including broadcasts), and introductions; and poems and Christmas cards. Entries for books give title-page transcriptions, collations, binding descriptions, and publication notes. Coverage extends from 1921 through 1989 and includes both published and unpublished materials but excludes Bates' reviews published in *Everyman, New Clarion, Morning Post*, and *John O'London's Weekly* from 1932 through 1940. Indexing is limited to titles. Also for a bibliography of works by and about Bates, see *NCBEL*, IV, pp. 520-21.

Ralph Bates, 1899-

Bibliographies

Munton and Young's *Seven Writers of the English Left*, pp. 83-115, describes Bates' publications from 1925 through 1966. For a bibliography of works by and about Bates, see *NCBEL*, IV, pp. 521-22.

L(yman) Frank Baum, 1856-1919
Bibliographies

74. Greene, Douglas G., and Peter E. Hanff. **Bibliographia Oziana: A Concise Bibliographical Checklist of the Oz Books by L. Frank Baum and His Successors.** Revised and enlarged ed. Kinderhook, IL: International Wizard of Oz Club, 1988. 146p. LC 89-190091.

Aimed at collectors, the revision of Hanff and Greene's *Bibliographia Oziana* (Kinderhook, IL: International Wizard of Oz Club, 1976) gives chronologically arranged descriptions of the Oz books by Baum, Ruth Plumly Thompson, John R. Neill, Jack Snow, and others. Bibliographic descriptions emphasize variants and textual points that distinguish editions, printings, and states. The 1988 edition adds new materials and reinterprets designations of states and editions, specifically for *The (Marvelous) Land of Oz* (Reilly & Britton), which Greene and Hanff now determine to all be part of one edition. Unindexed.

Baum's manuscripts are listed in Robbins' *American Literary Manuscripts*, p. 24. See *Bibliography of American Fiction, 1866-1918*, pp. 64-68, for Sarah Zavelle Marwil Lamstein's checklist of works by and about Baum.

Dictionaries, Encyclopedias, and Handbooks

75. Snow, Jack. **Who's Who in Oz.** New York: Peter Bedrick Books, 1988. 277p. LC 88-14822. ISBN 0-87226-188-3.

A juvenile title with better reference features than many similar writers' handbooks that are not intended to be read for fun. First published in 1954, Snow's companion (written in collaboration with "Professor H. M. Wogglebug, T. E., Dean of the Royal College of Oz") gives "informal introductions to over six hundred and thirty Oz Characters—people, animals, and creatures—with hints on the parts they play in the thirty-nine Oz books" (p. ix). Entries for the likes of Dorothy, Toto, and the two Wicked Witches give specific page references for their first appearances in *The Wizard of Oz*. Appends plot summaries of the 39 Oz books published from 1900 to 1951, with information on variant titles, editions, and collaborative authorship and biographies of Baum and the seven other authors and illustrators of the Oz books, including John R. Neill and Ruth Plumly Thompson. Maps of the Land of Oz on the binding's pastedowns and flyleaves. Unindexed.

Journals

76. **The Baum Bugle.** New York: International Wizard of Oz Club, 1957- . 3/yr. ISSN 0005-6677.

Contributions, generally bibliographic in nature and typically titled "Bibliographia Baumiana," treat the printing and publication history of Baum's works as well as his works as collectibles. Other articles have discussed Baum's sources, translations of Baum's works, and their media adaptations. The journal also publishes book reviews. *The Baum Bugle* is selectively indexed in *MLA* to 1990. Also available is Frederick E. Otto's *An Index to the Baum Bugle: The Journal of the International Wizard of Oz Club, Volumes 1-28, 1957-1984* (Kinderhook, IL: International Wizard of Oz Club, 1986).

Richard Baxter, 1615-1691
Bibliographies

For a bibliography of works by and about Baxter, see *NCBEL*, I, pp. 1,971-73. Roger Thomas' *The Baxter Treatises: A Catalogue of the Richard Baxter Papers (Other Than the Letters) in Dr. Williams's Library* (London: Dr. Williams's Trust, 1959), *Dr. Williams's Library Occasional Paper*, no. 8, chronologically organizes Baxter's papers from 1638 to 1691 and keys them to books in *Reliquae Baxterianae* and other Baxter publications, with a name index.

Rex (Ellingwood) Beach, 1877-1949
Bibliographies

See *Bibliography of American Fiction, 1866-1918*, pp. 68-69, for Gwen L. Nagel's checklist of works by and about Beach. Beach's manuscripts are listed in Robbins' *American Literary Manuscripts*, pp. 24-25.

Peter S(oyer) Beagle, 1939-
Bibliographies

For works by Beagle, see *First Printings of American Authors*, vol. 2, p. 33.

Aubrey Vincent Beardsley, 1872-1898
Bibliographies

77.   Gallatin, A. E. **Aubrey Beardsley: Catalogue of Drawings and Bibliography**. 1945; reprint Mamaroneck, NY: P. P. Appel, 1980. 141p. LC 80-22369. ISBN 0-911858-39-3.

First published by the Grolier Club of New York in 1945, Gallatin covers Beardsley's art and literary works and criticism of Beardsley in separate chapters. Full bibliographic descriptions of albums of drawings by Beardsley, other illustrated collections containing Beardsley's artworks, and Beardsley's literary works and collections of letters give title-page transcriptions, physical descriptions, and contents. Other chapters include a catalog of Beardsley's drawings, an unannotated list of studies on Beardsley in books and periodicals, and descriptions of catalogs of Beardsley exhibitions. Appendixes provide descriptions of collections at Harvard and elsewhere. Unindexed. For a bibliography of works by and about Beardsley, see *NCBEL*, III, pp. 610-11. Reviews of Beardsley's works in selected periodicals are identified in Wells' *The Literary Index to American Magazines, 1850-1900*, pp. 29-30.

Charles Beaumont, 1929-1967
Bibliographies

78.   Nolan, William F. **The Work of Charles Beaumont: An Annotated Bibliography & Guide**. 2d ed., revised and expanded. San Bernardino, CA: Borgo Press, 1990. 92p. (Bibliographies of Modern Authors, no. 6). LC 90-15043.

Builds on Nolan's *The Work of Charles Beaumont: An Annotated Bibliography & Guide* (San Bernardino, CA: Borgo Press, 1986), describing works by and about Beaumont in sections for books, short fiction, nonfiction, screenplays (both produced and unproduced), teleplays, and other miscellaneous materials, such as comics, letters, and unpublished stories. Gives data for contents and successive editions, with citations for reviews and criticisms. Section M lists 71 briefly annotated entries for reviews, entries in reference works, introductions mentioning Beaumont, and other secondary materials. Includes chronology of Beaumont's life and career and a list of biographies. Title index.

Francis Beaumont, 1584-1616, and John Fletcher, 1579-1625
Bibliographies

For a bibliography of works by and about Beaumont and Fletcher, see *NCBEL*, I, pp. 1,709-19. Beaumont and Fletcher's manuscripts are described in *Index of English Literary Manuscripts*, I, pt. 1:67-100, 565; and pt. 2:79-81. For modern editions and criticism of Beaumont and Fletcher, see the Tannenbaums' *Elizabethan Bibliographies*, vol. 1; and Charles A. Pennel and William P. Williams' *Elizabethan Bibliographies Supplements*, no. 8. Research on Beaumont and Fletcher is reviewed by Denzell S. Smith in Logan and Smith's *The Later Jacobean and Caroline Dramatists*, pp. 3-89; and by Michael Taylor in Wells' *English Drama*, pp. 100-12.

Samuel Barclay Beckett, 1906-1989
Bibliographies

79. Andonian, Cathleen Culotta. **Samuel Beckett: A Reference Guide**. Boston: G. K. Hall, 1989. 754p. (Reference Guide to Literature). LC 88-24501. ISBN 0-8161-8570-0.

The most comprehensive bibliography of Beckett studies in English. Chronologically arranges descriptively annotated entries for more than 3,500 critical works on Beckett's life and writings published from 1931 through 1984 in several separate listings, with the bulk (about 2,500 brief entries for scholarly studies) at the core of the guide. Slighter appendixes contain brief studies and notes, reviews, and parts of books; works that "briefly mention" Beckett; and periodicals and newspapers in which critical works have appeared. Unfortunately, Andonian excludes dissertations and theses. Critic and subject indexes offer broadly descriptive subject headings but fail to reference specific topics, themes, characters, and the like. Also for a bibliography of works by and about Beckett, see *NCBEL*, IV, pp. 885-906. Rolf Breuer, Harald Gundel, and Werner Huber's *Beckett Criticism in German: A Bibliography. Deutsche Beckett-Kritik: Eine Bibliographie* (Munchen: Wilhelm Fink Verlag, 1986) is a useful checklist of additional works on Beckett, including unannotated entries for 436 studies published from 1953 through 1984.

80. Federman, Raymond, and John Fletcher. **Samuel Beckett, His Works and His Critics: An Essay in Bibliography**. Berkeley, CA: University of California Press, 1970. 383p. LC 68-23782. ISBN 0-520-01475-8.

Federman and Fletcher offer essential coverage of Beckett's primary works, supplying full bibliographic descriptions of Beckett's published works in English and French and works translated into French and English; translations, manifestos, and miscellaneous writings (contributions, interviews, and the like); and known unpublished works. Entries give title-page transcriptions, collations, and references to reprintings. In addition, Federman and Fletcher describe critical studies, including dissertations and theses, through 1966. An appendix (pp. 323-24) briefly describes primary materials and manuscripts in special collections at Ohio State University and the University of Texas' Harry Ransom Humanities Research Center. Coverage of Beckett's published works is supplemented by R. J. Davis, J. R. Bryer, M. J. Friedman, and P. C. Hoy's *Samuel Beckett, 1 (2)* (Paris: Lettres Modernes, 1972), *Calepins de Bibliographie*, no. 2, which gives full bibliographic descriptions of Beckett's works from 1929 to 1966 and lists international criticism of Beckett to 1970; and Davis' *Samuel Beckett: A Checklist and Index of His Published Works, 1967-1976* (Stirling: The Compiler, 1979). Other useful descriptions of Beckett's primary materials are included in Carlton Lake, Linda Eichhorn, and Sally Leach's *No Symbols Where None Intended: A Catalogue of Books, Manuscripts, and Other Material Relating to Samuel Beckett in the Collections of the Humanities Research Center* (Austin, TX: Humanities Research Center, 1984); Sharon Bangert's *The Samuel Beckett Collection at Washington University Libraries: A Guide* (St. Louis, MO: Washington University Libraries, 1986); and the University of Reading's *The Samuel Beckett Collection: A Catalogue* (Reading, England: The Library, 1978). Richard L. Admussen's *The Samuel Beckett Manuscripts: A Study* (Boston: G. K. Hall, 1979) contains the most complete coverage of Beckett's manuscripts, reviewing collections at Washington University, Dartmouth College, Ohio State University, the University of Reading, and the University of Texas.

81. Murphy, P. J., Werner Huber, Rolf Breuer, and Konrad Schoell. **Critique of Beckett Criticism: A Guide to Research in English, French, and German**. Columbia, SC: Camden House, 1994. 173p. LC 94-595. ISBN 1-879751-93-3.

Offers excellent guidance to international scholarship on Beckett to 1994. Authoritative chapters survey research in English, French, and German, identifying the major bibliographies and other reference resources, editions, biographies, periodicals, collections of criticism, and studies of Beckett's works (by genre).

Appends chronology of Beckett's works and chronologically arranged bibliography of criticism (1951-94). Thoroughly indexed. Serves as a companion and supplement to Andonian's guide (entry 79). Additionally, Tjebbe Westendorp surveys works by and about Beckett in Schrank and Demastes' *Irish Playwrights, 1880-1995: A Research and Production Sourcebook*, pp. 3-22.

Dictionaries, Encyclopedias, and Handbooks

82.   Kenner, Hugh. **A Reader's Guide to Samuel Beckett**. London: Thames and Hudson, 1973. 208p. LC 73-174512. ISBN 0-5001-4018-9.

Kenner offers close, interpretive readings of Beckett's works. Beryl S. Fletcher's *A Student's Guide to the Plays of Samuel Beckett* (London: Faber and Faber, 1978) is useful for page-by-page explications of the text of Beckett's plays, analyses of stage histories, and appraisals of his international critical reception. Alan Astro's *Understanding Samuel Beckett* (Columbia, SC: University of South Carolina Press, 1990), contains introductory commentaries on Beckett's major and minor literary and theatrical works, with annotated bibliographies of criticism (pp. 209-16). Although more a collection of 13 original critical essays by authorities than a reference handbook, John Pilling's *The Cambridge Companion to Beckett* (Cambridge: Cambridge University Press, 1994) also includes a Beckett chronology with a selected bibliography of further readings.

Indexes and Concordances

83.   Barale, Michele Aina, and Rubin Rabinovitz. **A KWIC Concordance to Samuel Beckett's Trilogy: Molloy, Malone Dies, and The Unnamable**. New York: Garland, 1988. 2 vols. (Contextual Concordances; Garland Reference Library of the Humanities, vol. 753). LC 87-38471. ISBN 0-8240-8394-6.

A single, cumulative index to Beckett's texts in the New York: Grove Press editions of *Molloy* (1955), *Malone Dies* (1956), and *The Unnamable* (1958).

84.   Barale, Michele Aina, and Rubin Rabinovitz. **A KWIC Concordance to Samuel Beckett's Murphy**. New York: Garland, 1990. 497p. (Contextual Concordances; Garland Reference Library of the Humanities, vol. 1,079). LC 90-3312 ISBN 0-8240-4603-X.

Based on the New York: Grove Press 1957 edition of *Murphy*.

Journals

85.   **Beckett Circle: Newsletter of the Samuel Beckett Society**. Madison, WI: Samuel Beckett Society, 1978- . 2/yr. ISSN 0732-2224.

The membership journal of the Samuel Beckett Society, *Beckett Circle* is particularly valuable for accounts and reviews of stage and media productions and adaptations of Beckett's works in the United States and internationally. Issues also contain a selection of book reviews and a "New and Forthcoming" bibliography identifying editions and translations of Beckett's works and publications about Beckett. Other features announce upcoming festivals and conferences; describe projects; identify new addresses of members; and frequently request information, editorial, and other assistance related to Beckett. *Beckett Circle* is unindexed.

86.   **Beckettiana: Cuadernos del Seminario Beckett**. Buenos Aires: Facultad de Filosofia & Letras, Universidad de Buenos Aires, 1992-. Annual. ISSN 0327-7550.

Annual volumes contain four to six critical articles (in Spanish) on themes and other features in the full range of Beckett's works. Discussions of such topics as Beckett's treatment of hope and despair and time and space as well as Beckett's sources predominate. Occasional articles also discuss Latin American productions. A bibliographic contribution in 2 (1993): 41-42, describes the Reading University Library's Beckett collection. *Beckettiana* is indexed in *MLA*.

87.   **Journal of Beckett Studies**. Tallahassee, FL: Florida State University, 1976- . 2/yr. ISSN 0309-5207.

Previously published in London by John Calder and the Beckett Archive at the University of Reading. Scholarly studies and notes featured in *Journal of Beckett Studies* (about eight in each issue) focus on critical aspects of Beckett's works as well as topics related to their productions, such as translation, style, staging, and dramatic counterpoint. Others address broader interests, such as music and psychology in Beckett's works and textual studies of his manuscripts. Carla Locatelli's "An Outline of Beckett Criticism in Italy," in 3.1 (1993): 39-59, is an annotated bibliography of Italian scholarship. Occasional issues with guest editors have focused on a specific topic, such as "Beckett in France" in 4.1 (1994). Articles in both English and French are published. In addition, the journal includes selections of book reviews, reviews of productions and festivals, and letters to the editor. Past issues contained the interesting "Photographic Record of Recent Beckett Productions," which presented photos of actors and sets in productions; recent issues continue to include extensive numbers of black-and-white photographs of productions. *Journal of Beckett Studies* is indexed in *MHRA* and *MLA*.

Wortman's *A Guide to Serial Bibliographies for Modern Literatures*, p. 244, identifies other serial bibliographies for Beckett. Patterson's *Author Newsletters and Journals*, p. 359, describes other previously published journals for Beckett.

88.   **Samuel Beckett Today/Aujourd'hui: An Annual Bilingual Review/Revue Annuelle Bilingue**. Amsterdam: Rodopi, 1992- . Annual. OCLC 27369006.

Intends to be "a forum for the whole Beckett community in which it is not only called upon to listen but also to speak and write" (1 [1992]: 5). The first volume contains 16 papers from the 1991 Leiden Beckett Symposium "Beckett 1970-1989," addressing all aspects of Beckett's works. Vol. 2 covers the 1992 Hague International Symposium—"Beckett in the 1990s." *Samuel Beckett Today* is indexed in *MHRA* and *MLA*.

William Beckford, 1759-1844
Bibliographies

89.   Chapman, Guy, and John Hodgkin. **A Bibliography of William Beckford of Fonthill**. London: Constable, 1930. 127p. (Bibliographia). LC 30-33353.

Although badly dated, this remains the best guide to Beckford's primary materials, with full bibliographic descriptions (title-page transcriptions and facsimiles, physical descriptions, and notes on manuscripts and printing histories) for editions of Beckford's books, attributed works, unpublished prose works, translations, verse; music; and portraits of Beckford. Robert J. Gemmett's "An Annotated Checklist of the Works of William Beckford," *PBSA* 61 (1967): 243-58, supplies supplemental information. Also useful for descriptions of primary materials is Howard B. Gotlieb's *William Beckford of Fonthill: Writer, Traveller, Collector, Caliph, 1760-1844: A Brief Narrative and Catalogue of an Exhibition to Mark the Two Hundredth Anniversary of Beckford's Birth* (New Haven, CT: Yale University Press, 1969). Beckford's manuscripts are described in *Index of English Literary Manuscripts*, III, pt. 1:21-31. McNutt's *The Eighteenth-Century Gothic Novel*, pp. 265-310, contains a significant listing of works about Beckford. Reviews of Beckford's works in selected periodicals are identified in Wells' *The Literary Index to American Magazines, 1815-1865*, p. 8. Also for a bibliography of works by and about Beckford, see *NCBEL*, II, pp. 973-76. Robert Donald Spector reviews research on Beckford in *The English Gothic: A Bibliographic Guide to Writers from Horace Walpole to Mary Shelley*, pp. 153-204.

Thomas Lovell Beddoes, 1803-1849
Bibliographies

Beddoes' contributions to and reviews of Beddoes' works in selected periodicals are identified in Wells' *The Literary Index to American Magazines, 1850-1900*,

p. 30. For a bibliography of works by and about Beddoes, see *NCBEL*, III, pp. 409-11.

Bede, 673-735
Bibliographies

Greenfield and Robinson's *A Bibliography of Publications on Old English Literature to the End of 1972*, pp. 125, 298, 319-21, lists editions, translations, and studies of Bede, with citations for reviews. M. L. W. Laistner and H. H. King's *A Hand-List of Bede Manuscripts* (Ithaca, NY: Cornell University Press, 1943) identifies Bede's manuscripts copied before 950 and held in libraries and other depositories as of August 1939. Also for a bibliography of works by and about Bede, see *NCBEL*, I, pp. 345-49.

Thomas Beer, 1889-1940
Bibliographies

For works by Beer, see *First Printings of American Authors*, vol. 2, pp. 35-36. Beer's manuscripts are listed in Robbins' *American Literary Manuscripts*, p. 26. See *Bibliography of American Fiction, 1919-1988*, pp. 81-82, for Jackson R. Bryer's checklist of works by and about Beer.

(Sir Henry) Max(imilian) Beerbohm, 1872-1956
Bibliographies

90. Gallatin, A. E., and L. M. Oliver. **A Bibliography of the Works of Max Beerbohm.** Cambridge, MA: Harvard University Press, 1952. 60p. LC 52-9388.

Full bibliographic descriptions of Beerbohm's collected and separately published works. Originally published in *Harvard Library Bulletin* 5 (1951): 77-93, 221-41, and 338-61, the guide supersedes Gallatin's *Sir Max Beerbohm: Bibliographical Notes* (Cambridge, MA: Harvard University Press, 1944), which also described Beerbohm's contributions to books, uncollected and unpublished writings, caricatures, and other miscellaneous works and listed about 100 works on Beerbohm. Gallatin's major collection of Beerbohm materials is now located at Harvard. Another important, extensive primary and secondary bibliography appears in Jacobus Gerhardus Riewald's *Sir Max Beerbohm, Man and Writer* (The Hague: Nijhoff, 1953), pp. 213-343. Also for a bibliography of works by and about Beerbohm, see *NCBEL*, IV, pp. 1,000-1,003. Colette Lindroth surveys and identifies works by and about Beerbohm in Demastes and Kelly's *British Playwrights, 1880-1956*, pp. [37]-45.

Brendan Behan, 1923-1964
Bibliographies

91. Mikhail, E. H. **Brendan Behan: An Annotated Bibliography of Criticism.** Totowa, NJ: Barnes & Noble, 1980. 117p. LC 79-12337. ISBN 0-06-494826-9.

Mikhail briefly describes about 2,000 references to Behan in bibliographies and reference works; reviews of Behan's works (arranged by works); critical studies of Behan in books and chapters, articles, and dissertations; reviews of productions of Behan's plays (arranged by plays); sound recordings of Behan's works; and Behan's manuscripts located at Southern Illinois University and elsewhere (p. 104). Index headings under Behan's name for subjects such as "alleged homosexuality" and "trials and prisons" afford limited subject access. King's *Ten Modern Irish Playwrights*, pp. 1-33, gives brief bibliographic information for Behan's primary works and annotated entries for criticism of Behan, with a classified list of reviews. Maureen S. G. Hawkins surveys works by and about Behan in Schrank and Demastes' *Irish Playwrights, 1880-1995: A Research and Production Sourcebook*, pp. 23-42.

Aphra (Johnson) Behn, 1640?-1689

Bibliographies

92. O'Donnell, Mary Ann. **Aphra Behn: An Annotated Bibliography of Primary and Secondary Sources**. New York: Garland, 1986. 557p. (Garland Reference Library of the Humanities, vol. 505). LC 84-48023. ISBN 0-8240-8906-5.

The initial sections of O'Donnell's bibliography contain full bibliographic descriptions of early editions of Behn's writings. Chronologically arranged entries provide title-pages transcriptions, collations, and notes on publishing histories for 106 works written, edited, or translated by Behn; poetic contributions to other works; and works assigned to her. The remainder of the guide is an annotated listing of more than 600 works about Behn published from 1666 through 1983, covering books, chapters, articles, and essays. Appendixes and indexes reference names, primary titles, and subjects. O'Donnell's guide supersedes critical coverage of Behn offered in Armistead's *Four Restoration Playwrights* (entry 1177), which describes about 300 works on Behn to 1980. Also for a bibliography of works by and about Behn, see *NCBEL*, II, pp. 755-57. Behn's manuscripts are described in *Index of English Literary Manuscripts*, II, pt. 1:1-6.

Journals

"Recent Articles" in *The Scriblerian and the Kit Cats* (entry 1084) also regularly includes a selection of reviews of research on Behn.

S(amuel) N(athaniel) Behrman, 1893-1973

Bibliographies

93. Gross, Robert F. **S. N. Behrman: A Research and Production Sourcebook**. Westport, CT: Greenwood Press, 1992. 197p. (Modern Dramatists Research and Production Sourcebooks, no. 3). LC 92-26481. ISBN 0-31327-852-0.

Along with a chronology of Behrman's life and works and a critical introduction, Gross gives brief plot summaries, production histories and credits, citations to performance reviews, and critical overviews for each of the 52 plays; a bibliography of Behrman's publications in sections for drama, fiction, nonfiction, and archival sources; and separate, chronologically arranged sections of annotated entries for reviews (488 entries) and books, articles, and parts of books (156 entries) about Behrman published from 1926 through 1991. Entries for primary works give brief bibliographic data and contents summaries. Coverage of secondary works includes dissertations and newspaper features. General index of names, titles, and selected topics. Gross supersedes coverage of Behrman's primary and secondary works in William Klink's *Maxwell Anderson and S. N. Behrman: A Reference Guide* (Boston: G. K. Hall, 1977), which contains a checklist of Behrman's works and briefly describes about 200 studies on Behrman published from 1927 through 1973; and Klink's supplemental "Maxwell Anderson and S. N. Behrman: A Reference Guide Updated," *Resources for American Literary Study* 12 (1982): 195-214. Behrman's manuscripts are listed in Robbins' *American Literary Manuscripts*, p. 26. Robert F. Gross identifies works by and about Behrman in Demastes' *American Playwrights, 1880-1945*, pp. 40-56.

Jeremy Belknap, 1744-1798

Bibliographies

For works by Belknap, see *Bibliography of American Literature*, vol. 1, pp. 185-91. Belknap's manuscripts are listed in Robbins' *American Literary Manuscripts*, p. 27. See *Bibliography of American Fiction Through 1865*, pp. 52-53, for a checklist of works by and about Belknap.

Gertrude Margaret Lowthian Bell, 1868-1926
Bibliographies

For a bibliography of works by and about Bell, see *NCBEL*, IV, p. 1,311. Winifrid Cotterill Donkin's *Catalogue of the Gertrude Bell Collection in the Library of King's College, Newcastle upon Tyne* (Newcastle upon Tyne: University Library, 1960) gives brief information for the 2,000 volumes in Bell's personal library now located at King's College.

Edward Bellamy, 1850-1898
Bibliographies

94. Griffith, Nancy Snell. **Edward Bellamy: A Bibliography**. Metuchen, NJ: Scarecrow Press, 1986. 185p. (Scarecrow Author Bibliographies, no. 78). LC 86-17917. ISBN 0-8108-1932-5.

Although largely superseded by Widdicombe's *Edward Bellamy* (entry 95) for coverage of Bellamy criticism, Griffith's guide remains valuable for descriptions of Bellamy's fiction and nonfiction publications, including his contributions to newspapers, with some 505 entries arranged in separate listings for each format. Also lists more than 600 works about Bellamy's life, works, and ideas as well as reviews of his writings. Separate author, title, and subject indexes, with detailed topical headings. Also for works by Bellamy, see *Bibliography of American Literature*, vol. 1, pp. 192-96. Bellamy's contributions to and reviews of Bellamy's works in selected periodicals are identified in Wells' *The Literary Index to American Magazines, 1850-1900*, pp. 32-33. Bellamy's manuscripts are listed in Robbins' *American Literary Manuscripts*, pp. 27-28. See *Bibliography of American Fiction 1866-1918*, pp. 70-71, for Barbara L. Berman 's checklist of works by and about Bellamy.

95. Widdicombe, Richard Toby. **Edward Bellamy: An Annotated Bibliography of Secondary Criticism**. New York: Garland, 1988. 587p. (Garland Reference Library of the Humanities, vol. 827). LC 87-37686. ISBN 0-8240-8563-9.

Comprehensive international coverage of general and critical materials about Bellamy, with separate listings for books and chapters, journal and magazine articles, dissertations and theses, introductions, reviews, and miscellaneous references and citations, including non-English-language materials. Separate indexes reference authors, titles, sources, and subjects. Despite the guide's unreadability (resulting from reproduction of unsuitable camera-ready copy), Widdicombe's bibliography offers better coverage of secondary materials than Griffith's guide (entry 94).

Hilaire (Joseph Hilary Pierre) Belloc, 1870-1953
Bibliographies

96. Cahill, Patrick. **The English First Editions of Hilaire Belloc**. London: Cahill, 1953. 51p. LC 53-25907.

Cahill chronologically lists and describes 153 books and pamphlets by Belloc. Aimed at collectors, entries give title-page transcriptions and brief physical descriptions. Coverage of selected critical studies and additional information on primary material is provided in Renee Haynes's *Hilaire Belloc* (London: Longmans, Green, 1958), pp. 31-35. Also for a bibliography of works by and about Belloc, see *NCBEL*, IV, pp. 1,004-10.

Saul Bellow, 1915-
Bibliographies

97. Cronin, Gloria L., and Blaine H. Hall. **Saul Bellow: An Annotated Bibliography**. 2d ed. New York: Garland, 1987. 312p. (Garland Reference Library of the Humanities, vol. 679). LC 87-7607. ISBN 0-8240-9421-2.

Providing comprehensive coverage of works by and about Bellow published through 1985 (and somewhat through 1986), the first part of Cronin and Hall's guide contains separate listings for editions (with translations) of Bellow's novels, short fiction, plays, essays and miscellaneous writings, and interviews. The international popularity of Bellow's writings indicates a need for a full-scale descriptive bibliography. The second part of the guide gives annotated entries for 1,231 bibliographies and studies of Bellow's works and life in general (books and chapters, special journal issues, and the like), and studies of individual works, including reviews. The volume's useful author and subject indexing offers access by the names of critics as well as by such specific topics as "city," "imagery," and "Jewishness." Supersedes coverage of Bellow's primary and secondary works in Francine Lercangee's *Saul Bellow: A Bibliography of Secondary Sources* (Brussels: Center for American Studies, 1977); Robert G. Noreen's *Saul Bellow: A Reference Guide* (Boston: G. K. Hall, 1978), which lists Bellow criticism chronologically from 1944 through 1976, including non-English-language studies; and B. A. Sokoloff and Mark E. Posner's *Saul Bellow: A Comprehensive Bibliography* (Folcroft, PA: Folcroft Library Editions, 1974). See *Bibliography of American Fiction, 1919-1988*, pp. 82-86, for Keith Opdahl's checklist of works by and about Bellow. Cronin and Liela H. Goldman review research on Bellow in *Contemporary Authors: Bibliographical Series: Volume 1: American Novelists*, pp. 83-155.

98.   Nault, Marianne. **Saul Bellow: His Works and His Critics: An Annotated International Bibliography**. New York: Garland, 1977. 200p. (Garland Reference Library of the Humanities, vol. 59). LC 76-24738. ISBN 0-8240-9939-7.

A comprehensive bibliography of works by and about Bellow. Primarily useful for descriptions, with locations, of Bellow's published and unpublished writings through 1977, including major collections of manuscripts at the University of Chicago and the University of Texas' Harry Ransom Humanities Research Center (pp. 14-99). Nault also identifies interviews of Bellow and works by Bellow translated into other languages. Although Nault lists secondary materials, including reviews and dissertations produced in the United States and Great Britain, secondary coverage is superseded by Cronin and Hall's bibliography (entry 97). Bellow's manuscripts are listed in Robbins' *American Literary Manuscripts*, p. 28.

Journals

99.   **Saul Bellow Journal**. West Bloomfield, MI: Liela Goldman, 1981- . 2/yr. ISSN 0735-1550.

Issues typically include four to six articles that offer critical interpretations of Bellow's works, such as "The Hero as Sucker in Saul Bellow's Early Fiction" and "Atonement in Bellow's *Seize the Day*." Other articles have compared Bellow and Sophocles, Blake, Twain, and Dostoyevsky; surveyed the critical receptions of Bellow's works on Broadway or in Germany; and described Bellow's uses of Emerson and Poe. In addition, the journal features a current "Selected Annotated Critical Bibliography" of books, articles, dissertations, and other specialized secondary materials on Bellow's works. The bibliography for 1994, in 14.2 (Fall 1996): 72-102, was compiled by Gloria L. Cronin and Blaine H. Hall. Reviews of current publications on modern fiction and news items related to conferences, professional associations and societies, and research in progress are also included. *Saul Bellow Journal* is indexed in *AES, MHRA*, and *MLA*.

Park Benjamin, 1809-1864

Bibliographies

For works by Benjamin, see *Bibliography of American Literature*, vol.1, pp. 197-207. Benjamin's contributions to and reviews of Benjamin's works in selected periodicals are identified in Wells' *The Literary Index to American Magazines, 1815-1865*, pp. 8-9; and *The Literary Index to American Magazines, 1850-1900*, p. 33. Benjamin's manuscripts are listed in Robbins' *American Literary Manuscripts*, p. 29.

(Enoch) Arnold Bennett, 1867-1931
Bibliographies
100.   Miller, Anita. **Arnold Bennett: An Annotated Bibliography, 1887-1932.** New York: Garland, 1977. 787p. (Garland Reference Library of the Humanities, vol. 46). LC 75-42919. ISBN 0-8240-9954-0.

Miller identifies and describes Bennett's contributed articles in British and American periodicals and his books (novels, collections of stories, and nonfiction), edited journals, and published letters. The volume's bulk includes chronologically arranged descriptions of 2,815 periodical articles, reviews, and other writings published from 1887 through 1932. Annotations identify the contributions by types and summarize contents. Of the several indexes, the index of periodicals gives the most useful access to the entries. John D. Gordan's *Arnold Bennett: The Centenary of His Birth: An Exhibition in the Berg Collection* (New York: New York Public Library, 1968) offers useful descriptions of Bennett's works. Also for a bibliography of works by and about Bennett, see *NCBEL*, IV, pp. 429-36.

Journals
See Patterson's *Author Newsletters and Journals*, p. 19, for previously published journals for Bennett.

Emerson Bennett, 1822-1905
Bibliographies
For works by Bennett, see *Bibliography of American Literature*, vol. 1, pp. 208-15. Bennett's manuscripts are listed in Robbins' *American Literary Manuscripts*, p. 29. See *Bibliography of American Fiction Through 1865*, pp. 54-55, for a checklist of works by and about Bennett.

Beowulf, 8th century
Bibliographies
101.   Fry, Donald K. **Beowulf and The Fight at Finnsburh: A Bibliography.** Charlottesville, VA: University Press of Virginia, 1969. 222p. LC 70-947060. ISBN 0-8139-0268-1.

Comprehensive, alphabetically arranged author listing of 2,280 critical works (books, articles, dissertations, reviews, introductions to editions, and the like) in all languages about the poems through 1967. "Coded" entries ("alg" for allegory, "bibl" for bibliography, and "epc" for epic characters, for example) indicate topics covered in studies, with line references to the poems and citations for reviews. Indexes cross-reference both the subject codes and poems' lines. Short's bibliography (entry 103) updates *Beowulf* scholarship through 1978; Hasenfratz's *Beowulf Scholarship* (entry 102) extends coverage to 1990. Chauncey B. Tinker and Marijane Osborn's *The Translations of Beowulf: A Critical Bibliography* (1903; reprint Hamden, CT: Archon Books, 1974) reprints Tinker's chronologically arranged descriptions of translations of *Beowulf* through 1903, with additions through 1973.

102.   Hasenfratz, Robert J. **Beowulf Scholarship: An Annotated Bibliography, 1979-1990.** New York: Garland, 1993. 424p. (Garland Reference Library of the Humanities, vol. 1,422; Garland Medieval Bibliographies, vol. 14). LC 93-17683. ISBN 0-8153-0084-0.

A continuation of Short's *Beowulf Scholarship* (entry 103), which itself continues Fry's *Beowulf and The Fight at Finnsburh: A Bibliography* (entry 101). Chronologically arranging more than 600 annotated entries, Hasenfratz's guide offers international coverage of English and other translated editions (Danish, Dutch, Japanese, etc.) and of English and non-English-language criticism and reviews but excludes dissertations. Full and detailed annotations are descriptive and often cite reviews, with major studies described at length. Author, subject, word, and line indexes provide excellent access. Greenfield and Robinson's *A Bibliography of Publications on Old English Literature to the End of 1972*, pp. 125-97, lists reference works, editions, translations, and studies of *Beowulf,* with citations for reviews. Also for works about *Beowulf,* see *NCBEL,* I, pp. 244-67.

103.   Short, Douglas D. **Beowulf Scholarship: An Annotated Bibliography**. New York: Garland, 1980. 353p. (Garland Reference Library of the Humanities, vol. 193). LC 79-7924. ISBN 0-8240-9530-8.

Updates and offers addenda to Fry's bibliography (entry 101), providing chronologically arranged, annotated entries for more than 1,105 studies of *Beowulf* published from 1705 through 1978. Part 1 critically reviews 200 selected studies of *Beowulf* published before 1950. Short identifies these as "the central core of *Beowulf* scholarship" (p. vii). This list serves as a useful guide to essential studies of the poem. Part 2 is a comprehensive listing of studies from 1950 through 1978. Descriptive annotations review significant studies at length. A detailed, separate subject index enhances access.

Dictionaries, Encyclopedias, and Handbooks

104.   Bjork, Robert E., and John D. Niles. **A Beowulf Handbook**. Lincoln, NE: University of Nebraska Press, 1997. 466p. LC 96-41312. ISBN 0-8032-1237-2.

"Lays the foundation for up-to-date, nuanced approaches to *Beowulf* by supplying a succession of analyses of all major aspects of it from the beginnings to 1994" (preface). Eighteen parallel chapters by different experts give chronologies of major critical studies with accompanying surveys of scholarship. Chapters cover topics such as date, provenance, author, and audience; textual criticism; rhetoric and style; sources and analogues; Christian and pagan elements; myth and history; gender roles; and contemporary critical theory. Most consistently attempt to identify specific features of the poem with criticism. For example, the chapter on *Beowulf*'s "Digressions and Episodes" focuses discussion on three specific passages. Most quotations from the poem are taken from Friedrich Klaeber's *Beowulf and The Fight at Finnsburg,* 3d ed. (Boston: D. C. Heath, 1950). Includes a bibliography of bibliographies, editions, translations, adaptations and "imaginative re-creations," and studies and other works. Thorough index of names and topics.

Indexes and Concordances

105.   Bessinger, J. B., Jr. **A Concordance to Beowulf**. Ithaca, NY: Cornell University Press, 1969. 373p. (The Cornell Concordances). LC 67-23758.

Bessinger bases his concordance on the authoritative text in Elliot Van Kirk Dobbie's edition of *Beowulf and Judith* in vol. 4 of the *Anglo-Saxon Poetic Records* (New York: Columbia University Press, 1953). Includes a word-frequency list. Bessinger's concordance is superior to Albert S. Cook's *A Concordance to Beowulf* (1911; reprint New York: Haskell House, 1968), which is based on A. J. Wyatt's second edition of the text (Cambridge: Cambridge University Press, 1898).

Thomas (Louis) Berger, 1924-

Bibliographies

For works by Berger, see *First Printings of American Authors,* vol. 2, pp. 37-38. See *Bibliography of American Fiction, 1919-1988,* pp. 87-88, for Michael Adams' checklist of works by and about Berger. See Richard A. Betts's summary biography, critical assessment of major works, and selected primary and secondary bibliography for Berger in McCaffery's *Postmodern Fiction: A Bio-Bibliographical Guide,* pp. 275-77.

John Berryman, 1914-1972

Bibliographies

106.   Arpin, Gary Q. **John Berryman: A Reference Guide**. Boston: G. K. Hall, 1976. 158p. (Reference Guides in Literature, no. 8). LC 76-2491. ISBN 0-8161-7804-6.

Comprehensive, chronologically arranged bibliography of writings about Berryman published from 1935 through 1975, containing annotated entries for about 600 books, dissertations, periodical and newspaper articles, and reviews. Annotations are descriptive. Index headings under Berryman's name for selected topics (such as bibliography, biography, and interviews) give limited access. Arpin's work supersedes Richard Kelly's *John Berryman: A Checklist* (Metuchen, NJ: Scarecrow Press, 1972). Sonya Jones reviews research on Berryman in *Contemporary Authors: Bibliographical Series: Volume 2: American Poets*, pp. 3-33.

107. Stefanik, Ernest C., Jr. **John Berryman: A Descriptive Bibliography**. Pittsburgh, PA: University of Pittsburgh Press, 1974. 285p. (Pittsburgh Series in Bibliography). LC 74-4093. ISBN 0-8229-3281-4.

In his comprehensive bibliography of Berryman's writings, Stefanik describes in separate listings Berryman's books and separate publications, contributions to books, contributions to periodicals (some 279 entries), materials reprinted in collections and anthologies, interviews, recordings, dust-jacket blurbs, and selections of poetry in works of others. Entries give facsimiles of title and copyright pages; collations; contents; descriptions of paper, typography, and dust jackets; publishing histories; and copy locations. Also contains collations of variants. Appendixes list Berryman's writings chronologically and the titles of periodicals including Berryman's contributions. Also for works by Berryman, see *First Printings of American Authors*, vol. 1, pp. 31-34. Berryman's manuscripts are listed in Robbins' *American Literary Manuscripts*, p. 30.

Journals
See Patterson's *Author Newsletters and Journals*, p. 23, for previously published journals for Berryman.

Alfred Bester, 1913-1987
Bibliographies
See *Bibliography of American Fiction, 1919-1988*, pp. 89-90, for Carolyn Wendell's checklist of works by and about Bester.

John Betjeman, 1906-1984
Bibliographies
108. Stapleton, Margaret L. **Sir John Betjeman: A Bibliography of Writings by and About Him**. Metuchen, NJ: Scarecrow Press, 1974. 149p. (Scarecrow Author Bibliographies, no. 21). LC 74-14641. ISBN 0-8108-0758-0.

Stapleton describes works by and about Betjeman. Part 1 gives brief bibliographic information (with detailed summaries of contents) for Betjeman's writings in sections for his books of verse, prose works, edited works, contributions to books, introductions and prefaces, anthologies including his poems, poems in magazines, articles, reviews by Betjeman, and recordings. Part 2 lists unannotated entries for about 300 biographies, criticism in books and articles, and reviews of Betjeman's works. Pennie Denton's *An Exhibition of Works by Sir John Betjeman from the Collection of Ray Carter in the Art Gallery of St Paul's School, February-March, MCMLXXXIII* (London: Warren Editions, 1983) offers brief, supplementary bibliographic information on selected publications of Betjeman through 1982. Also for a bibliography of works by and about Betjeman, see *NCBEL*, IV, pp. 233-34.

Martha Gilbert Dickinson Bianchi, 1866-1943
Bibliographies
For works by Bianchi, see *First Printings of American Authors*, vol. 2, pp. 39-41.

Ambrose (Gwinett) Bierce, 1842-1914?

Bibliographies

109.   Gaer, Joseph. **Ambrose Gwinett Bierce: Bibliography and Biographical Data.** [s.l.: s.n., 1935]. 102 leaves. (California Literary Research Project: Monograph, no. 4). LC 35-27835.

Chronologically identifies and gives brief information for Bierce's separate publications, collected works, posthumous works, articles and essays, and other miscellaneous writings. Also available in a reprinted edition (New York: B. Franklin, 1968). Updated by George Monteiro's "Addenda to Gaer: Bierce in The Anto-Philistine," *PBSA* 66 (1972): 71-72; and "Addenda to Gaer: Reprintings of Bierce's Stories," *PBSA* 68 (1974): 330-31; William L. Andrews' "Some New Ambrose Bierce Fables," *American Literary Realism* 8 (1975): 349-52; and John C. Stubbs' "Ambrose Bierce's Contributions to Cosmopolitan: An Annotated Bibliography," *American Literary Realism* 4 (1971): 57-59. Also for works by Bierce, see *Bibliography of American Literature*, vol. 1, pp. 216-27. Bierce's manuscripts are listed in Robbins' *American Literary Manuscripts*, p. 31. The most comprehensive list of writings about Bierce is George F. Fortenberry's "Ambrose Bierce (1842-1914?): A Critical Bibliography of Secondary Comment," *American Literary Realism* 4 (1971): 11-56. Philip M. Rubens and Robert Jones' "Ambrose Bierce: A Bibliographic Essay and Bibliography," *American Literary Realism* 16 (1983): 73-91, reviews research. See *Bibliography of American Fiction, 1866-1918*, pp. 72-75, for M. E. Grenander's checklist of works by and about Bierce.

Earl Derr Biggers, 1884-1933

Bibliographies

110.   Koontz, Carole Ann. **An Earl Derr Biggers Checklist.** M.A. thesis, Columbus, OH: Ohio State University, 1982. 105 leaves. OCLC 9947409.

Useful because of its comprehensiveness and reliance on Biggers' collections in the Bobbs-Merrill papers in Indiana University's Lilly Library and other libraries. Gives brief bibliographic descriptions of Biggers' works, including non-English-language editions, in sections for verse, drama, and prose, and film based on Biggers' works. Also lists works about Biggers in sections for reviews, newspaper and magazine articles, and books. See *Bibliography of American Fiction, 1866-1918*, pp. 75-76, for Carl L. Boren's checklist of works by and about Biggers. Biggers' manuscripts are listed in Robbins' *American Literary Manuscripts*, p. 31.

Robert Montgomery Bird, 1806-1854

Bibliographies

For works by Bird, see *Bibliography of American Literature*, vol. 1, pp. 228-34. Bird's contributions to and reviews of Bird's works in selected periodicals are identified in Wells' *The Literary Index to American Magazines, 1815-1865*, pp. 9-10; and *The Literary Index to American Magazines, 1850-1900*, p. 36. Bird's manuscripts are listed in Robbins' *American Literary Manuscripts*, p. 32. See *Bibliography of American Fiction Through 1865*, pp. 56-58, for a checklist of works by and about Bird.

Elizabeth Bishop, 1911-1979

Bibliographies

111.   MacMahon, Candace W. **Elizabeth Bishop: A Bibliography, 1927-1979.** Charlottesville, VA: Published for the Bibliographical Society of the University of Virginia by the University Press of Virginia, 1980. 227p. LC 79-13063. ISBN 0-8139-0783-7.

MacMahon's comprehensive guide to Bishop's writings supplies detailed descriptions of Bishop's books and separate publications, contributions to books, contributions to periodicals, translations of Bishop's works (arranged by languages), recordings, and musical settings. Entries provide title- and copyright-page facsimiles;

collations; contents; descriptions of paper, typography, bindings, and dust jackets; publishing histories; and copy locations. Other listings cover books, journal issues, chapters, articles (32 entries), reviews (arranged by works), and miscellaneous writings about Bishop (such as biographical entries in reference works, poems dedicated to Bishop, and anthologized poems), as well as interviews and letters. An appendix lists unpublished poems, with their locations in libraries' special collections. Also for works by Bishop, see *First Printings of American Authors*, vol. 2, pp. 43-44. Bishop's manuscripts are listed in Robbins' *American Literary Manuscripts*, p. 32.

112.   Wyllie, Diana E. **Elizabeth Bishop and Howard Nemerov: A Reference Guide**. Boston: G. K. Hall, 1983. 196p. (Reference Guide to Literature). LC 82-15597. ISBN 0-8161-8527-1.
Wyllie provides separate checklists of works by Bishop and Nemerov and chronologically arranged, separate listings of annotated entries for works about them. Critical coverage for both Bishop and Nemerov includes books, parts of books, articles, reviews, and dissertations. Describes some 300 items for Bishop published from 1935 through 1981 and about 400 for Nemerov from 1947 through 1981. Comprehensive coverage of Bishop's primary materials is provided by MacMahon's bibliography (entry 111). For Nemerov, however, no other descriptive bibliography of primary writings exists. Wyllie lists Nemerov's books (fiction, nonfiction, poetry, drama, edited works, translations by Nemerov, and stage and screen adaptations), and first nonbook appearances of Nemerov's poems, short fiction, essays, articles, book reviews, translations, and other nonfiction. No subject indexing. Barbara Page reviews research on Bishop in *Contemporary Authors: Bibliographical Series: Volume 2: American Poets*, pp. 35-69.

Indexes and Concordances
113.   Greenhalgh, Anne Merrill. **A Concordance to Elizabeth Bishop's Poetry**. New York: Garland, 1985. 921p. (Garland Reference Library of the Humanities, vol. 508). LC 84-48021. ISBN 0-8240-8909-x.
Greenhalgh concords the text of *The Complete Poems, 1927-1979* (New York: Farrar, Straus & Giroux, 1979). An alphabetical word-frequency list completes the volume.

John Peale Bishop, 1892-1944
Bibliographies
For works by Bishop, see *First Printings of American Authors*, vol. 1, pp. 35-36. Bishop's manuscripts are listed in Robbins' *American Literary Manuscripts*, p. 32. Robert L. White surveys works by and about Bishop in Flora and Bain's *Fifty Southern Writers After 1900*, pp. 64-73.

MacKnight Black, 1896-1931
Bibliographies
For works by Black, see *First Printings of American Authors*, vol. 2, p. 45.

Paul Blackburn, 1926-1971
Bibliographies
114.   Woodward, Kathleen. **Paul Blackburn: A Checklist**. San Diego, CA: Archive for New Poetry, University of California, 1980. 92p. (Documents of New Poetry, no. 2). OCLC 6935650.
Brief bibliographic information for Blackburn's books, chapbooks, and broadsides of poetry and translations; poems published in little magazines (some 470 entries); poems in anthologies; translations in Provençal, Spanish, and other languages in little magazines and anthologies; and interviews and miscellaneous works. Descriptions based on materials in the University of California at San

Diego's Archive for New Poetry, which acquired the Paul Blackburn Archive of poetry manuscripts, journals, recordings, and published works in 1973.

Algernon Blackwood, 1869-1951
Bibliographies
115.　Ashley, Mike. **Algernon Blackwood: A Bio-Bibliography.** New York: Greenwood Press, 1987. 349p. (Bio-Bibliographies in World Literature, no. 1). LC 87-17808. ISBN 0-313-25158-4.

Comprehensively covers works by and about Blackwood. Ashley gives brief bibliographic information (with physical descriptions, contents, and publishing histories) for Blackwood's books; short and serialized fiction; nonfiction (essays, sketches, and book reviews); poetry and songs; plays and dramas (stage and radio); radio broadcasts (stories, talks, interviews, and discussions); television broadcasts; films; recorded works; manuscripts of unpublished and unbroadcast works; untraced items; adaptations of Blackwood's works for the stage, radio, and television; and recorded works and editions for the blind. Also lists works about Blackwood (criticisms, reviews, radio documentaries, and portraits and photographs). Appendixes cover translated and international editions and collections of Blackwood's books and manuscripts. Chronological and "locale and theme" indexes (with headings for such subjects as "lycanthropy" and "spirit travel") provide good topical access. Ashley's guide supersedes the coverage of John Robert Colombo's *Blackwood's Books: A Bibliography Devoted to Algernon Blackwood* (Toronto: Hounslow Press, 1981).

Hugh Blair, 1718-1800
Bibliographies
For a bibliography of works by and about Blair, see *NCBEL*, II, pp. 2,061-62.

Lillie Devereux Blake, 1833-1913
Bibliographies
See *Bibliography of American Fiction Through 1865*, p. 59, for a checklist of works by and about Blake.

William Blake, 1757-1827
Bibliographies
116.　Bentley, Gerald Eades. **Blake Books: Annotated Catalogues of William Blake's Writings in Illuminated Painting, in Conventional Typography and in Manuscript, and Reprints Thereof; Reproductions of His Designs; Books with His Engravings; Catalogues; Books He Owned; and Scholarly and Critical Works About Him.** Revised ed. Oxford: Clarendon Press, 1977. 1,079p. LC 77-363108. ISBN 0-19-818151-5.

The standard descriptive bibliography of Blake's works and works about him. A revised and expanded edition of Bentley and Martin Nurmi's *A Blake Bibliography* (Minneapolis, MN: University of Minnesota Press, 1964) and superseding Geoffrey Keynes' *Bibliography of William Blake* (New York: Grolier Club, 1921) and Keynes and Edwin Wolf's *William Blake's Illuminated Books: A Census* (New York: Grolier Club, 1953), Bentley's guide provides full descriptions in 218 entries for separate and collected editions of Blake's writings, reproductions of his drawings and engravings, and his commercial book engravings and artworks. Bibliographic entries give title-page transcriptions, extended descriptions of copies (with information for colors, designs, watermarks, plates, and sizes frequently cited in comparative tables), and detailed publishing histories. Also includes descriptive listings for 191 catalogs and bibliographies of Blake's literary and graphic works; books owned by Blake; and about 2,300 books and articles about Blake published through 1975 (briefly annotated). Comprehensive index provides thorough access.

Updated by:

116.1 Bentley, G. E., Jr. **Blake Books Supplement: A Bibliography of Publications and Discoveries About William Blake, 1971-1992, Being a Continuation of Blake Books.** Oxford: Clarendon Press, 1995. 789p. LC 93-43095. ISBN 0-1981-2354-X.

Introductory chapter "Blake Discoveries, Scholarship, and Criticism, 1971-1992" (pp. 10-30) affords excellent overview of bibliography, editions, and research. Following the scheme of *Blake Books*, Bentley gives full descriptions of editions of Blake's writings, reproductions of drawings and paintings, commercial book engravings, catalogs and bibliographies, and books owned by Blake, with an appendix of books owned by the "wrong" William Blake. Alphabetically lists more than 5,000 selectively annotated entries for works about Blake, including early works and contemporary allusions missed by Bentley's first compilation as well as recent criticism and comments. Covers the full range of secondary works, such as introductions in catalogs and editions, dissertations, and non-English-language works. Comprehensive index gives excellent access. Also useful for descriptions of primary materials are Robert N. Essick's *The Works of William Blake in the Huntington Collections: A Complete Catalog* (San Marino, CA: Huntington Library, Art Collections, Botanical Gardens, 1985); Christopher Heppner's *A Catalogue of the Lawrence Lande William Blake Collection in the Department of Rare Books and Special Collections of the McGill University Libraries/McLennan Library* (Montreal: McGill University, 1983); and Phyllis Goff's *William Blake: Catalogue of the Preston Blake Library, Presented by Kerrison Preston in 1967* (London: Westminster City Libraries, 1969). Donald Fitch's *Blake Set to Music: A Bibliography of Musical Settings of the Poems and Prose of William Blake* (Berkeley, CA: University of California Press, 1990) documents the use of Blake's poetry by composers, identifying 1,412 musical settings from the 1870s through 1989. Bentley's *Blake Records* (Oxford: Clarendon Press, 1969) attempts to calendar all contemporary references and allusions to Blake. Also for a bibliography of works by and about Blake compiled by Bentley, see *NCBEL*, II, pp. 615-36. Blake's manuscripts are described in *Index of English Literary Manuscripts*, III, pt. 1:33-34. Many of Blake's manuscript works have been facsimiled. Most recently, the William Blake Trust and Princeton University Press' series *Blake's Illuminated Books* (in progress) has produced excellent facsimile volumes.

117.   Natoli, Joseph P. **Twentieth-Century Blake Criticism: Northrop Frye to the Present.** New York: Garland, 1982. 327p. (Garland Reference Library of the Humanities, vol. 285). LC 85-15400. ISBN 0-8240-9326-7.

Covering English-language criticism of Blake from 1947 through 1981, Natoli's guide topically arranges 1,682 annotated entries for books, articles, reviews, and selected dissertations in separate listings for reference works and bibliographies; studies of Blake's reputation, influence, symbols and themes, style and form, and the like; and studies of individual works. Descriptive annotations attempt to relate trends in Blake criticism. Introductions for each section typically identify the most significant studies. Index headings for such subjects as "evil," "forgery," "the occult," and "simplicity" offer good access. Supplementing the critical coverage provided in Bentley's massive bibliography (entry 116), Natoli's guide offers a convenient starting point for research on Blake. Research on Blake is reviewed by Northrup Frye and Martin K. Nurmi in Houtchens and Houtchens' *The English Romantic Poets and Essayists*, pp. 1-36; David V. Erdman in Dyson's *English Poetry*, pp. 144-66; and Mary Lynn Johnson in Frank Jordan's *The English Romantic Poets*, pp. 113-254.

Dictionaries, Encyclopedias, and Handbooks

118.   Damon, S. Foster. **A Blake Dictionary: The Ideas and Symbols of William Blake.** Revised ed. Providence, RI: Brown University Press, 1988. 532p. LC 87-40509. ISBN 0-87451-436-1.

Regarded as an essential resource for Blake research since its first publication in 1965, Damon's dictionary remains an ideal starting point for anyone who needs to discover Blake's understanding of particular features in his works, such as "Hell," "Napoleon Bonaparte," and "sex." The "Revised edition with a new foreword and annotated bibliography" by Morris Eaves mainly adds an index to Damon's entries, permitting better access to the contents of entries that were previously buried by the eclectic arrangement of words, phrases, allusions, concepts, and themes.

Indexes and Concordances

119.   Erdman, David V. **A Concordance to the Writings of William Blake**. Ithaca, NY: Cornell University Press, 1967. 2 vols. (The Cornell Concordances). LC 66-18608.

Erdman bases this concordance on Geoffrey Keynes' edition of *The Complete Writings of William Blake: With All the Variant Readings* (London: Nonesuch Press, 1957), with incorporated additions and corrections. Appendixes list word frequencies and corrections and additions to Keynes' text.

Journals

120.   **Blake: An Illustrated Quarterly**. Rochester, NY: University of Rochester, 1967- . 4/yr. ISSN 0160-628x.

Continuing *Blake Newsletter* (1967-77), the well-illustrated quarto-size issues of this journal typically feature one or two major articles, briefer notes, and several extensive reviews. Articles largely focus on close readings of Blake's works, although the journal also has a distinctive bibliographic and technical orientation. A significant number of articles usually address printing and publishing history and editorial problems. Surveys of the sales of Blake materials—"Blake in the Marketplace"—are frequent. In addition, a regular feature is "Blake and His Circle: An Annotated Checklist of Recent Publications," an extensive, classified bibliography of books, articles, and reviews, with an index of authors, editors, and reviewers. The checklist for 1995, in 29.4 (Spring 1996): 131-68, was compiled by G. E. Bentley Jr. A "Newsletter" feature publishes notes on upcoming programs and meetings, recounts activities of Blake societies, announces publications and prizes, and the like. A lively section of letters to the editors usually includes rejoinders by authors who take issue with reviews of their books as well as questions and answers on points of Blake biography and criticism. *Blake: An Illustrated Quarterly* is indexed in *AES, AHI, A&HCI, MHRA,* and *MLA.*

Wortman's *A Guide to Serial Bibliographies for Modern Literatures,* p. 245, identifies other serial bibliographies for Blake. Patterson's *Author Newsletters and Journals,* pp. 25-28, describes other previously published journals for Blake.

Burt Blechman, 1932?-

Bibliographies

For works by Blechman, see *First Printings of American Authors,* vol. 2, p. 47.

Ann Eliza Bleecker, 1752-1783

Bibliographies

For works by Bleecker, see *First Printings of American Authors,* vol. 4, p. 33.

James Blish, 1921-1975

Bibliographies

121.   Blish, James. **The Tale That Wags the God**. Chicago, IL: Advent, 1987. 290p. ISBN 0-911682-29-5.

Evaluations of the science-fiction genre and modern science-fiction writers precede Judith L. Blish's classified "Bibliography of the Works of James Blish" (p. 201-277), giving brief bibliographic data for first and subsequent editions, translations, and reprintings of novels, short stories, anthologies edited by Blish, literary criticism, reviews, articles and interviews, introductions, poetry, and "Star Trek Books." Name and title indexes. See also *Bibliography of American Fiction, 1919-1988,* pp. 90-92, for Raymond J. Wilson III's checklist of works by and about Blish.

Judy Blume, 1938-
Bibliographies

See *Bibliography of American Fiction, 1919-1988*, pp. 92-93, for Alice Phoebe Naylor's checklist of works by and about Blume.

Edmund Charles Blunden, 1896-1974
Bibliographies

122. Fung, Sydney S. K., and Grace H. L. Chu. **Edmund Blunden: A Bibliography of Criticism.** Hong Kong: Kelly & Walsh, 1983. 118p. LC 84-103156. ISBN 962-7072-01-x.

Fung and Chu arrange selectively annotated descriptive entries for about 1,000 works about Blunden in separate listings for critical forms, including bibliographies, theses and dissertations, books and pamphlets, articles, biographic notices and obituaries, poems to and about Blunden, parodies, reviews, and portraits and photographs of Blunden, among others. Critical coverage, extending from 1920 through 1981, includes a few non-English-language works.

123. Kirkpatrick, B. J. **A Bibliography of Edmund Blunden.** Oxford: Clarendon Press, 1979. 725p. LC 77-30460. ISBN 0-19-8181704.

Kirkpatrick gives full bibliographic descriptions of Blunden's primary materials, covering books and pamphlets, contributions to books, contributions to periodicals and newspapers (some 3,370 entries); and translations of Blunden's works (arranged by languages). Entries give title-page transcriptions and facsimiles, physical descriptions, contents, and publishing histories. Appendixes list a broad variety of miscellaneous materials, such as quotations from Blunden's works in books and journals, testimonials, music scores and sound recordings, interviews, letters and announcements by Blunden in newspapers, and about 30 books and articles referring to Blunden and his works. Kirkpatrick (p. xvii) notes that Blunden's manuscripts of *Undertones of War*, poems, and letters are located in the Harry Ransom Humanities Research Center of the University of Texas. Also for a bibliography of works by and about Blunden, see *NCBEL*, IV, pp. 234-38.

Robert (Elwood) Bly, 1926-
Bibliographies

124. Roberson, William H. **Robert Bly: A Primary and Secondary Bibliography.** Metuchen, NJ: Scarecrow Press, 1986. 391p. (Scarecrow Author Bibliographies, no. 75). LC 86-939. ISBN 0-8108-1879-5.

Describes works by and about Bly. Part 1 gives detailed descriptions for Bly's books of poetry and prose, translations, and edited works; essays and nonfiction; reviews; letters; poems in journals (some 444 entries); translations in journals (some 410 entries); poems in books; translations in books; translations; sound recordings; video recordings; dust-jacket blurbs; dramas; notepapers; and a single musical setting. Entries give title-page transcriptions, physical descriptions, contents, and copy locations. Part 2 includes critically annotated entries for about 550 books, articles, reviews, dissertations, poems, and other works about Bly. An appendix (pp. 331-33) lists and locates Bly materials in libraries' special collections. The separate index for critical materials includes topical headings under Bly's name.

Manoah Bodman, 1765-1850
Bibliographies

For works by Bodman, see *First Printings of American Authors*, vol. 4, pp. 35-36.

Louise Bogan, 1897-1970
Bibliographies
125. Knox, Claire E. **Louise Bogan: A Reference Source**. Metuchen, NJ: Scarecrow Press, 1990. 315p. (Scarecrow Author Bibliographies, no. 86). LC 90-47804. ISBN 0-8108-2379-9.
  Covers works by and about Bogan. Part 1 chronologically and alphabetically lists, in short sections, works by Bogan published from 1915 to 1989 in sections for books (poetry collections, criticism, Bogan's writings arranged by others, bibliographies and anthologies by Bogan), *New Yorker* critical reviews and essays, critical reviews not in *New Yorker*, critical essays not in *New Yorker*, short stories and journals, translations, poems on records and tapes, talks and lectures, miscellaneous writings (introductions, forewords, afterwords; letters to the editor; collections of juvenilia, letters, papers, and books; and poems put to musical settings), uncollected poems, and anthologies. Entries for Bogan's six books of poems give brief publication data and emphasize first and subsequent appearances of individual poems. Annotations summarize contents of her three critical books and nearly 200 book reviews; her periodical contributions are more briefly described. Part 2 chronologically lists annotated entries for about 200 criticisms of Bogan from 1922 through 1989 in sections for books and their reviews, general criticisms, brief notices, reviews of Bogan's poetry and other books, dissertations, bibliographies and biographies, books and poems dedicated to Bogan, awards and appointments, and memorial speeches and obituaries. Indexes of personal names and titles. Knox's bibliography essentially incorporates and supersedes William Jay Smith's *Louise Bogan: A Woman's Words: A Lecture Delivered at the Library of Congress, May 4, 1970. With a Bibliography* (Washington, DC: Library of Congress, 1971) and Jane Couchman's "Louise Bogan: A Bibliography of Primary and Secondary Materials, 1915-1975: Part I," *Bulletin of Bibliography* 33 (February-March 1976): 73-77, 104; "Part II," 33 (April-June 1976): 111-26, 147; and "Part III," 33 (July-September 1976): 178-81. Although now the best bibliography for Bogan, Knox's guide lacks full bibliographic descriptions of Bogan's works and offers somewhat less than thorough indexing of criticisms. Also for works by Bogan, see *First Printings of American Authors*, vol. 1, pp. 37-38. Bogan's manuscripts are listed in Robbins' *American Literary Manuscripts*, p. 33. Andrew Kurtz's *Louise Bogan's Working Library: A Catalogue* (M.A. thesis, Oxford, OH: Miami University, 1987) is also useful for research on Bogan.

George Henry Boker, 1823-1890
Bibliographies
  For works by Boker, see *Bibliography of American Literature*, vol. 1, pp. 235-50. Boker's contributions to and reviews of Boker's works in selected periodicals are identified in Wells' *The Literary Index to American Magazines, 1815-1865*, p. 10; and *The Literary Index to American Magazines, 1850-1900*, pp. 40-41. Boker's manuscripts are listed in Robbins' *American Literary Manuscripts*, p. 34.

Henry St. John, 1st Viscount Bolingbroke, 1678-1751
Bibliographies
  For a bibliography of works by and about Bolingbroke by John Barnard, see *NCBEL*, II, pp. 1,119-22. Bolingbroke's manuscripts are described in *Index of English Literary Manuscripts*, III, pt. 1:35-38.

Robert Oxton Bolt, 1924-1995
Bibliographies
  King's *Twenty Modern British Playwrights*, pp. 35-42, lists works by Bolt and describes works about him.

Edward (Thomas) Bond, 1934-
Bibliographies
126.   Hay, Malcolm, and Philip Roberts. **Edward Bond: A Companion to the Plays**. London: TQ Publications, 1978. 100p. ISBN 0-904844-21-8.

Mainly useful for a classified bibliography of published plays, collected works, unpublished plays, translations and adaptations, published fiction, published nonfiction (in the United Kingdom), interviews and discussions, and about 100 selected critical books and articles in all languages on Bond (pp. 31-39). Additionally, Hay and Roberts separately list first and subsequent international productions of Bond's plays, with names of directors and designers and extensive citations to stage reviews (pp. [77]-100). The volume also contains a Bond chronology emphasizing performances and 17 "extracts" from Bond's previously unpublished letters and other material in theater programs by Bond about his works. Unindexed. King's *Twenty Modern British Playwrights*, pp. 43-54, also lists works by Bond and describes works about him.

Arna (Wendell) Bontemps, 1902-1973
Bibliographies
See Fleming's *James Weldon Johnson and Arna Wendell Bontemps* (entry 733). Bontemps' manuscripts are listed in Robbins' *American Literary Manuscripts*, p. 35.

Philip E. Booth, 1925-
Bibliographies
For works by Booth, see *First Printings of American Authors*, vol. 2, p. 49.

George Henry Borrow, 1803-1881
Bibliographies
127.   Collie, Michael, and Angus Fletcher. **George Borrow: A Bibliographical Study**. Winchester: St. Paul's Bibliographies, 1984. 231p. (St. Paul's Bibliographies, no. 9). ISBN 0-906795-24-9.

Superseding Thomas J. Wise's *A Bibliography of the Writings in Prose and Borrow* (London: Richard Clay, 1914; reprint London: Dawsons of Pall Mall, 1966), Collie and Fletcher supply full bibliographic descriptions for Borrow's works published in his lifetime, covering his books, translations by Borrow, anonymous publications, letters, pamphlets printed for T. J. Wise, privately printed pamphlets, John Murray's editions, collected editions, and contributions to periodicals. Other sections identify previously unpublished materials in books and periodicals (through 1981); nineteenth-century translations of Borrow's works; and other posthumous publications of Borrow's works, as well as about 50 bibliographies and bibliographical studies related to Borrow. Entries give title-page transcriptions, physical descriptions, and extensive notes on composition and publication histories. Manuscript sources are discussed throughout. Includes a list of collections of Borrow's manuscripts (pp. 15-16). Borrow's contributions to and reviews of Borrow's works in selected periodicals are identified in Wells' *The Literary Index to American Magazines, 1815-1865*, pp. 10-11; and *The Literary Index to American Magazines, 1850-1900*, p. 41. Also for a bibliography of works by and about Borrow, see *NCBEL*, III, pp. 851-55.

James Boswell, 1740-1795
Bibliographies
128.   Brown, Anthony E. **Boswellian Studies: A Bibliography**. 3d ed. Edinburgh, Scotland: Edinburgh University Press, 1991. 176p. LC 92-22454. ISBN 0-7486-0303-4.

Superseding and greatly expanding Brown's earlier *Boswellian Studies: A Bibliography* (2d ed., Hamden, CT: Archon Books, 1972), this is the most comprehensive guide to works by and about Boswell through 1989. The first section covers early and modern editions of Boswell's works, identifying all editions, including reprints and non-English-language translations from 1760 to 1989. Some 121 entries, most with sublistings, provide citations for contemporary notices, reviews, and commentaries in the likes of the *Monthly Review* and *Gentleman's Magazine*. Also notes reviews of modern scholarly editions. Other sections identify memorabilia and biographies of Boswell, with citations to contemporary and modern notices and reviews. The most substantial section covers general studies of Boswell through 1989, offering nearly 1,100 briefly annotated entries, with citations to reviews. Comprehensive coverage of criticism includes non-English-language scholarly studies and prefaces in editions as well as articles in newspapers and "whimsical sketches and parodies" (p. xiii). Separate sections list some 200 "newspaper and magazine paragraphs of the Eighteenth-century" (p. xiii); that is, articles and comments on Boswell in contemporary news publications, about 50 theses and dissertations (unannotated), and bibliographies. Addenda of several dozen items complete each section. An excellent comprehensive index of names, titles, and specific topics accesses the guide. Coverage is superior to Cochrane's *Boswell's Literary Art: An Annotated Bibliography of Critical Studies, 1900-1985* (entry 129), although Cochrane's annotations are more detailed. Likewise, Pottle's *The Literary Career of James Boswell, Esq.* (entry 130) offers the fullest bibliographic descriptions of Boswell's works.

129.   Cochrane, Hamilton E. **Boswell's Literary Art: An Annotated Bibliography of Critical Studies, 1900-1985**. New York: Garland, 1992. 162p. (Garland Reference Library of the Humanities, vol. 969). LC 91-30751. ISBN 0-8240-1516-9.

Chronologically arranges annotated entries for 685 major studies published from 1900 to 1985 in sections for biography; bibliography; studies of the Boswell papers; studies of individual works; general studies; and studies of Boswell and law, politics, and religion. Emphasis is on Boswell "as a writer and his major literary achievements: the *Life of Johnson* and *Tour to the Hebrides*, and the journals" (p. vii). Coverage excludes reviews, introductions in editions, and dramatizations; and unannotated entries for dissertations. Author and subject indexes offer detailed access.

130.   Pottle, Frederick Albert. **The Literary Career of James Boswell, Esq., Being the Bibliographical Materials for a Life of Boswell**. Oxford: Clarendon Press, 1929. 335p. LC 29-18372.

The standard bibliography of primary materials, Pottle's guide gives full bibliographic descriptions of Boswell's books, pamphlets, and broadsides; periodical publications; posthumous works; doubtful works; attributed works; and projected works, as well as contemporary reviews of Boswell's works. Entries include title-page transcriptions and facsimiles, collations, physical descriptions, contents, and publishing histories, with the most extensive coverage of Boswell's *Life of Johnson*. Available in a reprinted edition (Oxford: Clarendon Press, 1965). Also for a bibliography of works by and about Boswell compiled by Pottle, see *NCBEL*, II, pp. 1,210-49. Boswell's manuscripts are described in *Index of English Literary Manuscripts*, III, pt. 1:39-58. Marion S. Pottle, Claude Colleer Abbott, and Frederick A. Pottle's *Catalogue of the Papers of James Boswell at Yale University: For the Greater Part Formerly the Collection of Lieut.-Colonel Ralph Heyward Isham* (Edinburgh, Scotland: Edinburgh University Press; New Haven: Yale University Press, 1993) is also useful. Additionally of primary interest is the catalog of Boswell's library, *Bibliotheca Boswelliana* (London: Compton, 1825) and Donald D. Eddy's *Sale Catalogues of the Libraries of Samuel Johnson, Hester Lynch Thrale (Mrs. Piozzi) and James Boswell* (New Castle, DE: Oak Knoll Books, 1993).

Dion Boucicault, 1820-1890
Bibliographies

Boucicault's manuscripts are listed in Robbins' *American Literary Manuscripts*, pp. 35-36. Boucicault's contributions to and reviews of Boucicault's works in selected periodicals are identified in Wells' *The Literary Index to American Magazines, 1850-1900*, pp. 41-42. Research on Boucicault is reviewed by James F. Kilroy in Finneran's *Anglo-Irish Literature*, pp. 46-47.

Vance (Nye) Bourjaily, 1922-
Bibliographies

For works by Bourjaily, see *First Printings of American Authors*, vol. 1, pp. 39-40. Bourjaily's manuscripts are listed in Robbins' *American Literary Manuscripts*, p. 36.

Elizabeth (Dorothea Cole) Bowen, 1899-1973
Bibliographies

131. Sellery, J'nan M., and William O. Harris. **Elizabeth Bowen: A Bibliography**. Austin, TX: Humanities Research Center, University of Texas at Austin, 1981. 359p. (Tower Bibliographical Series, no. 16). LC 78-52676. ISBN 0-8795-9080-7.

Sellery and Harris cover works by and about Bowen, giving full bibliographic descriptions for first British and American editions of books and pamphlets; contributions to books; contributions to periodicals (some 667 entries); translations of Bowen's works (arranged by works); major collections of manuscripts located in the Harry Ransom Humanities Research Center, the Berg Collection of the New York Public Library, and the BBC Written Archives Centre (pp. 199-273); radio and television productions and appearances; and anthologies containing Bowen's works, as well as supplying unannotated entries for about 150 critical works (books, articles, dissertations, theses, and obituaries) about Bowen. Entries for primary materials include title-page transcriptions, collations, physical descriptions, contents, publishing histories, and references to reviews. Appends a list of Bowen's publishing contracts. Comprehensive indexing. Sellery and Harris' coverage of Bowen's primary works is more comprehensive than Stanton's *A Bibliography of Modern British Novelists*, pp. 135-79, 1,081, which contains classified, unannotated entries with brief bibliographic data for 144 works by Bowen and for 256 works about her (especially reviews), with an addendum. Also for a bibliography of works by and about Bowen, see *NCBEL*, IV, pp. 534-35.

George Bowering, 1935-
Bibliographies

132. Miki, Roy. **A Record of Writing: An Annotated and Illustrated Bibliography of George Bowering**. Vancouver, BC: Talonbooks, 1990. 401p. LC 90-176341. ISBN 0-889-22263-0.

Covers works by and about Bowering. Describes Bowering's works in sections for books and pamphlets; contributions to books; contributions to periodicals; other works, including broadsides, audio and video programs, advertisements, postcards, and ephemera; major manuscript collections; and translations of Bowering's works. Entries for separate publications give title-page transcriptions, with facsimiles of selected title pages, dust jackets, and other illustrations; collations; contents; and notes on publication histories. A final section chronologically lists more than 600 works about Bowering, including reviews and dissertations. The volume also includes a brief chronology of Bowering's life and career. Name and title index.

Jane Bowles, 1917-1973
Bibliographies

For works by Bowles, see *First Printings of American Authors*, vol. 5, pp. 35-36.

Paul Frederic Bowles, 1910-
Bibliographies

133. Miller, Jeffrey. **Paul Bowles: A Descriptive Bibliography**. Santa Barbara, CA: Black Sparrow Press, 1986. 323p. LC 84-10967. ISBN 0-87685-609-1.

Identifies Bowles' primary works, including detailed descriptions in separate listings for Bowles' books and pamphlets and translations by Bowles, contributions to books, contributions to periodicals (803 entries), translations of Bowles' works (arranged by languages), published and unpublished music, musical and literary recordings, and other miscellaneous materials (such as Bowles' writings in catalogs, broadsides, and film adaptations). Entries give title-page transcriptions, physical descriptions, and brief publishing histories, with facsimiles of selected title pages and dust jackets. Bowles' manuscripts are listed in Robbins' *American Literary Manuscripts*, p. 37. See *Bibliography of American Fiction 1919-1988*, pp. 95-97, for Richard Goldstone's checklist of works by and about Bowles.

James Boyd, 1888-1944
Bibliographies
See *Bibliography of American Fiction, 1919-1988*, p. 98, for Karen E. Antell's checklist of works by and about Bowles. Boyd's manuscripts are listed in Robbins' *American Literary Manuscripts*, p. 37.

John Boyd, 1912-
Bibliographies
King's *Ten Modern Irish Playwrights*, pp. 35-38, gives brief bibliographic information for Boyd's primary works and annotated entries for criticism of Boyd, with a classified list of reviews.

Hjalmar Hjorth Boyesen, 1848-1895
Bibliographies
For works by Boyesen, see *Bibliography of American Literature*, vol. 1, pp. 251-60. Boyesen's contributions to and reviews of Boyesen's works in selected periodicals are identified in Wells' *The Literary Index to American Magazines, 1850-1900*, pp. 42-44. Boyesen's manuscripts are listed in Robbins' *American Literary Manuscripts*, p. 37. See *Bibliography of American Fiction, 1866-1918*, pp. 78-79, for Clarence A. Glasrud's checklist of works by and about Boyesen.

Kay Boyle, 1903-1994
Bibliographies
Also for works by Boyle, see *First Printings of American Authors*, vol. 3, pp. 11-24. Boyle's manuscripts are listed in Robbins' *American Literary Manuscripts*, p. 37. See *Bibliography of American Fiction, 1919-1988*, pp. 99-100, for Byron K. Jackson's checklist of works by and about Boyle.

Robert Boyle, 1627-1691
Bibliographies
134.   Fulton, J. F. **A Bibliography of the Honourable Robert Boyle, Fellow of the Royal Society**. 2d ed. Oxford: Clarendon Press, 1961. 217p. LC 61-3930.
Originally published in the *Oxford Bibliographical Society Proceedings and Papers* 3.1 (1932): 1-172, with addenda in 3.3 (1933): 339-365; and *Oxford Bibliographical Society Publications*, new series, I (1947): 33-38. Fulton chronologically arranges full bibliographic descriptions of Boyle's works in sections for separate publications, contributions to other works (including *The Philosophical Transactions of the Royal Society*), and collections. Title-page transcriptions, collations, contents, and notes on publications histories and variants. Coverage includes editions and translations through the end of the nineteenth century. Also contains descriptions of 367 biographic and critical works about Boyle published through 1931, with appendixes for Boyle's lectures and sermons. Index. Also for a bibliography of works by and about Boyle, see *NCBEL*, I, p. 2,340.

Gerald Warner Brace, 1901-1978
Bibliographies

For works by Brace, see *First Printings of American Authors*, vol. 2, pp. 51-52. Brace's manuscripts are listed in Robbins' *American Literary Manuscripts*, p. 38.

Hugh Henry Brackenridge, 1748-1816
Bibliographies

135.   Heartman, Charles F. **A Bibliography of the Writings of Hugh Henry Brackenridge Prior to 1825.** 1917; reprint New York: Burt Franklin, 1968. 37p. (Burt Franklin Bibliography & Reference Series, no. 231). LC 68-56588.

Although not giving full bibliographic descriptions, Heartman supplements the standard account of works by Brackenridge in Blanck's *Bibliography of American Literature*, vol. 1, pp. 261-68. Heartman supplies chronologically arranged title-page transcriptions, pagination, and many copy locations for Brackenridge's writings published to 1825, including edited works, such as *The United States Magazine* and *The Tree of Liberty*, and a translation. Reviews of *Modern Chivalry* and comments on Brackenridge in selected periodicals are identified in Wells' *The Literary Index to American Magazines, 1815-1865*, p. 11. Brackenridge's manuscripts are listed in Robbins' *American Literary Manuscripts*, p. 38. See *Bibliography of American Fiction Through 1865*, pp. 60-63, for a checklist of works by and about Brackenridge.

Leigh Brackett, 1915-1978
Bibliographies

136.   Arbur, Rosemarie. **Leigh Brackett, Marion Zimmer Bradley, Anne McCaffrey: A Primary and Secondary Bibliography.** Boston: G. K. Hall, 1982. 277p. (Masters of Science Fiction and Fantasy). LC 81-4216. ISBN 0-8161-8120-9.

Arbur provides separate parallel lists for fiction; miscellaneous works, including screenplays, interviews, manuscripts in the Brackett Collection of Eastern New Mexico University (pp. 23-28), and the like; nonfiction works (with summaries); and critical works (mostly reviews) for these writers. Entries for primary works give brief bibliographic information, with references for separate, collected, and anthologized reprints. Critical coverage for Brackett includes 122 items from 1951 through 1980; for Bradley, 181 items from 1954 through 1980; and for McCaffrey, 165 items from 1968 through 1980. Annotations are descriptive. See *Bibliography of American Fiction, 1919-1988*, pp. 334-35, for Raymond H. Thompson's checklist of works by and about McCaffrey.

Ray (Douglas) Bradbury, 1920-1996
Bibliographies

137.   Nolan, William F. **The Ray Bradbury Companion: A Life and Career History, Photolog, and Comprehensive Checklist of Writings with Facsimiles from Ray Bradbury's Unpublished and Uncollected Work in All Media.** Detroit, MI: Gale, 1975. 339p. (A Bruccoli Clark Book). LC 74-10397. ISBN 0-8103-0930-0.

Chronologically arranged lists of works by Bradbury, covering his books, pamphlets, short fiction, nonfiction, poetry, miscellaneous writings (such as introductions, prefaces, and forewords), reviews, published speeches, plays, published letters, interviews, dedications, comic-book appearances, and contributions to anthologies, as well as radio and television adaptations, films, and recordings of his works. Entries for first editions give facsimiles of title pages and dust jackets, with collations, contents, and brief information on publishing histories for first and subsequent editions and printings. Nolan also includes selectively annotated entries for about 200 works about Bradbury, including dissertations and master's theses. Annotations are descriptive. Also for works by Bradbury, see *First Printings of American Authors*, vol. 1, pp. 41-47. Bradbury's manuscripts are listed in Robbins' *American Literary Manuscripts*, p. 38. See *Bibliography of American Fiction, 1919-1988*, pp. 101-103, for James L. Welsh's checklist of works by and about Bradbury.

William Bradford, 1590-1657
Bibliographies

138. Gallagher, Edward J., and Thomas Werge. **Early Puritan Writers: A Reference Guide: William Bradford, John Cotton, Thomas Hooker, Edward Johnson, Richard Mather, Thomas Shepard.** Boston: G. K. Hall, 1976. 207p. (Reference Guides in Literature). LC 76-2498. ISBN 0-8161-1196-0.

Brief descriptions of books, chapters and parts of books, articles, dissertations, and passing references in separate listings about each of the six writers. Identifies some 150 works published from 1669 through 1973 for Bradford; about 100 from 1658 through 1975 for Cotton; about 75 from 1695 through 1974 for Hooker; and about 50 each for Johnson (from 1814 through 1975), Mather (from 1670 through 1972), and Shepard (from 1702 through 1974). Descriptive annotations include extensive quotations, particularly from early works. Bibliographic entries for works treating more than one writer are duplicated throughout rather than cross-referenced. Index references selected topics (such as "nature," "chosen people," and others). For works by Bradford, see *First Printings of American Authors*, vol. 3, pp. 25-26. Bradford's manuscripts are listed in Robbins' *American Literary Manuscripts*, p. 38. Research on Bradford is reviewed by David Levin in Everett Emerson's *Major Writers of Early American Literature*, pp. 11-32.

Marion Zimmer Bradley, 1930-
Bibliographies

Arbur's *Leigh Brackett, Marion Zimmer Bradley, Anne McCaffrey* (entry 136) describes works about Bradley published from 1951 through 1980.

Dictionaries, Encyclopedias, and Handbooks

139. Breen, Walter. **The Darkover Concordance: A Reader's Guide**. Berkeley, CA: Pennyfarthing Press, 1979. 163p. LC 79-84472. ISBN 0-9308-0010-9.

Dictionary of "all families, individuals (including character sketches), officials, ranks, castes, positions, occupations, guilds, planetary origins, races, languages, buildings, settlements, Domains, geographical features, flora, fauna, artifacts, foodstuffs, drinkables, etc., as well as the various Gifts, technical terms and key concepts of matrix technology" (p. viii) mentioned in Bradley's "Darkover" novels, with summaries of plots and publishing histories of the 11 novels and genealogical tables.

Anne (Dudley) Bradstreet, c. 1612-1672
Bibliographies

140. Dolle, Raymond F. **Anne Bradstreet: A Reference Guide**. Boston: G. K. Hall, 1990. 145p. (Reference Guide to Literature). LC 89-26888. ISBN 0-8161-8974-9.

Chronologically arranges annotated entries for about 400 works about Bradstreet published from 1650 through 1989, with the vast majority published since 1900. International critical coverage includes introductions in editions, dissertations, and non-English-language works. Although descriptive, annotations provide significant works with extended reviews. Dolle's thorough introduction highlights important editions and studies. Indexing for subjects, persons, and titles offers detailed topical access. Oscar Wegelin's "A List of Editions of the Poems of Anne Bradstreet, with Several Additional Books Relating to Her," *American Book Collector* 4 (July 1933): 15-16, offers the fullest descriptive information for Bradstreet's primary works. Joseph R. McElrath Jr. and Allan P. Robbs's edition of *The Complete Works of Anne Bradstreet* (Boston: Twayne, 1981) gives supplemental information. Also for works by Bradstreet, see *First Printings of American Authors*, vol. 3, p. 27; and *NCBEL*, I, pp. 1,300-301. Bradstreet's manuscripts are listed in Robbins' *American Literary Manuscripts*, p. 39. Research on Bradstreet is reviewed by Ann Stanford in Everett Emerson's *Major Writers of Early American Literature*, pp. 33-58; and by Stanford in Duke, Bryer, and Inge's *American Women Writers*, pp. 3-20.

John Gardiner Calkins Brainard, 1796-1828
Bibliographies
For works by Brainard, see *Bibliography of American Literature*, vol. 1, pp. 269-74. Brainard's contributions to and reviews of Brainard's works in selected periodicals are identified in Wells' *The Literary Index to American Magazines, 1815-1865*, p. 11; and *The Literary Index to American Magazines, 1850-1900*, p. 44. Brainard's manuscripts are listed in Robbins' *American Literary Manuscripts*, p. 39.

John Gerard Braine, 1922-1986
Bibliographies
141.   Salwak, Dale. **John Braine and John Wain: A Reference Guide**. Boston: G. K. Hall, 1980. 195p. (Reference Publication in Literature). LC 79-19290. ISBN 0-8161-8232-9.

Separate lists of the primary works of Braine and Wain and chronologically arranged lists of annotated entries for works about them. Coverage for Braine (from 1957 through 1977) and Wain (from 1953 through 1977) includes books, articles, reviews, and dissertations. Annotations are descriptive.

Max Brand (Frederick Faust), 1892-1944
Bibliographies
142.   Nolan, William F. **Max Brand, Western Giant: The Life and Times of Frederick Schiller Faust**. Bowling Green, OH: Bowling Green State University Popular Press, 1985. 175p. LC 86-70192. ISBN 0-8797-2291-6.

An awkwardly organized guide to Faust's complete works from 1910 to 1985 and to works about Faust. "A Bibliographical Checklist of Works by and About Frederick Faust" (pp. 72-174) gives brief bibliographic information for 260 first and subsequent editions of Faust's books (subarranged by his pen names, which included "Max Brand," "Frank Austin," "George Owen Baxter," "Evan Evans," and others), with a comprehensive title listing of his books. Separate chronological listings of his fiction (Nolan attributes to him "nearly 700 stories," p. 114), plays and sketches, verse, nonfiction, silent- and sound-film adaptations, and radio, television, and stage adaptations supply brief data for publication histories, reprintings, credits, and so forth. Nolan also describes and gives the tables of contents for two books on Faust and identifies about 20 books (largely entries in biographic reference works) and 100 journal and magazine articles about Faust. In addition to a biographic introduction and several memorials and tributes, Nolan reprints in a separate section selected reviews and critical comments on Faust. Unindexed. Updated by listings in *The Max Brand Companion* (entry 143), pp. 143-282. See also *Bibliography of American Fiction, 1919-1988*, pp. 186-91, for David L. Fox's checklist of works by and about Faust. Faust's manuscripts are listed in Robbins' *American Literary Manuscripts*, p. 106. William Bloodworth surveys works by and about Brand in Erisman and Etulain's *Fifty Western Writers*, pp. 32-41.

Dictionaries, Encyclopedias, and Handbooks
143.   Tuska, Jon, Vicki Piekarski, and Darrell C. Richardson. **The Max Brand Companion**. Westport, CT: Greenwood Press, 1996. 547p. LC 96-18207. ISBN 0-313-29750-9.

In addition to contributed essays in sections "Biography and Tributes" and "Belles Lettres and Literary Criticism," Tuska, Piekarski, and Richardson's companion offers bibliographic features that can be used to update coverage of works by and about Faust in Nolan's *Max Brand, Western Giant* (entry 142). Includes a cumulative chronological checklist of Faust's published works (1910-92), with separate alphabetical and chronological lists of published books (to 1996); and Faust filmography (with brief credits for silent films and sound films). Entries give brief bibliographic information with citations for other appearances. Also includes an annotated listing of works about Faust (rather difficult to use in that entries are unnumbered and awkwardly formatted) in sections for books (four entries), parts of books, magazine and newspaper articles, and unpublished papers. Additional bibliographic features include a survey of fan publications and essays on Faust collecting. Index of names and titles.

Richard Brautigan, 1935-1984
Bibliographies

144.   Barber, John F. **Richard Brautigan: An Annotated Bibliography.** Jefferson, NC: McFarland, 1990. 236p. LC 89-43698. ISBN 0-899-50525-2.

Describes works by and about Brautigan published from 1956 through 1989. The first part contains 203 entries with brief bibliographic data for first and subsequent editions and translations and summaries of contents in sections for poems, novels, short stories, one collection, essays and articles, letters and papers, and recordings. The second part (with about 650 entries) describes general commentaries on Brautigan (in subsections for books, bibliographies, dissertations and theses, parodies, censorship litigation, and teaching experiences), criticism (general and general international, including non-English-language works), reviews of works by Brautigan (in sections, listed by work, for poetry, novels, short stories, and collections), "Mysterious and Erroneous Citations" (five entries), obituaries and eulogies, and sources (mostly indexes consulted by Barber). Descriptive annotations. Also includes chronology and biocritical overview. Comprehensive name and title index. See *Bibliography of American Fiction, 1919-1988*, pp. 104-105, for Michael Mullen's checklist of works by and about Brautigan. Craig Thompson gives a summary biography, critical assessment of major works, and selected primary and secondary bibliographies for Brautigan in McCaffery's *Postmodern Fiction: A Bio-Bibliographical Guide*, pp. 286-89.

Jimmy Breslin, 1930-
Bibliographies

For works by Breslin, see *First Printings of American Authors*, vol. 2, pp. 53-54.

Reginald Bretnor, 1911-
Bibliographies

145.   Burgess, Scott Alan, and Boden Clarke. **The Work of Reginald Bretnor: An Annotated Bibliography & Guide.** San Bernardino, CA: Borgo Press, 1989. 122p. (Bibliographies of Modern Authors, no. 8). LC 85-31405. ISBN 0-8937-0387-7.

Describes works by and about Bretnor in sections covering books, short fiction, nonfiction, "feghoots" (119 short tales on space and time travel featuring Ferdinand Feghoot), verse, edited works, unpublished works, honors and awards, 16 works about Bretnor, miscellanea (pen names, books dedicated to Bretnor, and so on), and selected quotes about Bretnor. The twenty-two entries for books give brief bibliographic information for first and subsequent editions, notes on contents, and citations for reviews. Also includes a chronology of Bretnor's life and career. Index of primary titles.

Nicholas Breton, 1555?-1626?
Bibliographies

For a bibliography of works by and about Breton, see *NCBEL*, I, pp. 565, 1,027-29. The Tannenbaums' *Elizabethan Bibliographies*, vol. 1, offers an unannotated list of modern editions and studies of Breton. Breton's manuscripts are described in *Index of English Literary Manuscripts*, I, pt. 1:101-14.

Robert (Seymour) Bridges, 1844-1930
Bibliographies
146.   Hamilton, Lee Templin. **Robert Bridges: An Annotated Bibliography, 1873-1988**. Newark, DE: University of Delaware Press, 1991. 243p. LC 88-40577. ISBN 0-87413-364-5.

Describes works by and about Bridges in chronologically arranged chapters for poems, dramas, and hymns by Bridges; for Bridges' prose writings, including critical essays, introductions, memoirs, and letters; and for about 700 reviews and criticisms of Bridges' works. Entries for separate, collected, anthologized, and excerpted editions of the primary works give brief bibliographic information, notes on contents, and references to reprintings, updating the coverage of McKay's *A Bibliography of Robert Bridges* (entry 147) through 1988. Secondary coverage is largely limited to English-language criticisms and excludes dissertations. Descriptive annotations note reprints. Separate indexes for primary titles, Bridges' works in anthologies, and criticisms, with listings for authors, titles, and detailed topics.

147.   McKay, George L. **A Bibliography of Robert Bridges**. New York: Columbia University Press, 1933. 215p. LC 33-31729.

McKay includes title-page transcriptions, physical descriptions, contents, and brief notes on publishing histories for Bridges' separate publications and contributions to books, journals, and newspapers. First line and general indexes are included. Available in a reprinted edition (New York: AMS Press, 1966). For a bibliography of works by and about Bridges, see *NCBEL*, III, pp. 593-97. Also useful, William S. Kable's *The Ewelme Collection of Robert Bridges: A Catalogue* (Columbia, SC: Department of English, University of South Carolina, 1967) supplements McKay with details on 109 separate publications as well as manuscripts, contributed works, and early responses to Bridges from a collection formed by Simon Nowell-Smith. See the review of research by Lionel Stevenson in Faverty's *The Victorian Poets*, pp. 375-79.

Charles Frederick Briggs, 1804-1877
Bibliographies
For works by Briggs, see *Bibliography of American Literature*, vol. 1, pp. 275-78. Briggs' contributions to and reviews of Briggs' works in selected periodicals are identified in Wells' *The Literary Index to American Magazines, 1815-1865*, p. 12. Briggs' manuscripts are listed in Robbins' *American Literary Manuscripts*, p. 40. See *Bibliography of American Fiction Through 1865*, p. 64, for a checklist of works by and about Briggs.

Paul Brodeur, 1931-
Bibliographies
For works by Brodeur, see *First Printings of American Authors*, vol. 1, p. 49.

Richard Brome, c.1590-1652/3
Bibliographies
For a bibliography of works by and about Brome, see *NCBEL*, I, pp. 1,733-34. See the review of research by Ann Haaker in Logan and Smith's *The Later Jacobean and Caroline Dramatists*, pp. 172-91, updated by Lidman's *Studies in Jacobean Drama, 1973-1984*, pp. 249-54.

Louis Bromfield, 1896-1956
Bibliographies
For works by Bromfield, see *First Printings of American Authors*, vol. 4, pp. 37-43. Bromfield's manuscripts are listed in Robbins' *American Literary Manuscripts*, p. 40. See *Bibliography of American Fiction, 1919-1988*, pp. 69-70, for Philip B. Eppard's checklist of works by and about Bromfield.

William Bronk, 1918-
Bibliographies

> For works by Bronk, see *First Printings of American Authors*, vol. 3, pp. 29-33.

The Brontes: Anne Bronte, 1820-1849; Charlotte Bronte, 1816-1855; Emily Bronte, 1818-1848; and Patrick Branwell Bronte, 1817-1848
Bibliographies

148.   Crump, R. W. **Charlotte and Emily Bronte, 1846-1915: A Reference Guide**. Boston: G. K. Hall, 1982. 194p. (Reference Guide to Literature). LC 82-1097. ISBN 0-8161-7953-0.

> Other volumes in this three-volume series include:

> 148.1. Crump, R. W. **Charlotte and Emily Bronte, 1916-1954: A Reference Guide**. Boston: G. K. Hall, 1985. 197p. (Reference Guide to Literature). LC 82-1097. ISBN 0-8161-8672-3.

> 148.2. Crump, R. W. **Charlotte and Emily Bronte, 1955-1983: A Reference Guide**. Boston: G. K. Hall, 1986. 319p. (Reference Guide to Literature). LC 82-1097. ISBN 0-8161-8797-5.

Crump offers comprehensive coverage of writings about Charlotte and Emily Bronte published from 1846 through 1983, chronologically arranging annotated entries for books, chapters and parts of books, articles, dissertations, and reviews in all languages about either or both Charlotte or Emily Bronte. The first and second volumes include about 1,000 entries each, with the third volume containing about 1,500. Works dealing exclusively with one of the writers are designated "C" or "E" for Charlotte or Emily. Annotations are descriptive, with significant studies receiving extended reviews. Subject indexing in the first volume is limited to broad topics (bibliography and biography) and headings under primary titles (for introductions, reviews, sources, and the like). Indexing in the other volumes is substantially improved, including a wider range of topical headings (for "Bronte manuscripts," "juvenilia," "Yorkshire, descriptions of," and the like). The coverage of Crump's bibliographies supersedes that provided by Anne Passel's *Charlotte and Emily Bronte: An Annotated Bibliography* (New York: Garland, 1979), which includes more than 1,300 entries in separate listings for Charlotte Bronte, Emily Bronte, the Bronte family, and bibliographies dating from 1846 through 1978. In addition, Crump's coverage of studies of Emily Bronte supersedes that of Janet M. Barclay's *Emily Bronte Criticism, 1900-1982: An Annotated Check List* (Westport, CT: Meckler Publishing, 1984), a revision of Barclay's *Emily Bronte Criticism 1900-1968: An Annotated Checklist* (New York: New York Public Library and Readex, 1974), which offers 1,021 brief, descriptive entries; as well as G. Anthony Yablon and John R. Turner's *A Bronte Bibliography* (Westport, CT: Meckler Books, 1978), which covers 646 biographical and critical works about the Brontes. Significant of the Bronte's international reputation, Tomoko Iijima's *Buronte Shimai* [transliterated title] (Tokyo: Nichigai Asoshietsu, Kinokuniya Shoten, 1994) is an extensive Japanese-language bibliography of editions and criticism of the Brontes. Research on the Brontes is reviewed by Mildred G. Christian in Stevenson's *Victorian Fiction*, pp. 214-44; Herbert J. Rosengarten in Ford's *Victorian Fiction*, pp. 172-203; and Miriam Allott in Dyson's *English Novel*, pp. 218-45.

149.   Wise, Thomas J. **A Bibliography of the Writings in Prose and Verse of the Members of the Bronte Family**. 1917; reprint London: Dawsons of Pall Mall, 1965. 255p. OCLC 1328253.

The major primary bibliography for the Brontes, Wise's guide gives full bibliographic descriptions for the separate publications and contributions to books and periodicals of Charlotte Bronte, Emily Bronte and Anne Bronte, Rev.

Patrick Bronte, and Patrick Branwell Bronte, in addition to describing 59 Bronteana. Entries give title-page transcriptions, physical descriptions, and publishing histories, with selected title-page facsimiles. Also available in a second reprinted edition (Folkestone: Dawsons of Pall Mall, 1972). For a bibliography of works by and about the Brontes, see *NCBEL*, III, pp. 863-73. The manuscripts of Anne, Charlotte, and Emily Bronte are described in *Index of English Literary Manuscripts*, IV, pt. 1:33-105. More specifically, Christine Alexander's *A Bibliography of the Manuscripts of Charlotte Bronte* (Westport, CT: Bronte Society in association with Meckler Publishing, 1982) describes 499 manuscripts of Charlotte Bronte's prose, poetry, business papers, and other writings (excluding letters). Victor A. Neufeldt's *A Bibliography of the Manuscripts of Patrick Branwell Bronte* (New York: Garland, 1993) supplies 289 entries for prose works, poetry, translations, and miscellaneous manuscripts. Arthur D. Walker's *The Correspondence of the Bronte Family: A Guide* (Didsbury, Manchester: E. J. Morton, 1982) calendars about 2,000 letters of the Brontes, with cross-references to locations of manuscripts and published versions. Additional descriptions of primary materials are included in the *Catalogue of the Bonnell Collection in the Bronte Parsonage Museum* (Haworth: Bronte Society, 1932).

Dictionaries, Encyclopedias, and Handbooks
150. Evans, Barbara, and Gareth Lloyd Evans. **Everyman's Companion to the Brontes**. London: J. M. Dent, 1982. 400p. LC 82-144255. ISBN 0-460-04455-9.

This is the most comprehensive handbook for information about the lives and works of the Brontes. The Evanses offer an extensive calendar of events from 1812 through 1861; brief biographies of Rev. Patrick and Maria Bronte, Charlotte Bronte, Emily Bronte, Anne Bronte and Aunt Branwell, and Patrick Branwell Bronte, with a dictionary of family, friends, and other associates; surveys of the Brontes' juvenilia and published writings, with dictionaries of characters, places, and plots; excerpts from contemporary comments and criticism on their works; maps; and much more. This is a solid starting point for study of the Brontes. More limited in coverage, Herbert E. Wroot's *The Persons and Places of the Bronte Novels* (1906; reprint New York: Burt Franklin, 1970) explains the plots and identifies the characters and places in the Brontes' works, while Glenda Leeming's *Who's Who in Jane Austen and the Brontes* (London: Elm Tree Books, 1974) covers characters only.

151. Pinion, F. G. **A Bronte Companion: Literary Assessment, Background, and Reference**. New York: Barnes and Noble, 1975. 394p. LC 75-3510. ISBN 0-06-495573-7.

In addition to biographical sketches of Charlotte, Emily, Anne, Rev. Patrick, and Patrick Branwell Bronte, Pinion offers critical introductory commentaries on their individual works, emphasizing traditional elements of plot and structure, characterization, theme, and imagery. A dictionary of "People and Places in the Novels," a "Glossary of Unusual Words," and a selective bibliography support the surveys. Appended list of films based on the Brontes' works.

Indexes and Concordances
152. Nakaoka, Hiroshi. **A Concordance to Wuthering Heights**. Tokyo: Kaibunsha, 1983. 426p. OCLC 11631514.

Concords the text of Hilda Marsden and Ian Jack's edition of *Wuthering Heights* in the standard *Clarendon Edition of the Novels of the Brontes* (Oxford: Clarendon Press, 1976). Nakaoka provides an index verborum to the appendixed text, with alphabetical and frequency lists. By comparison, following the model of volumes in Garland's Conrad Concordances (entry 293), C. Ruth Sabol and Todd K. Bender's *A Concordance to Bronte's Wuthering Heights* (New York: Garland, 1984) is an index verborum based on the field of reference that reproduces the 1847 text (London: Thomas Newby) of the novel.

153. Sabol, C. Ruth, and Todd K. Bender. **A Concordance to Bronte's Jane Eyre**. New York: Garland, 1981. 448p. (Garland Reference Library of the Humanities, vol. 290). LC 81-47016. ISBN 0-8240-9339-9.

Sabol and Bender produce a verbal index that cites pages and lines in the · field of reference based on the text of the second edition of *Jane Eyre: An Autobiography* (London: Smith, Elder, 1848). Appends an alphabetically arranged word-frequency table.

Journals

154. **Bronte Newsletter**. New York: Bronte Society, 1982- . Annual. ISSN 0737-6340.

Bronte Newsletter is chiefly valuable for information about upcoming conferences, conference reports, and reviews of new publications about the Brontes and of theatrical and media adaptations of their works. In addition, the newsletter typically publishes two to three brief, topical notes on such subjects as Byronic influences, Jane Eyre and the Cinderella story, and Branwell Bronte's masks. Vol. 11 (1995) includes a contributor index to vols. 1-11 (1982-1995). Although *MLA* cites any significant studies that appear in journal, the general contents of *Bronte Newsletter* are not indexed.

155. **Bronte Society Gazette**. Haworth, Keighley, West Yorkshire: Bronte Society, Bronte Parsonage Museum, 1990- . 2/yr. ISSN 1344-5960.

Membership newsletter of the Bronte Society. Contains information about activities, museums, the Brontes in the media, and membership. Unindexed.

156. **Bronte Society Transactions**. Haworth, Keighley, West Yorkshire: Bronte Society, Bronte Parsonage Museum, 1895- . Frequency has varied; most recently 2/yr. ISSN 0309-7795.

Sponsored by the Bronte Society, *Bronte Society Transactions* features brief scholarly critical and biographical articles on a full range of topics related to the Brontes, such as portraits of the Brontes, landscape symbolism and chronology in *Wuthering Heights*, the Brontes' borrowings from Scott and Dumas, and the poetry of Branwell Bronte. Many articles transcribe manuscripts and other documents. Others describe recent acquisitions (books, manuscripts, portraits, and realia) of the Bronte Parsonage Museum. Since 1970, the regularly featured brief checklist, "Bronte Reading List," identifies new editions and book-length critical works. In addition to selections of book reviews, the journal publishes announcements of activities (luncheons, programs for schoolchildren, walks, and the like) at the Bronte Parsonage, reports on affiliated international societies, such as its American Committee, and reviews research on the Brontes presented at conferences. *Bronte Society Transactions* is indexed in *AES*, *MHRA*, and *MLA*.

Rupert Chawner Brooke, 1887-1915

Bibliographies

157. Keynes, Geoffrey L. **A Bibliography of Rupert Brooke**. 3d ed., revised. London: Rupert Hart-Davis, 1964. 158p. (Soho Bibliographies, no. 4). OCLC 2504582.

First published in 1954 (London: R. Hart-Davis) and then in a revised second edition. (London: Rupert Hart-Davis, 1959), Keynes' guide supplies full bibliographic descriptions (title-page transcriptions, collations, contents, and publishing histories) for Brooke's separate editions of the poems: collected poems; contributions to books; selected poems; prose works; contributions to periodicals; and poems in manuscript (with locations). Also lists works about Brooke. The revisions of the third edition amount to "a few minor corrections" of the revised second edition. Indexes of titles and first lines and general index. John Schroder's *Catalogue of Books and Manuscripts by Rupert Brooke, Edward Marsh & Christopher Hassall* (Cambridge: Rampart Lions Press, 1970) offers additional information about Brooke's primary materials. For a bibliography of works by and about Brooke, see *NCBEL*, IV, pp. 241-43.

Charles T(imothy) Brooks, 1813-1883

Bibliographies

For works by Brooks, see *Bibliography of American Literature*, vol. 1, pp. 279-97. Brooks' manuscripts are listed in Robbins' *American Literary Manuscripts*, p. 41. Elizabeth R. McKinsey reviews research on Brooks in Myerson's *The Transcendentalists*, pp. 100-101. Fannie Mae Elliott and Lucy Clark's slim *The Barrett Library: Charles Timothy Brooks: A Checklist of Printed and Manuscript Works of Charles Timothy Brooks in the Library of the University of Virginia* (Charlottesville, VA: University of Virginia Press, 1960) is also available but offers little not already covered elsewhere.

Cleanth Brooks, 1906-

Bibliographies

158.   Walsh, John Michael. **Cleanth Brooks: An Annotated Bibliography**. New York: Garland, 1990. 438p. (Garland Bibliographies of Modern Critics and Critical Schools, vol. 14; Garland Reference Library of the Humanities, vol. 1,208). LC 89-23578. ISBN 0-8240-4941-1.

Describes works by and about Brooks in separate, classified sections. Part 1 covers primary sources with sections for books and collections of essays; edited books; essays and review articles; reviews; brief notes, letters, and replies; and panel discussions and interviews. Part 2 covers secondary works, with sections for books and essay collections; essays and review articles; reviews of Brooks' books; brief notes, replies, and letters; dissertations; reviews of books about Brooks; and miscellaneous works. Full annotations describe contents and note subsequent editions. Introduction surveys Brooks' career and ideas. Separate name indexes for writers on whom Brooks commented and who commented on Brooks. Brooks' manuscripts are listed in Robbins' *American Literary Manuscripts*, p. 41.

Gwendolyn Brooks, 1917-

Bibliographies

See Miller's *Langston Hughes and Gwendlyn Brooks* (entry 701). Brooks' manuscripts are listed in Robbins' *American Literary Manuscripts*, p. 41.

Maria Gowen Brooks, c.1794-1845

Bibliographies

For works by Brooks, see *Bibliography of American Literature*, vol. 1, pp. 298-301. Brooks' contributions to and reviews of Brooks' works in selected periodicals are identified in Wells' *The Literary Index to American Magazines, 1815-1865*, p. 14; and *The Literary Index to American Magazines, 1850-1900*, p. 47. Brooks' manuscripts are listed in Robbins' *American Literary Manuscripts*, p. 41.

Van Wyck Brooks, 1886-1963

Bibliographies

159.   Vitelli, James R. **Van Wyck Brooks: A Reference Guide**. Boston: G. K. Hall, 1977. 108p. (Reference Guides in Literature, no. 15). LC 76-21335. ISBN 0-8161-7978-6.

Chronologically arranged annotated entries for works about Brooks published from 1908 to 1974. Coverage identifies three books "wholly given over to Brooks" (p. ix), scholarly and popular articles, and (mostly) newspaper reviews and notices in the English language. Descriptive annotations quote extensively and note reprints. Comprehensive index allows detailed topical access. For works by Brooks, see *First Printings of American Authors*, vol. 5, pp. 37-46. Brooks' manuscripts are listed in Robbins' *American Literary Manuscripts*, p. 42.

Chandler Brossard, 1922-
Bibliographies

For works by Brossard, see *First Printings of American Authors*, vol. 2, pp. 55-56.

Alice Brown, 1857-1948
Bibliographies

For works by Brown, see *First Printings of American Authors*, vol. 3, pp. 35-41. Brown's contributions to and reviews of Brown's works in selected periodicals are identified in Wells' *The Literary Index to American Magazines, 1850-1900*, p. 47. Brown's manuscripts are listed in Robbins' *American Literary Manuscripts*, p. 43. See *Bibliography of American Fiction, 1866-1918*, pp. 80-81, for Philip B. Eppard's checklist of works by and about Brown.

Charles Brockden Brown, 1771-1810
Bibliographies

160.   Parker, Patricia L. **Charles Brockden Brown: A Reference Guide**. Boston: G. K. Hall, 1980. 132p. (Reference Publication in Literature). LC 79-24047. ISBN 0-8161-8450-x.

Parker describes about 650 works about Brown, including scholarly books, periodical and newspapers articles, general studies and reference works, dissertations, and textbooks in a chronological arrangement from 1796 to 1978. Items cite references to early reviews in *New York Weekly Magazine*, *Anti-Jacobin Review*, and *Port Folio*—serials now readily available in major microform collections, such as UMI's *American Periodicals* series. Annotations are descriptive, with significant works receiving detailed reviews. Subject indexing is largely nominal, offering a few subheadings under Brown for biographies, bibliographies, "as translator," and "use of Gothicism in," as well as for Brown's works. The most comprehensive bibliography of Brown scholarship, Parker's guide is updated by Charles A. Carpenter's "Selective Bibliography of Writings About Charles Brockden Brown," in Bernard Rosenthal's *Critical Essays on Charles Brockden Brown* (Boston: G. K. Hall, 1981), pp. 224-39. Several other bibliographies are valuable for information on Brown's primary bibliography, including Blanck's *Bibliography of American Literature*, vol. 1, pp. 302-309; Paul Witherington's "Charles Brockden Brown: A Bibliographical Essay," *Early American Literature* 9 (Fall 1974): 164-87, which describes manuscripts and letters; Charles E. Bennett's *The Charles Brockden Brown Canon* (Chapel Hill, NC: University of North Carolina, 1974) and "The Letters of Charles Brockden Brown: An Annotated Census," *Resources for American Literary Study* 6 (1976): 164-90; and Sydney J. Krause and Jane Nieset's "A Census of the Works of Charles Brockden Brown," *Serif* 3 (December 1966): 27-55, which lists early editions. Brown's manuscripts are also listed in Robbins' *American Literary Manuscripts*, p. 43. Research on Brown is reviewed by Donald A. Ringe in Everett Emerson's *Major Writers of Early American Literature*, pp. 273-94. See *Bibliography of American Fiction Through 1865*, pp. 65-67, for E. Kate Stewart's checklist of works by and about Brown.

George MacKay Brown, 1921-
Bibliographies

161.   Yamada, Osamu, Hilda D. Spear, and David S. Robb. **The Contribution to Literature of Orcadian Writer George MacKay Brown: An Introduction and a Bibliography**. Lewiston, NY: Edwin Mellen Press, 1991. 105p. (Studies in British Literature, vol. 16). LC 91-33423. ISBN 0773496513.

Covers works by and about Brown. The first part chronologically lists Brown's works in classified sections for books of poetry, short fiction, novels, drama, miscellaneous nonfiction, and children's books; contributions to books; contributions to periodicals and newspapers; and translations, librettos and texts for music, recordings, posters, and pamphlets. Entries give basic bibliographic data, with selected information about limited editions. The second part includes unannotated lists of works about Brown in sections for books, articles (mostly reviews), and theses; and works containing references to Brown. Introduction describes Brown's life on Scotland's Orkney islands and critically surveys his works. An appendix identifies dedicatees in Brown's works. Unindexed.

Thomas Brown, 1663-1704
Bibliographies
For a bibliography of works by and about Brown, see *NCBEL*, II, pp. 1,044-46.

William Hill Brown, 1765-1793
Bibliographies
For works by Brown, see *Bibliography of American Literature*, vol. 1, pp. 310-11; and *First Printings of American Authors*, vol. 1, p. 51. Brown's manuscripts are listed in Robbins' *American Literary Manuscripts*, p. 44. See *Bibliography of American Fiction Through 1865*, pp. 68-69, for a checklist of works by and about Brown.

William Wells Brown, 1816?-1884
Bibliographies
162. Ellison, Curtis W., and E. W. Metcalf, Jr. **William Wells Brown and Martin R. Delany: A Reference Guide.** Boston: G. K. Hall, 1978. 276p. (A Reference Publication in Literature). LC 77-25309. ISBN 0-8161-8025-3.

Ellison and Metcalf include separate introductions and separate, chronologically arranged listings of secondary works about Brown and Delany. Comprehensive coverage includes books, articles, reviews, newspaper stories, and anthologized materials for about 800 works about Brown published from 1844 through 1975 and for about 350 works about Delany from 1838 through 1975. Annotations are descriptive. Separate indexes supply headings for selected topics, such as "bibliography," "Africa," and "the south." See *Bibliography of American Fiction Through 1865*, pp. 70-71, for William E. Hull's checklist of works by and about Brown. Brown's manuscripts are listed in Robbins' *American Literary Manuscripts*, p. 44. Research on Brown and Delany is reviewed by Ruth Miller and Peter J. Katopes in Inge, Duke, and Bryer's *Black American Writers*, vol. I, pp. 133-60. John Sekora surveys works by and about Brown in Bain and Flora's *Fifty Southern Writers Before 1900*, pp. 44-54.

Charles Farrar Browne (Artemus Ward), 1834-1867
Bibliographies
For works by Browne, see *Bibliography of American Literature*, vol. 1, pp. 312-24. Browne's manuscripts are listed in Robbins' *American Literary Manuscripts*, p. 44. See *Bibliography of American Fiction, 1866-1918*, pp. 82, for Robert E. Adams' checklist of works by and about Browne.

Sir Thomas Browne, 1605-1682
Bibliographies
163. Donovan, Dennis G., Magaretha G. Hartley Herman, and Ann E. Imbrie. **Sir Thomas Browne and Robert Burton: A Reference Guide.** Boston: G. K. Hall, 1981. 530p. (A Reference Guide to Literature). LC 81-4263. ISBN 0-8161-8018-0.

Contains separate listings for Browne and Burton. Donovan and Herman provide 1,700 chronologically arranged, annotated entries for works by and about Browne, including editions, books, articles, dissertations, and reviews published from 1643 through 1977. Descriptive annotations identify significant studies. Imbrie includes 500 chronologically arranged annotated entries for Burton, covering editions and reprints of *Anatomy of Melancholy* as well as a similarly wide range of works about Burton published from 1621 through 1978. Separate indexes for each writer conclude the volume. These bibliographies supersede coverage in Dennis G. Donovan's *Elizabethan Bibliographies Supplements*, no. 10. Listings are updated by Andrea Sununu's "Recent Studies on Sir Thomas Browne (1979-1986)," *English Literary Renaissance* 19 (Winter 1989): 118-29; and Sununu's "Recent Studies of Burton and Walton," *English Literary Renaissance* 17 (Spring 1987): 243-55.

164. Keynes, Geoffrey. **A Bibliography of Sir Thomas Browne**. 2d ed., revised. Oxford: Clarendon, 1968. 293p. LC 68-111691. ISBN 0-1981-8130-2.

Standard bibliography of Browne's works, first published in 1924 (Cambridge: University Press). Keynes' guide gives full bibliographic descriptions for Browne's books and other writings, letters and collected and selected editions of his works, as well as a description of the sale catalog of Browne's library. Entries for primary works include title-page transcriptions and facsimiles, collations, contents, printing and publishing histories, and locations of copies for all editions (including translations). In addition, Keynes describes in full bibliographic detail 121 biographic and critical works about Browne published from 1633 through 1800 and briefly lists (with selective annotations) about 250 other secondary works about Browne from 1801 through 1966. Appendixes describe imitations of Browne's works. The index references printers, publishers, and booksellers. Also for a bibliography of works by and about Browne, see *NCBEL*, I, pp. 2,228-33. Browne's manuscripts are described in *Index of English Literary Manuscripts*, II, pt. 1:7-24. Also noteworthy, *A Catalogue of the Libraries of Sir Thomas Browne and Dr. Edward Browne, His Son: A Facsimile Reproduction* (Leiden: Published for the Sir Thomas Browne Institute by E. J. Brill/Leiden University Press, 1986), edited by Jeremiah S. Finch, reproduces the 1710 catalog of the Brownes' libraries.

William Browne, of Tavistock, 1590?-1645?

Bibliographies

For a bibliography of works by and about Browne, see *NCBEL*, I, p. 1,195. Browne's manuscripts are described in *Index of English Literary Manuscripts*, I, pt. 1:115-37, 565.

Henry Howard Brownell, 1820-1872

Bibliographies

For works by Brownell, see *Bibliography of American Literature*, vol.1, pp. 325-30. Brownell's contributions to and reviews of Brownell's works in selected periodicals are identified in Wells' *The Literary Index to American Magazines, 1850-1900*, p. 48. Brownell's manuscripts are listed in Robbins' *American Literary Manuscripts*, p. 44.

Elizabeth Barrett Browning, 1806-1861, and Robert Browning, 1812-1889

Bibliographies

165. Barnes, Warner. **A Bibliography of Elizabeth Barrett Browning**. Austin, TX: University of Texas and Baylor University, 1967. 179p. LC 67-64500.

Superseding Thomas J. Wise's *A Bibliography of the Writings in Prose and Verse of Elizabeth Barrett Browning* (1918; reprint Folkestone: Dawsons of Pall Mall, 1970), Barnes fully describes Browning's primary works in separate listings for first English and American editions and other editions of her works published during her life; posthumous works and Wise's forgeries; contributions to periodicals, newspapers, gift books, and anthologies; and editions of letters; and also gives a short title list of reprints. Entries provide title-page transcriptions; extensive physical descriptions of collations, typography, paper, and bindings; contents; and publishing histories. Textual collations of variants and facsimiles of selected title pages and bindings are also given. Barnes' coverage of editions of Browning's works is updated by Peterson's *Robert and Elizabeth Browning* (entry 169).

166.   Broughton, Leslie Nathan, Clark Sutherland Northup, and Robert Pearsall. **Robert Browning: A Bibliography, 1830-1950.** Ithaca, NY: Cornell University Press, 1953. 446p. (Cornell Studies in English, vol. 39). LC 54-7521.

The most important and comprehensive bibliography of works by and about Browning published from 1830 through 1950. Arranged in several separate sections, Broughton, Northup, and Pearsall's guide gives full bibliographic descriptions for Browning's primary works, including his books, contributions to periodicals, posthumous poems, anthologies and reprints, collected and selected works, single poems not published separately, dramatic and prose adaptations, and translations of Browning's works. Also includes annotated entries for reference works (bibliographies, handbooks, concordances, and indexes) and for 4,538 biographical and critical studies; descriptions of poems, appreciations, and parodies related to Browning; a calendar of about 2,000 of Browning's letters; and lists of musical settings to Browning's poems. Entries for primary works give title-page transcriptions, physical descriptions, publishing histories, and references to later editions and printings. This supersedes in reliability Thomas J. Wise's *A Complete Bibliography of the Writings in Prose and Verse of Robert Browning* (1897; reprint Folkstone: Dawsons of Pall Mall, 1971), which nonetheless offers additional physical details about primary works. Broughton, Northup, and Pearsall's guide is updated by Peterson (entry 169). The Brownings' manuscripts are described in *Index of English Literary Manuscripts*, IV, pt. 1:107-273, 825-27. Additionally, other valuable descriptions of the Brownings' primary materials are provided in Aurelia Brook's *Browningiana in Baylor University* (Waco, TX: Baylor University, 1921); Sally Keith Carrol East's *Browning Music: A Descriptive Catalog of the Music Related to Robert Browning and Elizabeth Barrett Browning in the Armstrong Browning Library: 1972* (Waco, TX: Armstrong Browning Library, 1973); Warner Barnes' *Catalogue of the Browning Collection* (Austin, TX: Humanities Research Center, 1966); and Philip Kelley and Betty A. Coley's *The Browning Collections: A Reconstruction with Other Memorabilia* (Winfield, KS: Wedgestone Press, 1984), which reconstructs the 1913 sale catalog for the Brownings' books, manuscripts, and other personal documents and identifies about 7,000 items in 237 collections, with appendixes for buyers and collections.

167.   Donaldson, Sandra. **Elizabeth Barrett Browning: An Annotated Bibliography of the Commentary and Criticism, 1826-1990.** New York: G. K. Hall, 1993. 642p. LC 92-24448. ISBN 0-8161-8910-2.

Incorporating materials for Elizabeth Barrett Browning from Peterson's *Robert and Elizabeth Browning: An Annotated Bibliography, 1951-1970* (entry 169), Donaldson's guide is comprehensive but does not attempt to be "exhaustive" (p. x). Donaldson chronologically arranges annotated entries for about 3,000 critical works on Elizabeth Browning published from 1826 to 1990. Coverage takes in major studies of all kinds, including dissertations and French- and Italian-language criticisms but excludes German and Japanese; likewise, Donaldson has attempted neither to identify every notice or mention of Browning in biographical dictionaries nor to include all reviews of criticism. Descriptive annotations cross-reference other studies and note reprints but do not offer much critical advice. The introduction, conversely, surveys Browning's critical reception (with cross-references to entries for major early studies as well as key works in the fields of textual and feminist scholarship, for example) and indicates areas for further research. Indexes for Browning's works and proper names of persons and places, secondary titles, and subjects— with many detailed subheadings—give excellent access. Coverage of Browning in Ehrsam's *Bibliographies of Twelve Victorian Authors*, pp. [47]-66, which cites international comments, criticism, and reviews for Browning through the early twentieth century, supplements Donaldson. Also for a bibliography of works by and about Elizabeth Browning, see *NCBEL*, III, pp. 435-39. Research on Elizabeth Browning is reviewed by Michael Timko in Faverty's *The Victorian Poets*, pp. 121-36.

168. Drew, Philip. **An Annotated Critical Bibliography of Robert Browning**. Brighton: Harvester Wheats, 1990. 106p. (Harvester Wheatsheaf Annotated Critical Bibliographies). LC 89-37701. ISBN 0-7108-0909-3.

A good starting point for research on Robert Browning and, to a lesser degree, on Elizabeth Barrett Browning. Drew's brief bibliography offers reliable critical guidance to editions of the primary works, reference works (bibliographies, handbooks, concordances, and the like), general biographical and critical studies, topical studies (of Browning and religion, politics, and music, among others), studies of individual works, and editions of letters. Annotations are detailed and evaluative. Drew clearly identifies the most significant studies. Solid indexing. Also for a bibliography of works by and about Robert Browning, see *NCBEL*, III, pp. 439-61. More specialized topical coverage is included in Vincent P. Anderson's *Robert Browning as a Religious Poet: An Annotated Bibliography of Criticism* (Troy, NY: Whitston, 1983). Research on Robert Browning is reviewed by Park Honan in Faverty's *The Victorian Poets*, pp. 81-120; as well as by Ian Jack in Dyson's *English Poetry*, pp. 284-315.

169. Peterson, William S. **Robert and Elizabeth Browning: An Annotated Bibliography, 1951-1970**. New York: Browning Institute, 1974. 209p. LC 74-24915.

Continues the bibliographies of Broughton, Northup, and Pearsall for Robert Browning (entry 166) and Barnes for Elizabeth Barrett Browning (entry 165); in turn, continued by the annual bibliographies included in *Browning Institute Studies*, now *Victorian Literature and Culture* (entry 176). Full bibliographic descriptions of editions of the Brownings' primary works and comprehensive coverage of secondary works. Arrangement follows the pattern established by Broughton, Northup, and Pearsall, describing about 1,000 works on the Brownings in detail, with references to reviews. A general index offers the full range of topical headings. Philip Kelley and Ronald Hudson's *The Brownings's Correspondence: A Checklist* (New York: Browning Institute, 1978) gives additional coverage of the Brownings' letters, with chronological, alphabetical, and location indexes for more than 10,000 items written by, and to, Robert and Elizabeth Browning.

Dictionaries, Encyclopedias, and Handbooks

170. DeVane, William Clyde. **A Browning Handbook**. 2d ed. New York: Appleton-Century-Crofts, 1955. 594p. LC 54-9558.

Authoritative accounts of the texts, publishing histories, composition, sources, influences, and reputation of Robert Browning's poetry. DeVane's discussions are more useful than those in Edward Berdoe's *Browning Cyclopedia: A Guide to the Study of the Works of Robert Browning* (London: Allen and Unwin, 1897); and Alexandra L. Orr's *Handbook to the Works of Robert Browning* (London: Bell, 1896). The older works, however, remain useful for near-contemporary readings of Browning's works. In addition to assessments of Browning's works with suggested further readings, Norton B. Crowell's *A Reader's Guide to Robert Browning* (Albuquerque, NM: University of New Mexico Press, 1972) contains an extensive chronology of Browning's life and a checklist of criticism published from 1945 to 1969 (pp. 243-65).

Indexes and Concordances

171. Broughton, Leslie N., and Benjamin F. Stelter. **A Concordance to the Poems of Robert Browning**. New York: G. E. Stechert, 1924-1925. 2 vols. LC 25-5042.

Until the publication of Shroyer and Collins' *A Concordance to the Poems and Plays of Robert Browning* (entry 173) this was the standard concordance to Browning's poetry. Based on Augustine Birrell's edition of *The Complete Poetical Works of Robert Browning* (New York: Macmillan, 1915), also referred to as the "New Globe Edition with Additional Poems." Also available in a reprinted edition (New York: Haskell House, 1970). A more specialized index is Cornelia Marschall Smith's *Browning's Proverb Lore* (Waco, TX: Baylor University Press, 1989), which identifies and locates some 1,315 uses of proverbs in Browning's complete works. Smith's references cite Augustine Birrell's edition of *The Complete Poetical Works* (New York: Macmillan, 1933). Marie Ada Molineux's *A Phrase Book from the Poetic and Dramatic Works of Robert Browning* (Boston: Houghton Mifflin, 1896) also serves as a word index to Browning.

172.   Hudson, Gladys W. **An Elizabeth Barrett Browning Concordance**. Detroit, MI: Gale, 1973. 4 vols. LC 73-5735.

Separate concordances, frequency tables, and appendixes for individual editions of Browning's works, corresponding to 13 segments of her poetry, including juvenilia, *Poems 1844*, *Poems 1850*, *Sonnets from the Portuguese*, *Aurora Leigh*, translations, and others. References cite titles and lines, with context lines. General appendixes cumulate word-frequency tables, headwords, and titles. Copy texts include Frederic G. Kenyon's edition of *The Poetical Works of Elizabeth Barrett Browning* (London: Smith, Elder, 1898), supplemented by previously unpublished texts in Kenyon's *New Poems of Robert Browning and Elizabeth Barrett Browning* (New York: Macmillan, 1915).

173.   Shroyer, Richard J., and Thomas J. Collins. **A Concordance to the Poems and Plays of Robert Browning**. New York: AMS Press, 1996. 7 vols. LC 93-4051. ISBN 0-404-61494-9.

Modern concordance to Browning's works computer produced using Oxford Concordance Program. Based on "the widely used and textually reliable poems and plays" in *Robert Browning: The Poems* (London: Penguin; New Haven, CT: Yale University Press, 1981), edited by John Pettigrew and T. J. Collins; *Robert Browning: The Ring and the Book* (London: Penguin, 1971; New Haven, CT: Yale University Press, 1981), edited by Richard Altick; and *The Plays of Robert Browning* (New York: Garland, 1988), edited by T. J. Collins and R. J. Shroyer. Appends frequency word list and statistics.

Journals

174.   **Browning Society Notes**. Windsor, Berkshire: Browning Society, 1970- . 2/yr. ISSN 0950-6349.

Sponsored by the Browning Society, issues feature substantial scholarly articles and reviews of new works about the lives and works of the Brownings as well as those of other Victorians (such as George Eliot, Alfred Tennyson, William Butler Yeats, Harrison Ainsworth, and Dante Gabriel Rossetti) and Victorian literature and culture in general. "Stirring a Dust of Figures: Elizabeth Barrett Browning and Love," "Robert Browning's London," and "Love of England: The Victorians and Patriotism" are characteristic contributions. Close readings of works, studies of specific characters and themes (women, morality, patriarchy, sexuality, reading), and discussions of biographical problems are common. "News and Comment" contains information about the membership, reports and announcements about projects, news of bibliographic discoveries, and the like. *Browning Society Notes* is indexed in *MHRA* and *MLA* (to vol. 21 for 1991-92).

175.   **Studies in Browning and His Circle: A Journal of Criticism, History, and Bibliography**. Waco, TX: Armstrong Browning Library, 1973- . Annual. ISSN 0095-4489.

Formerly *Browning Newsletter* (1968-72). Past issues have featured five to eight long, scholarly critical articles; six or more book reviews and reviews of the year's research; announcements of research in progress, conferences, fellowships; and a "Checklist of Publications" listing critical books, articles, reviews, and dissertations. Articles have focused specifically on aspects of the lives and works of the Brownings. More recent volumes (vols. 17-19 for 1989-93, the last of which was published in 1995-96) contain selected papers from the 1989 "Centennial Symposium: Robert Browning and Nineteenth Century Culture" and the 1993 "International Conference: Elizabeth Barrett Browning and Victorian Culture," Part I. Part II, continuing coverage of the 1993 conference, appears in vol. 20, published in 1996-97. These recent volumes resemble earlier *Studies of Browning and His Circle* in title only. The journal maintains a homepage at: http://www.baylor.edu/, under "Armstrong Browning Library." *Studies of Browning and His Circle* is indexed in *AHI*, *MHRA*, and *MLA*.

Wortman's *Guide to Serial Bibliographies for Modern Literatures*, pp. 246-47, describes other serial bibliographies for the Brownings. Patterson's *Author News-letters and Journals*, pp. 39-42, describes other previously published journals for the Brownings.

176. **Victorian Literature and Culture**. New York: AMS, 1973- . Annual. ISSN 0092-4725.

Until vol. 18 (1990), this was *Browning Institute Studies: An Annual of Victorian Literary and Cultural History*. Including about a dozen long, scholarly articles, volumes of *Victorian Literature and Culture* address topics related to the full range of Victorian writers and others of broad interest, with only a few about the lives and works of the Brownings. Earlier, occasional special volumes focused on specific topics, such as Victorian learning and Victorian popular culture. Notes also describe works in progress, such as Jerome McGann's "The Complete Writings and Pictures of Dante Gabriel Rossetti: A Hypermedia Research Archive," 22 (1994): 223-321. Review essays on scholarship on the Brownings and other writers and topics—including Victorian publishing history, women and the theater, and fairy tales—are also typical contributions. The journal continues to feature the important, annual "Robert and Elizabeth Barrett Browning: An Annotated Bibliography," which describes current editions, reference works, and critical studies and updates the coverage of Peterson's guide (entry 169). Volumes contain indexes. *Browning Institute Studies* is indexed in *MHRA* and *MLA*.

Orestes Augustus Brownson, 1803-1876
Bibliographies

For works by Brownson, see *First Printings of American Authors*, vol. 4, pp. 45-51. Comments on Brownson and reviews of Brownson's works in selected periodicals are identified in Wells' *The Literary Index to American Magazines, 1815-1865*, p. 17; and *The Literary Index to American Magazines, 1850-1900*, p. 54. Brownson's manuscripts are listed in Robbins' *American Literary Manuscripts*, p. 44. Thomas T. McAvoy and Lawrence J. Bradley's *Guide to the Microfilm Edition of the Orestes Augustus Brownson Papers* (Notre Dame, IN: University of Notre Dame Archives, 1966) is also available. Leonard Gilhooley reviews research on Brownson in Myerson's *The Transcendentalists*, pp. 303-309.

Brunanburh, c. 937
Bibliographies

Greenfield and Robinson's *A Bibliography of Publications on Old English Literature to the End of 1972*, pp. 116-19, lists editions, translations, and studies of the Old English *Battle of Brunanburh*, with citations for reviews.

C. D. B. Bryan, 1936-
Bibliographies

For works by Bryan, see *First Printings of American Authors*, vol. 2, p. 57.

William Cullen Bryant, 1794-1878
Bibliographies
177.   Boswell, Jeanetta. **The Schoolroom Poets: A Bibliography of Bryant, Holmes, Longfellow, Lowell, and Whittier with Selective Annotation**. Metuchen, NJ: Scarecrow Press, 1983. 303p. LC 83-19276. ISBN 0-8108-1659-8.

Separate, alphabetically arranged listings of works by and about each writer. Covering criticism published from 1900 through 1981, Boswell identifies about 400 works for Bryant, 500 for Holmes, 550 for Longfellow, 400 for Lowell, and 400 for Whittier. Largely limited to English-language books, articles, reviews, and dissertations. Descriptive annotations. Separate indexes for each writer include headings for specific subjects, such as "manuscripts," "poetic theory," and "politics," as well as for bibliography and biography. Boswell's coverage of Longfellow criticism is unique. Coverage of Bryant criticism complements Phair's guide (entry 178). Coverage of Holmes supplements Currier and Tilton's bibliography (entry 681). Coverage of Whittier updates Von Frank's guide (entry 1441). Coverage of Lowell continues Cooke's guide (entry 861).

178.   Phair, Judith Turner. **A Bibliography of William Cullen Bryant and His Circle, 1808-1972**. Troy, NY: Whitston, 1975. 188p. LC 74-18203. ISBN 0-8787-5064-9.

Phair describes about 750 works about Bryant, including annotated entries in sections for books, articles, news stories, reviews (arranged by works reviewed), non-English-language criticisms, and dissertations and theses (unannotated). Bryant's primary bibliography is described in Blanck's *Bibliography of American Literature*, vol. 1, pp. 331-84. Other useful descriptions of Bryant's primary materials include Motley V. Deakin's *The William Cullen Bryant Collection* in part 4 of Sidney Ives's *The Parkman Dexter Howe Library* (Gainesville, FL: University of Florida, 1986); and Thomas G. Voss' *William Cullen Bryant: An Annotated Checklist of the Exhibit Held in the Mullen Library of the Catholic University of America, October 30-November 10, 1967* (Washington, DC: Catholic University of America Libraries, 1967). Bryant's manuscripts, located in collections in more than 50 institutions, are described in Herman Spivey's "Manuscript Resources for the Study of William Cullen Bryant," *PBSA* 44 (1950): 254-68; and Charles H. Brown's *William Cullen Bryant* (New York: Scribner's, 1971). Bryant's manuscripts are also listed in Robbins' *American Literary Manuscripts*, pp. 44-45. James E. Rocks' useful essay in Harbert and Rees' *Fifteen American Authors Before 1900*, pp. 37-79, surveys primary and secondary scholarship.

John Buchan, 1st Baron Tweedsmuir, 1875-1940
Bibliographies
179.   Blanchard, Robert G. **The First Editions of John Buchan: A Collector's Bibliography**. Hamden, CT: Archon Books, 1981. 284p. LC 81-10902. ISBN 0-2080-1905-7.

Chronologically arranged full bibliographic descriptions of Buchan's works in sections for books and pamphlets, edited works, contributions to books, uncollected contributions to periodicals and public documents, and contributions to *The Spectator* (805 items from 1900 to 1934). Entries for 136 separate publications published from 1887 to 1947 contain title-page transcriptions; collations; physical details for format, paper, and binding; contents and variants; and notes on publication history of first and subsequent editions and printings. Index of names and titles. Although largely superseded by Blanchard's guide, Archibald Hanna's *John Buchan, 1875-1940: A Bibliography* (Hamden, CT: Shoe String Press, 1953) remains useful for brief bibliographic information for subsequent editions and translations of Buchan's writings and an unannotated checklist of forty works about Buchan. *A Checklist of Works by and About John Buchan in the John Buchan Collection, Queen's University* (Kingston, Ontario: Douglas Library, Queen's University, 1958), with a foreword by H. Pearson Gundy, describes Buchan's personal library that includes manuscripts "which he himself retained, with additions since the library came to Queen's" (foreword). Also for a bibliography of works by and about Buchan, see *NCBEL*, IV, pp. 540-44.

Dictionaries, Encyclopedias, and Handbooks
180.   Webb, Paul. **A Buchan Companion: A Guide to the Novels and Short Stories**. Far Thrupp: Alan Sutton, 1994. 126p. LC 94-60103. ISBN 0-86299-870-0.
        Provides plot summaries and character identifications for Buchan's works as well as more critically useful information about allusions and other selected topics in Buchan's works or related to Buchan, such as "America," "Class," and "Sex." Entries lack cross-references to appended secondary sources (pp. 125-26).

Journals
181.   **John Buchan Journal**. Edinburgh: John Buchan Society, 1980- . Annual. OCLC 10681614.
        Unseen. With 10 (1991) indexed in *MHRA*.

Pearl (Sydenstricker) Buck, 1892-1973
Bibliographies
        See *Bibliography of American Fiction 1919-1988*, pp. 108-10, for Paul A. Doyle's checklist of works by and about Buck. Buck's manuscripts are listed in Robbins' *American Literary Manuscripts*, p. 46. See the review of research by Samuel I. Bellman in Duke, Bryer, and Inge's *American Women Writers*, pp. 353-78.

(Carl) Frederick Buechner, 1926-
Bibliographies
        For works by Buechner, see *First Printings of American Authors*, vol. 1, pp. 53-54.

Charles Bukowski, 1920-1994
Bibliographies
182.   Dorbin, Sanford M. **A Bibliography of Charles Bukowski**. Los Angeles, CA: Black Sparrow Press, 1969. 93p. LC 72-11263.
        Dorbin gives full bibliographic descriptions for Bukowski's books and chapbooks, ephemeral and miscellaneous works (such as broadsides and recordings), poetry in periodicals and anthologies (441 entries), and prose contributions. Entries provide title-page transcriptions, physical descriptions, and contents. In addition, Dorbin selectively annotates 71 works about Bukowski (books, articles, and reviews). Dorbin supplements the listings in "Bukowski Bibliography Revisited" in Tony Quagliano's *Bukowski* (Paradise, CA: Dustbooks, 1973).

Thomas Bulfinch, 1796-1876
Bibliographies
        For works by Bulfinch, see *First Printings of American Authors*, vol. 4, pp. 53-54. Bulfinch's manuscripts are listed in Robbins' *American Literary Manuscripts*, p. 46.

Ed Bullins, 1935-
Bibliographies
        King's *Ten Modern American Playwrights*, pp. 137-54, gives brief bibliographic information for Bullins' primary works and annotated entries for criticism of Bullins, with a classified list of reviews.

Edward George Earle Lytton Bulwer-Lytton, 1st Barron Lytton, 1803-1873
Bibliographies
        For a bibliography of works by and about Bulwer-Lytton, see *NCBEL*, III, pp. 917-21. Bulwer-Lytton's contributions to and reviews of Bulwer-Lytton's

works in selected periodicals are identified in Wells' *The Literary Index to American Magazines, 1815-1865*, pp. 19-21; and *The Literary Index to American Magazines, 1850-1900*, pp. 56-57. See reviews of research by Curtis Dahl in Stevenson's *Victorian Fiction*, pp. 21-43; and by Dahl in Ford's *Victorian Fiction*, pp. 23-33.

H(enry) C(uyler) Bunner, 1855-1896
Bibliographies
    For works by Bunner, see *Bibliography of American Literature*, vol. 1, pp. 385-99. Bunner's contributions to and reviews of Bunner's works in selected periodicals are identified in Wells' *The Literary Index to American Magazines, 1850-1900*, pp. 57-58. Bunner's manuscripts are listed in Robbins' *American Literary Manuscripts*, p. 47. See *Bibliography of American Fiction, 1866-1918*, pp. 84-85, for Samuel I. Bellman's checklist of works by and about Bunner.

John Bunyan, 1628-1688
Bibliographies
183.   Forrest, James F., and Richard Lee Greaves. **John Bunyan: A Reference Guide**. Boston: G. K. Hall, 1982. 478p. (A Reference Guide to Literature). LC 82-15453. ISBN 0-8161-8267-1.
    Chronologically arranges annotated entries for about 2,000 works about Bunyan published from 1656 through 1981, with comprehensive coverage of books, parts of books, articles, and dissertations. Also covers selected prefaces and introductions in editions, anthologies, and standard textbooks; reviews of books about Bunyan; newspaper articles about major Bunyan celebrations; and passing references. Although generally descriptive, annotations clearly identify works of particular significance. A comprehensive index includes headings for names cited in annotations (such as Dante, Chaucer, and Shakespeare, among others) and a full range of topics under Bunyan's name (for "bibliography," "preaching," "psychology," and the like). Also for a bibliography of works by and about Bunyan by Roger Sharrock, see *NCBEL*, II, pp. 875-80. More specialized coverage of Bunyan scholarship is provided in Beatrice Batson's *John Bunyan's Grace Abounding and the Pilgrim's Progress: An Overview of Literary Studies, 1960-1987* (New York: Garland, 1988). Research on Bunyan is reviewed by Roger Sharrock in Dyson's *The English Novel*, pp. 1-15.

184.   Harrison, Frank M. **A Bibliography of the Works of John Bunyan**. Oxford: Bibliographical Society, 1932. 83p. LC 32-18825.
    The standard guide to Bunyan's primary works, published as *Supplement to the Bibliographical Society's Transactions*, no. 6 (for 1930). Chronologically arranged, full bibliographic descriptions for Bunyan's works published from 1656 to 1688 and posthumous works (1689-1765), also with descriptions of supposititious works. Entries intend to identify and confirm known, existing copies of Bunyan's works. Whereas Bunyan's earliest bibliographer, Charles Doe, in 1692 identified some "Sixty Pieces" by Bunyan, Harrison corrects this number to 57. Data include title-page transcriptions; collations; contents; paginations; details for headlines, page sizes, types, provenances, condition of copies, and identifying variants; brief notes on publication histories; citations to Doe's listing; and lists of known copies. Introduction offers a brief but solid publication history of Buyan's works. Appends list of copies of Bunyan's works saved from the 1865 fire that largely destroyed Bunyan collector George Offor's library. Additionally, *Catalogue of the John Bunyan Library (Frank Mott Harrison Collection)* (Bedford: Bedford Public Library, 1938) offers useful descriptions, with facsimiles, of Bunyan's works. Bunyan's manuscripts are described in *Index of English Literary Manuscripts*, II, pt. 1:25-30.

Journals

185. **Bunyan Studies: John Bunyan and His Times**. London: John Bunyan Society, 1988-. Annual. ISSN 0954-0970.

Focusing on Bunyan and other literary figures of the later seventeenth century, *Bunyan Studies* features close readings and interpretive studies of works by Bunyan and his contemporaries, including Milton, Dryden, Charles Sedley, and others. Influence and source studies have related Bunyan to the likes of John Foxe and Virginia Woolf. Of particular bibliographical interest are regular essays describing Bunyan collections in the Bedford Central Library, University of Alberta, Bunyan Museum Library, and the Vrije Universiteit of Amsterdam. Vols. 1-3 included "Recent Articles on Bunyan," a literature review updating Forrest and Greaves' guide (entry 183). In addition to book reviews, other departments publish information on conferences, calls for papers, and descriptions of research and progress. *Bunyan Studies* is indexed in *MLA*.

Robert Jones Burdette, 1844-1914

Bibliographies

For works by Burdette, see *Bibliography of American Literature*, vol. 1, pp. 400-12. Burdette's manuscripts are listed in Robbins' *American Literary Manuscripts*, p. 47.

Anthony Burgess (John Anthony Burgess Wilson), 1917-1994

Bibliographies

186. Boytinck, Paul. **Anthony Burgess: An Annotated Bibliography and Reference Guide**. New York: Garland, 1985. 349p. (Garland Reference Library of the Humanities, vol. 406). LC 82-49268. ISBN 0-8240-9135-3.

Emphasis in this awkwardly organized guide is on critical studies of Burgess. Expanding his previous *Anthony Burgess: An Enumerative Bibliography with Selected Annotations* (Norwood, PA: Norwood Editions, 1974), Boytinck integrates annotated entries for 1,791 works by and about Burgess in listings for fiction and nonfiction books and Burgess' other works (translations, edited works, introductions, adaptations, poems, stories, articles, essays, and reviews), with entries for their reviews, translated editions, and recordings. Listings for *A Clockwork Orange*, for example, identify reviews of the novel as well as film reviews. Entries for the play *Cyrano!* cite production reviews. Burgess' books are described in brief detail. The contents of his other works are summarized. Annotations for reviews, by comparison, are extensive. In addition, Boytinck describes about 200 bibliographies, dissertations, and critical books and articles about Burgess. The index offers access to the full range of topics under Burgess. Boytinck's guide is more comprehensive than Jeutonne Brewer's *Anthony Burgess: A Bibliography* (Metuchen, NJ: Scarecrow Press, 1980).

Thornton W(aldo) Burgess, 1874-1965

Bibliographies

See *Bibliography of American Fiction, 1866-1918*, pp. 85-87, for Lucien L. Agosta's checklist of works by and about Burgess.

Edmund Burke, 1729-1797

Bibliographies

187. Gandy, Clara I., and Peter J. Stanlis. **Edmund Burke: A Bibliography of Secondary Studies to 1982**. New York: Garland, 1983. 357p. (Garland Reference Library of the Humanities, vol. 358). LC 82-48284. ISBN 0-8240-9244-9.

Gandy and Stanlis provide comprehensive coverage of commentaries and critical studies of Burke, topically arranging annotated entries for 1,614 works in all languages published from 1797 through 1981. Separate listings for bibliographies, biographies, studies of sources, general studies, studies of Burke as a writer and speaker, studies of major works, broad topical studies (of Burke and politics, economics, America, Ireland, and India); and studies of Burke's reputation and influence, among others. Selective critical and evaluative annotations include citations to reviews. The index gives comprehensive subject access. Gandy and Stanlis' guide supersedes Francesco Cordasco's slim *Edmund Burke: A Handlist of Critical Notices & Studies* (Brooklyn, NY: Long Island University Press, Burt Frankin, 1950), *18th Century Bibliographical Pamphlets*, no. 12, which lists 106 selected works about Burke from 1812 to 1950, including works in French and German, with references to reviews.

188.   Todd, William B. **A Bibliography of Edmund Burke**. Godalming, Surrey: St. Paul's Bibliographies, 1982. 316p. (St. Paul's Bibliographies, no. 5). LC 81-25895. ISBN 0-9067-9503-6.
    Largely a reissue of Todd's earlier *A Bibliography of Edmund Burke* (London: Rupert Hart-Davis, 1964) with a few addenda, Todd gives full bibliographic descriptions of Burke's works published from 1748 through 1827 covering editions and selections, collected works, and works attributed to Burke; and imitations, parodies, and fictional works about Burke. Entries provide title-page transcriptions, detailed collations and physical descriptions (of paper, typography, press figures, and the like), locations of copies, and publishing histories. For a bibliography of works by and about Burke also compiled by Todd, see *NCBEL*, II, pp. 1,184-91. Burke's manuscripts are described in *Index of English Literary Manuscripts*, III, pt. 1:59-78. Leonard W. Cowie's *Edmund Burke, 1729-1797: A Bibliography* (Westport, CT: Greenwood Press, 1994), Bibliographies of British Statesmen, no. 19, usefully supplements both the guides of Todd and Gandy and Stanlis, offering particularly strong international coverage of manuscripts and special collections for Burke, contemporary allusions, and political and other background primary sources and critical studies.

Journals
    See Patterson's *Author Newsletters and Journals*, pp. 44-45, for previously published journals for Burke.

Frances (Eliza) Hodgson Burnett, 1849-1924
Bibliographies
    For works by Burnett, see *Bibliography of American Literature*, vol.1, pp. 413-32. Burnett's contributions to and reviews of Burnett's works in selected periodicals are identified in Wells' *The Literary Index to American Magazines, 1850-1900*, pp. 58-59. Burnett's manuscripts are listed in Robbins' *American Literary Manuscripts*, p. 48. See *Bibliography of American Fiction, 1866-1918*, pp. 88-90, for Sarah Zavelle Marwil Lamstein's checklist of works by and about Burnett.

Fanny Burney (Francis, Mme D'Arblay), 1752-1840
Bibliographies
189.   Grau, Joseph A. **Fanny Burney: An Annotated Bibliography**. New York: Garland, 1981. 210p. (Garland Reference Library of the Humanities, vol. 284). LC 80-9022. ISBN 0-8240-9325-9.
    Grau gives brief bibliographic information for Burney's works in separate listings for editions, excerpts, and translations; dramatic adaptations of Burney's works; works attributed to Burney; reviews of Burney's works (arranged by works); some 500 critical and biographical works about Burney, including dissertations; and about 100 reviews of works about Burney. Descriptive annotations quote sources extensively. Additionally, Joyce Hemlow's standard biography, *The History of Fanny Burney* (Oxford: Clarendon Press, 1958), pp. 496-502, lists Burney's manuscripts in the Berg Collection of the New York Public Library, the British Museum, and in other collections. Hemlow's *A Catalogue of the Burney Family Correspondence, 1749-1878* (New York: New York Public Library, 1971) also offers

coverage of primary materials. For a bibliography of works by and about Burney by Roger H. Lonsdale, see *NCBEL*, II, pp. 970-73. Burney's manuscripts are described in *Index of English Literary Manuscripts*, III, pt. 1:79-92.

Robert Burns, 1759-1796
Bibliographies

190.   Egerer, J. W. **A Bibliography of Robert Burns**. Edinburgh: Oliver & Boyd, 1964. 396p. LC 65-47700.

Full bibliographic descriptions of all editions and printings of Burns' works in sections for dated and undated editions, translations (arranged by languages), and first appearances in periodicals. Coverage extends from 1786 through 1956. Entries give title-page transcriptions, physical descriptions, contents, and publishing histories. Comments on Burns and reviews of Burns' works in selected periodicals are identified in Wells' *The Literary Index to American Magazines, 1815-1865*, p. 21. For a bibliography of works by and about Burns, see *NCBEL*, II, pp. 1,979-2,019. Burns' manuscripts are described in *Index of English Literary Manuscripts*, III, pt. 1:93-[193].

Dictionaries, Encyclopedias, and Handbooks

191.   Bold, Alan Norman. **A Burns Companion**. Basingstoke: Macmillan, 1991. 447p. (Macmillan Literary Companions). LC 90-889. ISBN 0-333-42270-8.

Six-part "biographical and critical guide to Burns, indicating the personal outlines and social background of the personality; and assessing the most important poems and songs" (p. xi). Part I contains a Burns chronology; biographical directory of family, friends, and associates; and a gazetteer of places in his life and writings. Part II, "Aspects of Burns," includes eight introductory essays on Burns' dialect and diction, religion, politics, philosophy, alcohol, the theater, sexuality, and poetic techniques and forms. Part III is a brief introduction to Burns' life and works that unifies topics covered in Part II. Part IV, the bulk of the volume, consists of entries for a wide selection of Burns' individual poems, verse epistles, songs, election ballads, epitaphs and epigrams, and letters, and two commonplace books. Entries reference the texts of standard editions, including James A. Mackay's *The Complete Works of Robert Burns* (Ayr: Alloway, 1986); identify details regarding composition, publication, and early critical reception; and give several pages-long critical readings and interpretations. Part V is a select, briefly annotated bibliography of reference works, manuscripts, editions, and biographical and critical studies. Part VI reprints prefaces from the Kilmarnock edition, Gilbert Burns' account of his brother, and other previously published historically significant documents for Burns. Glossary of English equivalents of Scottish words. Index of poems and a general index of names, titles, and topics.

192.   Lindsay, Maurice. **The Burns Encyclopedia**. 3d ed., revised and enlarged. New York: St. Martin's, 1980. 426p. LC 79-2534. ISBN 0-312-10866-4.

First published in 1959, Lindsay's work offers descriptive entries for characters, institutions ("Mauchline Conversation Society") , places, allusions ("Black Monday"), terminology, and other features of Burns' works, language, life, and times, including discussions of Burns's manuscripts, editions (Kilmarnock Edition), and other texts. Chronologically arranged by poems, W. B. Campbell's *A Burns' Companion, Being Everybody's Key to Burns's Poems* (Aberdeen: James Blair, 1953) remains useful for quick interpretations, including line-by-line readings and identifications of themes, persons, and first lines. John Dawson Ross' *Who's Who in Burns* (Stirling: Eneas Mackay, 1927) briefly identifies Burns' family, acquaintances, and other personal allusions.

Indexes and Concordances

193.   Reid, J. B. **A Complete Word and Phrase Concordance to the Poems and Songs of Robert Burns, Incorporating a Glossary of Scotch Words, with Notes, Index, and Appendix of Readings.** 1889; reprint New York: Burt Franklin, 1968. 568p. (Burt Franklin Bibliography & Reference Series, no. 252). LC 68-58477.

Reid concords the texts of "the First Editions, edited by the Poet himself" (preface).

Journals

See Patterson's *Author Newsletters and Journals*, pp. 45-46, which describes previously published journals for Burns.

Edgar Rice Burroughs, 1875-1950

Bibliographies

194.   Heins, Henry Hardy. **A Golden Anniversary Bibliography of Edgar Rice Burroughs.** Revised ed. West Kingston, RI: Donald M. Grant, 1964. 418p. LC 63-13900.

A collector's handbook and fan's biobibliography as well as a bibliography, Heins' guide integrates sections for primary and secondary works with various other features, such as a "who's who" of characters in Burroughs' books and a discussion of his writings during World War II. Heins gives detailed descriptions of editions and printings of Burroughs' works (with brief bibliographic information, title-page facsimiles, illustrations of bindings, and physical descriptions) in the Tarzan, Mars, Pellucidar, and Venus series, and his other fictional works, as well as descriptions of Burroughs' radio scripts, translations of his works, and other primary materials. In addition, Heins identifies Burroughsiana and other works about Burroughs, including bibliographies and fanzines. Burroughs' manuscripts are listed in Robbins' *American Literary Manuscripts*, p. 49. Aimed at collectors, Bradford M. Day's *Edgar Rice Burroughs: A Bibliography* (Woodhaven, NY: Science-Fiction & Fantasy Publications, 1962) gives "a complete listing" of Burroughs' "published works of fiction" (p. [6]), emphasizing bibliographic points and availability. George T. McWhorter's *Edgar Rice Burroughs Memorial Collection: A Catalog* (Vestal, NY: House of Greystoke, 1991) is a catalog of materials in the University of Louisville Library. Also see *Bibliography of American Fiction, 1866-1918*, pp. 91-93, for William Marderness' checklist of works by and about Burroughs.

Dictionaries, Encyclopedias, and Handbooks

195.   McWhorter, George T. **Burroughs Dictionary: An Alphabetical List of Proper Names, Words, Phrases, and Concepts Contained in the Published Works of Edgar Rice Burroughs.** Lanham, MD: University Press of America, 1987. 446p. LC 87-14266. ISBN 0-8191-6512-3.

An A-to-Z index of more than 5,000 real and fictional proper names, unusual words and phrases, concepts, numbers, and other allusions in the 77 published works of Burroughs, with citations to the work in which they appear. Succinct entries tend to use quotes in identifications. Appends brief Burroughs chronology.

196.   Roy, John Flint. **A Guide to Barsoom: Eleven Sections of References in One Volume Dealing with the Martian Stories Written by Edgar Rice Burroughs.** New York: Ballantine Books, 1976. 200p. LC 76-11849. ISBN 0-345-24722-1.

Roy's guide offers bibliographic details and plot summaries for Burroughs' Martian stories as well a dictionaries and gazetteers that identify and describe characters, places, and other features of the works, such as flora and fauna, language, religion, customs, and the like. Includes a bibliography of secondary sources.

Journals

See Patterson's *Author Newsletters and Journals*, pp. 46-47, 359, for previously published and popular journals for Burroughs.

John Burroughs, 1837-1921

Bibliographies

For works by Burroughs, see *Bibliography of American Literature*, vol.1, pp. 433-48. Burroughs' contributions to and reviews of Burroughs' works in selected periodicals are identified in Wells' *The Literary Index to American Magazines, 1850-1900*, pp. 59-61. Burroughs' manuscripts are listed in Robbins' *American Literary Manuscripts*, p. 49.

William S(eward) Burroughs, 1914-1997

Bibliographies

197.   Goodman, Michael B., and Lemuel B. Coley. **William S. Burroughs: A Reference and Research Guide**. New York: Garland, 1990. 270p. (Garland Reference Library of the Humanities, vol. 635). LC 89-26026. ISBN 0-8240-8642-2.

Superseding Goodman's *William S. Burroughs: An Annotated Bibliography of His Works and Criticism* (New York: Garland, 1975), this is the most comprehensive and up-to-date guide to Burroughs' primary and secondary materials and is particularly valuable for information about Burroughs' manuscripts and other materials in collections. Goodman and Coley give brief bibliographic information (with summaries of contents and references to reprints, excerpts, and translations) for books and articles, essays, and stories. In addition, other sections include annotated entries for 196 critical articles about Burroughs, 121 interviews and biographical items, miscellaneous works (such as adaptations and Burroughs' radio and television appearances), and secondary bibliographies. Goodman and Coley also summarize Burroughs' letters and contents of manuscripts, arranged by public and private collections, including those at Arizona State University (the largest institutional collection of Burroughs' materials), Columbia University, University of Kansas, and University of Texas, and in the privately owned William S. Burroughs Archive; describe materials related to Burroughs' in the Grove Press Collection at Syracuse University; and identify materials about the censorship of Burroughs' works (especially *The Naked Lunch*) in the ACLU Archives at the University of Chicago and Princeton University. Goodman and Coley's guide complements that of Maynard and Miles (entry 198). Burroughs' manuscripts are listed in Robbins' *American Literary Manuscripts*, p. 49. See *Bibliography of American Fiction, 1919-1988*, pp. 111-14, for Goodman's checklist of works by and about Burroughs. Additionally, the private William S. Burroughs Archive is described in *A Descriptive Catalogue of the William S. Burroughs Archive* (London: Covent Garden Press, 1973).

198.   Maynard, Joe, and Barry Miles. **William S. Burroughs: A Bibliography, 1953-1973**. Charlottesville, VA: University Press of Virginia, 1978. 242p. LC 77-2663. ISBN 0-8139-0710-1.

The most useful bibliography of Burroughs' published works, Maynard and Miles' guide gives full bibliographic descriptions for books and pamphlets, contributions to books and anthologies, contributions to periodicals, international editions (arranged by languages), interviews, miscellaneous works (such as postcards, letters, and quotations in catalogs), and recordings. Entries provide title-page transcriptions (with selected facsimiles), collations and other physical details (for paper and bindings), and publishing histories. Supplementary descriptions of primary materials through the late 1980s are included in Goodman and Coley's guide (entry 197). Also for works by Burroughs, see *First Printings of American Authors*, vol. 5, pp. 47-62.

Robert Burton, 1577-1640
Bibliographies

199.   Conn, Joey. **Robert Burton and the Anatomy of Melancholy: An Annotated Bibliography of Primary and Secondary Sources.** New York: Greenwood Press, 1988. 105p. (Bibliographies and Indexes in World Literature, no. 15). LC 88-24639. ISBN 0-313-26047-8.

An awkwardly arranged and marginally convenient listing of editions of *Anatomy of Melancholy* and guide to writings about Burton's major work through 1987. The first section supplies brief bibliographic data for 138 separate, selected, abridged, and translated editions and reprintings of *Anatomy of Melancholy* published from 1621 to 1985. Conn does not claim that this is a comprehensive listing; entries for early editions lack standard *STC* and *Wing* numbers. A second section is an unannotated list of 64 dissertations and theses, only a few of which specifically focus on *Anatomy of Melancholy*, with citations to *Dissertation Abstracts International*. The third listing alphabetically arranges annotated entries for 561 scholarly studies and other comments on Burton, covering books, articles, introductions and prefaces, reviews of editions and other works about Burton, letters to the editor, and features in popular magazines and newspapers. Annotations are descriptive. Indexes of dates and subjects-titles, with headings for names, forms, and topics such as "madness" and "borrowings." Conn does not supersede coverage of Burton's works in Jordan-Smith's *Bibliographia Burtoniana* (entry 200). Conn's guide is largely useful for updating Donovan, Herman, and Imbrie's *Sir Thomas Browne and Robert Burton* (entry 163), which describes criticism of Burton from 1621 through 1978, and Dennis G. Donovan's *Elizabethan Bibliographies Supplements*, no. 10.

200.   Jordan-Smith, Paul. **Bibliographia Burtoniana: A Study of Robert Burton's The Anatomy of Melancholy: With a Bibliography of Burton's Writings.** Stanford, CA: Stanford University Press, 1931. 120p. LC 31-19896.

Although largely a study of the influence of Burton's *Anatomy*, Jordan-Smith's guide is also the standard bibliography of Burton's works, providing full bibliographic descriptions of editions of his *Anatomy* published through 1676, with brief references to editions published after 1800 and descriptions of his other writings. Also useful for research on Burton's primary works are Nicholas K. Kiessling's *The Legacy of Democritus Junior, Robert Burton: An Exhibition to Commemorate the 350th Anniversary of the Death of Robert Burton (1577-1640)* (Oxford: Bodleian Library, 1990), which includes descriptions of selected published works, manuscripts (including Burton's will), and contemporary allusions; and Kiessling's *The Library of Robert Burton* (Oxford: Oxford Bibliographical Society, 1988). Also for a bibliography of works by and about Burton, see *NCBEL*, I, pp. 2,219-21. Burton's manuscripts are described in *Index of English Literary Manuscripts*, I, pt. 1:139-42.

Frederick Busch, 1941-
Bibliographies

For works by Busch, see *First Printings of American Authors*, vol. 2, p. 59. See Donald J. Greiner's summary biography, critical assessment of major works, and selected primary and secondary bibliography for Busch in McCaffery's *Postmodern Fiction: A Bio-Bibliographical Guide*, pp. 293-96.

Samuel Butler, 1613-1680
Bibliographies

201.   Wasserman, George. **Samuel Butler and the Earl of Rochester: A Reference Guide.** Boston: G. K. Hall, 1986. 176p. (A Reference Guide to Literature). LC 85-24885. ISBN 0-8161-8625-1.

Wasserman chronologically arranges in separate listings annotated entries for works about Butler (published from 1692 through 1984) and about Rochester (from 1680 through 1985). Coverage for Butler (about 300 items) and Rochester (about 450) includes early notices, prefaces, biographical sketches, non-English criticisms, and dissertations. Annotations describe significant studies in detail. Separate indexes for Butler and Rochester give topical headings under their names and for primary works. Coverage of Butler criticism updates James L. Thorson's "Samuel Butler (1612-1680): A Bibliography," *Bulletin of Bibliography* 30 (1973): 34-39. David M. Veith's bibliography (entry 1,137) offers better coverage (through 1984) of Rochester's primary and secondary bibliography. For a bibliography of works by and about Butler by John Wilders, see *NCBEL*, II, pp. 435-37. Butler's manuscripts are described in *Index of English Literary Manuscripts*, II, pt. 1:31-38.

Samuel Butler, 1835-1902
Bibliographies
202. Breuer, Hans-Peter, and Roger Parsell. **Samuel Butler: An Annotated Bibliography of Writings About Him**. New York: Garland, 1990. (Garland Reference Library of the Humanities, vol. 769; An Annotated Secondary Bibliography Series of English Literature in Transition, 1880-1920). LC 90-2749. ISBN 0-8240-2747-7.

Another volume in an outstanding series of secondary bibliographies formerly published by Northern Illinois University Press, Breuer and Parsell's guide offers comprehensive coverage of commentaries and criticisms of Butler, containing annotated entries for 1,462 works in all languages published from 1863 through 1988. Coverage includes books, articles, dissertations, reviews of Butler's works and of works about Butler, introductions in editions, and the like. Critical annotations give extensive detail and evaluation. Significant studies are identified. As in other volumes in the series, a comprehensive set of indexes provides solid access. Additionally, coverage of criticisms of Butler's travel writings is provided in Bethke's *Three Victorian Travel Writers* (entry 1,380). Breuer and Parsell's guide supersedes the coverage of Butler criticism in Alfred J. Hoppe's *A Bibliography of the Writings of Samuel Butler, Author of Erewhon, and of Writings About Him* (1925; reprint New York: Burt Franklin, 1967), although Hoppe's work remains the standard bibliography of Butler's primary materials, including full bibliographic descriptions for his books and contributions to books and periodicals. Also for a bibliography of works by and about Butler, see *NCBEL*, III, pp. 1,406-11. Butler's manuscripts are described in *Index of English Literary Manuscripts*, IV, pt. 1:275-94. Research on Butler is reviewed by Daniel F. Howard in Ford's *Victorian Fiction*, pp. 288-307.

Journals
See Patterson's *Author Newsletters and Journals*, pp. 288-307, for previously published journals for Butler.

William (Howard) Allen Butler, 1825-1902
Bibliographies
For works by Butler, see *Bibliography of American Literature*, vol.1, pp. 449-59. Butler's contributions to and reviews of Butler's works in selected periodicals are identified in Wells' *The Literary Index to American Magazines, 1815-1865*, pp. 21-22; and *The Literary Index to American Magazines, 1850-1900*, pp. 61-62.

Mather Byles, 1707-1788
Bibliographies
For works by Byles, see *First Printings of American Authors*, vol. 1, pp. 55-57. Byles' manuscripts are listed in Robbins' *American Literary Manuscripts*, p. 51.

Edwin Lassetter Bynner, 1842-1893
Bibliographies
203.   Clark, Lucy T. **The Barrett Library: Edwin Lassetter Bynner; A Checklist of Printed and Manuscript Works of Edwin Lassetter Bynner in the Library of the University of Virginia**. Charlottesville, VA: University of Virginia Press, 1961. 9p. LC 61-9484.

Checklist of 12 separate and contributed publications, with a list of manuscripts and autograph letters. Indexed. For full descriptions of Bynner's works, see *Bibliography of American Literature*, vol. 1, pp. 460-62. Bynner's contributions to and reviews of Bynner's works in selected periodicals are identified in Wells' *The Literary Index to American Magazines, 1850-1900*, p. 62. Bynner's manuscripts are listed in Robbins' *American Literary Manuscripts*, p. 51.

William Byrd II, 1674-1744
Bibliographies
For works by Byrd, see *First Printings of American Authors*, vol. 4, pp. 55-57. Byrd's manuscripts are listed in Robbins' *American Literary Manuscripts*, p. 51. See Cutting's *John and William Bartram, William Byrd II, and St. John de Crevecoeur* (entry 72) for works about Byrd through 1974. Research on Byrd is reviewed by Robert Bain in Bain and Flora's *Fifty Southern Writers Before 1900*, pp. 55-74; and by Richard Beale Davis in Everett Emerson's *Major Writers of Early American Literature*, pp. 151-78.

Marcus Lafayette Byrn,1826-1903
Bibliographies
See *Bibliography of American Fiction Through 1865*, pp. 72-73, for a checklist of works by and about Byrn.

(Brian Oswald) Donn Byrne, 1889-1928
Bibliographies
204.   Bannister, Henry S. **Donn Byrne: A Descriptive Bibliography, 1912-1935**. New York: Garland, 1982. 311p. (Garland Reference Library of the Humanities, vol. 226). LC 80-8485. ISBN 0-8240-9502-2.

The best descriptive bibliography of Byrne's primary works, Bannister's guide gives full bibliographic descriptions for books, "Various Works Not Previously Published in Book Form" (that is, Byrne's contributions to periodicals and newspapers and unpublished works), and letters. Bibliographic entries give title-page transcriptions, collations, contents, physical descriptions (of paper, typography, bindings, and the like), references to books and serial reprintings, manuscripts, locations of copies, and references to reviews. In addition, another section describes about 60 works about Byrne. Appendixes identify inscribed copies, dramatic and cinematic adaptations (with references to reviews), and special collections of manuscripts, letters, inscribed works, and other materials in the New York Public Library, Harvard University, University of Virginia, the Huntington Library, and the Library of Congress, among others (pp. 261-62). Additional descriptions of Byrne's primary works are included in Blanck's *Bibliography of American Literature*, vol. 1, pp. 463-70. Byrne's manuscripts are listed in Robbins' *American Literary Manuscripts*, p. 92. See *Bibliography of American Fiction, 1919-1988*, p. 115, for Bannister's checklist of works by and about Byrne.

George Gordon, (6th Baron) Byron, 1788-1824
Bibliographies
205.   Randolph, Francis Lewis. **Studies for a Byron Bibliography**. Lititz, PA: Sutter House, 1979. 123p. LC 79-13752. ISBN 0-915010-26-7.

Updating and correcting Thomas James Wise's *A Bibliography of the Writings in Verse and Prose of George Gordon Noel, Baron Byron* (1933; reprint London:

Dawsons of Pall Mall, 1963) without revising it, Randolph gives brief bibliographic information with full and detailed physical descriptions and publishing
histories for editions of Byron's works, contributions to works of others, and
privately printed and suppressed works. Throughout the guide Randolph relates
his descriptions to Wise's. Wise's personal collection (the basis of his descriptive
bibliography) is now in the Ashley Collection of the British Library. Byron's
manuscripts are described in *Index of English Literary Manuscripts*, IV, pt. 1:295-371,
827-28. More specifically, Willis W. Pratt's *Lord Byron and His Circle: A Calendar of
Manuscripts in the University of Texas Library* (1947; reprint New York: Haskell
House, 1970) describes the collection in the University of Texas' Harry Ransom
Humanities Research Center. *The Roe-Byron Collection, Newstead Abbey* (Nottingham: Corporation of Nottingham, 1937), describes one of the most significant
collections of first editions, manuscripts, and other materials.

206.   Santucho, Oscar Jose. **George Gordon, Lord Byron: A Comprehensive
Bibliography of Secondary Materials in English, 1807-1974.** Metuchen, NJ:
Scarecrow Press, 1977. 641p. (Scarecrow Author Bibliographies, no. 30). LC 76-
41006. ISBN 0-8108-0982-6.

The most comprehensive bibliography of secondary materials for Byron.
Santucho arranges entries for more than 5,000 works about Byron in English in
chronological sections that represent periods of Byron scholarship from 1807
through 1974, including periods of initial reception (1807 through 1824); develop-
ing critical interest (1824 through 1839); interest in Byron's centennial (1924-25);
and modern critical recognition (1935 through 1945), among others. Entries for
reviews of Byron's works are listed under his works in the first section; similarly,
entries for works about Byron give citations to reviews. Entries are largely unannotated. Extensive introductions for each chronological section critically review
Byron scholarship. Appendixes list dissertations, notices of sales of Byron materials and descriptions of library collections; works associated with Byron (such as
attacks, parodies, satires, and fictional works about Byron); and other miscellaneous materials. Santucho's guide lacks subject indexing. Coverage of non-English-
language criticisms of Byron is included in Ronald B. Hearn's *Byron Criticism Since
1952: A Bibliography* (Salzburg: Institut fur Anglistik und Amerikanistik, Universitat Salzburg, 1980). Also for a bibliography of works by and about Byron, see
NCBEL, III, pp. 270-309. Research on Byron is reviewed by John Jump in Dyson's
English Poetry, pp. 211-23; and John Clubbe in Frank Jordan's *The English Romantic
Poets*, pp. 465-592.

Dictionaries, Encyclopedias, and Handbooks

207.   Page, Norman. **A Byron Chronology.** Boston: G. K. Hall, 1988. 117p. LC
87-24776. ISBN 0-8161-8952-8.

Page attempts to provide a "record of Byron's life from year to year." The
chronology is based largely on Leslie A. Marchand's edition of *Byron's Letters and
Journals* (Cambridge: Harvard University Press, 1973-1981) and Page's *Byron:
Interviews and Recollections* (Atlantic Highlands, NJ: Humanities, 1985), although
cross-references to these sources are inconsistently provided. An appendix includes brief biographies of selected, significant Byron family members, associates,
and acquaintances. Separate indexes reference Byron's writings, personal names,
and selected topics.

Indexes and Concordances

208.   Hagelman, Charles W., Jr., and Robert J. Barnes. **A Concordance to Byron's
"Don Juan."** Ithaca, NY: Cornell University Press, 1967. 981p. (The Cornell Concordances). LC 67-19472.

Based on Truman Guy Steffan and Willis W. Pratt's *Byron's Don Juan: A
Variorum Edition* (Austin, TX: University of Texas Press, 1956). The volume includes frequency lists.

209. Young, Ione Dodson. **A Concordance to the Poetry of Byron**. Austin, TX: The Pemberton Press, 1965. 4 vols. LC 66-674.

Young concords the texts included in Paul Elmer More's edition of *The Complete Poetical Works of Byron* (Boston: Houghton Mifflin, 1905)—also referred to as the "Cambridge edition." A more specialized index is Travis Looper's *Byron and the Bible: A Compendium of Biblical Usage in the Poetry of Lord Byron* (Metuchen, NJ: Scarecrow Press, 1978), which records Byron's allusions and references to the Bible.

Journals

210. **The Byron Journal**. London: Byron Society, 1973-. Annual. ISSN 0301-7257.

Sponsored by the Byron Society, volumes of *The Byron Journal* reflect Byron's international reputation and romantic image, including announcements and reports of activities of affiliates of the Byron Society and conferences from around the world as well as advertisements from the likes of airlines and Greek banks. Typically 8 to 12 scholarly articles address biographical, historical, and critical topics, offering close readings of specific works or focusing on topics such as Byron's relationship with Austen, Coleridge, Pushkin, and Emerson. Occasional reviews of research (in China, Portugal, and elsewhere) also appear. Selections of a dozen or more book reviews, announcements of new publications, and descriptions of Byroniana in auctions and other sales are also provided. *The Byron Journal* is indexed in *AES* and *MLA*.

Patterson's *Author Newsletters and Journals*, pp. 49-50, 359, describes other previously published journals for Byron.

James Branch Cabell, 1879-1958

Bibliographies

211. Duke, Maurice. **James Branch Cabell: A Reference Guide**. Boston: G. K. Hall, 1979. 124p. (A Reference Publication in Literature). LC 78-25985. ISBN 0-8161-7838-0.

Duke chronologically arranges annotated entries for about 900 books, parts of books, articles, newspaper reviews, and introductions in anthologies about Cabell published from 1904 through 1975. Annotations are descriptive. Index headings reference such topics as "bibliography," "censorship," "the south," and primary titles. Also see *Bibliography of American Fiction, 1866-1918*, pp. 93-96, for Arvin R. Wells' checklist of works by and about Cabell. Research on Cabell is reviewed by Joseph M. Flora in Flora and Bain's *Fifty Southern Writers After 1900*, pp. 74-86.

212. Hall, James N. **James Branch Cabell: A Complete Bibliography**. New York: Revisionist Press, 1974. 245p. (James Branch Cabell Series). LC 74-23476. ISBN 0-8770-0208-8.

Hall gives detailed physical descriptions of editions and printings of Cabell's books, original contributions to books (introductions, published letters, and the like), reprinted materials in books, and selected contributions to periodicals, as well as descriptions of Cabelliana, including studies and bibliographies and books about Cabell's art. Information for Cabell's primary works supplements that provided in Frances Joan Brewer's *James Branch Cabell: A Bibliography of His Writings, Biography and Criticism* (Charlottesville, VA: University of Virginia Press, 1957), which gives full bibliographic descriptions of Cabell's works. A companion volume, Matthew J. Bruccoli's *Notes on the Cabell Collection of the University of Virginia: James Branch Cabell: A Bibliography: Part II* (Charlottesville, VA: University of Virginia Press, 1957), also offers useful descriptions. Also for works by Cabell, see *First Printings of American Authors*, vol. 2, pp. 61-81. Cabell's manuscripts are listed in Robbins' *American Literary Manuscripts*, pp. 51-52.

Journals

213. **Kalki: Studies in James Branch Cabell**. Commerce, TX: James Branch Cabell Society, 1965-. Irregular. ISSN 0022-7994.

Sponsored by the James Branch Cabell Society, issues of *Kalki* feature three to five articles and reviews of new publications related to Cabell's life and works. Close readings of Cabell's works and studies of characters, images, themes, and sources are typical, such as "Manuel as Savior of Poictesme" and *"The Duchess of Malfi* and *Jurgen*: The Shadow of Conscience" (which compares John Webster's and Cabell's works). Other articles have discussed Cabell's use of Shakespeare and Cabell's editing and revision. Particular attention has focused on Cabell's literary relations with William Faulkner, Sinclair Lewis, T. S. Eliot, and Kurt Vonnegut. Occasional bibliographic contributions include "The James Branch Cabell Suite," 9.4 (1991): 137-39, describing the James Branch Cabell Library collection. *Kalki* is indexed in *AHI*, *MHRA*, and *MLA*.

Patterson's *Author Newsletters and Journals*, pp. 50-51, describes other previously published journals for Cabell.

George Washington Cable, 1844-1925
Bibliographies

214. Roberson, William H. **George Washington Cable: An Annotated Bibliography**. Metuchen, NJ: Scarecrow Press, 1982. 255p. (Scarecrow Author Bibliographies, no. 62). LC 82-3201. ISBN 0-8108-1537-0.

Roberson describes works by and about Cable. Part 1 includes 416 entries for primary works by Cable in separate listings for books and pamphlets; short stories, serializations, and verse; articles, essays, and correspondence; and dates of appearances of "Drop Shot" columns in the New Orleans *Daily Picayune*. Part 2 chronologically arranges 891 selectively annotated entries for writings about Cable in listings for books, articles and parts of books, recordings, reviews, and dissertations and theses. Annotations are both descriptive and evaluative. An appendix (pp. 214-16) identifies special collections of Cable materials in 16 libraries, including the extensive collection of letters in Tulane University's Howard-Tilton Memorial Library. A comprehensive index for part 2 includes topical headings under Cable's name for "bibliography," "reform activities," "woman suffrage," and other subjects. Additional information on Cable's primary materials is provided in Blanck's *Bibliography of American Literature*, vol. 2, pp. 1-14. Cable's manuscripts are listed in Robbins' *American Literary Manuscripts*, p. 52. See *Bibliography of American Fiction, 1866-1918*, pp. 97-99, for John Lawrence Cleman's checklist of works by and about Cable. Research on Cable is reviewed by Robert O. Stephens in Bain and Flora's *Fifty Southern Writers Before 1900*, pp. 75-85.

Caedmon, fl. 670
Bibliographies

Greenfield and Robinson's *A Bibliography of Publications on Old English Literature to the End of 1972*, pp. 197-201, lists editions, translations, and studies of Caedmon and *Caedmon's Hymn*, with citations for reviews. See also Graham D. Caie's *Bibliography of Junius XI Manuscript: With Appendix on Caedmon's Hymn*, pp. 66-70, for unannotated checklists of international editions, translations, and criticisms of *Caedmon's Hymn*. Also available is a bibliography of works by and about Caedmon in *NCBEL*, I, pp. 268-69.

Abraham Cahan, 1860-1951
Bibliographies

For works by Cahan, see *First Printings of American Authors*, vol. 2, p. 83. Cahan's manuscripts are listed in Robbins' *American Literary Manuscripts*, p. 51. See *Bibliography of American Fiction, 1866-1918*, pp. 100-101, for Gerald R. Griffen's checklist of works by and about Cahan.

James M(allahan) Cain, 1892-1977
Bibliographies

For works by Cain, see *First Printings of American Authors*, vol. 1, pp. 59-61. Cain's manuscripts are listed in Robbins' *American Literary Manuscripts*, pp. 52-53. See *Bibliography of American Fiction, 1919-1988*, pp. 116-17, for Tom S. Reck's checklist of works by and about Cain.

Paul Cain (Peter Ruric), fl. 1933-1946
Bibliographies

For works by Cain, see *First Printings of American Authors*, vol. 4, p. 59.

Erskine (Preston) Caldwell, 1903-1987
Bibliographies

For works by Caldwell, see *First Printings of American Authors*, vol. 2, pp. 85-97. Caldwell's manuscripts are listed in Robbins' *American Literary Manuscripts*, p. 53. See *Bibliography of American Fiction, 1919-1988*, pp. 118-20, for Edwin T. Arnold's checklist of works by and about Caldwell. Ronald Wesley Hoag surveys works by and about Caldwell in Flora and Bain's *Fifty Southern Writers After 1900*, pp. 87-98.

Hortense Calisher, 1911-
Bibliographies

For works by Calisher, see *First Printings of American Authors*, vol. 2, pp. 89-101. Calisher's manuscripts are listed in Robbins' *American Literary Manuscripts*, p. 54. Marcia Littenberg reviews works by and about Calisher in Shapiro's *Jewish American Women Writers*, pp. 46-53.

George Henry Calvert, 1803-1889
Bibliographies

For works by Calvert, see *Bibliography of American Literature*, vol. 2, pp. 15-24. Calvert's contributions to selected periodicals and reviews of Calvert's works are identified in Wells' *The Literary Index to American Magazines, 1815-1865*, p. 23; and *The Literary Index to American Magazines, 1850-1900*, pp. 65-66. Calvert's manuscripts are listed in Robbins' *American Literary Manuscripts*, p. 54.

William Camden, 1551-1623
Bibliographies

For a bibliography of works by and about Camden, see *NCBEL*, I, pp. 2,213-14. Camden's manuscripts are described in *Index of English Literary Manuscripts*, I, pt. 1:143-65.

(Ignatius Royston Dunnachie) Roy Campbell, 1901-1957
Bibliographies

215. Parsons, D. S. J. **Roy Campbell: A Descriptive and Annotated Bibliography: With Notes on Unpublished Sources.** New York: Garland, 1981. 278p. (Garland Reference Library of the Humanities, vol. 197). LC 79-7930. ISBN 0-8240-9526-x.

Parsons gives full bibliographic descriptions (title-page transcriptions, physical descriptions, and contents) for Campbell's books of poetry, prose, and translations; prefaces and other contributions to books; contributions of poems to periodicals; published letters; broadcasts; incidental prose; and appearances in anthologies. In addition, Parsons lists about 300 works about Campbell; describes eight special collections of Campbell materials, including primary materials in the Berg Collection of the New York Public Library, the State University of New York at Buffalo, and the University of Texas' Harry Ransom Humanities Research Center (pp. 211-30); and lists 16 Campbell items (autographs and books) auctioned at Sotheby's on 18 July 1972. For a bibliography of works by and about Campbell, see *NCBEL*, IV, pp. 244-46.

Thomas Campbell, 1777-1844
Bibliographies

For a bibliography of works by and about Campbell, see *NCBEL*, III, pp. 261-63. Campbell's contributions to selected periodicals and reviews of Campbell's works are identified in Wells' *The Literary Index to American Magazines, 1815-1865*, p. 23. See the review of research by Hoover H. Jordan in Houtchens and Houtchens' *The English Romantic Poets and Essayists*, pp. 183-96.

Thomas Campion, 1567-1620
Bibliographies

For a bibliography of works by and about Campion, see *NCBEL*, I, pp. 1,069-71. Campion's manuscripts are described in *Index of English Literary Manuscripts*, I, pt. 1:167-89, 566.

Nash Candelaria, 1928-
Bibliographies

See *Bibliography of American Fiction, 1919-1988*, p. 121, for Ernesto Padilla's checklist of works by and about Candelaria.

Dorothy Canfield Fisher, 1879-1958
Bibliographies

See *Bibliography of American Fiction, 1866-1918*, pp. 168-70, for Philip B. Eppard's checklist of works by and about Fisher. Fisher's manuscripts are listed in Robbins' *American Literary Manuscripts*, p. 111.

Robert (Emmett) Cantwell, 1908-1978
Bibliographies

For works by Cantwell, see *First Printings of American Authors*, vol. 5, pp. 63-64.

Truman Capote, 1924-1984
Bibliographies

216.   Stanton, Robert J. **Truman Capote: A Primary and Secondary Bibliography.** Boston: G. K. Hall, 1980. 287p. (A Reference Publication in Literature). LC 79-20876. ISBN 0-8161-8108-X.

A checklist of editions, printings, and translations of Capote's primary materials, covering books, short stories, excerpts, nonfiction, television plays, films, stage plays, and collections of manuscripts and letters in the Library of Congress (p. 24) precedes chronologically arranged, annotated entries for about 1,200 books, articles, reviews, dissertations, published letters, passing references, interviews, and recordings in all languages about Capote published from 1946 through 1978. Annotations are critical. A comprehensive index includes headings for broad topics (such as bibliography and interviews) as well as topical subheadings under primary titles. Also for works by Capote, see *First Printings of American Authors*, vol. 5, pp. 65-69. Capote's manuscripts are listed in Robbins' *American Literary Manuscripts*, p. 55. See *Bibliography of American Fiction, 1919-1988*, pp. 122-24, for Craig M. Goad's checklist of works by and about Capote. Research on Capote is reviewed by Helen S. Garson in Flora and Bain's *Fifty Southern Writers After 1900*, pp. 99-110.

Thomas Carew, 1594/5-1640
Bibliographies

For a bibliography of works by and about Carew, see *NCBEL*, I, pp. 1207-1208. Carew's manuscripts are described in *Index of English Literary Manuscripts*, II, pt. 1:39-122. See McCarron and Shenk's *Lesser Metaphysical Poets*, pp. [14]-16, for works about Carew through 1980.

Henry Carey, 1687?-1743
Bibliographies

For a bibliography of works by and about Carey, see *NCBEL*, II, pp. 782-84. Carey's manuscripts are described in *Index of English Literary Manuscripts*, III, pt. 1:193-94.

Will(iam McKendree) Carleton, 1845-1912
Bibliographies

For works by Carleton, see *Bibliography of American Literature*, vol. 2, pp. 25-41. Carleton's contributions to selected periodicals and reviews of Carleton's works are identified in Wells' *The Literary Index to American Magazines, 1850-1900*, p. 66. Carleton's manuscripts are listed in Robbins' *American Literary Manuscripts*, p. 56.

Jane Baillie Welsh Carlyle, 1801-1866
Bibliographies

G. B. Tennyson reviews research on Jane Carlyle in DeLaura's *Victorian Prose*, pp. 105-111.

Thomas Carlyle, 1795-1881
Bibliographies

217. Tarr, Roger L. **Thomas Carlyle: A Bibliography of English-Language Criticism, 1824-1974**. Charlottesville, VA: Published for the Bibliographical Society of the University of Virginia by the University Press of Virginia, 1976. 295p. LC 76-10837. ISBN 0-8139-0695-4.

Tarr's chronologically arranged, unannotated list of 3,037 works provides comprehensive coverage of English-language criticisms of Carlyle. A separate subject index references the full range of topics. Research on Carlyle is reviewed by Carlisle Moore in Houtchens and Houtchens' *The English Romantic Poets and Essayists*, pp. 333-78. Also for a bibliography of works by and about Carlyle, see *NCBEL*, III, pp. 1,248-70. Research on Carlyle is reviewed by G. B. Tennyson in DeLaura's *Victorian Prose*, pp. 31-104.

218. Tarr, Roger L. **Thomas Carlyle: A Descriptive Bibliography**. Pittsburgh, PA: University of Pittsburgh Press, 1989. 543p. (Pittsburgh Series in Bibliography). LC 89-30016. ISBN 0-8229-3607-0.

Covering Carlyle's primary materials, Tarr gives full bibliographic descriptions for his separate publications, first book and pamphlet appearances, contributions to journals and newspapers, collected works, miscellaneous collections, works attributed to Carlyle, and the publications of Jane Welsh Carlyle. Entries provide title-page facsimiles for first editions and transcriptions for later ones; collations; contents; descriptions of type, paper, and bindings; publishing histories; and copy locations. Appendixes list unpublished works and works presumed lost as well as about 100 books about the Carlyles. Tarr's bibliography supersedes Isaac Watson Dyer's *A Bibliography of Thomas Carlyle's Writings and Ana* (Portland, ME: Southworth Press, 1928). Carlyle's manuscripts are described in *Index of English Literary Manuscripts*, IV, pt. 1:373-93, 828. Also available is *Carlyle, Books & Margins: Being a Catalogue of the Carlyle Holdings in the Norman and Charlotte Strouse Carlyle Collection and the University Library, with a Transcription of Carlyle's Marginalia in John Stuart Mill's Principles of Political Economy and an Interpretative Essay Thereon* (Santa Cruz, CA: University Library, University of California, 1980).

Journals

219. **Carlyle Studies Annual**. Flushing, NY: Queens College, City University of New York, 1979- . Annual. ISSN 1074-2670.

Formerly *The Carlyle Newsletter* (1979-88) and *The Carlyle Annual* (1989-94), the *Carlyle Studies Annual* publishes eight to 10 substantial, scholarly articles, notes, and reviews of new publications related to the lives and works of Thomas and Jane Welsh Carlyle. Typical contributions emphasize close readings and interpretations of Thomas Carlyle's works and discussions of primary biographical documents, such as "Carlyle, the Just War, and the Crimean War" and "Carlyle Makes His Will (1865-1871): New Documents Discovered." Previously undescribed manuscripts and recently found letters are also discussed. Other essays have reviewed Carlyle's reception in late nineteenth-century Poland and his impact on Romanian culture and identified both his sources and his influences on later writers and personalities (ranging from Thoreau to Jimi Hendrix). The journal featured Abigail Burnham Bloom's "Jane Welsh Carlyle: Review of Recent Research (1974-1987)," 10 (1989): 93-98. Other bibliographic contributions included Ian Campbell's "Carlyle House," 12 (1991): 65-90, describing a significant Carlyle collection. The annual also features "Years' Work in Carlyle Studies," a review of recent scholarship. The *Carlyle Studies Annual* is indexed in *MLA* and *MHRA*.

Patterson's *Author Newsletters and Journals*, pp. 54, 359-60, describes other previously published journals for Carlyle.

(William) Bliss Carman, 1861-1929
Bibliographies

For works by Carman, see *Bibliography of American Literature*, vol. 2, pp. 42-76. Carman's contributions to selected periodicals and reviews of Carman's works are identified in Wells' *The Literary Index to American Magazines, 1850-1900*, p. 70.

Paul Carroll, 1927-
Bibliographies

For works by Carroll, see *First Printings of American Authors*, vol. 2, p. 105. Carroll's manuscripts are listed in Robbins' *American Literary Manuscripts*, p. 56.

Hayden Carruth, 1921-
Bibliographies

For works by Carruth, see *First Printings of American Authors*, vol. 2, pp. 105-107. Carruth's manuscripts are listed in Robbins' *American Literary Manuscripts*, p. 57.

Guy Wetmore Carryl, 1873-1904
Bibliographies

For works by Carryl, see *Bibliography of American Literature*, vol. 2, pp. 77-80. Carryl's contributions to selected periodicals and reviews of Carryl's works are identified in Wells' *The Literary Index to American Magazines, 1850-1900*, p. 71. Carryl's manuscripts are listed in Robbins' *American Literary Manuscripts*, p. 57. See *Bibliography of American Fiction, 1866-1918*, p. 101, for Gwen L. Nagel's checklist of works by and about Carryl.

Rachel Carson, 1907-1964
Bibliographies

For works by Carson, see *First Printings of American Authors*, vol. 3, pp. 43-45. Carson's manuscripts are listed in Robbins' *American Literary Manuscripts*, p. 57.

Hodding Carter, 1907-1972
Bibliographies

For works by Carter, see *First Printings of American Authors*, vol. 4, pp. 61-67. Carter's manuscripts are listed in Robbins' *American Literary Manuscripts*, p. 57.

William Alexander Caruthers,1802-1846
Bibliographies

For works by Caruthers, see *Bibliography of American Literature*, vol. 2, pp. 81-82. Caruthers' contributions to selected periodicals and reviews of Caruthers' works are identified in Wells' *The Literary Index to American Magazines, 1815-1865*, pp. 24-25. Caruthers' manuscripts are listed in Robbins' *American Literary Manuscripts*, p. 57. See *Bibliography of American Fiction Through 1865*, pp. 74-75, for a checklist of works by and about Caruthers. Curtis Carroll Davis surveys works by and about Caruthers in Bain and Flora's *Fifty Southern Writers Before 1900*, pp. 86-95.

Raymond Carver, 1938-1989
Bibliographies

See *Bibliography of American Fiction, 1919-1988*, pp. 124-25, for Susan Gunter's checklist of works by and about Carver. See Cris Mazza's summary biography, critical assessment of major works, and selected primary and secondary bibliography for Carver in McCaffery's *Postmodern Fiction: A Bio-Bibliographical Guide*, pp. 300-302.

Alice Cary, 1820-1871
Bibliographies

For works by Cary, see *Bibliography of American Literature*, vol. 2, pp. 83-96. Cary's contributions to selected periodicals and reviews of Cary's works are identified in Wells' *The Literary Index to American Magazines, 1850-1900*, pp. 71-72. Cary's manuscripts are listed in Robbins' *American Literary Manuscripts*, p. 57. See *Bibliography of American Fiction Through 1865*, pp. 76-77, for a checklist of works by and about Cary.

(Arthur) Joyce (Lunel) Cary, 1888-1957
Bibliographies

220. Makinen, Merja. **Joyce Cary: A Descriptive Bibliography**. London: Mansell, 1989. 254p. LC 89-36542. ISBN 0-7201-1985-5.

Makinen offers comprehensive coverage of Cary's primary and secondary bibliography. The first section gives full bibliographic descriptions for Cary's novels, short stories, poetry, drama, screenplays, nonfiction books, essays, interviews, and letters. Entries include title-page transcriptions and brief physical descriptions. Descriptions of literary manuscripts in the Bodleian Library's Joyce Cary Collection are related throughout the descriptions. The second part arranges annotated entries for 592 works about Cary in separate listings for biographies, bibliographies, general studies, topical studies (of Cary's African experiences, the theme of social responsibility in his works, politics, religion, and others), and studies of individual works. Coverage includes books, articles, reviews, dissertations, introductions and prefaces. Annotations are critical and thorough. A separate subject index references entries for secondary works. Makinen's coverage supersedes that included in Susan Vander Closter's *Joyce Cary and Lawrence Durrell: A Reference Guide* (entry 434), which gives about 400 annotated entries for works about Cary from 1932 through 1983. Also for a bibliography of works by and about Cary, see *NCBEL*, IV, pp. 548-51.

Phoebe Cary, 1824-1871
Bibliographies

For works by Cary, see *Bibliography of American Literature*, vol. 2, pp. 97-106. Cary's contributions to selected periodicals and reviews of Cary's works are identified in Wells' *The Literary Index to American Magazines, 1850-1900*, p. 72. Cary's manuscripts are listed in Robbins' *American Literary Manuscripts*, p. 58.

Willa (Sibert) Cather, 1873-1947
Bibliographies

221.   Arnold, Marilyn. **Willa Cather: A Reference Guide**. Boston: G. K. Hall, 1986. 415p. (A Reference Guide to Literature). LC 86-14277. ISBN 0-8161-8654-5.

Arnold chronologically arranges from 1895 through 1984 annotated entries for about 1,800 writings on Cather, including books, periodical and newspaper articles, anonymous reviews, and dissertations. Particular attention is given to identifying criticisms in Japanese and Swedish. Articles in general encyclopedias and passing notices, reviews of secondary works, and creative works that refer to Cather are excluded. Annotations are severely descriptive: "they do not try to assess the worth or soundness of arguments or interpretations" (p. xii). As a result, little guidance to the best secondary studies is provided. Crane's descriptive bibliography of Cather's writings (entry 222), for example, is included but not described as significant or even useful. Includes separate author (critics) and subject indexes. The latter is most detailed, with subject headings for the usual forms of secondary works (bibliographies, biographies, etc.) and for literary terms, concepts, and topics ("Realism, realistic, realities in Cather's work" and "Theme, themes, motifs in Cather's work," for examples). The heading for "characters" includes subdivisions for individual characters, such as Crazy Ivar and Alexandra Bergson. Headings are also included for authors (Hemingway, Wolfe, Hawthorne). Subheadings for various, more eccentric topics, such as "artistic creed, principles, theories," "elusive" (whatever this is), "as conservative writer," "on cooking," and the like, are arranged under Cather's name. Other helpful subheadings are listed under the titles of primary works. For *My Antonia*, for example, "bibliographies of criticism," "Cliff's notes," and "Japanese criticism of" are cited. This very detailed indexing—once users overcome its complexity— makes Arnold's bibliography very useful. Other guides in G. K. Hall's series would do well to follow this model. Also see *Bibliography of American Fiction, 1866-1918*, pp. 102-109, for James Woodress' checklist of works by and about Cather. Research on Cather is reviewed by Bernice Slote in Bryer's *Sixteen Modern American Authors*, pp. 29-74; and the supplement by James Woodress in Bryer's *Sixteen Modern American Authors: Volume 2: A Survey of Research and Criticism Since 1972*, pp. 42-72; and by John J. Murphy in Erisman and Etulain's *Fifty Western Writers*, pp. 51-62.

222.   Crane, Joan. **Willa Cather: A Bibliography**. Lincoln, NE: University of Nebraska Press, 1982. 412p. LC 81-23134. ISBN 0-8032-1415-4.

This is the standard listing of Cather's primary bibliography. Entries in separate listings describe Cather's books (including reprintings and variants of separate and collected editions); poems; short fiction in books and periodicals; articles, reviews, and essays in newspapers and periodicals; translations of Cather's works into all languages; editions of Cather's works in large-type; editions in Braille; recordings of Cather's works for the blind; and books adapted for film and theater. Gives locations of the described copies. Crane's coverage of Cather's works supersedes P. M. Hutchinson's "The Writings of Willa Cather: A List of Works by and About Her," *Bulletin of the New York Public Library* 60 (June-August 1956): 263-88, 338-56, and 378-400; and JoAnna Lathrop's *Willa Cather: A Checklist of Her Published Writing* (Lincoln, NE: University of Nebraska Press, 1975). Margaret Anne O'Connor's "A Guide to the Letters of Willa Cather," *Resources for American Literary Study* 4 (1974): 145-72, which describes 900 letters in 43 locations, provides additional information about Cather's primary materials. Also for works by Cather, see *First Printings of American Authors*, vol. 4, pp. 69-76. Cather's manuscripts are listed in Robbins' *American Literary Manuscripts*, p. 58.

Dictionaries, Encyclopedias, and Handbooks

223.   March, John, Marilyn Arnold, and Debra Lynn Thornton. **A Reader's Companion to the Fiction of Willa Cather**. Westport, CT: Greenwood Press, 1993. 846p. LC 92-42434. ISBN 0-3132-8767-8.

March refers to this as "A Handbook of Willa Cather" (p. xii). While giving encyclopedic coverage of details in Cather's works—the people, places, sources, and other things in them—the volume lacks appropriate features that would increase both value and access. The volume does not offer plot summaries or publication histories of Cather's works; instead, alphabetically arranged entries try to place allusions in both their fictional and historical contexts, with references to the work or collection in which they originally appeared, while providing citations for relevant commentaries, criticisms, and other materials within the annotations. Entries explicate titles of Cather's works, translate passages in non-English languages, and identify quotations (subgrouped under Shakespeare, Wagner, Longfellow, and others). Although providing a list of primary sources with brief bibliographic information, the volume lacks a cumulative bibliography of works cited in annotations. The volume is unindexed.

224.   Meyering, Sheryl L. **A Reader's Guide to the Short Stories of Willa Cather**. New York: G. K. Hall, 1994. 286p. (Reference Publication in Literature). LC 93-10381. ISBN 0-8161-1834-5.

Meyering gives critical information for each of Cather's 61 short stories in narrative sections surveying publication and composition histories, thematic and technical relationships, and critical responses. Discussions conclude with selected bibliographies. Index of Cather's works and detailed general index that reference proper names and titles (Nebraska, Shakespeare, Lucretius' *De rerum natura*, and the like).

Journals

225.   **Cather Studies**. Lincoln, NE: University of Nebraska—Lincoln, and Willa Cather Pioneer Memorial & Educational Foundation, 1990-. Biennial. ISSN 1045-9871.

"A forum for Cather scholarship and criticism" (editorial policy), volumes of *Cather Studies* contain as many as a dozen substantial articles and notes on topics in Cather's works, her literary relations with other writers, and her critical reception. Occasional contributions discuss and describe newly discovered or previously unpublished Cather primary materials. Volumes include indexes. Indexed in *MLA*.

226.   **Willa Cather Pioneer Memorial Newsletter**. Red Cloud, NE: Willa Cather Pioneer Museum, 1957-. 4/yr. ISSN 0197-663x.

Typical issues of this now rather hefty, nearly 30-page newsletter, sponsored by the Willa Cather Pioneer Memorial and Educational Foundation, include reports and announcements related to past activities and upcoming events at the center, information about conferences, calls for papers, and brief reviews of new works about Cather. Additionally, most recent issues contain three to five brief, well-documented scholarly articles offering interpretations and close readings of Cather's works and the results of biographical investigations. An annual seminar and conference issue contains major papers. Since 1989 the newsletter has contained extensive bibliographic review essays on current scholarship, "Works on Cather," presently compiled by Virgil Albertini, which usefully update Arnold's *Willa Cather: A Reference Guide* (entry 221). *Willa Cather Pioneer Memorial Newsletter* is indexed in *MLA*.

Patterson's *Author Newsletters and Journals*, p. 55-56, describes other previously published journals for Cather.

Mary (Hartwell) Catherwood, 1847-1902
Bibliographies

For works by Catherwood, see *Bibliography of American Literature*, vol. 2, pp. 107-16. Catherwood's contributions to selected periodicals and reviews of Catherwood's works are identified in Wells' *The Literary Index to American Magazines, 1850-1900*, pp. 72-73. Catherwood's manuscripts are listed in Robbins' *American Literary Manuscripts*, p. 58. See *Bibliography of American Fiction, 1866-1918*, pp. 109-10, for Jane Atteridge Rose's checklist of works by and about Catherwood.

Christopher Caudwell (Christopher St. John Sprigg), 1907-1937
Bibliographies

Munton and Young's *Seven Writers of the English Left*, pp. 217-76, describes Caudwell's publications from 1925 through 1980 and manuscripts of Caudwell's published and unpublished works located at the University of Texas' Harry Ransom Humanities Research Center. Likewise, Jurgen Schmidt's *"That Paralysing Apparition. Beauty": Untersuchungen zu Christopher Caudwells Ideologie-und Widerspiegelungstheorie (mit einer Kommentierten Bibliographie im Anhang)* (Amsterdam: Verlag B.R. Gruner, 1982) offers a classified, annotated (in German) listing of works by and about Caudwell, including detailed descriptions of manuscripts and typescripts (pp. [413]-615). Also for a bibliography of works by and about Caudwell, see *NCBEL*, IV, pp. 1,016-17.

Madison (Julius) Cawein, 1865-1914
Bibliographies

For works by Cawein, see *Bibliography of American Literature*, vol. 2, pp. 117-28. Cawein's contributions to selected periodicals and reviews of Cawein's works are identified in Wells' *The Literary Index to American Magazines, 1850-1900*, p. 73. Cawein's manuscripts are listed in Robbins' *American Literary Manuscripts*, pp. 58-59.

William Caxton, c. 1422-1491
Bibliographies

227. Blake, N. F. **William Caxton: A Bibliographical Guide**. New York: Garland, 1985. 227p. (Garland Reference Library of the Humanities, vol. 524). LC 84-45396. ISBN 0-8240-8891-3.

Largely valuable as a classified guide to bibliographies and other reference works and critical comments related to Caxton and early printing, with alphabetically arranged, annotated checklists of separate editions and selections of works printed and published by Caxton and later reprintings, with standard reference numbers and summaries of contents. Entries for first editions of Caxton's works do not give full bibliographic details; emphasis is on modern editions. Provides sections for studies specifically on Caxton, language and style, literary-background studies, printing, typography, binding, bookselling, and historical backgrounds. Indexes of names, titles, and manuscripts. Robert H. Wilson offers a more comprehensive guide to Caxton's primary materials with a bibliography of editions and criticism in Severs and Hartung's *A Manual of the Writings in Middle English*, vol. III, pp. 771-807, 924-51. Also for a bibliography of works by and about Caxton, see *NCBEL*, I, pp. 667-74. Norman Blake reviews research on Caxton in Edwards' *Middle English Prose*, pp. 389-412.

Susannah Centlivre, 1669-1723
Bibliographies

For a bibliography of works by and about Centlivre, see *NCBEL*, II, pp. 781-82.

Journals

"Recent Articles" in *The Scriblerian and the Kit Cats* (entry 1084) regularly includes a selection of reviews of studies on Centlivre.

Robert W(illiam) Chambers, 1865-1933

Bibliographies

See *Bibliography of American Fiction, 1866-1918*, pp. 111-13, for Gwen L. Nagel's checklist of works by and about Chambers. Chambers' manuscripts are listed in Robbins' *American Literary Manuscripts*, p. 59.

Raymond Chandler, 1888-1959

Bibliographies

228. Bruccoli, Matthew J. **Raymond Chandler: A Descriptive Bibliography**. Pittsburgh, PA: University of Pittsburgh Press, 1979. 146p. (Pittsburgh Series in Bibliography). LC 78-4280. ISBN 0-8229-3382-9.

Bruccoli describes Chandler's primary works in full bibliographic detail in chronologically arranged sections for separately published and collected books and pamphlets; contributions to books; contributions to journals and newspapers; and miscellaneous writings, such as dust-jacket blurbs; and produced and unproduced screenplays and filmed adaptations of Chandler's works. Entries give title- and copyright-page facsimiles, collations, contents, physical descriptions (of paper, typography, bindings, and dust jackets), publishing histories, and copy locations. Selective list of five studies of Chandler. Skinner's *The Hard-Boiled Explicator* (entry 611) gives more thorough coverage of secondary materials for Chandler. Also for works by Chandler, see *First Printings of American Authors*, vol. 1, pp. 63-65. Chandler's manuscripts are listed in Robbins' *American Literary Manuscripts*, p. 59. See *Bibliography of American Fiction, 1919-1988*, pp. 126-27, for Bruccoli's checklist of works by and about Chandler.

William Ellery Channing, 1780-1842

Bibliographies

For works by Channing, see *First Printings of American Authors*, vol. 4, pp. 77-90. Criticism and reviews of Channing's works in selected periodicals are identified in Wells' *The Literary Index to American Magazines, 1815-1865*, pp. 25-26; and *The Literary Index to American Magazines, 1850-1900*, p. 75. Channing's manuscripts are listed in Robbins' *American Literary Manuscripts*, p. 60. David Robinson reviews research on Channing in Myerson's *The Transcendentalists*, pp. 310-16.

William Ellery Channing (II), 1818-1901

Bibliographies

For works by Channing II, see *Bibliography of American Literature*, vol. 2, pp. 129-33. Channing's contributions to selected periodicals and reviews of Channing's works are identified in Wells' *The Literary Index to American Magazines, 1815-1865*, p. 26; and *The Literary Index to American Magazines, 1850-1900*, p. 76. Channing's manuscripts are listed in Robbins' *American Literary Manuscripts*, p. 60. Francis B. Dedmond reviews research on Channing II in Myerson's *The Transcendentalists*, pp. 102-107.

William Henry Channing, 1810-1884

Bibliographies

Channing's manuscripts are listed in Robbins' *American Literary Manuscripts*, p. 60. Contributions by Channing and criticism and reviews of Channing's works in selected periodicals are identified in Wells' *The Literary Index to American Magazines, 1815-1865*, pp. 26-27; and *The Literary Index to American Magazines, 1850-1900*, p. 76. Elizabeth R. McKinsey reviews research on Channing in Myerson's *The Transcendentalists*, pp. 108-111.

George Chapman, 1559?-1634

Bibliographies

  For bibliographies of works by and about Chapman, see *NCBEL*, I, pp. 1,637-46, 1,765-66; Tannenbaums' *Elizabethan Bibliographies*, vol. 1; and Charles A. Pennel and William P. Williams' *Elizabethan Bibliographies Supplements*, no. 4. Chapman's manuscripts are described in *Index of English Literary Manuscripts*, I, pt. 1:191-95. See the reviews of research by Terrence P. Logan in Logan and Smith's *The New Intellectuals*, pp. 117-70, updated by Lidman's *Studies in Jacobean Drama, 1973-1984*, pp. 55-74; and by J. B. Bamborough in Wells' *English Drama*, pp. 54-68.

Indexes and Concordances

  229. Stagg, Charles Louis. **The Figurative Language of the Tragedies of Shakespeare's Chief 17th-Century Contemporaries: George Chapman, Thomas Heywood, Ben Jonson, John Marston, John Webster, Cyril Tourneur, Thomas Middleton: An Index**. 3d ed. New York: Garland, 1982. 549p. (Garland Reference Library of the Humanities, vol. 327). LC 81-48413. ISBN 0-8240-9382-8.

  A revision of Stagg's *Index to the Figurative Language of the Tragedies of Shakespeare's Chief Seventeenth-Century Contemporaries* (Memphis, TN: Memphis State University Press, 1977), this provides a separate concordance for each writer, citing context line, play, act, scene, and line. Standard editions serve as copy texts. Appendixes cumulate images relating to a broad range of subjects, including animals, the arts, daily life, and nature, among other topics.

Leslie Charteris, 1907-

Bibliographies

  230. Barer, Burl. **The Saint: A Complete History in Print, Radio, Film and Television of Leslie Charteris's Robin Hood of Modern Crime, Simon Templar, 1928-1992**. Jefferson, NC: McFarland, 1993. 419p. LC 92-53509. ISBN 0-89950-723-9.

  Based on the Leslie Charteris Collection at Boston University, Barer's narrative guide gives plot summaries and credits for radio productions, a filmography, script synopses, and other biographical and historical information about the development of the series. Mainly bibliographically useful for appended "Chronology of the Saint Writings" (pp. 384-403), with listings for short stories, separate publications as books, and French-language translations. Author, title, and subject index.

Jerome Charyn, 1937-

Bibliographies

  For works by Charyn, see *First Printings of American Authors*, vol. 2, pp. 109-110.

Thomas Chatterton, 1752-1770

Bibliographies

  231. Warren, Murray. **A Descriptive and Annotated Bibliography of Thomas Chatterton**. New York: Garland, 1977. 130p. (Garland Reference Library of the Humanities, vol. 49). LC 75-42872. ISBN 0-8240-9951-6.

  Warren chronologically arranges detailed descriptions of editions of Chatterton's works and his contributions to works of others published from 1770 through 1803 and topically arranges annotated entries for about 200 secondary works dealing with the Rowley controversy, Chatterton's biography, critical studies of his works, and adaptations, parodies, satires, and the like, from earliest notices to the 1970s. Entries for primary works give title-page transcriptions and facsimiles, collations, contents, physical descriptions, references to contemporary reviews, copy locations, and publishing histories. Critical annotations for secondary-works reference reviews. Chatterton's primary materials are described in E. R. Norris Mathew's *Bristol Bibliography, City and County of Bristol Municipal Public Libraries. A Catalogue of Books, Pamphlets, Collectanea* (Bristol: Libraries Committee, 1916). For a bibliography of works by and about Chatterton, see *NCBEL*, II, pp. 605-609, by Donald S. Taylor. Chatterton's manuscripts are described in *Index of English Literary Manuscripts*, III, pt.1:195-214.

Geoffrey Chaucer, c. 1343-1400
Bibliographies
232.   Allen, Mark, and John H. Fisher. **The Essential Chaucer: An Annotated Bibliography of Major Modern Studies**. Boston: G. K. Hall, 1987. 243p. (A Reference Publication in Literature). LC 87-17682. ISBN 0-8161-8739-8.

Allen and Fisher describe some 925 studies of Chaucer published from 1900 through 1984, arranged in about 100 separate listings for editions of Chaucer's works, manuscripts, reference works and bibliographies, and studies of the full range of subjects, such as Chaucer's life, language, and literary influences. Studies of each of *The Canterbury Tales* and a selection of themes from the *Tales* (such as pilgrimage and marriage) are also listed in separate sections. Studies of *Troilus and Criseyde* are contained in 13 sections. This complex scheme, outlined in a detailed table of contents, integrates subject indexing and the listings. Extensive cross-references interrelate studies on several topics, and an author-subject index indicates subjects not named in specific sections. Allen and Fisher's work is significantly more selective than either Baugh's (entry 234) or Leyerle and Quick's (entry 236) comparable works. On the other hand, Allen and Fisher's annotations are generally more detailed and better suited for undergraduate users. Although this guide cannot replace more comprehensive bibliographies, it offers a good point of departure for modern Chaucer criticism. Likewise, for a usefully convenient bibliography of works by and about Chaucer, see *NCBEL*, I, pp. 557-628, by Norman F. Blake. Research on Chaucer is reviewed by Traugott Lawler in Edwards' *Middle English Prose*, pp. 291-314; and J. A. Burrow in Dyson's *English Poetry*, pp. 1-14. *YWES* annually features a review essay on Chaucer scholarship.

233.   Baird-Lange, Lorrayne Y., and Hildegard Schnuttgen. **Bibliography of Chaucer, 1974-1985**. Hamden, CT: Archon, 1988. 344p. LC 87-35157. ISBN 0-208-02134-5.

This volume continues a series that provides comprehensive coverage of Chaucer's primary and secondary bibliography from the earliest works through the present. Other volumes include:

233.1. Baird, Lorrayne. **A Bibliography of Chaucer, 1964-1973**. Boston: G. K. Hall, 1977. 287p. (Reference Guides in Literature). LC 77-374. ISBN 0-8161-8005-9.

233.2. Crawford, William R. **Bibliography of Chaucer, 1954-63**. Seattle, WA: University of Washington Press, 1967. 144p. LC 66-29836.

233.3. Griffith, Dudley David. **Bibliography of Chaucer, 1908-1953**. Seattle, WA: University of Washington Press, 1955. 398p. (University of Washington Publications in Language and Literature, vol. 13). LC 26-27266.

233.4. Hammond, Eleanor Prescott. **Chaucer: A Bibliographical Manual**. 1908; reprint New York: Peter Smith, 1933. 579p. OCLC 13985705.

Hammond's handbook identifies and describes Chaucer's manuscripts, editions, translations, sources, and studies, with discussions of authorship, dating, and the narrative context of each work, through 1906. The other volumes follow a similar topical arrangement, including largely unannotated entries for bibliographies, editions, biographies, and studies of individual works. Baird's coverage for 1964 through 1973 contains about 2,200 entries. Baird-Lange and Schnuttgen's coverage for 1974 through 1985 includes nearly 3,000 entries, with additional listings for facsimile editions, studies of medieval women, and pedagogy. Both recent volumes include detailed topical indexes. Their coverage of modern scholarship will be superseded by the University of Toronto's *Chaucer Bibliographies* (entry 235).

234.   Baugh, Albert C. **Chaucer**. 2d ed. Arlington Heights, IL: AHM, 1977. 161p. (Goldentree Bibliographies in Language and Literature). LC 75-42975. ISBN 0-88295-563-2.

An updating of the 1968 edition, Baugh's *Chaucer* is regarded as a standard one-volume guide to Chaucer's modern primary and secondary bibliography. Including 3,205 items in separate listings for bibliographies and surveys, societies and journals, reference works, collected editions, critical texts, studies of language, versification, sources and influences, studies of individual works, and the like, Baugh identifies significant works with asterisks. No annotations are provided; however, notes describe the contents of otherwise nondescript titles. An index of authors, editors, and translators concludes the work. For undergraduate researchers, Allen and Fisher's guide (entry 232) is a better alternative.

235.   Colaianne, A. J., and R. M. Piersol, general eds. **The Chaucer Bibliographies**. Toronto: University of Toronto Press, 1983- . In progress. OCLC 18102961.

Individual volumes of "The Chaucer Bibliographies" series are the best and most comprehensive guides now available for modern scholarship on the particular works included. When completed, the series will supersede that continued by Baird-Lange and Schnuttgen (entry 233). Volumes in this series (by year of publication) include:

235.1. Peck, Russell A. **Chaucer's Lyrics and Anelida and Arcite: An Annotated Bibliography, 1900 to 1980**. Toronto: University of Toronto Press, 1983. 226p. LC 83-172594. ISBN 0-8020-2481-4.

Includes 575 topically and chronologically arranged entries. Although annotations are largely descriptive, Peck cites and comments on reviews of the more significant items. Cross-references and indexes are thoughtfully designed.

235.2. Peck, Russell A. **Chaucer's Romaunt of the Rose and Boece, Treatise on the Astrolabe, Equatorie of the Planetis, Lost Works, and Chaucerian Apocrypha: An Annotated Bibliography, 1900 to 1985**. Toronto: University of Toronto Press, 1988. 402p. LC 89-16118. ISBN 0-8020-2493-9.

With more than 750 topically and chronologically arranged entries, Peck's guide is particularly valuable for inclusion of background works. For example, listings for *Treatise on the Astrolabe* cite selected studies of medieval astronomy.

235.3. Eckhardt, Caroline D. **Chaucer's General Prologue to the Canterbury Tales: An Annotated Bibliography, 1900 to 1982**. Toronto: Published in association with the University of Rochester by University of Toronto Press, 1990. 468p. LC 89-90531. ISBN 0-8020-2592-7.

Topically and chronologically arranges 1,387 annotated entries arranged in sections for editions; bibliographies, indexes, and other reference sources; background studies and general criticisms; studies of language and metrics and manuscript and textual studies; studies of the "Springtime Setting," narrator, and the Tabbard (lines 1-42) and of the individual pilgrims (identified by lines). Coverage is international. Annotations are detailed. A comprehensive index references names, titles of selected primary works, and subjects.

235.4. McAlpine, Monica E. **Chaucer's Knight's Tale: An Annotated Bibliography, 1900 to 1985**. Toronto: University of Toronto Press, 1991. 432p. LC 92-129127. ISBN 0-8020-5913-9.

Topically and chronologically arranges 1,134 annotated entries in sections for modern editions and translations; background studies and general criticisms, including Chaucer and Italy, romance and romances, courtliness and courtly love,

Chaucer and women, paganism and the gods, Chaucer and science, estates and social status, chivalry, and miscellaneous subjects; source studies of *Teseida*, *Thebiad*, and *Roman de Thebes*; the character of the Knight in the "General Prologue" and the "Knight's Tale." Annotations generally indicate critical significance. Coverage is international in scope. Introduction surveys composition and revision, early appreciation, and modern responses, specifically in relation to Boethius, Boccaccio, Statius, and other works of Chaucer. A detailed index of names and subjects provides excellent access.

235.5. Burton, T. L., Rosemary Greentree, and David Briggs. **Chaucer's Miller's, Reeve's, and Cook's Tales**. Toronto: Published in association with the University of Rochester by University of Toronto Press, 1997. LC 96-932418. ISBN 0-8020-0874-7.

Unseen.

For convenience, selective guides by Allen and Fisher (entry 232), Baugh (entry 234), and Leyerle and Quick (entry 236) offer good alternatives. More specialized recently published bibliographies include Lynn King Morris' *Chaucer Source and Analogue Criticism: A Cross-Reference Guide* (New York: Garland, 1985), which cites some 1,400 secondary studies of Chaucer's sources and analogues published in books, articles, dissertations, and theses through 1981. Rossell Hope Robbins offers a comprehensive guide to primary materials of the Chaucer apocrypha with a bibliography of editions and criticism in Severs and Hartung's *A Manual of the Writings in Middle English*, vol. XI, pp. 1,061-1,101, 1,299-1,306.

236. Leyerle, John, and Anne Quick. **Chaucer: A Bibliographical Introduction**. Buffalo, NY: University of Toronto Press, 1986. 321p. (Toronto Medieval Bibliographies, no. 10). LC 86-232860. ISBN 0-8020-2375-4.

About 1,250 entries for secondary materials published through 1979-80 are included in separate listings for "Materials for the Study of Chaucer's Works," critical studies of the individual works, and background studies. Annotations are generally too brief to be greatly useful to the intended undergraduate users; those in Allen and Fisher's bibliography (entry 232) are preferable. On the other hand, Leyerle and Quick include entries for works published previous to 1900—something Allen and Fisher and, most unfortunately, volumes in *The Chaucer Bibliographies* (entry 235) exclude. Leyerle and Quick's bibliography can most effectively be used to supplement Baugh's standard selective guide to Chaucer's primary and secondary bibliography (entry 234).

Dictionaries, Encyclopedias, and Handbooks

237. Davis, Norman. **A Chaucer Glossary**. New York: Oxford University Press, 1979. 185p. LC 78-40245. ISBN 0-19-811168-1.

Davis and his associates have cumulated glosses from notable editions of Chaucer's works by Skeat, Robinson, and others; Tatlock and Kennedy's *Concordance* (entry 242); and specialized critical, philological, and linguistical studies of Chaucer's language and vocabulary; as well as from such standard works as the *OED* and *MED*. Entries cite a word's grammatical function, definition, and line references in Chaucer's works. Variant spellings are cross-referenced to main headwords, which are based on Skeat's edition of Chaucer's works (Oxford: Clarendon Press, 1915).

238. De Weever, Jacqueline. **Chaucer Name Dictionary: A Guide to Astrological, Literary, and Mythological Names in the Works of Geoffrey Chaucer**. New York: Garland, 1987. 402p. (Garland Reference Library of the Humanities, vol. 709). LC 87-21236. ISBN 0-8240-8306-7.

De Weever's dictionary is generally superior in detail and convenience to all previous Chaucerian personal-name dictionaries, including Hiram Corson's *Index of Proper Names and Subjects to Chaucer's Canterbury Tales* (1911; reprint New

York: Johnson Reprint, 1967); Bert Dillon's *Chaucer Dictionary: Proper Names and Allusions, Excluding Place Names* (Boston: G. K. Hall, 1974); and A. F. Scott's *Who's Who in Chaucer* (New York: Taplinger, 1974). For information on place names, scholars must continue to rely on F. P. Magoun Jr.'s *A Chaucer Gazetteer* (Chicago, IL: University of Chicago Press, 1961). Arrangement by Chaucerian spellings (as opposed to Dillon's by modern spellings) offers convenient access to De Weever's readable entries, which typically extend from a few lines to several pages (for significant personalities such as Seneca, Boethius, and Jean de Meun). De Weever's work will be very useful to students who need immediate explanations of Chaucer's allusions to the names of ancient and contemporary literary and political personalities; classical gods, nymphs, and monsters; prophets, saints, and popes; and other less romantic individuals, such as the Cook "Roger of Ware" and the Prioress "Eglentyne" who people his works. All occurrences of a name, for example, are referenced by work and line; additionally, occurrences in medial and final rhyming positions are indicated. De Weever's extensive bibliography of recent modern editions of classical and medieval sources is a real boon to the library intent on collecting primary materials.

239. Rowland, Beryl. **Companion to Chaucer Studies**. Revised ed. New York: Oxford University Press, 1979. 526p. LC 78-14542. ISBN 0-1950-2489-3.
　　Rowland assembles 22 bibliographic essays by authorities (Albert C. Baugh, Paul G. Ruggiers, D. W. Robertson Jr., among others) that survey scholarship on a broad range of topics and Chaucer's individual works. Discussions of similar topics are included in Robert D. French's *A Chaucer Handbook*, 2d ed. (New York: Crofts, 1957). The first volume of the "Oxford Guide to Chaucer," a series of more specialized handbooks, Helen Cooper's *The Canterbury Tales* (Oxford: Clarendon Press, 1989) surveys scholarship on dating, genre, sources, structure, themes, style, and "the tale in context" for each of the Canterbury tales.

Indexes and Concordances

240. Benson, Larry Dean. **A Glossarial Concordance to the Riverside Chaucer**. New York: Garland, 1993. 2 vols. (Garland Reference Library of the Humanities, vol. 1699). LC 93-8477. ISBN 0-8153-1290-3.
　　Offers more information about Chaucer's language than the concordances of Tatlock and Kennedy (entry 242) and Oizumi (entry 241). Based on 1986 (Boston: Houghton Mifflin) text edited by Benson. Each lemma (word entry) provides a headword, definition, references to the *OED* and *MED*, frequencies, and cross-references. Vol. 2 contains a supplementary concordance to "Fragments B and C of the Romaunt of the Rose, the Supplementary Propositions to the Astrolabe, and the lyrics Complaynt d'Armours and A Balade of Complaint" (p. xi) and indexes of spellings, modern-English equivalents, high-frequency spellings and words, and spelling and word frequencies.

241. Oizumi, Akio. **A Complete Concordance to the Works of Geoffrey Chaucer**. Hildesheim: Olms-Weidmann, 1991. 10 vols. (Alpha-Omega: Lexika, Indizes, Konkordanzen: Reihe C: Englische Autoren; Complete Concordance to the Works of Geoffrey Chaucer). ISSN 0175-9086.
　　Based on the text of the third edition (1987) of Larry Dean Benson's *The Riverside Chaucer* (Oxford: Oxford University Press, 1988), "with corrections" (p. vii), this supersedes Tatlock and Kennedy's *A Concordance to the Complete Works of Geoffrey Chaucer and to the Romaunt of the Rose* (entry 242). Consists of vol. I: *A KWIC Concordance to The Canterbury Tales, Part One*; vol. II: *A KWIC Concordance to The Canterbury Tales, Part Two*; vol. III: *A KWIC Concordance to The Canterbury Tales, Part Three, A Ranking Word-Frequency List of The Canterbury Tales, A Reverse-Word List of The Canterbury Tales, and A Hyphenated Word List of The Canterbury Tales*; vol. IV: *A General Word Index to The Canterbury Tales, and Word Indexes to Each Tale from The Canterbury Tales*; vol. V: *A Concordance to The Book of the Duchess, A Concordance to*

The House of Fame, A Concordance to Anelida and Arcite, and A Concordance to The Parliament of Fowls; vol. VI: *A Concordance to Boece;* vol. VII: *A Concordance to Troilus and Criseyde;* vol. VIII: *A Concordance to The Legend of Good Women, A Concordance to The Short Poems, A Concordance to "Poems Not Ascribed to Chaucer in the Manuscripts," and A Concordance to A Treatise on the Astrolabe;* vol. IX: *A Concordance to The Romaunt of the Rose;* and vol. X: *An Integrated Word Index to the Works of Geoffrey Chaucer.* Each concordance contains a KWIC concordance and appendixed word index, ranking word-frequency list, reverse-word list, and alphabetical list of hyphenated compounds. The 10-volume set is supplemented by:

241.1 Oizumi, Akio, and Hiroshi Yonekura. **A Rhyme Concordance to the Poetical Works of Geoffrey Chaucer.** Hildesheim: Olms-Weidmann, 1994. 2 vols. (Alpha-Omega: Lexika, Indizes, Konkordanzen: Reihe C: Englishe Autoren; Complete Concordance to the Works of Geoffrey Chaucer, vols. 11-12; Complete Concordance to the Works of Geoffrey Chaucer: Supplement Series, vols. 1-2.)

A "sequel" (p. v) to the KWIC concordances of vols. I-X separately lists for each of the works "all rhyme elements in alphabetical order, followed in each case by a complete listing of the rhyme words of that element," with rhyme word, rhyme scheme, and rhyme structure frequency and length order list.

242.   Tatlock, John S. P., and Arthur G. Kennedy. **A Concordance to the Complete Works of Geoffrey Chaucer and to the Romaunt of the Rose.** 1927; reprint Gloucester, MA: Peter Smith, 1963. 1,110p. LC 63-6086.

Long regarded as the standard concordance to Chaucer's work. Based on the dated Globe edition, edited by Alfred Pollard (London: Macmillan, 1913). More specialized indexes of Chaucer's language include Lawrence Besserman's *Chaucer and the Bible: A Critical Review of Research, Indexes, and Bibliography* (New York: Garland, 1988), which identifies and locates Chaucer's uses of the Bible or Biblical lore, including the uses of direct quotations, general references, glosses, Biblical authors, commonplace idioms and phrases, contemporary translations and paraphrases, misattributions, allusions of Biblical passages, and the like; and Thomas W. Ross' *Chaucer's Bawdy* (New York: E. P. Dutton, 1972).

Journals

243.   **Chaucer Newsletter.** Columbus, OH: New Chaucer Society, 1979-. 2/yr. OCLC 5105079.

Intended "primarily as a vehicle of Society business" (masthead). Gives brief information about conferences, programs, projects, and membership.

244.   **The Chaucer Review: A Journal of Medieval Studies and Literary Criticism.** University Park, PA: The Pennsylvania State University, 1966-. 4/yr. ISSN 0009-2002.

A major journal of medieval studies, sponsored by the Chaucer group of the MLA and the Pennsylvania State University. Issues feature four to eight major scholarly articles, ranging from the seemingly urbane "Was Chaucer's Knight Really a Mercenary?" to the more imposing "Medieval Optics and the Framed Narrative in Chaucer's *Troilus and Criseyde.*" Other recent studies have addressed Chaucer and toxicology, chess, the Bible, incest, and "the Rhetoric of the Body." Indeed, all varieties of topics that illustrate the expansiveness of scholarship on medieval history, politics, military science, science, art, music, law, education, and other subjects occupy this journal. In addition, the journal regularly publishes studies on other writers and works of medieval literature. Equally significant is the journal's contribution to Chaucer bibliography. Many major articles focus on manuscript and textual topics. James D. Johnson's "Identifying Chaucer Allusions, 1981-1990: An Annotated Bibliography," 29.2 (1994): 194-204, is a guide to references to Chaucer that updates Caroline Spurgeon's classic *Five Hundred Years of Chaucer Criticism and Allusions, 1357-1900* (Cambridge: Cambridge University

Press, 1925). Articles by Jackson Campbell Boswell and Sylvia Wallace Holton in 29.1 (1994): 93-109; and 29.3 (1995): 311-36 continue Johnson's bibliographic coverage of Chaucer allusions. Finally, the annual report on "Chaucer Research" is an extensive, classified, briefly annotated bibliography of bibliographies; editions, translations, and facsimiles; manuscript and textual studies; sources, analogues, and literary relations; language, rhetoric, and prosody; general studies; Chaucer and women's studies; and of studies of *The Canterbury Tales* and the other works. The bibliography identifies books, articles, and dissertations both completed and in progress. *Chaucer Review* is the premier journal of Chaucer scholarship and a major journal for medieval literature in general. Vol. 30.4 contains a useful 10-year contributor index. Also available is Peter G. Beidler and Martha A. Kalnin's *The Chaucer Review: An Indexed Bibliography of the First Thirty Volumes* (1966-96), a supplement to 31.2 (1996). *Chaucer Review* is indexed in *AES, HI, MHRA,* and *MLA.*

245.   **Chaucer Yearbook**. Woodbridge: Boydell and Brewer, 1992-. Annual. ISSN 1063-1836.

Representative articles in this new annual include "Reading Chaucer: What's Allowed in 'Aloud' " and "Metafiction and Chaucer's *Troilus.*" Substantial scholarly contributions emphasize modern critical approaches and interests in Chaucer and late medieval literature, examining such topics as narrative techniques, the treatment of gender and sexuality, and literary theory and criticism as applied to medieval literature. An extensive review section covers new titles in Chaucer and medieval studies. To date only vol. 1 of *Chaucer Yearbook* has been indexed in *MLA.*

246.   **Studies in the Age of Chaucer: The Yearbook of the New Chaucer Society**. Columbus, OH: New Chaucer Society, 1979-. Annual. ISSN 0190-2407.

Annual volumes feature four to six major scholarly contributions that "explore such concerns as the efficacy of various critical approaches to the art of Chaucer and his contemporaries, their literary relationships and reputations, and the artistic, economic, intellectual, religious, scientific, and social and historical backgrounds of their work" (masthead). Articles on the Pardoner's preaching and his pants, Chaucer's "victimized women," food imagery in the "Franklin's Tale," and Chaucer and time are typical. Other articles have dealt with Gower, Langland, and the works of the Sir Gawain-poet. Occasionally publishes bibliographical articles, such as Monica H. Green's "Obstetrical and Gynecological Texts in Middle English," 14 (1992): 53-88. In addition, the important "An Annotated Chaucer Bibliography," compiled (for the year 1994) in volume 19 (published in 1996) by Mark Allen and Bege K. Bowers, identifies recent editions and studies to update the comprehensive Chaucer bibliographies. Critical reviews of several dozen recent publications and a list of books received are also included. Volumes for alternate years contain society conference programs, addresses, and lectures. Each volume is indexed. *Studies in the Age of Chaucer* is indexed in *MHRA* and *MLA.*

Patterson's *Author Newsletters and Journals,* pp. 59-62, describes other previously published journals for Chaucer.

John Cheever, 1912-1982

Bibliographies

247.   Bosha, Francis J. **John Cheever: A Reference Guide**. Boston: G. K. Hall, 1981. 125p. (A Reference Guide to Literature). LC 80-27510. ISBN 0-8161-8447-X.

Contains chronologically arranged, annotated entries for about 600 books, articles, interviews, dissertations, and (mostly) reviews in all languages about Cheever published from 1943 through 1979. Annotations are descriptive. Index headings cover such topics as "awards," "bibliography," "public broadcasting," and the like. Bosha's work is more comprehensive than Deno Trakis' "John Cheever: An Annotated Secondary Bibliography," *Resources for American Literary Studies* 9 (1979): 181-99; and Dennis Coates' "John Cheever: A Checklist, 1930-1978,"

Bulletin of Bibliography 36 (1979): 1-13, 49. Bev Chaney Jr. and William Burton's "John Cheever: A Bibliographical Checklist," *American Book Collector* 7 (1986): 22-31 updates Bosha. Although Bosha's guide also includes a checklist of Cheever's primary materials, including his contributions to periodicals and adaptations, a definitive descriptive bibliography for Cheever remains to be provided. Also for works by Cheever, see *First Printings of American Authors*, vol. 5, pp. 71-74. Cheever's manuscripts are listed in Robbins' *American Literary Manuscripts*, p. 61. See *Bibliography of American Fiction, 1919-1988*, pp. 128-30, for Coates' checklist of works by and about Cheever. Robert A. Morace reviews research on Cheever in *Contemporary Authors: Bibliographical Series: Volume 1: American Novelists*, pp. 157-92.

Caroline Chesebro', 1825-1873
Bibliographies

See *Bibliography of American Fiction Through 1865*, p. 78, for a checklist of works by and about Chesebro'. Reviews of Chesebro's works and Chesebro's contributions to selected periodicals are identified in Wells' *The Literary Index to American Magazines, 1850-1900*, p. 77.

Charles W(addell) Chesnutt, 1858-1932
Bibliographies

248. Ellison, Curtis W., and E. W. Metcalf, Jr. **Charles W. Chesnutt: A Reference Guide**. Boston: G. K. Hall, 1977. 150p. (Reference Guides in Literature). LC 77-335. ISBN 0-8161-7825-9.

Ellison and Metcalf chronologically arrange annotated entries for about 700 secondary sources published from 1887 through 1975, including journal and newspaper articles, reviews, and dissertations. Annotations are descriptive. A thorough index includes topical headings for "bibliography," "dialect," "miscegenation," "the north," and other subjects. No comprehensive primary bibliography exists for Chesnutt. For works by Chesnutt, see *First Printings of American Authors*, vol. 3, pp. 47-49. Chesnutt's manuscripts are listed in Robbins' *American Literary Manuscripts*, p. 62. For additional coverage of Chesnutt's primary bibliography, researchers should consult William L. Andrews' "Charles Waddell Chesnutt: An Essay in Bibliography," *Resources for American Literary Study* 6 (1976): 3-22; and "The Works of Charles W. Chesnutt: A Checklist," *Bulletin of Bibliography* 34 (1976): 4-52, which surveys Chesnutt's editions, manuscripts, letters, and other primary materials as well as critical and biographical studies. Mildred Freeney and Mary T. Henry's *A List of Manuscripts, Published Works and Related Items in the Charles Waddell Chesnutt Collection of the Erastus Milo Cravath Memorial Library, Fisk University* (Nashville, TN: s.n., 1954) briefly lists Chesnutt's published works (books, contributions to books and journals, poems, short stories in books and journals, and speeches), manuscripts, correspondence, journals and scrapbooks, and other materials. Also see *Bibliography of American Fiction, 1866-1918*, pp. 113-15, for Kenneth Kinnamon's checklist of works by and about Chesnutt. Research on Chesnutt is reviewed by Ruth Miller and Peter J. Katopes in Inge, Duke, and Bryer's *Black American Writers*, vol. I, pp. 133-60; and William L. Andrews in Bain and Flora's *Fifty Southern Writers Before 1900*, pp. 107-17.

George Randolph Chester, 1869-1924
Bibliographies

See *Bibliography of American Fiction, 1866-1918*, p. 116, for Martha Bower's checklist of works by and about Chester. Chester's manuscripts are listed in Robbins' *American Literary Manuscripts*, p. 62.

Philip Dormer Stanhope, 4th Earl of Chesterfield, 1694-1773

Bibliographies

249.   Gulick, Sidney L. **A Chesterfield Bibliography to 1800**. 2d ed. Charlottesville, VA: Published for the Bibliographical Society of America by the University Press of Virginia, 1979. 255p. LC 78-25886. ISBN 0-8139-0815-9.

A revision of a guide first published as vol. 29 in *Papers of the Bibliographical Society of America* (1935), Gulick provides full bibliographic descriptions that primarily intend to resolve questions related to the authority of surviving bibliographic witnesses as well as the publication history of Chesterfield's *Letters to His Son*: "If the original letters were available, one would wish to determine—and restore—what Chesterfield actually wrote to his son" (p. 5). Chronologically arranged entries for authorized editions, Dodsley's octavo editions, and unauthorized editions in sections for preliminary publication; the letters; supplement; notes, index, and prospectus; and translations (including collected, selected, and other editions). Entries for first and subsequent early editions give title-page transcriptions, collations, contents, extensive details on variants and publication histories, and lists of examined copies. Other sections contain full information for adaptations and abridgments, burlesques, and other primary materials. Attesting to the work's popularity, more than half of Gulick's entries identify adaptations and abridgments. Also includes full bibliographic descriptions of about 20 contemporary works about Chesterfield. Appendixes supply cumulative data on variants and other topics related to publication history. Extensive indexes of editions, publishers, and general subjects. Also for a bibliography of works by and about Chesterfield, see *NCBEL*, II, pp. 1585-89, by Robert Halsband. Chesterfield's manuscripts are described in *Index of English Literary Manuscripts*, III, pt. 1:215-22.

G(ilbert) K(eith) Chesterton, 1874-1936

Bibliographies

250.   Sullivan, John. **G. K. Chesterton: A Bibliography**. London: University of London Press, 1958. 208p. LC 58-4090.

This volume is supplemented by:

250.1. Sullivan, John. **Chesterton Continued: A Bibliographical Supplement**. London: University of London Press, 1968. 120p. LC 72-370814. ISBN 0-340-09457-5.

Constitute the best listings of Chesterton's primary works, including full bibliographic descriptions of books and pamphlets, contributions to books, contributions to journals, books and journals containing Chesterton's illustrations, translated works, and other writings. Entries give title-page transcriptions, physical descriptions, and brief publishing histories. The first volume selectively describes about 120 works about Chesterton, with an additional 50 in the supplement. This secondary coverage is supplemented, in turn, by Sullivan's "Chesterton Bibliography Continued," *Chesterton Review* 2 (1975-1976): 94-98, and subsequent volumes. Also for a bibliography of works by and about Chesterton, see *NCBEL*, IV, pp. 1021-28.

Dictionaries, Encyclopedias, and Handbooks

251.   Marlin, George J., Richard P. Rabatin and John L. Swan. **The Quotable Chesterton: A Topical Compilation of the Wit, Wisdom and Satire of G. K. Chesterton**. San Francisco, CA: Ignatius Press, 1986. 391p. LC 86-80788. ISBN 0-89870-102-3.

Topically arranges approximately 1,200 passages representing "the best of G. K. C." (p. 14) from Chesterton's 73 works. Topics include Dickens, "Divorce," "Fairy-tales," "The Grotesque," and "Revolution." Keyed by page references to specific editions identified in the bibliography (pp. 375-78). Indexes of sources and topics.

Similarly useful is Joseph W. Sprug's *An Index to G. K. Chesterton* (Washington, DC: Catholic University of America Press, 1966), which serves as a subject index to allusions to persons, places, things, ideas, and themes—Americans, art, Communism, Adolf Hitler, Shakespeare, and so forth—in Chesterton's writings, with cross-references to selected editions.

Journals

252. **The Chesterton Review: The Journal of the Chesterton Society**. Saskatoon, SK: G. K. Chesterton Society, 1974-. 4/yr. ISSN 0317-0500.

Chesterton as a critic and satirist, primitive religion and Chesterton, and Chesterton's views on feminism are typical topics of the six to ten scholarly articles that appear in issues of *The Chesterton Review*. Other features describe recently discovered manuscripts and reprint Chesterton's uncollected articles and essays. Frequent special issues focus on specific topics, such as Chesterton and Christian writers in Japan and Chesterton and Austrian satirist Karl Kraus. The special issue "Chesterton's Schooldays," 21.3 (August 1995), contains several bibliographic articles on materials in the library of St. Paul's School, Chesterton's grammar school. In addition, issues include selections of book reviews as well as "News and Comments" about upcoming conferences and seminars, forthcoming publications, letters to the editor, and other membership activities. *The Chesterton Review* is indexed in *MHRA* and *MLA*.

Lydia Maria (Frances) Child, 1802-1880
Bibliographies

For works by Child, see *Bibliography of American Literature*, vol. 2, pp. 134-56. Contributions by Child and criticism and reviews of Child's works in selected periodicals are identified in Wells' *The Literary Index to American Magazines, 1815-1865*, p. 27; and *The Literary Index to American Magazines, 1850-1900*, p. 78. Child's manuscripts are listed in Robbins' *American Literary Manuscripts*, p. 62. Also useful is Patricia G. Holland, Milton Meltzer, and Francine Krasno's *The Collected Correspondence of Lydia Maria Child, 1817-1880: Guide and Index to the Microfiche Edition* (Millwood, NY: Kraus Microform, 1980). See *Bibliography of American Fiction Through 1865*, pp. 79-82, for a checklist of works by and about Child.

Thomas Holley Chivers, 1809-1858
Bibliographies

For works by Chivers, see *Bibliography of American Literature*, vol. 2, pp. 157-59. Contributions by Chivers and criticism and reviews of Chivers' works in selected periodicals are identified in Wells' *The Literary Index to American Magazines, 1815-1865*, p. 28; and *The Literary Index to American Magazines, 1850-1900*, p. 78. Chivers' manuscripts are listed in Robbins' *American Literary Manuscripts*, p. 63. Charles M. Lombard surveys works by and about Chivers in Bain and Flora's *Fifty Southern Writers Before 1900*, pp. 118-31.

Kate (O'Flaherty) Chopin, 1851-1904
Bibliographies

253. Springer, Marlene. **Edith Wharton and Kate Chopin: A Reference Guide**. Boston: G. K. Hall, 1976. 305p. (Reference Guides in Literature, no. 5). LC 76-1831. ISBN 0-8161-1099-9.

Although Springer's coverage of Wharton criticism has been superseded, her guide remains the most useful listing of criticism of Chopin, providing annotated entries for about 240 critical studies appearing from 1890 through 1973. Coverage includes dissertations and references to Chopin in dictionaries and literary histories. Annotations are descriptive. Topical index headings reference bibliographies, biographies, and studies of "local color," "the short story," and "women." Springer's guide is supplemented by her "Kate Chopin: A Reference

Guide Updated," *Resources for American Literary Study* 11 (Autumn 1981): 280-303; and Barbara C. Gannon's "Kate Chopin: A Secondary Bibliography," *American Literary Realism* 17 (Spring 1984): 124-29. For works by Chopin, see *Bibliography of American Literature*, vol. 2, pp. 160-61. Chopin's manuscripts are listed in Robbins' *American Literary Manuscripts*, p. 63. See *Bibliography of American Fiction, 1866-1918*, pp. 117-18, for Sandra L. Ballard's checklist of works by and about Chopin. Research on Chopin is reviewed in Bonner's "Bibliographic Essay," pp. 233-45, in *The Kate Chopin Companion* (entry 254) as well as by Tonette Bond Inge in Duke, Bryer, and Inge's *American Women Writers*, pp. 47-70; and Anne E. Rowe in Bain and Flora's *Fifty Southern Writers Before 1900*, pp. 132-43.

Dictionaries, Encyclopedias, and Handbooks
254.   Bonner, Thomas, Jr. **The Kate Chopin Companion: With Chopin's Translations from French Fiction**. New York: Greenwood Press, 1988. 245p. LC 88-15463. ISBN 0-313-25550-4.

The bulk of this work is a dictionary of about 900 fictional characters, real-life people, and 200 places, as well as titles and terms, from Chopin's life and writings. These include both named and unnamed characters, such as "the Acadian youth" from *The Awakening*, and the names of parishes, plantations, and country stores. Plot summaries of poems, short fiction, and novels present composition dates but little other bibliographic data. References to Chopin's texts cite Per Seyersted and Emily Toth's *A Kate Chopin Miscellany* (Natchitoches and Oslo, LA: Northwestern State University Press, 1979) and Seyersted's standard edition of *The Complete Works of Kate Chopin* (Baton Rouge, LA: Louisiana State University Press, 1969). In addition, the companion includes a brief Chopin chronology, Chopin's translations of one short tale by Adrien Vely and eight by Guy de Maupassant, and "period maps" of Louisiana, New Orleans, St. Louis, and Natchitoches. A useful "Bibliographic Essay" reviews works by and about Chopin, including bibliographies, editions, and criticisms of the individual works.

Journals
See Patterson's *Author Newsletters and Journals*, pp. 62-63, for previously published journals for Chopin.

Christ, c. 790-830
Bibliographies
Greenfield and Robinson's *A Bibliography of Publications on Old English Literature to the End of 1972*, pp. 201-205, lists editions, translations, and studies of the Old English *Christ*, with citations for reviews. *NCBEL*, I, pp. 269-70, also lists editions and studies.

Dame Agatha (Miller) Christie, 1890-1976
Dictionaries, Encyclopedias, and Handbooks
255.   Fitzgibbon, Russell H. **The Agatha Christie Companion**. Bowling Green, OH: Bowling Green State University Popular Press, 1980. 178p. LC 78-61075. ISBN 0-87972-137-5.

Guides, handbooks, and other bedside companions to Christie are legion. Those profiled here manifest bibliographic utility. A full descriptive bibliography of Christie remains to be completed. Fitzgibbon's guide offers checklists of Christie's writings, including fiction and alternate titles, short fiction, and characters, as well as analyses of major characters, such as Miss Marple and Hercule Poirot, with secondary bibliographies. Dramatic and film adaptations are also listed. The volume lacks an index. Also for a bibliography of works by and about Christie, see *NCBEL*, IV, pp. 552-54. More popularly oriented, Dick Riley and Pam McAllister's *The New Bedside, Bathtub & Armchair Companion to Agatha Christie* (New York: Ungar, 1986) gives lively plot summaries of individual works interspersed with recipes, quotations, and maps of murder locations in addition to annotated bibliographies and filmographies.

Appendixes list selected works about Christie, video adaptations, editions of Christie's works in print, and the like. Nancy Blue Wynne's *An Agatha Christie Chronology* (New York: Ace Books, 1976) contains separate, chronologically arranged surveys of Christie's novels and collections of stories, with several alphabetical listings of stories referenced to collections; other special chronological listings (of Miss Marple books, nonmystery books, plays, omnibus volumes, etc.); a cumulative chronological index; and a checklist of editions, translations, and reprintings. More descriptive identifications of characters are provided by Randall Toye's *The Agatha Christie Who's Who* (New York: Holt, Rinehart, and Winston, 1980); and Ben Morselt's *An A to Z of the Novels and Short Stories of Agatha Christie* (Hertfordshire: Phoenix, 1985). More recently, Dawn B. Sova's *Agatha Christie A to Z: The Essential Reference to Her Life and Writings* (New York: Facts on File, 1996) gives character identifications and plot summaries, with brief information on publishing and dramatization histories (useful for updating Fitzgibbon's filmography), and appends chronological and subject listings for Christie's works.

256. Sanders, Dennis, and Len Lovallo. **The Agatha Christie Companion: The Complete Guide to Agatha Christie's Life and Work.** New York: Delacorte Press, 1984. 523p. LC 83-5167. ISBN 0-3852-9285-6.

Generally more useful (and easier to use) than Fitzgibbon's guide (entry 255), this companion gives critical introductions (with references to reviews), plot summaries, lists of characters, bibliographic information for first British and American editions, and descriptions of stage, film, and television adaptations for Christie's novels, short fiction, and other writings. Additional sections describe these dramatic adaptations in detail, giving information on productions and critical receptions. Indexes list Christie's novels and short stories as well as those featuring Hercule Poirot, Miss Jane Marple, and others.

Charles Churchill, 1732-1764
Bibliographies

See Williams' *Seven XVIIIth Century Bibliographies* (entry 35), pp. [179]-205, for bibliographic descriptions of Churchill's works. For Arthur Sherbo's bibliography of works by and about Churchill, see *NCBEL*, II, pp. 593-95. Churchill's manuscripts are described in *Index of English Literary Manuscripts*, III, pt. 1:223-26.

Winston Churchill, 1871-1947
Bibliographies

257. Steinbaugh, Eric. **Winston Churchill: A Reference Guide.** Boston: G. K. Hall, 1985. 151p. (A Reference Guide to Literature). LC 84-28972. ISBN 0-8161-8427-5.

Following a brief checklist of Churchill's works, Steinbaugh chronologically arranges annotated entries for about 800 works about Churchill published from 1898 through 1981. A significant number of entries are for reviews of Churchill's works, although coverage also includes dissertations and newspaper articles. Annotations are descriptive. Topical indexing references subjects under Churchill, other authors, and places. Churchill's manuscripts are listed in Robbins' *American Literary Manuscripts*, p. 63. See *Bibliography of American Fiction, 1866-1918*, pp. 119-20, for Steven P. Ryan's checklist of works by and about Churchill.

John Ciardi, 1916-1985
Bibliographies

258. White, William. **John Ciardi: A Bibliography.** Detroit, MI: Wayne State University Press, 1959. 65p. LC 59-11552.

White includes full bibliographic descriptions for Ciardi's books, contributions to books, poems in periodicals, articles and reviews by Ciardi, and manuscripts and other materials in Wayne State University's Feinberg Collection (pp. 51-56). In addition, White describes 20 biographical and critical studies of Ciardi as well as reviews of Ciardi's books. Also for works by Ciardi, see *First Printings of American Authors*, vol. 2, pp. 111-15. Ciardi's manuscripts are listed in Robbins' *American Literary Manuscripts*, pp. 63-64.

Colley Cibber, 1671-1757
Bibliographies

For a bibliography of works by and about Cibber, see *NCBEL*, II, pp. 777-79.

Journals

"Recent Articles" in *The Scriblerian and the Kit Cats* (entry 1084) regularly includes a selection of reviews of studies on Cibber.

John Clare, 1793-1864
Bibliographies

259. Estermann, Barbara. **John Clare: An Annotated Primary and Secondary Bibliography**. New York: Garland, 1985. 303p. (Garland Reference Library of the Humanities, vol. 581). LC 84-48861. ISBN 0-8240-8754-2.

Covering works by and about Clare, Estermann gives brief bibliographic information and summarizes the contents and plots of Clare's primary materials. Presents very little information for physical descriptions and publishing histories. More useful and successful as a secondary guide, Estermann chronologically arranges extensively annotated entries for nearly 1,100 books, articles, dissertations, reviews, and reference works about Clare published from 1819 through 1984. Estermann's guide updates the coverage of Clare's primary works in David Powell's *A Bibliography of the Writings of John Clare* (London: University of London, 1953) and supersedes the critical coverage of H. O. Dendurent's *John Clare: A Reference Guide* (Boston: G. K. Hall, 1978), which describes about 700 works about Clare from 1820 through 1977. Clare's manuscripts are described in *Index of English Literary Manuscripts*, IV, pt. 1:421-58, 828-29. Additional coverage of Clare's primary works is included in Margaret Grainger's *A Descriptive Catalogue of the John Clare Collection in Peterborough Museum and Art Gallery* (Peterborough: Peterborough Museum and Art Gallery, 1973); A. J. V. Chapple's "Some Unpublished Poetical Manuscripts of John Clare," *Yale University Library Gazette* 31 (1956): 34-48; and David Powell's *Catalogue of the John Clare Collection in the Northampton Public Library* (Northampton: Northampton Public Library, 1964). Also for a bibliography of works by and about Clare, see *NCBEL*, III, pp. 356-58.

Journals

260. **John Clare Society Journal**. Nottingham: John Clare Society, 1982-. Annual. OCLC 11567684.

Sponsored by the John Clare Society, this annually features four to six articles and reviews of new works about the life and works of Clare. Typical features discuss themes and images in Clare's works, such as enclosure, rural life, class consciousness, and nature, as well as biographical problems, previously unpublished documents, and Clare's literary relations with the likes of Byron. Greg Crossan's "Clare's Debt to the Poets in His Library," 10 (1991): 41, usefully identifies some of Clare's sources. Crossan has also contributed "The Godfrey Collection of Clare Items in the Peterborough Museum," 3 (1984): 17-25. *John Clare Society Journal* is indexed in *MHRA* and *MLA*.

Edward Hyde, 1st Earl of Clarendon, 1609-1674
Bibliographies

For a bibliography of works by and about Hyde, see *NCBEL*, II, pp. 1678-82. Hyde's manuscripts are described in *Index of English Literary Manuscripts*, II, pt. 1:123-35.

Eleanor Clark, 1913-
Bibliographies

For works by Clark, see *First Printings of American Authors*, vol. 4, pp. 91-92.

Willis Gaylord Clark, 1808-1841
Bibliographies

For works by Clark, see *Bibliography of American Literature*, vol. 2, pp. 162-68. Contributions by Clark and criticism and reviews of Clark's works in selected periodicals are identified in Wells' *The Literary Index to American Magazines, 1815-1865*, p. 28-29. Clark's manuscripts are listed in Robbins' *American Literary Manuscripts*, p. 64.

Walter Van Tilburg Clark, 1909-1971
Bibliographies

For works by Clark, see *First Printings of American Authors*, vol. 5, pp. 75-77. Clark's manuscripts are listed in Robbins' *American Literary Manuscripts*, p. 64. See *Bibliography of American Fiction, 1919-1988*, pp. 131-32, for Ronald J. Nelson's checklist of works by and about Clark. Max Westbrook surveys works by and about Clark in Erisman and Etulain's *Fifty Western Writers*, pp. 63-70.

Arthur C(harles) Clarke, 1917-
Bibliographies

261. Samuelson, David N. Arthur. **Arthur C. Clarke: A Primary and Secondary Bibliography**. Boston: G. K. Hall, 1984. 256p. (Masters of Science Fiction and Fantasy). LC 84-10762. ISBN 0-8161-8111-x.

Samuelson offers a comprehensive listing of works by and about Clarke, giving brief bibliographic information for Clarke's fiction, miscellaneous works (interviews, recordings, and the like), and nonfiction works (some 702 entries), with references to reprintings, in addition to descriptions of about 300 biographical, bibliographic, and critical studies and a listing of about 800 (unannotated) reviews. Critical coverage extends from 1936 through 1980. Samuelson also describes special collections of Clarke's primary materials in the Mugar Memorial Library of Boston University and at Dene Court, Bishop's Lydeard, Taunton, Somerset (pp. 203-206).

Austin Clarke, 1896-1974
Bibliographies

262. Ricigliano, Lorraine. **Austin Clarke: A Reference Guide**. New York: G. K. Hall, 1993. 180p. (Reference Publication in Literature). LC 92-42514. ISBN 0-8161-7384-2.

Chronologically arranges descriptively annotated entries for approximately 700 works on Clarke published from 1918 to 1992. Covers chapters and parts of books, entries in reference works, dissertations, and reviews as well as non-English-language criticism. An introduction surveys Clarke's critical reception and identifies significant studies. Brief chronology of Clarke's major works and an appendix of titles of Clarke's plays and poems. Comprehensive author, title, and subject index offers good access. Also for a bibliography of works by and about Clarke, see *NCBEL*, IV, pp. 248-49. David J. Sorrells surveys works by and about Clarke in Schrank and Demastes' *Irish Playwrights, 1880-1995: A Research and Production Sourcebook*, pp. 57-68.

James Freeman Clarke, 1810-1888
Bibliographies

For works by Clarke, see *First Printings of American Authors*, vol. 4, pp. 93-107. Contributions by Clarke and criticism and reviews of Clarke's works in selected periodicals are identified in Wells' *The Literary Index to American Magazines, 1815-1865*, p. 29; and *The Literary Index to American Magazines, 1850-1900*, pp. 79-80. Clarke's manuscripts are listed in Robbins' *American Literary Manuscripts*, p. 65. Leonard Neufeldt reviews research on Clarke in Myerson's *The Transcendentalists*, pp. 112-16.

McDonald Clarke, 1798-1842

Bibliographies

For works by Clarke, see *Bibliography of American Literature*, vol. 2, pp. 169-72. Contributions by Clarke and criticism and reviews of Clarke's works in selected periodicals are identified in Wells' *The Literary Index to American Magazines, 1815-1865*, p. 29; and *The Literary Index to American Magazines, 1850-1900*, p. 80. Clarke's manuscripts are listed in Robbins' *American Literary Manuscripts*, p. 65.

John Cleland, 1709-1789

Bibliographies

For a bibliography of works by and about Cleland, see NCBEL, II, p. 145.

Indexes and Concordances

263.   Coleman, Samuel S., and Michael J. Preston. **A KWIC Concordance to John Cleland's Memoirs of a Woman of Pleasure**. New York: Garland, 1988. 627p. (Contextual Concordances; Garland Reference Library of the Humanities, vol. 829). LC 87-36615. ISBN 0-8240-8515-9.

Coleman and Preston concord the text of Peter Sabor's "World Classics" edition (New York: Oxford University Press, 1985). Frequency lists and a three-word concordance.

Journals

"Recent Articles" in *The Scriblerian and the Kit Cats* (entry 1084) regularly includes a selection of reviews of studies on Cleland.

Samuel Langhorne Clemens (Mark Twain), 1835-1910

Bibliographies

264.   Johnson, Merle. **A Bibliography of the Works of Mark Twain (Samuel Langhorne Clemens): A List of First Editions in Book Form and of First Printings in Periodicals and Occasional Publications of His Varied Literary Activities**. Revised ed. New York: Harper, 1935. 274p. LC 35-38122.

The standard guide to Twain's primary works (first published in 1910), Johnson gives full bibliographic entries for books, collections of speeches, letters published in books, contributions to books, broadsides and leaflets, poems and translations, plays and dramatizations, and other writings. Entries provide title-page transcriptions, collations, physical descriptions, contents, and publishing histories. Available in a reprinted edition (Westport, CT: Greenwood Press, 1972). Additional information is included in Blanck's *Bibliography of American Literature*, vol. 2, pp. 173-254. Other useful descriptions of Twain's primary materials are contained in Paul Machlis' *Union Catalog of Clemens Letters* (Berkeley, CA: University of California Press, 1986), and Machlis and Deborah Ann Turner's *Union Catalog of Letters to Clemens* (Berkeley, CA: University of California Press, 1992); Virginia Haviland and Margaret N. Coughlan's *Samuel Langhorne Clemens: A Centennial for Tom Sawyer, an Annotated, Selected Bibliography* (Washington, DC: Library of Congress, 1976); and William M. McBride's *Mark Twain: A Bibliography of the Collection of the Mark Twain Memorial and the Stowe-Day Foundation* (Hartford, CT: McBride, 1984). Although not intended as a comprehensive descriptive bibliography, McBride's guide cross-references entries in Johnson's and Blanck's bibliographies. Clemens' manuscripts are listed in Robbins' *American Literary Manuscripts*, pp. 65-66.

265.   Rodney, Robert M. **Mark Twain International: A Bibliography and Interpretation of His Worldwide Popularity**. Westport, CT: Greenwood Press, 1982. 275p. LC 81-13441. ISBN 0-313-23135-4.

Rodney identifies more than 5,300 editions in 73 languages from 55 countries. Entries are arranged in separate listings for domestic and other editions (by country of publication). A basic primary bibliography, Rodney's guide is most useful for the study of Twain's international reputation and influence. In addition, several more specialized bibliographies of Twain's primary materials include Louis J. Budd's *Interviews with Samuel L. Clemens, 1874-1910* (Arlington, TX: University of Texas at Arlington, 1977), which offers a checklist of newspaper and magazine interviews with Twain; and Alan Gribben's *Mark Twain's Library: A Reconstruction* (Boston: G. K. Hall, 1980), which describes Twain's books and notes and marginalia in them.

266. Tenney, Thomas Asa. **Mark Twain: A Reference Guide**. Boston: G. K. Hall, 1977. 443p. (Reference Guides in Literature). LC 76-41752. ISBN 0-8161-7966-2.
   This is the best secondary bibliography for Twain, chronologically arranging annotated entries for about 4,900 books, articles, and reviews about Twain published from 1858 through 1974. Annotations are descriptive, with significant studies receiving detailed reviews. The index gives detailed topical headings for a broad range of subjects, including names cited in annotations. Tenney's guide was updated in bibliographies annually featured in *American Literary Realism* to 1983. Recent coverage of other secondary works is provided in J. C. B. Kinch's *Mark Twain's German Critical Reception, 1875-1986: An Annotated Bibliography* (New York: Greenwood Press, 1989). Also see *Bibliography of American Fiction, 1866-1918*, pp. 121-31, for Alan Gribben's checklist of works by and about Twain. Research on Twain is reviewed by Harry Hayden Clark in Woodress' *Eight American Authors*, pp. 273-320; and Everett Emerson in Bain and Flora's *Fifty Southern Writers Before 1900*, pp. 144-64. *ALS* annually features a review essay on Twain scholarship.

Dictionaries, Encyclopedias, and Handbooks
267. LeMaster, J. R., James D. Wilson, and Christie Graves Hamric. **The Mark Twain Encyclopedia**. New York: Garland, 1993. 848p. (Garland Reference Library of the Humanities, vol. 1249). LC 92-45662. ISBN 0-8240-7212-X.
   About 740 signed, authoritative articles by some 180 contributing scholars cover all aspects of Twain's life and career. Entries for Twain's novels, short stories, and other writings summarize plots and contents, describe circumstances of composition and publication, and give critical assessments of characters, themes, and topics, with bibliographies. Other entries cover fictional characters and real persons, places, and topics, ranging from "Abolition" and "Racial Attitudes" (with "See also" references to articles on "Indians," "Jews," "Miscegenation," and related topics) to "Style" and "Bankruptcy." The two-page entry on the character of Jim in *Huckleberry Finn* notes Jim's antecedents and recurrences in other works of Twain, describes his role in each work, and indicates the responses of critics. Of particular bibliographic interest are entries for "Manuscript Collections" (pp. 487-90), with descriptions of collections; "Rare Books" (pp. 616-17), which surveys Twain collecting; and "Bibliographies" (pp. 77-80), which reviews and lists primary and secondary bibliographies for Twain. Other useful entries related to bibliography include "Auctions," "Homes and Literary Sites," and "Mark Twain Papers." The volume also gives a chronology of Twain's life and Twain family genealogy. A comprehensive index referencing names, titles, and specific topics offers good access.

268. Long, E. Hudson, and J. R. LeMaster. **The New Mark Twain Handbook**. New York: Garland, 1985. 254p. (Garland Reference Library of the Humanities, vol. 615). LC 85-45124. ISBN 0-8240-8667-8.
   An enlarged revision of *Mark Twain Handbook* (New York: Hendricks House, 1957), Long and LeMaster critically review and summarize the "most significant" scholarship (p. ix) on Twain's biography; literary backgrounds; literary and various professional careers; ideas, aesthetics, and techniques (including the use of folklore and literary sources, vocabulary, structure, and the like); and Twain's critical reception in the United States and abroad. In addition, James D. Wilson's

A Reader's Guide to the Short Stories of Mark Twain (Boston: G. K. Hall, 1987) is a bibliographic guide to the publication of Twain's short fiction.

269. Rasmussen, R. Kent. **Mark Twain A to Z: The Essential Reference to His Life and Writings**. New York: Facts on File, 1995. 552p. LC 94-39156. ISBN 0-8160-2845-1.

   Extensive, alphabetically arranged entries for Twain's individual works (notes on composition, chapter-by-chapter plot synopses for the novels or summaries of contents for other works, and publishing histories) and briefer entries for real and fictional persons, places, and things (billiards, cholera, German language, raft, science fiction, and steamboats) in his life and works. Entries reference Twain's works, particularly modern and scholarly editions and media adaptations, but contain little discussion of critical receptions and few references to critical studies. Includes an exceptionally full chronology detailing Twain's residences and travel; personal, business, and literary activities; and events in the lives of family and acquaintances. Complete with a map of Twain's American travels. Appends chronological list of Twain's books and list of secondary resources (pp. 527-31). Comprehensive index of names, titles, and detailed topics permits access to discussions of ubiquitous (and sometimes controversial) topics related to Twain, such as African Americans, imperialism, and slavery. Robert L. Gale's *Plots and Characters in the Works of Mark Twain* (Hamden, CT: Archon Books, 1973) remains valuable for simple identifications, providing brief plot summaries of Twain's works and identifications for more than 7,000 characters, including those who participate in the plots as well as those only alluded to (such as Stephen Dowling Bots).

Indexes and Concordances

270. Ramsay, Robert L., and Frances Guthrie Emberson. **A Mark Twain Lexicon**. 1938; reprint New York: Russell and Russell, 1963. 278p. LC 63-9325.

   "Towhead," "slick water," "Cherokee Strip," and "hump" (as in "Git up and hump yourself, Jim," from *Huckleberry Finn*) are examples of the several thousand words, terms, and expressions in Twain's vocabulary that Ramsay and Emberson describe in detail. Entries cover Twain's specialized vocabularies related to rivers and nautical navigation, travel and railroads, mining, printing and journalism, and other Americanisms and cross-reference related entries in the *OED* and other dictionaries. Useful for more familiar quotations, *Everyone's Mark Twain* (1948; reprint South Brunswick, NJ: A. S. Barnes, 1972), compiled by Caroline Thomas Harnsberger, topically arranges (under such headings as "weather," "women," "soap," "California," and "Theodore Roosevelt") passages from Twain's writings, with page references to *The Collected Works of Mark Twain*, "Author's National Edition" (New York: Harper and Row, 1899).

Journals

271. **Mark Twain Circular: Newsletter of the Mark Twain Circle of America**. Charleston, SC: The Citadel, 1987-. 4/yr. ISSN 1042-5357.

   Issued to subscribers of *Mark Twain Journal*, this stapled newsletter publishes information about conferences, calls for papers, notes and queries (largely biographical and bibliographic in nature), and announcements of new publications. In addition, "Current Books and Articles" has described international criticisms of Twain, continuing a bibliography previously included in *American Literary Realism* (1977-83). *Mark Twain Circular* is indexed in *MLA*.

272. **Mark Twain Journal**. Charleston, SC: College of Charleston, 1936-. 2/yr. ISSN 0025-3499.

   Founded by Cyril Clemens, "third cousin, twice removed" from Mark Twain, as *Mark Twain Quarterly* and sponsored by International Mark Twain Society, *Mark Twain Journal* publishes "well-documented factual articles and previously unknown material from Twain's own time," including materials such as cartoons and photographs, steamboat schedules, transcriptions or excerpts from manuscripts and letters, and the like. Studies employing critical or interpretive methods have been discouraged. Articles of these kinds, however, were common in issues published through 1985. An occasional issue contains a single feature devoted to a specific topic. The journal publishes no reviews, bibliographies, or information about its sponsoring society. According to its masthead: "The *Journal* tends to appear late, and begs your patient indulgence." Indeed, publication is at least three years behind schedule. The recto of the back cover of 30.1 (Spring 1992) gives a useful checklist of all volumes of *Mark Twain Quarterly* and *Mark Twain Journal* through 30.2 (Fall 1992). *Mark Twain Journal* is indexed in *AHI, A&HCI, MHRA,* and *MLA*.

Wortman's *A Guide to Serial Bibliographies for Modern Literatures,* p. 250, describes other serial bibliographies for Twain. Patterson's *Author Newsletters and Journals,* pp. 67-70, describes other previously published journals for Twain.

273.   **The Twainian.** Hannibal, MO: Mark Twain Research Foundation, 1939-1989, 1993-. 4/yr. ISSN 0041-4573.

Variously published in several fits and starts through its long history by the Mark Twain Society of Chicago, Mark Twain Association of America, and Mark Twain Research Foundation, past issues of *The Twainian* were "concerned with the wisdom of Mark Twain as taught by his life and writings" (masthead). The 1993 resuscitated *Twainian* is subtitled "(Discovering Mark Twain)." The contents of the single folded sheet remains much the same, including brief notes of biographical interest, such as the origins of the name "Mark Twain"; the source of the plot of *Huckleberry Finn*; tributes to Twain; reprintings of reminiscences, tributes, and reviews; and accounts of the activities of the foundation. According to 49.1 (30 November 1993): 1, the newsletter plans to "move, probably rather slowly, toward a format which will include more scholarly material." *The Twainian* is unindexed.

John Cleveland, 1613-1658
Bibliographies

274.   Morris, Brian. **John Cleveland (1613-1658): A Bibliography of His Poems.** London: The Bibliographical Society, 1967. 54p. LC 67-107421.

Morris offers full bibliographic descriptions for editions of Cleveland's works. Entries give title-page transcriptions, collations, contents, copy locations, and publishing histories. Emphasis is on identifying authoritative reprintings in subsequent editions. Coverage of criticisms of Cleveland's works to 1980 is included in McCarron and Shenk's *Lesser Metaphysical Poets,* pp. [16]-17. Also for a bibliography of works by and about Cleveland, see *NCBEL,* I, pp. 1304-1305.

Cloud of Unknowing, c.1350-1400
Bibliographies

Valerie M. Lagorio and Michael G. Sargent offer more comprehensive information about primary materials for Rolle and other English mystics with a bibliography of editions and criticism in Severs and Hartung's *A Manual of the Writings in Middle English,* vol. XXIII, pp. 3049-3137, 3405-71. Lagorio and Bradley's *The 14th-Century English Mystics* (entry 1143) covers modern criticism. Also see *NCBEL,* I, pp. 520-21, for works about the poem. Edwards' *Middle English Prose,* pp. 61-82, contains a review of research on Walter Hilton and *The Cloud of Unknowing* by Alastair Minnis.

Arthur Hugh Clough, 1819-1861
Bibliographies

275.   Golin, Richard M., Walter E. Houghton, and Michael Timko. **Arthur Hugh Clough: A Descriptive Catalogue.** New York: New York Public Library, 1967. 117p. LC 67-25798.

Reprinted from *Bulletin of the New York Public Library* 70 (1966): 554-85; 71 (1967): 55-58; and 71 (1967): 173-99, this is the standard descriptive bibliography of Clough's works. Entries give brief bibliographic information and summaries of contents for Clough's unpublished works, works published in his lifetime, and posthumously published poetry and prose. In addition, annotated entries for about 300 biographical and critical works about Clough published from 1829 through 1965 are arranged chronologically. Full bibliographic descriptions (presenting title-page transcriptions and physical descriptions) for editions and other separately published works by Clough, including juvenilia, through 1869 are provided in Patrick Greig Scott's *The Early Editions of Arthur Hugh Clough* (New York: Garland, 1977). Clough's manuscripts are described in *Index of English Literary Manuscripts*, IV, pt. 1:459-503. Supplemental coverage of works about Clough is provided in Ehrsam's *Bibliographies of Twelve Victorian Authors*, pp. [67]-75, which cites international comments, criticism, and reviews for Cough through the early twentieth century. Also for a bibliography of works by and about Clough, see *NCBEL*, III, p. 461. Research on Clough is reviewed by Michael Timko in Faverty's *The Victorian Poets*, pp. 149-226.

Robert M(yron) Coates, 1897-1973
Bibliographies

For works by Coates, see *First Printings of American Authors*, vol. 4, pp. 109-12.

Humphrey Cobb, 1899-1944
Bibliographies

For works by Cobb, see *First Printings of American Authors*, vol. 3, p. 51. Cobb's manuscripts are listed in Robbins' *American Literary Manuscripts*, p. 67.

Irvin S(hrewsbury) Cobb, 1876-1944
Bibliographies

See *Bibliography of American Fiction, 1866-1918*, pp. 131-33, for Gwen L. Nagel's checklist of works by and about Cobb. Cobb's manuscripts are listed in Robbins' *American Literary Manuscripts*, p. 67.

Sylvanus Cobb, Jr., 1823-1887
Bibliographies

See *Bibliography of American Fiction Through 1865*, pp. 83-85, for a checklist of works by and about Cobb. Cobb's manuscripts are listed in Robbins' *American Literary Manuscripts*, p. 67.

William Cobbett, 1763-1835
Bibliographies

276.   Pearl, M. L. **William Cobbett: A Bibliographical Account of His Life and Times**. 1953; reprint Westport, CT: Greenwood Press, 1971. LC 78-136079. ISBN 0-8371-5229-1.

Chronologically arranged descriptions of Cobbett's works in sections for "writings by or about Cobbett" (p. 15) published from 1792 to 1835; posthumously published selections, extracts, and other writings by or relating to Cobbett; and manuscripts and portraits of Cobbett mainly in the Cole Collection of Nuffield College. Entries supply title-page transcriptions, imprint data for first and subsequent editions and printings, with copy locations, and publication histories, but do not give physical descriptions. Pearl emphasizes "bio-bibliography" (p. 2), accounting for works attributed to or critical of Cobbett. Indexes of titles and persons. For a bibliography of works by and about Cobbett, see *NCBEL*, III, pp. 1199-1210.

J(ohn) M(ichael) Coetzee, 1940-
Bibliographies

277.   Goddard, Kevin, John Read, and Teresa Dovey. **J. M. Coetzee: A Bibliography.** Grahamstown: National English Literary Museum, 1990. 103p. (NELM Bibliographic Series, no. 3). ISBN 0-620-14768-7.

Largely unannotated listings of works by and about Coetzee through 1990. Part I presents chronologically arranged sections for Coetzee's separately published fiction, extracts from his books, translations of his works, separately published and contributed nonfiction, poetry, drama, translations by Coetzee, edited work, reviews, and interviews. Some 163 entries give brief bibliographic data and occasionally note contents and reprintings. In part II, Goddard, Read, and Dovey identify 474 works about Coetzee in sections for books and general critical articles and chapters, unpublished papers, and criticisms (largely reviews) of individual works. Coverage includes non-English-language studies. Contains Coetzee chronology. Awkward, separate indexes of reviewers, critics and anthologists, interviewers, and titles and kinds of works by Coetzee. Also see Ian Bernard's summary biography, critical assessment of major works, and selected primary and secondary bibliography for Coetzee in McCaffery's *Postmodern Fiction: A Bio-Bibliographical Guide*, pp. 305-308.

Elizabeth Boatwright Coker, 1909-
Bibliographies

For works by Coker, see *First Printings of American Authors*, vol. 4, pp. 113-15.

Samuel Taylor Coleridge, 1772-1834
Bibliographies

278.   Haven, Richard, Josephine Haven, and Maurianne Adams. **Samuel Taylor Coleridge: An Annotated Bibliography of Criticism and Scholarship: Volume 1: 1793-1899.** Boston: G. K. Hall, 1976. 382p. LC 75-40487. ISBN 0-8161-7829-1.

This volume is continued by a series of volumes, including:

278.1. Crawford, Walter B., and Edward S. Lauterbach. **Samuel Taylor Coleridge: An Annotated Bibliography of Criticism and Scholarship: Volume 2: 1900-1939; with Additional Entries for 1795-1899.** Boston: G. K. Hall, 1983. 812p. LC 75-40487. ISBN 0-8161-7866-6.

278.2. Crawford, Walter B. **Samuel Taylor Coleridge: An Annotated Bibliography of Criticism and Scholarship: Volume III: Part I, 1793-1994; Supplement to Volumes I and II, 1793-1939; Comprehensive Bibliography, 1940-1965; Selective Bibliography, 1966-1994; Part II, 1791-1993.** 946p. Boston: G. K. Hall, 1996. LC 75-40487. ISBN 0-8161-7829-1.

These constitute the most comprehensive, detailed, and extensively annotated listings of critical studies and works of other kinds about Coleridge. The first volume chronologically arranges entries for about 1,900 works of all varieties in all languages. The second volume includes entries for nearly 3,000 works on Coleridge. By far the largest and most complex volume in the set, the 1996 volume supplements and sometimes corrects the first two volumes in 680 entries; comprehensively covers criticism of Coleridge published from 1940 to 1965 in more than 2,200 entries; and selectively covers criticism from 1966 to 1994 in 669 entries. Additionally, Part II of the 1996 volume supplies more than 2,300 descriptions of works that allude to Coleridge in sections for fiction and drama, miscellanea (largely lectures, sermons, essays, and the like), verse, parodies and imitations, continuations and completions by other authors of Coleridge's uncompleted works, cartoons and comic strips, musical settings of Coleridge's works, other Coleridge-related music, audio and media production, portraits of Coleridge, and other art related to Coleridge. Chronologically arranged annotations are extensive, although description is emphasized over evaluation. Significant studies receive extended descriptions, with references to reviews. Volumes I and II include separate, comprehensive subject indexes. Volume III offers a more elaborate access system, with indexes for authors, titles, periodicals, book reviews (by reviewer and by periodical), subject proper names, subject titles, and subjects and categories. The latter is particularly complex: Users who quickly want to locate articles on bird images in *The Rime of the Ancient Mariner* will need to read the instructions and mine the listings. Perhaps an "Essential Coleridge," modeled on G. K. Hall's volumes for Chaucer, Shakespeare, and Milton, is now needed. Volume III supersedes Mary Lee Taylor Milton's *The Poetry of Samuel Taylor Coleridge: An Annotated Bibliography of Criticism, 1935-1970* (New York: Garland, 1981), which chronologically arranges 445 annotated entries for English-language books and articles about Coleridge and was previously the most useful guide to recent criticism. Coverage is also superior to that provided by Jefferson D. Caskey and Melinda M. Stapper's *Samuel Taylor Coleridge: A Selective Bibliography of Criticism, 1935-1977* (Westport, CT: Greenwood Press, 1978), which includes more than 2,000 briefly annotated entries for books and parts of books, articles, and dissertations. Also for a bibliography of works by and about Coleridge, see *NCBEL*, III, pp. 211-54. Research on Coleridge is reviewed by John Beer in Dyson's *English Poetry*, pp. 188-210; and Max F. Schulz in Jordan's *The English Romantic Poets*, pp. 341-464.

279. Wise, Thomas J. **A Bibliography of the Writings in Prose and Verse of Samuel Taylor Coleridge**. 1913; reprint Folkestone: Dawsons of Pall Mall, 1970. 316p. OCLC 3207893.

The standard primary bibliography, Wise's guide gives full bibliographic descriptions for Coleridge's books, prose and verse contributions to periodicals and other works and collected editions. Entries provide title-page transcriptions, collations, physical descriptions, and publishing histories. Wise's bibliography will be superseded by the descriptive bibliography to be included in a volume of the definitive edition of Coleridge's collected works. Coleridge's manuscripts are described in *Index of English Literary Manuscripts*, IV, pt. 1:505-661. Also of interest for research on Coleridge's primary bibliography is Ralph J. Coffman's *Coleridge's Library: A Bibliography of Books Owned or Read by Samuel Taylor Coleridge* (Boston: G. K. Hall, 1987); and William F. Taylor's *Critical Annotations: Being Marginal Notes Inscribed in Volumes Formerly in the Possession of Coleridge* (Harrow: W. F. Taylor, 1889).

Indexes and Concordances

280. Logan, Eugenia. **A Concordance to the Poetry of Samuel Taylor Coleridge**. Saint Mary-of-the-Woods, IN: Privately printed, 1940. 901p. LC 40-5258.

Logan bases this concordance on Ernest Hartley Coleridge's *The Poetical Works of Samuel Taylor Coleridge* (Oxford: Clarendon Press, 1912). More specialized indexing is provided in Patricia A. McEahern and Thomas F. Beckwith's *A Complete Concordance to the Lyrical Ballads of Samuel Taylor Coleridge and William Wordsworth, 1798 and 1800 Editions* (New York: Garland, 1987).

Jeremy Collier, 1650-1726
Bibliographies

For a bibliography of works by and about Collier, see *NCBEL*, II, pp. 721-24.

(William) Wilkie Collins, 1824-1889
Bibliographies

281. Beetz, Kirk H. **Wilkie Collins: An Annotated Bibliography, 1889-1976**. Metuchen, NJ: Scarecrow, 1978. 167p. (Scarecrow Author Bibliographies, no. 35). LC 77-26609. ISBN 0-8108-1103-0.

Beetz presents brief bibliographic information for editions and reprints of Collins' books (collected works, novels, plays, and anthologies) and contributions to periodicals, in addition to arranging annotated entries for about 300 critical studies (including dissertations) in separate, topical listings for biographies, bibliographies, studies of individual works, influence studies, studies of Collins' reputation, reviews of Collins' works and reviews of works about Collins. Annotations are descriptive. A separate subject index enhances access. Better coverage of Collins' primary materials is included in Parrish and Miller's bibliography (entry 282). Research on Collins and Reade is reviewed by Robert Ashley and Wayne Burns in Stevenson's *Victorian Fiction*, pp. 277-93; and on Collins by Ashley (pp. 223-29) and on Reade by Burns (pp. 230-33) in Ford's *Victorian Fiction*.

282.   Parrish, M. L., and Elizabeth V. Miller. **Wilkie Collins and Charles Reade: First Editions Described with Notes**. 1940; reprint New York: Burt Franklin, 1968. 355p. (Burt Franklin: Bibliography and Reference Series, no. 168). LC 68-4143.
　　　Parrish and Miller provide full bibliographic details for Collins' and Reade's primary works, including separate listings for each writer's books and posters and programs for plays, with (for Collins) an appendixed list of contributions to periodicals. Entries give title-page transcriptions, physical descriptions, and publishing histories. Collins' manuscripts are described in *Index of English Literary Manuscripts*, IV, pt. 1:663-79, 830. Other useful information about Reade's primary materials is provided in Robert B. Martin's "The Reade Collection," *Princeton University Library Chronicle* 17 (1956): 77-80; and "Manuscript Correspondence of Charles Reade," *Princeton University Library Chronicle* 19 (1957-58): 102-103. Also for a bibliography of works by and about Collins, see *NCBEL*, III, pp. 924-28.

Journals
283.   **Wilkie Collins Society Journal**. Davis, CA: Wilkie Collins Society, 1981-1987. Annual. ISSN 0897-2982.
　　　Sponsored by the Wilkie Collins Society, annual volumes publish articles and book reviews related to the life and works of Collins. Most contributions offer interpretations of images and themes or new information on Collins' biography, such as " 'A Terribly Strange Bed': Self-Subverting Gothicism" and " 'Everything to My Wife': The Inheritance Theme in *The Moonstone* and *Sense and Sensibility*" (which compares the use of the marriage theme in Collins' and Jane Austen's works). *Wilkie Collins Society Journal* was indexed in *MLA* through 1987.

William Collins, 1721-1759
Bibliographies
　　　See Williams' *Seven XVIIIth Century Bibliographies* (entry 35), pp. [99]-114, for full descriptions of Collins' works. For a bibliography of works by and about Collins, see *NCBEL*, II, pp. 585-89, by Roger H. Lonsdale. Collins' manuscripts are described in *Index of English Literary Manuscripts*, III, pt. 1:227-31.

Indexes and Concordances
284.   Booth, Bradford A., and Claude E. Jones. **A Concordance of the Poetical Works of William Collins**. Berkeley, CA: University of California Press, 1939. 126p. LC 40-344.
　　　Based on the Oxford "Standard Authors" edition, *The Poems of Gray and Collins*, 3d ed., revised (London: Oxford University Press, 1937); and *The Poems of William Collins* (London: F. Etchells & H. MacDonald, 1929), edited "with an introductory study" by Edmund Blunden.

George Colman, the Elder, 1732-1794
Bibliographies
　　　For a bibliography of works by and about Colman, see *NCBEL*, II, pp. 812-14.

George Colman, the Younger, 1762-1836
Bibliographies
　　　For a bibliography of works by and about Colman, see *NCBEL*, II, pp. 828-30.

Padraic Colum, 1881-1972

Bibliographies

For a bibliography of works by and about Colum, see *NCBEL*, III, pp. 1942-43. Colum's manuscripts are listed in Robbins' *American Literary Manuscripts*, p. 69. Additionally, Zack R. Bowen's *Annotated Catalogue and Bibliography for the Colum Collection of the Library of State University of New York at Binghamton* (Binghamton, NY: State University of New York, 1965) enumerates 464 items in the Binghamton collection, including 46 play manuscripts, 48 notebooks, galley and page proofs, letters, photographs, and other materials. Additionally, Kay S. Diviney surveys works by and about Colum in Schrank and Demastes' *Irish Playwrights, 1880-1995: A Research and Production Sourcebook*, pp. 69-79.

Richard Condon, 1915-

Bibliographies

For works by Condon, see *First Printings of American Authors*, vol. 2, pp. 117-18.

William Congreve, 1670-1729

Bibliographies

285. Bartlett, Laurence. **William Congreve: A Reference Guide**. Boston: G. K. Hall, 1979. 216p. (A Reference Publication in Literature). LC 79-19661. ISBN 0-8161-8142-x.

Updated and continued in:

285.1. Bartlett, Laurence. **William Congreve: An Annotated Bibliography, 1978-1994**. Lanham, MD: Scarecrow Press, 1996. 109p. (Scarecrow Author Bibliographies, no. 97). LC 96-11672. ISBN 0-8108-3166-X.

Bartlett's guides offer comprehensive international coverage of works by and about Congreve to 1994. The 1979 volume chronologically arranges annotated entries for about 1,300 editions of Congreve's works and critical comments and studies about Congreve published from 1729 through 1977. The 1996 volume contains chronologically arranged addenda of about 50 items for 1904-77 followed by entries for about 250 items published through 1994. Coverage includes books, articles, chapters, dissertations, and non-English-language studies; reviews are excluded. Entries for book-length works (editions and criticism) are listed together. Annotations are brief and descriptive. Indexes in both volumes include topical headings under the titles of Congreve's works—for "bibliography," "biography," "editions," "collections," and "criticisms." Coverage of Congreve's primary materials is provided in Albert M. Lyles and John Dobson's *The John C. Hodges Collection of William Congreve in the University of Tennessee Library: A Bibliographical Catalog* (Knoxville, TN: University of Tennessee Library, 1970). For a bibliography of works by and about Congreve, see *NCBEL*, II, pp. 750-53. Congreve's manuscripts are described in *Index of English Literary Manuscripts*, II, pt. 1:137-51. Research on Congreve is reviewed by John Barnard in Wells' *English Drama*, pp. 173-98.

Indexes and Concordances

286. Mann, David. **A Concordance to the Plays of William Congreve**. Ithaca, NY: Cornell University Press, 1973. 888p. (The Cornell Concordances). LC 72-13384. ISBN 0-8014-0767-2.

This is based on Herbert Davis' standard edition of *The Complete Plays of William Congreve* (Chicago, IL: University of Chicago Press, 1967). Mann provides indexes of stage directions, common words, and word frequencies.

Journals

"Recent Articles" in *The Scriblerian and the Kit Cats* (entry 1084) regularly includes a selection of reviews of studies on Congreve.

Evan S(helby) Connell, Jr., 1924-

Bibliographies

For works by Connell, see *First Printings of American Authors*, vol. 2, pp. 119-20. See *Bibliography of American Fiction, 1919-1988*, p. 133, for Robert C. Petersen's checklist of works by and about Connell.

Joseph Conrad (Jozef Teodor Konrad Korzeniowski), 1857-1924

Bibliographies

287.   Knowles, Owen. **An Annotated Critical Bibliography of Joseph Conrad.** New York: St. Martin's Press, 1992. 255p. (Annotated Critical Bibliographies). LC 91-37610. ISBN 0-7108-1265-5.

Annotated entries for selected works by Conrad and criticism of Conrad published from 1914 to 1990, emphasizing scholarship after 1975, chronologically arranged in sections for editions; bibliographies and surveys of criticism; letters; biographical studies and memoirs; reference and background works; anthologies of criticism; introductory studies; book-length studies; early fiction; the major individual novels; the late novels; shorter works of fiction; nonfictional prose; and 20 selected topics, including language and style, textual studies, Conrad and the sea, and Conrad and women. Annotations for nearly 600 entries clearly identify "invaluable," "indispensable," and otherwise significant research resources and studies. Separate indexes for critics, subjects, and Conrad's works offer good access, making this a handy starting point for research on Conrad.

288.   Teets, Bruce E., and Helmut E. Gerber. **Joseph Conrad: An Annotated Bibliography of Writings About Him.** DeKalb, IL: Northern Illinois University Press, 1971. 671p. (Annotated Secondary Bibliography Series on English Literature in Transition, 1880-1920). LC 70-146639. ISBN 0-8758-0020-3.

This volume, which Teets refers to as "Conrad I," is complemented by:

288.1. Teets, Bruce E. **Joseph Conrad: An Annotated Bibliography.** New York: Garland, 1990. 786p. (An Annotated Secondary Bibliography Series of English Literature in Transition, 1880-1920; Garland Reference Library of the Humanities, vol. 868). LC 88-24312. ISBN 0-8240-7037-2.

Comprehensive coverage of criticism of Conrad in all formats and languages. "Conrad I" includes annotated entries for 1,976 works published from 1895 through 1966. Its supplement, "Conrad II," contains entries for an additional 762 works through 1966 and for 1,389 works from 1967 through 1975. As in other volumes in this series formerly published by Northern Illinois University Press, thorough annotations describe significant studies in great detail, with references to reviews. Although lacking subject indexing, the volumes contain detailed indexes for primary titles and other indexes. These volumes supersede coverage of Conrad criticism included in Theodore G. Ehrsam's *A Bibliography of Joseph Conrad* (Metuchen, NJ: Scarecrow Press, 1969) and Kenneth A. Lohf and Eugene P. Sheehy's *Joseph Conrad at Mid-Century: Editions and Studies, 1895-1955* (Minneapolis, MN: University of Minnesota Press, 1957). More specialized secondary coverage is offered in Robert Secor and Debra Moddelmog's *Joseph Conrad and American Writers: A Bibliographical Study of Affinities, Influences, and Relations* (Westport, CT: Greenwood Press, 1985), which arranges 1,108 annotated entries in separate listings for studies of Conrad and American writers of the early and late nineteenth century and the twentieth century, "further listings" for studies of Conrad in relation to contemporary American writers, and lists of films based on Conrad's works. Wanda Perczak's *Polska Bibliografia Conradowska, 1896-1992* (Torun: Wydawnictwo Universytetu Mikolaj Kopernika, 1993) is valuable for lists of Polish-language criticisms of Conrad. Also for a bibliography of works by and about Conrad, see *NCBEL*, IV, pp. 395-417. Research on Conrad is reviewed by J. A. V. Chapple in Dyson's *The English Novel*, pp. 300-13.

289. Wise, Thomas J. **A Bibliography of the Writings of Joseph Conrad, 1895-1921**. 2d ed. 1921; reprint London: Dawsons of Pall Mall, 1964. 125p. OCLC 929598.

The basic bibliography of Conrad's primary materials, Wise's guide gives full bibliographic descriptions for Conrad's books and uncollected contributions to other works. Entries deliver title-page transcriptions, physical descriptions, and publishing histories. Based on Wise's personal collection, now largely in the British Library's Ashley Collection. Supplementary information for editions, reprints, serializations, and translations of Conrad's works is included in Kenneth A. Lohf and Eugene P. Sheehy's *Joseph Conrad at Mid-Century: Editions and Studies, 1895-1955* (Minneapolis, MN: University of Minnesota Press, 1957). Conrad's manuscripts are described and located in Gordon Lindstrand's "A Bibliographical Survey of Manuscripts of Joseph Conrad," *Conradiana* 2.1 (1969-70): 23-32; 2.2 (1969-70): 105-14; and 2.3 (1969-70): 153-62. Additionally, information on binding variants is provided in Walter E. Smith's *Joseph Conrad: A Bibliographical Catalogue of His Major First Editions with Facsimiles of Several Title Pages* (Long Beach, CA: Walter E. Smith, 1979). Major Conrad collections are described in George T. Keating's *A Conrad Memorial Library: The Collection of George T. Keating* (Garden City, NY: Doubleday, Doran, 1929), which details a collection now in Yale University's Beineke Library; and Flavio Fagnani's *Catalogo della Collezione Conradiana di Ugo Mursia* (Milan: Mursia, 1984), which describes materials at the Universita di Pisa in Italy. Also valuable is *The Robert C. Findlay Collection of Joseph Conrad, with Additions: An Annotated Catalogue of First Editions, Signed Books, Association and Holographic Material, Including an Original Manuscript* (Santa Barbara, CA: Randall House, 1993); and David W. Tutein's *Joseph Conrad's Reading: An Annotated Bibliography* (West Cornwall, CT: Locust Hill Press, 1990).

Dictionaries, Encyclopedias, and Handbooks

290. Knowles, Owen. **A Conrad Chronology**. Boston: G. K. Hall, 1990. 165p. (Macmillan Author Chronologies). LC 89-39750. ISBN 0-8161-1839-6.

Intended to provide "a clear and compact digest" of Conrad's life, Knowles' chronology emphasizes the significant facts related to the composition and publishing histories of Conrad's works from *Almayer's Folly* (1894) to the end of his literary career. Other themes, such as Conrad's reading and his concerns about deadlines and finances, are recurrent. A "Select Who's Who" briefly describes about 100 of Conrad's associates. Another appendix identifies locations and addresses of Conrad's residences. Several useful indexes cover people, places, organizations, Conrad's works, his reading, and other subjects, including his voyages, interviews, and homes. Emphasis on central themes of Conrad's career and detailed topical access make Knowles' chronology one of the more useful of the series.

291. Page, Norman. **A Conrad Companion**. London: Macmillan, 1986. 185p. ISBN 0-333-34598-3.

Chapters cover each of Conrad's novels, short stories, collaborations, nonfictional prose, and plays, including such topics as Conrad's languages and life and career in Poland, France, and Africa. Sections for writings give brief analyses of plots, characters, and themes and assess critical receptions. Includes a useful who's who in Conrad plus a chronology, filmography, and selected bibliography.

292. Stape, J. H., ed. **The Cambridge Companion to Joseph Conrad**. Cambridge: Cambridge University Press, 1996. 258p. (Cambridge Companions to Literature). ISBN 0-5214-8484-7.

Twelve critical essays by authorities, including Owen Knowles, Cedric Watt, and others on Conrad's life, short fiction, individual novels, narrative, "imperialism," "Modernism," and influence. Includes chronology, classified annotated bibliography of basic reference works and criticisms (p. 242-53). Indexed.

Indexes and Concordances

293. Parins, James W., Robert J. Dilligan, and Todd K. Bender. **A Concordance to Conrad's Lord Jim: Verbal Index Word Frequency Table and Field of Reference.** New York: Garland, 1976. 266p. (Garland Reference Library of the Humanities, vol. 210). LC 75-34972. ISBN 0-8240-9995-8.

The first volume of another informal series of concordances sometimes referred to as the "Garland Conrad Concordances," this represents a project begun in 1970 at the University of Wisconsin to concord all of Conrad's works. Most volumes are not really concordances but actually word indexes that cite page and line references of appended texts (usually identified as the "field of reference") that "mirror" pagination and lineation of the copy text. Exceptions to this format (which integrate the verbal indexes and lines of reference) are the concordances for *Heart of Darkness* (entry 293.2) and *Victory* (entry 293.4). The base texts for most of the volumes are the texts of the first British or American collected editions. Some volumes also provide word-frequency tables. Many of the volumes suffer from poor offset printing; despite the use of good acid-free paper, the print in several volumes is practically unreadable. The field of reference for *Lord Jim* is the 1921 edition (London: William Heinemann).

Other volumes in the series (by year of publication) include:

293.1. Briggum, Sue M., and Todd K. Bender. **A Concordance to Conrad's Almayer's Folly.** New York: Garland, 1978. 146p. (Garland Reference Library of the Humanities, vol. 101). LC 77-83408. ISBN 0-8240-9843-9.

This employs the text of the first British edition (London: Fisher Unwin, 1895) for the field of reference. The verbal index references pages and lines.

293.2. Bender, Todd K. **A Concordance to Conrad's Heart of Darkness.** New York: Garland, 1979. 507p. (Garland Reference Library of the Humanities, vol. 135). LC 78-68269. ISBN 0-8240-9809-9.

Concords the text of the 1921 (London: Heinemann) edition. Sybyl C. Jacobson, Robert J. Dilligan, and Bender's microfiche *Concordance to Joseph Conrad's Heart of Darkness* (Carbondale, IL: Southern Illinois University Press, 1973) is also available.

293.3. Bender, Todd K. **A Concordance to Conrad's The Secret Agent.** New York: Garland, 1979. 252p. (Garland Reference Library of the Humanities, vol. 134). LC 78-68258. ISBN 0-8240-9810-2.

Bender's volume indexes the text of the 1907 (London: Methuen) edition.

293.4. Parins, James W., Robert J. Dilligan, and Todd K. Bender. **A Concordance to Conrad's Victory.** New York: Garland, 1979. 486p. (Garland Reference Library of the Humanities, vol. 136). LC 78-68275. ISBN 0-8240-9808-0.

Concords the text of *Victory* (London: Heinemann, 1921).

293.5. Bender, Todd K. **Concordances to Conrad's The Shadow Line and Youth: A Narrative.** New York: Garland, 1980. 155p. (Garland Reference Library of the Humanities, vol. 204). LC 79-8416. ISBN 0-8240-9520-0.

Bender indexes the texts of *The Shadow Line* (Garden City, NY: Doubleday, Page, 1917) and *Youth: A Narrative and Two Other Stories* (London: William Blackwood and Sons, 1902).

293.6. Parins, James W., and Todd K. Bender. **A Concordance to Conrad's The Nigger of the Narcissus.** New York: Garland, 1981. 139p. (Garland Reference Library of the Humanities, vol. 205). LC 79-8417. ISBN 0-8240-9519-7.

Uses the text of the 1921 edition (London: William Heinemann) as the field of reference, with a verbal index cross-referencing pages and lines.

293.7. Gaston, Paul L., and Todd K. Bender. **A Concordance to Conrad's The Arrow of Gold**. New York: Garland, 1981. 255p. (Garland Reference Library of the Humanities, vol. 238). LC 80-8966. ISBN 0-8240-9370-4.

The field of reference is the text of the 1924 (New York: Doubleday, Dent) edition. The verbal index cites pages and lines. A word-frequency table is included.

293.8. Parins, James W., Robert J. Dilligan, and Todd K. Bender. **A Concordance to Conrad's Nostromo**. New York: Garland, 1984. 397p. (Garland Reference Library of the Humanities, vol. 262). LC 80-8967. ISBN 0-8240-9358-5.

The text of the 1926 (Garden City, NY: Doubleday, Page) edition is indexed.

293.9. Bender, Todd K. **A Concordance to Conrad's A Set of Six**. New York: Garland, 1981. 211p. (Garland Reference Library of the Humanities, vol. 291). LC 81-47287. ISBN 0-8240-9340-2.

Based on the text of the third edition (London: Methuen, 1908), which Bender identifies as an "unstable" text (p. viii). The verbal index cross-references pages and lines in the field of reference. A word-frequency list is also included.

293.10. Bender, Todd K. **Concordances to Conrad's Tales of Unrest and Tales of Hearsay**. New York: Garland, 1982. 261p. (Garland Reference Library of the Humanities, vol. 297). LC 81-43332. ISBN 0-8240-9297-X.

Bender indexes the texts of *Tales of Unrest* (London: T. Fisher Unwin, 1898) and *Tales of Hearsay* (Garden City, NY: Doubleday, Page, 1926).

293.11. Bender, Todd K., and Kirsten A. Bender. **Concordances to Conrad's Typhoon and Other Stories and Within the Tides**. New York: Garland, 1982. 368p. (Garland Reference Library of the Humanities, vol. 324). LC 81-48410. ISBN 0-8240-9379-8.

The Benders index the texts of the 1926 (Garden City, NY: Doubleday, Page) editions.

293.12. Higdon, David Leon, and Todd K. Bender. **A Concordance to Conrad's Under Western Eyes**. New York: Garland, 1983. 271p. (Garland Reference Library of the Humanities, vol. 363). LC 82-48434. ISBN 0-8240-9234-1.

Higdon and Bender index the text of the 1926 (Garden City, NY: Doubleday, Page) edition.

293.13. Bender, Todd K. **Concordances to Conrad's The Mirror of the Sea and The Inheritors**. New York: Garland, 1983. 160, 162p. (Garland Reference Library of the Humanities, vol. 426). LC 83-47608. ISBN 0-8240-9110-8.

The text of the 1926 (New York: Doubleday, Page) collected editions serve as the fields of reference, with verbal indexes cross-referencing pages and lines.

293.14. Bender, Todd K. **A Concordance to Conrad's An Outcast of the Islands**. New York: Garland, 1984. 250p. (Garland Reference Library of the Humanities, vol. 476). LC 83-49320. ISBN 0-8240-8991-X.

The field of reference is the text of the 1926 (New York: Doubleday, Page) edition.

293.15. Bender, Todd K., and James W. Parins. **A Concordance to Conrad's Romance**. New York: Garland, 1985. 406p. (Garland Reference Library of the Humanities, vol. 576). LC 84-48856. ISBN 0-8240-8760-7.

This employs the text of the 1921 (London: Heinemann) edition as the field of reference. The verbal index cites pages and lines. Alphabetical- and numerical-frequency tables are appendixed.

293.16. Bender, Todd K. **A Concordance to Conrad's The Rescue**. New York: Garland, 1985. 310p. (Garland Reference Library of the Humanities, vol. 577). LC 85-15974. ISBN 0-8240-8759-3.

Based on the text of the 1926 (Garden City, NY: Doubleday, Page) edition, providing a field of reference, verbal index, and frequency table.

293.17. Higdon, David Leon, and Todd K. Bender. **A Concordance to Conrad's The Rover**. New York: Garland, 1985. 212p. (Garland Reference Library of the Humanities, vol. 514). LC 84-45403. ISBN 0-8240-8896-4.

Verbal index that cites pages and lines and word-frequency tables. The field of reference is based on the text of the 1923 (New York: Sun-Dial) collected edition.

Journals

294. **The Conradian**. Dundee: Joseph Conrad Society, 1975-. 2/yr. ISSN 0951-2314.

Sponsored by the Joseph Conrad Society, this journal annually publishes eight to 14 scholarly articles, brief notes, and reviews of new publications related to Conrad's life and works. Typical contributions offer close, interpretive readings of works and discussions of biographical problems and primary documents, such as "Reflection and Self-Consumption in 'Youth' " and "Some Uncollected Letters from Joseph Conrad to T. Fisher Unwin." Other contributions have focused on film adaptations of Conrad's works and Conrad's literary relationships with other writers, such as Ford Madox Ford, Wyndham Lewis, T. S. Eliot, Louis Zukofsky, and Bertrand Russell. Bibliographic contributions describe important special collections of Conrad materials, such as Donald W. Rude's "Joseph Conrad's Letters to Eugene F. Saxton: A New Archive at Texas Tech University," 14: 1-2 (December 1989): 47-66. In addition, *Conradian* has regularly included two important bibliographic features: "Conrad in Some Recent General Studies and Collections," which briefly describes book-length works about Conrad; and "The Year's Work in Conrad Studies: A Survey of Periodical Literature." *The Conradian* is indexed in *MLA*.

295. **Conradiana: A Journal of Joseph Conrad Studies**. Lubbock, TX: Texas Tech University Press, 1968- . 3/yr. ISSN 0010-6356.

Conradiana publishes five to 10 articles per issue that discuss "all aspects and periods of the life and works of Joseph Conrad" (masthead). Articles such as "The Power of Culture in *Lord Jim*" and "Stylistic Variation in 'An Antichrist' " indicate the journal's interest in close readings and interpretations of allusions and images in particular works. In addition, a significant number of recent articles have presented the texts of previously unknown or unpublished Conrad letters or described otherwise unreported manuscripts and proofs, making the journal a source of valuable primary materials. The useful bibliographic feature, "Current Conrad Bibliography," covering 1987-88, last appeared in 22.1 (1990). Issues of *Conradiana* also include two to six book reviews. *Conradiana* is indexed in *AES*, *AHI*, *MHRA*, and *MLA*.

296. **L' Epoque Conradienne**. Limoges: Societe Conradienne Francaise, Faculte des Lettres & Sciences Humaines, 1975-. Annual. ISSN 0294-6904.

Articles in French and English have offered readings of specific works and interpretations of themes and images and more generally examined Conrad's relationship to European literary traditions. Typical contributions include "Betrayal and Corruptible Values in *Nostromo*" and "Joseph Conrad et le Cannibalisme Litteraire." Others have addressed the literary relations of Conrad and Shakespeare, Percy Bysshe Shelley, Dickens, Dostoyevsky, and Malcolm Lowry. Many articles pay particular attention to Conrad and Polish literature. *L' Epoque Conradienne* is indexed in *MLA*.

Patterson's *Author Newsletters and Journals*, pp. 72-75, describes other previously published journals for Conrad.

Jack (John Wesley) Conroy, 1899-1980
Bibliographies

For works by Conroy, see *First Printings of American Authors*, vol. 1, pp. 67-68. See *Bibliography of American Fiction, 1919-1988*, pp. 134-35, for Jon Christian Suggs and Douglas Wixson's checklist of works by and about Conroy.

Moncure Daniel Conway, 1832-1907
Bibliographies

Conway's manuscripts are listed in Robbins' *American Literary Manuscripts*, pp. 70-71. Conway's contributions to selected periodicals and reviews of Conway's works are identified in Wells' *The Literary Index to American Magazines, 1850-1900*, pp. 86-88. Robert E. Burkholder reviews research on Conway in Myerson's *The Transcendentalists*, pp. 117-22.

John Esten Cooke, 1830-1886
Bibliographies

For works by Cooke, see *Bibliography of American Literature*, vol. 2, pp. 255-65. Contributions by Cooke and criticism and reviews of Cooke's works in selected periodicals are identified in Wells' *The Literary Index to American Magazines, 1815-1865*, p. 31; and *The Literary Index to American Magazines, 1850-1900*, pp. 88-89. Cooke's manuscripts are listed in Robbins' *American Literary Manuscripts*, p. 71. See *Bibliography of American Fiction Through 1865*, pp. 85-87, for a checklist of works by and about Cooke. Ritchie D. Watson Jr., surveys works by and about Cooke in Bain and Flora's *Fifty Southern Writers Before 1900*, pp. 174-83.

Rose Terry Cooke, 1827-1892
Bibliographies

For works by Cooke, see *Bibliography of American Literature*, vol. 2, pp. 266-75. Cooke's contributions to selected periodicals and reviews of Cooke's works are identified in Wells' *The Literary Index to American Magazines, 1850-1900*, pp. 89-90. Cooke's manuscripts are listed in Robbins' *American Literary Manuscripts*, p. 71. See *Bibliography of American Fiction, 1866-1918*, pp. 134-35, for Cheryl Z. Oreovicz's checklist of works by and about Cooke.

James Fenimore Cooper, 1789-1851
Bibliographies

297. Dyer, Alan Frank. **James Fenimore Cooper: An Annotated Bibliography of Criticism**. New York: Greenwood, 1991. 293p. (Bibliographies and Indexes in American Literature, no. 16). LC 91-27084. ISBN 0-313-27919-5.

Arranges 1,943 descriptively annotated entries for books, dissertations, journal and newspaper articles, reviews, and editorials about Cooper published from 1820 through 1990 in sections for bibliography, biography, general studies (offering important coverage of contemporary reviews), frontier and Indian novels, literature of the sea, social and political writings, and miscellaneous publications, with subsections for specific forms, topics, and individual works. Introduction surveys critical responses to Cooper's writings. Indexes for authors and editors and for subjects.

298. Spiller, Robert E., and Philip C. Blackburn. **A Descriptive Bibliography of the Writings of James Fenimore Cooper**. 1903; reprint New York: Burt Franklin, 1968. 259p. (Burt Franklin Bibliography and Reference Series, vol. 242). LC 68-58431.

This remains the best bibliography of Cooper's writings, listing editions of Cooper's collected works, contributions to periodicals, and attributed and adapted works. Entries give title-page transcriptions, collations, physical descriptions, and publishing histories for first and subsequent editions, including translations. Additional information on Cooper's primary materials is included in Blanck's *Bibliography of American Literature*, vol. 2, pp. 276-310. Cooper's manuscripts are listed in Robbins' *American Literary Manuscripts*, p. 72. See *Bibliography of American Fiction Through 1865*, pp. 88-94, for James D. Wallace's checklist of works by and about Cooper. Research on Cooper is reviewed by James Franklin Beard in Harbert and Rees' *Fifteen American Authors Before 1900*, pp. 63-127.

Dictionaries, Encyclopedias, and Handbooks
  299. Walker, Warren S. **Plots and Characters in the Fiction of James Fenimore Cooper**. Hamden, CT: Archon Books, 1978. 346p. (The Plots and Characters Series). LC 78-9469. ISBN 0-208-01497-7.
  Walker summarizes plots and identifies characters in Cooper's novels and short stories. A cumulative list cross-references 1,286 characters (some 1,536 names) with the works. Lacking Walker's plot summaries but additionally useful nonetheless, Mitchell Eugene Summerlin's *A Dictionary to the Novels of James Fenimore Cooper* (Greenwood, FL: Penkevill, 1987) provides brief identifications (in an A-to-Z listing) of Cooper's characters—including unnamed characters, such as five different lieutenants and dozens of seamen and sentinels in several novels—as well as separate listings for Cooper's animal and nonhuman characters and ships.

Susan (Augusta) Fenimore Cooper, 1813-1894
Bibliographies
  For works by Cooper, see *Bibliography of American Literature*, vol. 2, pp. 311-15. Cooper's manuscripts are listed in Robbins' *American Literary Manuscripts*, p. 72.

Robert (Lowell) Coover, 1932-
Bibliographies
  For works by Coover, see *First Printings of American Authors*, vol. 1, pp. 69-70. See *Bibliography of American Fiction, 1919-1988*, pp. 135-36, for Matthew J. Bruccoli's checklist of works by and about Coover. See Larry McCaffery's summary biography, critical assessment of major works, and selected primary and secondary bibliography for Coover in McCaffery's *Postmodern Fiction: A Bio-Bibliographical Guide*, pp. 308-11.

A(lfred) E(dgar) Coppard, 1878-1957
Bibliographies
  300. Schwartz, Jacob. **The Writings of Alfred Edgar Coppard: A Bibliography**. London: The Ulysses Bookshop, 1931. 73p. LC 31-17551.
  Chronologically arranges full bibliographic descriptions of Coppard's 17 separate and collected works; anthologies, translations; reviews; unreprinted works; uncollected works; introductions, prefaces, and articles; and contributions to newspapers. Entries for books give title-page transcriptions, physical sizes, collations, paper and binding descriptions, notes on publication histories, and contents. Unindexed. Coppard participated in this less-than-comprehensive compilation. Although providing supplemental information for Coppard's separate publications and contributions to books, Gilbert H. Fabes' *The First Editions of A. E. Coppard, A. P. Herbert and Charles Morgan, with Values and Bibliographical Points* (London: Myers, 1933) does not supersede Schwartz's guide. Also for a bibliography of works by and about Coppard, see *NCBEL*, IV, pp. 556-57.

Richard Corbett, 1582-1635
Bibliographies

For a bibliography of works by and about Corbett, see *NCBEL*, I, p. 1306. Corbett's manuscripts are described in *Index of English Literary Manuscripts*, II, pt. 1:153-208.

Robert Cormier, 1925-
Bibliographies

See *Bibliography of American Fiction, 1919-1988*, pp. 136-37, for Sylvia Patterson Iskander's checklist of works by and about Cormier.

Charles Cotton, 1630-1687
Bibliographies

For John Wilders' bibliography of works by and about Cotton, see *NCBEL*, II, pp. 437-39. Cotton's manuscripts are described in *Index of English Literary Manuscripts*, II, pt. 1:209-33.

John Cotton, 1584-1652
Bibliographies

For works by Cotton, see *First Printings of American Authors*, vol. 4, pp. 117-27. Cotton's manuscripts are listed in Robbins' *American Literary Manuscripts*, pp. 73-74. Gallagher and Werge's *Early Puritan Writers* (entry 138) covers works about Cotton through 1975.

(Sir) Noel (Pierce) Coward, 1899-1973
Bibliographies

301.   Cole, Stephen. **Noel Coward: A Bio-Bibliography**. Westport, CT: Greenwood Press, 1993. 319p. (Bio-Bibliographies in the Performing Arts, no. 44). LC 93-28704. ISBN 0-313-28599-3.

Designing his guide as a "sourcebook" (p. [ix]) for Coward's life and works, Cole supplies a brief chronology of Coward's life and career and a biography; 227 entries for Coward's plays and stage appearances (with plot synopses, performance and cast information, and references to reviews); lists of appearances of Coward and/or productions of his works in film, radio (selected), television, and audio recordings (with production information, references to reviews, and other information); lists of Coward's awards and 13 miscellaneous projects "left unrealized or unproduced" (p. [259]); and an awkward "selected annotated bibliography of writings by and about Coward" (pp. 261-91) with 256 entries. Entries for Coward's separate publications, edited works, and contributions to books and periodicals (with brief bibliographic data and occasional summaries) are alphabetically interfiled with a "sampling" of works about Coward published from the 1920s to 1993. Indexed by name and title. Also for a bibliography of works by and about Coward, see *NCBEL*, IV, pp. 924-27. Sarah Duerden surveys and identifies works by and about Coward in Demastes and Kelly's *British Playwrights, 1880-1956*, pp. [81]-96.

Abraham Cowley, 1618-1667
Bibliographies

302.   Perkin, M. R. **Abraham Cowley: A Bibliography**. Folkestone: Dawson, 1977. 130p. (Pall Mall Bibliographies, no. 5). LC 77-366816. ISBN 0-7129-0697-5.

The standard bibliography of Cowley's works, Perkin's guide includes full bibliographic descriptions for separately published, collected, and selected editions of Cowley's works; first appearances of poems in other works; poems set to music; letters; and commendatory poems and elegies. Entries give title-page transcriptions, collations, contents, physical descriptions, publishing histories, copy locations, and cross-references to the standard bibliographies, such as the

STC. Coverage of works about Cowley is provided in McCarron and Shenk's *Lesser Metaphysical Poets*, pp. [18]-20. For a bibliography of works by and about Cowley, see *NCBEL*, I, pp. 1219-21. Cowley's manuscripts are described in *Index of English Literary Manuscripts*, II, pt. 1:235-65.

Malcolm Cowley, 1898-1989
Bibliographies
303.   Eisenberg, Diane U. **Malcolm Cowley: A Checklist of His Writings, 1916-1973**. Carbondale, IL: Southern Illinois University Press, 1975. 240p. LC 75-8953. ISBN 0-8093-0748-0.
    Eisenberg gives brief bibliographic entries for Cowley's books, edited books and introductions, and other contributions to books; translated books; contributions to periodicals, including book reviews (some 542 entries), essays and articles (337 entries), short fiction, translated prose, interviews, and other works; and separately published, collected, or translated poems. Entries include publishing histories and references to translations and subsequent editions. In addition, Eisenberg briefly describes 24 works about Cowley. Also for works by Cowley, see *First Printings of American Authors*, vol. 4, pp. 129-37. Cowley's manuscripts are listed in Robbins' *American Literary Manuscripts*, p. 74.

Journals
304.   **Horns of Plenty: Malcolm Cowley and His Generation**. Chicago, IL: William Butts and Yolanda Butts, eds., 1988-1990. 4/yr. ISSN 0896-9965.
    " 'The Twenties Were a Dancing': A Conversation with Malcolm Cowley" and "Malcolm Cowley and Edgar Allan Poe: A Critical Controversy of the 1920s" were typical contributions to *Horns of Plenty*. Studies of Cowley's influence predominated, with other articles focusing on such figures as Andrew Lytle, James T. Farrell, Kenneth Burke, and Lewis Mumford. Bibliographic contributions included Marice Wolfe's "The Andrew Nelson Lytle Papers at Vanderbilt University," 3.1 (Spring 1990): 37-39; and Jane Morley's "A 'Canvass of Possibilities': A Bibliographical Guide to Lewis Mumford's Life and Work," 2.3 (Fall 1989): 63-74. Queries about research problems and reviews of new publications also appeared. *Horns of Plenty* was indexed in *MLA*.

William Cowper, 1731-1800
Bibliographies
305.   Hartley, Lodowick C. **William Cowper: The Continuing Revaluation: An Essay and Bibliography of Cowperian Studies from 1895 to 1960**. Chapel Hill, NC: University of North Carolina Press, 1960. 159p. LC 60-16254.
    Following an extensive introduction, Hartley arranges annotated entries for about 400 books, articles, reviews, and dissertations in all languages in topical listings for bibliographies, editions and selections, biographical studies, general criticisms, and studies of individual works. Brief annotations are critical and evaluative and include references to reviews. For Norma H. Russell's bibliography of works by and about Cowper, see *NCBEL*, II, pp. 595-603. Cowper's manuscripts are described in *Index of English Literary Manuscripts*, III, pt. 1:233-92.

306.   Russell, Norma. **A Bibliography of William Cowper, to 1837**. Oxford: Clarendon Press, 1963. 339p. LC 63-23843.
    Russell gives full bibliographic descriptions for Cowper's primary works in classified listings for early writings, hymns, poems, Cowper's reviews in the *Analytical Review*, translations, posthumously published prose works, edited works, and collected works. Entries include title-page transcriptions, physical descriptions, and publishing histories. In addition, about 30 biographical and critical works about Cowper, Cowperiana (works dedicated to Cowper, imitations, and the like), and portraits of Cowper are described. An appendix lists American

editions of Cowper's works through 1837. Also published as *Oxford Bibliographical Society Publications* new series, 12 (1963).

Indexes and Concordances

307. Neve, John. **A Concordance to the Poetical Works of William Cowper.** 1887; reprint New York: Burt Franklin, 1969. 504p. LC 68-26363. ISBN 0-8383-0289-0.

Neve concords the texts of Cowper's works included in John Bruce's three-volume *The Poetical Works* in the "Aldine edition of the British Poets" (London: Bell and Daldy, 1865).

Frederick Swartwout Cozzens, 1818-1869

Bibliographies

For works by Cozzens, see *Bibliography of American Literature*, vol. 2, pp. 316-19. Contributions by Cozzens and criticism and reviews of Cozzens' works in selected periodicals are identified in Wells' *The Literary Index to American Magazines, 1815-1865*, pp. 36-37; and *The Literary Index to American Magazines, 1850-1900*, pp. 92-93. Cozzens' manuscripts are listed in Robbins' *American Literary Manuscripts*, p. 75. See *Bibliography of American Fiction Through 1865*, pp. 95-96, for a checklist of works by and about Cozzens.

James Gould Cozzens, 1903-1978

Bibliographies

308. Bruccoli, Matthew J. **James Gould Cozzens: A Descriptive Bibliography.** Pittsburgh, PA: University of Pittsburgh Press, 1981. 193p. (Pittsburgh Series in Bibliography). LC 80-24689. ISBN 0-8229-3435-2.

This is the most comprehensive listing of Cozzens' primary works, including detailed descriptions in separate listings for first and variant later editions of books and pamphlets; books edited by Cozzens; contributions to books; contributions to journals; unsigned contributions to student publications (juvenilia); original quotations in booksellers' or auction catalogs; and translations of Cozzens' works. Entries give facsimiles of title and copyright pages, collations, contents, physical descriptions (of typography, paper, bindings, and dust jackets), publishing histories, and copy locations. Textual collations of variants are also included. Appendixes identify two film adaptations of Cozzens' works as well as eight selected works about Cozzens. Bruccoli's work is more comprehensive than James B. Meriwether's *James Gould Cozzens: A Checklist* (Detroit, MI: Gale, 1972). Also for works by Cozzens, see *First Printings of American Authors*, vol. 1, pp. 71-74. Cozzens' manuscripts are listed in Robbins' *American Literary Manuscripts*, p. 75. See *Bibliography of American Fiction, 1919-1988*, pp. 138-39, for Bruccoli's checklist of works by and about Cozzens.

309. Michel, Pierre. **James Gould Cozzens: An Annotated Checklist.** Kent, OH: Kent State University Press, 1971. 123p. (The Serif Series: Bibliographies and Checklists, no. 22). LC 75-169068. ISBN 0-87338-122-x.

Michel critically describes about 350 works about Cozzens published as books, parts of books, articles, and reviews (241 entries). Annotations clearly identify significant works.

George Crabbe, 1754-1832

Bibliographies

310. Bareham, T., and S. Gatrell. **A Bibliography of George Crabbe.** Hamden, CT: Archon Books, 1978. 194p. LC 78-40052. ISBN 0-208-01723-2.

Tony Bareham and Simon Gatrell's guide provides the best listing of Crabbe's primary bibliography, including full bibliographic descriptions for first editions and brief descriptions for subsequent British and American editions through the 1970s. Entries for first editions give title-page transcriptions, physical descriptions, publishing histories, and copy locations. In addition, Bareham and Gatrell describe about

350 secondary works, including contemporary reviews, bibliographies and bibliographic studies, and biographical and critical studies. Annotations are descriptive. Appendixes list Crabbe's works in translations, non-English-language criticisms, and Crabbe's apocryphal works. Additionally, useful descriptions of Crabbe's primary works are provided in *George Crabbe, 1754-1832: Bicentenary Celebrations: Exhibition of Works and Manuscripts Held at Moot Hall, Aldeburgh* (Aldeburgh: Festival Committee and Suffolk Institute of Archaeology, 1954). For Norma H. Russell's bibliography of works by and about Crabbe, see *NCBEL*, II, pp. 609-15. Crabbe's manuscripts are described in *Index of English Literary Manuscripts*, III, pt. 1:293-330.

(Edward Henry) Gordon Craig, 1872-1966
Bibliographies
311.   Fletcher, Ifan Kyrle, and Arnold Rood. **Edward Gordon Craig: A Bibliography**. London: The Society for Theatre Research, 1967. 117p. OCLC 3312716.

Describes Craig's works published from 1898 through 1966 in chronologically arranged sections for books by Craig; contributions to books; books illustrated by Craig; texts of plays produced by Craig; periodicals edited by Craig (*The Page* and *The Mask*); contributions to periodicals (408 entries); one-man exhibitions; group exhibitions; and programs for plays designed, produced, or projected by Craig. Entries for 36 separate publications give brief bibliographic data for format, pagination, paper, binding, and contents for first and subsequent editions and translations. Unindexed. Also for a bibliography of works by and about Craig, see *NCBEL*, IV, pp. 1031-33. L. M. Newman's *Gordon Craig Archives: International Survey* (London: The Malkin Press, 1976), which includes "Resources for the Future Study of Edward Gordon Craig: The Seventh Annual Gordon Craig Memorial Lecture, Delivered in Venice on 14 Sept. 1974," describes and locates international resources for research on Craig, including manuscript notebooks and typescripts, scrapbooks and press cut books, theses, books owned by Craig, and selected editions and works about Craig. Newman also surveys in detail Craig collections in international research libraries and other centers.

Christopher Pearse Cranch, 1813-1892
Bibliographies
For works by Cranch, see *Bibliography of American Literature*, vol. 2, pp. 320-28. Contributions by Cranch and criticism and reviews of Cranch's works in selected periodicals are identified in Wells' *The Literary Index to American Magazines, 1815-1865*, p. 37; and *The Literary Index to American Magazines, 1850-1900*, p. 93. Cranch's manuscripts are listed in Robbins' *American Literary Manuscripts*, p. 75. David Robinson reviews research on Cranch in Myerson's *The Transcendentalists*, pp. 123-30.

(Harold) Hart Crane, 1899-1932
Bibliographies
312.   Schwartz, Joseph. **Hart Crane: A Reference Guide**. Boston: G. K. Hall, 1983. 251p. (Reference Guides in Literature). LC 82-18725. ISBN 0-8161-8493-3.

The best guide to studies of Crane, Schwartz chronologically arranges annotated entries for a comprehensive range of works published from 1919 through 1980, including dissertations and video and sound recordings. Descriptive and thorough annotations cite references to reviews. Schwartz reviews significant works in detail. A comprehensive index provides headings for selected broad and specific topics as well as a full range of topics under Crane, such as "manuscripts," "romanticism," and "technology and the machine." Schwartz's guide supersedes his earlier *Hart Crane: An Annotated Critical Bibliography* (New York: D. Lewis, 1970). Research on Crane is reviewed by Brom Weber in Bryer's *Sixteen Modern American Authors*, pp. 75-122; and Weber's supplement in Bryer's *Sixteen Modern American Authors: Volume 2: A Survey of Research and Criticism Since 1972*, pp. 73-119.

313.   Schwartz, Joseph, and Robert C. Schweik. **Hart Crane: A Descriptive Bibliography**. Pittsburgh, PA: University of Pittsburgh Press, 1972. 168p. (Pittsburgh Series in Bibliography). LC 73-151508. ISBN 0-8229-3228-8.

The standard descriptive bibliography of Crane's primary works, containing full bibliographic descriptions for books; contributions of poetry, prose, and letters to books and periodicals; drawings; translations; adaptations; and attributed works. Entries give facsimiles of title pages; collations; contents; physical descriptions of illustrations, typography, paper, bindings, and dust jackets; publishing histories; notes on textual variants; and copy locations. Additional coverage of Crane's writings is provided by Kenneth A. Lohf's *The Literary Manuscripts of Hart Crane* (Columbus, OH: Ohio State University Press, 1967), which identifies 278 manuscripts in 16 libraries and two private collections, including the Hart Crane Collection at Columbia University. This guide is supplemented by Lohf's "The Prose Manuscripts of Hart Crane: An Editorial Portfolio," *Proof*, 2 (1970): 1-60. Crane's manuscripts are also listed in Robbins' *American Literary Manuscripts*, p. 76. Additionally, Lohf's *The Library of Hart Crane* (Columbia, SC: University of South Carolina Press, 1973) is a descriptive bibliography of books owned by Crane. Also for works by Crane, see *First Printings of American Authors*, vol. 1, pp. 75-77.

Indexes and Concordances

314.   Lane, Gary. **A Concordance to the Poems of Hart Crane**. New York: Haskell House, 1972. 338p. LC 72-1872. ISBN 0-8383-1437-6.

Lane bases his concordance on Brom Weber's edition of *Complete Poems and Selected Letters and Prose of Hart Crane* (New York: Liveright, 1966). The volume also lists hyphenated words and word frequencies. These features (and perhaps a slimmer profile) make Lane's concordance preferable to Hilton Landry, Elaine Landry, and Robert DeMott's equally authoritative *A Concordance to the Poems of Hart Crane* (Metuchen, NJ: Scarecrow Press, 1973), which is also based on Weber's 1966 edition of Crane's *Complete Poems and Selected Letters and Prose*.

Journals

See Patterson's *Author Newsletters and Journals*, p. 77, for previously published journals for Crane.

Stephen Crane, 1871-1900
Bibliographies

315.   Dooley, Patrick K. **Stephen Crane: An Annotated Bibliography of Secondary Scholarship**. New York: G. K. Hall, 1992. 321p. LC 91-38132. ISBN 0-8161-7265-X.

Awkwardly organized although comprehensive guide to works about Crane, updating the secondary coverage of Stallman's work (entry 316). Dooley attempts "to locate, annotate, and sort by category everything written in English on Crane and his works from 1901 to 1991" (p. ix). Arranges about 1,900 annotated entries for books, book chapters, introductions, journal and newspaper articles, and dissertations (unannotated) about Crane in sections for biography; general criticism; poetry; style; collections, manuscripts, rare books, and first editions; letters; bibliography; and selected major works, such as *The Red Badge of Courage* and "The Open Boat," with other topically or chronologically organized sections for remaining major and minor works ("Bowery Works" includes sublistings for *Maggie, George's Mother*, and New York City Sketches, for example). "Overview" chapter introductions indicate the most significant studies and research resources; additionally, Dooley's useful critical annotations identify both important and minor works. Also includes a chronology of Crane's life. Appendixes contain additions to lists of contemporary reviews to update Stallman and lists of bibliographic sources consulted. Author index. Also see *Bibliography of American Fiction, 1866-1918*, pp. 135-40, for James B. Colvert's checklist of works by and about

Crane. Research on Crane is reviewed by Donald Pizer in Harbert and Rees' *Fifteen American Authors Before 1900*, pp. 97-184.

316.   Stallman, R. W. **Stephen Crane: A Critical Bibliography**. Ames, IA: Iowa State University Press, 1972. 642p. LC 79-103837. ISBN 0-8138-0357-8.
   The most comprehensive bibliography for Crane's works as well as for works about Crane. Stallman gives full bibliographic descriptions for Crane's books and contributions to books, ephemeral publications, and published letters, in addition to contemporary reviews of Crane's works and parodies (arranged by works). Entries include title-page transcriptions, collations, physical descriptions, and publishing histories. Perhaps the guide's most useful feature, an alphabetically arranged listing of Crane's works integrates entries for manuscripts, editions, reprintings, periodical appearances, and other writings, with cross-references to the full descriptions. In addition, Stallman chronologically arranges extensively annotated entries for critical works of all varieties in all languages about Crane published from 1888 through 1972. Descriptive annotations include references to reviews. A comprehensive index offers excellent topical access. Stallman's coverage of Crane's primary works supersedes that provided in Ames W. Williams and Vincent Starett's *Stephen Crane: A Bibliography* (Glendale, CA: J. Valentine, 1948) as well as Blanck's *Bibliography of American Literature*, vol. 2, pp. 329-38, and *First Printings of American Authors*, vol. 1, pp. 79-82. Similarly, Stallman's coverage of Crane scholarship is superior to that included in Theodore L. Gross and Stanley Wertheim's *Hawthorne, Melville, Stephen Crane: A Critical Bibliography* (New York: Free Press, 1971), which describes editions and about 100 studies of Crane. Crane's manuscripts are listed in Robbins' *American Literary Manuscripts*, p. 76. Other useful catalogs of Crane's primary materials include Matthew J. Bruccoli's *Stephen Crane, 1871-1900: An Exhibition from the Collection of Matthew J. Bruccoli* (Columbia, SC: Department of English, University of South Carolina, 1971); and *The Stephen Crane Collection from the Library of Prof. Matthew J. Bruccoli* (New York: Swann Galleries, 1974).

Dictionaries, Encyclopedias, and Handbooks
317.   Schaefer, Michael W. **A Reader's Guide to the Short Stories of Stephen Crane**. New York: G. K. Hall, 1996. 468p. (A Reference Publication in Literature). LC 96-10593. ISBN 0-8161-7285-4.
   Intends to distill "the large body of historical and critical information available as of the end of 1992" (p. ix) for 51 works by Crane that Schaefer defines as short stories. Alphabetically arranged chapters present overviews of publication and composition histories; sources and influences; relationships with Crane's other works, generally involving brief examinations of plots, characters, themes, and the like; and "significant critical interpretations" (p. xi) from the full range of perspectives, with "comprehensive" bibliographies for each story. Extensive chapters for "The Blue Hotel" and "The Open Boat." Index of Crane's works and a general index with selected topical headings for names and critical schools (existentialism, naturalism). Like other volumes in G. K. Hall's series, Schaefer's provides an excellent starting point for research.

Indexes and Concordances
318.   Crosland, Andrew T. **A Concordance to the Complete Poetry of Stephen Crane**. Detroit, MI: Gale, 1975. 189p. (A Bruccoli Clark Book). LC 74-30426. ISBN 0-8103-1006-6.
   Based on Fredson Bowers' CEAA-approved edition of *Poems and Literary Remains* (Charlottesville, VA: University of Virginia Press, 1975), vol. 10 of *The Works of Stephen Crane*. Appends alphabetical and ranked word frequency lists. Additionally, Herman Baron's *A Concordance to the Poems of Stephen Crane* (Boston: G. K. Hall, 1974) is based on Joseph Katz's revised edition of *The Poems of Stephen Crane: A Critical Edition* (New York: Cooper Square Publishers, 1972).

Journals

See Wortman's *Guide to Serial Bibliographies for Modern Literatures*, p. 252, for previously published serial bibliographies for Crane. Patterson's *Author Newsletters and Journals*, pp. 77-78, describes previously published journals for Crane.

Adelaide Crapsey, 1878-1914

Bibliographies

For works by Crapsey, see *Bibliography of American Literature*, vol. 2, pp. 339-40. Crapsey's manuscripts are listed in Robbins' *American Literary Manuscripts*, p. 76.

Richard Crashaw, 1612/13-1649

Bibliographies

319.   Roberts, John R. **Richard Crashaw: An Annotated Bibliography of Criticism, 1632-1980**. Columbia, MO: University of Missouri Press, 1985. 477p. LC 84-52264. ISBN 0-8262-0468-6.

Roberts chronologically arranges annotated entries for some 1,181 works by and about Crashaw published from 1632 through 1980, including editions and translations and studies published as books, parts of books (introductions in anthologies), and articles in all languages, as well as adaptations of Crashaw's works. Excludes unpublished dissertations and reviews of works about Crashaw. Annotations are thorough and descriptive. Significant works receive extensive review. Entries for early editions and works reference the *STC*, *Wing*, and other standard bibliographies. A separate subject index offers the full range of headings for topics and names, including "the Bible," "John Donne," "euphuism," "mysticism," and "St. Teresa of Avila." Roberts' guide supersedes the critical coverage provided in McCarron and Shenk's *Lesser Metaphysical Poets*, pp. [20]-25. Detailed descriptions of Crashaw's early editions are provided in A. F. Allison's *Four Metaphysical Poets* (entry 656), pp. [25]-32. For a bibliography of works by and about Crashaw, see *NCBEL*, I, pp. 1214-17. Crashaw's manuscripts are described in *Index of English Literary Manuscripts*, II, pt. 1:267-308.

Indexes and Concordances

320.   Cooper, Robert M. **A Concordance to the English Poetry of Richard Crashaw**. Troy, NY: Whitston, 1981. 477p. LC 80-51219. ISBN 0-87875-188-2.

Cooper bases this concordance on L. C. Martin's edition of *The Poems, English, Latin, and Greek, of Richard Crashaw*, 2d ed. (New York: Oxford University Press, 1957), with cross-references to George Walton Williams' edition of *The Complete Poetry of Richard Crashaw* (New York: Doubleday, 1970).

Francis Marion Crawford, 1854-1909

Dictionaries, Encyclopedias, and Handbooks

321.   Moran, John Charles. **An F. Marion Crawford Companion**. Westport, CT: Greenwood Press, 1981. 548p. LC 80-1707. ISBN 0-313-20926-X .

No comprehensive bibliographies of works by or about Crawford now exist. Moran's companion partially fills the need, providing checklists of first and subsequent editions of Crawford's separate publications (with notes on publishing histories and bibliographic points), contributions to books and periodicals, incomplete and unpublished works, and other Crawfordiana (pp. [441]-504). Entries do not give full bibliographic descriptions. Additionally, Moran offers a survey of Crawford's life and works; biographical and literary chronologies; and dictionaries of people associated with Crawford (from Thomas Bailey Aldrich to Oscar Wilde), real and fictional places, detailed plot summaries of the novels, fictional characters, and selected quotations. Author/subject and title indexes. For more detailed descriptions of first editions of Crawford's works, see *Bibliography of American Literature*, vol. 2, pp. 341-63. Crawford's contributions to selected periodicals and reviews of Crawford's works are identified in Wells' *The Literary Index to American Magazines, 1850-1900*, pp. 94-96. Crawford's manuscripts are listed in Robbins' *American Literary Manuscripts*, p. 76. See *Bibliography of American Fiction, 1866-1918*, pp. 141-42, for Randolph Lewis' checklist of works by and about Crawford.

Journals

322. **The Romantist**. Nashville, TN: F. Marion Crawford Memorial Society, 1977-. Irregular. ISSN 0161-682x.

Typical critical articles have focused on Crawford and other modern romantic and fantasy writers, including Algernon Blackwood, Lord Dunsany, Bram Stoker, Raymond Chandler, Sheridan LeFanu, H. P. Lovecraft, Lew Wallace, George Sterling, and Clark Ashton Smith. Biographic and interpretive studies predominate. The journal also often reprints Crawford's otherwise uncollected periodical contributions. Bibliographical contributions have included John C. Moran's "An F. Marion Crawford Companion: Addenda, &c.," 6-8 (1982-84): 55; and Moran's "Recent Interest in F. Marion Crawford: A Bibliographical Account," 1 (1977): 53-56. To date, *The Romantist* has been indexed in *MLA* through 1984.

Robert (White) Creeley, 1926-

Bibliographies

323. Fox, Willard. **Robert Creeley, Edward Dorn, and Robert Duncan: A Reference Guide**. Boston: G. K. Hall, 1989. (A Reference Guide to Literature). LC 88-24503. ISBN 0-8161-8604-9.

Fox provides comprehensive coverage of works about these writers, including separate, chronologically arranged listings of annotated entries for books, articles, reviews of Creeley's works, and dissertations in all languages. Excludes reviews of works about Creeley and creative works. Coverage for Creeley includes about 1,200 works published from 1951; for Dorn, about 300 works from 1959; and for Duncan, about 1,000 works from 1944, with a terminal date of 1987 for all. Annotations are descriptive. Besides separate indexes for primary works, a comprehensive author-subject index includes detailed headings for such topics as "development as writer," "the female figure," and "language," with coded entries ("C" for Creeley and so forth) to distinguish studies for each writer.

324. Novik, Mary. **Robert Creeley: An Inventory, 1945-1970**. Kent, OH: Kent State University Press, 1973. 210p. (The Serif Series: Bibliographies and Checklists, no. 28). LC 72-96943. ISBN 0-87338-139-4.

The most comprehensive bibliography of Creeley's primary works to date (and now out of date), Novik's guide gives brief bibliographic information (with contents, notes on publication, and references to reprintings, translations, manuscripts, and proofs) for Creeley's separately published poems, stories, novels, and contributions to other works; separately published and contributed nonfiction prose; and audiovisual materials, edited works, and works published by Creeley at the Divers Press. Creeley's unpublished works, proofs and advance copies, recordings, letters, and manuscripts in special collections at Washington University, Indiana University, and elsewhere are also described (pp. 135-67). A separate, alphabetical listing of Creeley's individual works gives detailed publishing histories and cross-references the descriptive entries for primary materials in both sections. In addition, Novik describes works about Creeley, including dissertations and media. More comprehensive coverage of Creeley criticism is provided in Fox's guide (entry 323). Also for works by Creeley, see *First Printings of American Authors*, vol. 3, pp. 53-69. Creeley's manuscripts are listed in Robbins' *American Literary Manuscripts*, p. 77.

Michel-Guillaume Jean de Crevecouer (J. Hector St. John de Crevecoeur), 1735-1813

Bibliographies

Crevecoeur's manuscripts are listed in Robbins' *American Literary Manuscripts*, p. 77. Cutting's *John and William Bartram, William Byrd II, and St. John de Crevecoeur* (entry 72) identifies works about Crevecoeur published through 1974.

Harry Crews, 1935-

Bibliographies

325.   Hargraves, Michael. **Harry Crews: A Bibliography**. Westport, CT: Meckler, 1986. 120p. LC 86-12885. ISBN 0-8873-6060-2.

Hargraves offers full bibliographic descriptions for Crews' works, covering books, contributions to books, contributions to journals, interviews, and miscellaneous writings (such as dust-jacket blurbs, screenplays, and the like), as well as annotated entries for 27 biographical and critical works about Crews, including a dissertation. Entries for primary materials give title-page descriptions; collations; contents; descriptions of paper, binding, and dust jackets; notes on publication histories; and references to reviews, with appended title-page facsimiles. Also for works by Crews, see *First Printings of American Authors*, vol. 2, pp. 121-22. Research on Crews is reviewed by Frank W. Shelton in Flora and Bain's *Fifty Southern Writers After 1900*, pp. 111-20.

A(rchibald) J(oseph) Cronin, 1896-1981

Bibliographies

326.   Salwak, Dale. **A. J. Cronin: A Reference Guide**. Boston: G. K. Hall, 1982. 185p. (A Reference Guide to Literature). LC 82-11954. ISBN 0-8161-8595-6.

Salwak chronologically arranges descriptively annotated entries for about 1,200 works related to Cronin published from 1931 through 1981. Identifies extensive numbers of local newspaper articles and reviews. Index headings under Cronin's name identify such broad subjects as bibliographies, biographies, and interviews. Also for a bibliography of works by and about Cronin, see *NCBEL*, IV, p. 557.

Caresse Crosby, 1892-1970

Bibliographies

For works by Crosby, see *First Printings of American Authors*, vol. 4, pp. 139-41. Crosby's manuscripts are listed in Robbins' *American Literary Manuscripts*, p. 77.

Harry Crosby, 1898-1929

Bibliographies

For works by Crosby, see *First Printings of American Authors*, vol. 2, pp. 123-29. Crosby's manuscripts are listed in Robbins' *American Literary Manuscripts*, p. 77.

Countee Cullen, 1903-1946

Bibliographies

327.   Perry, Margaret. **A Bio-Bibliography of Countee P. Cullen, 1903-1946**. Westport, CT: Greenwood, 1971. 134p. (Contributions in Afro-American and African Studies, no. 8). LC 75-105995. ISBN 0-8371-3325-1.

An extensive introduction to Cullen's life, works and critical reception precedes brief information for Cullen's major writings, covering books, articles, poems in periodicals, and miscellaneous writings (such as stories, plays, letters to editors, recordings of Cullen's works, and unpublished works). Entries include references to reviews. In addition, Perry identifies about 300 biographical and critical studies (including dissertations and master's theses), obituaries, and newspaper stories about Cullen. Coverage of Cullen is updated in Perry's *The*

Harlem Renaissance: An Annotated Bibliography and Commentary, pp. 64-75. Cullen's manuscripts are listed in Robbins' *American Literary Manuscripts*, p. 78. Research on Cullen is reviewed by Ruth Miller and Peter J. Katopes in Inge, Duke, and Bryer's *Black American Writers*, vol. I, pp. 161-86.

George Cumberland, 1754-1848
Bibliographies
328. Bentley, G. E., Jr. **A Bibliography of George Cumberland (1754-1848): Comprehending His Published Books (1780-1829) and Articles (1769-1847) and His Unrecorded Works in Manuscript Including a Novel (?1800), a Play (?1800), a Biography (?1823), a Long Poem (1802-3), and Works on Art (?1788, ?1816, ?1820)**. New York: Garland, 1975. 140p. (Garland Reference Library of the Humanities, vol. 11). LC 74-34010. ISBN 0-8240-1082-5.

Bentley describes Cumberland's primary works, including full bibliographic descriptions for books, contributions to books and periodicals, and "traced" and "untraced manuscripts." Entries give title-page transcriptions (with selected title-page facsimiles), notes on copies and locations, and composition and publishing histories.

Richard Cumberland, 1732-1811
Bibliographies
For a bibliography of works by and about Cumberland, see *NCBEL*, II, pp. 814-16.

E(dward) E(stlin) Cummings, 1894-1962
Bibliographies
329. Firmage, George J. **E. E. Cummings: A Bibliography**. Middletown, CT: Wesleyan University Press, 1960. 129p. LC 60-7257.

Firmage gives full bibliographic descriptions (title-page transcriptions, collations, and contents) for Cummings' books and pamphlets, contributions to periodicals, contributions to books and other works, translations, musical settings of poems, recordings of Cummings' readings, and reproductions of drawings and other artworks by Cummings. Cummings' manuscripts are listed in Robbins' *American Literary Manuscripts*, pp. 78-79.

330. Rotella, Guy L. **E. E. Cummings: A Reference Guide**. Boston: G. K. Hall, 1979. 212p. (A Reference Publication in Literature). LC 79-9873. ISBN 0-8161-8079-2.

Rottella provides comprehensive coverage of works about Cummings, chronologically arranging annotated entries for about 1,200 books, articles, reviews, dissertations, and entries in reference works in all languages published from 1927 through 1977. Annotations are descriptive. Significant studies receive extensive reviews. Index headings reference broad topics, such as "bibliography," "biography," "general studies," "linguistics," and "techniques," among others.

Indexes and Concordances
331. McBride, Katharine Winters. **A Concordance to the Complete Poems of E. E. Cummings**. Ithaca, NY: Cornell University Press, 1989. 1,006p. (The Cornell Concordances). LC 89-31058. ISBN 0-8014-2239-6.

Based on *E. E. Cummings: Complete Poems, 1913-1962* (New York: Harcourt, Brace, Jovanovich, 1972), McBride's concordance gives title, page, and line references, with context lines that include up to four words before and after each key word (for the most part), regardless of Cummings' unique lineation. To accommodate words that Cummings set down vertically (defying anything short of a horizontal rendering to make sense), McBride's concordance indicates that the actual text needs to be consulted.

Journals

332.   **Spring: The Journal of the E. E. Cummings Society.** Flushing, NY: E. E. Cummings Society, 1980-90; new series, 1992-. Annual. ISSN 0735-6889.

Issues of *Spring* publish critical studies of Cummings as well as selections of poems in imitation of Cummings. Many studies have explicated poems in relation to the other arts, particularly music and painting; others articles have discussed Cummings' illustrations and media adaptations of his works. A significant number of contributions emphasize Cummings' experimental poetic techniques (ranging from the uses of paradox to typography) and his sources in and influences on other writers. "Noise as Metaphor, Sound as Symbol: Charged Onomatopoeia in the Poetry of E. E. Cummings" and "Readable Silence: Blank Space in E. E. Cummings's Poetry" are typical of contributions. Occasional bibliographic features include Guy Rotella's useful "E. E. Cummings: A Reference Guide (Again) Updated: Part One (to 1986)," new series, 1.1 (1992): 127-43, an annotated guide to criticism (which remains to be continued), supplementing Rotella's guide (entry 330). *Spring* is indexed in *MLA*.

Maria Susanna Cummins, 1827-1866

Bibliographies

For works by Cummins, see *Bibliography of American Literature*, vol. 2, pp. 364-66. Cummins' manuscripts are listed in Robbins' *American Literary Manuscripts*, p. 79. See *Bibliography of American Fiction Through 1865*, pp. 96-97, for a checklist of works by and about Cummins.

J(ames) V(incent) Cunningham, 1911-1985

Bibliographies

333.   Gullans, Charles B. **A Bibliography of the Published Works of J. V. Cunningham.** Los Angeles, CA: University of California Library, 1973. 44p. LC 73-623222.

Gullans gives full bibliographic descriptions for Cunningham's books, edited works, and anthologies; contributions to books; and contributions to periodicals, with a detailed chronology of composition. Entries include title-page transcriptions, physical descriptions, and contents. Cunningham's manuscripts are listed in Robbins' *American Literary Manuscripts*, p. 79.

Robert Bontine Cunninghame Graham, 1852-1936

Bibliographies

For a bibliography of works by and about Graham, see *NCBEL*, IV, pp. 1318-19.

George William Curtis, 1824-1892

Bibliographies

For works by Curtis, see *Bibliography of American Literature*, vol. 2, pp. 367-93. Contributions by Curtis and criticism and reviews of Curtis' works in selected periodicals are identified in Wells' *The Literary Index to American Magazines, 1815-1865*, p. 39; and *The Literary Index to American Magazines, 1850-1900*, pp. 98-99. Curtis' manuscripts are listed in Robbins' *American Literary Manuscripts*, pp. 79-80. See *Bibliography of American Fiction Through 1865*, pp. 97-98, for a checklist of works by and about Curtis. W. Gordon Milne reviews research on Curtis in Myerson's *The Transcendentalists*, pp. 317-19.

James Oliver Curwood, 1878-1927

Bibliographies

See *Bibliography of American Fiction, 1866-1918*, pp. 143-44, for Judith A. Eldridge's checklist of works by and about Curwood. Curwood's manuscripts are listed in Robbins' *American Literary Manuscripts*, p. 80.

Eliza L. Cushing, b. 1794-
Bibliographies

For works by Cushing, see *First Printings of American Authors*, vol. 5, p. 79.

Cynewulf, late eighth or ninth century
Bibliographies

Greenfield and Robinson's *A Bibliography of Publications on Old English Literature to the End of 1972*, pp. 207-10, lists translations and studies of Cynewulf, with citations for reviews. Also for a bibliography of works by and about Cynewulf, see *NCBEL*, I, pp. 271-72. Several poems continue to be assigned to Cynewulf. For editions, translations, and studies of Old English *Elene*, with citations for reviews, see Greenfield and Robinson, pp. 219-222. For editions, translations, and studies of Old English *Juliana*, with citations for reviews, see Greenfield and Robinson, pp. 241-42.

James McBride Dabbs, 1896-1970
Bibliographies

For works by Dabbs, see *First Printings of American Authors*, vol. 4, pp. 143-46.

Edward Dahlberg, 1900-1977
Bibliographies

334.   Billings, Harold. **A Bibliography of Edward Dahlberg**. Austin, TX: Humanities Research Center, University of Texas at Austin, 1971. 122p. (Tower Bibliographical Series, no. 8). LC 75-633117.

Covering Dahlberg's works through 1970, Billings gives full bibliographic descriptions for books, contributions to books, contributions to periodicals, translations, and miscellaneous writings (one broadside and one offprint). Entries provide title-page transcriptions, collations, physical descriptions, and publishing histories. Includes an unannotated list of about 100 works about Dahlberg (mostly book reviews). Also for works by Dahlberg, see *First Printings of American Authors*, vol. 1, pp. 83-85. Dahlberg's manuscripts are listed in Robbins' *American Literary Manuscripts*, pp. 80-81. See *Bibliography of American Fiction, 1919-1988*, pp. 140-42, for Billings' checklist of works by and about Dahlberg.

Eneas Sweetland Dallas, 1829-1879
Bibliographies

Wendell V. Harris reviews research on Dallas in DeLaura's *Victorian Prose*, pp. 444-45.

Richard Henry Dana, Jr., 1815-1882
Bibliographies

335.   MacDonnell, Kevin B. **The Richard Henry Dana, Jr. Collection**. Gainesville, FL: University of Florida, 1986. 24p. (The Parkman Dexter Howe Library, Part III). LC 84-8702.

A volume in the series edited by Sidney Ives, MacDonnell gives descriptions of 46 items with cross-references to Blanck's *Bibliography of American Literature*, vol. 2, pp. 400-410 (which remains essential for basic bibliographic information about Dana's separate publications). MacDonnell's presentation emphasizes variants and provenances. Contributions by Dana and criticism and reviews of Dana's works in selected periodicals are identified in Wells' *The Literary Index to American Magazines, 1815-1865*, p. 40; and *The Literary Index to American Magazines, 1850-1900*, pp. 99-100. Dana's manuscripts are listed in Robbins' *American Literary Manuscripts*, p. 82. See *Bibliography of American Fiction Through 1865*, pp. 99-100, for Wesley T. Mott's checklist of works by and about Dana.

Richard Henry Dana, Sr., 1787-1879

Bibliographies

For works by Dana, see *Bibliography of American Literature*, vol. 2, pp. 394-99. Contributions by Dana and criticism and reviews of Dana's works in selected periodicals are identified in Wells' *The Literary Index to American Magazines, 1815-1865*, pp. 39-41; and *The Literary Index to American Magazines, 1850-1900*, p. 99. Dana's manuscripts are listed in Robbins' *American Literary Manuscripts*, p. 81.

Samuel Daniel, 1563-1619

Bibliographies

336. Harner, James L. **Samuel Daniel and Michael Drayton: A Reference Guide**. Boston: G. K. Hall, 1980. 338p. (A Reference Guide to Literature). LC 80-22655. ISBN 0-8161-8322-8.

Harner chronologically arranges separate listings of annotated entries for secondary materials for Daniel and Drayton. Coverage includes books, articles, and dissertations in all languages and extends from 1684 through 1979. About 800 entries for Daniel and about 1,000 for Drayton are included. Excludes general reference sources, introductions in editions, and master's theses. Annotations are descriptive. A separate subject index includes headings for such broad topics as "bibliography," "language," and "sources." This guide supersedes the coverage of Daniel and Drayton scholarship provided in the Tannenbaums' *Elizabethan Bibliographies*, vol. 2; and George Robert Guffey's *Elizabethan Bibliographies Supplements*, no. 7. Daniel's works are fully described in H. Sellers' "A Bibliography of the Works of Samuel Daniel, 1585-1623," *Oxford Bibliographical Society Proceedings & Papers* (for 1927-30) 2 (1930): 29-54; and "Supplementary Note," p. 341. Also for a bibliography of works by and about Daniel, see *NCBEL*, I, pp. 1061-65, 2235-37. Daniel's manuscripts are described in *Index of English Literary Manuscripts*, I, pt. 1:197-206, 566. Research on Daniel is reviewed by William L. Godshalk in Logan and Smith's *The New Intellectuals*, pp. 281-301.

Indexes and Concordances

337.   Donow, Herbert S. **A Concordance to the Sonnet Sequences of Daniel, Drayton, Shakespeare, Sidney, and Spenser**. Carbondale, IL: Southern Illinois University Press, 1969. 772p. LC 72-76188. ISBN 0-8093-0400-7.

Donow bases his concordance on the texts of Daniel's *Delia* in A. B. Gosart's *The Complete Works in Verse and Prose of Samuel Daniel* (London: Hazell, Watson, and Viney, 1885); Drayton's *Idea* in J. W. Hebel's *The Works of Michael Drayton* (Oxford: Basil Blackwell, 1931-1932); Shakespeare's *Sonnets* in Hyder E. Rollins' *A New Variorum Edition of Shakespeare: The Sonnets* (Philadelphia, PA: University of Pennsylvania Press, 1944); Sidney's *Astrophel and Stella* in William A. Ringler Jr.'s, *The Poems of Sir Philip Sidney* (Oxford: Clarendon Press, 1962); and Spenser's *Amoretti* in Charles Grosvenor Osgood and Henry Gibbons Lotspeich's *The Works of Edmund Spenser: A Variorum Edition: The Minor Poems* (Baltimore, MD: Johns Hopkins University Press, 1947). Separate frequency lists for each sequence. A more specialized index for Daniel's vocabulary is Stagg's *The Figurative Language of the Tragedies of Shakespeare's Chief 16th-Century Contemporaries* (entry 901).

Olive Tilford Dargan, 1869-1968

Bibliographies

See *Bibliography of American Fiction, 1866-1918*, pp. 144-45, for Kathy Cantley Ackerman's checklist of works by and about Dargan. Dargan's manuscripts are listed in Robbins' *American Literary Manuscripts*, p. 82.

Charles Robert Darwin, 1809-1882

Bibliographies

338.   Freeman, R. B. **The Works of Charles Darwin: An Annotated Bibliographical Handlist.** 2d ed., revised and enlarged. Folkestone: Dawson, Archon Books, 1977. 235p. LC 76-30002. ISBN 0-2080-1658-9.

The best listing of Darwin's works. The first part identifies "all the editions and issues of books, pamphlets and circulars, both British and non-English," of Darwin's writings published from 1835 to 1975 (p. 7). Lists more than 1,600 items in separate, chronologically arranged chapters for 46 separate publications and manuscript transcriptions, collections, and selections, giving brief bibliographic data and extensive discussions and information on composition and publication histories. The second part supplies brief data for about 150 "papers, notes and letters which were originally published in serials." Index of names and titles. Also for a bibliography of works by and about Darwin, see *NCBEL*, III, pp. 1364-68. Reviews of Darwin's works in selected periodicals are identified in Wells' *The Literary Index to American Magazines, 1815-1865*, p. 40; and *The Literary Index to American Magazines, 1850-1900*, pp. 100-103.

Indexes and Concordances

339.   Barrett, Paul H., Donald J. Weinshank, and Timothy T. Gottleber. **A Concordance to Darwin's Origin of Species, First Edition.** Ithaca, NY: Cornell University Press, 1981. 834p. LC 80-66893. ISBN 0- 8014-1319-2.

This and the following concordances constitute an untitled "series being produced by the editors to aid in the study of Charles Darwin's writings" (Preface). Based on the text of the first edition, *On the Origin of Species by Means of Natural Selection* (London: John Murray, 1859), with a supporting list of suppressed words and frequencies. Other volumes in the series include:

339.1.   Barrett, Paul H., Donald J. Weinshank, Paul Ruhlen, and Stephan J. Ozminski. **A Concordance to Darwin's The Descent of Man and Selection in Relation to Sex.** Ithaca, NY: Cornell University Press, 1987. 1,137p. LC 87-47699. ISBN 0-8014-2085-7.

Concords the "first issue of the first edition" (London: John Murray, 1871), which is also available in facsimile (Princeton, NJ: Princeton University Press, 1981). Provides a list of suppressed words and frequencies, a facsimile of Darwin's errata from vol. 2 of the 1871 edition, and a list of silently corrected typographic errors.

339.2.   Barrett, Paul H., Donald J. Weinshank, Paul Ruhlen, Stephan J. Ozminski, and Barbara N. Berhage. **A Concordance to Darwin's The Expression of the Emotions in Man and Animals.** Ithaca, NY: Cornell University Press, 1986. 515p. LC 86-47707. ISBN 0-8014-1990-5.

Uses as its source text the 1965 University of Chicago Press facsimile edition of the second printing (New York: Appleton, 1897). Appends frequency lists of suppressed words and headwords, with a list of corrections to the source text.

339.3.   Weinshank, Donald J., Stephan J. Ozminski, Paul Ruhlen, and Wilma M. Barrett. **A Concordance to Charles Darwin's Notebooks, 1836-1844.** Ithaca, NY: Cornell University Press, 1990. 739p. LC 89-45977. ISBN 0-8014-2352-X.

Based on the text of *Charles Darwin's Notebooks, 1836-1844: Geology, Transmutation of Species, Metaphysical Enquiries* (London: British Museum, Natural History; and Ithaca, NY: Cornell University Press, 1987), transcribed and edited by Paul H. Barrett, Peter J. Gautrey, Sandra Herbert, David Kohn, and Sydney Smith. Appends lists of word frequencies and variant spellings.

(Sir) William D'Avenant, 1606-1668
Bibliographies

340.   Blaydes, Sophia B., and Philip Bordinat. **Sir William Davenant: An Annotated Bibliography, 1629-1985**. New York: Garland, 1986. 370p. (Garland Reference Library of the Humanities, vol. 525). LC 84-45395. ISBN 0-8240-8874-3.

Blaydes and Bordinat list D'Avenant's separately published, collected, and miscellaneous works (prologues, commendatory poems, and the like), providing descriptions of contents and publishing histories, references to editions through the 1970s, and cross-references to standard bibliographies, such as the *STC*. In addition, they chronologically arrange annotated entries for about 900 works about D'Avenant published from 1639 through 1981, covering critical works of all varieties, including dissertations, introductions in editions, and reference works. Annotations are thorough and critical. A cumulative index references a wide selection of topics as well as names. For a bibliography of works by and about D'Avenant, see *NCBEL*, I, pp. 1208-10. D'Avenant's manuscripts are described in *Index of English Literary Manuscripts*, II, pt. 1:309-27. Research on D'Avenant is reviewed by H. Neville Davies in Wells' *English Drama*, pp. 150-72; and Michael V. DePorte in Logan and Smith's *The Later Jacobean and Caroline Dramatists*, pp. 192-209.

John Davidson, 1857-1909
Bibliographies

341.   Lester, John A. **John Davidson: A Grub Street Bibliography**. Charlottesville, VA: University of Virginia Press, 1958. 30p. (Secretary's News Sheet, The Bibliographical Society of the University of Virginia, no. 40 (Sept. 1958). OCLC 5372404.

Provides a checklist of "all John Davidson's writings which first appeared in periodicals, newspapers, and occasional volumes" (p. [9]), comprising 295 contributions to 33 different newspapers published from 1889 to 1906. Brief entries categorize contributions by form (poem, prose, etc.) and note subsequent appearances. See the review of research by Lionel Stevenson in Faverty's *The Victorian Poets*, pp. 385-86.

Donald Alfred Davie, 1922-
Bibliographies

342.   Wright, Stuart. **Donald Davie: A Checklist of His Writings, 1946-1988**. New York: Greenwood, 1991. 151p. (Bibliographies and Indexes in World Literature, no. 28). LC 90-47462. ISBN 0-313-27701-X.

Descriptive listing of Davie's works, arranged in sections for books, pamphlets, broadsides, and other separate publications; contributions to books; contributions to periodicals (687 chronologically arranged entries); interviews and published comments; translations; and recordings. Entries for 41 separate publications give brief bibliographic data; list subsequent editions, contents, and citations to reviews; and note publication histories. Index of personal names, publishers, and titles.

(Sir) John Davies, 1569-1626
Bibliographies

Klemp's *Fulke Greville and Sir John Davies* (entry 603) describes works by and about Davies. Also for a bibliography of works by and about Davies, see *NCBEL*, I, pp. 1071-74, by William A. Ringler. Davies' manuscripts are described in *Index of English Literary Manuscripts*, I, pt. 1:207-34, 566.

W(illiam) H(enry) Davies, 1871-1940
Bibliographies
343.   Harlow, Sylvia. **W. H. Davies: A Bibliography**. Winchester: St. Paul's Bibliographies, 1993. 260p. (Winchester Bibliographies of 20th Century Writers). LC 93-8210. ISBN 1-873040-00-8.

Offers full bibliographic descriptions of Davies' writings in chronologically arranged sections for books and pamphlets; works edited or compiled by Davies; introductions and epilogues by Davies; contributions to periodicals (298 brief citations); prose and poems appearing in anthologies; and broadcasts (323 entries for Davies' BBC programs, programs about Davies, and programs featuring Davies' works). The 53 entries for first and subsequent editions and impressions of the separate publications emphasize publication histories, giving title-page transcriptions; collations; contents; binding and dust-jacket descriptions; information on composition and corrections, with variants from manuscripts; notes on copies seen, with provenance; and citations for reviews and early notices. Also contains a list of 381 largely unannotated articles and books about Davies. Includes a chronology. Index of titles and first lines of poems and general index of names and other titles. Also for a bibliography of works by and about Davies, see *NCBEL*, IV, pp. 251-53 .

Charles Augustus Davis, 1795?-1868?
Bibliographies
For works by Davis, see *Bibliography of American Literature*, vol. 2, pp. 411-14. Davis' manuscripts are listed in Robbins' *American Literary Manuscripts*, pp. 83-84.

John Davis, 1775-1854
Bibliographies
See *Bibliography of American Fiction Through 1865*, pp. 101-102, for a checklist of works by and about Davis. Davis' manuscripts are listed in Robbins' *American Literary Manuscripts*, p. 84.

Rebecca Harding (Blaine) Davis, 1831-1910
Bibliographies
For works by Davis, see *First Printings of American Authors*, vol. 5, pp. 81-83. Davis' contributions to selected periodicals and reviews of Davis' works are identified in Wells' *The Literary Index to American Magazines, 1850-1900*, p. 105. Davis' manuscripts are listed in Robbins' *American Literary Manuscripts*, p. 84. See *Bibliography of American Fiction, 1866-1918*, pp. 145-46, for Jane Atteridge Rose's checklist of works by and about Davis.

Richard Harding Davis, 1864-1916
Bibliographies
344.   Quinby, Henry Cole. **Richard Harding Davis: A Bibliography, Being a Record of His Literary Life, of His Achievements as a Correspondent in Six Wars, and His Efforts in Behalf of the Allies in the Great War**. New York: E. P. Dutton, 1924. 294p. LC 24-31613.

Chronologically arranged full bibliographic descriptions of Davis' separate fiction publications; plays (with cast and production data), contributions to periodicals, translations, moving pictures, and books for the blind. Entries give title-page transcriptions, contents, and brief publication histories, with citations to reviews. Also includes a list of about 50 biographical and critical books and articles about Davis; a chronology of Davis' life and career; and an index of Davis' characters in fiction and plays. For works by Davis, see *Bibliography of American Literature*, vol. 2, pp. 415-27. Davis' manuscripts are listed in Robbins' *American*

Literary Manuscripts, pp. 84-85. Fannie Mae Elliott, Lucy Clark, and Marjorie Carver's *The Barrett Library: Richard Harding Davis: A Checklist of Printed and Manuscript Works of Richard Harding Davis in the Library of the University of Virginia* (Charlottesville, VA: University of Virginia Press, 1963) also offers useful descriptions of primary materials. Criticism and reviews of Davis' works in selected periodicals are identified in Wells' *The Literary Index to American Magazines, 1850-1900*, pp. 105-106. See *Bibliography of American Fiction, 1866-1918*, pp. 147-48, for Gary A. Best's checklist of works by and about Davis.

Rufus Dawes, 1803-1859

Bibliographies

For works by Dawes, see *Bibliography of American Literature*, vol. 2, pp. 428-31. Contributions by Dawes and criticism and reviews of Dawes' works in selected periodicals are identified in Wells' *The Literary Index to American Magazines, 1815-1865*, pp. 40-41. Dawes' manuscripts are listed in Robbins' *American Literary Manuscripts*, p. 85.

Fielding Dawson, 1930-

Bibliographies

For works by Dawson, see *First Printings of American Authors*, vol. 5, pp. 85-95.

Cecil Day-Lewis, 1904-1972

Bibliographies

345.   Handley-Taylor, Geoffrey, and Timothy D'Arch-Smith. **C. Day-Lewis, the Poet Laureate: A Bibliography**. Chicago: St. James, 1968. 42p. LC 73-1604.

A brief checklist of Day-Lewis' major works, describing first editions of books and pamphlets, contributions to books, and detective stories published under the pseudonym Nicholas Blake. Entries provide physical descriptions of size and format. Also for a bibliography of works by and about Day-Lewis, see *NCBEL*, IV, pp. 253-56.

Daniel Defoe, 1660-1731

Bibliographies

346.   Moore, John Robert. **A Checklist of the Writings of Daniel Defoe**. 2d ed. Hamden, CT: Archon Books, 1971. 281p. LC 70-122416. ISBN 0-2080-1886-6.

Moore describes Defoe's books, pamphlets, poems, and manuscripts; undated posthumously published works; and contributions to periodicals. Entries give physical descriptions of editions, publishing histories, and copy locations. Although regarded as the standard bibliography of Defoe's primary work, Moore's bibliography has recently been criticized as too inclusive. Finding "altogether unrealistic" (p. [vii]) Moore's attribution of 570 separate titles to Defoe, P. N. Furbank and W. R. Owens in *Defoe De-Attributions: A Critique of J. R. Moore's Checklist* (London and Rio Grande, OH: Hambledon Press, 1994) "systematically" reassess some 252 items and reattribute them to other writers. Other useful descriptions of Defoe's primary materials are included in John Alden's *A Catalog of the Defoe Collection of the Boston Public Library* (Boston: G. K. Hall, 1966). Robert W. Lovett and Charles C. Lovett's *Robinson Crusoe: A Bibliographical Checklist of English Language Editions (1719-1979)* (New York: Greenwood, 1991) chronologically arranges data for nearly 1,200 editions, "whether abridged, modified, adapted, or epitomized" (p. xiii), giving title-page and physical descriptions and brief publication histories. P. N. Furbank and W. R. Owens are preparing *A Critical Bibliography of Daniel Defoe* (London: Pickering and Chatto) for publication in 1998. For a bibliography of works by and about Defoe, see *NCBEL*, II, pp. 880-917, by Maximillian E. Novak. Defoe's manuscripts are described in *Index of English Literary Manuscripts*, III, pt. 1:331-36.

347. Peterson, Spiro. **Daniel Defoe: A Reference Guide, 1731-1924.** Boston: G. K. Hall, 1987. 455p. (A Reference Guide to Literature). LC 86-22963. ISBN 0-8161-8157-8.

Complementing Stoler's bibliography (item 348), Peterson offers a comprehensive, chronologically arranged listing of about 2,000 English-, French-, and German-language works about Defoe, including editions and translations; critical studies in books, articles, and dissertations; and miscellaneous works, such as verse and filmed adaptations, from 1731 through 1924. Annotations are descriptive, although significant studies receive extended reviews. A detailed subject index includes headings for a broad range of names, titles, and topics. Peterson's guide is most valuable for descriptions of early notices and responses. Peterson supplements coverage of early comments on Defoe with about 80 additional items in "Daniel Defoe: Supplement to Annotated Bibliography, 1731-1924," *Bulletin of Bibliography* 49.3 (1992): 215-33. Research on Defoe is reviewed by M. E. Novak in Dyson's *The English Novel*, pp. 16-35.

348. Stoler, John A. **Daniel Defoe: An Annotated Bibliography of Modern Criticism, 1900-1980.** New York: Garland, 1984. 424p. (Garland Reference Library of the Humanities, vol. 430). LC 83-48262. ISBN 0-8240-9086-1.

A comprehensive bibliography of modern editions and criticism of Defoe, Stoler arranges some 1,569 annotated entries for texts of Defoe's works as well as books, articles, dissertations, and citations in general reference works in all languages about him in separate topical listings for bibliographies, editions and collections, general studies, studies of the major novels and miscellaneous writings, criticisms in all languages, and dissertations. Annotations, limited largely to English-language works, are descriptive, with references to reviews. A separate subject index provides excellent topical access. Although Stoler's separate listing of editions is convenient, his annotations are not as informative as those in Peterson's guide (entry 347).

Dictionaries, Encyclopedias, and Handbooks

349. Hammond, J. R. **A Defoe Companion.** Lanham, MD: Barnes & Noble, 1993. 151p. LC 92-39387. ISBN 0-389-21006-4.

A handbook to Defoe's life and works, containing biographical and critical surveys, dictionaries of Defoe's works and of the characters and places in them, and detailed examinations of the shorter fiction and the eight principal works. Appendix lists major literary and film adaptations. Brief bibliography of modern editions and major studies (pp. 149-50). Index. See also Johnson's *Plots and Characters in the Fiction of Eighteenth-Century English Authors* (entry 1309).

Indexes and Concordances

350. Owens, W. R., and P. N. Furbank. **A KWIC Concordance to Daniel Defoe's Moll Flanders.** New York: Garland, 1985. 1,111p. (Garland Reference Library of the Humanities, vol. 620). LC 85-45128. ISBN 0-8240-8662-7.

Based on G. A. Starr's edition of *Moll Flanders* (New York: Oxford University Press, 1971), also reissued as a "World Classic" edition (New York: Oxford University Press, 1981), which Owen and Furbank call the "most scholarly and reliable text" (p. vii). Provides page and line references and context lines, with alphabetical and numerical word-frequency lists.

351. Spackman, I. J., W. R. Owens, and P. N. Furbank. **A KWIC Concordance to Daniel Defoe's Robinson Crusoe.** New York: Garland, 1987. 1,141p. (Contextual Concordances; Garland Reference Library of the Humanities, vol. 814). LC 87-19782. ISBN 0-8240-6338-4.

Concords the text of J. Donald Crowley's edition (New York: Oxford University Press, 1972).

Journals

"Recent Articles" in *The Scriblerian and the Kit Cats* (entry 1084) regularly includes a selection of reviews of studies on Defoe.

John William De Forest, 1826-1906

Bibliographies

For works by De Forest, see *Bibliography of American Literature*, vol. 2, pp. 432-37. Contributions by De Forest and criticism and reviews of De Forest's works in selected periodicals are identified in Wells' *The Literary Index to American Magazines, 1815-1865*, p. 41; and *The Literary Index to American Magazines, 1850-1900*, p. 107. De Forest's manuscripts are listed in Robbins' *American Literary Manuscripts*, p. 86. See *Bibliography of American Fiction, 1866-1918*, pp. 149-50, for George Monteiro's checklist of works by and about De Forest.

Thomas Dekker, 1570?-1632

Bibliographies

352.   Adler, Doris Ray. **Thomas Dekker: A Reference Guide**. Boston: G. K. Hall, 1983. 309p. (A Reference Guide to Literature). LC 83-5573. ISBN 0-8161-8384-8.

Adler chronologically arranges annotated entries for about 1,800 secondary materials about Dekker published from 1800 through 1980, including critical studies in books, articles, and dissertations, introductions in editions, and entries in reference works. Annotations are descriptive. An excellent cumulative index includes detailed headings for broad and specific subjects, individual works, and names. This guide complements the coverage of the Tannenbaums' *Elizabethan Bibliographies*, vol. 2, and Dennis Donovan's *Elizabethan Bibliographies Supplements*, no. 2. Research on Dekker is reviewed by Michael Taylor in Wells' *English Drama*, pp. 100-112; and M. L. Wine in Logan and Smith's *The Popular School*, pp. 3-50, updated by Lidman's *Studies in Jacobean Drama, 1973-1984*, pp. 77-92.

353.   Allison, A. F. **Thomas Dekker, c.1572-1632: A Bibliographical Catalogue of the Early Editions (to the End of the 17th Century)**. Folkestone: Dawsons of Pall Mall, 1972. 143p. (Pall Mall Bibliographies, no. 1). LC 72-170171. ISBN 0-7129-0537-5.

Allison gives full bibliographic descriptions for Dekker's dramatic and nondramatic works, providing facsimiles of title pages, collations, physical descriptions, publishing histories, copy locations, and references to standard bibliographies, such as the *STC* and W. W. Greg's *Bibliography of English Printed Drama* (1939; reprint London: Bibliographical Society, 1970). For a bibliography of works by and about Dekker, see *NCBEL*, I, pp. 1673-82. Dekker's manuscripts are described in *Index of English Literary Manuscripts*, I, pt. 1:235-40, 566.

Indexes and Concordances

354.   Small, V. A., R. P. Corballis, and J. M. Harding. **A Concordance to the Dramatic Works of Thomas Dekker**. Salzburg: Institut fur Anglistik und Amerikanistik, Universitat Salzburg, 1984. 890p. (Salzburg Studies in English Literature. Jacobean Drama Studies, vol. 82). OCLC 11238030.

A verbal index, citing play, act, scene, and line, for 11 of Dekker's plays—*If This Be Not a Good Play the Devil Is in It, The Honest Whore, Match Me in London, Sir Thomas More, Northward Ho, Old Fortunatus, Satiromastix, The Shoemakers Holiday, Westward Ho, The Wonder of a Kingdom*, and *The Whore of Babylon*—based on texts included in Fredson Bowers' standard four-volume edition, *The Dramatic Works of Thomas Dekker* (Cambridge: Cambridge University Press, 1953-1961). Coverage excludes Dekker's pageants, entertainments, and collaborative works.

Walter de la Mare, 1873-1956
Bibliographies
355. **Walter de la Mare: A Checklist Prepared on the Occasion of an Exhibition of His Books and Manuscripts at the National Book League, April 20 to May 19, 1956.** Cambridge: Cambridge University Press, 1956. LC 57-677.

This checklist offers brief bibliographic information (size and physical descriptions) for first and variant editions of de la Mare's books, contributions to books, contributions to periodicals, international editions, musical settings of his works, manuscripts, corrected typescripts, and proofs, as well as a list of 25 works about him. Additional information about de la Mare's primary materials is included in Leonard Clark's "A Handlist of the Writings in Book Form (1902-53) of Walter de la Mare," *Studies in Bibliography* 6 (1953): 197-217. Also for a bibliography of works by and about de la Mare, see *NCBEL*, IV, pp. 256-62.

Margaret(ta Wade Campbell) Deland, 1857-1945
Bibliographies
See *Bibliography of American Fiction, 1866-1918*, pp. 151-52, for Laraine Missory Olechowski's checklist of works by and about Deland. Deland's contributions to selected periodicals and reviews of Deland's works are identified in Wells' *The Literary Index to American Magazines, 1850-1900*, pp. 107-108. Deland's manuscripts are listed in Robbins' *American Literary Manuscripts*, p. 86.

Martin R(obinson) Delany, 1812-1885
Bibliographies
Delany's manuscripts are listed in Robbins' *American Literary Manuscripts*, p. 86. See Ellison and Metcalf's *William Wells Brown and Martin R. Delany* (entry 162) for comprehensive coverage of works about Delany through 1975. Research on Delany and Brown is reviewed by Ruth Miller and Peter J. Katopes in Inge, Duke, and Bryer's *Black American Writers*, vol. I, pp. 133-60.

Samuel R. Delany, 1942-
Bibliographies
356. Peplow, Michael W., and Robert S. Bravard. **Samuel R. Delany: A Primary and Secondary Bibliography: 1962-1979.** Boston: G. K. Hall, 1980. 178p. (Masters of Science Fiction and Fantasy). LC 80-20108. ISBN 0-8161-8054-7.

An extended introduction to Delany's life, works, and critical reception precedes Peplow and Bravard's chronologically arranged entries in separate listings for works by and about Delany. Entries cover his 140 different works of fiction and nonfiction, juvenilia, unpublished speeches, and other writings, as well as some 274 critical studies about him. Entries for primary materials give brief bibliographic information with references to subsequent editions and reprintings. Annotations for criticisms are descriptive. In addition, brief descriptions of materials in the Samuel R. Delany Collection in Boston University's Mugar Memorial Library are included (p. 160). See George Slusser's summary biography, critical assessment of major works, and selected primary and secondary bibliography for Delany in McCaffery's *Postmodern Fiction: A Bio-Bibliographical Guide*, pp. 320-23.

Don DeLillo, 1936-
Bibliographies
For works by DeLillo, see *First Printings of American Authors*, vol. 1, p. 87. See Michael Oriard's summary biography, critical assessment of major works, and selected primary and secondary bibliography for DeLillo in McCaffery's *Postmodern Fiction: A Bio-Bibliographical Guide*, pp. 323-26.

Floyd Dell, 1887-1969
Bibliographies

357. Nierman, Judith. **Floyd Dell: An Annotated Bibliography of Secondary Sources, 1910-1981.** Metuchen, NJ: Scarecrow, 1984. 178p. (Scarecrow Author Bibliographies, no. 69). LC 84-13852. ISBN 0-8108-1718-7.

Nierman chronologically arranges annotated entries for 1,099 English-language works about Dell published through 1981. Coverage includes critical books, articles, reviews, dissertations, and entries in reference works. Although generally descriptive, annotations also evaluate and clearly identify major studies. A cumulative index includes headings for a full range of topics under Dell's name as well as for other authors (such as Dreiser, Pound, and Sinclair). The most comprehensive listing of Dell's primary bibliography appears in G. Thomas Tanselle's Ph.D. dissertation, *Faun at the Barricades: The Life and Work of Floyd Dell* (Evanston, IL: Northwestern University, 1959). Also for works by Dell, see *First Printings of American Authors*, vol. 3, pp. 71-78. Dell's manuscripts are listed in Robbins' *American Literary Manuscripts*, pp. 86-87.

Thomas Deloney, 1560?-1600
Bibliographies

For a bibliography of works by and about Deloney, see *NCBEL*, I, pp. 1099, 2054-55, 2077, 2271. Deloney's manuscripts are described in *Index of English Literary Manuscripts*, I, pt. 1:241-42.

Lester Del Rey, 1915-1993
Bibliographies

See *Bibliography of American Fiction 1919-1988*, pp. 142-43, for Chris Pourteau's checklist of works by and about Del Rey.

(Sir) John Denham, 1615-1669
Bibliographies

For a bibliography of works by and about Denham, see *NCBEL*, I, pp. 1217-18. Denham's manuscripts are described in *Index of English Literary Manuscripts*, II, pt. 1:329-45.

Joseph Dennie, 1768-1812
Bibliographies

For works by Dennie, see *Bibliography of American Literature*, vol. 2, pp. 438-42. Dennie's manuscripts are listed in Robbins' *American Literary Manuscripts*, p. 87. Wells' *The Literary Index to American Magazines, 1815-1865*, p. 41, identifies comments on Dennie in selected periodicals.

John Dennis, 1657-1734
Bibliographies

For a bibliography of works by and about Dennis, see *NCBEL*, II, pp. 1041-44. Dennis' manuscripts are described in *Index of English Literary Manuscripts*, III, pt. 1:337-39.

Deor, ninth or tenth century
Bibliographies

Greenfield and Robinson's *A Bibliography of Publications on Old English Literature to the End of 1972*, pp. 211-13, lists editions, translations, and studies of the Old English *Deor*, with citations for reviews.

Thomas De Quincey, 1785-1859

Bibliographies

358. Dendurent, H. O. **Thomas De Quincey: A Reference Guide**. Boston: G. K. Hall, 1978. 166p. (Reference Guides in Literature). LC 77-6633. ISBN 0-8161-7840-2.

Dendurent chronologically arranges annotated entries for about 900 works about De Quincey published from 1821 through 1975. Comprehensive coverage includes anonymous reviews and notices, introductions to editions, unpublished lectures, dissertations, and critical studies in all languages. Annotations are brief and descriptive. Detailed subject access under De Quincey as well as under index headings for selected topics and names (such as "opium" and "Coleridge") is provided. The major listing of De Quincey's primary materials is J. A. Green's *Thomas De Quincey: A Bibliography Based upon the De Quincey Collection in the Moss Side Library* (1908; reprint New York: Burt Franklin, 1968), which describes separate and collected editions, manuscripts, and De Quinceyana. Also for a bibliography of works by and about De Quincey, see *NCBEL*, III, pp. 1238-47. De Quincey's manuscripts are described in *Index of English Literary Manuscripts*, IV, pt. 1:681-703, 830-31. Research on De Quincey is reviewed by John E. Jordan in Houtchens and Houtchens' *The English Romantic Poets and Essayists*, pp. 289-332.

George Horatio Derby, 1823-1861

Bibliographies

For works by Derby, see *Bibliography of American Literature*, vol. 2, pp. 443-45. Contributions by Derby and criticism and reviews of Derby's works in selected periodicals are identified in Wells' *The Literary Index to American Magazines, 1815-1865*, p. 42. See *Bibliography of American Fiction Through 1865*, p. 103, for a checklist of works by and about Derby.

August (William) Derleth, 1909-1971

Bibliographies

359. Wilson, Alison M. **August Derleth: A Bibliography**. Metuchen, NJ: Scarecrow, 1983. 229p. (Scarecrow Author Bibliographies, no. 59). LC 82-24020. ISBN 0-8108-1606-7.

Wilson gives a partial listing of Derleth's primary bibliography, including brief bibliographic information and summaries of contents in separate listings for his fictional writings (including science fiction, mystery, and horror short stories, collaborative works, 10 novels featuring Judge Peck, and edited works) and nonfiction writings (Sac Prairie short stories, novels, juvenile mysteries, and the like), and other works. Entries identify first and subsequent appearances. Derleth's poems, reviews, and unpublished writings are not described. Derleth's manuscripts are listed in Robbins' *American Literary Manuscripts*, p. 87.

Journals

See Patterson's *Author Newsletters and Journals*, p. 360, for previously published journals for Derleth.

Peter De Vries, 1910-1993

Bibliographies

360. Bowden, Edwin T. **Peter De Vries: A Bibliography, 1934-1977**. Austin, TX: Humanities Research Center, University of Texas, 1978. 72p. LC 76-620049. ISBN 0-87959-079-3.

Full bibliographic descriptions of De Vries' works chronologically arranged in sections for original books, original contributions to other books, and contributions to periodicals. Twenty-two entries for books and six for first appearances in books give title-page transcriptions, collations and paginations, contents, binding and dust-jacket descriptions, and brief notes on publication histories, with brief bibliographic information for subsequent editions, variants, and translations. Bowden lists 146 periodical appearances from 1934 to 1975. Title index. Also for works by De Vries, see *First Printings of American Authors*, vol. 4, pp. 147-53. De Vries' manuscripts are listed in Robbins' *American Literary Manuscripts*, p. 88. See *Bibliography of American Fiction, 1919-1988*, pp. 144-45, for Bowden's checklist of works by and about De Vries.

John Dewey, 1859-1952

Bibliographies

361. Levine, Barbara. **Works About John Dewey, 1886-1995.** Carbondale, IL: Southern Illinois University Press, 1996. 526p. LC 95-41509. ISBN 0-8093-2056-8.

Attempts to include "all the published works" (p. viii) about Dewey published from 1886 to April 1995, cumulating materials previously contained in Jo Ann Boydston and Kathleen Poulos' *Checklist of Writings About John Dewey, 1887-1973* (Carbondale, IL: Southern Illinois University Press, 1974) and the enlarged second edition. (Carbondale, IL: Southern Illinois University Press, 1978). Alphabetically arranges more than 5,000 selectively unannotated entries in sections for books and articles, with selective notes on contents and citations for reviews and reprints and reviews of Dewey's works. Identifies both scholarly and popular works. Author and title keyword indexes offer good access.

362. Thomas, Milton Halsey. **John Dewey: A Centennial Bibliography.** Chicago: University of Chicago Press, 1962. 370p. LC 62-12638.

A revision of Thomas and Herbert Wallace Schneider's *A Bibliography of John Dewey* (New York: Columbia University Press, 1929); and the second edition, revised and enlarged, *A Bibliography of John Dewey, 1882-1939* (New York: Columbia University Press, 1939), edited by Thomas. Also covering writings about Dewey, Thomas' 1962 guide is the standard bibliography of Dewey's works published to 1960. Offers comprehensive coverage of Dewey's separate publications and contributed works, including books; edited works; introductions and prefaces; articles; abstracts; reviews; letters to editor and other replies; published addresses and lectures; and collected, selected, anthologized, abridged, translated, large-print, Braille, and other versions. Chronologically arranged descriptions give data for paginations, contents, notes on subsequent appearances, and citations for abstracts and reviews. Includes brief chronology of Dewey. Thorough indexing. Thomas' international coverage of secondary materials is updated by Levine's more recent *Works About John Dewey* (entry 361). Also for works by Dewey, see *First Printings of American Authors*, vol. 1, pp. 89-91. Dewey's manuscripts are listed in Robbins' *American Literary Manuscripts*, pp. 88-89. Jo Ann Boydston's *John Dewey's Personal and Professional Library: A Checklist* (Carbondale, IL: Published for the Libraries, Southern Illinois University by Southern Illinois University Press, 1982) is also useful.

Philip K. Dick, 1928-1982

Bibliographies

363. Levack, Daniel J. H. **PKD: A Philip K. Dick Bibliography.** Westport, CT: Meckler, 1988. 156p. (Meckler's Bibliographies of Science Fiction, Fantasy, and Horror). LC 88-15597. ISBN 0-8873-6096-3.

"Attempts to cite all the published works of Phillip K. Dick through late 1984," including "non-English and English language publications," "fictional and non-fictional works and published interviews" (p. [11]). The bulk of the guide alphabetically arranges entries for 49 books and 152 stories that give brief bibliographic information for first and subsequent editions, translations, and reprintings; summaries of contents; and physical details about formats and other bibliographic points, with useful black-and-white illustrations of covers and title pages. A separate section lists Dick's works chronologically from 1952 to 1981.

Other sections identify and briefly describe unpublished manuscripts in the Special Collections of California State University at Fullerton libraries and media adaptations; and list Dick's pseudonyms, collaborations, connected stories and continuing characters, nonfiction, verse, and magazines containing Dick's work. Also provides an unannotated list of 17 works about Dick. Unindexed. See *Bibliography of American Fiction, 1919-1988*, pp. 146-49, for Hazel Pierce's checklist of works by and about Dick. Brian Stableford supplies a summary biography, critical assessment of major works, and selected primary and secondary bibliography for Dick in McCaffery's *Postmodern Fiction: A Bio-Bibliographical Guide*, pp. 332-35.

Charles (John Huffham) Dickens, 1812-1870
Bibliographies
364. **Garland Dickens Bibliographies**. Duane DeVries, general ed. New York: Garland, 1984- . In progress. OCLC 13917368.
   Volumes in this series offer the most comprehensive coverage of editions and criticisms of Dickens' individual works. Coverage includes (mostly English-language) books, parts of books, articles, and dissertations as well as contemporary reviews, prose adaptations, television, film, and stage adaptations, recordings, and the like, dating from the year of publication of Dickens' works to the present. Most volumes arrange entries in separate listings for editions, adaptations, critical genres and subjects, such as reviews, characters, literary sources, biographical sources, influence studies, and so forth. Volumes typically include about 700 to 1,000 entries. Glancy's *Dickens's Christmas Books, Christmas Stories, and Other Short Fiction* (entry 364.4) includes more than 2,200 entries; her *A Tale of Two Cities* (entry 364.12) contains 672 entries. Annotations are typically descriptive and extensive and often include citations for reviews. Significant texts and studies are usually clearly identified. All volumes include subject indexing. Several volumes, such as Paroissien's for *Oliver Twist* (entry 364.2) and Rice's for *Barnaby Rudge* (entry 364.6), provide separate, very detailed subject indexes. Volumes in the series supersede all previous bibliographies of Dickens criticism. Volumes to the present include:

   364.1. Vol. 1: Brattin, Joel J., and Bert G. Hornback. **Our Mutual Friend: An Annotated Bibliography**. New York: Garland, 1984. 197p. (Garland Reference Library of the Humanities, vol. 481). LC 83-49325. ISBN 0-8240-8986-3.

   364.2. Vol. 2: Paroissien, David. **Oliver Twist: An Annotated Bibliography**. New York: Garland, 1986. 313p. (Garland Reference Library of the Humanities, vol. 385). LC 82-49136. ISBN 0-8240-9198-1.

   364.3. Vol. 3: Manning, Sylvia. **Hard Times: An Annotated Bibliography**. New York: Garland, 1984. 296p. (Garland Reference Library of the Humanities, vol. 515). LC 84-45402. ISBN 0-8240-9985-6.

   364.4. Vol. 4: Glancy, Ruth F. **Dickens's Christmas Books, Christmas Stories, and Other Short Fiction: An Annotated Bibliography**. New York: Garland, 1985. 610p. (Garland Reference Library of the Humanities, vol. 479). LC 83-49323. ISBN 0-8240-8988-x.

   364.5. Vol. 5: Worth, George J. **Great Expectations: An Annotated Bibliography**. New York: Garland, 1986. 346p. (Garland Reference Library of the Humanities, vol. 555). LC 84-45369. ISBN 0-8240-8818-2.

   364.6. Vol. 6: Rice, Thomas Jackson. **Barnaby Rudge: An Annotated Bibliography**. New York: Garland, 1987. 351p. (Garland Reference Library of the Humanities, vol. 630). LC 85-45137. ISBN 0-8240-8652-x.

364.7. Vol. 7: Engel, Elliot D. **Pickwick Papers: An Annotated Bibliography.** New York: Garland, 1990. 345p. (Garland Reference Library of the Humanities, vol. 568). LC 89-71396. ISBN 0-8240-8766-6.

364.8. Vol. 8: Dunn, Richard J. **David Copperfield: An Annotated Bibliography.** New York: Garland, 1981. 256p. (Garland Reference Library of the Humanities, vol. 280.) LC 80-9023. ISBN 0-8240-9322-4.

364.9. Vol. 9: Schlicke, Priscilla. **Old Curiosity Shop: An Annotated Bibliography.** New York: Garland, 1988. 495p. (Garland Reference Library of the Humanities, vol. 708). LC 88-4359. ISBN 0-8240-8512-4.

364.10. Vol. 10: Lougy, Robert E. **Martin Chuzzlewit: An Annotated Bibliography.** New York: Garland, 1990. 290p. (Garland Reference Library of the Humanities, vol. 1083). LC 89-23263. ISBN 0-8240-4680-0.

364.11. Vol. 11: Not yet published.

364.12. Vol. 12: Glancy, Ruth F. **A Tale of Two Cities: An Annotated Bibliography.** New York: Garland, 1993. 236p. (Garland Reference Library of the Humanities, vol. 1339). LC 92-40546. ISBN 0-8240-7091-7.

365. Gold, Joseph. **The Stature of Dickens: A Centenary Bibliography.** Toronto: University of Toronto Press, 1971. 236p. LC 70-151368. ISBN 0-8020-3265-6.

The most comprehensive single-volume bibliography of works by and about Dickens. Gold provides unannotated entries for 3,625 editions of Dickens' works and critical studies. Coverage extends through 1968. Gold's guide is updated by Alan M. Cohn and K. K. Collins' *The Cumulated Dickens Checklist, 1970-1979* (Troy, NY: Whitston, 1982), which cumulates some 3,000 entries for editions and studies (including dissertations) listed in quarterly checklists featured in *Dickens Studies Newsletter* and continued through the present in *Dickens Quarterly* (entry 375). Less comprehensive (albeit annotated) coverage of Dickens criticism through the mid-1970s is provided in R. C. Churchill's *A Bibliography of Dickensian Criticism, 1836-1975* (New York: Garland, 1975) and John J. Fenstermaker's *Charles Dickens, 1940-1975: An Analytical Subject Index to Periodical Criticism of the Novels and Christmas Books* (Boston: G. K. Hall, 1979). All bibliographies of modern Dickens scholarship are (or will be) superseded by volumes in the *Garland Dickens Bibliographies* series (entry 364). A more specialized guide to Dickens' earliest critical reception, Kathryn Chittick's *The Critical Reception of Charles Dickens, 1833-1841* (New York: Garland, 1989), is an unannotated listing of reviews and notices of Dickens' works, with analyses of the reviewing periodicals. Also for a bibliography of works by and about Dickens, see *NCBEL*, III, pp. 779-850. Research on Dickens is reviewed by Ada Nisbet in Stevenson's *Victorian Fiction*, pp. 44-153; Philip Collins in Ford's *Victorian Fiction*, pp. 34-113; and Michael Slater in Dyson's *The English Novel*, pp. 179-99.

366. Hatton, Thomas, and Arthur H. Cleaver. **A Bibliography of the Periodical Works of Charles Dickens: Bibliographical, Analytical, and Statistical.** 1933; New York: Haskell House, 1973. 383p. LC 72-1271. ISBN 0-8383-1435-x.

The authoritative guide to first appearances of Dickens' novels. Hatton and Cleaver offer full bibliographic descriptions of all parts of Dickens' serialized works. Entries describe in detail the text, plates, wrappers, and advertisements. Numerous facsimiles of wrappers accompany the descriptions. Full bibliographic descriptions for the publications of Dickens' works in book form are included in Walter E. Smith's two-volume *Charles Dickens in the Original Cloth: A Bibliographical Catalogue of the First Appearance of His Writings in Book Form in England with Facsimiles of the Bindings and Titlepages* (Los Angeles, CA: Heritage Book Shop, 1982). Additional coverage related to Dickens' periodical publications is provided in Anne Lohrli's *Household Words: A Weekly Journal, 1850-1859* (Toronto: University of Toronto Press, 1973), which gives annotated tables of contents for issues of *Household Words*, with a directory of its contributors (including not only Dickens but also the likes of Wilkie Collins, Elizabeth Gaskell, and George Meredith); and Ella Ann Oppenlander's *Dickens's All the Year Round: Descriptive Index and Contributor List* (Troy, NY: Whitston, 1984), which gives annotated tables of contents for issues of *All the Year Round* published from 1859 through 1870, with indexes of contributors, titles, and keywords. Dickens' manuscripts are described in *Index of English Literary Manuscripts*, IV, pt. 1:705-42. *The Charles Dickens Research Collection: From The J. F. Dexter Collection in the British Library and Other Major Holdings in Great Britain and the United States of America: A Listing and Guide* (Cambridge and Alexandria, VA: Chadwyck-Healey, 1990) serves as a guide to a major microform research collection, also reprinting the British Library's catalog of the Dexter collection. Other useful descriptions of Dickens' primary materials are included in Sr. Mary Callista Carr's *Catalogue of the Dickens Collection at the University of Texas* (Austin, TX: Humanities Research Center, 1961), which describes the collection of Dickens' autographs and other manuscripts, books, journals, portraits, and other materials in the University of Texas' Harry Ransom Humanities Research Center; and John B. Podeschi's *Dickens and Dickensiana: A Catalogue of the Richard Gimbel Collection in the Yale University Library* (New Haven, CT: Yale University Library, 1980). Michael Pointer's *Charles Dickens on the Screen: The Film, Television, and Video Adaptations* (Lanham, MD: Scarecrow Press, 1996) gives a comprehensive, international listing of media adaptations of Dickens' works from 1897 through 1994.

Dictionaries, Encyclopedias, and Handbooks

367.   Bentley, Nicolas, Michael Slater, and Nina Burgis. **The Dickens Index**. Oxford: Oxford University Press, 1988. 308p. LC 88-19712. ISBN 0-19-211665-7.

The most comprehensive coverage of information about Dickens and his works. Brief, detailed entries are provided for all of Dickens' works, including novels, shorter fiction, plays, travel writings, journalistic pieces, edited periodicals, collected editions published in his lifetime; real persons professionally connected with Dickens; obsolete words and phrases from his works; named fictional characters; allusions to or quotations from myths, folklore, legends, history, and other sources; and real and fictional place names. Critical plot summaries for Dickens' works emphasize themes and other "unique features" (p. ix). Entries consistently cite texts and other sources. Coverage of Dickens' indebtedness to the works of other authors is particularly detailed. Additional coverage of characters and places in Dickens' works is provided in John Greaves' *Who's Who in Dickens* (London: Elm Tree Books, 1972); Mary Williams' *The Dickens Concordance: Being a Compendium of Names and Characters and Principal Places Mentioned in All the Works of Charles Dickens* (1907; reprint New York: Haskell House, 1970); Thomas Alexander Fyfe's *Who's Who in Dickens: A Complete Dickens Repertory in Dickens Own Words* (1912; reprint Ann Arbor, MI: Gryphon Books, 1971), which quotes Dickens' descriptions; Tony Lynch's *Dickens's England* (New York: Facts on File, 1986), which identifies approximately 200 London locations and other towns that appear in Dickens's works or were important in his life; and Alex J. Philip and W. Laurence Gadd's *A Dickens Dictionary*, 2d ed., revised (1928; reprint New York: Burt Franklin, 1970), which covers both characters and places (such as the Shooting Gallery, Marshalsea, and other public houses, pawnbrokers, and prisons) and lists originals and prototypes for Dickens' characters (such as the real Miss Havisham). A more specialized series, Unwin Hyman's Dickens Companions, includes volumes that identify and gloss allusions to current and historical events, issues, social customs, topographical features, and the like in individual works. Volumes include Michael Cotsell's *The Companion to Our Mutual Friend* (London: Unwin Hyman, 1986), Wendy S. Jacobson's *The Companion to The Mystery of Edwin Drood* (London: Unwin Hyman, 1986), Susan Shatto's *The Companion to Bleak House*

(London: Unwin Hyman, 1988), and Andrew Sanders's *The Companion Tale of Two Cities* (London: Unwin Hyman, 1988).

368. Hardwick, Michael, and Mollie Hardwick. **The Charles Dickens Encyclopedia**. 1973; reprint New York: Carol, 1993. 376p. ISBN 0-8065-1403-5.

First published in 1973 (Reading: Osprey), the Hardwicks' companion gives thorough summaries of the plots of Dickens' works and brief identifications of his characters and places as well as members of his circle of family, friends, and associates. This guide, however, lacks the bibliographic and critical strengths of Page's handbook (entry 373).

369. Hobsbaum, Philip. **A Reader's Guide to Charles Dickens**. New York: Farrar, Straus, Giroux, 1973. 318p. ISBN 0-500-14017-0.

Hobsbaum provides work-by-work critical introductions to the plots, structures, themes, and characters in Dickens' major works, with a selected bibliography of critical sources.

370. Levit, Fred. **Dickens Glossary**. New York: Garland, 1990. 450p. (Garland Reference Library of the Humanities, vol. 1210). LC 89-36390. ISBN 0-8240-5542-X.

Levit defines words, terms, and phrases ("Bandoline," "cock-loft," "firedamp," and several thousand others) that appear in Dickens' works, with cross-references to the texts. The dictionary offers excellent guidance to the Victorian urban vernacular. Additionally, Arthur Hayward's *Dickens Encyclopedia: An Alphabetical Dictionary of References to Every Character and Place Mentioned in the Works of Fiction, with Explanatory Notes on Obscure Allusions and Phrases* (London: George Routledge, 1924) provides complementary coverage of other Victorian terms and allusions not included in Levit's guide (such as "Morris," meaning "to move on"; "small-clothes"; and "The Ghost of Art").

371. Newlin, George. **Every Thing in Dickens: Ideas and Subjects Discussed by Charles Dickens in His Complete Works: A Topicon**. Westport, CT: Greenwood Press, 1996. 1,102p. LC 96-6347. ISBN 0-313-29874-2.

Topical concordance to subjects in Dickens' works. Places extended quotations from Dickens under 16 main (often seemingly allusive and narrow) chapters, including "Ages of Man"; "Body"; "Charles Dickens Revealed"; "Fellow Man, in Relation"; "First and last Things"; "Humankind, in Activity"; " Industry and Government"; "London"; "Letters and Communication"; "Mind"; "Nature"; "Spirit, and Moral Qualities"; "Three Professions: clergy, law, medical"; "Transportation and Travel"; and "The Rest of the World," with more elaborate subclassifications. Classes under "Body" include "Food and Drink," with specific divisions for "beer," "leg of mutton," and "sycophantic," for example. Indexes of words, phrases, and localities. Although tables of subclassifications precede each chapter, no comprehensive table or index cumulates all of the subclassifications, making the topical concordance rather difficult to use.

372. Newlin, George. **Everyone in Dickens**. Westport, CT: Greenwood Press, 1995. 3 vols. LC 95-2453. ISBN 0-313-29580-8.

Includes three separately titled volumes: vol. 1: *Plots, People, and Publishing Particulars in the Complete Works, 1833-1849*; vol. 2: *Plots, People, and Publishing Particulars in the Complete Works, 1850-1870*; and vol. 3: *Characteristics and Commentaries, Tables and Tabulations: A Taxonomy*, constituting vols. 1-3 of Newlin's *Windows in Dickens*; vol. 4 is Newlin's *Every Thing in Dickens* (entry 371). Identifies and describes, usually in extended quotations from Dickens, all named or otherwise mentioned persons in all of Dickens' works (a total of 588 works), except the speeches and some fragments. Self-contained entries for each work give a plot summary, a list of illustrations of characters, and list of all characters classified by significance (title roles, principals, supporting roles, and others), followed by descriptions of the individual characters. Vols. 1 and 2 conclude with classified indexes of characters and persons and indexes of subjects in nonfiction; vol. 3 consists of a series of 12 indexes for characters' surnames; given names; parodic, archetypal, and allegorical names and sobriquets; occupations and vocations of named males; occupations and vocations of named females; relationships of named characters; miscellaneous categories; generic figures in fiction and nonfiction; historical figures; occupations and vocations of historical figures; Biblical, literary, musical, and mythological references; and associations, boroughs, companies, hostelries, houses, newspapers, prisons, schools, and ships. Concludes with a useful chronology of Dickens' life and writings and a glossary. As Newlin advises, if one knows the character's name but not the work, consult the indexes in vols. 1 and 2 or the appropriate given or surname index in vol. 3. Although the most comprehensive dictionary of names in Dickens' works, Newlin's guide is not the most convenient place to get brief identifications of Dickens' characters.

373.   Page, Norman. **Dickens Chronology**. Boston: G. K. Hall, 1988. 156p. (Macmillan Author Chronologies). LC 87-25209. ISBN 0-8161-8949-8.
      Page heavily bases his chronology of Dickens' life on volumes 1-5 of *The Pilgrim Edition of the Letters of Charles Dickens* (Oxford: Clarendon Press, 1977-) as well as other primary works. Entries in the chronology give brief, factual details of events and activities and frequently seem quite perfunctory. Dickens appears to "dine at" successions of homes and little more. Indeed, Page notes that coverage of events varies in "density" (p. xi). This volume does not quote as extensively from sources as others in the series, such as the one for Byron (entry 207). Indexing is limited to works, persons, and places, with no topical access. Nonetheless, Page's chronology is superior to others, including the one in his handbook (entry 374) and in the Hardwicks' companion (entry 368).

374.   Page, Norman. **A Dickens Companion**. London: Macmillan, 1984. 369p. (Macmillan Literary Companions). LC 84-27568. ISBN 0-333-31539-1.
      Bibliographically and critically more substantial than other Dickens handbooks, the most useful features of Page's guide are its book-by-book descriptions of Dickens' writings, including his novels, readings and speeches, letters, plays and poems, and translations. Narrative entries survey and describe available editions, the composition of the work, serial and book publication, and critical reception. Entries conclude with detailed descriptions of characters in each work. In addition, Page gives brief identifications for members of Dickens' circle, illustrators of his works, and places associated with Dickens; a filmography and a list of early dramatizations of his works; and a substantial selected bibliography of primary and secondary works. Although very comprehensive, Page's guide lacks plot summaries.

Journals
375.   **Dickens Quarterly**. Amherst, MA: Dickens Society, 1970-. 4/yr. ISSN 0742-5473.
      Sponsored by the Dickens Society and formerly *Dickens Studies Newsletter* (1970-84), this is the most important journal devoted to Dickens. Issues include two to six scholarly critical and interpretive articles that address specific topics in individual works as well as biographical subjects. Studies of such topics as Dickens' views on class relations as evidenced in *Little Dorrit*, the uses of letters and correspondence in *Bleak House, All the Year Round* and Victorian psychiatry, Dickens and the Italian risorgimento, and the gothic plot of *Great Expectations* are typical. Volumes regularly publish studies focusing on individual works. Volumes have been devoted to *The Old Curiosity Shop* and *Nicholas Nickleby*. Occasional recent bibliographic features include surveys of French and Russian Dickens scholarship since 1970 in 12.4 (December 1995). The journal's most significant bibliographic contribution is a quarterly "Dickens Checklist," most recently compiled by Diane Hebert, that

identifies editions and studies (including dissertations), with references to reviews, as well as international criticism and media. In addition to publishing reviews, the journal includes announcements of seminars, reports on conferences, prizes, and other activities sponsored by the Dickens Society as well as research in progress. *Dickens Quarterly* is indexed in *AES, AHI, A&HCI, MHRA,* and *MLA.*

376. **Dickens Studies Annual: Essays in Victorian Fiction.** New York: AMS, 1970-. Annual. ISSN 0084-9812.

Volumes include a dozen substantial scholarly contributions on Dickens as well as other Victorian novelists and subjects related to fiction. Recent studies have compared Dickens and Twain, examined Dickens' views on America, reviewed Dickens' references to Longfellow, and focused on feminine discourses in *Hard Times.* Others articles have examined themes in the works of George Eliot, Thackeray, Wilkie Collins, Trollope, and the Brontes. In addition, since 1980 volumes include the bibliographic feature "Recent Dickens Studies," which reviews research on Dickens (usually two to three years out-of-date). Also publishes other similar reviews for any one or several Victorian novelists, including Thackeray, 23 (1995): 303-36; Trollope, 21 (1992): 281-312; Elizabeth Gaskell, 19 (1990): 345-69; the Brontes, 18 (1989): 381-402; and Thomas Hardy, 17 (1988): 249-84. All volumes include indexes and, through 21 (1992), contents list of all previous volumes. *Dickens Studies Annual* is indexed in *A&HCI, MHRA,* and *MLA.*

377. **The Dickensian.** London: The Dickens Fellowship, 1905-. 3/yr. ISSN 0012-2440.

Sponsored by the Dickens Fellowship, *The Dickensian* publishes two to six critical, biographical, and bibliographic studies and a few brief notes and book reviews. From 1968 to 1975, the journal featured an annual literature review, "Year's Work in Dickens Studies." As in *Dickens Quarterly,* features are limited to topics related to Dickens' works and life, such as the use of time in *Little Dorritt,* Dickens and van Gogh, descriptions of unpublished materials, and Shaw's comments on Dickens. The journal also publishes "Fellowship Notes and News" regarding activities of the society and its membership (obituaries, conference reports, etc.) as well as accounts of current stage, film, television, and other adaptations of Dickens' works. "Dickens Fellowship Diary" is a calendar of upcoming events. *The Dickensian* is indexed in *AES, A&HCI, MHRA,* and *MLA.*

Patterson's *Author Newsletters and Journals,* pp. 90-94, describes other previously published journals for Dickens.

James (Lafayette) Dickey, 1923-1997
Bibliographies

378. Bruccoli, Matthew J., and Judith S. Baughman. **James Dickey: A Descriptive Bibliography.** Pittsburgh, PA: University of Pittsburgh Press, 1990. 423p. (Pittsburgh Series in Bibliography). LC 89-16585. ISBN 0-8229-3629-1.

This is the best descriptive guide to Dickey's primary materials. Bruccoli and Baughman give full bibliographic descriptions for Dickey's books, pamphlets, and broadsides; contributions to books; contributions to journals and newspapers; interviews and articles including original quotes of Dickey; and later collections of Dickey's poems. Entries include title- and copyright-page facsimiles; collations; contents; descriptions of typography, paper, bindings, and dust jackets (with facsimiles); information on publishing histories, including references for press releases; and copy locations. Coverage includes first and subsequent editions. In addition, the guide lists about two dozen works about Dickey. Coverage of Dickey's publications in Bruccoli and Baughman's guide is superior to that provided in Elledge's guide (entry 379) and in Stuart Wright's *James Dickey: A Bibliography of His Books, Pamphlets, and Broadsides* (Dallas, TX: Pressworks, 1982). Also for works by Dickey, see *First Printings of American Authors,* vol. 1, pp. 93-95. Dickey's manuscripts are listed in Robbins' *American Literary Manuscripts,* p. 89.

379. Elledge, Jim. **James Dickey: A Bibliography, 1947-1974.** Metuchen, NJ: Scarecrow Press, 1979. 291p. (Scarecrow Author Bibliographies, no. 40). LC 79-10405. ISBN 0-8108-1218-5.

Including 1,242 entries, Elledge's guide gives separate listings for writings by and about Dickey. Entries cover Dickey's books and pamphlets, poetry and prose contributions to books and journals, film adaptations, published correspondence, recordings, special collections, and other miscellaneous primary materials, as well as books, articles, dissertations, interviews, and other secondary writings. Only the latter cite complete bibliographic data. Indexing is largely nominal, referencing critics, titles, and characters. Elledge's coverage of Dickey criticism supersedes that in Eileen Glancy's *James Dickey: The Critic as Poet: An Annotated Bibliography with an Introductory Essay* (Troy, NY: Whitston, 1971); and Franklin Ashley's *James Dickey: A Checklist* (Detroit, MI: Gale, 1972). Research on Dickey is reviewed by Richard J. Calhoun in Flora and Bain's *Fifty Southern Writers After 1900*, pp. 136-46, with a supplement in Bain and Flora's *Contemporary Poets, Dramatists, Essayists, and Novelists of the South*, pp. 564-65; and Ronald Baughman in *Contemporary Authors: Bibliographical Series: Volume 2: American Poets*, pp. 71-105.

Journals

380. **James Dickey Newsletter.** Atlanta, GA: James Dickey Society, 1984-. 2/yr. ISSN 0749-0291.

"Unifying the Energy and Balancing the Vision: Nature, Man, and Quest in James Dickey's *Deliverance* and *Alnilam*," " 'Stand waiting, my love, where you are': Women in James Dickey's Early Poetry," and "Postmodernism and *To the White Sea*" are typical of scholarly contributions to the photocopied and stapled *James Dickey Newsletter*. Other features offer close readings of works, interpretations of characters, and discussions of Dickey's uses of myths. Studies have also addressed Dickey's literary relations with Ann Sexton, Robinson Jeffers, Robert Browning, Anne Tyler, Old English poetry, and William Blake. Interviews with Dickey offer valuable primary information. A regular cover note and other occasional notes identify library acquisitions of Dickey materials and conference programs on Dickey. Useful bibliographic features include reviews of new works and a "Continuing Bibliography," an annual bibliography of editions, reference sources, critical studies, reviews, dissertations, and brief mentions. Vol. 11.2 (Spring 1995): 25-33, provides an index to vols. 1.1-10.2 (Fall 1984-Spring 1994). *James Dickey Newsletter* is indexed in *AHI* and *MLA*.

Emily (Elizabeth) Dickinson, 1830-1886

Bibliographies

381. Boswell, Jeanetta. **Emily Dickinson: A Bibliography of Secondary Sources, with Selective Annotations, 1890 Through 1987.** Jefferson, NC: McFarland, 1989. 418p. LC 89-8054. ISBN 0-89950-368-3.

Boswell alphabetically arranges critically annotated entries for about 2,500 English-language publications about Dickinson (including dissertations, theses, reviews, and newspaper articles). Helpful annotations clearly identify significant works. A separate subject index references names, titles, and such topics as "editions," "satire," and "women." Boswell's coverage of early reviews and notices of Dickinson is greatly supplemented by Willis J. Buckingham's *Emily Dickinson's Reception in the 1890's: A Documentary History* (Pittsburgh, PA: University of Pittsburgh Press, 1989), which excerpts nearly 600 (mostly anonymous) reviews. Likewise, coverage of non-English-language criticism is provided in Buckingham's *Emily Dickinson: An Annotated Bibliography* (Bloomington, IN: Indiana University Press, 1970). Boswell's guide is more useful than Karen Dandurand's limited *Dickinson Scholarship: An Annotated Bibliography, 1969-1985* (New York: Garland, 1988), which describes 795 secondary works; and Sheilah T. Clendenning's *Emily Dickinson: A Bibliography, 1850-1966* (Kent, OH: Kent State University Press, 1968). Research on Dickinson is reviewed by James Woodress in Harbert and Rees' *Fifteen American Authors Before 1900*, pp. 185-229; and Paul J. Ferlazzo in Myerson's *The Transcendentalists*, pp. 320-27. *ALS* annually features an review essay on Dickinson scholarship.

382.   Duchac, Joseph. **The Poems of Emily Dickinson: An Annotated Guide to Commentary Published in English, 1890-1977**. Boston: G. K. Hall, 1979. 658p. (A Reference Publication in Literature). LC 79-14196. ISBN 0-8161-7830-5.
     Continued and supplemented by:

382.1. Duchac, Joseph. **The Poems of Emily Dickinson: An Annotated Guide to Commentary Published in English, 1978-1989**. New York: G. K. Hall, 1993. 525p. (Reference Publication in Literature). LC 92-32694. ISBN 0-8161-7352-4.
     Covering the first 100 years of Dickinson criticism, Duchac's specialized indexes cross-reference individual poems, identified by title and number assigned by Thomas H. Johnson's edition of *The Poems of Emily Dickinson* (Cambridge, MA: Harvard University Press, 1955), with English-language critical studies. Together, the 1979 and 1993 volumes contain citations and brief descriptive entries for approximately 8,000 commentaries in approximately 1,400 books and articles published through 1989. Coverage excludes dissertations. Although Duchac's unique index offers the most direct access to close readings of Dickinson's individual poems, lack of subject indexing in the volumes makes topically focused research next to impossible. Boswell's less comprehensive guide (entry 381) remains useful for subject access.

383.   Myerson, Joel. **Emily Dickinson: A Descriptive Bibliography**. Pittsburgh, PA: University of Pittsburgh Press, 1984. 209p. (Pittsburgh Series in Bibliography). LC 83-21678. ISBN 0-8229-3491-4.
     The standard guide to Dickinson's primary works. Myerson gives full bibliographic descriptions in separate listings for separately published books and pamphlets and collected editions; contributions to books; contributions to journals and newspapers; and other materials attributed to her. Facsimiles of title and copyright pages; descriptions of collations, contents, bindings and dust jackets; printing and publishing histories; and locations of copies are included. An appendix lists about 50 works about Dickinson. A title and first-line index gives access. Emphasis is on recording the printing and publication histories of Dickinson's works. Myerson also describes Dickinson's primary materials in *The Emily Dickinson Collection* in part 4 in Sidney Ives' *The Parkman Dexter Howe Library* (Gainesville, FL: University of Florida, 1986). Also for works by Dickinson, see *Bibliography of American Literature*, vol. 2, pp. 446-54. Dickinson's manuscripts are listed in Robbins' *American Literary Manuscripts*, p. 89. Supplementary coverage of Dickinsoniana (including tributes, poetry about Dickinson, recordings of her works, and stage, film, and broadcast adaptations, and the like) is provided in Willis J. Buckingham's *Emily Dickinson: An Annotated Bibliography* (Bloomington, IN: Indiana University Press, 1970). Also valuable for research on Dickinson's primary materials are Jack L. Capp's *Emily Dickinson's Reading, 1836-1886* (Cambridge, MA: Harvard University Press, 1966) and Carlton Lowenberg's *Emily Dickinson's Textbooks* (Lafayette, LA: Lowenberg, 1986).

Indexes and Concordances
384.   Rosenbaum, S. P. **A Concordance to the Poems of Emily Dickinson**. Ithaca, NY: Cornell University Press, 1964. 899p. (The Cornell Concordances). LC 79-14196. ISBN 0-8161-7830-5.
     Concords the texts in Thomas H. Johnson's edition of *The Poems of Emily Dickinson* (Cambridge: Harvard University Press, 1955). A frequency list is included. Also following the numbering for poems provided by Johnson's standard edition, Fordyce R. Bennett's *A Reference Guide to the Bible in Emily Dickinson's Poetry* (Lanham, MD: Scarecrow Press, 1997) tracks and glosses "words, phrases,

and passages echoed or quoted from the Authorized Version of the Bible in the poems of Emily Dickinson" (p. [xi]).

Journals

385.   **Dickinson Studies: Emily Dickinson (1830-86), U.S. Poet**. Brentwood, MD: Emily Dickinson International Society, 1968-93. 2/yr. ISSN 0164-1492.

Formerly *The Emily Dickinson Bulletin* (1968-78), *Dickinson Studies* ceased in 1993. The slim journal featured brief notes, reviews, and information of interest about activities of the Emily Dickinson International Society and about scholarly activities abroad as reported by correspondents in Japan, Israel, Norway, Brazil, and elsewhere. Articles ranged from reminiscences to close readings and explications of poems, comparisons with such other poets as Robert Frost, and occasional bibliographies, including one identifying Russian studies (in Cyrillic) of Dickinson. *Dickinson Studies*'s irregularly featured "Current Bibliography" last appeared in no. 84 (December 1993). *Dickinson Studies* was indexed in *A&HCI, MHRA*, and *MLA*.

386.   **Emily Dickinson Journal**. Niwot, CO: Emily Dickinson International Society, 1992- . 2/yr. ISSN 1059-6879.

Sponsored by the Emily Dickinson International Society, *Emily Dickinson Journal* intends to create "a forum for scholarship on Dickinson and her relation to the tradition of American poetry and women's literature" (masthead). Six to ten articles and book-review essays in each issue cover the full range of topics in Dickinson—from why she did not title her manuscript fascicles to building a Dickinson hypermedia archive. Particular attention is given to editing Dickinson. Joel Myerson's "Supplement to *Emily Dickinson: A Descriptive Bibliography*," 4.2 (1995): 87-127, usefully extends the coverage of Myerson's standard guide (entry 383). A special conference volume, 5.2 (1996), contains more than 20 papers from the 1995 Emily Dickinson International Society in Innsbruck. *Emily Dickinson Journal* is indexed in *MHRA*.

Patterson's *Author Newsletters and Journals*, pp. 74, 360, describes other previously published journals for Dickinson.

387.   **Single Hound: The Poetry and Image of Emily Dickinson**. Newmarket, NH : Andrew Leibs, 1989-90. 2/yr. ISSN 1044-8934.

The short-lived *Single Hound* published brief articles on the "poetry or life of Emily Dickinson" (masthead). Issues contained interviews and (more often) brief comments on Dickinson by noted writers such as Isaac Asimov, Robert Bly, Maxine Kumin, Richard Wilbur, and Charles Simic. Tantalizingly titled contributions such as "Emily Dickinson in Japan" and "Dickinson and Her First Readers on the 'Breath' of Poetry" in fact amounted to brief reports. Occasional reviews were also featured. Some issues of *Single Hound* were indexed in *MLA*.

Gordon R. Dickson, 1923-

Bibliographies

388.   Thompson, Raymond H. **Gordon R. Dickson: A Primary and Secondary Bibliography**. Boston: G. K. Hall, 1983. 108p. (Masters of Science Fiction and Fantasy). LC 82-12126. ISBN 0-8161-8363-5.

Covering works by and about Dickson, Thompson includes checklists of Dickson's works of fiction, nonfiction, and miscellaneous primary materials, as well as a chronologically arranged listing of briefly annotated entries for 254 secondary works. Entries for primary works give brief bibliographic information and references to reprints and subsequent editions. Appendixes include a description of Dickson's papers in the University of Minnesota libraries (pp. 75-82); a chronological checklist of his novels, collections, and anthologies; and lists of his short stories (arranged by series), translated editions (arranged by language), and about 20 reviews of Dickson's works not listed elsewhere.

Joan Didion, 1934-
Bibliographies

For works by Didion, see *First Printings of American Authors,* vol. 2, p. 131. See *Bibliography of American Fiction, 1919-1988,* pp. 150-51, for Jean W. Cash's checklist of works by and about Didion. See C. Barry Chabot's summary biography, critical assessment of major works, and selected primary and secondary bibliography for Didion in McCaffery's *Postmodern Fiction: A Bio-Bibliographical Guide,* pp. 335-37.

Benjamin Disraeli, 1804-1881
Bibliographies

389.   Stewart, R. W. **Benjamin Disraeli: A List of Writings by Him and Writings About Him, with Notes.** Metuchen, NJ: Scarecrow Press, 1972. 278p. (Scarecrow Author Bibliographies, no. 7). LC 72-3906. ISBN 0-8108-0489-1.

Stewart describes Disraeli's works, including his separate publications; contributions to books; speeches, collected editions, edited works, and miscellaneous works; and attributed works, among others. Entries give brief bibliographic information, physical descriptions, publishing histories, references to later editions, and cross-references to standard bibliographies, such as Michael Sadlier's *XIX Century Fiction: A Bibliographical Record Based on His Own Collection* (1951; reprint New York: Cooper Square, 1969). In addition, Stewart arranges entries (mostly unannotated) for about 1,000 works about Disraeli in sections for books, articles, reviews, dissertations, creative works (novels, plays, and poems about Disraeli), and other materials. Index headings reference topics related to Disraeli's life. Disraeli's manuscripts are described in *Index of English Literary Manuscripts,* IV, pt. 1:743-56. R. W. Stewart's *Disraeli's Novels Reviewed, 1826-1968* (Metuchen, NJ: Scarecrow, 1975) reprints early notices and commentaries on Disraeli's works. Also for a bibliography of works by and about Disraeli, see *NCBEL,* III, pp. 771-79. Research on Disraeli is reviewed by Curtis Dahl in Stevenson's *Victorian Fiction,* pp. 21-43; and by Dahl in Ford's *Victorian Fiction,* pp. 21-27.

Journals

See Patterson's *Author Newsletters and Journals,* p. 95, for previously published journals for Disraeli.

Thomas Dixon, Jr., 1864-1946
Bibliographies

See *Bibliography of American Fiction, 1866-1918,* pp. 153-54, for Philip B. Eppard's checklist of works by and about Dixon. Dixon's manuscripts are listed in Robbins' *American Literary Manuscripts,* p. 90.

Henry Austin Dobson, 1840-1921
Bibliographies

390.   Dobson, Alban. **A Bibliography of the First Editions of Published and Privately Printed Books and Pamphlets by Austin Dobson.** London: The First Edition Club, 1925. 88p. LC 26-13772.

Also available in a reprinted edition (New York: Burt Franklin, 1970), Dobson chronologically arranges full descriptions of his father's separate works published from 1872 to 1923. Entries give title-page transcriptions, physical sizes, collations, descriptions of paper and bindings, British Museum shelf marks, and notes on variants and reprintings. Unindexed. Francis Edwin Murray's *A Bibliography of Austin Dobson* (Derby: Frank Murray, 1900) remains useful for bibliographic information on Dobson's edited works, contributions to books, and prose and verse contributions to periodicals through 1899. Also for a bibliography of works by and about Dobson, see *NCBEL,* III, pp. 1427-28. Criticism and reviews of Dobson's works in selected periodicals are identified in Wells' *The Literary Index to American Magazines, 1850-1900*, pp. 114-15.

E(dgar) L(awrence) Doctorow, 1931-
Bibliographies
391. Tokarczyk, Michelle M. **E. L. Doctorow: An Annotated Bibliography**. New York: Garland, 1988. 132p. (Garland Reference Library of the Humanities, vol. 811). LC 88-16106. ISBN 0-8240-7246-4.

Covers works by and about Doctorow. Part I gives brief bibliographic data (with selective descriptions of contents) for first appearances of Doctorow's works in sections for books, short fiction, political and cultural criticism, and literary essays. Part II provides annotated entries for works about Doctorow in sections for books (nine items), articles, dissertations (five items), interviews, book reviews, and film adaptations and film reviews. International critical coverage includes non-English language studies. Also contains a chronology and an annotated list of background materials on the Rosenberg case. Separate name and title indexes. Also for works by Doctorow, see *First Printings of American Authors*, vol. 1, pp. 97-98. See *Bibliography of American Fiction, 1919-1988*, p. 152, for Tokarczyk's checklist of works by and about Doctorow. See David S. Gross' summary biography, critical assessment of major works, and selected primary and secondary bibliography for Doctorow in McCaffery's *Postmodern Fiction: A Bio-Bibliographical Guide*, pp. 339-42.

Mary Abigail Dodge (Gail Hamilton), 1833-1896
Bibliographies
For works by Dodge, see *Bibliography of American Literature*, vol. 2, pp. 455-63. Dodge's contributions to selected periodicals and reviews of Dodge's works are identified in Wells' *The Literary Index to American Magazines, 1850-1900*, p. 116. Dodge's manuscripts are listed in Robbins' *American Literary Manuscripts*, p. 91.

Mary (Elizabeth) Mapes Dodge, 1831-1905
Bibliographies
For works by Dodge, see *Bibliography of American Literature*, vol. 2, pp. 464-73. Dodge's contributions to selected periodicals and reviews of Dodge's works are identified in Wells' *The Literary Index to American Magazines, 1850-1900*, pp. 116-17. Dodge's manuscripts are listed in Robbins' *American Literary Manuscripts*, p. 91. See *Bibliography of American Fiction, 1866-1918*, pp. 154-55, for Carol Acree and Jerome Griswold's checklist of works by and about Dodge.

Charles Lutwidge Dodgson (Lewis Carroll), 1832-1898
Bibliographies
392. Fordyce, Rachel. **Lewis Carroll: A Reference Guide**. Boston: G. K. Hall, 1988. 160p. (A Reference Guide to Literature). LC 88-16527. ISBN 0-8161-8925-0.

A selective guide to works by and about Carroll. Fordyce separately lists Carroll's works chronologically and alphabetically arranges annotated entries for 978 books, articles, dissertations, reviews, and other works about Carroll published since 1950 as well as selected earlier works, with brief critical annotations. A thorough index includes headings for primary works as well as for specific topics, such as "chess," "death as a theme," "fantasy," and "letters." No headings are included for bibliographies, handbooks, indexes, and similar research aids. More comprehensive in critical coverage (and subject indexing) but for a more limited period, Edward Guilliano's *Lewis Carroll: An Annotated International Bibliography, 1960-77* (Charlottesville, VA: Published for the Bibliographical Society of the University of Virginia and the Lewis Carroll Society of North America by the University Press of Virginia, 1980) describes reference works and bibliographies, biographies and critical studies, and miscellaneous writings about Carroll in all languages. Also for a bibliography of works by and about Carroll, see *NCBEL*, III, pp. 977-80.

393. Williams, Sidney Herbert, and Falconer Madan. **The Lewis Carroll Handbook**. Revised by Roger Lancelyn Green; further revised by Denis Crutch. Folkestone: Dawson, 1979. 340p. LC 79-323055. ISBN 0-7129-0906-0.

In this standard guide to Lewis Carroll's primary works, Williams and Madan give separate, chronologically arranged listings for Carroll's manuscripts, editions, and contributions to books and journals dating from 1845 through 1898 and for editions of *Alice's Adventures in Wonderland, Through the Looking-Glass,* and other works published from 1898 through 1978. Entries supply full bibliographic descriptions, including title-page transcriptions, contents, physical descriptions, and publishing histories. In addition, Williams and Madan describe about 200 biographical and critical works about Carroll. Also bibliographically useful are Selwyn H. Goodacre and Justin G. Schiller's *Alice's Adventures in Wonderland: An 1865 Printing Re-described and Newly Identified as the Publisher's 'File Copy': With a Revised and Expanded Census of the Suppressed 1865 'Alice' . . . To Which Is Added, a Short-Title Index Identifying and Locating the Original Preliminary Drawings by John Tenniel for Alice and Looking Glass* (New York: Privately printed for the Jabberwock, 1990); and Jeffrey Stern's *Lewis Carroll's Library: A Facsimile Edition of the Catalogue of the Auction Sale Following C. L. Dodgson's Death in 1898, with Facsimiles of Three Subsequent Bookseller's Catalogues Offering Books from Dodgson's Library* (Silver Spring, MD: Lewis Carroll Society of North America, 1981). Carroll's manuscripts are described in *Index of English Literary Manuscripts*, IV, pt. 1:395-420. Other useful bibliographies of Carroll's primary materials include Robert N. Taylor, Roy Flukinger, John O. Kirkpatrick, and Cinda Ann May's *Lewis Carroll at Texas: The Warren Weaver Collection and Related Dodgson Materials at the Harry Ransom Humanities Research Center* (Austin, TX: Harry Ransom Research Center, University of Texas at Austin, 1985), which partially catalogs materials at Texas, including printed works, manuscripts, and photographs; and Charles C. Lovett's *Lewis Carrol's Alice: An Annotated Checklist of the Lovett Collection* (Westport, CT: Meckler, 1990).

Indexes and Concordances

394. Preston, Michael J. **A Concordance to the Verse of Lewis Carroll**. New York: Garland, 1985. 344p. (Garland Reference Library of the Humanities, vol. 485). LC 83-49329. ISBN 0-8240-8982-0.

Based on the texts included in *The Humorous Verse of Lewis Carroll* (New York: Dover, 1960), which reprints the texts on *The Collected Verse of Lewis Carroll* (New York: Macmillan, 1933), the concordance cites pages, poems, and lines and provides context lines. Appends a word-frequency table and a reverse index of compound words.

395. Preston, Michael J. **A KWIC Concordance to Lewis Carroll's Alice's Adventures in Wonderland and Through the Looking-Glass**. New York: Garland, 1986. 628p. (Garland Reference Library of the Humanities, vol. 676). LC 86-9965. ISBN 0-8240-9914-1.

Concords the texts of Donald J. Gray's edition of *Alice's Adventures in Wonderland* and *Through the Looking-Glass and What Alice Found There* (New York: Norton, 1971); and Martin Gardner's *The Wasp in a Wig: A "Suppressed" Episode of "Through the Looking-Glass and What Alice Found There"* (New York: Potter, 1977). Appendixes include frequency lists and reverse, multiword, text-ordered, and italicized-word KWIC lists. More specialized indexing of a selection of Carroll's texts is provided by Charles A. Miller's *Isn't That Lewis Carroll?: A Guide to the Most Mimsy Words and Frabjous Quotations in Lewis Carroll's Alice's Adventures in Wonderland, Through the Looking-Glass, and The Hunting of the Snark* (New Market, VA: Trackaday, 1984), which is an index and dictionary of about 1,000 words and phrases from these works.

Journals

396. **Jabberwocky: The Journal of the Lewis Carroll Society.** Swadlincote, Derbyshire: Lewis Carroll Society, 1969-. Irregular. ISSN 0305-8182.

Critical studies in *Jabberwocky* address the larger issue of the fairy tale as literature as well as particular aspects of Carroll's works, particularly Carroll's sources. Typical contributions include "Dantean Allusions in Wonderland," which traces Carroll's uses of Dante; and "The Love-Gift of a Fairy Tale," which examines Carroll's works from the perspective of Bruno Bettelheim's *Uses of Enchantment*. Other articles have described previously unknown Carroll documents, illustrations, and publication histories. Issues also publish book reviews. To date *Jabberwocky* is indexed in *MLA* to 19 (1991).

See Patterson's *Author Newsletters and Journals*, pp. 96-97, for previously published journals for Carroll.

J(ames) P(atrick) Donleavy, 1926-

Bibliographies

For works by Donleavy, see *First Printings of American Authors*, vol. 2, pp. 133-35. Donleavy's manuscripts are listed in Robbins' *American Literary Manuscripts*, p. 92. See *Bibliography of American Fiction, 1919-1988*, pp. 153-54, for William E. Grant's checklist of works by and about Donleavy.

John Donne, 1572-1631

Bibliographies

397. Keynes, Geoffrey. **A Bibliography of Dr. John Donne, Dean of St. Paul's.** 4th ed. Oxford: Clarendon Press, 1973. 400p. LC 73-163884. ISBN 0-1981-8155-8.

First published in 1914 and revised and enlarged in 1932 and 1958, Keynes provides full bibliographic descriptions for Donne's prose and poetical works (including collections, selections, translations, and musical settings) as well as Walton's *Life of Donne*. Entries give facsimiles of title pages, collations, contents, physical descriptions, publishing histories, copy locations, and references to standard bibliographies, such as *STC*. Appendixes describe works by John Donne the younger, books dedicated to Donne, books in his library, images of Donne (portraits, miniatures, statues, and the like), and list selectively annotated entries for about 2,400 works about Donne published from 1594 through 1971. Keynes' coverage of early commentaries and criticisms on Donne is unique. For a bibliography of works by and about Donne, see *NCBEL*, I, pp. 1169-86. Donne's manuscripts are described in *Index of English Literary Manuscripts*, I, pt. 1:243-564, 566-68. Modern Donne scholarship is described in Roberts' guide (entry 398).

398. Roberts, John R. **John Donne: An Annotated Bibliography of Modern Criticism, 1912-1967.** Columbia, MO: University of Missouri Press, 1973. 323p. LC 72-93760. ISBN 0-8262-0136-9.

This is continued by:

398.1. Roberts, John R. **John Donne: An Annotated Bibliography of Modern Criticism, 1968-1978.** Columbia, MO: University of Missouri Press, 1982. 434p. LC 82-1849. ISBN 0-8262-0364-7.

Roberts' volumes are complementary. The first volume chronologically arranges annotated entries for 1,280 works about Donne through 1967. The 1982 edition chronologically arranges 1,044 entries through 1978. Coverage is comprehensive, although Roberts excludes unpublished dissertations. Annotations are thorough and descriptive. Significant studies and introductions in editions are described in detail. An excellent separate subject index offers topical access. Research on Donne is reviewed by W. Milgate in Dyson's *English Poetry*, pp. 40-59.

Dictionaries, Encyclopedias, and Handbooks

399.   Ray, Robert H. **A John Donne Companion**. New York: Garland, 1990. 414p. (Garland Reference Library of the Humanities, vol. 1070). LC 90-31981. ISBN 0-8240-4568-8.

Ray's detailed and critical entries offer excellent introductions and explications to some of the most important and well-known works of poetry and prose in English literature as well as accurate factual information about a wide range of elements related to Donne's life and times. Entries cover classical, Biblical, and historical allusions in Donne's works; place names; writers who influenced Donne (such as Aristotle, St. Augustine, and Calvin) and others who were his associates and contemporaries (such as Joseph Hall, Ben Jonson, and Francis Bacon); important critical concepts related to Donne, such as "New Philosophy" and "Dissociation of Sensibility"; and obscure or difficult words from Donne's poetic or colloquial vocabularies. The summary and critical analysis of "The Canonization" extends to four pages; the difficult poem, "Air and Angels," receives several paragraphs. In addition to a brief review of reference resources for research on Donne, a chronology of Donne's life, a short biography, and a checklist of his works, Ray's handbook provides an extensive, classified secondary bibliography.

Indexes and Concordances

400.   Combs, Homer Carroll, and Zay Rusk Sullens. **A Concordance to the English Poems of John Donne**. Chicago: Packard, 1940. 418p. LC 41-473.

Combs and Sullens concord the text of H. J. C. Grierson's revised one-volume edition of *The Poetical Works of John Donne* (London: Oxford University Press, 1929).

401.   Reeves, Troy D. **An Annotated Index to the Sermons of John Donne**. Salzburg: Institut fur Anglistik und Amerikanistik, Universitat Salzburg, 1979-81. 3 vols. (Salzburg Studies in English Literature. Elizabethan & Renaissance Studies, vol. 95). LC 80-515570.

Intended to complement the coverage of Combs and Sullens' concordance to Donne's poems (entry 400), Reeves indexes Donne's references to the Bible (based on the Authorized Version); proper names, including the names of Biblical, classical, and historical real and fictional persons and places, such as Cain, Aristotle, St. Jerome, Calvin, the Red Sea, Rome, and London; and a full range of detailed topics, such as "love," "sin," "punishment," and "sex." Entries reference volumes and pages of the text of George R. Potter and Evelyn M. Simpson's 10-volume edition of *The Sermons of John Donne* (Berkeley, CA: University of California Press, 1953-1962).

Journals

402.   **John Donne Journal: Studies in the Age of Donne**. Raleigh, NC: John Donne Society, 1982-. 2/yr. ISSN 0738-9655.

Articles in *John Donne Journal* mainly offer comments on specific works by Donne or his major contemporaries. Critical approaches are typically close readings or bibliographic and textual investigations of particular problems. The articles "Riders to the West: 'Good Friday, 1613' " and "A Note on the 1649/1650 Editions on Donne's *Poems*" are indicative of the ten to twelve articles that appear in each issue. Bibliographic articles such as John T. Shawcross's "Some Further Early Allusions to Donne," 10.1-2 (1991): 75-78, usefully update the standard bibliographies. Articles on George Herbert, Richard Crashaw, Robert Herrick, Aurelian Townshend, Andrew Marvell, Abraham Cowley, Philip Sidney, Thomas Carew, Edmund Spenser, and others also appear. In addition, occasional special issues (often double issues) are devoted to specific subjects: 14 (1995) was titled "New Uses of Biographical and Historical Evidence in Donne Studies"; 11.1-2 (1992) and focused on Donne's sermons; and 9.1 (1990) contained 12 articles on the poem "Air and Angels." Past issues have also included one or more extensive review essays or several book reviews as well as sections of news and announcements about meetings, conferences, publications, calls for papers, and projects in progress. Presently the journal is two years behind in its publication schedule. *John Donne Journal* is indexed in *MHRA* and *MLA*.

Ignatius (Loyola) Donnelly, 1831-1901

Bibliographies

For works by Donnelly see *Bibliography of American Literature*, vol. 2, pp. 474-79. Donnelly's manuscripts are listed in Robbins' *American Literary Manuscripts*, p. 92. Also available is Helen M. White's *Guide to a Microfilm Edition of the Ignatius Donnelly Papers* (St. Paul, MN: Minnesota Historical Society, 1968). See *Bibliography of American Fiction, 1866-1918*, pp. 156-57, for Stephen C. Brennan's checklist of works by and about Donnelly.

H(ilda) D(oolittle Aldington), 1886-1961

Bibliographies

403.   Boughn, Michael. **H. D.: A Bibliography, 1905-1990.** Charlottesville: Published for the Bibliographical Society of the University of Virginia by the University Press of Virginia, 1993. 229p. LC 92-28953. ISBN 0813914124.

Covers works by and about H. D. Part 1 chronologically arranges entries for H. D.'s works in sections for books, pamphlets, and broadsides; contributions to books and pamphlets; contributions to periodicals; translations; and miscellaneous works, such as recordings and musical settings. Data include title-page transcriptions for first and later editions, collations, paginations, contents, binding descriptions, publishing histories, and copy locations. Part 2 chronologically arranges entries for works about H. D. in sections for reviews of H. D.'s works (some 608 entries in subsections for each work); critical articles (307 entries); books and parts of books (246 entries); dissertations and theses; and miscellaneous works and H. D.-iana, including obituaries, photographs, published letters, etc. Indexes of primary titles and names and titles. H. D.'s manuscripts are listed in Robbins' *American Literary Manuscripts*, p. 9. Also useful for works by and about H. D., Susan Stanford Friedman and Rachel Blau DuPlessis' *Signets: Reading H. D.* (Madison, WI: University of Wisconsin Press, 1990) concludes with a checklist of H. D.'s published writings, manuscripts, letters, recordings, and books and articles about her (pp. 455-75). Michael King's *H. D., Woman and Poet* (Orono, ME: National Poetry Foundation, 1986) includes an "Annotated Bibliography of Works About H. D., 1969-1985" (pp. 393-511).

Journals

404.   **H. D. Newsletter.** Dallas, TX: Dallas Institute of the Humanities, 1987-1991. 2/yr. ISSN 1040-4015.

Contributions to this short-lived journal ranged from close readings of H. D.'s poetry to biographical investigations of her Moravian heritage, literary relations with Emily Dickinson, D. H. Lawrence, Ezra Pound, and Richard Aldington, and manuscript and textual studies. Issues also included listings of books, articles, and dissertations. *H. D. Newsletter* was indexed in *MLA*.

Ed(ward Merton) Dorn, 1929-

Bibliographies

405.   Streeter, David. **A Bibliography of Ed Dorn.** New York: The Phoenix Bookshop, 1973. 64p. LC 73-86694.

Streeter gives full bibliographic descriptions (title-page transcriptions, physical descriptions, and publishing histories) for Dorn's books, contributions to books and anthologies, contributions to periodicals, recordings, and ephemera, as well as selected works about Dorn. Also for works by Dorn, see *First Printings of American Authors*, vol. 3, pp. 79-86. Dorn's manuscripts are listed in Robbins' *American Literary Manuscripts*, p. 92. More comprehensive coverage of criticism of

Dorn is included in Fox's *Robert Creeley, Edward Dorn, and Robert Duncan* (entry 323).

John (Roderigo) Dos Passos, 1896-1970
Bibliographies

406. Rohrkemper, John. **John Dos Passos: A Reference Guide**. Boston: G. K. Hall, 1980. 300p. (A Reference Guide to Literature). LC 80-17591. ISBN 0-8161-8105-5.

Superseding Rohrkemper's "Criticism of John Dos Passos: A Selected Checklist," *Modern Fiction Studies* 26 (Fall 1980): 417-30, Rohrkemper includes about 1,700 annotated entries for books, parts of books, journal and newspaper articles, reviews of Dos Passos' works, dissertations, and passing references in general sources about Dos Passos published from 1921 through 1979. The guide's chronological arrangement and useful annotations complement more comprehensive coverage, particularly of non-English language criticisms, that is offered in Sanders' bibliography (entry 407). Indexing is limited to critics and primary titles.

407. Sanders, David. **John Dos Passos: A Comprehensive Bibliography**. New York: Garland, 1987. 511p. (Garland Reference Library of the Humanities, vol. 589). LC 84-48868. ISBN 0-8240-8738-0.

Sanders' bibliography provides separate listings for works by and about Dos Passos. The primary bibliography chronologically arranges 550 entries for Dos Passos' books, contributions to books and periodicals, letters, and holdings in 60 American libraries, including the major collection at the University of Virginia. Coverage of primary materials extends from 1911 through 1975. Full bibliographic descriptions include notes on later editions and translations. The secondary bibliography arranges by formats annotated entries for bibliographies, critical studies in books, journals, and newspapers, dissertations, and book reviews. Identifying criticisms in all languages, coverage extends through 1985. Sanders' coverage of primary materials supersedes Jack Potter's *A Bibliography of John Dos Passos* (1950; reprint Folcroft, PA: Folcroft Library Editions, 1976). Although surpassed by Sanders' in comprehensiveness, Rohrkemper's bibliography (entry 406) remains valuable for its annotations. Also useful for information about primary works, Anne Freudenberg and Elizabeth Fake's *John Dos Passos, Writer and Artist, 1896-1970: A Guide to the Exhibition at the University of Virginia Library, 1975* (Charlottesville, VA: University of Virginia Library, 1975) describes the large collection of Dos Passos' editions, notes, drafts, and typescripts of works, letters, and unpublished works in the Alderman Library. Also for works by Dos Passos, see *First Printings of American Authors*, vol. 1, pp. 99-105. Dos Passos' manuscripts are listed in Robbins' *American Literary Manuscripts*, p. 93. See *Bibliography of American Fiction, 1919-1988*, pp. 155-58, for Richard Layman's checklist of works by and about Dos Passos.

Gavin Douglas, 1475?-1522
Bibliographies

Florence H. Ridley offers a comprehensive guide to Douglas' primary materials with a bibliography of editions and criticism in "Middle Scots Writers" in Severs and Hartung's *A Manual of the Writings in Middle English*, vol. X, pp. 961-1060, 1123-1284. Douglas' manuscripts are also described in *Index of English Literary Manuscripts*, I, pt. 2: 3-5. Scheps and Looney's *Middle Scotts Poets* (entry 716) describes criticism of Douglas. Also for a bibliography of works by and about Douglas, see *NCBEL*, I, pp. 662-64, by Priscilla J. Bawcutt.

James Douglas, 1929-
Bibliographies

King's *Ten Modern Irish Playwrights*, pp. 39-42, gives brief bibliographic information for Douglas' primary works and annotated entries for criticism of Douglas, with a classified list of reviews.

Lloyd C(assel) Douglas, 1877-1951
Bibliographies
> See *Bibliography of American Fiction, 1919-1988*, p. 159, for Deborah Elwell Arfken's checklist of works by and about Douglas. Douglas' manuscripts are listed in Robbins' *American Literary Manuscripts*, p. 93.

(George) Norman Douglas, 1868-1952
Bibliographies
> 408.   Woolf, Cecil. **A Bibliography of Norman Douglas**. London: Rupert Hart-Davis, 1954. 201p. (Soho Bibliographies, no. 6). LC 54-10675.
> Woolf gives complete bibliographic descriptions of Douglas' writings, including books and pamphlets, contributions to books and journals, and translated editions. Coverage extends from 1892 through 1952. This supersedes Edward D. McDonald's *A Bibliography of the Writings of Norman Douglas* (Philadelphia, PA: Centaur Book Shop, 1927). Also for a bibliography of works by and about Douglas, see *NCBEL*, IV, pp. 563-65.

Frederick Douglass, 1817-1895
Bibliographies
> 409.   Petrie, William L. **Bibliography of the Frederick Douglass Library at Cedar Hill**. Fort Washington, MD: Silesia, 1995. 476p. ISBN 1-8871-8800-2.
> Amounts to topically arranged descriptions of more than 2,200 items that comprised Douglass' personal library. Classifies the collection in some 53 broad subjects, of which "well over half (some 1,300)" (p. xvii) of the items fit into five areas: government, literature, religion, biography, and history. Entries give brief bibliographic data, collection shelf marks, and notes on bindings and physical conditions. Separate, similarly formatted sections describe letters in the collection and Douglass' writings, speeches, and correspondence. The main section and the section for letters conclude with separate author listings. Appendixes identify newspapers, magazines, invitations in the collection and list other institutions holding Douglass' materials. Data in the main sections are poorly formatted; camera-ready reproduction is of poor quality; and the volume's original perfect binding is fragile. Contributions by Douglass and criticism and reviews of Douglass' works in selected periodicals are identified in Wells' *The Literary Index to American Magazines, 1850-1900*, p. 118. Douglass' manuscripts are listed in Robbins' *American Literary Manuscripts*, pp. 93-94. Also available are *Calendar of the Writings of Frederick Douglass in the Frederick Douglass Memorial Home, Anacostia, D.C.* (Washington: District of Columbia Historical Records Survey,1940); and *Frederick Douglass: A Register and Index of His Papers in the Library of Congress* (Washington: Library of Congress, 1976). See the review of research by W. Burghardt Turner in Inge, Duke, and Bryer's *Black American Writers*, vol. I, 47-132; and by Mary Kemp Davis in Bain and Flora's *Fifty Southern Writers Before 1900*, pp. 190-204.

Ernest Christopher Dowson, 1867-1900
Bibliographies
> 410.   Cevasco, G. A. **Three Decadent Poets: Ernest Dowson, John Gray, and Lionel Johnson: An Annotated Bibliography**. New York: Garland, 1990. 400p. (Garland Reference Library of the Humanities, vol. 968). LC 89-23712. ISBN 0-8240-3149-0.
> Cevasco provides separate introductions, checklists of major writings (with references to reprintings), and chronologically arranged listings of annotated entries for critical works about Dowson, Gray, and Johnson through 1988. Coverage for Dowson (some 382 works appearing from 1892), for Gray (211 works from 1892), and Johnson (319 works from 1893) is comprehensive, including dissertations and entries in reference sources. Annotations are descriptive. Separate indexes for each writer

offer topical access for names and subjects. Also for a bibliography of works by and about Dowson, see *NCBEL*, III, pp. 624-25. See the review of research by Lionel Stevenson in Faverty's *The Victorian Poets*, pp. 401-403.

Arthur Conan Doyle, 1859-1930

Bibliographies

411.   DeWaal, Ronald Burt. **The World Bibliography of Sherlock Holmes and Dr. Watson: A Classified and Annotated List of Materials Relating to Their Lives and Adventures.** Boston: New York Graphic Society, 1974. 526p. LC 72-80900. ISBN 0-8212-0420-3.

Encyclopedic in comprehensiveness, DeWaal's guide supplies more than 6,000 entries for the full range of primary and secondary materials related (albeit some very distantly) to Doyle's works. Coverage includes about 800 editions of primary works in English and some 1,000 in other languages. In addition to annotated entries for about 2,400 topically arranged critical works, DeWaal identifies works about Sherlockians (such as Isaac Asimov and Harry S. Truman) and their societies; memorials; adaptations for television, film, and ballet; parodies and imitations; and other ana. Manuscripts of Doyle's primary works are also described (pp. 41-45). An appendix identifies Holmes collections (pp. 463-4) and Sherlockian societies. DeWaal's guide is supplemented by:

411.1. DeWaal, Ronald Burt. **International Sherlock Holmes: A Companion Volume to The World Bibliography of Sherlock Holmes and Dr. Watson.** Hamden, CT: Archon Books, 1980. 621p. LC 79-24533.

This includes 6,135 entries for editions of works featuring Sherlock Holmes and also works about them (about 2,000 annotated entries) published from 1971 through 1978. Also useful for descriptions of primary materials, Donald A. Redmond's *A Checklist of the Arthur Conan Doyle Collection in the Metropolitan Toronto Library*, 2d ed. (Toronto: Metropolitan Toronto Library Board, 1977) describes materials in the most substantial institutional collection of Sherlockiana. Descriptions of items in this catalog cross-reference listings in DeWaal's 1974 guide.

412.   Green, Richard Lancelyn, and John Michael Gibson. **A Bibliography of A. Conan Doyle.** New York: Oxford University Press, 1983. 712p. (Soho Bibliographies, no. 23). LC 82-3541. ISBN 0-19-818190-6.

The comprehensive listing of Doyle's primary works, Green and Gibson's guide includes detailed, descriptive entries in separate listings for works of fiction (novels, plays, poetry, collected works, and others), miscellaneous works (such as histories, speeches, and psychic works), minor contributions (prefaces, introductions), and contributions to journals and newspapers. Entries give title-page transcriptions, collations, contents, physical descriptions, and publishing histories, covering English, British Colonial, American, Canadian, and continental editions. In addition, the guide lists biographic and critical materials published from 1882 through 1978. Appendixes list apocryphal and attributed works, musical settings, dramatic adaptations, bibliographies and bibliographical studies, and other works. Additional coverage of Doyle materials is provided in J. F. Whitt's *The Strand Magazine, 1891-1950: A Selective Checklist, Listing All Material Relating to Arthur Conan Doyle, All Stories by P. G. Wodehouse, and a Selection of Other Contributions, Mainly by Writers of Detective, Mystery, or Fantasy Fiction* (London: J. F. Whitt, 1979). Also for a bibliography of works by and about Doyle, see *NCBEL*, III, pp. 1046-49.

Dictionaries, Encyclopedias, and Handbooks

413.   Bunson, Matthew E. **Encyclopedia Sherlockiana: An A-to-Z Guide to the World of the Great Detective.** New York: Macmillan, 1994. 326p. LC 94-10714. ISBN 0-6717-9826-x.

Alphabetically arranged entries for individual works, fictional and real persons, places, things, and events, and other elements in works related to Holmes, including adaptations and parodies. Offers excellent coverage of film and television adaptations as well as actors. Also includes a "Chronology of Sherlockiana," covering real and fictional facts about Doyle, Holmes, and the works and bibliographies of the "published cases" of Holmes (pp. xv-xvii) and "unchronicled cases" (pp. xx-xxi). Appendixes include lists of the "writings" of Holmes, illustrators and artists of the works in the *Strand* and other publications, and film adaptations; give a brief biography of Doyle; and identify some 300 international Holmes societies and selected editions of works by and about Doyle and Holmes. Similarly useful for a "chronological sequence of the published cases" (p. 1) is John Hall's *I Remember the Date Very Well: A Chronology of the Sherlock Holmes Stories of Arthur Conan Doyle* (Ronford: Ian Henry Publications; Studio City, CA: Players Press, 1993).

414. Tracy, Jack. **The Encyclopedia Sherlockiana, or A Universal Dictionary of the State of Knowledge of Sherlock Holmes and His Biographer, John H. Watson, M.D**. Garden City, NY: Doubleday, 1977. 411p. LC 75-13394. ISBN 0-385-03061-4.

Tracy offers an alphabetical listing of about 3,500 entries that identify real and fictional persons, places, and selected subjects, terms, and things in stories featuring Sherlock Holmes. Emphasis on the historical backgrounds of Holmes' adventures makes this, in effect, a guidebook to English society through about 1914. Entries cover Victorian vocabulary and the real and fictional persons, places, and things of Holmes' "life" and times, including Queen Victoria, London, New York, and Scotland Yard. More than 20 pages detail Holmes' personal appearance, disguises, finances, and attitudes. Entries are cross-referenced to individual works. Still cited as authoritative and useful, Orlando Park's *Sherlock Holmes, Esq., and John H. Watson, M.D.: An Encyclopaedia of Their Affairs* (Evanston, IL: Northwestern University Press, 1962) supplies straightforward identifications of persons, places, and things "through the affairs" of Holmes and Watson (p. vii), with brief citations to *The Complete Sherlock Holmes* (New York: Doubleday, Doran, 1931). Tracy's handbook is more comprehensive than Scott R. Bullard and Michael Lee Collins' *Who's Who in Sherlock Holmes* (New York: Taplinger, 1980), which includes about 1,700 entries; and Christopher Redmond's *A Sherlock Holmes Handbook* (Toronto: Simon & Pierre, 1993).

Journals

415. **The Baker Street Journal: The Irregular Quarterly of Sherlockiana**. Hanover, PA: Baker Street Irregulars, 1946-. 4/yr. ISSN 0005-4070.

"Optics and Sherlock Holmes: A Detective's Tool" and "From Baker Street with Love: Being a Study of James Bond and His Illustrious Predecessor" suggest the range of the as many as 10 upbeat scholarly features regularly published in issues of *The Baker Street Journal*. Articles that track particular allusions across the Holmes canon—such as wine, telegrams, or astronomy—are typical. A few bibliographic features have appeared, including John Bennett Shaw's "The Basic Holmesiam Library," new series, 43.4 (December 1993): 224-33. Contributors are listed in "Who Dun It?" "Baker Street Inventory" and "Sherlockian Periodicals Received" provide brief reviews and other information for new books and journals. In addition to letters, obituaries, and news about conferences, papers, and research in progress, a special department recounts activities of worldwide Sherlockian societies. *The Baker Street Journal* is indexed in *AES, AHI, MHRA*, and *MLA*.

Patterson's *Author Newsletters and Journal*, pp. 98-116, describes other previously published and popular journals for Doyle and Sherlockiana.

Margaret Drabble, 1939-

Bibliographies

416.   Packer, Joan Garrett. **Margaret Drabble: An Annotated Bibliography**. New York: Garland, 1988. 189p. (Garland Reference Library of the Humanities, vol. 913). LC 88-23468. ISBN 0-8240-5937-9.

Following a brief checklist of Drabble's novels, short stories, plays, nonfiction and edited works, and reviews and essays (some 221 entries with summaries), Packer arranges annotated entries for more than 300 works about Drabble in sections for bibliographies, critical books and dissertations, articles, and reviews. Annotations are descriptive. Stanton's *A Bibliography of Modern British Novelists*, pp. 181-213, 1082, gives additional coverage of works by and about Drabble, with classified unannotated entries for 122 works by Drabble and 224 works about her, with an addendum.

Joseph Rodman Drake, 1795-1820

Bibliographies

For works by Drake, see *Bibliography of American Literature*, vol. 2, pp. 480-84. Contributions by Drake and criticism and reviews of Drake's works in selected periodicals are identified in Wells' *The Literary Index to American Magazines, 1815-1865*, pp. 45-46; and *The Literary Index to American Magazines, 1850-1900*, p. 120. Drake's manuscripts are listed in Robbins' *American Literary Manuscripts*, p. 94.

Michael Drayton, 1563-1631

Bibliographies

For a bibliography of works by and about Drayton, see *NCBEL*, I, pp. 1065-69. Drayton's manuscripts are described in *Index of English Literary Manuscripts*, I, pt. 2:7-15, 627. See Harner's *Samuel Daniel and Michael Drayton* (entry 336) for criticism of Drayton through 1979. Lists of editions and modern studies of Drayton are also included in the Tannenbaums' *Elizabethan Bibliographies*, vol. 2, and George Robert Guffey's *Elizabethan Bibliographies Supplements*, no. 7. Research on Drayton is reviewed by Richard F. Hardin in Logan and Smith's *The Popular School*, pp. 137-47.

Index

See Donow's *Concordance to the Sonnet Sequences* (entry 337) for a concordance to Drayton's *Idea*.

Dream of the Rood, c. 10th century

Bibliographies

Greenfield and Robinson's *A Bibliography of Publications on Old English Literature to the End of 1972*, pp. 214-17, lists editions, translations, and studies of the Old English *Dream of the Rood*, with citations for reviews.

Theodore Dreiser, 1871-1945

Bibliographies

417.   Boswell, Jeanetta. **Theodore Dreiser and the Critics, 1911-1982: A Bibliography with Selective Annotations**. Metuchen, NJ: Scarecrow, 1986. 305p. (Scarecrow Author Bibliographies, no. 73). LC 85-14405. ISBN 0-8108-1837-x.

Boswell alphabetically arranges 1,708 briefly annotated entries for books, parts of books and collections, articles, reviews of Dreiser's works, and dissertations in English published from 1901 through 1982. The brief annotations are descriptive. Subject indexing under broad topics, such as "biographical and critical studies" and "American life," and individual works without subdivisions make access difficult. Complementing the more comprehensive listings in Pizer's bibliography (entry 418), Boswell's guide is mainly valuable for its annotations.

418.   Pizer, Donald, Richard W. Dowell, and Frederic E. Rusch. **Theodore Dreiser: A Primary Bibliography and Reference Guide**. 2d ed. Boston: G. K. Hall, 1991. 308p. (Reference Guide to Literature). LC 91-25372. ISBN 0-8161-8976-5.

A thorough revision, updating, and expansion of Pizer, Dowell, and Rusch's earlier *Theodore Dreiser: A Primary and Secondary Bibliography* (Boston: G. K. Hall, 1975), this identifies more primary works and offers more details about them as well as extends coverage of Dreiser criticism to 1989 and describes it more specifically. The first part covers writings by Dreiser, giving chronologically arranged descriptions of books, pamphlets, leaflets, and broadsides; collected editions; contributions to books and pamphlets; contributions to periodicals; miscellaneous separate publications (mostly posthumous and translated works); published letters; speeches and interviews; productions and adaptations; and library holdings. Entries for separate editions give title-page transcriptions, pagination, and contents, with limited publication histories, and list subsequent English-language and translated editions. These lists are significantly updated from the 1975 bibliography. Likewise, Pizer, Dowell, and Rusch have identified many more of Dreiser's contributions to periodicals and other publications than in 1975. The second part of the guide, covering criticism, chronologically lists annotated entries for more than 4,300 books, parts of books, journal and newspaper articles, reviews, dissertations, and master's theses, in addition to nonprint and unpublished materials, from 1900 to 1989. Comprehensive international coverage includes non-English-language criticism. Descriptive annotations identify reprints. By comparison, the 1975 bibliography included only about 2,200 mostly unannotated entries. Separate indexes for primary materials and for secondary authors, editors, and translators, and for detailed subjects, including Dreiser's individual works (with topical subheadings), proper names, and topics such as "Chicago, Dreiser's portrayal of" and "Russian criticism" provide solid access. Like their 1975 bibliography, Pizer, Dowell, and Rusch's guide is the most important comprehensive bibliography of works by and about Dreiser, superseding Edward D. McDonald's *A Bibliography of the Writings of Theodore Dreiser* (Philadelphia, PA: Centaur Book Shop, 1928), which described works through 1917; and Hugh C. Atkinson's *Theodore Dreiser: A Checklist* (Kent, OH: Kent State University Press, 1971). Another useful catalog, *Theodore Dreiser Centenary Exhibition* (Philadelphia, PA: University of Pennsylvania, 1971), describes materials in the Theodore Dreiser Collection in the University of Pennsylvania's Charles Patterson Van Pelt Library, which includes manuscripts of books, collected and uncollected writings, drafts, notes, letters, clippings, and scrapbooks. Also for works by Dreiser, see *First Printings of American Authors*, vol. 4, pp. 155-71. Dreiser's manuscripts are listed in Robbins' *American Literary Manuscripts*, p. 94. See *Bibliography of American Fiction, 1866-1918*, pp. 158-62, for Pizer's checklist of works by and about Dreiser. Research on Dreiser is reviewed by Robert W. Elias in Bryer's *Sixteen Modern American Authors*, pp. 123-79; and its supplement by James L. W. West III in Bryer's *Sixteen Modern American Authors: Volume 2: A Survey of Research and Criticism Since 1972*, pp. 120-53.

Dictionaries, Encyclopedias, and Handbooks

419.   Gerber, Philip L. **Plots and Characters in the Fiction of Theodore Dreiser**. Hamden, CT: Archon, 1977. 153p. LC 76-54792. ISBN 0-208-01490-x.

Gerber gives plot summaries for Dreiser's novels and short stories and a separate listing of brief identifications for about 1,000 characters.

Journals

420.   **Dreiser Studies**. Terre Haute, IN: International Dreiser Society 1970-. 2/yr. ISSN 0996-6362.

Formerly *The Dreiser Newsletter* (1970-87), issues of *Dreiser Studies* feature three to six critical studies on specific topics related to Dreiser's life and works, reviews of new publications, and informational notes regarding society membership, Dreiser at conferences and in library collections, forthcoming publications, and other events of interest to Dreiser scholars.. Typical fare includes "Dreiser Looks at Longfellow" and "*Jennie Gerhardt*: A Daughteronomy of Desire." Occasional bibliographic features update the standard guide of Pizer, Dowell, and Rusch (entry 418), such as Shigeo Mizuguchi's "Addenda and Corrigenda to *Theodore Dreiser: A Primary Bibliography and Reference Guide*: English Language Instruction Texts Published in Japan," 25.1 (Spring 1994): 51-52. James M. Hutchinson describes Dreiser materials in "The Marguerite Tjader Collection at the Humanities Research Center," 25.2 (Fall 1994): 36-40. A special double issue in 24.1-2 (Spring-Fall 1993) offers a detailed register of the Theodore Dreiser Papers at the University of Pennsylvania, compiled by Julie Reahard and Lee Ann Draud. The annual "Dreiser Checklist" identifies and describes recent editions and studies, including dissertations. Vol. 26.1 (Spring 1995) provides an index to vols. 1-25. *Dreiser Studies* is indexed in *AHI, MHRA*, and *MLA*.

John Drinkwater, 1882-1937

Bibliographies

421.   Pearce, Michael. **John Drinkwater: A Comprehensive Bibliography of His Works**. New York: Garland, 1977. 157p. (Garland Reference Library of the Humanities, vol. 66). LC 76-24745. ISBN 0-8240-9932-x.

Including some 379 entries, Pearce's guide to Drinkwater's primary materials describes his books, contributions to books and journals, edited works, and films and pageants (for which Drinkwater wrote scripts). Indexes titles and first lines. Pearce's guide is based on the Drinkwater Collection located in the Brotherton Library of the University of Leeds. For a bibliography of works by and about Drinkwater, see *NCBEL*, IV, pp. 263-66.

William Drummond, of Hawthornden, 1585-1649

Bibliographies

For a bibliography of works by and about Drummond, see *NCBEL*, I, pp. 1188-90. Drummond's manuscripts are described in *Index of English Literary Manuscripts*, I, pt. 2:17-47. Robert H. MacDonald describes Drummond's library in *The Library of Drummond of Hawthornden* (Edinburgh: Edinburgh University Press, 1971).

John Dryden, 1631-1700

Bibliographies

422.   Hall, James M. **John Dryden: A Reference Guide**. Boston: G. K. Hall, 1984. 424p. (A Reference Guide to Literature). LC 83-10753. ISBN 0-8161-8088-1.

Presently the most comprehensive guide to Dryden scholarship. Hall chronologically arranges about 2,600 selectively annotated entries for criticisms of Dryden published from 1668 through 1980. Coverage includes books, parts of books, articles, and dissertations in all languages. Annotations are descriptive, although significant works receive extended descriptions. A comprehensive author, title, and subject index gives excellent access. Headings for individual works include detailed topical subheadings. Hall's guide covers more criticism than David J. Latt and Samuel Holt Monk's *John Dryden: A Survey and Bibliography of Critical Studies, 1895-1974* (Minneapolis, MN: University of Minnesota Press, 1976), which briefly describes works about Dryden published from 1895 through 1974 in classified listings for bibliography, editions, biography, general criticism, criticism of nondramatic poems, translations, Dryden's critical writings, drama, and international reputation; and John A. Zamonski's *An Annotated Bibliography of John Dryden: Texts and Studies, 1949-1973* (New York: Garland, 1975), which includes about 1,000 entries. Hall's guide, however, does not completely supersede them. The bibliographies of Latt and Monk and Zamonski remain valuable for their annotations. Research on Dryden's drama is reviewed by H. Neville Davies in Wells' *English Drama*, pp. 150-72. Research on his poetry is reviewed by James Kinsley in Dyson's *English Poetry*, pp. 111-27.

423.   MacDonald, Hugh. **John Dryden: A Bibliography of Early Editions and Drydeniana**. Oxford: Clarendon Press, 1939. 358p. LC 39-21174.

MacDonald describes editions of Dryden's works and commentaries on them published from 1649 through 1767. Separate listings cover Dryden's poems, miscellanies, collected editions of poems, plays, separate prologues and epilogues, collected editions of plays, contributed prologues and epilogues, prose, attributed works, letters, "Drydeniana," and "Poems on Affairs of State." Although its bibliographic descriptions are detailed, the bibliography's strongest features are accounts of printing and publishing histories of Dryden's works. Available in a reprinted edition (London: Dawsons of Pall Mall, 1966). Also for a bibliography of works by and about Dryden, see *NCBEL*, II, pp. 439-63, by John Barnard. Dryden's manuscripts are described in *Index of English Literary Manuscripts*, II, pt. 1:383-428.

Dictionaries, Encyclopedias, and Handbooks
424.   Aden, John M. **The Critical Opinions of John Dryden: A Dictionary**. Nashville, TN: Vanderbilt University Press, 1963. 290p. LC 63-9945.

Topical index of Dryden's critical works. Facilitates access to Dryden's comments regarding such subjects as invention, the epic, Horace, and Shakespeare. Additional coverage of Dryden's criticism is offered by H. James Jensen's *A Glossary of John Dryden's Critical Terms* (Minneapolis, MN: University of Minnesota Press, 1969), which alphabetically arranges a selection of words and phrases in Dryden's critical vocabulary, with explanations and textual references.

Indexes and Concordances
425.   Montgomery, Guy, and Lester A. Hubbard. **Concordance to the Poetical Works of John Dryden**. Berkeley, CA: University of California Press, 1957. 722p. LC 57-12394.

A very primitive index limited to Dryden's poetry, this concords the texts in George R. Noyes' edition of *The Poetical Works of John Dryden*, revised ed. (Boston: Houghton Mifflin, 1950), first published in 1909. Appearances are referenced by work and line, but the line is not quoted. Reprinted (London: Russell & Russell) in 1967. A new concordance based on the University of California Press' standard edition of Dryden's works is needed.

Journals
"Recent Articles" in *The Scriblerian and the Kit Cats* (entry 1084) regularly includes a selection of reviews of studies on Dryden.

W(illiam) E(dward) B(urghardt) DuBois, 1868-1963
Bibliographies
426.   Aptheker, Herbert. **Annotated Bibliography of the Published Writings of W. E. B. DuBois**. Millwood, NY: Kraus-Thomson, 1973. 626p. LC 73-13805.

Aptheker offers detailed summaries of the contents of DuBois' primary works, including 1,975 entries for his writings in magazines and newspapers edited by him or by others; newspaper columns; government publications and proceedings; contributions to books; edited works; and books, pamphlets, and leaflets. Bibliographic description is limited. Emphasis is on DuBois' ideas. An index of proper names includes topical headings for "Jim Crow," "NAACP," and "South Africa." A separate subject index is also included. Bibliographic information for DuBois' publications is included in Partington's bibliography (entry 427).

427.   Partington, Paul G. **W. E. B. DuBois: A Bibliography of His Published Writings**. Revised ed. Whittier, CA: Partington, 1979. 202p. LC 77-154520. ISBN 0-9602538-0-7.
This is supplemented by:

427.1. Partington, Paul G. **W. E. B. DuBois: A Bibliography of His Published Writings: Supplement**. Whittier, CA: Partington, 1984. 20p. ISBN 0-9602538-2-3.
The best bibliography of DuBois' primary materials, Partington gives bibliographic descriptions for DuBois' edited periodicals, newspaper contributions (including columns, letters, bylines, and the like), articles in magazines and newsletters, miscellaneous contributions, translations of DuBois' writings, book reviews, and books. Entries note reprints and translations. The supplement adds materials in the same classifications. Additionally, useful coverage of DuBois' primary materials is provided in Robert W. McDowell's guide to DuBois' papers at the University of Massachusetts, *The Papers of W. E. B. DuBois* (Sanford, NC: Microfilming Corporation of America, 1981). DuBois' manuscripts are also listed in Robbins' *American Literary Manuscripts*, p. 95. A sound listing of works about DuBois is Dan S. Green's "Bibliography of Writings About W. E. B. DuBois," *College Language Association Journal* 20 (1977): 410-21; and in Perry's *The Harlem Renaissance*, pp. 75-77. Research on DuBois is reviewed by W. Burghardt Turner in Inge, Duke, and Bryer's *Black American Writers*, vol. I, pp. 47-132.

Indexes and Concordances

428.   Weinberg, Meyer, ed. **The World of W. E. B. Du Bois: A Quotation Sourcebook**. Westport, CT: Greenwood Press, 1992. 282p. LC 92-15481. ISBN 0-313-28619-1.
Arranges 957 quotations (often extensive) from the full range of DuBois' published and unpublished writings in 20 imaginatively titled (and frequently overlapping) topical sections, including "The Trouble I've Seen" (covering poverty, lynching, Southern courts, and war) and "Reform, Radicalism, and Revolution" and others, such as "Racism" and "Women," whose contents are more readily comprehended. Entries supply full bibliographic citations for reference sources that are appended (p. [261]-263). Excellent index of names, DuBois' works, and more detailed topics.

Alan Dugan, 1923-
Bibliographies
For works by Dugan, see *First Printings of American Authors*, vol. 2, pp. 137-38. Dugan's manuscripts are listed in Robbins' *American Literary Manuscripts*, p. 95.

Augustine Joseph Hickey Duganne, 1823-1884
Bibliographies
For works by Duganne, see *Bibliography of American Literature*, vol. 2, pp. 485-97. Contributions by Duganne and criticism and reviews of Duganne's works in selected periodicals are identified in Wells' *The Literary Index to American Magazines, 1815-1865*, p. 46. Duganne's manuscripts are listed in Robbins' *American Literary Manuscripts*, p. 95.

Paul Laurence Dunbar, 1872-1906
Bibliographies
429.   Metcalf, E. W., Jr. **Paul Laurence Dunbar: A Bibliography**. Metuchen, NJ: Scarecrow Press, 1975. (Scarecrow Author Bibliographies, no. 23). LC 75-14466. ISBN 0-8108-0849-8.

Metcalf chronologically arranges briefly annotated entries in separate listings for works by and about Dunbar. Primary materials listed include Dunbar's novels, poems, short stories, articles, songs, dramatic works, correspondence from Dunbar and miscellanea. Secondary coverage is comprehensive, including books, articles, reviews of Dunbar's works, and significant passing references in general sources, as well as creative works (poems, plays, and songs) and films and radio programs about Dunbar, and correspondence to or about him. Metcalf describes microform collections of Dunbar's papers in the Schomberg Collection of the New York Public Library and in the Paul Laurence Dunbar Papers in the Ohio Historical Society. Indexing is limited to primary titles and personal names. For works by Dunbar, see *Bibliography of American Literature*, vol. 2, pp. 498-505. Dunbar's manuscripts are also listed in Robbins' *American Literary Manuscripts*, pp. 95-96. Additionally, Elli Bambakidis' *The Paul Laurence Dunbar Collection: A Special Collection of Historical Materials at the Dayton & Montgomery County Public Library*, revised ed. (Dayton, OH: Dayton and Montgomery County Public Library, 1995), first published in 1992, describes an important collection of books and manuscripts, with folder-by-folder information. Research on Dunbar is reviewed by Ruth Miller and Peter J. Katopes in Inge, Duke, and Bryer's *Black American Writers*, vol. I, pp. 133-60.

William Dunbar, 1456?-1513?
Bibliographies

Florence H. Ridley offers a comprehensive guide to Dunbar's primary materials with a bibliography of editions and criticism in "Middle Scots Writers" in Severs and Hartung's *A Manual of the Writings in Middle English*, vol. X, pp. 961-1060, 1123-1284. Dunbar's manuscripts are also described in *Index of English Literary Manuscripts*, I, pt. 2:49-67. Scheps and Looney's *Middle Scots Poets* (entry 716) describes criticism of Dunbar. Also for a bibliography of works by and about Dunbar, see *NCBEL*, I, pp. 660-62.

Alice Moore Dunbar-Nelson, 1875-1935
Bibliographies

See *Bibliography of American Fiction, 1866-1918*, pp. 162-63, for Joyce Hope Scott's checklist of works by and about Dunbar-Nelson. Dunbar-Nelson's manuscripts are listed in Robbins' *American Literary Manuscripts*, p. 233.

Robert (Edward) Duncan, 1919-1988
Bibliographies

430. Bertholf, Robert J. **Robert Duncan: A Descriptive Bibliography**. Santa Rosa, CA: Black Sparrow, 1986. 491p. LC 84-16740. ISBN 0-87685-620-2.

Bertholf lists Duncan's primary works, including detailed descriptions in separate listings for books, pamphlets, broadsides, and separate publications; contributions to books; contributions to periodicals; miscellaneous works (such as dust-jacket blurbs, drawings, and Christmas cards); letters; manuscripts; notebooks; translations; and tapes and records. In addition, Bertholf includes listings for 283 critical works about Duncan, biographical notices, photographs, and musical settings of his works. Also for works by Duncan, see *First Printings of American Authors*, vol. 3, pp. 87-99. Also with useful information on Duncan's works is Bertholf's *A Symposium of the Imagination: Robert Duncan in Word and Image* (Buffalo, NY: The Poetry/Rare Books Collection, The University at Buffalo, State University of New York, 1993). Duncan's manuscripts are listed in Robbins' *American Literary Manuscripts*, p. 96. More comprehensive coverage of criticism of Duncan is provided in Fox's *Robert Creeley, Edward Dorn, and Robert Duncan* (entry 323).

William Dunlap, 1766-1839
Bibliographies

431. Wegelin, Oscar. **A Bibliographical Checklist of the Plays and Miscellaneous Writings of William Dunlap (1766-1839).** New York: Charles F. Heartman, 1916. 76p. (Bibliographica Americana, vol. 1). LC 16-24828.

Wegelin gives full bibliographic descriptions of Dunlap's primary materials. More up-to-date coverage of his works is included in Blanck's *Bibliography of American Literature*, vol. 2, pp. 506-518. Contributions by Dunlap and criticism and reviews of Dunlap's works in selected periodicals are identified in Wells' *The Literary Index to American Magazines, 1815-1865*, p. 47. Dunlap's manuscripts are listed in Robbins' *American Literary Manuscripts*, p. 96.

Finley Peter Dunne, 1867-1936
Bibliographies

See *Bibliography of American Fiction, 1866-1918*, pp. 163-64, for William C. Hill's checklist of works by and about Dunne. Dunne's manuscripts are listed in Robbins' *American Literary Manuscripts*, p. 96.

Edward John Moreton Drax Plunkett, 18th Baron Dunsany, 1878-1957
Bibliographies

432. Joshi, S. T., and Darrell Schweitzer. **Lord Dunsany: A Bibliography.** Metuchen, NJ: Scarecrow Press, 1993. 365p. (Scarecrow Author Bibliographies, no. 90). LC 93-8453. ISBN 0-8108-271-4.

Part I covers Dunsany's works in English in sections for books; and contributions to books and periodicals, subarranged for fiction, essays, poetry, plays, book reviews, letters, and miscellany (including 12 chess problems and other items). Entries for 101 books give brief publication data for first and subsequent editions and information about contents; entries for contributed works largely cross-reference the contents information in the first section. Part II identifies non-English-language translations of Dunsany's books and contributed works, with brief bibliographic data and contents. Part III offers briefly and selectively annotated entries for approximately 400 works about Dunsany in sections for general reference works, bibliographies, books about Dunsany (with citations for reviews), criticisms in books and periodicals, theses and dissertations, reviews (sublisted under each of Dunsany's works), and "Unclassifiable Data," including creative works and parodies. Indexes of names, primary titles, and periodical titles. For a bibliography of works by and about Lord Dunsany, see *NCBEL*, III, pp. 1945-48.

Thomas D'Urfey, 1653-1723
Bibliographies

For a bibliography of works by and about D'Urfey, see *NCBEL*, II, pp. 761-64.

Lawrence George Durrell, 1912-1990
Bibliographies

433. Thomas, Alan G., and James A. Brigham. **Lawrence Durrell: An Illustrated Checklist.** Carbondale, IL: Southern Illinois University Press, 1983. 198p. LC 83-6782. ISBN 0-8093-1021-x.

This is a comprehensive listing of Durrell's primary works, including about 1,200 entries that describe Durrell's books; translations; prefaces; contributions to books and periodicals; recordings; musical settings; writings for radio, television, and film; and miscellaneous works (largely edited works, interviews, and biographical and autobiographical materials). Thomas gives full bibliographic descriptions, noting variant and subsequent editions and providing facsimiles of dust jackets. In addition, the work includes brief, descriptively annotated entries for about 500 works about Durrell. Coverage extends through 1981. Indexing is limited to names only. Shelley Cox's *"As Water into Language Flowing"*: *The Lawrence Durrell Papers at Southern Illinois University, Carbondale* (Carbondale, IL: Friends of Morris Library, Southern Illinois University at Carbondale, 1988) also offers useful descriptions of primary materials. For supplemental coverage of Durrell scholarship, researchers should consult Susan Vander Closter's *Joyce Cary and Lawrence Durrell* (entry 434).

434.   Vander Closter, Susan. **Joyce Cary and Lawrence Durrell: A Reference Guide**. Boston: G. K. Hall, 1985. 223p. (A Reference Guide to Literature). LC 85-5609. ISBN 0-8161-8627-8.

Separate, chronologically arranged listings for each writer include annotated entries for secondary materials, covering articles, books, reviews, and dissertations in English and other languages. About 400 entries for Cary range from 1932 through 1981; about 500 for Durrell range from 1937 through 1983. Annotations are evaluative. Significant studies receive extended reviews. Separate author, title, and subjects indexes for each writer. Makinen's *Joyce Cary* (entry 220) offers better coverage of works about Cary. Also for a bibliography of works by and about Durrell, see *NCBEL*, IV, pp. 266-71.

Journals
435.   **Deus Loci: The Laurence Durrell Journal**. New York: International Laurence Durrell Society, 1977-84; new series, 1992-93. Annual. ISSN 0707-9141.

Formerly *Lawrence Durrell Newsletter*, the two published volumes of the new series contained interviews, memorial tributes, seven or eight articles that offered close readings and other critical responses to Durrell's works, selections of poetry by Durrell and others, book reviews, and brief notes and queries. Additionally, the journal initiated a annual bibliography of primary and secondary materials, with volumes covering 1983 to 1985 and 1986 to 1988, respectively, compiled by Grove Koger and Susan S. MacNiven. *Deus Loci* was indexed in *MLA*.

See Patterson's *Author Newsletters and Journals*, p. 111, for previously published journals for Durrell.

John S(ullivan) Dwight, 1813-1893
Bibliographies
Contributions by Dwight and criticism and reviews of Dwight's works in selected periodicals are identified in Wells' *The Literary Index to American Magazines, 1815-1865*, pp. 48-49; and *The Literary Index to American Magazines, 1850-1900*, p. 123. Dwight's manuscripts are listed in Robbins' *American Literary Manuscripts*, p. 97. William G. Heath reviews research on Dwight in Myerson's *The Transcendentalists*, pp. 131-34.

Theodore Dwight, 1764-1846
Bibliographies
For works by Dwight, see *First Printings of American Authors*, vol. 1, pp. 107-108. Dwight's manuscripts are listed in Robbins' *American Literary Manuscripts*, p. 97.

Timothy Dwight, 1752-1817
Bibliographies
For works by Dwight, see *Bibliography of American Literature*, vol. 2, pp. 519-30. Criticism and reviews of Dwight's works in selected periodicals are identified in Wells' *The Literary Index to American Magazines, 1815-1865*, p. 49; and *The Literary Index to American Magazines, 1850-1900*, p. 123. Dwight's manuscripts are listed in Robbins' *American Literary Manuscripts*, p. 97.

John Dyer, 1699-1757
Bibliographies

For a bibliography of works by and about Dyer, see *NCBEL*, II, 545-46. Dyer's manuscripts are described in *Index of English Literary Manuscripts*, III, pt. 1: 341-53.

Wilma Dykeman, 1920-
Bibliographies

For works by Dykeman, see *First Printings of American Authors*, vol. 4, pp. 173-75. Patricia M. Gantt and Chip Jones survey works by and about Dykeman in Bain and Flora's *Contemporary Poets, Dramatists, Essayists, and Novelists of the South*, pp. 128-35.

John Earle, 1601?-1665
Bibliographies

For a bibliography of works by and about Earle, see *NCBEL*, I, pp. 2044-45. Earle's manuscripts are described in *Index of English Literary Manuscripts*, II, pt.1:429-41.

William Eastlake, 1917-
Bibliographies

For works by Eastlake, see *First Printings of American Authors*, vol. 2, p. 139. Eastlake's manuscripts are listed in Robbins' *American Literary Manuscripts*, p. 98. Gerald Haslam surveys works by and about Eastlake in Erisman and Etulain's *Fifty Western Writers*, pp. 89-99.

Richard (Ghormley) Eberhart, 1904-
Bibliographies

436.	Wright, Stuart. **Richard Eberhart: A Descriptive Bibliography, 1921-1987.** Westport, CT: Meckler, 1989. 438p. LC 89-12948. ISBN 0-88736-346-6.

Wright provides detailed descriptions of Eberhart's primary works, including entries in separate listings for 62 separate publications (books, pamphlets, and broadsides); 161 edited works and contributions to books; 859 contributions to periodicals, including juvenilia, poetry, prose, and criticisms; dust-jacket blurbs; interviews with Eberhart and published comments (with descriptions of contents); duplicated copies of typescript manuscripts; disc and tape sound recordings of Eberhart reading his works; unpublished musical settings of Eberhart's poems; translations of Eberhart's works (arranged by language); and miscellaneous works, including a recording of Eberhart reading works of others, a self-portrait, and original quotations on programs. Entries for first American and English editions include illustrations of title and copyright pages and notes on collations, typography, paper, binding, and printing and publication, with locations of copies. Wright's bibliography is based on the "Selected Bibliography" in Joel Roache's *Richard Eberhart: The Progress of an American Poet* (New York: Oxford University Press, 1971), pp. 263-88. Also for works by Eberhart, see *First Printings of American Authors*, vol. 1, pp. 109-13. Eberhart's manuscripts are listed in Robbins' *American Literary Manuscripts*, p. 99.

Maria Edgeworth, 1768-1849
Bibliographies

437.	Slade, Bertha Coolidge. **Maria Edgeworth, 1767-1849: A Bibliographical Tribute.** London: Constable, 1937. 253p. LC 38-6333.

Slade gives full bibliographic descriptions for Edgeworth's primary works, chronologically arranging entries in separate listings for first and variant editions of her books (including translations), contributions to books, and collected editions. In addition to a general index of names and titles, Slade provides an index of printers and publishers. Also for a bibliography of works by and about Edgeworth, see *NCBEL*, III, pp. 665-70. Edgeworth's manuscripts are described in *Index of English Literary Manuscripts*, IV, pt. 1:757-67. Wells' *The Literary Index to American Magazines, 1815-1865*, p. 49, identifies criticism and reviews of Edgeworth's works in selected periodicals. Research on Edgeworth is reviewed by James F. Kilroy in Finneran's *Anglo-Irish Literature*, pp. 25-30.

Walter D(umaux) Edmonds, 1903-
Bibliographies
See *Bibliography of American Fiction, 1919-1988*, pp. 160-61, for W. A. Wehmeyer's checklist of works by and about Edmonds. Edmonds' manuscripts are listed in Robbins' *American Literary Manuscripts*, pp. 99-100.

Jonathan Edwards, 1703-1758
Bibliographies
438.   Johnson, Thomas H. **The Printed Writings of Jonathan Edwards, 1703-1758: A Bibliography**. Princeton, NJ: Princeton University Press, 1940. LC 40-32578.

The standard listing of Edwards' primary works, including detailed descriptions of 346 first and subsequent editions, reprintings, and variants, as well as translations of Edwards' works. Coverage extends through 1925. Entries provide transcriptions of title pages and collations and locate copies in about 100 libraries. Also available in a reprinted edition (New York: B. Franklin, 1970). Edwards' manuscripts are listed in Robbins' *American Literary Manuscripts*, p. 100.

439.   Lesser, M. X. **Jonathan Edwards: A Reference Guide**. Boston: G. K. Hall, 1981. 421p. (A Reference Guide to Literature). LC 80-28540. ISBN 0-8161-7837-2.
Lesser extends coverage of works about Edwards in:

439.1.   Lesser, M. X. **Jonathan Edwards: An Annotated Bibliography, 1979-1993**. Westport, CT: Greenwood, 1994. 189p. (Bibliographies and Indexes in Religious Studies, no. 30). LC 94-31540. ISBN 0-313-29237-X.
Lesser's 1981 volume chronologically arranges annotated entries for about 1,800 secondary works on Edwards published from 1729 through 1978. The 1994 updating chronologically arranges an additional 700 entries. Coverage includes books, articles, dissertations, reviews of secondary works, and fugitive references and reprints. Extensive introductions in both volumes review Edwards' critical reputation and offer evaluations of major critical studies and biographies. Descriptive and nonevaluative annotations cross-reference other studies and note reprints. Comprehensive indexes provide subject access, consolidating subheadings under Edwards' name for critical forms (such as bibliographies, biographies, and dissertations); names of individual authors (Thomas Hooker, Nathaniel Hawthorne, Harriet Beecher Stowe, and Albert Einstein, for examples); and an extensive variety of topics, ranging from "absurdist view," "antichrist," "infant damnation," and "Jungian analysis" to the more traditional "imagery," "rhetoric," and "style." Additionally, Nancy Manspeaker's *Jonathan Edwards: Bibliographical Synopses* (Lewiston, NY: E. Mellen, 1981) selectively describes books, articles, and dissertations about Edwards from the eighteenth century through the present. Research on Edwards is reviewed by Everett Emerson in Harbert and Rees' *Fifteen American Authors Before 1900*, pp. 230-49; and by Daniel B. Shea, Jr., in Emerson's *Major Writers of Early American Literature*, pp. 179-204.

Edward Eggleston, 1837-1902
Bibliographies

For works by Eggleston, see *Bibliography of American Literature*, vol. 3, pp. 1-15. Eggleston's contributions to and reviews of Eggleston's works in selected periodicals are identified in Wells' *The Literary Index to American Magazines, 1850-1900*, pp. 124-25. Eggleston's manuscripts are listed in Robbins' *American Literary Manuscripts*, p. 100. See *Bibliography of American Fiction, 1866-1918*, pp. 165-66, for Tony Trigilio's checklist of works by and about Eggleston.

Larry Eigner, 1927-
Bibliographies

440. Leif, Irving P. **Larry Eigner: A Bibliography of His Works**. Metuchen, NJ: Scarecrow Press, 1989. 239p. (Scarecrow Author Bibliographies, no. 84). LC 88-27017. ISBN 0-8108-2210-5.

A listing of Eigner's primary works published through 1986, Leif's guide chronologically arranges descriptions of books and broadsides (52 entries from 1941 through 1986), contributions to books, periodical appearances (464 entries from 1937 through 1986), translations of Eigner's works, and recordings by Eigner. Entries for books include data for collations, bindings and dust jackets, contents, and notes on printing and publishing. A separate index for primary works includes references for forms (such as letters, interviews, and broadsides).

George Eliot (Mary Ann, later Marian, Evans), 1819-1880
Bibliographies

441. Fulmer, Constance Marie. **George Eliot: A Reference Guide**. Boston: G. K. Hall, 1977. 247p. (A Reference Guide to Literature). LC 76-58431. ISBN 0-8161-7859-3.

Fulmer provides a chronologically arranged listing of annotated entries for about 1,200 critical studies of Eliot published from 1858 through 1971, including books, articles, reviews, and dissertations both in English and other languages. The earliest entries identify anonymous reviews and notices. Annotations are selective, brief, and descriptive. Many merely cross-reference the listing for Eliot in the *NCBEL*, pp. 899-911, and offer neither detail nor guidance. Fulmer provides separate indexes, on the other hand, that offer solid access to critics, primary titles, secondary titles, and a variety of subjects, with headings for critical forms (bibliography, biography, dissertations); individual authors for "comparative studies" (Dickens, Emerson, Tolstoy); and topics ("morality," "theories of art").

442. Pangallo, Karen L. **George Eliot: A Reference Guide, 1972-1987**. Boston: G. K. Hall, 1990. 300p. (A Reference Guide to Literature). LC 89-35908. ISBN 0-8161-8973-0.

Complementing the coverage of Fulmer's guide (entry 441), Pangallo's bibliography chronologically arranges descriptively annotated entries for about 1,000 works about Eliot appearing from 1972 through 1987. Coverage includes books, articles, and dissertations, with a special emphasis on critical, biographical, and bibliographic analyses and feminist studies. Annotations are descriptive. Indexes for primary titles (with topical subheadings), critics, secondary titles, and subjects offer excellent access. A more selective guide, George Levine's *An Annotated Critical Bibliography of George Eliot* (Brighton: Harvester, 1988) topically arranges briefly annotated entries for critical studies of Eliot from 1945 through 1985. Also useful for research, William Baker's *The George Eliot-George Lewes Library: An Annotated Catalogue of Their Books at Dr. Williams's Library* (New York: Garland, 1977) and *The Libraries of George Eliot and George Henry Lewes* (Victoria, BC: University of Victoria, 1981) describe some 1,000 items in the libraries of George Eliot and George Henry Lewes (works ranging from science and medicine—about 50 percent of the collection—to modern and classical literature, philosophy, history, and biography) now located in Dr. Williams' Library, London. No standard guide to Eliot's primary works now exists. For a bibliography of works by and about Eliot, see *NCBEL*, III, pp. 899-912. Eliot's manuscripts are described in *Index of English Literary Manuscripts*, IV, pt. 1:769-82. Research on Eliot is reviewed by U. C. Knoepflmacher in Ford's *Victorian Fiction*, pp. 234-73; Jerome Beaty in Dyson's *The English Novel*, pp. 246-63; and W. J. Harvey in Stevenson's *Victorian Fiction*, pp. 294-323.

Dictionaries, Encyclopedias, and Handbooks

443. Hands, Timothy. **A George Eliot Chronology**. Boston: G. K. Hall, 1989. 195p. LC 88-1791. ISBN 0-8161-8983-8.

A volume in the "Macmillan Author Chronologies," Hands' chronology uses Eliot's fictional, critical, and autobiographical writings as well as standard biographical sources to provide a timetable to her life. Entries cross-reference resources that include J. W. Cross's three-volume *George Eliot's Life as Related in Her Letters and Journals* (Edinburgh: W. Blackwood and Sons, 1885), Gordon S. Haight's "standard and comprehensive" (p. xi) *George Eliot: A Biography* (Oxford: Oxford University Press, 1968) and the nine-volume *The George Eliot Letters* (New Haven, CT: Yale University Press, 1954-1978), and Thomas Pinney's *Essays of George Eliot* (London: Routledge and Kegan Paul, 1963). Hands emphasizes details of Eliot's reading, her thoughts on her career, and views on such topics as religion, politics, social reform, and the position of women. A cumulative index references names, works, and selected subjects, offering convenient access to information on Eliot's reading of classical authors and her interest in Italy. Also useful, Graham Handley's *George Eliot: A Guide Through the Critical Maze* (Bristol: Bristol Press, 1990) gives bibliographic survey essays on Eliot's modern critical reputation and biographical and critical scholarship (including feminist and other approaches).

444. Hartnoll, Phyllis. **Who's Who in George Eliot**. New York: Taplinger, 1977. 183p. LC 76-39621. ISBN 0-8008-8273-3.

Hartnoll's dictionary offers an alphabetically arranged listing of characters in 10 works by Eliot. Entries identify and describe the characters and locate them in the texts. Extensive analyses of such characters as Maggie Tulliver and Dorothea Brooke are included. A separate listing covers Eliot's animal characters. An appendix lists the characters by the individual novels, citing initial appearances by books and chapters. For minor characters Mudge and Sears' dictionary (entry 445) is more comprehensive.

445. Mudge, Isadore G., and M. E. Sears. **A George Eliot Dictionary: The Characters and Scenes of the Novels, Stories, and Poems Alphabetically Arranged**. London: Routledge, 1924. 260p. LC 24-20006.

Mudge and Sears supply synopses of Eliot's novels, stories, and poems and a dictionary of both historical and fictional characters, places, and things that appear in her works, with locations by work and chapter. Listings are most extensive for rivers, churches, convents, gates, hospitals, markets, squares, and so forth, both in domestic and exotic settings (in Florence, for example). In addition, Mudge and Sears include a list of books mentioned in Eliot's novels and stories and an index of real and fictional names. A useful supplement to Hartnoll's dictionary (entry 444).

446. Pinion, F. B. **A George Eliot Companion: Literary Achievement and Modern Significance**. Totowa, NJ: Barnes & Noble, 1981. 277p. LC 81-8044. ISBN 0-389-20208-8.

Pinion provides a useful guide to Eliot's life and works, including a brief chronology of Eliot's life and career; surveys of the individual works; lists of key people and places in the works; a glossary of Eliot's vocabulary; and a selected bibliography of primary and secondary materials. Maps and other illustrations are included.

Journals

447.   **George Eliot-George Henry Lewes Studies.** DeKalb, IL: Northern Illinois University, 1982- . 2/yr. ISSN 0953-0754.

Formerly *George Eliot-George Henry Lewes Newsletter* (1982-91), semiannual issues (more often annual volumes) of *George Eliot-George Henry Lewes Studies* contain as many as 10 substantial critical, biographical, and bibliographic contributions on George Eliot and Lewes. Particular attention has focused on George Eliot's influences, sources, and literary relations with other writers, including the likes of Theocritus, Goethe, Shakespeare, Cervantes, the Brontes, Robert Louis Stevenson, George Gissing, and Herbert Spencer, among others. Other articles have described previously unpublished primary materials. A double volume, 26-27 (September 1994): 36-81, presents a roundtable discussion on the BBC television adaptation of *Middlemarch*. Volumes publish a regular bibliographic feature, "George Eliot Articles," a review of current scholarship, as well as a selection of book reviews. *George Eliot-George Henry Lewes Studies* is indexed in *MLA*.

448.   **The George Eliot Review: Journal of the George Eliot Fellowship.** Coventry: George Eliot Fellowship, 1970-. Annual. ISSN 1358-345x.

Typical scholarly contributions to *The George Eliot Review*, formerly *The George Eliot Fellowship Review* (1970-91), include "*Romola* on the American Stage" and "Maggie's Sisters: Feminist Readings of *The Mill on the Floss*." Sponsored by the George Eliot Fellowship, issues provide close, interpretive readings of works; studies of images and themes (such as marriage, pilgrimage, the education of women), techniques (such as the use of metaphor), and characters; and discussions of literary relations, sources, and influences (including Eliot's uses of Greek tragedy, medieval saints' lives, and Chaucer). Other articles have described primary materials related to Eliot as well as biographical problems. Reviews and discussions of recent media adaptations of Eliot's works are now commonplace. Volumes also include book reviews. *The George Eliot Review* is indexed by *AES* and *MLA*.

T(homas) S(tearns) Eliot, 1888-1965

Bibliographies

449.   Gallup, Donald C. **T. S. Eliot: A Bibliography.** Revised and expanded ed. New York: Harcourt, Brace & World, 1969. 414p. LC 73-78883.

First published in 1947 and revised in 1952, this is the standard listing of Eliot's primary works, including full bibliographic descriptions of Eliot's books and pamphlets; edited works and contributions to books and pamphlets; anthologies and collections reprinting Eliot's poems and essays; contributions to periodicals (some 681 in number); and translations of his works. Appendixes list course syllabi, leaflets, broadsides, international editions, musical settings and recordings, and books announced but not published. Entries give title-page transcriptions, contents, physical descriptions, and publishing histories. Eliot's manuscripts are listed in Robbins' *American Literary Manuscripts*, p. 101. Also useful for coverage of Eliot's primary materials, Donald Gallup's *A Catalogue of English and American First Editions of Writings by T. S. Eliot, Exhibited in the Yale University Library, February 22 to March 20, 1937* (Portland, ME: Southworth-Anthoensen, 1937) describes materials at Yale University. Alexander Sackton's *The T. S. Eliot Collection of the University of Texas at Austin* (Austin, TX: Humanities Research Center, University of Texas at Austin, 1975) describes books, pamphlets, anthologies and collected editions, published letters, translations, correspondence, literary manuscripts, and works about Eliot in the University of Texas' Harry Ransom Humanities Research Center.

450. Knowles, Sebastian D. G., and Scott A. Leonard. **T. S. Eliot: Man and Poet, Volume 2: An Annotated Bibliography of a Decade of T. S. Eliot Criticism, 1977-1986**. Orono, ME: National Poetry Foundation, University of Maine, 1992. 425p. LC 88-62932. ISBN 0-943373-11-5.

Intends to "dovetail" with Ricks' *T. S. Eliot: A Bibliography of Secondary Works* (entry 452), "picking up roughly" (p. 12) from 1977 through 1986, with selected additions through 1989. Chronologically arranges 1,423 entries for books, chapters, articles, and non-English-language criticisms, with separate annual listings for dissertations. Selective annotations quote extensively from other reviews and abstracts. Introductions by Knowles and Leonard identify major critical responses. Separate indexes for critics, Eliot's works, and detailed subjects afford excellent access.

451. Malamud, Randy. **T. S. Eliot's Drama: A Research and Production Sourcebook**. New York: Greenwood Press, 1992. 314p. (Modern Dramatists Research and Production Sourcebooks, no. 2). LC 91-46960. ISBN 0-313-27813-X.

One of the more awkwardly organized volumes in this Greenwood series. Mainly valuable as a bibliographic companion for Eliot's seven plays and for Eliot's influential comments on drama. For the plays, Malamud provides plot summaries, production histories, overviews of critical scholarship and performance reviews, textual notes, and publication histories, with cross-references to entries in a classified section for "Secondary Sources," identifying more than 200 reviews and 400 general studies and studies of individual plays. In a separate listing Malamud identifies and describes 60 essays, interviews, and other comments by Eliot (published from 1919 to 1961) that "serve as an intriguing parallel—a guide or gloss, sometimes; a theoretical complement—to his poetry and plays" (p. 168). Appendixes identify media adaptations of Eliot's plays and give credits and casts for selected major productions. Also includes an Eliot chronology. Chronological index of secondary sources bibliography, with separate author and general indexes.

452. Ricks, Beatrice. **T. S. Eliot: A Bibliography of Secondary Works**. Metuchen, NJ: Scarecrow, 1980. 366p. (Scarecrow Author Bibliographies, no. 45). LC 79-21305. ISBN 0-8108-1262-2.

Ricks includes 4,319 entries for secondary studies (books, parts of books, and articles) arranged in separate listings for genres—drama, poetry, and criticism—with subdivisions for individual works and general studies. Coverage includes selected non-English-language materials. Annotations are very selective, brief, and descriptive. A separate subject index covers names and topics, such as "death," "objective correlative," and "Shakespeare." Ricks' work supersedes the coverage of Bradley Gunter's *The Merrill Checklist of T. S. Eliot* (Columbus, OH: Merrill, 1970), which is a handy list of primary and secondary works; and Mildred Martin's *A Half Century of Eliot Criticism* (Lewisburg, PA: Bucknell University Press, 1972), which chronologically arranges and annotates entries for about 2,700 English-language books and articles about Eliot published from 1919 through 1965. Also for a bibliography of works by and about Eliot, see *NCBEL*, IV, pp. 157-201. Research on Eliot is reviewed by Richard M. Ludwig in Bryer's *Sixteen Modern American Authors*, pp. 181-222, with a supplement by Stuart Y. McDougal in Bryer's *Sixteen Modern American Authors: Volume 2: A Survey of Research and Criticism Since 1972*, pp. 154-209; Anne Ridler in Dyson's *English Poetry*, pp. 360-76; and Randy Malamud in Demastes and Kelly's *British Playwrights, 1880-1956*, pp. [105]-16. *ALS* annually features a review essay on Eliot scholarship.

Dictionaries, Encyclopedias, and Handbooks

453. Behr, Caroline. **T. S. Eliot: A Chronology of His Life and Works**. London: Macmillan, 1983. 123p. LC 84-3854. ISBN 0-333-32827-2.

Behr charts the "main lines" of Eliot's life and works from 1888 through 1981. A list of sources is included but not cross-referenced.

454.   Williamson, George. **A Reader's Guide to T. S. Eliot: A Poem-by-Poem Analysis**. 2d ed. 1966; reprint New York: Octagon, 1974. 270p. LC 74-10531. ISBN 0-3749-8635-5.

Williamson offers background information and summaries of the thematic content for Eliot's works. B. C. Southam's *A Student's Guide to the Selected Poems of T. S. Eliot*, 6th ed. (1994; San Diego, CA: Harcourt Brace, 1996) provides introductory commentaries on Eliot's major poems. Lorraine Marie Kyle's *A Guide to the Major Criticism of T. S. Eliot* (Nashville, TN: Vanderbilt University, 1979) gives work-by-work analyses of Eliot's criticism.

Indexes and Concordances

455.   Dawson, J. L., P. D. Holland, and D. J. McKitterick. **A Concordance to the Complete Poems and Plays of T. S. Eliot**. Ithaca: Cornell University Press, 1995. 1,240p. (Cornell Concordances). LC 95-4884. ISBN 0-8014-1561-6.

Uses as copy text *The Complete Poems and Plays of T. S. Eliot* (London: Faber and Faber, 1969), regarded as "standard for all of the works it includes" (p. vii). Appends reverse index of word forms, statistical ranking list of word forms, lines containing numbers, and index of words containing hyphens or apostrophes.

Journals

456.   **Journal of the T. S. Eliot Society of Korea**. Seoul: T. S. Eliot Society of Korea, 1993-. Annual. ISSN 1225-5912.

Representative articles in English and Korean (with Korean or English summaries) include "The Political Thought of T. S. Eliot" and "Reading Process of *The Waste Land*: Filling Up the Gaps and Widening the Horizons." Contributions generally offer modern (poststructuralist and reader-response) critical approaches to Eliot, while others have discussed Eliot's writings in relationship to Christianity, Buddhism, Confucianism, and existentialism. *Journal of the T. S. Eliot Society of Korea* is indexed in *MLA*.

See also *Yeats Eliot Review* (entry 1521).

Patterson's *Author Newsletters and Journals*, pp. 113-14, describes other previously published journals for Eliot.

Stanley (Lawrence) Elkin, 1930-
Bibliographies

For works by Elkin, see *First Printings of American Authors*, vol. 1, pp. 115-16. See Peter J. Bailey's summary biography, critical assessment of major works, and selected primary and secondary bibliography for Elkin in McCaffery's *Postmodern Fiction: A Bio-Bibliographical Guide*, pp. 348-52.

George P(aul) Elliott, 1918-1980
Bibliographies

For works by Elliott, see *First Printings of American Authors*, vol. 4, pp. 177-79. Elliott's manuscripts are listed in Robbins' *American Literary Manuscripts*, p. 102.

William Elliot, 1788-1863
Bibliographies

For works by Elliot, see *First Printings of American Authors*, vol. 1, pp. 117-18. Reed Sanderlin surveys works by and about Elliot in Bain and Flora's *Fifty Southern Writers Before 1900*, pp. 205-11.

Ralph (Waldo) Ellison, 1914-1994
Bibliographies

457.   Covo, Jacqueline. **The Blinking Eye: Ralph Waldo Ellison and His American, French, German, and Italian Critics, 1952-1971: Bibliographic Essays and a Checklist**. Metuchen, NJ: Scarecrow, 1974. 214p. (Scarecrow Author Bibliographies, no. 18). LC 74-13042. ISBN 0-8108-0736-x.

Covo provides separate bibliographic surveys of bibliographies, reviews, and critical studies of Ellison in the United States, France, Germany, and Italy, with an accompanying checklist of about 600 entries for secondary works. Covo's reviews are critical and evaluative, emphasizing the sense of racial alienation in Ellison's writings and European misunderstanding. Joe Weixlmann and John O'Banion's "A Checklist of Ellison Criticism, 1972-1978," *Black American Literature Forum* 12 (1978): 51-55, updates Covo. R. S. Lillard's "A Ralph Waldo Ellison Bibliography (1914-1967)," *American Book Collector* 19 (November 1968): 18-22; and Carol Polsgrove's "Addenda to 'A Ralph Waldo Ellison Bibliography' 1914-1968," *American Book Collector* 20 (November-December 1969): 11-12, identify Ellison's works of fiction, reviews, essays, interviews, and speeches. Bernard Benoit and Michel Fabre's, "A Bibliography of Ralph Ellison's Published Writings," *Studies in Black Literature* 2 (Autumn 1971): 25-28, lists Ellison's works by genre. Also for works by Ellison, see *First Printings of American Authors*, vol. 3, p. 101. Ellison's manuscripts are listed in Robbins' *American Literary Manuscripts*, p. 102. See *Bibliography of American Fiction, 1919-1988*, pp. 161-66, for Leonard J. Deutsch's checklist of works by and about Ellison. Research on Ellison is reviewed by Joanne Giza in Inge, Duke, and Bryer's *Black American Writers*, vol. 2, pp. 47-71; and by J. Lee Greene in Flora and Bain's *Fifty Southern Writers After 1900*, pp. 147-57.

David Ely, 1927-
Bibliographies
For works by Ely, see *First Printings of American Authors*, vol. 2, p. 141.

Sir Thomas Elyot, c. 1490-1546
Bibliographies
458.   Dees, Jerome Steele. **Sir Thomas Elyot and Roger Ascham: A Reference Guide**. Boston: G. K. Hall, 1981. 186p. (A Reference Guide to Literature). LC 80-26951. ISBN 0-8161-8353-8.

Dees gives separate, chronologically arranged listings of annotated entries for about 500 critical materials about Ascham published from 1576 through 1981 and about 300 for Elyot published from 1662 through 1981. Comprehensive coverage includes dissertations, editions, reviews of works about Ascham and Elyot, and non-English-language criticisms. Annotations are critical, and significant studies are reviewed in detail. Separate subject indexes for each writer include headings under Ascham's and Elyot's names and for broad topics (biography and bibliography) and names (Xenophon and Sidney). Dees' coverage of Ascham supersedes that in the Tannenbaums' *Elizabethan Bibliographies*, vol. 1; and Robert Carl Johnson's *Elizabethan Bibliographies Supplements*, no. 9. For a bibliography of works by and about Elyot, see *NCBEL*, I, pp. 1818-19. Elyot's manuscripts are described in *Index of English Literary Manuscripts*, I, pt. 2: 69.

Ralph Waldo Emerson, 1803-1882
Bibliographies
459.   Burkholder, Robert E., and Joel Myerson. **Emerson: An Annotated Secondary Bibliography**. Pittsburgh, PA: University of Pittsburgh Press, 1985. 842p. (Pittsburgh Series in Bibliography). LC 84-15352. ISBN 0-8229-3502-3.

This is supplemented by:

459.1 Burkholder, Robert E., and Joel Myerson. **Ralph Waldo Emerson: An Annotated Bibliography of Criticism, 1980-1991**. Westport, CT: Greenwood, 1994. 234p. (Bibliographies and Indexes in American Literature, no. 18). LC 93-45954. ISBN 0-313-29150-0.

Burkholder and Myerson's two volumes provide the most comprehensive bibliography now available for secondary materials about Emerson. Materials in the 1985 volume are arranged in two disproportionate sections: the first, extending more than 700 pages, covers critical and biographical works; the second and smaller section, labeled "miscellaneous works," describes works that range from noncritical essays through parodies and references to Emerson in poetry, fiction, music, and the like. All major forms of critical works in all languages are included (books, articles, reviews, dissertations, and the like) but mostly excludes passing notices, references in general and literary encyclopedias, histories, and surveys, and references in similarly familiar sources. Putz's bibliography (entry 461) covers more of this variety. Coverage in the 1985 volume extends from notices of Emerson's orations, readings, and academic exercises in 1816 through criticisms in 1979, with Burkholder responsible for the nineteenth-century listings and Myerson for the twentieth-century. Some 2,590 entries date through 1900. The 1985 volume contains a total of 5,841 entries. The 1994 volume chronologically arranges annotated entries for 1,055 criticisms of Emerson published from 1980 through 1991. Annotations in both volumes are precisely descriptive and critical, although a significant number of the annotations indicate little with comments such as "general uninformative essay" and "general appreciative essay." Other descriptions are pointed: Comments such as "uninformative discussion," "now outdated," and "nothing on Emerson" warn off use. Both volumes describe in detail the most significant studies. Comprehensive cumulative indexes of names, titles, and selected subjects offer solid access. Burkholder and Myerson's bibliography supersedes Jeanetta Boswell's *Ralph Waldo Emerson and the Critics: A Checklist of Criticism, 1900-1977* (Metuchen, NJ: Scarecrow Press, 1979), which is described as adding "but a few titles to those available in earlier bibliographies, while perpetuating their errors and introducing new ones. Boswell clearly has not seen most of the items she lists, resulting in numerous errors, false leads, and nonexistent works" (A5598). A cumulative index references critics, journal titles, and a wide range of subjects. Headings under Emerson's name reference primary works, forms ("comments by," "letters to"), and topics ("imagery," "paganism," "the scholar [as concept]," and "trips to the west"). Separate headings are included for other writers, with subdivisions: for "Conrad Aiken"—"compared to Emerson"—and for "Francis Bacon"—"influence on Emerson." Also lists other topics, such as the "Atlantic Cable" and "French criticism of Emerson." The index's specificity makes the bibliography all the more useful. Burkholder and Myerson's bibliography supersedes Jackson R. Bryer and Robert A. Rees' *A Checklist of Emerson Criticism, 1951-1961* (Hartford, CT: Transcendental Books, 1964); and Alfred R. Ferguson's *The Merrill Checklist of Ralph Waldo Emerson* (Columbus, OH: Merrill, 1970). Going in the opposite direction, Kenneth Walter Cameron's *The Emerson Tertiary Bibliography with Researcher's Index* (Hartford, CT: Transcendental Books, 1986) and Cameron's *The Emerson Tertiary Bibliography with Researcher's Index: Supplement One* (Hartford, CT: Transcendental Books, 1995) identify (and selectively reproduce) more than 3,000 "tertiaries," largely passing references to Emerson in newspapers and non-English-language criticism beyond the near-exhaustive scope of Burkholder and Myerson. Research on Emerson is reviewed by Floyd Stovall in Woodress' *Eight American Authors*, pp. 37-83; and by Burkholder and Myerson in Myerson's *The Transcendentalists*, pp. 135-66. *ALS* annually features a review essay on Emerson scholarship.

460. Myerson, Joel. **Ralph Waldo Emerson: A Descriptive Bibliography**. Pittsburgh, PA: University of Pittsburgh Press, 1982. 802p. (Pittsburgh Series in Bibliography). LC 81-11502. ISBN 0-8229-3452-3.

This is the standard listing of Emerson's primary works, chronologically arranging in separate listings descriptions of Emerson's books, pamphlets, and broadsides; collected editions of Emerson's writings published through 1980 (46 entries); miscellaneous collections, including Emerson's writings through 1980 (177 entries); contributions to books (224 entries); contributions to American and English journals and newspapers through 1980 (316 entries); works edited by Emerson (seven entries); reprintings of Emerson's prose, poetry, and letters through 1882 (114 entries); materials attributed to Emerson (42 entries); and others possibly written by Emerson (21 entries). The section for separate publications (including 68 entries and extending more than 500 pages) includes all printings of all editions of Emerson's works published from 1832 through 1882 (suggestive of Emerson's contemporary popularity) in English and other languages, and in English through 1980. Descriptions of first and selected variant editions include illustrations of title pages, collations, contents, typography and paper, notes on printing and publishing, and locations of copies. Useful illustrations of variant bindings are also included (some 14 for *Nature*). Appends a brief list of selected works about Emerson. A cumulative index includes names of editors, critics, publishers, and individuals mentioned in notes; primary titles; and periodical titles. It is possible to identify all of Emerson's works published by the Riverside Press or in *The North American Review*. Myerson's bibliography supersedes George Willis Cooke's *A Bibliography of Ralph Waldo Emerson* (1908; reprint New York: Kraus, 1966). Myerson also describes Emerson's primary materials in *The Ralph Waldo Emerson Collection* in part 2 of Sidney Ives's *The Parkman Dexter Howe Library* (Gainesville: University of Florida, 1984). Also for works by Emerson, see *Bibliography of American Literature*, vol. 3, pp. 16-70; and *First Printings of American Authors*, vol. 2, pp. 143-61. Emerson's manuscripts are listed in Robbins' *American Literary Manuscripts*, pp. 102-103. A more specialized bibliography of interest is Walter Harding's *Emerson's Library* (Charlottesville, VA: University of Virginia Press, 1967).

461.   Putz, Manfred. **Ralph Waldo Emerson: A Bibliography of Twentieth-Century Criticism**. Frankfurt am Main: Verlag Peter Lang, 1986. 305p. (Sprache und Literatur: Regensburger Arbeiten zur Anglistik und Amerikanistik). LC 86-30236. ISBN 3-8204-8743-3.
     Putz's bibliography offers a useful supplement (for non-English-language criticisms) and update to Burkholder and Myerson's comprehensive bibliography (entry 459). A comprehensive listing for 1900 through 1985, Putz supplies unannotated entries for 2,941 books, articles, chapters and parts of books, introductions and prefaces to editions and anthologies, dissertations, and articles and notices in reference works and literary surveys. Newspaper articles and book reviews are excluded, except those about significant events (such as Emerson's centennial in 1903) or by significant critics. In addition, Putz's indexing complements that offered by Burkholder and Myerson, including headings for the usual critical forms (bibliography, biography, concordances, editions, essays, interviews, and the like), people and places (Beethoven, Melville, Creeley, Detroit, Cincinnati, and Indianapolis), and specific topics ("American Adam," "homosexuality," "science fiction," and "zen").

Dictionaries, Encyclopedias, and Handbooks
462.   Carpenter, Frederick Ives. **Emerson Handbook**. New York: Hendricks House, 1953. 268p. LC 53-2274.
     Mainly useful for background information, Carpenter provides survey chapters on Emerson's life, prose and poetry, ideas (such as transcendentalism, romanticism, and "Yankee realism"), classical sources, literary relationships, and influences on literature. Annotated, but dated, bibliographies accompany the discussions.

463.   Von Frank, Albert J. **An Emerson Chronology**. New York: G. K. Hall, 1994. 569p. LC 93-32317. ISBN 0-8161-7266-8.
     Detailed, annotated chronology of Emerson's life and career that is particularly useful for dating Emerson's reading and public performances (sermons, lectures, and readings). Summaries of each year's highlights precede the annual calenders. Von Frank cross-references standard editions, bibliographies, biographies, and other works. Also includes brief biographies of 68 prominent "recurrent figures" in Emerson's life. Comprehensive index of names of persons, places, and

things, titles, and events—ranging from the *Upanishads* to Galileo to Appomattox Court House—provides excellent access. Von Frank's Emerson chronology is exemplary.

Indexes and Concordances

464. Hubbell, George Shelton. **A Concordance to the Poems of Ralph Waldo Emerson**. New York: H. W. Wilson, 1932. 478p. LC 32-10875.

Based on the texts of poems in vol. 9 of Edward Waldo Emerson's Centenary Edition of Emerson's *Complete Works* (Boston: Houghton Mifflin, 1903-1904). Additionally, Kenneth Walter Cameron's *An Emerson Index* (Hartford, CT: Transcendental Books, 1950) indexes selected materials from journals, manuscripts, marginalia, and the like, while Cameron's *Index-Concordance to Emerson's Sermons with Homiletical Papers* (Hartford, CT: Transcendental Books, 1963) indexes 150 sermons.

465. Ihrig, Mary Alice. **Emerson's Transcendental Vocabulary: A Concordance**. New York: Garland, 1982. 290p. (Garland Reference Library of the Humanities, vol. 323). LC 81-47965. ISBN 0-8240-9264-3.

Indexes nine words—"beauty," "culture," "fate," "genius," "greatness-heroism," "nature," "prudence," "soul spirit," and "wealth/riches"—in the texts of Emerson's *Nature, Addresses and Lectures, Essays, First Series, Essays, Second Series, Representative Men, English Traits, The Conduct of Life,* and *Society and Solitude* is based on vols. 1-7 of Edward Waldo Emerson's edition of *The Complete Works of Ralph Waldo Emerson* (Boston: Houghton, Mifflin, 1903-1904).

466. Irey, Eugene F. **A Concordance to Five Essays of Ralph Waldo Emerson: Nature, The American Scholar, The Divinity School, Self-Reliance, Fate**. New York: Garland, 1981. 468p. (Contextual Concordances; Garland Reference Library of the Humanities, vol. 250). LC 80-8520. ISBN 0-8240-9464-6.

A companion to Ihrig's *Emerson's Transcendental Vocabulary* (entry 465) and based on the text of Emerson's *Works* (Boston: Houghton Mifflin, 1903), with cross-references to *The Complete Works of Ralph Waldo Emerson* (Boston: Houghton Mifflin, 1903-1904), Irey offers a limited index to nouns, main verbs, adverbs, and adjectives ("classes of words most significant in the author's statement of ideas as well as in style"). Of more general interest and application, Keith Weller Frome's *Hitch Your Wagon to a Star and Other Quotations from Ralph Waldo Emerson* (New York: Columbia University Press, 1996) offers some 750 quotations "from the major works" (p. [xiii]) of Emerson (with incomplete citations to editions), topically arranged under headings such as "Books," "Knowledge," "Property," and "Slavery."

Journals

467. **ESQ: A Journal of the American Renaissance**. Pullman, WA: Washington State University, 1955-. 4/yr. ISSN 0093-8297.

Formerly *Emerson Society Quarterly* (1955-68), typical issues of *ESQ* contain three scholarly studies on the full range of topics in nineteenth-century American literature, focusing on the Romantic transcendentalist tradition represented by Emerson as well as the likes of Charles Brockden Brown, Edgar Allan Poe, Henry David Thoreau, Herman Melville, Nathaniel Hawthorne, Walt Whitman, Washington Irving, and Emily Dickinson. Typical articles give critical or interpretive readings of specific writings or address particular elements in them. In addition, the journal has occasionally offered review essays, such as ones for Thoreau in 38.1 (1992): 71-86; Emerson in 38.3 (1992): 231-63; and James Fenimore Cooper in 39.1 (1993): 49-75. With 42.1 (1996) *ESQ* also features a few brief notes. From 1955-72 *ESQ* contained "Current Bibliography," which was continued in *American Transcendental Quarterly* (Kingston: University of Rhode Island, 1969-) from

1972-77, identifying criticisms and dissertations. *ESQ* is indexed in *AHI, A&HCI, MHRA,* and *MLA.*

Patterson's *Author Newsletters and Journals,* pp. 114-15, describes other previously published journals for Emerson.

(Sir) William Empson, 1906-1984
Bibliographies
468.　Day, Frank. **Sir William Empson: An Annotated Bibliography**. New York: Garland, 1984. 229p. (Garland Bibliographies of Modern Critics and Critical Schools, vol. 8; Garland Reference Library of the Humanities, vol. 376). LC 82-49130. ISBN 0-8240-9207-4.

Day lists works by Empson, including his books, articles, essays, poems, and reviews, in addition to describing about 250 works about him. Critical and evaluative annotations for both primary and secondary materials emphasize Empson's critical and aesthetic ideas. A separate subject index includes headings for such topics as "ambiguity," "intentional fallacy," and "zen," as well as names and titles. Also for a bibliography of works by and about Empson, see *NCBEL,* IV, pp. 272-74.

Thomas Dunn English, 1819-1902
Bibliographies
For works by English, see *Bibliography of American Literature,* vol. 3, pp. 71-81. English's contributions to and reviews of English's works in selected periodicals are identified in Wells' *The Literary Index to American Magazines, 1815-1865,* pp. 52-53; and *The Literary Index to American Magazines, 1850-1900,* p. 134. English's manuscripts are listed in Robbins' *American Literary Manuscripts,* pp. 103-104. See *Bibliography of American Fiction Through 1865,* pp.104-105, for a checklist of works by and about English.

Evangeline Walton Ensley, 1907-
Bibliographies
469.　Zahorski, Kenneth J., and Robert H. Boyer. **Lloyd Alexander, Evangeline Walton Ensley, Kenneth Morris: A Primary and Secondary Bibliography**. Boston: G. K. Hall, 1981. 291p. (Masters of Science Fiction and Fantasy). LC 81-6219. ISBN 0-8161-8055-5.

Contains separate introductions and lists of fiction, miscellaneous works (the only item in these sections is a recording of Alexander), nonfiction (some 338 poems, essays, and contributions to anthologies for Morris), and critical studies for the writers. Entries for primary works give brief bibliographic information, with references to editions and reprints. Critical coverage for Alexander includes 202 items published from 1955 through 1979; for Ensley, 33 items from 1936 through 1980; and for Morris, 32 items from 1914 through 1980. Annotations for secondary works are descriptive. Coverage of works by and about Alexander is superseded by Jacobs and Tunnell's *Lloyd Alexander: A Bio-Bibliography* (entry 16).

Seymour Epstein, 1917-
Bibliographies
For works by Epstein, see *First Printings of American Authors,* vol. 1, p. 119.

Clayton Eshleman, 1935-
Bibliographies
470.　Sattler, Martha J. **Clayton Eshleman: A Descriptive Bibliography**. Jefferson, NC: McFarland, 1988. 260p. (American Poetry Contemporary Bibliography Series, no. 4). LC 88-42647. ISBN 0-8995-0319-5.

Describes Eshleman's works through 1987 in chronologically arranged sections for books, broadsides, and separate publications; contributions to anthologies; contributions to periodicals; books and periodicals edited by Eshleman;

audiotape recordings of readings, introductions, comments, and the like by Eshleman; and manuscripts and ephemera. Entries for separate publications give title-page transcriptions, paginations and collations, contents, binding descriptions, and publication histories, with selected facsimiles of title pages and dust jackets. Also lists entries for 155 books, articles, and reviews about Eshleman. Includes prefatory chronology of Eshleman's life and career; appendixes of Eshleman's pseudonyms, information on manuscript collections in the Lilly Library, Indiana University; Fales Library, Elmer Holmes Bobst Library, New York University; and Mandeville Department of Special Collections at University of California, San Diego; and a facsimile of the typescript of "Dragon Rat Tail" with Eshleman's autograph corrections. Afterword by Eshleman. Useful index of names and titles. Also for works by Eshleman, see *First Printings of American Authors*, vol. 3, pp. 103-108. Eshleman's manuscripts are listed in Robbins' *American Literary Manuscripts*, p. 104.

(Sir) George Etherege, 1634?-1691
Bibliographies
471. Mann, David D. **Sir George Etherege: A Reference Guide**. Boston: G. K. Hall, 1981. 135p. (A Reference Guide to Literature). LC 81-4808. ISBN 0-8161-8171-3.

Following an introduction that surveys critical trends in Etherege scholarship, Mann chronologically arranges annotated entries for about 800 works by and about Etherege published mainly from 1664 through 1978, with some coverage of works through 1980. Entries for early editions give *Wing* numbers and references to reprinted editions. Coverage of primary works also includes translated editions. Coverage of secondary works includes dissertations and criticisms in all languages. Although annotations are objective, standard works are clearly identified. A cumulative index offers limited topical access under Etherege's name. For a bibliography of works by and about Etherege, see *NCBEL*, II, pp. 741-42. Etherege's manuscripts are described in *Index of English Literary Manuscripts*, II, pt. 1: 443-59. Research on Etherege is reviewed by John Barnard in Wells' *English Drama*, pp. 173-98.

Indexes and Concordances
472. Mann, David D. **A Concordance to the Plays and Poems of Sir George Etherege**. Westport, CT: Greenwood Press, 1985. 445p. LC 84-27917. ISBN 0-313-20976-6.

Mann concords the texts of Etherege's three plays and 30 poems, based on H. F. B. Brett-Smith's edition of *The Dramatic Works of Sir George Etherege* (Oxford: Basil Blackwell, 1927) and James Thorpe's *The Poems of Sir George Etherege* (Princeton, NJ: Princeton University Press, 1963), which are identified as the "most authoritative texts" (p. viii). References for plays identify characters, page numbers (in Brett-Smith's edition), acts, scenes, and lines, with context lines. References for poems give page numbers (in Thorpe's edition) and lines, with context lines. Appends a ranked frequency list.

John Evelyn, 1620-1706
Bibliographies
473. Keynes, Geoffrey. **John Evelyn: A Study in Bibliography with a Bibliography of His Writings**. 2d ed. Oxford: Clarendon Press, 1968. 313p. LC 68-131650.

A revision of a guide first published in 1937 (New York: Grolier Club), Keynes gives full bibliographic descriptions for Evelyn's separately published works, posthumous publications, contributions, and miscellaneous writings. Entries include title-page transcriptions, collations, contents, physical descriptions, publishing histories, and copy locations. Appendixes list the works of John Evelyn the younger and his son and describe Evelyn's library. Also for a bibliography of works by and about Evelyn, see *NCBEL*, II, pp. 1580-82. Evelyn's manuscripts are described in *Index of English Literary Manuscripts*, II, pt. 1: 461-87. Coverage of works about Evelyn is provided in Dennis G. Donovan's *Elizabethan Bibliographies Supplements*, no. 18. *John Evelyn in the British Library* (London: British Library, 1995) reprints essays by Nicholas Barker, Michael Hunter, Theodore Hoffman, and others on Evelyn's library and archives and collections related to Evelyn in the British Library first published in the *Book Collector* 44.2 (1995).

William Everson, 1912-1994
Bibliographies
474.   Bartlett, Lee, and Allan Campo. **William Everson: A Descriptive Bibliography, 1934-1976.** Metuchen, NJ: Scarecrow Press, 1977. 119p. (Scarecrow Author Bibliographies, no. 33). LC 77-5397. ISBN 0-8108-1037-9.
        Bartlett and Campo chronologically arrange full bibliographic descriptions in separate listings for Everson's books, pamphlets, broadsides; introductions contributed to books; poems contributed to periodicals; contributed prose pieces, including reviews, interviews, and published letters; anthologies including Everson's poems; and other miscellaneous writings. Entries give title-page transcriptions, physical descriptions, contents, and publishing histories. Appendixes list manuscripts of unpublished works and a selection of about 100 critical studies (unannotated) about Everson. Indexes arrange Everson's works alphabetically within each form. Everson's manuscripts are listed in Robbins' *American Literary Manuscripts*, p. 105.

Frederick Exley, 1929-
Bibliographies
        For works by Exley, see *First Printings of American Authors*, vol. 3, p. 109. See C. Barry Chabot's summary biography, critical assessment of major works, and selected primary and secondary bibliography for Exley in McCaffery's *Postmodern Fiction: A Bio-Bibliographical Guide*, pp. 352-53.

Exodus, c. early eighth century
Bibliographies
        Greenfield and Robinson's *A Bibliography of Publications on Old English Literature to the End of 1972*, pp. 222-25, lists editions, translations, and studies of the Old English *Exodus*, with citations for reviews. Graham D. Caie's *Bibliography of Junius XI Manuscript: With Appendix on Caedmon's Hymn*, pp. 51-59, contains unannotated checklists of international editions, translations, and criticisms of *Exodus*.

Edward Fairfax, d. 1635
Bibliographies
        For a bibliography of works by and about Fairfax, see *NCBEL*, I, p. 1103. Fairfax's manuscripts are described in *Index of English Literary Manuscripts*, I, pt. 2:71-73.

Sumner Lincoln Fairfield, 1803-1844
Bibliographies
        For works by Fairfield, see *Bibliography of American Literature*, vol. 3, pp. 82-85. Fairfield's manuscripts are listed in Robbins' *American Literary Manuscripts*, p. 105.

George Farquhar, 1677?-1707
Bibliographies
475.   James, Eugene Nelson. **George Farquhar: A Reference Guide**. Boston: G. K. Hall, 1986. 112p. (A Reference Guide to Literature). LC 85-16452. ISBN 0-8161-8182-9.

James chronologically arranges annotated entries for about 500 secondary works about Farquhar published from 1699 through 1979, including early notices, introductions in editions, dissertations, and non-English-language criticisms. Annotations are descriptive. Index headings under Farquhar's name offer access to editions and collections of primary works but no subject access. For a bibliography of works by and about Farquhar, see *NCBEL*, II, pp. 753-56. Farquhar's manuscripts are described in *Index of English Literary Manuscripts*, II, pt. 1: 489-92. Research on Farquhar is reviewed by John Barnard in Wells' *English Drama*, pp. 173-98.

James T(homas) Farrell, 1904-1979
Bibliographies
476.   Branch, Edgar. **A Bibliography of James T. Farrell's Writings, 1921-1957.** Philadelphia, PA: University of Pennsylvania Press, 1959. 142p. LC 58-10532.

Branch offers separate chronological checklists of Farrell's imaginative writings, covering novels and contributed short stories (with references to first appearances and reprints) and other prose writings (books, contributed essays and articles, reviews, prefaces, introductions, and the like). Appendixes list international first editions and tape recordings of Farrell's speeches. Branch supplements coverage of Farrell's primary works in several articles featured in the *American Book Collector* 11 (1961): 42-48; 17 (1967): 9-19; 21 (1971): 13-18; and 26 (1976): 17-22; and in *Bulletin of Bibliography* 39 (1982): 201-206. Jack Salzman's "James T. Farrell: An Essay in Bibliography," *Resources for American Literary Study* 6 (1976): 131-63, describes criticisms of Farrell. For works by Farrell, see *First Printings of American Authors*, vol. 5, pp. 97-113. Farrell's manuscripts are listed in Robbins' *American Literary Manuscripts*, p. 106. See *Bibliography of American Fiction, 1919-1988*, pp. 167-72, for Branch's checklist of works by and about Farrell.

William (Cuthbert) Faulkner, 1897-1962
Bibliographies
477.   Bassett, John Earl. **Faulkner: An Annotated Checklist of Criticism.** New York: David Lewis, 1972. 551p. LC 72-89960. ISBN 0-912012-13-8.
This is continued and updated by:

477.1. Bassett, John Earl. **Faulkner: An Annotated Checklist of Recent Criticism.** Kent, OH: Kent State University Press, 1983. 272p. (The Serif Series: Bibliographies and Checklists, no. 42). LC 83-11277. ISBN 0-87338-291-9.

477.2. Bassett, John E. **Faulkner in the Eighties: An Annotated Critical Bibliography.** Metuchen, NJ: Scarecrow, 1991. 322p. (Scarecrow Author Bibliographies, no. 88). LC 91-31218. ISBN 0-8108-2485-X.

Together Bassett's bibliographies offer comprehensive coverage of Faulkner criticism through 1990. All three volumes basically follow the same format, topically arranging selectively annotated entries in listings for general book-length studies; studies of each of the novels; studies of short stories, poetry, and other writings; topical studies, including studies of themes and techniques, biographical studies, and bibliographies and bibliographic studies; other materials, including reviews of works about Faulkner, periodical and newspaper articles, miscellaneous books, and American and British dissertations; and non-English-language commentaries. The 1972 volume covers about 5,000 works appearing through 1970. The 1983 volume covers criticisms from 1971 through 1982, with 1,950 entries. The third volume, *Faulkner in the Eighties*, includes some 1,816 entries. The latter volume more thoroughly annotates entries than the 1972 or 1983 volumes. Indexing in all is limited to the names of critics. Critical coverage complements that offered in Ricks' comprehensive guide (entry 479).

478.   Brodsky, Louis Daniel, and Robert W. Hamblin. **Faulkner: A Comprehensive Guide to the Brodsky Collection**. Jackson, MS: University Press of Mississippi, 1982-1985. 4 vols. (Center for the Study of Southern Culture Series). LC 82-6966. ISBN 0-87805-240-2.

A catalog of the private collection of Faulkner materials owned by Louis Daniel Brodsky (with supplementary information on Faulkner materials in other collections), this is the major descriptive listing of Faulkner's primary works. Vol. 1: *The Biobibliography* is a chronologically arranged (from 1871 through 1981) listing integrating annotated entries for manuscripts, letters, published works, editions (including reprints and translations), and other works related to Faulkner (such as Faulkner's juvenile cartoons, Christmas cards, and his will), as well as critical studies and reviews. Entries give bibliographic information, physical descriptions, and publishing histories, with selected facsimiles of title pages, dust jackets, and manuscripts, as well as photographs. Vol. 2: *The Letters* prints and annotates the texts of about 500 letters, memoranda, and telegrams to or from Faulkner (dating from 1924 through 1966), with cross-references to descriptive entries in vol. 1. Vols. 3 and 4 reprint the texts of Faulkner's "Battle Cry," "The DeGaulle Story," and other related documents. For works by Faulkner, also see *First Printings of American Authors*, vol. 1, pp. 121-26. Faulkner's manuscripts are listed in Robbins' *American Literary Manuscripts*, p. 106. Volumes in Garland's "William Faulkner Manuscripts" series provide facsimiles of Faulkner's literary holographs and typescripts, among other manuscripts. Additional guidance to Faulkner's primary bibliography is provided in James B. Meriwether's *William Faulkner: A Check List* (Princeton, NJ: Princeton University Press, 1957) and *The Literary Career of William Faulkner: A Bibliographical Study* (1961; reprint Columbia, SC: University of South Carolina Press, 1971), which give full bibliographic descriptions (title-page transcriptions, physical descriptions, and publishing histories); and Carl Petersen's *Each in Its Ordered Place: A Faulkner Collector's Notebook* (Ann Arbor, MI: Ardis, 1975), which identifies bibliographic points. Other useful descriptions of Faulkner's primary materials are included in Linton Reynolds Massey's *Man Working, 1919-1962: William Faulkner: A Catalogue of the William Faulkner Collection at the University of Virginia* (Charlottesville, VA: Bibliographical Society of the University of Virginia, 1968); Joan St. C. Crane and Anne E. H. Freudenberg's *Man Collecting: Manuscripts and Printed Works of William Faulkner in the University of Virginia Library* (Charlottesville, VA: University of Virginia, 1975); Thomas Bonner's *William Faulkner: The William B. Wisdom Collection in the Howard-Tilton Memorial Library, Tulane University* (New Orleans, LA: Tulane University Libraries, 1980); and Susan La Haye's *Faulkner: The Frank A. Von Der Haar Collection* (New Orleans, LA: Friends of the Library, University of New Orleans, 1983). Also useful is Joseph L. Blotner's *William Faulkner's Library: A Catalogue* (Charlottesville, VA: University Press of Virginia, 1964).

479.   Ricks, Beatrice. **William Faulkner: A Bibliography of Secondary Works**. Metuchen, NJ: Scarecrow Press, 1981. 657p. (Scarecrow Author Bibliographies, no. 49). LC 80-15251. ISBN 0-8108-1323-8.

Including 8,712 very briefly and selectively annotated entries arranged in separate listings for biographies, bibliographies, general studies, and studies of individual works, Ricks' guide provides comprehensive coverage of Faulkner scholarship. Coverage includes books, articles, and dissertations in all languages. A detailed topical index includes headings for names, places, and subjects such as "Dostoevsky," "Shakespeare," "the grotesque," "the negro and the negro problem," "textual studies," "Mississippi," and "the Soviet Union." The guides of Ricks and Bassett (entry 477) are complementary. Bassett offers slightly fuller annotations in topical sections but lacks subject indexing; Ricks' subject index, however, offers superior access. Both supersede Thomas L. McHaney's *William Faulkner: A Reference Guide* (Boston: G. K. Hall, 1976), which chronologically arranges annotated entries for (largely) English-language criticism published from 1924 through

1973. Additional coverage of dissertations is provided by Tetsumaro Hayashi's *William Faulkner: Research Opportunities and Dissertation Abstracts* (Jefferson, NC: McFarland, 1982), which identifies 415 dissertations on Faulkner published from 1941 through 1979. More specialized coverage of topics in Faulkner scholarship is included in Sensibar and Stegall's *Faulkner's Poetry: A Bibliographical Guide to Texts and Criticism* (entry 480) and Patricia E. Sweeney's *William Faulkner's Women Characters: An Annotated Bibliography of Criticism, 1930-1983* (Santa Barbara, CA: ABC-Clio, 1985), which identifies 2,336 critical books and articles that comment on Faulkner's female characters. See *Bibliography of American Fiction, 1919-1988*, pp. 173-85, for McHaney's checklist of works by and about Faulkner. Research on Faulkner is reviewed by James B. Meriwether in Bryer's *Sixteen Modern American Authors*, pp. 223-75; and its supplement by Philip G. Cohen in Bryer's *Sixteen Modern American Authors: Volume 2: A Survey of Research and Criticism Since 1972*, pp. 210-300; and by Thomas E. Dasher in Flora and Bain's *Fifty Southern Writers After 1900*, pp. 158-76. *ALS* annually features a review essay on Faulkner scholarship.

480.   Sensibar, Judith L., and Nancy L. Stegall. **Faulkner's Poetry: A Bibliographical Guide to Texts and Criticism.** Ann Arbor, MI: UMI Research Press, 1988. 147p. (Studies in Modern Literature, no. 94). LC 88-11077. ISBN 0-8357-1879-4.
     Sensibar and Stegall's guide is most important for its full bibliographic descriptions of all of Faulkner's "known extant poems" (p. [xiii]), supplementing coverage of Faulkner's primary works offered in Brodsky and Hamblin's *Faulkner: A Comprehensive Guide to the Brodsky Collection* (entry 478). Entries identify all versions of poems (including reproductions and transcriptions) and their extant typescripts or manuscripts, with copy locations and citations to Brodsky and Hamblin and other standard Faulkner bibliographies, in alphabetically arranged sections for published verse, unpublished verse, published and unpublished sequences and sequence fragments, and poem fragments. Indicates all manuscript variants (such as typescripts). The guide also includes facsimiles of manuscripts. Additionally, the guide includes an annotated bibliography of about 100 textual, biographical, and critical studies of Faulkner's poetry through 1987, supplementing coverage of scholarship of Faulkner's poetry in Ricks' *William Faulkner: A Bibliography of Secondary Works* (entry 479). Descriptions reference items cited in the primary bibliography. Title and first-line indexes. References and supersedes Keen Butterworth's "A Census of Manuscripts and Typescripts of William Faulkner's Poetry," *Mississippi Quarterly* 26 (1973): 33-59.

Dictionaries, Encyclopedias, and Handbooks
481.   Connolly, Thomas E. **Faulkner's World: A Directory of His People and Synopses of Actions in His Published Works.** Lanham, MD: University Press of America, 1988. 619p. LC 88-5439. ISBN 0-8191-5703-1.
     Connolly's guide is the most detailed of several works in the very competitive world of Faulkner character dictionaries. Approaching Faulkner's works chronologically, Connolly summarizes the plots of each work by giving synopses of the actions related to named and unnamed characters and place names. Cross-references cite several editions. Dasher's *William Faulkner's Characters* (entry 482) gives fewer details for characters who appear in Faulkner's works but covers a wider range of characters.

482.   Dasher, Thomas E. **William Faulkner's Characters: An Index to the Published and Unpublished Fiction.** New York: Garland, 1981. 427p. (Garland Reference Library of the Humanities, vol. 270). LC 80-9033. ISBN 0-8240-9305-4.
     The most comprehensive guide to Faulkner's characters, Dasher's index identifies the appearances and activities of each character by work, covering both named and unnamed characters as well as allusions to historical, Biblical, and mythic/literary characters. Information is very brief, indicating that Flem Snopes was somehow involved in a "goat deal" and a "horse auction" and "marries Eula

Varner." Entries reference standard editions. An index cumulates all characters. Dasher's dictionary complements Connolly's (entry 481) and supersedes Robert W. Kirk and Marvin Klotz's *Faulkner's People: A Complete Guide and Index* (Berkeley, CA: University of California Press, 1963) and Margaret Patricia Ford and Suzanne Kinkaid's *Who's Who in Faulkner* (Baton Rouge, LA: Louisiana State University Press, 1963). In addition to summarizing Faulkner's works and glossing his characters, Harry Runyon's *A Faulkner Glossary* (New York: The Citadel Press, 1964) includes a biographical sketch of Faulkner's life; bibliographic surveys of his poetry, nonfiction, and prose fiction; histories of the families of Yoknapatawpha County (the Varners and Snopeses, among others); a survey of the county's geography; and a list of Faulkner's works situated there.

483.   Gresset, Michel, and Arthur B. Scharff. **A Faulkner Chronology**. Jackson, MS: University Press of Mississippi, 1985. 120p. LC 84-50873. ISBN 0-87805-229-1.

Scharff's translation of Gresset's *Faulkner: Oeuvres Romanesques* (Paris: Editions Gallimard, 1977) offers a very detailed chronology of Faulkner's literary career, focusing on "main events in the *writer's* life" (p. xii), such as conception, composition, revision, publication, and further reworking and republication. Coverage is more extensive than that provided in volumes in Macmillan and G. K. Hall's "Author Chronologies" series. Gresset recounts events of the Indian settlement of Mississippi from about 1540 through the Faulkner Conference in Izu, Japan, in 1985. Details about Faulkner's personal life are not emphasized. Gresset relies heavily on Joseph Blotner's *Faulkner: A Biography* (New York: Random House, 1974) and his edition of *Selected Letters of William Faulkner* (New York: Random House, 1977).

484.   Jones, Diane Brown. **A Reader's Guide to the Short Stories of William Faulkner**. New York: G. K. Hall, 1994. 551p. (A Reference Publication in Literature). LC 93-36283. ISBN 0-8161-7272-2.

Thematically arranged chapters on 42 stories included in Faulkner's *Collected Stories* (New York: Random House, 1950) survey publication history; composition, sources, and influences; relationship to other Faulkner works; and critical reception, with supporting bibliographies. Index to Faulkner's works and general index. Jones' handbook is a very convenient starting point for discussions of such frequently studied works as "A Rose for Emily" and other Faulkner short stories.

485.   Volpe, Edmond Loris. **A Reader's Guide to William Faulkner**. New York: Farrar, Straus, 1964. 427p. LC 64-17120.

Volpe provides a convenient, one-volume guide to Faulkner's novels. Following an introduction to Faulkner's life and career, Volpe offers commentaries on the elements of character and theme, narrative structure and technique, and style in Faulkner's works in general. The novels are examined in detail in separate chapters. Appendixes include helpful chronologies of events in selected works, including *The Sound and the Fury* and *Absalom, Absalom!* as well as genealogical tables of the Faulkner family and of the Sartorises, McCaslins, Snopeses, and other fictional families. In addition to Jones' *A Reader's Guide to the Short Stories of William Faulkner* (entry 484), other similarly useful handbooks are Leland H. Cox's *William Faulkner: Biographical and Reference Guide: A Guide to His Life and Career* (Detroit, MI: Gale, 1982) and its companion volume, *William Faulkner: Critical Collection: A Guide to Critical Studies with Statements by Faulkner and Evaluative Essays on His Works* (Detroit, MI: Gale, 1982), which offer a biographical survey of Faulkner's life, plot summaries of his works, selected secondary bibliographies, and reprintings of selected interviews, essays, and addresses by Faulkner. Volumes in the recent "Reading Faulkner" series, such as James C. Hinkle and Robert McCoy's *Reading Faulkner: The Unvanquished: Glossary and Commentary* (Jackson, MS: University Press of Mississippi, 1995); and Stephen M. Ross and Noel Polk's *Reading*

Faulkner: The Sound and the Fury: Glossary and Commentary (Jackson, MS: University Press of Mississippi, 1996), intend to offer close readings of the individual works.

Indexes and Concordances

486. Brown, Calvin S. **A Glossary of Faulkner's South**. New Haven, CT: Yale University Press, 1976. 241p. LC 75-43308. ISBN 0-300-01944-0.

In this specialized index and guide to Faulkner's regional vocabulary, Brown identifies and glosses Southern words, phrases, and allusions. Coverage spans personal and place names, references based on fiction and history, and terms used for flora, fauna, tools and devices, and the like, such as "Bed Forrest" (for General Nathan Bedford Forrest), "Looeyvul" (for Louisville), and "peckerwood." Also explains such regional proverbial expressions as "New moon holding water" and "Another hog in this wallow."

487. **Faulkner Concordances**. Jack L. Capps, general ed. West Point, NY: Faulkner Concordance Advisory Board, U. S. Military Academy; Ann Arbor, MI: University Microfilms International, 1977-. In progress. ISSN 9050917.

An ambitious project begun in 1965 at the U.S. Military Academy and distributed by UMI, the "Faulkner Concordances" will concord all of Faulkner's works. Most volumes take as their base texts modern reprintings of first editions and include references to variants, particularly to typescripts in the Alderman Library of the University of Virginia. References give page and line numbers, with context lines. Volumes also include alphabetical and numerical frequency lists. Published volumes include:

487.1. Vol. 1: Capps, Jack L. **As I Lay Dying: A Concordance to the Novel**. West Point, NY: Faulkner Concordance Advisory Board, 1977. 428p. LC 77-298. ISBN 0-8357-0254-5.

This is based on 1967 Modern Library edition, which was reproduced from the 1964 (New York: Random House) edition.

487.2. Vol. 2: Capps, Jack L. **Go Down, Moses: A Concordance to the Novel**. West Point, NY; Faulkner Concordance Advisory Board, 1977. 2 vols. LC 77-15831. ISBN 0-8357-0279-0.

The base text is the 1955 Modern Library issue of the 1942 (New York: Random House) edition.

487.3. Vol. 3: Polk, Noel. **Requiem for a Nun: A Concordance to the Novel**. West Point, NY: Faulkner Concordance Advisory Board, 1979. 537p. LC 78-31191. ISBN 0-8357-0370-3.

Polk concords the text of the "fourth printing" of the first edition (New York: Random House, 1951).

487.4. Vol. 4: Capps, Jack L. **Light in August: A Concordance to the Novel**. West Point, NY: Faulkner Concordance Advisory Board, 1979. 2 vols. LC 79-9324. ISBN 0-8357-0429-7.

Capps bases this concordance on the text of the 1968 Modern Library edition, which was reprinted from the first printing of the first edition (New York: Smith & Haas, 1932).

487.5. Vol. 5: Polk, Noel, and Kenneth L. Privratsky. **The Sound and the Fury: A Concordance to the Novel**. West Point, NY: Faulkner Concordance Advisory Board, 1980. 2 vols. LC 80-12310. ISBN 0-8357-0513-7.

The base text is the 1963 Vintage Books edition, which was reproduced from the first printing of the first edition (New York: Jonathan Cape and Harrison Smith, 1929).

487.6. Vol. 6: Polk, Noel, and Kenneth L. Privratsky. **A Fable: A Concordance to the Novel**. Westpoint, NY: Faulkner Concordance Advisory Board, 1981. 2 vols. LC 81-3369. ISBN 0-8357-0587-0.

This is based on the first printing of the first edition of *The Fable* (New York: Random House, 1954), with variants from Faulkner's corrected typescript in the Alderman Library.

487.7. Vol. 7: Privratsky, Kenneth L. **The Wild Palms: A Concordance to the Novel**. West Point, NY: Faulkner Concordance Advisory Board, 1983. 767p. LC 83-1472. ISBN 0-8357-1049-1.

Based on the first printing of the first edition (New York: Random House, 1939), with variant readings from the typescript setting copy in the Alderman Library, this gives page and line references, with context lines, and includes appendixes of alphabetical and ranked word frequencies.

487.8. Vol. 8: Polk, Noel. **Intruder in the Dust: A Concordance to the Novel**. West Point, NY: Faulkner Concordance Advisory Board, 1983. 620p. LC 83-18270. ISBN 0-8357-0621-4.

Polk concords the text of the first printing of the first edition (New York: Random House, 1948).

487.9. Vol. 9: Polk, Noel, and Lawrence Z. Pizzi. **The Town: A Concordance to the Novel**. West Point, NY: Faulkner Concordance Advisory Board, 1985. 2 vols. LC 85-9841. ISBN 0-8357-0683-4.

This concords the text of the first printing of the first edition (New York: Random House, 1957), with variant readings from the typescript-setting copy in the Alderman Library and from the fourth printing (New York: Random House, 1964). References give page and line numbers, with context lines. Appendixes include alphabetical and ranked word frequencies.

487.10. Vol. 10: Polk, Noel, and John D. Hart. **Mansion: A Concordance to the Novel**. West Point, NY: Faulkner Concordance Advisory Board, 1988. 2 vols. LC 88-32704. ISBN 0-8357-0804-7.

Polk and Hart provide references to pages and lines, with context lines, based on the first printing of the first edition (New York: Random House, 1959), with variant readings from the typescript-setting copy in the Alderman Library and from the third edition (New York: Random House, 1964). Alphabetical and ranked frequency tables are appended.

487.11. Vol. 11: Polk, Noel, and John D. Hart. **Absalom, Absalom!: A Concordance to the Novel**. West Point, NY: Faulkner Concordance Advisory Board, 1989. 2 vols. LC 89-4921. ISBN 0-8357-0863-2.

Based on the corrected text of the 1986 (New York: Random House) edition, with variant readings from the typescript-setting copy, galley proofs, the manuscript in the Alderman Library, and the first edition (New York: Random House, 1936), this gives page and line references, with context lines. Alphabetical and ranked word frequency tables are appended.

487.12. Vol. 12: Polk, Noel, and John D. Hart. **Pylon: A Concordance to the Novel**. West Point, NY: Faulkner Concordance Advisory Board, 1989. 680p. LC 89-37165. ISBN 0-8357-0880-2.

Polk and Hart concord the text of *Pylon* included on pp. 779-992 of the first printing of Faulkner's *Novels 1930-1935* (New York: Library of America, 1985), with variant readings from the typescript copy in the Alderman Library. References give pages and lines, with context lines. Alphabetical and ranked frequency tables are appendixed.

487.13. Vol 13: Polk, Noel, and John D. Hart. **Collected Stories of William Faulkner: A Concordance to the Forty-Two Short Stories: With Statistical Summaries and Vocabulary Listings for Collected Stories, These 13, and Dr. Martino and Other Stories.** West Point, NY: Faulkner Concordance Advisory Board [forthcoming]. LC 90-10900. ISBN 0-8357-0920-5.

487.14. Vol. 14: Polk, Noel, and John D. Hart. **The Hamlet: A Concordance to the Novel.** West Point, NY: Faulkner Concordance Advisory Board, 1990. 2 vols. LC 90-38928. ISBN 0-8357-0867-5.
Based on the text provided on pp. 731-1,075 of the first printing of *Novels 1936-1940* (New York: Library of America, 1990), Polk and Hart give page and line references and context lines. Alphabetical and ranked word frequency tables are appended.

487.15. Vol. 15: Polk, Noel, and John D. Hart. **The Unvanquished: A Concordance to the Novel.** 509p. West Point, NY: Faulkner Concordance Advisory Board, 1989. LC 90-39453. ISBN 0-8357-0932-9.
Polk and Hart concord the text provided on pp. 321-492 of the first printing of *Novels 1936-1940* (New York: Library of America, 1990), giving page and line references and context lines, with appended alphabetical and ranked word frequency tables.

487.16. Vol. 16: Polk, Noel, and John D. Hart. **Sanctuary: The Original Text, 1981: A Concordance to the Novel.** West Point, NY: Faulkner Concordance Advisory Board, 1990. 690p. LC 90-13881. ISBN 0-8357-0938-8.
Concords the text of the first printing of the first edition (New York: Random House, 1981), edited by Noel Polk.

487.17. Vol. 17: Polk, Noel, and John D. Hart. **Sanctuary: Corrected First Edition Text, 1985: A Concordance to the Novel.** West Point, NY: Faulkner Concordance Advisory Board, 1990. 630p. LC 90-45544. ISBN 0-8357-0939-6.
Based on text of pp. 181-398 of the first printing of Faulkner's *Novels 1930-1935* (New York: Library of America, 1985).

487.18. Vol. 18: Polk, Noel, and John D. Hart. **Uncollected Stories of William Faulkner: Concordance of the Forty-Five Short Stories.** West Point, NY: Faulkner Concordance Advisory Board, 1990. 5 vols. LC 90-13857. ISBN 0-8357-0940-X.
Concords separately the texts of the 20 stories revised for later books (*The Unvanquished; The Hamlet; Go Down, Moses; Big Woods;* and *The Mansion*) and 25 stories appearing in the first edition of *Uncollected Stories of William Faulkner* (New York: Random House, 1959), with consolidated statistical summaries and vocabulary listings for previously published stories, stories first published in *Uncollected Stories*, and the complete set.

487.19. Vol. 19: Polk, Noel, and John D. Hart. **The Reivers: A Concordance to the Novel.** West Point, NY: Faulkner Concordance Advisory Board, 1990. 804p. LC 90-22949. ISBN 0-8357-0947-7.
Based on the first printing, first edition (New York: Random House, 1962), with variant readings from the typescript, plate changes, and Faulkner's emendations. Appended alphabetical and frequency lists.

Journals

488.   **The Faulkner Journal.** Akron, OH: University of Akron, 1985-. 2/yr. ISSN 0884-2949.
Recent issues of this scholarly journal regularly feature four or five substantial articles that examine Faulkner's life or offer critical readings of his works. "Anti-Semitism, Humor, and Rage in Faulkner's *The Hamlet*," "Familiar and Fantastic: Women in *Absolom! Absolom!*" and "Faulkner on Lynching" are typical

articles. Occasional special issues (with a more extensive number of articles) have focused on specific topics, such as Faulkner and the military or sexuality. A recent special double issue on Faulkner and Latin America contained several bibliographical contributions, including "William Faulkner's Works Translated into Spanish," 11.1-2 (Fall 1995/Spring 1996): 181-84. A special issue on Faulkner and masculinity is scheduled for 1998. *The Faulkner Journal* does not publish reviews. Issues are about one year behind schedule. *The Faulkner Journal* is indexed in *MLA*.

489.   **The Faulkner Newsletter & Yoknapatawpha Review**. Oxford, MS: Yoknapatawpha Review, 1981-. 4/yr. ISSN 0733-6357.
A newsletter that appeals to the practical interests of Faulkner scholars, this features reports related to Faulkner's biography, news about research in progress, announcements of new publications, a current "Checklist" of recent criticisms, information about conferences, obituaries, and the like. Increasing attention is paid to availability of Faulkner materials on the Internet. Vol. 26.6 (October-December 1996): 1, announces the URL for *The Faulkner Newsletter & Yoknapatawpha Review*: http://watervalley.net/yoknapatawphapress/index.htm. *The Faulkner Newsletter & Yoknapatawpha Review* is not indexed.
Wortman's *A Guide to Serial Bibliographies for Modern Literature*, pp. 256-57, describes other serial bibliographies for Faulkner. Patterson's *Author Newsletters and Journals*, pp. 119-20, describes other previously published journals for Faulkner.

490.   **Faulkner Studies**. Kyoto: Yamaguchi Publishing House, 1992-. 2/yr. ISSN 0917-4265.
"Devoted exclusively to commentary on William Faulkner" (masthead), issues of *Faulkner Studies* include four critical studies (in English by both American and Japanese scholars) and a few book reviews. Most articles focus on Faulkner's sources or offer close readings of particular works. Others have addressed Faulkner's literary relations with A. E. Housman and James Joyce. Issues also contain book reviews. *Faulkner Studies* is indexed in *MLA*.

Irvin Faust, 1924-
Bibliographies
For works by Faust, see *First Printings of American Authors*, vol. 1, p. 127. See *Bibliography of American Fiction, 1919-1988*, p. 191, for Faust's checklist of works by and about him.

Edgar Fawcett, 1847-1904
Bibliographies
For works by Fawcett, see *Bibliography of American Literature*, vol. 3, pp. 86-102. Fawcett's contributions to and reviews of Fawcett's works in selected periodicals are identified in Wells' *The Literary Index to American Magazines, 1850-1900*, pp. 135-36. Fawcett's manuscripts are listed in Robbins' *American Literary Manuscripts*, pp. 106-107. See *Bibliography of American Fiction, 1866-1918*, pp. 167-68, for Kevin S. Best's checklist of works by and about Fawcett.

Theodore Sedgwick Fay, 1807-1898
Bibliographies
For works by Fay, see *Bibliography of American Literature*, vol. 3, pp. 103-10. Fay's contributions to and reviews of Fay's works in selected periodicals are identified in Wells' *The Literary Index to American Magazines, 1815-1865*, pp. 54-55; and *The Literary Index to American Magazines, 1850-1900*, p. 136. Fay's manuscripts are listed in Robbins' *American Literary Manuscripts*, p. 107. See *Bibliography of American Fiction Through 1865*, pp.106-107, for a checklist of works by and about Fay.

Kenneth Fearing, 1902-1961
Bibliographies

For works by Fearing, see *First Printings of American Authors*, vol. 1, pp. 129-30. Fearing's manuscripts are listed in Robbins' *American Literary Manuscripts*, p. 107.

Edna Ferber, 1887-1968
Bibliographies

See *Bibliography of American Fiction, 1919-1988*, pp. 192-93, for Ellen Serlen Uffen's checklist of works by and about Ferber. Ferber's manuscripts are listed in Robbins' *American Literary Manuscripts*, p. 107. Daniel Walden reviews works by and about Ferber in Shapiro's *Jewish American Women Writers*, pp. 72-79.

Lawrence Ferlinghetti, 1920-
Bibliographies

491. Morgan, Bill. **Lawrence Ferlinghetti: A Comprehensive Bibliography to 1980**. New York: Garland, 1982. 397p. (Garland Reference Library of the Humanities, vol. 256). LC 80-8974. ISBN 0-8240-9362-3.

Covering both primary and secondary materials, Morgan gives full bibliographic descriptions for Ferlinghetti's books, pamphlets, and broadsides; works translated by Ferlinghetti and contributions to books; contributions to periodicals; interviews; translations of Ferlinghetti's writings; recordings of Ferlinghetti and his works; television and film appearances; and miscellaneous writings, such as cards, programs, and the like. Coverage excludes Ferlinghetti's edited works. Entries give facsimiles and transcriptions of title pages, contents, physical descriptions, publishing histories, and references to reviews. Other sections list unannotated entries for about 600 biographical and critical materials about Ferlinghetti as well as describe musical settings and stage productions of his works. Ferlinghetti's manuscripts are listed in Robbins' *American Literary Manuscripts*, p. 108.

Vincent Ferrini, 1913-
Bibliographies

For works by Ferrini, see *First Printings of American Authors*, vol. 3, pp. 111-16. Ferrini's manuscripts are listed in Robbins' *American Literary Manuscripts*, p. 108.

Eugene Field, 1850-1895
Bibliographies

For works by Field, see *Bibliography of American Literature*, vol. 3, pp. 111-14. Field's contributions to and reviews of Field's works in selected periodicals are identified in Wells' *The Literary Index to American Magazines, 1850-1900*, pp. 136-37. Field's manuscripts are listed in Robbins' *American Literary Manuscripts*, p. 109.

Henry Fielding, 1707-1754
Bibliographies

492. Morrissey, L. J. **Henry Fielding: A Reference Guide**. Boston: G. K. Hall, 1980. 560p. (A Reference Guide to Literature). LC 80-16396. ISBN 0-8161-8139-x.

Morrissey chronologically arranges annotated entries for about 3,000 works by and about Fielding published from 1755 through 1977. Coverage is comprehensive, including editions and translations of primary texts as well as early anonymous notices, dissertations, and criticisms in all languages. Annotations are detailed and critical, clearly identifying significant editions and studies and citing references to reviews. Indexing by critics and subjects references studies of individual works. This supersedes critical coverage of Fielding provided in Francesco Cordasco's *Henry Fielding: A List of Critical Studies Published from 1895 to 1946* (Brooklyn, NY: Long Island University Press, 1948). George H. Hahn's *Henry Fielding: An Annotated Bibliography* (Metuchen, NJ: Scarecrow Press, 1979), which includes entries for 962 works published from 1900 through 1978; and John A. Stoler and Richard D. Fulton's *Henry Fielding: An Annotated Bibliography of Twentieth-Century Criticism, 1900-1977* (New York: Garland, 1980), offer supplementary coverage of twentieth-century non-English-language criticisms. Coverage of Fielding's primary works is provided in Wilbur L. Cross' "Bibliography" in *The History of Henry Fielding* (New Haven, CT: Yale University Press, 1918), vol. 3, pp. 287-366. For a bibliography of works by and about Fielding, see *NCBEL*, II, pp. 925-48, by Martin C. Battestin. Fielding's manuscripts are described in *Index of English Literary Manuscripts*, III, pt. 1: 355-57. A facsimile of the 1755 auction catalog of Fielding's library (with copious descriptive notes, appendixes, and indexes), Frederick G. Ribble and Anne G. Ribble's *Fielding's Library: An Annotated Catalogue* (Charlottesville, VA: The Bibliographical Society of the University of Virginia, 1996), attempts "to understand Fielding as a reader through a study of the editions he owned and his intellectual response to them" (p. vii). Research on Fielding is reviewed by Martin C. Battestin in Dyson's *The English Novel*, pp. 71-89.

Dictionaries, Encyclopedias, and Handbooks
See Johnson's *Plots and Characters in the Fiction of Eighteenth-Century English Authors* (entry 1309) for plot summaries of Fielding's major works.

Indexes and Concordances

493.   Farringdon, Michael G. **A Concordance and Word-Lists to Henry Fielding's Joseph Andrews**. Swansea: Ariel House, 1984. 17 microfiche; 117p. ISBN 0-906948-03-7.
The microfiche concordance is based on Martin C. Battestin's text in *The Wesleyan Edition of the Works of Henry Fielding* (Middletown, CT: Wesleyan University Press, 1967). The accompanying printed guide includes appendixes of alphabetical and ranked word frequencies, hyphenated words, and the like.

494.   Farringdon, Michael G. **A Concordance and Word-Lists to Henry Fielding's Shamela**. Swansea: Ariel House, 1982. 4 microfiche; 16p. ISBN 0-906948-02-9.
Farringdon bases this concordance on the text of *An Apology for the Life of Mrs. Shamela Andrews* (Los Angeles, CA: Augustan Reprint Society, 1956). The accompanying paper guide includes lists of hyphenated words, words with missing letters, and statistical data.

Journals
"Recent Articles" in *The Scriblerian and the Kit Cats* (entry 1084) regularly includes a selection of reviews of studies on Fielding.

James T(homas) Fields, 1817-1881
Bibliographies
For works by Fields, see *Bibliography of American Literature*, vol. 3, pp. 142-58. Fields' contributions to and reviews of Fields' works in selected periodicals are identified in Wells' *The Literary Index to American Magazines, 1815-1865*, p. 55; and *The Literary Index to American Magazines, 1850-1900*, pp. 138-39. Fields' manuscripts are listed in Robbins' *American Literary Manuscripts*, p. 110-11.

Martha (Farquharson) Finley, 1828-1909
Bibliographies
See *Bibliography of American Fiction Through 1865*, pp.107-110, for a checklist of works by and about Finley.

The Fight at Finnsburh, c. 750
Bibliographies
Greenfield and Robinson's *A Bibliography of Publications on Old English Literature to the End of 1972*, pp. 119-21, lists editions, translations, and studies of

the Old English *Battle of Finnsburh*, with citations for reviews. Fry's *Beowulf and the Fight at Finnsburgh* (entry 101) describes criticism through 1967. Also for works about the *Battle of Finnsburh*, see *NCBEL*, I, pp. 240-41.

(Arthur Annesley) Ronald Firbank, 1886-1926
Bibliographies
495.   Benkovitz, Miriam J. **A Bibliography of Ronald Firbank**. 2d ed. New York: Oxford University Press, 1982. 106p. (The Soho Bibliographies, no. 16). ISBN 0-19-818188-4.

First published in 1963 (London: R. Hart-Davis), Benkovitz gives full bibliographic descriptions for Firbank's primary works, including his books and separate works; contributions to books; contributions to periodicals; and manuscripts and typescripts (pp. 87-93), with locations. Entries give title-page transcriptions, physical descriptions, and publishing histories. Also for a bibliography of works by and about Firbank, see *NCBEL*, IV, pp. 567-69.

496.   Moore, Steven. **Ronald Firbank: An Annotated Bibliography of Secondary Materials, 1905-1995.** Normal, IL: Dalkey Archive, Illinois State University, 1996. 154p. (Dalkey Archive Bibliography Series, vol. 3). LC 96-15667. ISBN 1-564-78133-x.

Comprehensively covering criticisms of Firbank, Moore offers approximately 850 unnumbered, annotated entries in sections for reviews (chronologically arranged by Firbank's books); books about Firbank, including annotated citations for their reviews; essays, parts of books, and other periodical contributions about Firbank; creative works mentioning or otherwise influenced by Firbank; dissertations and theses; and non-English-language materials. Entries for reviews in newspapers predominate. Critical and evaluative annotations typically excerpt criticisms. Index references names of critics and reviewers as well as persons cited in descriptions, such as Sappho, Laurence Sterne, and James Joyce, giving limited topical access.

Vardis (Alvero) Fisher, 1895-1968
Bibliographies
497.   Kellogg, George Alexis. **Vardis Fisher: A Bibliography**. Moscow, ID: The Library, University of Idaho, 1961. 19 leaves. OCLC 3688537.

Alphabetically arranged checklist of first and subsequent editions and translations of Fisher's books; works edited by Fisher; contributions to periodicals; and anthologized works, with an unannotated list of criticism and reviews of Fisher's writings. Unindexed. First published as a supplement to *The Bookmark* 13.3 (March 1961). See *Bibliography of American Fiction, 1919-1988*, pp. 193-95, for Joseph M. Flora's checklist of works by and about Fisher. Fisher's manuscripts are listed in Robbins' *American Literary Manuscripts*, p. 112. Flora surveys works by and about Fisher in Erisman and Etulain's *Fifty Western Writers*, pp. 110-20.

John Fiske, 1842-1901
Bibliographies
For works by Fiske, see *Bibliography of American Literature*, vol. 3, pp. 159-79. Fiske's contributions to and reviews of Fiske's works in selected periodicals are identified in Wells' *The Literary Index to American Magazines, 1850-1900*, pp. 139-40. Fiske's manuscripts are listed in Robbins' *American Literary Manuscripts*, p. 112.

(William) Clyde Fitch, 1865-1909
Bibliographies
For works by Fitch, see *Bibliography of American Literature*, vol. 3, pp. 180-86. Fitch's manuscripts are listed in Robbins' *American Literary Manuscripts*, pp. 112-13. Kim Marra identifies works by and about Fitch in Demastes' *American Playwrights, 1880-1945*, pp. 80-90.

Edward FitzGerald, 1809-1883
Bibliographies
498. Prideaux, W. F. **Notes for a Bibliography of Edward FitzGerald**. London: Frank Hollings, 1901. 88p. LC 1-25255.

Also available in a reprinted edition (New York: Burt Franklin, 1968), Prideaux chronologically arranges full bibliographic descriptions of FitzGerald's separate works, posthumous works, and contributions to books and periodicals. Entries give title-page transcriptions, collations, contents, binding descriptions, and details on variants and other bibliographic points. Unindexed. Also for a bibliography of works by and about FitzGerald, see *NCBEL*, III, pp. 483-86. FitzGerald's manuscripts are described in *Index of English Literary Manuscripts*, IV, pt. 1:783-803, 831. Ehrsam's *Bibliographies of Twelve Victorian Authors*, pp. [77]-90, identifies international comments, criticism, and reviews for FitzGerald through the early twentieth century. Reviews of FitzGerald's works in selected periodicals are also identified in Wells' *The Literary Index to American Magazines, 1850-1900*, p. 141. See the review of research by Michael Timko in Faverty's *The Victorian Poets*, pp. 137-48.

F(rancis) Scott (Key) Fitzgerald, 1896-1940
Bibliographies
499. Bruccoli, Matthew J. **F. Scott Fitzgerald: A Descriptive Bibliography**. Revised ed. Pittsburgh, PA: University of Pittsburgh Press, 1987. 479p. (Pittsburgh Series in Bibliography). LC 87-40220. ISBN 0-8229-3560-0.

The standard listing of Fitzgerald's primary works, this cumulates and revises Bruccoli's *F. Scott Fitzgerald: A Descriptive Bibliography* (Pittsburgh, PA: University of Pittsburgh Press, 1972); and *Supplement* (Pittsburgh, PA: University of Pittsburgh Press, 1980). Bruccoli gives full bibliographic descriptions for Fitzgerald's separate publications and collected editions, first-appearance contributions to books, first-appearance contributions to magazines and newspapers, keepsakes, interviews, articles that include original Fitzgerald materials, blurbs, English-language editions of story collections published in Japan, published plays based on his works, and Fitzgerald's movie work. Entries provide facsimiles of title and copyright pages, collations, contents; physical descriptions of paper and bindings, publishing histories, and copy locations. Appendixes list the publications of Zelda Fitzgerald and about 60 selected works about Fitzgerald. Also for works by Fitzgerald, see *First Printings of American Authors*, vol. 1, pp. 131-34. Fitzgerald's manuscripts are listed in Robbins' *American Literary Manuscripts*, p. 113. Additionally, the "F. Scott Fitzgerald Manuscripts" series (New York: Garland, 1990-1991), edited by Matthew J. Bruccoli, reproduces many of Fitzgerald's literary holographs and typescripts.

500. Bryer, Jackson R. **The Critical Reputation of F. Scott Fitzgerald: A Bibliographical Study**. Hamden, CT: Archon Books, 1967. 434p. LC 67-24031.
This is supplemented by:

500.1. Bryer, Jackson R. **The Critical Reputation of F. Scott Fitzgerald: A Bibliographical Study: Supplement One Through 1981**. Hamden, CT: Archon Books, 1984. 542p. LC 82-25536. ISBN 0-208-01489-6.

A comprehensive guide to criticisms of Fitzgerald, vol. 1 supplies annotated entries for about 2,000 critical materials on Fitzgerald published from 1912 through 1965. Vol. 2 adds about 2,500 items published through 1983. Separate listings in both volumes cover reviews of Fitzgerald's works (arranged by works), articles, books and parts of books, and dissertations and master's theses about Fitzgerald. Annotations are descriptive and critical. Significant studies are identified. Appendixes listing first appearances of works by Fitzgerald and Zelda Fitzgerald are superseded by Bruccoli's revised primary bibliography (entry 499). Topical indexing for names and subjects, arranged under Fitzgerald's name, give solid access, particularly in vol. 2. Editions and criticism of Fitzgerald's works outside the United States are described in Linda C. Stanley's *The Non-English Critical Reputation of F. Scott Fitzgerald: An Analysis and Annotated Bibliography* (Westport, CT: Greenwood, 1980). See *Bibliography of American Fiction, 1919-1988*, pp. 196-201, for Bruccoli's checklist of works by and about Fitzgerald. Research on Fitzgerald is reviewed by Bryer in his *Sixteen Modern American Authors*, pp. 277-321; and the supplement by Bryer in his *Sixteen Modern American Authors: Volume 2: A Survey of Research and Criticism Since 1972*, pp. 301-59. *ALS* annually features a review essay on Fitzgerald scholarship.

Indexes and Concordances

501.   Crosland, Andrew T. **A Concordance to F. Scott Fitzgerald's The Great Gatsby**. Detroit, MI: Gale, 1975. 425p. (A Bruccoli Clark Book). LC 74-11607. ISBN 0-8103-1005-8.

This is based on the text of the first printing of *The Great Gatsby* (New York: Scribner's, 1925), with emendations from Matthew J. Bruccoli's *Apparatus for a Definitive Edition of The Great Gatsby* (Columbia, SC: University of South Carolina Press, 1974) and references to the Scribner Library edition. Alphabetical and ranked word frequency lists.

Journals

502.   **The F. Scott Fitzgerald Society Newsletter**. Hempstead, NY: The F. Scott Fitzgerald Society, 1991-. Annual. ISSN 1072-5504.

Annual newsletter occasionally featuring one or two brief articles on topics related to Fitzgerald's works but mainly publishing four to six book reviews and descriptions of many conference programs related to Fitzgerald. Particular attention in 1996 focused on Fitzgerald centenaries. A regular bibliographic feature, "F. Scott Fitzgerald—Current Bibliography" is a checklist of editions and studies published as books, chapters, articles, dissertations, book reviews, and news features. *The F. Scott Fitzgerald Society Newsletter* is unindexed.

Wortman's *Guide to Serial Bibliographies for Modern Literatures*, p. 257, describes previously published serial bibliographies for Fitzgerald. See Patterson's *Author Newsletters and Journals*, pp. 121-22, for previously published journals for Fitzgerald.

Zelda Fitzgerald, 1899-1948

Bibliographies

For works by Fitzgerald, see *First Printings of American Authors*, vol. 2, p. 163. Fitzgerald's manuscripts are listed in Robbins' *American Literary Manuscripts*, p. 113. The bibliographies of Bruccoli (entry 499) and Bryer (entry 500) list works by and about Zelda Fitzgerald.

Janet Flanner, 1892-1978

Bibliographies

For works by Flanner, see *First Printings of American Authors*, vol. 4, pp. 181-84. Flanner's manuscripts are listed in Robbins' *American Literary Manuscripts*, p. 113.

Giles Fletcher, the Younger, 1585?-1623

Bibliographies

For a bibliography of works by and about Fletcher, see *NCBEL*, I, pp. 1190-91. Fletcher's manuscripts are described in *Index of English Literary Manuscripts*, I, pt. 2:75-77.

John Gould Fletcher, 1886-1950
Bibliographies

503. Morton, Bruce. **John Gould Fletcher: A Bibliography**. Kent, OH: Kent State University Press, 1979. 203p. (The Serif Series: Bibliographies and Checklists, no. 37). LC 79-10897. ISBN 0-87338-229-3.

Morton describes Fletcher's works in detail, covering his books; articles, poems, and reviews; editions and translations of his works; and miscellaneous works (such as recordings and musical settings). Entries offer title-page transcriptions, collations, contents, physical descriptions, and information on publishing histories. In addition, Morton describes about 250 books, articles, and dissertations about Fletcher. Fletcher's manuscripts are listed in Robbins' *American Literary Manuscripts*, p. 114. Research on Fletcher is reviewed by William Pratt in Flora and Bain's *Fifty Southern Writers After 1900*, pp. 177-87.

Phineas Fletcher, 1582-1650
Bibliographies

For a bibliography of works by and about Fletcher, see *NCBEL*, I, pp. 1187-88. Fletcher's manuscripts are described in *Index of English Literary Manuscripts*, I, pt. 2: 83-85.

Timothy Flint, 1780-1840
Bibliographies

For works by Flint, see *Bibliography of American Literature*, vol. 3, pp. 187-93. Contributions by Flint and criticism and reviews of Flint's works in selected periodicals are identified in Wells' *The Literary Index to American Magazines, 1815-1865*, p. 56. Flint's manuscripts are listed in Robbins' *American Literary Manuscripts*, p. 114. See *Bibliography of American Fiction Through 1865*, pp. 110-11, for a checklist of works by and about Flint.

John Florio, c. 1553-1625
Bibliographies

For a bibliography of works by and about Florio, see *NCBEL*, I, pp. 2029, 2137, 2150. Florio's manuscripts are described in *Index of English Literary Manuscripts*, I, pt. 2:87-88.

Mary Hallock Foote, 1847-1938
Bibliographies

See *Bibliography of American Fiction, 1866-1918*, pp. 170-71, for Gwen L. Nagel's checklist of works by and about Foote. Foote's manuscripts are listed in Robbins' *American Literary Manuscripts*, pp. 114-15. James H. Maguire surveys works by and about Foote in Erisman and Etulain's *Fifty Western Writers*, pp. 121-30.

Samuel Foote, 1720-1777
Bibliographies

For a bibliography of works by and about Foote, see *NCBEL*, II, pp. 809-11.

Shelby Foote, 1916-
Bibliographies

For works by Foote, see *First Printings of American Authors*, vol. 2, pp. 165-66. Foote's manuscripts are listed in Robbins' *American Literary Manuscripts*, p. 115. See *Bibliography of American Fiction, 1919-1988*, pp. 202-203, for Robert L. Phillips, Jr.'s checklist of works by and about Foote. See the review of research by Robert L. Phillips in Flora and Bain's *Fifty Southern Writers After 1900*, pp. 188-95; and supplemented in Bain and Flora's *Contemporary Poets, Dramatists, Essayists, and Novelists of the South*, p. 565.

Ford Madox Ford (Ford Hermann Hueffer), 1873-1939
Bibliographies

504. Harvey, David Dow. **Ford Madox Ford, 1873-1939: A Bibliography of Works and Criticism**. Princeton, NJ: Princeton University Press, 1962. 633p. LC 63-337.

The best listing of Ford's primary works, this includes detailed bibliographic descriptions in separate listings for Ford's books and collaborative works; contributions to books (including Ford's translations); manuscripts and letters, covering the extensive collection in Princeton University's Firestone Library (pp. 105-130), and miscellaneous works; and contributions to journals. Entries give title-page transcriptions, physical descriptions, contents, and publishing histories. Harvey also describes about 1,200 books and articles about Ford and reviews of his works. Also for a bibliography of works by and about Ford, see *NCBEL*, IV, pp. 569-75.

Indexes and Concordances

505. Sabol, C. Ruth, and Todd K. Bender. **A Concordance to Ford Madox Ford's The Good Soldier**. New York: Garland, 1981. 186p. (Garland Reference Library of the Humanities, vol. 283). LC 80-9003. ISBN 0-8240-9371-2.

Modeled on volumes in Garland's Conrad Concordance series (entry 293), this provides a field of reference that mirrors the pagination, lineation, spelling, and punctuation of *The Good Soldier/A Tale of Passion*, by Ford Madox Huefer (London: John Lane, 1915). A verbal index references pages and lines but does not cite context lines. Appends alphabetical word-frequency table.

Jesse Hill Ford, 1928-
Bibliographies

506. White, Helen. **Jesse Hill Ford: An Annotated Check List of His Published Works and of His Papers**. Memphis, TN: John Willard Brister Library, Memphis State University, 1974. 55p. (MVC Bulletin, no. 7). LC 74-623241.

This records the collection deposited in the Mississippi Valley Collection of Memphis State University's John Willard Brister Library, covering published works, manuscripts of published and unpublished works, miscellaneous writings, correspondence, and 19 biographical and critical materials. Entries for Ford's works give brief bibliographic data and summaries of contents.

John Ford, 1586-after 1639
Bibliographies

507. Tucker, Kenneth. **A Bibliography of Writings by and About John Ford and Cyril Tourneur**. Boston: G. K. Hall, 1977. 134p. LC 76-44005. ISBN 0-8161-7834-8.

Tucker surveys scholarship on both playwrights in his introduction and offers separate, alphabetically arranged lists of primary and secondary works. Coverage includes early and modern editions as well as early notices, dissertations, and passing references in general resources. Contains entries for about 500 critical works for Ford and about 400 for Tourneur. Selective annotations for criticisms do little more than identify their subjects. Tucker's coverage of Ford and Tourneur supersedes the coverage in the Tannenbaums' *Elizabethan Bibliographies*, vols. 2 and 10; and *Elizabethan Bibliographies Supplements*, nos. 8 and 2. For a bibliography of works by and about Ford, see *NCBEL*, I, pp. 1721-25. Ford's manuscripts are described in *Index of English Literary Manuscripts*, I, pt. 2: 89-91. Research on Ford and Tourneur is reviewed by Inga-Stina Ewbank in Wells' *English Drama*, pp. 113-33. Research on Ford is reviewed by Donald K. Anderson, Jr., in Logan and Smith's *The Later Jacobean and Caroline Dramatists*, pp. 120-51. Research on Tourneur is reviewed by Charles R. Forker in Logan and Smith's *The New Intellectuals*, pp. 248-80. Logan and Smith's reviews of research on Tourneur and Ford are updated by Lidman's *Studies in Jacobean Drama, 1973-1984*, pp. 107-21 and 233-46.

Paul Leicester Ford, 1865-1902
Bibliographies
    For works by Ford, see *Bibliography of American Literature*, vol. 3, pp. 194-210. Ford's contributions to and reviews of Ford's works in selected periodicals are identified in Wells' *The Literary Index to American Magazines, 1850-1900*, p. 142. Ford's manuscripts are listed in Robbins' *American Literary Manuscripts*, p. 115. See *Bibliography of American Fiction, 1866-1918*, pp. 172-73, for William F. Cash's checklist of works by and about Ford.

E(dward) M(organ) Forster, 1879-1970
Bibliographies
    508. Kirkpatrick, B. J. **A Bibliography of E. M. Forster**. 2d ed. New York: Oxford University Press, 1985. 327p. (The Soho Bibliographies, no. 19). LC 85-3081. ISBN 0-19-818191-4.
    The standard guide to Forster's primary works, Kirkpatrick gives detailed descriptions in separate listings for Forster's books and pamphlets; contributions to books and pamphlets; contributions to journals and newspapers; translations of Forster's works (arranged by languages); miscellaneous writings (including reported speeches, musical settings, and large-print editions); miscellaneous media (such as recordings, screen adaptations, and broadcasts in non-English languages); and manuscripts in a variety of collections, including the British Library, the Berg Collection of the New York Public Library, and the University of Texas' Harry Ransom Humanities Research Center. Forster's letters are not described. Entries give title-page transcriptions, physical descriptions, and publishing histories. Additional information on Forster's primary materials is available in Mary Lago's *Calendar of the Letters of E. M. Forster* (London: Mansell, 1985). Also for a bibliography of works by and about Forster, see *NCBEL*, IV, pp. 437-44.

    509. McDowell, Frederick P. W. **E. M. Forster: An Annotated Bibliography of Writings About Him**. DeKalb, IL: Northern Illinois University Press, 1976. 924p. (An Annotated Secondary Bibliography Series on English Literature in Transition, 1880-1920). LC 73-18797. ISBN 0-87580-046-7.
    The best listing of works about Forster, McDowell chronologically arranges annotated entries for 1,913 books, parts of books, articles, reviews, dissertations, articles in general reference works, letters to the editor in newspapers, and other critical materials published in all languages from 1905 through 1975. Annotations are descriptive, substantial, and scholarly and clearly identify important studies. As with other volumes in the series, a complex set of separate indexes references primary and secondary titles, languages, and names to offer comprehensive access. McDowell's guide is more useful than Alfred Borrello's *E. M. Forster: An Annotated Bibliography of Secondary Materials* (Metuchen, NJ: Scarecrow Press, 1973), which describes about 700 critical works. Research on Forster is reviewed by Malcolm Bradbury in Dyson's *The English Novel*, pp. 314-33.

    510. Summers, Claude J. **E. M. Forster: A Guide to Research**. New York: Garland, 1991. 405p. (Garland Reference Library of the Humanities, vol. 1101). LC 90-21293. ISBN 0-8240-4624-2.
    A selective guide to works by and about Forster published through 1990, complementing the more comprehensive coverage of Kirkpatrick (entry 508) and McDowell (entry 509). Part 1 briefly and critically describes Forster's novels, short fiction, and nonfiction; scholarly editions; and collections of letters and documents. In part 2, Summers evaluates nearly 1,300 works about Forster in sections for bibliographies; biographical materials; book-length studies and essay collections; general critical articles; and studies of the six individual novels, short fiction, and nonfiction. Thorough annotations indicate standard, essential, and otherwise important works. Detailed indexes for authors, subjects, and Forster's works. A very useful starting point for research.

Dictionaries, Encyclopedias, and Handbooks
511.   Borrello, Alfred. **An E. M. Forster Dictionary**. Metuchen, NJ: Scarecrow Press, 1971. 201p. LC 72-15109. ISBN 0-8108-0392-5.
The first volume in Borrello's Forster trilogy, this summarizes Forster's fiction and nonfiction works (excluding uncollected works) and identifies and describes characters and place names. An index lists characters by works. A second volume by Borrello, *An E. M. Forster Glossary* (Metuchen, NJ: Scarecrow Press, 1972), identifies and describes Forster's allusions (names, titles, and other references) to music, art, mythology, current events, and the like. Borrello's bibliography of criticism of Forster is superseded by McDowell's guide (entry 509). Aimed at novices or undergraduate readers, Nigel Messenger's *How to Study an E. M. Forster Novel* (Houndmills, Basingstoke: Macmillan, 1991), a volume in the "How to Study Literature" series, offers step-by-step advice on approaches to Forster.

512.   Stape, J. H. **An E. M. Forster Chronology**. Basingstoke: Macmillan, 1993. 198p. (Macmillan Author Chronologies). LC 93-20424. ISBN 0-333-54540-0.
Chronicles Forster's literary career and public activities. Fullest detail provided for 1914 to 1946, dependent on accessibility of Forster's papers in King's College, Cambridge (p. viii). Particular emphasis on Forster's early reading. Includes "Who's Who" of about fifty family and contemporaries, directory of locations and addresses, and selected bibliography (pp. 181-82). Indexes of names, Forster's works (major writings, lectures, selected broadcasts, and unpublished works but not reviews by Forster), and authors of Forster's reading. Absence of subject indexing, however, makes it impossible to track Forster's travels and holidays or identify when he gave an address or wrote a review.

Journals
See Patterson's *Author Newsletters and Journals*, p. 124, for previously published journals for Forster.

Hannah Webster Foster, 1758-1840
Bibliographies
For works by Foster, see *Bibliography of American Literature*, vol. 3, p. 211. See *Bibliography of American Fiction Through 1865*, pp.112-13, for a checklist of works by and about Foster.

John Robert Fowles, 1926-
Bibliographies
513.   Olshen, Barry N., and Toni A. Olshen. **John Fowles: A Reference Guide**. Boston: G. K. Hall, 1980. 88p. (Reference Guides to Literature). LC 80-10379. ISBN 0-8161-8187-x.
The Olshens provide a checklist of Fowles' primary works and a comprehensive bibliography of secondary works about Fowles published from 1963 through 1979. The checklist identifies Fowles' book-length fiction and nonfiction, stage and screen adaptations, poems and short fiction, essays, articles, and book reviews. A significant portion of the secondary materials consists of reviews in popular journals. Only a few books and dissertations were produced during this period. Annotations are generally descriptive; evaluative comments are limited. A cumulative index gives headings for forms (bibliography, biography, interviews) under Fowles' names, as well as headings for selected topics, such as "sources of fiction," "as novelist," and "literary influences on." Separate headings are also included for other writers, such as Vladimir Nabokov; primary works used by Fowles, such as Hardy's *A Pair of Blue Eyes* (as a source for *The French Lieutenant's Woman*); and broader subjects, such as "existentialism" and "games and game playing." An updated edition of this bibliography as well as a full descriptive bibliography of Fowles' primary works need to be completed. See

Ronald C. Dixon's summary biography, critical assessment of major works, and selected primary and secondary bibliography for Fowles in McCaffery's *Postmodern Fiction: A Bio-Bibliographical Guide*, pp. 363-66.

Dictionaries, Encyclopedias, and Handbooks

514.   Aubrey, James R. **John Fowles: A Reference Companion**. New York: Greenwood Press, 1991. 333p. LC 91-9553. ISBN 0-3132-6399-X.

This handbook includes a biography of Fowles and critical introductions to his writings. Entries for each of his works summarize plots, identify themes and characters, discuss critical receptions, and note film and other adaptations. A chapter identifies critical approaches to Fowles (historicist, deconstructive, biographical, and the like) and another glosses English- and non-English-language allusions in his works. An alphabetical list ("Census") of characters notes their appearances in the works. A classified bibliography of works by and about Fowles in part updates the coverage of criticism in the Olshens' *John Fowles: A Reference Guide* (entry 513) and fills the need for a descriptive guide to Fowles' primary works. Aubrey gives brief bibliographic data for Fowles' narrative fiction, poetry, drawings, screenplays, expository books and pamphlets, essays, book reviews, published letters, advertising copy, translations and adaptations, edited works, and excerpted works. Comprehensive index provides good access.

John (William) Fox, Jr., 1862-1919
Bibliographies

For works by Fox, see *Bibliography of American Literature*, vol. 3, pp. 212-16. Fox's manuscripts are listed in Robbins' *American Literary Manuscripts*, p. 116. See *Bibliography of American Fiction, 1866-1918*, pp. 174-75, for Sandra L. Ballard's checklist of works by and about Fox.

Ralph (Winston) Fox, 1900-1937
Bibliographies

Munton and Young's *Seven Writers of the English Left*, pp. 117-56, describes Fox's works published from 1920 through 1979, including non-English-language editions.

William Price Fox, 1926-
Bibliographies

For works by Fox, see *First Printings of American Authors*, vol. 1, p. 135.

John Foxe, 1516-1587
Bibliographies

For a bibliography of works by and about Foxe, see *NCBEL*, I, p. 2207. Foxe's manuscripts are described in *Index of English Literary Manuscripts*, I, pt. 2: 93-98, 627.

Convers Francis, 1795-1863
Bibliographies

Francis' manuscripts are listed in Robbins' *American Literary Manuscripts*, p. 116. Guy R. Woodall reviews research on Francis in Myerson's *The Transcendentalists*, pp. 167-70.

Benjamin Franklin, 1706-1790
Bibliographies

515.   Buxbaum, Melvin H. **Benjamin Franklin, 1721-1906: A Reference Guide**. Boston: G. K. Hall, 1983. 334p. (A Reference Publication in Literature). LC 82-12144. ISBN 0-8161-7985-9.

A companion volume is:

515.1. Buxbaum, Melvin H. **Benjamin Franklin, 1907-1983: A Reference Guide**. Boston: G. K. Hall, 1988. 796p. (A Reference Guide to Literature). LC 82-12144. ISBN 0-8161-8673-1.

Buxbaum's volumes provide comprehensive coverage of writings about Franklin. The 1983 volume chronologically arranges about 1,800 annotated entries, including some 270 from the eighteenth century. Coverage includes early notices of Franklin's scientific experiments and anonymous reviews of his satires; poems and dedications related to Franklin; and substantial numbers of commentaries on Franklin in French, German, Spanish, and Russian. The 1988 volume chronologically arranges about 4,000 entries, covering ephemeral pamphlets, advertisements, material about Franklin in reference works, dissertations, and non-English-language works. Annotations in both volumes are descriptive. Buxbaum describes significant works in great detail. Similarly, indexes in both volumes offer detailed subject access, including such topical subheadings under Franklin's name for "Benedict Arnold," "chess," "freemasonry," "money," and "religious views." Research on Franklin is reviewed by Bruce Granger in Harbert and Rees' *Fifteen American Authors Before 1900*, pp. 250-80; and by J. A. Leo LeMay in Everett Emerson's *Major Writers of Early American Literature*, pp. 205-44.

516. Ford, Paul Leicester. **Franklin Bibliography: A List of Books Written by, or Relating to Benjamin Franklin**. Brooklyn, NY: Historical Printing Club, 1889. 467p. LC 2-21672.

This is the standard guide to Franklin's primary works, including full bibliographic descriptions in about 1,000 entries. Available in a reprinted edition (New York: B. Franklin, 1968). Additional information on Franklin's primary bibliography is provided by C. William Miller's *Benjamin Franklin's Philadelphia Printing, 1728-1766: A Descriptive Bibliography* (Philadelphia, PA: American Philosophical Society, 1974); and J. A. Leo Lemay's *The Canon of Benjamin Franklin, 1722-1776: New Attributions and Reconsiderations* (Newark, DE: University of Delaware Press, 1986). Another useful guide, I. Minis Mays' *Calendar of the Papers of Benjamin Franklin in the Library of the American Philosophical Society* (Philadelphia, PA: University of Pennsylvania Press, 1908), describes the largest collection of Franklin materials, some 14,000 items, in the American Philosophical Society. Franklin's manuscripts are also listed in Robbins' *American Literary Manuscripts*, p. 117. James Green's *Poor Richard's Books: An Exhibition of Books Owned by Benjamin Franklin Now on the Shelves of the Library Company of Philadelphia* (Philadelphia, PA: The Library Company of Philadelphia, 1990) is also useful.

Dictionaries, Encyclopedias, and Handbooks

517. Barbour, Frances M. **A Concordance to the Sayings in Franklin's Poor Richard**. Detroit, MI: Gale, 1974. 245p. LC 73-20460. ISBN 0-8103-1009-0

Arranged under selected keywords from Franklin's sayings in his *Almanacks* (1733-58), entries give dates for the texts and references to standard dictionaries that contain them, including George Apperson's *English Proverbs and Proverbial Sayings* (1929; reprint Detroit, MI: Gale, 1969); William G. Smith's *The Oxford Dictionary of English Proverbs*, 2d ed. (New York: Oxford University Press, 1948); Burton Stevenson's *Home Book of Proverbs, Maxims, and Familiar Phrases* (New York: Macmillan, 1948); and Morris P. Tilley's *A Dictionary of Proverbs in England in the Sixteenth and Seventeenth Centuries* (Ann Arbor, MI: University of Michigan Press, 1950). The base texts are Paul Leicester Ford's edition of *The Sayings of Poor Richard* (New York: Putnam, 1890) and *Poor Richard: The Almanacks* (New York: Heritage Press, 1964). Indexing of keywords is quite selective. Of the phrase "Early to bed and early to rise/ Makes a man healthy, wealthy, and wise," only "bed" and "rise" appear as keywords.

518. Humes, James C. **The Wit & Wisdom of Benjamin Franklin: A Treasury of More Than 900 Quotations and Anecdotes**. New York: HarperCollins, 1995. 236p. LC 95-3174. ISBN 0-06-017172-3.

Topically arranges in seven chapters ("Sage Sayings," "Franklin Firsts," and the like) quotations from Franklin's writings, particularly *Poor Richard's Almanac* (on America, onions, old age, etc.), Franklin's observations on selected contemporaries (Benedict Arnold, Thomas Paine, George III), and anecdotes and other accounts of Franklin's life and works, covering his inventions, government service, and other fields of interest. Humes does not supply specific bibliographic references. Includes brief chronology and bibliography (p. 225-26). A detailed index pulls the collection together.

Harold Frederic, 1856-1898
Bibliographies
519. O'Donnell, Thomas F., Stanton Garner, and Robert H. Woodward. **A Bibliography of Writings by and About Harold Frederic**. Boston: G. K. Hall, 1975. 342p. (Research Bibliographies in American Literature, no. 4). LC 75-12827. ISBN 0-8161-1000-x.

This lists the first book and serialized appearances of Frederic's fiction and nonfiction writings, shorter works (contributions to journals and collections), journalistic writings (including contributions to the Utica *Observer*, *New York Times*, and *Manchester Guardian*), and collected editions, in addition to arranging brief, descriptively annotated entries for more than 1,000 works about Frederic in separate listings for bibliographies, reviews, and other forms, including dissertations. Other sections describe collections of Frederic's manuscripts in the New York Public Library, Columbia University, Cornell University, Princeton University, the Library of Congress, and other institutions (pp. 285-92). Additional coverage of Frederic's literary manuscripts, notes, correspondence, and papers in the Library of Congress is provided in Noel Polk's *The Literary Manuscripts of Harold Frederic: A Catalogue* (New York: Garland, 1979). Frederic's manuscripts are also listed in Robbins' *American Literary Manuscripts*, pp. 117-18. For published works by Frederic, see *Bibliography of American Literature*, vol. 3, pp. 217-23. See *Bibliography of American Fiction, 1866-1918*, pp. 175-77, for Stanton Garner's checklist of works by and about Frederic.

Journals
See Patterson's *Author Newsletters and Journals*, p. 125, for previously published journals for Frederic.

Mary E(leanor) Wilkins Freeman, 1852-1930
Bibliographies
For works by Freeman, see *Bibliography of American Literature*, vol. 3, pp. 224-43. Reviews of Freeman's works and Freeman's contributions to selected periodicals are identified in Wells' *The Literary Index to American Magazines, 1850-1900*, pp. 143-44. Freeman's manuscripts are listed in Robbins' *American Literary Manuscripts*, p. 118. See *Bibliography of American Fiction, 1866-1918*, pp. 178-80, for Shirley Marchalonis' checklist of works by and about Freeman. Research on Freeman is reviewed by Philip B. Eppard in Duke, Bryer, and Inge's *American Women Writers*, pp. 21-46.

Alice French (Octave Thanet), 1850-1934
Bibliographies
See *Bibliography of American Fiction, 1866-1918*, pp. 180-81, for Gwen L. Nagel's checklist of works by and about French. French's contributions to and reviews of French's works in selected periodicals are identified in Wells' *The Literary Index to American Magazines, 1850-1900*, p. 145. French's manuscripts are listed in Robbins' *American Literary Manuscripts*, p. 119.

Philip (Morin) Freneau, 1752-1832
Bibliographies

520. Paltsits, Victor Hugo. **A Bibliography of the Separate and Collected Works of Philip Freneau: Together with an Account of His Newspapers**. New York: Dodd, Mead, 1903. 96p. LC 4-1751.

Paltsits gives full bibliographic descriptions of Freneau's books, pamphlets, and broadsides, including title-page transcriptions (with selected facsimiles), physical descriptions, information on printing and publishing histories, and copy locations. Additional coverage of Freneau's collections of poetry is included in Blanck's *Bibliography of American Literature*, vol. 3, pp. 244-56. Largely an index to periodical prose, Philip Marsh's *Freneau's Published Prose: A Bibliography* (Metuchen, NJ: Scarecrow Press, 1970) attempts to distinguish about 1,100 of Freneau's contributions to such works as *The Monmouth Almanac* and *New-Jersey Gazette*. Judith R. Hiltner's *The Newspaper Verse of Philip Freneau: An Edition and Bibliographical Survey* (Troy, NY: Whitston, 1986) provides a critical edition of Freneau's newspaper verse, with bibliographies listing alphabetically and by city and state of publication all newspapers including Freneau's verse. Contributions by Freneau and criticism and reviews of Freneau's works in selected periodicals are identified in Wells' *The Literary Index to American Magazines, 1815-1865*, p. 58. Freneau's manuscripts are listed in Robbins' *American Literary Manuscripts*, p. 119. Research on Freneau is reviewed by Lewis Leary in Everett Emerson's *Major Writers of Early American Literature*, pp. 245-72.

Bruce Jay Friedman, 1930-
Bibliographies

For works by Friedman, see *First Printings of American Authors*, vol. 4, pp. 185-87. Friedman's manuscripts are listed in Robbins' *American Literary Manuscripts*, p. 119.

Brian Friel, 1929-
Bibliographies

521. O'Brien, George. **Brian Friel: A Reference Guide, 1962-1992**. New York: G. K. Hall, 1995. 136p. (Reference Guide to Literature). LC 94-30903. ISBN 0-8161-7273-0.

Chronologically arranged, annotated listing of about 1,000 biographical and critical studies of Friel from 1962 through 1992, including book reviews, newspaper articles, interviews, and entries in biographical dictionaries, as well as scholarly studies. Critical annotations offer guidance by identifying specific criticisms as important, substantial, hard-hitting, and the like. Includes lists of Friel's published works and production credits. Author and subject indexes offer good access, the latter including detailed headings. King's *Ten Modern Irish Playwrights*, pp. 43-53, gives brief bibliographic information for Friel's primary works and annotated entries for criticism of Friel, with a classified list of reviews. Danine Farquharson surveys works by and about Friel in Schrank and Demastes' *Irish Playwrights, 1880-1995: A Research and Production Sourcebook*, pp. 97-107.

Robert (Lee) Frost, 1874-1963
Bibliographies

522. Crane, Joan St. C. **Robert Frost: A Descriptive Catalog of Books and Manuscripts in the Clifton Waller Barrett Library, University of Virginia**. Charlottesville, VA: University Press of Virginia, 1974. 280p. LC 73-89904. ISBN 0-8139-0509-5.

The most comprehensive bibliography of Frost's primary materials, Crane gives full bibliographic descriptions for American and English editions of his books and pamphlets, Christmas cards, and contributed poetry and prose to books and journals. Entries provide title-page transcriptions; collations; contents; physical descriptions of paper, bindings, and variants; and publishing histories. In addition, Crane gives detailed descriptions and summaries of Frost's manuscripts and letters (pp. 159-257). This supersedes W. B. Shubrick Clymer and Charles R. Green's *Robert Frost: A Bibliography* (Amherst, MA: Jones Library, 1937); and Uma Parameswaran's "Robert Frost: A Bibliography of Articles and Books, 1958-1964," *Bulletin of Bibliography* 25 (January-April): 46-48; and 25 (May-August): 58, 69, 72. The catalog of *The Frank P. Piskor Collection of Robert Frost* (Canton, NY: Special Collections, Owen D. Young Library, St. Lawrence University, 1993) also contains useful descriptions of Frost's works and works related to him (such as Frost in art and the media), with cross-references to Crane and other standard bibliographies. Also for works by Frost, see *First Printings of American Authors*, vol. 1, pp. 137-43. Frost's manuscripts are listed in Robbins' *American Literary Manuscripts*, p. 120.

523. Lentricchia, Frank, and Melissa Christensen Lentricchia. **Robert Frost: A Bibliography, 1913-1974**. Metuchen, NJ: Scarecrow Press, 1976. 238p. (Scarecrow Author Bibliographies, no. 25). LC 75-44093. ISBN 0-8108-0896-x.

The Lentricchias include 1,164 entries for works by and about Frost. Primary materials described include selected and collected editions of Frost's poetry as well as his articles and plays, records and films, letters, interviews, and locations of manuscripts. Entries for Frost's book-length works give contents. Secondary coverage includes reviews of Frost's works (arranged by works), books and parts of books about Frost, scholarly and popular articles, commentaries in all languages, and dissertations. Coverage extends through 1974. Appendixes give bibliographic histories and note appearances of the poems, providing an index to the primary listings; list appearances of Frost's works in selected anthologies; and identify Frost's uncollected poems.

524. Van Egmond, Peter. **The Critical Reception of Robert Frost: An Annotated Bibliography of Secondary Comment**. Boston: G. K. Hall, 1974. 319p. (Research Bibliographies in American Literature, no. 1). LC 74-8210. ISBN 0-8161-1105-7.

Van Egmond includes brief, selectively annotated entries for about 3,000 works about Frost in separate listings for reviews, interviews and talks, news stories, bibliographies, critical studies (including dissertations), poems to and about Frost, and criticisms in all languages. The volume lacks subject indexing. Van Egmond updates coverage in:

524.1. Van Egmond, Peter. **Robert Frost: A Reference Guide, 1974-1990**. Boston: G. K. Hall, 1991. 148p. (Reference Guides to Literature). LC 91-13645. ISBN 0-8161-7271-4.

Chronologically arranged, annotated entries for about 800 criticisms of Frost from 1974 to 1990, including an addendum for 1970 through 1973 to update Van Egmond's 1974 volume. International coverage includes prefaces and other sections in books, memoirs, biographies, dissertations, and other works. Descriptive annotations identify contents of collections of criticisms. Indexes of critics and titles of Frost's works but no subject indexing. Van Egmond's guides also update coverage of the Lentricchias' *Robert Frost: A Bibliography, 1913-1974* (entry 523). Additional guidance to Frost scholarship is provided in Donald J. Greiner's narrative survey *Robert Frost: The Poet and His Critics* (Chicago, IL: American Library Association, 1974). Research on Frost is reviewed by Reginald L. Cook in Bryer's *Sixteen Modern American Authors*, pp. 323-66; and its supplement by Cook and John McWilliams in Bryer's *Sixteen Modern American Authors: Volume 2: A Survey of Research and Criticism Since 1972*, pp. 360-403.

Dictionaries, Encyclopedias, and Handbooks

525. Cramer, Jeffrey S. **Robert Frost Among His Poems: A Literary Companion to the Poet's Own Biographical Contexts and Associations**. Jefferson, NC: McFarland, 1996. 296p. LC 95-39536. ISBN 0-7864-0079-X

A handbook to Frost's poetic works. Covering Frost's collected published poetry, part one "attempts to identify Frost's intentions by placing each poem into the biographical, historical and geographical context of his life and time; by identifying conscious and unconscious points of association; by annotating words and phrases; and by dating, where possible, the composition of each poem and giving its place of first publication" (p. 2). Part two covers Frost's uncollected and unpublished poems. Appended entries identify spurious and doubtful poems. Includes brief chronology, bibliographic references (pp. 273-80), and index of names and titles.

Indexes and Concordances

526.   Lathem, Edward Connery. **A Concordance to the Poetry of Robert Frost.** New York: Holt Information Systems, 1971. 640p. LC 75-177494. ISBN 0-0309-1225-3.

This concords the text of Lathem's edition *The Poetry of Robert Frost* (New York: Holt, Rinehart & Winston, 1969). Lathem's concordance was reprinted (Guilford, CT: Jeffrey Norton, 1994).

Journals

527.   **Robert Frost Review.** Rock Hill, SC: Robert Frost Society, 1991- . Annual. ISSN 1062-6999.

A compact annual publishing the full range of scholarship on Frost, volumes of the *Robert Frost Review* contain transcriptions of otherwise unpublished primary materials, close readings and explications of specific poems, comparative studies of Frost and other writers, biographical and textual investigations, and other scholarly features in addition to a selection of book reviews. An irregular bibliographic feature, variously titled "Current Frost Scholarship" and "Robert Frost: A Current Bibliography," lists criticisms and dissertations on Frost, continuing a bibliography published from 1989-90 in *South Carolina Review*. The journal also includes occasional announcements and other informational notes about upcoming conference programs on Frost. *Robert Frost Review* is indexed in *MLA*.

Octavius Brooks Frothingham, 1822-1895

Bibliographies

Frothingham's manuscripts are listed in Robbins' *American Literary Manuscripts*, p. 120. Frothingham's contributions to and reviews of Frothingham's works in selected periodicals are identified in Wells' *The Literary Index to American Magazines, 1850-1900*, pp. 145-46. J. Wade Caruthers reviews research on Frothingham in Myerson's *The Transcendentalists*, pp. 171-74.

Christopher (Harris) Fry, 1907-

Bibliographies

For a bibliography of works by and about Fry, see *NCBEL*, IV, pp. 938-41. Jackie Tucker surveys and identifies works by and about Fry in Demastes and Kelly's *British Playwrights, 1880-1956*, pp. [117]-30.

Northrop Frye, 1912-1991

Bibliographies

528.   Denham, Robert D. **Northrop Frye: An Annotated Bibliography of Primary and Secondary Sources.** Toronto: University of Toronto Press, 1987. 449p. LC 87-94754. ISBN 0-8020-2630-3.

Continuing and greatly expanding his previous *Northrop Frye: An Enumerative Bibliography* (Metuchen, NJ: Scarecrow Press, 1974), Denham attempts to "present a comprehensive, annotated account of the critical writings by and about" Frye (p. [ix]). Coverage extends to 1987. Part one chronologically arranges entries in sections for Frye's books; edited books; separately published monographs; essays, introductions, review articles, and contributions to books; reviews; miscellaneous writings (including undergraduate writings, short fiction, editorials, letters to periodicals, etc.); interviews and dialogues; sound recordings, films, and videos; manuscripts (at the University of Toronto, Victoria University, and Queen's University); and unpublished correspondence, also in several special collections. Entries give brief bibliographic information for first and subsequent editions, translations, and reprintings, with detailed summaries of contents. Part two covers books and collections of essays; essays and parts of books (588 entries); reviews (subarranged under Frye's 22 major works); dissertations and theses; bibliographies; and miscellaneous works (including news items, biographical notices, etc.). Appends chronological listing of books and essays about Frye. Also includes chronology of Frye's life. Separate name and subject index and title index.

Journals

529.   **Northrop Frye Newsletter**. Salem, VA: Roanoke College, 1989- . Irregular. ISSN 1058-062x.

Presently "published occasionally and . . . distributed without charge to those who request it" (masthead), the newsletter has published occasional critical reviews and comments on Frye. Mostly the newsletter contains (often reprinted) interviews with Frye, excerpts from Frye's otherwise unpublished writings, a useful "Frye Bibliography" of works about Frye, and notices for new publications. To date, *Northrop Frye Newsletter* is indexed in *MLA* for 1991-1992 only.

Daniel Fuchs, 1909-

Bibliographies

For works by Fuchs, see *First Printings of American Authors*, vol. 1, p. 145. Fuchs' manuscripts are listed in Robbins' *American Literary Manuscripts*, p. 120. See *Bibliography of American Fiction, 1919-1988*, p. 204, for George P. Anderson's checklist of works by and about Fuchs.

Athol Fugard, 1932-

Bibliographies

530.   Read, John. **Athol Fugard: A Bibliography**. Grahamstown: National English Literary Museum, 1991. 336p. (NELM Bibliographic Series, no. 4). LC 92-128657. ISBN 0-9583156-1-2.

A comprehensive listing of published works by and about Fugard. Part I contains 193 chronologically arranged entries in sections for autobiography, drama, screenplays, fiction, nonfiction, unpublished works, and interviews, giving brief bibliographic data with selective annotations for first and subsequent printed appearances, translations, and performances. The bulk of the volume, part II, chronologically lists 3,540 works of criticism on Fugard in sections for general background articles, general criticism, unpublished papers, theses, and criticism of Fugard's 26 individual plays and 10 films, films and plays starring and/or directed by Fugard, bibliographies, reviews of works about Fugard, biography and secondary material on plays and actors, and censorship and Fugard. Entries for individual plays and films give place, date, director, and cast data for first and subsequent productions. International coverage includes materials in non-English languages. Also contains a Fugard chronology. Indexes for reviewers and primary and secondary titles (subindexed by forms; that is, books, journals, newspapers, articles, etc.).

Henry Blake Fuller, 1857-1929

Bibliographies

531.   Silet, Charles L. P. **Henry Blake Fuller and Hamlin Garland: A Reference Guide**. Boston: G. K. Hall, 1977. 148p. (Reference Guides in Literature). LC 76-21860. ISBN 0-8161-7988-3.

Silet offers separate, annotated listings of books, parts of books, and articles about Fuller (published from 1892 through 1975) and Garland (from 1891 through

1975). About 250 items for Fuller and about 350 for Garland are described. Separate indexes include headings for selected, broad topics (bibliography, biography, and the like) as well as primary titles. This is the best listing of works about Fuller, although coverage for Garland in Bryer and Harding's *Hamlin Garland and the Critics* (entry 541) is more comprehensive. See *Bibliography of American Fiction, 1866-1918*, pp. 182-83, for John Pilkington, Jr.'s checklist of works by and about Fuller. For works by Fuller, see *Bibliography of American Literature*, vol. 3, pp. 257-61. Fuller's manuscripts are listed in Robbins' *American Literary Manuscripts*, pp. 120-21.

(Sarah) Margaret Fuller (Marchesa d'Ossoli), 1810-1850
Bibliographies
532.   Myerson, Joel. **Margaret Fuller: An Annotated Secondary Bibliography.** New York: Burt Franklin, 1977. 272p. LC 77-3187. ISBN 0-89102-026-8.

Myerson chronologically arranges annotated entries for 1,245 criticisms and comments on Fuller published from 1834 through 1975. Comprehensive coverage includes entries in reference works, prefaces in editions, newspaper stories, dissertations, and master's theses. In addition, Myerson describes miscellaneous ana, such as fictional accounts of her life and poems dedicated to her and major collections of Fuller's manuscripts at Harvard University, the Boston Public Library, and the Fruitlands Museum (pp. 248-49). Critical and descriptive annotations identify significant works and studies. Coverage is updated by Myerson's "Supplement to *Margaret Fuller: An Annotated Secondary Bibliography*," *Studies in the American Renaissance 1984* (Charlottesville, VA: University Press of Virginia, 1984), pp. 331-85. Research on Fuller is reviewed by Robert N. Hudspeth in Myerson's *The Transcendentalists*, pp. 175-88.

533.   Myerson, Joel. **Margaret Fuller: A Descriptive Bibliography**. Pittsburgh, PA: University of Pittsburgh Press, 1978. 163p. (Pittsburgh Series in Bibliography). LC 78-4203. ISBN 0-8229-3381-0.

Myerson gives full bibliographic descriptions in sections for all editions of Fuller's books, pamphlets, and broadsides; contributions to books and collections, including translations; contributions to periodicals and newspapers; and miscellaneous writings (such as her anonymously published reviews). Entries provide title-page transcriptions; collations; contents; descriptions of paper, typography, and bindings; publishing histories; and copy locations. An appendix lists 18 selected works about Fuller. Also for works by Fuller, see *Bibliography of American Literature*, vol. 3, pp. 262-69; and *First Printings of American Authors*, vol. 1, pp. 147-48. Fuller's manuscripts are listed in Robbins' *American Literary Manuscripts*, p. 241.

Indexes and Concordances
534.   James, Laurie. **The Wit & Wisdom of Margaret Fuller Ossoli**. New York: Golden Heritage Press, 1988. 97p. LC 87-82467. ISBN 0-9443-8200-2.

"Volume 1 in a series on the life and works of Margaret Fuller Ossoli" (title page). Arranges selected quotes under topics such as "Truth," "Pain," "Prostitution," "Education," and "On Colleagues" (Poe, Washington Irving, Thomas Carlyle, and others), with title references to Fuller's works. Includes brief chronology and bibliography (pp. 95-97). Not a systematic index.

Thomas Fuller, 1608-1661
Bibliographies
535.   Gibson, Strickland. **A Bibliography of the Works of Thomas Fuller, D.D.** Oxford: University Press, 1936. pp. 63-162. (Oxford Bibliographical Society Proceedings and Papers, vol. 4 for 1935: Part I). OCLC 22122642.

Full bibliographic descriptions in sections for each of Fuller's separate works; selections from Fuller's works; contributed works; and 10 biographies of

Fuller. Entries give title-page transcriptions, collations, contents, notes on publication histories, and copy locations. Selected title-page facsimiles. Introduction by Geoffrey Keynes. Unindexed. Also for a bibliography of works by and about Fuller, see *NCBEL*, I, pp. 2233-35. Fuller's manuscripts are described in *Index of English Literary Manuscripts*, II, pt. 1: 493-97.

William Gaddis, 1922-
Bibliographies

For works by Gaddis, see *First Printings of American Authors*, vol. 1, p. 149. See *Bibliography of American Fiction, 1919-1988*, pp. 205-206, for Boyd E. Waltman's checklist of works by and about Gaddis. See Sarah E. Lauzen's summary biography, critical assessment of major works, and selected primary and secondary bibliography for Gaddis in McCaffery's *Postmodern Fiction: A Bio-Bibliographical Guide*, pp. 373-77.

Ernest J. Gaines, 1933-
Bibliographies

For works by Gaines, see *First Printings of American Authors*, vol. 1, p. 151. Gaines' manuscripts are listed in Robbins' *American Literary Manuscripts*, p. 121. See *Bibliography of American Fiction, 1919-1988*, pp. 207-208, for Jean W. Cash's checklist of works by and about Gaines. See the review of research by Frank W. Shelton in Flora and Bain's *Fifty Southern Writers After 1900*, pp. 196-205.

Zona Gale, 1874-1938
Bibliographies

See *Bibliography of American Fiction, 1866-1918*, pp. 184-85, for Vern L. Lindquist's checklist of works by and about Gale. Gale's manuscripts are listed in Robbins' *American Literary Manuscripts*, p. 121. Jan Balakian identifies works by and about Gale in Demastes' *American Playwrights, 1880-1945*, pp. 91-98.

William Davis Gallagher, 1808-1894
Bibliographies

For works by Gallagher, see *Bibliography of American Literature*, vol. 3, pp. 270-74. Gallagher's manuscripts are listed in Robbins' *American Literary Manuscripts*, p. 121.

John Galsworthy, 1867-1933
Bibliographies

536.   Marrot, H. V. **A Bibliography of the Works of John Galsworthy**. London: Elkin Matthews and Marrot, 1928. 252p. LC 29-5371.

Marrot gives full bibliographic descriptions for English and American editions of Galsworthy's novels and collections of stories, plays, poetry, essays, pamphlets, collected editions, contributions to books, contributions to journals, and translations. Entries provide title-page transcriptions, physical descriptions, and brief publishing histories. In addition, Marrot lists works about Galsworthy, including iconography. Available in a reprinted edition (New York: Burt Franklin, 1968). Also for a bibliography of works by and about Galsworthy, see *NCBEL*, IV, pp. 579-86. Lue Morgan Douthit surveys and identifies works by and about Galsworthy in Demastes and Kelly's *British Playwrights, 1880-1956*, pp. [131]-43.

537.   Stevens, Earl E., and H. Ray Stevens. **John Galsworthy: An Annotated Bibliography of Writings About Him**. DeKalb, IL: Northern Illinois University Press, 1980. 484p. (An Annotated Secondary Bibliography Series on English Literature in Transition, 1880-1920). LC 78-60456. ISBN 0-87580-073-4.

A comprehensive bibliography of writings about Galsworthy, this chronologically arranges annotated entries for 2,262 works published from 1897 through 1977, including books, parts of books (introductions, prefaces, and the like), articles, reviews, and dissertations in all languages. Annotations are descriptive, although significant studies receive substantial discussion. Indexes for critics, primary and secondary titles, periodical titles, and languages provide thorough access. Supersedes in coverage E. H. Mikhail's *John Galsworthy, the Dramatist: A Bibliography* (Troy, NY: Whitston, 1971).

Erle Stanley Gardner, 1889-1970
Bibliographies
538.   Mundell, E. H. **Erle Stanley Gardner: A Checklist**. Kent, OH: Kent State University Press, 1968. 91p. LC 70-97619. ISBN 0-87338-034-7.

Mundell gives a classified checklist of Gardner's short fiction, fiction in books, short nonfiction, book nonfiction, and miscellaneous works (including cartoon strips, media, and other works inspired by Gardner). Data limited to brief bibliographic information. Gardner's manuscripts are listed in Robbins' *American Literary Manuscripts*, p. 122. See *Bibliography of American Fiction, 1919-1988*, pp. 209-12, for Michael J. Pettengell's checklist of works by and about Gardner.

John (Champlin) Gardner, (Jr.), 1933-1982
Bibliographies
539.   Howell, John M. **John Gardner: A Bibliographical Profile**. Carbondale, IL: Southern Illinois University Press, 1980. 158p. LC 79-22167. ISBN 0-8093-0935-1.

In this descriptive listing of Gardner's primary works, Howell includes detailed entries in sections for Gardner's books; contributions to books; fiction, poetry, and other contributions (articles, essays, reviews, letters, and the like) to periodicals and newspapers; interviews; speeches; and miscellaneous writings (such as blurbs, cartoons, and edited journals). Entries give title- and copyright-page facsimiles, collations, contents, copy locations, and references to subsequent editions. In addition, Howell lists books and articles about Gardner as well as about 500 unannotated reviews of his works. Also for works by Gardner, see *First Printings of American Authors*, vol. 3, pp. 117-23.

540.   Morace, Robert A. **John Gardner: An Annotated Secondary Bibliography**. New York: Garland, 1984. 364p. (Garland Reference Library of the Humanities, vol. 434). LC 83-48266. ISBN 0-8240-9081-0.

Complementing Howell's primary bibliography (entry 539), Morace's guide offers comprehensive coverage of works about Gardner, including annotated entries for about 1,500 interviews and speeches; reviews and parts of reviews of Gardner's books; and books, articles, and other writings that mention Gardner (such as dissertations, newspaper stories, entries in reference works) in all languages. Critical coverage extends through 1982. Annotations are descriptive. In addition, Morace includes additions and corrections to Howell's guide. See *Bibliography of American Fiction, 1919-1988*, pp. 212-16, for Howell's checklist of works by and about Gardner. See Judy R. Smith's summary biography, critical assessment of major works, and selected primary and secondary bibliography for Gardner in McCaffery's *Postmodern Fiction: A Bio-Bibliographical Guide*, pp. 380-83.

(Hannibal) Hamlin Garland, 1860-1940
Bibliographies
541.   Bryer, Jackson R., and Eugene Harding. **Hamlin Garland and the Critics: An Annotated Bibliography**. Troy, NY: Whitston, 1973. 282p. LC 75-183300. ISBN 0-8787-5020-7.

The most extensive and reliable listing of secondary materials for Garland, describing more than 1,200 reviews, critical books, entries in reference works, articles, and dissertations (including non-English-language studies). Annotations are descriptive. Significant studies receive detailed reviews. A separate subject index gives access. Bryer and Harding's work is updated by Charles L. P. Silet and Robert E. Welch's "Further Additions to *Hamlin Garland and the Critics,*" *American Literary Realism* 9 (1976): 268-75; and "Corrections to *Hamlin Garland and the Critics,*" *PBSA* 72 (1978): 106-109. Coverage is superior to that for Garland in Silet's *Henry Blake Fuller and Hamlin Garland* (entry 531). Garland's primary bibliography is described in Joseph B. McCullough's *Hamlin Garland* (Boston: Twayne, 1978); Donald Pizer's "Hamlin Garland: A Bibliography of Newspaper and Periodical Publications, 1885-1895," *Bulletin of Bibliography* 22 (1957): 41-44; and Lloyd A. Arvidson's *Hamlin Garland: Centennial Tributes and a Checklist of the Hamlin Garland Papers in the University of Southern California Library* (Los Angeles, CA: University of Southern California Library Bulletin, no. 9, 1962). Garland's manuscripts are also listed in Robbins' *American Literary Manuscripts,* pp. 122-23. See *Bibliography of American Fiction, 1866-1918,* pp. 185-87, for James Nagel's checklist of works by and about Garland. Research on Garland is reviewed by Joseph McCullough in Erisman and Etulain's *Fifty Western Writers,* pp. 131-41.

George (Palmer) Garrett, (Jr.), 1929-

Bibliographies

For works by Garrett, see *First Printings of American Authors,* vol. 2, pp. 167-73. See *Bibliography of American Fiction, 1919-1988,* pp. 216-18, for Roy H. Andrews' checklist of works by and about Garrett. R. H. W. Dillard surveys works by and about Garrett in Bain and Flora's *Contemporary Poets, Dramatists, Essayists, and Novelists of the South,* pp. 184-96.

David Garrick, 1717-1779

Bibliographies

542.   Berkowitz, Gerald M. **David Garrick: A Reference Guide.** Boston: G. K. Hall, 1980. 309p. (A Reference Publication in Literature). LC 79-28317. ISBN 0-8161-8136-5.

A chronologically arranged listing of annotated entries for works by and about Garrick, Berkowitz's guide offers comprehensive coverage, including about 1,900 editions of Garrick's writings, early notices, dissertations and master's theses, and criticisms in all languages published from 1741 through 1979. Brief annotations are descriptive and critical, clearly identifying both significant and weak studies. The index offers detailed topical access under Garrick's name. Garrick's primary materials are described in Mary E. Knapp's *A Checklist of Verse by David Garrick* (Charlottesville, VA: University of Virginia Press, 1955), which covers published appearances and unpublished texts of writings (including prologues, epilogues, skits, and songs). Also for a bibliography of works by and about Garrick, see *NCBEL,* II, pp. 801-809.

George Gascoigne, c. 1534-1577

Bibliographies

For a bibliography of works by and about Gascoigne, see *NCBEL,* I, pp. 1025-27. Gascoigne's manuscripts are described in *Index of English Literary Manuscripts,* I, pt. 2: 99-100. The Tannenbaums' *Elizabethan Bibliographies,* vol. 2, and Robert Carl Johnson's *Elizabethan Bibliographies Supplements,* no. 9, list works about Gascoigne.

Indexes and Concordances

See Stagg's *Figurative Language of the Tragedies of Shakespeare's Chief 16th-Century Contemporaries* (entry 901) for an index of images in Gascoigne's works.

Elizabeth Cleghorn Gaskell, 1810-1865
Bibliographies

543. Selig, Robert L. **Elizabeth Gaskell: A Reference Guide**. Boston: G. K. Hall, 1977. 431p. (Reference Guides in Literature). LC 76-30505. ISBN 0-8161-7813-5.

Chronologically arranging annotated entries for about 2,200 writings about Gaskell published from 1848 through 1974, Selig's comprehensive coverage includes anonymous reviews, newspaper articles, dissertations, and non-English criticisms. Descriptive annotations identify significant studies, most paraphrasing or excerpting comments from the sources. Solid topical indexing includes detailed headings for subjects and names, such as "authors, women," "didactic literature," "emotions in literature," Jane Austen, and Thackeray. Selig's guide supersedes the coverage of Jeffrey Welch's *Elizabeth Gaskell: An Annotated Bibliography, 1929-1975* (New York: Garland, 1977), which chronologically arranges annotated entries for 237 books, articles, and dissertations published from 1929 through 1975. The standard bibliography of Gaskell's primary materials is Clark S. Northup's "A Bibliography," in Gerald DeWitt Sanders' *Elizabeth Gaskell* (New Haven, CT: Yale University Press, 1929), pp. 165-267. John Albert Green's *A Bibliographical Guide to the Gaskell Collection in the Moss Side Library* (Manchester: Reference Library, 1911) describes a major collection of Gaskell materials in the Manchester Central Library. Also for a bibliography of works by and about Gaskell, see *NCBEL*, III, pp. 873-78. Gaskell's manuscripts are described in *Index of English Literary Manuscripts*, IV, pt. 1:805-808. Research on Gaskell is reviewed by James D. Barry in Ford's *Victorian Fiction*, pp. 204-18: and by Barry in Stevenson's *Victorian Fiction*, pp. 245-76.

544. Weyant, Nancy S. **Elizabeth Gaskell: An Annotated Bibliography of English-Language Sources, 1976-1991**. Metuchen, NJ: Scarecrow Press, 1994. 209p. (Scarecrow Author Bibliographies, no. 91). LC 94-14735. ISBN 0-8108-2890-1.

Updates and supplements the bibliographies of Selig's guide (entry 543) and Jeffrey Welch's *Elizabeth Gaskell: An Annotated Bibliography, 1929-1975* (New York: Garland, 1977), identifying 339 works about Gaskell published from 1976 through 1991. Descriptively annotated entries arranged in sections for bibliographies, biographies, correspondence, criticism (including dissertations), and master's and honors theses (unannotated). Subject and author/critic indexes.

Journals

545. **Gaskell Society Journal**. Manchester: Gaskell Society, 1987-. Annual. ISSN 0951-7200.

Sponsored by the Gaskell Society, annual volumes feature articles, notes, and reviews of new publications related to Gaskell's life and works as well as those of her contemporaries, such as Margaret Oliphant, the Brontes, and Tennyson. Typical articles include "Faith and Family: Fundamental Values in *Mary Barton*" and "Elizabeth Gaskell and German Romanticism." Other articles have discussed narrative structure, sources, and images of social classes, education, gender, and Gaskell's reputation in Italy and Japan. Some recent attention has focused on Scottish publishing and authorship. Several contributions have described collections of Gaskell materials, such as those at Christ Church College, Canterbury, and the Manchester Central Library. Annual volumes conclude with brief notices and information of interest to society members. *Gaskell Society Journal* is indexed in *MLA* and *MHRA*.

William H(oward) Gass, 1924-
Bibliographies

For works by Gass, see *First Printings of American Authors*, vol. 4, pp. 189-90. See Richard J. Schneider's summary biography, critical assessment of major works, and selected primary and secondary bibliography for Gass in McCaffery's *Postmodern Fiction: A Bio-Bibliographical Guide*, pp. 383-85.

Sir Gawain and the Green Knight, c. 1375

Bibliographies

546.   Andrew, Malcolm. **The Gawain-Poet: An Annotated Bibliography, 1839-1977**. New York: Garland, 1979. 256p. (Garland Reference Library of the Humanities, vol. 129). LC 78-68243. ISBN 0-8240-9815-3.

Andrew provides about 1,300 annotated entries for editions and translations, critical studies (including reviews of editions, dissertations, and non-English-language criticisms), and reference works related to the works of the *Gawain*- or *Pearl*-Poet, providing separate listings for the *Pearl*, *Cleanness*, *Patience*, and *Sir Gawain and the Green Knight* (about 900 entries). Excludes coverage of *St. Erkenwald*. Critical coverage extends from 1839 through 1978. Annotations are detailed and descriptive, noting line references to passages in each work and including references to reviews. Significant editions and studies receive extended reviews. Separate indexes for each poem cross-reference studies of specific lines. Otherwise, no subject indexing is provided.

547.   Blanch, Robert J. **Sir Gawain and the Green Knight: A Reference Guide**. Troy, NY: Whitston, 1984. 298p. LC 82-50412. ISBN 0-87875-244-7.

Coverage is limited to studies of *Sir Gawain* only. Blanch chronologically arranges annotated entries for about 1,000 editions, translations, and critical studies (including dissertations) in all languages published from 1824 through 1980. Annotations are descriptive and critical. Significant studies receive extended discussion. A comprehensive index offers thorough subject access, including headings for "authorship controversy," "the beheading game," "bob and wheel," "character of Gawain," Dante, and the like. This detailed indexing makes Blanch's guide superior to Andrew's guide (entry 546) for coverage of *Sir Gawain* criticism. Stainsby's *Sir Gawain and the Green Knight* (entry 548) can be used to update both Blanch and Andrew.

548.   Stainsby, Meg. **Sir Gawain and the Green Knight: An Annotated Bibliography, 1978-1989**. New York : Garland, 1992. 197p. (Garland Reference Library of the Humanities, vol. 1495; Garland Medieval Bibliographies, vol. 13). LC 91-036810. ISBN 0-8153-0504-4.

Updating Andrew's *The Gawain-Poet* (entry 546), Stainsby offers 383 selectively annotated entries arranged in sections for editions, translations, adaptations and performances, reference works, general introductions and romance criticism, authorship and manuscript studies, alliteration and language studies, sources and analogues, and general criticism published from 1978 to 1989. Entries cite references to reviews. Coverage includes non-English-language studies but excludes dissertations and entries in general reference works. Introduction gives guidance to major critical approaches (feminist, psychological, etc.) to the poem. Author, detailed subject, line, and Middle English word indexes give excellent access. Also for earlier criticism, see Blanch's *Sir Gawain and the Green Knight* (entry 547) as well as Marie P. Hamilton's description of the Gawain/Pearl-Poet's primary materials with a bibliography of editions and criticism in Severs and Hartung's *A Manual of the Writings in Middle English*, vol. II, pp. 339-53, 503-16. Also see *NCBEL*, I, pp. 547-54, for Barbara Raw's list of works by and about the "Pearl Poet."

Dictionaries, Encyclopedias, and Handbooks

549.   Brewer, Derek, and Jonathan Gibson. **A Companion to the Gawain-Poet**. Woodbridge, Suffolk: D. S. Brewer, 1997. 442p. (Arthurian Studies, vol. 38). LC 96-32104. ISBN 0-85991-433-X.

Twenty-six essays—"stimulating introductions to a broad range of topics" (preface)—by different experts mix reference information with original (often joint) analyses of the poet's four works. Essays address rather controversial and novel topics, like "Gender and Sexual Transgression" and Sir Gawain in films, as well as more traditional ones, such as authorship, sources, allegory, symbolism, and Christian imagery. Others review research on selected major features in the works, such as castles, feasts, jewels, hunting, names, and greenness. A. S. G. Edwards presents an overview of the manuscript sources. Contributions also focus on the technical aspects of meter, dialect, and form. Extensive cumulative bibliography of cited editions, translations, and other sources (pp. [393]-427). Thorough subject and general indexes.

Indexes and Concordances

550.   Chapman, Coolidge Otis. **An Index of Names in Pearl, Purity, Patience, and Gawain**. 1951; reprint Westport, CT: Greenwood Press, 1978. 66p. LC 77-29259. ISBN 0-313-20213-3.

Chapman alphabetically arranges the names of persons, places, events, and other proper names in the works of the *Gawain-Poet*. Entries provide brief identifications and textual references, based on the texts of Charles G. Osgood, Jr.'s *Pearl* (Boston: Heath, 1906); Robert J. Menner's *Purity* [*Cleanness*] (New Haven, CT: Yale University Press, 1920); Hartley Bateson's *Patience* (London: Longman, 1918); and J. R. R. Tolkein and E. V. Gordon's *Sir Gawain and the Green Knight* (Oxford: Clarendon Press, 1930).

551.   Kottler, Barnet, and Alan M. Markham. **A Concordance to Five Middle English Poems: Cleanness, St. Erkenwald, Sir Gawain and the Green Knight, Patience, Pearl**. Pittsburgh, PA: University of Pittsburgh Press, 1966. 761p. LC 66-13311.

Kottler and Markham's standard concordance to the works of the *Gawain-Poet* is based on Israel Gollancz's Early English Texts Society editions of *Cleanness* (London: Oxford University Press, 1921); *St. Erkenwald* (London: Oxford University Press, 1922); *Sir Gawain and the Green Knight* (London: Oxford University Press, 1940); and *Patience* (London: Oxford University Press, 1913); and E. V. Gordon's *Pearl* (Oxford: Clarendon Press, 1953), with incorporated variants from editions used in Chapman's index (entry 550) and others. A frequency list is included.

John Gay, 1685-1732

Bibliographies

552.   Klein, Julie Thompson. **John Gay: An Annotated Checklist of Criticism**. Troy, NY: Whitston, 1974. 97p. LC 72-97234. ISBN 0-87875-041-x.

Klein critically describes major editions of Gay's works and about 600 biographies, editions of letters, general studies, studies of individual works, reviews of productions of *The Beggar's Opera*, and dissertations and theses. Coverage includes early anonymous notices and non-English-language criticisms. Important works are reviewed in detail. For a bibliography of works by and about Gay, see *NCBEL*, II, pp. 497-500, by John Fuller. Gay's manuscripts are described in *Index of English Literary Manuscripts*, III, pt. 2:3-13. Research on Gay is reviewed by Cecil Price in Wells' *English Drama*, pp. 199-212.

Journals

"Recent Articles" in *The Scriblerian and the Kit Cats* (entry 1084) regularly includes a selection of reviews of studies on Gay.

Theodor Seuss Geisel (Dr. Seuss, Theo. LeSieg), 1904-1991

Bibliographies

553.   **Dr. Seuss from Then to Now: A Catalogue of the Retrospective Exhibition Organized by the San Diego Museum of Art, San Diego, California**. New York: Random House, 1986. 95p. LC 87-4838. ISBN 0-394-89268-2.

A wonderfully illustrated catalog containing a chronological checklist (pp. 83-93) of 252 items, including published works, proofs and galleys, manuscripts, and original and reproduced illustrations that comprised the national exhibition, organized by San Diego Museum of Art, which appeared in San Diego, Cedar Rapids, Iowa, Pittsburgh, Dallas, Tampa, Baltimore, and New Orleans from May 1986 to April 1988. Substantially based on materials in the Theodor S. Geisel Collection in the Special Collections of University of California, Los Angeles, Libraries. The catalog also includes a Dr. Seuss chronology and a bibliography of Dr. Seuss' books and collaborations and selected works about Dr. Seuss (pp. 94-95). See *Bibliography of American Fiction, 1919-1988*, pp. 218-20, for Myra Kibler Chapman's checklist of works by and about Geisel.

Jack Gelber, 1932-

Bibliographies

King's *Ten Modern American Playwrights*, pp. 155-65, gives brief bibliographic information for Gelber's primary works and annotated entries for criticism of Gelber, with a classified list of reviews. Gelber's manuscripts are listed in Robbins' *American Literary Manuscripts*, p. 124.

Martha Gellhorn, 1908-

Bibliographies

For works by Gellhorn, see *First Printings of American Authors*, vol. 4, pp. 191-95. Gellhorn's manuscripts are listed in Robbins' *American Literary Manuscripts*, p. 124.

Genesis A and B, c. 8th century

Bibliographies

Greenfield and Robinson's *A Bibliography of Publications on Old English Literature to the End of 1972*, pp. 228-33, lists editions, translations, and studies of the Old English *Genesis*, with citations for reviews. Graham D. Caie's *Bibliography of Junius XI Manuscript: With Appendix on Caedmon's Hymn*, pp. 37-50, gives unannotated checklists of international editions, translations, and criticisms of *Genesis*.

Katharine Fullerton Gerould, 1879-1944

Bibliographies

See *Bibliography of American Fiction, 1866-1918*, p. 188, for Traci L. Hulsey's checklist of works by and about Gerould. Gerould's manuscripts are listed in Robbins' *American Literary Manuscripts*, p. 124.

Edward Gibbon, 1737-1794

Bibliographies

554. Craddock, Patricia B. **Edward Gibbon: A Reference Guide**. Boston: G. K. Hall, 1987. 476p. (A Reference Guide to Literature). LC 87-102. ISBN 0-8161-8217-5.

Aiming at comprehensive coverage of writings about Gibbon published from 1761 through 1985, Craddock chronologically arranges annotated entries for about 2,500 works, including early reviews and notices, reviews of works about Gibbon, entries in reference works, introductions in editions of Gibbon's works, dissertations, and non-English-language criticisms. Annotations are objective. Significant works receive detailed descriptions. A separate index of topics and allusions offers excellent access. Craddock's guide supersedes Francesco Cordasco's slim *Edward Gibbon: A Handlist of Critical Notices & Studies* (Brooklyn, NY: Long Island University Press, 1950), 18th Century Bibliographical Pamphlets, no. 10, which listed 40 selected titles, including works in French and German, with references to reviews.

555. Norton, J. E. **A Bibliography of the Works of Edward Gibbon**. 1940; reprint London: Oxford University Press, 1970. 256p. LC 77-121217.

The standard guide to Gibbon's primary works, Norton's work gives full bibliographic descriptions (title-page transcriptions, collations, physical descriptions, and locations of copies) and detailed publishing histories for editions and translations of Gibbon's works. Several chapters emphasize the publication history of *The Decline and Fall of the Roman Empire*. Appendixes list ana and other works about Gibbon, including contemporary attacks on him. For a bibliography of works by and about Gibbon, see *NCBEL*, II, pp. 1721-29. Gibbon's manuscripts are described in *Index of English Literary Manuscripts*, III, pt. 2:15-36. Also useful is *The Library of Edward Gibbon: A Catalogue*, 2d ed. (Godalming: St. Paul's Bibliographies, 1980), edited and introduced by Geoffrey Keynes.

Walter B. Gibson, 1897-
Bibliographies

556.   Cox, J. Randolph. **Man of Magic and Mystery : A Guide to the Work of Walter B. Gibson.** Metuchen, NJ: Scarecrow Press, 1988. 382p. LC 88-31917. ISBN 0-8108-2192-3.

Identifies Gibson's works in chronologically arranged sections for books, contributions to periodicals (950 items published from 1905 to 1984, with brief contents), contributions to books, syndicated features, comic strips, and radio scripts. The first eight chapters present brief bibliographic information on Gibson's 183 books, with summaries of contents, in an awkward, descriptive narrative embedding numbered entries in chatty paragraphs. Includes appendixes of pseudonyms, works by others under Gibson's name, biographical works, and filmed versions of his works. Title index.

William Gibson, 1914-
Bibliographies

For works by Gibson, see *First Printings of American Authors*, vol. 5, pp. 115-19. Gibson's manuscripts are listed in Robbins' *American Literary Manuscripts*, p. 124.

(Sir) William Schwenck Gilbert, 1836-1911
Bibliographies

557.   Searle, Townley. **A Bibliography of Sir William Schwenck Gilbert, with Bibliographical Adventures in the Gilbert & Sullivan Operas.** 1931; reprint New York: Burt Franklin, 1968. 107p. (Burt Franklin Bibliography and Reference Series, no.192). LC 68-5623.

An awkwardly organized guide, arranging descriptions of Schwenck's separate, collected, selected, and contributed published and unpublished dramatic and nondramatic works in a single chronological listing. Entries for separate and collected publications give title-page transcriptions, sizes, paginations, and descriptions of paper and bindings. All entries contain useful, although often rather anecdotal notes on composition and publishing histories and other information on locations of manuscripts. Entries for revised editions follow first editions (out of chronological order). Searle also offers separate listings of plays wrongly attributed to Gilbert, privately printed and advance proof copies, souvenir programs, books illustrated by Gilbert, uncollected "Bab" ballads, musical publications and illustrated title pages, books about Gilbert (about 30 brief items), contributions to magazines by Gilbert, magazine articles on Gilbert (another 30 items), miscellanea, and notes on first editions' rarity and value. Index of titles. Also for a bibliography of works by and about Gilbert, see *NCBEL*, III, pp. 1159-64. Mary Lindroth surveys and identifies works by and about Gilbert in Demastes and Kelly's *British Playwrights, 1880-1956*, pp. [144]-56.

Dictionaries, Encyclopedias, and Handbooks

558.   Benford, Harry. **The Gilbert and Sullivan Lexicon in Which Is Gilded the Philosophic Pill: Featuring New Illustrations and the Complete Libretto for The Zoo.** 2d ed., revised and enlarged. Ann Arbor, MI: Sarah Jennings Press, 1991. 270p. LC 90-24994. ISBN 0-9317-8108-6.

Offers brief plot summaries of 16 Gilbert and Sullivan operas and glosses of colloquial and non-English-language expressions and phrases, as well as terms for persons, places, and things "in their written order . . . one chapter for each opera, with those chapters placed in the sequence in which the operas were written, while the individual entries are listed in the order in which they first appear in the libretto" (p. 2). Entries cross-reference (by number) an extensive list of 208 sources (pp. 241-46), including the *OED*, and occasionally give pronunciations: "Etui {AY-twee}" in *Princess Ida* and "Gioco {JOE-co}" in *The Mikado*, for examples. Primarily based on the text of Gilbert's *The Savoy Operas* (London: Oxford University Press, 1962, 1963). Cumulative index of terms.

Concordances and Indexes

559.   Dixon, Geoffrey. **The Gilbert and Sullivan Concordance: A Word Index to W. S. Gilbert's Libretti for the Fourteen Savoy Operas.** New York: Garland,1987. 2 vols. (Garland Reference Library of the Humanities, vol. 702). LC 86-33484. ISBN 0-8240-8505-1.

Gives context lines, title abbreviations, and line references to words in *H. M. S. Pinafore, The Pirates of Penzance, The Mikado*, and other works that have made Gilbert "a national institution" (p. ix). Appends concordance to *Thespis*. Mainly based on the text of Gilbert's *The Savoy Operas* (London: Macmillan, 1926); base text for *Thespis* is from Gilbert's *Original Plays*, 4th series (London: Chatto and Windus, 1911). Supersedes F. J. Halton's *The Gilbert and Sullivan Operas: A Concordance* (New York: Bass, 1935), which amounts to a dictionary of allusions.

Frank B(unker) Gilbreth, Jr., 1911-
Bibliographies

For works by Gilbreth, see *First Printings of American Authors*, vol. 3, pp. 125-27.

Gildas, d. 570
Bibliographies

For a bibliography of works by and about Gildas, see *NCBEL*, I, pp. 337-39.

Richard Watson Gilder, 1844-1909
Bibliographies

For works by Gilder, see *Bibliography of American Literature*, vol. 3, pp. 275-88. Gilder's contributions to and reviews of Gilder's works in selected periodicals are identified in Wells' *The Literary Index to American Magazines, 1850-1900*, pp. 152-53. Gilder's manuscripts are listed in Robbins' *American Literary Manuscripts*, p. 125.

Charles Gildon, 1665-1724
Bibliographies

For a bibliography of works by and about Gildon, see *NCBEL*, II, pp. 1047-50.

(Arthur) Eric (Rowton) Gill, 1882-1940
Bibliographies

560.   Gill, Evan R., D. Steven Corey, and Julia MacKenzie. **Eric Gill: A Bibliography.** 2d ed. Winchester: St. Paul's Bibliographies; Detroit: Omnigraphics, 1991. 368p. LC 90-53251. ISBN 0-9067-9553-2.

Gill, Corey, and MacKenzie's revision updates and greatly expands Evan Gill's previous descriptive guide to works by and about his brother, *Bibliography of Eric Gill* (London: Casell, 1953). Full bibliographic descriptions chronologically arranged in sections for Gill's books, pamphlets, and separate publications; contributions to books and periodicals; books and other publications illustrated by Gill; books, periodicals, and other works about Gill; miscellanea (ephemeral descriptions of exhibitions, workshops, specimen sheets, catalogs, etc.); and posters and other items illustrated by Gill (a section not included in the 1953 edition). Entries for Gill's 54 separate publications from 1916 to 1953 give facsimiles of title pages; sizes; collations; paginations and contents; binding descriptions; and notes on publication histories (prices, edition sizes, and the like), citations for early notices, and details on variants and subsequent editions. Likewise, the approximately 140 works illustrated by Gill are fully described, and detailed descriptions of contents are supplied. Both this section and the one for works about Gill (with about 400 descriptively annotated entries) are selective, according to Gill, Corey, and MacKenzie. Appends cross-reference list of engraving numbers. Indexes of authors and titles. Also useful is David Peace's *Eric Gill, The Inscriptions: A Descriptive Catalogue* (London: Herbert Press, 1994). For a bibliography of works by and about Gill, see *NCBEL*, IV, pp. 1045-48.

Brendan Gill, 1914-
Bibliographies

For works by Gill, see *First Printings of American Authors*, vol. 3, pp. 129-32.

Charlotte Perkins Gilman, 1860-1935
Bibliographies

561.   Scharnhorst, Gary. **Charlotte Perkins Gilman: A Bibliography**. Metuchen, NJ: Scarecrow Press, 1985. 219p. (Scarecrow Author Bibliographies, no. 71). LC 84-27625. ISBN 0-8108-1780-2.

Scharnhorst chronologically arranges more than 2,250 entries within separate listings for Gilman's verse, fiction, dramatic, and nonfiction works and subsequent editions; "Selected Biographical Sources," such as lecture reports, biographical sketches, and obituaries; manuscripts in about 30 libraries; and miscellaneous writings. Entries give brief bibliographic information and identify reprintings, manuscript sources, and reviews. Also lists some 27 selected critical works about Gilman. Coverage extends from 1883 through 1982. Gilman's manuscripts are listed in Robbins' *American Literary Manuscripts*, p. 126. In addition, useful descriptions of Gilman's diaries, scrapbooks, and correspondence in Radcliffe College's Schlesinger Library are given in *The Schlesinger Library: The Manuscript Inventories and the Catalogs of the Manuscripts, Books, and Pictures*, 2d ed. (Boston: G. K. Hall, 1984), vol. 9, pp. 379-86. See *Bibliography of American Fiction 1866-1918*, pp. 189-91, for Sonja Launspach's checklist of works by and about Gilman.

Allen Ginsberg, 1926-1997
Bibliographies

562.   Kraus, Michelle P. **Allen Ginsberg: An Annotated Bibliography, 1969-1977**. Metuchen, NJ: Scarecrow Press, 1980. 328p. (Scarecrow Author Bibliographies, no. 46). LC 79-27132. ISBN 0-8108-1284-3.

Continuing George Dowden and Laurence McGilvery's *A Bibliography of Works by Allen Ginsberg, October, 1943 to July 1, 1967* (San Francisco, CA: City Lights Books, 1971), Kraus gives detailed descriptions of the contents of works by and about Ginsberg in separate listings for his separately published and collected works and translations (including audio and video recordings); and for about 800 critical studies and commentaries in all languages and videotapes, covering reviews (arranged by works), dissertations, and other miscellaneous works (such as letters to Ginsberg, poems mentioning him, dedications, and the like). Annotations for secondary works are critical, clearly identifying important works. An appendix describes the Allen Ginsberg Collection at Columbia University (pp. 253-56) and other primary materials.

563. Morgan, Bill. **The Response to Allen Ginsberg, 1926-1994: A Bibliography of Secondary Sources**. Westport, CT: Greenwood Press, 1996. 505p. (Bibliographies and Indexes in American Literature, no. 23). LC 95-26449. ISBN 0-313-29536-0.

This nominally continues and serves as a companion to Morgan's *The Works of Allen Ginsberg, 1941-1994: A Descriptive Bibliography* (entry 564). Following a "complete, comprehensive guide to the non-English language translations" (p. xiii) of Ginsberg's works, Morgan offers a "comprehensive history" of all writings about him. In sections for 42 different languages with subsections for books, anthologies, periodicals, and miscellaneous publications, Morgan gives brief publication and contents notes for 770 non-English-language translations of Ginsberg. International coverage of 5,830 works about Ginsberg consists of the full range of scholarly studies (books, articles, chapters, dissertations, reviews, and non-English-language comments) down to more mundane brief mentions, such as his 1926 birth announcement. Arrangement within each year is rigidly chronological, down to month and day of publication. About half of the entries contain very brief, three- or four-word descriptions that are not always helpful. Access is provided by a title and first-line index of Ginsberg's works and a general index of proper names of persons, places, organizations, events, and the like and other titles. No subject indexing. Includes a foreword by Allen Ginsberg. Although Morgan's coverage supersedes Kraus' *Allen Ginsberg: An Annotated Bibliography, 1969-1977* (entry 562), Kraus' annotations remain useful for critical guidance.

564. Morgan, Bill. **The Works of Allen Ginsberg, 1941-1994: A Descriptive Bibliography**. Westport, CT: Greenwood Press, 1995. 456p. (Bibliographies and Indexes in American Literature, no. 19). LC 94-41266. ISBN 0-313-29389-9.

Full bibliographic descriptions in chronologically arranged sections for Ginsberg's books and pamphlets; broadsides; contributions to books; contributions to periodicals (1,228 entries dating from 1941 through 1994); books, periodicals, and other publications that reproduce photographs taken by Ginsberg; miscellaneous publications, such as dust-jacket blurbs, catalogs, librettos, programs, and other ephemera containing writings or drawings by Ginsberg; commercially produced recordings of Ginsberg, including Ginsberg reading his works and those of others (in particular, works by William Blake); and commercially produced film, radio, and television appearances. The 66 entries for books give title-page transcriptions, collations and physical descriptions, and complete publication histories, with citations for all printings. Index of titles and first lines and general index offer excellent access. Includes a foreword by Allen Ginsberg. Morgan's guide supersedes in both scope and detail George Dowden and Laurence McGilvery's *A Bibliography of Works by Allen Ginsberg, October, 1943 to July 1, 1967* (San Francisco, CA: City Lights Books, 1971). Ginsberg's manuscripts are listed in Robbins' *American Literary Manuscripts*, p. 127. Ginsberg's most famous poem, *Howl*, has twice been reproduced, edited by Barry Miles, in *Howl: Original Draft Facsimile, Transcript & Variant Versions, Fully Annotated by Author, with Contemporaneous Correspondence, Account of First Public Reading, Legal Skirmishes, Precursor Texts & Bibliography* (New York: Harper & Row, 1986; and New York: Harper/Collins, 1995).

George (Robert) Gissing, 1857-1903
Bibliographies

565. Collie, Michael. **George Gissing: A Bibliographical Study**. Winchester: St. Paul's Bibliographies, 1985. 167p. (St. Paul's Bibliographies, no. 12). LC 86-121657. ISBN 0-906795-29-x.

This revises and supersedes Collie's *George Gissing: A Bibliography* (Buffalo, NY: University of Toronto Press, 1975), giving full bibliographic descriptions in separate listings for individual works published in Gissing's lifetime; first appearances of works published posthumously; posthumous contributions to books; letters; and short stories. Entries provide title-page transcriptions; collations; contents; physical descriptions of bindings, covers, and advertisements; and detailed publishing histories. Gissing's manuscripts for published works are described throughout. In addition, appendixes list critical studies of Gissing that update Wolff's bibliography (entry 566) and colonial reissues and early translations of Gissing's works. Gissing's manuscripts are also described in *Index of English Literary Manuscripts*, IV, pt. 1:809-24. More specifically, Arthur Freeman's *George Gissing, 1857-1903: An Exhibition of Books, Manuscripts and Letters from the Pforzheimer Collection in the Lilly Library* (Bloomington, IN: Lilly Library, Indiana University, 1994) contains extensive descriptions of Gissing's literary manuscripts and autograph letters. Also available is *George Gissing, 1857-1903: Books, Manuscripts and Letters: A Chronological Catalogue of the Pforzheimer Collection* (London: Bernard Quaritch, 1992). Likewise, descriptions of Gissing's manuscripts in the Berg Collection of the New York Public Library are included in John D. Gordon's *George Gissing, 1857-1903: An Exhibition of the Berg Collection* (New York: New York Public Library, 1954). Also providing useful information about Gissing's published works and manuscripts, John Spiers' *The Rediscovery of George Gissing: A Reader's Guide* (London: National Book League, 1971), an exhibition catalog, describes works by and about Gissing and his contemporaries.

566. Wolff, Joseph J. **George Gissing: An Annotated Bibliography of Writings About Him**. DeKalb, IL: Northern Illinois University Press, 1974. 293p. (Annotated Secondary Bibliography Series on English Literature in Transition, 1880-1920). LC 73-15093. ISBN 0-87580-038-6.

Wolff offers comprehensive coverage of works about Gissing, chronologically arranging detailed annotated entries for 1,196 critical studies, reviews, dissertations, reviews of works about Gissing, introductions, and other works in all languages published from 1880 through 1970. Annotations are descriptive and evaluative. Important works receive extended reviews. A complex set of indexes (for primary and secondary title, languages, and critics) gives access. Also for a bibliography of works by and about Gissing, see *NCBEL*, III, pp. 1000-1004. Research on Gissing is reviewed by Jacob Korg in Stevenson's *Victorian Fiction*, pp. 388-414; and by Korg in Ford's *Victorian Fiction*, pp. 360-74.

Journals
567. **The Gissing Journal**. Wakefield: Gissing Trust, 1965-. 4/yr. ISSN 0017-0615.

Formerly *The Gissing Newsletter* (1965-90), features published in *The Gissing Journal* emphasize bibliography, descriptions of new attributions to Gissing's canon, source studies, and studies of reputations and critical reception rather than close readings and studies of themes and images. Discussions of biographic problems, correspondence, and other documents are numerous. A bibliographical feature, "Recent Publications," has described new editions and recent criticisms of Gissing. Other essays routinely review Gissing's critical reputation in such places as Japan and Australia. Volumes also include book reviews. Volumes of *The Gissing Newsletter* were regularly indexed in *MLA* through 1990. *The Gissing Journal* is indexed in *MHRA* to date.

Ellen (Anderson Gholson) Glasgow, 1873-1945
Bibliographies
568. Kelly, William W. **Ellen Glasgow: A Bibliography**. Charlottesville, VA: Published for the Bibliographical Society of the University of Virginia by the University Press of Virginia, 1964. 330p. LC 64-4758.

In the first part of the standard guide to Glasgow's primary works, Kelly describes Glasgow's books; collected editions; stories, poems, and other contributions to periodicals; and contributions to books. Entries give brief bibliographic information, with descriptions of composition and references to reviews. The second part lists biographical and critical works about Glasgow, including American and other dissertations. The third section describes in extensive detail Glasgow's manuscripts in the University of Virginia's Alderman Library (pp. 193-301). Also of interest is Carrington C. Tutwiler, Jr.'s *Ellen Glasgow's Library* (Charlottesville: Bibliographical Society of the University of Virginia, 1967). Also for works by Glasgow, see *First Printings of American Authors*, vol. 2, pp. 175-85. Glasgow's manuscripts are listed in Robbins' *American Literary Manuscripts*, p. 127.

569.　MacDonald, Edgar E., and Tonette Bond Inge. **Ellen Glasgow: A Reference Guide**. Boston: G. K. Hall, 1986. (A Reference Guide to Literature). LC 85-27045. ISBN 0-8161-8218-3.
　　This chronologically arranges annotated entries for about 1,500 works about Glasgow published from 1897 through 1981, covering books, parts of books, articles, reviews, dissertations, interviews, and other miscellaneous publications. Annotations are descriptive. Detailed subject indexing, with specific headings for such topics as "female characters," "narrative techniques," and "social criticism," and for individual works, offers solid access. See *Bibliography of American Fiction, 1866-1918*, pp. 191-94, for Pamela R. Matthews' checklist of works by and about Glasgow. Research on Glasgow is reviewed by MacDonald in Duke, Bryer, and Inge's *American Women Writers*, pp. 167-200; and by Linda Wagner-Martin in Flora and Bain's *Fifty Southern Writers After 1900*, pp. 206-14.

Journals

570.　**The Ellen Glasgow Newsletter**. Austin, TX: Ellen Glasgow Society, 1974-. 2/yr. ISSN 0160-7545.
　　Sponsored by the Ellen Glasgow Society, the newsletter features articles, notes, and reviews of new publications related to the life and works of Glasgow as well as announcements and information about conferences and works in progress. Particular attention has been given to Glasgow's relations with her contemporaries, such as Marjorie Kinnan Rawlings, Gertrude Stein, and Allen Tate. Many articles discuss information included in Glasgow's correspondence. "The Eyes of the Sphinx," a transcription of Rebe Glasgow's travel journal of 1899, appears in installments in 35 (Fall 1995): 1, 7-10; 36 (Spring 1996): 3, 9-15; and 37 (Fall 1996): 3-59. Other articles have described collections of Glasgow's primary documents. Additionally, the journal includes important bibliographic contributions, such as Margaret Bauer's "Secondary Sources on Ellen Glasgow, 1986-1990," 26 (Spring 1991): 10-19, which reviews recent scholarship. Regular notices for recent criticism briefly describe works about Glasgow. Issue 35 (Fall 1995) contains an index to *The Ellen Glasgow Newsletter* from 1974 to 1995. *The Ellen Glasgow Newsletter* is indexed in *MLA*.

Susan Keating Glaspell, 1882-1948
Bibliographies

571.　Papke, Mary E. **Susan Glaspell: A Research and Production Sourcebook**. Westport, CT: Greenwood Press, 1993. 299p. (Modern Dramatists Research and Production Sourcebooks, no. 4). LC 92-42696. ISBN 0-313-27383-9.
　　Chronologically arranged entries for Glaspell's 14 plays give plot summaries, production details for first and subsequent major performances, and overviews of critical receptions, with cross-references to secondary sources. Separate classified listings for Glaspell's published dramatic works; novels; short stories and children's fiction; essays and nonfiction; nonprint sources (film, filmstrips, audiotapes); and special collections give brief bibliographic information for first and subsequent editions, translations, and reprintings, with plot summaries or descriptions of contents. Separate, chronologically arranged, critically annotated listings cover 195 reviews and 314 critical studies (covering books, chapters,

articles, and dissertations) published from 1916 to 1992. Includes biocritical introduction and a chronology. Author index. General index supplies detailed topical access. See also *Bibliography of American Fiction, 1866-1918*, pp. 194-95, for Lori J. Williams' checklist of works by and about Glaspell. Glaspell's manuscripts are listed in Robbins' *American Literary Manuscripts*, p. 127. J. Ellen Gainor identifies works by and about Glaspell in Demastes' *American Playwrights, 1880-1945*, pp. 109-120.

William Godwin, 1756-1836
Bibliographies

572. Pollin, Burton R. **Godwin Criticism: A Synoptic Bibliography**. Toronto: University of Toronto Press, 1967. 659p. LC 68-72137.

A (relatively early) computer-produced comprehensive listing of secondary materials, Pollin's guide alphabetically arranges annotated entries for about 4,200 works about Godwin in separate listings for books and articles published from 1783 through 1836 and from 1837 through 1966. Coverage of critical studies in all languages includes reviews, prefaces and introductions in editions, and dissertations. Annotations are descriptive. Separate indexes for names, reviews, dates of publication, and languages provide access. The all-upper-case text and its reproduction from computer printouts make for difficult reading. Pollin's guide supersedes Francesco Cordasco's slim *William Godwin: A Handlist of Critical Notices & Studies* (Brooklyn, NY: Long Island University Press, 1950), 18th Century Bibliographical Pamphlets, no. 9, which lists 30 selected works about Godwin, including works in French and German, with references to reviews. Coverage of Godwin's primary bibliography is provided in Jack W. Marken's "The Canon and Chronology of William Godwin's Early Works," *Modern Language Notes* 69 (1954): 176-80. For a bibliography of works by and about Godwin, see *NCBEL*, II, pp. 1249-54, by John Barnard. Godwin's manuscripts are described in *Index of English Literary Manuscripts*, III, pt. 2:37-62. Robert Donald Spector reviews research on Godwin in *The English Gothic: A Bibliographic Guide to Writers from Horace Walpole to Mary Shelley*, pp. 61-68.

Oliver Joseph St. John Gogarty, 1878-1957
Bibliographies

Research on Gogarty is reviewed by James F. Carrens in Finneran's *Anglo-Irish Literature*, pp. 452-59.

Herbert Gold, 1924-
Bibliographies

For works by Gold, see *First Printings of American Authors*, vol. 1, pp. 153-54. Gold's manuscripts are listed in Robbins' *American Literary Manuscripts*, p. 128.

Michael (Irwin Granich) Gold, 1893-1967
Bibliographies

See *Bibliography of American Fiction 1919-1988*, p. 221, for Alan D. Brasher's checklist of works by and about Gold.

Arthur Golding, 1536?-1605?
Bibliographies

For a bibliography of works by and about Golding, see *NCBEL*, I, pp. 1,107-8.

(Sir) William Golding, 1911-1993
Bibliographies

573. Gekoski, R. A., and P. A. Grogan. **William Golding: A Bibliography 1934-1993**. London: Andre Deutsch, 1994. 158p. ISBN 0-2339-8611-1.

Covering works by and about Golding, Gekoski and Grogan chronologically arrange full bibliographic descriptions of Golding's works in sections for first British and American editions of books and pamphlets; contributions to books; contributions to periodicals and newspapers; radio and television broadcasts by Golding or of his works; and translations of Golding's works, subarranged by country and language. The 20 main entries for separate publications and 17 entries for contributions to books give title-page transcriptions; collation, paper, and binding descriptions; contents; and extensive notes on publication histories. Gekoski and Grogan list 127 contributions to periodicals published from 1950 through 1993. Other sections identify works about Golding in separate listings (a total of 646 unannotated entries) covering book-length criticisms; chapters and parts of books; periodical articles; and reviews of books, plays, and broadcasts (632 unannotated entries). International coverage of criticisms includes dissertations, with separate listings for non-English-language scholarship. Index to names and primary titles. Foreword by Golding. Gekoski and Grogan's guide supersedes coverage of works by and about Golding in Stanton's *A Bibliography of Modern British Novelists*, pp. 215-79, 1083.

Oliver Goldsmith, 1730?-1774

Bibliographies

574. Scott, Temple. **Oliver Goldsmith Bibliographically and Biographically Considered**. New York: The Bowling Green Press, 1928. 368p. LC 29-913.

Although outdated, Scott's guide gives useful, full bibliographic descriptions (including title-page transcriptions, collations, accounts of printing and publishing histories) for first and later editions and translations of Goldsmith's works. Available in a reprinted edition (Folcroft, PA: Folcroft Library Editions, 1974). Additional listings of first editions of Goldsmith's works are included in Williams' *Seven XVIIIth Century Bibliographies* (entry 35), pp. [115]-77. Also for a bibliography of works by and about Goldsmith, see *NCBEL*, II, pp. 1191-1210, by Arthur Friedman. Katharine Canby Balderston's *A Census of the Manuscripts of Oliver Goldsmith* (1926; reprint Norwood, PA: Norwood, 1977) describes manuscript materials. Goldsmith's manuscripts are also described in *Index of English Literary Manuscripts*, III, pt. 2:63-70.

575. Woods, Samuel H., Jr. **Oliver Goldsmith: A Reference Guide**. Boston: G. K. Hall, 1982. 208p. (A Reference Guide to Literature). LC 81-23734. ISBN 0-8161-8339-2.

Woods chronologically arranges annotated entries for about 700 critical studies about Goldsmith, including anonymous reviews and notices, dissertations, introductions in editions, and the like in all languages published from 1759 through 1978. Annotations are full, descriptive, and evaluative, clearly identifying important works. The index offers limited subject access under Goldsmith's name. Research on Goldsmith is reviewed by Cecil Price in Wells' *English Drama*, pp. 199-212.

Dictionaries, Encyclopedias, and Handbooks

See Johnson's *Plots and Characters in the Fiction of Eighteenth-Century English Authors* (entry 1309) for plot summaries of Goldsmith's major works.

Indexes and Concordances

576. Paden, William Doremus, and Clyde Kenneth Hyder. **A Concordance to the Poems of Oliver Goldsmith**. 1940; reprint Gloucester, MA: Peter Smith, 1966. 180p. LC 66-9077.

Paden and Hyder concord the text of Austin Dobson's edition of *The Poetical Works of Oliver Goldsmith* (London: Oxford University Press, 1906).

Paul Goodman, 1911-1972
Bibliographies

577. Nicely, Tom. **Adam and His Work: A Bibliography of Sources by and About Paul Goodman (1911-1972).** Metuchen, NJ: Scarecrow Press, 1979. 336p. (Scarecrow Author Bibliographies, no. 42). LC 79-11662. ISBN 0-8108-1219-3.

Part I of Nicely's guide to works by and about Goodman is an integrated, chronologically arranged listing of Goodman's books, pamphlets, contributions to books (introductions, prefaces, and the like) and journals, and other writings. Entries for books give title-page transcriptions, collations, contents, physical descriptions, publishing histories, references to reprints and translations, and notes on manuscript sources. Entries for other works give full bibliographic information. Part II describes miscellaneous works, including sheet music and typescripts and manuscripts. Part III arranges in separate listings brief and selectively annotated entries for more than 1,000 biographies, bibliographies, general studies, dissertations, book and play reviews (arranged by work), and other secondary materials. The volume lacks subject indexing. Nicely's guide supersedes Eliot Glassheim's "Paul Goodman: A Checklist, 1913-1971," *Bulletin of Bibliography* 29 (April-June 1972): 61-72. Goodman's manuscripts are listed in Robbins' *American Literary Manuscripts*, p. 129.

Samuel Griswold Goodrich (Peter Parley), 1793-1860
Bibliographies

See *Bibliography of American Fiction Through 1865*, pp.113-17, for a checklist of works by and about Goodrich. Contributions by Goodrich and criticism and reviews of Goodrich's works in selected periodicals are identified in Wells' *The Literary Index to American Magazines, 1815-1865*, pp. 62-63. Goodrich's manuscripts are listed in Robbins' *American Literary Manuscripts*, p. 129.

Nadine Gordimer, 1923-
Bibliographies

578. Driver, Dorothy, Ann Dry, Craig MacKenzie, and John Read. **Nadine Gordimer: A Bibliography of Primary and Secondary Sources, 1937-1992.** London: Hans Zell, 1994. 341p. (Bibliographical Research in African Literatures, no. 4). LC 93-037446. ISBN 1-873836-26-0.

Part 1 contains chronologically arranged descriptions of works by Gordimer in sections for fiction, short stories in journals and newspapers, short stories in anthologies, drama, translations, extracts, nonfiction, reviews, and interviews (a total of 717 entries). Coverage includes Gordimer's English- and non-English-language writings. Twenty-five entries for Gordimer's novels give brief bibliographic data for first and subsequent editions and translations with contents. Part 2 covers works of criticism on Gordimer with more than 2,300 entries in sections for comments generally and specifically about Gordimer, theses and dissertations, reviews of Gordimer's works (arranged by work), reviews of works about Gordimer, film adaptations and criticism, biography and miscellaneous materials, and bibliographies. Also supplies a brief Gordimer chronology. Secondary coverage includes newspaper features and non-English-language criticism. Entries often indicate which Gordimer work is criticized and note reprintings but are not otherwise annotated. Eleven elaborate, separate indexes of personal names of reviewers; critics, anthologists, translators; interviewers; Gordimer's reviews; titles containing primary works; titles containing secondary works; and more.

Caroline Gordon, 1895-1981
Bibliographies

For works by Gordon, see *First Printings of American Authors*, vol. 1, pp. 155-57. Gordon's manuscripts are listed in Robbins' *American Literary Manuscripts*, p. 129. Golden and Sullivan's *Flannery O'Connor and Caroline Gordon* (entry 1024) describe criticism of Gordon through 1975. See *Bibliography of American Fiction 1919-1988*, pp. 222-23, for William J. Stuckey's checklist of works by and about Gordon. Research on Gordon is also reviewed by Ashley Brown in Flora and Bain's *Fifty Southern Writers After 1900*, pp. 215-24.

Joe Gores, 1931-

Bibliographies

For works by Gores, see *First Printings of American Authors*, vol. 3, pp. 133-35.

(Sir) Edmund (William) Gosse, 1849-1928

Bibliographies

Gosse's contributions to selected periodicals and reviews of Gosse's works are identified in Wells' *The Literary Index to American Magazines, 1850-1900*, pp. 158-60. Wendell V. Harris reviews research on Gosse in DeLaura's *Victorian Prose*, pp. 456-58.

Robert Gover, 1929-

Bibliographies

579.   Hargraves, Michael. **Robert Gover: A Descriptive Bibliography**. Westport, CT: Meckler, 1988. LC 87-16489. ISBN 0-88736-165-x.

Hargraves gives title-page transcriptions, collations, contents, physical descriptions, and references to reviews for Gover's books, contributions to books, contributions to periodicals, translations of Gover's works, and miscellaneous writings (such as dust-jacket blurbs and business cards). Appends facsimiles of title pages and briefly annotated entries for 22 biographical and critical works about Gover. Also for works by Gover, see *First Printings of American Authors*, vol. 2, pp. 187-88.

John Gower, 1330?-1408

Bibliographies

580.   Nicholson, Peter. **An Annotated Index to the Commentary on Gower's Confessio Amantis**. Binghamton, NY: Medieval & Renaissance Texts & Studies, 1989. 593p. (Medieval & Renaissance Texts & Studies, vol. 62). LC 88-8546. ISBN 0-86698-046-6.

Covers about 350 selected, mostly English-language editions and criticism published from 1900 through 1987. Entries arranged by book and line numbers in G. C. Macaulay's edition of *Confessio Amantis* in *The Complete Works of John Gower* (Oxford: Clarendon Press, 1899-1902), with cross-references to full bibliographic information for editions and criticism in "Works Cited" (pp. 571-89). Coverage excludes "purely linguistic or textual" (p. vii) studies and dissertations. While this particular presentation promotes close reading of Gower's work and facilitates identifying all studies of a particular passage, it also requires the user to have detailed knowledge of the critical sources. The extended introduction identifies the most significant studies and the major critical focuses.

581.   Yeager, Robert F. **John Gower Materials: A Bibliography Through 1979**. New York: Garland, 1981. (Garland Reference Library of the Humanities, vol. 266). LC 80-8983. ISBN 0-8240-9351-8.

Yeager chronologically arranges annotated entries for 797 works by and about Gower in sections for manuscript catalogs and descriptions, editions and translations of Gower's works, general studies, and topical studies, including studies of printing history, dating, language, literary influence and reputation, "courtly love," and other subjects. Coverage includes criticisms of all varieties (dissertations, introductions in editions, and the like) in all languages published through 1979. Descriptive annotations include references to reviews. A separate index references some 50 subjects, including names, topics, and works (such as Boethius, "rhetoric," and *De Planctu Naturae*). Additionally, Yeager, John H. Fisher,

R. Wayne Hamm, and Peter G. Beidler offer a comprehensive guide to Gower's primary materials with a bibliography of editions and criticism in Severs and Hartung's *A Manual of the Writings in Middle English*, vol. XVII, pp. 2195-2210, 2399-2418. Also for a bibliography of works by and about Gower, see *NCBEL*, I, pp. 553-56, by J. A. W. Bennett.

Indexes and Concordances

582.   Pickles, J. D., and J. L. Dawson. **A Concordance to John Gower's Confessio Amantis**. Woodbridge: D. S. Brewer, 1987. 1,124p. (Publications of the John Gower Society, no. 1). LC 87-21212. ISBN 0-85991-245-0.

Based on George Macaulay's text of Gower's *Complete Works* (London: Oxford University Press, 1899-1902), Pickles and Dawson provide separate concordances to the main text (excluding Gower's interspersed and side-noted Latin verses) and to variants, including "English passages that Macaulay identifies as authorial revisions and printed by Macaulay from manuscripts" (p. viii). Each concordance is accompanied by alphabetical and ranked word-frequency tables and reverse-word indexes. Appendixes include a concordance to four frequent words ("al," "alle," "love," and "man") ; a concordance to 146 other high-frequency words ("a," "ben," "for," and the like), with sample references and context lines; a rhyming index; and an index of capitalized words.

(Charles) William Goyen, 1915-1983

Bibliographies

583.   Wright, Stuart T. **William Goyen: A Descriptive Bibliography, 1938-1985**. Westport, CT: Meckler, 1986. 181p. LC 86-5213. ISBN 0-88736-057-2.

Wright gives detailed descriptions of Goyen's primary bibliography, including sections for editions of his separately published books, contributions to books, contributions to periodicals (including selections and excerpts), interviews and published comments, film and recorded adaptations, and translations (arranged by counties). Entries offer title-page transcriptions; collations; contents; descriptions of paper, bindings, and dust jackets; and publishing histories. Textual collations of variant texts are provided. Also for works by Goyen, see *First Printings of American Authors*, vol. 4, pp. 197-99.

Sheilah Graham, 1904?-1988

Bibliographies

For works by Graham, see *First Printings of American Authors*, vol. 3, pp. 137-38.

Shirley Ann Grau, 1929-

Bibliographies

For works by Grau, see *First Printings of American Authors*, vol. 4, pp. 201-202. Grau's manuscripts are listed in Robbins' *American Literary Manuscripts*, p. 130. See the review of research by Paul Schlueter in Flora and Bain's *Fifty Southern Writers After 1900*, pp. 225-34.

Richard Graves, 1715-1804

Bibliographies

For a bibliography of works by and about Graves, see *NCBEL*, II, pp. 1174-76, by John Barnard.

Robert van Ranke Graves, 1895-1985

Bibliographies

584.   Bryant, Hallman Bell. **Robert Graves: An Annotated Bibliography**. New York: Garland, 1986. 206p. (Garland Reference Library of the Humanities, vol. 671). LC 86-7669. ISBN 0-8240-8556-6.

Although its coverage of Graves' primary materials is superseded by Higginson and Williams' guide (entry 585), Bryant's bibliography provides the most comprehensive listing of materials about Graves. Sections include descriptively annotated entries for about 700 books and articles, selected reviews, dissertations, and collections and bibliographies in all languages published through 1985. The index provides limited topical access under Graves' name.

585. Higginson, Fred H., and William Proctor Williams. **A Bibliography of the Writings of Robert Graves**. 2d ed. Winchester: St. Paul's Bibliographies, 1987. 354p. (St. Paul's Bibliographies). ISBN 0-906795-16-8.

A revision of Higginson's *A Bibliography of the Works of Robert Graves* (Hamden, CT: Archon Books, 1966), this is the best listing of Graves' primary works, delivering full bibliographic descriptions of books, pamphlets, and collaborative, edited, and translated works by Graves; contributions to books; and contributions to journals and newspapers (some 959 entries). Entries give title-page transcriptions, collations, contents, physical descriptions, and publishing histories. Appendixes list translations of selections of Graves' works and briefly describe collections of Graves' manuscripts and printed works at Southern Illinois University, the University of Texas' Harry Ransom Humanities Research Center, the Berg Collection of the New York Public Library, and the Robert Graves Collection at the State University of New York at Buffalo (pp. 314-15). Also useful, John W. Presley's *The Robert Graves Manuscripts and Letters at Southern Illinois University: An Inventory* (Troy, NY: Whitston, 1976) describes Graves' letters and correspondence and literary manuscripts. Also for a bibliography of works by and about Graves, see *NCBEL*, IV, pp. 201-207.

Journals

586. **Focus on Robert Graves and His Contemporaries**. New York: University of Maryland University College, 1972-. 2/yr. ISSN 0190-650x.

Formerly *Focus on Robert Graves*, this describes itself in an editorial masthead first appearing in 2.2 (Spring 1994): 3 as "an international, interdisciplinary journal devoted to furthering discussion on the cultural consequences of the Great War." Features promote scholarship on Graves as well as his contemporaries, such as Paul Blackburn, Laura Riding, T. E. Lawrence, John Peale Bishop, William Empson, Siegfried Sassoon, Katherine Mansfield, Wildred Owen, and William Butler Yeats, as well as modern literature in general. Significant attention has focused on images of war in Graves' and others' works. Other contributions have described materials in the important Robert Graves Collection at Southern Illinois University and elsewhere. The journal also contains book-review essays, calls for papers, and notices of new publications. With 2.1 (Spring 1993), *Focus on Robert Graves and His Contemporaries* changed to a larger quarto-sized format. An index to vols. 1.7-2.3 is included in 2.4 (Winter 1995-96). *Focus on Robert Graves and His Contemporaries* is indexed in *AHI*, *MHRA*, and *MLA*.

587. **Gravesiana: The Journal of the Robert Graves Society**. Buffalo, NY: Robert Graves Society, 1996-. 2/yr. ISSN 1368-1095.

Gravesiana publishes critical and biographical articles and notes related to Graves, poetry in imitation of Graves, reviews of new publications, and news and information for society members. Bibliographic contributions include John Presley's "An Addendum to the Higginson Bibliography: Robert Graves, the Two Lawrences, and the FBI," 1.2 (December 1996): 174-76. A special issue coinciding with the publication of *The White Goddess* is planned. *Gravesiana* is indexed in *MLA*.

John Henry Gray, 1866-1934
Bibliographies

Cevasco's *Three Decadent Poets* (entry 410), pp. [163]-252, describes works about Gray through 1988. Also for a bibliography of works by and about Gray, see *NCBEL*, III, p. 628.

Simon James Holliday Gray, 1936-
Bibliographies
> King's *Twenty Modern British Playwrights*, pp. 55-58, lists works by Gray and describes works about him.

Thomas Gray, 1716-1771
Bibliographies
588.   McKenzie, Alan T. **Thomas Gray: A Reference Guide**. Boston: G. K. Hall, 1982. 334p. (A Reference Guide to Literature). LC 82-1074. ISBN 0-8161-8451-8.
> Attempting to "indicate the location and content of every substantial comment on Gray and his works since 1751" (p. xv), McKenzie chronologically arranges annotated entries for about 1,800 criticisms published in books, parts of books (including introductions in editions), articles, and dissertations in English and other languages appearing through 1981. Descriptive annotations note subsequent reprintings. Standard works, such as R. W. Ketton-Cremer's *Thomas Gray: A Biography* (Cambridge: Cambridge University Press, 1955) and others of particular significance receive detailed descriptions. Indexing for critics, editors, and subjects is adequate. References under Gray's name are topically subdivided for bibliography, biography, "and Dante," "and France," and so forth.

589.   Northup, Clark S. **A Bibliography of Thomas Gray**. New Haven, CT: Yale University Press, 1917. 296p. LC 17-10681.
> The standard guide to Gray's works (as well as to related ana, such as parodies and manuscript studies), Northup offers a classified descriptive listing of separately published and selected editions of Gray's poetry, prose, and translations. Entries give title-page transcriptions, collations, contents, and copy locations. Available in a reprinted edition (New York: Russell & Russell, 1970). Herbert W. Starr's *A Bibliography of Thomas Gray, 1917-1951* (Philadelphia, PA: University of Pennsylvania Press, 1953) continues Northup's coverage. For a bibliography of works by and about Gray, see *NCBEL*, II, pp. 577-85, by Roger H. Lonsdale. Gray's manuscripts are described in *Index of English Literary Manuscripts*, III, pt. 2:71-116.

Indexes and Concordances
590.   Cook, Albert S. **Concordance to the English Poems of Thomas Gray**. 1908; reprint Gloucester, MA: Peter Smith, 1967. 160p. LC 67-8967.
> This is based on Edmund Gosse's four-volume edition of *The Works of Thomas Gray in Prose and Verse* (London: Macmillan, 1884). Also reprinted (Norwood, PA: Norwood Editions, 1975).

Andrew M. Greeley, 1928-
Bibliographies
591.   Harrison, Elizabeth. **Andrew M. Greeley: An Annotated Bibliography**. Metuchen, NJ: Scarecrow, 1994. 389p. (Scarecrow Author Bibliographies, no. 92). LC 94-25619. ISBN 0-8108-2931-2.
> Covers works by and about Greeley published in the United States in English from 1956 through 1993. Part 1 arranges Greeley's publications by type, including books (nonfiction, novels, short stories, poems), contributions to books (essays, introductions, short stories), contributions to periodicals (articles, interviews, letters, short stories), newspaper columns (Catholic and secular), book and film reviews, unpublished papers and theses, newsletters, and miscellanea. Some 139 entries for Greeley's books give brief bibliographic data for first and subsequent editions (including recordings) with summaries of contents. Harrison briefly identifies Greeley's approximately 2,600 contributions to periodicals (including newspapers and reviews). Part 2 covers about 700 works about Greeley in sections for books; essays, parts of books, directories; periodical articles; news reports; and selected reviews of books (nonfiction, novels, short stories). Secondary

works are selectively annotated. Includes brief chronology and a list of Greeley's honors and awards Appendix classifies primary works in 10 subject categories (including education, the Irish, sociology of religion, and the like). Separate author and title indexes.

Anna Katharine Green, 1846-1935
Bibliographies

For works by Green, see *First Printings of American Authors*, vol. 4, pp. 203-209. Green's manuscripts are listed in Robbins' *American Literary Manuscripts*, p. 274. See *Bibliography of American Fiction, 1866-1918*, pp. 196-97, for Laura Plummer's checklist of works by and about Green.

Matthew Green, 1697-1737
Bibliographies

For a bibliography of works by and about Green, see *NCBEL*, II, 550, 1558, 1905. Green's manuscripts are described in *Index of English Literary Manuscripts*, III, pt. 2:117-19.

Paul (Eliot) Green, 1894-1981
Bibliographies

592.   Kimball, Sue Laslie, and Lynn Veach Sadler. **Paul Green's Celebration of Man, with a Bibliography**. Fayetteville, NC: Human Technology Interface, 1994. 125p. ISBN 187-8304-05-4

Unseen. Green's manuscripts are listed in Robbins' *American Literary Manuscripts*, p. 131. Laurence G. Avery surveys works by and about Green in Flora and Bain's *Fifty Southern Writers After 1900*, pp. 235-46. Mary Maddock identifies works by and about Green in Demastes' *American Playwrights, 1880-1945*, pp. 121-31.

Kate (Catherine) Greenaway, 1846-1901
Bibliographies

593.   Thomson, Susan Ruth. **Kate Greenaway: A Catalogue of the Kate Greenaway Collection, Rare Book Room, Detroit Public Library**. Detroit, MI: Published by Wayne State University Press for the Friends of the Detroit Public Library, 1977. 211p. LC 77-5222. ISBN 0-8143-1581-X.

Not intended to be the definitive Greenaway bibliography, Thomson's catalog arranges detailed descriptions of Greenaway materials (mainly from the John S. Newbery Gift Collection of Kate Greenaway and the estate of Robert Partidge) in four categories: books containing Greenaway's illustrations; magazines and annuals containing her illustrations; calendars, cards, invitations, programs, etc., containing her illustrations; and original Greenaway materials, including manuscript letters and drawings. Full descriptions for 188 books, alphabetically arranged by authors, give title-page transcriptions, sizes, paper and binding descriptions, contents, and provenance but do not attempt to identify "editio princeps" or bibliographic relationships. Appends descriptions of five awards given to Greenaway and an unannotated bibliography of about 30 works of "research value" on Greenaway in the collection (pp. [191]-96). Addenda. Index of names and titles. Another very useful catalog, Robert Kiger, Bernadette Gallery, Michael Stieber, James White, and Elizabeth Mosiman's *Kate Greenaway: Catalogue of an Exhibition of Original Artworks and Related Materials Selected from the Frances Hooper Collection at the Hunt Institute* (Pittsburgh, PA: The Hunt Institute for Botanical Documentation, Carnegie-Mellon University, 1980), contains a "Summary Register of the Francis Hooper Kate Greenaway Collection" (pp. 101-106), listing original artworks, applied designs, books and articles by Greenaway, and Greenaway records and papers, including manuscripts, correspondence, receipts, and miscellaneous materials. Also for a bibliography of works by and about Greenaway, see *NCBEL*, III, p. 1096.

Joanne Greenberg, 1932-

Bibliographies

For works by Greenberg, see *First Printings of American Authors*, vol. 2, pp. 189-90. Barbara Pitlick Lovenheim reviews works by and about Greenberg in Shapiro's *Jewish American Women Writers*, pp. 95-100.

(Henry) Graham Greene, 1904-1991

Bibliographies

594.   Cassis, A. F. **Graham Greene: An Annotated Bibliography of Criticism**. Metuchen, NJ: Scarecrow Press, 1981. 401p. (Scarecrow Author Bibliographies, no. 55). LC 81-770. ISBN 0-8108-1418-8.

Cassis offers a comprehensive, chronologically arranged annotated bibliography of about 2,200 works about Greene, including books, articles, reviews, dissertations, and miscellaneous writings in all languages published from 1929 through 1979. Annotations are descriptive and evaluative. A separate subject index references such topics as "allegory," "grace," and "social values" as well as individual works. Cassis' guide supersedes J. Don Vann's *Graham Greene: A Checklist of Criticism* (Kent, OH: Kent State University Press, 1970) and also the coverage of Greene's secondary materials provided in R. A. Wobbe's *Graham Greene: A Bibliography and Guide to Research* (entry 595).

595.   Wobbe, R. A. **Graham Greene: A Bibliography and Guide to Research**. New York: Garland, 1979. 440p. (Garland Reference Library of the Humanities, vol. 173). LC 78-68307. ISBN 0-8240-9760-2.

Although coverage of Greene scholarship is superseded by Cassis' work (entry 594), Wobbe's bibliography offers a comprehensive listing of Greene's primary works. Entries describe Greene's books, contributions to books, contributions to periodicals and newspapers (including film criticism), and miscellaneous writings (such as manuscripts, typescripts, letters, and films written in whole or part), providing title-page transcriptions, collations, contents, printing histories, and copy locations. In addition, Wobbe lists Greene's radio and television appearances and published and broadcasted interviews. Also covering Greene's primary materials, Robert H. Miller's *Graham Greene: A Descriptive Catalog* (Lexington, KY: University Press of Kentucky, 1979) describes Greene's letters and correspondence, radio scripts, pamphlets, and books at the University of Louisville. Also for a bibliography of works by and about Greene, see *NCBEL*, IV, pp. 503-12. Lawrence Jasper surveys and identifies works by and about Greene in Demastes and Kelly's *British Playwrights, 1880-1956*, pp. [172]-88.

Dictionaries, Encyclopedias, and Handbooks

596.   Hoskins, Robert. **Graham Greene: A Character Index and Guide**. New York: Garland, 1991. 512p. (Garland Reference Library of the Humanities, vol. 923). LC 91-002714. ISBN 0-8240-4111-9.

"A character index and guide to Graham Greene's fiction and drama" (p. xi), with more than 3,200 entries identifying named and unnamed characters, historical and literary allusions, place names, and non-English-language expressions and phrases in chronologically arranged sections (by publication date) for the novels, plays, and short fiction. Includes a list of editions used for the guide and a selected bibliography (p. 463). General index to the entries.

597.   Miller, R. H. **Understanding Graham Greene**. Columbia, SC: University of South Carolina Press, 1990. 195p. (Understanding Contemporary British Literature). LC 90-32677. ISBN 0-87249-704-6.

Miller provides introductory commentaries on Greene's life and writings as well as critical approaches to religion and politics in his works, with an annotated bibliography of secondary materials (pp. 177-88).

Journals

598.   **Essays in Graham Greene: An Annual Review**. St. Louis, MO: Lucas Hall Press, 1987-. Annual. ISSN 0738-0763.

Annual volumes include eight to ten features on biographical and critical topics, including themes, images, and structures; close readings of individual works; and reprintings of selected "landmark studies of Greene" from the previous 40 years. Bibliographic contributions have ranged from essay reviews of the year's work in Greene criticism to an annotated checklist of books, essays, and reviews. Also includes reviews of works by and about Greene. Vol. 3 appeared in 1992. To date, volumes of *Essays in Graham Greene* have not been indexed thoroughly in either *MLA* or *MHRA*.

Robert Greene, 1558-1592

Bibliographies

599.   Allison, A. F. **Robert Greene, 1558-1592: A Bibliographical Catalog of the Early Editions in English (to 1640)**. Folkestone: Dawson, 1975. 75p. (Pall Mall Bibliographies, no. 4). LC 76-350814. ISBN 0-7129-0659-2.

Allison gives detailed descriptions of Greene's writings, including collations, physical descriptions, lists of copies examined, cross-references to the *STC* and other standard catalogs, and publication histories for first and subsequent editions through 1640. Facsimiles of title pages appear in the volume's accompanying microfiche. An index of stationers (printers, publishers, booksellers, etc.) gives access. For a bibliography of works by and about Greene, see *NCBEL*, I, pp. 1437-43. Greene's manuscripts are described in *Index of English Literary Manuscripts*, I, pt. 2:101-102.

600.   Dean, James Seay. **Robert Greene: A Reference Guide**. Boston: G. K. Hall, 1984. 258p. (A Reference Guide to Literature). LC 84-4584. ISBN 0-8161-7854-2.

Dean chronologically arranges entries for about 1,000 studies and comments on Greene published from 1675 through 1979. Comprehensive coverage includes critical comments and studies (dissertations, introductions in editions, and the like) in all languages. Annotations are scholarly and evaluative. Subject indexing for broad topics and for specific ones under individual works (such as "authorship," "characterization," "structure," and the like in *Friar Bacon*) greatly increases the volume's usefulness. Dean's work supersedes Tetsumaro Hayashi's *Robert Greene Criticism: A Comprehensive Bibliography* (Metuchen, NJ: Scarecrow Press, 1971), which lists some 750 items; the Tannenbaums' *Elizabethan Bibliographies*, vol. 3; and Robert C. Johnson's *Elizabethan Bibliographies Supplements*, no. 5. Research on Greene is reviewed by William Nestrick in Logan and Smith's *The Predecessors of Shakespeare*, pp. 56-92.

Indexes and Concordances

See Stagg's *The Figurative Language of the Tragedies of Shakespeare's Chief 16th-Century Contemporaries* (entry 901) for an index of images in selected works by Greene.

Arthur Gregor, 1923-

Bibliographies

For works by Gregor, see *First Printings of American Authors*, vol. 2, pp. 191-92. Gregor's manuscripts are listed in Robbins' *American Literary Manuscripts*, p. 132.

(Isabella) Augusta (Persse), Lady Gregory, 1852-1932

Bibliographies

601.   Kopper, Edward A., Jr. **Lady Gregory: A Review of the Criticism**. Butler, PA: Edward A. Kopper, 1991. 39p. (Modern Irish Literature Monograph Series, vol. 2). OCLC 26096032.

"Synthesizes [approximately 150] writings about Lady Gregory's life and writings from about 1910 to the present" (p. 5). Narrative sections cover editions, letters, bibliography, and manuscripts; biography, personality, and relationships (with Wildred Scawen Blunt, John Quinn, Yeats, Gogarty, and others); books and shorter general commentary; plays; and prose. Identifies special collections for Lady Gregory in the New York Public Library's Berg Collection and elsewhere (p. 8). Unindexed. Kopper's work is by far the most up-to-date overview of current scholarship on Lady Gregory. Research on Lady Gregory is also reviewed by James F. Carens in Finneran's *Anglo-Irish Literature*, pp. 437-45; and by Tramble T. Turner in Schrank and Demastes' *Irish Playwrights, 1880-1995: A Research and Production Sourcebook*, pp. 108-23.

602. Mikhail, E. H. **Lady Gregory: An Annotated Bibliography of Criticism.** Troy, NY: Whitston, 1982. 258p. LC 80-51874. ISBN 0-87875-215-1.

Mikhail provides brief, selectively annotated entries for about 3,000 writings about Lady Gregory in topical listings for bibliographies, editions of Lady Gregory's works (with references to reviews), and critical works, including books, articles, dissertations, unpublished works, and reviews of play productions (arranged by plays). Coverage extends through 1979. Detailed topical indexing under Lady Gregory's name as well as for other subjects, such as James Joyce, Belfast Opera House, and "Irish Dramatic Movement," provides good access. Also for a bibliography of works by and about Lady Gregory, see *NCBEL*, III, pp. 1939-41.

(Sir) Fulke Greville, 1st Baron Brooke, 1554-1628
Bibliographies

603. Klemp, P. J. **Fulke Greville and Sir John Davies: A Reference Guide.** Boston: G. K. Hall, 1985. 128p. (A Reference Guide to Literature). LC 85-8150. ISBN 0-8161-8526-3.

Klemp delivers separate, chronologically arranged listings of annotated entries for works by and about Greville from 1581 through 1980 (about 400 items) and for Davies from 1590 through 1980 (about 400 items). Coverage is limited to printed editions (which is significant in that the early notices about each author refer to works that circulated only in manuscript). Entries for early editions provide basic bibliographic information but do not reference the *STC* or other standard catalogs. Coverage of secondary works includes dissertations and non-English-language criticisms. Annotations are descriptive and detailed, with significant studies receiving extended descriptions. Separate indexes for Greville and Davies offer excellent topical access, including headings for broad topics such as bibliographies, "Plato and platonism," and "Sources"; names of other writers, such as Shakespeare, Machiavelli, and Martial; and detailed topics under the names of Greville and Davies. For a bibliography of works by and about Greville, see *NCBEL*, I, pp. 1057-59. Greville's manuscripts are described in *Index of English Literary Manuscripts*, I, pt. 2:103-10, 627.

Zane Grey, 1872-1939
Bibliographies

604. Farley, G. M. **Zane Grey: A Documented Portrait: The Man, the Bibliography, the Filmography.** Tuscaloosa, AL: Portals Press, 1986. 128p. ISBN 0-916620-78-6.

A full, illustrated introductory account of Grey's life and career precedes a rather clumsily classified listings of works by and about Grey aimed more for the novice reader-collector than scholar. Entries give brief bibliographic data for works by Grey in sections covering books (listed by publication date and alphabetically), original editions in paperback, books in part by Grey, works reprinted as paperbacks, unabridged paperbacks with forewords by Loren Grey, anthologies containing Grey's writings, rare items by Grey, pamphlets by Grey, titles in the "Big Little Books" series, anthologies in paperback, abridgments attributed to (but not written by) Romer Zane Grey, and magazine and newspaper publications by Grey (arranged by periodical title). Unannotated listings of works about Grey include six books, 18 other books of interest to Grey fans, and approximately 50 articles about Grey by Farley, Norris F. Schneider (a Grey collector), and others. A concluding "Filmography of Zane Grey Movies," compiled by William C. Wilson, lists by year of first release movies based on Grey's works, with fuller entries (alphabetically arranged by titles) giving brief credits; fishing films starring Grey; and story sources of selected movies. Unindexed. Of slight research value, Charles G. Pfeiffer's 20-page pamphlet, *So You Want to Read Zane Grey—and Don't Know Where to Start: A Brief Guide to Make the Reading of Zane Grey's Novels More Pleasurable and Rewarding* (1989; revised ed. Columbia, SC: Charles G. Pfeiffer, 1994), classifies Grey's 58 adult romances of the American frontier by broad subjects and briefly gives for each Pfeiffer's "personal preferences at the moment" (p. 5). Also for works by Grey, see *First Printings of American Authors*, vol. 5, pp. 121-40. Grey's manuscripts are listed in Robbins' *American Literary Manuscripts*, p. 132.

605.   Scott, Kenneth William. **Zane Grey: Born to the West: A Reference Guide**. Boston: G. K. Hall, 1979. 179p. (A Reference Publication in Literature). LC 79-715. ISBN 0-8161-7875-5.

Following a list of film adaptations of Grey's works (with information about casts and productions), Scott chronologically arranges annotated entries for about 1,200 commentaries and criticisms of Grey published from 1904 through 1977. Comprehensive coverage includes reviews of Grey's books and film adaptations in popular magazines and newspapers, biographical and critical references in general sources, dissertations, and introductions in editions. Annotations are descriptive. Subject indexing is very limited, providing headings for "Indians" and a few names (such as Joseph Conrad and Hamlin Garland). See *Bibliography of American Fiction, 1866-1918*, pp. 198-202, for Robert L. Gale's checklist of works by and about Grey. Research on Grey is reviewed by Gary Topping in Erisman and Etulain's *Fifty Western Writers*, pp. 152-61.

Journals

See Patterson's *Author Newsletters and Journals*, p. 144, for previously published journals for Grey.

Sutton E(lbert) Griggs, 1872-1930

Bibliographies

See *Bibliography of American Fiction, 1866-1918*, pp. 202-203, for Betty E. Taylor Thompson's checklist of works by and about Griggs. Research on Griggs is reviewed by Ruth Miller and Peter J. Katopes in Inge, Duke, and Bryer's *Black American Writers*, vol. I, pp. 133-60.

Rufus Wilmot Griswold, 1815-1857

Bibliographies

For works by Griswold, see *Bibliography of American Literature*, vol. 3, pp. 289-304. Works about Griswold in selected periodicals are identified in Wells' *The Literary Index to American Magazines, 1815-1865*, pp. 64-66; and *The Literary Index to American Magazines, 1850-1900*, pp. 160-61. Griswold's manuscripts are listed in Robbins' *American Literary Manuscripts*, p. 133.

Alfred Grossman, 1927-

Bibliographies

For works by Grossman, see *First Printings of American Authors*, vol. 4, pp. 211-12.

Davis Grubb, 1919-1980
Bibliographies

> See *Bibliography of American Fiction, 1919-1988,* p. 224, for Edwin T. Arnold's checklist of works by and about Grubb.

Barbara Guest, 1920-
Bibliographies

> For works by Guest, see *First Printings of American Authors,* vol. 5, pp. 141-42.

Louise Imogen Guiney, 1861-1920
Bibliographies

> For works by Guiney, see *Bibliography of American Literature,* vol. 3, pp. 305-18. Guiney's contributions to selected periodicals and reviews of Guiney's works are identified in Wells' *The Literary Index to American Magazines, 1850-1900,* p. 161. Guiney's manuscripts are listed in Robbins' *American Literary Manuscripts,* pp. 133-34.

Neil Miller Gunn, 1891-1973

Bibliographies

> 606.   Stokoe, C. J. L. **A Bibliography of the Works of Neil M. Gunn.** Aberdeen: Published in association with Aberdeen City Libraries by Aberdeen University Press, 1987. 245p. ISBN 0-08-035079-8.
>
> Awkwardly arranges bibliographic descriptions of both separately published and contributed works by Gunn chronologically in sections for books and short stories; plays, adaptations, and film scripts; verse; articles in newspapers and periodicals; broadcast materials; and miscellanea, including contributed letters and forewords, speeches, and manuscripts in the National Library of Scotland. In all sections entries for books give title-page transcriptions, collations, contents, binding descriptions, notes for reprinted and subsequent editions, and summary contents. Entries for dramatic works note production information and credits and locate typescripts. Includes brief chronology of Gunn's life and works. Indexing limited to titles. Also for a bibliography of works by and about Gunn, see *NCBEL,* IV, p. 595.

Thom(son William) Gunn, 1929-
Bibliographies

> 607.   Hagstrom, Jack W. C., and George Bixby. **Thom Gunn: A Bibliography, 1940-1978.** London: Bertram Rota, 1979. 200p. LC 80-509352. ISBN 0-85400-021-6.
>
> Hagstrom and Bixby give full bibliographic descriptions for Gunn's books, pamphlets, and broadsides; edited works and contributions to books; contributions to periodicals and newspapers; translations (arranged by languages); interviews; recordings; and miscellaneous works (such as dust-jacket blurbs and quotations in dealer catalogs). Entries provide title-page transcriptions, collations, contents, descriptions of bindings, and publishing histories. Appendixes list Gunn's juvenilia and first lines of poems. Coverage of criticism of Gunn is provided in Shields' *Contemporary English Poetry,* pp. 71-91.

A(lfred) B(ertram) Guthrie, (Jr.), 1901-1991
Bibliographies

> See *Bibliography of American Fiction, 1919-1988,* pp. 225-26, for Richard W. Etulain's checklist of works by and about Guthrie. Guthrie's manuscripts are listed in Robbins' *American Literary Manuscripts,* p. 134. Fred Erisman surveys works by and about Guthrie in Erisman and Etulain's *Fifty Western Writers,* pp. 162-71.

William Habington, 1605-1654
Bibliographies

For a bibliography of works by and about Habington, see *NCBEL*, I, p. 1208. Habington's manuscripts are described in *Index of English Literary Manuscripts*, II, pt. 1: 499-506.

Sir H(enry) Rider Haggard, 1856-1925
Bibliographies

608.   Whatmore, D. E. **H. Rider Haggard: A Bibliography**. Westport, CT: Meckler, 1987. 187p. LC 86-33272. ISBN 0-88736-102-1.

Whatmore lists English-language editions of Haggard's works, including his fiction and nonfiction books; pamphlets and reports; contributions to *The African Review* and other periodicals and books; letters to editors; reports of Haggard's speeches; and film, stage, and radio adaptations of his works. Intended to identify bibliographic points of first editions, entries give title-page transcriptions; collations; descriptions of bindings, illustrations, and dust jackets; publishing histories; and references to reprintings and serializations. Also includes a checklist of about 350 works about Haggard (covering dissertations, parodies, and lampoons). Coverage of Haggard's primary materials supersedes J. E. Scott's *A Bibliography of the Works of Sir Henry Rider Haggard, 1856-1925* (Takeley: Elkin Mathews, 1947). Kriston Sites' catalog, *In and Out of Africa: The Adventures of H. Rider Haggard: An Exhibition* (Bloomington, IN: Lilly Library, 1995) gives detailed descriptions (with a selected bibliography) of 71 Haggard first editions, advertising and promotional materials, and artworks and films from the Lilly Library's extensive Haggard collection. Also for a bibliography of works by and about Haggard, see *NCBEL*, III, pp. 1055-56.

Richard Hakluyt, 1552-1616
Bibliographies

609.   Quinn, David B. **The Hakluyt Handbook**. London: Hakluyt Society, 1974. 2 vols. (Works Issued by the Hakluyt Society, 2d ser., no. 144-145). LC 72-87176. ISBN 0-521-20212-4.

Comprehensive companion and bibliography for the life and works of Hakluyt. Parts 1 and 2 consist of original essays by different authorities on historical and biographical backgrounds and Hakluyt's methods. Essays address Hakluyt's view of history, language, nautical terms, and maps, and especially his uses of primary materials and other accounts related to particular world regions, such as Russia, India, and North America. Part 3 is a detailed Hakluyt chronology cross-referenced to standard published and documentary sources. Part 4 attempts to identify and "assign all the items in Hakluyt's three documentary collections. to their sources," with information about subsequent appearances to 1600. Part 5 is "The Primary Hakluyt Bibliography" (pp. 461-575), compiled by Quinn, C. E. Armstrong, and R. A. Skelton, with full bibliographic descriptions of Hakluyt's works, works in which Hakluyt's influence is known or acknowledged and works that Hakluyt may have influenced. Entries supply title-page transcriptions (with facsimile illustrations), collations, and paginations, with detailed information about the contents of located variant copies in Britain and North America. L. E. Pennington's section "Secondary Works on Hakluyt and His Circle" (pp. 576-610) provides a classified bibliographic review of works about Hakluyt's life and works, covering international contemporary, early, and modern scholarship. Includes index of books and a comprehensive general index. Offers an excellent starting point for the study of Hakluyt and the Renaissance literature of travel and discovery. Also for a bibliography of works by and about Hakluyt, see *NCBEL*, I, pp. 2111, 2151, 2161, 2276.

Edward Everett Hale, 1822-1909
Bibliographies

See *Bibliography of American Fiction, 1866-1918*, pp. 203-206, for James L. Pettibone's checklist of works by and about Hale. Hale's contributions to and reviews of Hale's works in selected periodicals are identified in Wells' *The Literary Index to American Magazines, 1850-1900*, pp. 163-65. Hale's manuscripts are listed in Robbins' *American Literary Manuscripts*, pp. 135-36.

Lucretia Peabody Hale, 1820-1900
Bibliographies

See *Bibliography of American Fiction, 1866-1918*, p. 207, for Cheryl Z. Oreovicz's checklist of works by and about Hale.

Nancy Hale, 1908-1988
Bibliographies

For works by Hale, see *First Printings of American Authors*, vol. 1, pp. 159-60. Hale's manuscripts are listed in Robbins' *American Literary Manuscripts*, p. 136. See *Bibliography of American Fiction, 1919-1988*, pp. 226-27, for Laurie Ann Haynes' checklist of works by and about Hale.

Sarah Josepha (Buell) Hale, 1788-1879
Bibliographies

For works by Hale, see *Bibliography of American Literature*, vol. 3, pp. 319-40. Contributions by Hale and criticism and reviews of Hale's works in selected periodicals are identified in Wells' *The Literary Index to American Magazines, 1815-1865*, p. 66. Hale's manuscripts are listed in Robbins' *American Literary Manuscripts*, p. 136.

Thomas Chandler Haliburton, 1796-1865
Bibliographies

See *Bibliography of American Fiction Through 1865*, pp.117-18, for a checklist of works by and about Haliburton. Contributions by Haliburton and criticism and reviews of Haliburton's works in selected periodicals are identified in Wells' *The Literary Index to American Magazines, 1815-1865*, pp. 66-67. Haliburton's manuscripts are listed in Robbins' *American Literary Manuscripts*, p. 136.

George Savile, 1st Marquis of Halifax, 1633-1695
Bibliographies

For a bibliography of works by and about Savile, see *NCBEL*, II, pp. 1040-41. Savile's manuscripts are described in *Index of English Literary Manuscripts*, II, pt. 1:507-21.

Baynard Rush Hall, 1798-1863
Bibliographies

For works by Hall, see *Bibliography of American Literature*, vol. 3, pp. 341-43.

James Hall, 1793-1868
Bibliographies

For works by Hall, see *Bibliography of American Literature*, vol. 3, pp. 344-55. Contributions by Hall and criticism and reviews of Hall's works in selected periodicals are identified in Wells' *The Literary Index to American Magazines, 1815-1865*, p. 67. Hall's manuscripts are listed in Robbins' *American Literary Manuscripts*, pp. 136-37.

James Norman Hall, 1887-1951
Bibliographies

For works by Hall, see *First Printings of American Authors*, vol. 3, pp. 139-43. Hall's manuscripts are listed in Robbins' *American Literary Manuscripts*, p. 137.

Joseph Hall, 1574-1656
Bibliographies

For a bibliography of works by and about Hall, see *NCBEL*, I, pp. 1112-13. Hall's manuscripts are described in *Index of English Literary Manuscripts*, I, pt. 2:111-20, 627-28.

Arthur Henry Hallam, 1811-1833
Bibliographies

For a bibliography of works by and about Hallam, see *NCBEL*, III, pp. 1385-86.

FitzGreene Halleck, 1790-1867
Bibliographies

For works by Halleck, see *Bibliography of American Literature*, vol. 3, pp. 356-65. Works about Halleck in selected periodicals are identified in Wells' *The Literary Index to American Magazines, 1815-1865*, pp. 67-68; and *The Literary Index to American Magazines, 1850-1900*, pp. 165-66. Halleck's manuscripts are listed in Robbins' *American Literary Manuscripts*, p. 137.

Charles Graham Halpine (Miles O'Reilly), 1829-1868
Bibliographies

For works by Halpine, see *Bibliography of American Literature*, vol. 3, pp. 366-71. Halpine's manuscripts are listed in Robbins' *American Literary Manuscripts*, p. 137.

(Samuel) Dashiell Hammett, 1894-1961
Bibliographies

610.   Layman, Richard. **Dashiell Hammett: A Descriptive Bibliography**. Pittsburgh, PA: University of Pittsburgh Press, 1979. 185p. (Pittsburgh Series in Bibliography). LC 78-53600. ISBN 0-8229-3394-2.

This listing of Hammett's primary bibliography supplies full descriptions of editions and printings of Hammett's books, contributions to books, contributions to periodicals, contributions to newspapers (including published letters and petitions), movies for which Hammett provided the story or script, and miscellaneous writings (one dust-jacket blurb and a copy of a typed letter). Entries include facsimiles of title and copyright pages and dust jackets; collations; contents; descriptions of typography, paper, and bindings; publishing histories; and copy locations. Appendixes list ad copy written by Hammett for a San Francisco jewelry company from 1922 through 1926; stage, film, television, and radio adaptations of his works; syndications of his novels; and five selected works about Hammett. Coverage of Hammett's primary materials supersedes E. H. Mundell's *A List of the Original Appearances of Dashiel Hammett's Magazine Work* (Kent, OH: Kent State University Press, 1968). Also for works by Hammett, see *First Printings of American Authors*, vol. 1, pp. 161-63. Hammett's manuscripts are listed in Robbins' *American Literary Manuscripts*, p. 138.

611.   Skinner, Robert E. **The Hard-Boiled Explicator: A Guide to the Study of Dashiell Hammett, Raymond Chandler and Ross Macdonald**. Metuchen, NJ: Scarecrow Press, 1985. 125p. LC 84-20246. ISBN 0-8108-1749-7.

Skinner provides annotated entries for about 650 periodical and newspaper articles, essays in collections, books, dissertations, reviews, and other writings about one or more of these writers. Annotations are descriptive. A comprehensive index includes headings for "bibliographies," "biographies," "literary influence," and "symbolism," and the like (with subheadings for "Hammett," "Chandler," and "Macdonald") and for individual works. See *Bibliography of American Fiction, 1919-1988*, pp. 227-229, for Richard Layman's checklist of works by and about Hammett.

Jupiter Hammon, c. 1720-c. 1800
Bibliographies

Hammon's manuscripts are listed in Robbins' *American Literary Manuscripts*, p. 138. See the review of research by Jerome Klinkowitz in Inge, Duke, and Bryer's *Black American Writers*, vol. I, pp. 1-20.

Christopher Hampton, 1946-
Bibliographies

King's *Twenty Modern British Playwrights*, pp. 59-63, lists works by Hampton and describes works about him.

Lorraine Hansberry, 1930-1965
Bibliographies

Hansberry's manuscripts are listed in Robbins' *American Literary Manuscripts*, p. 138. Sharon Friedman reviews research on Hansberry in *Contemporary Authors: Bibliographical Series: Volume 3: American Dramatists*, pp. 69-89.

Arthur Sherburne Hardy, 1847-1930
Bibliographies

For works by Hardy, see *Bibliography of American Literature*, vol. 3, pp. 372-76. Hardy's manuscripts are listed in Robbins' *American Literary Manuscripts*, p. 139.

John Edward Hardy, 1922-
Bibliographies

For works by Hardy, see *First Printings of American Authors*, vol. 2, p. 193.

Thomas Hardy, 1840-1928
Bibliographies

612. Draper, Ronald R. **Annotated Critical Bibliography of Thomas Hardy**. Ann Arbor, MI: University of Michigan Press, 1989. 227p. LC 88-40557. ISBN 0-472-10116-1.

Draper delivers a handy, selective guide to 724 editions, collections, and critical studies of Hardy's works, arranged in separate listings for individual works and topics. Separate indexes for critics, subjects/names, and primary titles give convenient access. Selectivity makes this guide most useful to undergraduate researchers. Also for a bibliography of works by and about Hardy, see *NCBEL*, III, pp. 980-92. Research on Hardy is reviewed by Michael Millgate in Ford's *Victorian Fiction*, pp. 308-32; George S. Fayen, Jr., in Stevenson's *Victorian Fiction*, pp. 249-97: F. B. Pinion in Dyson's *The English Novel*, pp. 264-79; and Lionel Stevenson in Faverty's *The Victorian Poets*, pp. 367-75.

613. Gerber, Helmut E., and W. Eugene Davis. **Thomas Hardy: An Annotated Bibliography of Writings About Him**. DeKalb, IL: Northern Illinois University Press, 1973. 841p. (An Annotated Secondary Bibliography Series on English Literature in Transition, 1880-1920). LC 72-7514. ISBN 0-87580-039-4.

This volume, the first of two, includes materials for the period 1870-1968. It is continued and supplemented by:

613.1. Davis, W. Eugene, and Helmut E. Gerber. **Thomas Hardy: An Anno-tated Bibliography of Writings About Him: Volume II: 1970-1978 and Supple-ment for 1871-1969**. DeKalb, IL: Northern Illinois University Press, 1983. 735p. (An Annotated Secondary Bibliography Series on English Literature in Transition, 1880-1920). LC 72-7514. ISBN 0-87580-091-2.

Gerber and Davis' chronologically arranged volumes offer the most compre-hensive bibliography of materials about Hardy now available, including books and parts of books and articles in journals and newspapers in more than 20 languages. Annotations are uniformly descriptive and detailed but offer little critical guidance. Contains indexes for critics, titles of secondary works, and titles of Hardy's writings, the latter offering at least an alternative for a subject index. Both volumes include checklists of Hardy's works cited in the bibliography; neither, however, provides a comprehensive primary bibliography. For this guid-ance, scholars must refer to Purdy's bibliography (entry 614). Gerber and Davis' work supersedes Carl J. Weber's *The First Hundred Years of Thomas Hardy 1840-1940: A Centenary Bibliography of Hardiana* (New York: Russell and Russell, 1942) as well as coverage of Hardy in Ehrsam's *Bibliographies of Twelve Victorian Authors*, pp. [91]-125, which cites international comments, criticism, and reviews through the early twentieth century.

614.   Purdy, Richard Little. **Thomas Hardy: A Bibliographical Study**. 1954; reprint New York: Oxford University Press, 1978. 387p. ISBN 0-19-818131-0.

Purdy provides transcriptions of title pages and data for collations, bindings and variant bindings, notes on manuscripts sources, and notes on composition and publication of Hardy's canon in separate listings for "editiones principes," "collected editions," and "uncollected contributions to books, periodicals, and newspapers." The latter section covers poems, prefaces, notes, symposia lectures, addresses, obituaries, and the like but excludes personal letters not intended for publication. Appendixes include a calendar of letters of Hardy and publisher William Tinsley dating from 1869 though 1875, notes on the letters of Leslie Stephen regarding *Far from the Madding Crowd*, notes on dramatizations of the Wessex novels as performed by the "Hardy Players," and other materials. Purdy's volume is more detailed than A. P. Webb's *A Bibliography of the Works of Thomas Hardy* (London: Frank Hollings, 1966). Useful descriptions of Hardy's works are also provided in Charles C. Pettit's *A Catalogue of the Works of Thomas Hardy in Dorchester Reference Library* (Dorchester: Dorset County Library, 1984). Also useful for research on Hardy's primary materials is James Stevens-Cox's *Library of Thomas Hardy, O. M.* (St. Peter Port: Toucan Press, 1969). Hardy's manuscripts are de-scribed in *Index of English Literary Manuscripts*, IV, pt. 2:3.

615.   Weber, Carl J., and Clara Carter Weber. **Thomas Hardy's Correspondence at Max Gate: A Descriptive Check List**. Waterville, ME: Colby College Press, 1968. LC 76-6416.

The Webers chronologically list more than 5,000 pieces of correspondence "once retained in Hardy's files at Max Gate and now preserved in the Hardy Memorial Room in the Dorset County Museum at Dorchester" (p. 3). Some 4,187 are addressed to Hardy; 854 are from Hardy. Indexes of correspondents and of references to Hardy's works complete the volume. This index complements Purdy's bibliography (entry 614) as well as Purdy and Michael Millgate's edition of *The Collected Letters of Thomas Hardy* (Oxford: Clarendon Press, 1978-1988).

Dictionaries, Encyclopedias, and Handbooks

616.   Hands, Timothy. **A Hardy Chronology**. Houndmills, Basingstoke, Hamp-shire: Macmillan Press, 1992. 227p. (Macmillan Author Chronologies). LC 92-188458. ISBN 0-333-45914-8.

"Aims to tell the story of Hardy's life using Hardy's own words" (p. xi), extensively quoting from Richard Little Purdy and Michael Millgate's *Collected*

Letters of Thomas Hardy (New York: Oxford University Press, 1978-88) and other standard sources. Although limiting coverage of Hardy's publications to first editions and subsequent others of textual significance, Hands' record gives particular attention to Hardy's involvement in the literary business. Contains a bibliography of sources (p. 207). Comprehensive index of names, titles, and subjects identifies detailed topics under Hardy, including "architecture," "politics," "women's rights." Headings for countries and works by others, for example, allow tracking Hardy's travels, reading, and theatrical excursions.

617.　Leeming, Glenda. **Who's Who in Thomas Hardy**. New York: Taplinger, 1975. 134p. LC 74-24527. ISBN 0-8008-8271-7.

Alphabetically arranges descriptions of human and animal characters in Hardy's 14 novels but excludes characters in the short stories. Entries are more inclusive and comprehensive than those in Alan Hurst's *Hardy: An Illustrated Dictionary* (New York: St. Martin's, 1980). Leeming's coverage of cows and dairy herds is extraordinary. An index lists human characters for each novel, referencing where each first appears by books and chapters. Leeming's dictionary is not as comprehensive as Pinion's *A Thomas Hardy Dictionary* (entry 619), but is more convenient to use. Additional coverage of Hardy's characters is provided in F. Outwin Saxelby's *A Thomas Hardy Dictionary: The Characters and Scenes on the Novels and Poems Arranged and Described* (London: George Routledge, 1911).

618.　Pinion, F. B. **A Hardy Companion: A Guide to the Works of Thomas Hardy and Their Background**. London: Macmillan, 1968. 555p. LC 68-19810.

Pinion provides a solid starting point for research on Hardy, offering overviews of Hardy's life, career, works, and critical reputation. In addition, Pinion supplies a dictionary of people and places in Hardy's works and a glossary of dialect, literary terms, and words from non-English languages that appear in Hardy's works. J. O. Bailey's *The Poetry of Thomas Hardy: A Handbook and Commentary* (Chapel Hill, NC: University of North Carolina Press, 1970) offers more specialized introductory coverage.

619.　Pinion, F. B. **A Thomas Hardy Dictionary: With Maps and a Chronology**. London: Macmillan, 1989. 322p. LC 88-25454. ISBN 0-333-42873-0.

Pinion's objective in this dictionary is to try to answer questions about specific details that arise in the course of reading Hardy's poems, essays, plays, novels, and short stories. Pinion offers about 6,000 entries that briefly identify and explain Hardy's usage of specific English, classical, and non-English words, terms, and phrases; allusions and references to classical, Biblical, and other literary sources; fictional characters and places; and literary and philosophical influences. Covering a broad range of materials, this dictionary is more useful than Pinion's *Companion* (entry 618) and Leeming's *Who's Who* (entry 617) for facilitating close readings of Hardy's works.

Indexes and Concordances

620.　Preston, Cathy Lynn. **A KWIC Concordance to Thomas Hardy's Tess of the d'Urbervilles**. New York: Garland, 1989. 966p. (Contextual Concordances; Garland Reference Library of the Humanities, vol. 749). LC 89-1507. ISBN 0-8240-9076-4.

Concords the text of the *Norton Critical Edition*, 2d ed. (New York, 1965), edited by Scott Elledge, which is based on the 1912 Wessex Edition. Appends ranking frequency list.

Journals

621.　**Thomas Hardy Annual**. Atlantic Highlands, NJ: Humanities Press, 1983-1987. Annual. ISSN 0264-9454.

Ceasing in 1987, *Thomas Hardy Annual* published as many as 12 scholarly articles and six or more book reviews or review essays per issue, including particularly important bibliographic features. Articles typically offered critical readings and interpretations. Other contributions focused on specific images and allusions, editing and editorial problems, and comparative studies. The journal's most significant feature was an annual "Survey of Recent Hardy Studies," which evaluated editions, typographical studies, biographies, studies of Hardy's letters, and criticism in general. A complementary "A Hardy Bibliography" gave full bibliographic data for new editions, bibliographies, biographies, general critical studies and studies of individual works. *Thomas Hardy Annual* was indexed in *AES*.

622. **Thomas Hardy Journal.** Dorchester, Dorset: Thomas Hardy Society, 1985-. 3/yr. ISSN 0268-5418.

Sponsored by the Thomas Hardy Society, *Thomas Hardy Journal* publishes scholarly articles and reviews of new works about Hardy's life and works. Contributions present close readings of works; studies of Hardy's language, themes, and images, such as the family, fallen women, and sexuality; and discussions of Hardy's literary relations with other writers and artistic influences, including John Webster, William Wordsworth, Walter Scott, Marcel Proust, W. H. Auden, and Vaughan Williams. Typical articles are "Thomas Hardy's *Far from the Madding Crowd*: Perception and Understanding" and "Insects in Hardy's Fiction." Other features have discussed Hardy in translation and his modern critical reputation. Occasional bibliographic contributions include studies of composition and publication and lists of primary materials, such as Trevor Johnson's "Illustrated Versions of Hardy's Works: A Checklist 1872-1992," 9.3 (October 1993): 32-46. A review of the current Hardy scholarship is presented in "Periodical Articles on Hardy." *Thomas Hardy Journal* is indexed in *MLA* and *MHRA*.

623. **The Thomas Hardy Yearbook.** St. Sampson, Guernsey: Toucan Press, 1970-. Annual. ISSN 0082-416x.

This annual features "essays about the life, times, and works of Thomas Hardy; about the writer's environment; and about Dorset writers" (masthead) of the nineteenth and twentieth centuries. Four to 12 typically brief notes provide close readings of individual works, explicate allusions and images, record recollections, discuss Hardy's borrowings from Shakespeare, and so forth. Past issues have been heavily illustrated with photographs of Hardy, his contemporaries, and his surroundings. Recent textual studies have addressed the evolution of "To Please His Wife" and illustrations in *The Return of the Native*. The journal does not publish reviews but occasionally contains brief book notices. From 1970-77, the journal included "Thomas Hardy: A Bibliography," listing criticisms and dissertations. *The Thomas Hardy Year Book* is indexed in *MLA*.

Patterson's *Author Newsletters and Journals*, pp. 150-51, describes other previously published journals for Hardy.

Sir John Harington, c. 1561-1612

Bibliographies

For a bibliography of works by and about Harington, see *NCBEL*, I, pp. 2010-11. Harington's manuscripts are described in *Index of English Literary Manuscripts*, I, pt. 2:121-57, 628-29.

Henry Harland (Sidney Luska), 1861-1905

Bibliographies

For works by Harland, see *Bibliography of American Literature*, vol. 3, pp. 377-83. Harland's contributions to and reviews of Harland's works in selected periodicals are identified in Wells' *The Literary Index to American Magazines, 1850-1900*, pp. 167-68. Harland's manuscripts are listed in Robbins' *American Literary Manuscripts*, p. 139. See *Bibliography of American Fiction, 1866-1918*, pp. 208-209, for Jean Kowaleski's checklist of works by and about Harland.

Frances Ellen Watkins Harper, 1825-1911

Bibliographies

Harper's manuscripts are listed in Robbins' *American Literary Manuscripts*, p. 139. See the review of research by Ruth Miller and Peter J. Katopes in Inge, Duke, and Bryer's *Black American Writers*, vol. I, pp. 133-60.

James Harrington, 1611-1677

Bibliographies

For a bibliography of works by and about Harrington, see *NCBEL*, I, p. 2339. Harrington's manuscripts are described in *Index of English Literary Manuscripts*, II, pt. 1:523-26.

George Washington Harris, 1814-1869

Bibliographies

For works by Harris, see *Bibliography of American Literature*, vol. 3, pp. 384-86. Harris' manuscripts are listed in Robbins' *American Literary Manuscripts*, p. 140. See *Bibliography of American Fiction Through 1865*, pp.119-20, for a checklist of works by and about Harris. M. Thomas Inge surveys works by and about Harris in Bain and Flora's *Fifty Southern Writers Before 1900*, pp. 220-26.

Joel Chandler Harris, 1848-1908

Bibliographies

624. Bickley, R. Bruce, Jr. **Joel Chandler Harris: A Reference Guide**. Boston: G. K. Hall, 1978. 360p. (A Reference Publication in Literature). LC 77-15937. ISBN 0-8161-7873-9.

Bickley offers chronologically arranged, annotated entries for 1,442 English-language criticisms of Harris published from 1862 through 1976. Coverage includes books, parts of books, articles, anonymous reviews, and dissertations. Annotations are objective and extensive. Very comprehensive indexing covers critics, primary and secondary titles, and a wide variety of subjects, including names of characters (Brer Rabbit, Uncle Remus), critical forms (bibliography, biography, dissertations), and selected topics and themes—"linguistic dialect" and "Poor white, the," among others. Indexing is especially useful for identification of subjects in American and comparative folklore, offering headings for African, American Indian, European, Hindu, and Mexican folklores and for particular themes, such as "Golden Arm folktale" and the "Trickster." No separately published descriptive listing of Harris' primary bibliography now exists. This coverage is provided by Blanck's *Bibliography of American Literature*, vol. 3, pp. 387-401; Blanck's supplement, in *"BAL* Addendum: Joel Chandler Harris—entry 7115," *PBSA* 61 (1967): 266; and William Bradley Strickland's dissertation, *Joel Chandler Harris: A Bibliographical Study* (Athens, GA: University of Georgia, 1976). Harris' manuscripts are listed in Robbins' *American Literary Manuscripts*, p. 140. See *Bibliography of American Fiction, 1866-1918*, pp. 209-12, for Bickley's checklist of works by and about Harris. Research on Harris is reviewed by Lucinda H. MacKethan in Bain and Flora's *Fifty Southern Writers Before 1900*, pp. 227-39.

Mark Harris, 1922-

Bibliographies

For works by Harris, see *First Printings of American Authors*, vol. 1, pp. 165-66. Harris' manuscripts are listed in Robbins' *American Literary Manuscripts*, p. 140.

Constance Cary Harrison, 1843-1920

Bibliographies

For works by Harrison, see *Bibliography of American Literature*, vol. 3, pp. 402-11. Harrison's manuscripts are listed in Robbins' *American Literary Manuscripts*, p. 140.

See *Bibliography of American Fiction, 1866-1918*, pp. 213-14, for Joe Essid's checklist of works by and about Harrison.

Frederic Harrison, 1831-1923
Bibliographies
John W. Bicknell reviews research on Harrison in DeLaura's *Victorian Prose*, pp. 487-94.

Tony Harrison, 1937-
Bibliographies
625.   Kaiser, John R. **Tony Harrison: A Bibliography, 1957-1987**. London: Mansell, 1989. 105p. LC 89-36328. ISBN 0-7201-2024-1.

Kaiser offers full bibliographic descriptions for Harrison's books, pamphlets, and broadsides; first-appearance contributions to books and edited works; contributions to periodicals and newspapers; and miscellaneous works (including interviews, radio and television appearances, and translations of his works). Entries include title-page transcriptions, collations, contents, physical descriptions, and publishing histories. In addition, Kaiser lists 84 works about Harrison, with brief references to the primary works addressed.

Joseph C. Hart, 1798-1855
Bibliographies
See *Bibliography of American Fiction Through 1865*, p. 121, for a checklist of works by and about Hart. Wells' *The Literary Index to American Magazines, 1815-1865*, p. 68, identifies reviews of Hart's works in selected periodicals. Hart's manuscripts are listed in Robbins' *American Literary Manuscripts*, p. 141.

(Francis) Bret(t) Harte, 1836-1902
Bibliographies
626.   Barnett, Linda Diz. **Bret Harte: A Reference Guide**. Boston: G. K. Hall, 1980. 427p. (A Reference Publication in Literature). LC 79-21465. ISBN 0-8161-8197-7.

Barnett's comprehensive bibliography chronologically lists annotated entries for more than 2,300 books, articles, and dissertations, including selected German- and French-language works, about Harte published from 1865 through 1977. Annotations are critical, identifying significance as well as appropriateness. George R. Stewart, Jr.'s *Bret Harte: Argonaut and Exile* (Boston: Houghton, Mifflin, 1931), for example, is described as a "solid scholarly biography." Broad index headings reference critical forms such as bibliographies and biographies. Headings for Samuel Clemens and William Dean Howells, for example, offer subdivisions for "comments about" and "comments by." Nothing in the index, however, references either editions or thematic or technical elements of Harte's works. This guide supersedes Barnett's earlier "Bret Harte: An Annotated Bibliography of Secondary Comment," *American Literary Realism* 5 (Summer 1972): 189-320; and 5 (Fall 1972): 331-484.

627.   Scharnhorst, Gary. **Bret Harte: A Bibliography**. Lanham, MD: Scarecrow Press, 1995. 252p. (Scarecrow Author Bibliographies, no. 95). LC 95-38260. ISBN 0-8108-3067-1.

Although Scharnhorst provides a comprehensive guide to the full range of Harte's primary materials, a full descriptive bibliography remains to be published. Scharnhorst chronologically arranges brief bibliographic information for first and subsequent editions, reprintings, and translations of Harte's published and unpublished writings in sections for contributed verse, contributed prose, dramatic writings and productions, published letters (with contents notes), separate publications (books and edited works), and false and doubtful attributions. Other sections identify biographical sources, including interviews, lectures (with data for itineraries), and obituaries, as well as manuscripts and other documents (with locations and notes on contents). Coverage and features vary in each section. Scharnhorst identifies prose and verse contributions and collections of letters through 1994; entries for plays only give data for contemporary productions and performance reviews while those for books only cite contemporary reviews. Entries for verse give first lines; those for books cross-reference Lyle Henry Wright's *American Fiction, 1851-1875: A Contribution Toward a Bibliography* (San Marino, CA: Huntington Library, 1965); and *American Fiction, 1876-1900: A Contribution Toward a Bibliography* (San Marino, CA: Huntington Library, 1966). Indexing is limited to personal names. More detailed coverage of Harte's separate publications is provided by Blanck's *Bibliography of American Literature*, vol. 3, pp. 412-78; and updated and extended by George R. Stewart, Jr.'s "A Bibliography of the Writings of Bret Harte in the Magazines and Newspapers of California, 1857-1871," *University of California Publications in English* 3 (September 1933): 119-70; and Joseph Gaer's *Bret Harte: Bibliographical and Biographical Data* (1935; reprint New York: Burt Franklin, 1968). Additional descriptions of primary materials are included in Lucy Trimble Clark's *The Barrett Library of Bret Harte: A Checklist of Printed and Manuscript Works of Francis Bret Harte in the Library of the University of Virginia* (Charlottesville, VA: University of Virginia Press, 1957). Harte's manuscripts are also listed in Robbins' *American Literary Manuscripts*, p. 141. See *Bibliography of American Fiction, 1866-1918*, pp. 214-17, for Alfred Bendixen's checklist of works by and about Harte. Research on Harte is reviewed by Patrick D. Morrow in Erisman and Etulain's *Fifty Western Writers*, pp. 172-82.

Stephen Hawes, c. 1475-1511
Bibliographies
For a bibliography of works by and about Hawes, see *NCBEL*, I, pp. 650-51, 1114-15. Hawes' manuscripts are described in *Index of English Literary Manuscripts*, I, pt. 2:159-60.

John (Clendennin Burne) Hawkes, (Jr.), 1925-
Bibliographies
628. Hryciw-Wing, Carol A. **John Hawkes: A Research Guide**. New York: Garland, 1986. 396p. (Garland Reference Library of the Humanities, vol. 668). LC 86-14811. ISBN 0-8240-8560-4.

A comprehensive listing of primary and secondary materials, Hryciw-Wing's guide gives brief bibliographic information in separate listings for Hawkes' novels and novellas, short fiction, plays, poetry, critical pieces, unpublished materials (at Harvard University), and miscellaneous works, such as letters to editors and quotations in catalogs. In addition, Hryciw-Wing describes interviews with Hawkes and about 1,000 biographical materials, reviews of Hawkes' works and productions and critical studies (arranged by works), dissertations and master's theses, and bibliographies. Coverage includes studies in English and other languages published through 1985. Significant works receive extended descriptions, although entries for dissertations are not annotated. No subject indexing. Hryciw-Wing's work supersedes her earlier *John Hawkes: An Annotated Bibliography* (Metuchen, NJ: Scarecrow Press, 1977) as well as coverage of Hawkes in Robert M. Scotto's *Three Contemporary Novelists: An Annotated Bibliography of Works by and About John Hawkes, Joseph Heller, and Thomas Pynchon* (New York: Garland, 1977). Also for works by Hawkes, see *First Printings of American Authors*, vol. 1, pp. 167-68. Hawkes' manuscripts are listed in Robbins' *American Literary Manuscripts*, p. 142. See *Bibliography of American Fiction, 1919-1988*, pp. 230-32, for Donald J. Greiner's checklist of works by and about Hawkes.

Nathaniel Hawthorne, 1804-1864
Bibliographies

629.   Boswell, Jeanetta. **Nathaniel Hawthorne and the Critics: A Checklist of Criticism, 1900-1978.** Metuchen, NJ: Scarecrow Press, 1982. 273p. (Scarecrow Author Bibliographies, no. 57). LC 81-9398. ISBN 0-8108-1471-4.

Boswell offers the most comprehensive coverage of twentieth-century scholarship on Hawthorne presently available, providing an alphabetically arranged author listing of briefly annotated entries for about 2,800 books, parts of books, articles, and dissertations published largely in English. Limited subject indexing by broad topics provides unsatisfactory access. Coverage of contemporary criticisms of Hawthorne is available in Scharnhorst's bibliography (entry 631). These together supersede the coverage of Hawthorne criticism offered by Buford Jones' *A Checklist of Hawthorne Criticism, 1951-1966* (Hartford, CT: Transcendental Books, 1967) and its index in Kenneth Walter Cameron's *Hawthorne Index to Themes, Motifs, Topics, Archetypes, Sources and Key Words Dealt with in Recent Criticism* (Hartford, CT: Transcendental Books, 1968); Theodore L. Gross and Stanley Wertheim's *Hawthorne, Melville, Stephen Crane: A Critical Bibliography* (New York: Free Press, 1971); and Beatrice Ricks, Joseph D. Adams, and Jack O. Hazlerig's *Nathaniel Hawthorne: A Reference Bibliography, 1900-1971* (Boston: G. K. Hall, 1972). A more specialized guide, James C. Wilson's *The Hawthorne and Melville Friendship: An Annotated Bibliography, Biographical and Critical Essays, and Correspondence Between the Two* (Jefferson, NC: McFarland, 1991) contains Wilson's "An Essay in Bibliography" (pp. 19-39) and "An Annotated Bibliography: Major Discussions of the Relationship" (pp. 40-74). See *Bibliography of American Fiction through 1865*, pp.122-29, for John L. Idol, Jr.'s checklist of works by and about Hawthorne. Research on Hawthorne is reviewed by Walter Blair in Woodress' *Eight American Authors*, pp. 85-128; and Joel Myerson in Myerson's *The Transcendentalists*, pp. 328-35. *ALS* annually features a review essay on Hawthorne scholarship.

630.   Clark, C. E. Frazer, Jr. **Nathaniel Hawthorne: A Descriptive Bibliography**. Pittsburgh, PA: University of Pittsburgh Press, 1978. 478p. (Pittsburgh Series in Bibliography). LC 76-50885. ISBN 0-8229-3343-8.

The standard guide to Hawthorne's primary materials, Clark provides descriptive entries in separate listings for editions of Hawthorne's books published through 1883 and selected reprintings through 1975; collected editions; contributions to books and pamphlets; contributions to journals and newspapers; and other miscellaneous prose and verse writings by or attributed to Hawthorne (such as a manuscript Latin school composition). Entries give title- and copyright-page facsimiles; collations; contents; descriptions of typography, paper, and bindings; detailed publishing histories; and copy locations. Also supplies textual collations of variant texts and illustrations of bindings. Clark appends a list of 25 selected works about Hawthorne. Also for works by Hawthorne, see *Bibliography of American Literature*, vol. 4, pp. 1-36; and *First Printings of American Authors*, vol. 1, pp. 169-75. Clark's *Hawthorne at Auction, 1894-1971* (Detroit, MI: Gale, 1972) cumulates descriptions of early editions from sale catalogs. G. Thomas Tanselle describes a significant selection of primary materials in *A Descriptive Catalogue of the Nathaniel Hawthorne Collection*, in Part 6 of Sidney Ives's *The Parkman Dexter Howe Library* (Gainesville, FL: University of Florida, 1989), including Hawthorne's fair copy manuscript of "The Celestial Raid-road" (which the catalog reproduces in facsimile). Also available is *The Ulysses Sumner Milburn Collection of Hawthorniana* (Canton, NY: Special Collections, Owen D. Young Library, St. Lawrence University, 1989). For information on Hawthorne's manuscripts in collections, researchers should consult Kenneth Walter Cameron's "Inventory of Hawthorne Manuscripts, Part One," *Emerson Society Quarterly* 29 (1962): 5-20. Hawthorne's manuscripts are also listed in Robbins' *American Literary Manuscripts*, pp. 142-43.

631. Scharnhorst, Gary. **Nathaniel Hawthorne: An Annotated Bibliography of Comment and Criticism Before 1900.** Metuchen, NJ: Scarecrow Press, 1988. 404p. (Scarecrow Author Bibliographies, no. 82). LC 88-29221. ISBN 0-8108-2184-2.

Including 2,586 annotated entries chronologically arranged from 1828 through 1900, Scharnhorst's record of contemporary references, notices, reviews, editorials, and other comments on Hawthorne in dictionaries and encyclopedias as well newspapers and journals indicates trends in Hawthorne's early critical reputation. Entries cross-reference reprintings of criticism in standard sources, such as the *Centenary Edition* of Hawthorne's works. Contains indexes for critics, primary titles, and selected subjects, such as Brook Farm, Salem Custom House, and Shakespeare. References to works about *The Scarlet Letter*, for example, are subdivided by decades—that is, the 1850s, 1860s, and so forth—to assist the assessment of a particular work's critical recognition. Scharnhorst's bibliography serves as a useful and convenient guide to comments on Hawthorne in journals included in major microfilm collections, such as the American Periodicals Series, Early British Periodicals Series, and English Literary Periodicals Series.

Dictionaries, Encyclopedias, and Handbooks

632. Gale, Robert L. **A Nathaniel Hawthorne Encyclopedia.** New York: Greenwood Press, 1991. 583p. LC 90-47337. ISBN 0-313-26816-9.

Alphabetically arranged entries mainly locate and identify Hawthorne's individual works, characters, allusions, family, friends, and associates. Entries for novels and major works give plot summaries, publication and source information, and broad critical assessments. Although the five-page entry for *The Scarlet Letter* cross-references other entries for Dante, Spenser, and others, Gale does not provide a bibliography of specific sources. Other entries usefully identify and place allusions and characters (such as Aeolus in the short story "Circe's Palace" from *Tanglewood Tales*) but neglect to give references to the standard editions. Unlike other recent author encyclopedias, such as LeMaster, Wilson, and Hamric's *The Mark Twain Encyclopedia* (entry 267) or Hamilton's *The Spenser Encyclopedia* (entry 1259), Gale's encyclopedia offers entries neither for specific topics nor for broad subjects, such as biography, bibliography, language, or style. Multiple appendixes list Hawthorne's works by genre as well as historical and contemporary figures by relationship and profession, covering family; friends and professional associates; writers, editors, publishers, and journalists; painters, sculptors, graphic artists, and photographers; actors, actresses and singers; government officials, politicians, military and naval officers; educators; and religious figures: These appendixes essentially serve as the volume's index. The volume also includes a brief chronology of Hawthorne's life and career and a general bibliography (pp. 573-83).

633. Gale, Robert L. **Plots and Characters in the Fiction and Sketches of Nathaniel Hawthorne.** Hamden, CT: Archon Books, 1968. 259p. LC 68-25525.

Gale summarizes the plots of Hawthorne's novels, short stories, sketches, and other fictional works and identifies about 900 "named or namable characters" in them. *The Scarlet Letter* is reviewed in eight pages. Gale excludes names mentioned in Hawthorne's nonfiction works. For identifications of Hawthorne's references and allusions to historical, literary, or contemporary figures in his nonfiction writings (the likes of Shakespeare, Emerson, and others) as well as to place names and topics (such as Rome and "sin"), researchers should consult Evangeline M. O'Connor's *An Analytical Index to the Works of Nathaniel Hawthorne* (1882; reprint Detroit, MI: Gale, 1967).

634. Newman, Lea Bertani Vozar. **A Reader's Guide to the Short Stories of Nathaniel Hawthorne.** Boston: G. K. Hall, 1979. 380p. (A Reference Publication in Literature). LC 79-20100. ISBN 0-8161-8398-8.

Newman's guide offers individual chapters on each of Hawthorne's 54 stories, surveying composition, publication history, relationships with Hawthorne's other works, and subsequent criticism. Includes a bibliography of about 500 secondary materials related to Hawthorne's short fiction.

Indexes and Concordances

635. Byers, John R., and James Jarratt Owen. **A Concordance to the Five Novels of Nathaniel Hawthorne**. New York: Garland, 1980. 2 vols. (Garland Reference Library of the Humanities, vol. 182). LC 79-7910. ISBN 0-8240-9545-6.

Based on the standard *Centenary Edition of the Works of Nathaniel Hawthorne* (Columbus, OH: The Ohio State University Press, 1962-).

Journals

636. **The Nathaniel Hawthorne Review**. Pittsburgh, PA: Nathaniel Hawthorne Society, 1974-. 2/yr. ISSN 0980-4197.

Formerly *The Hawthorne Society Newsletter* (1974-85), *Nathaniel Hawthorne Review* features selections of three to five critical articles (on such topics as catechism in "Young Goodman Brown," Hawthorne in German translation, and Hawthorne iconography), six or more book reviews, and an annual, classified, annotated "Current Hawthorne Bibliography" that covers editions of primary materials, bibliographies and reference works, and critical studies, including dissertations. Despite a change from quarto newsletter-size to an octavo format more appropriate to a review, published studies remain focused on close readings of themes and characters in particular works, identifications of sources and analogues, and biographical investigations. Occasional bibliographic features have identified Spanish-language editions of *The Scarlet Letter*, in 20.2 (Fall 1994): 21-30; and additional contemporary reviews of Hawthorne, in 21.2 (Fall 1995): 24-28, to supplement Scharnhorst's *Nathaniel Hawthorne: An Annotated Bibliography of Comment and Criticism Before 1900* (entry 631). In addition, a regular department, "Along the Wayside," issues announcements of conferences and seminars, describes works in progress and forthcoming publications, and notes the discoveries, sales, and locations of unique Hawthorne materials. *The Nathaniel Hawthorne Review* is indexed in *AHI*, *MHRA*, and *MLA*.

Wortman's *A Guide to Serial Bibliographies for Modern Literatures*, pp. 259-60, describes other previously published serial bibliographies for Hawthorne. Patterson's *Author Newsletters and Journals*, pp. 152-53, describes other previously published journals for Hawthorne.

John (Milton) Hay, 1838-1905
Bibliographies

For works by Hay, see *Bibliography of American Literature*, vol. 4, pp. 37-63. Hay's contributions to and reviews of Hay's works in selected periodicals are identified in Wells' *The Literary Index to American Magazines, 1850-1900*, pp. 181-82. Hay's manuscripts are listed in Robbins' *American Literary Manuscripts*, pp. 143-44.

Ernest Haycox, 1899-1950
Bibliographies

See *Bibliography of American Fiction, 1919-1988*, pp. 233-34, for Richard W. Etulain's checklist of works by and about Haycox. Robert L. Gale surveys works by and about Haycox in Erisman and Etulain's *Fifty Western Writers*, pp. 183-93.

Robert Hayden, 1913-1980
Bibliographies

Hayden's manuscripts are listed in Robbins' *American Literary Manuscripts*, p. 144. Fred M. Fetrow reviews research on Hayden in *Contemporary Authors: Bibliographical Series: Volume 2: American Poets*, pp. 107-28.

Paul Hamilton Hayne, 1830-1886
Bibliographies

For works by Hayne, see *Bibliography of American Literature*, vol. 4, pp. 64-74. Hayne's contributions to and reviews of Hayne's works in selected periodicals are identified in Wells' *The Literary Index to American Magazines, 1815-1865*, p. 71; and *The Literary Index to American Magazines, 1850-1900*, p. 182. Hayne's manuscripts are listed in Robbins' *American Literary Manuscripts*, p. 144. See DeBellis' *Sidney Lanier, Henry Timrod, and Paul Hamilton Hayne* (entry 810) for criticisms of Hayne. Research on Hayne is reviewed by Rayburn S. Moore in Bain and Flora's *Fifty Southern Writers Before 1900*, pp. 240-49.

William Hazlitt, 1778-1830
Bibliographies

637.   Houck, James A. **William Hazlitt: A Reference Guide**. Boston: G. K. Hall, 1977. 268p. (Reference Guides in Literature). LC 77-5532. ISBN 0-8161-7826-7.

Houck chronologically arranges descriptively annotated entries for about 1,200 critical studies and comments about Hazlitt published from 1805 through 1973. Comprehensive coverage includes contemporary published letters, dissertations, introductions in editions, and non-English-language criticisms. A thorough index gives good topical access, offering subject headings for "bibliography" and "style" under Hazlitt's name, for names of other authors (such as Shakespeare, Napoleon, and Thomas Malthus), and for works (subdivided for reviews, editions, and the like). Research on Hazlitt is reviewed by Elisabeth W. Schneider in Houtchens and Houtchens' *The English Romantic Poets and Essayists*, pp. 75-114.

638.   Keynes, Geoffrey. **Bibliography of William Hazlitt**. 2d ed. Godalming: St. Paul's Bibliographies, 1981. 152p. (St. Paul's Bibliographies, no. 4). LC 80-142902. ISBN 0-906795-01-x.

A revision of the Keynes' work published in 1931, this provides facsimiles of title pages, collations, contents, binding descriptions, copy locations, and publishing histories for Hazlitt's books and selected works and letters, with a list of his complete and selected works published in the United States. Keynes' bibliography is the standard guide to Hazlitt's primary materials. For a bibliography of works by and about Hazlitt, see *NCBEL*, III, pp. 1230-38. Hazlitt's manuscripts are described in *Index of English Literary Manuscripts*, IV, pt. 2:225.

Samuel Hazo, 1928-
Bibliographies

For works by Hazo, see *First Printings of American Authors*, vol. 2, pp. 195-96.

Shirley Hazzard, 1931-
Bibliographies

For works by Hazzard, see *First Printings of American Authors*, vol. 4, pp. 213-14.

Seamus Heaney, 1939-
Bibliographies

639.   Durkan, Michael J., and Rand Brandes. **Seamus Heaney: A Reference Guide**. New York: G. K. Hall, 1996. 225 p. (A Reference Guide to Literature). LC 96-15049. ISBN 0-8161-7389-3.

Chronologically arranged, annotated entries for more than 1,000 works about Heaney published from 1965 through 1993. Comprehensive international coverage entails books; dissertations; essays in books; journal articles and reviews; newspaper articles, stories, and reviews; and interviews. Descriptive annotations give contents of collections and identify reprintings. Includes brief chronology and list of Heaney's major works. Index of names, titles, and subjects, with a few detailed topical headings under Heaney. Durkan's "Seamus Heaney: A Checklist for a Bibliography," *Irish University Review* 16.1 (Spring 1986): 48-76, contains a comprehensive but dated listing of Heaney's works.

Lafcadio Hearn, 1850-1904
Bibliographies
640. Perkins, P. D. and Ione Perkins. **Lafcadio Hearn: A Bibliography of His Writings.** Boston: Houghton Mifflin, 1934. 444p. LC 34-41793.

Full bibliographic descriptions of works by Hearn, with lists of works about him, in chronologically arranged sections for first editions, translations (sublisted by 15 languages), books about Hearn (sublisted by languages), American periodicals containing contributions by Hearn, newspapers containing contributions by Hearn, reviews and periodical articles about Hearn, reviews and newspaper articles about Hearn, non-English-language periodical articles about Hearn, unpublished materials by Hearn, unpublished manuscripts and lectures about Hearn, and music. Entries for first editions of Hearn's books give title-page transcriptions, collations, contents, variants, and notes on publication histories, with brief citations for subsequent editions and printings. Available in a reprinted edition (New York: Burt Franklin, 1968). Also for bibliographic descriptions of Hearn's works, see *Bibliography of American Literature*, vol. 4, pp. 75-106. Keyed by the Perkins' bibliography and *Bibliography of American Literature*, Ann S. Gwyn's *Lafcadio Hearn: A Catalogue of the Collection at the Howard-Tilton Memorial Library, Tulane University* (New Orleans, LA: Friends of the Tulane University Library, 1977) describes the most important collection of Hearn materials, giving brief bibliographic information for 294 works by Hearn in subsections for collected works, individual titles (some 237 items, substantially supplementing the Perkins' coverage of non-English-language editions), letters by Hearn, and articles and stories in magazines by Hearn (41 items, many supplementing Perkins' listings); some 97 works about Hearn; eight works by Hearn in Japanese and 28 in Japanese about him; 19 literary manuscripts, letters, and other manuscripts related to Hearn; and other Hearniana, including photographs, prints and drawings, plaques, and the like. A supplemental *Addenda to Lafcadio Hearn: A Catalogue of the Collection at the Howard-Tilton Memorial Library, Tulane University* (New Orleans, LA: Tulane University, 1990) has also appeared. Other descriptions of Hearn collections include *Catalogue of the Lafcadio Hearn Library at the Embassy of Ireland*, 2d ed. (Tokyo: Embassy of Ireland, Irish Literature Society of Japan, 1989); and Hisashi Kajitani's *Bibliotheca Hearniana: A Catalogue of the First Editions, Collected and Other Editions of the Works of Lafcadio Hearn, Together with a Selection of Studies and Bibliographical Materials, All Forming Part of the Collection of English Books in the Library of Kyoto University of Non-English Studies* (Kyoto: University Library, Kyoto University of Non-English Studies,1976). Hearn's manuscripts are listed in Robbins' *American Literary Manuscripts*, pp. 144-45. See *Bibliography of American Fiction, 1866-1918*, pp. 217-20, for Kristi Kibbe's checklist of works by and about Hearn.

Frederic Henry Hedge, 1805-1890
Bibliographies
For works by Hedge, see *First Printings of American Authors*, vol. 3, pp. 145-51. Hedge's contributions to and reviews of Hedge's works in selected periodicals are identified in Wells' *The Literary Index to American Magazines, 1815-1865*, p. 73; and *The Literary Index to American Magazines, 1850-1900*, pp. 183-84. Hedge's manuscripts are listed in Robbins' *American Literary Manuscripts*, p. 145. Leonard Neufeldt reviews research on Hedge in Myerson's *The Transcendentalists*, pp. 189-94.

Robert A(nson) Heinlein, 1907-1988
Bibliographies

641. Owings, Mark. **Robert A. Heinlein: A Bibliography**. Baltimore, MD: Croatan House, 1973. 23p. ISBN 0-88358-000-4.

Rather difficult to use alphabetical checklist of Heinlein's separate publications and contributed works because of cryptic abbreviations and arrangement. An updating would likely remedy these deficiencies. Compact entries give brief bibliographic information for first, subsequent, and translated editions, appearances in collections, and reprintings, with imprints, paginations, prices, and contents. See *Bibliography of American Fiction, 1919-1988*, pp. 235-37, for Edward Joseph Ingebretsen's checklist of works by and about Heinlein.

Joseph Heller, 1923-
Bibliographies

642. Keegan, Brenda M. **Joseph Heller: A Reference Guide**. Boston: G. K. Hall, 1978. 152p. (A Reference Publication in Literature). LC 78-6853. ISBN 0-8161-8143-8.

In addition to a checklist of Heller's primary works, including variant editions and reprintings of books, stories, essays, letters, and miscellaneous writings, the bulk of Keegan's guide is a chronologically arranged, annotated listing of about 800 works about Heller, including newspaper articles, anonymous reviews, and dissertations, published from 1961 through 1977. Annotations are largely descriptive. A cumulative author, title, and subject index offers solid access, including headings for critical forms (bibliographies, "biographical information"), the names of characters (Milo, Yossarian), authors and other primary works for comparative studies (Barth, Vonnegut, *Adventures of Huckleberry Finn*), and selected topics ("absurdity," "black humor," "*deja vu*"). Keegan's bibliography supersedes all other Heller bibliographies to date, including coverage of Heller in Robert M. Scotto's *Three Contemporary Novelists: An Annotated Bibliography of Works by and About John Hawkes, Joseph Heller, and Thomas Pynchon* (New York: Garland, 1977). For works by Heller, see *First Printings of American Authors*, vol. 2, pp. 197-98. Heller's manuscripts are listed in Robbins' *American Literary Manuscripts*, p. 146. Also see *Bibliography of American Fiction, 1919-1988*, pp. 237-39, for James Nagel's checklists of works by and about Heller. Nagel reviews research on Heller in *Contemporary Authors: Bibliographical Series: Volume 1: American Novelists*, pp. 193-218.

Lillian Hellman, 1905-1984
Bibliographies

643. Estrin, Mark. **Lillian Hellman—Plays, Films, Memoirs: A Reference Guide**. Boston: G. K. Hall, 1980. 378p. (A Reference Guide to Literature). LC 80-21307. ISBN 0-8161-7907-7.

Estrin offers brief checklists of Hellman's primary works, including original plays, adaptations, memoirs, edited books, screenplays, and miscellaneous writings (short stories, reviews, essays, reports, tributes, and interviews), in addition to adaptations of Hellman's works. In the bulk of the guide, Estrin chronologically arranges annotated entries for about 2,000 criticisms of Hellman published from 1934 through 1974, covering books, periodical and newspaper articles, dissertations, theses, publicity pieces, and brief notices. Access through the index of critics, primary titles, and selected subjects is limited. Subheadings are provided under primary titles (such as "films" and "plays") and under Hellman's name ("biographical items," "interviews," and "thematic surveys"). Other headings reference special topics, such as "House Committee on Un-American Activities/McCarthyism." On the other hand, no headings are included for bibliographies or for topics such as characterization, technique, and the like. Supplemental coverage of Hellman's secondary bibliography is provided by Steven Bills' *Lillian Hellman: An Annotated Bibliography* (New York: Garland, 1979), which describes criticisms through 1979 in sections for biographical materials; interviews, previews, and news; play reviews; critical studies; reviews in books; screenplay reviews; reviews of autobiographies; and theses and dissertations. Janet V. Haedicke identifies works by and about Hellman in Demastes' *American Playwrights, 1880-1945*, pp. 132-44. Research on Hellman is reviewed by Jacob H. Adler in Flora and Bain's *Fifty Southern Writers After 1900*, pp. 247-58; and by Bruce Henderson in Shapiro's *Jewish American Women Writers*, pp. 101-10.

644. Riordan, Mary Marguerite. **Lillian Hellman: A Bibliography, 1926-1978**. Metuchen, NJ: Scarecrow Press, 1980. 210p. (Scarecrow Author Bibliographies, no. 50). LC 80-16147. ISBN 0-8108-1320-3.

In addition to covering secondary materials, Riordan offers the best coverage of Hellman's primary materials, chronologically arranging descriptions in separate listings for plays and adaptations, authored and coauthored screenplays, books and edited works, contributions to newspapers and periodicals, unpublished works, letters and manuscripts in special collections, and recordings. Includes an extended chronology of Hellman's life and works. Chronologically arranged entries for primary materials give brief bibliographic information and contents. Also for works by Hellman, see *First Printings of American Authors*, vol. 2, pp. 199-201. Hellman's manuscripts are listed in Robbins' *American Literary Manuscripts*, p. 146. Additional information about Hellman's primary works is provided in Manfred Triesch's *The Lillian Hellman Collection at the University of Texas* (Austin, TX: University of Texas, 1966), which describes manuscripts of plays and filmscripts, notebooks, letters, and other materials in the Harry Ransom Humanities Research Center.

Ernest (Miller) Hemingway, 1899-1961

Bibliographies

645. Hanneman, Audrey. **Ernest Hemingway: A Comprehensive Bibliography**. Princeton, NJ: Princeton University Press, 1967. 568p. LC 67-14409.

This is the most comprehensive bibliography of Hemingway's primary and secondary materials. It is supplemented by:

645.1. Hanneman, Audrey. **Supplement to Ernest Hemingway: A Comprehensive Bibliography**. Princeton, NJ: Princeton University Press, 1975. 393p. LC 67-14409. ISBN 0-691-06284-6.

Covering works by and about Hemingway published through 1964, the first part of the 1967 volume gives full bibliographic descriptions of Hemingway's books and pamphlets, contributions to books, contributions to newspapers and periodicals, translations of Hemingway's works, anthologies, special collections (arranged by libraries) of Hemingway materials (pp. 249-55), published letters, and miscellaneous works. Entries provide title-page transcriptions, collations, contents, physical descriptions, and publishing histories. The second part offers brief, descriptively annotated entries for about 2,000 critical studies of Hemingway (including newspaper stories, dissertations, and reviews) in all languages. The 1975 supplement continues this two-part arrangement, covering primary materials, including special collections (pp. 103-110), as well as about 1,500 critical works. Coverage in the supplement extends from 1966 through 1973. Indexes in both volumes provide topical access for broad subjects (such as "manuscripts," "criticisms," and "allusions to") under individual works. Additional information on Hemingway's primary materials is provided in Matthew J. Bruccoli and C. E. Frazer Clark, Jr.'s *Hemingway at Auction, 1930-1973* (Detroit, MI: Gale, 1973). Also for works by Hemingway, see *First Printings of American Authors*, vol. 1, pp. 177-83. Also useful is James D. Brasch and Joseph Sigman's *Hemingway's Library: A Complete Record* (New York: Garland, 1981).

646. Wagner, Linda Welshimer. **Ernest Hemingway: A Reference Guide**. Boston: G. K. Hall, 1977. 363p. (Reference Guides in Literature, no. 13). LC 76-21821. ISBN 0-8161-7976-x.

Wagner's chronologically arranged, annotated listing of about 2,400 English-language criticisms published from 1923 through 1975 updates coverage of secondary materials in Hanneman's comprehensive bibliography (entry 645) through 1975. Although Wagner's annotations are more detailed than those in Hanneman's guide, the volume lacks subject indexing. Wagner's coverage of Hemingway criticisms is continued by:

646.1 Larson, Kelli A. **Ernest Hemingway: A Reference Guide, 1974-1989**. Boston: G. K. Hall, 1991. 318p. (Reference Guide to Literature). LC 90-43750. ISBN 0-8161-8944-7.

Chronologically arranges annotated entries for more than 1,700 works about Hemingway from 1974 through 1989. Attempts to identify "all serious contributions to Hemingway scholarship published in English": Coverage includes international imprints, reprints, introductions and chapters in books, reviews of editions of Hemingway's works and of works about Hemingway, and the like; excludes dissertations. Annotations are descriptive. Comprehensive index references names, primary titles, and selected subjects, such as biography, film studies, "Hemingway's influence ... on Bellow," "Source/influence studies," and others. See also *Bibliography of American Fiction, 1919-1988*, pp. 240-46, for Albert J. DeFazio's checklist of works by and about Hemingway. Research on Hemingway is reviewed by Frederick J. Hoffman and Melvin J. Friedman in Bryer's *Sixteen Modern American Authors*, pp. 367-416; and its supplement by Bruce Stark in Bryer's *Sixteen Modern American Authors: Volume 2: A Survey of Research and Criticism Since 1972*, pp. 404-79. *ALS* annually features a review essay on Hemingway scholarship. Additional coverage of dissertations is offered by Tetsumaro Hayashi's *Steinbeck and Hemingway: Dissertation Abstracts and Research Opportunities* (Metuchen, NJ: Scarecrow Press, 1980).

647. Young, Philip, and Charles W. Mann. **The Hemingway Manuscripts: An Inventory**. University Park, PA: Pennsylvania State University Press, 1969. 138p. LC 68-8189. ISBN 0-2710-0080-5.

In 324 entries Young describes the manuscripts of Hemingway's books, short fiction, journalistic nonfiction, poetry, fragments, letters, and other works in the possession of Mary Hemingway. Hemingway's manuscripts are also listed in Robbins' *American Literary Manuscripts*, p. 146. Other useful catalogs of primary materials include the *Catalog of the Ernest Hemingway Collection at the John F. Kennedy Library* (Boston: G. K. Hall, 1982), which describes manuscripts and correspondence, photographs, newspaper clippings, and other materials; and Bonnie D. Cherrin's *The Ernest Hemingway Collection of Charles D. Field: Catalogue* (Stanford, CA: Stanford University Libraries, 1985).

Dictionaries, Encyclopedias, and Handbooks

648. Mandel, Miriam B. **Reading Hemingway: The Facts in the Fictions**. Metuchen, NJ: Scarecrow Press, 1995. 592p. LC 94-14481. ISBN 0-8108-2870-7.

Useful guide to characters and named elements in Hemingway's novels. Mandel glosses names of real and fictional persons and characters, fictional and historical animals, named things (such as boats), and "cultural constructs" (p. 2), including titles of movies, names of organizations, and the like, in separate chapters for each of Hemingway's nine novels. Nameless characters are grouped and identified under headings for "barmen," "doctors," "drivers," "men and boys," etc. Index collects all entries into a single alphabetical listing.

649.   Reynolds, Michael S. **Hemingway: An Annotated Chronology: An Outline of the Author's Life and Career Detailing Significant Events, Friendships, Travels, and Achievements**. Detroit, MI: Omnigraphics, 1991. 155p. (Omni Chronology Series, no. 1). LC 90-24608. ISBN 1-55888-427-0.

A brief and sketchy chronology of Hemingway's life and works. Entries lack full and thorough details. Selective indexing limited to persons, works, and major or otherwise significant events. Index cites several bullfights but lists neither hunting expeditions nor Hemingway's reading.

650.   Smith, Paul. **A Reader's Guide to the Short Stories of Ernest Hemingway**. Boston: G. K. Hall, 1989. 407p. (A Reference Publication in Literature). LC 88-34944. ISBN 0-8161-8794-0.

Smith offers introductory discussions of the 55 short works of fiction published in Hemingway's lifetime. Chapters for individual stories describe composition histories (manuscripts and bibliographic studies), publishing histories, sources and influences (both biographical bases and analogues), and critical studies. Checklists of editions and criticisms accompany the discussions. Also useful, *New Critical Approaches to the Short Stories of Ernest Hemingway* (Durham, NC: Duke University Press, 1990), edited by Jackson J. Benson, includes "A Comprehensive Checklist of Hemingway Short Fiction Criticism, Explication, and Commentary, 1975-1990" (pp. 393-458).

651.   Waldhorn, Arthur. **Reader's Guide to Ernest Hemingway**. New York: Farrar, Straus & Giroux, 1972. 284p. LC 75-179795. ISBN 0-3742-4299-2.

Waldhorn provides introductory commentaries on Hemingway's life, his thoughts ("The World, the Hero, and the Code"), and his literary style, as well as close readings of the short stories and novels. A filmography and a selected primary and secondary bibliography conclude the guide.

Indexes and Concordances

652.   Hays, Peter L. **A Concordance to Hemingway's In Our Time**. Boston: G. K. Hall, 1990. 341p. LC 90-4575. ISBN 0-8161-9098-4.

This is based on the text of the first edition (New York: Boni & Liveright, 1925), with references to the texts of "On the Quai at Smyrna" and the 1930 second edition's version of "Mr. and Mrs. Eliot," which are included in appendixes.

Journals

653.   **The Hemingway Review**. Moscow, ID: Hemingway Society, 1979- . 2/yr. ISSN 0276-3362.

Sponsored by the Ernest Hemingway Foundation, *The Hemingway Review* publishes biographical as well as critical and interpretive articles, notes, book reviews, a current bibliography, letters to the editor, and other regular news features. "Gender-linked Miscommunication in 'Hills Like White Elephants,' " "Hemingway's Sun as Title and Metaphor," and "Fish Story: Ways of Telling in 'Big Two-Hearted River' " are typical contributions. Numerous articles and notes have dealt with bibliographical and textual topics and with issues relating to the conditions of publication and Hemingway's relations with his publishers. A good example is the article "Dear Mr. Scribner—About the Published Text of *The Sun Also Rises*." Special issues have focused on British criticism of Hemingway and the Spanish Civil War. A "Special European Issue," vol. 12 (1992), reviews Hemingway's reception in 10 western European countries. Additionally, *The Hemingway Review* continues to include in each issue a current "Hemingway Bibliography," which also appeared in its predecessor, *Hemingway Notes* (1971-81). "News from the Hemingway Collection" describes resources, programs, and ongoing projects at the John F. Kennedy Library. The "Bulletin Board" includes conference and program announcements, society news, and the like, with recent emphasis on

Hemingway resources on the Internet. *The Hemingway Review* is indexed in *HI*, *MHRA*, and *MLA*.

Wortman's *A Guide to Serial Bibliographies for Modern Literatures*, p. 261, describes previously published serial bibliographies for Hemingway. Patterson's *Author Newsletters and Journals*, p. 157, describes other previously published journals for Hemingway.

Beth Henley, 1952-

Bibliographies

Lisa J. McDonnell reviews research on Henley in *Contemporary Authors: Bibliographical Series: Volume 3: American Dramatists*, pp. 91-107.

W(illiam) E(rnest) Henley, 1849-1903

Bibliographies

See the review of research by Lionel Stevenson in Faverty's *The Victorian Poets*, pp. 379-80.

Robert Henryson, 1424?-1506?

Bibliographies

Florence H. Ridley offers a comprehensive guide to Henryson's primary materials with a bibliography of editions and criticism in "Middle Scots Writers" in Severs and Hartung's *A Manual of The Writings in Middle English Scots*, vol. X, pp. 961-1,060, 1,123-284. Henryson's manuscripts are also described in *Index of English Literary Manuscripts*, I, pt. 2:161-65. Scheps and Looney's *Middle Scots Poets* (entry 716) covers works about Henryson through 1978. Also for a bibliography of works by and about Henryson, see *NCBEL*, I, pp. 658-60.

Caroline Lee Hentz, 1800-1856

Bibliographies

See *Bibliography of American Fiction Through 1865*, pp. 130-31, for a checklist of works by and about Hentz.

Edward, Lord Herbert, of Cherbury, 1582-1648

Bibliographies

For a bibliography of works by and about Herbert, see *NCBEL*, I, pp. 1,311-12, 2,249-50, 2,333. Herbert's manuscripts are described in *Index of English Literary Manuscripts*, I, pt. 2:167-84. See McCarron and Shenk's *Lesser Metaphysical Poets*, pp. [26]-27, for works about Herbert through 1980.

Frank Herbert, 1920-1986

Bibliographies

654. Levack, Daniel J. H., and Mark Willard. **Dune Master: A Frank Herbert Bibliography**. Westport, CT: Meckler, 1988. 176p. (Meckler Publishing's Bibliographies on Science Fiction, Fantasy, and Horror, no. 2). LC 87-25034. ISBN 0-88736-099-8.

Levack provides separate listings for Herbert's books, contributions to books, contributions to periodicals, interviews, manuscripts (in the collection of the University of California at Fullerton), and pseudonymous and collaborative works. Descriptions of books include notes on subsequent editions and variant printings and plot summaries of each work. Separate indexes actually amount to checklists of Herbert's works arranged chronologically as well as by form (for fiction, nonfiction, verse, and media). An index of periodical titles is also included. Appends facsimiles of dust jackets of primary works and a list of works about Herbert. See *Bibliography of American Fiction, 1919-1988*, pp. 247-48, for William F. Touponce's checklist of works by and about Herbert.

Dictionaries, Encyclopedias, and Handbooks

655. McNelly, Willis E. **The Dune Encyclopedia**. New York: G. P. Putnam's Sons, 1984. 526p. LC 84-4824. ISBN 0-399-12950-2.

Intended for Dune enthusiasts. Herbert's foreword identifies the compilation as "rich background (and foreground) for the Dune Chronicles." Alphabetical compilation of biographies, histories, and accounts of major and minor figures and astronomical, biological, geological, mystical, and other terms used in the Dune series, with pronunciations, charts, tables, formulas, illustrations, and other features. Includes a source bibliography "classified according to the Library Confraternity system" (pp. 517-26).

George Herbert, 1593-1633

Bibliographies

656. Allison, A. F. **Four Metaphysical Poets: George Herbert, Richard Crashaw, Henry Vaughan, Andrew Marvell: A Bibliographical Catalogue of the Early Editions of Their Poetry and Prose (to the End of the 17th Century)**. Folkestone: Dawsons of Pall Mall, 1973. 134p. (Pall Mall Bibliographies). LC 74-168268. ISBN 0-7129-0599-5.

Allison gives separate, chronologically arranged listings of the works of these writers. Entries provide full bibliographic descriptions, including title-page facsimiles (appended), collations, physical descriptions, and summaries of contents, with *STC* and *Wing* numbers and copy locations. Herbert's works are described on pp. [11]-23. An index of printers and publishers references the entries. Also for a bibliography of works by and about Herbert, see *NCBEL*, I, pp. 1201-1206. Herbert's manuscripts are described in *Index of English Literary Manuscripts*, I, pt. 2:185-213, 629-30.

657. Roberts, John R. **George Herbert: An Annotated Bibliography of Modern Criticism, 1905-1984**. Revised ed. Columbia, MO: University of Missouri Press, 1988. 433p. LC 87-19095. ISBN 0-8262-0487-2.

A substantive revision of and improvement upon Roberts' *George Herbert: An Annotated Bibliography of Modern Criticism, 1905-1974* (Columbia, MO: University of Missouri Press, 1978), this is the definitive guide to criticism of Herbert, supplementing the original listing of 800 items with an additional 200 items published from 1905 through 1974 and about 450 items from the period 1975 through 1984. Includes critical works in all languages but excludes dissertations. Annotations offer detailed descriptions and cite bibliographic data for reprints, later editions, and the like. Very comprehensive and specific topical indexing provides subdivisions under "Bibliography," for example, for "autographs and holographs," "collected editions," "textual problems," and so forth. Roberts' coverage supersedes that in the Tannenbaums' *Elizabethan Bibliographies*, vol. 3. Research on Herbert is reviewed by Margaret Bottrall in Dyson's *English Poetry*, pp. 60-75.

Dictionaries, Encyclopedias, and Handbooks

658. Ray, Robert H. **A George Herbert Companion**. New York: Garland, 1995. 223p. (Garland Reference Library of the Humanities, vol. 921). LC 94-30947. ISBN 0-8240-4849-0.

Essentially amounts to a dictionary of Herbert's works; persons and other figures in Herbert's life and works (Ben Jonson, Izaak Walton, Johannes Kepler); places; characters, allusions, ideas, and concepts in Herbert; and literary terms. Entries for individual poems and prose works, such as "The Altar" and *The Church-Porch*, usefully identify themes, structures, and other features and offer close readings and explications. Rather shortsightedly, however, Ray's abundant brief entries for other terms (both allusions used by Herbert and concepts underlying his works) neglect to supply specific poem and line references or cite editions: the dictionary does not indicate where in fact "cockatrice" (p. 52) and

"Phlegm" (p. 125) appear in Herbert's writings. Also includes an introductory guide to resources, "Research in Herbert: Tools and Procedures" (pp. 3-6); a brief chronology of Herbert's life and works and a concise biography; and a selected bibliography of approximately 500 classified and briefly annotated works about Herbert published to 1993. Although most useful for readings of Herbert's individual writings, A. C. Hamilton's *Spenser Encyclopedia* (entry 1259) and Willam B. Hunter's *A Milton Encyclopedia* (entry 956) offer more detailed coverage of the intellectual and historical contexts of Herbert's life and works.

Indexes and Concordances

659.   DiCesare, Mario A., and Rigo Mignani, eds. **A Concordance to the Complete Writings of George Herbert**. Ithaca, NY: Cornell University Press, 1977. 1,319p. (The Cornell Concordances). LC 76-56642. ISBN 0-8014-1106-8.

Based on text of F. E. Hutchinson's edition of *The Works of George Herbert* (London: Oxford, 1941), this concordance provides separate indexes for Herbert's English vocabulary and Latin and Greek vocabulary, with word-frequency lists. For research purposes, DiCesare and Mignani's concordance is preferable to Cameron Mann's *A Concordance to the English Poems of George Herbert* (Boston: Houghton Mifflin, 1927; reprint St. Clair Shores, MI: Scholarly Press, 1972), which is based on George Herbert Palmer's *The English Works of George Herbert* (Boston: Houghton Mifflin, 1905), with selected additions.

Journals

660.   **George Herbert Journal**. Fairfield, CT: Sacred Heart University, 1977- . 2/yr. ISSN 0161-7435.

Issues feature three to five critical studies focusing on Herbert's life or works, selections of book reviews, and brief announcements of conferences, seminars, and the like. Biblical narratives and Herbert's dialogue poems, comparisons of Herbert with Sidney and Vaughan, and manuscripts of Herbert's works are topics of typical articles. Several studies have identified seventeenth-century allusions to Herbert's works. Recent, occasional special volumes devoted to specific topics are published as *George Herbert Journal Special Studies & Monographs*. Vol. 17.2 (Spring 1994) contains an index to all earlier volumes. *George Herbert Journal* is indexed in *AHI*, *MHRA*, and *MLA*.

Henry William Herbert (Frank Forester), 1807-1858

Bibliographies

661.   Van Winkle, William Mitchell, and David A. Randall. **Henry William Herbert [Frank Forester]: A Bibliography of His Writings, 1832-1858**. Portland, ME: Southworth-Anthoesen, 1936. 189p. OCLC 2204594.

Also available in a reprinted edition (New York: Burt Franklin, 1971), Van Winkle and Randall's guide contains full bibliographic descriptions chronologically arranged in sections for Herbert's separate publications, edited books, translations by Herbert, contributions to books, "Fugitive Writings" (contributions to periodicals), and attributed works. The 51 entries for first and subsequent editions and entries for Herbert's other book-length works include title-page transcriptions, collations, binding descriptions, and notes on publication histories. The volume is updated by Stephen Meats' "Addenda to Van Winkle: Henry William Herbert [Frank Forester]," *PBSA* 67 (1973): 69-73. Also for works by Herbert, see *Bibliography of American Literature*, vol. 4, pp. 107-38. Contributions by Herbert and criticism and reviews of Herbert's works in selected periodicals are identified in Wells' *The Literary Index to American Magazines, 1815-1865*, pp. 73-75; and *The Literary Index to American Magazines, 1850-1900*, p. 186. Herbert's manuscripts are listed in Robbins' *American Literary Manuscripts*, p. 147. Also useful for information about Herbert's primary materials is Paul S. Seybolt's *The First Editions of Henry William Herbert, "Frank Forester," 1807-1858* (Boston: Privately printed,

1932). See *Bibliography of American Fiction Through 1865*, pp. 132-34, for Robert Sattelmeyer's checklist of works by and about Herbert.

Josephine (Frey) Herbst, 1892-1969
Bibliographies

For works by Herbst, see *First Printings of American Authors*, vol. 1, p. 185. Herbst's manuscripts are listed in Robbins' *American Literary Manuscripts*, p. 147. See *Bibliography of American Fiction, 1919-1988*, p. 249, for Winifred Farrant Bevilacqua's checklist of works by and about Herbst.

Joseph Hergesheimer, 1880-1954
Bibliographies

662.   Stappenbeck, Herb. **A Catalogue of the Joseph Hergesheimer Collection at the University of Texas**. Austin, TX: University of Texas, 1974. 260p. (Tower Bibliographical Studies, no. 10). LC 78-169267.

Brief bibliographic descriptions of first and subsequent editions of Hergesheimer's books and pamphlets, contributions to books and pamphlets, contributions to periodicals, miscellaneous printed works, manuscripts of published works, manuscripts of unpublished and unlocated works, letters by Hergesheimer, letters to Hergesheimer, and miscellaneous letters. H. L. R. Swire's *A Bibliography of the Works of Joseph Hergesheimer* (Philadelphia, PA: Centaur Book Shop, 1922) gives full descriptions, including title-page transcriptions and collations, for Hergesheimer's works through 1922. Hergesheimer's manuscripts are listed in Robbins' *American Literary Manuscripts*, p. 147. See *Bibliography of American Fiction, 1866-1918*, pp. 221-22, for Richard J. Schrader's checklist of works by and about Hergesheimer.

James Leo Herlihy, 1927-
Bibliographies

For works by Herlihy, see *First Printings of American Authors*, vol. 5, pp. 143-44. Herlihy's manuscripts are listed in Robbins' *American Literary Manuscripts*, p. 147.

Robert Herrick, 1591-1674
Bibliographies

663.   Hageman, Elizabeth H. **Robert Herrick: A Reference Guide**. Boston: G. K. Hall, 1983. 245p. (A Reference Guide to Literature). LC 82-11763. ISBN 0-8161-8012-1.

Hageman chronologically arranges annotated entries for about 900 criticisms of Herrick published from 1648 through 1981. Coverage encompasses critical studies of all varieties, including reviews, dissertations, and entries in reference works in all languages. Annotations are descriptive. Important studies are described in detail. A separate subject index references names (St. Augustine, Donne) and topics ("carpe diem topos," "fairy poems"). Hageman's critical coverage supersedes that in the Tannenbaums' *Elizabethan Bibliographies*, vol. 3; and George Robert Guffey's *Elizabethan Bibliographies Supplements*, no. 3. Jay A. Gertzman's *Fantasy, Fashion, and Affection: Editions of Robert Herrick's Poetry for the Common Reader, 1810-1968* (Bowling Green, OH: Bowling Green State University Popular Press, 1986) includes an annotated checklist of Herrick's poetry published from 1810 to 1980 (pp. 193-236). For a bibliography of works by and about Herrick, see *NCBEL*, I, pp. 1196-98. Herrick's manuscripts are described in *Index of English Literary Manuscripts*, II, pt. 1:527-66.

Indexes and Concordances

664.   MacLeod, Malcolm. **A Concordance to the Poems of Robert Herrick**. New York: Oxford University Press, 1936. 299p. LC 36-24656. ISBN 0-8383-0991-7.

"Based upon F. W. Moorman's Oxford English Texts Edition of Robert Herrick's poems, published by the Oxford University Press, Oxford, 1915," which intends to reproduce the "original text" of *Hesperides* and *Noble Numbers* as published in 1648 and the texts of additional poems unpublished in 1648 (p. vii). References headwords by page in Moorman's edition and by Herrick's book, poem number, and line. Also available in reprinted editions (New York: Haskell House, 1971; and Folcroft, PA: Folcroft Library Editions, 1977).

Robert Herrick, 1868-1938

Bibliographies

See *Bibliography of American Fiction, 1866-1918*, pp. 223-24, for Jim Weber's checklist of works by and about Herrick. Herrick's contributions to and reviews of Herrick's works in selected periodicals are identified in Wells' *The Literary Index to American Magazines, 1850-1900*, p. 187. Herrick's manuscripts are listed in Robbins' *American Literary Manuscripts*, p. 148.

John (Richard) Hersey, 1914-1993

Bibliographies

665. Huse, Nancy Lyman. **John Hersey and James Agee: A Reference Guide**. Boston: G. K. Hall, 1978. 122p. (A Reference Publication in Literature). LC 78-15368. ISBN 0-8161-8019-9.

Huse gives separate introductions, checklists of primary works, and chronologically arranged, annotated listings of works (including dissertations) about Hersey and Agee. Coverage of Hersey (about 200 entries) extends from 1942 through 1977. Coverage of Agee (about 300 entries) extends from 1940 through 1977. Annotations are descriptive, with important works receiving detailed reviews. Works by Agee are described in Genevieve Fabre's "A Bibliography of the Works of James Agee," *Bulletin of Bibliography* 24 (1965): 145-48, 63-66. Huse's listing of works about Agee is updated by Steven Aulicino's "James Agee: Secondary Sources, 1935-1982," *Bulletin of Bibliography* 41 (1984): 64-72. Hersey's manuscripts are listed in Robbins' *American Literary Manuscripts*, p. 148. Additionally, Agee's literary manuscripts and correspondence in the University of Texas' Harry Ransom Humanities Research Center are described in Victor A. Kranmer's "James Agee's Papers at the University of Texas," *Library Chronicle of the University of Texas*, 8.2 (1966): 33-36. See *Bibliography of American Fiction, 1919-1988*, pp. 250-51, for Sally B. Young's checklist of works by and about Hersey.

William Heyen, 1940-

Bibliographies

666. Stefanik, Ernest, and Cis Stefanik. **William Heyen in Print**. Ruffsdale, PA: The Rook Press, 1978. 14p. OCLC 6152780.

Dealer's catalog containing checklists of Heyen's published and forthcoming books as of 1979, with information for ordering "in Print" and "Signed Editions" from Spring Church Book Company, Spring Church, Pennsylvania. Also reprints excerpts from several of Heyen's poems. Also for works by Heyen, see *First Printings of American Authors*, vol. 2, pp. 203-206. Also available is *William Heyen, Poet and Collector: An Exhibition, Department of Rare Books and Special Collections, the University of Rochester Library, 21 March-21 June 1982* (Rochester, NY: The Library, 1982).

DuBose Heyward, 1885-1940

Bibliographies

For works by Heyward, see *First Printings of American Authors*, vol. 3, pp. 153-56. Heyward's manuscripts are listed in Robbins' *American Literary Manuscripts*, p. 148. See *Bibliography of American Fiction, 1919-1988*, pp. 251-52, for James F. Smith's checklist of works by and about Heyward.

John Heywood, 1497?-1580?
Bibliographies

For a bibliography of works by and about Heywood, see *NCBEL*, I, pp. 1413-14. Heywood's manuscripts are described in *Index of English Literary Manuscripts*, I, pt. 2:215-17. See the Tannenbaums' *Elizabethan Bibliographies*, vol. 3; Robert Carl Johnson's *Elizabethan Bibliographies Supplements*, no. 9; and Philip C. Kolin's "Recent Studies in John Heywood," *English Literary Renaissance* 13.1 (Winter 1983): 113-23.

Indexes and Concordances

667. Canzler, David George. **A Concordance to the Dramatic Works of John Heywood**. Ph.D. dissertation, Eugene, OR: University of Oregon, 1961. 2 vols. OCLC 33071060.

Concords texts of *Play Called the Four PP; Play of Love; Witty and Witless; Play of the Weather; The Pardoner and the Friar; The Curate and Neighbor Prat; John John the Husband, Tib the Wife, and Sir John the Priest*, and three works that Canzler attributes to Heywood—*Gentleness and Nobility, Calisto and Melebea*, and *Thersites*. Uses "Tudor Facsimile Text," "Malone Society Reprints," and other old-spelling editions as base texts. Appends frequency list.

Thomas Heywood, 1574?-1641
Bibliographies

668. Wentworth, Michael. **Thomas Heywood: A Reference Guide**. Boston: G. K. Hall, 1986. 315p. (A Reference Guide to Literature). LC 86-4752. ISBN 0-8161-8575-1.

Wentworth chronologically arranges descriptively annotated entries for about 1,250 works about Heywood published from 1808 through 1981. Criticisms and comments on Heywood previous to 1800 are surveyed in the introduction. Coverage includes dissertations, introductions in editions, and studies in all languages. Annotations are descriptive. Significant works receive detailed reviews. A comprehensive index offers topical access under Heywood (with subheadings for "bibliographies," "characterization," and "historical drama") and for individual works. This supersedes the critical coverage in the Tannenbaums' *Elizabethan Bibliographies*, vol. 3, and Dennis Donovan's *Elizabethan Bibliographies Supplements*, no. 2. Heywood's works are fully described in Arthur Melville Clark's "A Bibliography of Thomas Heywood," *Oxford Bibliographical Society Papers & Proceedings* 1 (1927 [for 1922-1926]): 97-153. For a bibliography of works by and about Heywood, see *NCBEL*, I, pp. 1682-89. Heywood's manuscripts are described in *Index of English Literary Manuscripts*, I, pt. 2:219-21. Research on Heywood is reviewed by Michael Taylor in Wells' *English Drama*, pp. 100-12; and Joseph S. M. J. Chang and James P. Hammersmith in Logan and Smith's *The Popular School*, pp. 105-21, updated by Lidman's *Studies in Jacobean Drama, 1973-1984*, pp. 95-104.

Indexes and Concordances

See Stagg's *The Figurative Language of the Tragedies of Shakespeare's Chief 17th-Century Contemporaries* (entry 229).

George V. Higgins, 1939-
Bibliographies

For works by Higgins, see *First Printings of American Authors*, vol. 1, p. 187. See *Bibliography of American Fiction, 1919-1988*, p. 253, for Matthew J. Bruccoli's checklist of works by and about Higgins.

Thomas Wentworth Higginson, 1823-1911
Bibliographies

669. Mather, Winifred, and Eve G. Moore. **A Bibliography of Thomas Wentworth Higginson**. Cambridge: Cambridge Public Library, 1906. 47p. LC 7-16372.

Although Blanck's *Bibliography of American Literature*, vol. 4, pp. 139-84, offers fuller treatments of Higginson's separate publications, Mather and Moore's slim guide remains useful for brief, chronologically arranged information about contributions to books and periodicals to 1906 and for a selected listing of works about Higginson. Indexed. Higginson's contributions to and reviews of Higginson's works in selected periodicals are identified in Wells' *The Literary Index to American Magazines, 1815-1865*, p. 75; and *The Literary Index to American Magazines, 1850-1900*, pp. 187-190. Higginson's manuscripts are listed in Robbins' *American Literary Manuscripts*, p. 149. Howard N. Meyer reviews research on Higginson in Myerson's *The Transcendentalists*, pp. 195-203.

Richard Hildreth, 1807-1865
Bibliographies

See *Bibliography of American Fiction through 1865*, pp.135-36, for a checklist of works by and about Hildreth. Wells' *The Literary Index to American Magazines, 1815-1865*, p. 75, identifies comments on Hildreth in selected periodicals. Hildreth's manuscripts are listed in Robbins' *American Literary Manuscripts*, p. 149.

James Abraham Hillhouse, 1789-1841
Bibliographies

For works by Hillhouse, see *Bibliography of American Literature*, vol. 4, pp. 185-89. Wells' *The Literary Index to American Magazines, 1815-1865*, pp. 75-76, identifies comments on Hillhouse in selected periodicals. Hillhouse's manuscripts are listed in Robbins' *American Literary Manuscripts*, p. 150.

Walter Hilton, d. 1396
Bibliographies

Valerie M. Lagorio and Michael G. Sargent offer more comprehensive information about primary materials for Hilton and other English mystics with a bibliography of editions and criticism in Severs and Hartung's *A Manual of the Writings in Middle English*, vol. XXIII, pp. 3049-3137, 3405-71. Lagorio and Bradley's *The 14th-Century English Mystics* (entry 1143) covers modern criticism of Hilton. Also for a bibliography of works by and about Hilton, see *NCBEL*, I, pp. 521-22. Edwards' *Middle English Prose*, pp. 61-82, includes a review of research on Walter Hilton and *The Cloud of Unknowing* by Alastair Minnis.

Chester (Bonmar) Himes, 1909-1984
Bibliographies

670. Fabre, Michel, Robert E. Skinner, and Lester Sullivan. **Chester Himes: An Annotated Primary and Secondary Bibliography**. Westport, CT: Greenwood Press, 1992. 216p. (Bibliographies and Indexes in Afro-American and African Studies, no. 30). LC 92-18316. ISBN 0-313-28396-6.

Covers works by and about Himes. The first part describes Himes' writings in sections for fiction (novels, short fiction, contributions to periodicals, and collected short fiction), nonfiction (books, book appearances, and contributions to periodicals), manuscripts, and film adaptations of his works. Entries for book-length fiction give brief bibliographic data for U.S, U.K., and French editions and translations. Annotated entries for nonfiction works summarize contents and note reprintings; entries for manuscripts briefly describe contents of collections at Yale, Tulane, Fisk, and other institutions. The second part chronologically arranges annotated entries for 680 works about Himes published from 1945 to 1990, covering books, chapters, articles, dissertations, reviews, and non-English-language criticism. Introduction surveys Himes' career and critical reception. Includes a chronology of Himes' life and career. Author and title indexes. Himes' manuscripts are listed in Robbins' *American Literary Manuscripts*, p. 150. See *Bibliography of American Fiction, 1919-1988*, pp. 254-55, for Chris Ellery's checklist of works by and about Himes.

Rolando Hinojosa (-Smith), 1929-

Bibliographies

See *Bibliography of American Fiction, 1919-1988*, p. 256, for Salvador Rodriguez de Pino's checklist of works by and about Hinojosa-Smith.

Enos Hitchcock, 1744-1803

Bibliographies

See *Bibliography of American Fiction Through 1865*, p. 137, for a checklist of works by and about Hitchcock. Hitchcock's manuscripts are listed in Robbins' *American Literary Manuscripts*, p. 150.

Thomas Hobbes, 1588-1679

Bibliographies

671.   Garcia, Alfred. **Thomas Hobbes: Bibliographie Internationale de 1620 a 1986.** Caen: Centre de Philosophie Politique et Juridique, Universite de Caen, 1986. 267p. (Bibliotheque de Philosophie Politique et Juridique: Textes et Documents). OCLC 17655812.

Published to commemorate the 400th anniversary of Hobbes' birth, Garcia's bibliography offers both the most comprehensive listing of works about Hobbes to date as well as an important supplement to Macdonald and Hargreaves' standard *Thomas Hobbes* (entry 673), giving the most up-to-date guide to editions, reprintings, translations, and other appearances of Hobbes' works. Following a chronology of Hobbes' writings, Garcia supplies brief bibliographic information for their appearances in all languages, with the latest entries for 1983. The bulk of the volume alphabetically arranges more than 2,100 unannotated entries for international writings about Hobbes, covering books, chapters, introductions to editions, dissertations, and articles, with notes on translations and reprintings. Comprehensive index of names, titles of Hobbes' works, and subjects. Although Garcia's work essentially surpasses in scope Hinnant's *Thomas Hobbes* (entry 672), Hinnant's chronologically arranged, annotated guide in fact remains more readily accessible and useful. Also available and, to a degree, supplementing coverage of both the guides of Hinnant and Macdonald and Hargreaves is William Sacksteder's *Hobbes Studies (1879-1979): A Bibliography* (Bowling Green, OH: Philosophy Documentation Center, Bowling Green State University, 1982), an unannotated listing of editions, reprintings, and translations of Hobbes' works and of international critical scholarship through 1979.

672.   Hinnant, Charles H. **Thomas Hobbes: A Reference Guide.** Boston: G. K. Hall, 1980. 275p. (A Reference Publication in Literature). LC 79-28134. ISBN 0-8161-8173-x.

This chronologically arranges annotated entries for about 1,800 editions of Hobbes' works and criticisms in all languages published from 1679 through 1976. Coverage includes reviews of Hobbes' works and reviews of works about Hobbes, dissertations, and selected entries in reference works. Annotations are descriptive. Thorough topical indexing covers names (Aristotle, Shakespeare), individual works, broad subjects (such as "science, Hobbes's philosophy of" and "necessity, Hobbes's doctrine of"), and specific subjects under Hobbes' name, including "bibliography," "Hobbes and skepticism," and "Hobbes on power."

673. Macdonald, Hugh, and Mary Hargreaves. **Thomas Hobbes: A Bibliography**. London: The Bibliographical Society, 1952. 83p. LC 53-3337.

The standard descriptive guide to Hobbes' works. Gives full bibliographic descriptions of all editions of Hobbes' works published through 1725 as well as collected editions and translations. Entries provide title-page transcriptions, collations, contents, publishing histories, and copy locations, with selected title-page facsimiles. For a bibliography of works by and about Hobbes, see *NCBEL*, I, pp. 2325-30. Hobbes' manuscripts are described in *Index of English Literary Manuscripts*, II, pt. 1:567-86.

Dictionaries, Encyclopedias, and Handbooks

674. Martinich, A. P. **A Hobbes Dictionary**. Oxford: Blackwell Publishers, 1995. 336p. (The Blackwell Philosopher Dictionaries). LC 94-43256. ISBN 0-6311-9261-1.

Intends to identify and explain "the key concepts in Hobbes's thought and those subsidiary concepts that are important but not well known" (p. vii). Includes a biography of Hobbes in the context of seventeenth-century religious and political history; chronologies of Hobbes' life and works and events in seventeenth-century English history; 140 extended entries covering topics in philosophy, religion, linguistics, and politics, including "cause and effect," "Catholics and Presbyterians," and "motion," as well as Hobbes' major works; and a bibliography of editions and manuscripts of Hobbes' writings (with annotations), seventeenth-century philosophical works, and modern scholarship on Hobbes (pp. 317-30). Cross-referenced entries cite sections, chapters, and pages in Hobbes' works without references to particular editions. Comprehensive index of names and topics.

Thomas Hoccleve, 1369?-1426
Bibliographies

William Matthews offers a comprehensive guide to Hoccleve's primary materials with a bibliography of editions and criticism in Severs and Hartung's *A Manual of the Writings in Middle English*, vol. III, pp. 746-56, 903-908. Also for a bibliography of works by and about Hoccleve, see *NCBEL*, I, pp. 646-47.

Ralph Edwin Hodgson, 1871-1962
Bibliographies

675. Sweetser, Wesley D. **Ralph Hodgson: A Bibliography**. Revised and enlarged ed. New York: Garland, 1980. 148p. (Garland Reference Library of the Humanities, vol. 199). LC 79-7932. ISBN 0-8240-9524-3.

Sweetser gives full bibliographic descriptions for Hodgson's books, chapbooks, and broadsides; anthologies; contributions to periodicals; and miscellaneous works (three items). Entries for first editions of 32 separate publications offer title-page transcriptions, collations, contents, and physical descriptions. Gives brief information for Hodgson's more than 100 contributions to periodicals. In addition, Sweetser chronologically arranges brief descriptive entries for 190 works about Hodgson, including reviews of Hodgson's works, dissertations, introductions in editions, and entries in reference works. Name and title index.

Charles Fenno Hoffman, 1806-1884
Bibliographies

For works by Hoffman, see *Bibliography of American Literature*, vol. 4, pp. 190-203. Contributions by Hoffman and criticism and reviews of Hoffman's works in selected periodicals are identified in Wells' *The Literary Index to American Magazines, 1815-1865*, p. 76; and *The Literary Index to American Magazines, 1850-1900*, p. 190. Hoffman's manuscripts are listed in Robbins' *American Literary Manuscripts*, pp. 150-51. See *Bibliography of American Fiction Through 1865*, p. 138, for a checklist of works by and about Hoffman.

Daniel (Gerard) Hoffman, 1923-

Bibliographies

676.   Lowe, Michael. **Daniel Hoffman: A Comprehensive Bibliography**. Norwood, PA: Norwood Editions, 1973. 64 leaves. LC 73-11746.

Lowe's guide delivers less than thorough descriptions integrating coverage of works by and about Hoffman. Reprinted 1971 interview of Hoffman precedes separate, chronologically arranged listings of books, edited books, recordings (two entries), poems in periodicals, translations by Hoffman, poems in anthologies, articles in periodicals and anthologies, and reviews. Entries for Hoffman's 10 books give brief bibliographic information for first and subsequent editions and reprintings. Annotations entail extensive excerpts from reviews and other secondary works; for example, the annotation for Hoffman's *Poe Poe Poe Poe Poe Poe Poe* (1972) is lifted from John Hollander's review in the *New York Times Book Review* (13 February 1972): 7, 18. Entries for Hoffman's other publications essentially note contents and other appearances. Also includes unannotated list about 150 works about Hoffman (largely reviews subarranged by Hoffman's works). Unindexed. For works by Hoffman, see *First Printings of American Authors*, vol. 2, pp. 207-208. Hoffman's manuscripts are listed in Robbins' *American Literary Manuscripts*, p. 151.

James Hogg, 1770-1835

Bibliographies

677.   Adam, R. B. **Works, Letters and Manuscripts of James Hogg, "The Ettrick Shepherd."** Buffalo, NY: Privately Printed, 1930. Various pagings. OCLC 777676.

Chronologically arranged bibliographic descriptions of Hogg's separate, collected, and contributed published writings from 1801 to 1887 give title-page transcriptions and sizes (4to, 12mo, etc.), with a separate list of Hogg's literary manuscripts. Adam also provides transcriptions of Hogg's letters and other contemporary memorials and anecdotes related to Hogg. Unindexed. Title-page transcriptions and contents information for Hogg's prose and poetry are also contained in Edith C. Batho's *The Ettrick Shepherd* (Cambridge: Cambridge University Press, 1927), pp. 183-221; and Batho's supplement in "Note on the Bibliography of James Hogg, the Ettrick Shepherd," *Library*, 4th series, 16.4 (December 1935): 309-26. Also for a bibliography of works by and about Hogg, see *NCBEL*, III, pp. 267-70.

678.   Mack, Douglas S. **Hogg's Prose: An Annotated Listing**. Stirling: James Hogg Society, 1985. [215]-263pp. LC 87-47250. ISBN 0-9509-5772-0.

Reprinted from Mack's Ph.D. thesis, *Editing James Hogg* (Stirling: University of Stirling, 1984). Intends to provide a "useful sketch-map" (preface) identifying Hogg's published and unpublished prose writings. Entries in sections for books, pamphlets, and contributions to books; contributions to periodicals; contributions to annuals; and unpublished manuscripts give brief bibliographic information and notes on publication histories and contents. Short title index.

Journals

679.   **Studies in Hogg and His World**. Stirling: James Hogg Society, 1990- . Annual. ISSN 0960-6025.

In general, articles in this annual devoted to the Ettrick Shepherd attempt to locate Hogg in the various Scottish national literary traditions, ranging from folk literature and superstitions to Sir Walter Scott, as well as explicate typically Scottish images and themes in his works, such as the highlands and the border. A significant number of contributions describe manuscript sources and address editorial and textual problems, such as Peter Garside's "Vision and Revision: Hogg's MS Poems in the Turnbull Library," 5 (1994): 82-95. The annual has also published many new scholarly editions of Hogg's works. Valentina Bold and Douglas S. Mack provided an edition of Hogg's *The Royal Jubilee: A Scottish Mask*,

5 (1994): 102-51; and Garside and Mack collaborated on an edition of "A Sunday Pastoral by the Ettrick Shepherd," 4 (1993): 94-108. Other bibliographic contributions include Gordon Willis' "Hogg's Personal Library: Holdings in Stirling University Library," 3 (1992): 87-88. *Studies in Hogg and His World* is indexed in *MLA*.

Josiah Gilbert Holland (Timothy Titcomb), 1819-1881
Bibliographies

For works by Holland, see *Bibliography of American Literature*, vol. 4, pp. 204-18. Contributions by Holland and criticism and reviews of Holland's works in selected periodicals are identified in Wells' *The Literary Index to American Magazines, 1815-1865*, p. 77; and *The Literary Index to American Magazines, 1850-1900*, pp. 190-91. Holland's manuscripts are listed in Robbins' *American Literary Manuscripts*, p. 151.

Marietta Holley (Josiah Allen's Wife), 1836-1926
Bibliographies

For works by Holley, see *First Printings of American Authors*, vol. 5, pp. 145-51. Holley's manuscripts are listed in Robbins' *American Literary Manuscripts*, p. 151. See *Bibliography of American Fiction, 1866-1918*, pp. 225-26, for Kelly West's checklist of works by and about Holley.

John Holmes, 1904-1962
Bibliographies

For works by Holmes, see *First Printings of American Authors*, vol. 5, pp. 153-56. Holmes' manuscripts are listed in Robbins' *American Literary Manuscripts*, p. 152.

John Clellon Holmes, 1926-1988
Bibliographies

680.   Ardinger, Richard K. **An Annotated Bibliography of Works by John Clellon Holmes.** Pocatello, ID: Idaho State University Press, 1979. 26p. OCLC 6640036.

Full bibliographic descriptions of Holmes' works published from 1948 through 1978 in chronologically arranged sections for books, contributions to newspapers and periodicals, contributions to anthologies, translations of Holmes' works, and ephemera and library holdings (including recordings, excerpts and quotations in catalog, postcards, etc.). Entries for first editions of Holmes' five books give title-page transcriptions, collations, physical descriptions, contents, and notes on subsequent editions, reprintings, composition, and publication histories. Also contains brief descriptions of notebooks, drafts, and manuscripts in Holmes' Collection at Boston University. Unindexed. Also for works by Holmes, see *First Printings of American Authors*, vol. 2, p. 209.

Mary Jane (Hawes) Holmes, 1825-1907
Bibliographies

For works by Holmes, see *Bibliography of American Literature*, vol. 4, pp. 219-32. Holmes' manuscripts are listed in Robbins' *American Literary Manuscripts*, p. 152. See *Bibliography of American Fiction Through 1865*, pp.139-40, for a checklist of works by and about Holmes.

Oliver Wendell Holmes, 1809-1894
Bibliographies

681.   Currier, Thomas Franklin, and Eleanor M. Tilton. **A Bibliography of Oliver Wendell Holmes.** New York: New York University Press, 1953. 707p. LC 53-11420.

This is the standard descriptive guide to Holmes' primary materials, providing full bibliographic descriptions for his books and leaflets, poems, and prose works. Entries for books give title-page transcriptions, physical descriptions, publishing histories, and notes on manuscript sources. Entries for separate poems and prose pieces substantially relate publishing histories. Appendixes describe anonymous poems, Holmes' popular lectures, printed letters, and other miscellaneous primary materials, as well as list about 1,200 biographical and critical studies about Holmes, covering contemporary notices, reviews, letters to editors, theses and dissertations, and ana (such as poems and creative works to or about Holmes). Available in a reprinted edition (New York: Russell & Russell, 1971). Coverage of Holmes' primary materials is also included in Blanck's *Bibliography of American Literature*, vol. 4, pp. 233-339. Holmes' manuscripts are listed in Robbins' *American Literary Manuscripts*, pp. 152-53. Also useful is Anita Rutman, Lucy Clark, and Marjorie Carver's *The Barrett Library: Oliver Wendell Holmes: A Check List of Printed and Manuscript Works of Oliver Wendell Holmes in the Library of the University of Virginia* (Charlottesville: University of Virginia Press, 1969). Supplementing coverage of criticism of Holmes, Boswell's *The Schoolroom Poets* (entry 177) identifies works about Holmes from 1900 through 1981. Research on Holmes is reviewed by Barry Menikoff in Harbert and Rees' *Fifteen American Authors Before 1900*, pp. 281-305.

Homilies, Old English
Bibliographies
682.   Bately, James. **Anonymous Old English Homilies: A Preliminary Bibliography of Source Studies: Compiled for Fontes Anglo-Saxonici and Sources of Anglo-Saxon Literary Culture**. Binghamton, NY: Center for Medieval and Early Renaissance Studies, State University of New York at Binghamton, 1993. 76p. LC 94-5797.
Highly selective guide, intended to provide "a snap-shot of scholarship" (p. ii), to extant manuscripts, facsimiles, editions, and studies of Old English homilies, including the Blickling Homilies, Vercelli Homilies, and others. Greenfield and Robinson's *A Bibliography of Publications on Old English Literature to the End of 1972*, pp. 324-26, lists editions, translations, and studies of the Old English Blickling, Vercelli, and other homilies, with citations for reviews, as well as listings under Aelfric and Wulfstan. *NCBEL*, I, pp. 324-26, also lists editions and studies.

Thomas Hood, 1799-1845
Bibliographies
For a bibliography of works by and about Hood, see *NCBEL*, III, pp. 359-62. Contributions by Hood and criticism and reviews of Hood's works in selected periodicals are identified in Wells' *The Literary Index to American Magazines, 1815-1865*, p. 78; and *The Literary Index to American Magazines, 1850-1900*, p. 195.

Richard Hooker, 1554?-1600
Bibliographies
683.   Hill, W. Speed. **Richard Hooker: A Descriptive Bibliography of the Early Editions: 1593-1724**. Cleveland, OH: Press of Case Western Reserve University, 1970. 140p. LC 72-147090. ISBN 0-8295-0211-4.
Full bibliographic descriptions of early editions of Hooker's works. Intended to identify bibliographic witnesses in detail for the purpose of resolving questions of authority, entries contain title-page transcriptions; collations; detailed contents; descriptions of half titles, running titles, and typography, full notes on publication histories cross-referencing standard bibliographies such as the *STC* and *Wing*, and lists of examined and other known copies. Unindexed. Also for a bibliography of works by and about Hooker, see *NCBEL*, I, pp. 1949-58. Hooker's manuscripts are described in *Index of English Literary Manuscripts*, I, pt. 2:223-31.

Thomas Hooker, 1586-1647
Bibliographies

For works by Hooker, see *First Printings of American Authors*, vol. 4, pp. 215-21. Hooker's manuscripts are listed in Robbins' *American Literary Manuscripts*, pp. 153-54. Gallagher and Werge's *Early Puritan Writers* (entry 138) describes works about Hooker through 1974.

Johnson Jones Hooper, 1815-1862
Bibliographies

See *Bibliography of American Fiction Through 1865*, pp.141-42, for a checklist of works by and about Hooper. Wells' *The Literary Index to American Magazines, 1815-1865*, p. 78, identifies comments on Hooper in selected periodicals. Hooper's manuscripts are listed in Robbins' *American Literary Manuscripts*, p. 154. Robert L. Phillips surveys works by and about Hooper in Bain and Flora's *Fifty Southern Writers Before 1900*, pp. 250-56.

Gerard Manley Hopkins, 1844-1889
Bibliographies

684.   Dunne, Tom. **Gerard Manley Hopkins: A Comprehensive Bibliography**. Oxford: Clarendon Press, 1976. 394p. ISBN 0-19-818158-2.

Covering both Hopkins' primary and secondary materials, Dunne offers detailed descriptions of Hopkins' works, including separately published works of poetry and prose, works contributed to collections, translations, and other works attributed to him. Entries provide title-page transcriptions, collations, contents, brief publishing histories, and summaries of their reviews. In addition, Dunne describes about 1,800 works about Hopkins, covering bibliographies, biographies, books, parts of books, periodical articles and reviews, and dissertations in English and other languages published through 1970. Annotations are descriptive. Dunne also locates Hopkins' manuscripts and other special collections (pp. 359-62). The index offers topical access under Hopkins' name. An index of names and titles provides access. Dunne's work is more comprehensive than Edward H. Cohen's *Works and Criticism of Gerard Manley Hopkins: A Comprehensive Bibliography* (Washington, DC: Catholic University of America Press, 1969), which includes selectively annotated entries for 1,522 critical works about Hopkins but lacks subject indexing. Hopkins' manuscripts in the Bodleian Library and Campion Hall, Oxford, are described in D. Anthony Bischoff's "The Manuscripts of Gerard Manley Hopkins," *Thought* 26 (Winter 1951/52): 551-80. Ruth Seelhammer's *Hopkins Collected at Gonzaga* (Chicago, IL: Loyola University Press, 1970) also provides useful descriptions. For a bibliography of works by and about Hopkins, see *NCBEL*, III, pp. 581-93. Hopkins' manuscripts are described in *Index of English Literary Manuscripts*, IV, pt. 2:259. Research on Hopkins is reviewed by John Peck in Faverty's *The Victorian Poets*, pp. 317-52; and Graham Storey in Dyson's *English Poetry*, pp. 334-44.

Dictionaries, Encyclopedias, and Handbooks

685.   McDermott, John. **A Hopkins Chronology**. New York: St. Martin's Press, 1997. 161p. (Author Chronologies). LC 96-24546. ISBN 0-312-16167-0.

Detailed chronology identifying Hopkins' whereabouts and activities, depending heavily on the standard edition of Hopkins' works and correspondence. Also includes chronologies of Hopkins' poems, outline chronology of his life, and genealogical tree of Hopkins' family. Appends notes on "Tractarian Movement" (Oxford Movement) controversy, Society of Jesus (Jesuits), and Hopkins and Ireland; directory of the Hopkins circle, including family and acquaintances such as Robert Bridges, Walter Pater, and Katharine Tynan; and selected sources by and about Hopkins (pp. 149-52). Indexes of persons, places, Hopkins writings, and selected topics, such as music, Welsh language, and Hopkins' health. Listings under authors' names (Shakespeare, Keats, etc.) offer some insights on Hopkins' reading.

686.   MacKenzie, Norman H. **A Reader's Guide to Gerard Manley Hopkins**. Ithaca, NY: Cornell University Press, 1981. 256p. LC 80-69275. ISBN 0-8014-1349-4
   In this selective handbook, MacKenzie provides separate entries that survey the composition, publication, technique, themes, sources, and other topics for 158 works by Hopkins. A "Reference Section" is a dictionary offering brief identifications and discussions of Hopkins' contemporaries (such as Robert Bridges), literary techniques ("counterpoint"), and literary and philosophical influences (Duns Scotus). Selective primary and secondary bibliographies are included.

Indexes and Concordances
687.   Dilligan, Robert J., and Todd K. Bender. **A Concordance to the Poetry of Gerard Manley Hopkins**. Madison, WI: University of Wisconsin Press, 1970. 321p. LC 70-101504. ISBN 0-299-05330-x.
   Dilligan and Bender concord the text of W. H. Gardner and N. H. MacKenzie's fourth edition of *The Poems of Gerard Manley Hopkins* (London: Oxford University Press, 1967). Both alphabetical and ranked frequency lists are provided. In addition, Alfred Borrello's *A Concordance to the Poetry in English of Gerard Manly [sic] Hopkins* (Metuchen, NJ: Scarecrow Press, 1969) concords the text of the same edition and provides similar frequency tables. Although the computer-printout text of Dilligan and Bender's index is more difficult to read than Borrello's, it more faithfully renders Hopkins' text. Borrello omits all punctuation, as in "Now times Andromeda on this rock rude," whereas Dilligan and Bender give the more meaningful reading, "Now time's Andromeda."

688.   Foltz, William, and Todd K. Bender. **A Concordance to the Sermons of Gerard Manley Hopkins**. New York: Garland, 1989. 350p. (Garland Reference Library of the Humanities, vol. 1235). LC 89-31442. ISBN 0-8240-5699-X.
   Foltz and Bender provide a concordance to low-frequency words, giving page and line references and context lines, and a verbal index to high-frequency words, proving page and line references only. Separate appendixes for low- and high-frequency words are included. The base text is *Sermons and Devotional Writings* (London: Oxford University Press, 1959).

Journals
689.   **The Hopkins Quarterly**. Philadelphia, PA: International Hopkins Association, 1974-. 4/yr. ISSN 0094-9086.
   Subtitled "A Journal Devoted to Critical, Scholarly and Appreciative Responses to the Lives and Works of Gerard Manley Hopkins, S.J., and His Circle: Robert Bridges, Richard W. Dixon, and Coventry Patmore" and sponsored in part by the International Hopkins Association. Recent issues feature one to four critical studies and occasional book reviews. Lesley Higgins' "A New Catalogue of the Hopkins Collection at Campion Hall, Oxford," vol. 18.1-2 (April-July 1991): 9-44, is an important bibliographic contribution. Since 1989 some issues have featured an annual "Hopkins Bibliography," which identifies editions, critical studies, reviews, non-English-language scholarship, and other works related to Hopkins. Now badly dated, the bibliography for 1990 appears in vol. 21.1-2 (Winter-Spring 1994), published in 1996. A succession of double and special issues have struggled to bring the journal up to date. *The Hopkins Quarterly* is indexed in *AES*, *AHI*, *MHRA*, and *MLA*.

Wortman's *A Guide to Serial Bibliographies for Modern Literatures*, p. 262, describes other previously published serial bibliographies for Hopkins. Patterson's *Author Newsletters and Journals*, pp. 163-64, describes other previously published journals for Hopkins.

Pauline Hopkins, 1859-1930
Bibliographies

See *Bibliography of American Fiction, 1866-1918*, p. 227, for Jane Campbell's checklist of works by and about Hopkins.

Paul Horgan, 1903-1995
Bibliographies

See *Bibliography of American Fiction, 1919-1988*, pp. 257-58, for Robert F. Gish's checklist of works by and about Horgan. Horgan's manuscripts are listed in Robbins' *American Literary Manuscripts*, p. 155. Robert Gish surveys works by and about Horgan in Erisman and Etulain's *Fifty Western Writers*, pp. 194-204.

William H(owe) C(uyler) Hosmer, 1814-1877
Bibliographies

For works by Hosmer, see *Bibliography of American Literature*, vol. 4, pp. 340-44. Hosmer's manuscripts are listed in Robbins' *American Literary Manuscripts*, p. 155.

Emerson Hough, 1857-1923
Bibliographies

For works by Hough, see *Bibliography of American Literature*, vol. 4, pp. 345-55. Hough's manuscripts are listed in Robbins' *American Literary Manuscripts*, pp. 155-56. See *Bibliography of American Fiction, 1866-1918*, pp. 228-29, for Michael J. Sandle's checklist of works by and about Hough. Delbert E. Wylder surveys works by and about Hough in Erisman and Etulain's *Fifty Western Writers*, pp. 205-14.

A(lfred) E(dward) Housman, 1859-1936
Bibliographies

690. Carter, John, John Sparrow, and William White. **A. E. Housman: A Bibliography**. 2d ed. Godalming, UK: St. Paul's Bibliographies, 1982. 94p. (St. Paul's Bibliographies, no. 6). LC 82-231425. ISBN 0-906795-05-2.

A revision by White of Carter and Sparrow's *A. E. Housman: An Annotated Handlist* (London: Rupert Hart-Davis, 1952), this is the standard guide to Housman's primary materials, giving brief bibliographic information and publishing histories for Housman's books and pamphlets, contributions to books, contributions to periodicals, and translations of Housman's works, in addition to listing eight works about him. The first edition of the guide includes Carter's descriptions of Housman's manuscripts (pp. 50-54). Also for a bibliography of works by and about Housman, see *NCBEL*, III, pp. 601-606. See the review of research by Lionel Stevenson in Faverty's *The Victorian Poets*, pp. 391-97.

691. Ehrsam, Theodore G. **A Bibliography of Alfred Edward Housman**. Boston: F. W. Faxon, 1941. 44p. LC 41-6813.

Covering both critical studies and other ana related to Housman, Ehrsam lists about 200 reviews of Housman's works, reviews of works about Housman, news stories, poems influenced by Housman, photographs and other Housman iconography, and the like.

Indexes and Concordances

692.   Hyder, Clyde Kenneth. **A Concordance to the Poems of A. E. Housman**. Lawrence, KS: University of Kansas, 1940; reprint Gloucester, MA: Peter Smith, 1966. 133p. LC 66-9388.

Concords *A Shropshire Lad* and *Last Poems* (New York: Henry Holt, 1922); *More Poems* (New York: Knopf, 1936); verses in "Boyhood" in Katharine E. Symons' *Alfred Edward Housman* (New York: Henry Holt, 1937); verses in "A Memoir" and other sections in Laurence Housman's *My Brother, A. E. Housman* (New York: Scribner's, 1938); and all of the poems in *The Collected Poems* (London: Jonathan Cape, 1939), with a word list for "Fragment of a Greek Tragedy," *Yale Review* 17 (January 1928): 414-16. Yutaka Takeuchi's *Exhaustive Concordance to the Poems of A. E. Housman* (Tokyo: Shohakusha Publishing, 1971) limits indexing to the text of *The Collected Poems* (London: Jonathan Cape, 1939) and excludes Housman's three translations of Greek dramas.

Journals

693.   **Housman Society Journal**. Bromsgrove, Worcestershire: Housman Society, 1974-. Annual. ISSN 0305-926x.

Sponsored by the Housman Society, annual volumes publish eight to 10 articles, notes, and reviews of works about Housman's life, works, and family. Typical articles present close readings of works and interpretations of images and themes, such as the recent "Housman's 'Loveliest of Trees' " and "Housman as a Comic Writer." Other articles have discussed Housman and music; the treatment of male-male relations; use of pessimism; Housman's literary relations with Horace, Plautus, Matthew Arnold, Witter Bynner, Philip Larkin, and others; and the composition and publication histories of his works. Volumes of *Housman Society Journal* have been more thoroughly indexed in *MHRA* than in *MLA*.

Patterson's *Author Newsletters and Journals*, p. 164, describes other previously published journals for Housman.

Richard Hovey, 1864-1900

Bibliographies

For works by Hovey, see *Bibliography of American Literature*, vol. 4, pp. 356-62. Hovey's contributions to and reviews of Hovey's works in selected periodicals are identified in Wells' *The Literary Index to American Magazines, 1850-1900*, p. 196. Hovey's manuscripts are listed in Robbins' *American Literary Manuscripts*, p. 156.

E(dgar) W(atson) Howe, 1853-1937

Bibliographies

For works by Howe, see *First Printings of American Authors*, vol. 2, pp. 211-15. Howe's contributions to and reviews of Howe's works in selected periodicals are identified in Wells' *The Literary Index to American Magazines, 1850-1900*, pp. 196-97. Howe's manuscripts are listed in Robbins' *American Literary Manuscripts*, p. 156. See *Bibliography of American Fiction, 1866-1918*, pp. 230-31, for Stephen E. Hopkins' checklist of works by and about Howe.

Julia Ward Howe, 1819-1910

Bibliographies

For works by Howe, see *Bibliography of American Literature*, vol. 4, pp. 363-83. Howe's contributions to and reviews of Howe's works in selected periodicals are identified in Wells' *The Literary Index to American Magazines, 1850-1900*, p. 197. Howe's manuscripts are listed in Robbins' *American Literary Manuscripts*, pp. 156-57.

William Dean Howells, 1837-1920

Bibliographies

694.   Brenni, Vito J. **William Dean Howells: A Bibliography**. Metuchen, NJ: Scarecrow Press, 1973. 212p. (Scarecrow Author Bibliographies, no. 9). LC 73-4855. ISBN 0-8108-0620-7.

Brenni gives brief bibliographic information for Howell's primary materials, including his novels, short fiction, plays, poems, travel writings, and criticism, including his introductions, book and play reviews, speeches, interviews, letters, and the like. In addition, Brenni describes about 800 works about Howells. Critical coverage includes reviews, dissertations, and other ana, such as portraits of Howells and translations of his works. The index offers topical access to criticism under headings for Howells and broad subjects. Brenni's coverage of primary works supplements William Gibson and George Arms' *A Bibliography of William Dean Howells* (entry 696). See *Bibliography of American Fiction, 1866-1918*, pp. 232-39, for David J. Nordloh's checklist of works by and about Howells. Julie Bates Dock identifies works by and about Howells in Demastes' *American Playwrights, 1880-1945*, pp. 183-95. Research on Howells is also reviewed by Nordloh in Harbert and Rees' *Fifteen American Authors Before 1900*, pp. 306-29.

695.   Eichelberger, Clayton L. **Published Comment on William Dean Howells Through 1920: A Research Bibliography**. Boston: G. K. Hall, 1976. 330p. LC 76-2030. ISBN 0-8161-1078-6.

Eichelberger chronologically arranges annotated entries for 2,166 works about Howells published through 1920, including pamphlets, newspaper stories and editorials, reviews, interviews, cartoons, caricatures, and other materials. Annotations are descriptive. The volume lacks subject indexing.

696.   Gibson, William M., and George Arms. **A Bibliography of William Dean Howells**. New York: New York Public Library, 1948. 182p. LC 48-6028.

Also available in a reprinted edition (New York: New York Public Library, 1971), Gibson and Arms' guide gives full bibliographic descriptions of Howells' works in sections for separately published and contributed and edited books and contributions to periodicals and newspapers, with a list of selected works about Howells. Chronologically arranged entries contain title-page transcriptions, collations, binding descriptions, contents, with notes on first appearances and reprintings. Updated by Ulrich Halfmann's "Addenda to Gibson and Arms: Twenty-Three New Howell Items," *PBSA* 66 (1972): 174-77. Additional information about Howells' works is provided in Blanck's *Bibliography of American Literature*, vol. 4, pp. 384-448. Howells' manuscripts are listed in Robbins' *American Literary Manuscripts*, p. 158. Howells' primary materials at the University of Virginia are described in Fannie Mae Elliott and Lucy Clark's *The Barrett Library: W. D. Howells: A Checklist of Printed and Manuscript Works of William Dean Howells in the Library of the University of Virginia* (Charlottesville: University of Virginia Press, 1959). Another useful finding aid is John K. Reeves' "The Literary Manuscripts of William Dean Howells: A Descriptive Finding List," *Bulletin of the New York Public Library*. 62.6 (June 1958): 267-363. The standard descriptive guide to Howells' primary works will be included in the authoritative Indiana edition, *A Selected Edition of W. D. Howells* (Bloomington, IN: Indiana University Press, 1968-).

Dictionaries, Encyclopedias, and Handbooks

697.   Carrington, George C., Jr., and Ildiko de Papp Carrington. **Plots and Characters in the Fiction of William Dean Howells**. Hamden, CT: Archon Books, 1976. 306p. (The Plots and Characters Series). LC 75-45257. ISBN 0-208-01461-6.

Following a brief chronology of Howells' life and works and a chronological listing of his fiction, the Carringtons offer summaries of Howells' novels, short fiction, and miscellaneous imaginative prose works and include a dictionary with brief identifications of his named and unnamed characters. *A Hazard of New*

Fortunes is summarized in 10 pages. The persona of "The Editor's Easy Chair," which appeared in Howells' *Harper's Monthly* column of that title, is included among the characters.

Journals
    See Patterson's *Author Newsletters and Journals*, p. 165, for previously published journals for Howells.

W(illiam) H(enry) Hudson, 1841-1922
Bibliographies
    698.   Payne, John R. **W. H. Hudson: A Bibliography**. Folkestone: Dawson, 1977. 248p. LC 76-30003. ISBN 0-7129-0750-3.
    The best listing of Hudson's primary works, Payne gives full bibliographic descriptions for books, contributions to books, contributions to periodicals, and translations (arranged by languages). Entries provide title-page transcriptions, collations, contents, physical descriptions, references to reviews, publishing histories, and copy locations. Includes a list of about 40 books about Hudson. Payne's guide supersedes George F. Wilson's *A Bibliography of the Writings of W. H. Hudson* (London: Bookman's Journal, 1922). Also for a bibliography of works by and about Hudson, see *NCBEL*, III, pp. 1059-60.

(James) Langston Hughes, 1902-1967
Bibliographies
    699.   Dickinson, Donald C. **A Bio-Bibliography of Langston Hughes, 1902-1967**. 2d ed., revised Hamden, CT: Shoe String Press, 1972. 273p. LC 70-18177. ISBN 0-208-01269-9.
    A revision of the second edition (Hamden, CT: Archon Books, 1967). Following an examination of Hughes' life, works, and critical reputation, Dickinson gives separate listings for Hughes' books (including international and subsequent editions); works edited or translated by Hughes; works by Hughes not translated into English; collections including works by Hughes; and Hughes' prose, plays, and poems. Entries give full bibliographic information, including listings of contents and brief publishing histories. In addition, Dickinson lists about 250 works about Hughes, including reviews of his works. Coverage excludes radio and television scripts, song lyrics, and works subsequently published in Faith Berry's edition of *Good Morning Revolution* (New York: Lawrence Hill, 1973). Dickinson's coverage of secondary materials is updated by Mikolyzk's guide (entry 700). Also for works by Hughes, see *First Printings of American Authors*, vol. 3, pp. 157-81. Hughes' manuscripts are listed in Robbins' *American Literary Manuscripts*, pp. 159-60.

    700.   Mikolyzk, Thomas A. **Langston Hughes: A Bio-Bibliography**. New York: Greenwood Press, 1990. 295p. (Bio-Bibliographies in Afro-American and African Studies, no. 2). LC 90-3613. ISBN 0-313-26895-9.
    Covering works by and about Hughes, Mikolyzk gives bibliographic information and plot summaries and contents for Hughes' books and shorter works and descriptive annotations for about 700 critical works, including reviews, dissertations, and criticisms in all languages. A separate subject index references names, titles, and topics, such as "dialect," "protest," and "Harlem." Mikolyzk's guide supplements both Dickinson's guide (entry 699) for primary materials and Miller's (entry 701) for secondary. Richard K. Barksdale's *Langston Hughes* (Chicago, IL: American Library Association, 1977) assesses Hughes scholarship from early reviews to the late 1970s. Granger Babcock identifies works by and about Hughes in Demastes' *American Playwrights, 1880-1945*, pp. 196-205. Research on Hughes is reviewed by Blyden Jackson in Inge, Duke, and Bryer's *Black American Writers*, vol. 1, pp. 187-206.

701.   Miller, R. Baxter. **Langston Hughes and Gwendolyn Brooks: A Reference Guide**. Boston: G. K. Hall, 1978. 149p. (A Reference Publication in Literature). LC 78-8272. ISBN 0-8161-7810-0.

Miller provides separate introductions and chronologically arranged, annotated listings of comments and criticism on Hughes (about 350 items) published from 1924 through 1977 and on Brooks (about 300 items) from 1944 through 1977. Coverage includes books, articles, reviews, and dissertations. Annotations are descriptive. Significant works receive extended reviews. Separate indexes offer limited topical access under headings for "bibliographies," "biographies," and "poetry."

Indexes and Concordances

702.   Mandelik, Peter, and Stanley Schatt. **A Concordance to the Poetry of Langston Hughes**. Detroit, MI: Gale, 1975. 296p. LC 74-11251. ISBN 0-8103-1011-2.

Mandelik and Schatt concord the texts of some 572 poems by Hughes as they appear in 15 "most recent" editions, such as *Ask Your Mama* (New York: Knopf, 1961), *Langston Hughes Reader* (New York: Braziller, 1958), and *Selected Poems of Langston Hughes* (New York: Knopf, 1959). Entries reference collection, poem, and line, with the context line. A ranked word frequency table is appended.

Journals

703.   **The Langston Hughes Review**. Athens, GA: Langston Hughes Society, University of Georgia, 1982- . 2/yr. ISSN 0737-0555.

Features articles and reviews of works that focus on the life and writings of Hughes and other modern black American writers, including Zora Neale Hurston, Sterling A. Brown, and others. Typical contributions present close readings of works, discuss Hughes' literary relations with other writers, and assess Hughes' critical reception in the United States and abroad. Occasional special issues are devoted to single topics, such as 12.1 (Spring 1993), titled "Poets on Hughes." *The Langston Hughes Review* has also featured several bibliographic contributions, including Sharynn Owens Etheridge's "Langston Hughes: An Annotated Bibliography (1977-1986)," 11.1 (Spring 1992): 41-57; and Don Bertschman's "Jesse B. Sample and the Racial Mountain: A Bibliographic Essay," 13.2 (Winter/Summer 1995): 29-44. The journal contains brief notices for society activities and calls for papers. Publication is about one year behind schedule. *Langston Hughes Review* is indexed in *MLA*.

Ted (Edward James) Hughes, 1930-
Bibliographies

704.   Sagar, Keith, and Stephen Tabor. **Ted Hughes: A Bibliography, 1946-1980**. London: Mansell, 1983. 260p. LC 82-224260. ISBN 0-7201-1654-6.

Sagar and Tabor give a detailed descriptive listing of works by Hughes, including editions and reprints of his books, pamphlets, and broadsides; contributions to books; contributions to journals; translations; interviews; recordings; radio and television appearances; miscellaneous writings, such as dust jackets and programs; and musical settings. Entries offer title-page transcriptions; collations; contents; descriptions of paper, bindings, and dust jackets; brief publishing histories; and references to reviews. About 120 critical studies about Hughes, including books, articles, and dissertations, are also listed. Coverage extends through 1980. Additional coverage of criticism of Hughes is provided in Shields' *Contemporary English Poetry*, pp. 113-48.

William Humphrey, 1924-
Bibliographies

For works by Humphrey, see *First Printings of American Authors*, vol. 1, pp. 189-90. Humphrey's manuscripts are listed in Robbins' *American Literary Manuscripts*, p. 160.

James Gibbons Huneker, 1857-1921
Bibliographies

For works by Huneker, see *Bibliography of American Literature*, vol. 4, pp. 449-58. Huneker's contributions to and reviews of Huneker's works in selected periodicals are identified in Wells' *The Literary Index to American Magazines, 1850-1900*, p. 209. Huneker's manuscripts are listed in Robbins' *American Literary Manuscripts*, pp. 160-61.

(James Henry) Leigh Hunt, 1784-1859
Bibliographies

705. Lulofs, Timothy J., and Hans Ostrom. **Leigh Hunt: A Reference Guide**. Boston: G. K. Hall, 1985. 264p. (A Reference Guide to Literature). LC 85-811. ISBN 0-8161-8385-6.

Lulofs and Ostrom chronologically arrange annotated entries for about 1,100 works about Hunt published from 1800 through 1982. Comprehensive critical coverage includes early reviews and notices, dissertations, and introductions in editions in all languages. Although annotations are descriptive, some critical guidance is provided. Significant studies are reviewed in detail. Topical indexing references subjects under Hunt as well as other names (Shakespeare, Wordsworth) and individual works. Lulofs and Ostrom's guide offers more convenient and critical coverage than John L. Waltman and Gerald G. McDaniel's *Leigh Hunt: A Comprehensive Bibliography* (New York: Garland, 1985), which chronologically arranges by decades brief, descriptively annotated entries for about 1,300 critical works (excluding dissertations) about Hunt published from 1800 through 1979. A full descriptive bibliography of Hunt's primary materials does not exist. Alexander Mitchell's *A Bibliography of the Writings of Leigh Hunt: With Critical Notes* (London: Bookman's Journal, 1931); O. M. Brack and D. H. Stefanson's *A Catalogue of the Leigh Hunt Manuscripts in the University of Iowa Libraries* (Iowa City, IA: Friends of the University of Iowa Libraries, 1973); Luther A. Brewer's *My Leigh Hunt Library: The First Editions* (1932; reprint New York: Burt Franklin, 1967) provide information on Hunt's primary materials. Also for a bibliography of works by and about Hunt, see *NCBEL*, III, pp. 1216-23. Research on Hunt is reviewed by Carolyn W. and Lawrence H. Houtchens in Houtchens and Houtchens' *The English Romantic Poets and Essayists*, pp. 255-88.

Evan Hunter (Ed McBain), 1926-
Bibliographies

See *Bibliography of American Fiction, 1919-1988*, pp. 259-61, for Russell Wm. Hultgren's checklist of works by and about Hunter.

Zora Neale Hurston, 1901?-1960
Bibliographies

706. Newson, Adele S. **Zora Neale Hurston: A Reference Guide**. Boston: G. K. Hall, 1987. 90p. (Reference Guide to Literature). LC 87-8616. ISBN 0-8161-8902-1.

Newson chronologically arranges annotated entries for about 300 works about Hurston published from 1931 through 1986. Coverage includes articles in newspapers, miscellaneous news clippings, reviews of Hurston's works, and dissertations. Full annotations are both descriptive and evaluative. An appended "Finding List" locates and briefly describes manuscripts related to Hurston in special collections, including the New York Public Library's Schomberg Center for Research in Black Culture and the Library of Congress. Indexing is limited to proper names and primary titles. Newson's coverage supersedes that for Hurston in Perry's *The Harlem Renaissance*, pp. 100-107. Critical coverage is extended by Bonnie Carey Ryan's "Zora Neale Hurston—A Checklist of Secondary Sources," *Bulletin of Bibliography* 45 (1988): 33-39. For works by Hurston, see *First Printings of American Authors*, vol. 1, pp. 191-92. Hurston's manuscripts are listed in Robbins' *American Literary Manuscripts*, p. 161.

Laura K. Crawley and Joseph C. Hickerson's *Zora Neale Hurston: Recordings, Manuscripts, and Ephemera in the Archive of Folk Culture and Other Divisions of the Library of Congress* (Washington: Archive of Folk Culture, American Folklife Center, Library of Congress, 1992) is also available. See *Bibliography of American Fiction, 1919-1988*, pp. 262-64, for Ellen M. Millsap's checklist of works by and about Hurston. John Lowe identifies works by and about Hurston in Demastes' *American Playwrights, 1880-1945*, pp. 206-13. Research on Hurston is reviewed by Daryl C. Dance in Duke, Bryer, and Inge's *American Women Writers*, pp. 321-52; and by Elvin Holt in Flora and Bain's *Fifty Southern Writers After 1900*, pp. 259-69.

Journals

707.   **Zora Neale Hurston Forum**. Baltimore, MD: Zora Neale Hurston Society, 1986-. 2/yr. ISSN 1051-6867.

Sponsored by the Zora Neale Hurston Society, this journal has published articles and reviews of new publications about the life and works of Hurston. Particular attention has focused on Hurston's literary relations with other black American writers, such as Ishmael Reed, Alice Walker, and Jessie Redmon Fauset. Other contributions have discussed language, themes, images, and characters in Hurston's works. "Folk Humor as Comic Relief in Hurston's *Jonah's Gourd Vine*" and "A Sense of Wonder: The Pattern for Psychic Survival in *Their Eyes Were Watching* and *The Color Purple*" are typical. The last volume of *Zora Neale Hurston Forum* indexed in *MLA* dates from 6.1 (Fall 1991).

Richard Holt Hutton, 1826-1897
Bibliographies

Wendell V. Harris reviews research on Hutton in DeLaura's *Victorian Prose*, pp. 442-43.

Aldous Leonard Huxley, 1894-1963
Bibliographies

708.   Bass, Eben E. **Aldous Huxley: An Annotated Bibliography of Criticism**. New York: Garland, 1981. 221p. (Garland Reference Library of the Humanities, vol. 198). LC 79-7907. ISBN 0-8240-9525-1.

Bass arranges entries for some 651 works about Huxley in separate listings for biographical and critical works and dissertations. Studies in English and French receive extensive, descriptive annotations, including references to reviews. Studies in other languages and dissertations are unannotated. The volume lacks subject indexing. The best listing of Huxley's primary works is provided in Hanson R. Duval's *Aldous Huxley: A Bibliography* (New York: Arrow, 1939), which includes descriptions of Huxley's books (with references to their reviews), contributions to books and journals, reprinted editions, and other writings. It is supplemented and updated by Claire J. Eschelbach and Joyce Lee Shober's *Aldous Huxley: A Bibliography, 1916-1959* (Berkeley, CA: University of California Press, 1961), and Eschelbach and Shober's "Aldous Huxley: A Bibliography, 1914-1964 (A Supplementary Listing)," *Bulletin of Bibliography* 28 (1971): 114-17, which list both primary and secondary materials, including reviews of Huxley's works. Clair Shulz's *Aldous Huxley, 1894-1963: A Centenary Catalog* (Stevens Point, WI: Decline and Fall, 1994) is also available. Also for a bibliography of works by and about Huxley, see *NCBEL*, IV, pp. 609-17.

T(homas) H(enry) Huxley, 1825-1895
Bibliographies

Contributions by Huxley and criticism and reviews of Huxley's works in selected periodicals are identified in Wells' *The Literary Index to American Magazines, 1815-1865*, p. 80; and *The Literary Index to American Magazines, 1850-1900*, pp. 210-11. John W. Bicknell reviews research on Huxley in DeLaura's *Victorian Prose*, pp. 495-506.

Gilbert Imlay, c. 1754-1828
Bibliographies

See *NCBEL*, II, pp. 1010, 1474; and *Bibliography of American Fiction Through 1865*, pp.143-44, for checklists of works by and about Imlay.

Dean Ing, 1931-
Bibliographies

709.   Burgess, Scott Alan. **The Work of Dean Ing: An Annotated Bibliography & Guide**. San Bernardino, CA: Borgo Press, 1990. 82p (Bibliographies of Modern Authors, no. 11). LC 87-827. ISBN 0-8937-0495-4.

Describes works by and about Ing in separate sections for books, short fiction, nonfiction, unpublished works, editorial credits, radio and television appearances, honors and awards, works about Ing (27 entries, mostly unannotated, for interviews and citations in reference works), and miscellanea. Entries for books summarize plots and note citations for reviews. Also includes Ing chronology; selected quotes from critics; and "Afterword," by Ing. Title index.

William Inge, 1913-1973
Bibliographies

710.   Leeson, Richard M. **William Inge: A Research and Production Sourcebook**. Westport, CT: Greenwood Press, 1994. 221p. (Modern Dramatists Research and Production Sourcebooks, no. 5). LC 93-46360. ISBN 0-31327-407-X.

Following a chronology and introduction to Inge's life and career, Leeson delivers plot summaries, production information and credits, citations for both stage and film reviews, and critical overviews (with cross-references to critical studies) for each of the 29 plays and screenplays; chronologically lists television productions based on Inge's works; notes musical adaptations; describes Inge's publications in sections for drama, fiction, nonfiction, and archival sources; and gives separate, chronologically arranged lists of annotated entries for reviews (235 entries) and books, articles, and parts of books (89 entries, with a separate list of nine dissertations) about Inge published from 1950 to 1991. Entries for Inge's separate publications, anthologies, and collections give brief bibliographic data and contents information. Separate indexes for secondary authors and for proper names and Inge's works, but they lack topical headings.

711.   McClure, Arthur F., and C. David Rice. **A Bibliographical Guide to the Works of William Inge (1913-1973)**. Lewiston, NY: Edwin Mellen Press, 1991. 166p. (Studies in American Literature, vol. 14). LC 91-30669. ISBN 0-7734-9688-2.

Essentially updating and expanding McClure's *William Inge: A Bibliography* (New York: Garland, 1982), McClure and Rice describe works by and about Inge in five classified sections. Part I (primary materials) identifies Inge's thesis; prefaces, introductions, and forewords; published plays; collected plays; published screenplays; novels; articles; and reviews in the *St. Louis Star-Times* (1943-46). Entries give contents and brief data on publication histories. Part II (biographical materials) includes entries for book chapters and parts of books, articles, and entries in biographical dictionaries and other reference works (such as *Contemporary Authors* and *Oxford Companion to American Literature*); obituaries; and "postmortems" (mostly tributes). Part III (secondary materials) lists general articles and chapters and parts of books (about 50 selectively annotated items), reviews of Inge's plays (arranged by titles and additionally giving original cast and production information for Inge's eight plays), reviews of Inge's two novels, theses and dissertations on Inge, and bibliographies. Part IV separately lists cast and production information for film adaptations and for Inge's original screenplays and screen adaptations, with citations for reviews. Part V describes television adaptations of Inge's works. Appendixes briefly detail the Independence Community College Library's Inge Collection, which is also described in William Pfannenstiel's

William Inge Collection of Independence Junior College Library (Independence, Kansas: Independence Community College, 1986); and the William Inge Festival also held in Independence, KS. Also for works by Inge, see *First Printings of American Authors*, vol. 2, pp. 217-19. Inge's manuscripts are listed in Robbins' *American Literary Manuscripts*, p. 162.

Joseph Holt Ingraham, 1809-1860
Bibliographies

For works by Ingraham, see *Bibliography of American Literature*, vol. 4, pp. 459-91. Contributions by Ingraham and criticism and reviews of Ingraham's works in selected periodicals are identified in Wells' *The Literary Index to American Magazines, 1815-1865*, p. 81. Ingraham's manuscripts are listed in Robbins' *American Literary Manuscripts*, p. 163. See *Bibliography of American Fiction Through 1865*, pp.145-48, for a checklist of works by and about Ingraham.

Washington Irving, 1783-1859
Bibliographies

712.   Bowden, Edwin T. **Washington Irving Bibliography**. Boston, MA: Twayne, 1989. 761p. (Complete Works of Washington Irving, vol. 30). LC 88-31696. ISBN 0-8057-8526-4.

Standard descriptive bibliography of Irving's works, superseding William R. Langfeld and Philip C. Blackburn's *Washington Irving: A Bibliography* (New York: New York Public Library, 1933); and Stanley T. Williams and Mary Allen Edge's *A Bibliography of the Writings of Washington Irving: A Check List* (New York: Oxford University Press, 1936). Bowden chronologically arranges full bibliographic descriptions in sections for "Original Works" (starting with *Salmagundi*, which Bowden describes as neither originally a book nor a periodical, through *Life of Washington*), contributions to books, reprinted contributions, contributions to periodicals, and complete works. Entries in the first section cover first and subsequent American and international editions and translations and provide quasi-facsimile title-page transcriptions and data for collations, contents, bindings, publication histories, and copy locations. Indexed by titles of Irving's writings. Also for works by Irving, see *Bibliography of American Literature*, vol. 5, pp. 1-96. Irving's manuscripts are listed in Robbins' *American Literary Manuscripts*, pp. 163-64. Major research collections for Irving are at Yale University and the New York Public Library, the latter described in part in Andrew B. Myers' *The Worlds of Washington Irving, 1783-1859: From an Exhibition of Rare Books and Manuscript Materials in the Special Collections of the New York Public Library* (Tarrytown, NY: Sleepy Hollow Restorations, 1974).

713.   Springer, Haskell. **Washington Irving: A Reference Guide**. Boston: G. K. Hall, 1976. 235p. (Reference Guides in Literature, no. 6). LC 76-2489. ISBN 0-8161-1101-4.

Springer provides an annotated, chronological listing of about 1,000 comments and criticisms about Irving published from 1807 through 1974, including early anonymous reviews and notices, published letters, and dissertations in all languages. Coverage excludes masters theses, passing references in general sources, and the like. Annotations are descriptive. Topical indexing includes selected headings for such subjects as "bibliography," "biography," "folklore," "influence," and "sources," as well as for individual works. Springer and Raylene Penner's "Washington Irving: A Reference Guide Updated," *Resources for American Literary Study* 11 (1981): 257-79, updates listings for criticism to 1982. See *Bibliography of American Fiction Through 1865*, pp.149-54, for Edmund M. Hayes and Mary Jo Tate's checklist of works by and about Irving. Research on Irving is reviewed by James W. Tuttleton in Harbert and Rees' *Fifteen American Authors Before 1900*, pp. 330-56.

Journals
See Patterson's *Author Newsletters and Journals*, p. 361, for previously published journals for Irving.

Christopher Isherwood, 1904-1986
Bibliographies
714. Funk, Robert W. **Christopher Isherwood: A Reference Guide**. Boston: G. K. Hall, 1979. 196p. (A Reference Publication in Literature). LC 78-10199. ISBN 0-8161-8072-5.
Funk chronologically arranges annotated entries for about 1,100 works about Isherwood published from 1928 through 1977. Comprehensive coverage includes articles and reviews in local newspapers, entries in biographical dictionaries, dissertations, and non-English-language criticisms. Annotations are mostly brief excerpts from the sources. The index gives limited topical access, providing headings only for "bibliographies," "biographies," "interviews," and individual works. Coverage of Isherwood's primary works through 1967 is offered in Selmer Westby and Clayton M. Brown's *Christopher Isherwood: A Bibliography, 1923-1967* (Los Angeles, CA: California State College at Los Angeles Foundation, 1968), which gives brief bibliographic information (with references to editions and reprints) for Isherwood's separately published, contributed, collaborative, translated, and edited works. Also for a bibliography of works by and about Isherwood, see *NCBEL*, IV, pp. 619-20. Isherwood's manuscripts are listed in Robbins' *American Literary Manuscripts*, p. 164.

Sir Isumbras, before 1320
Indexes and Concordances
715.   Reichl, Karl, and Walter Sauer. **A Concordance to Six Middle English Tail-Rhyme Romances**. Frankfurt am Main: Peter Lang, 1993. 2 vols. LC 92-39411. ISBN 3-631-43026-4.
Cumulative KWIC concordance (using the Oxford Concordance Programme) to the texts of "a comparatively homogeneous group of non-cyclical Middle English romances . . . composed in tail-rhyme stanzas, sharing a common story pattern" (p. ii): *Sir Eglamour of Artois, Le Bone Florence, Sir Isumbras, Octavian, The King of Tars*, and *Syr Tryamowr*. Separate lemmas for 11 parts of speech and Latin and French words distinguish homonyms. Based on F. E. Richardson's Early English Text Society, no. 256, *Sir Eglamour of Artois* (London: Oxford University Press, 1965); C. F. Heffernan's Old and Middle English Texts *Le Bone Florence of Rome* (Manchester: Manchester University Press; New York: Barnes and Noble, 1976); M. Mills' editions of *Sir Isumbras* and *Octavian* in *Six Middle English Romances* (London: Dent, 1973); Judith Perryman's Middle English Texts, no. 12, *The King of Tars* (Heidelberg: C. Winter, 1980); and A. J. Erdmann Schmidt's *Syr Tryamowre: A Metrical Romance with Introduction, Glossary, and Notes* (Ph.D. thesis, Utrecht, 1937), with emended manuscript readings.

Charles (Reginald) Jackson, 1903-1968
Bibliographies
For works by Jackson, see *First Printings of American Authors*, vol. 3, pp. 183-84. Jackson's manuscripts are listed in Robbins' *American Literary Manuscripts*, p. 164. See *Bibliography of American Fiction, 1919-1988*, p. 265, for Dean H. Keller's checklist of works by and about Jackson.

Helen (Maria) Hunt Jackson (Saxe Holm), 1830-1885
Bibliographies
For works by Jackson, see *Bibliography of American Literature*, vol. 5, pp. 97-116. Jackson's contributions to and reviews of Jackson's works in selected periodicals are identified in Wells' *The Literary Index to American Magazines, 1850-1900*, pp. 215-16.

Jackson's manuscripts are listed in Robbins' *American Literary Manuscripts*, p. 165. See *Bibliography of American Fiction, 1866-1918*, pp. 239-41, for Alice Shukalo's checklist of works by and about Jackson.

Shirley (Hardie) Jackson, 1916-1965

Bibliographies

For works by Jackson, see *First Printings of American Authors*, vol. 2, pp. 221-23. Jackson's manuscripts are listed in Robbins' *American Literary Manuscripts*, p. 165. See *Bibliography of American Fiction, 1919-1988*, pp. 266-67, for Joan Wylie Hall's checklist of works by and about Jackson.

James I, King of Scotland, 1394-1437

Bibliographies

716.   Scheps, Walter, and J. Anna Looney. **Middle Scots Poets: A Reference Guide to James I of Scotland, Robert Henryson, William Dunbar, and Gavin Douglas.** Boston: G. K. Hall, 1986. 292p. (A Reference Guide to Literature). LC 85-24884. ISBN 0-8161-8356-2.

This offers separate, chronologically arranged listings of works about fifteenth- and sixteenth-century Scottish literature in general and about James I, Henryson, Dunbar, and Douglas. Coverage includes early notices, dissertations, introductions in editions, and reviews of works about the writers published from 1521 through 1978. About 200 works are listed for James, 300 for Douglas, and 400 each for Henryson and Dunbar. Brief, critical annotations identify standard, influential, or otherwise important works. Each listing is indexed separately. Detailed topical access is provided under the name of each writer. Florence H. Ridley offers a comprehensive guide to James I's primary materials with a bibliography of editions and criticism in "Middle Scots Writers" in Severs and Hartung's *A Manual of the Writings in Middle English*, vol. X, pp. 961-1060, 1123-1284. Also for a bibliography of works by and about James I, see *NCBEL*, I, pp. 654-56.

Henry James, (Jr.), 1843-1916

Bibliographies

717.   Budd, John. **Henry James: A Bibliography of Criticism, 1975-1981.** Westport, CT: Greenwood, 1983. LC 82-24163. ISBN 0-313-23515-5.

Alphabetically arranges descriptively annotated entries for more than 900 works about James in sections for dissertations and theses, books, chapters and parts of books, and articles. International coverage includes non-English-language criticisms (not all are annotated). Descriptions of books give citations for reviews. Although substantially superseded by Funston's *Henry James: A Reference Guide, 1975-1987* (entry 718), Budd remains useful for longer annotations and references to reviews of secondary works.

718.   Funston, Judith E. **Henry James: A Reference Guide, 1975-1987.** Boston: G. K. Hall, 1991. 571p. (Reference Guide to Literature). LC 90-48856. ISBN 0-8161-8953-6.

The most recent volume in a G. K. Hall series that constitutes the most comprehensive bibliography of James scholarship from 1866 through 1987. Other volumes are:

718.1. McColgan, Kristin Pruitt. **Henry James, 1917-1959: A Reference Guide.** Boston: G. K. Hall, 1979. (A Reference Publication in Literature). LC 78-27118. ISBN 0-8161-7851-8.

718.2. Scura, Dorothy McInnis. **Henry James, 1960-1974: A Reference Guide.** Boston: G. K. Hall, 1979. 490p. (A Reference Publication in Literature). LC 78-27143. ISBN 0-8161-7850-X.

718.3. Taylor, Linda J. **Henry James, 1866-1916: A Reference Guide**. Boston: G. K. Hall, 1982. 533p. (A Reference Guide to Literature). LC 82-979. ISBN 0-8161-7874-7.

Funston's bibliography largely supersedes John Budd's *Henry James: A Bibliography of Criticism, 1975-1981* (entry 717). Like the volumes of McColgan, Scura, and Taylor, Funston's guide chronologically arranges annotated entries for more than 2,300 studies of James. International coverage includes introductions, chapters, and parts of books; reviews of adaptations; selected book reviews; dissertations; and non-English-language criticisms (not all annotated). Brief annotations summarize and quote. Separate indexes for critics and subjects—the latter giving good access to names, specific topics, and titles of James' works and works of others—offer good access. McColgan chronologically arranges descriptively annotated entries for about 1,700 works about James, including reviews, dissertations, and foreign-language criticisms. The index includes subject headings under James' name. Scura chronologically arranges descriptive entries for about 2,000 items, including dissertations, reviews of works about James, articles dealing with adaptations of James' works, and non-English-language criticisms. The index references selected topics, including specific characters, such as Daisy Miller and Christina Light. Providing essential coverage of materials that reflect James' reputation during his lifetime, Taylor offers thorough coverage of early, anonymous reviews and notices in local newspapers and periodicals of James' works, including descriptive entries for some 2,600 items. Separate indexes for newspapers and periodicals as well as James' works offer useful access. Taylor in particular supersedes the coverage of James' early critical reception presented in Richard N. Foley's *Criticism in American Periodicals of the Works of Henry James from 1866 to 1916* (Washington, DC: Catholic University of America Press, 1944). A more critical and selective guide to James criticism, Nicola Bradbury's *An Annotated Critical Bibliography of Henry James* (New York: St. Martin's, 1987) highlights some 367 major critical studies of James (studies of "character," "irony," "James and Dickens," "James and Nabokov," and the like). Beatrice Ricks' *Henry James: A Bibliography of Secondary Works* (Metuchen, NJ: Scarecrow, 1975) topically arranges entries for about 4,600 English-language criticisms of James but offers little critical guidance. A more specialized bibliography, Thaddeo K. Babiiha's *The James-Hawthorne Relation: Bibliographical Essays* (Boston: G. K. Hall, 1980) surveys James' use of and comments on Hawthorne and its critical interpretation. See *Bibliography of American Fiction, 1866-1918*, pp. 242-50, for David Kirby's checklist of works by and about James. Jackie Tucker identifies works by and about James in Demastes' *American Playwrights, 1880-1945*, pp. 214-23. Research on James is reviewed by Robert L. Gale in Woodress' *Eight American Authors*, pp. 321-75; and S. Gorley Putt in Dyson's *The English Novel*, pp. 280-99. James scholarship is reviewed annually in *ALS*.

719. Edel, Leon, and Dan H. Laurence. **A Bibliography of Henry James**. 3d ed. Oxford: Clarendon Press, 1982. 428p. (Soho Bibliographies). LC 83-153876. ISBN 0-19-818186-8.

The best bibliography of James' primary materials, including full descriptions for James' books, contributions to books, published letters, contributions to periodicals (some 585 entries), translations of his works (arranged by languages), and miscellaneous writings, such as English-language international editions and book-club issues. In addition, Edel and Laurence describe James' manuscripts in collections at Yale, Harvard, the New York Public Library, and the University of Texas (pp. 390-93). Entries for books include title-page transcriptions, collations, contents, descriptions of bindings, references to serializations, and publishing histories. Also for works by James, see *Bibliography of American Literature*, vol. 5, pp. 117-81; and *NCBEL*, III, pp. 992-1000. James' manuscripts are listed in Robbins' *American Literary Manuscripts*, p. 166.

Dictionaries, Encyclopedias, and Handbooks

720.   Fogel, Daniel Mark. **A Companion to Henry James Studies**. Westport, CT: Greenwood, 1993. 545p. LC 92-1129. ISBN 0-313-25792-2.

Twenty contributed essays by different scholars address all of James' fiction and nonfiction works and the full range of topics related to James. Particularly useful is Richard A. Hocks' "From Literary Analysis to Postmodern Theory: A Historical Narrative of James Criticism" (pp. 3-24), which amounts to a review of scholarship on James. Appendixes chronologically describe James' principal book-length publications and identify "Landmarks of Henry James Criticism" (major critical studies from 1905 to 1991). Extensive bibliography of works cited (pp. 495-520). Thorough index of names, titles, and topics.

721.   Gale, Robert L. **Henry James Encyclopedia**. New York: Greenwood Press, 1989. 791p. LC 88-21338. ISBN 0-313-25846-5.

Gale offers about 3,000 brief, identifying entries for James' fiction and nonfiction works (mostly plot summaries), fictional characters, and real persons (including literary figures, critics, artists, actors, and others) associated with James or whom James commented on, and selected topics, such as James' income, "Sales Figures of Some of J's Books," and U.S. presidents commented on by James. *The American* receives a page-and-one-half summary. Nathaniel Hawthorne receives five pages. Gale's handbook supersedes coverage of James' characters in his previous *Plots and Characters in the Fiction of Henry James* (Hamden, CT: Archon Books, 1965). Likewise, Gale's handbook covers more characters than Glenda Leeming's *Who's Who in Henry James* (New York: Taplinger, 1976), although Leeming offers longer identifications. The most comprehensive coverage of allusions to literary figures and works and names of places and institutions that appear in James' critical writings (excluding his letters) is provided by William T. Stafford's *A Name, Title, and Place Index to the Critical Writings of Henry James* (Englewood, CO: Microcard Edition Books, 1975). At the other extreme is Louis Auchincloss' *Quotations from Henry James* (Charlottesville, VA: Published for the Associates of the University of Virginia Library by the University Press of Virginia, 1985), which offers about 300 excerpted "pictures of persons and places" (p. xi) from the full range of James' writings and is intended "not so much for scholars as for those who may find pleasure in a guided browsing in the Master's prose" (p. xiii). S. Gorley Putt's *Henry James: A Reader's Guide* (Ithaca, NY: Cornell University Press, 1966) offers introductory survey chapters on James' life and individual works.

Indexes and Concordances

722.   Bender, Todd K. **Concordances to the Works of Henry James**. New York: Garland, 1985- . In progress.

Following the model of Garland's "Conrad Concordances" series (entry 293), this project will index James' works included in the 24 volume "New York Edition" of *Novels and Tales of Henry James* (New York: Scribner's, 1907-1917). Volumes typically reproduce the copy text as a "field of reference" and separately index low- and high-frequency words, with appended frequency tables. References to low-frequency words include context lines and page and line references. References to high-frequency words omit context lines. Volumes include:

722.1. Bender, Todd K. **A Concordance to Henry James's Daisy Miller**. New York: Garland, 1987. 155p. (Garland Reference Library of the Humanities, vol. 578). LC 84-48858. ISBN 0-8240-8758-5.

The field of reference is the text included in *Daisy Miller, The Patagonian, and Other Tales* (New York: Scribner's, 1909).

722.2. Higdon, David Leon, and Todd K. Bender. **A Concordance to Henry James's The American**. New York: Garland, 1985. 336p. (Garland Reference Library of the Humanities, vol. 647). LC 85-45320. ISBN 0-8240-8599-x.

This indexes the text of the 1907 (New York: Scribner's) edition.

722.3. Bender, Claire E., and Todd K. Bender. **A Concordance to Henry James's The Turn of the Screw**. New York: Garland, 1988. 251p. (Garland Reference Library of the Humanities, vol. 828). LC 87-32834. ISBN 0-8240-4147-X.

The copy text is taken from *The Aspern Papers, The Turn of the Screw, The Liar, The Two Faces* (New York: Scribner's, 1908).

722.4. Bender, Todd K., and D. Leon Higdon. **Concordance to Henry James's The Spoils of Poynton**. New York: Garland, 1988. 400p. (Garland Reference Library of the Humanities, vol. 648). LC 88-12063. ISBN 0-8240-8598-1.

This is based on *The Spoils of Poynton, A London Life, The Chaperon* (New York: Scribner's, 1908).

722.5. Volume 5: Bender, Todd K. **A Concordance to Henry James's The Awkward Age**. New York: Garland, 1989. 691p. (Garland Reference Library of the Humanities, vol. 869). LC 89-1438. ISBN 0-8240-4437-1.

Bender indexes the text of the 1908 (New York: Scribner's) edition.

722.6. Volume 6: Hulpke, Erika. **A Concordance to Henry James's What Maisie Knew**. New York: Garland, 1989. 527p. (Garland Reference Library of the Humanities, vol. 915). LC 89-11983. ISBN 0-8240-4348-0.

Hulpke indexes the field of reference based on the 1908 (New York: Scribner's) edition.

Journals

723. **The Henry James Review**. Louisville, KY: Henry James Society, 1979- . 3/yr. ISSN 0273-0340.

Sponsored by the Henry James Society, whose offices are presently located at the University of Louisville, and distributed by the Johns Hopkins University Press, *The Henry James Review* publishes major scholarly articles on James and other features of interest to James scholars and readers. Issues include five to seven (and sometimes as many as 12) articles that offer close readings and interpretations of James' works; present interviews with other writers, such as James Baldwin and Louis Auchincloss, that relate James' contributions and influence; and relate bibliographic research on textual problems or previously unknown or unpublished texts of James' manuscripts and letters. Adeline R. Tintner's "Additions to the Library of Henry James Since 1987," 18 (1997): 97-98, supplements Leon Edel and Tintner's *The Library of Henry James* (Ann Arbor: UMI, 1987). Issues also include papers from recent conferences. In addition to regular book-review features and more extensive book-review essays, the journal also publishes occasional bibliographic essays that assess the present state of James scholarship. Frequent special issues devoted to particular subjects include 17.3 (Fall 1996) on teaching James and 16.1 (Fall 1995) on James and race. A double issue, 7.2-3 (Winter-Spring 1986), focused on *The Portrait of a Lady*, contains an extensive bibliography of primary materials and annotated criticism (pp. 164-95). A section of brief announcements, notes on conferences, calls for papers, reports on meetings, and descriptions of activities of the Henry James Society, new publications, and projects in progress also appears in each issue. *The Henry James Review* is indexed in *AES, MHRA*, and *MLA*.

Will(iam Roderick) James, 1892-1942
Bibliographies

See *Bibliography of American Fiction, 1919-1988*, pp. 268-69, for Glenna Bell's checklist of works by and about James. James' manuscripts are listed in Robbins' *American Literary Manuscripts*, p. 166.

Thomas Allibone Janvier, 1849-1913
Bibliographies

For works by Janvier, see *Bibliography of American Literature*, vol. 5, pp. 182-88. Janvier's contributions to and reviews of Janvier's works in selected periodicals are identified in Wells' *The Literary Index to American Magazines, 1850-1900*, p. 224. Janvier's manuscripts are listed in Robbins' *American Literary Manuscripts*, p. 167.

Randall Jarrell, 1914-1965
Bibliographies

724.   Wright, Stuart T. **Randall Jarrell: A Descriptive Bibliography, 1929-1983**. Charlottesville, VA: University Press of Virginia, 1986. 372p. LC 85-3132. ISBN 0-8139-1055-2.

Wright describes in detail Jarrell's primary works, including separately published works; contributions to books; contributions to periodicals; interviews and published comments; blurbs; and other miscellaneous works, such as musical settings, films, recordings, and translations. Entries give facsimiles of title and copyright pages; collations; contents; descriptions of typography, paper, bindings, and dust jackets; publishing histories, including extended excerpts from correspondence related to each work; and copy locations. Also for works by Jarrell, see *First Printings of American Authors*, vol. 4, pp. 223-30. Jarrell's manuscripts are listed in Robbins' *American Literary Manuscripts*, p. 167. Research on Jarrell is reviewed by George S. Lensing in Flora and Bain's *Fifty Southern Writers After 1900*, pp. 270-79; and Sr. Bernetta Quinn in *Contemporary Authors: Bibliographical Series: Volume 2: American Poets*, pp. 129-62.

Richard Jefferies, 1848-1887
Bibliographies

725.   Miller, George, and Hugoe Matthews. **Richard Jefferies: A Bibliographical Study**. Aldershot, Hants: Scolar Press, 1993. 787p. ISBN 0-8596-7918-7.

Covers works by and about Jefferies. Departs from descriptive bibliographic convention by providing separate listings first for Jefferies' contributions to periodicals, arranged alphabetically by periodical, followed by listings for his books and pamphlets, arranged chronologically, and contributions to anthologies and collections. Entries for books, including posthumous publications, give facsimiles of title pages, transcriptions of imprint data, collations, paginations, details on variants, binding and dust-jacket descriptions, and lengthy composition and publication histories, with copy locations. Another section describes 33 collections of manuscripts, letters, and other Jefferies papers in the British Library as well as other collections in the Richard Jefferies Museum, several U.S. and U.K. libraries, and private collections (pp. 726-47). Miller and Matthews conclude with a selectively and very briefly annotated, chronologically arranged list of about 200 works on Jefferies from 1887 to 1987. Includes a very brief chronology. Index of proper names, titles, and selected subjects. Also for a bibliography of works by and about Jefferies, see *NCBEL*, III, pp. 1060-62.

(John) Robinson Jeffers, 1887-1962
Bibliographies

726.   Albert, Sydney S. **A Bibliography of the Works of Robinson Jeffers**. 1933; reprint New York: Burt Franklin, 1968. 262p. LC 68-4089.

In this, the standard bibliography of Jeffers' primary works, Albert gives full descriptions for separately published works, contributions to books, contributions to periodicals and newspapers, and reprintings in anthologies. Entries provide title-page transcriptions, collations, physical descriptions, and information on publication histories. Also for works by Jeffers, see *First Printings of American Authors*, vol. 3, pp. 185-96. Jeffers' manuscripts are listed in Robbins' *American Literary Manuscripts*, pp. 167-68. Additional information on Jeffers' primary materials is provided in Ward Ritchie's *Theodore Lilienthal, Robinson Jeffers, and the Quercus Press: With a Checklist of the Lilienthal Jeffers Collection* (Los Angeles, CA: Mary Norton Clapp Library. 1974); Anita Rutman's *The Barrett Library: Robinson Jeffers: A Checklist of Printed and Manuscript Works of Robinson Jeffers in the Library of the University of Virginia* (Charlottesville, VA: University of Virginia Press, 1960); and Covington Rogers and John M. Meador, Jr.'s *The Robinson Jeffers Collection at the University of Houston: A Bibliographical Catalogue* (Houston, TX: The University, 1975).

727.   Boswell, Jeanetta. **Robinson Jeffers and the Critics, 1912-1983: A Bibliography of Secondary Sources with Selective Annotations**. Metuchen, NJ: Scarecrow Press, 1986. 170p. (Scarecrow Author Bibliographies, no. 77). LC 86-17862. ISBN 0-8108-1914-7.
        Boswell alphabetically arranges selectively annotated entries for 829 critical books, periodical and newspaper articles and reviews, dissertations, and passing references related to Jeffers. Annotations are descriptive. A separate subject index includes headings for such topics as "violence" and "T. S. Eliot"; individual works; and the like. Boswell's work updates and complements, but does not supersede, Alex A. Vardamis' more extensive *The Critical Reputation of Robinson Jeffers: A Bibliographical Study* (Hamden, CT: Archon Books, 1972), which briefly summarizes more than 1,000 books, periodical and newspaper articles, and reviews about Jeffers through 1972. Research on Jeffers is reviewed by Robert Brophy in Erisman and Etulain's *Fifty Western Writers*, pp. 215-27.

Journals
728.   **Robinson Jeffers Newsletter**. Los Angeles, CA: Robinson Jeffers Committee, Occidental College, 1962-. 4/yr. ISSN 0300-7936.
        Issues of the *Robinson Jeffers Newsletter* have published as many as a dozen articles, notes, and reviews of new publications about the life and works of Jeffers. Typical features offer close readings of individual works, trace sources and influences and discuss Jeffers' biography. In addition, particular attention focuses on bibliographic problems and resources. Articles have described Jeffers' manuscripts and unpublished works, letters, and textual variants of works. Other contributions have detailed collections of Jeffers' materials in the Harry Ransom Humanities Research Center of the University of Texas and in other locations. A wide range of Jeffers' manuscripts are surveyed in Robert Brophy's useful "An Index to Robinson Jeffers's Published Poems, Their First Appearances, and a Directory to Their Manuscripts," featured in a supplement to vol. 73 (June 1988). Past volumes of *Robinson Jeffers Newsletters* were thoroughly indexed in *MLA*; recent volumes have been indexed more selectively.

Thomas Jefferson, 1743-1826
729.   Shuffelton, Frank. **Thomas Jefferson: A Comprehensive Annotated Bibliography of Writings About Him (1826-1980)**. New York: Garland, 1984. 486p. (Garland Reference Library of Social Science, vol. 184). LC 83-48200. ISBN 0-8240-9078-0.
        Updated and continued by:

729.1 Shuffelton, Frank. **Thomas Jefferson, 1981-1990: An Annotated Bibliography**. New York: Garland, 1992. 238p. (Garland Reference Library of the Humanities, vol. 1217). LC 92-6846. ISBN 0-8240-5347-8.

Shuffelton's volumes offer the most comprehensive international coverage of writings about Jefferson from his death to the present. The 1984 volume includes briefly annotated entries for 3,447 works about Jefferson published through 1980 that are alphabetically arranged in sections for bibliography; biography; politics; philosophy and the history of ideas; and the practical and fine arts, science, and education. The 1992 volume adds another 87 pre-1981 items and chronologically arranges entries for 642 works about Jefferson published through 1990. Coverage of both volumes includes popular and scholarly books and parts of books, articles, dissertations, and non-English-language works dealing with Jefferson "in a substantial way" (1984, p. xii). Annotations in the 1992 update are generally more critical and evaluative than those in the 1984 volume. In both volumes separate, detailed subject indexes offer excellent topical access, with headings for names of individuals, places, institutions, and works, as well as for such topics as "architecture," "libraries," and "slavery." Headings for the *Declaration of Independence* and Monticello include detailed subdivisions. Shuffelton's guides far surpass the coverage of Eugene L. Huddleston's *Thomas Jefferson: A Reference Guide* (Boston: G. K. Hall, 1982), which chronologically arranges descriptively and critically annotated entries for a more limited range of about 1,400 works about Jefferson published from 1837 through 1980. Jefferson's manuscripts are listed in Robbins' *American Literary Manuscripts*, pp. 168-69. *Index to the Thomas Jefferson Papers* (Washington, DC: Library of Congress, Manuscript Division, 1976), Presidents' Papers Index Series, accesses the microform collection of *Thomas Jefferson Papers* (Washington, DC: Library of Congress, 1974). Also significant is *Thomas Jefferson's Library: A Catalog with the Entries in His Own Order* (Washington: Library of Congress, 1989), edited by James Gilreath and Douglas L. Wilson. Research on Jefferson is reviewed by William Peden in Bain and Flora's *Fifty Southern Writers Before 1900*, pp. 268-76.

Concordances and Indexes

730. Kaminski, John P. **Citizen Jefferson: The Wit and Wisdom of an American Sage**. Madison, WI: Madison House, 1994. 132p. LC 93-40661. ISBN 0-9456-1235-4.

Arranges selected and edited quotes from Jefferson's writings under about 150 topics, including "Education," "Liberty," and "Slavery." Although substantially based on Julian P. Boyd, Charles T. Cullen, and John Catanzariti's standard edition of *The Papers of Thomas Jefferson* (Princeton, NJ: Princeton University Press, 1950-), Kaminski only gives brief citations to the original publication or document and date. Includes Jefferson chronology. Comprehensive index of names and topics. More useful for bed and bath reading than for research.

(Patricia) Ann Jellicoe, 1927-

Bibliographies

King's *Twenty Modern British Playwrights*, pp. 65-68, lists works by Jellicoe and describes works about her.

Sarah Orne Jewett, 1849-1909

Bibliographies

731. Nagel, Gwen L., and James Nagel. **Sarah Orne Jewett: A Reference Guide**. Boston: G. K. Hall, 1977. 178p. (A Reference Publication in Literature). LC 77-7392. ISBN 0-8161-7848-8.

The Nagels offer the most comprehensive bibliography of secondary materials about Jewett, chronologically arranging annotated entries for about 800 early, anonymous notices and reviews, dissertations, introductions in editions, and the like published from 1873 through 1976. Annotations are descriptive and helpful. The index offers headings for such topics as "bibliography," "local color," "Guy de Maupassant," and "Jonathan Swift," as well as other topics listed under Jewett's name. The Nagels supplement their guide in *"Sarah Orne Jewett: A Reference Guide*: An Update," *American Literary Realism* 17 (1984): 228-63. See *Bibliography of American Fiction, 1866-1918*, pp. 250-52, for Gwen L. Nagel's checklist of works by and about Jewett. Research on Jewett is reviewed by Philip B. Eppard in Duke, Bryer, and Inge's *American Women Writers*, pp. 21-46.

732. Weber, Clara Carter, and Carl J. Weber. **A Bibliography of the Published Writings of Sarah Orne Jewett**. Waterville, ME: Colby College Press, 1949. 105p. LC 49-10893.

The standard bibliography of Jewett's primary works, this offers bibliographic information, physical descriptions, and publishing histories (with references to subsequent editions and reprintings) for Jewett's books, contributions to books, contributions to magazines and newspapers, reprintings in others' works, and translations of her works. In addition, the Webers describe non-English-language criticisms, reviews, and biographical and critical studies of Jewett. Also for works by Jewett, see *Bibliography of American Literature*, vol. 5, pp. 189-205. Jewett's manuscripts are listed in Robbins' *American Literary Manuscripts*, p. 170. Rosalie Murphy Baum describes Jewett's primary materials in *The Sarah Orne Jewett Collection* in part 3 of Sidney Ives' *The Parkman Dexter Howe Library* (Gainesville, FL: University of Florida, 1986).

Edward Johnson, 1598-1672
Bibliographies

Johnson's manuscripts are listed in Robbins' *American Literary Manuscripts*, p. 170. Gallagher and Werge's *Early Puritan Writers* (entry 138) describes works on Johnson through 1975.

James Weldon Johnson, 1871-1938
Bibliographies

733. Fleming, Robert E. **James Weldon Johnson and Arna Wendell Bontemps: A Reference Guide**. Boston: G. K. Hall, 1978. 149p. (A Reference Publication in Literature). LC 77-23874. ISBN 0-8161-7932-8.

For these writers Fleming gives separate introductions and chronologically arranged listings of critical studies, including reviews and dissertations. Coverage includes about 350 items each for Johnson (from 1905) and Bontemps (from 1926) published through 1976. Annotations are critical. A full range of index headings under Johnson's and Bontemps' names provides topical access. Additional coverage of works about Bontemps is provided in Perry's *The Harlem Renaissance*, pp. [59]-62. See *Bibliography of American Fiction, 1919-1988*, pp. 93-94, for Robert E. Fleming's checklist of works by and about Bontemps; and *Bibliography of American Fiction, 1866-1918*, pp. 253-54, for Kenneth Kinnamon's checklist of works by and about Johnson. Johnson's manuscripts are listed in Robbins' *American Literary Manuscripts*, p. 171. Research on Johnson and Bontemps is reviewed by Ruth Miller and Peter J. Katopes in Inge, Duke, and Bryer's *Black American Writers*, vol. I, pp. 161-86. Research on Johnson is also reviewed by Julian Mason in Flora and Bain's *Fifty Southern Writers After 1900*, pp. 280-89.

Josephine (Winslow) Johnson, 1910-
Bibliographies

For works by Johnson, see *First Printings of American Authors*, vol. 5, pp. 157-59. Johnson's manuscripts are listed in Robbins' *American Literary Manuscripts*, p. 171.

Lionel (Pigot) Johnson, 1867-1902
Bibliographies

Cevasco's *Three Decadent Poets* (entry 410), pp. [253]-376, identifies 320 works by and about Johnson to 1988. Also for a bibliography of works by and about Johnson, see *NCBEL*, III, pp. 633-34. See the review of research by Lionel Stevenson in Faverty's *The Victorian Poets*, pp. 399-400.

Owen (McMahon) Johnson, 1878-1952
Bibliographies

For works by Johnson, see *First Printings of American Authors*, vol. 5, pp. 161-65. Johnson's manuscripts are listed in Robbins' *American Literary Manuscripts*, p. 171. See *Bibliography of American Fiction, 1866-1918*, pp. 255-56, for Samuel I. Bellman's checklist of works by and about Johnson.

Samuel Johnson, 1709-1784
Bibliographies

734.   Courtney, William Prideaux, and David Nichol Smith. **A Bibliography of Samuel Johnson**. Oxford: Clarendon Press, 1915. 186p. LC 15-15044.

The standard guide to Johnson's primary works, Courtney and Smith describe editions of Johnson's separately published works, contributions, edited works, translations, and the like. Emphasis is on composition and publication histories rather than physical descriptions. The publishing history of Johnson's dictionary receives some 30 pages. Available in 1925 and 1968 reprinted editions (Oxford: Clarendon Press). This guide is supplemented by Robert W. Chapman and Allen T. Hazen's "Johnsonian Bibliography: A Supplement to Courtney," *Oxford Bibliographical Society* 5 (1938): 119-66. For a bibliography of works by and about Johnson, see *NCBEL*, II, pp. 1122-74. Johnson's manuscripts are described in *Index of English Literary Manuscripts*, III, pt. 2:121-78; and in J. D. Fleeman's *A Preliminary Handlist of Documents and Manuscripts of Samuel Johnson* (Oxford: Oxford Bibliographical Society, Bodleian Library, 1967). Also useful for research on Johnson's primary materials are Fleeman's *Preliminary Handlist of Copies of Books Associated with Dr. Samuel Johnson* (Oxford: Oxford Bibliographical Society, 1984) and *Sale Catalogue of Samuel Johnson's Library* (Victoria, BC: English Literary Studies, 1975); and Donald Greene's *Samuel Johnson's Library: An Annotated Guide* (Victoria, BC: English Literary Studies, 1975).

735.   Clifford, James L., and Donald Johnson Greene. **Samuel Johnson: A Survey and Bibliography of Critical Studies**. Minneapolis, MN: University of Minnesota Press, 1970. 333p. LC 74-109940. ISBN 0-8166-0572-6.

The most comprehensive guide to critical studies about Johnson, this cumulates and extends the coverage of Clifford's *Johnsonian Studies, 1887-1950: A Survey and Bibliography* (Minneapolis, MN: University of Minnesota Press, 1951) and Clifford and Greene's "A Bibliography of Johnsonian Studies, 1950-1960 (with Additions and Corrections to Johnsonian Studies, 1887-1950)," in Magdi Wahba's *Johnsonian Studies* (Cario: Oxford University Press, 1962), pp. 203-41. Clifford and Greene arrange about 5,000 largely unannotated entries in topical listings for bibliography (both enumerative and analytical), editions of Johnson's works (including selections and collections), biographical studies, studies related to Boswell, ana (such as parodies of Johnson, fictional works about him, and dedications to him), general criticisms, studies of specific topics (such as Johnson and the law, Johnson's prose style, and his attitudes toward science), and studies of individual works. A comprehensive index provides access to the full range of topics, with detailed subheadings. Clifford and Greene's guide is updated by Greene's *Bibliography of Johnsonian Studies, 1970-1985* (Victoria, BC: University of Victoria, Department of English, 1987). Helen Louise McGuffie's *Samuel Johnson in the British Press, 1749-1784: A Chronological Checklist* (New York: Garland, 1976) lists and describes more than 2,000 articles, notices, and other contemporary references to Johnson largely in London and Edinburgh newspapers but lacks indexing for newspaper titles.

Dictionaries, Encyclopedias, and Handbooks

See Johnson's *Plots and Characters in the Fiction of Eighteenth-Century English Authors* (entry 1309).

736.   Page, Norman. **A Dr. Johnson Chronology**. London: Macmillan, 1990. 136p. (Macmillan Author Chronologies). LC 89-12942. ISBN 0-333-45916-4.

Page emphasizes details of Johnson's "life, experiences, and friendships" (p. ix) after 1762 (he met Boswell in 1763), particularly those related to his major writings as well as the range of his social acquaintances and activities. The chronology recounts Johnson's endless visits, dinners, teas, and meetings; his early and late risings; the therapeutic uses of his diary; and his daily moods and health. Coverage of events from 1726 through 1761 and details about the conception and composition of such major works as Johnson's *Dictionary* and *The Vanity of Human Wishes* is very limited. An appendix includes very brief identifications of about 200 of Johnson's acquaintances. Separate indexes for people, places, and Johnson's writings provide limited access. Page's Johnson chronology lacks the great detail offered in other volumes in this series, such as Knowles' *A Conrad Chronology* (entry 290).

737.   Rogers, Pat. **The Samuel Johnson Encyclopedia**. Westport, CT: Greenwood Press, 1996. 483p. LC 95-33072. ISBN 0-313-29411-9.

Intends to gather together "all the essential facts regarding Johnson" (p. xi). Alphabetically arranged entries for topics (general, literary, social, and historical issues, concerns, and interests related to Johnson, such as health, law, bookselling, and Jacobitism); Johnson's works; individuals "with whom Johnson had significant contacts" literally or otherwise in his life (p. xiii), including family, close friends, and other associates as well as the likes of Shakespeare, Charles XII of Sweden, and Benjamin Franklin; and places. Entries include references to standard editions of Johnson's works and major biographies and critical studies. Includes a chronology and a classified bibliography of bibliographies, reference works, editions, biographies, and criticism. Thorough index references names of person and places, titles, and more specific topics in entries. Also useful as handbooks to Johnson's critical opinions are Richard L. Harp's *Dr. Johnson's Critical Vocabulary: A Selection from His Dictionary* (Lanham, MD: University Press of America, 1986), which reprints definitions and illustrative quotations for a selection of "words by which he surveyed and judged the whole range of English literature" (p. xiv); and Arthur Sherbo's Samuel Johnson's *Critical Opinions: A Reexamination* (Newark, DE: University of Delaware Press, 1995), which offers referenced quotes from Johnson's works on selected topics (dictionaries, imagination, poetry) and contemporaries' and others' works and lives (Shakespeare, most extensively).

Indexes and Concordances

738.   Naugle, Helen Harrold, and Peter B. Sherry. **A Concordance to the Poems of Samuel Johnson**. Ithaca, NY: Cornell University Press, 1973. 578p. (The Cornell Concordances). LC 72-13383. ISBN 0-8014-0769-9.

Naugle and Sherry provide separate concordances and frequency lists for Johnson's English and Latin poems and "Poems of Doubtful Attribution," based on texts in David Nichol Smith and Edward L. McAdam's edition of *The Poems of Samuel Johnson* (Oxford: Clarendon Press, 1941), with supplemental variants from McAdam and George Milne's vol. 6 of *The Yale Edition of the Works of Samuel Johnson* (New Haven, CT: Yale University Press, 1964).

Journals

739. **The Age of Johnson: A Scholarly Annual**. New York: AMS Press, 1987-. Annual. ISSN 0884-5816.

Age of Johnson publishes substantial features on "all aspects of the literature, history, and culture of the period of Samuel Johnson's literary career and primary influence, roughly the years from 1730 to 1810" (masthead). The annual's 10 to 20 scholarly contributions focus on Johnson and other literary figures of the Augustan period, such as James Boswell, Mary Wortley Montagu, Laurence Sterne, William Cowper, Jonathan Swift, Henry Fielding, Vicesimus Knox, and Charlotte Smith. Several essays usually address a single specific topic; vol. 7 (1996) contains five articles on Johnson and Jacobitism. Other features offer close readings of literary works; analyze sources, style, and techniques; and assess critical reputations and influence on the likes of Emerson and Virginia Woolf. A significant number of articles have addressed conditions of publication and authorship of the period. Vol. 6 (1994) is devoted to Johnson and America, containing papers from a 1993 symposium. Extensive selections of long reviews (often as many as 20) complete each volume. Volumes contain indexes. *Age of Johnson* is indexed in *MLA* and *MHRA*.

740. **Johnsonian News Letter**. New York: Columbia University, 1940-. Irregular. ISSN 0021-728x.

Although issues publish one or two significant scholarly articles (the latest focusing on editors of eighteenth-century literature), *Johnsonian News Letter* has been chiefly useful for its bibliographic coverage of works about Johnson and information of interest to scholars about conferences and other upcoming events. Common features include calls for papers, descriptions of conferences, and announcements of new publications and descriptions of research in progress, along with queries about research problems. A continuing bibliography, "Some Recent Books on Johnson," more recently titled "New Books and Articles on the Restoration and Eighteenth Century," reviews new books and articles on Johnson and other eighteenth-century writers and topics as well as briefly notes other works (books and articles) of interest. Additionally, "Precis of Articles on Johnson and Boswell" abstracts recent articles. The last published volume combining several issues, 52.2-4 (June, September, and December 1992) and 53.1-2 (March-June 1993), contains an apology from the editor for the journal's tardiness. Recent volumes of *Johnsonian News Letter* have not been indexed in either *MHRA* or *MLA*.

741. **New Rambler: Journal of the Johnson Society of London**. London: Johnson Society of London, 1941- . Annual. ISSN 0028-6540.

New Rambler publishes six to eight papers read at the society's annual meetings and as many as six occasional articles, book reviews, and notices for new publications. Papers and articles generally reflect biographical approaches to Johnson's life and works. Many have described Johnson's literary reputation and influence in his own and later times. *New Rambler* is unindexed.

742. **Transactions of the Samuel Johnson Society of the Northwest**. Calgary: University of Calgary, 1970-85. Annual. ISSN 0828-6515.

Sponsored by the Samuel Johnson Society of the Northwest, typical articles featured in this annual have focused on Johnson, his English and continental contemporaries, such as James Boswell, Sarah Fielding, and Denis Diderot, and the late eighteenth century in general. Typical articles included "*The Life of Savage* and Traditional Psychology" and "Boswell's Opinions Concerning Peculiarities of Dress." Volumes of *Transactions of the Samuel Johnson Society of the Northwest* through 1985 were indexed in *MLA*.

Patterson's *Author Newsletters and Journals*, pp. 169-72, describes other previously published journals for Johnson.

Samuel Johnson, 1822-1882
Bibliographies

For works by Johnson, see *First Printings of American Authors*, vol. 3, pp. 197-200. Johnson's manuscripts are listed in Robbins' *American Literary Manuscripts*, p. 172. Roger C. Mueller reviews research on Johnson in Myerson's *The Transcendentalists*, pp. 204-206.

Mary Johnston, 1870-1936
Bibliographies

743. Longest, George C. **Three Virginia Writers: Mary Johnston, Thomas Nelson Page, Amelie Rives Troubetzkoy: A Reference Guide**. Boston: G. K. Hall, 1978. 206p. (Reference Guide to Literature). LC 77-9566. ISBN 0-8161-7841-0.

Separate, chronologically arranged listings of writings about Johnston, Page, and Troubetzkoy, covering early reviews, newspaper features, scholarly books and articles, and dissertations. Coverage for Johnston extends from 1898 to 1976. Descriptive annotations. Separate name, title, and subject indexes. See *Bibliography of American Fiction, 1866-1918*, pp. 256-57, for Gwen L. Nagel's checklist of works by and about Johnston. Johnston's manuscripts are listed in Robbins' *American Literary Manuscripts*, p. 172.

Richard Malcolm Johnston, 1822-1898
Bibliographies

For works by Johnston, see *Bibliography of American Literature*, vol. 5, pp. 206-13. Reviews of Johnston's works and Johnston's contributions to selected periodicals are identified in Wells' *The Literary Index to American Magazines, 1850-1900*, pp. 227-28. Johnston's manuscripts are listed in Robbins' *American Literary Manuscripts*, pp. 172-73. See *Bibliography of American Fiction, 1866-1918*, pp. 258-59, for J. Arthur Bond's checklist of works by and about Johnston. L. Moody Simms, Jr., surveys works by and about Johnston in Bain and Flora's *Fifty Southern Writers Before 1900*, pp. 277-85.

David Michael Jones, 1895-1974
Bibliographies

744. Rees, Samuel. **David Jones: An Annotated Bibliography and Guide to Research**. New York: Garland, 1977. 97p. (Garland Reference Library of the Humanities, vol. 68). LC 76-24748. ISBN 0-8240-9929-X.

Covering works by and about Jones, Rees describes Jones' poetry, prose, published letters, recordings, and radio and television appearances. Entries identify reprintings and excerpts. In addition, Rees lists about 400 works about Jones, including critical books, periodical and newspaper articles and reviews, dissertations and theses, and passing references.

Henry Arthur Jones, 1851-1929
Bibliographies

For a bibliography of works by and about Jones, see *NCBEL*, III, pp. 1164-66.

James Jones, 1921-1977
Bibliographies

745. Hopkins, John R. **James Jones: A Checklist**. Detroit, MI: Gale, 1974. 67p. (Modern Authors Checklist Series/A Bruccoli Clark Book). LC 74-20824. ISBN 0-8103-0907-6.

Hopkins describes Jones' primary works, including his books, contributions to books and periodicals, interviews, and published letters. Entries give facsimiles of title pages, brief physical descriptions, and references to later printings and editions. Also for works by Jones, see *First Printings of American Authors*, vol. 1, pp. 193-95. Jones' manuscripts are listed in Robbins' *American Literary Manuscripts*, p. 173. Additional information on Jones' primary works is provided in Thomas J. Wood's *James Jones in Illinois: A Guide to the Handy Writers' Colony Collection in the Sangamon State University Library Archives* (Springfield, IL: Sangamon State University, 1989). See *Bibliography of American Fiction, 1919-1988*, pp. 269-70, for James R. Giles' checklist of works by and about Jones.

John Beauchamp Jones, 1810-1866
Bibliographies

For works by Jones, see *Bibliography of American Literature*, vol. 5, pp. 214-20. Jones' manuscripts are listed in Robbins' *American Literary Manuscripts*, p. 173. See *Bibliography of American Fiction Through 1865*, pp.155-56, for a checklist of works by and about Jones.

LeRoi Jones (Imamu Amiri Baraka), 1934-
Bibliographies

746.   Dace, Letitia. **LeRoi Jones (Imamu Amiri Baraka): A Checklist of Works by and About Him**. London: Nether Press, 1971. 196p. (Nether Press Bibliographies: Miscellaneous Series, no. 101). LC 72-181432.

Dace gives full bibliographic descriptions for Baraka's primary works, including books and pamphlets; contributions to books; contributions to periodicals (287 entries); anthologized reprints; and miscellaneous works, such as films adapted from his works and recordings. Entries give title-page transcriptions, contents, physical descriptions, publishing histories, and references to reviews. Also briefly describes special collections of Baraka's manuscripts and other materials in 14 institutional and private libraries, including major collections at Yale, Syracuse, and Indiana universities (pp. 87-88). In addition, Dace provides an unannotated list of about 1,000 works on Baraka in topical sections for biographies and general studies; Baraka and race, politics, and other subjects; Baraka as a poet and music critic; and works addressed to Baraka, among other subjects. Supplemental coverage of both works by and about Baraka is provided in King's *Ten Modern American Playwrights*, pp. 109-35. Also for works by Baraka, see *First Printings of American Authors*, vol. 1, pp. 197-207. Baraka's manuscripts are listed in Robbins' *American Literary Manuscripts*, p. 21. Research on Baraka is reviewed by Dace in Inge, Duke, and Bryer's *Black American Writers*, vol. 2, pp. 121-78; and Paul K. Jackson, Jr., in *Contemporary Authors: Bibliographical Series: Volume 3: American Dramatists*, pp. 49-68.

Madison Percy Jones, 1925-
Bibliographies

For works by Jones, see *First Printings of American Authors*, vol. 4, pp. 231-32. Jones' manuscripts are listed in Robbins' *American Literary Manuscripts*, p. 173.

Erica (Mann) Jong, 1942-
Bibliographies

For works by Jong, see *First Printings of American Authors*, vol. 1, p. 209. Bruce Henderson reviews works by and about Jong in Shapiro's *Jewish American Women Writers*, pp. 133-41.

Ben(jamin) Jonson, 1572/3-1637
Bibliographies

747.   Judkins, David C. **The Nondramatic Works of Ben Jonson: A Reference Guide**. Boston: G. K. Hall, 1982. 260p. (Reference Guides to Literature). LC 81-7257. ISBN 0-8161-8036-9.

No single comprehensive bibliography of criticism on Jonson now exists. Earlier bibliographies include volumes in the Tannenbaums' *Elizabethan Bibliographies*, vol. 4, and George Robert Guffey's *Elizabethan Bibliographies Supplements*, no. 3. More recently, D. Heyward Brock and James M. Welsh published *Ben Jonson: A Quadricentennial Bibliography, 1947-1972* (Metuchen, NJ: Scarecrow Press, 1974). Although restricted to the nondramatic poetry and prose, Judkins provides the widest coverage of Jonson criticism now available, including references to critical works published from 1615 through 1978. About 1,800 entries are chronologically arranged. Two thirds of the critical works were published since 1900. Annotations are largely concise and descriptive. Judkins also provides more extensive and evaluative reviews of significant critical works and does not hesitate to identify them as important, scholarly contributions or otherwise. Unfortunately, the subject indexing is nominal, largely limited to proper names and titles.

748.   Sarafinski, Dolores, Walter D. Lehrman, and Elizabeth Savage. **The Plays of Ben Jonson: A Reference Guide**. Boston: G. K. Hall, 1980. 311p. (Reference Guides to Literature). LC 80-22686. ISBN 0-8161-8112-8.
This guide identifies approximately 1,500 critical works published from 1911 to 1975 on Jonson's plays. The remaining dramatic works, Jonson's numerous masques and entertainments, are excluded. Arranged by formats and subjects, entries in the volume's first section cover book-length studies and collections of essays (as well as collected editions of Jonson's works). Sections follow for editions, criticism and commentaries, performance reviews, and so forth for the 18 plays. Concluding sections cover critical works on specific topics, such as Jonson's humor theory, influence and allusions, relations with Shakespeare and other contemporaries, and textual studies. An appendix lists dissertations. Extensive annotations, with citations for reviews of the book-length studies, are thoroughly descriptive and largely void of critical, scholarly evaluation. Excellent separate indexes reference authors and subjects, with the latter including references for the individual characters in the plays. Despite its limited scope, this is the most significant guide to Jonson scholarship. No full descriptive bibliography of Jonson's works now exists. For a bibliography of works by and about Jonson, see *NCBEL*, I, pp. 1655-73. H. L. Ford's *Collation of the Ben Jonson Folios, 1616-31—1640* (Oxford: Oxford University Press, 1932), also available in a reprinted edition (Folcroft, PA: Folcroft Press, 1969), describes variants of Jonson's early collected editions. Jonson's manuscripts are described in *Index of English Literary Manuscripts*, I, pt. 2:233-95, 630-31. Research on Jonson is reviewed by J. B. Bamborough in Wells' *English Drama*, pp. 54-68; and William L. Godshalk in Logan and Smith's *The New Intellectuals*, pp. 3-116.

Dictionaries, Encyclopedias, and Handbooks
749.   Brock, D. Heyward. **A Ben Jonson Companion**. Bloomington, IN: Indiana University Press, 1983. 307p. LC 81-48383. ISBN 0-2533-1159-4.
Brock's alphabetically arranged entries identify and detail Jonson's life and works. The most comprehensive entries are the plot summaries of Jonson's dramatic works, whose importance in the history of the English Renaissance stage is second only to those of Shakespeare. These analyses, however, provide little insight into the critical interest of the works and lack references to secondary studies. Additional entries are provided for Jonson's characters. For biographical information, this handbook is much more convenient than the existing biographies by Marchete Chute (1953) and by C. H. Herford and Percy and Evelyn Simpson in vol. I of *Ben Jonson* (Oxford: Clarendon Press, 1925). Brock's entries for Jonson's numerous personal and professional friends and enemies are most valuable. Brock is more selective in identifying and documenting Jonson's meticulous references to his beloved classical authorities. A thorough treatment of these

would have greatly enhanced the value of this handbook. A selected, unannotated bibliography of editions and book-length studies of Jonson concludes the volume. Coverage of streets, institutions, and other landmarks in Jonson's London is provided by Fran C. Chalfant's *Ben Jonson's London: A Jacobean Placename Dictionary* (Athens, GA: University of Georgia Press, 1978).

Indexes and Concordances

750. DiCesare, Mario A., and Ephim Fogel. **A Concordance to the Poems of Ben Jonson**. Ithaca, NY: Cornell University Press, 1978. 879p. (The Cornell Concordances). LC 78-59630. ISBN 0-8014-1217-X.

No concordances or indexes to Jonson's complete works or to any of his dramatic works have been published. This volume in the highly regarded Cornell Concordance series concords the texts in vol. VIII of the Herford and Simpson edition of Jonson's works, including the authoritative variant texts. Important features of Jonson's classical orthography, including Jonson's distinctive use of u/v initially and medially, are normalized. Several useful appendixes of indexed words by frequency and in alphabetical order, compound words ordered by second and third elements, words containing apostrophes in alphabetical order and ordered by second elements, and homographs conclude this index. Similarly, Steven L. Bates and Sidney D. Orr's *A Concordance to the Poems of Ben Jonson* (Athens, OH: Ohio University Press, 1978) concords Jonson's nondramatic English poetry, also based on the texts in Herford and Simpson's edition. A more specialized index of Jonson's language is Stagg's *The Figurative Language of the Tragedies of Shakespeare's Chief 17th-Century Contemporaries* (entry 229).

Journals

751. **Ben Jonson Journal: BJJ**. Reno, NV: University of Nevada Press, 1994-. Annual. ISSN 1079-3453.

Subtitled "Literary Contexts in the Age of Elizabeth, James, Charles," annual volumes of this new journal have featured as many as nine substantial articles. Contributions have focused on specific works of Jonson and his contemporaries, including Spenser, Marvell, Middleton, Donne, Milton, and Shakespeare, as well as on aspects of the Elizabethan and Stuart backgrounds. Bibliographic articles and other recent features of reference value include Neil Probst's "A Topical Index to Jonson's *Discoveries*," 3 (1996): 153-77. Additionally, the annual contains review essays and selections of reviews of new publications. *Ben Jonson Journal* is indexed in MLA.

Matthew Josephson, 1899-1978

Bibliographies

For works by Josephson, see *First Printings of American Authors*, vol. 1, pp. 211-13. Josephson's manuscripts are listed in Robbins' *American Literary Manuscripts*, p. 174.

James Augustine Aloysius Joyce, 1882-1941

Bibliographies

752. Deming, Robert H. **A Bibliography of James Joyce Studies**. 2d ed., revised and enlarged. Boston: G. K. Hall, 1977. 264p. (A Reference Publication in Literature). LC 77-9545. ISBN 0-8161-7969-7.

Deming arranges the most comprehensive listing of materials about Joyce by formats and subjects, including entries for some 5,500 books, articles, dissertations, reviews, recordings, musical settings, radio broadcasts, and dramatic adaptations in all languages published through 1973. This detailed arrangement is very convenient for identifying studies of such topics as Joyce and Faulkner, reviews of *Stephen Hero*, the censorship of *Ulysses* or studies of its individual episodes. Aside from listing contents (of essay collections and major works), annotations lack both descriptive and critical information. No subject indexing is included. Less comprehensive in scope, Thomas Jackson Rice's *James Joyce: A Guide to*

Research (New York: Garland, 1982) briefly but critically annotates entries for a selection of about 2,000 mostly English-language studies of Joyce published through 1981. Dissertations are excluded. Annotated coverage of dissertations is available in Tetsumaro Hayashi's *James Joyce: Research Opportunities and Dissertation Abstracts* (Jefferson, NC: McFarland, 1985).

753. Slocum, John J., and Herbert Cahoon. **A Bibliography of James Joyce, 1882-1941**. London: Rupert Hart-Davis, 1953. 195p. (The Soho Bibliographies, no. 5). LC 52-13968.

The standard guide to Joyce's primary works, this gives full bibliographic descriptions of his books and pamphlets, contributions to books, contributions to periodicals and newspapers, translations of Joyce's works (arranged by languages), manuscripts, musical settings, and miscellaneous materials (such as recordings, broadcasts, letters, and the like). Entries include title-page transcriptions, collations, pagination, binding descriptions, and brief information on publication histories. Coverage of Joyce's manuscripts is superseded by Michael Groden's *James Joyce's Manuscripts: An Index* (New York: Garland, 1980), which also serves as an index to Garland's *The James Joyce Archive* (1977-80), and is in turn updated by Groden's appendixed essay on Joyce's manuscripts in Zack Bowen and James F. Carens' *A Companion to Joyce Studies* (Westport, CT: Greenwood Press, 1984), pp. 783-85. Additional descriptive information for Joyce's primary works is available in various catalogs of Joyce materials in special collections, such as Arthur Mizener's *The Cornell Joyce Collection: Given to Cornell University by William G. Mennen* (Ithaca, NY: Cornell University Library, 1958); Robert E. Scholes' *The Cornell Joyce Collection: A Catalogue* (Ithaca, NY: Cornell University Press, 1961); and Steven Lund's *James Joyce: Letters, Manuscripts, and Photographs at Southern Illinois University* (Troy, NY: Whitston, 1983). Also useful is Thomas E. Connolly's *Personal Library of James Joyce: A Descriptive Bibliography*, 2d ed. (Buffalo, NY: University of Buffalo, 1957).

754. Staley, Thomas F. **An Annotated Critical Bibliography of James Joyce**. Brighton: Harvester Wheats, 1989. 182p. (Harvester Wheatsheaf Annotated Critical Bibliographies). LC 88-54011. ISBN 0-710-81012-1.

Staley offers excellent critical guidance to a topically arranged selection of about 600 of the most significant works about Joyce. Coverage includes bibliographies, biographies, source studies, general studies, and studies of poetry and minor works, and studies of *Dubliners, A Portrait of the Artist as a Young Man, Exiles, Ulysses,* and *Finnegans Wake.* Annotations identify major themes, focuses, and the like. No subject indexing. Also for a bibliography of works by and about Joyce, see *NCBEL,* IV, pp. 444-72. Research on Joyce is reviewed by A. Walton Litz in Dyson's *The English Novel,* pp. 349-69; and by Staley in Finneran's *Anglo-Irish Literature,* pp. 359-435.

Dictionaries, Encyclopedias, and Handbooks

755. Attridge, Derek. **The Cambridge Companion to James Joyce**. Cambridge: Cambridge University Press, 1990. 305p. LC 89-31421. ISBN 0-521-33014-9.

Intended more as a guide to reading and understanding Joyce than to identifying and interpreting specific features in his works, Attridge's companion addresses Joyce's Irish and continental sources, text, major individual works, feminism, and modernism, among other subjects. Bowen and Carens' *A Companion to Joyce Studies* (entry 753) is more a guide to research than a handbook, offering essays by different specialists who review the present state of research on textual, biographical, and critical problems and address opportunities for additional study of Joyce, with selective bibliographies. Aimed at undergraduates, William York Tindall's *A Reader's Guide to James Joyce* (New York: Farrar, Straus & Giroux, 1959; reprint Syracuse, NY: Syracuse University Press, 1995) provides interpretive chapters on Joyce's major works, including an episode-by-episode analysis of *Ulysses*. Tindall emphasizes such basic elements as plots, characters, settings, and themes. Similarly, Matthew Hodgart's *James Joyce: A Student's Guide* (London: Routledge & Kegan Paul, 1978) gives introductory commentaries on Joyce's major works. Limited to specific works, Tindall's *A Reader's Guide to Finnegans Wake* (New York: Farrar, Straus & Giroux, 1969) offers an episode-by-episode extended plot summary and informed reading of *Finnegans Wake*, cross-referenced by page and line to "every edition of the *Wake*, English, American, hardcover and paperback" (p. 3), while Joseph Campbell and Henry Morton Robinson's *A Skeleton Key to Finnegans Wake* (New York: Harcourt, Brace, 1944) traces the "fundamental narrative" structure of the work (p. x). Harry Blamires' *The Bloomsday Book: A Guide Through Joyce's Ulysses* (London: Methuen, 1970) provides similar analyses and readings for *Ulysses*, cross-referenced to the Bodley Head (1960) and New Random House (1961) editions. Similarly, Don Gifford and Robert J. Seidman's *Ulysses Annotated: Notes for James Joyce's Ulysses*, 2d ed. (Berkeley, CA: University of California Press, 1988); Weldon Thornton's *Allusions in Ulysses: An Annotated List* (Chapel Hill, NC: University of North Carolina Press, 1968); and Gifford's *Joyce Annotated: Notes for Dubliners and A Portrait of the Artist as a Young Man*, 2d ed. (Berkeley, CA: University of California Press, 1982) offer informed readings and explain Joyce's contemporary, historical, mythological, geographical, and autobiographical allusions. Jack McCarthy's *Joyce's Dublin: A Walking Guide to Ulysses* (Dublin: Wolfhound Press, 1986) offers even more specialized coverage of *Ulysses*, tracing the main routes of characters—"which characters took what paths in Dublin" (p. 6). John MacNicholas's *James Joyce's Exiles: A Textual Companion* (New York: Garland, 1979) provides "comprehensive information and commentary concerning the genesis, composition, and final authorial intention" in *Exiles* (p. xi).

756.   Benstock, Shari, and Bernard Benstock. **Who's He When He's at Home: A James Joyce Directory**. Urbana, IL: University of Illinois Press, 1980. 234p. LC 79-17947. ISBN 0-252-00756-5.

The Benstocks briefly identify and locate in Joyce's works more than 3,000 named and unnamed fictional, historical, mythical, animal, or inanimate characters or objects that are cited or otherwise alluded, referred, or "hallucinated" to, such as the boy in "Araby" and "the Nameless One" in "Cyclops." The guide is keyed to *Dubliners* (New York: Viking, 1967); *A Portrait of the Artist as a Young Man* (New York: Viking, 1964); *Exiles* (New York: Viking, 1951); *Stephen Hero*, 2d ed. revised (New York: New Directions, 1963); *Giacomo Joyce* (New York: Viking, 1968); and *Ulysses* (New York: Random House, 1961). Coverage excludes *Finnegans Wake*. A who's who for names appearing in this work is provided by Adaline Glasheen's encyclopedic *Third Census of Finnegans Wake: An Index of the Characters and Their Roles*, revised and expanded (Berkeley, CA: University of California, 1977), while Louis O. Mink's *A Finnegans Wake Gazetteer* (Bloomington, IN: Indiana University Press, 1978) identifies and explains nearly 8,000 place names appearing in this work. Roland McHugh's *Annotations to Finnegans Wake* (Baltimore, MD: Johns Hopkins University Press, 1980) offers line-by-line annotations to the text of *Finnegans Wake* (New York: Viking Press, 1945), supplementing information in these name dictionaries. David G. Wright's *Characters of Joyce* (Totowa, NJ: Barnes & Noble Books, 1983) gives additional, general coverage of names in Joyce's works.

757.   Fargnoli, A. Nicholas, and Michael Patrick Gillespie. **James Joyce A to Z: The Essential Reference to the Life and Work**. New York: Facts on File, 1995. 304p. LC 94-34660. ISBN 0-8160-2904-0.

Intended as a "clear and comprehensive companion to Joyce's works" for the "nonspecialist audience," Fargnoli and Gillespie emphasize "contextual and critical information of an introductory, wide-ranging, but not exhaustive, nature" (p. xi). Perhaps one half of the entries cover individual works, with the other half identifying real and fictional events, geographical locations, characters, and people; and ideas endorsed or manifested in Joyce's works (such as "parallax" and "Scholasticism"). Although entries cover each of Joyce's works, the most significant works receive the most substantial treatment. The *Finnegans Wake* entry extends 13 pages. A four-page entry for *Ulysses* reviews background, publication history, and structure, with a plot synopsis. Additionally, each of *Ulysses*'s 12 episodes receives detailed analysis in separate entries. Likewise, the entry for *Chamber Music* offers brief explications of each of the 36 constituent poems. The selection of fictional and historical people and places is rather eclectic, including both the expected (Molly Bloom, William Butler Yeats, Abbey Theatre, and Society of Jesus) and more curious: Fargnoli and Gillespie offer entries for such living Joyceans as Morris Beja and Thomas Staley; the "Gabler Edition" (of Hans Walter Gabler); Garland Publishing, Inc., which published the James Joyce Archives; and six journals devoted to Joyce. Although the cross-referenced entries are keyed to standard editions, no entries give bibliographic citations for relevant critical studies. Fargnoli and Gillespie also append a chronology of Joyce's writings and adaptations; a schema for the action in *Ulysses*, reproduced from Hugh Kenner's *Dublin's Joyce* (Bloomington, IN: Indiana University Press, 1956); a working outline for *Finnegans Wake*, reproduced from Bernard Benstock's *Joyce-Again's Wake* (Seattle, WA: University of Washington Press, 1965); a Joyce family tree; and a chronology of Joyce's life. Bibliographic appendixes identify Joyce journals and list works about Joyce (about 600 broadly classified, unannotated items). A comprehensive index offers detailed access to topics that are not the subjects of specific entries, such as "fatherhood," "narrative voice," and "sex and sexuality." Containing a sampling of just about everything possibly related to Joyce, Fargnoli and Gillespie's useful guide must nonetheless be supplemented by the several more comprehensive dictionaries of persons, places, things, allusions, and the like in Joyce.

Indexes and Concordances

758.　Anderson, Chester G. **A Word Index to James Joyce's Stephen Hero**. Ridgefield, CT: Ridgebury Press, 1958. 185p. LC 58-4937.

　　　Anderson indexes the text of the unrevised second edition (New York: New Directions, 1945).

759.　Bauerle, Ruth. **A Word List of James Joyce's Exiles**. New York: Garland, 1981. 217p. (Garland Reference Library of the Humanities, vol. 228). LC 80-4887. ISBN 0-8240-9500-6.

　　　Bauerle bases this index on the text of the 1951 (Harmondsworth: Penguin) edition of *Exiles*, with incorporated variants from manuscripts at Cornell University, and offers vocabulary and frequency listings, with additional alphabetical listing of words used 25 times or more.

760.　Doyle, Paul A. **A Concordance to the Collected Poems of James Joyce**. New York: Scarecrow Press, 1966. 218p. LC 66-13738.

　　　Doyle offers a word index to the texts of works included in *The Collected Poems* (New York: Viking, 1937), which includes *Chamber Music* (1907), *Poems Pennyeach* (1927), and *Ecce Puer* (1932), with two additional texts (originally published in broadside), *The Holy Office* (1904) and *Gas from a Burner* (1912), from *The Portable James Joyce* (New York: Viking, 1947).

761.　Fuger, Wilhelm. **Concordance to James Joyce's Dubliners: With a Reverse Index, a Frequency List, and a Conversion Table**. Hildesheim: Olms, 1980. 875p. LC 80-509693. ISBN 3-487-069504.

This KWIC-index is based on Robert Scholes' "Viking Compass Edition" (New York: Viking, 1967), with cross-references to the texts of the "Viking Critical Edition" (New York: Viking, 1969), the 1956 (Harmondsworth) Penguin edition, and the 1967 (London) Jonathan Cape edition. Gary Lane's *A Word Index to James Joyce's Dubliners* (New York: Haskell House, 1972) indexes the text of the 1968 (New York: Viking Press) edition. Additionally, Don Gifford's *Joyce Annotated: Notes for Dubliners and A Portrait of the Artist as a Young Man*, 2d ed. (Berkeley, CA: University of California Press, 1982) glosses difficult words, phrases, and passages in these works.

762.   Hancock, Leslie. **Word Index to James Joyce's Portrait of the Artist**. Carbondale, IL: Southern Illinois University Press, 1967. 145p. LC 67-13937.
    Hancock indexes the text of the 1964 (New York: Viking) edition.

763.   Hart, Clive. **A Concordance to Finnegans Wake**. Corrected edition. Mamaroneck, NY: Paul P. Appel, 1974. 516p. LC 73-80543.
    The most important resource for research on *Finnegans Wake*, this is a verbal index to 63,928 words occurring in Joyce's work, intended to "help the reader to trace the symbolic and thematic development of the intertwining verbal motifs out of which the book is constructed" (Introduction). Occurrences of some 141 common words are excluded. Arranged in three sections, the "Primary Index" references lines ("morphological fields"); the "Syllabifications" index alphabetically arranges inner elements of compound and portmanteau words; and the "Overtones" index lists English words suggested but "not orthographically present" in the text. The index is based on the text of the "first trade edition" (New York: Viking, 1945), "emended according to the 'Corrections of Misprints in *Finnegans Wake*.' " Additionally, Brendan O'Hehir and John M. Dillon's *A Classical Lexicon for Finnegans Wake: A Glossary of the Greek and Latin in the Major Works of Joyce Including Finnegans Wake, The Poems, Dubliners, Stephen Hero, A Portrait of the Artist as a Young Man, Exiles, and Ulysses* (Berkeley, CA: University of California, 1977) identifies and defines Greek and Latin phrases and variants in separate sections for *Finnegans Wake* and for Joyce's other works. Similarly, O'Hehir's *A Gaelic Lexicon for Finnegans Wake and Glossary for Joyce's Other Works* (Berkeley, CA: University of California Press, 1967) and Helmut Bonheim's *A Lexicon of the German in Finnegans Wake* (Berkeley, CA: University of California Press, 1967) cover other features of Joyce's vocabulary.

764.   Steppe, Wolfhard, and Hans Walter Gabler. **A Handlist to James Joyce's Ulysses: A Complete Alphabetical Index to the Critical Reading Text**. New York: Garland, 1985. 300p. (Garland Reference Library of the Humanities, vol. 582). LC 84-48862. ISBN 0-8240-8753-4.
    Steppe and Gabler provide an alphabetical index to all textual elements in Gabler, Steppe, and Claus Melchior's critical reading text of *Ulysses: A Critical and Synoptic Edition* (New York: Garland, 1984), including entries for separate and distinct words, letters, numerals, symbols, and the like in upper- and lowercases and in variant typefaces (italic, bold, and so forth). For example, Roman numeral "I," personal pronoun "I," and Italian article "i" are listed as distinct headwords. Also useful, Miles L. Hanley's *Word Index to James Joyce's Ulysses* (Madison, WI: University of Wisconsin Press, 1937) indexes the text of the 1934 (New York: Random House) edition. William M. Schutte's *Index of Recurrent Elements in James Joyce's Ulysses* (Carbondale, IL: Southern Illinois University Press, 1982), based on text of *Ulysses* (New York: Random House, 1961), cross-references all words (excluding proper names) in *Ulysses*. Weldon Thornton's *Allusions in Ulysses: An Annotated List* (Chapel Hill, NC: University of North Carolina Press, 1968) identifies and glosses names and phases, with page and line references to the 1961 and 1934 editions.

765.   Wall, Richard. **An Anglo-Irish Dialect Glossary for Joyce's Works**.
Syracuse, NY: Syracuse University Press, 1987. 131p. LC 86-30205. ISBN 0-8156-2399-2.
   The most complete guide to Joyce's Irish-English vocabulary, this identifies
and defines Anglo-Irish words and phrases used in Joyce's works, including
Stephen Hero (New York: New Directions, 1963), *Collected Poems* (New York: Viking
Press, 1957), *The Critical Writings of James Joyce* (New York: Viking Press, 1959), and
Richard Ellmann's edition of the *Selected Letters of James Joyce* (London: Faber and
Faber, 1975). Some of the allusions included, such as "Sinn Feiners," are obvious.
Others, such as "drisheens" (blood puddings) and "rossies" (brazen women) are
more obscure. An appendix cross-references pages and lines in the 1961 Random
House, 1984 Garland, and 1986 Bodley Head and Penguin editions of *Ulysses*.

Journals

766.   **A Finnegans Wake Circular**. Sandbach: Vincent Deane, editor, 1985-90.
4/yr. ISSN 0267-9612.
   A specialized, scholarly journal focusing exclusively on *Finnegans Wake*, this
attempted to replace *A Wake Newsletter* (1962-80). Typical features explicated and
interpreted allusions and passages in the work. *A Finnegans Wake Circular* was
selectively indexed in *MLA*.

767.   **James Joyce Broadsheet**. Leeds: James Joyce Broadsheet, University of
Leeds, 1980-. 3/yr. ISSN 0143-6333.
   James Joyce Broadsheet is one of several newsletters designed to provide
current information about conferences, research activities, and publications related to Joyce. Usually consisting of four broadside pages, *James Joyce Broadsheet*
substantially contains reviews of new publications about Joyce as well as information on upcoming symposia and conferences. Other departments supply accounts of conference papers and news about the activities of the numerous
international Joyce associations and their members. Letters and queries about
research problems are also published. *James Joyce Broadsheet* is unindexed.

768.   **James Joyce Literary Supplement**. Coral Gables, FL: University of Miami,
1987-. 2/yr. ISSN 0899-3114.
   James Joyce Literary Supplement features an extensive selection of reviews (often
as many as 20) of new publications about Joyce and occasionally his contemporaries
as well as notes and announcements for conferences, new publications, and programs
related to Joyce. *James Joyce Literary Supplement* is unindexed.

769.   **James Joyce Newestlatter**. Columbus, OH: International James Joyce Foundation, 1989-. 2/yr. OCLC 21957111.
   Formerly *James Joyce Foundation Newsletter* (1969-88), the eight to 12 page folded
newsletter provides detailed coverage of Joyce conferences, symposia, and other
programs, both past and future, in addition to information about new publications
(especially electronic sources) and society membership. The International James Joyce
Foundation maintains an Internet home page that links to electronic versions of the
James Joyce Newestlatter: http://www.cohums.ohio-state.edu/english/organiza-
tions/ijjf/. The *James Joyce Newestlatter* is unindexed.

770.   **James Joyce Quarterly**. Tulsa, OK: University of Tulsa, 1963- . 4/yr. ISSN
0021-4183.
   Close readings and interpretations of Joyce's works, explications of allusions
and images, analyses of literary relations and influences, and similar studies are
the standard fare in the five to six featured articles and various briefer notes
presented in *James Joyce Quarterly*, the most prestigious of Joyce journals. The
journal rejects "over three times" as many articles as it publishes. Representative

articles are *"Ulysses,* Chaos, and Complexity" and "The Gender of Travel in 'The Dead.' " Other articles have compared or related Joyce to Milton, Richard Wagner, Paul Claudel, Nietzsche, Pater, T. S. Eliot, Goethe, and Edouard Dujardin, among other writers, artists, and thinkers. The journal also publishes many textual, editorial, and bibliographic studies, including Ira B. Nadel's " 'Forget-Me-Not': Joycean Bibliography," 32.2 (Winter 1995): 243-59, which reviews the state of Joyce's primary and secondary bibliography. Equally significant is *James Joyce Quarterly's* important, regular bibliographic feature, "Current JJ Checklist," compiled by William S. Brockman of the University of Illinois at Urbana-Champaign, which offers comprehensive, international coverage of new editions of primary works and secondary materials of all varieties, including references to theatrical productions, musical settings, recordings, and the like. Occasional special issues (often double) focus on specific topics, such as Joyce and homosexuality in 31.3 (Spring 1994). The editor's "Preparatory to Anything Else" provides information on the activities of the Joyce Society, ongoing projects, highlights of the annual Bloomsday, and other announcements of interest to scholars and readers. Reviews (six or more) of recent publications, occasional review essays, and letters to the editor are also included. Amy M. Alt provides a 30-year index to vols. 1-30 of *James Joyce Quarterly* in 32.2 (Winter 1995): 261-437. *James Joyce Quarterly* is indexed in *AES, AHI, A&HCI, HI, MHRA,* and *MLA.*

771.   **Joyce Studies Annual**. Austin, TX: University of Texas, 1990-. Annual. ISSN 1049-0809.

Substantial, well-documented close readings and investigations of particular themes and other elements of Joyce's works, with a few briefer notes (often on textual or editorial questions), are the norm in *Joyce Studies Annual*. Occasional bibliographic features update standard guides and describe special collections for Joyce, including Richard B. Watson and Randolph Lewis' "The Joyce Calendar: A Chronological Listing of Unpublished and Ungathered Letters by James Joyce," 3 (1992): 141-79; and William Brockman's " 'Catalogue These Books': Joyce Bibliographies, Checklists, Catalogs, and Desiderata," 4 (1993): 119-36. Volume prefaces by editor Thomas F. Staley consistently identify Joyce collections and projects. Volumes through vol. 6 (1995) include an "Annual James Joyce Checklist," an unannotated listing of editions, criticism, and miscellaneous works, such as theatrical and media productions, electronic resources, and other materials related to Joyce. Volumes do not contain indexes. *Joyce Studies Annual* is indexed in *MLA.*

Wortman's *Guide to Serial Bibliographies for Modern Literatures,* p. 264, identifies other serial bibliographies for Joyce. Patterson's *Author Newsletters and Journals,* pp. 172-76, describes other previously published journals for Joyce.

Samuel B(enjamin) H(elbert) Judah, 1804-1876
Bibliographies

For works by Judah, see *Bibliography of American Literature,* vol. 5, pp. 221-33. Judah's manuscripts are listed in Robbins' *American Literary Manuscripts,* p. 174.

Sylvester Judd, 1813-1853
Bibliographies

For works by Judd, see *Bibliography of American Literature,* vol. 5, pp. 224-27. Judd's manuscripts are listed in Robbins' *American Literary Manuscripts,* p. 174. See *Bibliography of American Fiction Through 1865,* pp.156-57, for a checklist of works by and about Judd. Wells' *The Literary Index to American Magazines, 1815-1865,* p. 88; and *The Literary Index to American Magazines, 1850-1900,* p. 228, identifies comments and reviews for Judd in selected periodicals. Francis B. Dedmond reviews research on Judd in Myerson's *The Transcendentalists,* pp. 207-10.

Judith, late 9th century
Bibliographies

Greenfield and Robinson's *A Bibliography of Publications on Old English Literature to the End of 1972*, pp. 239-41, lists editions, translations, and studies of the Old English *Judith*, with citations for reviews.

Julian of Norwich, c. 1342-after 1416
Bibliographies

Ritamary Bradley gives comprehensive information about primary materials for Julian of Norwich with a bibliography of editions and criticism in Valerie M. Lagorio and Michael G. Sargent's "English Mystical Writings" in Severs and Hartung's *A Manual of the Writings in Middle English*, vol. XXIII, pp. 3082-84, 3438-444. Lagorio and Bradley's *The 14th-Century English Mystics* (entry 1143) covers twentieth-century criticism. Also for a bibliography of works by and about Dame Julian, see *NCBEL*, I, pp. 522-23. Edwards' *Middle English Prose*, pp. 97-108, includes a review of research on Julian of Norwich by Christina Von Nolcken.

"Junius," fl.1769-1772
Bibliographies

772.   Cordasco, Francesco. **Junius: A Bibliography of the Letters of Junius: With a Checklist of Junian Scholarship and Related Studies**. Fairview, NJ: Junius-Vaughn Press, 1986. 253p. LC 86-10697. ISBN 0-9401-9804-5.

Part I is an extensive introduction giving historical and political background and a survey of the Junian text. Part II provides separate, chronologically arranged listings of annotated entries for bibliographic resources, including general bibliographies and reference works, textual studies and bibliographical notes, and collections of Juniana; editions of the letters; and Junian scholarship and related studies (more than 400 entries). Entries for 184 editions note copy locations and bibliographic contents and significance. Coverage of critical works extends from 1790 to 1987, including anonymous reviews and notices in contemporary periodicals and dissertations. Appendixes list persons to whom letters have been attributed and about 100 selected works on historical and political background; and indexes articles on "Junius" featured in *Notes and Queries* from 1849-1915. Index of proper names and titles. Also for a bibliography of works by and about "Junius" by John Barnard, see *NCBEL*, II, pp. 1178-83.

Roger Kahn, 1927-
Bibliographies

For works by Kahn, see *First Printings of American Authors*, vol. 4, pp. 233-35.

MacKinlay Kantor, 1904-1977
Bibliographies

See *Bibliography of American Fiction, 1919-1988*, pp. 271-72, for Wilton Eckley's checklist of works by and about Kantor. Kantor's manuscripts are listed in Robbins' *American Literary Manuscripts*, p. 175.

Patrick Kavanagh, 1905-1967
Bibliographies

773.   Allison, Jonathan. **Patrick Kavanagh: A Reference Guide**. New York: G. K. Hall, 1996. 218p. (A Reference Guide to Literature). LC 96-29255. ISBN 0-8161-7286-2.

Chronologically arranged, brief, descriptively annotated entries for approximately 1,500 international works about Kavanagh published from 1935 to 1995, including books, introductions and selections in editions, chapters, journal and newspaper articles, reviews, letters to editors, dissertations, and radio and television broadcasts. Introduction surveys research on Kavanagh and identifies significant studies. Includes checklist of Kavanagh's major publications. Allison relies on newspaper files in the Kavanagh Archive at University College Dublin, Kavanagh files of *The Irish Times*, and sound archives of the BBC Northern Ireland and RTE Dublin. Separate indexes of critics and subjects. Peter Kavanagh's *Patrick Kavanagh: Man and Poet* (Orono, ME: National Poetry Foundation, University of Maine, 1986), pp. 425-86, also identifies works by and about Kavanagh. Mary M. Fitzgerald reviews research on Kavanagh in "Modern Poetry" in Finneran's *Recent Research on Anglo-Irish Writers*, pp. 299-334.

John B. Keane, 1928-
Bibliographies

King's *Ten Modern Irish Playwrights*, pp. 55-63, gives brief bibliographic information for Keane's primary works and annotated entries for criticism of Keane, with a classified list of reviews. Sr. Marie Hubert Kealy surveys works by and about Keane in Schrank and Demastes' *Irish Playwrights, 1880-1995: A Research and Production Sourcebook*, pp. 135-44.

John Keats, 1795-1821
Bibliographies

774. Green, David Bonnell, and Edwin Graves Wilson. **Keats, Shelley, Byron, Hunt, and Their Circles: A Bibliography: July 1, 1950-June 30, 1962.** Lincoln, NE: University of Nebraska Press, 1964. 323p. LC 64-15181.

This reprints the first 12 annual bibliographies originally published in *Keats-Shelley Journal* (entry 779) and provides a cumulative index. Offering briefly annotated entries (with references to reviews), coverage includes about 5,000 editions, reprints, translations, and similar primary materials, as well as critical materials published in books, articles, and dissertations. It is supplemented by:

774.1. Hartley, Robert A. **Keats, Shelley, Byron, Hunt, and Their Circles: A Bibliography, July 1, 1962-December 31, 1974.** Lincoln, NE: University of Nebraska Press, 1978. 487p. LC 78-16118. ISBN 0-8032-0960-6.

Reprints and indexes annual bibliographies originally published in vols. 13 to 25 of the *Keats-Shelley Journal*. Annotated entries for about 6,000 items are included. Cumulative indexes in both volumes reference names (Shakespeare, Milton, and the like) cited in entries. Ronald B. Hearn's *Keats Criticism Since 1954: A Bibliography* (Salzburg: Institut fur Anglistik und Amerikanistik, Universitat Salzburg, 1981) is a supplementary unannotated and unindexed list of about 600 books, articles, and dissertations about Keats. Research on Keats is reviewed by Robert Gittings in Dyson's *English Poetry*, pp. 251-64; and by Jack Stillinger in Frank Jordan's *The English Romantic Poets: A Review of Research and Criticism*, pp. 665-720.

775. MacGillivray, J. R. **Keats: A Bibliography and Reference Guide with an Essay on Keats' Reputation.** Toronto: University of Toronto Press, 1949. 210p. (Department of English Studies and Texts, no. 3). LC 50-12098.

The standard guide to Keats' primary materials, this gives full bibliographic descriptions for Keats' separate, selected, and collected poems, letters, and prose; contributions to periodicals; and contributions to anthologies; as well as describes the full range of ana, including contemporary reviews and early notices, translations of Keats' works, fiction and drama about Keats, and biographical and critical works about Keats. Entries for primary works include title-page transcriptions, collations, physical descriptions, and contents. Available in a reprinted edition (Toronto: University of Toronto Press, 1968). MacGillivray's comprehensive coverage of secondary materials is updated by Green and Wilson's cumulations (entry 774). For a bibliography of works by and about Keats, see *NCBEL*, III, pp. 344-56. Keats' manuscripts are described in *Index of English Literary Manuscripts*, IV, pt. 2:329. Many are reproduced in Garland's "The Manuscripts of the Younger Romantics" series, including *Endymion: A Facsimile of the Revised Holograph Manuscript* (New York: Garland, 1985), edited by Jack Stillinger. Also useful for research on Keats' primary materials is Frank N. Owing's *Keats' Library: A Descriptive Catalogue* (London: Keats-Shelley Memorial Association, 1978).

776.　Rhodes, Jack Wright. **Keats's Major Odes: An Annotated Bibliography of Criticism**. Westport, CT: Greenwood Press, 1984. 224p. LC 83-16634. ISBN 0-313-23809-X.

Rhodes provides solid access to criticisms of the most frequently read works of Keats. He chronologically arranges annotated entries for more than 700 English-language critical studies of Keats' odes, including early anonymous reviews and notices and dissertations, published from 1820 through 1980. Significant works receive extended descriptions. A separate subject index offers headings for such topics as "beauty," "nature," "truth," and other familiar themes.

Indexes and Concordances

777.　Becker, Michael G., Robert J. Dilligan, and Todd K. Bender. **A Concordance to the Poems of John Keats**. New York: Garland, 1981. 719p. (Garland Reference Library of the Humanities, vol. 137). LC 78-68264. ISBN 0-8240-9807-2.

The concordance is based on Jack Stillinger's edition of *The Poems of John Keats* (Cambridge: Harvard University Press, 1978), with incorporated manuscript variants. Alphabetical and ranked word frequency lists are appended. This is a most authoritative concordance of Keats' poetry, superseding Dane Lewis Baldwin, Leslie Nathan Broughton, Laura Cooper Evans, John William Hebel, Benjamin F. Steller, and Mary Rebecca Thayer's *A Concordance to the Poems of John Keats* (Washington, DC: The Carnegie Institution, 1971), which concords the text of Harry Buxton Forman's *The Complete Poetical Works of John Keats* (London: Oxford University Press, 1910), also referred to as the "Oxford edition."

778.　Pollard, David. **A KWIC Concordance to the Letters of John Keats**. Hove, East Sussex: Geraldson Imprints, 1989. 408p. ISBN 0-9514-4990-7.

Based on Hyder E. Rollins' edition of *The Letters of John Keats* (Cambridge: Harvard University Press, 1958), with cross-references to H. Buxton Forman's "Hampstead Edition" of *The Poeltical* [sic] *and Other Works of John Keats* (New York: Phaeton, 1970) and Frederick Page's *Letter* [sic] *of John Keats* (London: Oxford University Press, 1965).

Journals

779.　**Keats-Shelley Journal: Keats, Shelley, Byron, Hunt, and Their Circles**. New York: Keats-Shelley Association of America, 1952-. Annual. ISSN 0453-4387.

Sponsored by the Keats-Shelley Association of America, *Keats-Shelley Journal* annually features nearly a dozen substantial articles on the major English Romantics and the full range of their contemporaries. Typical contributions include "Keats and the Spiritual Economics of Gift Exchange," "The Evolution of the Surface Self: Byron's Poetic Career," and "An Early Response to Shelley's *The Necessity of Atheism*." Other articles offer close readings of specific works, evaluate sources, describe manuscripts, and focus on language and style. Vol. 42 (1993), devoted to Shelley, contained bibliographic reviews of studies of Shelley in Japan. In addition to six major articles, issues publish brief topical notes, news on society members and other scholars, accounts of meetings and conferences, notes on ana, and reviews of new publications, with particular attention to new editions. Of particular importance, the journal's annual "Current Bibliography" briefly describes editions of works by and studies about the writers of the Romantic period. Vol. 45 (1996) omits the annual bibliography for 1996 because of "circumstances beyond our control" but notes its availability upon completion on *Keats-Shelley Journal*'s WWW home page: http://www.luc.edu/publications/keats-shelley/ksjweb.htm. The 1996 bibliography is to be included in the 1997 issue of the journal. A major journal for the study and bibliography of the Romantic period, *Keats-Shelley Journal* is indexed in *AES, MHRA,* and *MLA.*

Patterson's *Author Newsletters and Journals*, pp. 177-79, describes other previously published journals for Keats.

780. **Keats-Shelley Review.** Windsor, Berks: Keats-Shelley Memorial Association, 1910-. Annual. ISSN 0453-4395.

Formerly *Keats-Shelley Memorial Bulletin* (1910-85), issues of *Keats-Shelley Review* publish four to six substantial articles, brief notes, and as many as a dozen reviews of new publications about the lives and works of Keats and Shelley, as well as those of members of their circle, including George Gordon Byron, Thomas Love Peacock, William Hazlitt, William Godwin, Mary Wollstonecraft, Leigh Hunt, and Walter Scott. Contributions present close readings of works; analyses and interpretations of sources, themes, images, language, and ideas; and discussions of biographical problems and information. Occasional literature reviews are also featured, such as Andrew Nicholson's "Recent Studies of Byron," 5 (1990): 118-28. Volumes for the early 1990s also included calendars of events related to anniversaries of Keats and Shelley, with 10 (1996) being a Keats "Bicentennial Issue." *Keats-Shelley Review* is indexed in *MHRA* and *MLA.*

Clarence Budington Kelland, 1881-1964
Bibliographies

See *Bibliography of American Fiction, 1866-1918,* pp. 259-61, for Beverly Brummett Klatt's checklist of works by and about Kelland. Kelland's manuscripts are listed in Robbins' *American Literary Manuscripts*, p. 175.

Edith Summers Kelley, 1884-1956
Bibliographies

For works by Kelley, see *First Printings of American Authors*, vol. 1, p. 215. See *Bibliography of American Fiction, 1919-1988,* p. 272, for Matthew J. Bruccoli's checklist of works by and about Kelley.

William Melvin Kelley, 1937-
Bibliographies

For works by Kelley, see *First Printings of American Authors*, vol. 2, p. 225.

Walt Kelly, 1913-1973
Bibliographies

For works by Kelly, see *First Printings of American Authors*, vol. 4, pp. 237-45.

Margery Kempe, c. 1373-c. 1439
Bibliographies

Valerie M. Lagorio and Michael G. Sargent offer a comprehensive guide to the primary materials of Kempe and other English mystics with a bibliography of editions and criticism in Severs and Hartung's *A Manual of the Writings in Middle English,* vol. XXIII, pp. 3049-3137, 3405-71. Also for a bibliography of works by and about Kempe, see *NCBEL,* I, p. 524. Lagorio and Bradley's *The 14th-Century English Mystics* (entry 1143) describes modern criticism. Edwards' *Middle English Prose* includes a review of research on Margery Kempe by John C. Hirsh (pp. 109-20).

Adrienne Kennedy, 1931-
Bibliographies

Lois More Overbeck reviews research on Kennedy in *Contemporary Authors: Bibliographical Series: Volume 3: American Dramatists*, pp. 109-24.

John Pendleton Kennedy, 1795-1870
Bibliographies

For works by Kennedy, see *Bibliography of American Literature*, vol. 5, pp. 228-42. Contributions by Kennedy and criticism and reviews of Kennedy's works in selected periodicals are identified in Wells' *The Literary Index to American Magazines, 1815-1865*, pp. 89-90; and *The Literary Index to American Magazines, 1850-1900*, p. 229. Kennedy's manuscripts are listed in Robbins' *American Literary Manuscripts*, pp. 177-78. See *Bibliography of American Fiction Through 1865*, pp.158-59, for a checklist of works by and about Kennedy. David O. Tomlinson surveys works by and about Kennedy in Bain and Flora's *Fifty Southern Writers Before 1900*, pp. 286-95.

William Kennedy, 1928-
Bibliographies

See *Bibliography of American Fiction, 1919-1988*, p. 273, for Mark Busby's checklist of works by and about Kennedy. See Elise Miller's summary biography, critical assessment of major works, and selected primary and secondary bibliography for Kennedy in McCaffery's *Postmodern Fiction: A Bio-Bibliographical Guide*, pp. 424-27.

X. J. Kennedy, 1929-
Bibliographies

For works by Kennedy, see *First Printings of American Authors*, vol. 2, pp. 227-28. Kennedy's manuscripts are listed in Robbins' *American Literary Manuscripts*, p. 178.

Jack Kerouac, 1922-1969
Bibliographies

781.   Charters, Ann. **A Bibliography of Works by Jack Kerouac (Jean Louis Lebris De Kerouac) 1939-1975.** Revised ed. New York: Phoenix Bookshop, 1975. 136p. (The Phoenix Bibliographies, no. 4). LC 75-30147. ISBN 0-9162-2806-1.

Charters offers full bibliographic descriptions for Kerouac's books, pamphlets, and broadsides; contributions to books; contributions to periodicals; translations of Kerouac's works (arranged by languages); recordings; musical settings; and interviews and articles containing quotations. Entries give title-page transcriptions, physical descriptions, and brief publishing histories, with supporting excerpts from correspondence and other documents. Also for works by Kerouac, see *First Printings of American Authors*, vol. 1, pp. 217-19. Kerouac's manuscripts are listed in Robbins' *American Literary Manuscripts*, p. 178.

782.   Milewski, Robert J. **Jack Kerouac: An Annotated Bibliography of Secondary Sources, 1944-1979.** Metuchen, NJ: Scarecrow Press, 1981. 225p. (Scarecrow Author Bibliographies, no. 52). LC 80-24477. ISBN 0-8108-1378-5.

Milewski provides (for the most part) briefly annotated entries in separate listings for about 800 ana, reviews, critical studies, and other works about Kerouac. Coverage includes English-language reviews of Kerouac's works (arranged by works); film adaptations of Kerouac's works, with references to film reviews; general studies of Kerouac in all languages, including dissertations and master's theses; interviews; parodies and imitations of Kerouac's works; bibliographies; reviews of works about Kerouac; and music, fiction, poetry, plays, and other creative works influenced by Kerouac. The index provides topical access under Kerouac and individual works. See *Bibliography of American Fiction, 1919-1988*, pp. 274-77, for William M. Gargan's checklist of works by and about Kerouac.

Journals

783. **Moody Street Irregulars: A Jack Kerouac Newsletter.** Clarence Center, NY: Moody Street Irregulars, 1978-. Irregular (2 or 3/yr.). ISSN 0196-2604.

Most recently subtitled "A Jack Kerouac Magazine," *Moody Street Irregulars* features a dozen or more biographical and critical contributions dealing with Kerouac and his contemporaries (such as John Clellon Holmes, Kenneth Rexroth, and Carolyn Cassady) as well as an equally wide selection of poems dedicated to or inspired by Kerouac. Typical articles are "Women Writers in the Beat Generation" and "Kerouac the 'Endless' Poet." Occasional bibliographic contributions include Michael Basinski's "John Montgomery—A Remembrance and A Report," 28 (Fall 1994): 27, describing Montgomery materials in the Poetry/Rare Books Collection at the State University of New York at Buffalo; and John Budan's "The Ultimate Kerouac Reading Experience," 18-19 (Fall 1987): 21-22, relating information about Kerouac materials in the University of Texas' Humanities Research Center. Other regular departments include reviews of new publications on modern American poetry and notes, queries, and announcements about services, publications, conferences, and the like of use to individuals interested in modern poetry. *Moody Street Irregulars* is indexed in *MLA*.

Ken Kesey, 1935-
Bibliographies

For works by Kesey, see *First Printings of American Authors*, vol. 1, p. 221. Kesey's manuscripts are listed in Robbins' *American Literary Manuscripts*, p. 178. See *Bibliography of American Fiction, 1919-1988*, pp. 278-80, for M. Gilbert Porter's checklist of works by and about Kesey. Robert Frank surveys works by and about Kesey in Erisman and Etulain's *Fifty Western Writers*, pp. 246-56.

Francis Scott Key, 1779-1843
Bibliographies

For works by Key, see *Bibliography of American Literature*, vol. 5, pp. 243-51. Key's manuscripts are listed in Robbins' *American Literary Manuscripts*, p. 179.

John Oliver Killens, 1916-1987
Bibliographies

For works by Killens, see *First Printings of American Authors*, vol. 2, p. 229. Killens' manuscripts are listed in Robbins' *American Literary Manuscripts*, p. 179. See *Bibliography of American Fiction, 1919-1988*, p. 281, for William H. Wiggins, Jr.'s checklist of works by and about Killens.

(Alfred) Joyce Kilmer, 1886-1918
Bibliographies

For works by Kilmer, see *Bibliography of American Literature*, vol. 5, pp. 252-59. Kilmer's manuscripts are listed in Robbins' *American Literary Manuscripts*, p. 179.

Thomas Kilroy, 1934-
Bibliographies

King's *Ten Modern Irish Playwrights*, pp. 65-69, gives brief bibliographic information for Kilroy's primary works and annotated entries for criticism of Kilroy, with a classified list of reviews.

Richard Burleigh Kimball, 1816-1892

Bibliographies

See *Bibliography of American Fiction Through 1865*, p. 160, for a checklist of works by and about Kimball. Contributions by Kimball and criticism and reviews of Kimball's works in selected periodicals are identified in Wells' *The Literary Index to American Magazines, 1815-1865*, pp. 90-91; and *The Literary Index to American Magazines, 1850-1900*, p. 230. Kimball's manuscripts are listed in Robbins' *American Literary Manuscripts*, p. 179.

Grace Elizabeth King, 1851-1932

Bibliographies

See *Bibliography of American Fiction, 1866-1918*, pp. 261-62, for Anne Pizziferri's checklist of works by and about King. King's contributions to and reviews of King's works in selected periodicals are identified in Wells' *The Literary Index to American Magazines, 1850-1900*, pp. 230-31. King's manuscripts are listed in Robbins' *American Literary Manuscripts*, p. 180. David Kirby surveys works by and about King in Bain and Flora's *Fifty Southern Writers Before 1900*, pp. 296-302.

Henry King, 1592-1669

Bibliographies

For a bibliography of works by and about King, see *NCBEL*, I, p. 1199. King's manuscripts are described in *Index of English Literary Manuscripts*, II, pt. 1:587-645. McCarron and Shenk's *Lesser Metaphysical Poets*, pp. [28]-29, covers criticism of King from 1960 through 1980.

Stephen King, 1947-

Bibliographies

784. Collings, Michael R. **The Work of Stephen King: An Annotated Bibliography & Guide.** San Bernardino, CA: Borgo Press, 1996. 480p. (Bibliographies of Modern Authors, no. 25). LC 93-16091. ISBN 0-8095-1520-7.

Although a thorough revision and vast improvement of Colling's earlier slim and unindexed *The Annotated Guide to Stephen King: A Primary and Secondary Bibliography of the Works of America's Premier Horror Writer* (Mercer Island, WA: Starmont House, 1986), as with other volumes in Borgo's series this one tries to pack in much that is self-promoting and only marginally valuable for research. International in scope and identifying works by and about King generally through 1994, Collings' guide provides chronologically arranged sections for King's book-length and collected fiction, short fiction, short nonfiction (including contributed introductions, forewords, letters, criticism, and reviews), poetry, screenplays, public and screen appearances, video adaptations, and audio adaptations. Entries for King's 50 books through *Los Langoliers* (New York: Signet, 1995) give brief bibliographic information, plot summaries, and critical comments for first and subsequent editions, translations, and reprintings, with references to critical studies and reviews. In general, all other entries indicate contents, note other appearances, and cite relevant reviews. Listings of reviews of video and audio adaptations are particularly extensive. In the second part, Collings attempts to organize a diverse range of works about King in sections for book-length studies (including 17 dissertations); newsletters; bibliographies and filmographies; profiles and bio-bibliographic sketches; interviews; scholarly articles (some 273 entries); articles in popular and news magazines; media and specialty magazines and fanzines; *Castle Rock: The Stephen King Newsletter* (1985-89); newspaper articles; articles in professional and trade journals; selected reviews of King's works; the Stephen King Archives of the University of Maine, Orono; unpublished works; parodies, pastiches, etc.; honors and awards; and miscellanea. Generally, all entries for secondary works are briefly and descriptively annotated. Entries for 45 books about King identify their reviews. Includes detailed chronology of King's life and works and selected quotations from criticism. Separate indexes for King's works, works about King, and names of critics.

Dictionaries, Encyclopedias, and Handbooks

785. Beahm, George. **The Stephen King Companion**. Kansas City, MO: Andrews and McMeel, 1995. 311p. LC 95-23170. ISBN 0-8362-0455-7.

A revision of Beahm's *The Stephen King Companion* (Kansas City, MO: Andrews and McMeel, 1989), the volume is aimed more at the fan than the scholar. Offering little bibliographic information, Beahm's revised companion provides plot summaries of King's works through *Insomnia* (1994). The 1989 edition, by comparison, gave basic bibliographic information about works by and about King, including media adaptations of his works, with brief information about primary materials in the Stephen King Collection of the University of Maine at Orono (pp. 297-300).

786. Spignesi, Stephen J. **The Shape Under the Sheet: The Complete Stephen King Encyclopedia: The Definitive Guide to the Works of America's Master of Horror**. Ann Arbor, MI: Popular Culture, Ink, 1991. 780p. LC 91-61010. ISBN 1-56075-018-9.

Part guide, dictionary, bibliography, and index, Spignesi's hefty volume suffers from disorganization likely reflecting the volume's many purposes. In addition to information on King's life and career, readership, filmed and recorded versions of his works, and unfinished works and works in progress, the core (or perhaps, cores) of Spignesi's work are separate lists of people, places, and things, with identifying information, for each published and unpublished work. A series of cumulative indexes is buried near the end of the volume (pp. 650-69). Also includes a bibliography of 27 books and articles about King (pp. 673-75).

William King, 1663-1712
Bibliographies

For a bibliography of works by and about King, see *NCBEL*, II, pp. 1046-47.

King Horn, c. 1225
Indexes and Concordances

787. Saito, Toshio, Mitsunori Imai, and Kunihiro Miki. **A Concordance to Middle English Metrical Romances**. Frankfurt am Main: Verlag Peter Lang, 1988. 2 vols. LC 88-19122. ISBN 3-8204-1196-8.

Vol. I concords works comprising "The Matter of England": *King Horn, Havelok the Dane, Athelston,* and *Gamelyn*. Vol. II concords "The Breton Lays": *Sir Degare, Sir Orfeo, Sir Launfal, The Earl of Toulouse, Emare, Lay le Freine,* and *Sir Gowther*. Copytext for all (with two exceptions) is Walter Hoyt French and Charles Brockway Hale's *Middle English Metrical Romances* (1930; New York: Russell & Russell, 1964). The text of *Lay le Freine* is based on Donald Sands' *Middle English Verse Romances* (New York: Holt, Rinehart and Winston, 1966). *Sir Gowther* is based on Maldwyn Mills' *Six Middle English Romances* (1973; London: Dent, 1982). Includes appended, cumulative word indexes and frequency lists as well as frequency lists for each individual work.

Charles Kingsley, 1819-1875
Bibliographies

788. Harris, Styron. **Charles Kingsley: A Reference Guide**. Boston: G. K. Hall, 1981. 163p. (A Reference Guide to Literature). LC 80-39701. ISBN 0-8161-8166-7.

Harris provides a chronologically arranged listing of briefly annotated entries for about 600 writings about Kinglsey, including early anonymous reviews and notices, books, journal and newspaper articles, and dissertations, published from 1848 through 1978. Coverage includes selected non-English-language materials. Annotations are descriptive. Subject indexing is limited to a few topical headings, such as "bibliography," "biography," and "Christian socialism." Also for a bibliography of works by and about Kinglsey, see *NCBEL*, III, pp. 935-39. Research on Kingsley is reviewed by James D. Barry in Stevenson's *Victorian Fiction*, pp. 245-76; and by Barry in Ford's *Victorian Fiction*, pp. 219-22. The standard guide to Kingsley's primary materials is Margaret Farrand Thorp's "Bibliography of Charles Kingsley's Works" in *Charles Kingsley, 1819-1875* (Princeton, NJ: Princeton University Press, 1937).

Galway Kinnell, 1927-

Bibliographies

For works by Kinnell, see *First Printings of American Authors*, vol. 2, pp. 231-33. Kinnell's manuscripts are listed in Robbins' *American Literary Manuscripts*, p. 181.

Rudyard Kipling, 1865-1936

Bibliographies

789.   Stewart, James McG. **Rudyard Kipling: A Bibliographical Catalogue**. Toronto: Dalhousie University Press and University of Toronto Press, 1959. 673p. LC 60-339.

Stewart provides detailed bibliographic descriptions of Kipling's writings, including entries for more than 700 editions as well as for contributions to books and journals and ana (such as quotations in sale catalogs, uncollected prose and verse, contributions to anthologies, collected sets, musical settings, and unauthorized editions). Entries give title-page transcriptions, physical descriptions, and contents. For a bibliography of works by and about Kipling, see *NCBEL*, III, pp. 1019-32. Kipling's manuscripts are described in *Index of English Literary Manuscripts*, IV, pt. 2:407. Ehrsam's *Bibliographies of Twelve Victorian Authors*, pp. [127]-160, cites international comments, criticism, and reviews for Kipling through the early twentieth century. See the review of research by Lionel Stevenson in Faverty's *The Victorian Poets*, pp. 397-98.

Dictionaries, Encyclopedias, and Handbooks

790.   Orel, Harold. **A Kipling Chronology**. Boston: G. K. Hall, 1990. 127p. (Macmillan Author Chronologies). LC 89-15513. ISBN 0-8161-9090-9.

This chronology emphasizes Kipling's earlier adventures and achievements as well as his major works, important meetings, and social activities, with more limited information on his routine travels and minor works. Cross-references to source materials are infrequent. Brief biographies of about 100 individuals who knew Kipling, including Baden-Powell, founder of the Boy Scouts, Walter Besant, and Theodore Roosevelt, are appended. An index references names of persons, places, and institutions, as well as titles of works.

791.   Page, Norman. **A Kipling Companion**. London: Macmillan, 1984. 202p. (Macmillan Literary Companions). LC 84-4480. ISBN 0-333-31538-3.

Following a brief chronology of Kipling's life, Page presents survey essays on Kipling's world (India, England, America, and South Africa); brief biographies of a very select group of family members and associates; publishing histories, textual and critical introductions, and plot summaries for the short stories, novels, miscellaneous prose, and verse; brief excerpts from critical studies of Kipling; a discussion of Kipling and freemasonry; and bibliographies of collected editions, reference works, and biographical and critical studies; and a filmography related to Kipling. Ralph Durand's *A Handbook to the Poetry of Rudyard Kipling* (Garden City, NY: Doubleday, Page, 1914) remains useful for line-by-line annotations and glosses for clichés, dialect words and regionalisms, expressions from military and nautical jargon, and the like in Kipling's poems, with alphabetical and general indexes.

792.   Young, W. Arthur, and John H. McGivering. **A Kipling Dictionary**. London: Macmillan, 1967. 230p. LC 67-11840.

A revision of Young's *A Dictionary of the Characters and Scenes in the Stories and Poems of Rudyard Kipling, 1886-1911* (London: G. Routledge, 1911), this briefly summarizes the plots of Kipling's books, stories, poems, and other writings and identifies their characters and places. *Kim* is reviewed in five columns. Daniel Dravot, on the other hand, is simply referenced to "The Man Who Would Be King."

Journals

793.   **The Kipling Journal**. London: The Kipling Society, 1927-. 4/yr. ISSN 0023-1738.

The Kipling Journal, according to its "Explanatory Note," is "not an austerely academic production." Sponsored by the Kipling Society, issues aim at featuring scholarly but readable and entertaining articles about Kipling's life and works, typically including two to three biographical, historical, or critical articles (on such works and subjects as *Captains Courageous* or Kipling and the Bible, medicine, the law, or golf), in addition to information on previously unpublished or relatively unknown Kipling materials, such as "unfamiliar photographs; fresh light on people and places that Kipling wrote about; [and] unpublished letters." Only occasional features have covered bibliographic topics, such as Sue Ogetrop's description of Kipling materials at the University of Cape Town in 67 (June 1993): 14-29. A few reviews of new publications and information and news about the Kipling Society members are also published. *The Kipling Journal* is indexed in *AHI*, *MHRA*, and *MLA*.

Patterson's *Author Newsletters and Journals*, pp. 180-81, describes other previously published journals for Kipling.

Caroline (Matilda) Stansbury Kirkland (Mary Clavers), 1801-1864
Bibliographies

For works by Kirkland, see *Bibliography of American Literature*, vol. 5, pp. 260-69. Contributions by Kirkland and criticism and reviews of Kirkland's works in selected periodicals are identified in Wells' *The Literary Index to American Magazines, 1815-1865*, pp. 91-92; and *The Literary Index to American Magazines, 1850-1900*, p. 234. Kirkland's manuscripts are listed in Robbins' *American Literary Manuscripts*, p. 181. See *Bibliography of American Fiction Through 1865*, pp.161-62, for a checklist of works by and about Kirkland.

Joseph Kirkland, 1830-1894
Bibliographies

For works by Kirkland, see *Bibliography of American Literature*, vol. 5, pp. 270-73. Kirkland's contributions to and reviews of Kirkland's works in selected periodicals are identified in Wells' *The Literary Index to American Magazines, 1850-1900*, p. 234. Kirkland's manuscripts are listed in Robbins' *American Literary Manuscripts*, pp. 181-82. See *Bibliography of American Fiction, 1866-1918*, pp. 263-64, for Calvin Gibson's checklist of works by and about Kirkland.

Sarah Kemble Knight, 1666-1727
Bibliographies

For a bibliography of works by and about Knight, see *NCBEL*, II, p. 1458. Knight's manuscripts are listed in Robbins' *American Literary Manuscripts*, p. 182.

See the review of research by Ann Stanford in Duke, Bryer, and Inge's *American Women Writers*, pp. 3-20.

John Knowles, 1926-
Bibliographies
> For works by Knowles, see *First Printings of American Authors*, vol. 3, pp. 201-202. Knowles' manuscripts are listed in Robbins' *American Literary Manuscripts*, p. 182.

Arthur Koestler, 1905-1983
Bibliographies
> 794. Day, Frank. **Arthur Koestler: A Guide to Research**. New York: Garland, 1987. 248p. (Garland Reference Library of the Humanities, vol. 612). LC 85-45122. ISBN 0-8240-8670-8.
> Day provides extensive descriptions of works by and about Koestler. Entries for first appearances of Koestler's novels, dramas, autobiographies, books and collections of essays, contributions to books, contributions to periodicals, interviews, symposia, lectures, broadcasts, and miscellaneous works give brief bibliographic information and summaries of plots and contents. Secondary coverage includes annotated entries for about 500 works about Koestler arranged in separate listings for books and essay collections, essays and articles, reviews of Koestler's works, reviews of works about Koestler, miscellaneous works (mostly non-English-language criticisms), and dissertations. Annotations are descriptive. A separate subject index accesses primary works but not criticisms. Day's guide complements Reed Merrill and Thomas Frazier's *Arthur Koestler: An International Bibliography* (Ann Arbor, MI: Ardis Publishers, 1979), which offers broader coverage of Koestler's primary materials (including translations, editions, and the like) but extends only through 1978. Also for a bibliography of works by and about Koestler, see *NCBEL*, IV, pp. 628-29. Koestler's manuscripts are described in *The Koestler Archive in Edinburgh University Library: A Checklist* (Edinburgh: Edinburgh University Library, 1987).

Arthur L. Kopit, 1937-
Bibliographies
> King's *Ten Modern American Playwrights*, pp. 167-78, gives brief bibliographic information for Kopit's primary works and annotated entries for criticism of Kopit, with a classified list of reviews. Doris Auerbach reviews research on Kopit in *Contemporary Authors: Bibliographical Series: Volume 3: American Dramatists*, pp. 125-39.

Jerzy (Nikodem) Kosinski, 1933-1991
Bibliographies
> 795. Cronin, Gloria L., and Blaine H. Hall. **Jerzy Kosinski: An Annotated Bibliography**. New York: Greenwood Press, 1991. 104p. (Bibliographies and Indexes in American Literature, no. 15). LC 91-21555. ISBN 0-313-27442-8.
> Lists works by and about Kosinski through 1991. Part 1 arranges 76 entries for primary works in sections for novels, short stories, miscellaneous writings (articles, books, recordings, and reviews), and interviews (annotated). Part 2 includes selectively, descriptively annotated entries for about 400 secondary works in sections for bibliographies, books and monographs (six entries), biographies, criticisms and reviews (subarranged in sections for general articles and chapters and individual works, reviews of nonfiction, and non-English-language sources), and dissertations. Includes brief chronology. Separate author and subject indexes, the latter referencing personal names, titles, and topics, such as absurdist hero, narrative technique, and pornography. Also for works by Kosinski, see *First Printings of American Authors*, vol. 4, pp. 247-48. Kosinski's manuscripts are listed in Robbins' *American Literary Manuscripts*, p. 183.

796. Walsh, Thomas P., and Cameron Northouse. **John Barth, Jerzy Kosinski, and Thomas Pynchon: A Reference Guide**. Boston: G. K. Hall, 1977. 145p. (A Reference Publication in Literature). LC 77-10918. ISBN 0-8161-7910-7.

Although coverage for Barth and Pynchon is superseded by other sources, including Weixlmann's *John Barth* (entry 70) and Mead's *Thomas Pynchon* (entry 1109), this remains valuable for annotated coverage of secondary materials about Kosinski. Walsh and Northouse chronologically arrange annotated entries for studies about Barth, Kosinski, and Pynchon in separate sections. Coverage of Barth (about 200 items) extends from 1956 through 1973; of Kosinski (about 150), from 1960 through 1973; and of Pynchon (about 200), from 1963 through 1975, covering reviews, introductions in editions, dissertations, and entries in reference works. Annotations are descriptive. Separate indexes for Barth, Kosinski, and Pynchon give limited topical access under the titles of major works. See Welch D. Everman's summary biography, critical assessment of major works, and selected primary and secondary bibliography for Kosinski in McCaffery's *Postmodern Fiction: A Bio-Bibliographical Guide*, pp. 434-37.

Stanley J(asspon) Kunitz, 1905-
Bibliographies

For works by Kunitz, see *First Printings of American Authors*, vol. 2, pp. 235-36. Kunitz's manuscripts are listed in Robbins' *American Literary Manuscripts*, pp. 183-84.

Thomas Kyd, 1558-1594
Bibliographies

For a bibliography of works by and about Kyd, see *NCBEL*, I, pp. 1427-31; the Tannenbaums' *Elizabethan Bibliographies*, vol. 4; and Robert Carl Johnson's *Elizabethan Bibliographies Supplements*, no. 9. Kyd's manuscripts are described in *Index of English Literary Manuscripts*, I, pt. 2:297-98. Dickie A. Spurgeon reviews research on Kyd in Logan and Smith's *The Predecessors of Shakespeare*, pp. 93-106.

Indexes and Concordances

See Stagg's *The Figurative Language of the Tragedies of Shakespeare's Chief 16th-Century Contemporaries* (entry 901). Also available is Charles Crawford's *A Concordance to the Works of Thomas Kyd* (1911-32; reprint Nendeln: Kraus Reprint, 1967).

Peter B(ernard) Kyne, 1880-1957
Bibliographies

797. Williams, Susan Johnson, and Danielle Lanier. **Two San Francisco Writers: Inventory of the Papers of Dean S. Jennings and Inventory of the Papers of Peter B. Kyne**. Eugene, OR: University of Oregon Library, 1974. 38, 23p. (University of Oregon Library Occasional Paper, no. 6). OCLC 12906571.

Contains Lanier's separately compiled inventory of the University of Oregon's Kyne collection of 3,401 letters, 133 manuscripts of novels, serials and short stories, and 11 radio scripts and film and novel synopses dating from 1917 to 1957, giving brief information for kinds (carbon-typed draft, holograph revisions, etc.), size, and persons mentioned in each document. A list of 12 published books by Kyne gives no significant bibliographic information. Unindexed. Susan Johnson Williams compiled the inventory for Jennings. Kyne's manuscripts are also listed in Robbins' *American Literary Manuscripts*, p. 184. See *Bibliography of American Fiction, 1866-1918*, pp. 264-65, for Robert T. Kelley's checklist of works by and about Kyne.

Charles Lamb, 1775-1834
Bibliographies
798. Thomson, J. C. **Bibliography of the Writings of Charles and Mary Lamb: A Literary History**. Hull: J. R. Tutin, 1908. 141p. LC 8-20572.

Thomson provides a single, chronologically arranged listing of books and contributions to periodicals by the Lambs. Entries give title-page transcriptions, physical details, and publishing histories. Also for a bibliography of works by and about Charles Lamb, see *NCBEL*, III, pp. 1223-30. Wells' *The Literary Index to American Magazines, 1815-1865*, pp. 93-94; and *The Literary Index to American Magazines, 1850-1900*, pp. 235-36, identifies reviews of Charles Lamb in selected periodicals. Lamb's manuscripts are described in *Index of English Literary Manuscripts*, IV, pt. 2:655. Research on Lamb is reviewed by George L. Barnett and Stuart M. Tave in Houtchens and Houtchens' *The English Romantic Poets and Essayists*, pp. 37-74.

Dictionaries, Encyclopedias, and Handbooks
799. Prance, Claude A. **Companion to Charles Lamb: A Guide to People and Places 1760-1847**. London: Mansell, 1983. 392p. LC 83-216694. ISBN 0-7201-1657-0.

Prance provides in about 1,000 entries brief summaries of Lamb's works; biographies of members of Lamb's family, friends, and associates, ranging from the likes of Coleridge to Dash (Thomas Hood's dog), to modern scholars, including Prance himself; and descriptions of places and institutions known by Lamb, such as South Sea House and the Amicable Society of Blues; as well as selected topics. These include entries on "Religion and Charles Lamb" and "Coaching" (describing Lamb's coach journeys) and lists of plays about Lamb and of portraits of Lamb. In addition to a chronology of the lives of the Charles and Mary Lamb, several family trees, and maps of London, the volume includes useful indexes for persons connected with the theater, the fine arts, Lamb's contemporaries, nineteenth- and twentieth-century commentators on the period, and nonbiographical topics. The dictionary is an excellent starting point for research on Lamb and his contemporaries.

Journals
800. **Charles Lamb Bulletin**. London: Charles Lamb Society, 1973-. 4/yr. ISSN 0308-0951.

Sponsored by the Charles Lamb Society, *Charles Lamb Bulletin* features articles and reviews of new publications related to the life and works of Lamb and his contemporaries, including Robert Southey, Leigh Hunt, William Wordsworth, and Samuel Taylor Coleridge. Studies of Byron, Keats, and Shelley are specifically excluded. Substantial contributions offer close readings and interpretations of specific works and themes, evaluate critical receptions, provide new biographical information, and describe primary materials in special collections. "The Pleasure of Early Enlightenment: The Lamb Tales from Shakespeare," "The Cultural Foundations of Wordsworth's Literary Criticism," and "The Ancient Mariner Controversy" are representative. The journal also publishes occasional bibliographic features as supplements, such as Deborah K. Hedgecock's *A Handlist to the Charles Lamb Society Collection at Guildhall Library* (London: Charles Lamb Society, 1995), issued with 89 (January 1995). "Society Notes and News" describes conferences, programs, and membership activities. *Charles Lamb Bulletin* is indexed in *AES*, *MHRA*, and *MLA*.

Patterson's *Author Newsletters and Journals*, pp. 187-89, describes other previously published journals for Lamb.

Louis (Dearborn) L'Amour, 1910?-1988
Bibliographies
801. Hall, Halbert W. **The Work of Louis L'Amour: An Annotated Bibliography and Guide**. San Bernardino, CA: Borgo Press, 1991. 192p. (Bibliographies of Modern Authors, no. 15). LC 88-034678. ISBN 0-8095-0510-X.

Lists works by and about L'Amour through 1991. Descriptive entries for L'Amour's 130 books, including reprint and non-English editions, nonfiction works, and autobiographies; short fiction; nonfiction; poetry; audio recordings; and film adaptations, give plot synopses and references to reviews and adaptations. Identifies about 200 book chapters, journal and newspaper articles, essays, and other criticisms about L'Amour. Also includes the text of a 1985 interview with L'Amour and lists of novels in series. Subject index. See *Bibliography of American Fiction, 1919-1988*, pp. 282-84, for Robert L. Gale's checklist of works by and about L'Amour. Michael T. Marsden surveys works by and about L'Amour in Erisman and Etulain's *Fifty Western Writers*, pp. 257-67.

Dictionaries, Encyclopedias, and Handbooks

802. L'Amour, Louis. **The Sackett Companion: A Personal Guide to the Sackett Novels**. New York: Bantam Books, 1988. 341p. LC 88-47530. ISBN 0-5530-5305-1.

Prepared to answer frequently asked questions about his writings, L'Amour gives brief notes and descriptions of persons, places, and things in his 17 Sackett novels. Also contains a Sackett genealogy and family tree and a cumulative glossary of entries (fictional and historical characters; places; ranches and brands; saloons, taverns, restaurants, inns, and hotels; rifles and pistols; books; ships; songs; narrators; and chronology). Indexed.

Melville De Lancey Landon (Eli Perkins), 1839-1910

Bibliographies

For works by Landon, see *Bibliography of American Literature*, vol. 5, pp. 274-79. London's manuscripts are listed in Robbins' *American Literary Manuscripts*, p. 185.

Walter Savage Landor, 1775-1864

Bibliographies

803. Wise, Thomas James, and Stephen Wheeler. **A Bibliography of the Writings in Prose and Verse of Walter Savage Landor**. London: Bibliographical Society, 1919. 426p. LC 21-673.

Wise and Wheeler give full bibliographic descriptions in listings for published, lost, and attributed editions; contributions of verse and prose to periodicals, books, and annuals; collected editions; and Landoriana and works about Landor through 1919. Available in reprinted edition (Folkestone: Dawsons of Pall Mall, 1971). Contributions by Landor and criticism and reviews of Lender's works in selected periodicals are identified in Wells' *The Literary Index to American Magazines, 1815-1865*, p. 94; and *The Literary Index to American Magazines, 1850-1900*, pp. 236-37. Also for a bibliography of works by and about Landor, see *NCBEL*, III, pp. 1210-16. Research on Landor is reviewed by R. H. Super in Houtchens and Houtchens' *The English Romantic Poets and Essayists*, pp. 221-54. Although not exclusively the subject of an author journal, Landor is among the writers frequently covered in *Wordsworth Circle* (entry 1500).

Charles Lane, fl. 1840s

Bibliographies

Joel Myerson reviews research on Lane in Myerson's *The Transcendentalists*, pp. 211-13.

William Langland, perhaps c. 1330-c. 1386

Bibliographies

804. DiMarco, Vincent. **Piers Plowman: A Reference Guide**. Boston, MA: G. K. Hall, 1982. 384p. (A Reference Guide to Literature). LC 82-3137. ISBN 0-8161-8309-0.

DiMarco chronologically arranges annotated entries for about 1,000 critical studies of Langland's poem, including dissertations and non-English-language works, dating from 1395 through 1979. Excluded are contemporary adaptations of *Piers Plowman* or parodies in the *"Piers Plowman* tradition," modernized editions, or non-English-language translations of the work. DiMarco's annotations are especially valuable. Although the annotations are descriptive, evaluation is implicit in length. Significant studies receive extensive comments. The description of George Kane and E. Talbot Donaldson's edition of *Piers Plowman: The B Version* (London: University of London, Athlone Press, 1975) extends three full pages. Those for seminal works, such as Guy Bourquim's *Piers Plowman: Etudes sur la Genese Litteraire des Trois Versions* (Paris: Honore Champion, 1978) and Willi Erzgraber's *William Langland's Piers Plowman: Eine Interpretation des C-Textes* (Heidelberg: Carl Winter, 1957) are equally extensive. A cumulative index includes critics and names, secondary titles, and selected subjects. Headings provided for Chaucer, Dante, and Gower, for example, encourage comparative studies. Subordinate headings for such topics as "biography" and "authorship" are arranged under Langland's name. Topical headings under *Piers Plowman* include "allegory," "antichrist," "dating," and "righteous heathen," among others. DiMarco's work is comprehensive but not definitive. Anne Middleton offers a comprehensive guide to primary materials for *Piers Plowman* with a bibliography of editions and criticism in Severs and Hartung's *A Manual of the Writings in Middle English*, vol. XVII, pp. 2211-34, 2419-48. Additional guidance to Langland scholarship is available in A. J. Colaianne's topically arranged *Piers Plowman: An Annotated Bibliography of Editions and Criticism, 1550-1977* (New York: Garland, 1978).

805.   Pearsall, Derek. **An Annotated Critical Bibliography of Langland**. Ann Arbor: University of Michigan Press, 1990. 295p. (Harvester Annotated Critical Bibliographies). ISBN 0-7108-0943-3.

More appropriate for undergraduate requirements than DiMarco's work (entry 804), Pearsall's selective (about 600 entries), topically arranged bibliography offers excellent guidance to editions of the text and the most significant English-language studies of topics perennially associated with *Piers Plowman* published from 1900 through 1988, such as authorship, dating, social and historical contexts, the dream vision, and allegory. Evaluative annotations clearly indicate major scholarly studies. Thorough indexing readily identifies studies of imagery, language and poetry, satire, and other specific topics. Also for a bibliography of works by and about Langland, see *NCBEL*, I, pp. 533-44.

Dictionaries, Encyclopedias, and Handbooks

806.   Alford, John A. **A Companion to Piers Plowman**. Berkeley, CA: University of California Press, 1988. 286p. LC 87-24873.

Alford provides a selection of essays that survey *Piers Plowman* scholarship on subjects of significant historical and critical interest, including the poem's historical backgrounds, allegory, satire, the medieval sermon, textual problems, grammar and language, the alliterative style, and the like. Chapters include extensive bibliographies. Alford's *Piers Plowman: A Glossary of Legal Diction* (Cambridge: D. S. Brewer, 1988) offers a guide to a specialized aspect of the poem's language.

807.   Alford, John A. **Piers Plowman: A Guide to the Quotations**. Binghamton, NY: Medieval & Renaissance Texts & Studies, 1992. 153p. (Medieval & Renaissance Texts & Studies, vol. 77). LC 91-31220. ISBN 0-86698-088-1.

Arranged by passus and line, Alford's guide provides translations and commentaries on some 600 Latin and French-language quotations in the A, B, and C texts of *Piers Plowman*, based on the Athlone editions of the poem: George Kane's *Piers Plowman: The A Version* (London: Athlone, 1960); Kane and E. Talbot Donaldson's *Piers Plowman: The B Version* (London: Athlone, 1975); and George Russell and Kane's *Piers Plowman: The C Version* (London: Athlone, 1997). Entries offer extensive citations for sources and analogs and other critical studies of particular aspects of the poem. Introduction traces textual transmission of quotations. Indexes for Biblical quotations, listed by book, chapter, and verse; and alphabetical lists of all quotations.

Journals

808.   **Yearbook of Langland Studies**. East Lansing, MI: Colleagues Press, 1987- . Annual. ISSN 0890-2917.

The annual features as many as 15 scholarly articles and notes on Langland, his contemporaries (including Wyclif and Dante) and anonymous contemporary works, and medieval English literature in general. Articles that offer close readings or interpretations of *Piers Plowman* or its allegorical or Christian symbols are typical. Many other contributions have focused on textual and editorial problems or described manuscript sources. Peter Barney's "Line-Number Index to the Athlone Edition of *Piers Plowman*," 7 (1993): 97-114, is among the useful reference contributions. In addition, an "Annual Bibliography" of Langland studies, presently compiled by Vincent DiMarco, describes recent criticisms, dissertations, and reviews. The annual also includes a selection of reviews of new publications. *Yearbook of Langland Studies* is indexed in *MLA*.

Sidney Lanier, 1842-1881

Bibliographies

809.   Boswell, Jeanetta. **Spokesmen for the Minority: A Bibliography of Sidney Lanier, William Vaughan Moody, Frederick Goddard Tuckerman, and Jones Very: With Selective Annotations**. Metuchen, NJ: Scarecrow Press, 1987. 296p. LC 86-24823. ISBN 0-8108-1944-9.

Covering works about these writers, Boswell provides separate, alphabetically arranged listings of selectively annotated entries for reviews, criticisms, and biographical studies published in books, parts of books, articles, reviews, and dissertations. About half of the entries (some 906) are for Lanier, with about 360 for Moody, 200 for Henry Timrod (not mentioned in the subtitle), 50 for Tuckerman, and 200 for Very. Separate subject indexes are included for each writer. Boswell's coverage of Lanier criticism is more current than that in DeBellis' bibliography (entry 810). A partial list of Lanier's primary bibliography (books, collections of reprints, sheet music, and contributions to books) is included in Blanck's *Bibliography of American Literature*, vol. 5, pp. 280-98. Wells' *The Literary Index to American Magazines, 1850-1900*, pp. 240-41, identifies Lanier's contributions to selected periodicals. Lanier's manuscripts are listed in Robbins' *American Literary Manuscripts*, p. 185. Boswell's coverage of secondary materials for Very, Moody, and Tuckerman is unique. Research on Lanier is reviewed by Jane S. Gabin (pp. 303-11), and research on Timrod is reviewed by Jack DeBellis (pp. 464-72) in Bain and Flora's *Fifty Southern Writers Before 1900*. Research on Very is reviewed by David Robinson in Myerson's *The Transcendentalists*, pp. 286-94.

810.   DeBellis, Jack. **Sidney Lanier, Henry Timrod, and Paul Hamilton Hayne: A Reference Guide**. Boston: G. K. Hall, 1978. 213p. (A Reference Publication in Literature). LC 77-17203. ISBN 0-8161-7967-0.

DeBellis chronologically lists in separate listings annotated entries for books and articles about Lanier published from 1868 through 1976, for Timrod from 1860 through 1974, and for Hayne from 1855 through 1974. Annotations are largely descriptive. Separate indexes include subject headings for general topics ("bibliography" and "biography") as well as names (Poe and Wordsworth). DeBellis' annotations complement Boswell's (entry 809) more up-to-date coverage for Lanier and Timrod. Coverage of Hayne is unique.

Indexes and Concordances

811.   Graham, Philip, and Joseph Jones. **A Concordance to the Poems of Sidney Lanier, Including the Poem Outlines and Certain Uncollected Items**. Austin, TX: University of Texas Press, 1939. 447p. LC 39-29630.

Based on the texts of the *Poems of Sidney Lanier*, edited by Mary Day Lanier (New York: Scribner's, 1929), *Poem Outlines*, edited by H. W. L[anier] (New York: Scribner's, 1908), and texts for 15 uncollected items ("listed on page vi") that appeared in collections, periodicals, or were unpublished. Available in a reprinted edition (New York: Johnson Reprint Corp., 1969).

Lucy Larcom, 1824-1893
Bibliographies

For works by Larcom, see *Bibliography of American Literature*, vol. 5, pp. 299-325. Larcom's contributions to and reviews of Larcom's works in selected periodicals are identified in Wells' *The Literary Index to American Magazines, 1850-1900*, pp. 241-42. Larcom's manuscripts are listed in Robbins' *American Literary Manuscripts*, p. 186.

Ring(old) W(ilmer) Lardner, 1885-1933
Bibliographies

812.   Bruccoli, Matthew J., and Richard Layman. **Ring W. Lardner: A Descriptive Bibliography**. Pittsburgh, PA: University of Pittsburgh Press, 1976. 424p. (Pittsburgh Series in Bibliography). LC 75-9126. ISBN 0-8229-3306-3.

Bruccoli and Layman give descriptions of Lardner's primary works in separate listings for Lardner's separately published and collected works, sheet music, contributions to books, contributions to journals, contributions to newspapers, filmscripts and dramatic works, interviews, and dust-jacket blurbs. Illustrations of covers and data for contents, collations, typography, paper, bindings and jackets, printing and publishing histories, and copy locations are provided. An appendix lists selected works about Lardner. Also for works by Lardner, see *First Printings of American Authors*, vol. 1, pp. 223-26. Lardner's manuscripts are listed in Robbins' *American Literary Manuscripts*, p. 186. See *Bibliography of American Fiction, 1919-1988*, pp. 285-86, for Richard Layman's checklist of works by and about Lardner.

Philip Arthur Larkin, 1922-1985
Bibliographies

813.   Bloomfield, B. C. **Philip Larkin: A Bibliography**. London: Faber and Faber, 1979. 187p. LC 80-670086. ISBN 0-517-11447-4.

Modeled on Bloomfield and Mendelson's bibliography of Auden (entry 49), Bloomfield provides descriptions of Larkin's works in separate listings for books and pamphlets; works edited or contributed to by Larkin; contributions to periodicals (some 449 items from 1933); writings (largely reports) by Larkin in the "course of his duties as librarian at the University of Hull" (1955-76); interviews (some 20 entries); published and unpublished recordings; radio and television appearances (twenty-nine entries for readings and interviews); "Odds and ends," such as notes on record sleeves, slide/tape library tours, and the like; manuscripts in the British Library (p. 139); published letters; translations into 11 languages; and anthologies (some 32 entries). The section for books, chronologically arranged from 1945, offers full descriptions for first impressions of first editions; including transcriptions of title pages; data on collations, contents, binding, and paper; and notes on printing and publishing histories. Only the significant bibliographic points for subsequent editions are noted. Also provides references to selected reviews. An appendix includes a bibliography of some 96 critical studies of Larkin's works, citing books, articles, theses, and dissertations. An index of names, primary titles, periodical titles, and institutions concludes the volume. Additional coverage of works about Larkin is provided in Shields' *Contemporary English Poetry*, pp. 151-83.

Indexes and Concordances

814. Watt, R. J. C. **Philip Larkin: A Concordance to the Poetry of Philip Larkin**. Hildesheim: Olms-Weidmann, 1995. 660p. (Alpha-Omega: Lexika, Indizes, Konkordanzen: Reihe C: Englishe Autoren, vol. 3). ISBN 3-4870-9801-6.

Based on the text of the revised paperback edition of *Collected Poems* (London: Marvell Press and Faber and Faber, 1990), edited by Anthony Thwaite. Appends verbal, word-frequency, and reverse-word lists.

Jeremy Larner, 1937-
Bibliographies

For works by Larner, see *First Printings of American Authors*, vol. 2, p. 237.

George Parsons Lathrop, 1851-1898
Bibliographies

For works by Lathrop, see *Bibliography of American Literature*, vol. 5, pp. 326-39. Lathrop's contributions to and reviews of Lathrop's works in selected periodicals are identified in Wells' *The Literary Index to American Magazines, 1850-1900*, pp. 242-44. Lathrop's manuscripts are listed in Robbins' *American Literary Manuscripts*, p. 186.

D(avid) H(erbert) Lawrence, 1885-1930
Bibliographies

815. Cowan, James C. **D. H. Lawrence: An Annotated Bibliography of Writings About Him. Volume I**. De Kalb, IL: Northern Illinois University Press, 1985. 612p. (Annotated Secondary Bibliography Series on English Literature in Transition, 1880-1920). LC 80-8664. ISBN 0-87580-077-7.

This volume is complemented by:

815.1. Cowan, James C. **D. H. Lawrence: An Annotated Bibliography of Writings About Him. Volume II**. De Kalb, IL: Northern Illinois University Press, 1985. 768p. (Annotated Secondary Bibliography Series on English Literature in Transition, 1880-1920). LC 80-8664. ISBN 0-87580-105-6.

These volumes constitute the most comprehensive bibliography of works about Lawrence in all formats and languages. Vol. I contains 2,061 chronologically arranged, annotated entries for writings about Lawrence published from 1909 through 1960 in 11 languages. Vol. II includes 2,566 entries for 1961 through 1975 in 15 languages. Coverage includes books, parts of books, articles in journals and newspapers, dissertations, reviews, brief notices, letters to editors, adaptations of Lawrence's works in other media, and other materials. Annotations are descriptive. Indexes for critics, titles of secondary works, periodical and newspaper titles, languages, and titles of Lawrence's works. Cowan's work supersedes William White's *D. H. Lawrence: A Checklist: Writings About D. H. Lawrence, 1931-1950* (Detroit, MI: Wayne State University Press, 1950).

816. Rice, Thomas Jackson. **D. H. Lawrence: A Guide to Research**. New York: Garland, 1983. 484p. (Garland Reference Library of the Humanities, vol. 412). LC 82-49260. ISBN 0-8240-9127-2.

Although lacking the comprehensiveness of Cowan's definitive bibliography (entry 815), Rice's work offers a wide selection of Lawrence studies—some 2,123 annotated entries—published through 1983. Indeed, according to Rice, the volume includes "all English and Foreign-language books, essay collections, monographs, pamphlets, and special periodical issues" concerned with Lawrence and his works, with more selective coverage of articles and chapters. Dissertations and newspaper articles are excluded. Annotations are evaluative. A section for primary works lists editions, collections, and letters, offering "basic initial publication information" for first English, American, or other international editions and later critical editions of the novels, stories, plays, miscellaneous writings, anthologies and collections, and letters.

A section of secondary studies in English includes bibliographies, biographies, and criticisms. Appendixes list non-English-language criticisms. Rice's author, title, and subject indexes complement those provided by Cowan's bibliographies. Headings are provided for such topics as "Bible and biblical allusions," "characterization," "T. S. Eliot," "form and structure," "morality in literature," and "women in literature," among others. Rice's listing is more useful than John E. Stoll's *D. H. Lawrence: A Bibliography, 1911-1975* (Troy, NY: Whitston, 1977). Also for a bibliography of works by and about Lawrence, see *NCBEL*, IV, pp. 481-503. Research on Lawrence is reviewed by Mark Spilka in Dyson's *The English Novel*, pp. 334-48; and Robert Wilcher in Demastes and Kelly's *British Playwrights, 1880-1956*, pp. [251]-67.

817.   Roberts, Warren. **A Bibliography of D. H. Lawrence**. 2d ed. Cambridge: Cambridge University Press, 1982. 626p. LC 81-10149. ISBN 0-521-22295-8.
        The definitive listing of Lawrence's primary works, including separate listings for all appearances of Lawrence's works in books and pamphlets, contributions to books, contributions to periodicals, translations of Lawrence's works, and manuscripts in the University of Texas' Harry Ransom Humanities Research Center and 40 other collections (pp. 431-540). Entries for books provide transcriptions of title pages of first and variant editions, collations, contents, notes on publishing histories, notes on bibliographic points, and citations for reviews. Some 11 editions of *Lady Chatterley's Lover* are described. An unannotated listing of secondary works (books and pamphlets) about Lawrence is also included. Appendixes list parodies of *Lady Chatterley's Lover* and spurious works. An index of names, primary titles, and secondary titles concludes the volume. The second edition is a substantive revision of Roberts' *A Bibliography of D. H. Lawrence* (London: Hart Davis, 1963). New entries and new information is provided in all categories. Some 20 additional contributions to books and 30 to periodicals are noted. The number of locations of Lawrence's manuscripts is tripled. This coverage of manuscripts supersedes that of Sagar's work (entry 822). Roberts' bibliography supersedes all other descriptive bibliographies of Lawrence's primary works, including Edward McDonald's *A Bibliography of the Writings of D. H. Lawrence* (Philadelphia, PA: Centaur Bookshop, 1925) and *The Writings of D. H. Lawrence, 1925-30: A Bibliographical Supplement* (Philadelphia, PA: Centaur Bookshop, 1931); and Richard Aldington's *Lawrence: A Complete List of His Works: Together with Critical Appraisal* (London: William Heinemann, 1935). Additional coverage of editions of *Lady Chatterley* is available in Jay A. Gertzman's *Descriptive Bibliography of Lady Chatterley's Lover: With Essays Toward a Publishing History of the Novel* (Westport, CT: Greenwood Press, 1990).

Dictionaries, Encyclopedias, and Handbooks

818.   Holderness, Graham. **Who's Who in D. H. Lawrence**. New York: Taplinger, 1976. 136p. LC 75-37482. ISBN 0-8008-8272-5.
        Holderness identifies, describes, and locates significant characters in 20 works by Lawrence, including the novels and selected novellas and short stories. Characters of all varieties are covered, such as "The Man Who Died" in *The Man Who Died*, as well as Lawrence's animal and nonhuman characters (in a separate section), such as the Aztec god of the wind, Quetzacoatl, in *The Plumed Serpent*. Some entries are extensive, examining a character's psychology as well as actions and role in the plot. The description of Captain Alexander Hepburn extends for three pages, for example. An index lists the characters by individual works, books, and chapters in which each first appears.

819.   Pinion, F. B. **A D. H. Lawrence Companion: Life, Thought, and Works**. London: Macmillan, 1978. 316p. LC 79-300993. ISBN 0-333-17983-8.
        Chapters offer details and survey discussions of Lawrence's life, "thought-adventures" (ideas), poetry, 10 major novels (in individual chapters), short stories,

and other writings (fragments, travel works, plays, and literary criticism). Illustrations include maps and photographs. A dictionary of people and places in the novels, a selected bibliography of primary and secondary sources, and a checklist of film adaptations of Lawrence's works are appendixed. An index of names, primary works, and subjects concludes this handy volume. Supplemental information on such topics as Lawrence's mining terminology as well as the locations depicted in his works is provided by contributing specialists in Keith Sagar's *A D. H. Lawrence Handbook* (New York: Barnes & Noble, 1982).

820. Poplawski, Paul. **D. H. Lawrence: A Reference Companion**. Westport, CT: Greenwood Press, 1996. 714p. LC 95-38654 . ISBN 0-313-28637-X.

In Part I, along with a biography by John Worthen that includes a chronology of Lawrence's life and works, Poplawski offers chapters that survey biographical scholarship and criticism, and give overviews on the social and geographical contexts of Lawrence's works. Part II covers Lawrence's works, giving composition and publication histories, plot summaries and details about characters and settings, and critical bibliographies in sections for each the novels, short stories, poems, plays, and other works. Part III is a general guide to criticism on Lawrence, identifying major bibliographies and reference works and scholarly studies, works about Lawrence arranged by critical approaches (historicist, psychoanalytic, linguistic, etc.), and Lawrence and the mass media. Poplawski's descriptions of research resources, editions, and scholarship are evaluative. Part IV amounts to a master list of all works cited in the guide, with checklists of journals and special issues devoted to Lawerence and Lawrence's works. Detailed indexes for Lawrence's life and works, Lawrence and film, and names offer excellent access.

821. Preston, Peter. **A D. H. Lawrence Chronology**. New York: St. Martin's Press, 1994. 208p. LC 93-43707. ISBN 0-3121-2114-8.

A straightforward chronology of Lawrence's life and works that ably complements Sagar's more extensive guide (entry 822) to Lawrence's creative development. Preston's emphasis is on dating and establishing "the context of Lawrence's relationship with an individual or his work on a text" (p. xi). The chronology also records all reading that is evidenced in Lawrence's work. Preston notes Lawrence's whereabouts and movements. Based extensively on the first 21 published volumes of the Cambridge University Press edition of Lawrence's works. Corrects some of Sagar's conclusions based on subsequent editorial work. Includes a directory of frequently mentioned people and a bibliography (pp. 170-74). Detailed indexes of Lawrence's works and a general index enable tracking composition, revision, and publication of particular works and Lawrence's travels and residences.

822. Sagar, Keith. **D. H. Lawrence: A Calendar of His Works**. Austin, TX: University of Texas Press, 1979. 294p. LC 78-65562. ISBN 0-292-71519-6.

Sagar provides a calendar of Lawrence's life and career from 1897 through 1930. Emphasizing Lawrence's creative development, Sagar quotes extensively from an extensive variety of primary sources, including Edward Nehl's *D. H. Lawrence: A Composite Biography* (Madison, WI: University of Wisconsin Press, 1957-59); Harry T. Moore's *The Priest of Love* (London: Heinemann, 1974); and Vivian de Sola Pinto and Warren Roberts' edition of *The Complete Poems of D. H. Lawrence* (New York: Viking, 1971). Also contains Lindeth Vasey's "A Checklist of the Manuscripts of D. H. Lawrence," locating Lawrence's manuscripts in 40 private and academic collections: This is now superseded by Roberts' definitive bibliography (entry 817).

Indexes and Concordances

823. Garcia, Reloy, and James Karabatsos. **A Concordance to the Poems of D. H. Lawrence**. Lincoln, NE: University of Nebraska Press, 1970. 523p. LC 70-120277. ISBN 0-8032-0768-9.

This is based on Vivian de Sola Pinto and Warren Roberts' first edition of *The Complete Poems* (New York: Viking, 1964).

824. Garcia, Reloy, and James Karabatsos. **A Concordance to the Short Fiction of D. H. Lawrence**. Lincoln, NE: University of Nebraska Press, 1972. 474p. LC 72-77195. ISBN 0-8032-0807-3.

Based on the American paperback edition of *The Complete Short Stories* (New York: Viking, 1961), which Rice (entry 816), p. 32, calls a flawed text; *Four Short Novels of D. H. Lawrence* (New York: Viking, 1965); *St. Mawr* and *The Man Who Died* (New York: Knopf, 1953); and "The Virgin and the Gypsy" in *The Short Novels of D. H. Lawrence* (London: Heinemann, 1956).

Journals

825. **D. H. Lawrence: The Journal of the D. H. Lawrence Society**. Nottingham: D. H. Lawrence Society, 1976-. Annual. No ISSN or OCLC.

This irregularly published "annual" of the D. H. Lawrence Society features a few critical and biographical studies of Lawrence and his writings. A number of contributions have discussed editorial problems and textual revisions of *Women in Love*. The annual also publishes selections of reviews of new publications, which *MHRA* comprehensively indexes. To date, indexing of *D. H. Lawrence* in *MLA* has been inconsistent, extending to 1992.

826. **The D. H. Lawrence Review**. Austin, TX: University of Texas at Austin, 1968-. 3/yr. ISSN 0011-4936.

Providing "a forum for criticism, scholarship, reviews, and bibliography of the works of D. H. Lawrence and his circle" (masthead) typical articles published in *The D. H. Lawrence Review* offer close readings of Lawrence's works, compare or relate Lawrence and his writings to the works of other artists, or investigate particular bibliographic or textual problems. Pedagogical articles intended to enliven classroom instruction frequently appear as well as occasional special issues devoted to specific topics, such as Lawrence in the Southwest, Lawrence and women, and Lawrence's sources. In addition, the journal regularly features several significant enumerative bibliographies. A "Checklist of D. H. Lawrence Criticism and Scholarship," last appearing in 24.3 (Fall 1992), lists international criticisms and dissertations. Other bibliographies have covered master's theses and studies and editions of Lawrence in Korea and Japan. Issues usually include eight to 12 reviews, although as many as 40 might fill some issues. "Laurentiana" gives information and notes on activities of the D. H. Lawrence Society of North America and of other associations throughout the world; new publications; research in progress and on the progress of major projects, such as the Cambridge edition of the works; personal notices on scholars, collectors, and readers; and similar reports of interest. *The D. H. Lawrence Review* is indexed in *AHI, A&HCI, MHRA*, and *MLA*.

Patterson's *Author Newsletters and Journals*, pp. 190-91, describes other previously published journals for Lawrence.

827. **Etudes Lawrenciennes**. Nanterre: Universite de Paris X—Nanterre, 1986-. Annual. ISSN 0994-5490.

Typical contributions (mostly in French) address images and themes in Lawrence's works and identify Lawrence's sources and literary relations (particularly with modern continental writers). A number of articles have addressed textual revisions, especially in *Women in Love*. A special issue, "Humour et Satire," in 6 (1991), contained English and French studies on parody, irony, and satire in Lawrence's poetry and long and short prose works. To date, *Etudes Lawrenciennes* is indexed in *MLA* to 1991.

T(homas) E(dward) Lawrence, 1888-1935

Bibliographies

828. O'Brien, Philip M. **T. E. Lawrence: A Bibliography**. Boston: G. K. Hall, 1988. 724p. LC 87-11993. ISBN 0-8161-8945-5.

Although no Lawrence bibliography to date is completely satisfactory, O'Brien's perhaps comes the closest for Lawrence's primary materials. An ambitious guide, O'Brien attempts "to give, in as complete a fashion as is possible, full reference to all works by and about" Lawrence (p. [ix]). Part 1 supplies full bibliographic descriptions of Lawrence's works in chronologically arranged sections for books and contributions to books (262 items published from 1914 to 1977, including prefaces, forewords, book reviews, dust-wrapper blurbs, translations, and other works); contributions to periodicals, including posthumously published letters; newspaper articles; and other books reprinting Lawrence's writings. Entries for separate publications and contributions to books contain title-page transcriptions; collations; contents; data on format, type, paper, and binding; notes of publication histories; and copy locations. Part 2 likewise gives chronologically arranged, full bibliographic descriptions (aimed at collectors) of 407 books about Lawrence published through 1987 followed by separate, alphabetical and unannotated listings of 1,187 "incidental books containing references to Lawrence" (p. xi), 1,708 periodical articles (including book reviews), and 1,292 newspaper articles. No entries indicate the critical contents of works about Lawrence. Index of authors, titles, periodicals, newspapers, and publishers. An integrated, chronologically arranged and annotated presentation of works about Lawrence would be preferred. O'Brien's guide largely supersedes Elizabeth W. Duval's *T. E. Lawrence: A Bibliography* (New York: Arrow Edition, 1938), which gives full bibliographic descriptions for Lawrence's books, introductions and prefaces, contributions to journals and newspapers, miscellaneous writings (such as dust-jacket blurbs), and published letters; Frank Clements' *T. E. Lawrence: A Reader's Guide* (Newton Abbot: David & Charles, 1972), which gives full bibliographic descriptions for Lawrence's primary works and detailed physical descriptions of works about Lawrence, general works on the Middle East War that refer to Lawrence, and Arabic sources; and Jeffrey Meyers' *T. E. Lawrence: A Bibliography* (New York: Garland, 1974), which gives a checklist of primary materials followed by 700 unannotated and unindexed entries for works about Lawrence, covering books, parts of books, articles, and selected reviews. Also for a bibliography of works by and about Lawrence, see *NCBEL*, IV, pp. 1181-85.

Journals

829. **Journal of the T. E. Lawrence Society**. Oxford: T. E. Lawrence Society, 1991-. 2/yr. ISSN 0963-1747.

Previously published as *T. E. Lawrence Studies* (1976-90). Substantial articles, some representing papers given at the society's meetings, have addressed Lawrence and classical translation and topics in publication history. Bibliographic contributions include Clifford Irwin's "A Comprehensive Listing and Index of T. E. Lawrence's Letters," 4.1 (1994): 14-28. The journal maintains a home page, with a list of published articles: http://www.bodley.ox.ac.uk/users/jf/teweb/journals/jtelsoc.htm. Indexed in *MHRA*.

830. **T. E. Notes: A T. E. Lawrence Newsletter**. Honesdale, PA: Denis W. McDonnell, 1990- . 10/yr. ISSN 1054-514X.

Generally brief articles in this newsletter have focused on Lawrence's biography, although others have addressed Lawrence and the Japanese and publication history, as well as topics in popular culture, such as Lawrence's literary relationship to "The Young Indiana Jones Chronicles" comic book and television series. The newsletter also publishes book reviews. Maintains a home page: http://www.denismcd.com/tensub.html. *T. E. Notes* is indexed in *MLA*.

See Patterson's *Author Newsletters and Journals*, p. 192, which describes previously published journals for Lawrence.

Emma Lazarus, 1849-1887
Bibliographies
For works by Lazarus, see *Bibliography of American Literature*, vol. 5, pp. 340-46. Lazarus' contributions to and reviews of Lazarus' works in selected periodicals are identified in Wells' *The Literary Index to American Magazines, 1850-1900*, pp. 244-45. Lazarus' manuscripts are listed in Robbins' *American Literary Manuscripts*, p. 188. Diane Lichtenstein reviews works by and about Lazarus in Shapiro's *Jewish American Women Writers*, pp. 189-196.

Edward Lear, 1812-1888
Bibliographies
For a bibliography of works by and about Lear, see *NCBEL*, III, p. 1091.

F(rank) R(aymond) Leavis, 1895-1978
831.   Kinch, M. B., William Baker, and John Kimber. **F. R. Leavis and Q. D. Leavis: An Annotated Bibliography**. New York: Garland, 1989. 531p. (Garland Reference Library of the Humanities, vol. 521; Garland Bibliographies of Modern Critics and Critical Schools, vol. 12). LC 88-16561. ISBN 0-8240-8894-8.

Covers both primary and secondary works published from 1924 through 1986 in separate sections for the Leavises' books, edited books, essays, reviews, and letters and for juvenilia and books and parts of books, essays, reviews of works about them, theses, and fictional works about them. Introduction indicates major critical responses. Appendixes give a chronology of published critical exchanges between the Leavises and others, details on revisions of *The Great Tradition* and *Dickens the Novelist*, and a list of F. R. Leavis' writings on T. S. Eliot and D. H. Lawrence. Author, title, and subject index. Also for a bibliography of works by and about F. R. Leavis, see *NCBEL*, IV, pp. 1070-72; for Q. D. Leavis, see *NCBEL*, IV, p. 1073.

John Le Carré (David John Moore Cornwell), 1931-
Dictionaries, Encyclopedias, and Handbooks
832.   Monaghan, David. **Smiley's Circus: A Guide to the Secret World of John Le Carré**. New York: St. Martin's, 1986. 207p. LC 86-6447. ISBN 0-312-73014-4.

Monaghan gives chronologies of the plots, summary descriptions of the "cases" and "operations" of Le Carré's series of novels, organizational profiles of the "Circus" (the British Intelligence Service) and its sections, and a dictionary that identifies and explicates names of characters (such as Smiley and Deathwich the Hun), places and institutions (Oxford and Moscow Centre), and jargon ("fragged" and "frighten the game") that occur in Le Carré's works. Entries reference appearances in the novels. Maps and other illustrations are also included.

Harper (Nelle) Lee, 1926-
Bibliographies
See *Bibliography of American Fiction, 1919-1988*, p. 287, for Verbie Lovorn Prevost's checklist of works by and about Lee. Lee's manuscripts are listed in Robbins' *American Literary Manuscripts*, p. 189.

Nathaniel Lee, 1649?-1692
Bibliographies
For a bibliography of works by and about Lee, see *NCBEL*, II, pp. 746-47. Lee's manuscripts are described in *Index of English Literary Manuscripts*, II, pt. 2:3-8. Armistead's *Four Restoration Playwrights* (entry 1177) describes works about Lee through 1980.

Vernon Lee (Violet Paget), 1856-1935

Bibliographies

Wendell V. Harris reviews research on Lee in DeLaura's *Victorian Prose*, pp. 445-46.

J(oseph) S(heridan) LeFanu, 1814-1873

Bibliographies

833.   Crawford, Gary William. **J. Sheridan Le Fanu: A Bio-Bibliography**. Westport, CT: Greenwood Press, 1995. 155p. (Bio-Bibliographies in World Literature, no. 3). LC 94-38419. ISBN 0-313-28515-2.

Chronologically arranges brief bibliographic information, with summaries of contents and notes on composition and publication histories, in sections for contributions to magazines (subarranged by periodicals); books; anthologies; and manuscript collections. Coverage extends from 1838. Entries for books identify first and subsequent editions and reprints from 1845 through 1992 but exclude non-English-language editions. A brief research overview precedes annotated entries for 300 works about LeFanu in sections for books (five entries), essays (chapters), general studies, introductions, articles, reviews, and dissertations. Entries are critical. Coverage includes non-English-language criticism. Crawford also supplies a brief biography and chronology of LeFanu. Appends descriptions and credits for stage, film, and television adaptations of LeFanu's works from 1931 to 1990. Indexes of primary titles and secondary authors. Research on LeFanu is also reviewed by James F. Kilroy in Finneran's *Anglo-Irish Literature*, pp. 35-38.

Ursula K. LeGuin, 1929-

Bibliographies

834.   Cogell, Elizabeth Cummins. **Ursula K. LeGuin: A Primary and Secondary Bibliography**. Boston: G. K. Hall, 1983. 244p. (Masters of Science Fiction and Fantasy). LC 82-12071. ISBN 0-8161-8155-1.

Cogell lists brief bibliographic information (with notes on contents and subsequent appearances) for works by LeGuin in separate listings for fiction; poetry, translations, and media adaptations; and nonfiction (such as book reviews, letters, and introductions). Primary coverage extends from 1951 through 1981. In addition, Cogell chronologically arranges annotated entries for 761 books, articles, reviews, and dissertations about LeGuin. Annotations are descriptive. Significant studies receive detailed reviews. Subject indexing is limited to personal names and titles cited in the annotations. See *Bibliography of American Fiction, 1919-1988*, pp. 288-90, for Lorraine A. Jean's checklist of works by and about LeGuin. See Donald G. Keller's summary biography, critical assessment of major works, and selected primary and secondary bibliography for LeGuin in McCaffery's *Postmodern Fiction: A Bio-Bibliographical Guide*, pp. 449-53.

Fritz Leiber, 1910-

Bibliographies

835.   Morgan, Chris. **Fritz Leiber: A Bibliography, 1935-1979**. Birmingham: Morgenstern, 1979. 36p. OCLC 8182971.

Major sections chronologically list brief bibliographic information (with notes on contents, dust jackets, and prices) for first and subsequent U.S. and U.K. editions of Leiber's 37 books, 64 articles in books and journals, and 206 contributed stories and poems. Smaller sections identify other Leiber bibliographies, special magazine issues, awards, and four media adaptations of Leiber's works and three interviews. Includes black-and-white illustrations of dust jackets. Index of primary titles. See also *Bibliography of American Fiction, 1919-1988*, pp. 291-92, for Bruce Byfield's checklist of works by and about Leiber.

Charles Godfrey Leland (Hans Breitmann), 1824-1903
Bibliographies

For works by Leland, see *Bibliography of American Literature*, vol. 5, pp. 347-98. Contributions by Leland and criticism and reviews of Leland's works in selected periodicals are identified in Wells' *The Literary Index to American Magazines, 1815-1865*, pp. 95-96; and *The Literary Index to American Magazines, 1850-1900*, pp. 246-47. Leland's manuscripts are listed in Robbins' *American Literary Manuscripts*, p. 190.

John Leland, c. 1503-1552
Bibliographies

For a bibliography of works by and about Leland, see *NCBEL*, I, p. 2204. Leland's manuscripts are described in *Index of English Literary Manuscripts*, I, pt. 2:299-310.

Madeleine L'Engle, 1918-
Bibliographies

See *Bibliography of American Fiction, 1919-1988*, pp. 293-94, for Deborah Elwell Arfken's checklist of works by and about L'Engle. L'Engle's manuscripts are listed in Robbins' *American Literary Manuscripts*, p. 190.

Charlotte (Ramsay) Lennox, 1720-1804
Bibliographies

For a bibliography of works by and about Lennox, see *NCBEL*, II, p. 848. Lennox's manuscripts are listed in Robbins' *American Literary Manuscripts*, p. 191.

Journals

"Recent Articles" in *The Scriblerian and the Kit Cats* (entry 1084) regularly includes a selection of reviews of studies on Lennox.

Hugh Leonard (John Keyes Byrne), 1926-
Bibliographies

King's *Ten Modern Irish Playwrights*, pp. 71-82, gives brief bibliographic information for Leonard's primary works and annotated entries for criticism of Leonard, with a classified list of reviews. Sandra Manoogian Pearce surveys works by and about Leonard in Schrank and Demastes' *Irish Playwrights, 1880-1995: A Research and Production Sourcebook*, pp. 145-58.

Eliza Leslie, 1787-1858
Bibliographies

See *Bibliography of American Fiction Through 1865*, pp.163-64, for a checklist of works by and about Leslie. Leslie's manuscripts are listed in Robbins' *American Literary Manuscripts*, p. 191.

Doris May Taylor Lessing, 1919-
Bibliographies

836. Seligman, Dee. **Doris Lessing: An Annotated Bibliography of Criticism.** Westport, CT: Greenwood Press, 1981. 139p. LC 80-24540. ISBN 0-313-21270-8.

This covers Lessing's primary works, translations of her works, and works about her in three main sections. In the first section Seligman offers brief bibliographic information for Lessing's primary works in separate listings for novels, short-story collections, short stories in periodicals, short stories in other collections, plays, poems. Autobiographies, essays, reportage, reviews, letters, tape recordings, television scripts, and theater criticisms. A second section lists translations of Lessing's works (arranged by country). The third section includes critically annotated entries for more than 800 works about her arranged in subsections for biographies, interviews, book reviews (arranged by works), and dissertations, among other materials. Seligman clearly identifies significant works in extended reviews. Coverage extends through 1978. Separate indexes of primary titles and proper names give access. Coverage supersedes Selma R. Burkom and Margaret Williams' *Doris Lessing: A Checklist of Primary and Secondary Sources* (Troy, NY: Whitston, 1973); and Stanton's *A Bibliography of Modern British Novelists*, pp. 471-534, 1087-88. Aimed at the collector of first editions, Eric T. Brueck's *Doris Lessing: A Bibliography of Her First Editions* (London: Metropolis Antiquarian Books, 1984) gives brief information for British and American editions of Lessing's books and pamphlets, collections, first separate appearances, contributions to books, and photographs and tape recordings.

Journals

837. **Doris Lessing Newsletter**. Oakland, CA: Doris Lessing Society, 1977- . 2/yr. ISSN 0882-486x.

Sponsored by the Doris Lessing Society, this journal publishes brief, scholarly articles and notes, bibliographies, reviews and announcements of new publications, abstracts of presentations, notices of research in progress, reports on conferences, obituaries of notable scholars, and the like. "Budding Profanity in 'A Sunrise on the Veld,' " "The Spanish Confusion: The Reception of Doris Lessing in Spain," "Garments of the Mind: Clothing and Appearance in the Fiction of Doris Lessing," and "The Politics of Motherhood" are typical contributions. Interviews with Lessing, reviews of research in other countries, and comparative studies (of Milton and Lessing, for example) predominate. "New Items on Doris Lessing" is a regular checklist of new editions and criticisms. *Doris Lessing Newsletter* is indexed in *AHI* and *MLA*.

(Sir) Roger L'Estrange, 1616-1704

Bibliographies

For a bibliography of works by and about L'Estrange, see *NCBEL*, II, pp. 1035-38.

Denise Levertov, 1923-

Bibliographies

838. Sakelliou-Schultz, Liana. **Denise Levertov: An Annotated Primary and Secondary Bibliography**. New York: Garland, 1988. 321p. (Garland Reference Library of the Humanities, vol. 856). LC 88-21766. ISBN 0-8240-5746-5.

Covering primary and secondary materials published from 1940 through 1988, Sakelliou-Schultz gives brief bibliographic information, with descriptions of contents and critical summaries, for Levertov's books; contributions to books and translations by Levertov (with selective critical evaluations); and contributed articles and poems in periodicals (some 473 entries). Secondary coverage consists of a classified listing of annotated entries for 115 books, dissertations, and parts of books; 114 articles; and reviews (some 254 entries, arranged by works); and bibliographic and biographical entries in reference works. Appendixes list and describe recordings, manuscripts of letters in libraries, and selected anthologies, and chronologically list book and periodical criticisms. Annotations for books and articles are critical. Important works receive detailed reviews. Index headings for "dreams," "myths," "political," "Vietnam," and the like offer good subject access. Coverage of primary materials supersedes that in Robert A. Wilson's *A Bibliography of Denise Levertov* (New York: Phoenix Book Shop, 1972), which lists American and British editions, translations, and selected miscellaneous writings published from 1940 through 1972. Also for works by Levertov, see *First Printings of American Authors*, vol. 3, pp. 203-208. Levertov's manuscripts are listed in Robbins' *American Literary Manuscripts*, p. 192.

Ira Levin, 1929-
Bibliographies
> For works by Levin, see *First Printings of American Authors*, vol. 2, pp. 239-40.

G(eorge) H(enry) Lewes, 1817-1878
Bibliographies
> Works about Lewes in selected periodicals are identified in Wells' *The Literary Index to American Magazines, 1815-1865*, p. 96; and *The Literary Index to American Magazines, 1850-1900*, pp. 247-48. Wendell V. Harris reviews research on Lewes in DeLaura's *Victorian Prose*, pp. 439-40.

Journals
> See *George Eliot-George Henry Lewes Studies* (entry 447).

Alfred Henry Lewis, c. 1858-1914
Bibliographies
> For works by Lewis, see *Bibliography of American Literature*, vol. 5, pp. 399-404. Lewis' manuscripts are listed in Robbins' *American Literary Manuscripts*, p. 192. See *Bibliography of American Fiction, 1866-1918*, p. 266, for Laura Plummer's checklist of works by and about Lewis.

C(live) S(taples) Lewis, 1898-1963
Bibliographies
> 839. Christopher, Joe R., and Joan K. Ostling. **C. S. Lewis: An Annotated Checklist of Writings About Him and His Works**. Kent, OH: Kent State University Press, 1973. 389p. (The Serif Series: Bibliographies and Checklists, no. 30). LC 73-76556. ISBN 0-87338-138-6.
>
> Christopher and Ostling topically arrange annotated entries for works about Lewis in separate listings for general studies, biographies, individual works of fiction and poetry, religion and ethics (with subsections for culture, science, and others), literary criticism (with sections for allegory, Milton, children's literature, and others), and book reviews (arranged by works). Annotations are descriptive and critical, with extensive reviews of important studies. Coverage extends through 1972. Separate indexes for master's theses, Ph.D. dissertations; and primary works cited in the entries provide access. Coverage of Lewis' primary bibliography is included in Walter Hooper's "A Bibliography of the Writings of C. S. Lewis" (pp. 801-83) in his *C. S. Lewis: A Companion & Guide* (entry 842). In addition, Christopher and Ostling's guide describes the Wheaton College Library's collection of published works, 900 holograph letters, holographs of poems and other works, and copies of other manuscripts, as well as works about Lewis (p. xii). This collection is also described in Margaret Hannay's "C. S. Lewis Collection at Wheaton College," *Mythlore* 2 (Winter 1962): 20.
>
> 840. Lowenberg, Susan. **C. S. Lewis: A Reference Guide, 1972-1988**. New York: G. K. Hall, 1993. 304p. (Reference Guide to Literature). LC 92-42316. ISBN 0-8161-1846-9.
>
> Lowenberg's guide updates Christopher and Ostling's *C. S. Lewis: An Annotated Checklist of Writings About Him and His Works* (entry 839), chronologically arranging annotated entries for English-language criticisms of Lewis published from 1972 to 1988. Coverage includes books and book chapters, essays, articles, dissertations; the most notable exclusions are book reviews and adaptations. The often extensive annotations summarize criticisms and sometimes provide some evaluation; annotations also note reprints and cross-reference other entries. Introduction surveys Lewis' life and works and lists Lewis' writings with brief bibliographic data (pp. 11-15). A comprehensive and detailed index of names, primary titles, and topics (many of which are more specifically subheaded) gives excellent

access. Also for a bibliography of works by and about Lewis, see *NCBEL*, IV, pp. 1073-78.

Dictionaries, Encyclopedias, and Handbooks

841. Duriez, Colin. **The C. S. Lewis Handbook**. Eastbourne: Monarch, 1990. 255p. LC 90-4050. ISBN 1-85424-013-7.

Straight forward A-to-Z listing of entries with brief information related to Lewis' life and works, including real and fictional persons, places, and things. "Reference guide" (pp. 246-55) usefully classifies entries under "life," "works," "literary criticism," "themes," "thought," "science fiction," "*The Screwtape Letters*," "*Till We Have Faces*," and "Narnia." Also includes "Books by C. S. Lewis" (pp. 235-39) and "Books About C. S. Lewis" (pp. 240-45). More convenient for brief character identifications than Hooper's comprehensive companion (entry 842). More limited in scope are Paul F. Ford's *Companion to Narnia* (New York: Harper & Row, 1980), which identifies and defines characters, places, things, events, and themes that appear in Lewis' "Narnia" novels, with a bibliography of secondary resources; and Martha Sammons' *A Guide Through Narnia* (Wheaton, IL: H. Shaw, 1979).

842. Hooper, Walter. **C. S. Lewis: A Companion & Guide**. San Francisco: HarperSanFrancisco, 1996. 940p. ISBN 0-06-063879-6.

An excellent, comprehensive guide to Lewis' life, works, and ideas that also includes the most comprehensive bibliography of Lewis' works. Extensive entries for individual works give background information, summaries of plots or contents, and overviews of early critical receptions, with citations to reviews. Dictionary of "Key Ideas" defines at length such terms as "Allegory" and "Mere Christianity" and tracks them through Lewis' works. Other dictionaries identify Lewis' acquaintances and places and things associated with him. Extended biography of Lewis, with a separate chronology, cross-references entries for works, places, things, ideas, and the like. "A Bibliography of the Writings of C. S. Lewis" (pp. 801-83) gives descriptive information (title-page transcriptions and imprints for UK and U.S. editions and reprintings) for Lewis' books; short stories; edited works and contributions to books; essay contributions to pamphlets, periodicals and miscellaneous pieces; single short poems; book reviews; and published letters. Detailed index of proper names, titles, and selected topics. Hooper's coverage of Lewis' primary bibliography updates his listing in *Light on C. S. Lewis*, ed. Jocelyn Gibb (London: Geoffrey Bles, 1965), pp. 117-60.

Indexes and Concordances

843. Martindale, Wayne, and Jerry Root. **The Quotable Lewis**. Wheaton, IL: Tyndale House Publishers, 1989. 651p. LC 89-50921. ISBN 0-84235-115-9.

Draws on all of Lewis' published works (excluding uncollected letters and book reviews) to compile "an encyclopedic selection of [1,565] quotes" (dust jacket). Alphabetically arranges entries under such topics as "Absolute values," "Free will," Plato, and Shakespeare. Entries cite Lewis' work by chapters and page numbers, with sources listed in a bibliography (pp. 629-31). Detailed index of other names, titles, and topics affords additional access. An excellent index to Lewis' ideas.

844. McLaughlin, Sara Park, and Mark O. Webb. **Word Index to the Poetry of C. S. Lewis**. West Cornwall, CT: Locust Hill Press, 1988. 232p. LC 88-17562. ISBN 0-933951-21-3.

McLaughlin provides an index verborum to Lewis' English vocabulary in poems included in *Spirits of Bondage* (New York: Harcourt, 1984), *Poems* (New York: Harcourt, 1977), and *Narrative Poems* (New York: Harcourt, 1979).

Journals

845.   **CSL: The Bulletin of the New York C. S. Lewis Society**. Glendale, NY: New York C. S. Lewis Society, 1969-. 12/yr. ISSN 0883-9980.

Studies of Lewis as a fantasy writer, literary critic, and Christian apologist predominate in this scholarly journal, sponsored by the New York C. S. Lewis Society. "C. S. Lewis on the Disappearance of the Individual," "Secularism, the Academy, the Arts and C. S. Lewis," and "Paradox in Narnia: Unconscious but Inevitable" are typical contributions. Other articles have commented on Lewis' associations as an "Inkling"; assessed his literary relations with Edmund Spenser, G. K. Chesterton, Dorothy Sayers, Winston Churchill, and George MacDonald; and offered biographical information. Issues also publish book reviews. To date *CSL: The Bulletin of the New York C. S. Lewis Society* is indexed in *MLA* through 1992.

Also for Lewis, see *Mythlore* (entry 1371).

Patterson's *Author Newsletters and Journals*, pp. 195-96, describes other previously published and popular journals on Lewis.

Janet Lewis, 1899-
Bibliographies

For works by Lewis, see *First Printings of American Authors*, vol. 4, pp. 249-52. Lewis' manuscripts are listed in Robbins' *American Literary Manuscripts*, p. 192.

M(atthew) G(regory) Lewis, 1775-1818
Bibliographies

For a bibliography of works by and about Lewis, see *NCBEL*, III, pp. 742-44. Robert Donald Spector reviews research on Lewis in *The English Gothic: A Bibliographic Guide to Writers from Horace Walpole to Mary Shelley*, pp. 153-204.

(Harry) Sinclair Lewis, 1885-1951
Bibliographies

846.   Fleming, Robert E. **Sinclair Lewis: A Reference Guide**. Boston: G. K. Hall, 1980. 240p. (A Reference Publication in Literature). LC 79-24048. ISBN 0-8161-8094-6.

Some 1,400 entries for secondary works about Lewis are chronologically arranged from 1914 through 1978. Coverage is substantial, including both American and international criticisms. Brief annotations are largely descriptive; some, however, are clearly evaluative. Mark Schorer's *Sinclair Lewis: An American Life* (New York: McGraw Hill, 1961) is called "definitive," for example. An effective index cites critics and other personal names, primary and secondary titles, and selected subjects. Headings refer to critical forms, such as "bibliographies" and "biographies," and topics, such as "characterization," "satire," and "social criticism," among others. The heading for "reputation" is subdivided nationally—for Italy, Russia, France, Latin America, and the like. Fleming's coverage of criticisms supersedes James Lundquist's *Merrill Checklist of Sinclair Lewis* (Columbus, OH: Merrill, 1970). Fleming extends secondary coverage with "Recent Research on Sinclair Lewis," *Modern Fiction Studies* 31 (1985): 609-16. For works by Lewis, see *First Printings of American Authors*, vol. 3, pp. 209-24. Lewis' manuscripts are listed in Robbins' *American Literary Manuscripts*, pp. 192-93. Also useful is *Sinclair Lewis: An Exhibition from the Grace Hegger Lewis-Sinclair Lewis Collection* (Austin, TX: Humanities Research Center, University of Texas, 1960). See *Bibliography of American Fiction, 1919-1988*, pp. 295-99, for Denise Kasinec and James S. Measell's checklist of works by and about Lewis.

(Percy) Wyndham Lewis, 1882-1957
Bibliographies

847.   Morrow, Bradford, and Bernard Lafourcade. **A Bibliography of the Writings of Wyndham Lewis**. Santa Barbara, CA: Black Sparrow Press, 1978. 373p. LC 78-12757. ISBN 0-87685-419-6.

This is the most generally useful, although not the definitive, listing of works by and about Lewis. The guide includes descriptions of Lewis' primary works in separate listings for books and other separate publications, contributions to books, edited periodicals, contributions to journals, translations of Lewis' works, and miscellaneous writings. Descriptions give transcriptions of title pages and data for collations, pagination, paper, bindings, and printing and publishing histories. Illustrations of dust jackets are also included. No coverage of Lewis' radio and television broadcasts and appearances. In addition, Morrow and Lafourcade also chronologically arrange briefly annotated entries for about 1,900 critical studies. Coverage extends from 1912 through 1977. Coverage of Lewis' primary materials, including media appearances, is available in Omar S. Pound and Philip Grover's *Wyndham Lewis: A Descriptive Bibliography* (Hamden, CT: Archon Books, 1978). Lewis' primary and secondary materials are described in Mary F. Daniels' *Wyndham Lewis: A Descriptive Catalogue of the Manuscript Material in the Department of Rare Books, Cornell University Library* (Ithaca, NY: Cornell University Library, 1972); and William K. Rose's *Wyndham Lewis at Cornell: A Review of the Lewis Papers Presented to the University by William G. Mennen* (Ithaca, NY: Cornell University Library, 1961). Coverage of secondary works is supplemented by Jeffrey Meyers' "Wyndham Lewis: A Bibliography of Criticism, 1912-1980," *Bulletin of Bibliography* 37 (1980): 33-52, which lists more than 900 items in various languages. Also for a bibliography of works by and about Lewis, see *NCBEL*, IV, pp. 631-64.

Journals
848. **Wyndham Lewis Annual**. Bath: Wyndham Lewis Society, 1994- . Annual. ISSN 0142-6214.

Unseen. Formerly *Enemy News: Newsletter of the Wyndham Lewis Society* (1978-93). See Patterson's *Author Newsletters and Journals*, pp. 196-97, for previously published journals for Lewis.

George Lillo, 1693-1739
Bibliographies
For a bibliography of works by and about Lillo, see *NCBEL*, II, pp. 794-95.

Joseph C(rosby) Lincoln, 1870-1944
Bibliographies
849. Rex, Percy Fielitz, Fredrika A. Burrows, and Stephen W. Sullwold. **The Prolific Pencil: A Biography of Joseph Crosby Lincoln, Litt. D.** Taunton, MA: W. S. Sullwold, 1980. 322p. LC 80-51482. ISBN 0-8849-2037-2.

Biography of Lincoln precedes "A Descriptive Bibliography of Joseph C. Lincoln First Editions" (pp. 181-311), compiled by Sullwold. Chronologically arranged sections for contributed poetry, short stories, books, sheet music, plays, and movies. Entries for 56 first editions of Lincoln's works published from 1902 to 1959 supply title-page transcriptions, collations and paginations, contents, binding and dust jacket descriptions, and brief notes on publication histories (with selected facsimile illustrations of title pages, bindings, and jackets). Bibliography is unindexed. Also see *Bibliography of American Fiction, 1866-1918*, pp. 267-68, for Gwen L. Nagel's checklist of works by and about Lincoln. Lincoln's manuscripts are listed in Robbins' *American Literary Manuscripts*, p. 194.

Sir David Lindsay, c. 1486-1555
Bibliographies
For a bibliography of works by and about Lindsay, see *NCBEL*, I, pp. 2426-27. Lindsay's manuscripts are described in *Index of English Literary Manuscripts*, I, pt. 2:311-14.

George Lippard, 1822-1854
Bibliographies

For works by Lippard, see *Bibliography of American Literature*, vol. 5, pp. 405-18. Lippard's manuscripts are listed in Robbins' *American Literary Manuscripts*, p. 195. See *Bibliography of American Fiction through 1865*, pp.166-68, for a checklist of works by and about Lippard. Wells' *The Literary Index to American Magazines, 1815-1865*, p. 97, identifies reviews of Lippard in selected periodicals.

David Ross Locke (Petroleum Vesuvius Nasby), 1833-1888
Bibliographies

For works by Locke, see *Bibliography of American Literature*, vol. 5, pp. 419-30. Locke's contributions to and reviews of Locke's works in selected periodicals are identified in Wells' *The Literary Index to American Magazines, 1850-1900*, p. 249. Locke's manuscripts are listed in Robbins' *American Literary Manuscripts*, pp. 196-97. See *Bibliography of American Fiction 1866-1918*, pp. 269-70, for Judith Yaross Lee's checklist of works by and about Locke.

Ross (Franklin) Lockridge, Jr., 1914-1948
Bibliographies

See *Bibliography of American Fiction 1919-1988*, pp. 299-300, for Laurence S. Lockridge and George Thompson's checklist of works by and about Lockridge. Lockridge's manuscripts are listed in Robbins' *American Literary Manuscripts*, p. 197.

George Cabot Lodge, 1873-1909
Bibliographies

For works by Lodge, see *First Printings of American Authors*, vol. 1, pp. 227-28. Lodge's manuscripts are listed in Robbins' *American Literary Manuscripts*, p. 197.

Thomas Lodge, 1558-1625
Bibliographies

850.   Allison, A. F. **Thomas Lodge, 1558-1625: A Bibliographical Catalogue of the Early Editions (to the End of the 17th Century).** Folkestone: Dawsons of Pall Mall, 1973. 98p. (Pall Mall Bibliographies, no. 2). LC 73-164856. ISBN 0-7129-0538-3.

Allison gives title page transcriptions, collations, contents, copy locations, publishing histories, and references to the *STC* and other catalogs for fifty editions of Lodge's works appearing through 1692. Also for a bibliography of works by and about Lodge, see *NCBEL*, I, pp. 1434-37. Lodge's manuscripts are described in *Index of English Literary Manuscripts*, I, pt. 2:315-18. Coverage of Lodge scholarship is provided in the Tannenbaums' *Elizabethan Bibliographies*, vol. 4, and Robert C. Johnson's *Elizabethan Bibliographies Supplements*, no. 5. Research on Lodge is reviewed by Joseph W. Houppert in Logan and Smith's *The Predecessors of Shakespeare*, pp. 153-60.

Indexes and Concordances

See Stagg's *The Figurative Language of the Tragedies of Shakespeare's Chief 16th-Century Contemporaries* (entry 901).

Harold Loeb, 1891-1974
Bibliographies

For works by Loeb, see *First Printings of American Authors*, vol. 1, p. 229.

Jack (John Griffith) London, 1876-1916
Bibliographies

851.   Sherman, Joan R. **Jack London: A Reference Guide**. Boston, MA: G. K. Hall, 1977. 323p. (Reference Guides in Literature). LC 76-54639. ISBN 0-8161-7849-6.

Sherman chronologically arranges annotated entries for about 1,500 books, parts of books, articles, reviews, selected introductions, and dissertations about London published from 1900 through 1976. Non-English-language criticism is excluded. Separate lists of poems and M.A. theses about London as well as descriptions of manuscript collections, including the Jack London Collection (of London's personal and professional papers) and the Jack London and Charmian (Kittredge) London Collection in the Huntington Library, as well as other collections (pp. 293-97), are appended. Annotations are descriptive, although significant works (particularly biographical studies) receive extended descriptions. Index headings for broad topics ("bibliography," "biography," and "criticism") give limited subject access. Sherman's guide generally supersedes coverage of criticism in Woodbridge, London, and Tweney's bibliography (entry 852), although the latter remains valuable for coverage of non-English language criticisms. See *Bibliography of American Fiction 1866-1918*, pp. 271-76, for Earle Labor's checklist of works by and about London. Research on London is also reviewed by Labor in Erisman and Etulain's *Fifty Western Writers*, pp. 268-79.

852.   Woodbridge, Hensley C., John London, and George H. Tweney. **Jack London: A Bibliography**. Enlarged ed. Millwood, NY: Kraus Reprint, 1973. 554p. LC 73-5921. ISBN 0-527-97860-4.

First published in 1966 (Georgetown, CA: Talisman), this is a comprehensive bibliography of primary and secondary materials, including non-English-language criticism, published through 1971. Woodbridge, London, and Tweney give full bibliographic descriptions in separate listings for London's books; collected works in English; anthologies in English; non-English language collections; short stories; contributions to periodicals; contributions to newspapers; introductions and prefaces; separate ephemera; spurious works; and films based on London's works. In addition, other sections list books, articles, dissertations, reviews (arranged by works) in English and other languages. Supplemental listings for 1966 through 1971 follow the same arrangement. Additional information on London's primary materials is provided in James E. Sisson, III, and Robert W. Martens's *Jack London First Editions: A Chronological Reference Guide* (Oakland, CA: Star Rover House, 1979), which provides notes on points of identification for first editions; Dale L. Walker and Sisson's *The Fiction of Jack London: A Chronological Bibliography* (El Paso, TX: Texas Western Press, 1972); and Blanck's *Bibliography of American Literature*, vol. 5, pp. 431-67. London's manuscripts are listed in Robbins' *American Literary Manuscripts*, p. 198. Also of interest for the study of London's primary materials, David Mike Hamilton's *"The Tools of My Trade": The Annotated Books in Jack London's Library* (Seattle, WA: University of Washington Press, 1986) identifies about 400 books (from London's library of 15,000 volumes) that London annotated, marked, or quoted in his works, with descriptions of London's annotations and copy locations, as well as a list of books given to London.

Journals

853.   **The Call: The Official Newsletter of the Jack London Society**. San Antonio, TX: Jack London Society, 1991- . 2/yr. ISSN 1083-6799.

Intends to keep members "up to date on Jack London events, scholarly presentations at conferences, publications, and book collecting" (masthead). Features a few notes on topics like Valley wineries and London acquisitions in libraries as well as a few book reviews. "News Briefs and Research Notes" reports on projects and conferences, issues calls for papers, and gives membership information.

854.   **Jack London Newsletter**. Carbondale, IL: Southern Illinois University, 1967-1988. 3/yr. ISSN 0021-3837.

"Jack London's Use of Joseph Conrad's 'The End of the Tether' in *The Sea Wolf* " and "Jack London and the Spanish American Short Story" were typical features in this newsletter. Emphasis was on close interpretive readings of London's works, biographical problems, media adaptations of London's works, and London's influence and reputation abroad. Reviews of new works also appeared. From 1974-1981 the journal featured bibliographies of editions, translations, and criticisms that updated Woodbridge, London, and Tweney's *Jack London: A Bibliography* (entry 852). Other bibliographical contributions included Kevin J. Harty's "Dissertations on Jack London, 1936-1987: Evidence for Canonicity," 20: 2-3 (May-December 1987): 58-62. *Jack London Newsletter* was indexed in *AES, AHI, MHRA*, and *MLA*.

Patterson's *Author Newsletters and Journals*, pp. 197-98, describes other previously published journals for London.

Haniel Long, 1888-1956
Bibliographies

For works by Long, see *First Printings of American Authors*, vol. 5, pp. 167-70.

Henry Wadsworth Longfellow, 1807-1882
Bibliographies

855.   Livingston, Luther S. **A Bibliography of the First Editions in Book Form of the Writings of Henry Wadsworth Longfellow**. 1908; reprint New York: Burt Franklin, 1968. 131p. (Burt Franklin: Bibliography and Reference Series, vol. 182). LC 8-31655.

Livingston provides title page transcriptions, physical details, contents, and publishing histories for Longfellow's books published from 1826 through 1907. More comprehensive coverage of Longfellow's books, contributions to books, musical settings, dated and undated reprints, reprints in anthologies, collected works, and sheet music is offered in Blanck's *Bibliography of American Literature*, vol. 5, pp. 468-640. Longfellow's manuscripts are listed in Robbins' *American Literary Manuscripts*, pp. 198-99. David L. O'Neal and Mary T. O'Neal describe Longfellow's primary materials in *The Henry Wadsworth Longfellow Collection* in part 3 of Sidney Ives's *The Parkman Dexter Howe Library* (Gainesville, FL: University of Florida, 1986). Longfellow's contributions to and reviews of Longfellow's works in selected periodicals are identified in Wells' *The Literary Index to American Magazines, 1850-1900*, pp. 251-55. Coverage of Longfellow criticism from 1900 through 1981 is included in Boswell's *The Schoolroom Poets* (entry 177). Research on Longfellow is reviewed by Richard Dilworth Rust in Harbert and Rees's *Fifteen American Authors Before 1900*, pp. 357-78. The collection of Longfellow materials at Bowdoin College is described in Richard Harwell's *Hawthorne and Longfellow* (Brunswick, ME: Bowdoin College, 1966).

Samuel Longfellow, 1819-1892
Bibliographies

For works by Longfellow, see *First Printings of American Authors*, vol. 3, pp. 225-28. Longfellow's manuscripts are listed in Robbins' *American Literary Manuscripts*, p. 199.

Augustus Baldwin Longstreet, 1790-1870
Bibliographies

For works by Longstreet, see *Bibliography of American Literature*, vol. 6, pp. 1-5; and *First Printings of American Authors*, vol. 1, pp. 231-33. Wells' *The Literary Index to American Magazines, 1815-1865*, p. 100; and *The Literary Index to American Magazines, 1850-1900*, p. 255, identifies reviews of Longstreet in selected periodicals. Longstreet's manuscripts are listed in Robbins' *American Literary Manuscripts*, p. 199. See *Bibliography of American Fiction Through 1865*, pp.168-70, for a checklist of works by and about Longstreet. William E. Lenz surveys works by and about Longstreet in Bain and Flora's *Fifty Southern Writers Before 1900*, pp. 312-22.

Anita Loos, 1888-1981
Bibliographies

For works by Loos, see *First Printings of American Authors*, vol. 3, pp. 229-31. Loos' manuscripts are listed in Robbins' *American Literary Manuscripts*, p. 200. See *Bibliography of American Fiction 1919-1988*, pp. 300-301, for Richard J. Schrader's checklist of works by and about Loos.

Harriett Mulford Stone Lothrop (Margaret Sidney), 1844-1924
Bibliographies

See *Bibliography of American Fiction 1866-1918*, pp. 277-78, for Janice M. Alberghene's checklist of works by and about Lothrop. Lothrop's manuscripts are listed in Robbins' *American Literary Manuscripts*, p. 200.

H(oward) P(hillips) Lovecraft, 1890-1937
Bibliographies

856.	Joshi, S. T. **H. P. Lovecraft and Lovecraft Criticism: An Annotated Bibliography**. Kent, OH: Kent State University Press, 1981. 473p. (The Serif Series: Bibliographies and Checklists, no. 38). LC 80-84662. ISBN 0-87338-248-x.

Separate listings in Joshi's guide cover works by Lovecraft, translations of his works, and works about Lovecraft. The first section provides full bibliographic descriptions for Lovecraft's works in English, covering his books; contributions of fiction, nonfiction, poetry, revisions, collaborative works, and letters to periodicals; contributions to books; edited books and periodicals; and apocryphal and miscellaneous writings, including lost works, destroyed works, and others. The second section lists and describes translations of Lovecraft's works in books, periodicals, and collections. The third section includes selectively annotated entries in lists for books, articles, brief notices in general and reference works, bibliographies and glossaries, dissertations, book reviews of Lovecraft's works in English and non-English languages, unpublished critical studies, and other works about Lovecraft. Separate indexes reference primary and secondary titles, names, periodical titles, and non-English languages. Joshi's guide does not cover manuscripts, media, or other adaptations of Lovecraft's works.

Dictionaries, Encyclopedias, and Handbooks

857.	Joshi, S. T. **An Index to the Selected Letters of H. P. Lovecraft**. West Warwick, RI: Necronomicon Press, 1980. 78p. OCLC 9501097.

An index to "individual people, places, titles, and subjects" as well as, to a lesser degree, "broader and more abstract . . . concepts as art, aesthetics, civilisation, literature, and the like" (p. [9]), with volume and page references to *Selected Letters of H. P. Lovecraft* (Sauk City, WI: Arkham House, 1965-1976), which Joshi regards the "single greatest landmark in Lovecraft studies." Identifies specific references to Lovecraft's compositional practices, library, and reading. Appends brief Lovecraft chronology and list of correspondents, including the likes of August Derleth. Joshi relied on Lovecraft Collection in Brown University's John Hay Library.

858.	Shreffler, Philip A. **The H. P. Lovecraft Companion**. Westport, CT: Greenwood Press, 1977. 198p. LC 76-52605. ISBN 0-8371-9482-2.

Offers summaries of Lovecraft's works, identifies and describes real and fictional characters, and includes bibliographies of works by and about Lovecraft.

Journals

859.	**Lovecraft Studies**. West Warwick, RI: Necronomicon Press, 1979-. 2/yr. ISSN 0899-8361.

Close readings of Lovecraft's works; studies of sources, themes, characters, myths, and images; and assessments of Lovecraft's literary relationships (with such writers as Edgar Allan Poe, William Butler Yeats, James Joyce, George Willard

Kirk, and Sylvia Plath) and critical reception are published in this journal. "The Genesis of 'The Shadow Out of Time' " and "A Gothic Approach to Lovecraft's Sense of Outsideness" are typical critical features. Other contributions have evaluated biographical writing on Lovecraft and described special collections of Lovecraft's primary materials. Several bibliographical contributions have reviewed scholarship on Lovecraft, including Steve J. Mariconda's " 'Expect Great Revelations': Lovecraft Criticism in His Centennial Year," 24 (Spring 1991): 24-29. *Lovecraft Studies* is indexed in *MLA*.

Richard Lovelace, 1618-1657/8
Bibliographies

For a bibliography of works by and about Lovelace, see *NCBEL*, I, pp. 1221-22. Lovelace's manuscripts are described in *Index of English Literary Manuscripts*, II, pt. 2:9-16.

Amy (Lawrence) Lowell, 1874-1925
Bibliographies

860.   Hurff, Carmen Russell. **A Descriptive Catalogue of the Amy Lowell Collection**. Gainesville, FL: University Press of Florida, 1992. 98p.

Unseen. For works by Lowell, see *Bibliography of American Literature*, vol. 6, pp. 6-20. Lowell's manuscripts are listed in Robbins' *American Literary Manuscripts*, p. 201.

James Russell Lowell, 1819-1891
Bibliographies

861.   Cooke, George Willis. **A Bibliography of James Russell Lowell**. Boston, MA: Houghton Mifflin, 1906. 208p. LC 6-39795.

Following a chronological list of Lowell's works, Cooke alphabetically lists Lowell's works, including his separate publications as well as contributions to books and periodicals. Other sections include descriptions of separate works, collected works, selections and anthologies, edited works, addresses and speeches, published letters and biographical materials, as well as works about Lowell. Available in a reprinted edition (Boston: Milford House, 1972). Although dated, Cooke's comprehensive bibliography remains useful, covering Lowell's periodical publications and nineteenth-century critical materials not included in Blanck's *Bibliography of American Literature*, vol. 6, pp. 21-105, nor in Boswell's *The Schoolroom Poets* (entry 177). Luther S. Livingston's *A Bibliography of the First Editions in Book Form of the Writings of James Russell Lowell* (New York: Privately printed, 1914) offers additional physical information for Lowell's books. Contributions by Lowell and criticism and reviews of Lowell's works in selected periodicals are identified in Wells' *The Literary Index to American Magazines, 1815-1865*, pp. 100-101; and *The Literary Index to American Magazines, 1850-1900*, pp. 255-59. Lowell's manuscripts are listed in Robbins' *American Literary Manuscripts*, p. 201. Research on Lowell is reviewed by Robert A. Rees in Harbert and Rees's *Fifteen American Authors Before 1900*, pp. 379-401; and Thomas Wortham in Myerson's *The Transcendentalists*, pp. 336-42.

Robert Traill Spence Lowell, 1816-1891
Bibliographies

For works by Lowell, see *Bibliography of American Literature*, vol. 6, pp. 106-11. Lowell's manuscripts are listed in Robbins' *American Literary Manuscripts*, p. 202.

Robert (Traill Spence) Lowell, (Jr.), 1917-1977
Bibliographies

862.   Axelrod, Steven Gould, and Helen Deese. **Robert Lowell: A Reference Guide**. Boston, MA: G. K. Hall, 1982. 445p. (A Reference Guide to Literature). LC 81-13282. ISBN 0-8161-7814-3.

Axelrod and Deese provide a comprehensive, but not definitive, chronologically-arranged listing of annotated entries for 1,736 English-language works about Lowell published from 1943 through 1980, including books, chapters in books, articles, reviews, dissertations, and references to Lowell in general works or works about others. Creative works about Lowell and reviews of secondary works are excluded. An extensive introduction offers evaluative comments on biographical and critical studies. Annotations are descriptive. The volume's indexing is complex but effective. Critics and names, periodical titles for anonymous works, and selected subjects are included. Headings reference writers like Shakespeare, T. S. Eliot, and Randall Jarrell, facilitating comparative studies. Other subjects are arranged and subarranged in topical categories under Lowell's name. "Kinds of studies of," for example, includes subordinate topical references for "American studies approach," "formalist or New Critical approach," and "rhetorical or reader-response approach," in addition "bibliography" and "biography." "Works of" subarranges studies under the individual works. Axelrod and Deese's work supersedes the coverage of secondary materials offered by Mazzaro's *The Achievement of Robert Lowell* (entry 863) and its supplements. Supplemental coverage of non-English language criticisms is provided in Annamaria Zin's "Italian Bibliography of Robert Lowell," in *Robert Lowell: A Tribute*, ed. Rolando Anzilotti (Pisa: Nistri-Lischi Editori, 1979), pp. 172-80. Norma Procopiow's *Robert Lowell: The Poet and His Critics* (Chicago, IL: American Library Association, 1984) reviews critical responses to Lowell as both a writer and a critic. Axelrod reviews research on Lowell in *Contemporary Authors: Bibliographical Series: Volume 2: American Poets*, pp. 163-202.

863.   Mazzaro, James. **The Achievement of Robert Lowell, 1939-1959**. Detroit, MI: University of Detroit Press, 1960. 41p. LC 61-469.

This remains the best available descriptive listing of Lowell's primary bibliography, including entries for books and contributions of periodicals, individual works (poems, articles, letters, and the like). Mazzaro also lists secondary materials. The listings are supplemented by Mazzaro's "A Checklist of Materials on Robert Lowell, 1939-1968," in Michael London and Robert Boyer's *Robert Lowell: A Portrait of the Artist in His Time* (New York: D. Lewis, 1970). Also for works by Lowell, see *First Printings of American Authors*, vol. 1, pp. 235-38. Lowell's manuscripts are listed in Robbins' *American Literary Manuscripts*, p. 202. Also useful is Patrick K. Miehe's *Robert Lowell Papers at the Houghton Library, Harvard University: A Guide to the Collection* (New York: Greenwood, 1990), which describes family and literary correspondence previous to 1971, literary manuscripts of early poems from about 1935 through *Notebooks*, and uncollected poems from about 1970.

Dictionaries, Encyclopedia, and Handbooks

864.   Hobsbaum, Philip. **A Reader's Guide to Robert Lowell**. London: Thames and Hudson, 1988. 184p. LC 88-50133. ISBN 0-5001-5020-6.

Hobsbaum gives introductions to Lowell's life and major works, with a selected bibliography of primary and secondary materials.

Indexes and Concordances

865.   Rehor, Rosalind. **This Round Dome: An Analysis of Theme and Style in the Poetry of Robert Lowell**. Ph.D. dissertation, Cleveland, OH: Case Western Reserve University, 1972. 747p. OCLC 19003991.

Appendixed to this study of Lowell's prosody and themes in his elegiac works is a concordance to fifty-four poems.

(Clarence) Malcolm Lowry, 1909-1957
Bibliographies

866.   New, William H. **Malcolm Lowry: A Reference Guide**. Boston, MA: G. K. Hall, 1978. 162p. (A Reference Publication in Literature). LC 77-28579. ISBN 0-8161-7884-4.

This is the best listing of critical studies of Lowry. New chronologically arranges annotated entries for about 1,000 books and "shorter writings" about Lowry published from 1927 through 1976. Coverage attempts comprehensiveness, including books, articles, dissertations, "substantive" reviews, conference papers, newspaper reports, and films and broadcasts in English as well as in non-English languages. Annotations are largely descriptive. A cumulative index of critics and names, primary and secondary titles, and selected subjects offers excellent access to the listings. Broad subject headings are included for "alcoholism," "bibliography," "Canadian literature," and other topics. Multiple topical subdivisions are provided as well. Studies of individual works, such as *Under the Volcano*, are classified and referenced as "general studies," "adaptations of," "themes in," and the like. Studies by or about Conrad Aiken (in relation to Lowry, of course) are referenced under Aiken both "as author" and "as subject." The volume also identifies collections of Lowry's manuscripts at the University of British Columbia, the University of California at Berkeley, University of Texas at Austin, City of Liverpool Library, and the University of Virginia; and lists Lowry's major writings, with later editions, and translations of Lowry's works. Another useful catalog, Judith O. Combs' *Malcolm Lowry, 1909-1957: An Inventory of His Papers in the Library of the University of British Columbia* (Vancouver, BC: University of British Columbia Library, 1973) describes manuscripts and other drafts of published and unpublished works of poetry, prose, and music; letters; notes and notebooks; financial records; photographs and memorabilia; works from Lowry's library; and critical works about Lowry.

867.   Woolmer, J. Howard. **Malcolm Lowry: A Bibliography**. Revere, PA: Woolmer Brotherson, 1983. 183p. LC 82-050810. ISBN 0-913506-12-5.

Modeled on volumes in the Pittsburgh Bibliography series, this is the most comprehensive listing of Lowry's primary works. Separate listings include entries for Lowry's books and pamphlets; contributions to books; contributions to periodicals (some 224 entries, including two interviews in British newspapers as well as quotations from Lowry that appeared in booksellers and auction catalogues); translations of Lowry's works (books, anthologies, and articles) into nineteen non-English languages; radio, television, and film adaptations; song lyrics and musical recordings; and recordings made by Graham Collier. The section for books covers American, British, and Canadian first and subsequent editions appearing since 1933. Descriptions include illustrations of title pages and versos and data on bindings, dust jackets, and printing and publishing histories. An index of names, primary titles, and periodical titles is provided. Also for a bibliography of works by and about Lowry, see *NCBEL*, IV, pp. 640-42.

Dictionaries, Encyclopedias, and Handbooks

868.   Ackerley, Chris, and Lawrence J. Clipper. **A Companion to Under the Volcano**. Vancouver, BC: University of British Columbia Press, 1984. 476p. LC 84-231488. ISBN 0-7748-0199-9.

In a chapter-by-chapter, line-by-line arrangement, Ackerley and Clipper identify and explicate Lowry's allusions and references to people, books, places, films, and historical events. About 1,600 notes cover 7,000 particular points. Entries cross reference the text of the Penguin edition (Harmondsworth: 1986). A glossary of frequently occurring Spanish words, a diagram of *The Cabbala*, and maps are also included.

Journals

869.   **The Malcolm Lowry Review**. Waterloo, ON: Wilfred Laurier University, 1977-. 2/yr. ISSN 0828-5020.

Issues of *The Malcolm Lowry Review* feature close readings of Lowry's works; interpretive studies of sources, themes, and literary relations; discussions of biographical and bibliographical interest; checklists of publications, like Norman Amor's "Malcolm Lowry/A Checklist," 34-35 (Spring-Fall 1994): 8-235, one of several supplements by Amor to New's *Malcolm Lowry: A Reference Guide* (entry 866) and Woolmer's *Malcolm Lowry: A Bibliography* (entry 867); and reviews of new publications about Lowry. "Color in Malcolm Lowry's *Under the Volcano*" and "Malcolm Lowry's 'Tender Is the Night': Form, Structure, Spirit" are representative. Other articles have focused on Lowry's narrative structure and use of despair and assessed his literary relations with Nikolai Gogol, Eugene O'Neill, James Joyce, and Christopher Marlowe. Occasional bibliographical contributions describing Lowry's letters and collections of other primary materials include Patrick A. McCarthy's "The La Mordida Drafts and Notes at UBC [University of British Columbia Library]," 28 (Spring 1991): 6-12. *The Malcolm Lowry Review* is indexed in *MLA*.

E(dward) V(errall) Lucas, 1868-1938

Bibliographies

870.   Prance, Claude A. **E. V. Lucas and His Books**. West Cornwall, CT: Locust Hill Press, 1988. 243p. LC 88-15728. ISBN 0-933951-19-1.

Prance provides brief bibliographic information and descriptions of contents for Lucas' books and pamphlets (including edited works and contributions to books); contributions to periodicals; and selected reprintings of Lucas' works; in addition to annotated entries for some 266 works about Lucas. Also for a bibliography of works by and about Lucas, see *NCBEL*, IV, pp. 1079-82.

Grace Lumpkin, 1903?-1980

Bibliographies

For works by Lumpkin, see *First Printings of American Authors*, vol. 2, pp. 241-42. Lumpkin's manuscripts are listed in Robbins' *American Literary Manuscripts*, p. 204. See *Bibliography of American Fiction 1919-1988*, p. 302, for Gina D. Peterman's checklist of works by and about Lumpkin.

Alison Lurie, 1926-

Bibliographies

For works by Lurie, see *First Printings of American Authors*, vol. 5, pp. 171-73.

John Lydgate, 1370?-1449

Bibliographies

Alain Renoir and C. David Benson offer a comprehensive guide to Lydgate's primary materials with a bibliography of editions and criticism in Severs and Hartung's *A Manual of Writings in Middle English*, vol. VI, pp. 1809-1920, 2011-2175. Also for a bibliography of works by and about Lydgate, see *NCBEL*, I, pp. 639-46.

Journals

See Patterson's *Author Newsletters and Journals*, p. 200, for previously published journals for Lydgate.

John Lyly, 1554?-1606

Bibliographies

For a bibliography of works by and about Lyly, see *NCBEL*, I, pp. 1423-27; the Tannenbaums' *Elizabethan Bibliographies*, vol. 5; and Robert C. Johnson's *Elizabethan Bibliographies Supplements*, no. 5. Lyly's manuscripts are described in *Index of English Literary Manuscripts*, I, pt. 2:319-21, 631. Joseph W. Houppert reviews research on Lyly in Logan and Smith's *The Predecessors of Shakespeare*, pp. 125-42.

Indexes and Concordances

871.   Mittermann, Harald, and Herbert Schendl. **A Complete Concordance to the Novels of John Lyly**. Hildesheim: G. Olms, 1986. 879p. (Elizabethan Concordance Series, no. 2). ISBN 3-487-07564-4.

Mittermann and Schendl concord the texts of the first editions of *Euphues* (1578) and *Euphues and His England* (1580) as edited by R. W. Bond in *The Complete Works of John Lyly* (1902; reprint Oxford: Clarendon Press, 1967). Alphabetical and frequency lists for headwords and variant spellings are included.

Harris Merton Lyon, 1883-1916
Bibliographies

For works by Lyon, see *First Printings of American Authors*, vol. 4, p. 253.

Andrew Nelson Lytle, 1902-1995
Bibliographies

872.   Kramer, Victor A., Patricia A. Bailey, Carol G. Dana, and Carl H. Griffin. **Andrew Lytle, Walker Percy, Peter Taylor: A Reference Guide**. Boston, MA: G. K. Hall, 1983. 278p. (A Reference Guide to Literature). LC 82-15748. ISBN 0-8161-8399-6.

Each writer receives a separate introductory essay, a list of primary materials, and a chronologically-arranged list of annotated entries for secondary works. Including books, parts of books, articles, reviews, dissertations, introductions, and entries in reference works, coverage for Lytle extends from 1931 through 1980 (about 250 entries); for Percy, from 1961 through 1980 (about 500 entries); and for Taylor, from 1948 through 1980 (about 200 entries). Separate lists of M.A. theses for the three writers are also included. Reviews from regional newspapers and other brief notices are typically excluded. Separate indexes for the writers complete the guide. Flora and Bain's *Fifty Southern Writers After 1900* includes reviews of research on Lytle by Mark T. Lucas (pp. 290-300), on Percy by Mark Johnson (pp. 345-55), and on Taylor by Lynn Z. Bloom (pp. 469-78).

873.   Wright, Stuart. **Andrew Nelson Lytle: A Bibliography, 1920-1982**. Sewanee, TN: University of the South, 1982. 131p. LC 83-123561.

Covering Lytle's primary materials, Wright provides full descriptions in separate listings for books and pamphlets; contributions to books and edited works; poems; short fiction, essays, reviews, and tributes; and selected interviews and published articles including original comments by Lytle. Entries give facsimiles of title and copyright pages; collations; contents; descriptions of typography, paper, and bindings (illustrations of bindings are appended); and printing histories. Textual collations of variants are also included. In addition, Wright selectively describes about 100 secondary works. Also for works by Lytle, see *First Printings of American Authors* , vol. 1, pp. 239-40. Lytle's manuscripts are listed in Robbins' *American Literary Manuscripts*, p. 204.

Edward Robert Bulwer Lytton, 1st Earl of Lytton, 1831-1891
Bibliographies

For a bibliography of works by and about Lytton, see *NCBEL*, III, pp. 636-37. Works about Lytton in selected periodicals are identified in Wells' *The Literary Index to American Magazines, 1850-1900*, p. 260.

Robert McAlmon, 1896-1956

Bibliographies

For works by McAlmon, see *First Printings of American Authors*, vol. 1, pp. 251-52. McAlmon's manuscripts are listed in Robbins' *American Literary Manuscripts*, pp. 204-205. See *Bibliography of American Fiction, 1919-1988*, p. 333, for Hugh Ford's checklist of works by and about McAlmon.

Thomas Babington Macaulay, 1800-1859

Bibliographies

For a bibliography of works by and about Macaulay, see *NCBEL*, III, pp. 1463-68. Macaulay's contributions to and reviews of Macaulay's works in selected periodicals are identified in Wells' *The Literary Index to American Magazines, 1815-1865*, p. 101; and *The Literary Index to American Magazines, 1850-1900*, pp. 261-62. See the review of research by John Clive and Thomas Pinney in DeLaura's *Victorian Prose*, pp. 17-30.

Anne McCaffrey, 1926-

Bibliographies

See Arbur's *Leigh Brackett, Marion Zimmer Bradley, Anne McCaffrey* (entry 136) for works about McCaffrey published from 1968 through 1980.

Dictionaries, Encyclopedias, and Handbooks

874.   Nye, Jody Lynn, and Anne McCaffrey. **The Dragonlover's Guide to Pern**. New York: Ballantine Books, 1989. 178p. LC 89-6715. ISBN 0-3453-5424-9.

Black-and-white illustrated "companion volume to [McCaffrey's] work, intended to help you visualize the setting and background of her chronicles" (p. xi). A potpourri of descriptions largely of things (not persons) related to Pern, including native, imported, and adapted flora and fauna; dragons and dragonets, especially their care, feeding, and training; fighting tactics; typical oaths and maledictions; currency and exchange rates; craft knitting patterns; recipes for favorite dishes; and much more. Appends a pronunciation guide to names on Pern and a bibliography (pp. 177-78). Unindexed.

Cormac McCarthy, 1933-

Bibliographies

For works by McCarthy, see *First Printings of American Authors*, vol. 2, p. 249.

Mary (Therese) McCarthy, 1912-1989

Bibliographies

875.   Bennett, Joy, and Gabriella Hochmann. **Mary McCarthy: An Annotated Bibliography**. New York: Garland, 1992. 442p. (Garland Reference Library of the Humanities, vol. 1251). LC 91-47702. ISBN 0-8240-7028-3.

Covers works by and about McCarthy. Part 1 (with 289 entries) lists works by McCarthy in sections for books and edited books; essays; short stories, book reviews; theater and film reviews; translations; letters to the editor; miscellanea (two entries); and interviews. Entries for books give brief bibliographic information for first and subsequent editions and translations, with content notes and citations for first appearances. Part 2 covers works about McCarthy, including descriptively annotated entries for nearly 1,500 general criticisms, reviews (arranged by McCarthy's works), dissertations and theses, biographies and biographical sources, and obituaries. Descriptive annotations. Indexes of secondary authors and of names and titles. No subject indexing. Bennett and Hochmann produce a comprehensive guide to works about McCarthy. While complementing Goldman's primary bibliography (entry 876) with listings of paperback, British editions, and translations, Bennett and Hochmann's guide lacks Goldman's bibliographic detail. See also *Bibliography of*

American Fiction, 1919-1988, pp. 335-36, for James W. Hipp's checklist of works by and about McCarthy.

876.   Goldman, Sherli Evens. **Mary McCarthy: A Bibliography**. New York: Harcourt, Brace & World, 1968. 80p. LC 68-12574.

Goldman gives full bibliographic descriptions of McCarthy's books; contributions to books; contributions to periodicals; translations of McCarthy's works (arranged by languages); and miscellaneous primary materials, such as interviews, McCarthy's translations of others' works, editions for the blind, and the like. Entries include title-page transcriptions, physical descriptions, and contents. Also for works by McCarthy, see *First Printings of American Authors*, vol. 4, pp. 255-60. McCarthy's manuscripts are listed in Robbins' *American Literary Manuscripts*, p. 205.

Horace McCoy, 1897-1955
Bibliographies

For works by McCoy, see *First Printings of American Authors*, vol. 1, pp. 253-54. McCoy's manuscripts are listed in Robbins' *American Literary Manuscripts*, p. 205. See *Bibliography of American Fiction, 1919-1988*, pp. 337-38, for Mark Royden Winchell's checklist of works by and about McCoy.

Carson (Smith) McCullers, 1917-1967
Bibliographies

877.   Shapiro, Adrian M., Jackson R. Bryer, and Kathleen Field. **Carson McCullers: A Descriptive Listing and Annotated Bibliography of Criticism**. New York: Garland, 1980. 315p. (Garland Reference Library of the Humanities, vol. 142). LC 79-7909. ISBN 0-8240-9534-0.

Full bibliographic details for McCullers' works in separate listings for books (with facsimiles of title and copyright pages, physical descriptions, copy locations, publication histories, and references to later printings); contributions to books; contributions to periodicals and newspapers; and adaptations, recordings, and international English-language editions of McCullers' works. In addition, Shapiro, Bryer, and Field give annotated entries for about 900 works about McCullers published in books and parts of books, periodical and newspaper articles, reviews of McCullers' books (arranged by works); reviews of play productions (arranged by plays); dissertations; and non-English language criticisms. Coverage of secondary materials for McCullers is better than that provided in Kiernan's *Katherine Anne Porter and Carson McCullers* (entry 1086). George Bixby's "Carson McCullers: A Bibliographical Checklist," *American Book Collector* 5 (1984): 38-43, updates Shapiro, Bryer, and Field's coverage of primary materials. Also for works by McCullers, see *First Printings of American Authors*, vol. 2, pp. 251-52. McCullers' manuscripts are listed in Robbins' *American Literary Manuscripts*, p. 206. See *Bibliography of American Fiction 1919-1988*, pp. 338-39, for Virginia Spencer Carr's checklist of works by and about McCullers. Research on McCullers is reviewed by Carr and Joseph R. Millichap in Duke, Bryer, and Inge's *American Women Writers*, pp. 297-320; Carr in Flora and Bain's *Fifty Southern Writers After 1900*, pp. 301-12; and Carr in *Contemporary Authors: Bibliographical Series: Volume 1: American Novelists*, pp. 293-345; and by Margaret B. McDowell in *Contemporary Authors: Bibliographical Series: Volume 3: American Dramatists*, pp. 171-88.

George Barr McCutcheon, 1866-1928
Bibliographies

For works by McCutcheon, see *Bibliography of American Literature*, vol. 6, pp. 112-27. McCutcheon's manuscripts are listed in Robbins' *American Literary Manuscripts*, p. 206. See *Bibliography of American Fiction, 1866-1918*, pp. 284-85, for John Cavin's checklist of works by and about McCutcheon.

Hugh MacDiarmid (Christopher Murray Grieve), 1892-1978
Bibliographies

878.   National Library of Scotland. **Hugh MacDiarmid**. Edinburgh: The Library, 1967. 39p. (National Library of Scotland Catalogue, no. 7). LC 70-445538.

Catalog of National Library of Scotland exhibition in honor of MacDiarmid's 75th birthday. Supplies brief bibliographic descriptions, with full captions, for selected works by and about MacDiarmid, including separate publications, collected and selected editions, first book and periodical appearances, letters, literary manuscripts, portraits and photographs, tributes and other ana. Also includes a brief MacDiarmid chronology. For a bibliography of works by and about MacDiarmid, see *NCBEL*, IV, pp. 299-303. A full, descriptive bibliography for MacDiarmid remains to be completed.

John D(ann) MacDonald, 1916-1986
Bibliographies

879.   Shine, Walter, and Jean Shine. **A Bibliography of the Published Works of John D. MacDonald with Selected Biographical Materials and Critical Essays**. Gainesville, FL: Patrons of the Libraries, University of Florida, 1980. 209p. LC 80-22673.

Covers works by and about MacDonald. The first part supplies a chronology of published works and sections for books (with chronological and alphabetical lists of titles and separate lists of American, British, and translated editions); magazine and newspaper fiction; anthologized and collected fiction; nonfiction (subarranged lists for articles on art, letters to the editor, speeches, and other types of publications); and motion-picture, television, and radio appearances. Offers only brief bibliographic information for primary works. The second part separately classifies biographical articles and information (honors and awards, education, military career, employment, and the like) and critical works (essays, book reviews, and features in the *JDM Bibliophile*) on MacDonald. Unannotated. Index of titles. See *Bibliography of American Fiction, 1919-1988*, pp. 303-305, for Jan Tillery's checklist of works by and about MacDonald.

880.   Shine, Walter, and Jean Shine. **A MacDonald Potpourri: Being a Miscellany of Post-Perusal Pleasures of the John D. MacDonald Books for Bibliophiles, Bibliographers, and Bibliomaniacs**. Gainesville, FL: University of Florida Libraries, 1988. 219p. LC 88-14419. ISBN 0-929595-00-9.

Generally supplements and updates the Shines' *A Bibliography of the Published Works of John D. MacDonald* (entry 879), although essentially aimed at collectors. Provides separate checklists of bibliographic points (explained in Part I) to identify "80% of . . . nearly 1300 printings of MacDonald's work in hardcover and paperback . . . [to] early 1988" (p. xi), with cumulative data. Part II contains chronological, alphabetical, publisher, best-seller, non-English-language, and other checklists of MacDonald's works. Part III lists works by typographical and other errors in printings, epigraphs, dedications, cover artists and jacket designers, and the like. Part III cumulates the several bibliographical points for all printings of each work. Part IV cumulates for each of MacDonald's works the several distinguishing bibliographic points for all printings to 1988. Selected bibliography (pp. 217-19) on book collecting. Unindexed.

Ross Macdonald (Kenneth Millar), 1915-1983
Bibliographies

881.   Bruccoli, Matthew J. **Ross Macdonald/Kenneth Millar: A Descriptive Bibliography**. Pittsburgh, PA: University of Pittsburgh Press, 1983. 259p. (Pittsburgh Series in Bibliography). LC 83-1398. ISBN 0-8229-3482-5.

Bruccoli gives full bibliographic details (including facsimiles of title and copyright pages and dust jackets) for Macdonald's primary materials, covering separate publications, collected novels, contributions to books, contributions to periodicals and newspapers, and dust-jacket blurbs. Entries also give notes on contents, typography, paper, bindings, publishing histories, and copy locations. A selective list of four works about Macdonald is also included. Better coverage of criticisms and comments about Macdonald is available in Skinner's *The Hard-Boiled Explicator* (entry 611). Also for works by Macdonald, see *First Printings of American Authors*, vol. 1, pp. 259-63. See *Bibliography of American Fiction, 1919-1988*, pp. 346-48, for Matthew J. Bruccoli's checklist of works by and about Macdonald.

Katherine (Sherwood Bonner) MacDowell, 1849-1883
Bibliographies

See *Bibliography of American Fiction, 1866-1918*, pp. 77-78, for Hubert H. McAlexander's checklist of works by and about MacDowell. MacDowell's contributions to and reviews of MacDowell's works in selected periodicals are identified in Wells' *The Literary Index to American Magazines, 1850-1900*, p. 263. MacDowell's manuscripts are listed in Robbins' *American Literary Manuscripts*, p. 206.

William (Morley Punshon) McFee, 1881-1966
Bibliographies

882. Babb, James T. **A Bibliography of the Writings of William McFee**. Garden City, NY: Doubleday, Doran, 1931. 126p. LC 32-1167.

With an introduction and notes throughout by McFee, Babb's guide chronologically arranges full bibliographic descriptions of McFee's books, uncollected contributions to periodicals, and contributions to books to May 1931, with a list of about 40 works about McFee. Entries give title-page transcriptions; collation and pagination; contents, paper, typography, binding, and jacket information; and notes on publication history, with brief descriptions of subsequent issues and editions. Indexed. McFee's manuscripts are listed in Robbins' *American Literary Manuscripts*, p. 206. See *Bibliography of American Fiction, 1866-1918*, pp. 286-87, for Jean Kowaleski's checklist of works by and about McFee.

Thomas (Francis) McGuane (III), 1939-
Bibliographies

For works by McGuane, see *First Printings of American Authors*, vol. 5, pp. 191-93. See Carlton Smith's summary biography, critical assessment of major works, and selected primary and secondary bibliography for McGuane in McCaffery's *Postmodern Fiction: A Bio-Bibliographical Guide*, pp. 462-64.

Arthur Llewelyn Machen, 1863-1947
Bibliographies

883. Danielson, Henry. **Arthur Machen: A Bibliography**. 1923; reprint New York: Haskell House, 1970. 59p. LC 74-130267. ISBN 0-8383-1174-1.

Offers dated but still useful chronologically arranged bibliographic descriptions of Machen's books published from 1881 to 1915. Provides title-page transcriptions, collations, contents, binding descriptions, and "Biographical and Critical" notes on composition and publication histories by Machen. Unindexed. Also for a bibliography of works by and about Machen, see *NCBEL*, IV, pp. 644-48.

James McHenry (Solomon Secondsight), 1785-1845
Bibliographies

For works by McHenry, see *Bibliography of American Literature*, vol. 6, pp. 128-36. McHenry's manuscripts are listed in Robbins' *American Literary Manuscripts*, p. 207. See *Bibliography of American Fiction Through 1865*, pp. 173-74, for a checklist of works by and about McHenry.

Claude McKay, 1890-1948

Bibliographies

Limited coverage of works by and about McKay is provided in Perry's *The Harlem Renaissance*, pp. 118-30. McKay's manuscripts are listed in Robbins' *American Literary Manuscripts*, p. 207. See the review of research by Ruth Miller and Pater J. Katopes in Inge, Duke, and Bryer's *Black American Writers*, vol. I, pp. 161-86.

James McKenna, 1933-

Bibliographies

King's *Ten Modern Irish Playwrights*, pp. 83-86, gives brief bibliographic information for McKenna's primary works and annotated entries for criticism of McKenna, with a classified list of reviews.

Henry MacKenzie, 1745-1831

Bibliographies

For a bibliography of works by and about MacKenzie, see *NCBEL*, II, pp. 148, 184, 1003, 1004, 1005, 1371.

Archibald MacLeish, 1892-1982

Bibliographies

884.   Ellis, Helen E., Bernard A. Drabeck, and Margaret E. C. Howland. **Archibald MacLeish: A Selectively Annotated Bibliography**. Lanham, MD: Scarecrow Press, 1995. 344p. LC 95-22926. ISBN 0-8108-3022-1.

Covers works by and about MacLeish in alphabetically arranged sections for MacLeish's books, booklets, and pamphlets; contributions to periodicals; books and parts of books about MacLeish; and articles about MacLeish (853 largely unannotated entries); *New York Times* articles featuring MacLeish; dissertations and master's theses; recordings and media adaptations of MacLeish's works; and recordings and other media about MacLeish. For primary works there are 295 entries, including first and subsequent editions, reprintings, and translations, with brief bibliographic information with notes on contents. Entries for MacLeish's more than 550 articles note reprintings and sometimes indicate the subject but are not otherwise annotated. Includes chronology. Comprehensive author, title, and subject indexes offer detailed topical access. Although superseding coverage of MacLeish's primary works in Edward J. Mullaly's *Archibald MacLeish: A Checklist* (Kent, OH: Kent State University Press, 1973), Ellis, Drabeck, and Howland's guide is not a definitive primary bibliography. More detailed descriptions of first editions of MacLeish's works and contributions to periodicals through 1938 are provided in Arthur Mizener's *A Catalogue of the First Editions of Archibald MacLeish* (New Haven, CT: Yale University Press, 1938). MacLeish's manuscripts are listed in Robbins' *American Literary Manuscripts*, pp. 208-209.

Larry (Jeff) McMurtry, 1936-

Bibliographies

For works by McMurtry, see *First Printings of American Authors*, vol. 4, pp. 261-63. McMurtry's manuscripts are listed in Robbins' *American Literary Manuscripts*, p. 209. See *Bibliography of American Fiction, 1919-1988*, pp. 342-43, for Mark Busby's checklist of works by and about McMurtry. Kerry Ahearn surveys works by and about McMurtry in Erisman and Etulain's *Fifty Western Writers*, pp. 280-90.

(Frederick) Louis MacNeice, 1907-1963

Bibliographies

885.   Armitage, Christopher M., and Neil Clark. **A Bibliography of the Works of Louis MacNeice**. London: Kaye and Ward, 1973. 136p. LC 73-180536. ISBN 0-7182-0934-6.

Armitage and Clark provide full bibliographic descriptions of MacNeice's primary materials—including listings for separate publications, translations, edited, and coauthored works—and his contributions to books and periodicals (320 entries). In addition, Armitage gives an unannotated checklist of 254 works about MacNeice published through 1971 and descriptions of miscellaneous works, including collections of manuscripts in the University of Texas' Harry Ransom Humanities Research Center, the Berg Collection of the New York Public Library, at Ohio State University, and at the State University of New York at Buffalo (pp. 104-105); scripts of MacNeice's Radio Play Library for the BBC; and recordings of his poems. Entries for books give title-page transcriptions, physical descriptions, and contents. An alphabetical list of published poems details publication histories.

James MacPherson, 1736-1796

Bibliographies

886. Black, George Fraser. **Macpherson's Ossian and the Ossianic Controversy. A Contribution Towards a Bibliography**. New York: The New York Public Library, 1926. 41p. LC 27-19887.

Brief, chronologically arranged bibliographic descriptions of first and subsequent editions, translations, and reprintings of MacPherson's works (with notes on contents) in sections for Fragments, Poems of Ossian (English editions, Gaelic text, and translations), 11 individual poems, and selections. Also includes alphabetically arranged, annotated entries for about 250 international works about the Ossianic controversy published from the 1760s to the early twentieth century. Unindexed. Also for a bibliography of works by and about MacPherson, see *NCBEL*, II, pp. 603-605, by Donald S. Taylor. MacPherson's manuscripts are described in *Index of English Literary Manuscripts*, III, pt. 2:179-83.

Norman Mailer, 1923-

Bibliographies

887. Adams, Laura. **Norman Mailer: A Comprehensive Bibliography**. Metuchen, NJ: Scarecrow Press, 1974. 131p. (Scarecrow Author Bibliographies, no. 20). LC 74-17163. ISBN 0-8108-0771-8.

In addition to brief, chronologically arranged checklists of Mailer's books, contributions to books (prefaces) and periodicals, contributions to selected anthologies and excerpts from his works, films and plays, and unpublished works, Adams provides checklists of works about Mailer in separate listings for articles and reviews (arranged by works), reviews of works about Mailer, dissertations, interviews, nonprint media, bibliographies, and other types of secondary materials. Adams' guide supersedes the coverage of Benjamin Aaron Sokoloff's *A Bibliography of Norman Mailer* (Darby, PA: Darby Books, 1969). Also for works by Mailer, see *First Printings of American Authors*, vol. 5, pp. 175-85. Mailer's manuscripts are listed in Robbins' *American Literary Manuscripts*, p. 210. See *Bibliography of American Fiction, 1919-1988*, pp. 306-10, for J. Michael Lennon's checklist of works by and about Mailer. Lennon reviews research on Mailer in *Contemporary Authors: Bibliographical Series: Volume 1: American Novelists*, pp. 219-60.

Charles Major, 1856-1913

Bibliographies

For works by Major, see *Bibliography of American Literature*, vol. 6, pp. 137-40. Major's manuscripts are listed in Robbins' *American Literary Manuscripts*, p. 210. See *Bibliography of American Fiction, 1866-1918*, p. 279, for William Burriss' checklist of works by and about Major.

Bernard Malamud, 1914-1986

Bibliographies

888. Kosofsky, Rita N. **Bernard Malamud: A Descriptive Bibliography**. New York: Greenwood, 1991. 263p (Bibliographies and Indexes in American Literature, no. 13). LC 90-19915. ISBN 0-313-27694-3.

Describes works by and about Malamud. The first part gives brief bibliographic information and contents for Malamud's works in sections for books, contributions to periodicals, other writings, juvenilia, and translations (arranged by work and language). Secondary coverage includes nearly 1,000 alphabetically arranged, annotated entries for studies published in books and articles, reviews (arranged by work), and dissertations published through 1990. Extensive introduction reviews Malamud's critical reception and trends in criticism, with references to specific studies. Also includes chronology of Malamud's life and career. Author, title, and subject index. General index includes headings for Malamud's works and selected topics. This supersedes coverage of primary works in Kosofsky's earlier *Bernard Malamud: An Annotated Checklist* (Kent, OH: Kent State University Press, 1969) and secondary coverage in Joel Salzberg's *Bernard Malamud: A Reference Guide* (Boston: G. K. Hall, 1985), which chronologically arranges annotated entries for about 900 works about Malamud published from 1952 through 1983. Also for works by Malamud, see *First Printings of American Authors*, vol. 5, pp. 187-89. Malamud's manuscripts are listed in Robbins' *American Literary Manuscripts*, p. 210. For works by and about Malamud, see Salzberg's checklist in *Bibliography of American Fiction, 1919-1988*, pp. 311-14. Robert D. Habich reviews research on Malamud in *Contemporary Authors: Bibliographical Series: Volume 1: American Novelists*, pp. 261-91. Richard R. O'Keefe surveys research on Malamud through 1988 in "Bibliographical Essay: Bernard Malamud," *Studies in American Jewish Literature* 7 (Fall 1988): 240-50.

(Battle of) Maldon, c. 1000

Bibliographies

Greenfield and Robinson's *A Bibliography of Publications on Old English Literature to the End of 1972*, pp. 121-24, lists editions, translations, and studies of the Old English *Battle of Maldon*, with citations for reviews. Also for works about the *Battle of Maldon*, see *NCBEL*, I, pp. 241-43.

Sir Thomas Malory, d. 1471

Bibliographies

889. Gaines, Barry. **Sir Thomas Malory: An Anecdotal Bibliography of Editions, 1485-1985**. New York: AMS, 1990. 172p. (AMS Studies in the Middle Ages, no. 10). LC 89-018429. ISBN 0-4046-1440-X.

This is not a comprehensive bibliography of Malory's primary works. Based on the 1979 Grolier Club exhibition of Gaines' collection (and others) of editions of Malory, Gaines offers descriptive entries in chronologically arranged sections for 29 separate editions of the complete works published from 1485 to 1983; abridgments, selections, and single tales; adaptations; and translations. Data include colophon and other transcriptions and collations, with *STC* numbers. "Anecdotal" notes address composition and publication history; the provenance of notable individual copies; the uses of particular copies in producing modern editions; and distinguished editors, adapters, illustrators, and translators. Index of names and series titles. Robert H. Wilson offers a comprehensive guide to Malory's primary materials with a bibliography of editions and criticism in Severs and Hartung's *A Manual of the Writings in Middle English*, vol. III, pp. 757-71, 909-24. Malory's manuscripts are described in *Index of English Literary Manuscripts*, I, pt. 2:323-24.

890. Life, Page West. **Sir Thomas Malory and the Morte Darthur: A Survey of Scholarship and Annotated Bibliography**. Charlottesville, VA: Published for the Bibliographical Society of the University of Virginia by the University of Virginia Press, 1980. 297p. LC 80-16180. ISBN 0-8139-0868-x.

Following an extensive survey of Malory scholarship, Life provides a comprehensive, topically arranged listing of annotated entries for 922 works about Malory and *Morte Darthur* published through 1978. Chapters cover descriptive bibliographies; editions and translations of English, Spanish, and French sources and analogues; manuscripts and editions of *Morte Darthur* (including translations, adaptations, and recordings); bibliographies of the Arthurian legend and *Morte Darthur*; and studies of *Morte Darthur* and Malory. Annotations are descriptive, with significant works (such as Eugene Vinaver's scholarly edition) receiving detailed reviews. A comprehensive index includes headings for specific topics, such as the names of characters and things (such as Excalibur) as well as topics (such as "Marvellous elements" and "Marxist interpretation"). This cumulation supplements the listings for Malory in *NCBEL*, I, pp. 674-78.

Dictionaries, Encyclopedias, and Handbooks

891. Archibald, Elizabeth, and A. S. G. Edwards. **A Companion to Malory**. Cambridge: D. S. Brewer, 1996. 262p. (Arthurian Studies, vol. 37). LC 96-22491. ISBN 0-85991-443-7.

Contributing authorities offer state-of-the art reviews of topics related to Malory, including textual studies, sources, language, the role of women, chivalry, and life records; individual chapters and episodes in the *Morte Darthur*; and Malory's critical reception from earliest times to the present, with a selective bibliography of editions, reference works, biographies, and studies of Malory (pp. 253-55). Comprehensive index.

892. Dillon, Bert. **A Malory Handbook**. Boston: G. K. Hall, 1978. 196p. (A Reference Publication in Literature). LC 77-26240. ISBN 0-8161-7964-6.

Dillon offers plot summaries for the chapter divisions in *Le Morte Darthur* as established in the text of Eugene Vinaver's edition of *The Works of Sir Thomas Malory* (Oxford: Clarendon, 1967), with cross-references to the text of H. O. Sommer's edition of Caxton's *Le Morte Darthur* (London: D. Nutt, 1889-91. Contains unannotated bibliography of secondary sources. Lack of indexing limits usefulness. One must know where a character appears to identify his or her role in the narrative. Wider coverage of the Arthurian legend in all languages and periods is available in Charles Moorman and Ruth Moorman's *An Arthurian Dictionary* (Oxford, MS: University Press of Mississippi, 1978); Norris J. Lacy's *The Arthurian Encyclopedia* (New York: Garland, 1986); and Phyllis Ann Karr's *The King Arthur Companion: The Legendary World of Camelot and the Round Table as Revealed by the Tales Themselves, Discussed and Related by the Authoress with Warm Concern, the Greatest and the Humblest in the Realm, Interpreted in Hundreds of Entries Arranged Alphabetically for Convenient, Secure Reference and Pleasure* (Reston, VA: Reston Publishing, 1983).

Indexes and Concordances

893. Kato, Tomomi. **A Concordance to the Works of Sir Thomas Malory**. Tokyo: University of Tokyo Press, 1974. 1,659p. LC 74-182274. ISBN 0-86008-100-1.

Kato concords the text of Eugene Vinaver's second edition of *The Works of Sir Thomas Malory* (Oxford: Clarendon Press, 1967). The index includes frequency lists.

David (Alan) Mamet, 1947-
Bibliographies

King's *Ten Modern American Playwrights*, pp.179-96, gives brief bibliographic information for Mamet's primary works and annotated entries for criticism of Mamet, with a classified list of reviews. June Schlueter reviews research on Mamet in *Contemporary Authors: Bibliographical Series: Volume 3: American Dramatists*, pp. 141-69.

Journals

894. **The David Mamet Review: The Newsletter of the David Mamet Society**. Las Vegas, NV: David Mamet Society, 1994- . Annual. OCLC 34674269.

Publishes reviews of theatrical and media performances, book reviews, and conference reports. "New and Forthcoming" identifies upcoming productions, films, publications, and conferences. "David Mamet Bibliography," compiled by David K. Sauer and Janice A. Sauer, covers works by and about Mamet, including books, articles, reviews, performances, and media adaptations. *David Mamet Review* is presently unindexed.

Bernard de Mandeville, 1670-1733
Bibliographies

For a bibliography of works by and about Mandeville, see *NCBEL*, II, pp. 1095-98, by Donald A. Low. Other bibliographies include F. B. Kaye's "The Writings of Bernard Mandeville: A Bibliographical Survey," *JEGP* 20 (1921): 419-67, which is updated in Michael Boyd Wood's "Bernard Mandeville: Sources," *Bulletin of Bibliography* 40 (1983): 103-107. Mandeville's manuscripts are described in *Index of English Literary Manuscripts*, III, pt. 2:185.

Journals

"Recent Articles" in *The Scriblerian and the Kit Cats* (entry 1084) regularly includes a selection of reviews of studies on Mandeville.

Sir John Mandeville, fl. 1356/7
Bibliographies

Ralph Hanna III reviews research on *Mandeville's Travels* in Edwards' *Middle English Prose*, pp. 121-32.

Frederick Manfred (Feike Feikema), 1912-
Bibliographies

895. Mulder, Rodney J., and John H. Timmerman. **Frederick Manfred: A Bibliography and Publishing History**. Sioux Falls, SD: Center for Western Studies, Augustana College, 1981. 139p. LC 81-67077. ISBN 0-931170-15-x.

Covers works by and about Manfred in chronologically arranged sections for Manfred's original books; other works (including student writings, short stories, poems, nonfiction articles and published letters, reviews, and interviews); critical studies of Manfred (about 100 items in subsections for articles and books, news reports and miscellaneous items, and dissertations and theses); and book reviews (subarranged by work), with a narrative interview. Twenty-five entries give full bibliographic descriptions for Manfred's books, supplying title-page transcriptions, collation and pagination, contents, binding and jacket information, and notes on publication history, with brief bibliographic information and notes on variants for subsequent editions and printings. Descriptive annotations for critical books and articles only. Unindexed. George Kellogg's *Frederick Manfred: A Bibliography* (Denver, CO: Swallow, 1965) also lists works by and about Manfred. Manfred's manuscripts are listed in Robbins' *American Literary Manuscripts*, p. 211. See *Bibliography of American Fiction, 1919-1988*, pp. 315-17, for Joseph M. Flora's checklist of works by and about Manfred. Dick Harrison surveys works by and about Manfred in Erisman and Etulain's *Fifty Western Writers*, pp. 291-302.

Katherine Mansfield (Kathleen Mansfield Beauchamp), 1888-1923
Bibliographies

896.   Kirkpatrick, B. J. **A Bibliography of Katherine Mansfield**. Oxford: Clarendon Press, 1989. 396p. (The Soho Bibliographies). LC 89-30191. ISBN 0-19-818401-8.

Kirkpatrick gives full bibliographic descriptions for Mansfield's primary works in separate listings for books and pamphlets; contributions to books and books translated by Mansfield; contributions to periodicals and newspapers, including doubtful and attributed works; selected editions; translations of Mansfield's books and articles in some 29 languages (arranged by languages); non-U.S or U.K. editions of Mansfield's works in English; educational and shorthand editions; large print, Braille, embossed, and talking-book editions; original quotations from unpublished letters, journals, and other primary works; reported speeches; music; stage and film scripts; sound recordings; radio and television productions; ballet, musical, and stage productions; and manuscripts in the Alexander Turnbull Library, the Harry Ransom Humanities Research Center of the University of Texas, the Newberry Library, and elsewhere. Entries for books include title-page transcriptions (with selected facsimiles), collations, contents, binding descriptions, printing and publishing histories, and reference to reviews. This is the standard guide to Mansfield's works. Also for a bibliography of works by and about Mansfield, see *NCBEL*, IV, pp. 653-59.

William Edward March (William Edward March Campbell), 1893-1954
Bibliographies

897.   Simmonds, Roy S. **William March: An Annotated Checklist**. Tuscaloosa: University of Alabama Press, 1988. 191p. LC 86-30786. ISBN 0-8173-0361-8.

Comprehensively covers works by and about March. The first part chronologically arranges brief bibliographic information on March's works (with detailed notes on contents) in sections for first editions of March's books (novels, short stories, and anthologies), contributed short stories, contributed fables, and miscellaneous contributed writings (containing four entries for a published letter, poem, etc.). Entries for March's books list subsequent editions, translations, and other reprintings. Identifying 13 subsequent editions of *Company K* through 1984 and some 18 of *The Bad Seed*, Simmonds offers valuable information about March's continuing and international recognition. The second part, covering works about March, contains descriptively annotated entries in sections for plays and films (mostly giving information about several productions of *The Bad Seed*), biographical and critical articles and dissertations (alphabetically arranged entries for about 200 books, chapters, entries in reference works, introductions, and articles in scholarly and popular journals and newspapers), and selected contemporary reviews (more than 300 entries subarranged under each of March's works). Unindexed. Also for works by March, see *First Printings of American Authors*, vol. 3, pp. 233-35.

Wallace Markfield, 1926-
Bibliographies

For works by Markfield, see *First Printings of American Authors*, vol. 1, p. 241. See *Bibliography of American Fiction, 1919-1988*, pp. 317-18, for Matthew J. Bruccoli's checklist of works by and about Markfield.

Christopher Marlowe, 1564-1593
Bibliographies

898.   Brandt, Bruce E. **Christopher Marlowe in the Eighties: An Annotated Bibliography of Marlowe Criticism from 1978 Through 1989**. West Cornwall, CT: Locust Hill Press, 1992. 215p. LC 91-32885. ISBN 0-9339-5145-0.

Continuing the coverage of Kenneth Friedenreich's *Christopher Marlowe: An Annotated Bibliography of Criticism Since 1950* (Metuchen, NJ: Scarecrow Press, 1979) and Chan's *Marlowe Criticism* (entry 899), Brandt describes more than 500 works about Marlowe through 1989. Descriptively annotated entries in sections for editions, bibliographies, and concordances; general critical and biographical studies; criticisms of the individual plays; criticisms of poetry and translations; fictional works based on Marlowe's life; and non-English-language research on Marlowe. Coverage includes dissertations. The introduction and annotations for editions identify the most significant scholarly works. Author and subject indexes give good access, the latter containing headings for specific topics, such as "androgyny," "blank verse," and "plot," as well as personal names and titles of others' works.

899. Chan, Lois Mai. **Marlowe Criticism: A Bibliography**. Boston: G. K. Hall, 1978. 226p. (A Reference Publication in Literature Series). LC 78-5464. ISBN 0-8161-7835-6.

Chan chronologically arranges about 2,500 largely unannotated entries for works about Marlowe in separate classified listings for bibliographic studies, biographical studies and general criticisms, and studies of the individual plays and poems. Coverage is comprehensive, including dissertations, literary works based on Marlowe's life, and reviews of productions, as well as non-English-language criticisms (listed separately). Indexes for critics and subjects include subheadings for topics such as "characterization," "themes," and the like. Chan's bibliography surpasses in coverage Kenneth Friedenreich's *Christopher Marlowe: An Annotated Bibliography of Criticism Since 1950* (Metuchen, NJ: Scarecrow Press, 1979), which offers separate listings of annotated entries for selected editions (pp. 20-29) and about 600 general and specialized studies of the individual works. Friedenreich's annotations are better than Chan's, but his volume lacks subject indexing. Chan's guide supersedes the Tannenbaums' *Elizabethan Bibliographies*, vol. 5; and Robert C. Johnson's *Elizabethan Bibliographies Supplements*, no. 6. Chan's coverage is updated by Ronald Levao's "Recent Studies in Marlowe (1977-1986)," *English Literary Renaissance* 18.2 (Spring 1988): 329-42; and by Brandt's guide (entry 898). For a bibliography of works by and about Marlowe, see *NCBEL*, I, pp. 1443-56. Marlowe's manuscripts are described in *Index of English Literary Manuscripts*, I, pt. 2:325-28, 631. Research on Marlowe is reviewed by D. J. Palmer in Wells' *English Drama*, pp. 42-53; and Robert Kimbrough in Logan and Smith's *The Predecessors of Shakespeare*, pp. 3-55.

Indexes and Concordances

900. Fehrenbach, Robert J., Lea Ann Boone, and Mario A. Di Cesare. **A Concordance to the Plays, Poems, and Translations of Christopher Marlowe**. Ithaca, NY: Cornell University Press, 1982. 1,681p. (The Cornell Concordances). LC 81-67175. ISBN 0-8014-1420-2.

This is based on the text of Fredson Bowers' critical old-spelling edition of *The Complete Works of Christopher Marlowe*, 2d ed. (Cambridge: Cambridge University Press, 1981). Separately concords stage directions. Appends alphabetical and frequency lists and lists of compounds, words with apostrophes, non-English words, and the like. This concordance supersedes in authority Louis Ule's *A Concordance to the Works of Christopher Marlowe* (Hildesheim: Olms, 1979), which concords a modernized version of C. F. Tucker Brooke's edition of *The Works of Christopher Marlowe* (Oxford: Clarendon Press, 1962); and Charles Crawford's *The Marlowe Concordance* (1911-32; reprint New York: Burt Franklin, 1964).

901. Stagg, Louis Charles. **The Figurative Language of the Tragedies of Shakespeare's Chief 16th-Century Contemporaries: Christopher Marlowe, Thomas Kyd, George Peele, Thomas Lodge, Samuel Daniel, Countess of Pembroke/Robert Garnier, Thomas Preston, Thomas Sackville & Thomas Norton,**

Robert Wilmot/Inner Temple, Robert Greene, George Gascoigne/Francis Kin-
welmersh/Christopher Yelverton, Thomas Hughes, and Anonymous Authors of
Shakespeare Apocrypha: An Index. New York: Garland, 1984. 1,030p. (Garland
Reference Library of the Humanities, vol. 393). LC 82-49173. ISBN 0-8240-9176-0.

Based on standard modern editions, this offers separate concordances of
images in the works of each writer, citing context line, plays, acts, scenes, and lines.
Indexes cumulate images for the full range of topics, such as animals, the body
and bodily action, daily life, learning, nature, and other subjects. Included among
the important anonymous tragedies that have been attributed to Shakespeare are
Arden of Feversham, Locrine, and Parts I and II of *The Troublesome Reign of King John.*

Journals

902. **MSAN: Marlowe Society of America Newsletter/MSA Book Reviews.**
Tampa, FL: Marlowe Society of America, 1982- . 2/yr. LC 93-646203.

Membership in the Marlowe Society of America brings *MSAN Newsletter* and
MSA Book Reviews, issued and edited separately in different places. *MSAN Newsletter* (Brookings, SD: South Dakota State University) publishes reviews of productions; descriptions of conference papers; news relevant to Marlowe and
Renaissance scholars; and an unannotated checklist of "Recent Studies in Marlowe," covering books, articles, and dissertations. *MSA Book Reviews* (West Lafayette, Indiana) typically contains as many as six extensive reviews of works
about Marlowe and other Renaissance writers. Unindexed.

J(ohn) P(hillips) Marquand, 1893-1960
Bibliographies

For works by Marquand, see *First Printings of American Authors*, vol. 1, pp.
243-47. Marquand's manuscripts are listed in Robbins' *American Literary Manuscripts*, p. 213. See *Bibliography of American Fiction, 1919-1988*, pp. 318-19, for Paul
H. Carlton's checklist of works by and about Marquand.

Don(ald Robert Perry) Marquis, 1878-1937
Bibliographies

See *Bibliography of American Fiction, 1866-1918*, pp. 280-81, for Gwen L.
Nagel's checklist of works by and about Marquis. Marquis' manuscripts are listed
in Robbins' *American Literary Manuscripts*, p. 213.

(Captain) Frederick Marryat, 1792-1848
Bibliographies

For a bibliography of works by and about Marryat, see *NCBEL*, III, pp.
704-708.

James Marsh, 1794-1842
Bibliographies

Marsh's manuscripts are listed in Robbins' *American Literary Manuscripts*, p.
213. Douglas McCready Greenwood reviews research on Marsh in Myerson's *The
Transcendentalists*, pp. 343-47.

John Marston, 1577?-1634
Bibliographies

903. Tucker, Kenneth. **John Marston: A Reference Guide**. Boston: G. K. Hall,
1985. 204p. (A Reference Guide to Literature). LC 85-941. ISBN 0-8161-8355-4.

Tucker chronologically arranges briefly annotated entries for editions and about
1,100 commentaries and criticisms of Marston. Coverage extends from 1598 through
1981, although about 1,000 entries date from 1900 to the present. Annotations are very
uneven, ranging from scholarly and evaluative to nearly useless. Selective indexing references broad subjects ("Comedy," "War of the Theaters," and the like).

Coverage supersedes that of the Tannenbaums' *Elizabethan Bibliographies*, vol. 5, and Charles A. Pennel and William P. Williams' *Elizabethan Bibliographies Supplements*, no. 4. For a bibliography of works by and about Marston, see *NCBEL*, I, pp. 1689-94. Marston's manuscripts are described in *Index of English Literary Manuscripts*, I, pt. 2:329-33. Research on Marston is reviewed by Samuel Schoenbaum in Wells' *English Drama*, pp. 69-99; and Cecil M. McCulley in Logan and Smith's *The New Intellectuals*, pp. 171-247, updated by Lidman's *Studies in Jacobean Drama, 1973-1984*, pp. 125-44.

Indexes and Concordances

904.   Ward, James X. **A Concordance to The Malcontent**. Salzburg: Institut fur Anglistik und Amerikanistik Universitat Salzburg, 1988. (Salzburg Studies in English Literature: Jacobean Drama Studies, vol. 25). OCLC 19113381.

Concords the text of G. K. Hunter's "Revels Plays" edition (London: Methuen, 1975). Appends word-frequency list. Also see Stagg's *The Figurative Language of the Tragedies of Shakespeare's Chief 17th-Century Contemporaries* (entry 229).

Andrew Marvell, 1621-1678

Bibliographies

905.   Collins, Dan S. **Andrew Marvell: A Reference Guide**. Boston: G. K. Hall, 1981. 449p. (A Reference Guide to Literature). LC 81-5017. ISBN 0-8161-8017-2.

Collins calls this "an annual register, with annotations, of the writings" about Marvell published from 1641 through 1980 (p. vii). Arrangement of the approximately 1,000 entries is chronological within sections for centuries. Some 800 studies of Marvell have appeared since 1900. Annotations are remarkably descriptive and evaluative. For example, Pierre Legois' *Andre Marvell, Poete, Puritain, Patriote, 1621-1678* (London: Oxford University Press, 1928) is clearly identified as a definitive study. Descriptions of other significant works, such as Legois and E. E. Duncan-Jones' revised edition of *The Poems and Letters of Andrew Marvell*, 3d ed. (Oxford: Clarendon Press, 1971), are equally extensive. Citations for reviews conclude the annotations. Dissertations and bibliographies are listed in a separate section. The index of authors, titles, and selected subjects is very specific, offering under Marvell's name a variety of subdivided headings, such as "Attitudes and allegiances toward..." the likes of "Anglicanism," "Machiavellianism," and "Trimming." The main heading, "Relationships with other authors...," identifies a wide range of writers who influenced or were influenced by Marvell, including Horace, Chaucer, Shakespeare, Emerson, Melville, and John Crowe Ransom. This supersedes the coverage of Marvell in Dennis G. Donovan's *Elizabethan Bibliographies Supplements*, no. 12. Coverage of editions of Marvell's primary materials is provided in Allison's *Four Metaphysical Poets* (entry 656), pp. [43]-59. Also for a bibliography of works by and about Marvell, see *NCBEL*, I, pp. 1222-29. Marvell's manuscripts are described in *Index of English Literary Manuscripts*, II, pt. 2:17-67. Additionally, Hilton Kelliher's *Andrew Marvell, Poet & Politician, 1621-78: An Exhibition to Commemorate the Tercentenary of His Death, British Library Reference Division, 14 July-1 October 1978* (London: British Museum Publications for the British Library, 1978) draws on a wide array of British Library resources to document Marvell's life and career, including manuscripts, portraits, seals, and maps, with many facsimiles and a useful selected bibliography of major editions and secondary resources (pp. [126]-28). Research on Marvell is reviewed by D. I. B. Smith in Dyson's *English Poetry*, pp. 96-110.

Indexes and Concordances

906.   Guffey, George R. **A Concordance to the English Poems of Andrew Marvell**. Chapel Hill, NC: University of North Carolina Press, 1974. 623p. LC 73-21550. ISBN 0-8078-1230-7.

"Based on a copy of Volume I of the second edition of H. M. Margoliouth's *The Poems & Letters of Andrew Marvell*, 2 vols. (Oxford: Clarendon Press, 1952)" (p. [v]) that Guffey describes more accurately as a second issue of the 1927 edition. Also notes significant variants between Margoliouth's second edition and his third edition (Oxford: Clarendon Press, 1971). Appends list of words in order of frequency.

John Edward Masefield, 1878-1967

Bibliographies

907.   Simmons, Charles H. **A Bibliography of the Works of John Masefield**. New York: Columbia University Press, 1930. 171p. LC 30-33002.

Simmons gives title-page transcriptions, physical descriptions, and contents for Masefield's books and contributions to books, journals, and other works, as well as brief, selectively annotated entries for about 100 books and articles about Masefield. Descriptions of Masefield's works through 1960 are provided in Geoffrey Hadley-Taylor's *John Masefield, O.M.: The Queen's Poet Laureate: A Bibliography and Eighty-First Birthday Tribute* (London: Cranbrook Tower Press, 1960). In addition, Hadley-Taylor (pp. 19-25) describes Masefield collections at Yale University, the Berg Collection of the New York Public Library, Fisk University, and elsewhere. Also available is Crocker Wight's *John Masefield: A Bibliographical Description of His First, Limited, Signed, and Special Editions* (Boston: Library of the Boston Athenaeum, 1986). For a bibliography of works by and about Masefield, see *NCBEL*, IV, 306-13. Ronald E. Shields surveys and identifies works by and about Masefield in Demastes and Kelly's *British Playwrights, 1880-1956*, pp. [268]-77.

Philip Massinger, 1583-1640

Bibliographies

For bibliographies of works by and about Massinger, see *NCBEL*, I, pp. 1703-1709; the Tannenbaums' *Elizabethan Bibliographies*, vol. 6; and Charles A. Pennel and William P. Williams' *Elizabethan Bibliographies Supplements*, no. 8. Massinger's manuscripts are described in *Index of English Literary Manuscripts*, I, pt. 2:335-40, 631. Samuel Schoenbaum reviews research on Massinger in Wells' *English Drama*, pp. 69-99; and Terence P. Logan reviews research in Logan and Smith's *The Later Jacobean and Caroline Dramatists*, pp. 90-119, updated by Lidman's *Studies in Jacobean Drama, 1973-1984*, pp. 219-29.

Edgar Lee Masters, 1868?-1950

Bibliographies

For works by Masters, see *First Printings of American Authors*, vol. 2, pp. 243-48. Masters' manuscripts are listed in Robbins' *American Literary Manuscripts*, p. 214.

Cotton Mather, 1663-1728

Bibliographies

908.   Holmes, Thomas James. **Cotton Mather: A Bibliography of His Works**. Cambridge: Harvard University Press, 1940. 3 vols. LC 40-32579.

Describes Mather's completed works and fragments. Following a chronological list of Mather's works published from 1682 through 1728, Holmes gives title-page transcriptions and facsimiles, physical information, contents, printing and publishing histories, and notes on copy locations for more than 400 works.

Mather's manuscripts in the American Antiquarian Society and elsewhere are described (pp. 1301-11). Indexes for titles, non-English-language titles, names, subjects, and scriptural passages. Mather's manuscripts are also listed in Robbins' *American Literary Manuscripts*, pp. 214-15. Research on Mather is reviewed by Sacvan Bercovitch in Everett Emerson's *Major Writers of Early American Literature*, pp. 93-150.

Richard Mather, 1596-1669
Bibliographies

Mather's manuscripts are listed in Robbins' *American Literary Manuscripts*, p. 215. See Gallagher and Werge's *Early Puritan Writers* (entry 138) for works about Mather through 1972.

Cornelius Mathews, 1817-1889
Bibliographies

For works by Mathews, see *Bibliography of American Literature*, vol. 6, pp. 141-51. Contributions by Mathews and criticism and reviews of Mathews' works in selected periodicals are identified in Wells' *The Literary Index to American Magazines, 1815-1865*, pp. 103-104. Mathews' manuscripts are listed in Robbins' *American Literary Manuscripts*, p. 215. See *Bibliography of American Fiction Through 1865*, pp. 170-71, for a checklist of works by and about Mathews.

(James) Brander Matthews, 1852-1929
Bibliographies

909.   Columbia University Libraries. **The Bookshelf of Brander Matthews**. New York: Columbia University Press, 1931. 114p. LC 31-9544.

A descriptive catalog of books and papers of Brander Matthews bequeathed to the Columbia University Library (also reprinted New York: AMS Press, 1966). Briefly identifies volumes dedicated to Matthews; presentation and association copies; 122 book-length writings of Matthews; and Matthews' prefaces, introductions, and other contributions to books. Does not give full bibliographic information. Matthews' contributions to and reviews of Matthews' works in selected periodicals are identified in Wells' *The Literary Index to American Magazines, 1850-1900*, pp. 264-66. Matthews' manuscripts are listed in Robbins' *American Literary Manuscripts*, p. 215. See *Bibliography of American Fiction, 1866-1918*, pp. 282-84, for Lawrence J. Oliver's checklist of works by and about Matthews.

Peter Matthiessen, 1927-
Bibliographies

910.   Nicholas, D. **Peter Matthiessen: A Bibliography, 1951-1979**. Canoga Park, CA: Orirana, 1979. 63p. OCLC 6303392.

Chronologically arranged bibliographic descriptions in sections for Matthiessen's books; short fiction, nonfiction, and essays contributed to periodicals and books; reviews of Matthiessen's books (about 200 unannotated entries alphabetically subarranged under individual works); and miscellanea (ranging from Matthiessen's translations to entries for him in *Current Biography* and a few critical studies). Entries for first and subsequent editions and translations give brief data for imprints, paginations, sizes, prices, and bindings, with plot summaries or contents and notes on publishing histories. Entries for contributed works identify other appearances. Selected facsimiles of title pages. Also contains a Matthiessen chronology. Introduction by William Styron. Unindexed.

Also for works by Matthiessen, see *First Printings of American Authors*, vol. 1, pp. 249-50. See *Bibliography of American Fiction, 1919-1988*, pp. 331-32, for Gina D. Peterman and Timothy C. Lundy's checklist of works by and about Matthiessen.

Charles Robert Maturin, 1782-1824
Bibliographies

For a bibliography of works by and about Maturin, see *NCBEL*, II, pp. 746-47. For reviews of research on Maturin, see Robert Donald Spector's *The English Gothic: A Bibliographic Guide to Writers from Horace Walpole to Mary Shelley*, pp. 205-62; and by James F. Kilroy in Finneran's *Anglo-Irish Literature*, pp. 35-38.

W(illiam) Somerset Maugham, 1874-1965
Bibliographies

911. Sanders, Charles. **W. Somerset Maugham: An Annotated Bibliography of Writings About Him**. De Kalb, IL: Northern Illinois University Press, 1970. 436p. (An Annotated Secondary Bibliography Series on English Literature in Transition, 1880-1920). LC 79-11628. ISBN 0-87580-015-7.

Sanders gives comprehensive international coverage of criticism of Maugham published from 1897 through 1968, including descriptive annotations for some 2,355 works. Coverage includes books, parts of books, articles, reviews of Maugham's works, reviews of works about Maugham, and dissertations, as well as works in non-English languages. Significant studies receive extended reviews. As in other bibliographies in this series, indexing is exceptional. Separate indexes reference critics and editors, secondary titles, primary titles, periodicals and newspapers, and languages.

912. Toole-Stott, Raymond. **A Bibliography of W. Somerset Maugham**. Revised and extended ed. London: Kay & Ward, 1973. 320p. LC 73-175351. ISBN 0-7182-0950-8.

First published in 1956 (London: Bertram Rota), Toole-Stott's guide describes Maugham's primary materials, including separate listings for books and pamphlets, collected editions, contributions to books and edited works, contributions to periodicals, and "novelized plays" and "dramatized novels." Additional brief, selectively annotated entries describe about 200 works about Maugham. Entries for Maugham's books give title-page transcriptions, physical descriptions, and publishing histories. Appendixes describe manuscripts of published works, miscellaneous manuscripts (collections of letters), and unpublished works in the University of Texas' Harry Ransom Humanities Research Center, which owns the manuscripts of several published works and a large collection of Maugham's letters, as well as collections in other institutions (pp. 266-306). Also for a bibliography of works by and about Maugham, see *NCBEL*, IV, pp. 661-68. Robert F. Gross surveys and identifies works by and about Maugham in Demastes and Kelly's *British Playwrights, 1880-1956*, pp. [278]-95.

Dictionaries, Encyclopedias, and Handbooks

913. Hewetson, Cecil. **The Sayings of Somerset Maugham**. London: Duckworth, 1992. 63p. ISBN 0-7156-2440-7.

Brief quotations from Maugham's writings are arranged in 11 categories, including women, art, writing, manners, and "The World." Deficient in references to sources and, therefore, not immediately useful for research.

Julian May, 1931-
Bibliographies

914. Dikty, Thaddeus, and R. Reginald. **The Work of Julian May: An Annotated Bibliography & Guide**. San Bernardino, CA: Borgo Press, 1985. 66p. (Bibliographies of Modern Authors, no. 3). LC 84-21705. ISBN 0-89370-382-6.

Gives brief bibliographic information for May's science-fiction works, works for children, professional writings, miscellaneous works (such as study prints, audio recordings, kits, unpublished works, maps, and so forth), and 10 works about May. Entries for May's substantial works give summaries of contents.

Dictionaries, Encyclopedias, and Handbooks
915.   May, Julian. **A Pliocene Companion: Being a Reader's Guide to The Many-Colored Land, The Golden Torc, The Nonborn King, The Adversary.** Boston: Houghton Mifflin, 1984. 219p. LC 84-9124. ISBN 0-395-36516-3.

Lists and identifies characters and places and offers the fictional chronology of the action in May's saga, with an extensive family tree of the Remillards, in addition to including transcriptions of interviews with May and a bibliography of background materials.

Julian Mayfield, 1928-1984

Bibliographies

See *Bibliography of American Fiction, 1919-1988*, p. 332, for Philip Richard's checklist of works by and about Mayfield.

William Starbuck Mayo, 1811-1895

Bibliographies

See *Bibliography of American Fiction Through 1865*, p. 172, for a checklist of works by and about Mayo. Contributions by Mayo and criticism and reviews of Mayo's works in selected periodicals are identified in Wells' *The Literary Index to American Magazines, 1815-1865*, pp. 104-105. Mayo's manuscripts are listed in Robbins' *American Literary Manuscripts*, p. 217.

Henry Medwall, fl. 1486

Bibliographies

For a bibliography of works by and about Medwall, see *NCBEL*, I, pp. 1405, 1412.

Herman Melville, 1819-1891

Bibliographies

916.   Higgins, Brian. **Herman Melville: An Annotated Bibliography, Volume I: 1846-1930.** Boston: G. K. Hall, 1979. 397p. (A Reference Publication in Literature). LC 78-23446. ISBN 0-8161-7843-7.

In the first volume of a proposed three-volume bibliography of critical studies of Melville, Higgins chronologically arranges entries for approximately 1,500 book-length and shorter writings published largely in the United States through 1930. The bulk of the studies through 1900 consists of anonymous reviews appearing in popular literary magazines. This cumulation, therefore, provides an important record of Melville's contemporary critical reception. Although the annotations are generally very extensive (with some a few pages in length), they are strictly descriptive and provide little critical guidance. An excellent cumulative index of authors, titles, and subjects, including Melville's characters as well as broader topics, concludes the volume. An important listing of many previously unrecorded comments on Melville. Important supplemental coverage of early reviews and general notices is provided in Kevin J. Hayes and Hershel Parker's *Checklist of Melville Reviews* (Evanston, IL: Northwestern University Press, 1991), a revision of Steven Mailloux and Parker's earlier checklist (Los Angeles, CA: The Melville Society, 1975). Hayes and Parker identify and very briefly describe about 1,500 reviews dating from 1846 through 1889 in sections for each of Melville's works. Higgins' coverage of Melville scholarship is continued by:

916.1.   Higgins, Brian. **Herman Melville: A Reference Guide, 1931-1960.** Boston, MA: G. K. Hall, 1987. 531p. (Reference Guide to Literature). LC 87-19630. ISBN 0-8161-8671-5.

Higgins follows the pattern established in the 1979 volume, chronologically arranging descriptively annotated entries for books, periodical articles, and other secondary materials. Dissertations and non-English-language criticisms (for the most part) are excluded. For coverage of these, researchers should consult such cumulations as Tetsumaro Hayashi's *Herman Melville: Research Opportunities and Dissertation Abstracts* (Jefferson, NC: McFarland, 1987), which abstracts 565 American and international dissertations completed from 1932 through 1984; John Bryant's *Melville Dissertations, 1924-1980: An Annotated Bibliography and Subject Index* (Westport, CT: Greenwood Press, 1983), which abstracts 531 dissertations from 1924 through 1980; or proceed directly to *Dissertation Abstracts International* for the most recent dissertations. International criticism of Melville is covered in Phelps and McCullough's guide (entry 917). In general, Higgins' bibliographies offer more convenient and contextualized (because of the annotations) access to Melville criticism than Jeanetta Boswell's *Herman Melville and the Critics: A Checklist of Criticism, 1900-1978* (Metuchen, NJ: Scarecrow Press, 1981). Despite the fact that Boswell's listings extend through 1978, arrangement by authors makes use as a supplement to Higgins very difficult. See *Bibliography of American Fiction Through 1865*, pp.175-84, for Sanford E. Marovitz's checklist of works by and about Melville. Also, a more specialized guide, James C. Wilson's *The Hawthorne and Melville Friendship: An Annotated Bibliography, Biographical and Critical Essays, and Correspondence Between the Two* (Jefferson, NC: McFarland, 1991) contains Wilson's "An Essay in Bibliography" (pp. 19-39) and "An Annotated Bibliography: Major Discussions of the Relationship" (pp. 40-74). Research on Melville is reviewed by Nathalia Wright in Woodress' *Eight American Authors*, pp. 173-224, and by Higgins in Myerson's *The Transcendentalists*, pp. 348-61. *ALS* annually features a review essay on Melville scholarship.

917.   Phelps, Leland R., and Kathleen McCullough. **Herman Melville's Non-English Reputation: A Research Guide**. Boston: G. K. Hall, 1983. 331p. (A Reference Publication in Literature). LC 82-23320.

Including about 3,400 unannotated entries for editions and studies of Melville's works published outside the United States in 48 languages, including English, from 1847 through 1981, Phelps and McCullough document and chronicle Melville's enormous international popularity. Introductory essays on Melville translation as well as international scholarly interest and an appendix showing the chronological and lingual distribution of translations of the individual works of Melville are insightful. An author index concludes the volume. Few similar bibliographies exist for American or English writers of Melville's significance, causing even the most knowledgeable scholar to consider the variety of scholarship produced in the non-English-speaking parts of the critical world.

918.   Tanselle, G. Thomas. **A Checklist of Editions of Moby-Dick 1851-1976: Issued on the Occasion of an Exhibition at the Newberry Library Commemorating the 125th Anniversary of Its Original Publication**. Evanston, IL: Northwestern University Press; Chicago: The Newberry Library, 1976. 50p. LC 76-150913.

Describes an exhibition of 126 editions and printings of Melville's work at the Newberry Library. Tanselle attempts to list all editions, abridgments, and selections in English of *Moby Dick*. Emphasis is on publishing histories rather than physical descriptions. Additional coverage of Melville's books, reprints, and contributions to books is included in Blanck's *Bibliography of American Literature*, vol. 6, pp. 152-81. Melville's manuscripts are listed in Robbins' *American Literary Manuscripts*, p. 217. Also significant is Tanselle's *A Descriptive Catalogue of the Herman Melville Collection*, in Part 6 of Sidney Ives' *The Parkman Dexter Howe Library* (Gainesville, FL: University of Florida, 1989), with descriptions of 115 printed items and one manuscript leaf. The definitive primary bibliography of Melville, also compiled by Tanselle, is to be published as vol. 16 of the Northwestern-Newberry edition, *The Writings of Herman Melville* (Evanston, IL: Northwestern University Press, 1968-). Additional coverage related to Melville's primary bibliography is afforded by Merton M. Sealts, Jr.'s *Melville's Reading* (Madison, WI: University of Wisconsin Press, 1966), which lists books used or owned by Melville; and Mary K. Bercaw's *Melville's Sources* (Evanston, IL: Northwestern University Press, 1987).

Dictionaries, Encyclopedias, and Handbooks

919.   Bryant, John. **A Companion to Melville Studies**. Westport, CT: Greenwood Press, 1986. 906p. LC 86-361. ISBN 0-313-23874-X.

Bryant offers 25 essays by different authorities that give textual and topical information for the full range of interests in Melville's life and works. Essays for individual works give plot summaries; survey sources, manuscripts, and scholarly and popular editions and texts and give their composition, publication, and reception histories; and review modern scholarly studies. Melville's biographies, aesthetics, language, religion, and international reputation are subjects of specific chapters. A final section, "Melville and the World of Books" (pp. 781-835), by G. Thomas Tanselle, surveys Melville and authorship as well as gives a history of the bibliographic study of Melville and the editing of his works. All chapters append extensive bibliographies. Comprehensive general index.

920.   Coffler, Gail H. **Melville's Classical Allusions: A Comprehensive Index and Glossary**. Westport, CT: Greenwood Press, 1985. 153p. (Bibliographies and Indexes in American Literature, no. 2). LC 84-22513. ISBN 0-3132-4626-2.

Coffler provides several valuable indexes to Melville's allusions and references to the classics, including ancient philosophy, art, history, literature, mythology, religion, politics, and military affairs, among others. The first index is an alphabetically arranged master index to all classical allusions in Melville's complete writings. Separate indexes alphabetically and sequentially list the allusions occurring in the individual works as well. A supplementary index identifies allusions in Melville's letters and travel journals. All references in these indexes are to the definitive editions of Melville's writings, including the Northwestern-Newberry editions of *Moby-Dick* and *The Piazza Tales* that were not available to the general public in 1985. Indexes to the then-current definitive editions of these works are appended. The Hendricks House editions of *The Collected Poems* and *Clarel* and the Hayford-Sealts edition of *Billy Budd* were also indexed. A glossary of Melville's classical allusions is provided.

921.   Gale, Robert L. **A Herman Melville Encyclopedia**. Westport, CT: Greenwood Press, 1995. 536p. LC 94-29837. ISBN 0-313-29011-3.

Broader in scope and more generally useful than Kier's *A Melville Encyclopedia: The Novels* (entry 923), Gale gives plot summaries for each of Melville's works, identifies real and fictional characters in his life and writings, and explicates dominant allusions and other elements in the works. No substantial coverage of specific subjects or topics in Melville. Thoroughly cross-referenced entries cite works for further reading. Includes a brief chronology and a "General Bibliography" (pp. 505-507) that lists editions and major critical studies.

922.   Gale, Robert L. **Plots and Characters in the Fiction and Narrative Poetry of Herman Melville**. Hamden, CT: Archon Press, 1969. 273p. LC 70-82690. ISBN 0-208-00906-x.

Gale summarizes plots and identifies characters in Melville's works. *Moby Dick* receives a 10-page description. Coverage includes characters that are mentioned but do not appear, such as Queequeg's father, the King of Kokovoko, and

Jonah, the hero of Father Mapple's sermon. James E. Miller, Jr.'s *A Reader's Guide to Herman Melville* (New York: Farrar, Straus, Cudahy, 1962), surveys the plots, themes, and other elements of Melville's major works.

923.   Kier, Kathleen E. **A Melville Encyclopedia: The Novels**. 2d ed. Troy, NY: Whitston, 1994. 1,220p. LC 90-70385. ISBN 0-8787-5453-9.

Reprints without any changes or additions *A Melville Encyclopedia: The Novels* (Troy, NY: Whitston, 1990) and is published in two continuously paged volumes. Intended as a "book of facts" (p. ix), giving paragraph-length identifications of real and fictional people, places, events, and ideas mentioned or alluded to in Melville's novels. References cite chapters rather than pages. Topical entries cover such subjects as Melville's lectures, piracy and pirates, and Melville's knowledge of Hebrew. Coverage of such places as Malacca and Martha's Vineyard is most useful. More generally useful for specific allusions in the novels than Gale's *A Herman Melville Encyclopedia* (entry 921) but not so inclusive.

924.   Leyda, Jay. **The Melville Log: A Documentary Life of Herman Mellvile, 1819-1891**. 1951; reprint New York: Gordian Press, 1969. 2 vols. LC 73-81564.

Leyda chronologically arranges extended excerpts from Melville's letters, diaries, journals, works, and other documents and provides brief editorial explanations. Sources are noted throughout. A comprehensive index of names and titles provides access.

925.   Maeno, Shigeru. **A Melville Dictionary**. Tokyo: Kaibunsha, 1976. 277p. LC 76-365367.

Maeno's dictionary covers mythological, classical, Biblical, literary, religious, historical, and geographical references and allusions as well as "hard words" (pp. iii) in Melville's works. These include the likes of Boccaccio, Mozart, Blue-Beard, and Bruin (the bear in "Reynard the Fox"), and the Bunker Hill Monument, Capella (the star), and Cape Tormentoto (Cape of Good Hope). Entries reference passages in standard editions.

Indexes and Concordances

926.   Irey, Eugene F. **A Concordance to Herman Melville's Moby Dick**. New York: Garland, 1982. 2 vols. (Garland Reference Library of the Humanities, vol. 340). LC 82-9387. ISBN 0-8240-9398-4.

The first volume in an informal series of concordances of Melville's works published by Garland. Uses as a base text Luther S. Mansfield and Howard P. Vincent's 1952 Hendricks House edition. Irey appends lists of nouns, verbs, adverbs, adjectives, hyphenated words, and word frequencies. In Irey's choice of copy text, his concordance is superior to Hennig Cohen and James Cahalan's *A Concordance to Melville's Moby Dick* (Glassboro, NJ: Melville Society, 1978), which employed Charles Feidelson, Jr.'s edition (Indianapolis, IN: Bobbs-Merrill, 1964) as the base text. Other volumes in the series include:

926.1. Wegener, Larry Edward. **A Concordance to Herman Melville's The Confidence-Man, His Masquerade**. New York: Garland, 1987. 1,123p. (Garland Reference Library of the Humanities, vol. 733). LC 86-31997. ISBN 0-8240-9492-1.
Based on the Northwestern-Newberry edition of *The Confidence-Man* (1984).

926.2. Wegener, Larry Edward. **A Concordance to Herman Melville's Pierre; Or, The Ambiguities**. New York: Garland, 1985. 2 vols. (Garland Reference Library of the Humanities, vol. 392). LC 84-48871. ISBN 0-8240-8734-8.
Concords the texts established in the standard Northwestern-Newberry edition of *Pierre* (1971).

926.3. Wegener, Larry Edward. **A Concordance to Herman Melville's Mardi, and A Voyage Thither**. New York: Garland, 1991. 2 vols. (Contextual Concordances; Garland Reference Library of the Humanities, vol. 1116). LC 91-8008. ISBN 0-8240-6694-4.

Based on the Northwestern-Newberry edition of *Mardi* (1970), with a critical introduction and appendixes for capitalized words and phrases, hyphenated words, deleted words, italicized words, and numbers and special characters. Also concords 23 satellite poems of songs of *Mardi* and a list of variant readings.

Other useful concordances to Melville, not part of Garland's series, include Wegener's *A Concordance to Herman Melville's Clarel: A Poem and Pilgrimage in the Holy Land* (Glassboro, NJ: Melville Society, 1979), based on the first American edition of *Clarel* (New York: G. P. Putnam, 1876); Charles J. Murray's Ph.D. dissertation, *A Concordance to Melville's Billy Budd* (Oxford, OH: Miami University, 1979), a computer-produced index to Harrison Hayford and Merton M. Sealts, Jr.'s *Billy Budd, Sailor* (Chicago, IL: University of Chicago Press, 1962); and William D. Richardson's *Melville's "Benito Cereno": An Interpretation, with Annotated Text and Concordance* (Durham, NC: Carolina Academic Press, 1987), which concords the text that appeared as part of *The Piazza Tales* (New York: Dix and Edwards, 1856), which incorporates "some rather extensive emendations that Melville made in the earlier 1855 version" (p. x). A specialized index of Melville's sea language, Jill B. Gidmark's *Melville Sea Dictionary: A Glossed Concordance and Analysis of the Sea Language in Melville's Nautical Novels* (Westport, CT: Greenwood Press, 1982) analyzes Melville's use of 345 words. Complementing Gidmark's work, Shigeru Maeno and Kaneaki Inazumi's *A Melville Lexicon* (Tokyo: Kaibunsha, 1984) identifies and briefly defines some 8,000 words in Melville's works. Coverage emphasizes Melville's nautical and whaling terms.

Journals

927. **Melville Society Extracts**. Hempstead, NY: Melville Society of America, 1969- . 4/yr. ISSN 0193-8991.

This newsletter publishes one or two substantial articles and a few brief notes and miscellaneous comments concerning the life, times, writings, reputation, and associates of Melville (including reviews and descriptions of new books and reports on Melville research in progress) and includes notices and other information about the society's activities. Critical features trace allusions and sources, discuss Melville's methods of composition and revision, and provide close interpretive readings of specific works and characters. Other studies have tracked Melville allusions in such contemporary sources as the *New York Critic* and *New York Christian Inquirer* and presented annotated lists of references. Many contributions identify and describe recently discovered Melville materials, such as Gary Scharnhorst's "More Uncollected Melville Reviews and Notices," no. 106 (September 1996): 12-14, supplementing the standard bibliographies. A special issue, "Melville and the Lathers Collection," in no. 99 (December 1994), includes a catalog of the collection. *Melville Society Extracts* is indexed in *AES*, *AHI*, and *MLA*.

Patterson's *Author Newsletters and Journals*, pp. 211-12, describes other previously published journals for Melville.

H(enry) L(ouis) Mencken, 1880-1956

Bibliographies

928. Adler, Betty. **H. L. M.: The Mencken Bibliography**. Baltimore, MD: Johns Hopkins University Press, 1961. 367p. LC 61-15699.

Adler provides comprehensive coverage of Mencken's primary and secondary materials, giving brief bibliographic information, with summaries of contents and notes on reprintings, for Mencken's books and pamphlets; contributions to books and pamphlets; newspaper work; magazine articles; book reviews; speeches, talks, and radio addresses; and correspondence. Coverage of works about Mencken includes books and pamphlets; parts of books; articles; portraits and caricatures; and miscellaneous works, such as musical settings of Mencken's works, works dedicated to Mencken, works inspired by Mencken, and others. Adler's coverage is supplemented by:

928.1. Adler, Betty. **H. L. M.: The Mencken Bibliography: A Ten-Year Supplement, 1962-1971**. Baltimore, MD: Enoch Pratt Free Library, 1971. 84p. OCLC 19651301.

928.2. Fitzpatrick, Vincent. **H. L. M.: The Mencken Bibliography: A Second Ten-Year Supplement, 1972-1981**. Baltimore, MD: Enoch Free Library Press, 1981. 177p. ISBN 0-910556-253.
    The supplements follow the arrangement established in Adler's first volume. Coverage of both primary and secondary works surpasses that attempted in Allison Blusterbaum's selective *H. L. Mencken: A Research Guide* (New York: Garland, 1988), which gives brief information for Mencken's works and topically arranges about 800 works about Mencken; as well as William H. Nolte's *The Merrill Checklist of H. L. Mencken* (Columbus, OH: Charles E. Merrill, 1969). Mencken's manuscripts are listed in Robbins' *American Literary Manuscripts*, p. 217. Also available is Betty Adler's *Man of Letters: A Census of the Correspondence of H. L. Mencken* (Baltimore, MD: Enoch Pratt Free Library, 1969). Research on Mencken is reviewed by Fred Hobson in Flora and Bain's *Fifty Southern Writers After 1900*, pp. 313-23.

Indexes and Concordances
929.   DuBasky, Mayo. **The Gist of Mencken: Quotations from America's Critic: Gleaned from Newspapers, Magazines, Books, Letters, and Manuscripts**. Metuchen, NJ: Scarecrow Press, 1990. 862p. LC 89-6385. ISBN 0-8108-2150-8.
    Thematically arranged dictionary of quotations from Mencken. Excerpts from the entire range of Mencken's works, in particular from *Smart Set* and *American Mercury* magazines and the Baltimore *Evening Sun,* assembled in "three categories stressed throughout Mencken's work: the American people, their government, and their aesthetics" (p. xiii). "Bibliography" (pp. 787-94) lists the base texts. A comprehensive subject index of proper names, titles, and specific topics accesses the compilation.

Journals
930.   **Menckeniana: A Quarterly Review**. Baltimore, MD: Enoch Pratt Free Library, 1962-. 4/yr. ISSN 0025-9233.
    Sponsored by the Mencken Society, issues of this slim, 16-page quarterly typically feature a few scholarly articles and brief notes on Mencken's life (including recollections by his contemporaries) as well as critical and comparative studies. In addition to the occasional "Books on HLM," which contains reviews of new publications, the journal publishes news about activities of the society, letters to the editor, descriptions of research in progress, and information about Menckeniana and Mencken collections. A useful regular "Bibliographic Check List" offers annotated entries for recent editions of Mencken's works and works about him (including newspaper articles), updating Adler's guide (entry 928) and its supplements. *Menckeniana* is indexed in *AHI, MHRA,* and *MLA.*

Miguel Mendez M., 1930-
Bibliographies
    See *Bibliography of American Fiction, 1919-1988*, p. 344, for Salvador Rodriguez del Pino's checklist of works by and about Mendez M.

George Meredith, 1828-1909

Bibliographies

931. Collie, Michael. **George Meredith: A Bibliography**. Toronto: University of Toronto Press, 1974. 290p. LC 73-85962. ISBN 0-8020-2106-9.

Collie gives full bibliographic descriptions for Meredith's primary materials, including in separate listings for Meredith's novels and short stories in books, prose contributions to books, collected letters, prose contributions to periodicals and newspapers, poems in books (with first-line and title indexes), collected editions, and translations of Meredith's works (arranged by languages). Entries include title-page transcriptions, physical descriptions, contents, and publishing histories, with particular attention to the bibliographic relationships of serializations, dramatizations, and manuscript sources with first editions. Meredith's surviving manuscripts are described throughout the guide. Collie's bibliography supersedes Maurice Buxton Forman's *A Bibliography of the Writings in Prose and Verse of George Meredith* (1922; reprint New York: Haskell House, 1971). For a bibliography of works by and about Meredith, see *NCBEL*, III, pp. 889-99.

932. Olmsted, John Charles. **George Meredith: An Annotated Bibliography of Criticism, 1925-1975**. New York: Garland, 1978. 158p. (Garland Reference Library of the Humanities, vol. 99). LC 77-83354. ISBN 0-8240-9841-2.

Olmsted chronologically arranges 585 annotated entries for books, parts of books, articles, reviews of works about Meredith, and dissertations about Meredith published from 1925 through 1975. Coverage includes significant works published abroad. Annotations are descriptive and quote works extensively. Olmsted's guide complements the coverage of Maurice Buxton Forman's *Meredethiana* (1924; reprint New York: Haskell House, 1971), which covers earlier criticism. Meredith's contributions to and reviews of Meredith's works in selected periodicals are identified in Wells' *The Literary Index to American Magazines, 1850-1900*, pp. 268-69. Research on Meredith is reviewed by Gillian Beer in Ford's *Victorian Fiction*, pp. 274-87; C. L. Cline in Stevenson's *Victorian Fiction*, pp. 324-48; and Lionel Stevenson in Faverty's *The Victorian Poets*, pp. 360-64.

Dictionaries, Encyclopedias, and Handbooks

933. McCullen, Maurice, and Lewis Sawin. **A Dictionary of the Characters in George Meredith's Fiction**. New York: Garland, 1977. 194p. (Garland Reference Library of the Humanities, vol. 48). LC 75-42886. ISBN 0-8240-9952-4.

The characters appearing or mentioned in Meredith's published, unpublished, and attributed novels, short fiction, and dramatic works are briefly identified and referenced to their appearances in the works. An appendix lists the characters under the works in which they appear.

Indexes and Concordances

934. Hogan, Rebecca S., Lewis Sawin, and Lynn L. Merrill. **A Concordance to the Poetry of George Meredith**. New York: Garland, 1982. 2 vols. (Garland Reference Library of the Humanities, vol. 203). LC 79-7923. ISBN 0-8240-9521-9.

Based on Phyllis B. Bartlett's edition of *The Poems of George Meredith* (New Haven, CT: Yale University Press, 1978). Includes lists of hyphenated words and frequencies.

William (Morris) Meredith, 1919-

Bibliographies

For works by Meredith, see *First Printings of American Authors*, vol. 2, pp. 253-55. Also available is *Reasons for Poetry: William Meredith: Exhibit at the Egbert Starr Library, Middlebury College, August 1988-February 1989; and a Bibliography of the Meredith Manuscript Materials in the Abernethy Library of American Literature: with an Introductory Essay* (Middlebury, VT: Abernethy Library, Middlebury College, 1989).

James (Ingram) Merrill, 1926-1995

Bibliographies

For works by Merrill, see *First Printings of American Authors*, vol. 2, pp. 257-62. Merrill's manuscripts are listed in Robbins' *American Literary Manuscripts*, p. 219. Also available is Laurence Copel and Jessy Randall's *J. I. M.'s Book: A Collection of Works by James Ingram Merrill: The Collection of Dennis M. Silverman* (New York: Glenn Horowitz Bookseller, 1995).

Thomas Merton, 1915-1969

Bibliographies

935. Breit, Marquita E., and Robert E. Daggy. **Thomas Merton: A Comprehensive Bibliography**. New ed. New York: Garland, 1986. 710p. (Garland Reference Library of the Humanities, vol. 659). LC 85-31167. ISBN 0-8240-8920-0.

Breit and Daggy give comprehensive coverage of works by and about Merton, integrating alphabetically arranged lists of Merton's books, pamphlets, and limited editions; shorter prose works (some 1,263 entries); poetry (580 entries); 58 books, pamphlets, and tape recordings about Merton; 91 theses; 985 articles, essays, poems, and reviews about Merton; and media presentations and sound recordings by and about Merton. Coverage extends through 1985. Entries for primary works include brief bibliographic information, summaries of contents, references to subsequent editions and translations, and references to their criticisms and reviews. Extremely brief annotations offer cryptic descriptions. This supersedes Breit's earlier *Thomas Merton: A Bibliography* (Metuchen, NJ: Scarecrow Press, 1974) and Frank Dell'Isola's *Thomas Merton: A Bibliography* (Kent, OH: Kent State University Press, 1975). Merton's manuscripts are listed in Robbins' *American Literary Manuscripts*, p. 219.

Journals

936. **Merton Annual: Studies in Culture, Spirituality and Social Concerns**. New York: AMS, 1988-. Annual. ISSN 0894-4857.

Formerly subtitled *"Studies in Thomas Merton, Religion, Culture, Literature & Social Concerns,"* annual volumes of the *Merton Annual* focus on Merton as a writer and a monk. Contributed scholarly articles—as many as 15 in each volume—offer close readings of Merton's works, thematic and stylistic analyses, and comparisons of Merton's ideas with those of others. In addition to reviews of new publications, the annual also contains a variously titled bibliographic survey of recent editions and international criticisms and dissertations. Volumes contain indexes. To date the *MLA* has indexed the *Merton Annual* through vol. 3 (1990).

W(illiam) S(tanley) Merwin, 1927-

Bibliographies

For works by Merwin, see *First Printings of American Authors*, vol. 1, pp. 255-58. Merwin's manuscripts are listed in Robbins' *American Literary Manuscripts*, p. 219.

Paul Metcalf, 1917-

Bibliographies

For works by Metcalf, see *First Printings of American Authors*, vol. 3, pp. 237-39.

Oscar Micheaux, 1884-1951

Bibliographies

See *Bibliography of American Fiction, 1866-1918*, p. 287, for J. Randall Woodland's checklist of works by and about Micheaux.

James A(lbert) Michener, 1907-1997
Bibliographies

937. Groseclose, David A. **James A. Michener: A Bibliography**. Austin, TX: State House Press, 1996. 315p. LC 95-13090. ISBN 1-880510-23-5.

Full bibliographic descriptions of Michener's works chronologically arranged in sections for first editions, with a subsection listing first printings and subsequent editions and reprintings; contributions to anthologies, collections, and other books; forewords, introductions, and miscellaneous commentary; magazine articles; newspaper articles; books about or related to Michener (some 146 brief, descriptively annotated entries); video materials; and audio materials. Entries for Michener's 69 separate publications from 1939 through *Ventures in Editing* (Huntington Beach, CA: James Cahill, 1995) give title-page and copyright-page transcriptions (with selected illustrative facsimiles), contents, collations, binding and jacket descriptions, and notes on prices and publication histories. International coverage of subsequent editions excludes translations; selected appearances of contributed works in non-English languages, however, are indicated. Appends separate, selectively annotated listings for about 800 works about Michener, including magazine and newspaper articles and reviews (chronologically listed under each of Michener's works). Contains foreword by Michener. Introduction notes special collections of manuscripts. Also includes chronologies of Michener's published writings and of his life. Indexes of names, periodical titles, publishers, titles, and topics of Michener's works offer excellent access. Groseclose's coverage of both primary and secondary works for Michener is more comprehensive, detailed, up-to-date, and better organized than that offered in F. X. Roberts and C. D. Rhine's *James A. Michener: A Checklist of His Works, with a Selected, Annotated Bibliography* (Westport, CT: Greenwood Press, 1995), which provides separate, alphabetically arranged lists for Michener's books, parts of books and stories, articles to 1993 (with brief bibliographic information); and for 326 books, parts of books, articles, and book reviews about Michener. Unfortunately, like Groseclose's guide, Roberts and Rhine's also lacks coverage of non-English-language editions of Michener's works. See also *Bibliography of American Fiction, 1919-1988*, pp. 345-46, for A. Grove Day's checklist of works by and about Michener. Michener's manuscripts are listed in Robbins' *American Literary Manuscripts*, p. 219.

Thomas Middleton, 1580-1627
Bibliographies

938. Steen, Sara Jayne. **Thomas Middleton: A Reference Guide**. Boston: G. K. Hall, 1984. 297p. (A Reference Guide to Literature). LC 83-26505. ISBN 0-8161-8340-6.

Steen arranges 1,939 annotated entries for studies of Middleton in classified listings for bibliography, biography, general studies (dealing with four or more works), drama, pageants or entertainments, poetry, prose, and "Uncertain Ascriptions," with sublistings for individual works. Coverage extends through 1978. Duplication of entries in several sections greatly inflates the listings. Annotations are brief and descriptive. Subject indexing is limited to selected broad topics (such as "printing" and "biography"). Despite this guide's shortcomings, it is superior to Dorothy Wolff's awkwardly organized, selectively annotated, and poorly indexed *Thomas Middleton: An Annotated Bibliography* (New York: Garland, 1985), which covers Middleton criticism through 1983. Coverage also supersedes that in the Tannenbaums' *Elizabethan Bibliographies*, vol. 5, and Dennis Donovan's *Elizabethan Bibliographies Supplements*, no. 1. For a bibliography of works by and about Middleton, see *NCBEL*, I, pp. 1646-54. Middleton's manuscripts are described in *Index of English Literary Manuscripts*, I, pt. 2:341-46, 632. Research on Middleton is reviewed by Samuel Schoenbaum in Wells' *English Drama*, pp. 69-99; and John B. Brooks in Logan and Smith's *The Popular School*, pp. 51-84, updated by Lidman's *Studies in Jacobean Drama, 1973-1984*, pp. 147-84.

Indexes and Concordances
See Stagg's *The Figurative Language of the Tragedies of Shakespeare's Chief 17th-Century Contemporaries* (entry 229).

John Stuart Mill, 1806-1873
Bibliographies
939.   Laine, Michael. **Bibliography of Works on John Stuart Mill**. Toronto: University of Toronto Press, 1982. 173p. LC 82-216844. ISBN 0-8020-2414-9.

Building on the earlier lists of Dudley L. Hascall and John M. Robson that appeared in *Mill News Letter* (Toronto: University of Toronto Press) from 1965 through 1970 and Keitaro Amano's *John Stuart Mill: Bibliography of the Classical Economists*, Volume III, Part 4 (Tokyo: Science Council of Japan, 1964), Laine provides brief, selectively annotated entries for 1,971 works about Mill published through 1978. Appendixes list miscellaneous works about Mill, including poems, cartoons, portraits, and other representations. A detailed index includes headings for broad topics ("bibliography," "education," "religion," and the like), other writers and figures (Wordsworth, Shaw, Plato), and Mill's individual works. Also for a bibliography of works by and about Mill, see *NCBEL*, III, pp. 1551-76. Research on Mill is reviewed by John M. Robson in DeLaura's *Victorian Prose*, pp. 185-218.

940.   MacMinn, Ney, J. R. Hainds, and James McNab McCrimmon. **Bibliography of the Published Writings of John Stuart Mill**. Evanston, IL: Northwestern University, 1945. 101p. (Northwestern University Studies in the Humanities, no. 12). LC 45-5303.

No complete, fully descriptive bibliography of Mill's works now exists. MacMinn, Hainds, and McCrimmon's guide amounts to an annotated, chronological checklist of Mill's writings from 1822 to 1873 based on Mill's own records. Entries briefly identify contents and other appearances but do not provide full bibliographic descriptions. Unindexed. Available in reprinted editions (New York: AMS Press; 1970; and Bristol: Thoemmes, 1990).

Journals
See Wortman's *A Guide to Serial Bibliographies for Modern Literatures*, p. 268, for a description of the previously published serial bibliography in *Mill News Letter* (1965-88). Patterson's *Author Newsletters and Journals*, p. 214, describes previously published journals for Mill.

Edna St. Vincent Millay, 1892-1950
Bibliographies
941.   Nierman, Judith. **Edna St. Vincent Millay: A Reference Guide**. Boston: G. K. Hall, 1977. 191p. (Reference Guides in Literature). LC 77-5400. ISBN 0-8161-7950-6.

Nierman chronologically arranges descriptive entries for about 1,000 books, articles, reviews, and dissertations about Millay published from 1918 through 1973. Annotations are brief and descriptive but occasionally include critical comments. A comprehensive index includes topical subheadings under Millay's name (for "appraisal," "bibliography," and the like) as well as under individual works. Also for works by Millay, see *First Printings of American Authors*, vol. 4, pp. 265-75. Millay's manuscripts are listed in Robbins' *American Literary Manuscripts*, p. 220.

942.   Yost, Karl. **A Bibliography of the Works of Edna St. Vincent Millay**. New York and London: Harper & Brothers, 1937. 248p. LC 37-6505.

Full bibliographic descriptions of Millay's primary materials, including sections for books (1912-36), appearances in anthologies and collections, poems set to music, contributions to periodicals, and portraits of Millay. Entries give title-page transcriptions, collations, binding descriptions, contents, and notes on publication histories. Also identifies about 70 books and articles about Millay.

Indexed. Includes an essay in appreciation by Harold Lewis Cook, introductions and three poems by Edna St. Vincent Millay. Available in a reprinted edition (New York: Burt Franklin, 1968).

Journals

943.   **Tamarack: Journal of the Edna St. Vincent Millay Society**. Cambridge: Edna St. Vincent Millay Society, 1981-86. Annual. OCLC 11861771.

Sponsored by the Edna St. Vincent Millay Society, annual issues of *Tamarack* featured articles, notes, and reviews of new publications about Millay. Articles, such as "The Variety of Language in Millay's Verse Plays," provided close readings and interpretations of Millay's works. Others focused on Millay's life as well as productions of Millay's works and discussed Millay's literary relations with the likes of Dante. Irene R. Fairley's "Millay in Feminist Perspective: Critical Trends of the 70's," 1.1 (Spring 1981): 28-31, reviewed modern responses to Millay. *Tamarack* was indexed in *MLA*.

Arthur Miller, 1915-

Bibliographies

944.   Ferres, John H. **Arthur Miller: A Reference Guide**. Boston: G. K. Hall, 1979. 225p. (A Reference Publication in Literature). LC 79-10121. ISBN 0-8161-7822-4.

Ferres offers an annotated, chronologically arranged listing of about 1,200 works about Miller published from 1944 through 1978. Coverage includes books, parts of books, articles, reviews, and dissertations. Excludes non-English-language criticisms. Annotations are descriptive. Index headings for Miller (with subheadings for "divorce" and "Jewishness," among others), his works (with subheadings for films, productions, and published versions), and selected names (such as T. S. Eliot and Lillian Hellman) give good topical access. Supersedes Tetsumaro Hayashi's *An Index to Arthur Miller Criticism*, 2d ed. (Metuchen, NJ: Scarecrow Press, 1976); and Sidney White's *The Merrill Guide to Arthur Miller* (Columbus, OH: Charles E. Merrill, 1970). Additional coverage of dissertations about Miller (through 1980) is provided in Hayashi's *Arthur Miller and Tennessee Williams: Research Opportunities and Dissertation Abstracts* (Jefferson, NC: McFarland, 1983). June Schlueter reviews research on Miller in *Contemporary Authors: Bibliographical Series: Volume 3: American Dramatists*, pp. 189-270.

945.   Jensen, George H. **Arthur Miller: A Bibliographical Checklist**. Columbia, SC: J. Faust, 1976. 146p. (Bibliographical Checklist Series, no. 1). ISBN 0-915188-12-0.

Jensen gives a comprehensive record of Miller's primary bibliography, offering facsimiles of title and copyright pages, brief physical descriptions, copy locations, and publishing histories for Miller's books; contributions to books; contributions to periodicals; speeches; interviews; three testimonies (one for a divorce and two before the House Committee on Un-American Activities); recordings; and attributed works. Also for works by Miller, see *First Printings of American Authors*, vol. 1, pp. 265-67. Miller's manuscripts are listed in Robbins' *American Literary Manuscripts*, p. 220.

Henry Miller, 1891-1980

Bibliographies

946.   Shifreen, Lawrence J., and Roger Jackson. **Henry Miller: A Bibliography of Primary Sources, with an Original Preface by Henry Miller**. Chelsea, MI: The Authors, 1993. 1,022p. ISBN 0-9634136-0-0.

The most comprehensive guide to Miller's works. Full bibliographic descriptions of Miller's works in chronologically arranged sections for books, pamphlets, broadsides, and watercolor reproductions; contributions to books and pamphlets; contributions to periodicals (807 entries from 1919 through 1992); non-English-language translations; audiotapes and records; and video appearances. Coverage includes all editions of books through 1990, identifying some 55 editions of *Tropic of Cancer*. The 283 entries for books, including translations of Miller's books, and 404 contributions to books give title-page transcriptions, paginations, binding descriptions, and notes on publication histories. Appendixes include a list of titles never published by Miller or erroneously attributed to Miller; "*Opus Pistorum* and Henry Miller" (historical background) and a character key to *Tropic of Cancer*, compiled by Jackson; a resource guide listing Miller associations and collections; and a list of book dealers specializing in Miller. Includes glossy illustrations of title pages, dust jackets, and other contributions, with a separate index. Comprehensive index of names and titles. Miller's manuscripts are listed in Robbins' *American Literary Manuscripts*, p. 221. Aimed at collectors, Michael Hargraves' *Henry Miller Bibliography: A Humble Listing of His Major First Editions with Some Additions, Plus a Complete Discography* (San Francisco, CA: Hargraves, 1980) gives brief bibliographic information for first editions and appearances of Miller's works (91 entries), with a list of 21 recordings of Miller's readings and interviews. Also useful is *Descriptive Catalogue of the Dr. James F. O'Roark Collection of the Works of Henry Miller* (Santa Barbara, CA: Joseph the Provider, n.d.).

947. Shifreen, Lawrence J. **Henry Miller: A Bibliography of Secondary Sources**. Metuchen, NJ: Scarecrow Press, 1979. 477p. (Scarecrow Author Bibliographies, no. 38). LC 78-12518. ISBN 0-8108-1171-5.

Shifreen briefly describes works about Miller in all languages in separate chronologically arranged listings covering 74 books; 392 parts of books, 17 dissertations, 125 passing references in books about others, and 4,093 articles and reviews (the great bulk). Annotations are descriptive. Significant works receive extended descriptions. Coverage extends from 1925 through 1977. Subject access is limited to indexing for primary works. See *Bibliography of American Fiction, 1919-1988*, pp. 348-51, for Mary Dearborn and Margaret Donovan DuPriest's checklist of works by and about Miller.

Dictionaries, Encyclopedias, and Handbooks

948. Fielding, Blair. **Nothing but the Marvelous: Wisdoms of Henry Miller**. Santa Barbara, CA: Capra Press, 1991. 83p. LC 89-48703. ISBN 0-8849-6313-6.

Topically arranged, selected quotations from Miller's works in sections for "The Man," "The Artist," and "The Spirit." Entries for "Angels," "Censorship," "Individuality," "Parenting," etc., cite works by titles but do not give specific citations. "Acknowledgments" lists sources.

Journals

See Patterson's *Author Newsletters and Journals*, pp. 214-15, for previously published journals for Miller.

Joaquin Miller (Cincinnatus Hiner Miller), 1841?-1913

Bibliographies

949. Longtin, Ray C. **Three Writers of the Far West: A Reference Guide**. Boston: G. K. Hall, 1980. 296p. (A Reference Guide to Literature). LC 80-19537. ISBN 0-8161-7832-1.

For Joaquin Miller, Charles Warren Stoddard, and George Sterling, Longtin provides separate biographical introductions, brief checklists of primary materials, and chronologically arranged, annotated listings of secondary works (books, parts of books, articles, reviews, and dissertations). Coverage for Miller includes about 500 entries published from 1870 through 1978; for Stoddard, about 250 entries from 1863 through 1979; and for Sterling, about 250 entries from 1903 through 1979. Annotations are brief and descriptive. Separate indexes for each author include headings for "bibliography" and "biography." Coverage of Miller's primary materials is included in Blanck's *Bibliography of American Literature*, vol. 6, pp. 182-217. Wells' *The Literary Index to American Magazines, 1850-1900*, pp. 271-72, identifies Miller's contributions to selected periodicals. Miller's manuscripts are listed in Robbins' *American Literary Manuscripts*, pp. 220-21. Research on Miller is reviewed by Alan Rosenus in Erisman and Etulain's *Fifty Western Writers*, pp. 303-12.

Walter M. Miller, Jr., 1923-

Bibliographies

950.   Roberson, William H., and Robert L. Battenfeld. **Walter M. Miller, Jr.: A Bio-Bibliography**. Westport, CT: Greenwood Press, 1992. 149p. (Bio-Bibliographies in American Literature, no. 3). LC 92-7335. ISBN 0-313-27651-X.

Covers works by and about Miller. Part 1 chronologically lists Miller's works in sections for books (sublisted for English and "Non-English Language" editions), short fiction in periodicals, short fiction in anthologies, nonfiction, adaptations, and television scripts. Entries for eight U.S. and U.K. English-language editions give title-page transcriptions, collations, paginations, binding descriptions, contents, and brief data on publication histories. Entries for periodical fiction and nonfiction summarize contents and identify characters. Part 2 chronologically lists annotated entries in sections for 130 critical articles, 72 book reviews (subarranged by works), and six dissertations. Evaluative annotations cross-reference other works. Also includes glossary of characters, terms, allusions, and other references in Miller's *A Canticle for Leibowitz* and a brief chronology. Introduction surveys Miller's career and critical reception. Separate indexes for names, titles, and characters in Part 1 and names, titles, and subjects in Part 2.

A(lan) A(lexander) Milne, 1882-1956

Bibliographies

951.   Haring-Smith, Tori. **A. A. Milne: A Critical Bibliography**. New York: Garland, 1982. 344p. (Garland Reference Library of the Humanities, vol. 305). LC 81-43350. ISBN 0-8240-9282-1.

Offers separate listings for Milne's writings (books, plays, children's literature, poems, short stories, essays, parodies, autobiographies, reviews, and published letters), giving brief bibliographic information, references to later editions, and selectively annotated entries for their reviews. In addition, Haring-Smith covers critical and biographical works about Milne, including published interviews and bibliographies; media and other adaptations of Milne's "Pooh" characters; and writings of the Milne family, including Christopher Robin Milne, Kenneth J. Milne, and Dorothy DeSelincourt Milne. Also for a bibliography of works by and about Milne, see *NCBEL*, IV, pp. 671-73.

Indexes and Concordances

952.   Sibley, Brian. **The Pooh Book of Quotations: In Which Will Be Found Some Useful Information and Sustaining Thoughts by Winnie-the-Pooh and His Friends**. New York: Dutton Children's Books, 1991. 120p. LC 91-2628. ISBN 0-5254-4824-1.

Of limited reference value. A collection of quotations in prose and poetry, apparently based on the (New York: E. P. Dutton) editions of *Winnie-the-Pooh* (1926), *The House at Pooh Corner* (1928), *When We Were Very Young* (1924), and *Now We Are Six* (1927), grouped by 25 topics, such as weather, food, misunderstanding, and bravery. Entries do not give specific references to editions. Index of names and more limited topics. Originally published (London: Methuen Children's Books) in 1986.

John Milton, 1608-1674
Bibliographies

953. Huckabay, Calvin. **John Milton: An Annotated Bibliography, 1929-1968.**
Revised ed. Pittsburgh, PA: Duquesne University Press, 1969. 392p. (Duquesne
Studies: Philological Series, no. 1). LC 73-98551.
    This is continued by:

953.1. Huckabay, Calvin, and Paul J. Klemp. **John Milton: An Annotated
Bibliography, 1968-1988.** Pittsburgh, PA: Duquesne University Press, 1996. 535p.
LC 95-49712. ISBN 0-8207-0272-2.
    The standard, comprehensive bibliographies of Milton scholarship, both of
Huckabay's volumes chronologically arrange briefly annotated entries in topical
sections for bibliography and reference works; editions of Milton's collected and
individual works; translations; general critical and biographical studies; studies
of the individual works; and topical listings covering studies of style and versification, editions, translations, illustrations, and fame and influence. International
coverage includes dissertations, non-English-language criticisms, reprints, listings in reference works, and many other kinds of items. The volume for Milton
scholarship from 1929 to 1968 includes 3,932 annotated entries; the volume covering 1968 to 1988 offers 4,571 annotated entries. Brief, descriptive annotations
typically cite references to reviews. The volume for 1929 to 1968 limits indexing
to names of critics and very selective subjects (under Milton); the volume for 1968
to 1988 provides more thorough indexing for proper names (such as Virgil,
Spenser, and Mark Twain), titles of Milton's works, and subjects, such as "Arian-
ism," "Music," and "Women" (still listed under Milton). Although Huckabay's
bibliographies are essential resources for advanced Milton scholarship, Klemp's
more selective *Essential Milton: An Annotated Bibliography of Major Modern Studies*
(entry 954) offers better guidance for students to recent scholarship. Huckabay's
guide supplements David H. Stevens' *Reference Guide to Milton: From 1800 to the
Present Day* (Chicago: University of Chicago Press, 1930), which topically arranges
2,850 briefly annotated entries for editions, translations, and studies through 1928;
and Harris Francis Fletcher's *Contributions to a Milton Bibliography, 1800-1930:
Being a List of Addenda to Stevens's Reference Guide to Milton* (Urbana, IL: University
of Illinois Press, 1931), which chronologically arranges about 1,000 entries for
editions, translations, and studies.

954. Klemp, P. J. **Essential Milton: An Annotated Bibliography of Major Modern Studies.** Boston: G. K. Hall, 1989. 474p. (Reference Publication in Literature).
LC 89-30984. ISBN 0-8161-8730-4.
    The best starting point for research on Milton, Klemp's guide identifies 1,021
editions of primary texts, reference works, and critical studies about Milton
published from 1900 through 1987. Descriptive and detailed annotations in classified listings cover background works; editions; biographies; bibliographies;
reference works; studies of reputation and influence; studies of translations,
illustrations, and adaptations; criticism of Milton's critics; general studies; and
studies of individual works and their major topics and themes, such as style,
narrative technique, Hell, and Earth in *Paradise Lost*. Unfortunately, Klemp's
annotations are rigidly objective and offer little helpful guidance beyond selectivity. Equally selective coverage of Milton scholarship, but lacking detailed annotations, is provided by C. A. Patrides' *An Annotated Critical Bibliography of John Milton*
(New York: St. Martin's, 1987). Patrides includes about 1,200 studies. Both Klemp
and Patrides update the selective coverage of James Holly Hanford and William
A. McQueen's reliable *Milton*, 2d ed. (Arlington Heights, IL: AHM, 1979), a volume
in the Goldentree Bibliographies in Language and Literature series. Graduate
students will find all three very useful. Additionally, William C. Johnson's *Milton*

Criticism: A Subject Index (Kent: Dawson, 1978) topically indexes a selection of 150 books about Milton. Klemp's selective guide is partially supplemented by his *Paradise Lost: An Annotated Bibliography* (Lanham, MD: Scarecrow Press and Pasadena, CA: Salem Press, 1996), which describes some 450 twentieth-century criticisms of *Paradise Lost*. Edward Jones' selective *Milton's Sonnets: An Annotated Bibliography, 1900-1992* (Binghamton, NY: Medieval & Renaissance Texts & Studies, 1994) includes 516 annotated entries for general studies and studies of the individual English and Italian sonnets and non-English-language translations. Also for a bibliography of works by and about Milton, see *NCBEL*, I, pp. 1237-96, by C. A. Patrides. Research on Milton is reviewed by Douglas Bush in Dyson's *English Poetry*, pp. 76-95. *YWES* annually features a review essay on Milton scholarship.

955.   Shawcross, John T. **Milton: A Bibliography for the Years 1624-1700**. Binghamton, NY: Medieval & Renaissance Texts & Studies, State University of New York, 1984. 452p. (Medieval & Renaissance Texts & Studies, vol. 30). LC 84-653. ISBN 0-86698-064-4.
   This is updated by:

   955.1. Shawcross, John T. **Milton: A Bibliography for the Years 1624-1700: Addenda and Corrigenda**. Binghamton, NY: Medieval & Renaissance Texts & Studies, 1990. 30p. (Medieval & Renaissance Texts & Studies, vol. 30A). LC 89-14584. ISBN 0-86698-081-4.
   Shawcross offers the most comprehensive listing of primary and contemporary materials by and about Milton, "bring[ing] together all manuscripts and editions of the works and all studies and critical statements concerning Milton's life and works, all allusions and quotations, and all significant imitations during the years 1624-1700" (p. ix). In the first part, Shawcross chronologically arranges detailed descriptions for 416 editions and variants of Milton's publications, giving title-page transcriptions, collations, locations of copies, and *STC* and *Wing* numbers. In the second part, Shawcross chronologically arranges briefly annotated entries for 1,753 contemporary secondary works, including books, broadsides, dedications, manuscripts, letters, documents, and other materials. Detailed, separate indexes for primary titles and subjects (such as "divorce," "education theory," and "letters"); state papers; secondary and other cited titles; editors and authors of non-Miltonic works (Virgil and Shakespeare); printers, publishers, and booksellers; and locations of printed copies and manuscripts give comprehensive access. The 1990 *Addenda and Corrigenda* introduces about 150 additions, deletions, changes, and corrections to the 1984 volume listed by original Shawcross numbers. Shawcross' guide, along with Huckabay's bibliographies (entry 953), is a cornerstone of Milton bibliography. Additional coverage of Milton's primary bibliography is provided by Jackson Campbell Boswell's *Milton's Library: A Catalogue of the Remains of John Milton's Library and an Annotated Reconstruction of Milton's Library and Ancillary Readings* (New York: Garland, 1975), which describes 1,500 books related to Milton's reading. Other useful descriptions of Milton's primary materials are included in K. A. Coleridge's *A Descriptive Catalogue of the Milton Collection in the Alexander Turnbull Library, Wellington, New Zealand: Describing Works Printed Before 1801 Held in the Library at December 1975* (Oxford: Published for the Alexander Turnbull Library, National Library of New Zealand by Oxford University Press, 1980). Milton's manuscripts are described in *Index of English Literary Manuscripts*, II, pt. 2:69-104.

Dictionaries, Encyclopedias, and Handbooks
956.   Hunter, Willam B., general ed. **A Milton Encyclopedia**. Cranbury, NJ: Associated University Presses, 1978-84. 9 vols. LC 75-21896. ISBN 0-8387-1834-5.
   Authoritative articles by contributing specialists survey topics related to the life, works, and times of Milton. "Lycidas" is surveyed in 18 pages. Milton's

numerous allusions to the Bible and classics receive significant attention. In many other instances, however, the work amounts to an encyclopedia of the latter seventeenth century. Entries review the lives and accomplishments of Milton's contemporaries in the arts, politics, and society and cover Milton's indebtedness to and influences on earlier and later writers. Extended articles cover Milton and the "Arts of Design" and "Debate" as well as Milton's literary relationships with Robert Burton, William Blake, and Robert Bridges. Vol. 9 supplies brief, selected supporting bibliographies for limited topics as well as indexes for names and topics. Edward S. LeComte's *A Milton Dictionary* (New York: AMS Press, 1969) offers briefer identifications of real and fictional persons, places, and things and difficult words that appear in Milton's works. Allan H. Gilbert's *A Geographical Dictionary of Milton* (New Haven, CT: Yale University Press, 1919) identifies place names in Milton's writings. More specialized coverage of Milton's allusions and other features of his works is offered in Edward LeComte's *Dictionary of Puns in Milton's English Poetry* (New York: Columbia University Press, 1981), which glosses of 1,630 puns; and M. Christopher Pecheux's *Milton: A Topographical Guide* (Washington, DC: University Press of America, 1981), which identifies real places in Milton's England.

Indexes and Concordances

957.   Hudson, Gladys W. **Paradise Lost: A Concordance**. Detroit, MI: Gale, 1970. 361p. LC 74-127413.

This is based on the facsimile and old-spelling text of the second edition (1674) of *Paradise Lost*, edited by Harris Francis Fletcher (Urbana, IL: University of Illinois Press, 1948). The 1674 edition is also the base text for Frank Allen Patterson's edition of *Paradise Lost*, which is vol. 2 of *The Works of John Milton* (New York: Columbia University Press, 1931). Includes word frequencies. For scholarly research, Hudson's concordance is superior to Celia Floren's *John Milton: A Concordance of Paradise Lost* (Hildesheim: Olms-Weidmann, 1992), a KWIC index based on the modern spelling "edition of Douglas Bush, Oxford University Press, 1966" (Preface); and Linda D. Misek's *Context Concordance to John Milton's Paradise Lost* (Cleveland, OH: Andrew R. Jennings Computing Center, Case Western Reserve University, 1971), which is a KWIC index based on Henry J. Todd's edition (London: Johnson, 1809) of the second 1674 edition.

958.   Ingram, William, and Kathleen Swaim. **A Concordance to Milton's English Poetry**. Oxford: Clarendon Press, 1972. 683p. LC 72-186436. ISBN 0-1981-1138-X.

Ingram and Swaim concord the texts of early editions, manuscripts, fragments, and variants of Milton's English poems. It supersedes John Bradshaw's *Concordance to the Poetical Works of John Milton* (New York: Macmillan, 1894; reprint Hamden, CT: Archon Books, 1965; and St. Clair Shores, MI: Scholarly Press, 1972); and Charles Dexter Cleveland's *Complete Concordance to the Poetical Works of John Milton* (London: Low, Son, and Marston, 1867; reprint Norwood, PA: Norwood Editions, 1977). Lane Cooper's *A Concordance of the Latin, Greek, and Italian Poems of John Milton* (Halle: Max Niemeyer, 1926; reprint New York: Kraus, 1971) gives separate indexes for Latin, Greek, and Italian poems included (for the most part) in H. C. Beeching's *The Poetical Works of John Milton* (Oxford: Clarendon Press, 1900). Laura E. Lockwood's *Lexicon to the English Poetical Works of John Milton* (New York: Macmillan, 1907) defines words in Milton's poetical vocabulary. Another more specialized index, Samuel J. Rogal's *An Index to the Biblical References, Parallels, and Allusions in the Poetry and Prose of John Milton* (Lewiston, NY: Edwin Mellen Press, 1994) cross-references Milton's writings with Old and New Testament books, chapters, and verses.

959.   Sterne, Laurence, and Harold H. Kollmeier. **A Concordance to the English Prose of John Milton**. Binghamton, NY: Center for Medieval & Early Renaissance

Studies, State University of New York, 1985. 1,491p. (Medieval & Renaissance Texts & Studies, vol. 35). LC 85-4881. ISBN 0-86698-068-7.

Sterne and Kollmeier give an old-spelling concordance to texts in Don M. Wolfe's eight-volume edition of the *Complete Prose Works of John Milton* (New Haven, CT: Yale University Press, 1953-82), excluding Milton's translations of Latin prose as well as a few works in English.

Journals

960.   **Milton Quarterly**. Binghamton, NY: Milton Society of America, 1967- . 4/yr. ISSN 0026-4326.

The unassuming appearance of *Milton Quarterly* is deceptive. Sponsored by the Milton Society of America, typical issues publish a few major scholarly notes in addition to news about the activities of the society. The cover's verso contains the journal's table of contents. Although many notes are necessarily brief and specific, their range of interest is extensive, including analyses and interpretations of images and allusions, comments on sources and analogues, discussions of biographical and textual problems, and the like. "Bees and Fallen Angels: A Note on *Paradise Lost*," "Milton and the Early Mormon Defense of Polygamy," "The Name of Jesus in *Paradise Lost*," and "Free Will, Predestination, and Ghost-Busting" are sufficiently suggestive of the journal's range. Occasional issues containing a single feature devoted to specific topics nearly amount to monographs: 30.2 (May 1996) is James Patrick McHenry's "A Milton Herbal," an indexed dictionary of Milton's plants and trees that supplements this topic's coverage in Hunter's *A Milton Encyclopedia* (entry 956); and 28.4 (December 1994) is Norman Postlethwaite and Gordon Campbell's "Edward King, Milton's 'Lycidas': Poems and Documents," an edition of King's Latin poems and poems about King, with facsimiles of primary materials and an extensive bibliography. Additionally, *Milton Quarterly* publishes letters containing "news of any sort interesting to Miltonists" and research queries and questions. Reviews of new works, review articles, abstracts of conference papers, and miscellaneous notes on upcoming conferences, papers, performances, and the like round out most issues. *Milton Quarterly* is indexed in *AES, AHI, A&HCI, MHRA,* and *MLA*.

961.   **Milton Studies**. Pittsburgh, PA: University of Pittsburgh Press, 1969- . Annual. ISSN 0076-8820.

The most prestigious journal of Milton studies. Each 300-page volume typically includes nine or more substantial articles that reflect the full range of literary scholarship, including biographical and historical background studies, bibliographic analyses, critical and interpretive readings, studies of sources and influences, and more. Typical articles include "The Lyric Dimensions of *Paradise Lost*," "Donne, Milton, and Holy Sex," "Opposites of Wifehood: Eve and Dalila," and "The Iconography of Eden." In addition, *Milton Studies* maintains a balanced presentation of scholarship for all of Milton's works, with most volumes featuring several (four or five) articles on *Paradise Lost*, a few (two to three) on Milton's other longer works, such as *Comus, Paradise Regained,* and *Samson Agonistes,* and the remainder on such works as "L'Allegro" and "Il Penseroso," the sonnets, and his other writings. An occasional volume is devoted to a specific topic, such as "The Miltonic Samson," focusing on *Samson Agonistes,* in 33 (1996), published in 1997. *Milton Studies* has not included literature reviews nor other bibliographic features, such as reviews. The volumes do not include indexes. *Milton Studies* is indexed in *A&HCI, MHRA,* and *MLA*.

Patterson's *Author Newsletters and Journals,* pp. 216-18, describes other previously published journals for Milton.

Donald Grant Mitchell (Ik. Marvel), 1822-1908

Bibliographies

962.   Seybolt, Paul S. **The First Editions of Donald Grant Mitchell, "Ik Marvel": A Checklist**. Boston: Privately printed, 1930. OCLC 13348649.

Unseen. For works by Mitchell, see *Bibliography of American Literature*, vol. 6, pp. 218-43. Contributions by Mitchell and criticism and reviews of Mitchell's works in selected periodicals are identified in Wells' *The Literary Index to American Magazines, 1815-1865*, pp. 106-107; and *The Literary Index to American Magazines, 1850-1900*, pp. 272-73. Mitchell's manuscripts are listed in Robbins' *American Literary Manuscripts*, p. 222. See *Bibliography of American Fiction Through 1865*, pp. 185-86, for a checklist of works by and about Mitchell.

Isaac Mitchell, c. 1759-1812

Bibliographies

For works by Mitchell, see *Bibliography of American Literature*, vol. 6, pp. 244-45. See *Bibliography of American Fiction Through 1865*, p. 187, for a checklist of works by and about Mitchell.

John Ames Mitchell, 1845-1918

Bibliographies

For works by Mitchell, see *Bibliography of American Literature*, vol. 6, pp. 246-50. Mitchell's manuscripts are listed in Robbins' *American Literary Manuscripts*, p. 222.

Margaret Mitchell, 1900-1949

Bibliographies

963.   Jelks, Joyce E., Martha Sue Farmer, and Sarah H. Alexander. **A Literary Guide for the Study of Margaret Mitchell and Gone with the Wind**. Atlanta, GA: Atlanta-Fulton Public Library, 1984. 44p. OCLC 16123251.

Unseen. Mitchell's manuscripts are listed in Robbins' *American Literary Manuscripts*, p. 223. See *Bibliography of American Fiction, 1919-1988*, pp. 352-54, for Judith S. Baughman's checklist of works by and about Mitchell. See the review of research by Samuel I. Bellman in Duke, Bryer, and Inge's *American Women Writers*, pp. 353-78; and Darden Asbury Pyron in Flora and Bain's *Fifty Southern Writers After 1900*, pp. 224-33.

S(ilas) Weir Mitchell, 1829-1914

Bibliographies

964.   Mumey, Nolie. **Silas Weir Mitchell: The Versatile Physician (1829-1914): A Sketch of His Life and His Literary Contributions**. Denver, CO: The Range Press, 1935. 201p. LC 35-16578.

Contains chapters that chronologically arrange brief bibliographic descriptions of first editions of Mitchell's books, medical and scientific articles (approximately 300 contributions from 1851 to 1914), literary articles, and poems (to 1927). Covering Mitchell's separately published scientific and medical writings (including translated works), entries give pagination, size, and notes on contents. Concluding "Reference" chapter (pp. [189]-96) identifies approximately 50 items about Mitchell, including entries in encyclopedias, biographical articles, and published photographs. Also contains facsimile plates of manuscripts and letters. Indexed. Although Blanck's *Bibliography of American Literature*, vol. 6, pp. 251-99, gives more detail for Mitchell's separately published literary works, Mumey's guide remains significant for information about the separately published and contributed scientific and medical writings. Mitchell's contributions to selected periodicals and reviews of Mitchell's works are also identified in Wells' *The Literary Index to American Magazines, 1850-1900*, pp. 273-74. Mitchell's manuscripts are listed in Robbins' *American Literary Manuscripts*, p. 223. See *Bibliography of American Fiction,*

1866-1918, pp. 288-89, for Paul Leslie Ross' checklist of works by (excluding most on scientific and medical subjects) and about Mitchell.

Robert Molloy, 1906-1977
Bibliographies

For works by Molloy, see *First Printings of American Authors*, vol. 4, pp. 277-80.

N(avarre) Scott Momaday, 1934-
Bibliographies

Momaday's manuscripts are listed in Robbins' *American Literary Manuscripts*, p. 224. See *Bibliography of American Fiction, 1919-1988*, pp. 354-55, for Susan Elizabeth Gunter's checklist of works by and about Momaday. Martha Scott Trimble surveys works by and about Momaday in Erisman and Etulain's *Fifty Western Writers*, pp. 313-24.

Lady Mary Wortley Montagu (Pierrepoint), 1689-1762
Bibliographies

For a bibliography of works by and about Montagu, see *NCBEL*, II, pp. 1584-85, by Robert Halsband. Montagu's manuscripts are described in *Index of English Literary Manuscripts*, III, pt. 2:187-233.

Journals

"Recent Articles" in *The Scriblerian and the Kit Cats* (entry 1084) regularly includes a selection of reviews of studies on Montagu.

William Vaughan Moody, 1869-1910
Bibliographies

For works by Moody, see *Bibliography of American Literature*, vol. 6, pp. 300-309. Moody's manuscripts are listed in Robbins' *American Literary Manuscripts*, p. 224. Moody's contributions to and reviews of Moody's works in selected periodicals are identified in Wells' *The Literary Index to American Magazines, 1850-1900*, p. 275. See Boswell's *Spokesmen for the Minority* (entry 809) for criticism of Moody. Lincoln Konkle identifies works by and about Moody in Demastes' *American Playwrights, 1880-1945*, pp. 302-309.

Clement Clarke Moore, 1779-1863
Bibliographies

For works by Moore, see *Bibliography of American Literature*, vol. 6, pp. 310-14. Also available is George H. M. Lawrence's *"The Night Before Christmas": An Exhibition Catalogue* (Pittsburgh, PA: Pittsburgh Bibliophiles, 1964). Moore's manuscripts are listed in Robbins' *American Literary Manuscripts*, p. 225.

George Augustus Moore, 1852-1933
Bibliographies

965. Gilcher, Edwin. **A Bibliography of George Moore**. DeKalb, IL: Northern Illinois University Press, 1970. 274p. LC 72-125334. ISBN 0-87580-017-3.
This is supplemented by:

965.1. Gilcher, Edwin **Supplement to A Bibliography of George Moore**. Westport, CT: Meckler, 1988. 95p. LC 87-18593. ISBN 0-8873-6199-4.
Gilcher gives full bibliographic descriptions for Moore's primary materials, including sections for books and pamphlets; contributions to books, including letters and excerpts; contributions to periodicals; translations of Moore's works (arranged by languages); and miscellaneous works, such as apocrypha, lost works, and plays produced by Moore. Entries include title-page transcriptions,

physical descriptions, contents, and brief publishing histories. Also for a bibliography of works by and about Moore, see *NCBEL*, III, pp. 1014-19.

966.   Langenfeld, Robert. **George Moore: An Annotated Secondary Bibliography of Writings About Him**. New York: AMS Press, 1987. 531p. (AMS Studies in Modern Literature, no. 13). LC 84-48436. ISBN 0-404-61583-x.

Langenfeld chronologically arranges annotated entries for 2,355 works in English and other languages about Moore published from 1878 through 1987, covering books, parts of books, articles, reviews, and passing references in all languages. Dissertations are unannotated. Annotations are descriptive and evaluative. Significant works receive extensive descriptions. A comprehensive index includes detailed topical subheadings under Moore's name (for "interviews," "Irish Literary Movement," and "realism") as well as headings for names (Joyce and Shakespeare), "dissertations," and languages. Research on Moore is reviewed by Jacob Korg in Ford's *Victorian Fiction*, pp. 348-59; by Korg in Stevenson's *Victorian Fiction*, pp. 388-414; by Wendell V. Harris in Delaura's *Victorian Prose*, pp. 451-53; and by Helmut E. Gerber in Finneran's *Anglo-Irish Literature*, pp. 138-66.

Marianne (Craig) Moore, 1887-1972

Bibliographies

967.   Abbott, Craig S. **Marianne Moore: A Descriptive Bibliography**. Pittsburgh, PA: University of Pittsburgh Press, 1977. 265p. (Pittsburgh Series in Bibliography). LC 76-5922. ISBN 0-8229-3319-5.

Abbott provides detailed descriptions of Moore's writings, including listings for separately published works, first-appearance contributions to books, contributions to books and periodicals, letters, drawings, edited works, recordings, and translations of Moore's works. Entries give illustrations of title and copyright pages and bindings, physical descriptions, publishing histories, and copy locations. A selected list of about 50 secondary works is appended. This supersedes in coverage Eugene P. Sheehy and Kenneth A. Lohf's *The Achievement of Marianne Moore: A Bibliography, 1907-1957* (New York: New York Public Library, 1958). Also for works by Moore, see *First Printings of American Authors*, vol. 1, pp. 269-72. Moore's manuscripts are listed in Robbins' *American Literary Manuscripts*, p. 225.

968.   Abbott, Craig S. **Marianne Moore: A Reference Guide**. Boston: G. K. Hall, 1978. (A Reference Publication in Literature). 153p. LC 78-14318. ISBN 0-8161-8061-x.

Chronologically arranged, annotated entries describe secondary materials (books, parts of books, articles, reviews of Moore's works and of works about Moore, and dissertations) about Moore published from 1916 through 1976. Annotations are descriptive, with significant works receiving detailed reviews. Index headings for names and works appearing in the annotations (Robert Browning, Francis Bacon) and broad subjects ("bibliographies," "interviews," and "manuscripts") offer good access. Chronologically covering major critical studies as well as dissertations and non-English-language criticism, Bonnie Honigsblum's "An Annotated Bibliography of Works About Marianne Moore, 1977-1990," in Patricia C. Willis' *Marianne Moore, Woman and Poet* (Orono, ME: National Poetry Foundation, University of Maine, 1990), pp. [443]-620, updates and supplements Abbott's guide. Research on Moore is reviewed by Cindy Hoffman, Carol Duane, Katharen Soule, and Linda Wagner in Duke, Bryer, and Inge's *American Women Writers*, pp. 379-402.

Indexes and Concordances

969.   Lane, Gary. **A Concordance to the Poems of Marianne Moore**. New York: Haskell House, 1972. 526p. LC 72-6438. ISBN 0-8383-1588-7.

Lane concords the texts in *The Complete Poems* (New York: Viking, 1967) and appends word-frequency lists.

Journals

See Wortman's *A Guide to Serial Bibliographies for Modern Literatures*, p. 269, for a description of the previously published serial bibliography in *Marianne Moore Newsletter* (1977-83). Patterson's *Author Newsletters and Journals*, p. 221, describes previously published journals for Moore.

Thomas Moore, 1779-1852

Bibliographies

For a bibliography of works by and about Moore, see *NCBEL*, III, pp. 263-67. Contributions by Moore and criticism and reviews of Moore's works in selected periodicals are identified in Wells' *The Literary Index to American Magazines, 1815-1865*, pp. 107-108; and *The Literary Index to American Magazines, 1850-1900*, pp. 275-76. See the review of research by Hoover H. Jordan in Houtchens and Houtchens' *The English Romantic Poets and Essayists*, pp. 197-220; and by James F. Kilroy in Finneran's *Anglo-Irish Literature*, pp. 41-43.

Henry More, 1614-1687

Bibliographies

For a bibliography of works by and about More, see *NCBEL*, I, pp. 2334-36. More's manuscripts are described in *Index of English Literary Manuscripts*, II, pt. 2:105-107.

Sir Thomas More, 1477?-1535

Bibliographies

970.   Boswell, Jackson Campbell, and Anne Lake Prescott. **Sir Thomas More in the English Renaissance: An Annotated Catalogue.** Binghamton, NY: Medieval & Renaissance Texts & Studies, 1994. 362p. (Medieval & Renaissance Texts & Studies, vol. 83). LC 91-9356. ISBN 0-8669-8093-8.

Supplements coverage of contemporary and early allusions to More offered in Gibson's standard bibliography (entry 971). Identifies by authors, short titles, imprints, and *STC* numbers some 706 works published through 1640 that "include references or allusions" to More (p. vii). Based on the *STC*'s coverage (that is, excludes continental imprints other than English-language works as well as all manuscripts). Entries quote primary sources extensively (in old spellings), with detailed glosses and explications. Most useful for comparisons of the treatment of More in the writings of Erasmus, John Bale, John Foxe, William Tyndale, and others. Chronological index of works.

971.   Gibson, R. W. **St. Thomas More: A Preliminary Bibliography of His Works and of Moreana to the Year 1750.** New Haven, CT: Yale University Press, 1961. 499p. LC 61-7190.

The standard descriptive bibliography of More's writings. Gibson gives full bibliographic descriptions of works by More and Moreana in separate listings for *Utopia*; other separate works; collected works; More's translations of Lucian; prayers; lives of More; letters; and Moreana, including some 441 entries for contemporary allusions, attributed works, and documents relating to More. Other sections describe works on "utopias and dystopias" and portraits of More dating from 1500 through 1700. Entries for primary works include facsimiles of title pages, collations, and locations. Supplemental information for More's primary works is listed in Constance Smith's *An Updating of R. W. Gibson's St. Thomas More: A Preliminary Bibliography* (St. Louis, MO: Center for Reformation Research, 1981) as well as in numerous articles published in *Moreana* (entry 974). Other sources for updating Gibson are identified in Wentworth's *The Essential Sir Thomas More* (entry 972), item 1. Also for a bibliography of works by and about More, see *NCBEL*, I, pp. 1792-1809, 2329. More's manuscripts are described in *Index of English Literary Manuscripts*, I, pt. 2:347-54.

972. Wentworth, Michael D. **The Essential Sir Thomas More: An Annotated Bibliography of Major Modern Studies**. New York: G. K. Hall, 1995. 351p. (Reference Publication in Literature). LC 95-13088. ISBN 0-8161-8942-0.

Intends to "provide a convenient annotated survey of twentieth-century scholarship on More published in English through the year 1991" (p. ix). Covers both books and articles. With "taxonomic consistency" (p. x) in mind, Wentworth alphabetically lists annotated entries for 805 works by and about More in seven major topical sections covering general reference works; biographical studies; More's writings in general; his humanist, polemical, and devotional writings; and his correspondence. Parallel subsections identify more specialized reference sources, editions, and criticisms for collected and individual works. Biographical sublistings focus on More's personal relations, public and legal careers, iconography, and other topics. Although generally descriptive, Wentworth's substantial and thorough annotations are particularly evaluative of editions. His introduction identifies major non-English-language studies. A comprehensive index with detailed subjects provides excellent access. Wentworth's guide complements and selectively updates the more comprehensive coverage of works about More through the mid-1980s supplied in Frank Sullivan and Majie Padberg Sullivan's *Moreana, 1478-1945: A Preliminary Check List of Materials by and About Saint Thomas More* (Kansas City, MO: Rockhurst College, 1946) and *Moreana: Materials for the Study of Saint Thomas More* (Los Angeles, CA: Loyola University of Los Angeles, 1964-65); and in Majie Padberg Sullivan's *Moreana: Materials for the Study of Saint Thomas More: Supplement and Chronology to 1800* (Los Angeles, CA: Loyola Marymount University, 1977) and *Moreana: Materials for the Study of Saint Thomas More. Supplement II* (Los Angeles, CA: Loyola Marymount University, 1985).

Indexes and Concordances

973. Bolchazy, Ladislaus J., Gregory Gichan, and Frederick Theobald. **A Concordance to the Utopia of St. Thomas More and a Frequency Word List**. Hildesheim: Georg Olms, 1978. 332, 56 p. (Alpha-Omega: Reihe B: Indizes, Konkordanzen, Statistische Studien zur Mittellateinischen Philologie, vol. 2). ISBN 3-4870-6514-2.

"Based on and referenced to the Yale edition of Edward Surtz, S. J. and J. H. Hexter in *The Yale Edition of the Complete Works of St. Thomas More*, Volume 4 (Yale University Press, New Haven and London, 1965)" (Introduction). Contains every word in the edition; does not lemmatize forms (that is, *sum, est*, and *fuit* are listed alphabetically).

Journals

974. **Moreana: Bulletin Thomas More**. Angers Cedex, France: Amici Thomae Mori, 1963-. 3/yr. ISSN 0047-8105.

Sponsored by Amici Thomae Mori, an international association of More scholars, *Moreana* features substantial scholarly articles (in French and English) on the life and writings of More and other humanists (such as Erasmus, Martin Luther, and William Tyndale). Studies address More as an influential political and historical figure, a religious and political writer, and a saint and otherwise legendary figure. Typical contributions offer close readings and interpretations of works and ideas, trace More's sources and identify contemporary allusions to More, and account More's critical reputation and influence. Occasional bibliographic articles offer literature reviews, such as Francisco Lopez Estrada's review of scholarship on More in Spain and Latin America in 33 (June 1996): 41-50. In addition, issues publish reviews of new books about More, announce conferences and calls for papers, and describe activities of the association. Quite in character of this very learned journal, issues also include a "Libri Recensendi." *Moreana* is indexed in *MHRA* and *MLA*.

Patterson's *Author Newsletters and Journals*, pp. 221-22, describes other previously published journals for More.

Christopher (Darlington) Morley, 1890-1957

Bibliographies

975. Lee, Alfred P. **A Bibliography of Christopher Morley**. Garden City, NY: Doubleday, Doran, 1935. 277p. LC 35-38125.

Full bibliographic descriptions in sections for Morley's separate works, contributions and introductions, and "Morleyana" (works containing information about Morley). Entries offer title-page transcriptions, collations and paginations, descriptions of paper and bindings, data for variants and notes on publication histories, and bibliographic information for subsequent editions. Appendix identifies Morley's contributed works.

976. Lyle, Guy R., and H. Tatnall Brown, Jr. **A Bibliography of Christopher Morley**. Washington, DC: Scarecrow, 1952. 198p. LC 53-5976.

Provides supplemental information for works by and about Morley to update Lee's *A Bibliography of Christopher Morley* (entry 975). Contains separate sections for Morley's books and pamphlets, ephemeral publications, Morley's contributions to books, books about Morley, Morley's contributions to periodicals, and articles about Morley. Entries for Morley's separate publications give title-page transcriptions, collations and paginations, contents, and binding and jacket descriptions, with notes on publication histories. Identifies about 50 works about Morley. Morley's manuscripts are listed in Robbins' *American Literary Manuscripts*, pp. 226-27. *An Exhibition of CDM: Manuscripts and First Editions at the Humanities Research Center, The University of Texas, Austin, Texas, December 1961-February 1962* (Austin, TX: Humanities Research Center, University of Texas, 1961) offers useful notes on primary materials, with facsimiles of selected manuscripts, typescripts, and other works at Texas. Also useful is J. Terry Bender's *Christopher Morley: A Comprehensive Exhibition* (Freeport, NY: Hofstra University Library, 1970). See *Bibliography of American Fiction, 1919-1988*, pp. 356-58, for Mark I. Wallach's checklist of works by and about Morley.

John Morley, 1838-1923

Bibliographies

John W. Bicknell reviews research on Morley in DeLaura's *Victorian Prose*, pp. 506-16.

George Pope Morris, 1802-1864

Bibliographies

For works by Morris, see *Bibliography of American Literature*, vol. 6, pp. 315-50. Morris' contributions to and reviews of Morris' works in selected periodicals are identified in Wells' *The Literary Index to American Magazines, 1815-1865*, p. 108; and *The Literary Index to American Magazines, 1850-1900*, p. 276. Morris' manuscripts are listed in Robbins' *American Literary Manuscripts*, p. 227.

William Morris, 1834-1896

Bibliographies

977. Latham, David, and Sheila Latham. **An Annotated Critical Bibliography of William Morris**. London: Harvester Wheatsheaf, 1991. 423p. LC 90-047281. ISBN 0-7108-1153-5.

The most convenient guide to works about Morris. Chronologically arranged, annotated entries for 1,408 works by and about Morris published from 1854 through 1990 in sections for Morris' books and pamphlets (editions, translations, popular editions and collections, and letters and manuscripts); bibliographies and catalogs; surveys and biographies; Morris' individual works of poetry, prose, and translations; and selected subjects, such as aesthetic philosophy, decorative arts (paintings and murals, stained glass, textiles, and others), book design (calligraphy, Kelmscott Press, and so on), and politics. Critical annotations evaluate editions and scholarship and identify standard and otherwise important works. Thorough author and subject indexing provide excellent access. Also for a bibliography of works by and about Morris, see *NCBEL*, III, pp. 563-71.

978. Aho, Gary L. **William Morris: A Reference Guide**. Boston: G. K. Hall, 1985. 428p. (A Reference Guide to Literature). LC 85-17708. ISBN 0-8161-8449-6.

Aho chronologically arranges annotated entries for about 1,900 books, parts of books, articles, dissertations, and miscellaneous publications (such as exhibition catalogs) about Morris in English and other languages. Reviews are excluded. Coverage extends from 1897 through 1982. Annotations are critical and evaluative. Important works are described in detail. A unique subject index classifies topical subheadings in broad sections for "Morris and...," "Contemporaries," "Influenced by," and "Places," among other subjects. Coverage of Morris in Ehrsam's *Bibliographies of Twelve Victorian Authors*, pp. [161]-87, cites international comments, criticism, and reviews for Morris through the early twentieth century. Reviews of Morris' works in selected periodicals are also identified in Wells' *The Literary Index to American Magazines, 1850-1900*, pp. 276-78. See the review of research by William E. Fredeman in Faverty's *The Victorian Poets*, pp. 293-307.

979. Peterson, William S. **A Bibliography of the Kelmscott Press**. Oxford: Clarendon Press, 1984. 217p. (Soho Bibliographies, no. 24). LC 83-25017. ISBN 0-1981-8199-x.

Peterson gives full bibliographic descriptions for works from the Kelmscott Press, including listings for published works, unfinished works, advertising circulars, ephemera (such as spine labels and greeting cards), and contracts and memoranda. Entries give transcriptions of title pages and colophons; collations; descriptions of paper, dimensions, typography, ornaments, contents, and bindings; publication histories; and descriptions of related materials (such as proofs, presentation copies, and the like). Indexes for association copies and for collections supplement the general index. Peterson's bibliography is more comprehensive than John J. Walsdorf's *William Morris in Private Press and Limited Editions: A Descriptive Bibliography of Books by and About William Morris, 1891-1981* (Phoenix, AZ: Oryx Press, 1983). Also available is *The Work of William Morris: An Exhibition Arranged by the William Morris Society* (London: Published for the William Morris Society by the Times Bookshop, 1962). K. L. Goodwin's *A Preliminary Handlist of Manuscripts and Documents of William Morris* (London: William Morris Society, 1983) is a detailed and comprehensive guide to international depositories containing Morris' "literary, artistic, and political manuscripts" (p. iv) and, to a lesser degree, Morris' autograph letters. The geographically arranged and well-indexed inventory describes holdings in the United States, the United Kingdom, Canada, Australia, republics of the former Soviet Union, France, Iceland, and the Netherlands.

Journals

980. **Journal of the William Morris Society**. London: William Morris Society and Kelmscott Fellowship, 1961-. 2/yr. ISSN 0084-0254.

Sponsored by the William Morris Society, issues feature articles and reviews of new publications about the life and works of Morris. Typical contributions offer interpretations of themes and characters in Morris' works and present new biographical and bibliographic information and primary documents. Particular recent attention addresses the working conditions at the Kelmscott Press. A "Special Education Issue," in 11.1 (Autumn 1994), contained eight features on Morris and literacy, the English curriculum, and educational reform, among other topics. In addition, the journal has published several annotated checklists that update the standard guide to Morris scholarship. David Latham and Sheila Latham annually contribute "William Morris: An Annotated Bibliography," a classified and indexed listing covering editions and general studies and studies in the areas of literature, decorative arts, book design, and politics. *Journal of the William Morris Society* is indexed in *MHRA*.

Patterson's *Author Newsletters and Journals*, pp. 222-23, describes other previously published journals for Morris.

981. **William Morris Society Newsletter**. Hammersmith, London: William Morris Society and Kelmscott Fellowship, 1984-. 4/yr. OCLC 11990620.

This stapled 10-page newsletter, usually rather handsomely illustrated, publishes brief letters, notes on activities of the society's membership, reviews of new books and recent journal issues that offer information about Morris, and descriptions of annual and special programs related to Morris. The physically more substantial *William Morris Society in the United States Newsletter*, published as a supplement, includes much the same fare, with an emphasis on American library collections and exhibitions related to Morris and, most recently, materials on Morris and other Victorian writers available on the WWW. Unindexed.

Wright Morris, 1910-
Bibliographies
982. Knoll, Robert E. **Conversations with Wright Morris: Critical Views and Responses**. Lincoln, NE: University of Nebraska Press, 1977. 211p. LC 76-25497. ISBN 0-8032-0904-5.

In addition to commentaries on and interviews with Morris, Knoll's volume contains Robert L. Boyce's unannotated, classified "A Wright Morris Bibliography" (pp. 169-206). Covers "all significant publications by or about Morris and his work through 1975, including dissertations and selected newspaper articles" (p. 169) in chronologically arranged sections for Morris' books and their reviews, short stories, articles and reviews by Morris, photo-text material and photographs, general and critical works about Morris, and biographical and bibliographic material. Brief bibliographic entries for Morris' books note subsequent editions and printings. Also for works by Morris, see *First Printings of American Authors*, vol. 5, pp. 195-202. Morris' manuscripts are listed in Robbins' *American Literary Manuscripts*, p. 227. See *Bibliography of American Fiction, 1919-1988*, pp. 358-61, for Michael Adams' checklist of works by and about Morris. G. B. Crump surveys works by and about Morris in Erisman and Etulain's *Fifty Western Writers*, pp. 325-35.

Toni Morrison, 1931-
Bibliographies
983. Middleton, David L. **Toni Morrison: An Annotated Bibliography**. New York: Garland, 1987. 186p. (Garland Reference Library of the Humanities, vol. 767). LC 87-15031. ISBN 0-8240-7970-1.

This guide tries to make more of works by and about Morrison than perhaps their numbers merit. The result is an ill-balanced, awkwardly organized guide. Middleton lists Morrison's four novels; summaries of her poetry, dramas, editions, essays and reviews, and interviews; and describes in great detail some 170 general works about Morrison and studies of her individual works. Other sections list Morrison's awards and honors; anthologies and recordings of her works, selected biographical and bibliographic entries in reference works, and Morrison's memberships in organizations. Index headings for such topics as "feminism," "quest," and "urban values" offer good subject access. See *Bibliography of American Fiction, 1919-1988*, pp. 361-64, for Marilyn Sanders Mobley's checklist of works by and about Morrison. See Nancy Carol Joyner's summary biography, critical assessment of major works, and selected primary and secondary bibliography for Morrison in McCaffery's *Postmodern Fiction: A Bio-Bibliographical Guide*, pp. 473-75.

Sarah Wentworth Morton, 1759-1846

Bibliographies

For works by Morton, see *Bibliography of American Literature*, vol. 6, pp. 351-54; and *First Printings of American Authors*, vol. 2, p. 263. Morton's manuscripts are listed in Robbins' *American Literary Manuscripts*, p. 229.

Howard Moss, 1922-1987

Bibliographies

For works by Moss, see *First Printings of American Authors*, vol. 2, pp. 265-66. Moss' manuscripts are listed in Robbins' *American Literary Manuscripts*, p. 229.

John Lothrop Motley, 1814-1877

Bibliographies

For works by Motley, see *Bibliography of American Literature*, vol. 6, pp. 355-67. Contributions by Motley and criticism and reviews of Motley's works in selected periodicals are identified in Wells' *The Literary Index to American Magazines, 1815-1865*, p. 109; and *The Literary Index to American Magazines, 1850-1900*, p. 278. Motley's manuscripts are listed in Robbins' *American Literary Manuscripts*, p. 229.

Willard Motley, 1912-1965

Bibliographies

For works by Motley, see *First Printings of American Authors*, vol. 2, pp. 267-68. Motley's manuscripts are listed in Robbins' *American Literary Manuscripts*, pp. 229-30. See *Bibliography of American Fiction, 1919-1988*, p. 365, for Michael Mullen's checklist of works by and about Motley.

(Ellen) Louise Chandler Moulton, 1835-1908

Bibliographies

For works by Moulton, see *Bibliography of American Literature*, vol. 6, pp. 368-86. Moulton's contributions to and reviews of Moulton's works in selected periodicals are identified in Wells' *The Literary Index to American Magazines, 1850-1900*, pp. 278-79. Moulton's manuscripts are listed in Robbins' *American Literary Manuscripts*, p. 230.

Edwin Muir, 1887-1959

Bibliographies

984.   Hoy, Peter C., and Elgin W. Mellown. **A Checklist of Writings About Edwin Muir**. Troy, NY: Whitston, 1971. 80p. LC 70-150336. ISBN 0-8787-5012-6.

Hoy and Mellown offer unannotated listings of works about Muir, including sections for bibliographies, books (with citations for reviews), parts of books, articles and reviews, unpublished dissertations, and poems about Muir. No index of any sort is provided.

985.   Mellown, Elgin W. **Bibliography of the Writings of Edwin Muir**. University, AL: University of Alabama, 1964. 139p. LC 64-8393.

This is supplemented by: .

985.1. Mellown, Elgin W. **Supplement to Bibliography of the Writings of Edwin Muir**. University, AL: University of Alabama, 1970. 28p. LC 64-8393. ISBN 0-8173-9510-5.

Mellown gives full bibliographic descriptions in separate listings for the first English and American editions of Muir's books and pamphlets, contributions to books (excluding selections reprinted in anthologies and the like), contributions to periodicals and newspapers (some 1,128 entries), and translations by Edwin and Willa Muir. Also for a bibliography of works by and about Muir, see *NCBEL*, IV, pp. 316-19.

John Muir, 1838-1914
Bibliographies

986. Kimes, William F., and Maymie B. Kimes. **John Muir: A Reading Bibliography**. Fresno, CA: Panorama West Books, 1986. 179p. LC 86-60765. ISBN 0-9143-3089-6.

Enlarging on the Kimes' previous *John Muir: A Reading Bibliography* (Palo Alto, CA: W. P. Wreden, 1977) "by 40 percent—[with] 192 new entries" (p. xv), the revision intends to show the enduring popularity of Muir as an environmental writer. Comprehensively covers Muir's writings from 1866 through 1986. Chronologically integrates bibliographic descriptions of 515 first and subsequent editions, reprintings, and other appearances of Muir's separate publications (books, government documents), edited works, and contributions to books and periodicals (articles in magazines and newspapers, letters to editors, tributes, entries in catalogs, etc.). Coverage also includes excerpts and selections in collections and anthologies. Entries quote Muir's writings extensively and cross-reference other reprintings and appearances of the same work. Appends reports on lectures and interviews (39 entries). Includes brief chronology of Muir's life and writings. Index of names, titles, and topics. Headings under Muir identify works by their formats and genres. For full bibliographic descriptions of works by Muir, see *Bibliography of American Literature*, vol. 6, pp. 387-403. Muir's manuscripts are listed in Robbins' *American Literary Manuscripts*, p. 230. Ronald H. Limbaugh and Kirsten E. Lewis' *The Guide and Index to the Microform Edition of the John Muir Papers, 1858-1957* (Alexandria, VA: Chadwyck-Healey Inc., 1986) describes Muir's papers at the University of the Pacific and more than 40 other repositories, with more than 19,000 entries as well as a detailed chronology of Muir's life and works.

Clarence E(dward) Mulford, 1883-1956
Bibliographies

See *Bibliography of American Fiction, 1866-1918*, pp. 290-91, for Gwen L. Nagel's checklist of works by and about Mulford.

Lewis Mumford, 1895-1990
Bibliography

987. Morley, Jane. **On Lewis Mumford: An Annotated Bibliography**. Philadelphia, PA: Interdisciplinary Seminar on Technology and Culture, Program for Assessing and Revitalizing the Social Sciences, School of Arts and Sciences, University of Pennsylvania, 1985. 43 leaves. OCLC 16110637.

Intends to "provide a more or less comprehensive compilation of the interdisciplinary body of secondary work which has been done on Mumford in the humanities and the social sciences (including architecture and city planning) since roughly 1950" (p. iv). Following listings for Mumford's primary works, editions, manuscripts at the University of Pennsylvania, and Newman's bibliography (entry 988), Morley alphabetically arranges descriptively annotated entries for approximately 150 "largely Anglo-American sources" about Mumford in sections for books and chapters, journal articles, and dissertations (in subsections for biographical and analytical studies, general interpretations, and applications of Mumford's thought). Appendixes reprint entries for Mumford and listings for reviews of Mumford's works from several standard reference sources. Unindexed.

988. Newman, Elmer S. **Lewis Mumford: A Bibliography, 1914-1970**. New York: Harcourt Brace Jovanovich, 1971. 167p. LC 72-160407. ISBN 0-1515-4750-5.

Newman gives brief bibliographic information, with notes on reprints, for Mumford's books and pamphlets; writings in periodicals (636 entries); book reviews; collaborative writings and contributions to editions; letters to editors; prefaces, forewords, introductions, and epilogues; miscellaneous works, such as cartoons and testimonies; British editions of books; and non-English-language editions. An appendix (pp. 125-27) lists collections of Mumford's manuscripts, including the significant collection in the New York Public Library. Mumford's manuscripts are listed in Robbins' *American Literary Manuscripts*, pp. 230-31.

Anthony Munday, 1560-1633

Bibliographies

For bibliographies of works by and about Munday, see *NCBEL*, I, pp. 1464-67; the Tannenbaums' *Elizabethan Bibliographies*, vol. 6; and Robert Carl Johnson's *Elizabethan Bibliographies Supplements*, no. 9. Ann Haaker reviews research on Munday in Logan and Smith's *The Popular School*, pp. 122-36.

Dame Iris Jean Murdoch, 1919-

Bibliography

989. Fletcher, John, and Cheryl Bove. **Iris Murdoch: A Descriptive Primary and Annotated Secondary Bibliography**. New York: Garland, 1994. 915p. (Garland Reference Library of the Humanities, vol. 506). LC 93-50597. ISBN 0-8240-8910-3.

Covers works by and about Murdoch. Part 1 gives full bibliographic descriptions of Murdoch's works in chronologically arranged sections for separately published works and critical essays, reviews, contributions to books, letters, and poems by Murdoch. Alphabetically arranged entries for first editions of books give title-page transcriptions, collations, paginations, contents, binding and jacket descriptions, with brief notes on publication history and brief bibliographic data for subsequent editions and translations. Describes 118 contributed works by Murdoch from 1933 to 1993, with summary contents and references to reprintings. Part 2 includes annotated entries for criticism of Murdoch in sections for interviews; books and journals entirely on Murdoch; books partly on Murdoch; dissertations and theses; notes, allusions, and brief items; articles; broadcasts featuring, or about, Murdoch; reviews of works by and about Murdoch (more than 3,000 entries); selected biographical sources; and bibliographies. Appendixes list Murdoch's principal works, manuscripts and correspondence (pp. 811-28), translations, and periodicals and newspapers in which Murdoch's works appeared. Indexes of names and works. Fletcher and Bove's comprehensive guide supersedes all previous bibliographies for Murdoch, including Kate Begnal's *Iris Murdoch: A Reference Guide* (Boston: G. K. Hall, 1987), which covered about 1,200 works on Murdoch published from 1953 through 1983; Thomas T. Tominaga and Wilma Schneidermeyer's *Iris Murdoch and Muriel Spark: A Bibliography* (entry 1253), which offered the most comprehensive listings of primary works of Murdoch published through 1975; and Stanton's *A Bibliography of Modern British Novelists*, pp. 569-619, 1091-92, which listed 59 works by and 448 works (mostly reviews) about Murdoch, with an addendum.

Dictionaries, Encyclopedias, and Handbooks

990. Bove, Cheryl Browning. **A Character Index and Guide to the Fiction of Iris Murdoch**. New York: Garland, 1986. 272p. (Garland Reference Library of the Humanities, vol. 607). LC 85-45151. ISBN 0-8240-8675-9.

Bove identifies and explicates characters, place names, references, and other allusions in each of Murdoch's works through 1985, with an alphabetical index to all entries.

Mary Noailles Murfree (Charles Egbert Craddock), 1850-1922

Bibliographies

For works by Murfree, see *Bibliography of American Literature*, vol. 6, pp. 404-11. Murfree's contributions to and reviews of Murfree's works in selected periodicals are identified in Wells' *The Literary Index to American Magazines, 1850-1900*, pp. 279-80. Murfree's manuscripts are listed in Robbins' *American Literary Manuscripts*, p. 231. See *Bibliography of American Fiction, 1866-1918*, pp. 291-92, for Kathryn Thompson Presley's checklist of works by and about Murfree. Research on Murfree is reviewed by Philip B. Eppard in Duke, Bryer, and Inge's *American Women Writers*, pp. 21-46; and Allison R. Ensor in Bain and Flora's *Fifty Southern Writers Before 1900*, pp. 336-47.

Arthur Murphy, 1727-1805
Bibliographies

For a bibliography of works by and about Murphy, see *NCBEL*, II, pp. 851-53.

Thomas Murphy, 1935-
Bibliographies

King's *Ten Modern Irish Playwrights*, pp. 87-94, gives brief bibliographic information for Murphy's primary works and annotated entries for criticism of Murphy, with a classified list of reviews.

John Middleton Murry, 1889-1957
Bibliographies

991.   Lilley, George P. **A Bibliography of John Middleton Murry, 1889-1957**. London: Dawsons of Pall Mall, 1974. 226p. LC 75-312451. ISBN 0-7129-0619-3.

A comprehensive listing of Murry's primary bibliography, Lilley's guide includes descriptions of books, contributions to books, contributions to periodicals (some 1,544 entries), and works of uncertain authorship. Entries give brief bibliographic information, summaries of contents, and references to subsequent printings. Also for a bibliography of works by and about Murry, see *NCBEL*, IV, pp. 1092-96.

Peter Hamilton Myers, 1812-1878
Bibliographies

For works by Myers, see *Bibliography of American Literature*, vol. 6, pp. 412-16. Myers' manuscripts are listed in Robbins' *American Literary Manuscripts*, p. 232. See *Bibliography of American Fiction Through 1865*, p. 188, for a checklist of works by and about Myers.

Mystery Plays, thirteenth-sixteenth centuries
Indexes and Concordances

992.   Kinneavy, Gerald Byron. **A Concordance to the Towneley Plays**. New York: Garland, 1990. 705p. (Contextual Concordances; Garland Reference Library of the Humanities, vol. 750). LC 89-48682. ISBN 0-8240-8392-X.

Concords the texts in George England's Early English Text Society edition of *The Towneley Plays* (London: Oxford University Press, 1897), which was based on the Towneley manuscript in the Huntington Library. Preserves England's printed signals that reflect the manuscript. Contains a word-frequency list and "Reverse Index" (words arranged by endings).

993.   Pfleiderer, Jean D., and Michael J. Preston. **A Complete Concordance to The Chester Mystery Plays**. New York: Garland, 1981. 513p. (Garland Reference Library of the Humanities, vol. 249). LC 80-8519. ISBN 0-8240-9465-4.

"Based upon the R. M. Lumiansky and David Mills edition, *The Chester Mystery Cycle*, Vol. I. (London: Oxford University Press, 1974), in the Early English Text Society series" (p. ix). Gives cumulative word-frequency data for the 25 plays, with play, speaker, cited line number, and context line for each use.

994.   Preston, Michael J., and Jean D. Pfleiderer. **A KWIC Concordance to The Plays of the Wakefield Master**. New York: Garland, 1982. 472p. (Garland Reference Library of the Humanities, vol. 248). LC 80-8518. ISBN 0-8240-9466-2.

Preston and Pfleiderer concord the texts of *Mactacio Abel, Processus noe cum filiis, Prima pastorum, Secunda pastorum, Magnus Herodes*, and *Coliphizacio* included in A. C. Cawley's *The Wakefield Pageants in the Towneley Cycle* (Manchester: Manchester University Press, 1958).

Vladimir Nabokov, 1899-1977

Bibliographies

995. Juliar, Michael. **Vladimir Nabokov: A Descriptive Bibliography**. New York: Garland, 1986. 780p. (Garland Reference Library of the Humanities, vol. 656). LC 86-7585. ISBN 0-8240-8590-6.

Juliar provides a comprehensive listing of Nabokov's works in Russian and English and translated into other languages appearing through 1985. Separate listings cover separately published editions of works in Russian, English, and other languages; scientific works (largely reprints); contributions of books (poems, essays, short stories, and the like); contributions to periodicals (some 702 entries), with separate indexes of periodical titles, languages, and kind of articles (a letter, a solution to a "chess problem," and so forth); translations of Nabokov's works, arranged by works (with indexes of languages, countries of origin, and dates); prepublication copies; editions for the blind and recorded editions; adaptations of Nabokov's works; interviews; drawings and ephemera; and piracies. Entries for Nabokov's books give Romanized title-page transcriptions (with facsimiles of title pages), physical descriptions, contents, and references for subsequent editions. Juliar also lists about 60 unannotated works about Nabokov. Appendixes include chronologies of Nabokov's career and the publication history of *Lolita* as well as a statistical summary of translations, and they list Nabokov collections, including Nabokov materials in the University of Texas' Harry Ransom Humanities Research Center, which Juliar describes as "the most complete collection I have seen anywhere" (pp. 697-98). Also for works by Nabokov published in English, see *First Printings of American Authors*, vol. 5, pp. 203-16. Nabokov's manuscripts are listed in Robbins' *American Literary Manuscripts*, p. 232. See *Bibliography of American Fiction, 1919-1988*, pp. 366-76, for Juliar's checklist of works by and about Nabokov.

996. Schuman, Samuel. **Vladimir Nabokov: A Reference Guide**. Boston: G. K. Hall, 1979. 214p. (A Reference Publication in Literature). LC 79-18355. ISBN 0-8161-8134-9.

Schuman chronologically arranges descriptive entries for about 800 English and selected non-English-language criticisms of Nabokov published from 1931 through 1977, covering books, parts of books, articles, reviews, news stories, and dissertations. Entries are descriptive. Significant works are reviewed in detail. Appends lists of reviews of film adaptations of *Lolita* and *Laughter in the Dark* and Russian émigré criticisms of Nabokov. A comprehensive index includes headings for such topics as "chess" and "butterflies"; Nabokov's works and their characters, such as Krug and Humbert Humbert; and other persons, including Poe and Shakespeare.

Dictionaries, Encyclopedias, and Handbooks

997. Alexandrov, Vladimir E. **The Garland Companion to Vladimir Nabokov**. New York: Garland, 1995. 798p. (Garland Reference Library of the Humanities, vol. 1474). LC 94-37409. ISBN 0-8153-0354-8.

"Conceived as a kind of encyclopedia" (p. [xiii]), more than 40 contributing international authorities provide detailed and thorough critical overviews (but not plot summaries) in chapters for Nabokov's major works and other writings (correspondence, Lepidoptera studies, plays, poetry, Russian short stories, and uncollected critical writings) and a wide range of topics, including "Bilingualism," "Humor," and "Politics." Entries for major works emphasize critical responses rather than composition and publication history. Other chapters focus on Nabokov and specific writers, including Chekhov, Dostoyevski, Joyce, Shakespeare (in both English and Russian), Poe, Updike, and other English and American writers. Of particular note are different chapters on Nabokov's library and manuscripts. Stephen Jan Parker's "Critical Reception" (pp. 67-75) identifies major general studies and studies of Nabokov's individual works, with some coverage of reference resources (guides, special journal issues, and bibliographies). Includes a bibliography of works by and about Nabokov (pp. 741-82) and a detailed comprehensive index.

998.   Nakhimovsky, Alexander D., and S. Paperno. **An English-Russian Dictionary of Nabokov's Lolita.** Ann Arbor, MI: Ardis, 1982. 204p. LC 82-11645. ISBN 0-8823-3443-3.

Nakhimovsky and Paperno list about 3,000 English words from *Lolita* (synonyms, phrases, idioms, etc., not usually included in English or Russian dictionaries) with their Russian translations. Entries are keyed to the Russian-language edition of *Lolita* (New York: Phaedra, 1967; reprint Ann Arbor, MI: Ardis, 1976). Also useful for the study of *Lolita* are Alfred Appel, Jr.'s *The Annotated Lolita* (1970; revised New York: Vintage, 1991) and Carl Proffer's *Keys to Lolita* (Bloomington, IN: Indiana University Press, 1968). Bobie Ann Mason's *Nabokov's Garden: A Guide to Ada* (Ann Arbor, MI: Ardis, 1974) and Gennady Barabtarlo's *Phantom of Fact: A Guide to Nabokov's Pnin* (Ann Arbor, MI: Ardis, 1989) also offer good starting points.

Journals

999.   **The Nabokovian.** Lawrence, KS: The Vladimir Nabokov Society, 1978-. 2/yr. ISSN 0894-7120.

Sponsored by the Vladimir Nabokov Society, *The Nabokovian*, formerly *Vladimir Nabokov Research Newsletter* (1978-84), features articles and reviews of new publications about the life and works of Nabokov. Typical articles offer close readings and interpretations of Nabokov's works; discuss Nabokov's literary relations with other writers; and assess Nabokov's critical reception throughout the world. "*Laughter in the Dark* and *Othello*" and "Nabokov's Cardiology" (on Nabokov's treatment of heart trouble) are representative. Other articles have focused on Nabokov's relationships with Edgar Allan Poe and James Joyce. Among recent, numerous bibliographic contributions are Peter Evans' "Nabokov in Japan: 1985-1992," 32 (Spring 1994): 76-84; Roy Flannagan and Edward A. Malone's "Nabokov in Letters: An Annotated Bibliography," 32 (Spring 1994): 20-23; and "The New York Public Library Acquires Vladimir Nabokov Archive," 27 (Fall 1991): 13-18, describing materials in the Berg Collection. In addition, the journal includes an annual bibliography of Nabokov scholarship. *The Nabokovian* is indexed in *MHRA* and *MLA*.

(Sir) V(idiadhar) S(urajprasad) Naipaul, 1932-

Bibliographies

1000.   Jarvis, Kelvin. **V. S. Naipaul: A Selective Bibliography with Annotations, 1957-1987.** Metuchen, NJ: Scarecrow Press, 1989. 205p. (Scarecrow Author Bibliographies, no. 83). LC 89-10056. ISBN 0-8108-2190-7.

Jarvis gives brief bibliographic information, with lists of subsequent editions and translations, for Naipaul's books and translations (novels, short fiction, and nonfiction); and contributed articles and short stories to books, anthologies, and periodicals; as well as selectively annotated entries for about 800 works (bibliographies, critical studies in books and articles, interviews, dissertations, and book reviews) about Naipaul. Index headings for "colonialism," "rastafarianism," and "leitmotiv," and the like provide subject access. Jarvis' work supersedes the coverage of works by and about Naipaul provided in Stanton's *A Bibliography of Modern British Novelists*, pp. 621-64, 1093, which gives classified, unannotated lists of 124 works by and 311 works about Naipaul, with an addendum.

Ogden Nash, 1902-1971

Bibliographies

1001.   Crandell, George W. **Ogden Nash: A Descriptive Bibliography**. Metuchen, NJ: Scarecrow Press, 1990. LC 90-33726. ISBN 0-8108-2332-2.

Crandell gives full bibliographic descriptions for Nash's separately published and collected works; works edited by Nash; contributions to books; contributions to periodicals (some 1,289 entries); sheet music; published letters; interviews; and other miscellaneous writings, such as dust-jacket blurbs, greeting cards, translations, and screenplays. Entries provide title-page transcriptions; collations; contents; descriptions of typography, paper, and dust jackets; publishing histories; and copy locations. Also for works by Nash, see *First Printings of American Authors*, vol. 3, pp. 241-54. Nash's manuscripts are listed in Robbins' *American Literary Manuscripts*, p. 232.

Indexes and Concordances

1002.   Axford, Lavonne. **An Index to the Poems of Ogden Nash**. Metuchen, NJ: Scarecrow Press, 1972. 139p. LC 72-7266. ISBN 0-8108-0547-2.

Intended as a finding aid to Nash's individual poems. Provides a unique symbol for each publication in which a poem appears, with combined symbols indicating multiple appearances. Axford makes no effort to cover all appearances nor to identify standard or otherwise authoritative editions.

Thomas Nashe, 1567-1601

Bibliographies

For bibliographies of works by and about Nashe, see *NCBEL*, I, pp. 1456-60; the Tannenbaums' *Elizabethan Bibliographies*, vol. 6; Robert C. Johnson's *Elizabethan Bibliographies Supplements*, no. 5; and Robert J. Fehrenbach's "Recent Studies in Nashe (1968-1979)," *English Literary Renaissance*, 11.3 (Autumn 1981): 844-50. Nashe's manuscripts are described in *Index of English Literary Manuscripts*, I, pt. 2:355-57. Fehrenbach reviews research on Nashe in Logan and Smith's *The Predecessors of Shakespeare*, pp. 107-24.

Robert (Gruntal) Nathan, 1894-1985

Bibliographies

1003.   Laurence, Dan H. **Robert Nathan: A Bibliography**. New Haven, CT: Yale University Library, 1960. 97p. OCLC 1059134.

Full bibliographic descriptions of Nathan's works chronologically arranged in sections for books and pamphlets; contributions to books; contributions to periodicals; non-English-language editions of Nathan's works; and musical contributions. Forty-four entries for first and subsequent editions and reprintings and 19 book contributions give title-page transcriptions, collations, sizes, original prices, binding and dust-jacket descriptions, dates of publication, numbers of copies, contents, and other notes on publication history. Laurence identifies 207 periodical contributions. Introduction locates Nathan's literary manuscripts in collections at Texas, Rutgers, UCLA, SUNY Buffalo, and Yale. Index of first lines of poetry and general index of names and titles. Laurence's standard guide is updated by Darrell Schweitzer's "A Robert Nathan Checklist," in *Exploring Fantasy Worlds: Essays on Fantastic Literature* (San Bernardino, CA: Borgo, 1985), pp. 94-96. Also for works by Nathan, see *First Printings of American Authors*, vol. 2, pp. 269-76. Nathan's manuscripts are listed in Robbins' *American Literary Manuscripts*, p. 232. See *Bibliography of American Fiction, 1919-1988*, pp. 377-78, for Kenneth Womack's checklist of works by and about Nathan.

John Neal (Jehu O'Cataract), 1793-1876
Bibliographies

For works by Neal, see *Bibliography of American Literature*, vol. 6, pp. 417-34. Contributions by Neal and criticism and reviews of Neal's works in selected periodicals are identified in Wells' *The Literary Index to American Magazines, 1815-1865*, p. 109; and *The Literary Index to American Magazines, 1850-1900*, p. 281. Neal's manuscripts are listed in Robbins' *American Literary Manuscripts*, p. 233. See *Bibliography of American Fiction Through 1865*, pp. 189-90, for a checklist of works by and about Neal.

Joseph Clay Neal, 1807-1847
Bibliographies

For works by Neal, see *Bibliography of American Literature*, vol. 6, pp. 435-38. Contributions by Neal and criticism and reviews of Neal's works in selected periodicals are identified in Wells' *The Literary Index to American Magazines, 1815-1865*, pp. 109-10. Neal's manuscripts are listed in Robbins' *American Literary Manuscripts*, p. 233. See *Bibliography of American Fiction Through 1865*, p. 191, for a checklist of works by and about Neal.

John G(neisenau) Neihardt, 1881-1973
Bibliographies

1004. Richards, John Thomas. **Rawhide Laureate, John G. Neihardt: A Selected, Annotated Bibliography**. Metuchen, NJ: Scarecrow Press, 1983. 169p. (Scarecrow Author Bibliographies, no. 65). LC 83-10117. ISBN 0-8108-1640-7.

Richards describes 492 works by Neihardt, with detailed summaries of plots and contents, in separate listings for Neihardt's separately published poems, short stories, plays; books; articles, essays, reviews, and literary criticisms; recordings by Neihardt; and films about his life; as well as books (nine annotated entries) and dissertations and theses about him. A comprehensive index includes headings for such specific topics as "hunting," "pornography," and "psychical research." Neihardt's manuscripts are listed in Robbins' *American Literary Manuscripts*, p. 233. Research on Neihardt is reviewed by Lucile F. Aly in Erisman and Etulain's *Fifty Western Writers*, pp. 336-46.

Howard Nemerov, 1920-
Bibliographies

For works by Nemerov, see *First Printings of American Authors*, vol. 2, pp. 277-80. Nemerov's manuscripts are listed in Robbins' *American Literary Manuscripts*, p. 234. Wyllie's *Elizabeth Bishop and Howard Nemerov* (entry 112) describes works about Nemerov through 1981. Deborah S. Murphy and Gloria Young review research on Nemerov in *Contemporary Authors: Bibliographical Series: Volume 2: American Poets*, pp. 203-32.

Jay Neugeboren, 1938-
Bibliographies

For works by Neugeboren, see *First Printings of American Authors*, vol. 5, pp. 217-18.

Margaret (Cavendish), Duchess of Newcastle, 1623-1723
Bibliographies

For a bibliography of works by and about Cavendish, see *NCBEL*, I, pp. 1303, 1736, 2252.

Charles King Newcomb, 1820-1894
Bibliographies

Newcomb's manuscripts are listed in Robbins' *American Literary Manuscripts*, p. 234. Joel Myerson reviews research on Newcomb in Myerson's *The Transcendentalists*, pp. 214-15.

Robert Henry Newell (Orpheus C. Kerr), 1836-1901
Bibliographies

For works by Newell, see *Bibliography of American Literature*, vol. 6, pp. 439-46. Newell's manuscripts are listed in Robbins' *American Literary Manuscripts*, p. 234. See *Bibliography of American Fiction Through 1865*, pp. 192-93, for a checklist of works by and about Newell.

Edward Newhouse, 1911-
Bibliographies

For works by Newhouse, see *First Printings of American Authors*, vol. 2, pp. 281-82.

Frances Newman, 1888-1928
Bibliographies

For works by Newman, see *First Printings of American Authors*, vol. 1, p. 273. Newman's manuscripts are listed in Robbins' *American Literary Manuscripts*, p. 234.

John Henry Newman, 1801-1890
Bibliographies

1005. Blehl, Vincent Ferrer. **John Henry Newman: A Bibliographical Catalogue of His Writings**. Charlottesville, VA: Published for the Bibliographical Society of the University of Virginia by the University Press of Virginia, 1978. 148p. LC 77-12141. ISBN 0-8139-0738-1.

Blehl gives brief bibliographic information and notes on the contents for Newman's primary materials, including separate listings for books, broadsides, collections, pamphlets, and postscripts; publications in periodicals and newspapers; contributions to books, including edited works and translations; and posthumous publications. Additionally, James David Earnest and Gerard Tracey's *John Henry Newman: An Annotated Bibliography of His Tracts and Pamphlet Collection* (New York: Garland, 1984) describes about 2,000 tracts and pamphlets in Newman's library of 17,500 volumes. Also available is David E. Horn's *The Newman Collection: Catalogue of the J. Harry Lynch Memorial Cardinal Newman Collection* (Boston: Newman Preparatory School, 1965). For a bibliography of works by and about Newman, see *NCBEL*, III, pp. 1311-40.

1006. Griffin, John R. **Newman: A Bibliography of Secondary Studies**. Front Royal, VA: Christendom Publications, 1980. 145p. LC 80-68760. ISBN 0-9318-8804-2.

Griffin alphabetically lists in topical sections about 2,000 unannotated entries for books, parts of books, articles, reviews, dissertations, and other materials in all languages about Newman and his works. Chapters cover such topics as Newman and the Oxford Movement, Newman and history, "Newman's Poetry," "Newman and the Laity," and press coverage of Newman, as well as studies of individual works. No index whatsoever is provided. Research on Newman is reviewed by Martin J. Svaglic and Charles Stephen Dessain in DeLaura's *Victorian Prose*, pp. 113-84.

Indexes and Concordances

    1006a. Artz, Johannes. **Newman-Lexikon: Zugleich Registerband zu den Ausgewahlten Werken von John Henry Kardinal Newman.** Mainz: Matthias-Grunewald-Verlag, 1975. 1,274 pages (columns). (Ausgewahlten Werke von John Henry Newman, Band 9). LC 77-460005. ISBN 3-7867-0171-7.

    Index of proper names of persons, places, and things (King David, Shakespeare, Mary Shelley, Theological Library) and topics (Islam, "Katechismus," "Konversion") with very brief identifications and chapter and page cross-references to English and German editions of Newman's published works as well as selected manuscripts. Appends chronology of Newman's life and works. Topical index. Less comprehensive than Artz's index, Joseph Rickaby's *An Index to the Works of John Henry Cardinal Newman* (London: Longman's, 1914; reprint Westminster, MD: Christian Classics, 1977) is also an A-to-Z listing of identifications of names and ideas, with specific citations to Newman's published works.

Journals

    1007. **Internationale Cardinal Newman Studien.** Sigmaringendorf: Glock, 1988- . Irregular. ISSN 0934-7259.

    Unseen. Formerly *Newman Studien* (1948-80). Wortman's *A Guide to Serial Bibliographies for Modern Literatures,* p. 270, cites a "Newman-Bibliographie" listing new editions, translations, and criticisms.

    See Patterson's *Author Newsletters and Journals,* p. 226, for previously published journals for Newman.

Peter Richard Nichols, 1927-

Bibliographies

    King's *Twenty Modern British Playwrights,* pp. 69-75, lists works by Nichols and describes works about him.

Meredith Nicholson, 1866-1947

Bibliographies

    1008. Russo, Dorothy R., and Thelma Lois Sullivan. **Bibliographical Studies of Seven Authors of Crawfordsville, Indiana: Lew and Susan Wallace, Maurice and Will Thompson, Mary Hannah and Caroline Virginia Krout, and Meredith Nicholson.** Indianapolis, IN: Indiana Historical Society, 1952. 486p. LC 52-14852.

    Full bibliographic descriptions of first editions of separate publications, contributions to books, contributions to periodicals, and ephemera chronologically arranged in separate sections for each author. Entries for books give title-page transcriptions, collations, descriptions of illustrations and bindings, contents, and notes on publishing histories. Nicholson's section (pp. [69]-172) describes first editions published from 1890 to 1923 and first contributed book appearances to 1945. The section for Maurice Thompson (pp. [173]-283) covers books published from 1875 to 1928. Lew Wallace's section (pp. [305]-416) covers first editions from 1873 to 1906. Contributions to periodicals in all sections are arranged by periodical title. A general index must be used to sort out the entries. Also see *Bibliography of American Fiction, 1866-1918,* pp. 293-94, for Susan B. Egenolf's checklist of works by and about Nicholson. Nicholson's manuscripts are listed in Robbins' *American Literary Manuscripts,* pp. 234-35.

J(ohn) F(rederick) Nims, 1913-

Bibliographies

    For works by Nims, see *First Printings of American Authors,* vol. 4, pp. 281-82. Nims' manuscripts are listed in Robbins' *American Literary Manuscripts,* p. 235.

Anais Nin, 1903-1977
Bibliography

1009. Cutting, Rose Marie. **Anais Nin: A Reference Guide**. Boston: G. K. Hall, 1978. 218p. (A Reference Publication in Literature). LC 78-13505. ISBN 0-8161-8001-6.

Cutting chronologically arranges about 800 studies of Nin published from 1937 through 1977, covering books, parts of books, articles, reviews of Nin's works and of works about Nin (including the brief ones published in *Choice*), and dissertations. Annotations are descriptive but typically quite extensive. Broad topical headings as well as other subheadings under Nin's name give good subject access. See *Bibliography of American Fiction, 1919-1988*, pp. 379-81, for Benjamin Franklin V's checklist of works by and about Nin. Research on Nin is reviewed by Barbara J. Griffin in Duke, Bryer, and Inge's *American Women Writers*, pp. 135-66.

1010. Franklin, Benjamin, V. **Anais Nin: A Bibliography**. Kent, OH: Kent State University Press, 1973. 115p. (The Serif Series: Bibliographies and Checklists, no. 29). LC 72-619701. ISBN 0-87338-137-8.

Franklin gives full bibliographic descriptions for Nin's books and pamphlets; contributions to books; contributions to periodicals; recordings of Nin's works; and edited periodicals and letters to Nin. Entries include title-page transcriptions, physical descriptions, contents, and brief notes on publishing histories. Also for works by Nin, see *First Printings of American Authors*, vol. 1, pp. 275-79. Nin's manuscripts are listed in Robbins' *American Literary Manuscripts*, p. 235.

Journals

1011. **Anais: An International Journal**. Los Angeles, CA: Anais Nin Foundation, 1983-. Annual. ISSN 8755-3910.

Sponsored by the Anais Nin Foundation, *Anais* publishes critical and biographical articles and reviews of new publications about the life and works of Nin and members of her circle, especially Henry Miller. Typical critical features focus on interpretations of recurrent themes in her works, such as marriage, feminism, gender, and sexuality. Other articles have discussed Nin and narrative, Japanese No drama, Marcel Proust, George Sand, and D. H. Lawrence. *Anais* also includes selections of poetry and short fiction. Since 1987 a bibliographic feature, "Readings," lists new publications related to Nin and her associates. The "Fifteenth Anniversary Issue," 15 (1997), contains an index to vols. 11-15 (1993-97). *Anais* is indexed in *AHI* and *MLA*.

Wortman's *A Guide to Serial Bibliographies for Modern Literatures*, pp. 270-71, describes the serial bibliography for Nin previously published in *Under the Sign of Pisces* (1970-81). Patterson's *Author Newsletters and Journals*, pp. 228-29, describes other previously published journals for Nin.

Mordecai Manuel Noah, 1785-1851
Bibliographies

For works by Noah, see *Bibliography of American Literature*, vol. 6, pp. 447-54. Contributions by Noah and criticism and reviews of Noah's works in selected periodicals are identified in Wells' *The Literary Index to American Magazines, 1815-1865*, p. 111. Noah's manuscripts are listed in Robbins' *American Literary Manuscripts*, p. 235.

Charles Bernard Nordhoff, 1887-1947
Bibliographies

For works by Nordhoff, see *First Printings of American Authors*, vol. 3, pp. 255-59. Nordhoff's contributions to and reviews of Nordhoff's works in selected periodicals are identified in Wells' *The Literary Index to American Magazines, 1850-1900*, pp. 283-84.

Nordhoff's manuscripts are listed in Robbins' *American Literary Manuscripts*, p. 236.

Marsha Norman, 1947-
Bibliographies

Linda L. Hubert reviews research on Norman in *Contemporary Authors: Bibliographical Series: Volume 3: American Dramatists*, pp. 271-87.

(Benjamin) Frank(lin) Norris, 1870-1902
Bibliographies

1012.   Crisler, Jesse S., and Joseph R. McElrath, Jr. **Frank Norris: A Reference Guide**. Boston: G. K. Hall, 1974. 131p. (Reference Guides in Literature, no. 3). LC 74-14956. ISBN 0-8161-1097-2.

Crisler and McElrath chronologically arrange about 700 entries for works about Norris in separate listings for critical studies in English (annotated), dissertations, and non-English-language publications. Coverage extends from 1891 through 1973. Annotations are descriptive. Subject access is limited to a few broad topics ("biography" and "bibliography") and primary titles.

1013.   McElrath, Joseph R., Jr. **Frank Norris: A Descriptive Bibliography**. Pittsburgh, PA: University of Pittsburgh Press, 1992. 355p. (Pittsburgh Series in Bibliography). LC 92-7198. ISBN 0-8229-3712-3.

The standard listing of Norris' works. Chronologically arranges full bibliographic descriptions in sections for separate publications (books and pamphlets and collected editions), first-appearance contributions to books, first-appearance contributions to periodicals, "Keepsakes," and works misattributed to Norris. Covers 1899 through 1990. Entries for 18 first editions of separate works give facsimiles of title and copyright pages; collation; pagination; data on variants; typography, paper, binding, and dust-jacket descriptions; notes on composition and publication history, with citations for reviews and early notices; and copy locations, as well as brief, descriptive information on selected subsequent editions and printings. Lists brief bibliographic information for 298 contributions to magazines and newspapers, with citations for reprintings, and for 519 misattributions and dubious attributions. Appendixes reprint revisions of *McTeague* and *A Man's Woman*; and list selected works about Norris. Thorough index of names and titles. See *Bibliography of American Fiction, 1866-1918*, pp. 294-97, for McElrath's checklist of works by and about Norris. McElrath's guide supersedes Kenneth A. Lohf and Eugene P. Sheehy's *Frank Norris: A Bibliography* (Los Gatos, CA: Talisman Press, 1959), which gives full bibliographic descriptions for Norris' collected works; individual works; dramatizations; film adaptations; and contributions to periodicals, including serializations, poetry, short stories, articles, sketches, and translations; as well as unannotated entries for about 300 criticisms and reviews (arranged by works) about Norris. Lohf and Sheehy's guide remains useful for brief descriptions of the Frank Norris Collection in the Bancroft Library of the University of California at Berkeley, which contains letters, fragments of the manuscript of *McTeague*, notes for other works, and other miscellaneous manuscripts (pp. xiv-xv). Blanck's *Bibliography of American Literature*, vol. 6, 455-67, provides additional coverage of Norris' works. Norris' manuscripts are listed in Robbins' *American Literary Manuscripts*, p. 236. Likewise, McElrath's *Frank Norris and the Wave: A Bibliography* (New York: Garland, 1988) gives supplemental coverage of Norris' contributions to *The Wave*, a San Francisco weekly magazine, from 1891 through 1898. Research on Norris is reviewed by William B. Dillingham in Harbert and Rees' *Fifteen American Authors Before 1900*, pp. 402-38; and Warren French in Erisman and Etulain's *Fifty Western Writers*, pp. 347-57.

Journals

1014.   **Frank Norris Studies**. Tallahassee, FL: Frank Norris Society, 1986-. 2/yr. OCLC 15325184.

"Supernatural Naturalism: Norris's Spiritualism in *The Octopus*" and "Frank Norris's *The Pit*: 'A Romance of Chicago' and 'A Story of Chicago' " are representative of the articles, notes, and reviews of new works about the life and works of Norris featured in this journal, sponsored by the Frank Norris Society. Most contributions offer close, interpretive readings of Norris' works or new biographical information. Other features have assessed Norris' critical reception and discussed musical and media adaptations of Norris' works. Occasional bibliographic contributions include Ronnie D. Carter's "Polish Academic Writing on Frank Norris," 18 (Autumn 1994): 4-5, a brief review of Polish dissertations on Norris; Charles L. Crow's "Recent Trends in McTeague Scholarship," 13 (Spring 1992): 1-5; and Jesse S. Crisler's "Norris's 'Library,' " 5 (Spring 1988): 1-11. In addition, the journal includes "Current Publications Update," a checklist of Norris scholarship compiled by Thomas K. Dean, which updates the coverage of Crisler and McElrath's standard guide (entry 1012). A special issue, "Perverted Tales," in 15 (Spring 1993), contains papers from the 1992 Norris Society Conference in San Diego, California. *Frank Norris Studies* is indexed in *MLA*.

Andre Norton, 1912-

Bibliographies

1015.   Schlobin, Roger C., and Irene R. Harrison. **Andre Norton: A Primary and Secondary Bibliography**. Framingham, MA: NESFA, 1994. 92p. LC 94-69292. ISBN 0-915368-64-1.

A much enlarged revision of Schlobin's *Andre Norton: A Primary and Secondary Bibliography* (Boston: G. K. Hall, 1980), with a preface by Norton, Schlobin, and Harrison, chronologically lists works by and about Norton in sections for Norton's fiction; miscellaneous media (four poems and a paper); nonfiction (126 reviews, articles, introductions, etc.); and descriptively annotated entries for some 131 criticisms, biographical entries, and selected reviews of Norton's works. Coverage extends from 1934 to 1994. Entries for primary works give brief bibliographic information, with citations for reprintings and subsequent appearances. In addition to a discussion of Norton's "phantom" names and pseudonyms, appendixes classify Norton's works by genres and series, sequels, and related works. Separate indexes of primary and secondary works. Schlobin's 1980 edition identified only 57 critical and biographical works about Norton and reviews of her works. Also see *Bibliography of American Fiction, 1919-1988*, pp. 382-84, for Schlobin's checklist of works by and about Norton.

Bill (Edgar Wilson) Nye, 1850-1896

Bibliographies

For works by Nye, see *Bibliography of American Literature*, vol. 6, pp. 468-82. Nye's contributions to and reviews of Nye's works in selected periodicals are identified in Wells' *The Literary Index to American Magazines, 1850-1900*, p. 288. Nye's manuscripts are listed in Robbins' *American Literary Manuscripts*, p. 237. See *Bibliography of American Fiction, 1866-1918*, pp. 298-300, for David B. Kesterson's checklist of works by and about Nye.

Joyce Carol Oates, 1938-

Bibliographies

1016.   Lercangee, Francine. **Joyce Carol Oates: An Annotated Bibliography**. New York: Garland, 1986. 272p. (Garland Reference Library of the Humanities, vol. 509). LC 84-48022. ISBN 0-8240-8908-1.

This covers works by and about Oates. In the first part Lercangee provides 1,084 brief bibliographic descriptions (titles, publishers, dates, and pagination) for Oates' primary works published through 1986, including sections for novels, short fiction, poems, plays, anthologies, essays and nonfiction, and interviews. The second part includes annotated entries for nearly 2,000 secondary works arranged in separate listings for bibliographies, books, articles and parts of books, reviews and essays, and dissertations. Separate indexes for names, primary and secondary titles, and subjects (of criticism written by Oates only) conclude the volume. For works by Oates, see *First Printings of American Authors*, vol. 5, pp. 219-30. Oates' manuscripts are listed in Robbins' *American Literary Manuscripts*, p. 237. See *Bibliography of American Fiction, 1919-1988*, pp. 385-88, for Judith S. Baughman's checklist of works by and about Oates.

Edna O'Brien, 1932-
Bibliographies

King's *Ten Modern Irish Playwrights*, pp. 95-105, gives brief bibliographic information for O'Brien's primary works and annotated entries for criticism of O'Brien, with a classified list of reviews.

Fitz-James O'Brien, c. 1828-1862
Bibliographies

For works by O'Brien, see *Bibliography of American Literature*, vol. 6, pp. 483-91. Contributions by O'Brien and criticism and reviews of O'Brien's works in selected periodicals are identified in Wells' *The Literary Index to American Magazines, 1815-1865*, p. 113; and *The Literary Index to American Magazines, 1850-1900*, p. 288. O'Brien's manuscripts are listed in Robbins' *American Literary Manuscripts*, p. 238. See *Bibliography of American Fiction Through 1865*, pp. 193-94, for a checklist of works by and about O'Brien.

Sean O'Casey (John Casey), 1880-1964
Bibliographies

1017.   Ayling, Ronald, and Michael J. Durkan. **Sean O'Casey: A Bibliography**. Seattle, WA: University of Washington Press, 1979. 411p. LC 77-83181. ISBN 0-295-95566-x.

Ayling and Durkan chronologically arrange O'Casey's writings in separate listings for books and pamphlets; contributions to books; contributions to periodicals; translations of O'Casey's works; manuscripts, typescripts, proofs, and other unpublished materials; first stage productions and major revivals; adaptations and recordings; radio and television broadcasts; and motion pictures. Entries give detailed descriptions of first and later printings, with significant publication data. In addition, Ayling and Durkan describe manuscripts in the Berg Collection of the New York Public Library, which includes the Sean O'Casey and Fergus O'Connor Papers, the largest collection of O'Casey materials, as well as manuscripts in other collections (pp. 299-340). This is the definitive descriptive guide for O'Casey's works. Schrank's *Sean O'Casey* (entry 1019) updates Ayling and Durkan's coverage of English-language editions of O'Casey's works.

1018.   Mikhail, E. H. **Sean O'Casey and His Critics: An Annotated Bibliography, 1916-1982**. Metuchen, NJ: Scarecrow Press, 1985. 348p. (Scarecrow Author Bibliographies, no. 67). LC 84-14166. ISBN 0-8108-1747-0.

A thorough revision of his *Sean O'Casey: A Bibliography of Criticism* (Seattle, WA: University of Washington Press, 1972), Mikhail's bibliography is chiefly valuable for coverage of criticism through 1982, although it also covers a full range of primary materials, such as collected and separate editions, manuscripts (p. 305), and recordings. The bulk of the 4,379 briefly annotated entries describes criticism in separate listings for reference works, books, parts of books, articles, reviews of play productions, reviews of staged autobiographies, film reviews, and dissertations. Schrank's *Sean O'Casey* (entry 1019) selectively updates Mikhail's guide.

1019.   Schrank, Bernice. **Sean O'Casey: A Research and Production Sourcebook**. Westport, CT: Greenwood Press, 1996. 298p. (Modern Dramatists Research and Production Sourcebooks, no. 11). LC 96-5254. ISBN 0-313-27844-X

More valuable for production data and plot summaries than for bibliography, Schrank's guide selectively updates but supersedes neither Ayling and Durkan's *Sean O'Casey: A Bibliography* (entry 1017) for works by O'Casey nor Mikhail's *Sean O'Casey and His Critics* (entry 1018) for works about him. A chronology and brief biography of O'Casey precede alphabetically arranged plot summaries and "critical overviews" (with cross-references to full entries for productions and reviews and criticism) for O'Casey's 23 plays. "Primary Bibliography" supplies brief bibliographic information for first and subsequent individual and collected editions of O'Casey's published writings in separate listings for nondramatic and dramatic works. Schrank does not cover translations. A third listing gives brief details for four special collections of unpublished materials. "Secondary Bibliography" chronologically arranges critically annotated entries for 1,286 works about O'Casey published from 1923 to 1993 (in subsections for reviews; articles, chapters, and sections; and book-length studies). Coverage includes production reviews in newspapers and popular magazines, but excludes dissertations and non-English-language criticism. A final section contains credits and other data for first U.S. productions and selected productions in Ireland and England, with cross-references to reviews. Indexes of critics and scholars and general index of names, titles, theaters, and "Easter Rising" of 1916. Also for a bibliography of works by and about O'Casey, see *NCBEL*, IV, pp. 879-85. Research on O'Casey is reviewed by David Krause in Finneran's *Anglo-Irish Literature*, pp. 470-517; and by Schrank in Schrank and Demastes' *Irish Playwrights, 1880-1995: A Research and Production Sourcebook*, pp. 253-69.

Dictionaries, Encyclopedias, and Handbooks

1020.   O'Riordan, John. **A Guide to O'Casey's Plays: From the Plough to the Stars**. London: Macmillan, 1984. 419p. (Macmillan Studies in Anglo-Irish Literature). LC 84-21211. ISBN 0-333-36428-7.

Covering all of O'Casey's 23 plays, O'Riordan accounts the facts of composition and stage production; summarizes plots, identifies characters, and assesses major themes and elements; and notes later productions. Interest is more in describing backgrounds than evaluating critical reception.

Indexes and Concordances

1021.   Lowery, Robert G. **Sean O'Casey's Autobiographies: An Annotated Index**. Westport, CT: Greenwood Press, 1983. 487p. LC 83-826. ISBN 0-313-23765-4.

Lowery indexes two editions of O'Casey's autobiographies, *Mirror in My House* (New York: Macmillan, 1956) and *Autobiographies* (London: Pan, 1971-73).

Journals

1022.   **O'Casey Annual**. Atlantic Highlands, NJ: Humanities Press, 1982-85. Annual. ISSN 0278-5641.

This featured scholarly articles on O'Casey's life and themes and images in his works as well as reviews of new publications. Contributions compared O'Casey to Joyce and Brecht and tracked his reception in China. Robert G. Lowery's "Music in the Autobiographies: An Index," 2 (1983): 27-69, identified O'Casey's allusions to music. In addition, volumes included "Sean O'Casey: An Annual Bibliography," compiled by E. H. Mikhail (and others), covering secondary works. *O'Casey Annual* was indexed in *MLA*.

Wortman's *A Guide to Serial Bibliographies for Modern Literatures*, p. 271, describes serial bibliographies previously featured in *O'Casey Annual* (1982-85) and *Sean O'Casey Review* (1974-82). Patterson's *Author Newsletters and Journals*, pp. 29-30, describes other previously published journals for O'Casey.

Edwin O'Connor, 1918-1968
Bibliographies

For works by O'Connor, see *First Printings of American Authors*, vol. 5, pp. 231-32. O'Connor's manuscripts are listed in Robbins' *American Literary Manuscripts*, p. 238. See *Bibliography of American Fiction, 1919-1988*, p. 389, for Hugh Rank's checklist of works by and about O'Connor.

Flannery O'Connor, 1925-1964
Bibliographies

1023.   Farmer, David. **Flannery O'Connor: A Descriptive Bibliography**. New York: Garland, 1981. 132p. (Garland Reference Library of the Humanities, vol. 221). LC 80-8480. ISBN 0-8240-9493-x.

Farmer offers a detailed descriptive bibliography of O'Connor's primary works through *Habit of Being* (1981), including entries for first and later printings of books, first-appearance contributions to books and periodicals, reviews, translations, letters, film and television adaptations, and early published works of art. A comprehensive index references names, titles, translated languages, publishers, and the like. Also for published works by O'Connor, see *First Printings of American Authors*. vol. 1, pp. 281-83. O'Connor's manuscripts are listed in Robbins' *American Literary Manuscripts*, p. 238. Stephen G. Driggers, Robert J. Dunn, and Sarah Gordon's *The Manuscripts of Flannery O'Connor at Georgia College* (Athens, GA: University of Georgia Press, 1989) is a chronologically arranged catalog and finding aid (with detailed descriptions) for the Flannery O'Connor Collection, which includes manuscripts, drafts, and notes for *Wise Blood, A Good Man Is Hard to Find, The Violent Bear It Away, Everything That Rises Must Converge, Why Do the Heathen Rage?* and other works. O'Connor's library, also housed in the collection, is described in Arthur F. Kinney's *Flannery O'Connor's Library: Resources of Being* (Athens, GA: University of Georgia Press, 1985).

1024.   Golden, Robert E., and Mary C. Sullivan. **Flannery O'Connor and Caroline Gordon: A Reference Guide**. Boston: G. K. Hall, 1977. 342p. (Reference Guides in Literature). LC 76-44334. ISBN 0-8161-7845-3.

Separate bibliographies chronologically arrange and index annotated entries for critical books, articles, and reviews (with appendixes for dissertations) about O'Connor (covering 1952 through 1976) and about Gordon (covering 1931 through 1975). Annotations are descriptive. Subject indexing is limited to headings for "bibliographies" and "biographies." Also see *Bibliography of American Fiction, 1919-1988*, pp. 390-93, for David H. Payne's checklist of works by and about O'Connor. Research on O'Connor is reviewed by Martha E. Cook in Duke, Bryer, and Inge's *American Women Writers*, pp. 269-96; and Martha Stephens in Flora and Bain's *Fifty Southern Writers After 1900*, pp. 334-44.

Dictionaries, Encyclopedias, and Handbooks

1025.   Grimshaw, James A., Jr. **The Flannery O'Connor Companion**. Westport, CT: Greenwood Press, 1981. 133p. LC 80-26828. ISBN 0-313-21086-1.

Grimshaw briefly introduces significant events and facts of O'Connor's life and works; summarizes nonfiction and fiction works; and identifies and describes fictional characters (the likes of Red Sammy and the Misfit). An appendix identifies Catholic and Christian figures whose works or ideas O'Connor knew. A selective, classified secondary bibliography completes the guide.

Journals
1026. **The Flannery O'Connor Bulletin**. Milledgeville, GA: Georgia College, 1972- . Annual. ISSN 0091-4924.

Annual volumes usually feature eight to 12 articles that offer critical readings and interpretations of O'Connor's works, discuss her literary relations with other writers, or account biographical reminiscences and recollections. Studies of images and themes in O'Connor's works (particularly spirituality), uses of military terms and knowledge of music, and the demonstration of O'Connor's works as reflective of Southern culture are typical. The works of Thomas Merton, Joyce Carol Oates, Yeats, Poe, Alice Walker, Walker Percy, Dickens, and Dostoyevsky have also been discussed in relation to O'Connor's writings. Past annual volumes have featured significant bibliographical contributions. Volumes also include selections of book reviews. *The Flannery O'Connor Bulletin* is indexed in *AES*, *MHRA*, and *MLA*.

Clifford Odets, 1906-1963
Bibliographies
1027. Cooperman, Robert. **Clifford Odets: An Annotated Bibliography, 1935-1989**. Westport, CT: Meckler, 1990. 147p. LC 88-27299. ISBN 0-88736-326-1.

Cooperman provides brief descriptive entries for works by and about Odets in an awkward organizational scheme that makes it difficult to distinguish primary and secondary works. The volume includes a chronology of Odets' career; a bibliographic essay on bibliographies; and separate listings for manuscripts of published plays, unpublished scripts, diaries, and journals in the New York Public Library's Lincoln Center collection (pp. 3-10); texts; criticism; primary works, play productions, screenplays, and teleplays; annotated listings for articles by Odets; Odets' journals and letters; general critical studies and studies of individual works; dissertations; studies of Odets and Group Theatre; and studies of Odets and the House Un-American Activities Committee. Limited indexing attempts to pull all this together. Odets' manuscripts are also listed in Robbins' *American Literary Manuscripts*, p. 239.

1028. Demastes, William W. **Clifford Odets: A Research and Production Sourcebook**. Westport, CT: Greenwood, 1991. 209p. (Modern Dramatists Research and Production Sourcebooks, no. 1). LC 91-3757. ISBN 0-313-26294-2.

"More than an annotated bibliography" (p. vii), identifying characters, summarizing plots, and providing critical overviews of Odets' 21 stage plays and three radio plays produced from 1926 to 1964, with separate listings of credits for major New York and regional productions. Primary bibliography of Odets' nondramatic, nonfiction works; dramatic publications; and unpublished collected materials. Chronologically arranged "Annotated Secondary Bibliography" describes 608 reviews, articles, parts of books, and book-length studies on Odets from 1935 to 1990. Evaluative descriptions and the introductory "Life and Career" indicate major critical studies. Includes brief chronology. Useful general index of names, titles, and selected topics. Demastes also identifies works by and about Odets in Demastes' *American Playwrights, 1880-1945*, pp. 310-22.

Liam O'Flaherty, 1896-1984
Bibliographies
1029. Doyle, Paul A. **Liam O'Flaherty: An Annotated Bibliography**. Troy, NY: Whitston, 1972. 68p. LC 71-161085. ISBN 0-87875-017-7.

Although superseded by Jefferson's descriptive guide (entry 1030) to O'Flaherty's works, Doyle's work remains useful for coverage of works about O'Flaherty to about 1970. Doyle gives brief bibliographic information (with selective notes on contents) in listings for O'Flaherty's books, a serialized novel, poems, a translation of a short story into Gaelic, essays and articles, book reviews, letters to editors, contributed short stories in periodicals, and a play published in a periodical. In addition, Doyle identifies two dissertations and about 75 critical works about O'Flaherty. Also for a bibliography of works by and about O'Flaherty, see *NCBEL*, IV, pp. 686-87.

1030. Jefferson, George. **Liam O'Flaherty: A Descriptive Bibliography of His Works**. Dublin: Wolfhound Press, 1993. 176p. ISBN 0-86327-188-X.

Chronologically arranged, full bibliographic descriptions of O'Flaherty's works in sections for novels, short stories (individual appearances, collections, and children's and students' editions), booklets, biography and autobiography, introductions, articles, reviews, letters to the press, writings in Gaelic, theater and film adaptations, radio and television adaptations and appearances by O'Flaherty and a sound recording, manuscripts of published and unpublished works, manuscripts of letters (arranged by repository), and translations. Entries for first and subsequent U.K., U.S., and Irish editions of the novels published from 1923 to 1992 and other separate publications give title-page transcriptions, contents and collations, binding descriptions, and notes on publication history. Entries for other books and periodical appearances and media adaptations emphasize contents and credits. Index of names and titles.

Frank O'Hara, 1926-1966
Bibliographies

1031. Smith, Alexander, Jr. **Frank O'Hara: A Comprehensive Bibliography**. New York: Garland, 1979. 323p. (Garland Reference Library of the Humanities, vol. 107). LC 77-83403. ISBN 0-8240-9833-1.

Smith describes O'Hara's primary materials in detail, providing separate listings for his books, pamphlets, and broadsides; contributions to books and edited and translated works; contributions to periodicals and newspapers, including his translations; miscellaneous works (such as playscripts, recordings, artworks, musical settings, and the like); and translations of O'Hara's works. Entries give full bibliographic descriptions, including title-page transcriptions (with facsimiles of title pages); physical descriptions; contents; and notes on publication, composition, and manuscripts. In addition, gives annotated entries for 232 writings about O'Hara published from 1951 through 1985. Secondary coverage includes memoirs, poetry and fictional works related to O'Hara, reviews, and dissertations. Entries for works of art and music about or relating to O'Hara are listed in a separate section. Appendixes describe two unpublished collections of O'Hara's poetry, listing their contents; recount O'Hara's participation in art exhibitions; and briefly list the contents of collections of O'Hara's manuscripts in 23 institutions, including the major collection at the University of Connecticut at Storrs. The index offers limited topical access to both primary and secondary materials under O'Hara's name. Also for works by O'Hara, see *First Printings of American Authors*, vol. 4, pp. 283-88. O'Hara's manuscripts are listed in Robbins' *American Literary Manuscripts*, p. 239.

John (Henry) O'Hara, 1905-1970
Bibliographies

1032. Bruccoli, Matthew J. **John O'Hara: A Descriptive Bibliography**. Pittsburgh, PA: University of Pittsburgh Press, 1978. 324p. (Pittsburgh Series in Bibliography). LC 77-15737. ISBN 0-8229-3349-7.

Superseding Bruccoli's *John O'Hara: A Checklist* (New York: Random House, 1972), this detailed, descriptive bibliography chronologically arranges entries for O'Hara's writings in separate listings covering all editions and variants of English-language books and pamphlets, first appearances of short fiction in books and periodicals, appearances of nonfiction works (letters, articles, reviews, and the like) in magazines and newspapers, newspaper and magazine columns, and dust-jacket blurbs. Entries locate copies. Appendixes identify O'Hara's jobs as a journalist and movie writer as well as list selected works about O'Hara. Also for works by O'Hara, see *First Printings of American Authors*, vol. 1, pp. 285-89. O'Hara's manuscripts are listed in Robbins' *American Literary Manuscripts*, p. 239. See *Bibliography of American Fiction, 1919-1988*, pp. 394-95, for Matthew J. Bruccoli's checklist of works by and about O'Hara.

Journals

See Patterson's *Author Newsletters and Journals*, pp. 231-32, for previously published journals for O'Hara.

Chad Oliver, 1928-

Bibliographies

1033.   Hall, Halbert W. **Work of Chad Oliver: An Annotated Bibliography and Guide**. San Bernardino, CA: Borgo Press, 1989. 88p. (Bibliographies of Modern Authors, no. 12). LC 86-2288. ISBN 0-89370-391-5.

Covering works by and about Oliver, Hall gives brief bibliographic information in separate listings for Oliver's books (with notes on editions and translations, plot summaries, publishing histories, and references to secondary studies and reviews), short-fiction contributions to collections and periodicals, nonfiction, letters, media appearances, and an unpublished work (Oliver's master's thesis). Hall also identifies about 80 works about Oliver (including passing references in encyclopedias), news releases mentioning Oliver, and other biographical materials related to him.

Charles Olson, 1910-1970

Bibliographies

1034.   Butterick, George F., and Albert Glover. **A Bibliography of Works by Charles Olson**. New York: Phoenix Book Shop, 1967. 90p. LC 67-20817.

Full bibliographic details for Olson's works in sections for books, pamphlets, and broadsides; contributions to books; contributions to periodicals; translations; and recordings and miscellaneous works. Gives title-page transcriptions, contents, physical descriptions, and brief notes on publication histories for Olson's books published from 1947 to 1965.

1035.   McPheron, William. **Charles Olson: The Critical Reception, 1941-1983. A Bibliographic Guide**. New York: Garland, 1986. 427p. (Garland Reference Library of the Humanities, vol. 619). LC 85-45127. ISBN 0-8240-8663-5.

McPheron gives comprehensive coverage of writings about Olson, chronologically arranging annotated entries for 1,630 critical books and articles in English and other languages; reviews of Olson's works and of works about Olson; American, Canadian, and British dissertations and theses; entries in reference works and anthologies and other passing references; and interviews with and works by other writers that mention or credit Olson. Annotations are descriptive, with significant studies receiving extended reviews. Coverage extends from 1938 through 1970. In addition to indexes for primary and periodical titles, a names index (with headings for Shakespeare, Jung, Joyce, and others mentioned in annotations) offers limited subject access. For works by Olson, see *First Printings of American Authors*, vol. 3, pp. 261-73. Olson's manuscripts are listed in Robbins' *American Literary Manuscripts*, p. 240. Alan Golding reviews research on Olson in *Contemporary Authors: Bibliographical Series: Volume 2: American Poets*, pp. 233-68.

Dictionaries, Encyclopedias, and Handbooks

1036.   Butterick, George F. **A Guide to The Maximus Poems of Charles Olson**. Berkeley, CA: University of California Press, 1978. 816p. LC 75-27921. ISBN 0-520-03140-7.

Butterick provides line-by-line glosses and explications of the names of persons, places, and things; words, phrases, and quotations in English and other languages; and sources, references, allusions, and other elements in Olson's work—that, for example, "Brer Fox" is Ezra Pound and "the Gulf of Maine" is a section of the Atlantic Ocean. The index is keyed to *The Maximus Poems* (New York: Jargon/Corinth, 1960), *Maximus Poems IV, V, VI* (London: Cape, Goliard, 1968), and *The Maximus Poems: Volume Three* (New York: Grossman, 1975). A bibliography of Olson's sources is included.

Journals

See Patterson's *Author Newsletters and Journals*, p. 231, for previously published journals for Olson.

Elder (James) Olson, 1909-

Bibliographies

1037. Battersby, James L. **Elder Olson: An Annotated Bibliography**. New York: Garland, 1983. 289p. (Garland Bibliographies of Modern Critics and Critical Schools, vol. 5; Garland Reference Library of the Humanities, vol. 349). LC 82-48273. ISBN 0-8240-9254-6.

Battersby presents a comprehensive bibliography of works by and about Olson, including separate listings for his books and collections of essays, books of poetry, edited works, essays, introductions, articles, reviews, poems, plays, and notes and lectures, as well as for secondary books, articles, reviews, dissertations, and passing references. Separate indexes for primary works, critics, and subjects conclude the volume. Olson's manuscripts are listed in Robbins' *American Literary Manuscripts*, p. 240.

Eugene (Gladstone) O'Neill, 1888-1953

Bibliographies

1038. Atkinson, Jennifer McCabe. **Eugene O'Neill: A Descriptive Bibliography**. Pittsburgh, PA: University of Pittsburgh Press, 1974. 410p. (Pittsburgh Series in Bibliography). LC 73-13312. ISBN 0-8229-3279-2.

The definitive listing of O'Neill's primary bibliography, Atkinson offers detailed descriptions of O'Neill's published writings, including separate, chronologically arranged listings for all first English-language editions of plays, broadsides, and other separate publications; first appearances of letters, interviews, conversations, and the like in books by others; appearances in periodicals and newspapers; promotional blurbs on dust jackets and advertisements; original quotations from O'Neill in catalogs; and collections and anthologies of plays. A very brief appendix lists film, radio, and musical adaptations of plays. An index of names, titles, theaters, and publishers provides access. Atkinson's bibliography largely supersedes Ralph Sanborn and Barrett H. Clark's *A Bibliography of the Works of Eugene O'Neill, Together with the Collected Poems of Eugene O'Neill* (1931; reprint New York: Benjamin Blom, 1965), which retains value for details about O'Neill's periodical appearances. Also for works by O'Neill, see *First Printings of American Authors*, vol. 1, pp. 291-96. O'Neill's manuscripts are listed in Robbins' *American Literary Manuscripts*, p. 240.

1039. Miller, Jordan Y. **Eugene O'Neill and the American Critic: A Bibliographical Checklist**. 2d ed. Hamden, CT: Archon Books, 1973. 553p. LC 72-122403. ISBN 0-208-00939-6.

As much a handbook as a bibliography, Miller's work provides significant data about O'Neill's life and career as well as evaluative descriptions of criticism of O'Neill published through 1972. The volume includes a detailed "Life Chronology" and "Chronology of Composition," entries for major productions (with information on performances and casts), and synopses of nondramatic works (letters, poems, essays), in addition to entries for general studies in books, articles, and reviews; studies of individual works; and theses and dissertations. Indexing by names, titles, and subjects (especially under O'Neill's name) is very thorough. Miller's work is exemplary. Additional information on 139 dissertations on O'Neill produced from 1928 through 1980 is provided by Tetsumaro Hayashi's *Eugene O'Neill: Research Opportunities and Dissertation Abstracts* (Jefferson, NC: McFarland, 1983). Margaret Loftus Ranald identifies works by and about O'Neill in Demastes' *American Playwrights, 1880-1945*, pp. 323-47. Research on O'Neill is reviewed by John H. Raleigh in Bryer's *Sixteen Modern American Authors*, pp. 417-43; and its supplement by Raleigh in Bryer's *Sixteen Modern American Authors: Volume 2: A Survey of Research and Criticism Since 1972*, pp. 480-518.

1040.   Smith, Madeline. **Eugene O'Neill: An Annotated Bibliography**. New York: Garland, 1988. 320p. (Garland Reference Library of the Humanities, vol. 860). LC 88-11264. ISBN 0-8240-0691-7.

Intended to update Miller's bibliography (entry 1039) for 1973 through 1985 and extend coverage for international criticism, Smith provides a complex arrangement of descriptively annotated entries in separate listings for books and parts of books in English; dissertations; articles in English; non-English-language publications; English-language productions and reviews; non-English-language productions and reviews; adaptations, television and radio productions, audio and film recordings, and fictional representations of O'Neill's life; editions of primary works; and translations. Although Smith offers details about productions and casts and a solid index of names and titles, these features are not nearly as thorough as those provided in Miller's bibliography.

Dictionaries, Encyclopedias, and Handbooks

1041.   Ranald, Margaret Loftus. **The Eugene O'Neill Companion**. Westport, CT: Greenwood Press, 1984. 827p. LC 83-22671. ISBN 0-313-22551-6.

Ranald's very useful handbook gives detailed and extensive summaries of O'Neill's writings, including information about productions, casts, and publication histories; identifications of characters; and biographies of O'Neill's family members and associates. Entries include bibliographic references. A "Bibliographic Essay" (pp. 765-89) surveys reference sources, manuscripts, texts, and criticism. A thorough index of names, titles, and subjects is very helpful.

Indexes and Concordances

1042.   Bryan, George B., and Wolfgang Mieder. **The Proverbial Eugene O'Neill: An Index to Proverbs in the Works of Eugene Gladstone O'Neill**. Westport, CT: Greenwood Press, 1995. 359p. (Bibliographies and Indexes in American Literature, no. 21). LC 95-36073. ISBN 0-313-29794-0.

Key-word index to more than 2,500 proverbs, clichés, and other catchphrases in the full range of O'Neill's writings based on standard editions, including *Complete Plays of Eugene O'Neill* (New York: Library of America, 1988) and other editions (listed on pp. 79-84). Introductory essay characterizing O'Neill's use of proverbs as a "preoccupation" (p. 4) also serves as primer on types of proverbs in O'Neill. Appends tables of data on distribution and frequency.

1043.   Reaver, J. Russell. **An O'Neill Concordance**. Detroit, MI: Gale, 1969. 3 vols. LC 73-75960.

Reaver concords the texts of 28 plays published after 1924, including selected works from *The Plays of Eugene O'Neill* (New York: Random House, 1951), *A Moon for the Misbegotten* (New York: Random House, 1952), *Long Days Journey into Night* (New Haven, CT: Yale University Press, 1956), *A Touch of the Poet* (New Haven, CT: Yale University Press, 1957), *Hughie* (New Haven, CT: Yale University Press, 1959), and *More Stately Mansions* (New Haven, CT: Yale University Press, 1964). As such, the concordance offers only limited data on O'Neill's language.

Journals

1044. **The Eugene O'Neill Review**. Boston: Eugene O'Neill Society, Suffolk University, 1977-. 2/yr. ISSN 1040-9843.

Sponsored by the Eugene O'Neill Society and formerly the *Eugene O'Neill Newsletter* (1977-88), recent (mostly double) issues of this journal typically feature more than a dozen substantial critical articles as well as news about the activities of the society and information about other events of interest to both O'Neill scholars and persons associated with the theater. Articles have included biographical and interpretive studies of O'Neill's works or their productions, transcriptions of texts of O'Neill's letters, and studies of O'Neill's influence on, or literary relationships with, writers such as Shakespeare, Lillian Hellman, Albee, Sherwood Anderson, Strindberg, Hemingway, Susan Glaspell, Kipling, and Faulkner, as well as interviews with O'Neill's associates, actors, and directors of productions. Occasional special issues focus on specific topics, such as "O'Neill and Gender" in 19.1-2 (Spring-Fall 1995). The journal has not recently published any formal supplemental bibliographies or checklists. Reports and reviews of productions of O'Neill's works throughout the world and reviews and abstracts of new books, however, make the journal an important source for primary and secondary bibliographic data. A section of news, notes, queries, and comments announces conferences, calls for papers, readings, new publications, and other editions and critical works in progress. *The Eugene O'Neill Review* is indexed in *MHRA* and *MLA*.

Joel Oppenheimer, 1930-

Bibliographies

For works by Oppenheimer, see *First Printings of American Authors*, vol. 3, pp. 275-78. Also available is George F. Butterick's *Joel Oppenheimer: A Checklist of His Writings* (Storrs, CT: University of Connecticut Library, 1975).

John Boyle O'Reilly, 1844-1890

Bibliographies

For works by O'Reilly, see *Bibliography of American Literature*, vol. 6, pp. 492-504. O'Reilly's contributions to and reviews of O'Reilly's works in selected periodicals are identified in Wells' *The Literary Index to American Magazines, 1850-1900*, p. 289. O'Reilly's manuscripts are listed in Robbins' *American Literary Manuscripts*, pp. 240-41.

Joe Orton, 1933-1967

Bibliographies

King's *Twenty Modern British Playwrights*, pp. 77-83, lists works by Orton and describes works about him.

George Orwell (Eric Arthur Blair), 1903-1950

Bibliographies

1045. Meyers, Jeffrey and Valerie Meyers. **George Orwell: An Annotated Bibliography of Criticism**. New York: Garland, 1977. 132p. (Garland Reference Library of the Humanities, vol. 54). LC 75-42887. ISBN 0-8240-9955-9.

The Meyers alphabetically arrange descriptively annotated entries for about 500 secondary writings (excluding dissertations) about Orwell published from 1903 through 1950. Coverage includes books, articles, and reviews in all languages. No index whatsoever is provided. For a bibliography of works by and about Orwell, see *NCBEL*, IV, pp. 690-96. Indicative of Orwell's international reputation, Kentaro Oishi and Hideaki Sagara's *Joji Oweru* [transliterated title] (Tokyo: Nichigai Asoshietsu, Kinokuniya Shoten,1995) is an annotated Japanese-language guide to Orwell editions and criticism.

Dictionaries, Encyclopedias, and Handbooks

1046.   Hammond, J. R. **A George Orwell Companion**. London: Macmillan, 1982. 278p. ISBN 0-333-28668-5.

Hammond surveys the career and literary reputation of Orwell and provides brief publication information and summaries for his books, essays, poems, and book reviews. Extensive chapters review themes, characterization, structures, and other features of Orwell's nine major works, including *Animal Farm* and *Nineteen Eighty-Four*, as well as (to a lesser degree) Orwell's essays. A dictionary identifies and describes Orwell's fictional characters. A selective, annotated bibliography completes the guide. Hammond's companion is more extensive than Jeffrey Meyers' *A Reader's Guide to George Orwell* (London: Thames and Hudson, 1975).

John James Osborne, 1929-1994

Bibliographies

1047.   Northouse, Cameron, and Thomas P. Walsh. **John Osborne: A Reference Guide**. Boston: G. K. Hall, 1974. 158p. (Reference Guides in American Literature, no. 2). LC 74-14966. ISBN 0-8161-1152-9.

Northouse and Walsh chronologically arrange descriptively annotated entries for English-language studies of Osborne appearing from 1956 through 1972, with a separate list of unannotated non-English-language criticisms. Indexing is limited to critics and primary works. Additionally, King's *Twenty Modern British Playwrights*, pp. 85-124, lists Osborne's works and describes about 175 international scholarly studies and dissertations on Osborne, with a classified list of reviews.

Frances Sargent (Locke) Osgood, 1811-1850

Bibliographies

For works by Osgood, see *Bibliography of American Literature*, vol. 6, pp. 505-22. Contributions by Osgood and criticism and reviews of Osgood's works in selected periodicals are identified in Wells' *The Literary Index to American Magazines, 1815-1865*, p. 113. Osgood's manuscripts are listed in Robbins' *American Literary Manuscripts*, p. 241.

Thomas Otway, 1652-1685

Bibliographies

For a bibliography of works by and about Otway, see *NCBEL*, II, pp. 747-49. Otway's manuscripts are described in *Index of English Literary Manuscripts*, II, pt. 2:109-11. Armistead's *Four Restoration Playwrights* (entry 1177) describes criticism of Otway through 1980. Wells' *English Drama*, pp. 150-72, includes reviews of research on Nathaniel Lee and Otway by H. Neville Davies.

Wilfred Owen, 1893-1918

Bibliographies

1048.   White, William. **Wilfred Owen, 1893-1918: A Bibliography**. Kent, OH: Kent State University Press, 1967. (The Serif Series in Bibliography, no. 1). 41p. LC 66-28409.

White provides a descriptive checklist (with brief bibliographic data) for Owen's uncollected and collected poems, letters, and reviews and lists criticisms and biographical accounts of Owen. Also for a bibliography of works by and about Owen, see *NCBEL*, IV, pp. 324-26.

Indexes and Concordances

1049.   Heneghan, Donald A. **A Concordance to the Poems and Fragments of Wilfred Owen**. Boston: G. K. Hall, 1979. 226p. (A Reference Publication in Literature). LC 79-9221. ISBN 0-8161-8371-6.

Heneghan concords the text of the third printing of C. Day Lewis' amended edition of *The Collected Poems of Wilfred Owen* (New York: New Directions, 1964). Word-frequency lists are included.

Cynthia Ozick, 1928-
Bibliographies

See *Bibliography of American Fiction, 1919-1988*, pp. 396-97, for Barbara L. Scrafford and Elaine M. Kauvar's checklist of works by and about Ozick. S. Lillian Kremer reviews works by and about Ozick in Shapiro's *Jewish American Women Writers*, pp. 265-77.

Thomas Nelson Page, 1853-1922
Bibliographies

For works by Page, see *Bibliography of American Literature*, vol. 6, pp. 523-40. Page's contributions to and reviews of Page's works in selected periodicals are identified in Wells' *The Literary Index to American Magazines, 1850-1900*, pp. 290-91. Page's manuscripts are listed in Robbins' *American Literary Manuscripts*, pp. 242-43. Longest's *Three Virginia Writers* (entry 743) describes criticism of Page published from 1886 through 1976. See *Bibliography of American Fiction, 1866-1918*, pp. 300-301, for Kathryn Lee Seidel's checklist of works by and about Page. Harriet R. Holman surveys works by and about Page in Bain and Flora's *Fifty Southern Writers Before 1900*, pp. 348-58.

Albert Bigelow Paine, 1861-1937
Bibliographies

For works by Paine, see *First Printings of American Authors*, vol. 5, pp. 233-44. Reviews of Paine's works and Paine's contributions to selected periodicals are identified in Wells' *The Literary Index to American Magazines, 1850-1900*, pp. 291-92. Paine's manuscripts are listed in Robbins' *American Literary Manuscripts*, p. 243.

Thomas Paine, 1737-1809
Bibliographies

1050.   Gimbel, Richard. **The Resurgence of Thomas Paine: With the Catalogue of an Exhibition: Thomas Paine Fights for Freedom in Three Worlds**. Worcester, MA: American Antiquarian Society, 1961. Various pagings. OCLC 5358057.

Reprinted from the *Proceedings of the American Antiquarian Society* (October 1959-October 1960), Gimbel's catalog is the most comprehensive, descriptive guide to Paine's works, chronologically arranging entries in sections for separate works, letters, and manuscripts; collected works; portraits and engravings; caricatures; tokens; and celebrations. No full bibliographic descriptions provided. Notes describe circumstances of composition and publication and indicate significance.

1051.   Gimbel, Richard. **Thomas Paine: A Bibliographical Check List of Common Sense: With an Account of Its Publication**. New Haven, CT: Yale University Press, 1956. 124p. LC 56-5942.

Gimbel provides an extensive publication history of *Common Sense* and chronological listings of detailed descriptions of printings of the work in Philadelphia and elsewhere. A list of contemporary works related to *Common Sense* is also included. Paine's manuscripts are listed in Robbins' *American Literary Manuscripts*, p. 244.

Journals

See Patterson's *Author Newsletters and Journals*, p. 232, for previously published journals for Paine.

Grace Paley, 1922-
Bibliographies

For works by Paley, see *First Printings of American Authors*, vol. 2, p. 283. Victoria Aarons reviews works by and about Paley in Shapiro's *Jewish American Women Writers*, pp. 278-87.

Dorothy (Rothschild) Parker, 1893-1967
Bibliographies

1052.   Calhoun, Randall. **Dorothy Parker: A Bio-Bibliography**. Westport, CT: Greenwood Press, 1993. 174p. (Bio-Bibliographies in American Literature, no. 4). LC 92-30882 ISBN 0-313-26507-0.

Covers works by and about Parker. The first part chronologically arranges entries for Parker's writings in sections for books, short fiction, screenplays, interviews, miscellaneous works (incidental essays, poems, and critical prose), and individual pieces from magazines and newspapers (arranged by publication and classified by type). Twenty entries for books supply brief bibliographic information, with a note on composition and publication history and citations for reviews; 39 entries for screenplays identify reviews only, without production credits. Prefaced by a brief narrative surveying Parker's critical reception, the second part chronologically arranges annotated entries for 196 criticisms of Parker from 1922 to 1992, including entries in reference works, newspaper articles, unpublished conference papers, and dissertations. Annotations for books give citations for reviews. Appended reprinted biographical sketches by Richard E. Lauterbach (1944), Wyatt Cooper (1968), and Joseph Bryan III (1985). Classified index for primary works and general index of names and selected titles; no subject indexing. For works by Parker, see *First Printings of American Authors*, vol. 4, pp. 289-93. Parker's manuscripts are listed in Robbins' *American Literary Manuscripts*, p. 245. See *Bibliography of American Fiction, 1919-1988*, pp. 397-98, for Arthur F. Kinney's checklist of works by and about Parker.

Theodore Parker, 1810-1860
Bibliographies

1053.   Myerson, Joel. **Theodore Parker: A Descriptive Bibliography**. New York: Garland, 1981. 225p. (Garland Reference Library of the Humanities, vol. 307). LC 81-43354. ISBN 0-8240-9279-1.

Full bibliographic descriptions of Parker's published writings chronologically arranged in separate sections for books, pamphlets, and broadsides; collected editions; Parker's contributions to collections and selections of his works; books edited by Parker; and works attributed to Parker. Coverage is limited to English-language publications. Entries for Parker's 68 separate publications give title-page transcriptions; paginations; collations; descriptions of typography, paper, and binding; notes on printing history; and copy locations for first and subsequent editions and printings through 1980. Entries for collected, selected, and contributed works indicate contents. Thorough index of titles, names, and publishers. Also for works by Parker, see *First Printings of American Authors*, vol. 4, pp. 295-312. Contributions by Parker and criticism and reviews of Parker's works in selected periodicals are identified in Wells' *The Literary Index to American Magazines, 1815-1865*, p. 114; and *The Literary Index to American Magazines, 1850-1900*, pp. 292-93. Parker's manuscripts are listed in Robbins' *American Literary Manuscripts*, p. 245.

Francis Parkman, 1823-1893
Bibliographies

For works by Parkman, see *Bibliography of American Literature*, vol. 6, pp. 541-56. Contributions by Parkman and criticism and reviews of Parkman's works in selected periodicals are identified in Wells' *The Literary Index to American Magazines, 1815-1865*, p. 115; and *The Literary Index to American Magazines, 1850-1900*, pp. 293-94. Parkman's manuscripts are listed in Robbins' *American Literary Manuscripts*, pp. 245-46. Gary L. Collison reviews research on Parkman in Myerson's *The Transcendentalists*, pp. 216-32.

Thomas Parnell, 1679-1718
Bibliographies

For a bibliography of works by and about Parnell, see *NCBEL*, II, p. 561. Parnell's manuscripts are described in *Index of English Literary Manuscripts*, III, pt. 2:235-51.

Anne Parrish, 1888-1957
Bibliographies

For works by Parrish, see *First Printings of American Authors*, vol. 4, pp. 313-17. Parrish's manuscripts are listed in Robbins' *American Literary Manuscripts*, p. 246.

Thomas Williams Parsons, 1819-1892
Bibliographies

For works by Parsons, see *Bibliography of American Literature*, vol. 6, pp. 557-90. Parsons' contributions to and reviews of Parsons' works in selected periodicals are identified in Wells' *The Literary Index to American Magazines, 1850-1900*, p. 294. Parsons' manuscripts are listed in Robbins' *American Literary Manuscripts*, p. 246.

Sara Payson Willis Parton (Fanny Fern), 1811-1872
Bibliographies

See *Bibliography of American Fiction through 1865*, pp. 194-95, for a checklist of works by and about Parton. Comments on and reviews of Parton's works in selected periodicals are identified in Wells' *The Literary Index to American Magazines, 1815-1865*, pp. 54-55; and *The Literary Index to American Magazines, 1850-1900*, p. 295. Parton's manuscripts are listed in Robbins' *American Literary Manuscripts*, pp. 246-47.

Kenneth Patchen, 1911-1972
Bibliographies

1054. Morgan, Richard G. **Kenneth Patchen: An Annotated, Descriptive Bibliography with Cross-Referenced Index**. Mamaroneck, NY: Paul P. Appel, 1979. 174p. LC 78-15376. ISBN 0-911858-36-9.

This is a comprehensive bibliography of works by and about Patchen. Morgan chronologically arranges full bibliographic descriptions of Patchen's writings published from 1928 through 1973 in separate listings for American and British editions of books and pamphlets; cards, broadsides, and folios; contributions to books and pamphlets; contributions to periodicals; plays; recordings; and musical and film adaptations. Illustrations of title pages and variants are useful. In addition, Morgan identifies books, parts of books, dissertations, articles, reviews of individual works, manuscripts, correspondence, and ephemera about Patchen. Contains a particularly useful description of the Kenneth Patchen Archives at the University of California at Santa Cruz, which includes copies of published works, literary manuscripts, papers, scrapbooks, and ephemera (pp. 122-23). Primary and secondary materials are indexed separately. Also available is William E. Mullane's *Kenneth Patchen: An Exhibition of Painted Poems, Books, Sculptures, and Documentation of Kenneth's Early Years in Warren, Ohio, March 7-April 5, 1987: Kenneth Patchen Literary Festival, April 27-30, 1989* (Warren, OH: Kenneth Patchen Literary Festival Committee and Trumbull Art Gallery & Pig Iron Press, 1989). Patchen's manuscripts are also listed in Robbins' *American Literary Manuscripts*, p. 247.

Walter Horatio Pater, 1839-1894
Bibliographies

1055. Court, Franklin E. **Walter Pater: An Annotated Bibliography of Writings About Him**. DeKalb, IL: Northern Illinois University Press, 1980. 411p. (Annotated Secondary Bibliography Series on English Literature in Transition, 1880-1920). LC 78-56125. ISBN 0-87580-072-6.

Court gives comprehensive and international coverage of works about Pater, chronologically arranging entries for books, parts of books, articles, reviews, biographical studies, dissertations, and passing references published from 1871 through 1973. Annotations are descriptive, with the most significant studies receiving extensive discussion. Indexes for critics, secondary titles, periodical and newspaper titles, languages, and primary titles enhance access.

1056. Wright, Samuel. **A Bibliography of the Writings of Walter H. Pater**. New York: Garland, 1975. 190p. (Garland Reference Library of the Humanities, vol. 6). LC 74-30448. ISBN 0-8240-1062-0.

Wright provides full bibliographic descriptions of Pater's published and unpublished writings dating from 1856 through 1931, covering his books, periodical publications, and manuscripts of his published and unpublished works, including the significant collection at Harvard University (pp. 135-38, 144-47). A prefatory chronology of Pater's works provides access. No index whatsoever is included. More specialized coverage related to Pater's primary works is provided in Billie Andrew Inman's *Walter Pater's Reading: A Bibliography of His Library Borrowings and Literary References, 1858-1873* (New York: Garland, 1981) and *Walter Pater and His Reading, 1874-1877: With a Bibliography of His Library Borrowings, 1878-1894* (New York: Garland, 1990), which identifies Pater's bibliographic resources. Also for a bibliography of works by and about Pater, see *NCBEL*, III, pp. 1412-16. Research on Pater is reviewed by Lawrence Evans in DeLaura's *Victorian Prose*, pp. 321-60.

Indexes and Concordances

1057. Wright, Samuel. **An Informative Index to the Writings of Walter H. Pater**. West Cornwall, CT: Locust Hill Press, 1987. 460p. LC 87-22852. ISBN 0-9339-5111-6.

Wright seemingly attempts to compensate for the absence of indexing in his primary bibliography (entry 1056) by compiling this guide to topics; names of persons, places, and things; sources; and other elements in Pater's works. The index is keyed to works included in the "New Library Edition" of *The Works of Walter Pater* (London: Macmillan, 1910), Pater's *Uncollected Essays* (Portland, ME: Thomas B. Mosher, 1903), Albert Mordell's edition of *Sketches and Reviews* (New York: Boni and Liveright, 1919), and Pater's six uncollected articles. A very convenient guide to Pater's writings, Wright's handy index identifies passages in which Pater comments on all varieties of topics, such as Plato, flowers, and Paris.

Coventry Kersey Dighton Patmore, 1823-1896
Bibliographies

For a bibliography of works by and about Patmore, see *NCBEL*, III, pp. 486-89. Criticism and reviews of Patmore's works in selected periodicals are identified in Wells' *The Literary Index to American Magazines, 1850-1900*, p. 296. See the review of research by Lionel Stevenson in Faverty's *The Victorian Poets*, pp. 355-60.

Elliott Harold Paul, 1891-1958
Bibliographies

For works by Paul, see *First Printings of American Authors*, vol. 5, pp. 245-50. Paul's manuscripts are listed in Robbins' *American Literary Manuscripts*, p. 247.

James Kirke Paulding (Launcelot Langstaff), 1778-1860
Bibliographies

For works by Paulding, see *Bibliography of American Literature*, vol. 7, pp. 1-22. Contributions by Paulding and criticism and reviews of Paulding's works in selected periodicals are identified in Wells' *The Literary Index to American Magazines, 1815-1865*, pp. 115-16; and *The Literary Index to American Magazines, 1850-1900*, pp. 296. Paulding's manuscripts are listed in Robbins' *American Literary Manuscripts*, p. 247-48. See *Bibliography of American Fiction Through 1865*, pp. 196-98, for a checklist of works by and about Paulding.

John Howard Payne, 1791-1852
Bibliographies

For works by Payne, see *Bibliography of American Literature*, vol. 7, pp. 23-53. Contributions by Payne and criticism and reviews of Payne's works in selected periodicals are identified in Wells' *The Literary Index to American Magazines, 1815-1865*, p. 116; and *The Literary Index to American Magazines, 1850-1900*, p. 297. Payne's manuscripts are listed in Robbins' *American Literary Manuscripts*, p. 248.

Elizabeth Palmer Peabody, 1804-1894
Bibliographies

For works by Peabody, see *First Printings of American Authors*, vol. 3, pp. 279-84. Contributions by Peabody and criticism and reviews of Peabody's works in selected periodicals are identified in Wells' *The Literary Index to American Magazines, 1815-1865*, pp. 116-17; and *The Literary Index to American Magazines, 1850-1900*, p. 297. Peabody's manuscripts are listed in Robbins' *American Literary Manuscripts*, pp. 248-49. Margaret Neussendorfer reviews research on Peabody in Myerson's *The Transcendentalists*, pp. 233-41.

Thomas Love Peacock, 1785-1866
Bibliographies

1058.   Prance, Claude A. **The Characters in the Novels of Thomas Love Peacock, 1785-1866, with Bibliographical Lists.** Lewiston, NY: Mellen, 1992. 303p. LC 92-5982. ISBN 0-7734-9510-X.

A poorly organized and mistitled guide to works by and about Peacock with separate dictionaries of characters in his novels and plays and of his contemporaries. Buried in part 4 are annotated bibliographies of selected introductions to Peacock, first and later editions of Peacock's works, and about 300 critical studies of Peacock published to 1990. Includes chronology of Peacock's life and writings. Separate indexes of characters, poems and songs in the plays and novels, and names, titles, and selected topics. Also for a bibliography of works by and about Peacock, see *NCBEL*, III, pp. 700-704.

Mervyn Laurence Peake, 1911-1968
Bibliographies

1059.   The National Book League. **Mervyn Peake, 1911-1968: Exhibition Arranged by the National Book League.** London: National Book League, 1972. 43p. (Word and Image, no. 3). LC 73-160901. ISBN 0-85353-132-3.

Heavily illustrated exhibit catalog, with an introduction by Maeve Gilmore, listing 69 editions and manuscripts of Peake's published and unpublished works and 89 artworks (oils, watercolors, drawings, etc.), with a Peake chronology.

Journals

1060.   **Peake Studies.** Orzens, Switzerland: G. P. Winnington, 1988- . 2/yr. ISSN 1013-1191.

Typical contributions are "Peake's Fantastic Realism in the Titus Books" and "The Impact of Mervyn Peake on His Readers." Other articles have addressed imagery in Peake's works, discussed publication history, focused on Peake's illustrations, and examined Peake's relationship to China. Biographically oriented features have provided editions of otherwise unpublished works, such as Peter G. Winnington's "Mervyn Peake's Correspondence with the Ministry of Information During World War II," 2.2 (Summer 1991): 3-42. Other useful bibliographical features include Winnington's "Recent and Forthcoming Publications," 1.1 (Autumn 1988): 31-36; and Gerard Neill's "Peake at the Imperial War Museum," 1.4 (Summer 1990): 29-34, a London exhibition description. *Peake Studies* is indexed in *MLA*.

George Peele, 1556-1596

Bibliographies

For a bibliography of works by and about Peele, see *NCBEL*, I, pp. 1431-34. See also the Tannenbaums' *Elizabethan Bibliographies*, vol. 6, and Robert C. Johnson's *Elizabethan Bibliographies Supplements*, no. 5. Peele's manuscripts are described in *Index of English Literary Manuscripts*, I, pt. 2:359-62, 632. Charles W. Daves reviews research on Peele in Logan and Smith's *The Predecessors of Shakespeare*, pp. 143-52.

Indexes and Concordances

See Stagg's *The Figurative Language of the Tragedies of Shakespeare's Chief 16th-Century Contemporaries* (entry 901).

Samuel Pepys, 1633-1703

Bibliographies

For a bibliography of works by and about Pepys, see *NCBEL*, II, pp. 1582-84. See also Dennis G. Donovan's *Elizabethan Bibliographies Supplements*, no. 18. Pepys' manuscripts are described in *Index of English Literary Manuscripts*, II, pt. 2:113-23.

James Gates Percival, 1795-1856

Bibliographies

For works by Percival, see *Bibliography of American Literature*, vol. 7, pp. 54-73. Contributions by Percival and criticism and reviews of Percival's works in selected periodicals are identified in Wells' *The Literary Index to American Magazines, 1815-1865*, pp. 117-18; and *The Literary Index to American Magazines, 1850-1900*, p. 298. Percival's manuscripts are listed in Robbins' *American Literary Manuscripts*, pp. 250-51.

Thomas Percy, 1729-1811

Bibliographies

For a bibliography of works by and about Percy, see *NCBEL*, II, pp. 242-45. Also available is *The Thomas Percy Collection: Gift of Professor Bertram H. Davis: Catalogue of the Exhibition and Gift, April 15-May 15, 1985* (Tallahassee, FL: Florida State University, Robert Manning Strozier Library, 1985). Percy's manuscripts are described in *Index of English Literary Manuscripts*, III, pt. 2:253-339.

Walker Percy, 1916-1990

Bibliographies

1061. Hobson, Linda Whitney. **Walker Percy: A Comprehensive Descriptive Bibliography**. New Orleans, LA: Faust, 1988. 115p. LC 87-80959. ISBN 0-917905-05-9.

This offers comprehensive coverage of works by and about Percy. Hobson gives full descriptions for Percy's primary works, covering book-length works, including speeches and essays, in English and in translations; contributed reviews and review essays published in periodicals; contributed articles, introductions, essays, and excerpts; interviews, speeches, and panels; and records, tapes, and miscellaneous works. Entries give illustrations of title pages and dust jackets; collations; contents; descriptions of typography, paper, bindings, and dust jackets; publication information about price, numbers of copies, and the like; and references to subsequent editions and translations. In addition, Hobson offers separate, unannotated listings of books (with references to their reviews), bibliographies, dissertations, and theses; parts of books and articles (arranged under Percy's works); and reviews and articles in newspapers and magazines (also arranged under Percy's works). No indexing of any variety is provided. Hobson's guide supersedes Stuart Wright's *Walker Percy, a Bibliography: 1930-1984: Based on the Collection of the Compiler, Including Books, Pamphlets, Magazines, Journals, Newspapers, Etc.* (Westport, CT: Meckler, 1986), which gives full bibliographic information (title-page transcriptions and physical descriptions) for Percy's separate publications, contributions to books and periodicals, interviews and published comments, and miscellaneous writings. Also for works by Percy, see *First Printings of American Authors*, vol. 2, pp. 285-86. Percy's manuscripts are listed in Robbins' *American Literary Manuscripts*, p. 251. Kramer's *Andrew Lytle, Walker Percy, Peter Taylor* (entry 872) offers more descriptive coverage of works about Percy. See *Bibliography of American Fiction, 1919-1988*, pp. 398-400, for Hobson's checklist of works by and about Percy.

William Alexander Percy, 1885-1942

Bibliographies

For works by Percy, see *First Printings of American Authors*, vol. 2, pp. 287-88. Percy's manuscripts are listed in Robbins' *American Literary Manuscripts*, p. 251.

S(idney) J(oseph) Perelman, 1904-1979

Bibliographies

1062.   Gale, Steven H. **S. J. Perelman: An Annotated Bibliography**. New York: Garland, 1985. 162p. (Garland Reference Library of the Humanities, vol. 531). LC 84-45389. ISBN 0-8240-8845-8.

Covers works by and about Perelman. Gale gives brief, identifying information for Perelman's single novel; plays; films; television scripts; sound recordings; articles and short stories (some 621 entries); and published letters, with cross-references to their appearances in collections. In addition, Gale gives selectively annotated entries for about 400 biographies, interviews, bibliographies, and critical books, articles, and reviews about him. Gale's guide is particularly valuable for descriptions of the University of Pittsburgh's Curtis Theatre Collection of Perelman's scripts and papers related to *The Beauty Part* (pp. 149-53). Perelman's manuscripts are also listed in Robbins' *American Literary Manuscripts*, p. 251.

Julia (Mood) Peterkin, 1880-1961

Bibliographies

For works by Peterkin, see *First Printings of American Authors*, vol. 1, pp. 297-98. Peterkin's manuscripts are listed in Robbins' *American Literary Manuscripts*, p. 252. See *Bibliography of American Fiction, 1919-1988*, p. 401, for Susan Millar Williams' checklist of works by and about Peterkin.

Ann Petry, 1911-

Bibliographies

1063.   Ervin, Hazel Arnett. **Ann Petry: A Bio-Bibliography**. New York: G. K. Hall, 1993. 115p. LC 92-36575. ISBN 0-8161-7278-1.

Covers works by and about Petry. The first part presents brief bibliographic information and contents for 62 separate, collected, and contributed works by Petry subarranged by forms (fiction, children, juvenile, poetry, collection, autobiography, nonfiction). The second part alphabetically lists annotated entries for 336 works about Petry, covering articles, entries in reference works, reviews, and newspaper articles. Appends an interview with Petry. Introduction identifies Petry's critical reception. Includes chronology of Petry's life and works. Index of names, titles, and subjects. Also for works by Petry, see *First Printings of American Authors*, vol. 1, p. 299. Petry's manuscripts are listed in Robbins' *American Literary Manuscripts*, p. 252. See *Bibliography of American Fiction, 1919-1988*, pp. 402-403, for Verbie Lovorn Prevost's checklist of works by and about Petry.

Elizabeth (Stuart) Phelps (H. Trusta), 1815-1852
Bibliographies

See *Bibliography of American Fiction Through 1865*, p. 199, for a checklist of works by and about Phelps. Phelps' contributions to and reviews of Phelps' works in selected periodicals are identified in Wells' *The Literary Index to American Magazines, 1850-1900*, pp. 300-302. Phelps' manuscripts are listed in Robbins' *American Literary Manuscripts*, p. 252.

Charles Philbrick, 1922-1971
Bibliographies

For works by Philbrick, see *First Printings of American Authors*, vol. 5, pp. 251-52.

Ambrose Philips, 1674-1749
Bibliographies

For a bibliography of works by and about Philips, see *NCBEL*, II, pp. 562-63. Philips' manuscripts are described in *Index of English Literary Manuscripts*, III, pt. 2:341-45.

Katherine Philips, 1631-1664
Bibliographies

For a bibliography of works by and about Philips, see *NCBEL*, II, p. 480. McCarron and Shenk's *Lesser Metaphysical Poets*, p. 29, identifies criticism of Philips from 1960 through 1980. Philips' manuscripts are described in *Index of English Literary Manuscripts*, II, pt. 2:125-81.

David Graham Phillips, 1867-1911
Bibliographies

For works by Phillips, see *Bibliography of American Literature*, vol. 7, pp. 74-81. Phillips' manuscripts are listed in Robbins' *American Literary Manuscripts*, p. 253. See *Bibliography of American Fiction, 1866-1918*, pp. 302-303, for Lawrence J. Oliver's checklist of works by and about Phillips.

Phoenix, later ninth century
Bibliographies

Greenfield and Robinson's *A Bibliography of Publications on Old English Literature to the End of 1972*, pp. 252-54, lists editions, translations, and studies of Old English *Phoenix*, with citations for reviews.

John James Piatt, 1835-1917
Bibliographies

For works by Piatt, see *Bibliography of American Literature*, vol. 7, pp. 82-91. Piatt's contributions to and reviews of Piatt's works in selected periodicals are identified in Wells' *The Literary Index to American Magazines, 1850-1900*, pp. 302-303. Piatt's manuscripts are listed in Robbins' *American Literary Manuscripts*, pp. 253-54.

Albert Pike, 1809-1891
Bibliographies

1064. Boyden, William Llewellyn, and Ray Baker Harris. **Bibliography of the Writings of Albert Pike**. Centennial ed. Washington, DC: Supreme Council 33, Ancient and Accepted Scottish Rite of Freemasonry, Southern Jurisdiction, 1957. 109p. LC 57-13911.

A revision of Boyden's previous descriptive guide to Pike's writings (Privately printed, 1933). The first part arranges brief bibliographic information for Pike's separate and contributed writings in sections for general works, biography, language, law, military, newspapers, politics and economics, poetry, miscellaneous, and manuscripts. Entries indicate other appearances. The second part is limited to Pike's Masonic works, including entries for addresses and reports, obituaries by Pike, official letters and notices, "Cerneau Controversy" or writings about "irregular masonry" (p. 16), ritualistic and ceremonial writings, miscellaneous, and manuscripts. Manuscripts are located in the library of the Supreme Council at Washington and elsewhere. Unindexed. For full bibliographic descriptions of works by Pike, see *Bibliography of American Literature*, vol. 7, pp. 92-108. Pike's manuscripts are also listed in Robbins' *American Literary Manuscripts*, pp. 254-55.

Josephine Pinckney, 1895-1957
Bibliographies

For works by Pinckney, see *First Printings of American Authors*, vol. 2, p. 289. Pinckney's manuscripts are listed in Robbins' *American Literary Manuscripts*, p. 255.

Sir Arthur Wing Pinero, 1855-1934
Bibliographies

For a bibliography of works by and about Pinero, see *NCBEL*, III, pp. 1166-69. Arthur Gewirtz surveys and identifies works by and about Pinero in Demastes and Kelly's *British Playwrights, 1880-1956*, pp. [305]-26.

Edward Coote Pinkney, 1802-1828
Bibliographies

For works by Pinkney, see *Bibliography of American Literature*, vol. 7, pp. 109-14. Pinkney's manuscripts are listed in Robbins' *American Literary Manuscripts*, p. 255. Contributions by Pinkney and criticism and reviews of Pinkney's works in selected periodicals are identified in Wells' *The Literary Index to American Magazines, 1815-1865*, p. 118; and *The Literary Index to American Magazines, 1850-1900*, p. 303. C. Michael Smith surveys works by and about Pinkney in Bain and Flora's *Fifty Southern Writers Before 1900*, pp. 359-64.

Harold Pinter, 1930-
Bibliographies

1065. Gale, Steven H. **Harold Pinter: An Annotated Bibliography**. Boston: G. K. Hall, 1978. 244p. (A Reference Publication in Literature). LC 78-2782. ISBN 0-8161-8014-8.

In this, the most comprehensive bibliography of writings by and about Pinter, Gale provides 2,048 descriptively annotated entries. Pinter's plays, film scripts, shorter writings, short stories, poems, and translations of his works in other languages are described in 133 entries, with the volume's bulk covering studies of Pinter, including articles, reviews, and dissertations. Appendixes chronologically list Pinter's works, first performances, productions directed by Pinter, and awards given to him. A solid index of critics, primary titles, and subjects provides access. Gale's coverage is more comprehensive than Rudiger Imhof's *Pinter: A Bibliography: His Works and Occasional Writings with a Comprehensive*

Checklist of Criticism and Reviews of the London Productions, 2d ed. revised (London: TQ Publications, 1976), Herman T. Schroll's *Harold Pinter: A Study of His Reputation (1958-1969) and a Checklist* (Metuchen, NJ: Scarecrow Press, 1971), and the listings for Pinter in King's *Twenty Modern British Playwrights*, pp. 125-95.

Journals

1066. **Pinter Review**. Tampa, FL: Harold Pinter Society, 1987- . Annual. ISSN 0895-9706.

Sponsored by the Harold Pinter Society, annual volumes publish six to 10 critical studies, reviews of stage and media productions of Pinter's works, book reviews, and a comprehensive bibliography of works by and about Pinter. Recent features cover the full range of Pinter's works, offering excerpts from Pinter's unpublished works; discussing themes in his stage and screenplays and novels, such as sexual politics and rituals; and examining staging, filming, and other production techniques. Bibliographic contributions include Susan Hollis Merritt's "The Harold Pinter Archive in the British Library," 7 (1994): 14-55. The annual "Harold Pinter Bibliography," also presently compiled by Merritt, is a classified listing with editions and translations of Pinter's works; stage productions; film, television, and other media adaptations; reviews of stage and media productions and adaptations; and books, articles, essays, dissertations, and works in progress about Pinter that substantially updates the coverage of Gale's *Harold Pinter: An Annotated Bibliography* (entry 1065). Publication is about a year behind schedule. · The 1992-93 volume contained cumulative author and title indexes for the annual from 1987 to 1991. The *Pinter Review* is indexed in *MLA*.

Sylvia Plath, 1932-1963

Bibliographies

1067. Meyerling, Sheryll. **Sylvia Plath: A Reference Guide, 1973-1988**. Boston: G. K. Hall, 1990. 203p. (A Reference Guide to Literature). LC 89-39238. ISBN 0-8161-8929-3.

Superseding the coverage of secondary works on Plath in Gary Lane and Maria Stevens' *Sylvia Plath: A Bibliography* (Metuchen, NJ: Scarecrow Press, 1978) and Cameron Northouse and Thomas P. Walsh's *Sylvia Plath and Anne Sexton* (entry 1176), Meyerling's guide chronologically arranges about 800 descriptively annotated entries. No subject indexing is provided. Research on Plath is reviewed by Cindy Hoffman, Carol Duane, Katharen Soule, and Linda Wagner in Duke, Bryer, and Inge's *American Women Writers*, pp. 379-402.

1068. Tabor, Stephen. **Sylvia Plath: An Analytical Bibliography**. Westport, CT: Meckler, 1987. 268p. LC 86-8625. ISBN 0-88736-100-5.

The best and most detailed descriptive bibliography of Plath's primary works as well as a solid listing of works about Plath. Separate sections chronologically list first and later editions and variants of Plath's separately published works, contributions to books and edited works, contributions to periodicals, recordings by Plath (both commercial and unpublished sessions), broadcasts, manuscripts, translations of Plath's works, and musical and dramatic adaptations. About 950 critical studies (books, articles, reviews, and dissertations) about Plath are briefly annotated. Tabor also describes Indiana University's Lilly Library's two collections of Plath materials (Plath MSS and Plath MSS II), which contain papers from Plath's early life and career, including correspondence, memorabilia, juvenilia, and literary manuscripts of poems and prose, as well as collections at Smith College, Washington University in St. Louis, the British Library, and the University of Texas' Harry Ransom Humanities Research Center. An index of names and primary titles provides access. Tabor's bibliography largely supersedes the coverage of Eric Homberger's *A Chronological Checklist of the Periodical Publications of Sylvia Plath* (Exeter: University of Exeter, 1970), which lists Plath's contributions to journals. Also for published works by Plath, see *First Printings of American*

Authors, vol. 2, pp. 291-95. Plath's manuscripts are also listed in Robbins' *American Literary Manuscripts*, p. 255.

Indexes and Concordances

1069.   Matovich, Richard M. **A Concordance to the Collected Poems of Sylvia Plath**. New York: Garland, 1986. 623p. (Garland Reference Library of the Humanities, vol. 618). LC 85-45126. ISBN 0-8240-8664-3.

Matovich concords Plath's *Collected Poems* (London: Faber & Faber, 1981), providing alphabetical and ranked frequency lists.

Edgar Allan Poe, 1809-1849

Bibliographies

1070.   Dameron, J. Lasley, and Irby B. Cauthen, Jr. **Edgar Allan Poe: A Bibliography of Criticism, 1827-1967**. Charlottesville, VA: University Press of Virginia, 1974. 386p. LC 73-89824. ISBN 0-8139-0498-6.

Dameron and Cauthen provide a comprehensive, annotated listing of about 3,000 criticisms of Poe published from 1827 through 1968 in separate listings for English and other languages. Brief annotations are critical. A comprehensive name, title, and subject index concludes the volume. Esther F. Hyneman's *Edgar Allan Poe: An Annotated Bibliography of Books and Articles in English, 1827-1973* (Boston: G. K. Hall, 1974) is slightly more up-to-date but covers and provides descriptive annotations for fewer studies in a classified arrangement. Albert J. Robbins' *The Merrill Checklist of Edgar Allan Poe* (Columbus, OH: Merrill, 1969) is substantially dated. Leona Rasmussen Phillips' *Edgar Allan Poe: An Annotated Bibliography* (New York: Gordon Press, 1978) affords very limited guidance. See *Bibliography of American Fiction Through 1865*, pp. 200-208, for Kent P. Ljungquist's checklist of works by and about Poe. Research on Poe is reviewed by Jay B. Hubbell in Woodress' *Eight American Authors*, pp. 3-36; Ottavio M. Casale in Myerson's *The Transcendentalists*, pp. 362-71; and Eric W. Carlson in Bain and Flora's *Fifty Southern Writers Before 1900*, pp. 365-88. *ALS* annually features a review essay on Poe scholarship.

1071.   Heartman, Charles F., and James R. Canny. **A Bibliography of First Printings of the Writings of Edgar Allan Poe: Together with a Record of First and Contemporary Later Printings of His Contributions to Annuals, Anthologies, Periodicals, and Newspapers Issued During His Lifetime: Also Some Spurious Poeana and Fakes**. Revised ed. Hattiesburg, MS: The Book Farm, 1943. 294p. LC 44-7988.

Although badly dated, this gives title-page transcriptions, physical descriptions, and publishing histories for Poe's primary materials. Additional supplemental information on Poe's books and contributions is provided in Blanck's *Bibliography of American Literature*, vol. 7, pp. 115-54. Poe's manuscripts are listed in Robbins' *American Literary Manuscripts*, p. 256. The most important collections of letters, manuscripts, photographs, and other primary materials for Poe are described in John E. Reilly's *John Henry Ingram's Poe Collection at the University of Virginia: A Calendar and Index of Letters and Other Manuscripts, Photographs, Printed Matter, and Biographical Source Materials Concerning Edgar Allan Poe Assembled by John Henry Ingram, With Prefatory Essay by John Carl Miller on Ingram as a Poe Editor and Biographer and as a Collector of Poe Materials*, 2d ed. (Charlottesville: University of Virginia Library, 1994), a fully descriptive and indexed revision of John Carl Miller's *John Henry Ingram's Poe Collection at the University of Virginia* (Charlottesville, VA: University of Virginia, 1960); Joseph J. Moldenhauer's *A Descriptive Catalog of Edgar Allan Poe Manuscripts in the Humanities Research Center Library, University of Texas at Austin* (Austin, TX: University of Texas, 1973); and Arthur Hobson Quinn and Richard H. Hart's *Edgar Allan Poe: Letters and Documents in the Enoch Pratt Free Library* (New York: Scholar's Facsimiles and Reprints, 1941). Also available is *The Poe Catalogue: A Descriptive Catalogue of the Stephan Loewentheil*

Collection of Edgar Allan Poe Material (Baltimore, MD: The 19th Century Shop, 1992). Burton R. Pollin's *Images of Poe's Works : A Comprehensive Descriptive Catalogue of Illustrations* (New York: Greenwood, 1989) is an extensive, descriptive international bibliography of books, portfolios, prints, paintings, and other representations of Poe's works or works inspired by Poe, with a 300-entry filmography of motion pictures and television films based on Poe's works.

Dictionaries, Encyclopedias, and Handbooks

1072.   Carlson, Eric W. **A Companion to Poe Studies**. Westport, CT: Greenwood Press, 1996. 604p. LC 95-40034. ISBN 0-313-26506-2.

Twenty-five chapters by different authorities offer overviews of Poe's writings (covering sources, publication history, early and recent reception, and critical approaches) and evaluate specific issues related to Poe's life and times, thought, art, and influence. Two chapters cover the poems, and six address the tales. Other chapters focus on Poe's long fiction, essays and marginalia, reviews, and science fiction and landscape sketches. Includes a bibliography (pp. 560-76) and a comprehensive index with detailed topical headings.

1073.   Gale, Robert L. **Plots and Characters in the Fiction and Poetry of Edgar Allan Poe**. Hamden, CT: Archon Books, 1970. 190p. LC 76-113809. ISBN 0-208-00974-4.

Gale offers plot summaries of Poe's prose and poetry as well as identifications of 523 named or namable characters. The plot of *Eureka* is described in eight pages, *The Narrative of Arthur Gordon Pym* in 11. "The Pit and the Pendulum" and "The Raven" receive long paragraphs. Coverage of characters includes personified abstractions, such as "Death" and "Shadow"; historical persons in fictionalized parts, such as Kepler in *Eureka*; and anonymous narrators (listed under "Persona").

1074.   Hammond, J. R. **An Edgar Allan Poe Companion: A Guide to the Short Stories, Romances and Essays**. Totowa, NJ: Barnes & Noble, 1981. 205p. LC 81-167695. ISBN 0-389-20172-3.

Essays survey details of Poe's life and literary reputation and summarize the plots and themes of his writings. Separate dictionaries identify characters and place names in Poe's works and describe his writings. An appendix lists film versions of Poe's life and works produced since 1909. A selected bibliography of primary and secondary materials and an index of names, titles, and topics complete the volume. Additional coverage of plots, characters, and places of Poe's works is provided in Robert L. Gale's *Plots and Characters in the Fiction and Poetry of Edgar Allan Poe* (Hamden, CT: Archon Books, 1970).

1075.   Thomas, Dwight, and David K. Jackson. **The Poe Log: A Documentary Life of Edgar Allan Poe, 1809-1949**. Boston: G. K. Hall, 1987. 919p. (American Author Log Series). LC 86-19319. ISBN 0-8161-8734-7.

Relying extensively on both published and unpublished primary materials, Thomas and Jackson provide an exemplary chronology of Poe's life and literary career. Substantial quotations and references to sources are included throughout the work. Biographical sketches of persons mentioned and a detailed index of names, titles, and subjects are also provided. Extensive list of sources (pp. 855-76). Detailed name, title, and subject index provides excellent access.

Indexes and Concordances

1076.   Pollin, Burton R. **Word Index to Poe's Fiction**. Staten Island, NY: Gordian Press, 1982. 485p. LC 82-2869. ISBN 0-87752-225-1.

Pollin lists all of the words and variants in Poe's fictional works included in volumes 2 and 3 for *Tales and Sketches* of the *Collected Works of Edgar Allan Poe* (Cambridge: Harvard University Press, 1978) and the *Collected Writings of Edgar Allan Poe: Volume 1: The Imaginary Voyages* (Boston: Twayne, 1981). Pollin includes frequency lists. This index complements Wiley's concordance (entry 1077) for Poe's poems.

1077.   Wiley, Elizabeth. **Concordance to the Poetry of Edgar Allan Poe**. Selinsgrove, PA: Susquehanna University Press, 1989. 745p. LC 87-43350. ISBN 0-941664-96-1.

Wiley concords the texts of poems included in vol. 1 of Thomas Ollive Mannott's *Collected Works of Edgar Allan Poe* (Cambridge: Harvard University Press, 1969). The volume includes frequency lists. Wiley's concordance supersedes Bradford A. Booth and Claude E. Jones' *A Concordance of the Poetical Works of Edgar Allan Poe* (Baltimore, MD: Johns Hopkins University Press, 1941), which was based on Killis Campbell's edition of *The Poems of Edgar Allan Poe* (1917; reprint New York: Russell & Russell, 1962). A more specialized index, Burton R. Pollin's *Dictionary of Names and Titles in Poe's Collected Works* (New York: DaCapo Press, 1968) provides separate indexes for names and titles (of real and fictional persons, places, and things) in references and allusions in Poe's writings. Pollin's work is based on James A. Harrison's edition of *Complete Works* (1902; reprint New York: AMS, 1965). J. Lasley Dameron and Louis Charles Stagg's *An Index to Poe's Critical Vocabulary* (Hartford, CT: Transcendental Books, 1966) covers another more specialized aspect of Poe's writings.

Journals

1078.   **The Poe Messenger**. Richmond, VA: Poe Foundation, 1969-. Annual. ISSN 0276-3737.

Issues of *The Poe Messenger* feature a dozen or more brief notes on Poe's life, works, and reputation, including such topics as Poe's portraits, Poe and other writers, and Poe and nature. Reprints of previously published reviews and commentaries and reminiscences about Poe are also published. In addition to reports on the activities of the Poe Foundation, the newsletter lists new works acquired by the Poe Museum, including books, journals, art, media, and realia. Reviews of new publications about Poe also appear. Although not as important for research on Poe as *Poe Studies* (entry 1079), *Poe Messenger* nonetheless offers useful information for scholars. Annual volumes are usually a year or more behind publication schedule. *Poe Messenger* is unindexed.

1079.   **Poe Studies: Dark Romanticism: History, Theory, Interpretation**. Pullman, WA: Washington State University Press, 1968-. 2/yr. ISSN 0090-5224.

Sponsored by the Poe Studies Association, issues of *Poe Studies* and its predecessor, the *Poe Newsletter* (1968-70), typically feature news about the activities of the society in addition to one to three articles and book reviews. Studies generally offer close readings of specific works, identify allusions and sources, and assess critical responses to Poe. Past issues have included bibliographic reviews of Romanian translations of "The Raven" and Poe criticism in France. A significant number of other recent, briefer articles, in a section called "Marginalia," have addressed textual issues or identified and described primary materials and library collections. *Poe Studies* annually features the important "International Poe Bibliography," which offers brief annotations for recent editions and criticisms and dissertations. Vol. 24.1-2 (June/December 1991): 1-48 includes Jana L. Argersinger and Steven Gregg's "Subject Index to 'International Poe Bibliography': Poe Scholarship and Criticism, 1983-1988." The journal also announces meetings, conferences, new publications, and ongoing research activities. *Poe Studies* is indexed in *A&HCI*, *MHRA*, and *MLA*.

Patterson's *Author Newsletters and Journals*, pp. 240-42, describes other previously published journals for Poe.

Frederik Pohl, 1919-
Bibliographies
>   See *Bibliography of American Fiction, 1919-1988*, pp. 403-405, for Stephen H. Goldman's checklist of works by and about Pohl.

Francis Pollini, 1930-
Bibliographies
>   For works by Pollini, see *First Printings of American Authors*, vol. 2, pp. 297-98.

Maria Louise Pool, 1841-1898
Bibliographies
>   For works by Pool, see *First Printings of American Authors*, vol. 5, pp. 253-55. Pool's manuscripts are listed in Robbins' *American Literary Manuscripts*, p. 256.

Ernest Poole, 1880-1950
Bibliographies
>   See *Bibliography of American Fiction, 1866-1918*, pp. 303-304, for Gary Beason's checklist of works by and about Poole. Poole's manuscripts are listed in Robbins' *American Literary Manuscripts*, pp. 256-57.

Alexander Pope, 1688-1744
Bibliographies
>   1080.   Griffith, Reginald Harvey. **Alexander Pope: A Bibliography**. Austin, TX: University of Texas Press, 1922. 2 vols. LC 23-573.
>   The best descriptive listing of editions of Pope's works published in his lifetime (although, as Griffith admits, not without shortcomings), Griffith's work provides full bibliographic detail for editions and variants from 1709 through 1751. Emphasis is on bibliographic points. Available in a reprinted edition (New York: AMS Press, 1975). Supplemental detail for selected editions is available in Thomas James Wise's *A Pope Library: A Catalogue of Plays, Poems, and Prose Writings by Alexander Pope* (1931; reprint Folkestone: Dawsons of Pall Mall, 1973). A new primary bibliography of Pope based on modern principles is needed. For a bibliography of works by and about Pope, see *NCBEL*, II, pp. 500-27, by Vinton A. Dearing. Pope's manuscripts are described in *Index of English Literary Manuscripts*, III, pt. 3:1-78.

>   1081.   Kowalk, Wolfgang. **Alexander Pope: An Annotated Bibliography of Twentieth Century Criticism, 1900-1979**. Frankfurt am Main: Lang, 1981. 371p. LC 86-672118. ISBN 3-8204-5881-6.
>   Of several existing bibliographies covering criticism of Pope, this is the most comprehensive. Kowalk arranges some 2,000 selectively annotated entries in separate topical sections (for "Pope as Critic" and "Biography," for examples) and for individual works. A thorough index of primary works, critics, and subjects offers solid access. Listings here supersede those in James Tobin's *Alexander Pope: A List of Critical Studies Published from 1895-1944* (New York: Cosmopolitan Science and Art Service, 1945); and Cecilia L. Lopez's *Alexander Pope: An Annotated Bibliography, 1945-1967* (Gainesville, FL: University of Florida Press, 1970), which provides about 700 annotated entries. Research on Pope is reviewed by Geoffrey Tillotson in Dyson's *English Poetry*, pp. 128-43.

Dictionaries, Encyclopedias, and Handbooks
>   1082.   Berry, Reginald. **A Pope Chronology**. Boston: G. K. Hall, 1988. 221p. LC 87-24772. ISBN 0-8161-8951-x.
>   Berry gives a day-by-day account of Pope's life and career. Major sources of information include George Sherburn's five-volume edition of *The Correspondence*

of *Alexander Pope* (Oxford: Clarendon Press, 1956) and Maynard Mack's *Alexander Pope: A Life* (New Haven, CT: Yale University Press, 1985). In addition, dictionaries briefly identify persons and places connected with Pope. A thorough index provides access to the chronology by Pope's works as well as detailed subjects (listed under Pope's name), such as "attacks published against" and "investment matters."

Indexes and Concordances
1083.   Bedford, Emmett G., and Robert J. Dilligan. **A Concordance to the Poems of Alexander Pope in Two Volumes**. Detroit, MI: Gale, 1974. 2 vols. LC 74-852. ISBN 0-8103-1008-2.

Based on John Butt's *The Twickenham Edition of the Poems of Alexander Pope* (New Haven, CT: Yale University Press, 1939-69), Bedford and Dilligan's concordance provides line, page, and volume references. This supersedes Edwin Abbot's *A Concordance to the Works of Alexander Pope* (New York: D. Appleton, 1875; reprint New York: Kraus Reprint, 1965), which was based on the 1751 Warburton edition.

Journals
1084.   **The Scriblerian and the Kit Cats: A Newsjournal Devoted to Pope, Swift, and Their Circle**. Philadelphia: Temple University, 1968-. 2/yr. ISSN 0036-9640.

Formerly *The Scriblerian* (1968-71), this journal is more significant for its bibliographic features than for critical ones. Issues typically publish one or two brief notes of biographical or textual interest, generally facsimiles or transcriptions of previously unreported letters or minor works of Pope, Defoe, Thomas Warton the Elder, and many minor writers. More important, the *Scriblerian* regularly features "Recent Articles," a current bibliography (with abstracts) of scholarship on the full range of both major and minor eighteenth-century writers—from Addison, Collier, Congreve, and Defoe to Richardson, Smollett, and Steele. The bibliography offers particularly valuable coverage of criticism for the likes of Mary Barber, Jane Barker, Sarah Butler, Anne Finch, Eliza Haywood, Mary Pix, and many other women writers not covered in individual bibliographies. Issues also include extensive selections (a dozen or more) of book reviews. "Scribleriana" gives information on research in progress, conferences, and other news of interest to specialists. All issues append a detailed table of contents. *The Scriblerian and the Kit Cats* is indexed in *AHI, A&HCI, MHRA*, and *MLA*.

Eleanor Hodgman Porter, 1868-1920
Bibliographies
See *Bibliography of American Fiction, 1866-1918*, p. 305, for Shirley Marchalonis' checklist of works by and about Porter.

Katherine Anne Porter, 1890-1980
Bibliographies
1085.   Hilt, Kathryn, and Ruth M. Alvarez. **Katherine Anne Porter: An Annotated Bibliography**. New York: Garland, 1990. 354p. (Garland Reference Library of the Humanities, vol. 507). LC 90-43628. ISBN 0-8240-8912-x.

Covering both primary and secondary works, Hilt and Alvarez supplement and update the guides of Waldrip and Bauer (entry 1087) and Kiernan (entry 1086). Part 1 describes Porter's works in sections for her books; translations; stories contributed to books and periodicals; essays, letters, poems; journalism; and book reviews. Entries for separate publications give brief bibliographic information, summary contents, and notes on composition and publication history, with citations for subsequent editions. Entries for contributed works emphasize contents and composition history and cite reprintings. Part 2 describes approximately 600 works about Porter published through 1990 in sections for bibliographies; biographies and interviews; general critical studies; studies of individual works; books reviews, arranged by work; and dissertations. Author and title indexes. Also for works by Porter, see *First Printings of American Authors*, vol. 2, pp. 299-303. Porter's manuscripts are listed in Robbins' *American Literary Manuscripts*, p. 257. Supplemental bibliographic detail for Porter's works is provided in Edward Schwartz's *Katherine Anne Porter: A Critical Bibliography* (1953; reprint New York: Norwood Editions, 1977), originally published in *Bulletin of the New York Public Library* 57 (May 1953): 211-47; and George Bixby's "Katherine Anne Porter: A Bibliographical Checklist," *American Book Collector* 1 (1980): 19-33.

1086. Kiernan, Robert F. **Katherine Anne Porter and Carson McCullers: A Reference Guide**. Boston: G. K. Hall, 1976. 194p. (Reference Guides in Literature, no. 9). LC 76-2357. ISBN 0-8161-7806-2.
    Kiernan chronologically arranges entries in separate listings for criticism appearing in books, articles, reviews, and dissertations. Coverage of Porter extends from 1924 through 1974. Coverage of McCullers extends from 1940 through 1975. About 500 entries for Porter are provided, including selected non-English studies. Annotations are descriptive. Critics, titles, and selected topics are separately indexed. Detailed subheadings are listed for primary titles. See *Bibliography of American Fiction, 1919-1988*, pp. 406-408, for Darlene Harbour Unrue's checklist of works by and about Porter. Research on Porter is reviewed by Joan Givner, Jane DeMouy, and Ruth M. Alvarez in Duke, Bryer, and Inge's *American Women Writers*, pp. 201-32; and by Givner in Flora and Bain's *Fifty Southern Writers After 1900*, pp. 356-67.

1087. Waldrip, Louise, and Shirley Ann Bauer. **A Bibliography of the Works of Katherine Anne Porter, and a Bibliography of the Criticism of the Works of Katherine Anne Porter**. Metuchen, NJ: Scarecrow Press, 1969. 219p. LC 70-6835. ISBN 0-8108-0275-9.
    The most comprehensive, descriptive listing of Porter's primary works, Waldrip and Bauer chronologically arrange entries in listings for separate publications, contributions to books, contributions to periodicals, and translations of Porter's works. Coverage extends through 1968. Full bibliographic descriptions of Porter's 17 separate works and collections give title-page transcriptions, pagination and collations, contents, binding and jacket information, and notes on publication history, with bibliographic information for other editions and citations for first appearances. Hilt and Alvarez's *Katherine Anne Porter* (entry 1085) contributes supplemental descriptions of more recent primary materials.

Peter Neville Frederick Porter, 1929-
Bibliographies
1088. Kaiser, John R. **Peter Porter: A Bibliography, 1954-1986**. London and New York: Mansell, 1990. 211p. LC 89-13943. ISBN 0-7201-2032-2.
    Provides chronologically arranged full bibliographic descriptions of Porter's works in sections for books, pamphlets, and broadsides; contributions to books and edited works; contributions to periodicals; interviews; recordings; and addenda. Entries for separate publications and book contributions give title-page transcriptions, collations, paginations, binding descriptions, contents, prices, numbers of copies printed, and notes on publication histories. Title index.

William Sydney Porter (O. Henry), 1862-1910
Bibliographies
1089. Clarkson, Paul S. **A Bibliography of William Sydney Porter (O. Henry)**. Caldwell, ID: Caxton Printers, 1938. 161p. LC 39-735.
    Clarkson gives full bibliographic descriptions (title-page transcriptions, physical details, and publishing histories) for Porter's books; contributions to books; collected editions; dramatizations; and contributions to periodicals. Also contains a list of biographical and critical writings about him. Supplemental details for Porter's works are provided in Blanck's *Bibliography of American Literature*, vol. 7, pp. 155-69. Porter's manuscripts are listed in Robbins' *American Literary Manuscripts*, pp. 257-58.

1090. Harris, Richard C. **William Sydney Porter (O. Henry): A Reference Guide**. Boston: G. K. Hall, 1980. 229p. (A Reference Guide to Literature). LC 80-19508. ISBN 0-8161-8006-7.

Harris chronologically arranges annotated entries for writings about Porter published from 1904 through 1978. Coverage is comprehensive, including books, parts of books, articles, and dissertations, although Harris notes limited inclusion of non-English-language materials. Annotations are descriptive. A subject index, employing headings such as "Language, slang, dialect in stories" and "Mark Twain," gives topical access. See *Bibliography of American Fiction, 1866-1918*, pp. 307-309, for Luther S. Luedtke's checklist of works by and about Porter. Research on Porter is reviewed by Eugene Current-Garcia in Flora and Bain's *Fifty Southern Writers After 1900*, pp. 368-81.

Charles (McColl) Portis, 1933-
Bibliographies

For works by Portis, see *First Printings of American Authors*, vol. 4, p. 319.

Ezra (Weston Loomis) Pound, 1885-1972
Bibliographies

1091. Gallup, Donald. **Ezra Pound: A Bibliography**. Charlottesville, VA: Published for the Bibliographical Society of the University of Virginia by the University of Virginia Press, 1983. 548p. LC 82-15995. ISBN 0-8139-0976-7.

A revision of Gallup's *A Bibliography of Ezra Pound* (London: Rupert Hart-Davis, 1963), this is the best descriptive listing of Pound's primary works. Gallup gives full bibliographic descriptions in separate listings for Pound's books and pamphlets and translations by Pound (106 entries dating from 1908); edited books and contributions to books; contributions to periodicals (some 1,989 entries from 1902); translations of Pound's works (arranged by languages); and miscellaneous writings, such as syllabi, leaflets and broadsides, international editions, music and musical settings, recordings, and books contracted but never published. Entries give title-page transcriptions, physical descriptions, and publishing histories. A comprehensive name and title index gives access. Pound's manuscripts are listed in Robbins' *American Literary Manuscripts*, pp. 258-59.

1092. Ricks, Beatrice. **Ezra Pound: A Bibliography of Secondary Works**. Metuchen, NJ: Scarecrow Press, 1986. 281p. (Scarecrow Author Bibliographies, no. 74). LC 85-26140. ISBN 0-8108-1862-0.

Ricks arranges unannotated entries for 3,696 books, parts of books, journal and newspaper articles, and dissertations about Pound in topical sections (for biographies, general criticism, interviews, letters, bibliographies, and the like) as well as for Pound's works. Both English- and non-English-language materials are covered. An index for topics (such as "imagism," "politics and poetry," and "vorticism") includes names (Confucius, Dante, and T. S. Eliot), providing excellent access. Ricks' guide is more useful than Volker Bischoff's *Ezra Pound Criticism, 1905-1985: A Chronological Listing of Publications in English* (Marburg: Universitatsbibliothek Marburg, 1991), which amounts to an unannotated list of 5,390 works about Pound to December 1985. Research on Pound is reviewed by John J. Espey in Bryer's *Sixteen Modern American Authors*, pp. 445-71; and its supplement by Espey in Bryer's *Sixteen Modern American Authors: Volume 2: A Survey of Research and Criticism Since 1972*, pp. 519-57. *ALS* annually features a review essay on Pound scholarship.

Dictionaries, Encyclopedias, and Handbooks

1093. Terrell, Carroll Franklin. **A Companion to the Cantos of Ezra Pound**. Berkeley, CA: University of California Press, 1980, 1985. 2 vols. LC 78-54802. ISBN 0-520-03687-5 (vol. 1); 0-520-04731-1 (vol. 2).

Terrell gives a canto-by-canto, allusion-by-allusion account of Pound's complex work. Entries identify Pound's sources; list additional background and critical studies; and gloss all references to persons and places in Pound's text, translate non-English-language words and phrases, and comment on the text. Vol. 1 covers cantos 1 through 71; vol. 2 covers cantos 74 through 117. A selected bibliography and an index of topics, non-English words, and Chinese characters complete vol. 2. The work supersedes John Hamilton Edwards and William W. Varse's *Annotated Index to the Cantos of Ezra Pound: Cantos 1-84* (Berkeley, CA: University of California Press, 1957), which briefly glosses allusions to persons, places, and things; English-language quotations; non-English-language expressions; and the like, with appendixes for Greek and Chinese words and characters, chronology (which indexes dates), sources, and more. Edwards and Varse reference the 1948 (New York) New Directions edition. A more limited introduction is provided in George Kearns' *Guide to Ezra Pound's Selected Cantos* (New Brunswick, NJ: Rutgers University Press, 1980).

Indexes and Concordances

1094.   Dilligan, Robert J., James W. Parins, and Todd K. Bender. **A Concordance to Ezra Pound's Cantos**. New York: Garland, 1981. 612p. (Garland Reference Library of the Humanities, vol. 106). LC 77-83375. ISBN 0-8240-9837-4.

This concords *The Cantos of Ezra Pound* (New York: New Directions, 1975), referencing canto, line, and page numbers. Provides separate lists for Pound's English and non-English vocabularies as well as word frequencies.

1095.   Lane, Gary. **A Concordance to Personae: The Shorter Poems of Ezra Pound**. New York: Haskell House, 1972. 546p. LC 72-6462. ISBN 0-8383-1613-1.

Lane concords the texts of the shorter poems (excluding the Cantos) that Pound included in *Personae: The Collected Poems of Ezra Pound* (New York: Boni and Liveright, 1926). Frequency lists are included. Similar to Terrell's guide to the Cantos (entry 1093), K. K. Ruthven's *A Guide to Ezra Pound's Personae (1926)* (Berkeley, CA: University of California Press, 1969) offers a title-by-title account of allusions and references in *Personae*.

Journals

1096.   **Paideuma: A Journal Devoted to Ezra Pound Scholarship**. Orono, ME: National Poetry Foundation, 1972-. 3/yr. ISSN 0090-5674.

Sponsored in part by the National Poetry Foundation, *Paideuma* reflects the complexity of Pound's work. Issues have typically been variously divided into several distinct sections, each with its specific function. "The Periplum" generally includes four to six long articles that constitute the bulk of the journal. Significant space is given to studies that pay close attention to Pound's relationships with other writers and artists as well as to the influences of Pound on others and of others on Pound. Other articles have discussed Pound and Japanese cosmography, John Ruskin, T. S. Eliot, John Milton, Ivan Turgenev, Charles Olson, Wyndham Lewis, Ford Madox Ford, Chinese philosophy, Arabic literature, Amy Lowell, James Dickey, and Walt Whitman, among other subjects. Paul Wellen's "Analytical Dictionary of Ezra Pound's Chinese Characters," 25.3 (Winter 1996): 59-100, usefully complements concordances to Pound's works. "The Explicator" includes three to six briefer, more specific notes, including excerpts from Pound's critical writings. Past issues included "The Documentary" department, which published analyses of textual problems, transcriptions of manuscripts and letters, and translations of Pound's works and sources. In addition, several bibliographic checklists and literature reviews have also appeared, such as Massimo Bacigalupo's "Pound Studies in Italy, 1991," 22.1-2 (Spring-Fall 1993): 11-34. In recent issues, "The Departments" includes reports on activities of Pound scholars, conferences, calls for papers, abstracts, and the like, with a "Bulletin Board" that notes works, research, and other projects in progress. "The Reviewer," of course, includes reviews of new works. "Books Received" abstracts other new titles. Issues have also featured a useful section, "The Bibliographer," that published checklists and survey reviews, such as Elizabeth J. Bell and Mary Barnard's "Bibliographic Record of Periodical and Book Publication," 23.1 (Spring 1994): 187-98, that updates Gallup's *Ezra Pound: A Bibliography* (entry 1091). Occasional special issues have focused on specific topics: 24.2-3 (Fall-Winter 1995), containing papers from the 1994 NEH Seminar "Pound and His Contemporaries," included Dannah Edwards' "Addendum to the Preliminary Catalog of Ezra Pound's Library" (pp. 51-55), supplementing Tim Redman's "Pound's Library: A Preliminary Catalog," 15.2-3 (Fall-Winter 1986): 213-37. *Paideuma* is indexed in *AHI*, *MHRA*, and *MLA*.

Patterson's *Author Newsletters and Journals*, pp. 244-46, 364, describes other previously published journals for Pound.

Anthony Dymoke Powell, 1905-

Bibliographies

1097. Lilley, George P. **Anthony Powell: A Bibliography**. Winchester, UK: St. Paul's Bibliographies, 1993. 253p. (Winchester Bibliographies of 20th Century Writers). LC 93-28193. ISBN 0-9387-6846-8.

Describes works by Powell, chronologically arranging full bibliographic entries in sections for first and subsequent editions of books, edited books and contributions to books, contributions to periodicals, radio and television appearances, and published interviews. Coverage extends from 1922 to 1992. Thirty-three extensive entries for Powell's separate publications and 28 for book contributions give title-page transcriptions; collations; binding, paper, and dust-jacket descriptions; detailed textual notes on states and publication history; and citations for early notices and reviews. Lilley identifies and briefly describes some 1,488 periodical contributions from 1922 to 1984. Section F, "Miscellanea and some out-of-the-way Powell criticism" (with 17 entries) and an addenda (with five entries) should be consulted with some care in that Lilley mixes both primary and secondary materials, including reviews and book contributions by Powell, apocrypha, and criticisms and reviews of Powell's works. Includes brief chronology of Powell's life and career. The index references personal names and titles of books and contributed books listed in the first three sections. Lilley's coverage of Powell's primary materials supersedes Stanton's *A Bibliography of Modern British Novelists*, pp. 665-751, 1094-95, which contains classified unannotated entries for 440 works by Powell and 511 works about him, with an addendum.

Dictionaries, Encyclopedias, and Handbooks

1098. Spurling, Hilary. **Handbook to Anthony Powell's Music of Time**. London: Heinemann, 1977. 329p. ISBN 1-434-72410-6.

Intended as both a reference guide and a "pleasant bedside companion" (p. ix) to Powell's 12-volume novel. Separate indexes for characters, books (and authors), paintings (and artists), and places. Appends synopses and chronologies of the individual novels. Keyed by work and page to the London (Heinemann) and Boston (Little, Brown) first editions identified by abbreviations (p. xx). Unindexed. Published in the United States as *Invitation to the Dance: A Guide to Anthony Powell's Dance to the Music of Time* (Boston: Little, Brown, 1977).

Dawn Powell, 1897-1965

Bibliographies

For works by Powell, see *First Printings of American Authors*, vol. 5, pp. 257-59. Powell's manuscripts are listed in Robbins' *American Literary Manuscripts*, p. 259.

J(ames) F(arl) Powers, 1917-
Bibliographies

For works by Powers, see *First Printings of American Authors*, vol. 5, pp. 261-62. Powers' manuscripts are listed in Robbins' *American Literary Manuscripts*, p. 259. See *Bibliography of American Fiction, 1919-1988*, pp. 409-10, for Philip B. Eppards' checklist of works by and about Powers.

John Cowper Powys, 1872-1963
Bibliographies

1099.   Thomas, Dante. **A Bibliography of the Writings of John Cowper Powys: 1872-1963**. Mamaroneck, NY: Paul P. Appel, 1975. 192p. LC 73-80544. ISBN 0-911858-28-8.

Thomas gives full bibliographic descriptions in listings for Powys' books; contributions to books; and contributions to periodicals, in addition to listing about 40 books about Powys published from 1931 through 1974. Entries for primary materials include title-page transcriptions, physical descriptions, contents, and publishing histories, with illustrations of title pages and bindings. Appendixes list syllabi, collaborative works, sketches, and other miscellaneous writings. Also for a bibliography of works by and about Powys, see *NCBEL*, IV, pp. 706-10.

Journals

1100.   **The Powys Journal**. Lampeter, Wales: Powys Society, 1991- . Annual. ISSN 0962-7057.

"Aims to publish original material by the Powys family—in particular, John Cowper Powys, Theodore Francis Powys and Llewelyn Powys—and scholarly articles and other materials relating to them and their circle" (masthead). The hefty annual volumes of *The Powys Journal* features as many as 15 selections of writings by the many Powyses (including mostly previously unpublished letters, selections from diaries and journals, and reminiscences) and critical and biographic studies by others (usually offering close readings or interpretations of themes and images), with review articles and book reviews. Occasional bibliographical contributions include Peter J. Foss' "The Bissell Collection," 4 (1994): 191-99, describing manuscripts and books of the Powys family now housed at the Dorset County Museum Powys Centre. *The Powys Journal* is indexed in *MHRA*.

1101.   **Powys Notes**. Hamilton, NY: Powys Society of North America, 1985- . 2/yr. ISSN 1058-7691.

Both substantial and brief review articles and notes on biographical and bibliographic topics are common fare in *Powys Notes*. Studies on publishing history and editorial problems frequently include descriptions of previously unpublished primary materials. *Powys Notes* is indexed in *MLA* and *MHRA*.

1102.   **The Powys Review**. Lampeter, Wales: Powys Society, 1977-. 2/yr. ISSN 0309-1619.

The six to eight featured scholarly articles in *The Powys Review* cover the full range of topics related to John Cowper Powys, Theodore Francis Powys, and Llewelyn Powys. Recent close readings and explications of themes and allusions in *Owen Glendower, Mandragora*. and *A Glastonbury Romance* are typical. Biographical, source, and textual studies predominate, with many discussing the Powys' and Thomas Hardy's Wessex roots. Articles often reproduce primary documents. Recent bibliographic contributions include J. Lawrence Mitchell's "In Search of T. F. Powys," nos. 27-28 (1992-93): 3-15, which contains a checklist of drawings, paintings, and photographic portraits. In addition, the journal includes extensive selections of book reviews. In 1992 the Powys Society published a separate index to vols. 1-26, compiled by Stephen Powys Marks. *The Powys Review* is indexed in *A&HCI* and *MLA*.

Llewelyn Powys, 1884-1939

Bibliographies

For a bibliography of works by and about Powys, see *NCBEL*, IV, pp. 1105-1107.

T(heodore) F(rancis) Powys, 1875-1953

Bibliographies

For a bibliography of works by and about Powys, see *NCBEL*, IV, pp. 710-12.

Winthrop Macworth Praed, 1802-1839

Bibliographies

For a bibliography of works by and about Praed, see *NCBEL*, III, pp. 411-12.

William Hickling Prescott, 1796-1859

Bibliographies

1103.   Gardiner, C. Harvey. **William Hickling Prescott: An Annotated Bibliography of Published Works, Prepared for the Library of Congress**. Washington, DC: Hispanic Foundation, Reference Department, Library of Congress, 1958. 275p. (Hispanic Foundation Bibliographical Series, no. 4). LC 59-60031.

Reflects an effort "to locate and describe copies of every issue of the [six] book-length works" of Prescott (p. v). Emphasis is on providing extensive bibliographic information relevant to the popularity of Prescott's works. Entries give title-page transcriptions, collations, paginations, contents, binding descriptions, detailed notes on publication histories, and locations of examined copies for first and subsequent editions, translations, and reprintings. Identifies 200 editions of the *History of the Conquest of Mexico*, including 29 translations in nine different languages. Appends descriptions of adaptations of Prescott's works. Comprehensive index. Also for works by Prescott, see *Bibliography of American Literature*, vol. 7, pp. 170-82. Criticism and reviews of Prescott's works in selected periodicals are identified in Wells' *The Literary Index to American Magazines, 1815-1865*, pp. 123-24; and *The Literary Index to American Magazines, 1850-1900*, pp. 307-308. Prescott's manuscripts are listed in Robbins' *American Literary Manuscripts*, pp. 259-60.

Reynolds Price, 1933-

Bibliographies

1104.   Wright, Stuart, and James L. West, III. **Reynolds Price: A Bibliography, 1949-1984**. Charlottesville, VA: University Press of Virginia, 1986. 122p. LC 85-29463. ISBN 0-8139-1092-7.

Full bibliographic descriptions of Price's works in sections for books, pamphlets, and broadsides; contributions to books; appearances in periodicals and newspapers; translations; interviews, published discussions, and published comments on Price (109 annotated entries) published from 1956 to 1983; and two miscellaneous items. Entries for 39 separate publications give title-page and copyright-page transcriptions; collations; contents; information on paper, typography, binding, and jackets; and notes on publication histories. Entries for 165 first periodical appearances offer brief bibliographic information. Index of names and titles. Also for works by Price, see *First Printings of American Authors*, vol. 1, pp. 301-303. Price's manuscripts are listed in Robbins' *American Literary Manuscripts*, p. 260. Sue Laslie Kimball and Lynn Veach Sadler's collection of essays, *Reynolds Price: From A Long and Happy Life to Good Hearts, with a Bibliography* (Fayetteville, NC: Methodist College Press, 1989), supply supplemental coverage of works by and about Price published through 1988, with unannotated checklists of more than 200 critical studies and reviews (largely from regional newspapers). See *Bibliography of American Fiction, 1919-1988*, pp. 411-21, for Margaret Donovan DuPriest's checklist of works by and about Price. David Marion

Holman surveys works by and about Price in Flora and Bain's *Fifty Southern Writers After 1900*, pp. 382-90.

Richard Price, 1723-1791
Bibliographies
> 1105.   Thomas, D. O., John Stephens, and P. A. L. Jones. **A Bibliography of the Works of Richard Price**. Aldershot, Hants: Scolar, 1993. 221p. ISBN 0-85967-916-0.
>   Covers works by and about Price. Chronologically arranged entries for Price's primary works emphasize composition and publication histories. Forty full bibliographic descriptions of first and subsequent early editions of Price's books give title-page transcriptions, collation, pagination, information on press figures, paper, typography, publication history, citations to early notices and reviews, and lists of copies. Other entries give extensive lists of textual variants. Also separately lists 137 books and pamphlets, 74 articles, and 58 other works about Price published from 1772 to 1992, with a note on Price's manuscripts (pp. 206-208). Title and name index and index of printers, publishers, and booksellers.

J(ohn) B(oynton) Priestley, 1894-1984
Bibliographies
> 1106.   Day, Alan Edwin. **J. B. Priestley: An Annotated Bibliography**. New York: Garland, 1980. 360p. (Garland Reference Library of the Humanities, vol. 145). LC 78-68251. ISBN 0-8240-9798-x.
>   Day gives brief bibliographic information and contents for Priestley's primary materials, covering books and pamphlets; contributions to books; contributions to journals and newspapers (some 2,318 entries dating from 1912 through 1979); miscellaneous writings (including theater programs and advertisements); and stage, television, and screen adaptations, and other media. In addition, Day includes entries for about 120 works (unannotated) about Priestley in classified listings for bibliographies, general studies, studies of Priestley's family, "Priestleiana," and other materials. A separate index identifies books reviewed by Priestley. Useful descriptions of Priestley's primary materials are also included in *J. B. Priestley: A Exhibition of Manuscripts and Books* (Austin, TX: Humanities Research Center, 1963), which describes 156 items in the University of Texas' Harry Ransom Humanities Research Center. Also for a bibliography of works by and about Priestley, see *NCBEL*, II, pp. 1890-91. Lincoln Konkle surveys and identifies works by and about Priestley in Demastes and Kelly's *British Playwrights, 1880-1956*, pp. [327]-38.

Elizabeth Waties Allston Pringle (Patience Pennington), 1845-1921
Bibliographies
> For works by Pringle, see *First Printings of American Authors*, vol. 2, p. 305.

Matthew Prior, 1664-1721
Bibliographies
> For a bibliography of works by and about Prior, see *NCBEL*, II, pp. 489-92, by John Fuller. Prior's manuscripts are described in *Index of English Literary Manuscripts*, III, pt. 3:79-166.

Journals
> "Recent Articles" in *The Scriblerian and the Kit Cats* (entry 1084) regularly includes a selection of reviews of studies on Prior.

Proverbs, Precepts, and Monitory Pieces, Middle English
Bibliographies
> Cameron Louis offers a comprehensive guide to primary materials for Middle English proverbs and precepts with a bibliography of editions and criticism in Severs

and Hartung's *A Manual of the Writings in Middle English*, vol. XXI, pp. 2957-3048, 3349-3404.

James Purdy, 1923-
Bibliographies

For works by Purdy, see *First Printings of American Authors*, vol. 2, pp. 307-309. Purdy's manuscripts are listed in Robbins' *American Literary Manuscripts*, p. 261.

Howard Phelps Putnam, 1894-1948
Bibliographies

For works by Putnam, see *First Printings of American Authors*, vol. 2, p. 311. Putnam's manuscripts are listed in Robbins' *American Literary Manuscripts*, p. 262.

George Puttenham, c. 1529-1591
Bibliographies

For a bibliography of works by and about Puttenham, see *NCBEL*, I, p. 2312. Puttenham's manuscripts are described in *Index of English Literary Manuscripts*, I, pt. 2:363-64.

Mario Puzo, 1920-
Bibliographies

For works by Puzo, see *First Printings of American Authors*, vol. 5, pp. 263-64.

Howard Pyle, 1853-1911
Bibliographies

1107.   Morse, Willard Samuel, and Gertrude Brinckle. **Howard Pyle: A Record of His Illustrations and Writings**. 1921; reprint Detroit, MI: Singing Tree Press, 1969. 242p. LC 68-31099.

First published in 1921 by the Wilmington, Delaware, Society of the Fine Arts, Morse and Brinckle's guide describes Pyle's contributed writings and illustrations in periodicals (arranged by journal), Pyle's books, contributions to books, and miscellaneous works (including programs, book plates, posters, murals, and paintings). Chronologically arranged entries for Pyle's books give title-page transcriptions, collations, paginations, paper and binding information, contents, and brief notes on publishing histories, with citations for other appearances. Includes facsimiles of selected illustrations. Subject index of illustrations and general index of names and titles. Also for works by Pyle, see *Bibliography of American Literature*, vol. 7, pp. 183-91. Pyle's manuscripts are listed in Robbins' *American Literary Manuscripts*, p. 262. Criticism and reviews of Pyle's works in selected periodicals are identified in Wells' *The Literary Index to American Magazines, 1850-1900*, pp. 308-309. See *Bibliography of American Fiction 1866-1918*, pp. 310-11, for Mary Evelyn Tielking's checklist of works by and about Pyle.

Barbara Mary Crampton Pym, 1913-1980
Bibliographies

1108.   Salwak, Dale. **Barbara Pym: A Reference Guide**. Boston: G. K. Hall, 1991. 162p. (Reference Guide to Literature). LC 91-13044. ISBN 0-8161-9076-3.

Chronologically arranges descriptively annotated entries for about 750 writings about Pym from 1950 to 1991. Reviews of Pym's works published in newspapers constitute the bulk of the entries, although Salwak also identifies entries in reference works, interviews, and dissertations as well as scholarly books and articles. Index of authors, titles of works by and about Pym, and subjects offers good access, with references under headings for Jane Austen and Henry James as well as for bibliographies, biographies, and interviews under Pym. Also for a bibliography of works by and about Pym, see *NCBEL*, IV, p. 718.

Thomas Pynchon, 1937-

Bibliographies

1109.   Mead, Clifford. **Thomas Pynchon: A Bibliography of Primary and Secondary Materials**. Elmwood Park, IL: Dalkey Archive Press, 1989. 176p. LC 88-30415. ISBN 0-916583-37-6.

Covering works by and about Pynchon, Mead offers brief imprint information (with illustrations of dust jackets and details about bibliographic points) for Pynchon's books published from *V* (1963) through *Slow Learner* (1984), contributions to books and periodicals (including Pynchon's articles published in his high-school newspaper and appearances of his works in anthologies), unauthorized editions, translations, and dust-jacket blurbs and other advertisements (with selected excerpts). No detailed bibliographic descriptions are provided. In addition, Mead gives unannotated listings of about 1,500 works about Pynchon published from 1962 through 1988, covering reviews of Pynchon's works, conference papers, dissertations, non-English-language criticisms, and American, Canadian, and British dissertations and theses. An appendix reprints a selection of Pynchon's contributions to his high-school newspaper, with photographs of Pynchon from his school yearbook (which he edited). No indexing of any sort is provided. Mead's coverage of secondary works supersedes that offered in Robert M. Scotto's *Three Contemporary Novelists: An Annotated Bibliography of Works by and About John Hawkes, Joseph Heller, and Thomas Pynchon* (New York: Garland, 1977) and Thomas P. Walsh and Cameron Northouse's *John Barth, Jerzy Kosinski, and Thomas Pynchon: A Reference Guide* (entry 796). Also for published works by Pynchon, see *First Printings of American Authors*, vol. 1, p. 305. Pynchon's manuscripts are listed in Robbins' *American Literary Manuscripts*, p. 262. See *Bibliography of American Fiction, 1919-1988*, pp. 413-14, for Robert D. Newman's checklist of works by and about Pynchon. Khachig Tololyan gives a summary biography, critical assessment of major works, and selected primary and secondary bibliography for Pynchon in McCaffery's *Postmodern Fiction: A Bio-Bibliographical Guide*, pp. 488-91.

Journals

1110.   **Pynchon Notes**. Eau Claire, WI: University of Wisconsin—Eau Claire, 1979-. 2/yr. ISSN 0278-1891.

Most of the as many as 15 articles contained in issues (often double) of *Pynchon Notes* offer close readings of works and interpretations of themes, images, sources, allusions, and techniques. Contributions have also compared Pynchon and Salman Rushdie, Don DeLillo, and Vassily Aksyonov and examined the influences of Glenn Miller and Foucault. In addition, issues include a current bibliography of Pynchon scholarship (covering both publications and works in progress), with a list of other books received, and "Notes" about projects and forthcoming meetings. Publication is more than a year behind, and double issues are now the norm, reflecting an effort to bring the journal up to schedule. *Pynchon Notes* is indexed in *MLA*.

Francis Quarles, 1592-1644

Bibliographies

1111.   Horden, John. **Francis Quarles (1592-1644): A Bibliography of His Works to the Year 1800**. Oxford: Oxford Bibliographical Society, 1953. 83p. (Oxford Bibliographical Society Publications, new series, vol. 2 [for 1948]). LC 54-3638.

Chronologically arranges full bibliographic descriptions of first and subsequent editions and printings of Quarles' 29 separate works, terminating coverage at 1800 "to exclude the substantial numbers of nineteenth-century editions of *Emblemes*" (preface). Also excludes coverage of selected editions, works including contributions by Quarles, and chapbook versions and translations of Quarles' works. Entries give title-page transcriptions; collations; contents; details on variants; and brief notes on publication histories, with locations of examined copies.

Identifies 26 editions and variants of *Argalus and Parthenia* and 20 of *Emblemes and Hieroglyphikes*. Unindexed. Also for a bibliography of works by and about Quarles, see *NCBEL*, I, pp. 1199-1201.

David (William) Rabe, 1940-
Bibliographies

1112.   Kolin, Philip C. **David Rabe: A Stage History and a Primary and Secondary Bibliography**. New York: Garland, 1988. 273p. (Garland Reference Library of the Humanities, vol. 795). LC 87-21155.

Covers both works by and about Rabe. Following a brief account of Rabe's life and an introductory stage history for his works, Kolin lists brief information (bibliographic and stage production) for Rabe's plays; screenplays; novels; short stories; poems; prefaces and afterwords; newspaper articles; book, play, and movie reviews; miscellaneous writings, such as blurbs, advertisements, and lyrics; translations of Rabe's works; and interviews. In addition, Kolin arranges entries for about 1,100 works about Rabe in separate listings for bibliographies, biographies, critical studies (about 100 annotated entries), and production reviews (arranged by plays). A comprehensive index references such topics as "military life" and "myths" in relation to Rabe's works. Kolin's coverage supersedes that provided in King's *Ten Modern American Playwrights*, pp. 187-96. Rodney Simard reviews research on Rabe in *Contemporary Authors: Bibliographical Series: Volume 3: American Dramatists*, pp. 289-303.

Arthur Rackham, 1867-1939
Bibliographies

1113.   Riall, Richard. **A New Bibliography of Arthur Rackham**. Bath: Ross, 1994. 245p. LC 94-44941. ISBN 0-9523-3530-1.

Comprehensive international coverage of Rackham's published works from 1884 to the present (latest entry from 1981). Chronologically arranged biblio-graphic descriptions of works containing illustrations by Rackham in sections for books; miscellaneous books; contributions to periodicals (sublistings for *Cassell's Magazine*, *St. Nicholas Magazine*, *Little Folks*, and others); Haddon Hall Library trade editions; deluxe and limited editions; dust wrappers with original or added drawings; commercial work; theatrical work; ephemera (bookplates, greeting cards, etc.); "A Quandary," regarding an attribution to Rackham; and non-English-language editions. Entries for first and subsequent editions of Rackham's books give title-page transcriptions, binding and dust-jacket descriptions, and notes on publication histories. Descriptions of contents emphasize details related to Rackham's illustrations. Numerous color and other facsimile illustrations from Rackham's books and other works. Index of names and titles. Supersedes Sarah Briggs Latimore and Grace Clark Haskell's *Arthur Rackham: A Bibliography* (1936; reprint New York: Burt Franklin, 1970; Jacksonville, FL: Michael Blauer, San Marco Bookstore, 1987), which covered Rackham's works from 1896 to 1936, acknowledging that Rackham reported that his earliest work dated from the magazine *Scraps* in 1884 (p. [vii]). Also for a bibliography of works by and about Rackham, see *NCBEL*, III, p. 67.

Ann Radcliffe, 1764-1823
Bibliographies

1114.   Rogers, Deborah D. **Ann Radcliffe: A Bio-Bibliography**. Westport, CT: Greenwood Press, 1996. 209p. (Bio-Bibliographies in World Literature, no. 4). LC 95-41982. ISBN 0-313-28379-6.

A very brief chronology and the life of Radcliffe precede sections containing brief bibliographic information for editions and translations and chronologically arranged descriptions of early reviews and notices (subarranged by work for the period 1789-1826) and criticism through 1994, with separate, annotated listings for full-length works, dissertations, and bibliographies. Coverage includes non-English-language materials. Annotations readily identify major critical studies. Appends lists of adaptations and abridgments, with citations for reviews; parodies and imitations; and spurious attributions. Index of names, with the full range of topical subheadings under Radcliffe. Also for a bibliography of works by and about Radcliffe, see *NCBEL*, II, pp. 758-60. Radcliffe's manuscripts are described in *Index of English Literary Manuscripts*, III, pt. 3:167-68. Robert Donald Spector reviews research on Radcliffe in *The English Gothic: A Bibliographic Guide to Writers from Horace Walpole to Mary Shelley*, pp. 111-52.

Sir Walter Ralegh, 1554?-1618

Bibliographies

1115.   Armitage, Christopher M. **Sir Walter Ralegh: An Annotated Bibliography**. Chapel Hill, NC: University of North Carolina Press, 1987. 236p. LC 87-40134. ISBN 0-8078-1757-0.

This is the most comprehensive listing of works by and about Ralegh, including 1,967 entries for works appearing from 1576 through 1986. Armitage arranges entries in separate listings for works by or attributed to Ralegh; biographical studies; studies of Ralegh in relation to Britain, Europe, and the Old World; studies of Ralegh in relation to America and the New World; literary history and criticism; literature, music, and the visual arts; and bibliographies. Brief annotations are descriptive. An index of names enhances subject access. Supplemental coverage of modern scholarship on Ralegh is provided in Jerry Leath Mills' *Sir Walter Ralegh: A Reference Guide* (Boston: G. K. Hall, 1986), which chronologically arranges annotated entries for about 500 studies of Ralegh published from 1901 through 1984. In addition to longer descriptive annotations, Mills' work offers a detailed subject index. Both Armitage's and Mills' works complement T. N. Brushfield's *A Bibliography of Sir Walter Ralegh, Knt.*, 2d ed. (1908; reprint New York: Burt Franklin, 1968) and supersede coverage of Ralegh in Humphrey Tonkin's *Elizabethan Bibliographies Supplements*, no. 17. For a bibliography of works by and about Ralegh, see *NCBEL*, I, pp. 2214-19. Raleigh's manuscripts are described in *Index of English Literary Manuscripts*, I, pt. 2:365-445, 632-33.

Allan Ramsay, 1686-1758

Bibliographies

For a bibliography of works by and about Ramsay, see *NCBEL*, II, pp. 1965-73. Ramsay's manuscripts are described in *Index of English Literary Manuscripts*, III, pt. 3:169-261.

Ayn Rand, 1905-1982

Bibliographies

1116.   Perinn, Vincent L. **Ayn Rand: First Descriptive Bibliography**. Rockville, MD: Quill & Brush, 1990. 92p. LC 91-117230. ISBN 0-9610-4948-0.

Full bibliographic descriptions of works by Rand, chronologically arranged in sections for books; manuscripts, plays, and contributions to books; periodicals and pamphlets; magazine and newspapers articles and interviews; and audio and video recordings and radio and television programs. Data for separate publications include title-page and copyright-page transcriptions, collations, binding and dust-jacket descriptions, and notes on publication histories. Index for primary titles only. Rand's manuscripts are listed in Robbins' *American Literary Manuscripts*, p. 263. See *Bibliography of American Fiction, 1919-1988*, pp. 415-16, for Mimi Reisel Gladstein's checklist of works by and about Rand.

Dictionaries, Encyclopedias, and Handbooks

1117.   Binswanger, Harry. **Ayn Rand Lexicon: Objectivism from A to Z**. New York: New American Library, 1986. 535p. LC 86-8665. ISBN 0-453-00528-4.

Excerpts passages from Rand's philosophical writings and selected philosophical passages from Rand's fiction, with citations to each work and a "Conceptual Index" classifying the entries.

Thomas Randolph, 1605-1635
Bibliographies

For a bibliography of works by and about Randolph, see *NCBEL*, I, p. 1773. Randolph's manuscripts are described in *Index of English Literary Manuscripts*, II, pt. 2:183-223. See the Tannenbaums' *Elizabethan Bibliographies*, vol. 6, and George Robert Guffey's *Elizabethan Bibliographies Supplements*, no. 3.

John Crowe Ransom, 1888-1974
Bibliographies

1118.   Young, Thomas Daniel. **John Crowe Ransom: An Annotated Bibliography.** New York: Garland, 1982. 187p. (Garland Bibliographies of Modern Critics and Critical Schools, vol. 3; Garland Reference Library of the Humanities, vol. 354). LC 82-48279. ISBN 0-8240-9249-X.

Young arranges about 900 descriptively annotated entries for works by and about Ransom in separate listings, including books, poems, essays, reviews in periodicals, miscellanea, and biographical and critical materials (books, parts of books, articles, and dissertations). Coverage extends through the 1970s. For works by Ransom, see *First Printings of American Authors*, vol. 5, pp. 265-69. Ransom's manuscripts are listed in Robbins' *American Literary Manuscripts*, pp. 263-64. Research on Ransom is reviewed by John J. Hindle in Flora and Bain's *Fifty Southern Writers After 1900*, pp. 391-400.

Marjorie Kinnan Rawlings, 1896-1953
Bibliographies

1119.   Tarr, Rodger L. **Marjorie Kinnan Rawlings: A Descriptive Bibliography.** Pittsburgh, PA: University of Pittsburgh Press, 1996. 283p. (Pittsburgh Series in Bibliography). LC 95-24171. ISBN 0-822903920-7.

The standard guide to Rawlings' published writings. Tarr offers full bibliographic descriptions of Rawlings' works in chronologically arranged sections for separate publications, collections, contributions to books and pamphlets, contributions to serials (650 items published from 1910 to 1975), blurbs, and translations (130 items). Entries for 11 books (covering all printings of all editions in English through 1994) supply facsimiles of title and copyright pages; paginations; collations; contents; descriptions of typography, paper, bindings, and dust jackets; and extensive notes on publication histories and variants, with copy locations. Appendixes identify Rawlings' two movie scripts, five film adaptations of Rawlings' works, a radio address, and an unlocated poem. Also appends a list of five principal books about Rawlings. Thorough index of proper names and titles. Also for works by Rawlings, see *First Printings of American Authors*, vol. 2, pp. 313-14. Rawlings' manuscripts are listed in Robbins' *American Literary Manuscripts*, p. 264. See *Bibliography of American Fiction, 1919-1988*, pp. 417-18, for Tarr's checklist of works by and about Rawlings. See the review of research by Samuel I. Bellman in Duke, Bryer, and Inge's *American Women Writers*, pp. 353-78; and Owen Gilman in Flora and Bain's *Fifty Southern Writers After 1900*, pp. 401-10.

Journals

1120.   **The Marjorie Kinnan Rawlings Journal of Florida Literature**. Normal, IL: Marjorie Kinnan Rawlings Society/Journal of Florida Literature, 1988- . Annual. ISSN 1060-3409.

The journal's title belies the contents of the former *Rawlings Journal* (1988-89) in that the annual usually focuses on far more than Rawlings and Florida literature. Articles have examined the works of Rawlings in addition to those of the likes of James Weldon Johnson, Alice Walker, Zora Neale Hurston, and Richard Wright. Typical articles include "Gender and Mothering in *The Yearling*" and "Engendering Fictions: Rawlings and a Female Tradition of Southern Writing." Other articles have examined depictions of Florida and the South in the works of James Branch Cabell, Ernest Hemingway, and Ring Lardner. Occasional bibliographic contributions describe collections in libraries in Florida. *The Marjorie Kinnan Rawlings Journal of Florida Literature* is indexed in *MLA*.

Thomas Buchanan Read, 1822-1872
Bibliographies
　　　For works by Read, see *Bibliography of American Literature*, vol. 7, pp. 192-212. Contributions by Read and criticism and reviews of Read's works in selected periodicals are identified in Wells' *The Literary Index to American Magazines, 1815-1865*, pp. 125-26; and *The Literary Index to American Magazines, 1850-1900*, pp. 309-10. Read's manuscripts are listed in Robbins' *American Literary Manuscripts*, p. 265.

Charles Reade, 1814-1884
Bibliographies
　　　Parrish and Miller's *Wilkie Collins and Charles Reade* (entry 282) gives full bibliographic descriptions of Reade's works. Contributions by Reade and criticism and reviews of Reade's works in selected periodicals are identified in Wells' *The Literary Index to American Magazines, 1815-1865*, p. 126; and *The Literary Index to American Magazines, 1850-1900*, pp. 310-11. Also for a bibliography of works by and about Read, see *NCBEL*, III, pp. 878-82.

John (Francisco) Rechy, 1934-
Bibliographies
　　　For works by Rechy, see *First Printings of American Authors*, vol. 3, pp. 285-86.

Ishmael (Scott) Reed, 1938-
Bibliographies
1121.　Settle, Elizabeth A., and Thomas A. Settle. **Ishmael Reed: A Primary and Secondary Bibliography**. Boston: G. K. Hall, 1982. 155p. (A Reference Publication in Afro-American Studies). LC 81-20035. ISBN 0-8161-8514-X.
　　　The Settles describe works by and about Reed in separate listings. Entries for primary materials published from 1967 through 1981 cover Reed's novels; edited works; excerpts and shorter works; articles, reviews, and interviews (with summaries); poems in anthologies; poems published separately; and sound and videotape recordings. Descriptively annotated entries for about 700 books, parts of books, articles, reviews, and dissertations in all languages about Reed are also included. Significant studies receive detailed descriptions. The Settles' guide supersedes their earlier *Ishmael Reed: An Annotated Checklist* (Dominguez Hills, CA: California State College, 1977), which covers Reed's works through 1977. Also for works by Reed, see *First Printings of American Authors*, vol. 2, pp. 315-16. See *Bibliography of American Fiction, 1919-1988*, pp. 418-19, for Reginald Martin and Margaret Donovan DuPriest's checklist of works by and about Reed. Jerry W. Ward, Jr., surveys works by and about Reed in Bain and Flora's *Contemporary Poets, Dramatists, Essayists, and Novelists of the South*, pp. 407-17.

Sampson Reed, 1800-1880
Bibliographies
　　　Reed's manuscripts are listed in Robbins' *American Literary Manuscripts*, p. 266. Elizabeth A. Meese reviews research on Reed in Myerson's *The Transcendentalists*, pp. 372-74.

Clara Reeve, 1729-1807
Bibliographies

For a bibliography of works by and about Reeve, see *NCBEL*, II, p. 149. Robert Donald Spector reviews research on Reeve in *The English Gothic: A Bibliographic Guide to Writers from Horace Walpole to Mary Shelley*, pp. 83-110.

Robert Reginald (Michael Burgess, Boden Clarke), 1948-
Bibliographies

1122.   Burgess, Michael. **The Work of Robert Reginald: An Annotated Bibliography & Guide**. 2d ed., revised and expanded. San Bernardino, CA: Borgo Press, 1992. 176p. (Bibliographies of Modern Authors, no. 5). LC 87-6306. ISBN 0-8095-0505-3.

A self-authored and self-published book. Describes works by and about Reginald in separate sections for books, short nonfiction, short fiction, editorial credits, documents, catalogs, book production and design, unpublished works, juvenilia, public appearances, works about Reginald (56 entries, mostly unannotated, for citations in reference works), honors and awards, and miscellanea. Entries for 87 books (including those by others under Boden Clarke's general editorship) note publication histories, summarize plots and contents, and give citations for reviews. Also includes a Reginald chronology; selected quotes from critics; and an "Afterword," by Jack Dann. Title index.

Frederic Sackrider Remington, 1861-1909
Bibliographies

1123.   McCracken, Harold. **Frederic Remington, Artist of the Old West: With a Bibliographical Check List of Remington Pictures and Books**. Philadelphia, PA: J. B. Lippincott, 1947. 157p. LC 47-11799.

Contains "Bibliographic Check List of Remingtoniana" (pp. 123-57), "intended primarily as a complete record of Frederic Remington's pictures and the publications in which they have appeared" (p. 123). Identifies first appearances of 2,739 Remington pictures in classified listings for periodicals (by name of publication), books written and illustrated by Remington, books and portfolios of Remington's pictures, books illustrated entirely or in part, books containing references to Remington or his works (21 items), and Remington's bronzes. Entries for books give contents and size and binding descriptions. Also for works by Remington, see *Bibliography of American Literature*, vol. 7, pp. 213-17. Remington's contributions to and reviews of Remington's works in selected periodicals are identified in Wells' *The Literary Index to American Magazines, 1850-1900*, p. 311. Remington's manuscripts are listed in Robbins' *American Literary Manuscripts*, p. 267. Ben Merchant Vorpahl surveys works by and about Remington in Erisman and Etulain's *Fifty Western Writers*, pp. 358-68.

Sir Joshua Reynolds, 1723-1792
Bibliographies

For a bibliography of works by and about Reynolds, see *NCBEL*, II, pp. 1176-78, by John Barnard. Also available is Frederick W. Hilles' catalog, *An Exhibition of Books, Manuscripts & Prints Pertaining to Sir Joshua Reynolds: On the Two Hundred and Fiftieth Anniversary of His Birth: The Beinecke Rare Book & Manuscript Library and Sterling Memorial Library, Yale University, May-July, 1973* (New Haven, CT: Yale University Library, 1973), containing 218 brief, descriptive entries chronologically arranged in sections for correspondence to and from Reynolds (including letters to Samuel Johnson, Edmund Burke, and James Boswell), 11 notebooks and commonplace books, miscellaneous manuscripts (largely notes and drafts on the likes of Pope, Johnson, and various topics), related manuscripts and letters, Reynolds' published writings (including many presentation copies), books from Reynolds' library, publications associated with Reynolds, and Reynolds' drawings and engravings. Described materials are substantially from collections at Yale.

Eugene Manlove Rhodes, 1869-1934
Bibliographies
1124.   Hutchinson, W. H. **A Bar Cross Liar: Bibliography of Eugene Manlove Rhodes Who Loved the West-That-Was When He Was Young.** Stillwater, OK: Redlands Press, 1959. 94p. LC 60-17854.

Covers works by and about Rhodes. Chronologically arranges bibliographic information for magazine appearances, with notes on contents and reprintings; Rhodes' 16 books; booklets; book and booklet notes; Henry Wallace Phillips' Books; an unfinished manuscript, now in the Rhodes Collection of the Huntington Library; and motion-picture adaptations. Entries for books give brief bibliographic information, notes on other editions and publication histories, and excerpts from selected contemporary reviews. Also contains annotated entries for about 100 major reviews and critical opinions of Rhodes' works (largely from newspapers). Other sections identify works that include passing references and miscellaneous notices for Rhodes. Additionally, Hutchinson provides several brief dictionary listings for selected characters, real and fictional places, "cow outfits," and expressions in Rhodes' writings. Unindexed. See *Bibliography of American Fiction, 1866-1918*, pp. 311-12, for Gwen L. Nagel's checklist of works by and about Rhodes. Rhodes' manuscripts are listed in Robbins' *American Literary Manuscripts*, p. 267. Edwin W. Gaston, Jr., surveys works by and about Rhodes in Erisman and Etulain's *Fifty Western Writers*, pp. 369-78.

Jean Rhys (Ella Gwendolyn Rees Williams), 1890?-1979
Bibliographies
1125.   Mellown, Elgin W. **Jean Rhys: A Descriptive and Annotated Bibliography of Works and Criticism.** New York: Garland, 1984. 218p. (Garland Reference Library of the Humanities, vol. 435). LC 83-48267. ISBN 0-8240-9079-9.

Mellown provides separate listings of Rhys' books and separate publications (with citations to reviews); contributions to books; contributions to periodicals; translations of others' writings about Rhys; television, radio, and film adaptations of works; musical adaptations; and recordings; in addition to descriptively annotated entries for writings about Rhys in books, parts of books, and articles. Entries for primary materials include title-page transcriptions, collations, contents, and publishing histories. Mellown's coverage of works by and about Rhys supersedes Stanton's *A Bibliography of Modern British Novelists*, pp. 753-69, 1096.

Journals
1126.   **Jean Rhys Review.** New York: Jean Rhys Review, 1986-. 2/yr. ISSN 0889-7596.

Now published in double issues through vol. 10 (in an attempt to bring the journal back up to date), *Jean Rhys Review* features critical, biographical, and comparative studies of Rhys' life and works and reviews of new publications. In addition, issues regularly include a bibliography of recent editions and international criticism, reviews, and dissertations. Also contains a section of queries and announcements regarding projects and conferences. *Jean Rhys Review* is indexed in *MLA*.

Alice Hegan (Caldwell) Rice, 1870-1942
Bibliographies
See *Bibliography of American Fiction, 1866-1918*, p. 313, for Thomas L. Wilmeth's checklist of works by and about Rice. Rice's manuscripts are listed in Robbins' *American Literary Manuscripts*, p. 268.

Elmer Rice (Elmer Reizenstein), 1892-1967
Bibliographies
1127. Vanden Heuvel, Michael. **Elmer Rice: A Research and Production Sourcebook**. Westport, CT: Greenwood Press, 1996. 242p. (Modern Dramatists Research and Production Sourcebooks, no. 9). LC 95-39030. ISBN 0-313-27431-2.

Vanden Heuvel summarizes the plots of Rice's 35 plays, with references to reviews and critical assessments; briefly identifies Rice's published and unpublished works in sections for nondramatic writings, dramatic publications, and unpublished collected materials in the University of Texas' Humanities Research Center, Library of Congress, and New York Public Library's Billy Rose Collection; and separately lists chronologically arranged annotated entries for 376 reviews and 161 critical works (including dissertations) from 1914 to 1994. Also gives credits for major productions, with references to reviews. Index of names, titles, and selected topics. Rice's manuscripts are also listed in Robbins' *American Literary Manuscripts*, p. 268. Vanden Heuvel identifies works by and about Rice in Demastes' *American Playwrights, 1880-1945*, pp. 348-61.

Dorothy Miller Richardson, 1873-1957
Bibliographies
For a bibliography of works by and about Richardson, see *NCBEL*, IV, pp. 721-22.

Samuel Richardson, 1689-1761
Bibliographies
1128. Sale, William M., Jr. **Samuel Richardson: A Bibliographical Record of His Literary Career**. New Haven, CT: Yale University Press, 1936. 165p. LC 37-1046.

Sale offers full bibliographic descriptions of English editions of Richardson's books as well as his contributions to periodicals. A comprehensive primary bibliography covering international editions of Richardson's writings needs to be completed. Available in a reprinted edition (Hamden, CT: Archon Books, 1969). Also for John Carroll's bibliography of works by and about Richardson, see *NCBEL*, II, pp. 917-25. Richardson's manuscripts are described in *Index of English Literary Manuscripts*, III, pt. 3:263-72.

1129. Smith, Sarah W. R. **Samuel Richardson: A Reference Guide**. Boston: G. K. Hall, 1984. 425p. (A Reference Guide to Literature). LC 83-18557. ISBN 0-8161-8170-5.

Superseding Francesco Cordasco's *Samuel Richardson: A List of Critical Studies Published from 1896 to 1946* (Brooklyn, NY: Long Island University Press, 1948), Smith chronologically arranges (from 1723 through 1978) annotated entries for about 1,800 works by and about Richardson. Coverage of early and international editions is notable. Annotations are selective and generally objective. Important works are described in detail. Dissertations are unannotated. Several appendixes list novels, plays, juvenilia, and poetry influenced by Richardson. The comprehensive index offers broad subheadings that make topical access difficult. Several "look-ups" are needed to locate studies on similar specific topics. Richard Gordon Hannaford's *Samuel Richardson: An Annotated Bibliography of Critical Studies* (New York: Garland, 1980) offers similar coverage of Richardson scholarship in a topical arrangement. Research on Richardson is reviewed by John Carroll in Dyson's *The English Novel*, pp. 56-70.

Dictionaries, Encyclopedias, and Handbooks

See Johnson's *Plots and Characters in the Fiction of Eighteenth-Century English Authors* (entry 1309).

Journals

"Recent Articles" in *The Scriblerian and the Kit Cats* (entry 1084) regularly includes a selection of reviews of studies on Richardson.

Conrad (Michael) Richter, 1890-1968

Bibliographies

For works by Richter, see *First Printings of American Authors*, vol. 1, pp. 307-309. Richter's manuscripts are listed in Robbins' *American Literary Manuscripts*, p. 269. See *Bibliography of American Fiction, 1919-1988*, pp. 420-21, for Charles W. Mann's checklist of works by and about Richter. William T. Pilkington surveys works by and about Richter in Erisman and Etulain's *Fifty Western Writers*, pp. 379-88.

Edgell Rickword, 1898-1982

Bibliographies

Munton and Young's *Seven Writers of the English Left*, pp. 25-81, chronologically arranges descriptions of Rickword's publications, including non-English-language editions, from 1919 through 1980. Also for a bibliography of works by and about Rickword, see *NCBEL*, IV, p. 1366.

Riddles, Old English

Bibliographies

Greenfield and Robinson's *A Bibliography of Publications on Old English Literature to the End of 1972*, pp. 256-62, lists editions, translations, and studies of the Old English *Riddles*, with citations for reviews. *NCBEL*, I, pp. 296-99, also lists editions and studies.

Laura Riding (Laura Reichenthal), 1901-1991

Bibliographies

1130.   Wexler, Joyce Piell. **Laura Riding: A Bibliography**. New York: Garland, 1981. 173p. (Garland Reference Library of the Humanities, vol. 224). LC 80-8481. ISBN 0-8240-9476-x.

Wexler gives full bibliographic descriptions (title-page transcriptions, physical details, and publishing histories, with selective illustrations) of Riding's writings in separate, chronologically arranged listings for her major works, including books, periodicals, collaborative works, and translations; contributed poetry in books and periodicals; contributed prose in books and periodicals; poems in anthologies; entries in reference works; collections of manuscripts and letters; and broadcasts and recordings; in addition to listing descriptions of 165 works about Riding. Also for a bibliography of published works by and about Riding, see *NCBEL*, IV, p. 1371. Riding's manuscripts are listed in Robbins' *American Literary Manuscripts*, p. 269.

James Whitcomb Riley, 1849-1916

Bibliographies

1131.   Russo, Anthony J., and Dorothy Russo. **A Bibliography of James Whitcomb Riley**. Indianapolis, IN: Indiana Historical Society, 1944. 351p. LC 44-41917. ISBN 0-8383-1418-x.

The standard bibliography of Riley's primary materials, the Russos' guide gives full bibliographic details in separate listings for Riley's books, ephemeral publications (broadsides, leaflets, cards, music, and the like), contributions to books and journals, reprint editions, sheet music, collected works, and attributed works. Also contains listings for Rileyana and other works about Riley. Entries for books give title-page transcriptions, physical descriptions, and publication histories, with illustrations of title pages and bindings. Additional information about Riley's works is provided in Blanck's *Bibliography of American Literature*, vol. 7, pp. 218-72. Criticism and reviews of Riley's works in selected periodicals are identified in Wells' *The Literary Index to American Magazines, 1850-1900*, pp. 312-13. Riley's manuscripts are listed in Robbins' *American Literary Manuscripts*, p. 270.

Journals

See Patterson's *Author Newsletters and Journals*, p. 260, for previously published journals for Riley.

Mary Roberts Rinehart, 1876-1958
Bibliographies

See *Bibliography of American Fiction, 1866-1918*, pp. 314-15, for Nancy W. Shankle's checklist of works by and about Rinehart. Rinehart's manuscripts are listed in Robbins' *American Literary Manuscripts*, p. 270.

George Ripley, 1802-1880
Bibliographies

For works by Ripley, see *First Printings of American Authors*, vol. 3, pp. 287-89. Contributions by Ripley and criticism and reviews of Ripley's works in selected periodicals are identified in Wells' *The Literary Index to American Magazines, 1815-1865*, pp. 127-28; and *The Literary Index to American Magazines, 1850-1900*, p. 313. Ripley's manuscripts are listed in Robbins' *American Literary Manuscripts*, pp. 270-71. Charles Crowe reviews research on Ripley in Myerson's *The Transcendentalists*, pp. 242-49.

Sophia Dana Ripley, fl. 1820s-1847?
Bibliographies

Charles Crowe reviews research on Sophia Ripley in Myerson's *The Transcendentalists*, pp. 250-52.

Tomas Rivera, 1935-1984
Bibliographies

See *Bibliography of American Fiction, 1919-1988*, pp. 421-23, for Oscar Samoza's checklist of works by and about Rivera.

Amelie Rives, Princess Troubetzkoy, 1863-1945
Bibliographies

Contributions by Troubetzkoy and reviews of Troubetzkoy's works in selected periodicals are identified in Wells' *The Literary Index to American Magazines, 1850-1900*, pp. 313-14. Longest's *Three Virginia Writers* (entry 743) chronologically describes writings about Troubetzkoy published from 1887 to 1974.

Elizabeth Madox Roberts, 1881-1941
Bibliographies

For works by Roberts, see *First Printings of American Authors*, vol. 2, pp. 317-19. Roberts' manuscripts are listed in Robbins' *American Literary Manuscripts*, p. 271. See *Bibliography of American Fiction 1866-1918*, pp. 316-17, for Gwen L. Nagel's checklist of works by and about Roberts. Research on Roberts is reviewed by William H. Slavick in Flora and Bain's *Fifty Southern Writers After 1900*, pp. 411-22.

Kenneth (Lewis) Roberts, 1885-1957

Bibliographies

1132. Bales, Jack. **Kenneth Roberts: The Man and His Works**. Metuchen, NJ: Scarecrow Press, 1989. 312p. (Scarecrow Author Bibliographies, no. 85). LC 89-34008. ISBN 0-8108-2227-X.

Following an extensive biographical introduction, Bales describes 988 works about Roberts in separate listings for book reviews (some 456 entries arranged by works reviewed), biographies and bibliographies, parts of books and passing references, journal and newspaper articles, theses and dissertations, film reviews, and other miscellaneous writings. Appendixes list editions and translations of Roberts' novels, special collections (pp. 267-75), and other primary materials. Also for works by Roberts, see *First Printings of American Authors*, vol. 2, pp. 321-32. Roberts' manuscripts are listed in Robbins' *American Literary Manuscripts*, pp. 271-72. See *Bibliography of American Fiction, 1919-1988*, pp. 424-26, for Bales' checklist of works by and about Roberts.

T(homas) W(illiam) Robertson, 1829-1871

Bibliographies

For a bibliography of works by and about Robertson, see *NCBEL*, III, pp. 1141-44.

Edwin Arlington Robinson, 1869-1935

Bibliographies

1133. Hogan, Charles Beecher. **A Bibliography of Edwin Arlington Robinson**. New Haven, CT: Yale University Press, 1936. 221p. LC 37-1224.

The standard bibliography of Robinson's primary works, Hogan's guide gives full bibliographic details in separate listings for Robinson's separately published books and pamphlets, contributions to periodicals and newspapers, uncollected works, translations, and attributed works, in addition to listing secondary biographical and critical writings about Robinson. Also available in a reprinted edition (Folcroft, PA: Folcroft Press, 1969). Hogan's "Edwin Arlington Robinson: New Bibliographical Notes," *PBSA* 35 (1941): 115-44; and William White's *Edwin Arlington Robinson: A Supplementary Bibliography* (Kent, OH: Kent State University Press, 1971) correct and update the bibliography through 1970. Also for works by Robinson, see *First Printings of American Authors*, vol. 2, pp. 333-44. Robinson's manuscripts are listed in Robbins' *American Literary Manuscripts*, p. 272. A. Carl Bredahl describes Robinson's primary works in *The Edwin Arlington Robinson Collection* in part 4 in Sidney Ives' *The Parkman Dexter Howe Library* (Gainesville, FL: University of Florida, 1986). In addition, James Humphrey III's *The Library of Edwin Arlington Robinson: A Descriptive Catalogue* (Waterville, ME: Colby College Press, 1950); and Richard Cary's "Robinson Books and Periodicals: I," *Colby Library Quarterly* 8 (March 1969): 266-77; "Robinson Books and Periodicals: II," *Colby Library Quarterly* 8 (June 1969): 334-43; "Robinson Books and Periodicals: III," *Colby Library Quarterly* 8 (September 1969): 399-413; and "Robinson's Manuscripts and Letters," *Colby Library Quarterly* 8 (December 1969): 479-87, describe Robinson materials at Colby College.

1134. Joyner, Nancy Carol. **Edwin Arlington Robinson: A Reference Guide**. Boston: G. K. Hall, 1978. 223p. (Reference Publications in Literature). LC 77-25280. ISBN 0-8161-7807-0.

Joyner provides a chronologically arranged, annotated listing of about 1,400 criticisms of Robinson published from 1894 through 1976. Coverage includes reviews and dissertations. Although annotations are objective, Joyner consistently indicates important or standard works. Thorough and useful indexing for critics, primary titles, secondary book titles, and selected subjects (mainly concentrated as subheadings under Robinson's name). Research on Robinson is reviewed by Ellsworth Barnard in Bryer's *Sixteen Modern American Authors*, pp. 473-98; and its supplement by Barnard in Bryer's *Sixteen Modern American Authors: Volume 2: A Survey of Research and Criticism Since 1972*, pp. 558-81.

Indexes and Concordances

1135.   Sundermeir, Michael William. **A Concordance to the Poetry of Edwin Arlington Robinson**. Ph.D. dissertation, Lincoln, NE: University of Nebraska, 1972. 4 vols. OCLC 3987808.

The concordance is based on the *Collected Poems of Edwin Arlington Robinson* (New York: Macmillan, 1937).

Rowland Evans Robinson, 1833-1900

Bibliographies

For works by Robinson, see *Bibliography of American Literature*, vol. 7, pp. 273-78. Robinson's manuscripts are listed in Robbins' *American Literary Manuscripts*, p. 272.

John Wilmot, 2nd Earl of Rochester, 1647-1680

Bibliographies

1136.   Prinz, Johannes. **John Wilmot, Earl of Rochester: His Life and Writings, with His Lordship's Private Correspondence, Various Other Documents, and a Bibliography of His Works and of the Literature on Him**. Leipzig: Mayer & Muller, 1927. 460p. (Palaestra, Band 154). LC 28-11527.

Contains a technically dated but very detailed "Bibliographical Appendix" of Rochester's published works and manuscripts and works about Rochester through 1927 (pp. [303]-443), with transcriptions of manuscripts and otherwise unpublished documents. Entries in Part I for Rochester's works give title-page transcriptions, collations, contents, bibliographic notes, and shelf marks (in the British Museum, Bodleian, Bibliotheque Nationale in Paris, etc.) in consecutively (but confusingly) numbered separate listings for: (a) six poems separately published as broadsides and pamphlets; poems in contemporary collections and miscellanies, in modern anthologies (from Ritson's collection published in 1783 to 1923), and in "various" other works, including dramatic prologues and epilogues, selections in modern collections of quotations and proverbs, and excerpted lines in literary biographies and histories; collected editions of the poems to 1821; translations of the poems; and poems in manuscripts; (b) separate, selected, modern, and translated editions and manuscripts of the two plays; (c) separate and selected editions and manuscripts of the letters; (d) other prose writings; and (e) spurious publications. Includes many facsimiles of title pages and manuscripts. Part II, "The Literature of the Earl of Rochester," classifies approximately 300 contemporary allusions and more recent scholarship in sections for historiography (contemporary and early sources, modern biography and criticism), fiction (including nineteenth-century historical and romantic novels based on Rochester's life); and elegies. Most entries note subsequent appearances, contents, manuscripts, and shelf marks. Unindexed. Extremely useful for descriptions of works by and early works about Rochester.

1137.   Veith, David M. **Rochester Studies, 1925-1982: An Annotated Bibliography**. New York: Garland, 1984. 174p. (Garland Reference Library of the Humanities, vol. 457). LC 83-49078. ISBN 0-8240-9022-5.

The most comprehensive bibliography of works about Rochester, Veith's volume separately lists editions of Rochester's works and extensive and detailed descriptions of about 400 general bibliographies, criticisms of individual poems, and studies of prose, drama, and biography. Appends annotated entries for dissertations and theses. A comprehensive index of titles, first lines, and names gives access. Coverage is superior to that provided by George Wasserman's *Samuel Butler and the Earl of Rochester* (entry 201), which covers Rochester scholarship through 1983. For a bibliography of works by and about Rochester, see *NCBEL*, II, 464-66, by Curt A. Zimansky. Rochester's manuscripts are described in *Index of English Literary Manuscripts*, II, pt. 2:225-87.

Indexes and Concordances

1138.   Moehlmann, John Frederick. **A Concordance to the Complete Poems of John Wilmot, Earl of Rochester**. Troy, NY: Whitston, 1979. 338p. LC 78-69872. ISBN 0-87875-164-5.

Moehlmann bases the concordance on David M. Veith's *The Complete Poems of John Wilmot, Earl of Rochester* (New Haven, CT: Yale University Press, 1968), the standard edition of Rochester's poetry.

Journals

"Recent Articles" in *The Scriblerian and the Kit Cats* (entry 1084) regularly includes a selection of reviews of studies on Wilmot (Rochester).

Ross Rocklynne, 1913-

Bibliographies

1139.   Menville, Douglas. **The Work of Ross Rocklynne: An Annotated Bibliography & Guide**. San Bernardino, CA: Borgo Press, 1989. 70p. (Bibliographies of Modern Authors, no. 17). LC 88-34360. ISBN 0-8095-0511-8.

Describes works by and about Rocklynne in separate sections for books, short fiction, nonfiction, fanzine contributions, radio productions, juvenilia, works about Rocklynne (25 selectively annotated entries), unpublished works, and miscellanea. Entries for Rocklynne's two books give brief publication histories, describe contents, and note reviews. Entries for other primary works contain selective annotations. Also includes an introduction, a Rocklynne chronology, and selected quotes from critics. Title index.

E(dward) P(ayson) Roe, 1838-1888

Bibliographies

For works by Roe, see *Bibliography of American Literature*, vol. 7, pp. 279-91. Roe's contributions to and reviews of Roe's works in selected periodicals are identified in Wells' *The Literary Index to American Magazines, 1850-1900*, pp. 314-15. Roe's manuscripts are listed in Robbins' *American Literary Manuscripts*, p. 273. See *Bibliography of American Fiction, 1866-1918*, pp. 317-18, for Yanwing Leung's checklist of works by and about Roe.

Theodore Roethke, 1908-1963

Bibliographies

1140.   McLeod, James Richard. **Theodore Roethke: A Bibliography**. Kent, OH: Kent State University Press, 1973. 241p. (The Serif Series: Bibliographies and Checklists, no. 27). LC 72-158715. ISBN 0-8733-8100-9.

McLeod gives full bibliographic details for Roethke's works in separate listings for books, contributions to books, contributions to periodicals (some 262 entries), international editions and translations, films and recordings, and musical backgrounds and settings. Entries provide title-page transcriptions, collations, contents, and publishing histories. In addition, McLeod arranges secondary works by formats (bibliographies, biographies, criticism and reviews, dedications, and the like). Of particular value is a list of non-English-language criticisms. McLeod's bibliography offers the best coverage of Roethke's primary materials as well as secondary materials in all languages. Also for works by Roethke, see *First Printings of American Authors*, vol. 1, pp. 311-13. Roethke's manuscripts are listed in Robbins' *American Literary Manuscripts*, p. 273. McLeod's *Theodore Roethke: A Manuscript Checklist* (Kent, OH: Kent State University Press, 1971) identifies collections of Roethke's manuscripts, including the important collection at the University of Washington. Coverage of secondary materials in English is superseded by Moul's guide (entry 1141).

1141.   Moul, Keith R. **Theodore Roethke's Career: An Annotated Bibliography**. Boston: G. K. Hall, 1977. 254p. (Reference Guides in Literature). LC 76-50593. ISBN 0-8161-7892-2.

Following an extensive, classified checklist of Roethke's primary materials, Moul chronologically arranges annotated entries for about 1,500 works about Roethke published from 1922 through 1973. Coverage includes books, parts of books, journal and newspaper articles and reviews, and dissertations. Annotations are descriptive and critical. Important works receive detailed reviews. Research on Roethke is reviewed by Rosemary Sullivan in Erisman and Etulain's *Fifty Western Writers*, pp. 389-401; and James R. McLeod and Judith A. Sylte in *Contemporary Authors: Bibliographical Series: Volume 2: American Poets*, pp. 269-305.

Indexes and Concordances

1142.   Lane, Gary. **A Concordance to the Poems of Theodore Roethke**. Metuchen, NJ: Scarecrow Press, 1972. 484p. LC 77-188503. ISBN 0-8108-0514-6.

Concords texts of 209 poems published in *The Collected Poems of Theodore Roethke* (New York: Doubleday, 1966; and London: Faber and Faber, 1968). Table of word frequencies.

Samuel Rogers, 1763-1855
Bibliographies

For a bibliography of works by and about Rogers, see *NCBEL*, III, pp. 181-82.

Richard Rolle, c. 1300-1349
Bibliographies

1143.   Lagorio, Valerie Marie, and Ritamary Bradley. **The 14th-Century English Mystics: A Comprehensive Annotated Bibliography**. New York: Garland, 1981. 197p. (Garland Reference Library of the Humanities, vol. 190). LC 79-7922. ISBN 0-8240-9535-9.

Lagorio and Bradley describe twentieth-century general background and critical studies of medieval English religious mysticism as well as editions and studies of five prominent mystical writers, including Rolle, Walter Hilton, Julian of Norwich, Margery Kempe, and the author of *The Cloud of Unknowing*. Provides about 150 entries for Rolle; 40 for *The Cloud*; 60 for Hilton; 120 for Dame Julian; and 27 for Mistress Kemp. Annotations are critical and evaluative. This supersedes in coverage Michael E. Sawyer's *A Bibliographical Index of Five English Mystics* (Pittsburgh, PA: The Clifford E. Barbour Library, Pittsburgh Theological Seminary, 1978), which describes editions and studies of these writers through 1976. Lagorio and Michael G. Sargent offer more comprehensive information about primary materials for Rolle and other English mystics with a bibliography of editions and criticism in Severs and Hartung's *A Manual of the Writings in Middle English*, vol. XXIII, pp. 3049-3137, 3405-71. Also available is Hope Emily Allen's *Writings Ascribed to Richard Roole, Hermit of Hampole and Materials for His Biography* (New York: Modern Language Association of America, 1927; reprint New York: Kraus Reprint, 1966). For a bibliography of works by and about Rolle, see *NCBEL*, I, pp. 517-20. Edwards' *Middle English Prose* includes reviews of research on Rolle by John A. Alford (pp. 35-60); on Walter Hilton and *The Cloud of Unknowing* by Alastair Minnis (pp. 61-82); on Julian of Norwich by Christina Von Nolcken (pp. 97-108); and on Margery Kempe by John C. Hirsh (pp. 109-20).

O(le) E(dvart) Rolvaag, 1876-1931

Bibliographies

     See *Bibliography of American Fiction, 1919-1988*, pp. 426-28, for Gerald Thorson's checklist of works by and about Rolvaag. Barbara Howard Meldrum surveys works by and about Rolvaag in Erisman and Etulain's *Fifty Western Writers*, pp. 402-14.

Christina Georgina Rossetti, 1830-1894

Bibliographies

    1144. Crump, Rebecca W. **Christina Rossetti: A Reference Guide**. Boston: G. K. Hall, 1976. 172p. (Reference Guides in Literature). LC 75-28008. ISBN 0-8161-7847-x.

    Crump briefly describes about 450 biographical and critical materials about Rossetti published in books, parts of books, articles, reviews of Rossetti's works and of works about Rossetti, introductions in editions and anthologies, and dissertations from 1862 through 1973. Annotations are descriptive. Subject headings in the author-title index reference broad topics, such as "bibliography," "biography," and "obituaries." Ehrsam's *Bibliographies of Twelve Victorian Authors*, pp. [189]-99, cites international comments, criticism, and reviews for Rossetti through the early twentieth century. For a bibliography of works by and about Rossetti, see *NCBEL*, III, pp. 496-500. See the review of research by William E. Fredeman in Faverty's *The Victorian Poets*, pp. 284-93.

Indexes and Concordances

    1145. Jimenez, Nilda. **The Bible and the Poetry of Christina Rossetti: A Concordance**. Westport, CT: Greenwood Press, 1979. 258p. LC 78-74651. ISBN 0-313-21196-5.

    Jimenez gives parallel texts of passages from Rossetti's works and the King James version of the Bible. The index is based on dated poems included in the *Poetical Works* (London: Macmillan, 1928), *New Poems* (London: Macmillan, 1896), and other selected editions.

Dante Gabriel Rossetti, 1828-1882

Bibliographies

    1146. Fennell, Francis L. **Dante Gabriel Rossetti: An Annotated Bibliography**. New York: Garland, 1982. 282p. (Garland Reference Library of the Humanities, vol. 286). LC 80-9034. ISBN 0-8240-9327-5.

    Covering works by and about Rossetti, Fennell provides classified listings of annotated entries for bibliographies; "Source Materials for Literary Works," describing first and later editions and manuscripts; "Source Materials for Artistic Works"; editions of Rossetti's published letters; biographies and biographical studies; general criticisms and critical studies of individual works; critical studies of Rossetti as an artist; "Studies of Rossetti as a Poet-Painter"; and dissertations. Descriptive annotations are provided for all items except non-English-language criticisms and dissertations. Fennell critically describes significant works in detail. Identifying about 1,000 secondary works published from Rossetti's death in 1882 through 1980, Fennell's guide attempts to supersede coverage of Rossetti in William E. Fredeman's *Pre-Raphaelitism: A Bibliocritical Study* (Cambridge: Harvard University Press, 1965). Supplementing coverage of Rossetti's primary works, William Michael Rossetti's *Bibliography of the Works of Dante Gabriel Rossetti* (London: Ellis, 1905; reprint New York: AMS, 1971) contains full bibliographic descriptions of Rossetti's separate and contributed writings and illustrations. Also available is Charles Edwyn Vaughn's *Bibliographies of Swinburne, Morris and Rossetti* (London: English Association, 1914; reprint Folcroft, PA: Folcroft Press, 1969). Ehrsam's *Bibliographies of Twelve Victorian Authors*, pp. [201]-25, cites international comments, criticism, and reviews for Rossetti through the early twentieth century. Reviews of Rossetti's works in selected periodicals are also identified in Wells' *The Literary Index to American Magazines, 1850-1900*, pp. 317-18. For a bibliography of works by and about Rossetti, see *NCBEL*, III, pp. 490-96. Also available is Paul Franklin Baum's *Dante Gabriel Rossetti: An Analytical List of Manuscripts in the Duke University Library, With Hitherto Unpublished Verse and Prose* (Durham, NC: Duke University Press, 1931; reprint New York: AMS Press, 1966). See the review of research by William E. Fredeman in Faverty's *The Victorian Poets*, pp. 262-84.

Henry Roth, 1906?-

Bibliographies

See *Bibliography of American Fiction, 1919-1988*, pp. 428-29, for Todd H. Stebbins' checklist of works by and about Roth.

Philip Roth, 1933-

Bibliographies

1147.   Rodgers, Bernard F., Jr. **Philip Roth: A Bibliography**. 2d ed. Metuchen, NJ: Scarecrow Press, 1984. 386p. (Scarecrow Author Bibliographies, no. 19). LC 84-5452. ISBN 0-8108-1699-7.

First published (Metuchen, NJ: Scarecrow Press) in 1974. Covering works by and about Roth, Rodgers lists brief bibliographic information for Roth's books (including international editions); juvenilia; short fiction and excerpts; reviews; essays; interviews, plays, screenplays, and adaptations; works edited by Roth; and letters to editors. In addition, Rodgers provides unannotated entries for nine books and annotated entries for dissertations, reviews (about 820 entries, arranged by works), articles, parts of books, bibliographies, adaptations, and other writings about Roth. Critical coverage extends from 1954 through 1984. Indexing is limited to critics. Roth's manuscripts are listed in Robbins' *American Literary Manuscripts*, p. 277. Useful coverage of the Library of Congress' extensive collection of Roth's literary manuscripts and correspondence in provided in "Philip Roth Papers," *Quarterly Journal of the Library of Congress* 27 (1970): 343-44. See *Bibliography of American Fiction, 1919-1988*, pp. 429-31, for Murray Baumgarten and Barbara Gottfried's checklist of works by and about Roth.

Jerome Rothenberg, 1931-

Bibliographies

1148.   Polkinhorn, Harry. **Jerome Rothenberg: A Descriptive Bibliography**. Jefferson, NC: McFarland, 1988. 179p. (American Poetry Contemporary Bibliography Series, no. 3). LC 88-42648. ISBN 0-89950-317-9.

Polkinhorn includes detailed bibliographic descriptions in separate listings for Rothenberg's books, pamphlets, and broadsides; edited, coauthored, and translated works; contributions to periodicals (some 311 entries); anthologies; prefaces and blurbs; musical lyrics; and sound and videotape recordings; as well as lists of secondary materials in 38 books (predominantly entries in reference works and passing references) and 156 periodical articles (substantially reviews). Also for works by Rothenberg, see *First Printings of American Authors*, vol. 4, pp. 321-26.

Constance (Mayfield) Rourke, 1885-1941

Bibliographies

Rourke's manuscripts are listed in Robbins' *American Literary Manuscripts*, p. 277. See the review of research by Samuel I. Bellman in Duke, Bryer, and Inge's *American Women Writers*, pp. 353-78.

Nicholas Rowe, 1674-1718

Bibliographies

For a bibliography of works by and about Rowe, see *NCBEL*, II, pp. 780-81.

Journals

"Recent Articles" in *The Scriblerian and the Kit Cats* (entry 1084) regularly includes a selection of reviews of studies on Rowe.

Mary (White) Rowlandson, c. 1635-c. 1678

Bibliographies

See the review of research by Ann Stanford in Duke, Bryer, and Inge's *American Women Writers*, pp. 3-20.

William Rowley, 1585?-1626

Bibliographies

For a bibliography of works by and about Rowley, see *NCBEL*, I, pp. 1719-21.

Susanna (Haswell) Rowson, c. 1762- 1824

Bibliographies

For works by Rowson, see *Bibliography of American Literature*, vol. 7, pp. 292-310. See *Bibliography of American Fiction Through 1865*, pp. 209-11, for a checklist of works by and about Rowson.

Anne Newport Royall, 1769-1854

Bibliographies

For works by Royall, see *Bibliography of American Literature*, vol. 7, pp. 311-12. Royall's manuscripts are listed in Robbins' *American Literary Manuscripts*, p. 277.

Michael Rumaker, 1932-

Bibliographies

For works by Rumaker, see *First Printings of American Authors*, vol. 3, pp. 291-92.

(Alfred) Damon Runyon, 1880-1946

Bibliographies

See *Bibliography of American Fiction, 1919-1988*, pp. 432-33, for Guy Szuberla's checklist of works by and about Runyon. Runyon's manuscripts are listed in Robbins' *American Literary Manuscripts*, p. 278.

(Ahmed) Salman Rushdie, 1947-

Bibliographies

1149. Kuortti, Joel. **The Salman Rushdie Bibliography: A Bibliography of Salman Rushdie's Work and Rushdie Criticism**. Frankfurt am Main: Peter Lang, 1997. 241p. LC 96-51176. ISBN 3-631-31094-3.

Part I chronologically arranges entries for Rushdie's works in sections for books; short stories and parts of novels; essays, articles, and letters; reviews; interviews and discussions; poems; television, radio, and video; life and works, including entries in biobibliographies and reference sources; and three miscellaneous items. Entries for Rushdie's 10 books to 1995 give brief bibliographic data for English-language hard- and paperbound editions, with references to serialized, excerpted, and other appearances and extensive cross-references to reviews and critical studies. Part II chronologically arranges more than 2,400 unannotated entries in sections for books and chapters and for articles (including both criticism and reviews and news features) on Rushdie and his works from 1975 to part of

1996. Kuortti identifies more than 900 items for 1989, the year of the *Satanic Verses* incident. Indexes for names and titles of journals, periodicals, and newspapers. A final section lists "Some Related World Wide Web Sites" for Rushdie and modern literature, without additional details.

John Ruskin, 1819-1900

Bibliographies

1150.   Cate, George Allan. **John Ruskin: A Reference Guide: A Selective Guide to Significant and Representative Works About Him.** Boston, MA: G. K. Hall, 1988. 146p. (A Reference Guide to Literature). LC 88-19158. ISBN 0-8161-8908-0.

Cate chronologically arranges annotated entries for books, parts of books, articles, dissertations, introductions, and contemporary reviews, including major critical works in German and French, about Ruskin published from 1843 through 1987. Annotations are both descriptive and critical. Cate's guide largely supersedes Kirk H. Beetz's *John Ruskin: A Bibliography, 1900-1974* (Metuchen, NJ: Scarecrow Press, 1976), which includes mostly unannotated entries for about 1,000 works about Ruskin. More specialized is Robert B. Harmon's brief *The Impact of John Ruskin on Architecture: A Selected Bibliography* (Monticello, IL: Vance Bibliographies, 1982). The most reliable information about Ruskin's primary materials is included in Edward T. Cook and A. D. O. Weddeburn's "Bibliography" in vol. 38 of their edition of *The Works of John Ruskin* (London: G. Allen, 1912). This largely supersedes the coverage of Thomas J. Wise and James P. Smart's *Complete Bibliography of the Writings in Prose and Verse of John Ruskin, LL.D.: With a List of the More Important Ruskiniana* (1893; reprint London: Dawsons of Pall Mall, 1964). Also for a bibliography of works by and about Ruskin, see *NCBEL*, III, pp. 1340-64. Research on Ruskin is reviewed by Francis G. Townsend in DeLaura's *Victorian Prose*, pp. 219-48.

Dictionaries, Encyclopedias, and Handbooks

1151.   Bradley, J. L. **A Ruskin Chronology.** New York: St. Martin's Press, 1997. 129p. (Author Chronologies). LC 96-8459. ISBN 0-312-16159-X.

Straightforward, but rather thin, chronology of "the significant movements and activities of a man arguably the most distinguished art and social critic of his time" (p. xi), generally neglecting to specifically reference the "vast and complex" sources for Ruskin. Bradley often buries substantial analyses linking Ruskin's intellectual and psychological dispositions to his writings in paragraph- and page-long entries for specific periods (such as January-May 1860). Includes selected bibliography (pp. 121-22) and indexes of Ruskin's writings and selected names and titles. Indexing does not permit tracing Ruskin's travels, lectures, reading, and the like. Unlike other volumes in the series, Bradley's lacks a directory of family, associates, and others in Ruskin's circle.

1152.   Gibbs, Mary, and Ellen Gibbs. **The Bible References of John Ruskin.** Folcroft, PA: Folcroft Library Editions, 1977. 303p. LC 77-13181. ISBN 0-8414-4608-3.

Reprinting of the 1898 edition (New York: Henry Frowde). Alphabetical arrangement of Biblical subjects and other allusions cross-referenced to extensive excerpts from Ruskin's works. Cites specific chapter and verse and work and page references.

Journals

1153.   **Ruskin Gazette.** Oxford: Ruskin Society of London, 1987- . Annual. ISSN 0915-0158.

Generally brief biographical contributions have addressed Ruskin's relationships with Byron, Shelley, Swinburne, and other writers, artists, and architects and discussed Ruskin in relation to philosophy, aesthetics, art history, and criticism. The annual also publishes book reviews. *Ruskin Gazette* is indexed in *MLA* to 1990 and in *MHRA* to date.

1154.   **Ruskin Newsletter**. Isle of Wight: Ruskin Association, 1969-. 2/yr. ISSN 0953-1130.

Sponsored by the Ruskin Association, this newsletter has published brief notes and reviews of new works about Ruskin. Features mainly have focused on Ruskin's biography and his relations with contemporaries. Other contributions have described unpublished Ruskin letters. "Recent Books and Articles" has identified new publications. *Ruskin Newsletter* was indexed in *MLA* through 1986.

Joanna Russ, 1937-
Bibliographies

See *Bibliography of American Fiction, 1919-1988*, pp. 433-34, for Diane Parkin-Speer's checklist of works by and about Russ.

George William Russell (AE), 1867-1935
Bibliographies

1155.   Denson, Alan. **Printed Writings by George W. Russell (AE): A Bibliography, with Some Notes on His Pictures and Portraits**. Evanston, IL: Northwestern University Press, 1961. 255p. LC 61-16862.

Full bibliographic descriptions of AE's literary and art works in chronologically or alphabetically arranged sections for books and pamphlets; symposia (works in collections); books prefaced by AE; reports of oral evidence to Parliamentary Committees; contributions to periodicals in selected journals; other articles by AE; poems by AE set to music; other periodical contributions of poems and prose; other contributions to books by others; letters and manuscripts (pp. 161-66), particularly materials in Indiana University's Lilly Library; public sales of books by or owned by AE; selected books known to AE in youth; biographical and critical allusions to AE (about 300 unannotated items); poems addressed to AE; books dedicated to AE; recordings of AE's voice; exhibitions of paintings; present owners; printed reproductions; portraits by AE; and portraits of AE. Entries for 60 books give title-page transcriptions, collations and paginations, physical descriptions of bindings, and notes on publication histories for first and subsequent editions and printings. Also includes extensive chronology of AE's life and works and a list of major publications, a foreword by Padraic Colum, reminiscences of AE by M. J. Bonn, and a note on AE and painting by Thomas Bodkin. Selective index of names and titles. Also for a bibliography of works by and about AE, see *NCBEL*, III, pp. 1912-16. Research on AE is reviewed by James F. Carrens in Finneran's *Anglo-Irish Literature*, pp. 446-52.

Irwin Russell, 1853-1879
Bibliographies

For works by Russell, see *Bibliography of American Literature*, vol. 7, pp. 313-17. Russell's manuscripts are listed in Robbins' *American Literary Manuscripts*, p. 278. Marlene Youmans surveys works by and about Russell in Bain and Flora's *Fifty Southern Writers Before 1900*, pp. 389-94.

Abram Joseph Ryan, 1838-1886
Bibliographies

For works by Ryan, see *Bibliography of American Literature*, vol. 7, pp. 318-25. Ryan's manuscripts are listed in Robbins' *American Literary Manuscripts*, p. 279.

Charles Sackville, Lord Buckhurst, later 6th Earl of Dorset, 1638-1706

Bibliographies

For a bibliography of works by and about Sackville, see *NCBEL*, II, p. 472. Sackville's manuscripts are described in *Index of English Literary Manuscripts*, II, pt. 1:347-81.

Thomas Sackville, 1st Earl of Dorset, Baron Buckhurst, 1536-1608

Bibliographies

For a bibliography of works by and about Sackville, see *NCBEL*, I, pp. 1024-25, 1141-42, 1722. Sackville's manuscripts are described in *Index of English Literary Manuscripts*, I, pt. 2:447-48.

George Edward Bateman Saintsbury, 1845-1933

Bibliographies

Reviews of Saintsbury's works in selected periodicals are identified in Wells' *The Literary Index to American Magazines, 1850-1900*, pp. 323-24. Wendell V. Harris reviews research on Saintsbury in DeLaura's *Victorian Prose*, pp. 454-56.

Floyd Salas, 1931-

Bibliographies

See *Bibliography of American Fiction, 1919-1988*, p. 434, for Gerald W. Haslam's checklist of works by and about Salas.

J(erome) D(avid) Salinger, 1919-

Bibliographies

1156.   Sublette, Jack R. **J. D. Salinger: An Annotated Bibliography, 1938-1981.** New York: Garland, 1984. 257p. (Garland Reference Library of the Humanities, vol. 436). LC 83-48268. ISBN 0-8240-9077-2.

Superseding in coverage Kenneth Starosciark's *J. D. Salinger: A Thirty-Year Bibliography, 1938-1968* (s. l.: The Croixside Press, 1971), Sublette's guide covers works by and about Salinger. Entries for primary works identify editions and reprintings, unpublished short stories, letters, and other manuscripts. Annotated entries for some 1,462 works are chronologically arranged in classified listings for biographical studies, Whit Burnett's letters to Salinger, bibliographies and entries in reference works, critical studies, dissertations and theses, reviews of Salinger's works (arranged by works), translations, and non-English-language criticisms. Annotations are descriptive. No subject indexing is provided. Also for works by Salinger, see *First Printings of American Authors*, vol. 1, p. 315. Salinger's manuscripts are listed in Robbins' *American Literary Manuscripts*, p. 279. See *Bibliography of American Fiction, 1919-1988*, pp. 435-37, for Warren French's checklist of works by and about Salinger.

Edgar Evertson Saltus, 1855-1921

Bibliographies

For works by Saltus, see *Bibliography of American Literature*, vol. 7, pp. 326-37. Saltus' contributions to and reviews of Saltus' works in selected periodicals are identified in Wells' *The Literary Index to American Magazines, 1850-1900*, pp. 324-35. Saltus' manuscripts are listed in Robbins' *American Literary Manuscripts*, p. 279. See *Bibliography of American Fiction, 1866-1918*, pp. 319-20, for Lori Correll's checklist of works by and about Saltus.

Franklin Benjamin Sanborn, 1831-1917

Bibliographies

1157.   Cameron, Kenneth Walter. **Parameters of American Romanticism and Transcendentalism: A Chronological Ordering of Sanborn's 700 Recently Gathered**

Literary Papers (Critical, Historical, and Biographical) With a Locating Index.
Hartford, CT: Transcendental Books, 1981. 35 leaves. LC 81-187658.

Chronologically lists and briefly identifies by title Sanborn's "literary papers and table talk" (largely contributed writings such as reviews, introductions, and the like) in seven collections reprinted by Cameron, including *Transcendental Eye* (Hartford, CT: Transcendental Books, 1980) and *Transcendental Writers and Heroes* (Hartford, CT: Transcendental Books, 1978). Indexed. Also for works by Sanborn, see *First Printings of American Authors*, vol. 4, pp. 327-33. Sanborn's contributions to and reviews of Sanborn's works in selected periodicals are identified in Wells' *The Literary Index to American Magazines, 1850-1900*, pp. 325-26. Sanborn's manuscripts are listed in Robbins' *American Literary Manuscripts*, p. 279. Robert E. Burkholder reviews research on Sanborn in Myerson's *The Transcendentalists*, pp. 253-59.

Carl (August) Sandburg, 1878-1967

Bibliographies

1158.   Salwak, Dale. **Carl Sandburg: A Reference Guide**. Boston: G. K. Hall, 1988. 175p. (Reference Guide to Literature). LC 88-12048. ISBN 0-8161-8821-1.

Salwak chronologically arranges brief, descriptive entries for works about Sandburg published from 1904 through 1986. Coverage includes dissertations. A comprehensive index offers subject access. Coverage of Sandburg's primary bibliography is provided by Mark Van Doren's *Carl Sandburg: With a Bibliography of Sandburg Materials in the Collection of the Library of Congress* (Washington, DC: Library of Congress, 1969). Joan St. C. Crane's *Carl Sandburg, Philip Green Wright, and the Asgard Press, 1900-1910: A Descriptive Bibliography of Early Books, Manuscripts, and Letters in the Clifton Waller Barrett Library* (Charlottesville, VA: University Press of Virginia, 1975) also describes Sandburg's primary materials. Also available is John T. Flanagan and Leslie W. Dunlap's *The Sandburg Range: An Exhibit of Materials from Carl Sandburg's Library Placed on Display in the University of Illinois Library on January 6, 1958* (Urbana-Champaign, IL: University of Illinois Library, 1958). Sandburg's manuscripts are listed in Robbins' *American Literary Manuscripts*, pp. 279-80.

Mari Sandoz, 1896-1966

Bibliographies

1159.   Greenwell, Scott L. **Descriptive Guide to the Mari Sandoz Collection**. Lincoln, NE: University of Nebraska Press, 1980. 109p. (University of Nebraska Studies: New series, no. 63). LC 80-52644.

A box-by-box inventory of the collection (measuring 200 linear feet) donated by Sandoz to University of Nebraska-Lincoln. Includes her personal library, research files, manuscripts and publications, personal files, maps, awards, paintings, and other materials. Entries for publications give brief bibliographic information. Also for works by Sandoz, see *First Printings of American Authors*, vol. 2, pp. 345-48. Sandoz's manuscripts are listed in Robbins' *American Literary Manuscripts*, p. 280. Rosemary Whitaker and Myro Jo Moon's "A Bibliography of Works by and About Mari Sandoz," *Bulletin of Bibliography* 38 (1981): 82-91, identifies criticism of Sandoz. See *Bibliography of American Fiction, 1919-1988*, pp. 437-39, for Barbara Wright Rippey's checklist of works by and about Sandoz. Helen Stauffer surveys works by and about Sandoz in Erisman and Etulain's *Fifty Western Writers*, pp. 415-23.

Stephen Sandy, 1934-

Bibliographies

For works by Sandy, see *First Printings of American Authors*, vol. 5, pp. 271-76.

George Sandys, 1578-1644
Bibliographies

1160.   Bowers, Fredson Thayer, and Richard Beale Davis. **George Sandys: A Bibliographical Catalogue of Printed Editions in England to 1700**. New York: New York Public Library, 1950. 53p. LC 50-6572.

Full chronologically arranged bibliographic descriptions of first and subsequent editions and issues of Sandys' six works to 1700, supplying title-page transcriptions, collations, contents, and notes on variants and publication histories. Reprinted from the *Bulletin of the New York Public Library* 54.4-6 (April-June 1950): 159-81, 223-44, 280-86. Also for a bibliography of works by and about Sandys, see *NCBEL*, I, pp. 1186-87. Sandys' manuscripts are described in *Index of English Literary Manuscripts*, II, pt. 2:289-98.

Epes Sargent, 1813-1880
Bibliographies

For works by Sargent, see *Bibliography of American Literature*, vol. 7, pp. 338-62. Contributions by Sargent and criticism and reviews of Sargent's works in selected periodicals are identified in Wells' *The Literary Index to American Magazines, 1815-1865*, p. 130; and *The Literary Index to American Magazines, 1850-1900*, p. 328. Sargent's manuscripts are listed in Robbins' *American Literary Manuscripts*, p. 281.

Pamela Sargent, 1948-
Bibliographies

1161.   Elliot, Jeffrey M. **The Work of Pamela Sargent: An Annotated Bibliography & Literary Guide**. 2d ed., revised and expanded. San Bernardino, CA: Borgo Press, 1996. 144p. (Bibliographies of Modern Authors, no. 13). LC 96-15693. ISBN 0-8937-0396-6.

A revision and expansion of Elliot and Boden Clarke's *The Work of Pamela Sargent: An Annotated Bibliography & Guide* (San Bernardino, CA: Borgo Press, 1990). Describes works by and about Sargent in sections for books; short fiction; short nonfiction; unpublished works; works edited by Sargent; other media (two radio and television adaptations and a CD-ROM); juvenilia; public appearances; honors and awards; works about Sargent (56 briefly annotated items, many for entries in collective biographies); and miscellanea, ranging from the Sargent Papers at Temple University to a Sargent World Wide Web site. Entries for 30 books give brief bibliographic data for first and subsequent editions and translations, with contents (or plot summaries) and lists of secondary works and reviews. Also includes a Sargent chronology; selected quotes from critics; and two reprinted articles and an afterword by Sargent. Index of titles and selected names.

William Saroyan, 1908-1981
Bibliographies

1162.   Kherdian, David. **A Bibliography of William Saroyan, 1934-1964**. San Francisco, CA: Roger Beacham, 1965. 188p. LC 66-3154.

This is mainly useful as a listing of Saroyan's primary works, including descriptive entries for books, contributions to books, and contributions to periodicals, as well as for sheet music, piano-voice scores, recordings, and other ana through the mid-1960s. Entries give title-page transcriptions (with facsimiles), collations, pagination, descriptions of bindings and dust jackets, and information on publishing histories. Whitmore's *William Saroyan* (entry 1163) supplements Kherdian with brief bibliographic information for first and subsequent appearances of Saroyan's works through the early 1990s and descriptions of special collections for Saroyan. A thorough and up-to-date descriptive bibliography of Saroyan's works remains to be published. Saroyan's manuscripts are also listed in Robbins' *American Literary Manuscripts*, p. 281. Listings for secondary materials are superseded by coverage in Whitmore's guide.

1163.   Whitmore, Jon. **William Saroyan: A Research and Production Sourcebook**. Westport, CT: Greenwood Press, 1994. 268p. (Modern Dramatists Research and Production Sourcebooks, no. 6). LC 94-34224. ISBN 0-313-29250-7.

Three-part guide to works by and about Saroyan. The first part gives plot summaries, information and credits for selected productions (with cross-references to reviews), and critical overviews for Saroyan's 49 plays from 1935 to 1980 and brief information for Saroyan's other dramatic dialogues, screenplays, teleplays, and radio plays. Identifies 20 productions of *The Time of Your Life* from 1939 to 1991. The second part supplies brief bibliographic information for Saroyan's writings arranged in sections for published plays, dramatic dialogues, fiction, and nonfiction. Entries for published works cite subsequent appearances in collections and anthologies but exclude non-English-language editions. A subsection covering archival sources (arranged by holding institutions) contains an extensive list of scripts in the William Saroyan Collection of the Bancroft Library, University of California at Berkeley. The third part provides separate, chronologically arranged, descriptively annotated entries for approximately 800 reviews and books, chapters, and articles about Saroyan published from 1935 to 1993. International English-language coverage includes newspaper and popular magazine articles and dissertations. Whitmore also offers a chronology and an introduction surveying Saroyan's life and critical reception. Index of authors and critics and detailed subject index, with headings for Saroyan's works and topics including "Armenian heritage," "commedia dell'arte," and Shakespeare. One of the best volumes yet published in Greenwood's series, Whitmore's guide is more comprehensive than Elizabeth C. Foard's *William Saroyan: A Reference Guide* (Boston: G. K. Hall, 1989), covering writings about Saroyan published from 1934 through 1986 but excluding dissertations. Foard's very brief annotations, however, are generally more critical than Whitmore's. Whitmore's coverage of works by Saroyan selectively updates but does not supersede Kherdian's *A Bibliography of William Saroyan* (entry 1162). Also see *Bibliography of American Fiction, 1919-1988*, pp. 439-42, for Leo Hamalian's checklist of works by and about Saroyan. Pamela Jean Monaco identifies works by and about Saroyan in Demastes' *American Playwrights, 1880-1945*, pp. 362-73.

(Eleanor) May Sarton, 1912-
Bibliographies

1164.   Blouin, Lenora P. **May Sarton: A Bibliography**. Metuchen, NJ: Scarecrow Press, 1978. 236p. (Scarecrow Author Bibliographies, no. 34). LC 77-14311. ISBN 0-8108-1054-9.

Covering works by and about Sarton, Blouin provides detailed descriptions of Sarton's books of poetry, novels, nonfiction, essays and articles, short stories, separately published and anthologized poems, translations, film and stage adaptations, recordings, and manuscript collections (pp. 79-80). Entries give brief information for editions and list or summarize contents. In addition, Blouin describes about 400 reviews and other criticisms (arranged by Sarton's works) and biographical studies. Annotations are descriptive. An appendix lists Sarton's individual poems. Indexing is limited to critics. Sarton's manuscripts are listed in Robbins' *American Literary Manuscripts*, p. 282. See *Bibliography of American Fiction, 1919-1988*, pp. 442-44, for Ronald J. Nelson's checklist of works by and about Sarton.

Siegfried Loraine Sassoon, 1886-1967
Bibliographies

1165.   Keynes, Geoffrey. **A Bibliography of Siegfried Sassoon**. London: Rupert Hart-Davis, 1962. 199p. LC 63-3445.

This is the best listing of Sassoon's primary works, including descriptions of poetry and prose and contributions to books and journals. Entries give title-page transcriptions (with selected facsimiles), physical descriptions, contents, and brief information about publishing histories. Coverage is supplemented by David Farmer's "Addenda to Keynes's Bibliography of Siegfried Sassoon," *PBSA* 63 (1969): 310-17. Additionally, other primary materials in the University of Texas' Harry Ransom Humanities Research Center are described in David Farmer's *Seigfried Sassoon: A Memorial Exhibition* (Austin, TX: University of Texas, 1969); and in the auction catalog, *The Library of the Late Siegfried Sassoon: Comprising a Large Collection of His Own Original Manuscripts and Printed Books, Together with Books (Many Presentation Copies), Manuscripts and Autograph Letters from Other Important Writers, the Property of George Sassoon, Esq.* (London: Christie, Manson & Woods, 1975). Also for a bibliography of works by and about Sassoon, see *NCBEL*, IV, pp. 337-40.

John Godfrey Saxe, 1816-1887
Bibliographies

For works by Saxe, see *Bibliography of American Literature*, vol. 7, pp. 363-79. Contributions by Saxe and criticism and reviews of Saxe's works in selected periodicals are identified in Wells' *The Literary Index to American Magazines, 1815-1865*, p. 131; and *The Literary Index to American Magazines, 1850-1900*, p. 329. Saxe's manuscripts are listed in Robbins' *American Literary Manuscripts*, pp. 282-83.

Dorothy L(eigh) Sayers, 1893-1957
Bibliographies

1166.   Gilbert, Colleen B. **A Bibliography of the Works of Dorothy L. Sayers**. Hamden, CT: Archon Books, 1978. 263p. LC 78-18795. ISBN 0-208-01755-0.

A comprehensive bibliography of Sayers' primary materials, Gilbert gives detailed bibliographic descriptions in listings for separately published British and American editions of Sayers' books, pamphlets, cards, and ephemera (including edited, translated, and collaborative works), with lists of later editions; contributions to books; contributions to periodicals and newspapers; book reviews by Sayers; broadcasts, stage productions, film adaptations, and recordings; lectures; and manuscript collections at the University of Texas, Wheaton College, the Bodleian Library, and the Dorothy Sayers Society (pp. 223-37). Entries give title-page transcriptions, collations, contents, and brief information on publishing histories. Gilbert's bibliography supersedes the coverage of Sayers' primary materials in Robert B. Harmon and Margaret A. Burger's *An Annotated Guide to the Works of Dorothy L. Sayers* (New York: Garland, 1977), although Harmon and Burger's guide offers more detailed descriptions of Sayers' papers in the Marion E. Wade Collection at Wheaton (pp. 249-63). Also for a bibliography of works by and about Sayers, see *NCBEL*, IV, pp. 730-31.

1167.   Youngberg, Ruth Tanis. **Dorothy L. Sayers: A Reference Guide**. Boston: G. K. Hall, 1982. 178p. (A Reference Guide to Literature). LC 81-6992. ISBN 0-8161-8198-5.

Youngberg chronologically arranges descriptively annotated entries for more than 900 works about Sayers published from 1917 through 1981. Coverage includes the earliest notices and reviews of Sayers' works in local newspapers, reviews of works about Sayers, introductions in editions, entries in reference works, and dissertations. Annotations are descriptive. Subject indexing is limited to broad topics and primary works.

Dictionaries, Encyclopedias, and Handbooks
1168.   Clarke, Stephan P. **The Lord Peter Wimsey Companion**. New York: Mysterious Press, 1985. 563p. LC 85-60072. ISBN 0-8929-6850-8.

Glosses more than 7,500 names, allusions, and other words and phrases in Sayers' short stories and 11 novels, citing works by titles and chapters. Selected bibliography (pp. 535-44). Separate index for each work. Black-and-white illustrations and maps.

Journals

1169.   **Sayers Review.** Los Angeles, CA: Christie McMenomy, 1976-81. 3/yr. OCLC 6994742.

Issues included several features notable for reference value, such as Joe R. Christopher's "Dorothy Leigh Sayers: A Chronology," 1.1 (1976): 1-12, as well as checklists of primary and secondary materials and works in progress about Sayers. Not listed in Patterson's *Author Newsletters and Journals*. Only volumes for 1980-81 were indexed in *MLA*.

Jack Schaefer, 1907-1991

Bibliographies

See *Bibliography of American Fiction, 1919-1988*, pp. 445-46, for Barbara A. Looney's checklist of works by and about Schaefer. Michael Cleary surveys works by and about Schaefer in Erisman and Etulain's *Fifty Western Writers*, pp. 424-33.

Budd (Wilson) Schulberg, 1914-

Bibliographies

For works by Schulberg, see *First Printings of American Authors*, vol. 1, pp. 317-18. Schulberg's manuscripts are listed in Robbins' *American Literary Manuscripts*, p. 284. See *Bibliography of American Fiction, 1919-1988*, p. 447, for Richard Fine's checklist of works by and about Schulberg.

Delmore Schwartz, 1913-1966

Bibliographies

For works by Schwartz, see *First Printings of American Authors*, vol. 1, pp. 319-20. Schwartz's manuscripts are listed in Robbins' *American Literary Manuscripts*, p. 284.

Evelyn Scott, 1893-1963

Bibliographies

For works by Scott, see *First Printings of American Authors*, vol. 5, pp. 277-80. Scott's manuscripts are listed in Robbins' *American Literary Manuscripts*, p. 285. See *Bibliography of American Fiction, 1919-1988*, pp. 48-49, for Henry E. Turlington's checklist of works by and about Scott.

Sir Walter Scott, 1771-1832

Bibliographies

1170.   Bolton, H. Philip. **Scott Dramatized**. London; New York: Mansell, 1992. 579p. (Novels on Stage, vol. 2). ISBN 0-7201-2060-8.

"A calendar of dramatic performances and a bibliography of published texts and unpublished manuscripts derived from the novels, tales, and narrative poems" (p. vii). In separate sections for each of Scott's works, Bolton chronologically arranges descriptions of about 4,500 dramatic adaptations, including film and video productions, from 1810 to the present. Following details about the dramatic and dramatized features of each work, Bolton describes published versions and identifies performances, with data for production dates, cast lists, surviving playbills, etc.

1171.   Corson, James C. **A Bibliography of Sir Walter Scott: A Classified and Annotated List of Books and Articles Relating to His Life and Works, 1797-1940**. London: Oliver and Boyd, 1943. 428p. LC 44-27734.

Corson lists about 3,000 secondary works in classified listings for bibliographies, biographies, general critical studies, studies of genres, studies of individual works, and topical studies (such as politics, the supernatural, and topography). Descriptive annotations note reprintings and reviews. Reprinted (New York: Burt Franklin, 1968). Corson's coverage is continued by Rubenstein's guide (entry 1172). A comprehensive, descriptive guide for Scott's primary works does not exist. William Ruff's "A Bibliography of the Poetical Works of Sir Walter Scott, 1796-1832," *Edinburgh Bibliographical Society Transactions* 1.2 (1937): 99-239, with "Additions and Corrections," 1.3 (1938): 277-81; and Charles A. Webbert's *Scottiana Idahoensis: A Descriptive Catalog of the Earl J. Larrison Collection of Sir Walter Scott in the University of Idaho Library* (Moscow, ID: University Press of Idaho, 1978), offer detailed descriptions of Scott's works. Also useful is the *Catalogue of the Library at Abbotsford, Edinburgh, 1838* (New York: AMS Press, 1971), which describes Scott's library. Also for a bibliography of works by and about Scott, see *NCBEL*, III, pp. 670-92.

1172.   Rubenstein, Jill. **Sir Walter Scott: A Reference Guide**. Boston: G. K. Hall, 1978. 344p. (A Reference Publication in Literature). LC 77-26785. ISBN 0-8161-7868-2.
Continued by:

1172.1. Rubenstein, Jill. **Sir Walter Scott: An Annotated Bibliography of Scholarship and Criticism, 1975-1990**. Aberdeen: Association for Scottish Literary Studies, 1994. 124p. (The Association for Scottish Literary Studies, Occasional Papers, no. 11). LC 94-91292. ISBN 0-9488-7725-1.
Rubenstein offers the most thorough coverage of major scholarship on Scott. Continuing the coverage of Corson's guide (entry 1171), Rubenstein's 1978 volume describes about 1,500 works about Scott published from 1832 through 1977. International coverage includes criticisms, comments, and reviews of all varieties, including editions and dissertations. Annotations are descriptive. A comprehensive index offers detailed topical access, providing headings for "ballads," "medievalism," "religion," and the like. Following a survey of recent Scott criticism, Rubenstein's 1994 supplement chronologically arranges descriptively annotated entries for more than 700 works about Scott published from 1975 to 1990, including books, chapters, articles, introductions in editions, and non-English-language studies but excluding unpublished dissertations, newspaper articles, and reviews. Like the earlier volume, the 1994 supplement offers a comprehensive index of names, titles, and detailed topics. Research on Scott is reviewed by James T. Hillhouse and Alexander Welsh in Houtchens and Houtchens' *The English Romantic Poets and Essayists*, pp. 115-54; and W. E. K. Anderson in Dyson's *The English Novel*, pp. 128-44.

Dictionaries, Encyclopedias, and Handbooks

1173.   Bradley, Philip. **An Index to the Waverly Novels**. Metuchen, NJ: Scarecrow Press, 1975. 681p. LC 75-6838. ISBN 0-8108-0812-9.
Bradley identifies and locates selected persons, places, things, words, phrases, and topics that appear in Scott's text and notes, based on Alexander Lang's edition of the *Waverly Novels* (London: Macmillan, 1900), usually referred to as the Border edition. Topical entries cover animals, churches, fairies, food, London, witches, and the like. Descriptions are more detailed than those in M. F. A. Husband's *A Dictionary of the Characters in The Waverly Novels of Sir Walter Scott* (1910; reprint New York: Humanities Press, 1962). Henry Grey's *A Key to The Waverly Novels in Chronological Sequence: With an Index of the Principal Characters* (1882; reprint New York: Haskell House, 1973) also offers brief plot summaries and character identifications.

Journals

See Patterson's *Author Newsletters and Journals*, p. 278, for previously published journals for Scott.

Winfield Townley Scott, 1910-1968

Bibliographies

For works by Scott, see *First Printings of American Authors*, vol. 5, pp. 281-84. Scott's manuscripts are listed in Robbins' *American Literary Manuscripts*, p. 285.

Seafarer, before about 940

Bibliographies

Greenfield and Robinson's *A Bibliography of Publications on Old English Literature to the End of 1972*, pp. 267-70, lists editions, translations, and studies of the *Seafarer*, with citations for reviews.

Charles Sealsfield (Karl Postl), 1793-1864

Bibliographies

1174. Heller, Otto, and Theodore H. Leon. **Charles Sealsfield: Bibliography of His Writings Together with a Classified and Annotated Catalogue of Literature Relating to His Works and His Life**. St. Louis, MO: Washington University, 1939. 88p. (Washington University Studies. New Series. Language and Literature, no. 8). LC 40-5412.

Covers works by and about Sealsfield. Part 1 gives brief bibliographic information for Sealsfield's works in listings for editions, posthumously published works, translations, retranslations into German, contributions to periodicals, "works allegedly destroyed," and letters. Part 2 offers selectively annotated entries for works about Sealsfield in sections for books and essays, general studies, articles, and studies specifically on aspects of Sealsfield's life and works. Part 3 briefly describes manuscripts, pictures, and other memorabilia. Alexander Ritter's "Sealsfield-Bibliographie, 1976-1986," in *Schriftenreihe der Charles-Sealsfield-Gesellschaft*, 1 (1987): 50-65, a classified unannotated listing (of about 150 entries) for bibliographies (largely German-language), editions and selections of Sealsfield's writings and for books, chapters, and articles about Sealsfield, continues previous compilations, including Ritter's *Sealsfield-Bibliographie, 1966-1975* (Stuttgart: Charles Sealsfield-Gesellschaft, 1976), and Felix Bornemann and Hans Freising's *Sealsfield-Bibliographie, 1945-1965* (Stuttgart: Charles Sealsfield-Gesellschaft, 1966). See *Bibliography of American Fiction Through 1865*, pp. 211-14, for Walter Grunzweig's checklist of works by and about Sealsfield. Sealsfield's manuscripts are listed in Robbins' *American Literary Manuscripts*, p. 258.

Catharine Maria Sedgwick, 1789-1867

Bibliographies

For works by Sedgwick, see *Bibliography of American Literature*, vol. 7, pp. 380-96. Contributions by Sedgwick and criticism and reviews of Sedgwick's works in selected periodicals are identified in Wells' *The Literary Index to American Magazines, 1815-1865*, pp. 134-35; and *The Literary Index to American Magazines, 1850-1900*, p. 334. Sedgwick's manuscripts are listed in Robbins' *American Literary Manuscripts*, p. 286. See *Bibliography of American Fiction Through 1865*, pp. 215-16, for a checklist of works by and about Sedgwick.

Sir Charles Sedley, 1639?-1701

Bibliographies

For a bibliography of works by and about Sedley, see *NCBEL*, II, pp. 463-64, by Curt A. Zimansky. Sedley's manuscripts are described in *Index of English Literary Manuscripts*, II, pt. 2:299-314.

Alan Seeger, 1888-1916
Bibliographies

For works by Seeger, see *Bibliography of American Literature*, vol. 7, pp. 397-98. Seeger's manuscripts are listed in Robbins' *American Literary Manuscripts*, p. 287.

Maurice (Bernard) Sendak, 1928-
Bibliographies

1175.   Hanrahan, Joyce Y. **Works of Maurice Sendak, 1947-1994: A Collection with Comments**. Portsmouth, NH: P. E. Randall, 1995. 93p. OCLC 32398966.

Chronologically arranges full bibliographic descriptions of Sendak's works in sections for first editions, ephemera and related books and periodicals, and visuals and posters. Aimed at collectors, entries contain title-page transcriptions, brief physical details, and notes on bibliographic points, with valuations. Indexed. See *Bibliography of American Fiction, 1919-1988*, pp. 449-52, for Geraldine DeLuca's checklist of works by and about Sendak.

Mary Lee Settle, 1918-
Bibliographies

See *Bibliography of American Fiction, 1919-1988*, pp. 452-53, for Margaret Donovan DuPriest and Beverly Brummert Klatt's checklist of works by and about Settle.

Anne Sexton, 1928-1974
Bibliographies

1176.   Northouse, Cameron, and Thomas P. Walsh. **Sylvia Plath and Anne Sexton: A Reference Guide**. Boston: G. K. Hall, 1974. 143p. (Reference Guides in American Literature, no. 1). LC 74-14965. ISBN 0-8161-1146-4.

Although coverage for Plath is superseded in the guides of Meyerling (entry 1067) and Tabor (entry 1068), Northouse and Walsh's guide remains valuable for its separate lists of works by and about Sexton. Coverage of criticism (about 100 annotated entries for works published from 1960 through 1971) largely includes parts of books and periodical and newspaper articles and reviews. Annotations are descriptive. A separate index for Sexton provides limited topical access under primary titles. Sexton's manuscripts are listed in Robbins' *American Literary Manuscripts*, p. 289. Research on Sexton is reviewed by Cindy Hoffman, Carol Duane, Katharen Soule, and Linda Wagner in Duke, Bryer, and Inge's *American Women Writers*, pp. 379-402; and Diana Hume George in *Contemporary Authors: Bibliographical Series: Volume 2: American Poets*, pp. 307-334.

Thomas Shadwell, 1642?-1692
Bibliographies

1177.   Armistead, J. M. **Four Restoration Playwrights: A Reference Guide to Thomas Shadwell, Aphra Behn, Nathaniel Lee and Thomas Otway**. Boston: G. K. Hall, 1984. 448p. (A Reference Guide to Literature). LC 83-18384. ISBN 0-8161-8289-2.

Armistead provides, in separate, chronologically arranged listings, annotated entries for 450 works about Shadwell, 300 about Behn, 450 about Lee, and 600 about Otway. Coverage of books, parts of books, articles, and dissertations extends from the earliest notices through 1980. Annotations are scholarly and evaluative. Significant works receive detailed descriptions. A single author and title index includes coded references ("B" for Behn and so forth) that assist access. O'Donnell's *Aphra Behn* (entry 92) affords better coverage of criticism; for Lee, Otway, and Shadwell, however, Armistead's guide is the best available bibliography. For a bibliography of works by and about Shadwell, see *NCBEL*, II, pp. 744-46. Shadwell's manuscripts are described in *Index of English Literary Manuscripts*, II, pt. 2:315-22. Wells' *English Drama* includes reviews of research on Lee and Otway by H. Neville Davies (pp. 150-72) and on Shadwell by John Barnard (pp. 173-98).

Journals
   "Recent Articles" in *The Scriblerian and the Kit Cats* (entry 1084) regularly includes a selection of reviews of studies on Shadwell.

Anthony Shaffer, 1926- , and Peter Levin Shaffer, 1926-
Bibliographies
   1178.   Thomas, Eberle. **Peter Shaffer: An Annotated Bibliography.** New York: Garland, 1991. 270p. (Garland Reference Library of the Humanities, vol. 916). LC 90-14052. ISBN 0-8240-7645-1.
   Some 35 awkwardly and complexly organized sections cover general works (bibliographies, book-length criticisms, biographies, separately published and collected criticisms of individual or several plays, and dissertations); interviews; and early works and individual works, from *Five Finger Exercises* to *Lettice and Lovage*, with sublistings for published editions and film versions, reviews of specific stage productions and film adaptations, newspaper features and articles, scholarly studies, and letters to the editor about productions and films. Extending from 1956 through 1900, coverage in the section for general studies is a mixture of substantial scholarly works, reviews, newspaper articles, and comments on film adaptations, as well as repetitive entries in standard reference works. Descriptive annotations indicate if a particular review was positive or negative. Includes a chronology of Shaffer's works. Comprehensive index covers proper names and selected topics. Thomas offers more comprehensive coverage of works by and about Shaffer than King's *Twenty Modern British Playwrights*, pp. 197-205.

   1179.   Klein, Dennis A. **Peter and Anthony Shaffer: A Reference Guide.** Boston: G. K. Hall, 1982. 110p. (A Reference Guide to Literature). LC 82-2962. ISBN 0-8161-8574-3.
   Klein's guide gives separate, chronologically arranged listings of annotated entries for works about Peter Shaffer (about 500 items) and Anthony Shaffer (about 100 items) published from 1956 through 1980. Coverage includes a few books, selected entries in reference works, articles in popular and scholarly journals and newspapers, and reviews of the Shaffers' works. Annotations are descriptive. Separate indexes offer limited topical access.

Anthony Ashley Cooper, 3rd Earl of Shaftesbury, 1671-1713
Bibliographies
   For a bibliography of works by and about Cooper, see *NCBEL*, II, pp. 1865-67. Cooper's manuscripts are described in *Index of English Literary Manuscripts*, III, pt. 3:273-92.

William Shakespeare, 1564-1616
Bibliographies
   1180.   Bartlett, Henrietta C., and Alfred W. Pollard. **A Census of Shakespeare's Plays in Quarto, 1594-1709.** Revised and extended ed. New Haven, CT: Yale University Press, 1939. 165p. LC 39-24284.
   Bartlett and Pollard describe surviving copies of quarto and other separate editions of Shakespeare's plays dating through 1709, providing title-page transcriptions, collations, and other physical information, as well as extensive notes on printing and publishing histories, physical condition, and locations. This is the basic primary bibliography for Shakespeare. Complementing Bartlett and Pollard's guide, Harold M. Otness' *Shakespeare Folio Handbook and Census* (New York: Greenwood Press, 1990) locates copies of Shakespeare's First, Second, Third, and Fourth folio editions in American institutions, with information on provenances and sales of particular copies. Also for a bibliography of works by and about

Shakespeare, see *NCBEL*, I, pp. 1473-1636, by T. S. Dorsch. Manuscripts are described in *Index of English Literary Manuscripts*, I, pt. 2:449-63, 633.

1181.   Champion, Larry S. **The Essential Shakespeare: An Annotated Bibliography of Major Modern Studies**. 2d ed. New York: G. K. Hall, 1993. 568p. (Reference Publication in Literature). LC 92-39078. ISBN 0-8161-7332-X.

A revision and expansion of his *The Essential Shakespeare: An Annotated Bibliography of Major Modern Studies* (Boston: G. K. Hall, 1986), Champion's work—despite more than 1,800 entries—remains a usefully succinct guide to recent Shakespeare scholarship through 1991 and the best single-volume general guide for Shakespeare scholarship. Champion continues to helpfully organize frequently critically annotated entries in the kinds of topical sections and subsections that students will readily comprehend and access: General studies (reference works and bibliographies; collected editions; biographies; history of criticism; dating and textual studies; sources; background studies; language and style; staging, stage histories, and film; and thematic and topical studies, with nearly 200 entries); the poems and sonnets (reference works, editions, and separate listings of criticisms of individual works); and the English history plays, comedies, tragedies, and romances, with separate listings for general studies of each genre and of reference works, editions, textual studies, and criticisms of each individual play. Annotations offer extensive detail and critical guidance; descriptions of bibliographies and other reference works are helpfully evaluative. Champion's information about modern editions is also valuable. Champion does not hesitate to note a work's strengths and weaknesses. The introduction also identifies the most important recent scholarly studies. The comprehensive index of proper names and primary titles, with detailed subheadings for characters in the plays and more specific topics (such as "identity of W. H." and "feminist studies") offers good access. Chronological arrangement and detailed indexing contribute to making Champion's guide superior to Joseph Rosenblum's *Shakespeare: An Annotated Bibliography* (entry 1185). Aimed at advanced undergraduates, David M. Bergeron and Geraldo U. de Sousa's *Shakespeare: A Study and Research Guide*, 2d ed. (Lawrence, KS: University Press of Kansas, 1987), surveys a wide range of critical approaches (historical, genre, psychological, mythic, feminist and gender, and textual, among others) to Shakespeare; evaluates bibliographies and reference works, editions, critical studies, periodicals, and biographies; and describes the processes of researching and writing a research paper on Shakespeare. Advanced scholars should be directed to the more comprehensive "Garland Shakespeare Bibliographies" (entry 1182) and the *World Shakespeare Bibliography* in *Shakespeare Quarterly* (entry 1202). Also giving useful guidance more appropriate for advanced scholars is Stanley Wells' *Shakespeare: A Bibliographical Guide* (entry 1188). *YWES* annually features a review essay on Shakespeare research.

1182.   **Garland Shakespeare Bibliographies**. New York: Garland, 1980- . In progress. OCLC 10626526.

Volumes in this ambitious project aim at providing comprehensive coverage of modern Shakespearean scholarship (generally since the 1930s and 1940s) and intend to bring up to date the coverage of the standard bibliographies of Jaggard, Ebisch and Schucking, and Gordon Ross Smith (entry 1187). Volumes focus on editions and studies of individual plays, with most including about 1,000 to 1,500 descriptively annotated entries. Champion's volume for *King Lear* (entry 1182.1) and Roberts' for *Richard II* (entry 1182.14) include more than 2,500 entries. Metz's volume for plays attributed to Shakespeare (entry 1182.2) includes only 280. Providing classified listings, volumes include divisions and sections for standard textual and topical research focuses (such as bibliographies and bibliographic studies, individual and collected editions and translations, and general criticism) and for topics of more limited interests, including sources and background, dating and authorship, influence, language and vocabulary, characterization, and stage history and film adaptation. Although coverage of English-language criticism predominates, coverage of materials in non-English-languages is also extensive. Cross-references and a comprehensive index of critics and subjects are also included in each volume. Topical indexing is very specific, offering detailed subheadings for such subjects as Richard III "as a businessman" or "compared to Hitler" and Cordelia as "a figure of Christian redemption" or "her speech pattern." Students will find this specificity most valuable. Volumes published include:

1182.1. Vol. 1: Champion, Larry S. **King Lear: An Annotated Bibliography**. New York: Garland, 1980. 2 vols. (Garland Reference Library of the Humanities, vol. 230). LC 80-8489. ISBN 0-8240-9498-0.

1182.2. Vol. 2: Metz, G. Harold. **Four Plays Ascribed to Shakespeare: The Reign of King Edward III, Sir Thomas More, The History of Cardenio, The Two Noble Kinsmen: An Annotated Bibliography**. New York: Garland, 1982. 193p. (Garland Reference Library of the Humanities, vol. 236). LC 81-13357. ISBN 0-8240-9488-3.

1182.3. Vol. 3: Jacobs, Henry E. **Cymbeline: An Annotated Bibliography**. New York: Garland, 1982. 591p. (Garland Reference Library of the Humanities, vol. 347). LC 82-48082. ISBN 0-8240-9258-9.

1182.4. Vol. 4: Candido, Joseph, and Charles R. Forker. **Henry V: An Annotated Bibliography**. New York: Garland, 1983. 815p. (Garland Reference Library of the Humanities, vol. 281). LC 80-9051. ISBN 0-8240-9232-2.

1182.5. Vol. 5: Hinchcliffe, Judith. **King Henry VI, Parts 1, 2, and 3: An Annotated Bibliography**. New York: Garland, 1984. 368p. (Garland Reference Library of the Humanities, vol. 422). LC 83-47607. ISBN 0-8240-9115-9.

1182.6. Vol. 6: Harvey, Nancy Lenz, and Anna Kirwan Carey. **Love's Labor's Lost: An Annotated Bibliography**. New York: Garland, 1984. 220p. (Garland Reference Library of the Humanities, vol. 365). LC 82-48478. ISBN 0-8240-9231-7.

1182.7. Vol. 7: Robinson, Randal F. **Hamlet in the 1950s: An Annotated Bibliography**. New York: Garland, 1984. 383p. (Garland Reference Library of the Humanities, vol. 417). LC 82-49289. ISBN 0-8240-9119-1.

1182.8. Vol. 8: Halio, Jay L., and Barbara C. Millard. **As You Like It: An Annotated Bibliography, 1940-1980**. New York: Garland, 1985. 744p. (Garland Reference Library of the Humanities, vol. 443). LC 83-48275. ISBN 0-8240-9071-3.

1182.9. Vol. 9: Wheeler, Thomas. **The Merchant of Venice: An Annotated Bibliography**. New York: Garland, 1985. 386p. (Garland Reference Library of the Humanities, vol. 423). LC 83-47606. ISBN 0-8240-9114-0.

1182.10. Vol. 10: Ruszkiewicz, John J. **Timon of Athens: An Annotated Bibliography**. New York: Garland, 1986. 274p. (Garland Reference Library of the Humanities, vol. 388). LC 82-49112. ISBN 0-8240-9195-7.

1182.11. Vol. 11: Moore, James A. **Richard III: An Annotated Bibliography**. New York: Garland, 1986. 867p. (Garland Reference Library of the Humanities, vol. 425). LC 83-47604. ISBN 0-8240-9112-4.

1182.12. Vol. 12: Carroll, D. Allen, and Gary Jay Williams. **A Midsummer's Night's Dream: An Annotated Bibliography**. New York: Garland, 1986. 641p. (Garland Reference Library of the Humanities, vol. 440). LC 86-4469. ISBN 0-8240-9073-X.

1182.13. Vol. 13: Michael, Nancy C. **Pericles: An Annotated Bibliography**. New York: Garland, 1988. 289p. (Garland Reference Library of the Humanities, vol. 424). LC 87-17295. ISBN 0-8240-9113-2.

1182.14. Vol. 14: Roberts, Josephine A. **Richard II: An Annotated Bibliography**. New York: Garland, 1988. 2 vols. (Garland Reference Library of the Humanities, vol. 14). LC 88-2697. ISBN 0-8240-8588-4.

1182.15. Vol. 15: Micheli, Linda McJ. **Henry VIII: An Annotated Bibliography**. New York: Garland, 1988. 444p. (Garland Reference Library of the Humanities, vol. 540). LC 84-45381. ISBN 0-8240-8836-0.

1182.16. Vol. 16: Pearson, D'Orsay W. **Two Gentlemen of Verona: An Annotated Bibliography**. New York: Garland, 1988. 251p. (Garland Reference Library of the Humanities, vol. 847). LC 88-16544. ISBN 0-8240-5641-8.

1182.17. Vol. 17: Leggatt, Alexander. **Coriolanus: An Annotated Bibliography**. New York: Garland, 1989. 738p. (Garland Reference Library of the Humanities, vol. 483). LC 89-16786. ISBN 0-8240-8984-7.

1182.18. Vol. 18: Dietrich, Julia. **Hamlet in the 1960's: An Annotated Bibliography**. New York: Garland, 1992. 771p. (Garland Reference Library of the Humanities, vol. 477). LC 91-29683. ISBN 0-8240-8990-1.

1182.19. Vol. 19: Owen, Trevor A. **Troilus and Cressida: An Annotated Bibliography**. New York: Garland [forthcoming].

1182.20. Vol. 20: Mikesell, Margaret Lael, and Virginia Mason Vaughan. **Othello: An Annotated Bibliography**. New York: Garland, 1990. 941p. (Garland Reference Library of the Humanities, vol. 964). LC 89-25852. ISBN 0-8240-2749-3.
Additionally, John Hazel Smith's *Shakespeare's Othello: A Bibliography* (New York: AMS, 1988) topically arranges more than 4,000 mostly unannotated entries for international criticisms of Othello through 1984 (and partially 1985).

1182.21. Vol. 21: Harvey, Nancy Lenz. **The Taming of the Shrew: An Annotated Bibliography**. New York: Garland, 1994. 310p. (Garland Reference Library of the Humanities, vol. 523). LC 94-6493. ISBN 0824088921.

1182.22. Vol. 22: Wheeler, Thomas. **Macbeth: An Annotated Bibliography**. New York: Garland, 1990. 1,001p. (Garland Reference Library of the Humanities, vol. 522). LC 89-71465. ISBN 0-8240-8893-X.

1182.23. Vol. 23: Curren-Aquino, Deborah T. **King John: An Annotated Bibliography**. New York: Garland, 1994. 894p. (Garland Reference Library of the Humanities, vol. 770). LC 93-47107. ISBN 0-8240-6626-X.

1182.24. Vol 24: Yet to be published.

1182.25. Vol. 25: Yet to be published.

1182.26. Vol. 26: Gira, Catherine, and Adele Seeff. **Henry IV, Parts 1 and 2: An Annotated Bibliography**. New York: Garland, 1994. 576p. (Garland Reference Library of the Humanities, vol. 1334). LC 94-5075. ISBN 0-8240-7097-6.
International bibliographic coverage of studies and other materials on themes, influences, and topics not confined to individual plays is available in a variety of other compilations. In addition to Kolin's *Shakespeare and Feminist Criticism* (entry 1184), a selection of recent bibliographies for specialized topics includes William R. Elton's *Shakespeare's World: Renaissance Intellectual Contexts: A Selective, Annotated Guide, 1966-1971* (New York: Garland, 1979); Henry E. Jacobs

and Claudia D. Johnson's *An Annotated Bibliography of Shakespearean Burlesques, Parodies, and Travesties* (New York: Garland, 1976); and J. Paul McRoberts' *Shakespeare and the Medieval Tradition: An Annotated Bibliography* (New York: Garland, 1985). Bibliographical and textual studies are identified in Trevor H. Howard-Hill's *Shakespearian Bibliography and Textual Criticism: A Bibliography* (Oxford: Clarendon Press, 1971), vol. 2 of *Index to British Literary Bibliography*. Hansjurgen Blinn's *The German Shakespeare: An Annotated Bibliography of the Shakespeare Reception in German-Speaking Countries (Literature, Theatre, Mass Media, Music, Fine Arts)/Der deutsche Shakespeare: Eine annotierte Bibliographie zur Shakespeare-Rezeption des deutschsprachigen Kulturraums (Literatur, Theater, Film, Funk, Fernsehen, Musik und bildende Kunst)* (Berlin: Schmidt, 1993) offers an important, classified, unannotated listing of approximately 4,500 mostly German-language studies of Shakespeare, with an index of plays, names, and subjects.

1183. Harris, Laurie Lanzen. **Shakespearean Criticism: Excerpts from the Criticism of William Shakespeare's Plays and Poetry**. Detroit, MI: Gale, 1984-. LC 84-4010. ISSN 0883-9123.

Similar to other series in Gale's "Literary Criticism" family anchored by *Contemporary Literary Criticism*, volumes present excerpts of comments and criticisms from the sixteenth century through the present on each of Shakespeare's works. The series has gone through several permutations that have both increased and redefined its scope. Early volumes generally focus on three to four works; for example, vol. 1 covers *1* and *2 Henry IV, The Comedy of Errors, Hamlet, Timon of Athens*, and *Twelfth Night*; and vol. 7, *All's Well That Ends Well, Julius Caesar*, and *The Winter's Tale*. With vol. 11, emphasis in the series is on tracing "the history of Shakespeare's plays on the stage and in important films through reviews and retrospective evaluations of individual productions, comparisons of major interpretations, and discussions of staging issues" (p. vii). Vol. 11 covers *King Lear, Othello*, and *Romeo and Juliet*; and vol. 12, *The Merchant of Venice, A Midsummer's Night's Dream, The Taming of the Shrew*, and *The Two Gentlemen of Verona*. In addition to excerpts, sections for each work include critical introductions and supplemental, annotated bibliographies. Representing another change in emphasis, vol. 13 is subtitled *Yearbook 1989: A Selection of the Year's Most Noteworthy Studies of William Shakespeare's Plays and Poetry*. One volume per year now reprints full texts of about 40 to 50 book chapters and articles on selected topics for Shakespeare's plays. Other yearbook volumes are 16 (1990), 19 (1991), 22 (1992), 25 (1993), 28 (1994), and 32 (1995). In vol. 27 (1995), *Shakespearean Criticism* limits coverage to criticism published after 1960, "with a view to providing the reader with the most significant modern critical approaches" (preface). The same volume introduces special topical coverage for "Shakespeare and Classical Civilization" along with excerpts for selected plays. Topical coverage of subsequent volumes has included magic and the supernatural, politics and power, women, sexuality, and appearance versus reality. With vol. 6, all volumes provide a cumulative subject index (for each work) and a cumulative index of critics. As a bibliography of works about Shakespeare, volumes in the series are helpful for identifying the canonical critical highpoints in Shakespeare scholarship and are of far greater value to undergraduate students than to scholars.

1184. Kolin, Philip C. **Shakespeare and Feminist Criticism: An Annotated Bibliography and Commentary**. New York: Garland, 1991. 420p. (Garland Reference Library of the Humanities, vol. 1345). LC 91-27900. ISBN 0-8240-7386-X.

Kolin chronologically arranges descriptively annotated entries for 439 feminist criticisms of Shakespeare in English from 1975 to 1988, including books, chapters, articles, notes, and dissertations (unannotated). Lengthy (with a few for books extending to four pages) and thorough annotations wonderfully identify and summarize major points; entries for books also cite book reviews. Detailed introduction surveys feminist perspectives in relationship to other critical approaches.

Separate author, play/poem, and detailed subject indexes. Supplementing the "Garland Shakespeare Bibliographies" (entry 1182) in coverage and detail, Kolin's guide makes the substantial and important body of feminist criticism on Shakespeare more directly accessible.

1185. Rosenblum, Joseph. **Shakespeare: An Annotated Bibliography**. Pasadena, CA: Salem Press, 1992. 307p. (Magill Bibliographies). LC 92-4863. ISBN 0-89356-676-4.

Evaluative descriptions of approximately 1,200 selected modern works about Shakespeare alphabetically arranged in chapters for bibliographies and other reference sources, editions, biographies, stage productions and performances, general studies (of sources, text, language, themes and topics, comedies, histories, and tragedies), and the individual plays and poems. Annotations indicate particular studies as outstanding, useful, and otherwise important. Name index. Lack of subject indexing limits usefulness for the intended undergraduate audience. Champion's *The Essential Shakespeare* (entry 1181) and Sajdak's *Shakespeare Index* (entry 1186) are more convenient starting points for research on popular Shakespearean topics.

1186. Sajdak, Bruce T. **Shakespeare Index: An Annotated Bibliography of Critical Articles on the Plays, 1959-1983**. Millwood, NY: Kraus International Publications, 1992. 2 vols. LC 91-28335. ISBN 0-5277-8932-1.

"Because of its thorough indexing of critical articles by subject, character, and scene, *Shakespeare Index* is a new concept in literary bibliography" (p. xi). In fact, *Shakespeare Index* often offers the quickest and most efficient guidance to major recent criticisms of Shakespeare's plays. Vol. 1 (*Citations and Author Index*) chronologically arranges from 1959 to 1983 annotated entries for more than 7,000 studies in 48 topical sections for political, economic, social, and cultural background; Shakespeare's life, knowledge, and sources; general textual studies; language; Elizabethan and Jacobean theater and stage practices; studies of theme, character, and other general topics; studies of the plays by period; studies of the plays by genres (with separate chapters for comedies, histories, romances, tragedies, and pastoral, problem, Roman, and other plays); studies of each of the 35 individual plays, the apocrypha, *Book of Sir Thomas More, Edward III*, and *Two Noble Kinsman*. Limited to major English-language scholarship published in periodicals, coverage for each play, although more limited than that offered in volumes in the *Garland Shakespeare Bibliographies* (entry 1182), is nonetheless adequate for most undergraduate uses and for some plays considerably more. While listing only 29 studies of *Merry Wives of Windsor*, Sajdak includes some 160 for *Romeo and Juliet* and 800 for *Hamlet*. Brief, detailed annotations cross-reference other studies in the listings. Vol. 1 concludes with an index of critics. Vol. 2 (*Character, Scene, and Subject Indexes*) offers detailed and systematic indexing of the entries in vol. 1. The separate indexes make it convenient to identify studies of audience response to Cordelia in *King Lear*, act 1, scene 1; of feminist views of the character Gregory in *Romeo and Juliet*; and of the imagery of blood not only in *Macbeth* but in *Hamlet, Measure for Measure, Richard II*, and other plays as well. The elaborate and very specific indexing makes *Shakespeare Index* a useful supplement to less generously indexed bibliographies of recent criticisms.

1187. Smith, Gordon Ross. **A Classified Shakespeare Bibliography, 1936-1958**. State College, PA: Pennsylvania State University Press, 1963. 784p. LC 63-17265.

The most comprehensive and accessible listing of secondary materials on Shakespeare previous to volumes in the *Garland Shakespeare Bibliographies* series (entry 1182), this topically arranges brief, unannotated entries for more than 20,000 works about Shakespeare's life and times, texts, sources, techniques and other elements in his works, and literary reputation and influence. Separate sections also list general studies as well as studies of individual works. The extremely detailed "Table of Contents" (pp. vi-xli) must be studied carefully before attempting to use this guide. No other indexing is provided. To identify references to studies of Shakespeare's influence on Joyce, for example, users are compelled to dig deep within sections, subsections, and sub-subsections: "XIII. Shakespeare's Influence Through the Centuries"; "2. Shakespeare's Influence in England"; "b. Shakespeare's Significance for Various English Authors"; "5. Twentieth Century"; "b. Studies of the Attitudes of Authors Toward Shakespeare"; and "iii. Joyce." Equally arduous is locating studies of Pasternak's Russian translations of Shakespeare. Finding studies of individual plays or studies of their characters is slightly more straightforward. Before the publication of the Garland bibliographies for the individual plays or Sajdak's *Shakespeare Index* (entry 1186), Smith's guide was the most convenient source to identify studies of particular characters, themes, and allusions. And until the completion of the Garland bibliographies, Smith's listings will remain absolutely essential for research. Smith's bibliography continues Walter Ebisch and L. L. Schucking's *Shakespeare Bibliography* (Oxford: Clarendon Press, 1931) and its *Supplement for the Years 1930-1935* (Oxford: Clarendon Press, 1937); and William Jaggard's *Shakespeare Bibliography: A Dictionary of Every Known Issue of the Writings of Our National Poet and of Recorded Opinion Thereon in the English Language: With Historical Introduction* (Stratford-on-Avon: Shakespeare Press, 1911). These three works, typically referred to simply as "Gordon Ross Smith," "Ebisch and Schucking," and "Jaggard," constitute the standard bibliographies of Shakespeare criticism through the mid-twentieth century. More limited coverage of twentieth-century Shakespearean studies is available in James G. McManaway and Jeanne Addison Roberts' *A Selective Bibliography of Shakespeare Editions, Textual Studies, Commentary* (Charlottesville, VA: Published for the Folger Shakespeare Library by the University Press of Virginia, 1975), which lists about 4,500 editions, general and specialized studies, and studies of individual works since 1930. David Bevington's *Shakespeare* (Arlington Heights, IL: AHM, 1978), a volume in the Goldentree Bibliographies series, similarly classifies about 4,600 unannotated entries for editions and critical studies.

1188.   Wells, Stanley. **Shakespeare: A Bibliographical Guide**. 2d ed. Oxford: Clarendon, 1990. 430p. LC 89-72129. ISBN 0-19-871036-4

Assembles 19 survey essays by specialists, including Kenneth Muir, Norman Sanders, and Maurice Charney, on scholarship on Shakespeare's text, performance, individual works, and recent critical themes and approaches, such as cultural materialism, feminism and gender, and new historicism, with supporting critical bibliographies of editions and studies. Wells' "The Study of Shakespeare" (pp. 1-15) surveys reference works for Shakespeare. Unindexed.

Dictionaries, Encyclopedias, and Handbooks
1189.   Boyce, Charles. **Shakespeare A to Z: The Essential Reference to His Plays, His Poems, His Life and Times, and More**. New York: Facts on File, 1990. 742p. LC 90-31239. ISBN 0-8160-1805-7.

A straight forward and effective guide to Shakespeare's works intended for the "information and entertainment of the student and the general reader" (p. ix). The majority of the entries cover characters in the plays. Entries for individual plays give a plot summary, commentary on themes and characters, and information on stage history, sources, and textual history, with numerous cross-references to other entries. Line citations are taken from volumes of the *New Arden Shakespeare* (London: Methuen, 1951-84). Unlike Campbell and Quinn's *The Reader's Encyclopedia of Shakespeare* (entry 1190), Boyce largely refrains from quoting sources and authorities. Entries lack bibliographies; the volume concludes with a selective list for "Suggested Reading" (pp. 725-28). The volume also includes black-and-white illustrations of actors, productions, title pages, and the like. Elaborate appendixes, serving as indexes to the entries, identify entries for actors and other theatrical figures; fictional characters; Shakespeare's historical contemporaries; "Documents and Artifacts," such as the

First Folio and "Pied Bull Quarto"; historical events and places; the individual plays and poems; related works of others (mostly sources and analogues); Shakespeare's family; scholars, authors, translators, artists, printers, and publishers; and a very limited number of theatrical and literary terms.

1190. Campbell, Oscar James, and Edward G. Quinn. **The Reader's Encyclopedia of Shakespeare**. New York: Thomas Y. Crowell, 1966. 1,014p. LC 66-11946.

Campbell and Quinn's companion is the best guide for identifying the factual details in the life, works, and times of Shakespeare. This gives thorough introductions to the texts, background and sources, plots and characters, and stage and critical histories of the plays and poems. Entries for Shakespeare's works also include extended excerpts from major critical studies as well as brief supporting bibliographies. In addition, Campbell and Quinn offer entries for Shakespeare's characters and for real people associated with his life and works, such as Philip Henslowe, Edwin Booth, and Franco Zeffirelli. Boyce's *Shakespeare A to Z* (entry 1189) gives equally useful information on Shakespearean performers and performances. Entries in Campbell and Quinn for places, including the Hope Theatre and New Place, and for such topics as "homosexuality," "military life," and "language and characterization" also offer solid information and cite primary sources. Includes chronology of Shakespeare's life and works, transcripts of selected primary documents, and a selected classified bibliography (pp. 983-1014). Other similar Shakespeare companions and handbooks are legion. They include Harley Granville-Barker and G. B. Harrison's *A Companion to Shakespeare Studies* (Cambridge: Cambridge University Press, 1934); Alfred Harbage's *William Shakespeare: A Reader's Guide* (New York: Noonday Press, 1963); F. E. Halliday's *A Shakespeare Companion*, revised ed. (New York: Penguin, 1964); Gareth Evans and Barbara Lloyd Evans' *The Shakespeare Companion* (New York: Scribner's, 1978); Stanley Wells' *Shakespeare: An Illustrated Dictionary* (New York: Oxford University Press, 1978); Kenneth Muir and Samuel Schoenbaum's *A New Companion to Shakespeare Studies* (Cambridge: Cambridge University Press, 1971); Marguerite Alexander's *Shakespeare and His Contemporaries: A Reader's Guide* (New York: Barnes & Noble, 1979); and Levi Fox's *The Shakespeare Handbook* (Boston: G. K. Hall, 1988).

1191. Davis, J. Madison, and A. Daniel Frankforter. **The Shakespeare Name Dictionary**. New York: Garland, 1995. 533p. (Garland Reference Library of the Humanities, vol. 976). LC 94-13784. ISBN 0-8240-6341-4.

A comprehensive index of proper names for real and fictional persons, places, and things—and much more—in Shakespeare's works. More comprehensive than Stokes' *Dictionary of the Characters and Proper Names in the Works of Shakespeare* (entry 1192) largely because Davis and Frankforter identify a substantial number of words that are used like, or substituted for, proper names such as "Jakes" (meaning privy), "Jack-priest," "King's Peace," "King's English," and even the oaths "Zounds" (for "God's wounds") and "Bodykins" (for "by God's body"). Entries neatly place the proper names in Shakespeare's works, with line citations to Stanley Wells and Gary Taylor's *William Shakespeare: The Complete Works* (New York: Oxford University Press, 1986), but lack the references to classical and other sources and analogues provided by Stokes' more scholarly and still valuable resource. Bibliography of works consulted (pp. 521-33). Less comprehensive than *The Shakespeare Name Dictionary*, Kenneth McLeish's *Shakespeare's Characters: A Players Press Guide: Who's Who of Shakespeare* (Studio City, CA: Players Press, 1992) alphabetically lists summaries of the plays and identifications of all characters in them. Emphasis is on explaining a character's dramatic significance.

1192. Stokes, Francis Griffin. **Dictionary of the Characters and Proper Names in the Works of Shakespeare, with Notes on the Sources and Dates of the Plays and Poems**. 1924; reprint New York: Peter Smith, 1949. 359p. OCLC 2592163.

Stokes offers coverage of names in Shakespeare's works that is uniquely valuable for research on sources, including the likes of Ovid, Higden's *Polychronicon*, Hollinshed, Cinthio, and Michelangelo Florio. In addition to providing brief, basic information on the dating, publication, and sources of the plots for Shakespeare's plays, Stokes references and describes the sources for characters, place names, and miscellaneous personifications that are listed in the *dramatis personae* or only referenced in allusions. Coverage includes characters based on medieval history (Hotspur, Macbeth), classical myth and history (Ulysses, Cleopatra), and fiction (Ariel, Othello). Entries are cross-referenced to text, act, scene, and line. Additional coverage of names is provided by Walter Jerrold's *A Descriptive Index to Shakespeare's Characters in Shakespeare's Words* (1932; reprint Detroit, MI: Gale, 1975). Place names are explained in Edward H. Sugden's *A Topographical Dictionary to the Works of Shakespeare and His Fellow Dramatists* (New York: Longmans, 1925).

Indexes and Concordances

1193.   Onions, C. T., and Robert D. Eagleson. **A Shakespeare Glossary**. New York: Oxford University Press, 1986. 326p. LC 84-7912. ISBN 0-19-812521-6.

A third revision of Onions' classic dictionary by Robert D. Eagleson, this relies on modern linguistic scholarship to bring definitions of Shakespeare's vocabulary up to date. Illustrations of usage (usually three per word), based on the text of G. Blakemore Evans' edition of *The Riverside Shakespeare* (Boston: Houghton Mifflin, 1974), support entries for about 25,000 words used by Shakespeare, including such obsolete words as "acture," "whiffler," and "eke" and altered modern words such as "silly," "wake," and "politician." Onions' dictionary is as fundamental as the *Oxford English Dictionary* for the study of Shakespeare's vocabulary, although even Onions' guide is less comprehensive than the two-volume third edition of Alexander Schmidt and Gregor Sarrazin's *Shakespeare-Lexicon: A Complete Dictionary of All the English Words, Phrases and Constructions in the Works of the Poet* (Berlin: Georg Reimer, 1902). Eugene F. Shewmaker's *Shakespeare's Language: A Glossary of Unfamiliar Words in Shakespeare's Plays and Poems* (New York: Facts on File, 1996), based on a combination of several standard editions, usefully supplements information in Onions' guide. Helge Kokeritz's *Shakespeare's Pronunciation* (New Haven, CT: Yale University Press, 1953) and *Shakespeare's Names: A Pronouncing Dictionary* (New Haven, CT: Yale University Press, 1959) also provide useful explanations and guidance for Shakespeare's language. Michael Rheta Martin and Richard C. Harris' *The Concise Encyclopedic Guide to Shakespeare* (New York: Horizon Press, 1971) identify and define a wide range of words, terms, names, and allusions in Shakespeare's works, with cross-references to George Lyman Kittredge's *The Complete Works of Shakespeare* (Boston: Ginn, 1936).

1194.   Spevack, Marvin. **A Complete and Systematic Concordance to the Works of Shakespeare**. Hildesheim: Georg Olms Verlagsbuchhandlung, 1968-80. 9 vols. LC 68-108766.

Based on the modern-spelling text of G. Blakemore Evans' *The Riverside Shakespeare* (Boston: Houghton Mifflin, 1974), Spevack's index consists of "a series of interlocking concordances to individual plays, to the characters, to the poems (singly and together), and to the complete works—in which all the words are indexed in exactly the form in which they appear in the text of Shakespeare, together with primary statistical data, as well as the indication of homographs and departures from the respective copy texts" (vol. 1, p. vii). Vols. 1 through 3 index the characters' lines by the individual works, with vols. 4 through 6 alphabetically concording the complete works. Vol. 7 concords stage directions and speech prefixes, and vol. 8 indexes bad quartos of individual works, with vol. 9 listing substantive variants from the copytexts. *The Harvard Concordance to Shakespeare* (Cambridge: Harvard University Press, 1973) represents a convenient abridgment of the contents of vols. 4 through 7. Coverage is supplemented by Louis Ule's *A*

Concordance to the Shakespeare Apocrypha (Hildesheim: Olms, 1987). Trevor H. Howard-Hill's 37-volume *Oxford Shakespeare Concordances* (Oxford: Clarendon Press, 1969-72) provides an old-spelling index. Donow's *Concordance to the Sonnet Sequences* (entry 337) offers more limited indexing to the vocabulary of Shakespeare's sonnets.

1195. Spevack, Marvin. **A Shakespeare Thesaurus.** Hildesheim: Georg Olms, 1993. 541p. (Shakespeare Database). ISBN 3-487-09775-3.

A companion to Spevack's *A Complete and Systematic Concordance to the Works of Shakespeare,* Spevack assigns each of Shakespeare's words, including proper names of persons, places, things, events, and the like, to one of 37 main categories containing 897 subgroups. Categories and subgroups (given in standard British spelling) resemble dictionary headwords, representing the physical world; plants; animals; humans, family, friendship; life, birth, death; body, bodily functions; health, medicine; dwellings, furnishings; food; clothing; basic manual acts; sense perception; emotions; qualities; mind, thought; sociopolitical structure; solidarity; power; opposition; warfare; law; trade, possession; occupations, tools; communication; education; arts, leisure; pastimes, games; religion, superstition; existence, relation; manner; quantity; time; space; motion; ships, navigation; names: persons and places; and names: fictional characters. Entries indicate parts of speech for each word. Entries for malapropisms and characters with the same names give act-scene-line references to Spevack's concordance. An alphabetical index to all entries cross-references the categories and subgroups.

1196. Stevenson, Burton. **Stevenson's Book of Shakespeare Quotations: Being Also a Concordance & a Glossary of the Unique Words & Phrases in the Plays & Poems.** London: Cassell, 1969. 2,055p. OCLC 13265713.

Difficult-to-identify lines are identifiable by consulting Spevack's concordance (entry 1194). Shakespeare's more familiar lines are topically arranged in Stevenson's dictionary, first published in 1937 as *The Home Book of Shakespeare Quotations. The Folger Book of Shakespeare Quotations* (Washington, DC: Folger Shakespeare Library, 1979) is an abridgment of Stevenson's handbook. Other significant, more specialized indexes of Shakespeare's language include R. W. Dent's *Shakespeare's Proverbial Language: An Index* (Berkeley, CA: University of California Press, 1981) and Eric Partridge's *Shakespeare's Bawdy* (London: Routledge, 1947). First published in 1985, Trevor R. Griffiths and Trevor A. Joscelyn's *Shakespeare's Quotations: A Players Press Guide* (Studio City, CA: Players Press, 1992) places some 2,000 quotations, arranged by plays and poems, in plain-English contexts with glosses and explanations and is based on the New Penguin Shakespeare. Michael Macrone's *Brush Up Your Shakespeare!* (New York: Harper & Row, 1990) glosses a very selective set of frequently used phrases from Shakespeare, based on the Riverside edition. Among the many collections intended to help writers and speakers find just the right quote for any occasion is Louis Marder and Kathy Wagner's *Speak the Speech: The Shakespeare Quotation Book* (New York: HarperCollins, 1994), which arranges more than 3,000 quotations (based on the Shakespeare Data Bank) in some 500 topical sections, ranging from "Absence" to "Youth," and includes a glossary of early modern words used in quotes and indexes. Margaret Miner and Hugh Rawson's *A Dictionary of Quotations from Shakespeare: A Topical Guide to over 3,000 Great Passages from the Plays, Sonnets, and Narrative Poems* (New York: Dutton, 1992) is based on Sylvan Barnet's *The Complete Signet Classic Shakespeare* (New York: Harcourt Brace Jovanovich, 1972).

Journals

1197. **Hamlet Studies: An International Journal of Research on The Tragedie of Hamlet, Prince of Denmarke.** New Delhi: R. W. Desai, 1979-. 2/yr. ISSN 0256-2480.

A very specialized scholarly journal—"the first journal devoted to a single literary work" (masthead)—*Hamlet Studies* focuses exclusively on *Hamlet*. Each issue is packed with as many as a dozen articles, notes, and other comments reflecting scholarly attention to ghosts, revenge, madness, procrastination, and other features of the play. Such articles as "Hamnet or Hamlet, That Is the Question" and "Taboo, or Not Taboo? The Text, Dating, and Authorship of *Hamlet*, 1589-1623" are representative. Other features have addressed the play's influence on contemporary and later English and Continental drama and literature. In addition, the journal publishes reviews of recent productions and new publications. A regular bibliographic feature, "A Review of Periodical Articles," abstracts selected articles on *Hamlet* published in other scholarly journals. *Hamlet Studies* is indexed in *AES* and *MLA*.

1198. **Shakespeare Bulletin: A Journal of Performance Criticism and Scholarship**. Easton, PA: Lafayette College, 1982-. 4/yr. ISSN 0748-2558.

Incorporating *Shakespeare on Film Newsletter* (1976-92), *Shakespeare Bulletin* "provides commentary on Shakespeare and Renaissance drama" (masthead) in the form of a few feature articles on topics of current interest (such as the restoration of the Globe and Kenneth Branagh's several productions) and extensive reviews of stage and media productions of Shakespeare in United States and around the world. An excellently illustrated record of current global interest in Shakespeare. Calendar of events identifies productions and conferences and announces opportunities for study and new publications. Also includes selection of book reviews. Indexed in *MLA*.

1199. **Shakespeare in Southern Africa: Journal of the Shakespeare Society of Southern Africa**. Grahamstown, SA: Shakespeare Society of Southern Africa, Rhodes University, 1987-. Annual. ISSN 1011-582X.

Substantial scholarly features focus on thematic and other specific aspects of Shakespeare's works, examine current and historical theatrical productions both in South Africa and elsewhere, and identify Shakespeare's influences on the likes of Verdi, Shaw, and T. S. Eliot. A significant number of articles have examined Shakespeare in relation to South African politics. Articles such as Peter Mtuze's "Mdledle's Xhosa Translation of *Julius Caesar*," 4 (1990-91): 65-72, and others on translations into other African languages, afford unique perspectives on Shakespeare. Occasional bibliographic contributions include Laurence Wright's "A Checklist of South African Theses and Dissertations on Shakespeare," 6 (1993): 88-92; and the Durban Municipal Library's "A Bibliography of Translations of Shakespeare's Plays into Southern African Languages," 2 (1988): 124-30. The annual also publishes a regular bibliographic feature, "A Shakespeare Bibliography of Periodical Publications in South Africa," compiled by Cecilia Blight. Volumes contain a few book reviews. *Shakespeare in Southern Africa* is indexed in *MLA* and *MHRA*.

1200. **Shakespeare Jahrbuch**. Wiemar: Verlag Hermann Bohlaus Nachfolger, 1925-. Annual. ISSN 0080-9128.

Shakespeare Jahrbuch features major critical studies (mostly in German but also in English) on the full range of topics related to Shakespeare and his works. A particular focus is textual studies and bibliography, but vol. 130 (1993) contained 12 features on Shakespeare and the media. The annual regularly publishes reviews of international productions, with a significant bibliography of current performance reviews and criticism. *Shakespeare Jahrbuch* also offers an extensive selection of book reviews. Formerly *Jahrbuch der Deutschen Shakespeare-Gesellschaft* (1865-24) and issued by several publishers over its long history, recent publication history is more complicated. *Shakespeare Jahrbuch* was absorbed by Deutsche Shakespeare-Gesellschaft West and issued as *Jahrbuch 1991* (1990) and *Jahrbuch 1992* (1992). These volumes, in fact, constitute *Shakespeare Jahrbuch*'s vols. 129 and 130 in that

Shakespeare Jahrbuch in turn, in 1993, absorbed *Deutsche Shakespeare-Gesellschaft* (1904-1993), resuming its former title. All volumes contain indexes. *Shakespeare Jahrbuch* is indexed in *MLA*.

1201. Shakespeare Newsletter. New Rochelle, NY: Iona College, 1951- . 4/yr. ISSN 0037-3214.

The practical usefulness of this journal to "Shakespeareans"—literary scholars, theater professionals, and lovers of Shakespeare's works—cannot be overestimated. *Shakespeare Newsletter* offers comprehensive coverage of current news and information about Shakespeare, much like a local newspaper. Emphasis is on current and upcoming events, providing calendars of festivals and conferences and announcing new discoveries, productions, and publications. Likewise, regular departments describe and digest conference papers, lectures, productions, books, dissertations, and scholarly articles. A few feature articles in each issue address more topical interests, such as the latest Kenneth Branagh production, progress in the development of the Shakespeare Data Bank, and perennial controversies about the authorship of Shakespeare's works. Obituaries for and tributes to leading Shakespeare scholars also appear. Although students in need of studies of themes and characterizations in Shakespeare's works will not find many of them here, they will find ample evidence that there is much ado about Shakespeare. *Shakespeare Newsletter* is indexed in *AES* and *MLA*.

1202. Shakespeare Quarterly. Washington, DC: Folger Shakespeare Library, 1950- . 4/yr. ISSN 0037-3222.

A prestigious scholarly journal sponsored by the Folger Shakespeare Library, issues of *Shakespeare Quarterly* regularly feature as many as six major research articles and several brief scholarly notes. These represent the full range of interests and critical approaches. Most studies focus on specific aspects of Shakespeare's works rather than biography or cultural backgrounds. Studies of sources and texts and interpretations of characterizations are common. Rhetorical, psychological, and feminist critical methods are represented. A recent special issue, "Teaching Judith Shakespeare" 47.4 (Winter 1996), addressed topics on Shakespeare and women. Issues of *Shakespeare Quarterly* also publish selections of five to 15 reviews of new publications. In addition, the journal includes several other important features. "Shakespeare Performed" reviews recent stage productions in the United States and abroad. An additional issue, published in December, is an annual, classified "World Shakespeare Bibliography" that covers editions, general and specialized studies, and studies of individual works, including stage and media production and performance reviews. Recent listings have included about 5,000 briefly annotated entries. This bibliography makes *Shakespeare Quarterly* the most important journal for research on Shakespeare. The cumulated annual bibliography, covering 1900-date, is available electronically in *World Shakespeare Bibliography on CD-ROM* (Cambridge: Cambridge University Press, 1996-). *Shakespeare Quarterly* is indexed in *AES, A&HCI, HI, MHRA,* and *MLA*.

Wortman's *A Guide to Serial Bibliographies for Modern Literatures*, pp. 276-79, describes other current and previously published serial bibliographies for Shakespeare. Patterson's *Author Newsletters and Journals*, pp. 279-96, describes other previously published journals for Shakespeare.

1203. Shakespeare Studies. Tokyo: Shakespeare Society of Japan, 1962- . Annual. ISSN 0582-9402.

Substantial English-language articles (largely by Japanese scholars) on Shakespeare and his contemporaries, especially Christopher Marlowe and Ben Jonson most recently, predominate in *Shakespeare Studies*. Studies represent diverse critical approaches (feminist, sociopolitical, psychological, new historicist, and the like) and span the full range of topics and interests—from themes and images, Shakespeare's sources, and the printing histories of the quartos and folios to staging Shakespearean productions in Japanese. Early volumes included several noteworthy bibliographic studies. Presently *Shakespeare Studies* is indexed in *MLA* through 1992.

1204.   **Shakespeare Studies: An Annual Gathering of Research, Criticism, and Reviews**. Cranbury, NJ: Associated University Presses, 1965-. Annual. ISSN 0582-9399.

To vol. 23 (1995), annual volumes have featured as many as 20 substantial, scholarly articles as well as five to 10 reviews of new publications. Contributions have reflected a wider range of interests in the English Renaissance than either *Shakespeare Quarterly* (entry 1202) or *Shakespeare Survey* (entry 1205), including articles on Shakespeare's society as well as his life and works. With vol. 24 (1996), the traditional fare of *Shakespeare Studies* moves in "new directions," according to editor Leeds Barroll, with a "new emphasis on theoretical issues" (p. 9). Special features in the volume focus on editing early modern texts (covering both Shakespeare and other writers, especially women), with review articles. The remainder of the volume continues to offer scholarly studies on the full range of Shakespearean and Renaissance topics and a extensive selection of book reviews. Each volume includes an index. *Shakespeare Studies* is indexed in *HI*, *MHRA*, and *MLA*.

1205.   **Shakespeare Survey: An Annual Survey of Shakespearian Study and Production**. New York: Cambridge University Press, 1948-. Annual. ISSN 0080-9152.

An annual collection of 20 or more scholarly, heavily illustrated research articles by major scholars, volumes of *Shakespeare Survey* focus on special topics, including such individual works as *Romeo and Juliet* (vol. 49), *King Lear* (vols. 13 and 33) and *Hamlet* (vol. 9). Other volumes have been devoted to such subjects as characterization, film and television adaptation, stages and staging, and language. Future volumes will be devoted to Shakespeare and language (vol. 50) and Shakespeare in the eighteenth century (vol. 51). In addition, regular features review stage productions in Great Britain and "The Year's Contributions to Shakespearian Study," a survey of recent critical, biographical, and textual studies of Shakespeare's life and works. Editors of this important journal have included such significant scholars as Allardyce Nicoll, Kenneth Muir, and Stanley Wells. Volumes include indexes. *Shakespeare Survey* is indexed in *HI*, *MHRA*, and *MLA*.

1206.   **Shakespeare Yearbook: An Interdisciplinary Annual Dealing With All Influences on the Shakespearean Corpus and Culture**. Lewiston, NY: Edwin Mellen Press, 1990-. Annual. ISSN 1045-9456.

Shakespeare Yearbook publishes articles "dealing with all aspects of Shakespeare and his period, with particular emphasis on theater-oriented, comparative, and interdisciplinary studies" (masthead). Vols. 1-3 offered scholarly articles on the full range of topics in Shakespeare and the Renaissance. With vol. 4 (1994), volumes are to focus on "a main theme" but will also include "independent contributions" on more general topics. Vol. 4 is devoted to Shakespeare and opera, including nearly 20 articles and a selection of book reviews. "Shakespeare and France," vol. 5 (1997), for 1994, contains 20 substantial contributions, including Jean-Marie Maguin's "Shakespeare Studies in France Since 1960" (pp. 359-73). Several years behind publication schedule, proposed volumes include "Shakespeare, the Tudor Myth, and Modern Historiography" in vol. 6, for 1995; "Shakespeare in Hungary" in vol. 7, for 1996; "Hamlet on Screen in vol. 8, for 1997; "Shakespeare and Japan" in vol. 9, for 1998; and "Shakespeare and Italy" in vol. 10, for 1999. Volumes do not contain indexes. *Shakespeare Yearbook* is indexed in *MLA*.

1207.   **Upstart Crow**. Springfield, MO: Drury College, 1987-. Annual. ISSN 0886-2168.

Both long and brief scholarly articles and notes address the full range of topics in Shakespeare. Typical features include "Shakespeare's Christianity: The Future for Scholarship" and "A Macbeth for Our Time." Studies of specific literary images and themes, characterization, manuscript sources, language, and current and historical stage and media productions predominate. Past volumes have regularly reviewed productions at the Alabama Shakespeare Festival. Volumes also publish book reviews. *Upstart Crow* is indexed in MLA.

Ntozake Shange, 1948-

Bibliographies

Catherine Carr Lee reviews research on Shange in *Contemporary Authors: Bibliographical Series: Volume 3: American Dramatists*, pp. 305-24.

Karl (Jay) Shapiro, 1913-

Bibliographies

1208.   Bartlett, Lee. **Karl Shapiro: A Descriptive Bibliography, 1933-1977**. New York: Garland, 1979. 194p. (Garland Reference Library of the Humanities, vol. 131). LC 78-68245. ISBN 0-8240-9812-9.

This gives detailed bibliographic descriptions for Shapiro's primary materials published from 1933 through 1977, including entries for separately published books, pamphlets, and broadsides; collaborative and edited works and books introduced by Shapiro; contributions to periodicals; appearances in anthologies; and translations of Shapiro's works. Entries give title-page transcriptions, collations, physical descriptions (of pagination, bindings, and dust jackets), contents, and information on publishing histories. An appendix lists selected reviews and studies of Shapiro. Bartlett's guide offers more detail than William White's *Karl Shapiro: A Bibliography* (Detroit, MI: Wayne State University Press, 1960), although White's guide provides useful descriptions of Shapiro's manuscripts in the collection of Charles Feinberg. Also for works by Shapiro, see *First Printings of American Authors*, vol. 1, pp. 321-24. Shapiro's manuscripts are listed in Robbins' *American Literary Manuscripts*, p. 289.

(George) Bernard Shaw, 1856-1950

Bibliographies

1209.   Laurence, Dan H. **Bernard Shaw: A Bibliography**. New York: Oxford University Press, 1983. 2 vols. (Soho Bibliographies, no. 22). LC 81-22454. ISBN 0-19-818179-5.

The standard bibliography of Shaw's primary materials, Laurence's guide provides detailed entries for Shaw's books and other separate publications, proofs and rehearsal copies, contributions to books, works edited by Shaw, contributions to periodicals (some 3,975 entries), miscellaneous writings (such as postcards and blurbs), and broadcasts and recordings of Shaw's voice and of his works. Laurence also describes Shaw's manuscripts at the University of Texas, Cornell University, the Berg Collection of the New York Public Library, the National Library of Ireland, and elsewhere (pp. 891-95), and identifies works misattributed to Shaw. Entries include title-page transcriptions, detailed collations and physical descriptions, contents, and publishing histories for editions and later printings. A separate, selected list of works about Shaw through 1982 is also included. A very detailed, comprehensive index offers access. Also for a bibliography of works by and about Shaw, see *NCBEL*, III, pp. 1169-82.

1210.   Wearing, J. P. **G. B. Shaw: An Annotated Bibliography of Writings About Him. Volume I: 1871-1930**. DeKalb, IL: Northern Illinois University Press, 1986. 562p. (Annotated Secondary Bibliography Series on English Literature in Transition, 1880-1920). LC 86-8649. ISBN 0-87580-125-0.

Other volumes in this three-volume comprehensive bibliography of writings about Shaw include:

1210.1. Adams, Elsie B., and Donald C. Haberman. **G. B. Shaw: An Anno-tated Bibliography of Writings about Him. Volume II: 1931-1956**. DeKalb, IL: Northern Illinois University Press, 1987. 667p. (Annotated Secondary Bibliography Series on English Literature in Transition, 1880-1920). LC 86-8649. ISBN 0-87580-121-8.

1210.2. Haberman, Donald C. **G. B. Shaw: An Annotated Bibliography of Writings About Him. Volume III: 1957-1978**. DeKalb, IL: Northern Illinois University Press, 1986. 824p. (Annotated Secondary Bibliography Series on English Literature in Transition, 1880-1920). LC 86-12477. ISBN 0-87580-111-0.

Combined volumes give comprehensive coverage of writings about Shaw through the late-1970s, chronologically arranging annotated entries for a total of about 8,500 criticisms and comments on Shaw in books, parts of books, articles, reviews of Shaw's works and of selected works about Shaw, dissertations, letters to editors, news items, and the like in all languages. Wearing includes about 3,600 entries; Adams and Haberman, 2,394 entries; and Haberman, 2,677 entries. Annotations are both descriptive and critical, with significant works receiving extended reviews. Volumes include sets of indexes for critics, titles, periodicals and newspapers, languages, and primary titles that offer solid access.

1211. Weintraub, Stanley. **Bernard Shaw: A Guide to Research**. University Park: Pennsylvania State University Press, 1992. 154p. LC 91-41779. ISBN 0-2710-0831-8.

A "subjective overview by one scholar" (p. 2)—a leading authority on Shaw—of research resources and criticisms for Shaw. Extensive discussions of particular bibliographic resources in topical sections covering provenance and copyright; bibliographies; editions; biographies and autobiographies; early criticisms; general criticisms; criticisms of novels and other fiction; early musical, dramatic, and literary journalism; criticisms of individual plays; non-English-language criticisms; fictional works about Shaw; and influence and reputation. Weintraub does not hesitate to identify works as either standard or biased. Author, title, and subject indexes offer excellent access. Weintraub essentially updates and greatly expands his previous review of research on Shaw in Finneran's *Anglo-Irish Literature*, pp. 167-215. Weintraub's guide affords an excellent model that should be emulated for other writers. Research on Shaw is also reviewed by Margery M. Morgan in Wells' *English Drama*, pp. 231-47; and Tramble T. Turner in Demastes and Kelly's *British Playwrights, 1880-1956*, pp. [364]-80, and in Schrank and Demastes' *Irish Playwrights, 1880-1995: A Research and Production Sourcebook*, pp. 322-40.

Dictionaries, Encyclopedias, and Handbooks

1212. Hardwick, Michael, and Mollie Hardwick. **The Bernard Shaw Companion**. London: John Murray, 1973. 193p. LC 73-175405. ISBN 0-7195-2717-1.

The Hardwicks summarize the plots of Shaw's plays, identify characters in a "Who's Who," topically arrange notable quotations from Shaw's works (under such categories as "England," "Mankind and Society," and "The Arts"), and provide a brief biography of Shaw. Descriptions of characters are not as informative as those included in Hartnoll's guide (entry 1213). Also useful, C. Lewis Broad and Violet M. Broad's *Dictionary to the Plays and Novels of Bernard Shaw: With Bibliography of His Works and of the Literature Concerning Him, with a Record of the Principal Shavian Play Productions* (1929; reprint St. Clair Shores, MI: Scholarly Press, 1972) offers synopses of plots. The Broads' information on play productions and coverage of Shaw's primary and secondary bibliography is superseded in the bibliographies of Laurence (entry 1209) and Wearing (entry 1210). C. B. Purdom's *A Guide to the Plays of Bernard Shaw* (London: Methuen, 1963) and Edward Wagenknecht's *Guide to Bernard Shaw* (New York: Russell & Russell, 1971) provide survey introductions to Shaw's works.

1213.   Hartnoll, Phyllis. **Who's Who in Shaw**. London: Elm Tree Books, 1975. 247p. LC 75-321146. ISBN 0-241-89097-7.

Hartnoll's guide gives detailed, identifying entries for about 900 characters in Shaw's plays, with an accompanying play-by-play listing of their appearances. The information provided is fuller than that included in several other dictionaries.

Indexes and Concordances

1214.   Bevan, E. Dean. **A Concordance to the Plays and Prefaces of Bernard Shaw**. Detroit, MI: Gale, 1971. 10 vols. LC 77-166191.

Based on the *Standard Edition of the Works of Bernard Shaw* (New York: Constable, 1930-50), this is a keyword-in-context concordance to Shaw's dramatic works (excluding only a few "playlets"), citing plays, acts, scenes, and lines. Also useful for the study of Shaw's vocabulary, Paul Kozelka's *A Glossary to the Plays of Bernard Shaw* (New York: Teachers College, Columbia University, 1959) identifies and glosses more than 860 words and phrases (including stage directions and allusions) that Kozelka considers "uniquely Shavian or peculiarly British" (Introduction). George B. Bryan and Wolfgang Mieder's *The Proverbial Bernard Shaw: An Index to Proverbs in the Works of George Bernard Shaw* (Westport, CT: Greenwood Press, 1994) claims to be a comprehensive index to some 2,000 proverbs, proverbial expressions, and proverbial comparisons discovered in Shaw's works, based on a variety of standard and readily available editions of the plays, letters, diaries, book reviews, and other published and unpublished works, including *Complete Plays with Prefaces* (New York: Dodd, Mead, 1963).

Journals

1215.   **Independent Shavian**. New York: The Bernard Shaw Society, 1957-. 3/yr. ISSN 0019-3763.

Sponsored by the Bernard Shaw Society, formerly the New York Shavians, issues include a few brief biographical and critical articles (of two to eight pages), several less substantial notes on such topics as productions of Shaw's works and minor Shaviana, and excerpts from Shaw's works. In addition to reviews of new publications, the journal publishes membership news, reports on the society's activities, obituaries, and announcements. Indexed in *AES* and *MHRA*.

Patterson's *Author Newsletters and Journals*, pp. 296-301, describes other previously published journals for Shaw.

1216.   **Shavian: The Journal of the Shaw Society**. Stone, Staffordshire: Bernard Shaw Society, 1946-. Annual. ISSN 0037-3346.

Recent typically brief features include "The Intelligent Person's Guide to Shaw's Comic Art" and "Shaw's Fabian Tracts and His Political Plays." Most contributions offer interpretations of themes and characters, although occasional articles have addressed publication and production history. Formerly *Bernard Shaw Society Bulletin* (1946-53), volumes have also featured a "Literary Survey" essay covering criticisms of Shaw. The annual also publishes reviews of new publications. *Shavian* is indexed in *MLA* to 1988 and in *MHRA* to date.

1217.   **Shaw: The Annual of Bernard Shaw Studies**. University Park, PA: Pennsylvania State University Press, 1951- . Annual. ISSN 0741-5842.

The most substantial and important journal for Shaw scholarship. Continuing *Shaw Bulletin* (1951-58) and *Shaw Review* (1958-80), *Shaw* publishes 10 long scholarly and critical articles that offer close readings and interpretations of individual works, examine influences on Shaw and Shaw's influence on other writers, and discuss the text and language of his works or their stage productions. Recent volumes (with guest editors) have focused on broad themes, including Shaw and other playwrights (vol. 13), the first 100 years of Shaw criticism (vol. 14), and the unpublished Shaw (vol. 16). Forthcoming volumes will address speculative fiction (vol. 17) and Shaw and history (vol. 19). Publishes occasional bibliographic articles. In addition to including several reviews of new publications, the annual features an important "Continuing Checklist of Shaviana," which briefly describes recent editions of Shaw's works; critical books, articles, and dissertations about Shaw; and recordings and other media related to Shaw. *Shaw* is indexed in *MHRA* and *MLA*.

Henry Wheeler Shaw (Josh Billings), 1818-1885
Bibliographies

For works by Shaw, see *Bibliography of American Literature*, vol. 7, pp. 399-409. Shaw's manuscripts are listed in Robbins' *American Literary Manuscripts*, p. 289. See *Bibliography of American Fiction, 1866-1918*, pp. 321-22, for Kreg A. Abshire's checklist of works by and about Shaw.

Irwin Shaw, 1913-1984
Bibliographies

For works by Shaw, see *First Printings of American Authors*, vol. 5, pp. 285-91. Shaw's manuscripts are listed in Robbins' *American Literary Manuscripts*, p. 289. See *Bibliography of American Fiction, 1919-1988*, pp. 454-55, for James R. Giles' checklist of works by and about Shaw. Walter H. Placzek identifies works by and about Shaw in Demastes' *American Playwrights, 1880-1945*, pp. 374-79.

Wilfred (John Joseph) Sheed, 1930-
Bibliographies

For works by Sheed, see *First Printings of American Authors*, vol. 4, pp. 335-37.

Mary Wollstonecraft Shelley, 1797-1851
Bibliography

1218. Lyles, W. H. **Mary Shelley: An Annotated Bibliography**. New York: Garland, 1975. 297p. (Garland Reference Library of the Humanities, vol. 22). LC 75-17713. ISBN 0-8240-9993-1.

Covering works by and about Shelley, Lyles provides separate listings for Shelley's letters and journals, novels, plays, short fiction, poems, travel works, biographies, articles and reviews, and edited works, in addition to listing about 900 books, articles, reviews, dissertations, works in non-English languages, and fictional works (including screenplays) about Shelley. Entries for primary works give brief bibliographic information and describe contents. Critical annotations for secondary materials indicate significant and important works. Appendixes chronologically list primary works; reprint the text of "The Legend of George Frankenstein"; list stage, television, and film adaptations of *Frankenstein;* and identify prices of Shelley's works at auctions and sales. More detailed coverage of adaptations and other works based on *Frankenstein* is provided in Donald F. Glut's *The Frankenstein Catalog: Being a Comprehensive Listing of Novels, Translations, Adaptations, Stories, Critical Works, Popular Articles, Series, Fumetti, Verse, Stage Plays, Films, Cartoons, Puppetry, Radio & Television Programs, Comics, Satire & Humor, Spoken & Musical Recordings, Tapes, and Sheet Music Featuring Frankenstein's Monster and/or Descended from Shelley's Novel* (Jefferson, NC: McFarland, 1984). Also for a bibliography of works by and about Shelley, see *NCBEL*, III, pp. 761-64. Robert Donald Spector reviews research on Shelley in *The English Gothic: A Bibliographic Guide to Writers from Horace Walpole to Mary Shelley*, pp. 205-62.

Journals

See *Keats-Shelley Journal* (entry 779).

Percy Bysshe Shelley, 1792-1822

Bibliographies

1219. Dunbar, Clement. **A Bibliography of Shelley Studies: 1823-1950**. New York: Garland, 1976. 320p. (Garland Reference Library of the Humanities, vol. 32). LC 75-24097. ISBN 0-8240-9980-X.

Dunbar chronologically arranges entries for 3,238 entries for English-language works about Shelley, including early anonymous reviews and comments and selected major editions, published from 1823 through 1950. Annotation is reduced to codes that identify critical studies, textual studies, and the like. Topical indexing is limited to names. Coverage of works about Shelley is continued by listings in *Keats-Shelley Journal* (entry 779). More detailed specialized coverage of early commentaries on Shelley is provided in Karsten Klejs Engelberg's *The Making of the Shelley Myth: An Annotated Bibliography of Criticism of Percy Bysshe Shelley, 1822-1860* (Westport, CT: Meckler, 1988), which chronologically arranges briefly annotated entries for about 1,800 poems, dedications, letters, reviews, and other notices that are the critical bases for Shelley's contemporary reputation. Research on Shelley is reviewed by Stuart Curran in Frank Jordan's *The English Romantic Poets: A Review of Research and Criticism*, pp. 593-664; and by R. B. Woodings in Dyson's *English Poetry*, pp. 224-50.

1220. Forman, H. Buxton. **Shelley's Own Books, Pamphlets & Broadsides, Posthumous Separate Issues, and Posthumous Books Wholly or Mainly by Him**. 1886; New York: Haskell House, 1971. 127p. LC 78-116794. ISBN 0-8383-1036-2.

Forman gives title-page transcriptions, physical descriptions, and information on publishing histories for Shelley's primary works. Although valuable for detail, Forman's guide is based on outdated principles. Similarly valuable (and outdated), Thomas James Wise's *A Shelley Library: A Catalogue of Printed Books, Manuscripts and Autograph Letters by Percy Bysshe Shelley, Harriet Shelley, and Mary Wollstonecraft Shelley* (1924; reprint New York: Haskell House, 1971) gives title-page transcriptions, collations, contents, and information on publishing histories for Shelley's works. Other useful information on Shelley's works is provided in Ruth S. Grannis' *A Descriptive Catalogue of the First Editions in Book Form of the Writings of Percy Bysshe Shelley* (New York: Grolier Club, 1922). Also for a bibliography of works by and about Shelley, see *NCBEL*, III, pp. 309-43.

Dictionaries, Encyclopedias, and Handbooks

1221. Bradley, J. L. **A Shelley Chronology**. Basingstoke: Macmillan, 1993. 93p. (Macmillan Author Chronologies). LC 93-58347. ISBN 0-333-55770-0.

Amounts to a sketchy accounting of Shelley's life and works based on (but without specific citations to) Frederick L. Jones' *The Letters of Percy Bysshe Shelley* (Oxford: Clarendon Press, 1964) and other standard sources. Infrequently notes, for example, that Shelley attended plays or read books. Includes biographies for family members, acquaintances, and others and a selected bibliography (pp. 87-88). Limited (and sometimes ineffective) indexing for major writings of Shelley and Mary Shelley; selected, rather broad topics, such as "Finances," "Health," and "Social Unrest," make it difficult to identify the composition and revision of individual writings, track Shelley's travels in England and on the continent, and the like. Lacks fullness of detail of other volumes in Macmillan's series.

Indexes and Concordances

1222. Ellis, F. S. **Lexical Concordance to the Poetical Works of Percy Bysshe Shelley: An Attempt to Classify Every Word Found Therein According to Its Significance**. London: Quaritch, 1892. 818p. LC 13-24598.

Based on H. B. Forman's two-volume edition of *The Poetical Works* (London: Reeves and Turner, 1882), Ellis references Shelley's vocabulary by context line. Entries indicate the usage and part of speech for each headword. Also available in a reprinted edition (New York: Burt Franklin, 1968).

Journals
See *Keats-Shelley Journal* (entry 779).

William Shenstone, 1714-1763
Bibliographies
Williams' *Seven XVIIIth Century Bibliographies* (entry 35), pp. [38]-71, gives full bibliographic descriptions of Shenstone's works. For a bibliography of works by and about Shenstone, see *NCBEL*, II, pp. 531-34, by John Fuller. Shenstone's manuscripts are described in *Index of English Literary Manuscripts*, III, pt. 3:293-316.

Sam Shepard (Samuel Shepard Rogers Jr.), 1943-
Bibliographies
King's *Ten Modern American Playwrights*, pp. 197-213, gives brief bibliographic information for Shepard's primary works and annotated entries for criticism of Shepard, with a classified list of reviews. Lynda Hart reviews research on Shepard in *Contemporary Authors: Bibliographical Series: Volume 3: American Dramatists*, pp. 325-60.

Thomas Shepard, 1605-1649
Bibliographies
Shepard's manuscripts are listed in Robbins' *American Literary Manuscripts*, p. 290. See Gallagher and Werge's *Early Puritan Writers* (entry 138) for works about Shepard published to 1974.

Richard Brinsley Sheridan, 1751-1816
Bibliographies
1223.   Durant, Jack D. **Richard Brinsley Sheridan: A Reference Guide**. Boston: G. K. Hall, 1981. 312p. (A Reference Publication in Literature). LC 80-28053. ISBN 0-8161-8146-2.
Following an introduction to Sheridan's career and a brief listing of primary materials, Durant chronologically arranges annotated entries for about 1,200 works about Sheridan published from 1816 through 1979. Coverage includes reviews, introductions in editions, dissertations, and critical studies in all languages. Annotations are detailed and evaluative, identifying standard editions, major critical works, and the like. Topical indexing provides detailed headings for such subjects as "bibliography," "Sheridan's funeral," "speeches," and individual works, with subheadings for characters, texts, stage histories, and so forth. Coverage of Sheridan's primary materials is provided in John P. Anderson's checklist in Lloyd C. Sanders' *The Life of Richard Brinsley Sheridan* (London: W. Scott, 1891), pp. i-xi; Walter S. Sichel's "Bibliography of Sheridan's Works, Published and Unpublished," in *Sheridan* (London: Constable, 1909), vol. 2, pp. 445-59; and Williams' *Seven XVIIIth Century Bibliographies*, pp. [207]-39, which includes full bibliographic descriptions of Sheridan's primary works. Also for a bibliography of works by and about Sheridan, see *NCBEL*, II, pp. 816-24. Sheridan's manuscripts are described in *Index of English Literary Manuscripts*, III, pt. 3:317-74. Research on Sheridan is reviewed by Cecil Price in Wells' *English Drama*, pp. 199-212.

Frank Dempster Sherman, 1860-1916
Bibliographies
For works by Sherman, see *Bibliography of American Literature*, vol. 7, pp. 410-16. Sherman's contributions to and reviews of Sherman's works in selected periodicals are identified in Wells' *The Literary Index to American Magazines, 1850-1900*, p. 341. Sherman's manuscripts are listed in Robbins' *American Literary Manuscripts*, p. 290.

Benjamin Penhallow Shillaber, 1814-1890

Bibliographies

For works by Shillaber, see *Bibliography of American Literature*, vol. 7, pp. 417-31. Shillaber's manuscripts are listed in Robbins' *American Literary Manuscripts*, p. 291. See *Bibliography of American Fiction Through 1865*, pp. 217-18, for a checklist of works by and about Shillaber. Wells' *The Literary Index to American Magazines, 1815-1865*, p. 137; and *The Literary Index to American Magazines, 1850-1900*, p. 141, identifies reviews of Shillaber in selected periodicals.

James Shirley, 1596-1666

Bibliographies

1224.   Zimmer, Ruth K. **James Shirley: A Reference Guide**. Boston: G. K. Hall, 1980. 132p. (A Reference Publication in Literature). LC 79-27573. ISBN 0-8161-7974-3.

A comprehensive listing of works by and about Shirley, Zimmer's guide describes separate, collected, and selected editions of Shirley's plays and poems through the present. Entries recount sources and publication histories as well as identify major thematic features. In addition, Zimmer describes about 400 works about Shirley published through 1978, including separate listings for bibliographies; critical books and articles; parts of larger works, including criticisms of Shirley; dissertations; and poems dealing with Shirley. Selected annotations are thorough and critical. Index headings for such broad topics as "authorship problems," "comedy," "prologues and epiloges," and Shakespeare provide access. Coverage supersedes that provided in the Tannenbaums' *Elizabethan Bibliographies*, vol. 9; and Charles A. Pennel and William P. Williams' *Elizabethan Bibliographies Supplements*, no. 8. For a bibliography of works by and about Shirley, see *NCBEL*, I, pp. 1725-30. Shirley's manuscripts are described in *Index of English Literary Manuscripts*, II, pt. 2:323-50. Research on Shirley is reviewed by Albert Wertheim in Logan and Smith's *The Later Jacobean and Caroline Dramatists*, pp. 152-71, updated by Lidman's *Studies in Jacobean Drama, 1973-1984*, pp. 257-67.

Luke Short (Frederick Glidden), 1908-1975

Bibliographies

See *Bibliography of American Fiction, 1919-1988*, pp. 455-57, for Robert L. Gale's checklist of works by and about Short. Richard W. Etulain surveys works by and about Short in Erisman and Etulain's *Fifty Western Writers*, pp. 434-43.

Sir Philip Sidney, 1554-1586

Bibliographies

1225.   Stump, Donald V., Jerome S. Dees, and C. Stuart Hunter. **Sir Philip Sidney: An Annotated Bibliography of Texts and Criticism (1554-1984)**. New York: G. K. Hall, 1994. 834p. (Reference Publication in Literature). LC 93-12829. ISBN 0-8161-8238-8.

Annotated entries for 2,845 primary and secondary works published from 1584 to 1984 in chapters for editions and translations, bibliography, general criticisms, biography, and studies of *Arcadia*, *Defense of Poetry*, minor works, poetry, correspondence, and literary works about Sidney. Offers comprehensive coverage of early editions of Sidney's works as well as of non-English-language criticism, dissertations, reviews of critical studies, fictional and other literary works about Sidney, and works misattributed to Sidney. All annotations are thorough. A critical work's importance is indicated by an annotation's fullness and length (often a full page or more). Separate indexes for authors in main entries, names in annotations, and very detailed subjects, including elaborate references for proper names, titles, specific literary terms under particular works, and the like. Superseding coverage of Sidney in the Tannenbaums' *Elizabethan Bibliographies*, vol. 9; and George Robert Guffey's *Elizabethan Bibliographies Supplements*, no. 7, this is an exemplary secondary bibliography. Also for a bibliography of works by and about Sidney, see *NCBEL*, I, pp. 1047-57. Sidney's manuscripts are described in *Index of English Literary Manuscripts*, I, pt. 2:465-88, 633-34.

Indexes and Concordances

1226. Donow, Herbert S. **A Concordance to the Poems of Sir Philip Sidney.** Ithaca, NY: Cornell University Press, 1975. 624p. (The Cornell Concordances). LC 73-20816. ISBN 0-8014-0805-9.

Based on William A. Ringler, Jr.'s standard edition of *The Poems of Sir Philip Sidney* (New York: Oxford University Press, 1962), Donow's concordance also includes indexes of modern spellings and word frequencies. Donow's *Concordance to the Sonnet Sequences* (entry 337) offers additional coverage of Sidney's sonnets.

Journals

1227. **Sidney Newsletter and Journal.** Guelph, ON: University of Guelph, 1980-. 2/yr. ISSN 0227-826x.

Formerly *Sidney Newsletter* (1980-90). Issues offer two to four critical articles and notes in addition to reviews of new works about the life and writings of Sidney, his circle, and the English Renaissance. Typical features are interpretive readings of themes, allusions, sources, and images in Sidney's works. In the past, other contributions have discussed Fulke Greville, Ben Jonson, Mary Wroth, and John Milton and published annotated bibliographies. In addition, the journal includes extensive information on conferences and symposia and calls for papers. *Sidney Newsletter and Journal* is indexed in *MLA*.

Lydia Huntley Sigourney, 1791-1865

Bibliographies

For works by Sigourney, see *Bibliography of American Literature*, vol. 7, pp. 432-99. Contributions by Sigourney and criticism and reviews of Sigourney's works in selected periodicals are identified in Wells' *The Literary Index to American Magazines, 1815-1865*, pp. 137-39; and *The Literary Index to American Magazines, 1850-1900*, p. 342. Sigourney's manuscripts are listed in Robbins' *American Literary Manuscripts*, pp. 291-92.

Edward Rowland Sill, 1841-1887

Bibliographies

For works by Sill, see *Bibliography of American Literature*, vol. 7, pp. 500-508. Reviews of Sill's works and Sill's contributions to selected periodicals are identified in Wells' *The Literary Index to American Magazines, 1850-1900*, p. 342. Sill's manuscripts are listed in Robbins' *American Literary Manuscripts*, p. 292.

Alan Sillitoe, 1928-

Bibliographies

1228. Gerard, David. **Alan Sillitoe: A Bibliography.** Westport, CT: Meckler, 1988. 175p. LC 87-34748. ISBN 0-88736-104-8.

A comprehensive bibliography of Sillitoe's primary materials, Gerard's guide gives detailed bibliographic descriptions in separate listings covering first editions of Sillitoe's books; contributions of short stories, essays, poems, recipes, and letters in books and periodicals; critical and biographical materials about Sillitoe (295 entries); reviews of Sillitoe's works (arranged by individual works); stage and film adaptations (with citations for film reviews, publication, and critical studies); and radio, television, and recorded appearances (including Sillitoe's readings and interviews as well as recordings of his works). Coverage extends from 1950 through 1987. Gerard's identification of subsequent and translated editions of Sillitoe's works is impressive. More than 30 editions of *The Loneliness of the Long-Distance Runner* dating through 1985 in English, Serbo-Croatian, and Lettish, among other languages, are listed. Additional coverage of works by and about Sillitoe is provided in Stanton's *A Bibliography of Modern British Novelists*, pp. 771-806, 1097.

Robert Silverberg, 1935-
Bibliographies

1229. Clareson, Thomas D. **Robert Silverberg: A Primary and Secondary Bibliography**. Boston: G. K. Hall, 1983. (Masters of Science Fiction and Fantasy). LC 83-154. ISBN 0-8161-8118-7.

Clareson chronologically lists Silverberg's primary materials, including separate listings for science-fiction novels and short fiction, other fiction works, edited anthologies, nonfiction works (including Silverberg's comments on science-fiction writing), and selected audiovisual materials. In addition, Clareson describes about 800 works (mostly reviews) about Silverberg published through 1981. Coverage excludes non-English-language materials. Annotations typically excerpt sources. Appendixes identify Silverberg's pseudonymous works, awards, and contributions to *Bulletin of the Science Fiction Writers of America*. A separate index references primary works; no subject indexing is included.

Clifford D. Simak, 1904-1988
Bibliographies

1230. Becker, Muriel R. **Clifford D. Simak: A Primary and Secondary Bibliography**. Boston: G. K. Hall, 1980. 149p. (Masters of Science Fiction and Fantasy). LC 79-18124. ISBN 0-8161-8063-6.

Becker identifies Simak's publications dating from 1931 through 1978, covering his science-fiction novels, short fiction, collections, and anthologies; non-science-fiction works and adaptations; and nonfiction. In addition, Becker chronologically lists and describes 193 criticisms and commentaries on Simak (mostly reviews) published from 1939 through 1977. Annotations excerpt sources. Subject indexing is limited to broad topics. Also see *Bibliography of American Fiction, 1919-1988*, pp. 457-58, for Becker's checklist of works by and about Simak.

William Gilmore Simms (Frank Cooper), 1806-1870
Bibliographies

1231. Butterworth, Keen, and James E. Kibler, Jr. **William Gilmore Simms: A Reference Guide**. Boston: G. K. Hall, 1980. 213p. (A Reference Guide to Literature). LC 80-13079. ISBN 0-8161-1059-x.

Butterworth and Kibler chronologically arrange annotated entries for about 1,200 writings about Simms published from 1825 through 1979, including early anonymous reviews and notices in local newspapers and journals, introductions in editions, and dissertations. Annotations are descriptive. Subject indexing is limited to selected broad topics, such as "bibliography," "Indians in Simms's works," and "revolutionary romances." Kibler provides coverage of Simms' primary works in *The Poetry of William Gilmore Simms: An Introduction and Bibliography* (Spartanburg, SC: Published for the Southern Studies Program, University of South Carolina, by Reprint, 1979), which lists and describes in detail 1,830 poems written by Simms in separate listings for anthologies, poems, and attributed poems, with indexes for titles and first lines; and in *Pseudonymous Publications of William Gilmore Simms* (Athens, GA: University of Georgia Press, 1976). Also for works by Simms, see *Bibliography of American Literature*, vol. 7, pp. 509-42; and *First Printings of American Authors*, vol. 1, pp. 325-34. Simms' manuscripts are listed in Robbins' *American Literary Manuscripts*, pp. 292-93. Oscar Wegelin's *A Bibliography of the Separate Writings of William Gilmore Simms of South Carolina, 1806-1870*, 3d ed. (Hattiesburg, MS: Book Farm, 1941) supplies title-page transcriptions and brief bibliographic descriptions of 86 books, with copy locations. See *Bibliography of American Fiction Through 1865*, pp. 218-25, for Butterworth's checklist of works by and about Simms. Research on Simms is reviewed by Mary Ann Wimsatt in Bain and Flora's *Fifty Southern Writers Before 1900*, pp. 395-415.

Neil Simon, 1927-
Bibliographies

King's *Ten Modern American Playwrights*, pp. 215-33, gives brief bibliographic information for Simon's primary works and annotated entries for criticism of Simon, with a classified list of reviews.

Louis (Aston Marantz) Simpson, 1923-
Bibliographies

1232.   Roberson, William H. **Louis Simpson: A Reference Guide**. Boston: G. K. Hall, 1980. 172p. (A Reference Guide to Literature). LC 80-17654. ISBN 0-7161-8494-1.

Identifying works by and about Simpson, Roberson's bibliography chronologically arranges entries for Simpson's writings by genre, covering books and broadsides, poems contributed to periodicals, short stories, plays, translations, essays and nonfiction, reviews, letters, recordings, and poems contributed to books. Entries give bibliographic information and describe contents. In addition, Roberson chronologically lists briefly annotated entries for about 400 studies and comments on Simpson published from 1949 through 1979. Coverage includes reviews in local newspapers and journals and one book-length study. Annotations are descriptive. A separate author, title, and subject index for secondary works provides broad topical access. Also for works by Simpson, see *First Printings of American Authors*, vol. 2, pp. 349-50. Simpson's manuscripts are listed in Robbins' *American Literary Manuscripts*, p. 293.

N(orman) F(rederick) Simpson, 1919-
Bibliographies

King's *Twenty Modern British Playwrights*, pp. 207-15, lists works by Simpson and describes works about him.

Upton (Beall) Sinclair, 1878-1968
Bibliographies

1233.   Ahouse, John B. **Upton Sinclair: A Descriptive, Annotated Bibliography**. Los Angeles, CA: Mercer & Aitchison, 1994. 167p. ISBN 0923980-35-0.

Ahouse directly supplements Gottesman's guide (entry 1234) by describing in full bibliographic detail "all of [Sinclair's] first editions and recording all known American reprints of his books" (p. xii). Entries in chronologically arranged sections for books (92 items), pamphlets, and books with introductions and forewords by Sinclair supply title-page transcriptions, collations and paginations, physical and binding descriptions, and extensive notes on composition and publication histories, with specific details (including variants) for subsequent editions and printings. Ahouse identifies 23 editions and reprintings of *The Jungle* from 1906 to 1988. Index of names and titles. Despite Ahouse's detail, Gottesman's guide remains most important for coverage of international editions of Sinclair's works. No existing guide gives a full account of Sinclair's contributed works.

1234.   Gottesman, Ronald. **Upton Sinclair: An Annotated Checklist**. Kent, OH: Kent State University Press, 1973. 544p. (The Serif Series: Bibliographies and Checklists, no. 24). LC 72-634010. ISBN 0-87338-114-9.

Gottesman covers works by and about Sinclair, including separate listings for his writings; recordings and media adaptations of his works; translations and international editions (arranged by languages); selected secondary bibliographies; reviews of Sinclair's works; and critical books, articles, and unpublished works. Entries for primary materials give brief bibliographic information. Selected entries for secondary works include descriptive annotations. For a selective list of the works by Sinclair (excluding ephemeral materials such as broadsides, works of less than 16 pages, and translations of Sinclair's books), see *First Printings of American Authors*, vol. 5, pp. 293-319. Sinclair's manuscripts are listed in Robbins' *American Literary Manuscripts*, p. 293. Gottesman and Charles L. P. Silet provide detailed descriptions of Sinclair's manuscripts, largely in Indiana University's Lilly Library, in *The Literary Manuscripts of Upton Sinclair* (Columbus, OH: Ohio State University Press, 1972). See *Bibliography of American Fiction 1866-1918*, pp. 322-27, for John Ahouse and Cheryl Z. Oreovicz's checklist of works by and about Sinclair.

Isaac Bashevis Singer, 1904-1991
Bibliographies
1235.   Miller, David Neal. **Bibliography of Isaac Bashevis Singer, 1924-1949**. New York: Peter Lang, 1983. 315p. LC 83-47647. ISBN 0-8204-0002-5.

Miller provides full bibliographic descriptions for Singer's books; contributions to newspapers, periodicals, and anthologies; and translations of his works. Coverage includes his short stories, novellas, serialized novels, interviews, literary criticisms, book reviews, works of popular history and science, sketches, and miscellaneous essays. Entries give title-page transcriptions, collations, and contents, with transliterated and translated titles. Singer's manuscripts are listed in Robbins' *American Literary Manuscripts*, p. 293. Also see *Bibliography of American Fiction, 1919-1988*, pp. 459-61, for Lawrence S. Friedman's checklist of works by and about Singer.

Dame Edith Louisa Sitwell, 1887-1964
Bibliographies
1236.   Fifoot, Richard. **A Bibliography of Edith, Osbert and Sacheverell Sitwell**. 2d ed., revised. London: Rupert Hart-Davis, 1971. 432p. (Soho Bibliographies, no. 11). LC 75-31654. ISBN 0-208-012338.

First published in 1963 (London: Hart-Davis), Fifoot's guide provides full bibliographic descriptions for the separate publications, contributions to books, contributions to periodicals, unpublished works, translations, musical settings, and recordings of the works of Edith, Osbert, and Sacheverell Sitwell. Entries give title-page transcriptions, physical descriptions, contents, and brief information on publishing histories for first and later editions. Fifoot's bibliography supersedes Thomas Balston's *Sitwelliana, 1915-1927* (London: Duckworth, 1928). Also for a bibliography of works by and about Sitwell, see *NCBEL*, IV, pp. 342-46.

John Skelton, 1460?-1529
Bibliographies
1237.   Kinsman, Robert. **John Skelton, Early Tudor Laureate: An Annotated Bibliography, c.1488-1977**. Boston: G. K. Hall, 1979. 179p. (A Reference Publication in Literature). LC 78-13239. ISBN 0-8161-8125-x.

Following a thorough survey of nearly 500 years of Skelton scholarship, Kinsman chronologically arranges annotated entries for about 700 editions and critical works about Skelton dating through 1977. Coverage includes early editions and manuscript sources, modern editions, dissertations, master's theses, and criticisms in non-English languages. Annotations are both detailed and critical. Significant works received extended reviews. An elaborate, classified index includes subsections for bibliography, biography, general criticism, criticism of individual works, textual studies, portraits of Skelton, and other topics.

1238.   Kinsman, Robert, and Theodore Yonge. **John Skelton: Canon and Census**. New York: Published for the Renaissance Society of America by the Monographic Press, 1967. 88p. (Renaissance Society of America: Bibliographies and Indexes, no. 4). OCLC 2220071.

Kinsman and Yonge give full descriptions of manuscripts and printed editions of Skelton's writings published through 1600. Entries for manuscripts transcribe first lines, describe texts and metrics, and note locations of copies. Entries for books include title-page and colophon transcriptions; physical descriptions of typography and paper, contents, cross-references to the *STC* and other standard catalogs, and notes on publishing histories. For a bibliography of works by and about Skelton, see *NCBEL*, I, pp. 1015-19. Skelton's manuscripts are described in *Index of English Literary Manuscripts*, I, pt. 2:489-94, 634.

Indexes and Concordances

1239. Fox, Alistair, and Gregory Waite. **A Concordance to the Complete English Poems of John Skelton**. Ithaca, NY: Cornell University Press, 1987. 1,001p. (The Cornell Concordances). LC 87-47552. ISBN 0-8014-1944-1.

Fox and Waite base this concordance on John Scattergood's edition of *John Skelton: The Complete English Poems* (New Haven, CT: Yale University Press, 1983). The concordance excludes Skelton's Latin, Greek, French, and other non-English-language works. Indexes for word frequencies, modern spellings, and compound words are provided.

Christopher Smart, 1722-1771

Bibliographies

1240. Mahony, Robert, and Betty W. Rizzo. **Christopher Smart: An Annotated Bibliography, 1743-1983**. New York: Garland, 1984. 671p. (Garland Reference Library of the Humanities, vol. 214). LC 82-48498. ISBN 0-8240-9226-0.

Mahony and Rizzo's intention is to identify "every appearance in any printed form of Smart's work, textually complete or not, and every recorded reference to him or his writings" appearing through 1900 and selectively thereafter. Mahony and Rizzo chronologically arrange annotated entries in separate listings for works by Smart and other works and documents related to the publishing histories of his works, including textual studies, Smart's separate publications, his contributions to books and journals, and about 500 critical and biographical studies of Smart and his works. Appendixes include a census of Smart's manuscripts (pp. 545-48), with locations as well as a cumulative alphabetical list of his publications. Entries for primary works give bibliographic information, publishing histories, and references to reviews. Secondary coverage includes letters, early anonymous notices and reviews, and dissertations. Thorough annotations are descriptive. Topical indexing under Smart's name and names of others provides access. This supersedes George J. Gray's "A Bibliography of the Writings of Christopher Smart with Biographical References," *Transactions of the Bibliographical Society* 6 (1903): 269-303. Also for a bibliography of works by and about Smart, see *NCBEL*, II, pp. 589-93, by Arthur Sherbo. Smart's manuscripts are described in *Index of English Literary Manuscripts*, III, pt. 3:375-84.

Betty (Wehner) Smith, 1904-1972

Bibliographies

For works by Smith, see *First Printings of American Authors*, vol. 3, pp. 293-98. Smith's manuscripts are listed in Robbins' *American Literary Manuscripts*, p. 294.

Charles Henry Smith, 1826-1903

Bibliographies

See *Bibliography of American Fiction, 1866-1918*, pp. 328-29, for William E. Lenz's checklist of works by and about Smith. Smith's manuscripts are listed in Robbins' *American Literary Manuscripts*, p. 294. James C. Austin surveys works by and about Smith in Bain and Flora's *Fifty Southern Writers Before 1900*, pp. 416-26.

Charlotte Smith, 1748-1806
Bibliographies

For a bibliography of works by and about Smith, see *NCBEL*, II, pp. 683-84. Robert Donald Spector reviews research on Smith in *The English Gothic: A Bibliographic Guide to Writers from Horace Walpole to Mary Shelley*, pp. 111-52.

Cordwainer Smith (Paul Myron Anthony Linebarger), 1913-1966
Bibliographies

See *Bibliography of American Fiction, 1919-1988*, pp. 461-62, for Alan C. Elms' checklist of works by and about Smith.

Dictionaries, Encyclopedias, and Handbooks

1241. Lewis, Anthony R. **Concordance to Cordwainer Smith**. Cambridge: New England Science Fiction Association, 1984. 90p. LC 84-236060. ISBN 0-915368-24-2.

Admittedly incomplete and less-than-comprehensive index of "all the people, places, things, concepts in the science fiction works of Cordwainer Smith together with exegetical comments (in some cases, highly speculative)" (preface). Cross-references some 45 of Smith's works. Unindexed.

Elihu Hubbard Smith, 1771-1798
Bibliographies

For works by Smith, see *First Printings of American Authors*, vol. 1, pp. 335-36. Smith's manuscripts are listed in Robbins' *American Literary Manuscripts*, p. 294.

Francis Hopkinson Smith, 1838-1915
Bibliographies

For works by Smith, see *Bibliography of American Literature*, vol. 7, pp. 543-57. Smith's contributions to and reviews of Smith's works in selected periodicals are identified in Wells' *The Literary Index to American Magazines, 1850-1900*, pp. 343-44. Smith's manuscripts are listed in Robbins' *American Literary Manuscripts*, p. 295. See *Bibliography of American Fiction, 1866-1918*, pp. 330-31, for Chryseis O. Fox's checklist of works by and about Smith.

Captain John Smith, 1580-1631
Bibliographies

1242. Hayes, Kevin J. **Captain John Smith: A Reference Guide**. Boston: G. K. Hall, 1991. 245p. (Reference Guide to Literature). LC 90-49128. ISBN 0-8161-7275-7.

Chronologically arranges annotated entries for approximately 1,000 English-language works about Smith and his writings published from 1613 to 1988, ranging from allusions and passing references in contemporary literary and historical works to modern scholarly studies, popular accounts, and fictional adaptations, with separate entries for their reviews. The listing is also inflated with entries for Smith in bibliographies, encyclopedias, and other reference works. Includes brief checklist of Smith's writings. Introduction summarizes critical, literary, and historical responses to Smith. Critic, title, and selected subject index. Smith's manuscripts are listed in Robbins' *American Literary Manuscripts*, p. 295. Jennifer R. Goodman surveys works by and about Smith in Bain and Flora's *Fifty Southern Writers Before 1900*, pp. 427-34.

Richard Penn Smith, 1799-1854
Bibliographies

For works by Smith, see *Bibliography of American Literature*, vol. 7, pp. 558-62. Smith's manuscripts are listed in Robbins' *American Literary Manuscripts*, p. 296.

Samuel Francis Smith, 1808-1895
Bibliographies

For works by Smith, see *Bibliography of American Literature*, vol. 7, pp. 563-75. Smith's manuscripts are listed in Robbins' *American Literary Manuscripts*, p. 296.

Seba Smith, 1792-1868
Bibliographies

For works by Smith, see *Bibliography of American Literature*, vol. 7, pp. 576-83. Contributions by Smith and criticism and reviews of Smith's works in selected periodicals are identified in Wells' *The Literary Index to American Magazines, 1815-1865*, p. 144. Smith's manuscripts are listed in Robbins' *American Literary Manuscripts*, p. 296. See *Bibliography of American Fiction Through 1865*, pp. 226-27, for a checklist of works by and about Smith.

Stevie (Florence Margaret) Smith, 1902-1971
Bibliographies

1243.   Barbera, Jack, William McBrien, and Helen Bajan. **Stevie Smith: A Bibliography**. Westport, CT: Meckler, 1987. 183p. LC 86-23738. ISBN 0-88736-101-3.

Covering works by and about Smith, Part A gives bibliographic information for Smith's primary materials, including entries in separate listings for collected and uncollected verse, novels, nonfiction books, stories, essays, Smith's book reviews, uncollected letters, and miscellaneous writings. Part B includes published interviews, with Part D describing recordings of Smith's works and Part E covering Smith's materials in special collections in Great Britain and the United States (pp. 119-24). Part C is an unannotated listing of about 400 English-language works about Smith published through 1985, including two book-length studies, articles, and reviews. No subject indexing is provided.

William Gardner Smith, 1927-
Bibliographies

For works by Smith, see *First Printings of American Authors*, vol. 2, p. 351.

Tobias George Smollett, 1721-1771
Bibliographies

1244.   Spector, Robert D. **Tobias Smollett: A Reference Guide**. Boston: G. K. Hall, 1980. 341p. (A Reference Publication in Literature). LC 79-28423. ISBN 0-8161-7960-3.

Spector chronologically arranges annotated entries for about 2,500 works about Smollett. Coverage extends from 1746 through 1978. Although Spector claims only representative coverage, the listings are most comprehensive, including early anonymous notices and reviews as well as dissertations and non-English-language criticism. Although his annotations are generally descriptive, Spector does not hesitate to describe works as "vigorous" or "uninformative." A comprehensive index gives solid access, including headings for the names of characters and topics ("Gothic," "picaresque"), with extensive subheadings listed under Smollett's name. As the best guide to Smollett scholarship, Spector's bibliography supersedes the coverage of Francesco Cordasco's *Tobias George Smollett: A Bibliographical Guide* (New York: AMS Press, 1978), which reprints *Smollett Criticism, 1770-1924: A Bibliography Enumerative and Annotative* (Brooklyn, NY: Long Island University Press, 1948), and *Smollett Criticism, 1925-1945: A Compilation* (Brooklyn, NY: Long Island University Press, 1947); as well as Donald M. Korte's *An Annotated Bibliography of Smollett Scholarship, 1946-68* (Toronto: University of Toronto Press, 1969). Research on Smollett is reviewed by Lewis M. Knapp in Dyson's *The English Novel*, pp. 112-27.

1245. Wagoner, Mary. **Tobias Smollett: A Checklist of Editions of His Works and an Annotated Secondary Bibliography.** New York: Garland, 1984. 753p. (Garland Reference Library of the Humanities, vol. 431). LC 83-48263. ISBN 0-8240-9085-3.

A full descriptive bibliography of Smollett's primary works has yet to be published. L. F. Norwood's *A Descriptive Bibliography of the Creative Works of Tobias Smollett* (Ph.D. dissertation, New Haven, CT: Yale University, 1931) remains the most detailed guide presently available. By comparison, Wagoner's guide provides a useful checklist of Smollett's primary works, including collected editions of novels, selected works, *Travels Through France and Italy*, histories, plays, poems, *An Essay on the External Use of Water*, translations, compilations, journals edited or contributed to by Smollett, *Habbakkuk Hilding*, attributed works, other works edited by Smollett, letters, and adaptations and imitations of Smollett's works. Entries give bibliographic information for editions, reprintings, and translations published through 1982, with selected notes on publishing histories and references to reviews. In addition, Wagoner arranges annotated entries for about 2,700 works about Smollett in classified listings for bibliographic and biographical studies, general critical studies and studies of individual works, dissertations, and studies of illustrations. Annotations are descriptive, lacking the critical and evaluative content of those in Spector's guide (entry 1244). Detailed subject indexing provides excellent access. Also for Lewis M. Knapp's bibliography of works by and about Smollett, see *NCBEL*, II, pp. 962-70. Smollett's manuscripts are described in *Index of English Literary Manuscripts*, III, pt. 3:385-88.

Dictionaries, Encyclopedias, and Handbooks

1246. Bulckaen, Denise. **A Dictionary of Characters in Tobias Smollett's Novels.** Nancy: Presses Universitaires de Nancy, Editions Universitaires de Dijon, 1993. 153p. (Collection Litteratures Anglaise et Americaine). ISBN 2-86480-790-4.

Identifies real and fictional individual characters and groups of characters named, unnamed, mentioned, or otherwise alluded to (such as "Lord B———") in Smollett's five novels with cross-references to pages in the Oxford University Press and other recent editions. Intends to be complete, hoping that "no footman or stray onlooker has been forgotten" (p. [5]). Index of "main categories" of characters, including "Aristocrats," "Catholics," "French," and "Upstarts." Appends bibliography of editions, reference works, and critical studies (pp. 147-53). See also Johnson's *Plots and Characters in the Fiction of Eighteenth-Century English Authors* (entry 1309).

Journals

"Recent Articles" in *The Scriblerian and the Kit Cats* (entry 1084) regularly includes a selection of reviews of studies on Smollett.

William Joseph Snelling, 1804-1848
Bibliographies

For works by Snelling, see *Bibliography of American Literature*, vol. 7, pp. 584-89. Snelling's manuscripts are listed in Robbins' *American Literary Manuscripts*, p. 297. See *Bibliography of American Fiction Through 1865*, pp. 228-29, for a checklist of works by and about Snelling.

W(illiam) D(eWitt) Snodgrass, 1926-
Bibliographies

1247. White, William. **W. D. Snodgrass: A Bibliography.** Detroit: Wayne State University Library, 1960. 32p. LC 60-15662.

Badly dated guide to Snodgrass' works. Full bibliographic descriptions of Snodgrass' writings in sections for one book, *Heart's Needle* (1959); contributions to books; poems contributed to periodicals; translations by Snodgrass in periodicals; essays and reviews by Snodgrass; and reprintings of Snodgrass' poems.

Also identifies about 20 studies and reviews of Snodgrass. Includes a note by W. D. Snodgrass and a brief chronology. Title index. For works by Snodgrass, see *First Printings of American Authors*, vol. 1, pp. 337-38. Snodgrass' manuscripts are listed in Robbins' *American Literary Manuscripts*, p. 297.

C(harles) P(ercy) Snow, 1905-1980

Bibliographies

1248.   Boytinck, Paul. **C. P. Snow: A Reference Guide**. Boston: G. K. Hall, 1980. 381p. (Reference Guides to Literature). LC 79-27529. ISBN 0-8161-8357-0.

Boytinck offers a thorough checklist of editions and translations of Snow's primary materials, including his novels, pamphlets, essays, reviews, and published letters; contributions to books and periodicals; and about 1,000 book reviews. In addition, Boytinck chronologically arranges annotated entries for about 900 criticisms and commentaries about Snow, including separate listings for books, articles, parts of books, dissertations, and reviews in all languages. Coverage extends from 1944 through 1978. Annotations are descriptive and detailed. Significant works receive extended reviews. An appendix outlines references to Snow in *The Times* of London (1945-76) and the *New York Times* (1955-77). Topical indexing under Snow's name offers subject access. This supersedes Boytinck's earlier *C. P. Snow: A Bibliography: Works by and About Him Complete with Selected Annotations* (Norwood, PA: Norwood Editions, 1977). Additional coverage of works by and about Snow is provided in Stanton's *A Bibliography of Modern British Novelists*, pp. 807-933, 1098-110, with 484 entries for Snow's works and 815 for works about him and an addendum.

Gary (Sherman) Snyder, 1930-

Bibliographies

1249.   McNeill, Katherine. **Gary Snyder: A Bibliography**. New York: Phoenix Bookshop, 1983. 247p. LC 84-103483. ISBN 0-916228-12-6.

McNeill arranges full bibliographic descriptions of Snyder's works in separate listings for books and broadsides; contributions to books; contributions to periodicals (some 537 entries); translations of Snyder's works (arranged by languages); miscellaneous writings, such as news releases and sheet music; and recordings of Snyder's works. Entries give title-page transcriptions (with selected facsimiles), physical descriptions, contents, and brief information on publishing histories. An unannotated checklist of 173 works about Snyder (including dissertations) concludes the guide. First-line and title indexes offer access. Snyder's manuscripts are listed in Robbins' *American Literary Manuscripts*, p. 298. Research on Snyder is reviewed by Bert Almon in Erisman and Etulain's *Fifty Western Writers*, pp. 444-53.

Susan Sontag, 1933-

Bibliographies

For works by Sontag, see *First Printings of American Authors*, vol. 1, pp. 339-40. Sherry Lee Linkon reviews works by and about Sontag in Shapiro's *Jewish American Women Writers*, pp. 415-22. Sontag's manuscripts are listed in Robbins' *American Literary Manuscripts*, p. 298.

Gilbert Sorrentino, 1929-

Bibliographies

1250.   McPheron, William. **Gilbert Sorrentino: A Descriptive Bibliography**. Elmwood Park, IL: Dalkey Archive, 1991. 241p. (Dalkey Archive Bibliography Series, vol. 2). LC 90-3674. ISBN 0-916583-67-8.

Covers works by and about Sorrentino published from 1956 to 1990. Full bibliographic descriptions of works by Sorrentino chronologically arranged in sections for books and other separate publications, contributions to books, contributions to periodicals, dust-jacket blurbs and publishers' advertisements, and 15 interviews and recordings. Entries for all issues of first editions of 24 books supply title-page transcriptions; data for collation, contents, paper, bindings, and dust jackets; and notes on publication history. McPheron gives brief bibliographic information and summary information for 324 first periodical appearances. Separate listings of reviews of Sorrentino's books (357 annotated entries sublisted for 20 books) and criticism (113 annotated entries) of Sorrentino, including books, articles, dissertations, and non-English-language studies. Index references Sorrentino's works, other titles, and names (Joyce, Faulkner, Freud, etc.). Also for works by Sorrentino, see *First Printings of American Authors*, vol. 1, p. 341. Maria Vittoria D'Amico gives a summary biography, critical assessment of major works, and selected primary and secondary bibliography for Sorrentino in McCaffery's *Postmodern Fiction: A Bio-Bibliographical Guide*, pp. 505-508.

Robert Southey, 1774-1843

Bibliographies

1251.   Curry, Kenneth. **Robert Southey: A Reference Guide**. Boston: G. K. Hall, 1977. 95p. (Reference Guides in Literature). LC 76-51435. ISBN 0-8161-7831-3.

Following a checklist of editions of Southey's books, edited works, translations of his works, and collected letters, Curry chronologically arranges annotated entries for about 400 comments and criticisms about Southey published from 1796 through 1975. Coverage includes early anonymous reviews, introductions in editions, dissertations, and non-English-language criticisms. Annotations are critical and evaluative. Index headings for primary titles and names (such as Coleridge and Wordsworth) and detailed topical subheadings under Southey's name provide subject access. Also available is Jane Britton's *Catalogue of the Bertram R. Davis "Robert Southey" Collection* (Waterloo, ON: University of Waterloo Library, 1990), listing materials by and about Southey and Thomas Chatterton. For a bibliography of works by and about Southey, see *NCBEL*, III, pp. 254-61. Research on Southey is reviewed by Kenneth Curry in Houtchens and Houtchens' *The English Romantic Poets and Essayists*, pp. 155-82.

Saint Robert Southwell, 1561?-1595

Bibliographies

1252.   McDonald, James H. **The Poems and Prose Writings of Robert Southwell, S.J.: A Bibliographical Study**. Oxford: Printed for Presentation to Members of the Roxburghe Club at the University Press, 1937. 161p. LC 41-377.

An excellent descriptive bibliography of Southwell's works. A detailed apparatus analyzing the complicated printing history of Southwell's poems precedes full bibliographic descriptions of Southwell's works in sections covering literary manuscripts (arranged by repository and manuscript collection), manuscripts of letters, 20 early editions of Southwell's poems, 28 early editions of prose works, six works attributed to Southwell, later editions of the works (to 1931), early allusions to Southwell's writings, and 30 general books and articles about Southwell. Thirty-one entries for manuscripts give contents, citing selected variants with published editions, and note modern appearances. Entries for books give quasi-facsimile title-page transcriptions, *STC* numbers, sizes, collations, contents, multiple copy locations, citations for later editions, and substantial information about printing histories, including details on variants distinguishing particular copies. Also contains selected illustrations of title pages. Appendixes reprint selected manuscript fragments and previously published works. Unindexed. Also for a bibliography of works by and about Southwell, see *NCBEL*, I, pp. 1059-61, 1933-34. Southwell's manuscripts are described in *Index of English Literary Manuscripts*, I, pt. 2:495-522.

E(mma) D(orothy) E(liza) N(evitte) Southworth, 1819-1899

Bibliographies

See *Bibliography of American Fiction Through 1865*, pp. 229-33, for a checklist of works by and about Southworth. Southworth's manuscripts are listed in Robbins' *American Literary Manuscripts*, p. 298. Wells' *The Literary Index to American Magazines, 1815-1865*, p. 146; and *The Literary Index to American Magazines, 1850-1900*, p. 345, identifies reviews of Southworth in selected periodicals.

Dame Muriel Sarah Camberg Spark, 1918-

Bibliographies

1253. Tominaga, Thomas T., and Wilma Schneidermeyer. **Iris Murdoch and Muriel Spark: A Bibliography**. Metuchen, NJ: Scarecrow Press, 1976. 237p. (Scarecrow Author Bibliographies, no. 27). LC 76-909. ISBN 0-8108-0907-9.

Although superseded for coverage of Murdoch's works by Fletcher and Bove's *Iris Murdoch* (entry 989), Tominaga and Schneidermeyer's guide remains useful for coverage of Spark's primary works through 1975. Includes entries for Spark's novels (with references to translations and reviews), critical essays, autobiographical essays, plays, poems, short stories, children's books, literary criticism, book reviews, editorials, collected works, and works edited or translated by Spark. About 400 secondary works (including books, essays, interviews, biographies, bibliographies, and works about the filmed adaptation of *The Prime of Miss Jean Brodie*) are also listed. No annotations are provided. A single subject index, covering both Murdoch and Spark, provides access under such specific headings as "dryness," "miracles," and "religion." Additional coverage of works by and about Spark is provided in Stanton's *A Bibliography of Modern British Novelists*, pp. 935-96, 1101-1109. Also for a bibliography of works by and about Spark, see *NCBEL*, IV, pp. 1359, 1379.

John Speicher, 1934-

Bibliographies

For works by Speicher, see *First Printings of American Authors*, vol. 2, p. 353.

Elizabeth Spencer, 1921-

Bibliographies

See *Bibliography of American Fiction, 1919-1988*, pp. 463-64, for Verbie Lovorn Prevost's checklist of works by and about Spencer. Spencer's manuscripts are listed in Robbins' *American Literary Manuscripts*, p. 299. Peggy Whitman Prenshaw surveys works by and about Spencer in Flora and Bain's *Fifty Southern Writers After 1900*, pp. 423-32.

Sir Stephen Harold Spender, 1909-

Bibliographies

1254. Kulkarni, H. B. **Stephen Spender: Works and Criticism: An Annotated Bibliography**. New York: Garland, 1976. 264p. (Garland Reference Library of the Humanities, vol. 43). LC 75-24090. ISBN 0-8240-9960-5.

Kulkarni offers full bibliographic descriptions of Spender's writings published from 1925 through 1975, including separate listings for first and variant editions of separately published works, edited and translated works and contributions to books, anthologies and collections of poetry and prose containing works by Spender, contributions to periodicals, Spender's manuscripts located at the University of California at Berkeley and the University of Texas' Harry Ransom Humanities Research Center; manuscripts of individual poems; and recordings of Spender reading his works. Entries give title-page transcriptions, physical descriptions, contents, and information on publishing histories. In addition, Kulkarni briefly describes about 150 critical studies about Spender, including reviews and dissertations. Indexing is limited to primary titles. Also for a bibliography of works by and about Spender, see *NCBEL*, IV, pp. 355-77.

Edmund Spenser, c. 1552-1599

Bibliographies

1255. Heffner, Ray, Dorothy E. Mason, Frederick M. Padelford, and William Wells. **Spenser Allusions in the Sixteenth and Seventeenth Centuries**. Chapel Hill, NC: University of North Carolina Press, 1972. 351p. LC 72-167739.

First published in installments in *Studies in Philology*, "Part I: 1580-1625," 48.5 (December 1971); and "Part II: 1626-1700," 49.5 (December 1972), this identifies and excerpts allusions to Spenser's works from contemporary and other sources dating through 1700. An enormously valuable bibliographic guide for tracing Spenser's contemporary influence and reputation.

1256. Johnson, Francis R. **A Critical Bibliography of the Works of Edmund Spenser Printed Before 1700**. Baltimore, MD: Johns Hopkins Press, 1933. 61p. LC 33-38177.

Johnson gives full bibliographic descriptions of early editions of Spenser's works, including title-page and colophon transcriptions and facsimiles, collations, contents, copy locations, and information on publishing histories. Available in a reprinted edition (London: Dawsons of Pall Mall, 1966). Also for a bibliography of works by and about Spenser, see *NCBEL*, I, pp. 1029-47, by A. C. Hamilton. Spenser's manuscripts are described in *Index of English Literary Manuscripts*, I, pt. 2:523-31, 634.

1257. McNeir, Waldo F., and Foster Provost. **Edmund Spenser: An Annotated Bibliography, 1937-1972**. 2d ed. Pittsburgh, PA: Duquesne University Press, 1975. 490p. (Duquesne Studies: Philological Series, vol. 17). LC 75-33311. ISBN 0-391-00395-x.

McNeir and Provost provide comprehensive coverage of works about Spenser published from 1937 through 1972, arranging about 2,600 annotated entries in topical listings for biography, editions and selections of Spenser's works, general critical studies, studies of *The Faerie Queene, The Shepheardes Calendar*, the minor poems, and prose works. Coverage includes selected reviews of works about Spenser, dissertations, and non-English-language criticisms. Annotations are descriptive and detailed. A comprehensive index includes headings for primary works, names (Aristotle, Chaucer, and Shakespeare), and the full range of topics, such as "allegory," "classicism and neoclassicism," and "imagery." Additionally, Richard C. Frushell and Bernard J. Vondersmith's *Contemporary Thought on Edmund Spenser: With a Bibliography of Criticism of The Faerie Queene, 1900-1970* (Carbondale, IL: Southern Illinois University Press, 1975) gives an unannotated listing of modern studies of the epic poem, with essays on trends in research on its themes, text, structure, and the like. Research on Spenser is reviewed by Peter Bayley in Dyson's *English Poetry*, pp. 15-39.

1258. Sipple, William L. **Edmund Spenser 1900-1936: A Reference Guide**. Boston: G. K. Hall, 1984. 244p. (A Reference Guide to Literature). LC 83-10745. ISBN 0-8161-8007-5.

Complementing the coverage of later Spenser criticism by McNeir and Provost's bibliography (entry 1257), Sipple offers an annotated, chronologically arranged listing of about 1,400 studies of Spenser and his works published from 1900 through 1936. Coverage includes introductions in editions, dissertations, master's theses, and non-English-language criticisms. Significant works receive extended descriptions. A detailed index references the full rage of topics. The works of Sipple and McNeir and Provost supersede the coverage of twentieth-century criticism of Spenser included in Frederic I. Carpenter's *A Reference Guide to Edmund Spenser* (Chicago, IL: University of Chicago Press, 1923) and Dorothy F. Atkinson's *Edmund Spenser: A*

Bibliographical Supplement (Baltimore, MD: Johns Hopkins University Press, 1937), although both Carpenter's and Atkinson's works remain useful for coverage of editions and criticisms of Spenser previous to 1900.

Dictionaries, Encyclopedias, and Handbooks

1259.   Hamilton, A. C., general ed. **The Spenser Encyclopedia**. Toronto: University of Toronto Press, 1990. 858p. LC 90-95007. ISBN 0-8020-2676-1.

An exemplary, scholarly, encyclopedic companion to Spenser's works and his age and an essential reference resource for the Renaissance. Contributing authorities (listed on pp. xiii-xxi, with their entries) is a who's who of Renaissance expertise. Offers alphabetically arranged, long signed entries for each of Spenser's works, with particular emphasis on *The Faerie Queene*; historical and literary persons and characters, places, and things; themes and topics in Spenser and Renaissance literature in general, such as classical and native mythologies; other fields in the Renaissance, such as the arts, science, and religion; Spenser's sources and antecedents as well as Spenser's influences from earliest notices through the twentieth century in England and internationally; and Spenser research and scholarship. Elaborate "Classification of Articles" (pp. vii-x) identifies main categories and related entries. Particular attention is given to topics related to "Women, marriage, sexuality." Entries cite Spenser's and others' works and give detailed references as well as lists of further readings. Appendix of black-and-white illustrations. General bibliography (pp. 789-809). A thorough subject index includes proper names, titles, and detailed topics.

1260.   Jones, H. S. V. **A Spenser Handbook**. New York: Crofts, 1930. 419p. LC 31-3371.

Jones' standard handbook provides introductory essays on the life and times of Spenser and on his individual works, emphasizing the several books of *The Faerie Queene*. In addition, Mark Rose's *Spenser's Art: A Companion to Book One of the Faerie Queene* (Cambridge: Harvard University Press, 1975) offers an undergraduate guide to the plot and themes of Book I of *The Faerie Queene*.

1261.   Maley, Willy. **A Spenser Chronology**. Lanham, MD: Macmillan, Barnes & Noble, 1994. 120p. (Author Chronologies). LC 93-2455. ISBN 0-389-21010-2.

Attempts to reconcile accounts of Spenser in "English Renaissance literary biography with the early modern Irish historiography" to give "a clearer picture of Spenser's whereabouts and activities than has hitherto been available" (pp. xiii-xiv). Emphasis on both political events in Ireland, where Spenser spent "almost his entire literary career," and Spenser's literary activities. Entries specifically cite *Calendar of State Papers*, *STC*, and other published and manuscript primary sources. Identifies mentions of and allusions to Spenser in publications of others. Includes biographical directory of "The Spenser Circle" integrating members of the "Leicester-Sidney Circle," Irish administrators, and other contemporaries. Selected bibliography of general references sources, biographies, and studies of Spenser in Ireland (pp. 111-15). Index limited to personal names.

Indexes and Concordances

1262.   Osgood, Charles Grosvenor. **A Concordance to the Poems of Edmund Spenser**. 1915; reprint Gloucester, MA: Peter Smith, 1963. 997p. LC 63-6151.

Osgood concords the texts of Richard Morris and John W. Hales' "Globe Edition" of the *Complete Works* (London: Macmillan, 1869), R. E. Neil Dodge's "Cambridge Edition" of *Complete Poetical Works* (Boston: Houghton Mifflin, 1907), and Ernest De Selincourt's edition of the *Poetical Works* (London: Oxford University Press, 1910). Also based on Dodge's "Cambridge Edition," Charles Huntington Whitman's *A Subject-Index to the Poems of Edmund Spenser* (New Haven, CT: Yale University Press, 1918) cumulates Spenser's references (with context lines) to proper names and more generic terms for persons, places, and things, ranging from Queen Elizabeth and Mary, Queen of Scots, to allusions to altars, death, and wrestling. Henry Lotspeich's *Classical Mythology in the Poetry of Edmund Spenser* (1932; reprint New York: Octagon, 1965) identifies and glosses Spenser's allusions to characters and concepts based on classical mythology, such as "Hades," "The Furies," and "mutability." Einar Bjorvand's *A Concordance to Spenser's Fowre Hymnes* (Oslo: Universitetsforlaget, 1973), based on the text of C. G. Osgood and H. G. Lotspeich's *The Works of Edmund Spenser: A Variorum Edition*, vol. VII: *The Minor Poems*, vol. I (Baltimore, MD: Johns Hopkins University Press, 1943), supplements Osgood's concordance, providing useful appendixes for frequencies, rhymes, end-stopped and run-on lines, homographs, and other elements of Spenser's work. Naseeb Shaheen's *Biblical References in The Faerie Queene* (Memphis, TN: Memphis State University Press, 1976) lists and analyzes Biblical illusions in Spenser's text. Donow's *Concordance to the Sonnet Sequences* (entry 337) offers additional coverage of Spenser's *Amoretti*.

Journals

1263. **Spenser Newsletter.** Manhattan, KS: Kansas State University, 1968- . 3/yr. ISSN 0038-7347.

Complementing *Spenser Studies* (entry 1264), issues of *Spenser Newsletter* include "news of any sort which would be of interest to Spenserians" (masthead). Consequently, the newsletter typically offers several short critical, biographical, or bibliographic notes in addition to reviews and notices of four or five new books, abstracts of a dozen or more articles, and announcements and information on upcoming meetings related to Spenser and various research centers. "Spenser Bibliography Update" is a current bibliography of Spenser studies that complements the coverage of McNeir and Provost's *Edmund Spenser: An Annotated Bibliography* (entry 1257). *Spenser Newsletter* is indexed in *MHRA* and *MLA*.

1264. **Spenser Studies: A Renaissance Poetry Annual.** New York: AMS Press, 1980- . Annual. ISSN 0195-9468.

Formerly published at the University of Pittsburgh Press, annual volumes of *Spenser Studies* usually feature eight to 12 long, often illustrated, scholarly articles on Spenser and a wide selection of his contemporaries, including Shakespeare, Tasso, Giordano Bruno, Lady Mary Wroth, Campion, Skelton, Sidney, and Ralegh, to name only a few. Close readings or interpretations of Spenser's works, biographical studies, and analyses or investigations of the sources of allusions predominate. Articles on Spenser's contemporaries recount Spenser's influences or literary relations with them—and vice versa—or their literary contributions alone. Occasional bibliographic contributions to *Spenser Studies* include Willy Maley's "Spenser and Ireland: A Select Bibliography," 9 (1991 [for 1988]): 22-42. The annual has published no reviews to date. Publication is badly behind schedule: vol. 11 for 1990 was published in 1994. Volumes contain indexes, with vol. 11 giving the contents of previous volumes (pp. 243-50). *Spenser Studies* is indexed in *MHRA* and *MLA*.

Mickey Spillane (Frank Morrison), 1918-
Bibliographies

See *Bibliography of American Fiction, 1919-1988*, pp. 464-65, for Max Allan Collins and James L. Traylor's checklist of works by and about Spillane.

Harriet (Elizabeth) Prescott Spofford, 1835-1921
Bibliographies

For works by Spofford, see *Bibliography of American Literature*, vol. 7, pp. 590-608. Spofford's contributions to and reviews of Spofford's works in selected periodicals are identified in Wells' *The Literary Index to American Magazines, 1850-1900*, pp. 346-48. Spofford's manuscripts are listed in Robbins' *American Literary*

Manuscripts, pp. 299-300. See *Bibliography of American Fiction, 1866-1918*, pp. 331-32, for Heather Stone's checklist of works by and about Spofford.

Elliott White Springs, 1896-1959

Bibliographies

> For works by Springs, see *First Printings of American Authors*, vol. 1, pp. 343-44.

David Stacton, 1923-1968

Bibliographies

> For works by Stacton, see *First Printings of American Authors*, vol. 3, pp. 299-308.

Jean Stafford, 1915-1979

Bibliographies

> 1265. Avila, Wanda. **Jean Stafford: A Comprehensive Bibliography.** New York: Garland, 1983. 195p. (Garland Reference Library of the Humanities, vol. 377). LC 82-49127. ISBN 0-8240-9210-4.
>
> A bibliography of works by and about Stafford, Avila's guide provides annotated listings for Stafford's book-length fiction, nonfiction, and collected works; short stories; contributions to books and periodicals; reviews; and miscellaneous writings, such as blurbs, letters, recordings, and the like. Entries give brief bibliographic information for first and later editions, including translations. Entries for contributed works and reviews summarize contents. In addition, Avila briefly describes about 400 critical and biographical studies, reviews, entries in reference works, and news items about Stafford. A comprehensive index includes headings for primary titles and selected topics. Stafford's manuscripts are listed in Robbins' *American Literary Manuscripts*, p. 300. Also see *Bibliography of American Fiction, 1919-1988*, pp. 466-67, for Sappho Human's checklist of works by and about Stafford.

Ann Stanford, 1916-

Bibliographies

> For works by Stanford, see *First Printings of American Authors*, vol. 2, pp. 355-56.

Olaf Stapledon, 1886-1950

Bibliographies

> 1266. Satty, Harvey J., and Curtis C. Smith. **Olaf Stapledon: A Bibliography.** Westport, CT: Greenwood Press, 1984. 167p. (Bibliographies and Indexes in World Literature, no. 2). LC 84-6549. ISBN 0-313-24099-x.
>
> This gives full bibliographic descriptions of first and selected later editions and reprintings of Stapledon's separately published works; collected editions; contributions to books, periodicals, and newspapers; manuscripts of published and unpublished works; and translations of Stapledon's works, in addition to listing bibliographies and about 100 selected works about Stapledon. Entries for Stapledon's books give title-page transcriptions; collations; contents; descriptions of paper, typography, and bindings; information on publishing histories; and copy locations. Entries for contributions include summaries of contents.

Edmund Clarence Stedman, 1833-1908

Bibliographies

> For works by Stedman, see *Bibliography of American Literature*, vol. 7, pp. 609-41. Contributions by Stedman and criticism and reviews of Stedman's works in selected periodicals are identified in Wells' *The Literary Index to American Magazines, 1815-1865*,

p. 148; and *The Literary Index to American Magazines, 1850-1900*, pp. 348-50. Stedman's manuscripts are listed in Robbins' *American Literary Manuscripts*, pp. 301-302.

Sir Richard Steele, 1672-1729
Bibliographies
For works by and about Steele, see Donald F. Bond's bibliography in *NCBEL*, II, pp. 1112-119. Steele's manuscripts are described in *Index of English Literary Manuscripts*, III, pt. 3:389-412. Knight's *Joseph Addison and Richard Steele* (entry 5) is a comprehensive guide to works about Steele published from 1730 through 1991. Evans and Wall's *A Guide to Prose Fiction in the Tatler and the Spectator* (entry 4) account for Steele's contributions and list of works about them.

Wilbur Daniel Steele, 1886-1970
Bibliographies
See *Bibliography of American Fiction, 1919-1988*, p. 469, for Martin Bucco's checklist of works by and about Steele. Steele's manuscripts are listed in Robbins' *American Literary Manuscripts*, p. 302.

Wallace (Earle) Stegner, 1909-1993
Bibliographies
1267.   Colberg, Nancy. **Wallace Stegner: A Descriptive Bibliography**. Lewiston, ID: Confluence Press, 1990. 280p. (Confluence American Authors Series, vol. 3). LC 89-82163. ISBN 0-917652-80-0.

Full bibliographic descriptions of Stegner's works published from 1930 through October 1988 chronologically arranged in sections for separate publications; contributions to books and edited works; articles in periodicals and newspapers; short stories in periodicals and newspapers; miscellaneous works, including postcards, keepsakes, etc.; 24 non-English-language editions of Stegner's works; and manuscripts and special collections (pp. 254-60) at the universities of Iowa, Utah, Nevada—Reno, and Stanford University. Entries for first and subsequent editions and printings of Stegner's 34 books give title-page transcriptions; pagination; collation; contents; details on paper, binding, and dust jackets; notes on publication history, and copy locations. Brief bibliographic information for Stegner's 242 articles and 57 short stories in periodicals, with citations for other appearances. Appendix lists 68 selected unannotated works on Stegner. Includes brief chronology of Stegner's career. Comprehensive index of names, titles, publishers, and the like. Stegner's manuscripts are also listed in Robbins' *American Literary Manuscripts*, p. 302. Merrill Lewis surveys works by and about Stegner in Erisman and Etulain's *Fifty Western Writers*, pp. 465-76.

Gertrude Stein, 1874-1946, and Alice B(abette) Toklas, 1877-1967
Bibliographies
1268.   White, Ray Lewis. **Gertrude Stein and Alice B. Toklas: A Reference Guide**. Boston: G. K. Hall, 1984. 282p. (A Reference Guide to Literature). LC 83-12896. ISBN 0-8161-8057-1.

White provides the most comprehensive listing of works about Stein and Toklas, chronologically arranging 1,920 briefly annotated entries for books, articles, reviews in local newspapers, news items, dissertations, and non-English-language criticisms published from 1909 through 1981. Annotations are descriptive. Subject indexing is limited to primary works (with subheadings for reviews, analyses, and the like) and names, such as Shakespeare, Poe, and Joyce. Critical coverage supersedes Maureen R. Liston's *Gertrude Stein: An Annotated Critical Bibliography* (Kent, OH: Kent State University Press, 1979). See *Bibliography of American Fiction, 1919-1988*, pp. 470-76, for Liston and Gina D. Peterman's checklist of works by and about Stein. Mark Fearnow identifies works by and about Stein in Demastes' *American Playwrights, 1880-1945*, pp. 408-16. Research on Stein is reviewed by Jayne L.

Walker in Duke, Bryer, and Inge's *American Women Writers*, pp. 109-34; and Linda Wagner-Martin in Shapiro's *Jewish American Women Writers*, pp. 431-39.

1269.   Wilson, Robert A. **Gertrude Stein: A Bibliography**. New York: Phoenix Bookshop, 1974. 227p. LC 73-85937.

The best descriptive listing of Stein's primary materials, Wilson's work gives full bibliographic descriptions in separate listings for Stein's books and pamphlets; contributions to books; contributions to periodicals; translations; musical settings; recordings; miscellaneous and ephemeral works, such as dust-jacket blurbs and quotations in sale catalogs, and works attributed to Stein. A listing of Alice B. Toklas' primary works is also included. Entries give title-page transcriptions, physical descriptions, and brief information on publishing histories for Stein's and Toklas' works. In addition, Wilson provides an annotated list of about 150 selected critical and biographical works about Stein. Also for works by Stein, see *First Printings of American Authors*, vol. 1, pp. 345-52. Stein's manuscripts are listed in Robbins' *American Literary Manuscripts*, p. 302. Robert Bartlett Haas and Donald Clifford Gallup's *A Catalogue of the Published and Unpublished Writings of Gertrude Stein Exhibited in the Yale University Library 22 February to 29 March 1941* (New Haven, CT: Yale University Library, 1941; reprint Folcroft, PA: Folcroft Press, 1971) also supplies full bibliographic descriptions of Stein's works.

Dictionaries, Encyclopedias, and Handbooks

1270.   Kellner, Bruce. **Gertrude Stein Companion: Content with the Example**. New York: Greenwood Press, 1988. 368p. LC 88-3126. ISBN 0-313-25078-2.

An all-purpose handbook of information about Stein's life, works, and works about her. Kellner provides introductory advice on reading Stein; summaries of her published works, with commentaries on their composition and publishing histories; critical approaches to Stein as part of the American literary tradition, her manuscripts, and language and style; a biographical dictionary of Stein's "Friends and Enemies," including such personalities as Virgil Thompson and Carl Van Vechten; quotations from Stein's works on such topics as age, families, and (of course) roses; and descriptions of about 60 critical works about Stein.

Journals

See Patterson's *Author Newsletters and Journals*, pp. 303-304, for previously published journals for Stein.

John (Ernst) Steinbeck, 1902-1968

Bibliographies

1271.   Goldstone, Adrian H., and John R. Payne. **John Steinbeck: A Bibliographical Catalogue of the Adrian H. Goldstone Collection**. Austin, TX: Humanities Research Center, University of Texas at Austin, 1974. 240p. (Tower Bibliographical Series, no. 13). LC 73-620234.

Although a catalog of collections in the Harry Ransom Humanities Research Center as well as in private collections, Goldstone and Payne's bibliography constitutes the best descriptive listing of Steinbeck's primary materials. Separate listings include detailed bibliographic entries for first English-language editions and selected other editions of Steinbeck's separately published books; contributions to books; contributions to periodicals; translations of his works into 58 different languages; and stage, film, television, and radio adaptations, in addition to works about Steinbeck. An appendix identifies miscellaneous writings, such as blurbs, recordings, and the like. An index of names and primary and periodical titles offers access. Also for works by Steinbeck, see *First Printings of American Authors*, vol. 1, pp. 353-57. Steinbeck's manuscripts are listed in Robbins' *American Literary Manuscripts*, p. 303. William B. Todd's *John Steinbeck: An Exhibition of American and Non-English Editions* (Austin, TX: Humanities Research Center, University of Texas, 1963) also describes materials at Texas. Additionally, Susan F.

Riggs' *A Catalogue of the John Steinbeck Collection at Stanford University* (Stanford, CA: Stanford University Libraries, 1980) describes more than 1,000 letters by Steinbeck as well as editions of his books (and other related materials, such as typescripts and proofs), screenplays, works based on Steinbeck's fiction, and Steinbeck memorabilia. Other important finding aids for primary materials include Bradford Morrow's *John Steinbeck: A Collection of Books and Manuscripts Formed by Harry Valentine of Pacific Grove, California* (Santa Barbara, CA: Morrow, 1980); John Gross and Lee Richard Hayman's *John Steinbeck: A Guide to the Collection of the Salinas Public Library* (Salinas, CA: Salinas Public Library, 1979); and Robert H. Woodward's *The Steinbeck Research Center at San Jose State University: A Descriptive Catalogue* (San Jose, CA: San Jose State University, 1985). Tetsumaro Hayashi's *A Handbook for Steinbeck Collectors, Librarians, and Scholars* (Muncie, IN: Steinbeck Society of America, 1981), pp. 29-46, describes Steinbeck materials at the University of California at Berkeley, the University of Virginia, the Library of Congress, and the Pierpont Morgan Library. Robert B. Harmon's *The Collectible John Steinbeck: A Practical Guide* (Jefferson, NC: McFarland, 1986) provides additional details about original prices as well as bibliographic points. Research on Steinbeck is reviewed by Warren French in Bryer's *Sixteen Modern American Authors*, pp. 499-527; and its supplement by French in Bryer's *Sixteen Modern American Authors: Volume 2: A Survey of Research and Criticism Since 1972*, pp. 582-622; and by Richard Astro in Erisman and Etulain's *Fifty Western Writers*, pp. 477-87.

1272.   Harmon, Robert B., and John F. Early. **The Grapes of Wrath: A Fifty Year Bibliographic Survey.** San Jose, CA: Steinbeck Research Center, San Jose State University, 1990. 325p. OCLC 21718522.

A handy bibliographic casebook for the study of Steinbeck's novel both as literary masterpiece and international social phenomenon. Provides annotated entries in either chronologically or alphabetically arranged sections for Steinbeck's "series of writings" (articles in *The Nation* and *San Francisco News* and the books *Their Blood Is Strong* and *The Harvest Gypsies*), which appeared between 1936 and 1938 anticipating the novel; texts of *The Grapes of Wrath*, including the holograph manuscript, typescript, and proofs, and U.S., U.K., non-English-language, pirated, collected, and excerpted editions; critical studies (775 entries), including book reviews, scholarship from 1939 to 1949 and 1950 to 1989, collections of criticisms, news articles, reminiscences, theses and dissertations, and study guides; audiovisual materials (mostly educational study aids); bibliographies; miscellanea (largely citations to articles in the popular press); materials related to the 1940 film, including citations for the screenplay, motion picture, and video versions and for early film reviews and recent scholarly criticisms; and stage adaptations, including citations for the scripts and stage reviews. Entries for selected primary materials indicate availability in Steinbeck Research Center and San Jose State University libraries. Introduction by Susan Shillinglaw. Separate name, title, and subject indexes.

1273.   Harmon, Robert B. **John Steinbeck: An Annotated Guide to Biographical Sources.** Lanham, MD: Scarecrow Press, 1996. 288p. LC 96-5417. ISBN 0-8108-3174-0.

Similarly exhaustive and at the same time almost as tangential to the bibliographic needs of most researchers as his *Steinbeck Bibliographies* (entry 1274), Harmon's guide describes separately published, collected, serial, and audiovisual biographical and autobiographical materials for Steinbeck. Harmon interfiles descriptions of book- and article-length studies of Steinbeck's life with entries for him in the likes of *Contemporary Authors* and *Current Biography*. Other sections identify obituaries and entries for Steinbeck in biographical dictionaries and encyclopedias. A section for audiovisual materials includes audiotapes, filmstrips, videos, and motion pictures, with valuable information on oral-history tapes in the Steinbeck Research Center at San Jose State University and the Steinbeck Library of Salinas, California. Harmon also provides a detailed Steinbeck chronology. Indexes of names/subjects and titles.

1274.   Harmon, Robert B. **Steinbeck Bibliographies: An Annotated Guide**. Metuchen, NJ: Scarecrow Press, 1987. 137p. LC 86-33830. ISBN 0-8108-1963-5.

Whether scholars and students actually need a bibliography of Steinbeck bibliographies is irrelevant. This book is an argument against them. Harmon has identified references to materials related to Steinbeck in some 200 different sources, ranging from the *MLA* to Goldstone and Payne's standard bibliography (entry 1271). Detailed annotations describe their uses. Most of this information experienced scholars should already know. It is most optimistic that the average student would go to such lengths to identify bibliographies just for *The Grapes of Wrath*, for example, when such resources as Hayashi's guide (entry 1275) and the electronic *MLA* are so much more conveniently immediate.

1275.   Hayashi, Tetsumaro. **A New Steinbeck Bibliography: 1929-1971**. Metuchen, NJ: Scarecrow Press, 1973. 225p. (Scarecrow Author Bibliographies, no. 1). LC 73-9982.

A revision of his previous *John Steinbeck: A Concise Bibliography, 1930-1965* (New York: Scarecrow Press, 1967), Hayashi provides descriptive listings of works by and about Steinbeck. Separate listings for Steinbeck's primary bibliography include 379 brief, identifying entries (largely notes on contents) for his novels, short stories, plays, filmscripts, nonfiction books, nonfiction articles, published letters, published speeches, verse, adaptations, excerpts, anthologized works, and unpublished manuscripts. Sections for secondary materials include some 1,800 cryptically annotated entries (typically just noting the primary work discussed) for books and other separate publications, dissertations, poems about Steinbeck, audiovisual materials, film reviews, critical and biographical studies and reviews published as articles and parts of books, and bibliographies. A thorough author, title, and subject index gives solid access. This volume is continued by:

1275.1. Hayashi, Tetsumaro. **A New Steinbeck Bibliography: 1971-1981**. Metuchen, NJ: Scarecrow Press, 1983. 147p. (Scarecrow Author Bibliographies, no. 64). LC 82-24077. ISBN 0-8108-1610-5.

Organized in approximately the same fashion as the previous volume, this gives brief entries for 282 primary and about 700 secondary works. In general, Hayashi's *New Steinbeck Bibliography* offers the most comprehensive coverage of materials about Steinbeck. Although Goldstone and Payne's bibliography (entry 1271) offers better descriptions of Steinbeck's primary materials, Hayashi's survey of manuscripts (pp. 39-53) is very informative. Additional coverage of dissertations on Steinbeck is contained in Hayashi and Beverly K. Simpson's *John Steinbeck: Dissertation Abstracts and Research Opportunities* (Metuchen, NJ: Scarecrow, 1994). Useful, more specialized listings of materials for research on Steinbeck include Robert J. DeMott's *Steinbeck's Reading: A Catalogue of Books Owned and Borrowed* (New York: Garland, 1984). See *Bibliography of American Fiction, 1919-1988*, pp. 476-81, for Susan Shillinglaw's checklist of works by and about Steinbeck.

Dictionaries, Encyclopedias, and Handbooks

1276.   Hayashi, Tetsumaro. **John Steinbeck: A Dictionary of His Fictional Characters**. Metuchen, NJ: Scarecrow Press, 1976. 22p. LC 76-14803. ISBN 0-8108-0948-6.

Hayashi's dictionary offers excellent and insightful identifications of characters in Steinbeck's major works of fiction. Contributed entries provide physical, psychological, and sociological descriptions and explanations for the likes Ma Joad of *The Grapes of Wrath* and George Milton of *Of Mice and Men*. Jim Casy is identified as a parallel to Christ (p. 45), while Connie Rivers is described as an irresponsible "foil to the Joad family" (p. 164).

1277. Hughes, R. S. **Beyond the Red Pony: A Reader's Companion to Steinbeck's Complete Short Stories**. Metuchen, NJ: Scarecrow Press, 1987. 164p. LC 86-31567. ISBN 0-8108-1970-8.

Intended as "a practical handbook" with discussions of all of Steinbeck's published and unpublished short fiction and "an up-to-date and complete bibliography of these stories" (p. ix). Mainly valuable for chronologically arranged chapters emphasizing elements associated with close readings (such as plots, themes, characterization, style, imagery, and point of view). Seldom presents full overviews of critical receptions. Very selective unannotated bibliography (pp. 142-55) is, in fact, neither up-to-date nor comprehensive. Names and topics indexes. Aimed at classroom teachers, librarians, and students, Tetsumaro Hayashi's two-volume *A Study Guide to Steinbeck: A Handbook to His Major Works* (Metuchen, NJ: Scarecrow Press, 1974, 1979) contains background information, plot summaries, critiques, selected annotated bibliographies of critical studies, and suggestions for discussion and student research on Steinbeck's works.

Journals

1278. **Steinbeck Quarterly**. Muncie, IN: International John Steinbeck Society, 1968- . 2/yr. ISSN 0039-100x.

Sponsored by Ball State University and the International Steinbeck Society, issues of *Steinbeck Quarterly*, formerly *Steinbeck Newsletter* (1968) include critical and biographical articles and reviews of new publications about the life and works of Steinbeck. Studies of Steinbeck's characters (such as Jim Casy in *The Grapes of Wrath* and Molly Morden in *The Moon Is Down*), images and symbolism (of women and animals in "The Chrysanthemums," for example), techniques (particularly narrative), critical reception (in the U.S.S.R. and Japan), and biographical problems are typical. Other studies have compared Steinbeck with John Dos Passos, Edward Albee, and Ernest Hemingway and identified literary relations with Charles Darwin and Adlai Stevenson. Recent bibliographic contributions include Tetsumaro Hayashi's "The A-B-C's of Steinbeck Studies: A Bibliographic Guide for English Majors," 26.3-4 (Summer-Fall 1993): 117-27; and Robert DeMott's "East of Eden: A Bibliographical Checklist (For Roy S. Simmonds and Preston Beyer)," 25.1-2 (Winter-Spring 1992): 14-28. *Steinbeck Quarterly* is indexed in *AHI, A&HCI, MHRA*, and *MLA*.

Patterson's *Author Newsletters and Journals*, pp. 304-305, describes other previously published journals for Steinbeck.

Sir Leslie Stephen, 1832-1904

Bibliographies

1279. Fraser, Gillian. **Leslie Stephen's Life in Letters: A Bibliographical Study**. Aldershot, Hants: Scolar Press, 1993. 436p. ISBN 0-8596-7912-8.

Covers works by and about Stephen. Full bibliographic descriptions of Stephen's works in chronologically arranged chapters for books; pamphlets, booklets, and bound offprints; translations; contributions to periodicals; *Dictionary of National Biography*; contributions to books and books edited by Stephen; principal, posthumously published works; miscellaneous writings; and published letters. Includes chronology of major events and publications. Entries for first and subsequent editions of Stephen's 18 separate publications give title-page transcriptions, collations, contents, information on bindings and dust jackets, citations for contemporary notices and reviews, and extensive notes and discussions on composition and publication history. Fraser identifies Stephen's 462 contributions to periodicals and 283 *Dictionary of National Biography* entries. Appendixes list Stephen's income from 1855 to 1903; locate collections of Stephen's manuscripts and other resource material in several dozen U.S. and U.K. libraries; identify Stephen's autograph inscriptions, annotations, sketches, and other marginalia in books in the Leonard and Virginia Woolf Collection at Washington State University; note more than 200 excerpts from Stephen's books contained in the *Library of*

Literary Criticism of English and American Authors (New York: Malkan, 1902); and list about 100 selected works about Stephen. Comprehensive index of proper names and titles. Criticism and reviews of Stephen's works in selected periodicals are identified in Wells' *The Literary Index to American Magazines, 1850-1900*, pp. 350-51. Also for a bibliography of works by and about Stephen, see *NCBEL*, III, pp. 1405-1406. John W. Bicknell reviews research on Stephen in DeLaura's *Victorian Prose*, pp. 516-27.

James Stephens, 1882-1950

Bibliographies

1280.   Bramsback, Birgit. **James Stephens: A Literary and Bibliographical Study**. Upsala: A.-B. Lundequistska Bokhandeln, 1959. 209p. (Upsala Irish Studies, no. 4). OCLC 304320.

A comprehensive guide to works by and about Stephens. Part I covers Stephens' literary (poetry and prose) manuscripts and unpublished letters to, from, and about Stephens. Chronologically arranged entries for 280 manuscripts indicate contents, listings in standard catalogs, and locations (mostly in Harvard's Houghton Library or the New York Public Library's Berg Collection). Part II contains separate, chronologically arranged listings of Stephens' separate poetry and prose publications; contributions to books; contributions to periodicals and newspapers; and biographical and critical works about Stephens, subarranged in sections for books and chapters (some 104 entries) and for articles and reviews in newspapers and periodicals. Entries for Stephens' works give brief bibliographic data, format and binding notes, citations for subsequent editions, translations, reprintings, and information on publication history, with detailed contents. Selectively annotated entries for works about Stephens. Appends addendum of 28 manuscripts and primary works; chronological table of Stephens' separate publications; list of newspapers and periodicals; and list of 21 BBC recordings of Stephens reading his works and those of Joyce, Blake, and others. Extended introduction to Stephens' works and critical reception. Comprehensive index. Supplementing Bramsback and other listings for Stephens, Richard J. Finneran's standard edition, *Letters of James Stephens: With an Appendix Listing Stephens's Published Writings* (London: Macmillan, 1974), pp. [420]-58, gives brief bibliographic descriptions, with contents, for 130 items (books, contributions to books, and contributions to periodicals) from 1905 to 1972, with a Stephens' chronology. Research on Stephens is reviewed by James F. Carrens in Finneran's *Anglo-Irish Literature*, pp. 459-69.

George Sterling, 1869-1926

Bibliographies

1281.   Johnson, Cecil. **A Bibliography of the Writings of George Sterling**. San Francisco, CA: Windsor Press, 1931. 63p. LC 31-19395.

Johnson includes full bibliographic descriptions of Sterling's books and contributions to books and periodicals. Entries give title-page transcriptions, collations, contents, and brief information on publishing histories. Reprinted edition available (Folcroft, PA: Folcroft, 1969). Also for works by Sterling, see *Bibliography of American Literature*, vol. 7, pp. 642-59. Sterling's manuscripts are listed in Robbins' *American Literary Manuscripts*, p. 304. Coverage of critical works on Sterling through 1979 is provided in Longtin's *Three Writers of the Far West* (entry 949).

Laurence Sterne, 1713-1768

Bibliographies

1282.   Hartley, Lodwick. **Laurence Sterne: An Annotated Bibliography, 1965-1977: With an Introductory Essay-Review of the Scholarship**. Boston: G. K. Hall, 1978. 103p. (A Reference Publication in Literature). LC 78-153. ISBN 0-8161-8167-5.

In addition to an extended survey of recent Sterne scholarship, Hartley offers about 400 annotated entries in separate listings for bibliographic aids; editions and selections of primary texts; biography; general criticism and criticism of *Tristram Shandy*, *A Sentimental Journey*; Sterne's sermons, letters, and minor works; and studies of literary influence and reputation. Annotations for editions and significant critical works are detailed and critical. Indexing is limited to critics. This intends to update Hartley's *Laurence Sterne in the Twentieth Century: An Essay and a Bibliography of Sternean Studies, 1900-1965* (Chapel Hill, NC: University of North Carolina Press, 1966), a standard survey of trends in Sterne scholarship. Both of Hartley's guides supersede Francesco Cordasco's *Laurence Sterne: A List of Critical Studies Published from 1896 to 1946* (Brooklyn, NY: Long Island University Press, Burt Frankin, 1948), *18th Century Bibliographical Pamphlets*, no. 4, listing 154 selected works about Sterne, including studies in French and German and with references to reviews, in sections for bibliography, biography and general criticism, *Tristram Shandy*, *Sentimental Journey*, Sterne's letters, non-English influence and reputation, and miscellaneous articles (largely memorials). Also for J. C. T. Oates' bibliography of works by and about Sterne, see *NCBEL*, II, pp. 948-62. Research on Sterne is reviewed by Duncan Isles in Dyson's *The English Novel*, pp. 90-111. Also useful for research on Sterne's primary materials is the *Facsimile Reproduction of a Unique Catalogue of Laurence Sterne's Library* (London: J. Tregaskis, 1930).

Dictionaries, Encyclopedias, and Handbooks

See Johnson's *Plots and Characters in the Fiction of Eighteenth-Century English Authors* (entry 1309).

Indexes and Concordances

1283. Graves, Patricia Hogan. **A Computer-Generated Concordance to Sterne's Tristram Shandy**. Ph.D. dissertation, Atlanta, GA: Emory University. 4 vols. OCLC 8767738.

Graves concords the text of James A. Work's edition (New York: Odyssey Press, 1940).

1284. Pasta, Betty B., David J. Pasta, and John R. Pasta. **A Short Concordance to Laurence Sterne's A Sentimental Journey Through France and Italy by Mr. Yorick.** Urbana, IL: Department of Computer Science, University of Illinois at Urbana-Champaign, 1974. 2 vols. (Report No. UIUCDCS-R-74-676). OCLC 2499411.

The Pastas provide a KWIC concordance to the text of Gardner Stout, Jr.'s edition (Berkeley, CA: University of California Press, 1967).

Journals

1285. **The Shandean: An Annual Volume Devoted to Laurence Sterne and His Works.** Coxwold, York: Laurence Sterne Trust, 1989-. Annual. ISSN 0956-3083.

The Shandean publishes "factual notes and queries as well as scholarly contributions relating to the life and works of Laurence Sterne" (masthead). Substantial, well-documented studies of textual issues and topics related to Sterne's works, particularly their printing history and illustration, are the norm. A significant number of articles discussing Sterne's international reputation have contained extensive bibliographies of translations and contemporary allusions. Major bibliographic contributions include Judith Hawley's " 'Hints and Documents' I: A Bibliography for Tristram Shandy," 3 (1991): 9-36; and " 'Hints and Documents' 2: A Bibliography for Tristram Shandy," 4 (1992): 49-65; and Kenneth Monkman's "Towards a Bibliography of Sterne's Sermons," 5 (1993): 32-109; and "Towards a Bibliography of Sterne's Sermons: Some Corrections and Slight Additions," 7 (1995): 101-103 (with a corrected addendum published with the issue). Descriptions of previously unknown Sterne documents, Sterne's library, and collections of materials related to Sterne appear regularly. Especially noteworthy is *The Shandean's* excellent facsimile illustrations, often folding and in color; vol. 6 (1994) published a set of extra illustrations of R. Dighton's 12 scenes from *Tristram Shandy*. Annual volumes also contain reviews of new publications, program announcements and calls for papers, and advertisements. *The Shandean* is indexed in *MLA*.

"Recent Articles" in *The Scriblerian and the Kit Cats* (entry 1084) also regularly includes a selection of reviews of studies on Sterne.

See Patterson's *Author Newsletters and Journals*, p. 306, for previously published journals for Sterne.

Wallace Stevens, 1879-1955
Bibliographies

1286.   Edelstein, J. M. **Wallace Stevens: A Descriptive Bibliography**. Pittsburgh, PA: University of Pittsburgh Press, 1973. 429p. LC 72-91106. ISBN 0-8229-3268-7.

In this, the most comprehensive listing of Stevens' primary materials, Edelstein gives full and detailed bibliographic descriptions in separate listings for Stevens' books and separate publications, including subsequent and reprinted editions, published from 1923 through 1971; contributions to books, including juvenilia; contributions to periodicals; miscellaneous publications, such as dust-jacket blurbs and quotations in catalogs; translations of Stevens' writings published in books, anthologies, and periodicals; musical settings; and recordings of Stevens reading his works. Entries for books include illustrations of title pages and versos, collations and other notes on printing and publishing, and locations of copies. Other sections cover secondary materials, including dedicatory poems and other poems referring to Stevens, and references to about 700 books, parts of books, articles, and dissertations about Stevens through 1972 and citations for reviews of Stevens' books. An appendix describes "an unauthorized printing" of *Tea* (1939). The comprehensive index references names (critics, editors, personalities, publishers, and the like) and primary and periodical titles. Edelstein's guide supersedes Samuel French Morse, Jackson R. Bryer, and Joseph N. Riddel's *Wallace Stevens Checklist and Bibliography of Stevens Criticism* (Denver, CO: Alan Swallow, 1963). Also for works by Stevens, see *First Printings of American Authors*, vol. 1, pp. 359-63. Stevens' manuscripts are listed in Robbins' *American Literary Manuscripts*, p. 304.

1287.   Serio, John N. **Wallace Stevens: An Annotated Secondary Bibliography**. Pittsburgh, PA: University of Pittsburgh Press, 1994. 435p. (Pittsburgh Series in Bibliography). LC 93-1005. ISBN 0-8229-3836-7.

Intended to complement Edelstein's primary bibliography (entry 1286), Serio's guide chronologically arranges annotated entries for 1,875 criticisms of Stevens published from 1916 through 1990. After 1953 entries are subgrouped for articles, books, and dissertations. International coverage includes early notices, reviews of Stevens' works and of works about Stevens, introductions and parts of books, and non-English-language scholarship. Annotations are full and descriptive. Indexes for authors, journals, detailed subjects (such as "Hedonism," "Emerson," "Source studies"), and titles cited in annotations. Willard's *Wallace Stevens: The Poet and His Critics* (entry 1289) offers evaluations of criticisms of Stevens through the mid-1970s. Research on Stevens is reviewed by Joseph N. Riddell in Bryer's *Sixteen Modern American Authors*, pp. 529-71; and its supplement by Riddell in Bryer's *Sixteen Modern American Authors: Volume 2: A Survey of Research and Criticism Since 1972*, pp. 623-74.

Dictionaries, Encyclopedias, and Handbooks

1288.   Sukenick, Ronald. **Wallace Stevens: Musing the Obscure: Readings, Interpretation, and a Guide to the Collected Poetry**. New York: New York University Press, 1967. 234p. LC 67-25041.

Following an introduction to Stevens' poetic ideas and techniques, Sukenick gives brief readings ("paraphrases") of his works in the order of appearance in *The Collected Poems* (New York: Knopf, 1954) and Samuel French Morse's edition of *Opus Posthumous* (New York: Knopf, 1957).

1289. Willard, Abbie F. **Wallace Stevens: The Poet and His Critics**. Chicago: American Library Association, 1978. 270p. (The Poet and His Critics). LC 78-8150. ISBN 0-8389-0267-7.

Willard provides detailed essays that survey and review scholarship on Stevens. Essays, with supporting bibliographies, address literary and historical backgrounds of Stevens' works, particularly in relation to Continental forces, American transcendentalism, and other literary movements and specific writers; Stevens and the fine arts, music, and philosophy; and his literary, critical, and aesthetic theories. Most useful for evaluative summaries of close critical readings and interpretations of Stevens' individual works.

Indexes and Concordances

1290. Walsh, Thomas F. **Concordance to the Poetry of Wallace Stevens**. University Park, PA: Pennsylvania State University Press, 1963. 341p. LC 63-18744.

Walsh gives context lines and line references to the texts of works in *The Collected Poems of Wallace Stevens* (New York: Knopf, 1954), *The Necessary Angel* (New York: Knopf, 1951), and Samuel French Morse's edition of *Opus Posthumous* (New York: Knopf, 1957).

Journals

1291. **The Wallace Stevens Journal**. Potsdam, NY: The Wallace Stevens Society, 1977- . 2/yr. ISSN 0148-7132.

Sponsored by the Wallace Stevens Society, issues typically feature four to six substantial articles that provide close readings and interpretive studies of individual works and comparative and biographical studies. Contributions have examined Stevens and Longfellow, Mallarme, Bakhtin, Paul Klee, and Wassily Kadinsky. Features also offer transcriptions of previously unpublished Stevens' letters and other primary materials. In addition, occasional special issues have focused on such topics as Stevens and politics and women. Included in 17.1 (Spring 1993), "Poets Reading Stevens," are contributions by the likes of Theodore Roethke, John Berryman, Donald Justice, Robert Pinsky, Robert Creeley, Charles Wright, and other poets. Poems in imitation of Stevens; reviews of three or four new publications; news and comments on upcoming conferences, library acquisitions, research in progress, and forthcoming publications; and a "Current Bibliography" of books, articles, dissertations, and media related to Stevens complete each issue. *The Wallace Stevens Journal* is indexed in *AES*, *A&HCI*, *MHRA*, and *MLA*.

Patterson's *Author Newsletters and Journals*, pp. 306-307, describes other previously published journals for Stevens.

Robert Louis Balfour Stevenson, 1850-1894

Bibliographies

1292. Prideaux, W. F., and Mrs. Luther S. [Frances V.] Livingston. **Bibliography of the Works of Robert Louis Stevenson**. London: Frank Hollings, 1917. 401p. LC 17-31675.

Mrs. Livingston's revision of Prideaux's guide (London: F. Hollings; New York: Scribner's, 1903) offers descriptive entries for Stevenson's primary writings, covering books, contributions to books, contributions to periodicals, collected editions, and selected editions. Entries give title-page transcriptions, collations, physical descriptions, and notes on publishing histories for first and later editions. In addition, appendixes describe biographical and critical works about Stevenson. Reprinted edition available (New York: Burt Franklin, 1968). Additionally, George

L. McKay's six-volume *A Stevenson Library Catalogue of a Collection of Writings by and About Robert Louis Stevenson Formed by Edwin J. Beinecke* (New Haven, CT: Yale University Library, 1951-64) gives full descriptions of books, manuscripts, and ana by and related to Stevenson. More a handbook than a bibliography of Stevenson's writings, Roger G. Swearingen's *The Prose Writings of Robert Louis Stevenson: A Guide* (Hamden, CT: Archon Books, 1980) arranges Stevenson's published and unpublished prose works by earliest date of composition from the 1850s through 1894, providing information on composition, publication history, locations of manuscripts, publication in standard editions, and the like. Ehrsam's *Bibliographies of Twelve Victorian Authors*, pp. [227]-61, cites international comments, criticism, and reviews for Stevenson through the early twentieth century. More specialized coverage of criticism of Stevenson's travel writings is provided in Bethke's *Three Victorian Travel Writers* (entry 1380). Also for a bibliography of works by and about Stevenson, see *NCBEL*, III, pp. 1004-14. Research on Stevenson is reviewed by Robert Kiely in Ford's *Victorian Fiction*, pp. 333-47; and Lionel Stevenson in Faverty's *The Victorian Poets*, pp. 381-83.

Dictionaries, Encyclopedias, and Handbooks

1293.   Hammond, J. R. **Robert Louis Stevenson Companion: A Guide to the Novels, Essays, and Short Stories**. London: Macmillan, 1984. 252p. (Macmillan Author Companions). LC 85-6522. ISBN 0-333-31906-0.

Emphasis in this handbook is on summarizing the plots and identifying the characters in Stevenson's works. Separate, complementary dictionaries summarize the individual short stories and essays, with cross-references to the collections in which they appear; survey these essay and short-story collections; summarize and critically introduce the novels; and identify the characters in the novels and short stories. Introductory chapters review Stevenson's life and literary achievement. Appendixes list film versions of Stevenson's works. Harry M. Geduld's *The Definitive Dr. Jekyll and Mr. Hyde Companion* (New York: Garland, 1983) offers more specialized introductory commentaries on sources, themes, and critical approaches to Stevenson's novel, with bibliographies and filmographies.

1294.   Knight, Alanna. **The Robert Louis Stevenson Treasury**. London: Shepeard-Walwyn, 1985. 359p. LC 82-10226. ISBN 0-85683-052-6.

More ambitious than Hammond's handbook (entry 1293) and somewhat more difficult to use, Knight's guide attempts to cumulate into one volume "as much as possible of the material which has accumulated on the life and work" of Stevenson (p. xv). A handbook of both Stevenson's life and career, Knight provides an extensive dictionary of persons (including critics), places, writings, and selected topics (such as children, marriage, and social customs) associated with Stevenson; descriptions of Stevenson's manuscripts and unpublished materials (with locations); identifications of his fictional characters and places; an index, with detailed descriptions, of Stevenson's letters, arranged by recipients; an index of his poems and musical settings; a listing of television, film, and radio adaptations of his works; and classified lists of published primary and secondary materials.

Donald Ogden Stewart, 1894-1980

Bibliographies

For works by Stewart, see *First Printings of American Authors*, vol. 1, p. 365. See *Bibliography of American Fiction, 1919-1988*, p. 482, for Rodney Rather's checklist of works by and about Stewart.

George R(ippey) Stewart, 1895-1980

Bibliographies

See *Bibliography of American Fiction, 1919-1988*, pp. 483-84, for John Caldwell's checklist of works by and about Stewart. Stewart's manuscripts are listed in Robbins' *American Literary Manuscripts*, p. 305. John Caldwell surveys works by and about Stewart in Erisman and Etulain's *Fifty Western Writers*, pp. 488-97.

Frank (Francis) R(ichard) Stockton, 1834-1902

Bibliographies

1295. Clark, Lucy T., and Marjorie D. Carver. **The Barrett Library: Frank Stocktons [sic]: A Checklist of Printed and Manuscript Works of Frank Richard Stockton in the Library of the University of Virginia.** Charlottesville, VA: University of Virginia Press, 1963. 24p. LC 63-1099.

Alphabetically arranged bibliographic descriptions of Stockton's published works in the Barrett Library, with a chronological index. Also identifies holdings of literary manuscripts and autograph letters. Name and title index. For works by Stockton, see *Bibliography of American Literature*, vol. 7, pp. 660-81. Stockton's contributions to and reviews of Stockton's works in selected periodicals are identified in Wells' *The Literary Index to American Magazines, 1850-1900*, pp. 354-56. Stockton's manuscripts are listed in Robbins' *American Literary Manuscripts*, p. 305. See *Bibliography of American Fiction, 1866-1918*, pp. 333-34, for David C. Owen's checklist of works by and about Stockton.

Charles Warren Stoddard, 1843-1909

Bibliographies

For works by Stoddard, see *Bibliography of American Literature*, vol. 8, pp. 1-10. Stoddard's contributions to and reviews of Stoddard's works in selected periodicals are identified in Wells' *The Literary Index to American Magazines, 1850-1900*, pp. 356-57. Stoddard's manuscripts are listed in Robbins' *American Literary Manuscripts*, p. 306. See Longtin's *Three Writers of the Far West* (entry 949) for criticisms of Stoddard.

Elizabeth Drew (Barstow) Stoddard, 1823-1902

Bibliographies

For works by Stoddard, see *Bibliography of American Literature*, vol. 8, pp. 11-15. Stoddard's contributions to and reviews of Stoddard's works in selected periodicals are identified in Wells' *The Literary Index to American Magazines, 1850-1900*, p. 357. Stoddard's manuscripts are listed in Robbins' *American Literary Manuscripts*, p. 306. See *Bibliography of American Fiction Through 1865*, pp. 234-35, for a checklist of works by and about Stoddard.

Richard Henry Stoddard, 1825-1903

Bibliographies

For works by Stoddard, see *Bibliography of American Literature*, vol. 8, pp. 16-49. Contributions by Stoddard and criticism and reviews of Stoddard's works in selected periodicals are identified in Wells' *The Literary Index to American Magazines, 1815-1865*, p. 148; and *The Literary Index to American Magazines, 1850-1900*, pp. 357-59. Stoddard's manuscripts are listed in Robbins' *American Literary Manuscripts*, p. 306.

William Leete Stone, 1792-1844

Bibliographies

See *Bibliography of American Fiction Through 1865*, pp. 236-37, for a checklist of works by and about Stone. Contributions by Stone and criticism and reviews of Stone's works in selected periodicals are identified in Wells' *The Literary Index to American Magazines, 1815-1865*, pp. 148-49; and *The Literary Index to American Magazines, 1850-1900*, pp. 360-61. Stone's manuscripts are listed in Robbins' *American Literary Manuscripts*, p. 307.

Tom Stoppard, 1937-

Bibliographies

1296. Bratt, David. **Tom Stoppard: A Reference Guide**. Boston: G. K. Hall, 1982. 264p. (A Reference Guide to Literature). LC 82-11739. ISBN 0-8161-8576-x.

Following a brief checklist of Stoppard's primary materials, Bratt chronologically arranges annotated entries for about 2,000 works about Stoppard published from 1964 through 1980, including books, newspaper and journal articles and production reviews, dissertations, and non-English-language criticisms, with an appendix of "incomplete" miscellanea (such as publicity clippings). Annotations are descriptive. A detailed index of names, titles, and subjects affords excellent access. Additional coverage of works by Stoppard as well as descriptions of works about him are provided in King's *Twenty Modern British Playwrights*, pp. 217-30.

David Malcolm Storey, 1933-

Bibliographies

King's *Twenty Modern British Playwrights*, pp. 231-40, lists works by Storey and describes works about him.

William Wetmore Story, 1819-1895

Bibliographies

For works by Story, see *Bibliography of American Literature*, vol. 8, pp. 50-69. Contributions by Story and criticism and reviews of Story's works in selected periodicals are identified in Wells' *The Literary Index to American Magazines, 1815-1865*, p. 149; and *The Literary Index to American Magazines, 1850-1900*, pp. 361-62.

Rex Stout, 1886-1975

Bibliography

1297. Townsend, Guy M., John J. McAleer, Judson C. Sapp, and Arriean Schemer. **Rex Stout: An Annotated Primary and Secondary Bibliography**. New York: Garland, 1980. 199p. (Garland Reference Library of the Humanities, vol. 239). LC 80-8507. ISBN 0-8240-9479-4.

Townsend and his associates give bibliographic information, brief data about publishing histories, and plot summaries for Stout's novels, separately published short stories, collections and anthologies containing his works, articles, reviews, poetry, contributions to books, edited volumes, broadcasts, movies, interviews, and other miscellaneous works, in addition to annotated entries for 112 selected works about Stout. Entries for Stout's book-length works give bibliographic information for editions and translations, plot summaries, and references to reviews. Entries for contributed works summarize contents. No topical indexing is provided. Stout's manuscripts are listed in Robbins' *American Literary Manuscripts*, p. 308. See *Bibliography of American Fiction, 1919-1988*, pp. 485-88, for John McAleer's checklist of works by and about Stout.

Harriet (Elizabeth) Beecher Stowe (Christopher Crowfield), 1811-1896

Bibliographies

1298. Ashton, Jean W. **Harriet Beecher Stowe: A Reference Guide**. Boston: G. K. Hall, 1977. 168p. (Reference Guides in Literature). LC 76-51433. ISBN 0-8161-7833-x.

Ashton's annotated, chronologically arranged listing covers about 800 comments and criticisms about Stowe published from 1843 through 1974. Comprehensive coverage includes published letters about Stowe, early anonymous reviews and notices, introductions in editions, and dissertations. Appendixes list fictional works based on *Uncle Tom's Cabin* and plays based on Stowe's life. Annotations are descriptive, not critical. Indexing under Stowe's name offers detailed subject access. See *Bibliography of American Fiction Through 1865*, pp. 238-44, for E. Bruce Kirkham's checklist of works by and about Stowe.

1299.   Hildreth, Margaret Holbrook. **Harriet Beecher Stowe: A Bibliography**. Hamden, CT: Archon Books, 1976. 257p. LC 76-14425. ISBN 0-208-01596-6.

Hildreth provides the best listing of Stowe's primary materials, chronologically arranging entries for English- and non-English-language editions of Stowe's works, abridgments, dramatic and film adaptations, microform editions, Stowe's collaborative works, contributions to periodicals, contributions to books, collected works and anthologies, and poetry set to music. Entries give brief bibliographic information. Hildreth also offers comprehensive coverage of creative and critical writings about Stowe or inspired by her, including plays and music based on Stowe's life and works, news items, theses and dissertations, and non-English-language criticisms. Secondary coverage in Ashton's guide (entry 1298) is more useful. John D. Haskell, Jr.'s "Addenda to Hildreth: Harriet Beecher Stowe," *PBSA* 72 (1978): 348, supplements coverage. Additional coverage of Stowe's primary materials is included in *Bibliography of American Literature*, vol. 8, pp. 70-133. Stowe's manuscripts are listed in Robbins' *American Literary Manuscripts*, pp. 308-309. Margaret Granville Mair's *The Papers of Harriet Beecher Stowe: A Bibliography of the Manuscripts in the Stowe-Day Memorial Library* (Hartford, CT: Stowe-Day Foundation, 1977) briefly describes 211 letters, 28 manuscripts, and other miscellaneous primary works in the collection. Also useful is Chester E. Jorgenson's *Uncle Tom's Cabin as Book and Legend: A Guide to an Exhibition* (Detroit: Friends of the Detroit Public Library, 1952).

(Giles) Lytton Strachey, 1880-1932
Bibliographies

1300.   Edmonds, Michael. **Lytton Strachey: A Bibliography**. New York: Garland, 1981. 157p. (Garland Reference Library of the Humanities, vol. 231). LC 80-8493. ISBN 0-8240-9494-8.

The best listing of Strachey's primary works, Edmonds' guide gives detailed descriptions for separately published English and American editions of Strachey's books and pamphlets, contributions to books, contributions to journals, collected editions, non-English-language editions (arranged by languages), and manuscripts and letters located at the University of Texas, the Berg Collection of the New York Public Library, and elsewhere. Entries for first editions give title-page transcriptions, with facsimiles; collations; descriptions of paper and bindings; and publishing histories; as well as brief information for later editions. In addition, Edmonds describes 14 selected works about Strachey. The most comprehensive listing of works about Strachey is Martin Kallich's "Lytton Strachey: An Annotated Bibliography of Writings About Him," *English Fiction in Transition* 5.3 (1962): 1-77; as well as Rae Gallant Robbins' *The Bloomsbury Group: A Selective Bibliography* (Kenmore, WA: Price Guide Publishers, 1978), pp. 143-59. Also for a bibliography of works by and about Strachey, see *NCBEL*, IV, pp. 1215-18.

Gene(va Grace) Stratton-Porter, 1863-1924
Bibliographies

1301.   MacLean, David G. **Gene Stratton Porter: A Bibliography and Collector's Guide**. 119p. Decatur, IN: Americana Books, 1976. LC 76-47355. ISBN 0-917902-01-7.

Gives brief bibliographic data (imprint, pagination, and size) for Porter's works, with descriptions or summaries of contents and citations to reviews and early notices, in sections for books, contributions to books, contributions to periodicals, books by Jeannette (Porter) Meehan, contributions to periodicals by Meehan, non-English-language translations, Braille and talking books, and miscellaneous works (about a dozen entries for a manuscript, postcards, and other ephemera). Emphasis is on bibliographic points and variants. Concluding chapter relates comparative values of editions. Also lists about 40 books and articles relating to Porter. See *Bibliography of American Fiction, 1866-1918*, p. 306-307, for

Mary Beth Butler's checklist of works by and about Porter. Porter's manuscripts are listed in Robbins' *American Literary Manuscripts*, p. 257.

Thomas Sigismund Stribling, 1881-1965
Bibliographies

For works by Stribling, see *First Printings of American Authors*, vol. 4, pp. 339-41. Stribling's manuscripts are listed in Robbins' *American Literary Manuscripts*, p. 309. See *Bibliography of American Fiction, 1919-1988*, pp. 489-90, for Edward J. Piacentino's checklist of works by and about Stribling.

William Strode, 1602-1645
Bibliographies

For a bibliography of works by and about Strode, see *NCBEL*, I, pp. 1320, 1774, 2002. Strode's manuscripts are described in *Index of English Literary Manuscripts*, II, pt. 2:351-444.

Jesse (Hilton) Stuart, 1907-1984
Bibliographies

1302.   LeMaster, J. R. **Jesse Stuart: A Reference Guide**. Boston: G. K. Hall, 1979. 206p. (A Reference Publication in Literature). LC 78-31883. ISBN 0-8161-8041-5.

LeMaster chronologically arranges annotated entries for about 1,500 writings about Stuart published from 1934 through 1977, including books, parts of books, entries in reference works, and articles and reviews in journals and local newspapers. Annotations are descriptive. No subject indexing is provided. LeMaster has relied extensively on clipping files located in the Stuart Collection at Murray State University. LeMaster updates coverage in "Jesse Stuart: A Bibliographical Supplement," *Register of the Kentucky Historical Society* 86 (1988): 142-65.

1303.   Woodbridge, Hensley C. **Jesse and Jane Stuart: A Bibliography**. 3d ed. Murray, KY: Murray State University Press, 1979. 221p. OCLC 8605755.

This gives separate listings for works by and about the father and daughter Stuarts. Although LeMaster's guide (entry 1302) gives more convenient coverage of secondary materials for Jesse Stuart, Woodbridge's listings for primary materials are more detailed. Intended for the collector, Jerry A. Herndon and George Brosi, with James M. Gifford and Jim Wayne Miller, provide brief bibliographic descriptions of Jesse Stuart's works (with information on bibliographic points, condition, prices, and such) in *Jesse Stuart, The Man & His Books: A Bibliography & Purchase Guide* (Ashland, KY: Jesse Stuart Foundation, 1988). The handbook also contains a brief biography and chronology for Stuart. Supplemental checklists for the Stuarts have appeared in *Jack London Newsletter* through vol. 15 (1982). Also for works by Jesse Stuart, see *First Printings of American Authors*, vol. 4, pp. 343-56. Stuart's manuscripts are listed in Robbins' *American Literary Manuscripts*, p. 310. See *Bibliography of American Fiction, 1919-1988*, pp. 490-93, for Woodbridge's checklist of works by and about Stuart. Research on Stuart is reviewed by Ruel E. Foster in Flora and Bain's *Fifty Southern Writers After 1900*, pp. 433-43.

Journals

See Patterson's *Author Newsletters and Journals*, p. 311, for previously published journals for Stuart.

Theodore (Hamilton) Sturgeon, 1918-1985
Bibliography

1304.   Diskin, Lahna F. **Theodore Sturgeon: A Primary and Secondary Bibliography**. Boston: G. K. Hall, 1980. 105p. (Masters of Science Fiction and Fantasy). LC 79-18120. ISBN 0-8161-8046-6.

Diskin gives a four-part chronologically arranged bibliography of publications by and about Sturgeon, recording Sturgeon's short fiction in periodicals, collections, and edited anthologies; poetry and work in nonprint media (radio, television, films, and recordings); book reviews, articles, and essays (including introductions and postscripts by Sturgeon in his own and others' works); and 116 entries for works in books and periodicals about Sturgeon. Coverage extends from 1939 through 1977. Each section is separately indexed. Critical materials are indexed by authors, titles, and subjects.

William (Clark) Styron, 1925-
Bibliographies

1305. Bryer, Jackson R. **William Styron: A Reference Guide**. Boston: G. K. Hall, 1978. 155p. (A Reference Publication in Literature). LC 78-8265. ISBN 0-8161-8042-3.

Bryer chronologically arranges annotated entries for about 1,200 works about Styron published from 1946 through 1978. Coverage includes reviews in journals and newspapers, dissertations, and non-English-language criticisms. Annotations are descriptive. Indexing under primary works and names of authors and titles (such as Updike and *Uncle Tom's Cabin*) provides access. Bryer updates and corrects his guide as well as supplements West's *William Styron* (entry 1306) in "William Styron: A Bibliography," pp. 299-382, in Robert K. Morris and Irving Malin's *The Achievement of William Styron*, revised ed. (Athens, GA: University of Georgia Press, 1981). Bryer's guide must be compared with Philip W. Leon's *William Styron: An Annotated Bibliography of Criticism* (Westport, CT: Greenwood Press, 1978), which gives selected descriptive and critical annotations for an equally comprehensive range of works about Styron and includes more useful topical indexing. See *Bibliography of American Fiction, 1919-1988*, pp. 494-96, for Keen Butterworth's checklist of works by and about Styron. Research on Styron is reviewed by Melvin J. Friedman in Flora and Bain's *Fifty Southern Writers After 1900*, pp. 444-56.

1306. West, James L. W., III. **William Styron: A Descriptive Bibliography**. Boston: G. K. Hall, 1977. 252p. (Reference Guides in Literature). LC 77-5581. ISBN 0-8161-7968-9.

This detailed, descriptive bibliography covers Styron's published and un-published materials, including separate listings for books, translations into French and other languages, contributions to books, reprintings, contributions to periodicals and newspapers, published letters, blurbs, interviews, discussions, comments, and miscellaneous works. Entries give full bibliographic descriptions for first and subsequent editions and reprintings, including title- and copyright-page transcriptions; detailed descriptions of paper, typography, bindings, and dust jackets; and information on publishing histories. Textual collations for variants are included. This is the best guide to Styron's primary works. Also for works by Styron, see *First Printings of American Authors*, vol. 4, pp. 357-59. Styron's manuscripts are listed in Robbins' *American Literary Manuscripts*, p. 310.

Sir John Suckling, 1609-1642
Bibliographies

For a bibliography of works by and about Suckling, see *NCBEL*, I, pp. 1213-14. Suckling's manuscripts are described in *Index of English Literary Manuscripts*, II, pt. 2:445-65.

Ruth Suckow, 1892-1960
Bibliographies

See *Bibliography of American Fiction, 1919-1988*, pp. 497-98, for Susan Goodman's checklist of works by and about Suckow. Suckow's manuscripts are listed in Robbins' *American Literary Manuscripts*, p. 311. Leedice Kissane surveys works by and about Suckow in Erisman and Etulain's *Fifty Western Writers*, pp. 498-508.

Hollis Summers, 1916-
Bibliographies

For works by Summers, see *First Printings of American Authors*, vol. 2, pp. 357-58. Summers' manuscripts are listed in Robbins' *American Literary Manuscripts*, p. 311.

Henry Howard, Earl of Surrey, 1517?-1547
Bibliographies

For a bibliography of works by and about Howard, see *NCBEL*, I, pp. 1023-24. Howard's manuscripts are described in *Index of English Literary Manuscripts*, I, pt. 2:533-42, 634-35. Jentoft's *Sir Thomas Wyatt and Henry Howard* (entry 1507) describes works about Howard to 1975.

Jonathan Swift, 1667-1745
Bibliographies

1307.   Rodino, Richard H. **Swift Studies, 1965-1980: An Annotated Bibliography.** New York: Garland, 1984. 252p. (Garland Reference Library of the Humanities, vol. 386). LC 82-49113. ISBN 0-8240-9197-3.

Rodino's work continues the coverage of Louis A. Landa and James E. Tobin's *Jonathan Swift: A List of Critical Studies Published from 1895-1945: To Which Is Added Remarks on Some Swift Manuscripts in the United States by Herbert Davis* (1945; reprint New York: Octagon, 1974), which gives a classified checklist of unannotated entries; and James J. Stathis' *A Bibliography of Swift Studies, 1945-1965* (Nashville, TN: Vanderbilt University Press, 1967), which gives a classified arrangement of 659 briefly annotated entries. Rodino provides comprehensive coverage of writings about Swift published from 1965 through 1980, including annotated entries for 1,500 critical books, articles, reviews, and dissertations in English and other languages as well as modern editions. Separate listings cover biography, general criticism, poetry, prose, and *Gulliver's Travels*. David M. Vieth's *Swift's Poetry, 1900-1980: An Annotated Bibliography of Studies* (New York: Garland, 1982) provides more limited coverage of modern scholarship, including 582 annotated entries for works about Swift's poetry. In addition, Milton Voight's *Swift and the Twentieth Century* (Detroit, MI: Wayne State University Press, 1964) reviews nineteenth-century views on Swift and surveys modern textual criticism, critical scholarship on *A Tale of a Tub* and *Gulliver's Travels*, and research on Swift's biography, as well as Swift and religion, satire, politics, and other topics. Research on Swift is reviewed by Louis A. Landa in Dyson's *The English Novel*, pp. 36-55.

1308.   Teerink, Herman, and Arthur H. Scouten. **A Bibliography of the Writings of Jonathan Swift.** 2d ed., revised and corrected. Philadelphia, PA: University of Pennsylvania Press, 1965. 453p. LC 62-11270.

First published as *A Bibliography of the Writings in Prose and Verse of Jonathan Swift, D.D.* (The Hague: Martinus Nijhoff, 1937), Scouten's revision of Teerink's bibliography is the standard listing of Swift's primary materials. Awkward organization blurs distinctions about the formats of Swift's works. Detailed entries give full bibliographic descriptions of collected works, "smaller collections," *A Tale of a Tub*, *Gulliver's Travels*, separate works, and doubtful works. In addition, a selection of critical and biographic studies published from 1709 through 1895 is listed. Teerink and Scouten's bibliography must be updated by consulting numerous more recent bibliographical studies of Swift's works. For Oliver W. Ferguson's bibliography of works by and about Swift, see *NCBEL*, II, pp. 1054-91. Useful for research on Swift's contemporary reception, Jeanne K. Welcher's *An Annotated List of Gulliveriana, 1721-1800* (Delmar, NY: Scholar's Facsimiles & Reprints, 1988) chronologically arranges detailed descriptions of approximately 1,800 published and unpublished allusions or other references to *Gulliver's Travels*, including analogues, imitations, artworks and illustrations, stage adaptations, maps, correspondence, and other works. International in scope. Welcher's entries reference standard editions and bibliographies and briefly explain "Gulliverian features" of each work. An extensive introduction emphasizes responses to and imitations of *Gulliver's Travels* as an international literary phenomenon (p. 51). Also important for research on Swift is Harold H. Williams' *Dean Swift's Library: With a Facsimile of the Original Sale Catalogue and Some Account of Two Manuscript Lists of His Books* (Cambridge: Cambridge University Press, 1932).

Dictionaries, Encyclopedia, and Handbooks

1309. Johnson, Clifford R. **Plots and Characters in the Fiction of Eighteenth-Century English Authors. Volume I: Jonathan Swift, Daniel Defoe, and Samuel Richardson. Volume II: Henry Fielding, Tobias Smollett, Laurence Sterne, Samuel Johnson, and Oliver Goldsmith.** Hamden, CT: Archon Books, 1977-78. 2 vols. (The Plots and Characters Series). LC 77-2572. ISBN 0-7129-0762-9 (vol. 1); 0-7129-0763-7 (vol. 2).

Plot summaries and brief character identifications for the fictional works of these major writers, including such works as *Clarissa*, *Rasselas*, and *Jonathan Wild*. Dramatic works are excluded. The plot of *Tom Jones* is summarized in 18 pages; *The Vicar of Wakefield* in six. Covers a total of 3,370 central characters. For further coverage of Swift, Paul Odell Clark's *A Gulliver Dictionary* (1953; reprint New York: Haskell House, 1972) gives brief explanations for names and other words in the "non-English" Brobdingnagian, Houyhnhnmian, and similar languages.

Indexes and Concordances

1310. Kelling, Harold D., and Cathy Lynn Preston. **A KWIC Concordance to Jonathan Swift's A Tale of a Tub, The Battle of the Books, and A Discourse Concerning the Mechanical Operation of the Spirit, a Fragment.** New York: Garland, 1984. 1,017p. (Garland Reference Library of the Humanities, vol. 461). LC 83-49083. ISBN 0-8240-9014-4.

Based on the standard text of Swift's works included in Herbert Davis' edition of *The Prose Writings of Jonathan Swift* (Oxford: Basil Blackwell, 1965). Every word in the texts is indexed; no stop list.

1311. Shinagel, Michael. **A Concordance to the Poems of Jonathan Swift.** Ithaca, NY: Cornell University Press, 1972. 977p. LC 72-4870. ISBN 0-8014-0747-8.

This is based on Harold Williams' edition of *The Poems of Jonathan Swift*, 2d ed. (Oxford: Clarendon Press, 1958).

Journals

1312. **Swift Studies: The Annual of the Ehrenpreis Center.** Munster: Forderkreis des Ehrenpreis Instituts fur Swift Studien, 1986-. Annual. ISSN 0938-8036.

Articles and brief notes offer close readings and focus on biographical problems and sources of the works of Swift and his contemporaries, including Alexander Pope, Sir William Temple, Mary Goddard, and Laetitia Pilkington. Studies have also described the literary relationships of Swift with Horace, Christopher Smart, Richard Steele, and William Collins. In addition, numerous features have addressed manuscripts and textual problems, examined topics in publishing history, described holdings related to Swift in special collections, and reviewed critical scholarship about Swift. Recent bibliographic contributions include Michael During's "Swift in Russia: An Annotated Bibliography, I," 9 (1994): 100-12, and "Swift in Russia: An Annotated Bibliography, II," 10 (1995): 89-101; and James O'Toole's "A New Book from Swift's Library," 9 (1994): 113-17. *Swift Studies* is indexed in *MHRA* and *MLA*.

"Recent Articles" in *The Scriblerian and the Kit Cats* (entry 1084) also regularly includes a selection of reviews of studies on Swift.

Algernon Charles Swinburne, 1837-1909
Bibliographies
1313.   Beetz, Kirk H. **Algernon Charles Swinburne: A Bibliography of Secondary Works, 1861-1980**. Metuchen, NJ: Scarecrow Press, 1982. 227p. (Scarecrow Author Bibliographies, no. 61). LC 82-3359. ISBN 0-8108-1541-9.

The most complete bibliography of secondary materials about Swinburne, Beetz's guide chronologically arranges selectively annotated entries for 2,300 books, parts of books, articles, reviews, dissertations, and non-English-language criticisms published from 1861 through 1980. Brief introductions in each annual listing describe Swinburne's critical reception and its scholarly context, as well as identify significant works of the year by other major writers. Selective annotations are descriptive. A separate subject index includes headings for Swinburne (with topical subheadings), primary works, and names. Additionally, Ehrsam's *Bibliographies of Twelve Victorian Authors*, pp. [263]-97, cites international comments, criticism, and reviews for Swinburne through the early twentieth century. Research on Swinburne is reviewed by Clyde K. Hyder in Faverty's *The Victorian Poets*, pp. 227-50; and Wendell V. Harris in DeLaura's *Victorian Prose*, pp. 446-48.

1314.   Wise, Thomas J. **A Bibliography of the Writings in Prose and Verse of Algernon Charles Swinburne**. 1919; reprint London: Dawsons of Pall Mall, 1966. 2 vols. LC 68-76793.

Wise gives detailed descriptions of Swinburne's primary materials, covering separately published works (194 entries); poems, prose pieces, and letters contributed to periodicals and books (404 entries); "works wrongly attributed to Swinburne"; and unpublished writings. Entries give title-page transcriptions and facsimiles, collations, contents, and information about the publishing histories of first and subsequent editions. Additionally, 43 selected "Swinburneiana" (that is, early critical and biographical works about Swinburne) are listed. Also for a bibliography of works by and about Swinburne, see *NCBEL*, III, pp. 571-79.

John Addington Symonds, 1840-1893
Bibliographies
1315.   Babington, Percy Lancelot. **Bibliography of the Writings of John Addington Symonds**. London: John Castle, 1925. 244p. LC 26-7363.

Full bibliographic descriptions of Symonds' works chronologically arranged in chapters for first editions; edited books and contributions to books; contributions to "British and Non-English" periodicals (subarranged by periodical titles and covering Symonds' 14 contributions to the ninth edition of *The Encyclopaedia Britannica*); later editions and reprints, 1895-1925; "Some American Issues of Books, Articles, Etc. by Symonds"; and European translations and reprints, 1879-1905. Entries for 67 first editions supply title-page transcriptions, collations, contents, binding descriptions, and notes on variants and publication histories. Also includes entries for about 40 biographical and critical books, articles, and other notices about Symonds published from 1890 to 1925. Name and title index. Also available in a reprinted edition (New York: Burt Franklin, 1968). Criticism and reviews of Symonds' works in selected periodicals are identified in Wells' *The Literary Index to American Magazines, 1850-1900*, pp. 367-68. Wendell V. Harris reviews research on Symonds in DeLaura's *Victorian Prose*, pp. 449-51.

Arthur William Symons, 1865-1945
Bibliographies
1316.   Beckson, Karl, Ian Fletcher, Lawrence W. Markert, and John Stokes. **Arthur Symons: A Bibliography**. Greensboro, NC: ELT Press, 1990. 330p. (1880-1920 British Authors Series, no. 5). LC 89-84406. ISBN 0-9443-1804-5.

Describes works by Symons in sections for books and pamphlets, edited books and contributions to books, contributions to periodicals and newspapers, and translations. Chronologically arranged bibliographic descriptions for first and subsequent editions and printings of Symons' 64 books published through 1989 give title-page transcriptions, pagination, brief details about format and bindings, contents, and notes on publication history. Gives brief bibliographic citations, with notes on reprintings, for nearly 2,000 periodical contributions (including posthumous works) published from 1882 to 1989. Introduction notes manuscripts and archival collections (pp. xi-xii). Author and title index. Also for a bibliography of works by and about Symons, see *NCBEL*, III, pp. 649-71. Wendell V. Harris reviews research on Symons in DeLaura's *Victorian Prose*, pp. 464-67.

(Edmund) John Millington Synge, 1871-1909
Bibliographies
1317.　Kopper, Edward A., Jr. **Synge: A Review of the Criticism**. Lyndora, PA: Edward A. Kopper, Jr., 1990. 65p. (Modern Irish Literature Monograph Series, vol. 1). OCLC 25966296.

A narrative "assessment of Synge criticism . . . complete through 1989, with a few items included from 1990" (p. 5). Selective coverage of approximately 300 items, including non-English-language publications, in sections for bibliography (with notes on Synge's manuscripts and special collections), editions, correspondence, biography, general critical studies, studies of the six individual plays, the poetry, *The Aran Islands* and other nondramatic prose, and language. Kopper clearly identifies standard works as well as critical strengths, weaknesses, and desiderata. Unindexed. Research on Synge is also reviewed by Weldon Thornton in Finneran's *Anglo-Irish Literature*, pp. 315-65; and by Richard Jones in Schrank and Demastes' *Irish Playwrights, 1880-1995: A Research and Production Sourcebook*, pp. 356-66.

1318.　Kopper, Edward A. **John Millington Synge: A Reference Guide**. Boston: G. K. Hall, 1979. 199p. (A Reference Publication in Literature). LC 78-21968. ISBN 0-8161-8119-5.

The most convenient listing of works about Synge, Kopper's bibliography chronologically arranges annotated entries for about 1,000 comments and criticisms of Synge published from 1900 through 1976. Coverage includes anonymous reviews and notices in newspapers, published letters, dissertations, and entries in reference works. Descriptive annotations quote extensively from sources. Important works are clearly identified. Topical indexing is limited to headings for primary works and for bibliography and biography. Kopper's guide supersedes Paul M. Levitt's *J. M. Synge: A Bibliography of Published Criticism* (New York: Barnes & Noble, 1974); and E. H. Mikhail's *J. M. Synge: A Bibliography of Criticism* (Totowa, NJ: Rowman and Littlefield, 1975). For a bibliography of works by and about Synge, see *NCBEL*, III, pp. 1934-38.

Dictionaries, Encyclopedias, and Handbooks
1319.　Kopper, Edward A., Jr. **J. M. Synge Literary Companion**. Westport, CT: Greenwood Press, 1988. 268p. LC 87-32295. ISBN 0-313-25173-8.

Kopper assembles contributed survey essays by different specialists on Synge's life, individual works, and other topics, such as Irish mythology, the Irish Literary Renaissance, and Synge's language and female characters. In addition to brief stage histories of the plays and a selected secondary bibliography, the volume includes a brief dictionary of characters, place names, and themes and images (such as aging, drinking, and wandering), with cross-references to Robin Skelton's four-volume edition of *J. M. Synge: Collected Works* (London: Oxford University Press, 1962-1968).

John B(anister) Tabb, 1845-1909
Bibliographies

For works by Tabb, see *Bibliography of American Literature*, vol. 8, pp. 134-43. Tabb's manuscripts are listed in Robbins' *American Literary Manuscripts*, p. 312.

Genevieve Taggard, 1894-1948
Bibliographies

For works by Taggard, see *First Printings of American Authors*, vol. 1, pp. 367-68. Taggard's manuscripts are listed in Robbins' *American Literary Manuscripts*, pp. 312-13.

Tales, Middle English
Bibliographies

Thomas D. Cooke offers a comprehensive guide to primary materials for Middle English tales with a bibliography of editions and criticism in Severs and Hartung's *A Manual of the Writings in Middle English*, vol. XXIV, pp. 3138-3328, 3472-3570. *NCBEL*, I, pp. 455-60, also gives a bibliography of editions and studies.

Harden E(dwards) Taliaferro, 1818-1875
Bibliographies

1320.   Walser, Richard. **Biblio-Biography of Skitt Taliaferro**. Raleigh, NC: North Carolina Historical Review, 1978. [375]-95p. OCLC 18210160.

Reprinted from the *North Carolina Historical Review* 55.4 (October 1978): [375]-95. Brief narrative account of Taliaferro's life and writings with bibliographic references to published and manuscript sources. See *Bibliography of American Fiction Through 1865*, p. 245, for a checklist of works by and about Taliaferro.

(Newton) Booth Tarkington, 1869-1946
Bibliographies

1321.   Russo, Dorothy Ritter, and Thelma L. Sullivan. **A Bibliography of Booth Tarkington**. Indianapolis, IN: Indiana Historical Society, 1949. 303p. LC 49-50289.

Russo and Sullivan offer detailed descriptions of first editions or publications of Tarkington's books, "ephemera" (drawings, programs, broadsides, cards, and the like), and contributions to books of others; reprint editions; secondary works (books, pamphlets, leaflets, and periodical articles); and Tarkington's contributions to newspapers and journals. Entries include title-page transcriptions, collations, notes on bindings (with illustrations), and other bibliographic data. Also for works by Tarkington, see *First Printings of American Authors*, vol. 1, pp. 369-75. Tarkington's manuscripts are listed in Robbins' *American Literary Manuscripts*, p. 313. See *Bibliography of American Fiction, 1866-1918*, pp. 335-37, for Mark E. Williams' checklist of works by and about Tarkington.

(John Orley) Allen Tate, 1899-1979
Bibliographies

1322.   Fallwell, Marshall, Jr. **Allen Tate: A Bibliography**. New York: D. Lewis, 1969. 112p. LC 75-7563. ISBN 0-8103-2017-7.

Covering works by and about Tate appearing through 1967, Fallwell's checklist gives brief identifying information (not full bibliographic descriptions) for Tate's books, poems, essays and articles, book reviews, reviews in the *Nashville Tennessean*, and miscellaneous primary materials (such as forewords, interviews, and comments in newspaper columns). Entries for about 200 books; articles in scholarly journals, popular magazines, and newspapers; and dissertations include brief descriptive annotations. Unindexed. Also for works by Tate, see *First Printings of American Authors*, vol. 4, pp. 361-72. Tate's manuscripts are listed in Robbins' *American Literary Manuscripts*, p. 314. Research on Tate is reviewed by Thomas Daniel Young in Flora and Bain's *Fifty Southern Writers After 1900*, pp. 457-68.

James (Vincent) Tate, 1943-
Bibliographies
> For works by Tate, see *First Printings of American Authors*, vol. 2, pp. 359-61.

(James) Bayard Taylor, 1825-1878
Bibliographies
> For works by Taylor, see *Bibliography of American Literature*, vol. 8, pp. 144-95. Contributions by Taylor and criticism and reviews of Taylor's works in selected periodicals are identified in Wells' *The Literary Index to American Magazines, 1815-1865*, pp. 151-52; and *The Literary Index to American Magazines, 1850-1900*, pp. 369-71. Taylor's manuscripts are listed in Robbins' *American Literary Manuscripts*, p. 314.

Edward Taylor, c. 1644-1729
Bibliographies
> 1323. Gefvert, Constance J. **Edward Taylor: An Annotated Bibliography, 1668-1970.** Kent, OH: Kent State University Press, 1971. 82p. (The Serif Series: Bibliographies and Checklists, no. 19). LC 70-144811. ISBN 0-87338-113-0.
>
> Gefvert offers full bibliographic descriptions for Taylor's primary materials, including editions of poems and sermons, letters, poems first published in others' works, first editions of other works (Taylor's diary and fragments), and manuscripts, in addition to a solid introductory survey of Taylor scholarship from 1937 through 1970 and briefly annotated entries for about 250 works about Taylor (books, parts of books, articles, and dissertations) in English and other languages. Describes the collection of Taylor's literary manuscripts of poetry, drafts, fragments, and notebooks in Yale University's Beinecke Library, in addition to those of the Massachusetts Historical Society, Westfield Athenaeum, the Redwood Library and Athenaeum, and Prince Library of the Boston Public Library (pp. 15-19). An index of names offers only limited access. Also for works by Taylor, see *First Printings of American Authors*, vol. 5, pp. 321-22. Taylor's manuscripts are listed in Robbins' *American Literary Manuscripts*, p. 315. For a bibliography of works by and about Taylor, see *NCBEL*, I, pp. 1321-23. Research on Taylor is reviewed by Norman S. Grabo and Jane Wainwright in Harbert and Rees' *Fifteen American Authors Before 1900*, pp. 439-67; and Donald E. Stanford in Everett Emerson's *Major Writers of Early American Literature*, pp. 59-92.

Indexes and Concordances
> 1324. Craig, Raymond A. **A Concordance to the Minor Poetry of Edward Taylor (1642?-1729), American Colonial Poet.** Lewiston, NY: Edwin Mellen Press, 1992. 2 vols. LC 92-3910. ISBN 0-7734-9632-7 (vol. 1); 0-7734-9633-5 (vol. 2).
>
> Craig concords 145 poems included in Thomas M. Davis and Virginia L. Davis' *Edward Taylor's Minor Poetry* (Boston: Twayne, 1981), which excludes "Metrical History of Christianity." Includes frequency index and a list and index of omitted words.

> 1325. Russell, Gene. **A Concordance to the Poems of Edward Taylor.** Washington, DC: Microcard Editions, 1973. 413p. LC 72-96374. ISBN 0-9109-7235-4.
>
> This concordance is based on the texts of *Preparatory Meditations, God's Determinations Touching His Elect* and miscellaneous poems in Donald E. Stanford's edition of *The Poems* (New Haven, CT: Yale University Press, 1960).

Jeremy Taylor, 1613-1667
Bibliographies
> 1326. Williams, William Proctor. **Jeremy Taylor, 1700-1976: An Annotated Checklist.** New York: Garland, 1979. 76p. (Garland Reference Library of the Humanities, vol. 177). LC 78-68302. ISBN 0-8240-9756-4.

Covering works by and about Taylor published after 1700, Williams' check-list complements the coverage of Gathorne-Hardy and Williams' earlier primary bibliography (entry 1327). Williams gives brief identifying information in separate listings for Taylor's individual works, abridged works, collected editions, and collections including selections of Taylor's works. Most copies are located in the British Library; for several, however, Williams notes that no copies are available. In addition, listings present about 270 briefly annotated entries for biographical, theological, and literary and general studies of Taylor's works. Separate indexes of authors and primary titles give good access.

1327.   Gathorne-Hardy, Robert, and William Proctor Williams. **A Bibliography of the Writings of Jeremy Taylor to 1700: With a Section of Tayloriana**. DeKalb, IL: Northern Illinois University Press, 1971. 159p. LC 71-149932. ISBN 0-87580-023-8.
The bulk of the volume gives full bibliographic descriptions of all editions, printings, and issues of Taylor's works published through 1700, including title-page transcriptions, collations, contents, and extensive bibliographic notes, with *STC* and *Wing* numbers. In addition, sections list Taylor's contributed works, printings of Taylor's letters (through the present), "Tayloriana" (works attributed to Taylor), contemporary critical and biographical materials about Taylor, and contemporary attacks on Taylor's works. For a bibliography of works by and about Taylor, see *NCBEL*, I, pp. 1984-87. Taylor's manuscripts are described in *Index of English Literary Manuscripts*, II, pt. 2:467-76.

Dictionaries, Encyclopedias, and Handbooks
1328.   Smith, Logan Pearsall, ed. **The Golden Grove: Selected Passages from the Sermons and Writings of Jeremy Taylor**. Oxford: Clarendon Press, 1930. 330p. LC 31-3379.
Selection of 180 extended passages from Taylor's writings, based on the texts of "the first editions of the works in which they appear" ("Note") and arranged under such headings as "Angry Prayer," "Tears," "Men's Notions," "Friendship and Fancy," and "Joan of Arc." Entries give page citations, textual notes, and glosses but are otherwise unindexed. Appends "A Bibliography of Jeremy Taylor" (pp. [297]-330, compiled by Robert Gathorne-Hardy), giving full bibliographic descriptions of 56 works.

John Taylor, 1578?-1653
Bibliographies
For a bibliography of works by and about Taylor, see *NCBEL*, I, pp. 2014-20.

Peter (Hillsman) Taylor, 1917-1994
Bibliographies
1329.   Wright, Stuart T. **Peter Taylor: A Descriptive Bibliography, 1934-1987**. Charlottesville, VA: University of Virginia Press, 1989. LC 87-32044. ISBN 0-8139-1168-0.
Provides full bibliographic descriptions of Taylor's primary materials, in-cluding American and English editions of books and pamphlets (with locations of copies); contributions to books and edited works; contributed poems, stories, plays, and juvenilia in periodicals (with collations for variant texts); interviews and published comments; dust-jacket blurbs; recordings of Taylor reading his works; translations of Taylor's stories; and a self-portrait drawing by Taylor. Illustrations of title and copyright pages accompany title-page transcriptions, collations, contents, and bibliographic notes. Kramer's guide to Lytle, Percy, and Taylor (entry 872) offers coverage of Taylor scholarship from 1948 through 1980. Also for works by Taylor, see *First Printings of American Authors*, vol. 1, p. 378. Taylor's manuscripts are listed in Robbins' *American Literary Manuscripts*, p. 315.

See *Bibliography of American Fiction, 1919-1988*, pp. 498-99, for Sappho Human's checklist of works by and about Taylor.

Sir William Temple, 1628-1699
Bibliographies

For a bibliography of works by and about Temple, see *NCBEL*, II, pp. 1038-40.

Tabitha (Gilman) Tenney, 1762-1837
Bibliographies

See *Bibliography of American Fiction Through 1865*, p. 246, for a checklist of works by and about Tenney. Tenney's manuscripts are listed in Robbins' *American Literary Manuscripts*, p. 315.

Alfred Tennyson, 1809-1892
Bibliographies

1330. Beetz, Kirk H. **Tennyson: A Bibliography, 1887-1982**. Metuchen, NJ: Scarecrow Press, 1984. 528p. (Scarecrow Author Bibliographies, no. 68). LC 84-1274. ISBN 0-8108-1687-3.

The most comprehensive listing of works by and about Tennyson, Beetz's guide chronologically arranges more than 5,000 entries. Coverage includes books, articles, and dissertations and extends from 1827 through 1982. Annotations are descriptive, with works of particular importance receiving extended reviews. Beetz's bibliography supersedes coverage of Tennyson's primary and secondary works provided in Charles Tennyson and Christine Fall's *Alfred Tennyson: An Annotated Bibliography* (Athens, GA: University of Georgia Press, 1967) and complements the coverage of Wise's primary bibliography (entry 1332). Beetz's coverage is also more comprehensive than Ehrsam's *Bibliographies of Twelve Victorian Authors*, pp. [299]-362, which cites international comments, criticism, and reviews through the early twentieth century. Providing a detailed overview of early critical responses, Aletha Andrew's *An Annotated Bibliography and Study of the Contemporary Criticism of Tennyson's Idylls of the King: 1859-1886* (New York: Peter Lang, 1993) is a fully and critically annotated and indexed guide to contemporary criticism and reviews of Tennyson's *Idylls*, greatly supplementing early coverage in the guides of Shaw and Snaith (entry 1331) and Beetz. Also for a bibliography of works by and about Tennyson, see *NCBEL*, III, pp. 412-35. Research on Tennyson is reviewed by E. D. H. Johnson in Faverty's *The Victorian Poets*, pp. 33-80; and John Dixon Hunt in Dyson's *English Poetry*, pp. 265-84.

1331. Shaw, Marion, and Clifton U. Snaith. **An Annotated Critical Bibliography of Alfred, Lord Tennyson**. London: Harvester Wheatsheaf, 1989. 134p. (Harvester Annotated Critical Bibliographies). LC 89-35427. ISBN 0-3120-1962-9.

Annotated entries for about 400 selected criticisms of Tennyson, chronologically arranged in major sections for biography; bibliography, including manuscript and textual studies and reference works; and criticism of the poems in general (with subdivisions for book-length studies and articles, studies of context and reputation, Romantic influences, religion, philosophy, science, style, and other topics), the early poetry, individual poems (in separate listings), and the plays. Intended for the general audience, annotations are evaluative and clearly identify important editions and other resources. Includes a chronology of Tennyson's life and publications. Indexes for authors, editors, and other names; poems and plays; and subjects. Shaw and Snaith's guide can be used to selectively update the more comprehensive coverage of Beetz's *Tennyson: A Bibliography, 1887-1982* (entry 1330).

1332. Wise, Thomas J. **A Bibliography of the Writings of Alfred, Lord Tennyson.**
1908; reprint London: Dawsons, 1967. 363, 209p. in 1 vol. LC 67-106005.

Despite Wise's reputation for forgeries, this is the standard descriptive
bibliography of Tennyson and still regarded as the most nearly complete listing
of Tennyson's primary materials. Vol. 1 of Wise's bibliography gives detailed
bibliographic data (title-page transcriptions, collations, and notes) for first and
later editions of Tennyson's writings. Vol. 2 covers Tennyson's contributions to
periodicals, annuals, books, collections, and works by others; pirated issues;
collected editions; and book-length biographical and critical works. Indexing is
limited to primary titles. Although a source of good data, Wise's work needs to be
updated according to modern principles of description. For Wise's forgeries, see
William B. Todd's "A Handlist of Thomas J. Wise," in *Thomas J. Wise: Centenary
Studies* (Austin, TX: University of Texas Press, 1959). Also of interest for research
on Tennyson's primary materials, Nancie Campbell's *Tennyson in Lincoln: A Catalogue of the Collections in the Research Center* (Lincoln: Tennyson Society, 1971-73)
describes the collection of the Tennyson Research Center, Central Library, containing the personal libraries of members of the Tennyson family, including Alfred
Tennyson; his father, Dr. George Clayton Tennyson; Charles Tennyson Turner; and
Hallam, Lord Tennyson, among others; as well as editions, proofs, trial books,
illustrative materials, and biographical and critical materials. Also useful is Sian
Allsobrook and Peter Revell's *A Catalogue of the Tennyson Collection in the Library
of the University College, Cardiff* (Cardiff: University College, 1972), which describes
416 items formerly in the estate of Cyril Brett.

Dictionaries, Encyclopedia, and Handbooks

1333. Marshall, George O., Jr. **A Tennyson Handbook.** New York: Twayne, 1963.
291p. LC 63-17403.

Gives a chronology of Tennyson's life and career and work-by-work summary data on composition, analyses of techniques (metrics, themes, and the like),
and publication history. A selective, concluding bibliography lists basic primary
and secondary materials. Arthur E. Baker's *A Tennyson Dictionary: The Characters
and Place-Names Contained in the Poetical and Dramatic Works of the Poet, Alphabetically Arranged and Described with Synopses of the Poems and Plays* (1916; reprint New
York: Haskell House, 1967) summarizes the plots of each of Tennyson's works and
identifies characters and places.

1334. Pinion, F. B. **A Tennyson Chronology.** London: Macmillan, 1990. 209p.
(Macmillan Author Chronologies). LC 89-31429. ISBN 0-333-460200.

Based on the letters, diaries, and biographies of Tennyson and his contemporaries, Pinion's chronology is event oriented. Appends brief sketches of about
50 "Persons of Importance in Tennyson's Life." Separate indexes of persons,
places, and institutions (such as Shakespeare and the Metaphysical Society) and
of Tennyson's plays and poems provide access. No topical indexing.

Indexes and Concordances

1335. Baker, Arthur E. **A Concordance to the Poetical and Dramatic Works of
Alfred, Lord Tennyson.** 1914; reprint New York: Barnes & Noble, 1966. 1,212p. LC
66-2700.

Baker separately concords Tennyson's poems and plays included in *The
Works of Alfred Lord Tennyson* ("The Complete Edition") (London: Macmillan,
1894); poems included in *Alfred Lord Tennyson: A Memoir* ("Life of Lord Tennyson")
(London: Macmillan, 1898); and J. C. Thomson's edition of the *Suppressed Poems of
Alfred Lord Tennyson, 1830-1868* (London: Sands, 1910). In addition, Baker also
produced *A Concordance to The Devil and the Lady: Being a Supplement to the
"Concordance to the Works of the Late Lord Tennyson"* (London: Golden Vista, 1931;
reprinted New York: Kraus, 1971). Baker's concordances are superior to Daniel
Barron Brightwell's *A Concordance to the Entire Works of Alfred Tennyson* (London:

E. Moxon, Son, 1869), which is limited to the poetry, and its updating, *A Concordance to the Works of Alfred Tennyson, Poet Laureate* (London: Strahan and Co., 1870).

Journals

1336. **Tennyson Research Bulletin**. Lincoln: Tennyson Society, 1967- . Annual. ISSN 0082-2841.

Sponsored by the Tennyson Society, *Tennyson Research Bulletin* features scholarly articles and notes on the life, works, and times of Tennyson and his contemporaries. Emphasis is on bibliographic and biographical studies, although critical and interpretive features also appear. Facsimiles of letters and other primary documents are commonly included. In addition, issues offer extensive coverage of papers and other research reports on Tennyson at conferences, notices of recent acquisitions by the Tennyson Research Center, reviews of new publications and announcements of others, and obituaries. The journal features a variously titled bibliography of the year's international scholarship on Tennyson in volumes through 6.1 (1992) and hopefully beyond. *Tennyson Research Bulletin* is indexed in *MHRA* and *MLA*.

Patterson's *Author Newsletters and Journals*, pp. 318-20, describes other previously published journals for Tennyson.

Madison Tensas, M.D. (Henry Clay Lewis), 1825-1850
Bibliographies

See *Bibliography of American Fiction Through 1865,* p. 165, for a checklist of works by and about Lewis.

Mary Virginia Terhune (Marion Harland), 1830-1922
Bibliographies

See *Bibliography of American Fiction Through 1865,* pp. 247-49, for a checklist of works by and about Terhune. Terhune's manuscripts are listed in Robbins' *American Literary Manuscripts*, p. 315.

Megan Terry, 1932-
Bibliographies

Karen L. Laughlin reviews research on Terry in *Contemporary Authors: Bibliographical Series: Volume 3: American Dramatists*, pp. 361-78.

William Makepeace Thackeray, 1811-1863
Bibliographies

1337. Goldfarb, Sheldon. **William Makepeace Thackeray: An Annotated Bibliography, 1976-1987**. New York: Garland, 1989. 175p. (Garland Reference Library of the Humanities, vol. 857). LC 89-1482. ISBN 0-8240-1212-7.

Goldfarb provides detailed, descriptive annotations for about 450 studies of Thackeray published from 1976 through 1987, including non-English-language criticisms and dissertations (listed separately), in addition to addenda to the bibliography of Olmsted (entry 1338). Significant works receive extended descriptions. Index for critics, Thackeray's works, characters, and topics offers comprehensive access.

1338. Olmsted, John Charles. **Thackeray and His Twentieth-Century Critics: An Annotated Bibliography 1900-1975**. New York: Garland, 1977. 249p. (Garland Reference Library of the Humanities, vol. 62). LC 76-24394. ISBN 0-8240-9915-X.

Olmsted chronologically arranges evaluative entries for about 850 studies of Thackeray, including books and articles. Dissertations are listed separately. Coverage is largely limited to American and British publications. Coverage excludes newspaper articles, passing references, and master's theses. Significant studies receive extended descriptions with citations to reviews. Indexes for critics, primary titles, and subjects provide access. Olmsted's guide extends the coverage of commentaries and criticisms on Thackeray offered by Dudley Flamm's *Thackeray's Critics: An Annotated Bibliography of British and American Criticism, 1836-1901* (Chapel Hill, NC: University of North Carolina Press, 1967). Research on Thackeray is reviewed by Robert A. Colby in Ford's *Victorian Fiction*, pp. 114-42; Lionel Stevenson in Stevenson's *Victorian Fiction*, pp. 154-87; and Arthur Pollard in Dyson's *The English Novel*, pp. 164-78.

1339.   Van Duzer, Henry Sayre. **A Thackeray Library: First Editions and First Publications, Portraits, Water Colors, Etchings, Drawings, and Manuscripts.** 1919; reprint Port Washington, NY: Kennikat Press, 1965. 198p. LC 65-18612.

This reprinting, with an introduction by Lionel Stevenson, provides comprehensive coverage of Thackeray's primary materials. The volume's organization and descriptions, however, reflect Victorian principles and need to be updated. Van Duzer describes Thackeray's published and unpublished illustrations (accompanied by facsimiles) as well as his books; contributions to periodicals and newspapers; and contributions to *Fraser's Magazine*, *Punch*, and *Cornhill Magazine*. Entries supply title-page transcriptions, collations, contents, and publishing histories. A chronological index of primary titles (the volume's only index) and selected "Thackerayana" (works about or related to Thackeray) complete the guide. Also for a bibliography of works by and about Thackeray, see *NCBEL*, III, pp. 855-64.

Dictionaries, Encyclopedias, and Handbooks
1340.   Mudge, Isadore Gilbert, and M. Earl Sears. **A Thackeray Dictionary: The Characters and Scenes of the Novels and Short Stories Alphabetically Arranged.** 1910; reprint New York: Humanities Press, 1962. 304p. (Dictionaries of Famous Authors). LC 62-6137.

Mudge and Sears provide work-by-work summaries of Thackeray's writings (complete with family trees for the Esmonds in *Henry Esmond* and *The Virginians* and other characters) as well as an alphabetically arranged dictionary of characters with cross-references to the works in which they appear. Becky Sharp gets a full page description. An "Index of Originals" matches real persons, places, and things with Thackeray's fictional counterparts.

1341.   Harden, Edgar F. **Annotations for the Selected Works of William Makepeace Thackeray: The Complete Novels, the Major Non-Fictional Prose, and Selected Shorter Pieces.** New York: Garland, 1990. 2 vols. (Garland Reference Library of the Humanities, vol. 1000). LC 89-16914. ISBN 0-8240-3140-7.

Harden glosses Victorian and non-English-language vocabulary and identifies allusions to real and fictional persons, places, things, events, and sources of quotations. Annotations are keyed to chapter numbers and cite standard reference sources. Comprehensive index of abbreviations and names and titles. John Sutherland and Oscar Mandel's *Annotations to Vanity Fair*, 2d ed. (Lanham, MD: University Press of America, 1989) offers a similar service for terms, characters, places, historical events, and the like, including French, German, and Greek words, in *Vanity Fair*.

Journals
1342.   **Thackeray Newsletter.** Mississippi State, MS: Mississippi State University, 1977-. 2/yr. ISSN 1064-2463.

Brief scholarly contributions to *Thackeray Newsletter* have discussed Thackeray's narrative techniques; pointed out allusions to Milton, Tennyson, and other writers and Thackeray's influence on literature; and delved into the publication histories of specific works. A bibliographic feature, "Thackeray Studies: Recent and Forthcoming," lists international criticisms. The journal also notes conference proceedings and research in progress and abstracts dissertations. *Thackeray Newsletter* is indexed in *MLA*.

See Patterson's *Author Newsletters and Journals*, p. 320, for previously published journals for Thackeray.

Celia (Laighton) Thaxter, 1835-1894
Bibliographies
For works by Thaxter, see *Bibliography of American Literature*, vol. 8, pp. 196-214. Thaxter's contributions to selected periodicals and reviews of Thaxter's works are identified in Wells' *The Literary Index to American Magazines, 1850-1900*, pp. 378-79. Thaxter's manuscripts are listed in Robbins' *American Literary Manuscripts*, p. 316.

Dylan Marlais Thomas, 1914-1953
Bibliographies
1343.   Gaston, Georg M. A. **Dylan Thomas: A Reference Guide**. Boston: G. K. Hall, 1987. 213p. (Reference Guide to Literature). LC 87-8552. ISBN 0-8161-8779-7.

Gaston claims to identify all "truly important and useful critical and descriptive pieces" about Thomas and includes about 1,500 chronologically arranged and objectively annotated entries. Coverage extends from 1934 through 1985, excluding passing references, brief notices, and entries in reference works. The index references critics, titles of book-length studies, and selected subjects.

1344.   Maud, Ralph. **Dylan Thomas in Print: A Bibliographical History**. Pittsburgh, PA: University of Pittsburgh Press, 1970. 261p. LC 78-101190. ISBN 0-8229-3201-6.

Despite its awkward organization, Maud's guide is the most comprehensive and complete descriptive bibliography of Thomas' primary materials. Intending to list everything published by or about Thomas during his lifetime or posthumously, Maud provides separate, chronologically arranged listings for books, anthologies, dissertations, Welsh periodicals and newspapers, London periodicals and newspapers, U.S. and Canadian periodicals and newspapers, and non-English-language publications. Although giving comprehensive coverage, Maud's entries lack full details: Bibliographic descriptions are incomplete. For more detailed descriptions of Thomas' primary materials, researchers should consult Rolph's bibliography (entry 1345).

1345.   Rolph, J. Alexander. **Dylan Thomas: A Bibliography**. London: J. M. Dent, 1956. 108p. LC 56-13348.

Rolph presents full bibliographic descriptions, with collations for textual variants, in separate listings for Thomas' books and pamphlets, contributions to periodicals, contributions to books, translations of Thomas' books, and recordings by Thomas and of his works. Not as complete as Maud's work (entry 1344) although better organized and, therefore, easier to use, Rolph's listings give more fully descriptive information. Available in a reprinted edition (Westport, CT: Greenwood, 1974). Also for a bibliography of works by and about Thomas, see *NCBEL*, IV, pp. 220-30.

Dictionaries, Encyclopedias, and Handbooks
1346.   Tindall, William York. **A Reader's Guide to Dylan Thomas**. New York: Farrar, Strauss & Giroux, 1962. 306p. LC 62-11525.

Tindall briefly explicates works in the *Collected Poems, 1934-1952* (London: J. M. Dent, 1952) and surveys Thomas' critical reception and specific aspects (political, religious, and Welsh themes, among others) of his works. More in the way of original critical readings of Thomas' life and works than Tindall's companion, John Ackerman's *A Dylan Thomas Companion* (Basingstoke: Macmillan, 1991) contains chapters on Thomas' life, poetry, prose, film scripts, broadcasts, last stories, letters, and *Under Milk Wood*, with a selective bibliography of editions, reference sources, and critical studies of Thomas (pp. 297-300).

Indexes and Concordances

1347.   Lane, Gary. **A Concordance to the Poems of Dylan Thomas**. Metuchen, NJ: Scarecrow Press, 1976. 697p. (Scarecrow Concordances, no. 5). LC 76-18078. ISBN 0-8108-0971-0.

Using *Dylan Thomas: The Poems* (London: J. M. Dent, 1971) as the base text, Lane's concordance supersedes Robert Coleman Williams' *A Concordance to the Collected Poems of Dylan Thomas* (Lincoln, NE: University of Nebraska Press, 1967), which supplied page and line references to the 1952 London edition and the 1953 American edition of the *Collected Poems of Dylan Thomas*. Also available are Jillian M. Farringdon and Michael G. Farringdon's microfiche *A Concordance and Word-Lists to the Poems of Dylan Thomas* (Oxford: Oxford Microform Publications; Swansea: Ariel House Publications, 1980), based on the Daniel Jones' edition of *Dylan Thomas: The Poems* (London: Dent, 1978); and Michael G. Farringdon's microfiche *A Concordance and Word-Lists to Dylan Thomas's Under Milk Wood* (Swansea: Ariel House, 1982).

Frederick William Thomas, 1806-1866

Bibliographies

For works by Thomas, see *Bibliography of American Literature*, vol. 8, pp. 215-19. Contributions by Thomas and criticism and reviews of Thomas' works in selected periodicals are identified in Wells' *The Literary Index to American Magazines, 1815-1865*, p. 155. Thomas' manuscripts are listed in Robbins' *American Literary Manuscripts*, p. 317. See *Bibliography of American Fiction Through 1865*, p. 251, for a checklist of works by and about Thomas.

Daniel Pierce Thompson, 1795-1868

Bibliographies

For works by Thompson, see *Bibliography of American Literature*, vol. 8, pp. 220-25. Thompson's manuscripts are listed in Robbins' *American Literary Manuscripts*, p. 317. See *Bibliography of American Fiction Through 1865*, pp. 252-53, for a checklist of works by and about Thompson.

Francis Thompson, 1859-1907

Bibliographies

1348.   Connolly, Terence L. **An Account of Books and Manuscripts of Francis Thompson**. Chestnut Hill, MA: Boston College, 1937. 79p. LC 37-33887.

Contains 50 entries (with subentries and appendix) detailing contents of Boston College's Seymour Adelman Collection, including Thompson's literary manuscripts and correspondence, manuscripts of Coventry Patmore, Ernest Dowson, and others on matters related (and unrelated) to Thompson, and editions and translations of Thompson's and others' works. Does not give full bibliographic descriptions. Unindexed. Also for a bibliography of works by and about Thompson, see *NCBEL*, III, pp. 597-601. See the review of research by Lionel Stevenson in Faverty's *The Victorian Poets*, pp. 387-91.

(James) Maurice Thompson, 1844-1901

Bibliographies

Dorothy R. Russo and Thelma Lois Sullivan's *Bibliographical Studies of Seven Authors of Crawfordsville, Indiana* (entry 1008), pp. [173]-283, offers chronologically arranged, full bibliographic descriptions of first editions of separate publications, contributions to books, contributions to periodicals, and ephemera by Thompson. Also for works by Thompson, see *Bibliography of American Literature*, vol. 8, pp. 226-42. Thompson's contributions to selected periodicals and reviews of Thompson's works are identified in Wells' *The Literary Index to American Magazines, 1850-1900*, pp. 380-81. Thompson's manuscripts are listed in Robbins' *American*

Literary Manuscripts, p. 318. See *Bibliography of American Fiction, 1866-1918*, pp. 338-39, for James Nagel's checklist of works by and about Thompson.

William Tappan Thompson, 1812-1882

Bibliographies

For works by Thompson, see *Bibliography of American Literature*, vol. 8, pp. 243-47. Thompson's manuscripts are listed in Robbins' *American Literary Manuscripts*, p. 318. See *Bibliography of American Fiction Through 1865*, pp. 253-54, for a checklist of works by and about Thompson. Herbert Shippey surveys works by and about Thompson in Bain and Flora's *Fifty Southern Writers Before 1900*, pp. 440-51.

James Thomson, 1700-1748

Bibliographies

1349.   Campbell, Hilbert H. **James Thomson (1700-1748): An Annotated Bibliography of Selected Editions and the Important Criticism**. New York: Garland, 1976. 157p. (Garland Reference Library of the Humanities, vol. 33). LC 75-24092. ISBN 0-8240-9979-6.

Campbell briefly describes the publication histories of 34 contemporary and modern editions of Thomson's works and arranges within sections (for forms and periods from the eighteenth century to the twentieth) annotated entries for 571 primary and secondary bibliographies, reviews, bibliographic and textual studies, critical and biographical studies, studies of individual works, studies of reputation and influence, general books and articles, dissertations, and theses. Annotations are critical and evaluative. Campbell clearly identifies significant and important studies. In addition, Campbell briefly notes locations of Thomson's manuscripts. An index of critics and names cited in annotations (Aeschylus, Shakespeare, and Wordsworth, among others) provides good access. Also for a bibliography of works by and about Thomson, see *NCBEL*, II, pp. 527-31, by John Fuller.

Journals

"Recent Articles" in *The Scriblerian and the Kit Cats* (entry 1084) also regularly includes a selection of reviews of studies on Thomson.

James Thomson (B. V.), 1834-1882

Bibliographies

For a bibliography of works by and about Thomson, see *NCBEL*, III, pp. 579-81. See the review of research by Lionel Stevenson in Faverty's *The Victorian Poets*, pp. 364-67.

Mortimer Neal Thomson, 1831-1875

Bibliographies

For works by Thomson, see *Bibliography of American Literature*, vol. 8, pp. 248-52. Contributions by Thomson and criticism and reviews of Thomson's works in selected periodicals are identified in Wells' *The Literary Index to American Magazines, 1815-1865*, pp. 155-56. Thomson's manuscripts are listed in Robbins' *American Literary Manuscripts*, p. 318. See *Bibliography of American Fiction Through 1865*, p. 255, for a checklist of works by and about Thomson.

Henry David Thoreau, 1817-1862

Bibliographies

1350.   Borst, Raymond R. **Henry David Thoreau: A Descriptive Bibliography**. Pittsburgh, PA: University of Pittsburgh Press, 1982. 232p. (Pittsburgh Series in Bibliography). LC 81-50638. ISBN 0-8229-3445-0.

The standard bibliography of Thoreau's primary materials, this describes all printings in English through 1880 (and selectively thereafter through 1980) of Thoreau's separate publications (books, pamphlets, broadsides, and the like) and selected reprintings, collected works, contributions to books and pamphlets, and contributions to journals and newspapers. Entries provide full bibliographic details, including title-page transcriptions, illustrations of title and copyright pages, collations, and notes on typography, paper, and other bibliographic points, with copy locations. Appendixes contain supplementary bibliographic notes and list selected works about Thoreau. A comprehensive index references primary titles, periodical titles, names, and publishers. Borst also describes Thoreau's primary materials in *The Henry David Thoreau Collection* in part 2 of Sidney Ives' *The Parkman Dexter Howe Library* (Gainesville, FL: University of Florida, 1984). Additionally, for works by Thoreau, see *Bibliography of American Literature*, vol. 8, pp. 253-85; and *First Printings of American Authors*, vol. 3, pp. 309-16. Also of bibliographic interest are Walter Harding's *Thoreau's Library* (Charlottesville, VA: University of Virginia Press, 1957), which lists books from Thoreau's library, with locations of copies; and Robert Sattelmeyer's *Thoreau's Reading: A Study in Intellectual History with a Bibliographical Catalogue* (Princeton, NJ: Princeton University Press, 1988).

1351.   Borst, Raymond R. **Henry David Thoreau: A Reference Guide, 1835-1899.** Boston: G. K. Hall, 1987. 147p. (A Reference Guide to Literature). LC 87-7420. ISBN 0-8161-8822-x.

Borst chronologically arranges annotated entries for 737 books, book reviews, journal and newspaper articles, and miscellaneous publications (lecture notes, announcements, and the like) about Thoreau that appeared from 1835 through 1899. A significant portion of the material is biographical in nature (such as references to Thoreau's activities at Concord Academy and other early notices). Annotations are generally descriptive, although Borst critically evaluates works that influenced Thoreau's later reputation. Subject indexing is limited, with headings for major literary figures and institutions (Emerson and the "Concord School of Philosophy," for examples). Borst's compilation supersedes Francis A. Allen's *A Bibliography of Henry David Thoreau* (Boston: Houghton Mifflin, 1908). Borst's coverage is supplemented by Kenneth Walter Cameron's *Toward a Thoreau Tertiary Bibliography (1833-1899)* (Hartford, CT: Transcendental Books, 1988), which offers addenda and a supplemental index to Borst's listings; and Scharnhorst's *Henry David Thoreau: An Annotated Bibliography of Comment and Criticism Before 1900* (entry 1354).

1352.   Boswell, Jeanetta, and Sarah Crouch. **Henry David Thoreau and the Critics: A Checklist of Criticism, 1900-1978.** Metuchen, NJ: Scarecrow Press, 1981. 204p. (The Scarecrow Author Bibliographies, no. 56). LC 81-929. ISBN 0-8108-1416-1.

Boswell and Crouch alphabetically arrange (by author) largely unannotated entries for 2,150 English-language works (for the most part) about Thoreau appearing from 1900 through 1978. The brief subject index is inadequate. This supersedes Walter Harding and Cameron Advena's *A Bibliography of the Thoreau Society Bulletin Bibliographies* (Troy, NY: Whitston, 1971) but is far from comprehensive and complete. Coverage complements that provided for nineteenth-century comments and criticisms in the guides of Borst (entry 1351) and Scharnhorst (entry 1354). Research on Thoreau is reviewed by Lewis Leary in Woodress' *Eight American Authors*, pp. 129-72; and Michael Meyer in Myerson's *The Transcendentalists*, pp. 260-85. *ALS* annually features a review essay on Thoreau scholarship.

1353.   Howarth, William L. **The Literary Manuscripts of Henry David Thoreau.** Columbus, OH: The Ohio State University Press, 1974. 408p. LC 73-8476. ISBN 0-8142-0179-2.

Supplementing Borst's definitive listing of Thoreau's published works, Howarth offers descriptions of his manuscripts and a comprehensive census of their locations. Coverage includes Thoreau's student writings, poems and translations, lectures and essays, individual major writings, journals dating from 1837 through 1861, notes and notebooks, and other writings, in addition to identifying unlocated manuscripts. Of its several indexes, the one for private and institutional repositories is most valuable. Thoreau's manuscripts are listed in Robbins' *American Literary Manuscripts*, pp. 318-19.

1354.   Scharnhorst, Gary. **Henry David Thoreau: An Annotated Bibliography of Comment and Criticism Before 1900**. New York: Garland, 1992. 386p. (Garland Reference Library of the Humanities, vol. 1218). LC 92-15648. ISBN 0-8240-5349-4.

Like Borst's *Henry David Thoreau: A Reference Guide* (entry 1351), Scharnhorst's guide is valuable for tracking Thoreau's early reception. Some 2,087 chronologically arranged, annotated entries record comments, criticisms, and allusions to Thoreau and reviews of his works published from 1840 through 1900. Scharnhorst offers particularly useful coverage of stories and other features in contemporary local newspapers. Annotations cite reprintings in standard collections. Comprehensive index references critics, Thoreau's works, and a wide range of subjects. Also useful are Kenneth Walter Cameron's *Toward a Thoreau Tertiary Bibliography (1833-1899)* (Hartford, CT: Transcendental Books, 1988); and Cameron's *Thoreau Secondary Bibliography: Supplement Two (1836-1940)* (Hartford, CT: Transcendental Books, 1997), which identifies 1,513 additional items to supplement both Borst and Scharnhorst.

Dictionaries, Encyclopedias, and Handbooks

1355.   Borst, Raymond R. **The Thoreau Log: A Documentary Life of Henry David Thoreau, 1817-1862**. New York: G. K. Hall, 1992. 654p. (American Authors Log Series). LC 91-34885. ISBN 0-8161-8985-4.

A model chronology. Massive and comprehensive day-by-day (and frequently hour-by-hour) record of "factual information" (p. xviii) about Thoreau's life, "based primarily on his own two-million-word *Journal* (p. xvii). Integrates personal events with detailed information relevant to the composition, revision, and publication of Thoreau's writings: "what he was reading, where he walked, who he met and talked to, what he observed and found significant in the natural world around him, where he lectured and surveyed, etc." Entries quote extensively from Thoreau's writings and give specific citations. Includes biographical directory of about 50 frequently mentioned family members, acquaintances, and contemporaries. Includes extensive bibliography of published and unpublished primary sources (pp. 613-22). Comprehensive index of works, persons, places, and things.

1356.   Harding, Walter, and Michael Meyer. **The New Thoreau Handbook**. New York: New York University Press, 1980. 238p. LC 79-53078. ISBN 0-8147-3401-4.

A revision of Harding's *A Thoreau Handbook* (New York: New York University Press, 1959), chapters survey studies of Thoreau's biography; summarize his works and identify themes and topics; and evaluate studies of sources, ideas, techniques, and reputation. A more specialized handbook, Robert F. Stowell's *A Thoreau Gazeteer* (Princeton, NJ: Princeton University Press, 1970), documents Thoreau's travels from 1831 through 1861 (excluding his Minnesota journey), with facsimiles of contemporary illustrations and maps. The volume serves as a geographical supplement to the standard edition of *The Writings of Henry D. Thoreau* (Princeton, NJ: Princeton University Press, 1971-). More a collection of new readings and original critical studies than a reference handbook, Joel Myerson's *The Cambridge Companion to Henry David Thoreau* (Cambridge: Cambridge University Press, 1995) contains 13 essays by contributing experts on Thoreau's individual works and selected topics of perennial interest (such as Thoreau, Emerson, and

Concord) and more novel ones (such as Thoreau and his audience and Thoreau and the natural environment).

Indexes and Concordances

1357.   Karabatsos, James. **A Word-Index to A Week on the Concord and Merrimack Rivers**. Hartford, CT: Transcendental Books, 1971. 99 leaves. LC 79-31438.

"Based on the standard *Walden* edition" (Introduction). Appends indexes classifying keywords for proper names, poetic allusions, poetry, ethics, philosophy, religion, topography, mythology, and history.

1358.   Ogden, Marlene A., and Clifton Keller. **Walden: A Concordance**. New York: Garland, 1985. 261p. (Garland Reference Library of the Humanities, vol. 557). LC 84-48402. ISBN 0-8240-8786-0.

Ogden and Keller's concordance is based on the standard text of *Walden* in vol. 1 of *The Writings of Henry D. Thoreau* (Princeton, NJ: Princeton University Press, 1971). Other indexes of *Walden* include Joseph Jones' *Index to Walden with Notes, Map, and Vocabulary Lists* (Austin, TX: Hemphill, 1955); and Stephen J. Sherwin and Richard C. Reynolds' *A Word Index to Walden with Textual Notes*, 2d ed., corrected (Hartford, CT: Emerson Society, 1969), which is based on Brooks Atkinson's Modern Library edition of *Walden and Other Writings of Henry David Thoreau* (New York: Random House, 1950).

1359.   Van Anglen, Kevin P. **Simplify, Simplify and Other Quotations from Henry David Thoreau**. New York: Columbia University Press, 1996. 196p. LC 95-47962. ISBN 0-231-10388-3.

Arranges extended quotations from Thoreau's works, with page citations, under about 300 topics, including "Imagination," "Independence," "The Mind," "Nature versus Civilization," and others. Based on *The Writings of Henry David Thoreau* (Boston: Houghton Mifflin, 1906), with silent corrections from *The Writings of Henry D. Thoreau* (Princeton: Princeton University Press, 1971-). Introduction identifies Thoreau as "one of the most frequently quoted American authors" (p. [xv]). Includes selected bibliography of editions, reference works, and critical sources (pp. [xxiii]-xxvi). Unindexed.

Journals

1360.   **Concord Saunterer**. Concord, MA: Thoreau Lyceum, original series, 1966-1988; new series, 1993-. Annual. ISSN 1068-5359.

Sponsored by the Thoreau Society, issues of the *Concord Saunterer* publish six to 10 substantial "historical, textual, bibliographical, and interpretive [articles about] Thoreau and his associates, Concord, and Transcendentalism" (masthead). In addition to typical articles on *Walden* and such topics as nature, domestic economy, and nonviolence, the journal has published articles on Emerson, John Muir, and Thomas Wentworth Higginson, among others. To date the journal has featured no reviews or bibliographic articles. *Concord Saunterer* is indexed in *AHI* and *MLA*.

1361.   **The Thoreau Quarterly: A Journal of Literary and Philosophic Studies**. Minneapolis, MN: University of Minnesota, 1969-85. 4/yr. ISSN 0730-868x.

Offering a wider fare than *The Thoreau Society Bulletin* (entry 1362), this journal published scholarly articles and notes on the works, life, and times of Thoreau as well as those of his contemporaries (such as Emerson and Hawthorne), the Transcendentalist movement, and the American literary renaissance. The journal also offered reviews of new publications. *The Thoreau Quarterly* was indexed in *AHI*, *MHRA*, and *MLA*.

1362.   **The Thoreau Society Bulletin**. Concord, MA: The Thoreau Society, 1941- . 4/yr. ISSN 0040-6406.

The Thoreau Society Bulletin, sponsored by the Thoreau Society, features a few brief articles on Thoreau's life and works, reviews of new publications, and notices of research and other projects in progress. A regular bibliographic feature, "Additions to the Thoreau Bibliography," presently compiled by Thomas S. Harris, lists international criticism in books, scholarly and popular articles, and newspapers. Jean C. Advena's *A Bibliography of the Thoreau Society Bulletin Bibliographies, 1941-1969* (Troy, NY: Whitston, 1971) has cumulated them. Occasional bibliographic contributions include Kent P. Ljungquist's "Additions to Nineteenth-Century Comment on Thoreau," no. 211 (Spring-Summer 1995): 12-13, supplementing Scharnhorst's *Henry David Thoreau: An Annotated Bibliography of Comment and Criticism Before 1900* (entry 1354). In addition, the journal includes announcements of programs at the Thoreau Lyceum and other membership information. "Notes and Queries" contains Thoreauiana. *The Thoreau Society Bulletin* is indexed in *AES, AHI, MHRA,* and *MLA.*

Patterson's *Author Newsletters and Journals,* pp. 321-23, describes other previously published journals for Thoreau.

T(homas) B(angs) Thorpe, 1815-1878
Bibliographies

For works by Thorpe, see *Bibliography of American Literature,* vol. 8, pp. 286-92. Contributions by Thorpe and criticism and reviews of Thorpe's works in selected periodicals are identified in Wells' *The Literary Index to American Magazines, 1815-1865,* p. 156; and *The Literary Index to American Magazines, 1850-1900,* p. 383. Thorpe's manuscripts are listed in Robbins' *American Literary Manuscripts,* p. 319. See *Bibliography of American Fiction Through 1865,* pp. 256-57, for a checklist of works by and about Thorpe. Eugene Current-Garcia surveys works by and about Thorpe in Bain and Flora's *Fifty Southern Writers Before 1900,* pp. 452-63.

James (Grover) Thurber, 1894-1961
Bibliographies

1363. Bowden, Edwin T. **James Thurber: A Bibliography**. Columbus, OH: The Ohio State University Press, 1968. 353p. LC 68-20365.

The definitive, descriptive bibliography of Thurber's primary works, giving detailed entries in listings for his separate works, contributions to journals (both his writings and 626 drawings), contributions to books, and translations of Thurber's works into more than 20 languages. Presents extensive information on variants and significant textual collations. Indexes for titles of writings and captions of drawings. Also for works by Thurber, see *First Printings of American Authors,* vol. 1, pp. 379-83. Thurber's manuscripts are listed in Robbins' *American Literary Manuscripts,* p. 319.

1364. Toombs, Sarah Eleanora. **James Thurber: An Annotated Bibliography of Criticism**. New York: Garland, 1987. 258p. (Garland Reference Library of the Humanities, vol. 634). LC 86-31866. ISBN 0-8240-8643-0.

Toombs arranges selectively annotated entries for 1,150 English-language works about Thurber in separate listings for biographical materials, general criticisms, studies of single collections, and reviews of plays and productions. Coverage includes reviews of Thurber's works as well as newspaper articles about Thurber. Selected significant works receive extensive assessments. Appendixes list non-English-language studies and theses and dissertations. A thorough index references all of Thurber's writings and drawings. Also see *Bibliography of American Fiction, 1919-1988,* pp. 500-503, for Toombs' checklist of works by and about Thurber.

Wallace Thurman, 1902-1934
Bibliographies

For works by Thurman, see *First Printings of American Authors*, vol. 4, p. 373. Thurman's manuscripts are listed in Robbins' *American Literary Manuscripts*, p. 319. For works by and about Thurman, see Perry's *The Harlem Renaissance*, pp. 135-38; and Dorothy Jean Palmer McIver's checklist in *Bibliography of American Fiction, 1919-1988*, pp. 503-504.

Henry Timrod, 1828-1867
Bibliographies

For works by Timrod, see *Bibliography of American Literature*, vol. 8, pp. 293-99; and *First Printings of American Authors*, vol. 1, p. 385-86. Contributions by Timrod and criticism and reviews of Timrod's works in selected periodicals are identified in Wells' *The Literary Index to American Magazines, 1815-1865*, p. 157; and *The Literary Index to American Magazines, 1850-1900*, p. 384. Timrod's manuscripts are listed in Robbins' *American Literary Manuscripts*, p. 320. See Boswell's *Spokesmen for the Minority* (entry 809) for criticisms of Timrod. Jack De Bellis surveys works by and about Timrod in Bain and Flora's *Fifty Southern Writers Before 1900*, pp. 464-72.

J(ohn) R(onald) R(euel) Tolkien, 1892-1973
Bibliographies

1365.   Hammond, Wayne G., and Douglas A. Anderson. **J. R. R. Tolkien: A Descriptive Bibliography**. Winchester: St. Paul's, 1993. 434p. (Winchester Bibliographies of 20th Century Writers). LC 92-35912. ISBN 1-873040-11-3.

The standard bibliography of Tolkien's works. Provides superior bibliographic information in chronologically arranged entries within separate, classified sections covering Tolkien's books and separate publications; edited and translated books and contributions to books; contributions to periodicals; published letters and extracts; art (published drawing, photographs, posters, etc.); miscellaneous works, including audio recordings, published interviews, manuscripts excerpted in booksellers' catalogs, and the like; and translations of Tolkien's works into about two dozen languages. The first two sections focus on British and American trade editions, with entries giving quasi-facsimile transcriptions of title pages (illustrations of selected pages), paginations, contents, collations, binding and dust-jacket descriptions, data on paper and typography, and extensive publication histories. Also includes brief Tolkien chronology and a section of "Selected References" (pp. 411-12). Comprehensive index references proper names (persons, places, publishers, organizations) and titles (primary, translated, series, etc.). This is a model of modern bibliography. Also for a bibliography of works by and about Tolkien, see *NCBEL*, IV, pp. 748-49.

1366.   Johnson, Judith A. **J. R. R. Tolkien: Six Decades of Criticism**. Westport, CT: Greenwood Press, 1986. 266p. (Bibliographies and Indexes in World Literature, no. 6). LC 85-27248. ISBN 0-313-25005-7.

The arrangement of this volume is unique and quite effective. Johnson chronologically arranges (within decades) annotated entries in parallel listings for 93 works by Tolkien (including his scholarly and fictional books, edited works, and articles) and 1,649 popular and scholarly works about Tolkien. Coverage extends from 1922 through 1984. Annotations are descriptive. Emphasis is on Tolkien's creative works rather than his pioneering efforts in Old and Middle English scholarship. Johnson's guide updates Richard C. West's *Tolkien Criticism: An Annotated Checklist*, revised ed. (Kent, OH: Kent State University Press, 1981).

Dictionaries, Encyclopedias, and Handbooks

1367. Day, David. **Tolkien: The Illustrated Encyclopedia**. New York: Macmillan, 1991. 279p. LC 91-12921. ISBN 0-02-533431-X.

A very usable, excellently illustrated "reader's guide to" the "Middle-earth and the Undying Lands . . . the world of J. R. R. Tolkien" (p. 6), although with some limitations for scholarly study. Arranged in five major sections (history, geography, sociology, natural history, and biography). History offers time lines and explanations for the "eight major epochs, from the creation of the Third Age of the Sun" (p. 13). The geographical gazetteer is an A to Z listing of "cities, countries, mountain ranges, forests, rivers, lakes and seas" (p. 45), with maps. "All the racial, national, and tribal categories of men, elves, dwarves, hobbits, ents, maiar, and valar" (p. 125) are explained in the sociology section, which includes genealogical charts and illustrations of representative individuals. Likewise, the natural history section is an illustrated dictionary of Middle-earth and Undying Lands' flora ("olvar") and fauna ("kelvar"), also covering "supernatural spirits, spectres, ghosts, demons, and monsters" (p. 189). Finally, the biographical section amounts to an "illustrated Who's Who" in Tolkien, giving "lineage, physical appearance, personal attributes, dates of birth and death, and major events of each life" (p. 235). Covers both human and nonhuman characters that may have been treated elsewhere, including Smaug the Golden who is also covered in the natural history section under "Dragons." Also includes a chronology of Tolkien's life and works. General index of main entries. Day does not provide plot summaries of particular works, and entries lack specific references, although an "Index of Principal Sources" relates Day's individual entries to parts, chapters, and sections in unspecified editions of Tolkien's texts.

1368. Duriez, Colin. **The J. R. R. Tolkien Handbook: A Comprehensive Guide to His Life, Writings, and World of Middle-earth**. Grand Rapids, MI: Baker Book House, 1992. 316p. LC 92-13612. ISBN 0-8010-3014-5.

Duriez's work is perhaps the most useful of several selective dictionaries of Tolkien's works, proper names of real and fictional persons, places, and things, and topics. Entries for Tolkien's novels give plot summaries, with many cross-references. Those for such topics as "Death," "The Hero," and "Evil" identify critical works on the subject. Includes checklists of works by and about Tolkien (pp. 294-302) and topical index to the entries. Among other useful, selective companions and dictionaries are Karen Wynn Fonstad's *The Atlas of the Middle-Earth* (Boston: Houghton Mifflin, 1981), which identifies, chronicles, and maps a comprehensive selection of features, events, and elements of Tolkien's world, with cross-references Tolkien's works; and Robert Foster's *The Complete Guide to the Middle-Earth: From The Hobbit to The Silmarillion* (New York: Ballantine Books, 1978), an enlarged revision of *A Guide to Middle-Earth* (New York: Ballantine, 1971), providing brief explanations and identifications for characters and other features in Tolkien's works, with cross-references to the text. These guides are generally more thorough, scholarly, and valuable than J. E. A. Tyler's *The New Tolkien Companion* (New York: St. Martin's, 1979); and Barbara Strachey's *Journeys of Frodo: An Atlas of J. R. R. Tolkien's The Lord of the Rings* (New York: Ballantine, 1981).

Indexes and Concordances

1369. Blackwelder, Richard E. **A Tolkien Thesaurus**. New York: Garland, 1990. 277p. (Garland Reference Library of the Humanities, vol. 1326). LC 90-31755. ISBN 0-8240-5296-X.

Concordance to *Lord of the Ring* trilogy (*The Fellowship of the Ring*, *The Two Towers*, and *The Return of the King*), based on the "Houghton Mifflin second edition (hardbound) [1967] and the Ballantine Books revised editions (paperback) [1965]" (Introduction), with a reference table for other editions. Among the legion dictionaries of Tolkien's Middle-earth vocabulary are Ruth S. Noel's *The Languages of Tolkien's Middle-Earth* (Boston: Houghton Mifflin, 1980); and Paul Nolan Hyde's *A*

Working Concordance: Being a Compilation of Names, Places, Things and Language Elements Together with Volume and Page Number of Every Occurrence in the Following Works of J. R. R. Tolkien (Simi Valley, CA: s. n., 1987); and Hyde's *A Working Reverse Dictionary (with Meanings): Being an Alphabetical Listing of Reverse-Spelled Morphological Elements in the Languages of Middle-Earth Together* (Simi Valley, CA: s. n., 1989).

Journals

1370. **Mallorn: The Journal of the Tolkien Society.** High Wycombe, Bucks: Tolkien Society, 1970- . 1-2/yr. ISSN 0308-6674.

Sponsored by the Tolkien Society, *Mallorn* features articles on the life and works of Tolkien and occasionally on other writers and works of fantasy. Studies give close readings of Tolkien's works; interpretations of themes, symbols, sources (including the likes of Shakespeare and Beethoven), and allusions; and discussions of biographical information. "Celtic Influences on the History of the First Age" and "An Ethnically Cleansed Faery? Tolkien and the Matter of Britain" are recent representative features. Other articles have focused on Tolkien as a translator, linguist, lexicographer, and editor. Occasional bibliographic contributions include Maria Kamenkovich's "The Secret War and the End of the First Age: Tolkien in the (Former) U.S.S.R.," 29 (August 1992): 33-38, on Russian-language translations of Tolkien. In addition, the journal includes reviews of new publications and reports on the activities of the society. *Mallorn* is indexed in *MLA*.

1371. **Mythlore: A Journal of J. R. R. Tolkien, C. S. Lewis, Charles Williams, General Fantasy and Mythic Studies.** Altadena, CA: Mythopoeic Society, 1969- . 4/yr. ISSN 0146-9339.

Sponsored by the Mythopoeic Society, *Mythlore* features critical and explicative studies of themes, characters, topography, images, ecology, and other elements in the works of these major fantasy writers as well as in fantasy literature in general. Studies have focused on Apuleius, the Arthurian legend, *Sir Gawain and the Green Knight*, Dante, George Herbert, H. G. Wells, Owen Barfield, J. M. Barrie, Frances Hodgson Burnett, T. H. White, Anne Sexton, and Ursula K. Le Guin. "The Witch Woman: A Recurring Motif in Recent Fantasy Writing for Young Readers," "Dance as Metaphor and Myth in Lewis, Tolkien, and Williams," and "Husbands and Gods as Shadowbrutes: 'Beauty and the Beast' from Apuleius to C. S. Lewis" are typical. A regular feature, "Quenti Lambardillion: A Column of Middle-Earth Linguistics," focuses on etymology, language, runic inscriptions, and the like that appear in Tolkien's works. In addition, the journal publishes "The Inklings Bibliography," presently compiled by Joe R. Christopher and Wayne G. Hammond, listing criticisms of Tolkien, Lewis, and Williams. *Mythlore* is indexed in *MHRA* and *MLA*.

Patterson's *Author Newsletters and Journals*, pp. 323-26, and Johnson's bibliography (entry 1366), pp. 337-39, describe other previously published and popular journals on Tolkien.

1372. **Vinyar Tengwar.** Crofton, MD: C. F. Hostetter, 1988- . 6/yr. ISSN 1054-7606.

" 'Si man i$2fyulmar n(g)win enquatuva': A Newly-Discovered Tengwar Inscription" is rather typical of the largely linguistic and lexical studies of Tolkien's creative and scholarly works. A significant number of contributions focus on real and invented languages, particularly the names of characters in Tolkien. A regular feature, "Transitions in Translations," discusses translation of Tolkien's works into other languages and Tolkien's views on translation. *Vinyar Tengwar* is indexed in *MLA*.

Jean Toomer, 1894-1967
Bibliographies

For works by and about Toomer, see Perry's *The Harlem Renaissance*, pp. 138-58; and Frederik L. Rusch's checklist in *Bibliography of American Fiction, 1919-1988*, pp. 504-506. Toomer's manuscripts are listed in Robbins' *American Literary Manuscripts*, p. 321. See reviews of research on Toomer by Ruth Miller and Peter J. Katopes in Inge, Duke, and Bryer's *Black American Writers*, vol. I, pp. 161-86; and by John M. Reilly in Flora and Bain's *Fifty Southern Writers After 1900*, pp. 479-90.

Bradford Torrey, 1843-1912
Bibliographies

For works by Torrey, see *First Printings of American Authors*, vol. 3, pp. 317-18. Torrey's contributions to selected periodicals and reviews of Torrey's works are identified in Wells' *The Literary Index to American Magazines, 1850-1900*, p. 387. Torrey's manuscripts are listed in Robbins' *American Literary Manuscripts*, p. 321.

Albion W(inegar) Tourgee, 1838-1905
Bibliographies

For works by Tourgee, see *Bibliography of American Literature*, vol. 8, pp. 300-12; and *First Printings of American Authors*, vol. 1, pp. 387-90. Tourgee's contributions to selected periodicals and reviews of Tourgee's works are identified in Wells' *The Literary Index to American Magazines, 1850-1900*, pp. 387-88. Tourgee's manuscripts are listed in Robbins' *American Literary Manuscripts*, p. 322. Also available is Dean H. Keller's *An Index to the Albion W. Tourgee Papers in the Chautauqua County Historical Society, Westfield, N.Y.* (Kent, OH: Kent State University, 1964). See *Bibliography of American Fiction, 1866-1918*, pp. 339-41, for Troy L. Headrick's checklist of works by and about Tourgee.

Cyril Tourneur, 1575?-1626
Bibliographies

For a bibliography of works by and about Tourneur, see *NCBEL*, I, pp. 1694-97. Tourneur's manuscripts are described in *Index of English Literary Manuscripts*, I, pt. 2:547-48. See Tucker's *A Bibliography of Writings by and About John Ford and Cyril Tourneur* (entry 507).

Indexes and Concordances

See Stagg's *The Figurative Language of the Tragedies of Shakespeare's Chief 17th-Century Contemporaries* (entry 229).

Thomas Traherne, 1637-1674
Bibliographies

For bibliographies of works by and about Traherne, see *NCBEL*, I, pp. 1235-38; and George Robert Guffey's *Elizabethan Bibliographies Supplements*, no. 11. See McCarron and Shenk's *Lesser Metaphysical Poets*, pp. [30]-35, for works about Traherne through 1980. Traherne's manuscripts are described in *Index of English Literary Manuscripts*, II, pt. 2:477-506.

Indexes and Concordances

1373.   Guffey, George Robert. **A Concordance to the Poetry of Thomas Traherne**. Berkeley, CA: University of California Press, 1974. 521p. LC 73-76112. ISBN 0-520-02449-4.

Based on H. M. Margoliouth's edition, *Centuries, Poems, and Thanksgivings* (Oxford: Clarendon Press, 1958). Appends table of words in order of frequency.

B. Traven, 1882?-1969

Bibliographies

For works by Traven, see *First Printings of American Authors*, vol. 1, pp. 391-93. Traven's manuscripts are listed in Robbins' *American Literary Manuscripts*, p. 323.

John Trevisa, 1340?-1402

Bibliographies

Anthony S. G. Edwards reviews research on Trevisa in Edwards' *Middle English Prose*, pp. 133-46.

Lionel Trilling, 1905-1975

Bibliographies

1374.   Leitch, Thomas M. **Lionel Trilling: An Annotated Bibliography**. New York: Garland, 1992. 626p. (Garland Reference Library of the Humanities, vol. 1303; Garland Bibliographies of Modern Critics and Critical Schools, vol. 19). LC 92-23192. ISBN 0-8240-7128-X.

Covers works by and about Trilling. First part provides 419 annotated entries for Trilling's writings in sections for books and essay collections; prefaces and edited books; essays, stories, poems, and review articles; reviews; and symposia, interviews, and miscellanea. Entries for primary works identify subsequent printings and translated editions and emphasize contents rather than bibliographic details. Second part includes 661 annotated entries for criticism of Trilling in sections for books, essay collections, and special journal issues; review articles; reviews of books by Trilling; reviews of Trilling's writings; dissertations; miscellaneous comments (letters to editor, etc.); and (in a separate third part) background studies published as books, essays, dissertations, and other works. Introduction surveys Trilling's career and offers a critical assessment. Indexes of authors (including the likes of John Donne and James Joyce as well as Trilling's critics) and titles give reasonable access. Also for works by Trilling, see *First Printings of American Authors*, vol. 5, pp. 323-28. Trilling's manuscripts are listed in Robbins' *American Literary Manuscripts*, p. 323.

Anthony Trollope, 1815-1882

Bibliographies

1375.   Olmsted, John Charles, and Jeffrey Egan Welch. **The Reputation of Trollope: An Annotated Bibliography, 1925-1975**. New York: Garland, 1978. 212p. (Garland Reference Library of the Humanities, vol. 88). LC 76-52683. ISBN 0-8240-9885-4.

Olmsted and Welch offer thoroughly descriptive annotations for 652 mostly English-language critical works about Trollope, including books, articles, and dissertations. Annotations usually excerpt from the works themselves. Limited coverage of nineteenth-century criticisms of Trollope in 53 selected American and British periodicals is provided by Anne K. Lyons' *Anthony Trollope: An Annotated Bibliography of Periodical Works by and About Him in the United States and Great Britain to 1900* (Greenwood, FL: Penkevill, 1985). Lyons describes 302 contemporary commentaries and criticisms of Trollope as well as 64 essays by Trollope. Likewise, Trollope's contributions to selected periodicals and reviews of Trollope's works are identified in Wells' *The Literary Index to American Magazines, 1850-1900*, pp. 389-90. Research on Trollope is reviewed by Ruth apRoberts in Ford's *Victorian Fiction*, pp. 143-71; Donald Smalley in Stevenson's *Victorian Fiction*, pp. 188-213; and Bradford A. Booth in Dyson's *The English Novel*, pp. 200-17.

1376.   Sadlier, Michael. **Trollope: A Bibliography**. 1928; reprint London: Dawsons of Pall Mall, 1964. 322p. LC 78-108718.

Superseding Mary Leslie Irwin's *Anthony Trollope: A Bibliography* (New York: H.W. Wilson, 1926), Sadlier gives detailed descriptions for Trollope's books and separately published works, undated private issues, contributions to books, contributions to periodicals, writings published in *St. Pauls Magazine* under Trollope's editorship, and collected editions. Entries for first British and American editions present title-page transcriptions, collations, contents, and binding descriptions, with illustrations. A concluding chapter discusses the business of collecting editions of Trollope. Reprinted editions available (Folkestone: Dawson's, 1964 and 1977). Lance O. Tingay's *The Trollope Collector: A Record of Writings by and About Anthony Trollope* (London: Silverbridge Press, 1985) gives supplemental information for primary materials, with references to Michael Sadlier's standard bibliography of Victorian fiction, *XIX Fiction: A Bibliographical Record Based on His Own Collection* (1951; reprint New York: Cooper Square, 1969). Also for a bibliography of works by and about Trollope, see *NCBEL*, III, pp. 882-89.

Dictionaries, Encyclopedias, and Handbooks

1377. Daniels, Mary L. **Trollope-to-Reader: A Topical Guide to Digressions in the Novels of Anthony Trollope**. Westport, CT: Greenwood Press, 1983. 393p. LC 83-10873. ISBN 0-313-23877-4.

Daniels' helpful, specialized guide topically indexes digressions in Trollope's 45 novels published from 1845 through 1882, intending to help trace the development of his views on various subjects of social and historical interest, such as aging, Americans, famine and famine relief, marriage, writing, and the like. A shorter index cites Trollope's digressions about contemporary and historical figures. Excerpts are referenced to modern editions.

1378. Gerould, Winifred Gregory, and James Thayer Gerould. **A Guide to Trollope**. London: Oxford University Press, 1948. 256p. OCLC 7609001.

A dictionary of persons, places, and things in Trollope that offers useful plot summaries and contents of Trollope's separately published and contributed works. Entries locate characters by work and chapters in first editions. Includes maps of Barsetshire, Dillsborough, and other locations. Also supplies chronological list of Trollope's novels and stories, a bibliography of major works on Trollope, an interesting "Classification of the Novels and Stories" (political, psychological, burlesque, Irish, etc.), and conversion table for chapters in first and selected other editions. Not indexed. Available in reprinted editions (Westport, CT: Greenwood Press, 1970; and London: The Trollope Society by arrangement with Princeton University Press, 1988).

1379. Terry, R. C. **A Trollope Chronology**. London: Macmillan, 1989. 167p. (Macmillan Author Chronologies). LC 88-5133. ISBN 0-333-39914-5.

Terry describes Trollope as "a man who could not keep still" (p. xi), and this chronology attempts to keep up with him, accounting for the daily rituals of Trollope's two careers as postal service administrator and writer as well as his full personal and social life of family and friends. Information is heavily indebted to Michael Sadlier's *Trollope: A Commentary* (London: Constable, 1927) and N. John Hall's two-volume edition of *The Letters of Anthony Trollope* (Stanford, CA: Stanford University Press, 1983), in addition to collections of manuscript notebooks and family papers at Princeton University, the University of Illinois, and the Bodleian Library. Appendixes identify Trollope's numerous lectures and speeches from 1861 through 1879 and Trollope's role in the formation of the Post Office Library and list contemporary reviews of Trollope's novels and *Autobiography*. Indexing is limited to names and places. No subject access is provided.

Journals

See Patterson's *Author Newsletters and Journals*, p. 327, for previously published journals for Trollope.

Frances Trollope, 1780-1863
Bibliographies
1380. Bethke, Frederick John. **Three Victorian Travel Writers: An Annotated Bibliography of Criticism on Mrs. Frances Milton Trollope, Samuel Butler, and Robert Louis Stevenson.** Boston: G. K. Hall, 1977. 203p. (Reference Guides in Literature). LC 76-55023. ISBN 0-8161-7852-6.

Following separate introductions for each writer, Bethke separately lists their primary materials and chronologically arranges entries for secondary works about Mrs. Trollope (covering works published from 1832 through 1972), Butler (from 1863 through 1974), and Stevenson (from 1878 through 1974). Annotations for secondary works are descriptive. Separate indexes for each writer cover primary titles, names, and selected broad topics, such as bibliography and biography. More thorough and comprehensive coverage of criticisms of Butler is provided in Breuer and Parsell's *Samuel Butler* (entry 202). Also for a bibliography of works by and about Mrs. Trollope, see *NCBEL*, III, pp. 769-70.

J(ohn) T(ownsend) Trowbridge, 1827-1916
Bibliographies
For works by Trowbridge, see *Bibliography of American Literature*, vol. 8, pp. 313-44. Trowbridge's contributions to selected periodicals and reviews of Trowbridge's works are identified in Wells' *The Literary Index to American Magazines, 1850-1900*, pp. 390-92. Trowbridge's manuscripts are listed in Robbins' *American Literary Manuscripts*, p. 324. See *Bibliography of American Fiction Through 1865*, pp. 258-60, for a checklist of works by and about Trowbridge.

John Trumbull, 1750-1831
Bibliographies
For works by Trumbull, see *Bibliography of American Literature*, vol. 8, pp. 345-57; and *First Printings of American Authors*, vol. 4, pp. 375-78. Wells' *The Literary Index to American Magazines, 1815-1865*, p. 158, identifies comments on Trumbull in selected periodicals. Trumbull's manuscripts are listed in Robbins' *American Literary Manuscripts*, p. 324.

George Tucker, 1775-1861
Bibliographies
See *Bibliography of American Fiction Through 1865*, pp. 260-61, for a checklist of works by and about Tucker. Contributions by Tucker and criticism and reviews of Tucker's works in selected periodicals are identified in Wells' *The Literary Index to American Magazines, 1815-1865*, p. 158. Tucker's manuscripts are listed in Robbins' *American Literary Manuscripts*, p. 325. Donald R. Noble surveys works by and about Tucker in Bain and Flora's *Fifty Southern Writers Before 1900*, pp. 473-82.

Nathaniel Beverley Tucker (Edward William Sidney), 1784-1851
Bibliographies
For works by Tucker, see *Bibliography of American Literature*, vol. 8, pp. 358-62. Tucker's manuscripts are listed in Robbins' *American Literary Manuscripts*, p. 325. See *Bibliography of American Fiction Through 1865*, pp. 262-63, for a checklist of works by and about Tucker. J. V. Ridgely surveys works by and about Tucker in Bain and Flora's *Fifty Southern Writers Before 1900*, pp. 483-91.

St. George Tucker, 1752-1827
Bibliographies
For works by Tucker, see *First Printings of American Authors*, vol. 4, pp. 379-80. Tucker's manuscripts are listed in Robbins' *American Literary Manuscripts*, p. 325. Carl R. Dolmetsch surveys works by and about Tucker in Bain and Flora's *Fifty Southern Writers Before 1900*, pp. 492-501.

Frederick Goddard Tuckerman, 1821-1873
Bibliographies

Tuckerman's manuscripts are listed in Robbins' *American Literary Manuscripts*, p. 325. Contributions by Tuckerman and criticism and reviews of Tuckerman's works in selected periodicals are identified in Wells' *The Literary Index to American Magazines, 1815-1865*, pp. 159-60. See Boswell's *Spokesmen for the Minority* (entry 809) for works about Tuckerman.

Henry Theodore Tuckerman, 1813-1871
Bibliographies

For works by Tuckerman, see *Bibliography of American Literature*, vol. 8, pp. 363-86. Reviews of Tuckerman's works and Tuckerman's contributions to selected periodicals are identified in Wells' *The Literary Index to American Magazines, 1850-1900*, pp. 392-93. Tuckerman's manuscripts are listed in Robbins' *American Literary Manuscripts*, p. 325.

John R. Tunis, 1889-1975
Bibliographies

See *Bibliography of American Fiction 1919-1988*, pp. 506-507, for Philip B. Eppard's checklist of works by and about Tunis.

Anne Tyler, 1941-
Bibliographies

1381. Croft, Robert William. **Anne Tyler: A Bio-Bibliography**. Westport, CT: Greenwood Press, 1995. 172p. (Bio-Bibliographies in American Literature, no. 5). LC 94-42115. ISBN 0-313-28952-2.

Extensive and full critical biography (with discussions of each of Tyler's works) precedes separate listings of works by and about Tyler. Croft chronologically arranges brief bibliographic information in separate checklists for first editions of Tyler's novels, short stories, nonfiction (with summary contents), poetry, children's books, and book reviews (259 entries). Provides brief information on manuscripts, typescripts, holographs, correspondence, and other materials in Anne Tyler Papers at Duke University. Also includes critically annotated entries for works about Tyler in sections for books (six entries); chapters in books, articles and interviews in journals (80 entries); dissertations and theses; and reviews (unannotated) of Tyler's novels (298 entries subarranged by works). Name, title, and subject index. See the review of research by Anne R. Zahlan in Flora and Bain's *Fifty Southern Writers After 1900*, pp. 491-504.

Royall Tyler, 1757-1826
Bibliographies

For works by Tyler, see *Bibliography of American Literature*, vol. 8, pp. 387-96; and *First Printings of American Authors*, vol. 4, pp. 381-83. Tyler's manuscripts are listed in Robbins' *American Literary Manuscripts*, p. 326. See *Bibliography of American Fiction Through 1865*, pp. 264-66, for a checklist of works by and about Tyler.

William Tyndale, c. 1495-1536
Bibliographies

For a bibliography of works by and about Tyndale, see *NCBEL*, I, pp. 1809-11, 1829-32. Tyndale's manuscripts are described in *Index of English Literary Manuscripts*, I, pt. 2:543-45.

Nicholas Udall, c. 1504-1556

Bibliographies

For a bibliography of works by and about Udall, see *NCBEL*, I, pp. 1414-16. Udall's manuscripts are described in *Index of English Literary Manuscripts*, I, pt. 2:549-51.

John (Hoyer) Updike, 1932-

Bibliographies

1382.　De Bellis, Jack. **John Updike: A Bibliography, 1967-1993.** Westport, CT: Greenwood Press, 1994. 335p. (Bibliographies and Indexes in American Literature, no. 17). LC 93-28538. ISBN 0-3132-8861-5.

Continues and sometimes corrects C. Clarke Taylor's *John Updike: A Bibliography* (Kent, OH: Kent State University Press, 1968), which covered works by and about Updike to 1967. In part 1, De Bellis chronologically lists Updike's works (totaling 1,336 entries) in sections for books; plays; short fiction; poetry; articles and essays; reviews; interviews in printed, broadcasted, and other recorded media; letters and manuscripts, including brief notes on repositories; translations by Updike; and graphics and readings. Entries for primary works give brief imprint data and note contents and reprintings, without substantial bibliographic information on composition or publication history. Part 2 lists 1,748 works about Updike in sections for general criticisms; criticisms of individual works; other media, covering recorded readings, film and video adaptations, musical settings, and the like; dissertations and theses; and parodies and caricatures. Entries for criticism are unannotated. Appendixes list translations of Updike's works and periodicals in which Updike's works have appeared. Author and title index with selected subjects listed under primary titles. Foreword by John Updike. Also for works by Updike, see *First Printings of American Authors*, vol. 5, pp. 329-43. Updike's manuscripts are listed in Robbins' *American Literary Manuscripts*, pp. 327-28. Also important is Elizabeth A. Falsey's *The Art of Adding and the Art of Taking Away: An Exhibition of John Updike's Manuscripts at the Houghton Library* (Cambridge: Harvard College Library, 1987).

1383.　Gearhart, Elizabeth A. **John Updike: A Comprehensive Bibliography with Selected Annotations.** Norwood, PA: Norwood Editions, 1978. 128p. LC 78-11800. ISBN 0-8482-4174-6.

Gearhart provides entries for about 1,200 primary and secondary materials published through 1975, chronologically arranging separate listings for fiction; translations of Updike's works, short stories, poems, articles and essays, and reviews by Updike. Entries give brief bibliographic information (title, place, publisher, and date). Coverage of secondary works (unannotated) includes books, parts of books, dissertations, interviews, articles, and reviews. Unindexed. Gearhart's work updates B. A. Sokoloff and David E. Aronson's *John Updike: A Comprehensive Bibliography* (Norwood, PA: Norwood Editions, 1972) and complements Michael A. Olivas' *An Annotated Bibliography of John Updike Criticism, 1967-1973, and a Checklist of His Works* (New York: Garland, 1975), which frequently provides more detailed descriptions. Several more recent works update these cumulations, including Ray A. Roberts' "John Updike: A Bibliographical Checklist," *American Book Collector* new series 1 (January-February 1980): 5-12, 40-44; and 1 (March-April 1980): 39-47; and Donald J. Greiner's "Selected Checklist," in his *The Other John Updike: Poems/Short Stories/Plays* (Athens, OH: Ohio University Press, 1981). See *Bibliography of American Fiction, 1919-1988*, pp. 507-10, for Greiner's checklist of works by and about Updike. Greiner reviews research on Updike in *Contemporary Authors: Bibliographical Series: Volume 1: American Novelists*, pp. 347-82.

Edward Falaise Upward, 1903-
Bibliographies

Munton and Young's *Seven Writers of the English Left*, pp. 157-68, describes Upward's writings published from 1920 through 1980.

Leon Uris, 1924-
Bibliographies

For works by Uris, see *First Printings of American Authors*, vol. 4, pp. 385-87.

Sir Thomas Urquhart, 1611-1660
Bibliographies

For a bibliography of works by and about Urquhart, see *NCBEL*, I, p. 2236. Urquhart's manuscripts are described in *Index of English Literary Manuscripts*, II, pt. 2:507-10.

Sir John Vanbrugh, 1664-1726
Bibliographies

1384. McCormick, Frank. **Sir John Vanbrugh: A Reference Guide**. New York: G. K. Hall, 1992. 228p. (Reference Guide to Literature). LC 92-13099. ISBN 0-8161-8990-0.

Chronologically arranges annotated entries for about 800 works about Vanbrugh—"every substantial discussion of Vanbrugh's life and his work as architect and dramatist published between 1694 and 1990" (p. vii). International coverage includes parts of books, dissertations, and non-English-language scholarship, with more selective coverage of performance reviews. Particularly thorough coverage of contemporary and early notices and mentions. Introduction identifies standard biographies, editions, and studies. Separate indexes for names and titles and for topics and allusions, with detailed subheadings under Vanbrugh. Also for a bibliography of works by and about Vanbrugh, see *NCBEL*, II, pp. 749-50. Vanbrugh's manuscripts are described in *Index of English Literary Manuscripts*, II, pt. 2:511-40. See the review of research by John Barnard in Wells' *English Drama*, pp. 173-98.

Journals

"Recent Articles" in *The Scriblerian and the Kit Cats* (entry 1084) also regularly includes a selection of reviews of studies on Vanbrugh.

Jack Vance, 1916-
Bibliographies

1385. Hewett, Jerry, and Daryl F. Mallett. **The Work of Jack Vance: An Annotated Bibliography & Guide**. San Bernardino, CA: Borgo Press, 1994. 293p. (Bibliographies of Modern Authors, no. 29). LC 92-28056. ISBN 0-8095-0509-6.

Chronologically arranges entries for Vance's works, works about Vance, and other information related to Vance in sections for books, short fiction, verse and poetry, nonfiction, other media, interviews, maps and drawings, "Phantom Editions and Works" (nonexistent and misattributed works), unpublished manuscripts, honors and awards, guest-of-honor appearances; interviews with Vance; secondary sources (169 selective briefly annotated entries); and miscellanea (including notes on Vance collections at Boston University and the University of California, Riverside). Full bibliographic descriptions for first editions of Vance's 86 books give title-page transcriptions, contents; collations; binding descriptions; and notes on publication histories, with brief bibliographic information for subsequent editions, translations, and reprintings and citations for criticism and reviews. Includes a Vance chronology. Separate indexes of Vance's works, artists, translators, publishers, critics and reviewers, etc. Substantially improves on Daniel J. H. Levack and Tim Underwood's *Fantasms: A Bibliography of the Literature of Jack Vance* (San Francisco, CA: Underwood-Miller, 1978), which covers Vance's English-language writings published from 1945 through 1978. Also see *Bibliography of American Fiction, 1919-1988*, pp. 511-13, for Russell Letson's checklist of works by and about Vance.

Henry Van Dyke, 1852-1933
Bibliographies

For works by Van Dyke, see *First Printings of American Authors*, vol. 2, p. 263. Van Dyke's contributions to selected periodicals and reviews of Van Dyke's works are identified in Wells' *The Literary Index to American Magazines, 1850-1900*, pp. 395-96. Van Dyke's manuscripts are listed in Robbins' *American Literary Manuscripts*, p. 329.

Carl Van Vechten, 1880-1964
Bibliographies

1386. Kellner, Bruce. **A Bibliography of the Work of Carl Van Vechten**. Westport, CT: Greenwood Press, 1980. 258p. LC 79-8409. ISBN 0-313-20767-4.

A comprehensive, descriptive listing of Van Vechten's primary and secondary materials, Kellner's guide supplies entries in separate listings for Van Vechten's separately published books and pamphlets in English and other languages, edited works, and books with introductions by Van Vechten; contributions to books and pamphlets; contributions to journals; contributions to newspapers; ephemeral works (such as dust-jacket blurbs, comments on programs, and the like); and photographs. Kellner also chronologically arranges unannotated entries for biographical, bibliographic, and critical studies; reviews of Van Vechten's works (some 442 unannotated entries); and collections of Van Vechten's writings and photographs. Briefly describes the New York Public Library's Carl Van Vechten Collection and Van Vechten materials in the Berg Collection, as well as several other major and minor collections elsewhere (pp. 244-45). Critical coverage extends from 1912 through 1979. Van Vechten's manuscripts are also listed in Robbins' *American Literary Manuscripts*, p. 330.

A(lfred) E(lton) Van Vogt, 1912-
Bibliographies

1387. Van Vogt, A. E. **Reflections of A. E. Van Vogt: The Autobiography of a Science Fiction Giant: With a Complete Bibliography**. Lakemont, GA: Fictioneer Books, 1975. 136p. LC 73-94037.

Contains bibliography (pp. [123]-36) of Van Vogt's science fiction, fantasy, and other contributions to periodicals and of his separately published and collected works. Entries give brief titles, imprints, and word counts, with notes on contents. See *Bibliography of American Fiction, 1919-1988*, pp. 513-15, for Edward Joseph Ingebretsen's checklist of works by and about Van Vogt.

Henry Vaughan, 1621-1695
Bibliographies

1388. Marilla, E. L. **A Comprehensive Bibliography of Henry Vaughan**. Tuscaloosa, AL: University of Alabama Press, 1948. 44p. (University of Alabama Studies, no. 3). OCLC 379316.

Describes contemporary and early biographical sources, early and modern editions, and more than 200 critical studies of Vaughan. International coverage includes books, parts of books, articles, dissertations, and non-English-language scholarship. Critical annotations indicate importance, usefulness, or the opposite. Unindexed. Also available in a reprinted edition (New York: Haskell House Publishers, 1972). Continued by:

1388.1. Marilla, E. L., and James D. Simmonds. **Henry Vaughan: A Bibliographical Supplement, 1946-1960**. University, AL: University of Alabama, 1963. 20p. (University of Alabama Studies, no. 16). LC 63-17400.

"Inclusive survey of scholarship and criticism" (preface) from 1945 to 1960 supplementing Marilla's previous volume. Contains 127 alphabetically arranged, critically annotated entries for modern editions, books, chapters, articles, dissertations, substantial reviews, and non-English-language studies. Unindexed. Also for a bibliography of works by and about Vaughan, see *NCBEL*, I, pp. 1230-34. See also Allison's *Four Metaphysical Poets* (entry 656), pp. [33]-41; and McCarron and Shenk's *Lesser Metaphysical Poets*, pp. [36]-45. Vaughan's manuscripts are described in *Index of English Literary Manuscripts*, II, pt. 2:541-45.

Indexes and Concordances

1389. Tuttle, Imilda. **Concordance to Vaughan's Silix Scintillans**. University Park, PA: The Pennsylvania State University Press, 1969. 238p. LC 75-79843. ISBN 0-271-00095-3.

The concordance is based on French Fogle's edition of *The Complete Poetry of Henry Vaughan* (Garden City, NY: Doubleday, 1964).

Jones Very, 1813-1880
Bibliographies

For works by Very, see *Bibliography of American Literature*, vol. 8, pp. 397-405; and *First Printings of American Authors*, vol. 3, pp. 319-20. Contributions by Very and criticism and reviews of Very's works in selected periodicals are identified in Wells' *The Literary Index to American Magazines, 1815-1865*, p. 161; and *The Literary Index to American Magazines, 1850-1900*, p. 397. Very's manuscripts are listed in Robbins' *American Literary Manuscripts*, p. 331. See Boswell's *Spokesmen for the Minority* (entry 809) for criticisms of Very. David Robinson reviews research on Very in Myerson's *The Transcendentalists*, pp. 286-94.

Gore Vidal, 1925-
Bibliographies

1390. Stanton, Robert J. **Gore Vidal: A Primary and Secondary Bibliography**. Boston: G. K. Hall, 1978. 226p. (A Reference Publication in Literature). LC 78-11553. ISBN 0-8161-8109-8.

The first extensive bibliography for Vidal, this gives brief, identifying entries in separate listings for Vidal's poems; short stories and excerpts from his novels; collected short stories; television plays; collected television plays; films; stage plays (with details on production, publication, and references to reviews); collected stage plays; novels (with notes on translations and subsequent printings); collected novels and short stories; detective novels (written under the pseudonym Edgar Box); essays, reviews, published letters, and miscellaneous writings (with descriptions of contents); collected essays and reviews; and manuscripts and letters. Stanton also chronologically arranges annotated entries for about 1,000 writings about Vidal published from 1946 through 1978. Although secondary materials consist mostly of reviews, entries cover books, articles, notes, published letters, interviews, and fictional works featuring Vidal as a character. A comprehensive author, title, and subject index, with subheadings under Vidal's name, references the entries. Also for works by Vidal, see *First Printings of American Authors*, vol. 3, pp. 321-33. Vidal's manuscripts are listed in Robbins' *American Literary Manuscripts*, p. 331.

Jose Antonio Villarreal, 1924-
Bibliographies

See *Bibliography of American Fiction, 1919-1988*, pp. 515-16, for Roberta Fernandez's checklist of works by and about Villarreal.

John Donaldson Voelker (Robert Traver), 1903-

Bibliographies

For works by Voelker, see *First Printings of American Authors*, vol. 3, pp. 335-37.

Kurt Vonnegut, Jr., 1922-

Bibliographies

1391.   Pieratt, Asa B., Julie Huffman Klinkowitz, and Jerome Klinkowitz. **Kurt Vonnegut: A Comprehensive Bibliography**. Hamden, CT: Archon Books/Shoe String Press, 1987. 289p. LC 86-32108. ISBN 0-208-02071-3.

The most comprehensive bibliography of primary and secondary materials for Vonnegut. Delivers descriptive entries in separate listings for first editions of Vonnegut's books, plays, short stories, essays, reviews, published speeches, interviews, and juvenilia published from 1950 through 1985. In addition, other sections list selected criticism of Vonnegut, dissertations, and reviews. Coverage of primary and secondary materials supersedes that provided by the compilers' previous *Kurt Vonnegut, Jr.: A Descriptive Bibliography and Annotated Secondary Checklist* (Hamden, CT: Archon Books, 1974); and Betty Lenhardt Hudgens' *Kurt Vonnegut, Jr.: A Checklist* (Detroit, MI: Gale, 1972). Also for works by Vonnegut, see *First Printings of American Authors*, vol. 1, pp. 395-97. Vonnegut's manuscripts are listed in Robbins' *American Literary Manuscripts*, p. 332. See *Bibliography of American Fiction, 1919-1988*, pp. 516-18, for Peter Reed's checklist of works by and about Vonnegut. For a summary biography, critical assessment of major works, and selected primary and secondary bibliography, see Peter J. Reed's entry for Vonnegut in McCaffery's *Postmodern Fiction: A Bio-Bibliographical Guide*, pp. 533-35.

Dictionaries, Encyclopedias, and Handbooks

1392.   Leeds, Marc. **The Vonnegut Encyclopedia: An Authorized Compendium**. Westport, CT: Greenwood Press, 1995. 693p. LC 94-16122. ISBN 0-313-29230-2.

Intends "to organize and identify a good portion of Vonnegut's most frequently reappearing images and all his characters" (p. xii) in his novels and short fiction. Separate entries for novels offer brief plot summaries. The majority of the entries locate specific fictional and real persons, places, and things in Vonnegut's works and provide extended quotations, with page references to first editions. The entries for the planet "Tralfamadore" in *The Sirens of Titan* and *Slaughterhouse-Five* and for the topic "science fiction" both extend more than two full pages. Includes foreword by Vonnegut and table of editions cited. Comprehensive index of names of fictional and real persons, places and things, titles, and subjects supplies headings for "A-bomb," "schizophrenia," "virtue," and the like. An excellent companion to Vonnegut's writings, but lacks some features commonplace in similar encyclopedias (such as a chronology and bibliography of selected secondary resources).

John Barrington Wain, 1925-1994

Bibliographies

1393.   Gerard, David. **John Wain: A Bibliography**. Westport, CT: Meckler, 1987. 235p. LC 87-7059. ISBN 0-88736-103-x.

Gerard gives detailed descriptions of Wain's primary materials, covering first editions in English (with notes on later printings), contributions to books and periodicals, and radio, television, and sound recordings (175 entries), in addition to listing reviews of Wain's works and providing annotated entries for about 300 critical and biographical works about Wain published from 1972 through 1986. Coverage of primary materials extends from 1939 through 1986 and includes Wain's juvenilia. Names, primary titles, and periodical titles are indexed. Salwak's *John Braine and John Wain* (entry 141) chronologically arranges critical studies of

Wain from 1953 through 1977. Also for a bibliography of works by and about Wain, see *NCBEL*, IV, p. 1376.

Diane Wakoski, 1937-
Bibliographies

1394. Newton, Robert. **Diane Wakoski: A Descriptive Bibliography.** Jefferson, NC: McFarland, 1987. 136p. (American Poetry Contemporary Bibliography Series, no. 1). LC 87-43065. ISBN 0-89950-297-0.

Newton provides detailed descriptions of Wakoski's primary materials, including separate listings for books, pamphlets, broadsides, recordings, and postcards (66 works published from 1959 through 1985); coauthored publications; contributions to periodicals; appearances in anthologies; poems translated into non-English languages; and published interviews. An appendix lists 91 reviews and criticisms of Wakoski's works. Entries give title-page transcriptions (with illustrations), collations, pagination, binding descriptions, and publication notes. Indexing is limited to titles only.

Waldere, before late tenth century
Bibliographies

Greenfield and Robinson's *A Bibliography of Publications on Old English Literature to the End of 1972*, pp. 274-77, lists editions, translations, and studies of the Old English *Waldere*, with citations for reviews.

Alice (Malsenior) Walker, 1944-
Bibliographies

1395. Banks, Erma Davis, and Keith Byerman. **Alice Walker: An Annotated Bibliography: 1968-1986.** New York: Garland, 1989. 210p. (Garland Reference Library of the Humanities, vol. 889). LC 89-1251. ISBN 0-8240-5731-1.

In addition to listing bibliographic information, with summaries of contents, for Walker's books, essays, poetry, short stories, and miscellaneous writings, this describes about 700 works about Walker in separate listings for general studies and reference works, interviews, studies of individual works, and bibliographies. Coverage includes dissertations, reviews, and newspaper articles. Annotations are descriptive. Indexing is limited to primary titles. Banks and Byerman's guide is more comprehensive than Louis H. Pratt and Darnell D. Pratt's *Alice Malsenior Walker: An Annotated Bibliography: 1968-1986* (Westport, CT: Meckler, 1988), which describes about 400 works about Walker. Also for works by Walker, see *First Printings of American Authors*, vol. 2, pp. 365-66. See Martha J. McGowan's summary biography, critical assessment of major works, and selected primary and secondary bibliography for Walker in McCaffery's *Postmodern Fiction: A Bio-Bibliographical Guide*, pp. 537-39.

David Walker, 1785?-1830
Bibliographies

Walker's manuscripts are listed in Robbins' *American Literary Manuscripts*, p. 333. See the review of research by W. Burghardt Turner in Inge, Duke, and Bryer's *Black American Writers*, vol. I, pp. 47-132.

Margaret Abigail Walker, 1915-
Bibliographies

For works by Walker, see *First Printings of American Authors*, vol. 2, pp. 367-68. Mary Hughes Brookhart surveys works by and about Walker in Bain and Flora's *Contemporary Poets, Dramatists, Essayists, and Novelists of the South*, pp. 504-14.

Horace Binney Wallace, 1817-1852
Bibliographies

See *Bibliography of American Fiction Through 1865*, p. 266, for a checklist of works by and about Wallace. Wallace's manuscripts are listed in Robbins' *American Literary Manuscripts*, p. 333.

Lew(is) Wallace, 1827-1905
Bibliographies

Dorothy R. Russo and Thelma Lois Sullivan's *Bibliographical Studies of Seven Authors of Crawfordsville, Indiana* (entry 1008), pp. [305]-416, chronologically arranges full bibliographic descriptions of first editions of Wallace's separate publications, contributions to books, contributions to periodicals, and ephemera. Also for works by Wallace, see *Bibliography of American Literature*, vol. 8, pp. 406-19. Wallace's contributions to selected periodicals and reviews of Wallace's works are identified in Wells' *The Literary Index to American Magazines, 1850-1900*, p. 399. Wallace's manuscripts are listed in Robbins' *American Literary Manuscripts*, p. 333. See *Bibliography of American Fiction, 1866-1918*, pp. 342-43, for J. Pritchard's checklist of works by and about Wallace.

Edward Lewis Wallant, 1926-1962
Bibliographies

For works by Wallant, see *First Printings of American Authors*, vol. 1, p. 399. See *Bibliography of American Fiction, 1919-1988*, pp. 519-20, for M. Gilbert Porter's checklist of works by and about Wallant.

Edmund Waller, 1606-1687
Bibliographies

For a bibliography of works by and about Waller, see *NCBEL*, I, pp. 1211-13. Waller's manuscripts are described in *Index of English Literary Manuscripts*, II, pt. 2:547-619.

Horace Walpole, 1717-1797
Bibliographies

1396.   Hazen, Allen T. **A Bibliography of Horace Walpole**. 1948; reprint Folkestone: Dawsons of Pall Mall, 1973. 189p. LC 73-173383. ISBN 0-06-492760-1.

First published by the Yale University Press in 1948, Hazen's standard bibliography of Walpole's primary materials gives facsimiles of title pages (no title page transcriptions are included), collations, pagination, and extensive notes on states and variants in separate listings for Walpole's books, books with editorial contributions by Walpole, verse and essay contributions to periodicals and newspapers, books dedicated to Walpole, apocrypha (including letters and verse), and unpublished manuscripts. Also relevant for primary materials, Hazen's *A Catalogue of Horace Walpole's Library* (New Haven, CT: Yale University Press, 1969) describes books and manuscripts owned by Walpole. Hazen also supplies a bibliography of works by and about Walpole in *NCBEL*, II, pp. 1588-94.

1397.   Sabor, Peter. **Horace Walpole: A Reference Guide**. Boston: G. K. Hall, 1984. 270p. (A Reference Guide to Literature). LC 84-6748. ISBN 0-8161-8578-6.

Sabor's solid secondary bibliography chronologically arranges annotated entries for about 1,600 works about Walpole published from 1757 through 1983, providing comprehensive coverage of anonymous eighteenth- and nineteenth-century reviews, English-language as well as French and German works, and dissertations. Passing references, twentieth-century reviews, and works in Spanish, Italian, Danish, Russian, and Polish receive selective attention. Although generally descriptive, annotations for significant critical and biographical studies are particularly evaluative. Separate indexes for names of critics, editors, translators, and the like; and for general and specific subjects, with detailed headings (for "biography," "editions," "Gothicism," "America," and the like); individual works, and prominent literary figures (such as "George III" and "Samuel Johnson") provide excellent access. Robert Donald Spector reviews research on Walpole in *The English Gothic: A Bibliographic Guide to Writers from Horace Walpole to Mary Shelley*, pp. 83-110.

Izaak Walton, 1593-1683
Bibliographies

1398. Horne, Bernard S. **The Compleat Angler, 1653-1967: A New Bibliography**. Pittsburgh, PA: The Pittsburgh Bibliophiles, 1970. 350p. LC 73-118263. ISBN 0-8229-4036-1.

Horne describes nearly 400 editions and separate issues of *The Compleat Angler*, giving substantial bibliographic information for important editions (with illustrations of title pages) and briefer descriptions of variants. Appendixes identify repositories, trace the lineage of reprints and editions, and list selected additional primary and secondary materials. The comprehensive index references illustrators, booksellers, artists, publishers, editors, translators, variant titles, languages of translations, places of publication, and more. Andrea Sununu's "Recent Studies in Burton and Walton," *English Literary Renaissance* 17.2 (Spring 1987): 243-55, covers secondary materials on Walton. For a bibliography of works by and about Walton, see *NCBEL*, I, pp. 2222-23. Walton's manuscripts are described in *Index of English Literary Manuscripts*, II, pt. 2:621-35.

Joseph Wambaugh, 1937-
Bibliographies

For works by Wambaugh, see *First Printings of American Authors*, vol. 5, pp. 345-47. See *Bibliography of American Fiction, 1919-1988*, p. 521, for David K. Jeffrey's checklist of works by and about Wambaugh.

Wanderer, before about 940
Bibliographies

Greenfield and Robinson's *A Bibliography of Publications on Old English Literature to the End of 1972*, pp. 277-80, lists editions, translations, and studies of the *Wanderer*, with citations for reviews. Also for works about the *Wanderer*, see *NCBEL*, I, pp. 306-308.

Edward (Ned) Ward, 1667-1731
Bibliographies

For a bibliography of works by and about Ward, see *NCBEL*, II, pp. 1091-95.

Elizabeth Stuart Phelps Ward, 1844-1911
Bibliographies

For works by Ward, see *Bibliography of American Literature*, vol. 8, pp. 420-51. Ward's manuscripts are listed in Robbins' *American Literary Manuscripts*, p. 334. See *Bibliography of American Fiction, 1866-1918*, pp. 343-45, for Pamela R. Matthews' checklist of works by and about Ward.

William Ware, 1797-1852
Bibliographies

For works by Ware, see *Bibliography of American Literature*, vol. 8, pp. 452-57. Contributions by Ware and criticism and reviews of Ware's works in selected periodicals are identified in Wells' *The Literary Index to American Magazines, 1815-1865*, pp. 161-62; and *The Literary Index to American Magazines, 1850-1900*, p. 399. Ware's manuscripts are listed in Robbins' *American Literary Manuscripts*, p. 335. See *Bibliography of American Fiction Through 1865*, pp. 267-68, for a checklist of works by and about Ware.

Anna Bartlett Warner (Amy Lothrop), 1827-1915

Bibliographies

1399.   Sanderson, Dorothy Hurlbut. **They Wrote for a Living: A Bibliography of the Works of Susan Bogert Warner and Anna Bartlett Warner**. West Point, NY: Constitution Island Association, 1976. 44p. LC 76-11294.

Contains alphabetically arranged, separate listings of the works of Susan Bogert Warner (Elizabeth Wetherell), Anna Bartlett Warner (Amy Lothrop), collaborative works by the Warners, and approximately 60 works about the Warners, ranging from contemporary reviews to entries in *Who's Who of Childrens' Literature* (1968). Entries for primary materials, including fictional and nonfictional works (biographies, autobiographies, and companions to gardening), children's and devotional books, and contributions to books and periodicals, give brief titles and imprint data for first and subsequent editions, translations, and series, with plot summaries and contents. Sanderson identifies more than 100 editions of Susan Warner's *The Wide, Wide World*, published from 1851 to 1972. Unindexed. Sanderson's guide supplements coverage of works by Warner in Blanck's *Bibliography of American Literature*, vol. 8, pp. 458-76. Warner's manuscripts are listed in Robbins' *American Literary Manuscripts*, p. 335. See *Bibliography of American Fiction Through 1865*, pp. 269-71, for a checklist of works by and about Warner.

Charles Dudley Warner, 1829-1900

Bibliographies

For works by Warner, see *Bibliography of American Literature*, vol. 8, pp. 477-500. Warner's contributions to selected periodicals and reviews of Warner's works are identified in Wells' *The Literary Index to American Magazines, 1850-1900*, pp. 399-401. Warner's manuscripts are listed in Robbins' *American Literary Manuscripts*, pp. 335-36.

Rex (Reginald Ernest) Warner, 1905-1986

Bibliographies

Munton and Young's *Seven Writers of the English Left*, pp. 169-215, describes Warner's publications from 1926 through 1980. For a bibliography of works by and about Warner, see *NCBEL*, IV, pp. 761-62.

Indexes and Concordances

1400.   McLeod, A. L., and Eleanor Wyland. **A Concordance to the Poems of Rex Warner**. Trenton, NJ: A. L. McLeod, 1966. 45p. OCLC 886008.

Index verborum to 57 poems collected in Warner's *Poems* (London: Boriswood, 1937; New York: Alfred A. Knopf, 1938) and *Poems and Contradictions* (London: John Lane; New York: Alfred A. Knopf, 1945), and "The Tourist Looks at Spain," in *New Writing: Number 4* (London: John Lehman, 1937), pp. 229-31, and "Arms in Spain," in *Poems for Spain* (London: Hogarth Press; New York: Macmillan, 1939), p. 28. References 2,675 different words by poems and line numbers. Lists stop words.

Susan Bogert Warner (Elizabeth Wetherell), 1819-1885

Bibliographies

Sanderson's *They Wrote for a Living: A Bibliography of the Works of Susan Bogert Warner and Anna Bartlett Warner* (entry 1399) supplements coverage of works by Warner in Blanck's *Bibliography of American Literature*, vol. 8, pp. 501-16. Warner's manuscripts are listed in Robbins' *American Literary Manuscripts*, p. 336. See *Bibliography of American Fiction Through 1865*, pp. 272-74, for a checklist of works by and about Warner.

Caroline Matilda (Thayer) Warren, 1787?-1844
Bibliographies

See *Bibliography of American Fiction Through 1865*, p. 250, for a checklist of works by and about Warren.

Mercy Otis Warren, 1728-1814
Bibliographies

For works by Warren, see *First Printings of American Authors*, vol. 3, pp. 339-40. Warren's manuscripts are listed in Robbins' *American Literary Manuscripts*, p. 336.

Robert Penn Warren, 1905-1989
Bibliographies

1401.   Grimshaw, James A. **Robert Penn Warren: A Descriptive Bibliography, 1922-79**. Charlottesville, VA: University Press of Virginia, 1982. 494p. LC 81-3003. ISBN 0-8139-0891-4.

In this comprehensive, descriptive bibliography of Warren's primary and secondary materials, Grimshaw includes detailed entries for American and English editions of Warren's separately published works; coauthored, edited, and otherwise collaborative works; printing histories of individual poems, short stories, plays, essays, and reviews; contributions to anthologies; unpublished works; and translations of Warren's works. Entries contain title-page transcriptions, collations, contents, and details on publication, with copy locations. In addition, Grimshaw's coverage of secondary materials (unannotated) includes books, parts of books, articles, reviews, biographical sketches and interviews, news releases, master's theses and dissertations, and bibliographies. An appendix (pp. 397-414) identifies collections of Warren's manuscripts at Yale University, the University of Kentucky, and Louisiana State University. Other appendixes list Warren's works set to music and recordings. Also for works by Warren, see *First Printings of American Authors*, vol. 1, pp. 401-406. Warren's manuscripts are listed in Robbins' *American Literary Manuscripts*, p. 336. Another important primary bibliography is Susan E. Allen, James A. Birchfield, and Catherine High's *Robert Penn Warren: An Exhibition on the Occasion of the 75th Birthday Symposium at the University of Kentucky* (Lexington, KY: University of Kentucky Library Associates, 1980). Grimshaw's guide updates coverage of Warren criticism in Neil Nakadate's *Robert Penn Warren: A Reference Guide* (Boston: G. K. Hall, 1977), which chronologically arranges annotated entries for scholarship from 1925 through 1975. Also see *Bibliography of American Fiction, 1919-1988*, pp. 522-26, for Grimshaw's checklist of works by and about Warren. Research on Warren is reviewed by James H. Justus in Flora and Bain's *Fifty Southern Writers After 1900*, pp. 505-15.

Joseph Warton, 1722-1800, and Thomas Warton, 1728-1790
Bibliographies

1402.   Vance, John A. **Joseph and Thomas Warton: An Annotated Bibliography**. New York: Garland, 1983. 190p. (Garland Reference Library of the Humanities, vol. 359). LC 82-48285. ISBN 0-8240-9243-0.

Vance elaborately arranges in separate chronological and topical listings annotated entries for some 88 first and subsequent editions of works by the Wartons and about 300 works (including books, articles, and dissertations) about them. Coverage extends from the earliest eighteenth-century anonymous reviews. Appendixes identify and locate collections of manuscripts at Trinity College, Oxford, as well as collections in other institutions (pp. 175-76), and list works in progress related to Thomas Warton (as of 1983). Indexing is limited to names and primary titles. Also for a bibliography of works by and about Joseph Warton, see *NCBEL*, II, pp. 689-90; for a bibliography of works by and about Thomas Warton, see *NCBEL*, II, pp. 690-92.

Booker T(aliaferro) Washington, 1856-1915
Bibliographies

Washington's contributions to selected periodicals and reviews of Washington's works are identified in Wells' *The Literary Index to American Magazines, 1850-1900*, p. 402. Washington's manuscripts are listed in Robbins' *American Literary Manuscripts*, pp. 336-37. Also available is *Booker T. Washington: A Register of His Papers in the Library of Congress* (Washington, DC: Library of Congress, 1958). See the review of research by W. Burghardt Turner in Inge, Duke, and Bryer's *Black American Writers*, vol. I, pp. 47-132; and Sondra O'Neale in Bain and Flora's *Fifty Southern Writers Before 1900*, pp. 502-13.

Wendy Wasserstein, 1950-1995
Bibliographies

Patricia R. Schroeder reviews research on Wasserstein in *Contemporary Authors: Bibliographical Series: Volume 3: American Dramatists*, pp. 379-84.

Frank Waters, 1902-1995
Bibliographies

1403.   Tanner, Terence A. **Frank Waters: A Bibliography with Relevant Selections from His Correspondence**. Glenwood, IL: Meyerbooks, 1983. 356p. ISBN 0-916638-07-3.

Full bibliographic descriptions of Waters' works published from 1916 to 1981 in chronologically arranged sections for books; pamphlets; contributions to books; contributions to the *Encyclopedia Americana*; contributions to periodicals; contributions to the Taos, New Mexico, bilingual newspaper *El Crepusculo*, including editorials and other articles; articles by others containing material by Waters, including interviews; dust-jacket blurbs and publishers' announcements; non-English-language translations of Waters' works, with a selected list of 32 works about Waters. Entries for first and subsequent editions and printings of Waters' 22 books give title-page transcriptions; collation; pagination; contents; binding, dust-jacket, and illustration descriptions; and extensive notes on variants and composition and publication history, with citations for reviews and early notices; and copy locations. Tanner's full descriptions of Waters' pamphlets and first book appearances give less information on publication history. Brief bibliographic entries for 70 first periodical appearances present summary contents and citations for reprintings. Includes brief chronology of Waters' career. Index of proper names and titles. Also see *Bibliography of American Fiction, 1919-1988*, pp. 527-28, for Tanner's checklist of works by and about Waters. Waters' manuscripts are listed in Robbins' *American Literary Manuscripts*, p. 338. Thomas J. Lyon surveys works by and about Waters in Erisman and Etulain's *Fifty Western Writers*, pp. 509-18.

Ian Watson, 1943-
Bibliographies

1404.   Mackey, Douglas A. **The Work of Ian Watson: An Annotated Bibliography & Guide**. San Bernardino, CA: Borgo Press, 1989. 148p. (Bibliographies of Modern Authors, no. 18). LC 88-036646. ISBN 0-8095-0512-6.

Identifies works by and about Watson through 1989 in sections for books, short fiction, nonfiction, letters, poetry, campaign literature (two items), other media (television episodes, games, recordings), unpublished manuscripts, awards, editorial posts, public appearances, 22 interviews, and 29 works about Watson. Entries for books give brief bibliographic information for first and subsequent editions and translations, with summary contents and citations for criticism and reviews. Includes chronology, selected quotations from critics, and Watson's "Dancing on a Tightrope." Title index.

George Watterson, 1783-1854
Bibliographies

See *Bibliography of American Fiction Through 1865*, pp. 275-76, for a checklist of works by and about Watterson.

Isaac Watts, 1674-1748
Bibliographies

1405. Bishop, Selma L. **Isaac Watts's Hymns and Spiritual Songs (1707): A Publishing History and a Bibliography.** Ann Arbor, MI: Pierian Press, 1974. 479p. LC 73-78316. ISBN 0-8765-0033-5.

Bishop describes editions and printings of Watts' works as well as their bibliographic relationships. Entries give detailed information, including title-page transcriptions, collations and other physical data, and publishing histories, with copy locations. Several equally detailed indexes for variant titles, printers and publishers, holding libraries, and the like give comprehensive access.

Evelyn (Arthur St. John) Waugh, 1903-1966
Bibliographies

1406. Davis, Robert Murray. **Bibliography of Evelyn Waugh.** Troy, NY: Whitston, 1986. 473p. LC 85-51386. ISBN 0-87875-313-3.

Superseding his *Evelyn Waugh: A Checklist of Primary and Secondary Material* (Troy, NY: Whitston, 1972), Davis offers a chronologically arranged listing of about 3,000 entries for writings by and about Waugh, with separate listings for reviews of books about Waugh and Waugh's reviews published posthumously. Translations of Waugh's works are excluded. Descriptive annotations are extensive. Although not comprehensive, this is the best bibliography of Waugh's primary materials that is now available. Additionally, Davis' *A Catalogue of the Evelyn Waugh Collection at the Humanities Research Center, The University of Texas at Austin* (Troy, NY: Whitston, 1981) provides valuable descriptions of materials in the University of Texas' Harry Ransom Humanities Research Center, the largest collection of Waugh material, which includes Waugh's literary manuscripts, about 1,400 letters, copies and proofs of published works, unpublished works and fragments, diaries, and miscellaneous materials, such as photos, clippings, and realia. Information about Waugh criticism from 1919 through 1983 is provided in Margaret Morriss and D. J. Dooley's *Evelyn Waugh: A Reference Guide* (Boston: G. K. Hall, 1984). Also for a bibliography of works by and about Waugh, see *NCBEL*, IV, pp. 764-68.

Dictionaries, Encyclopedias, and Handbooks

1407. Doyle, Paul. **Reader's Companion to the Novels and Short Stories of Evelyn Waugh: An Annotated Glossary of the Narratives, a Who's Who Among the Characters, a Gazetteer of the Principal Places, a Description of the Important Proper Names, and a Explanation of Abbreviations Used in the Stories.** Norman, OK: Pilgrim Books, 1989. 233p. LC 88-2407. ISBN 0-937664-78-2.

Doyle gives a work-by-work account of biographical, historical, and cultural allusions and references in Waugh's novels and short stories (that, for example, "1700" hours is 5:00 PM in *Men at Arms* and "The Rock" is Gibraltar in *The Ordeal of Gilbert Pinfold*); separate dictionaries of characters and places; and a selected bibliography of primary and secondary materials. Indexing is limited to entries for allusions.

1408. Gale, Iain. **Waugh's World: A Guide to the Novels of Evelyn Waugh.** London: Sidgwick & Jackson, 1990. 335p. LC 90-41058. ISBN 0-283-99835-0.

Gale supplements coverage of persons, places, and things in Waugh's novels provided by Doyle's more comprehensive and thorough *Reader's Companion to the Novels and Short Stories of Evelyn Waugh* (entry 1407). Additionally, alphabetically arranged entries citing work and page numbers offer unique coverage of an interesting range of topics in Waugh, including "Abortion," "Shooting," and "Suicide." Other "generic headings" include "Dress, Drink, Food, Battles, Games, Cars, Churches, Clubs, Expressions, Schools, Hotels and Newspapers" (p. viii). Designed as "a bedside book," lack of indexing limits usefulness.

Journals

1409. **Evelyn Waugh Newsletter and Studies**. Garden City, NY: Evelyn Waugh Society, 1967-. 3/yr. ISSN 0014-3693.

Formerly the *Evelyn Waugh Newsletter* (1967-89), *Evelyn Waugh Newsletter and Studies* is "designed to stimulate interest and continue interest in the life and writings of Evelyn Waugh." The journal features brief articles and notes about Waugh's life and works as well as reports and announcements of new publications and works in progress. Studies have ranged from examinations of Waugh's Biblical sources to the PBS television adaptation of *Brideshead Revisited*. Others have addressed Waugh's treatment of images and themes, including homosexuality, modernity, the hero, and anti-Semitism. A few have looked at textual problems. Recent bibliographic features include Carlos Villar Flor's "Waugh in Spain: Translations," 27.3 (Winter 1993): 7-8. The journal continues to publish a regular bibliography, "Evelyn Waugh: A Supplementary Checklist of Criticism," presently compiled by Gerhard Wolk, listing international scholarship. *Evelyn Waugh Newsletter and Studies* is indexed in *AHI*, *MHRA*, and *MLA*.

John V(an) A(lstyn) Weaver, 1893-1938

Bibliographies

For works by Weaver, see *First Printings of American Authors*, vol. 5, pp. 349-51. Weaver's manuscripts are listed in Robbins' *American Literary Manuscripts*, p. 338.

Frank J. Webb, fl. 1857-1870

Bibliographies

See the review of research by Ruth Miller and Peter J. Katopes in Inge, Duke, and Bryer's *Black American Writers*, vol. I, pp. 133-60.

Charles Wilkins Webber, 1819-1856

Bibliographies

See *Bibliography of American Fiction Through 1865*, pp. 276-77, for a checklist of works by and about Webber. Contributions by Webber and criticism and reviews of Webber's works in selected periodicals are identified in Wells' *The Literary Index to American Magazines, 1815-1865*, p. 162. Webber's manuscripts are listed in Robbins' *American Literary Manuscripts*, p. 339.

John Webster, c. 1578-c. 1632

Bibliographies

1410. Schuman, Samuel. **John Webster: A Reference Guide**. Boston: G. K. Hall, 1985. 280p. (A Reference Guide to Literature). LC 85-5570. ISBN 0-8161-8433-X.

Schuman chronologically arranges annotated entries for about 1,200 critical studies of Webster, including major studies as well as passing comments in reference works. Annotations are detailed, critical, and evaluative. The guide's thorough subject index offers headings for "imagery," "plot," "structure," and the like for studies of Webster's individual works. Schuman supersedes the coverage of Webster scholarship in the Tannenbaums' *Elizabethan Bibliographies*, vol. 10, and Dennis Donovan's *Elizabethan Bibliographies Supplements*, no. 1. Additional coverage of editions and selections of Webster's works as well as criticism is provided in William E. Mahaney's *John Webster: A Classified Bibliography* (Salzburg: University of Salzburg, Institut fur Englische Sprache und Literatur, 1973), with more than 1,700 unannotated entries. For a bibliography of works by and about Webster, see *NCBEL*, I, pp. 1697-1703. Webster's manuscripts are described in *Index of English Literary Manuscripts*, I, pt. 2:553-55. Research on Webster is reviewed by Inga-Stina Ewbank in Wells' *English Drama*, pp. 113-33; and Don D. Moore in Logan and Smith's *The Popular School*, pp. 85-104, updated by Lidman's *Studies in Jacobean Drama, 1973-1984*, pp. 189-216.

Indexes and Concordances

1411. Corballis, Richard, and J. M. Harding. **A Concordance to the Works of John Webster**. Salzburg: Institut fur Englische Sprache und Literatur, Universitat Salzburg, 1978-81. 4 vols. (Salzburg Studies in English Literature: Jacobean Drama Studies, vol. 70). OCLC 4201924.

Old-spelling concordance based on texts selected from F. L. Lucas' *The Complete Works of John Webster*, 2d ed. (Cambridge: Cambridge University Press, 1966), "the only 'complete' edition of Webster's works" (p. ii), with additions of Webster's dramatic contributions to works assigned to Thomas Dekker—*Northward Ho, Westward Ho*, and *Sir Thomas Wyatt*—from Fredson Bowers' *The Dramatic Works of Thomas Dekker* (Cambridge: Cambridge University Press, 1953-61); and from Bernard M. Wagner's "New Verses by John Webster," *Modern Language Notes* 46 (1931): 403-405. Issued in parts (vol. 1, parts 1-4; vol. 2, parts 1-4; vol. 3, parts 1-4; and vol. 4, appendix). See also Stagg's *The Figurative Language of the Tragedies of Shakespeare's Chief 17th-Century Contemporaries* (entry 229).

John Weiss, 1818-1879

Bibliographies

Robert E. Burkholder reviews research on Weiss in Myerson's *The Transcendentalists*, pp. 295-98.

H(erbert) G(eorge) Wells, 1866-1946

Bibliographies

1412. Hammond, J. R. **Herbert George Wells: An Annotated Bibliography of His Works**. New York: Garland, 1977. 257p. (Garland Reference Library of the Humanities, vol. 84). LC 76-52667. ISBN 0-8240-9889-7.

The best listing of Wells' primary works, Hammond's guide supplies full bibliographic details in separate listings for first editions of Wells' fiction (novels, romances, and collected short stories) and collected essays, nonfiction books and pamphlets, works included in collected editions, posthumously published works through 1975, collected letters, prefaces contributed to books of others, other contributions to books of others (introductions and the like), and books by Wells or others including Wells' illustrations. Appendixes chronologically arrange Wells' writings published from 1892 through 1945; note unreprinted works; list selected critical, biographical, and bibliographic secondary materials (unannotated); describe collections of Wells' materials in the University of Illinois Wells Archive (pp. 226-29) and the Bromley Central Library (pp. 229-30); and recount the history of the H. G. Wells Society. Hammond's guide contains more bibliographic detail than *H. G. Wells: A Comprehensive Bibliography*, 2d ed. (London: H. G. Wells Society, 1968), compiled by the H. G. Wells Society (with a foreword by Kingsley Martin), which gives brief descriptions of Wells' 156 separate publications and checklists of contributed short stories, other contributed and selected works, and stage and film adaptations. Other descriptions of materials in the Wells Archive are also included in A. H. Watkins' *Catalogue of the H. G. Wells Collection in the Bromley Public Libraries* (Bromley: London Borough of Bromley Public Libraries, 1974). The University of Illinois Wells Archive is described in *Catalog of the Wells Collection* (Urbana, IL: University of Illinois Library, 1972). Also for a bibliography of works by and about Wells, see *NCBEL*, IV, pp. 417-28.

1413.   Scheick, William J., and J. Randolph Cox. **H. G. Wells: A Reference Guide**. Boston: G. K. Hall, 1988. 430p. (A Reference Guide to Literature). LC 88-5220. ISBN 0-8161-8946-3.

Aiming at coverage of a "broadly representative portion" of critical commentary, Scheick and Cox provide annotated entries for 3,019 books; parts of books; articles, reviews of Wells' books, films, and works about Wells; dissertations; (unannotated) letters to editors; and introductions in editions published from 1895 through 1986. Coverage includes early anonymous notices in general magazines as well as materials in Polish, German, Russian, Italian, and French. In addition, an extensive checklist of primary works is included. Indexing is only adequate. An index of critics, editors, translators, and names of writers (Plato, Swift, Poe, Vonnegut, and the like) does not compensate for the lack of subject indexing.

Dictionaries, Encyclopedias, and Handbooks

1414.   Hammond, J. R. **An H. G. Wells Companion: A Guide to the Novels, Romances, and Short Stories**. New York: Barnes and Noble, 1979. 288p. ISBN 0-06-492674-5.

Hammond offers plot summaries and critical introductions for Wells' romances, short stories, and novels; essays on Wells' biography, critical reputation, and works in general; and dictionaries of characters and places appearing in his writings. Selected bibliographies identify major primary and secondary materials. Coverage of Wells' characters is superior to that offered in Brian Ash's *Who's Who in H. G. Wells* (North Pomfret, VT: Hamish Hamilton, 1979), which identifies characters but lacks plot summaries of Wells' works.

Journals

1415.   **Wellsian: The Journal of the H. G. Wells Society**. Luton: H. G. Wells Society, 1960- . Annual. ISSN 0308-1397.

Sponsored by the H. G. Wells Society, *The Wellsian* is the most important of several journals that have been devoted to Wells. Typical articles focus on critical and biographical topics, assess Wells' contemporary critical reception, and review the present state of textual and critical scholarship (particularly related to science fiction and fantasy). "The Narrative Voice in *Tono-Bungay*" and "On the Contemporary Relevance of Wells' Conception of History" are representative. Studies have also assessed the literary relations of Wells with Aldous Huxley and John Buchan. Vol. 15 (1992) contains several features on Wells, socialist utopias, and the fall of the former Soviet Union, including David C. Smith's literature review, "H. G. Wells and Eastern Europe" (pp. 3-15). *Wellsian* also features "Recent Books and Articles on Wells," a checklist of current Wells scholarship. *Wellsian* is indexed in *MLA*.

Patterson's *Author Newsletters and Journals*, pp. 337-40, describes other previously published journals for Wells.

Eudora Welty, 1909-

Bibliographies

1416.   Polk, Noel. **Eudora Welty: A Bibliography of Her Work**. Jackson, MS: University Press of Mississippi, 1994. 517p. LC 92-28491. ISBN 0-87805-566-5.

Superseding his earlier "A Eudora Welty Checklist," *Mississippi Quarterly* 26 (Fall 1973): 663-93, as the best available basic primary bibliography, Polk gives full bibliographic descriptions of Welty's works chronologically arranged in sections for American separate publications; works compiled by others to which Welty contributed; English- and non-English-language editions of Welty's works; the collected edition, *The Complete Works of Eudora Welty* (Kyoto: Rinsen, 1988); catalogs of exhibitions containing Welty material; and shorter works in subsections for fiction, nonfiction prose, book reviews, poetry, blurbs, occasional pieces, and other miscellaneous works; early publications; photographs; interviews; lost or unidentified titles; translations; "Welty on Record" (four recordings of Welty or her works); 10 adaptations of Welty's works; three works edited by Welty; and other first book appearances. In addition to facsimiles of title pages, entries for first and subsequent American editions and printings of Welty's 36 books give title-page transcriptions; collation; contents; data for paper, typography, page layout, bindings, and dust jackets; and notes on publication history, with copy locations. Entries for shorter works note composition and contents and identify reprintings. "A Publishing Log" (pp. 433-81) is an extensive chronology of Welty's life and publications. Separate indexes of titles and proper names. Also for works by Welty, see *First Printings of American Authors*, vol. 1, pp. 407-409. Welty's manuscripts are listed in Robbins' *American Literary Manuscripts*, p. 341. Suzanne Marrs' *Welty Collection: A Guide to the Eudora Welty Manuscripts and Documents at the Mississippi Department of Archives and History* (Jackson, MS: University Press of Mississippi, 1988) offers additional information about Welty's primary materials in the Mississippi Department of Archives and History, including manuscripts of Welty's books, uncollected works, and unpublished works; photographic prints and negatives; correspondence; published works; and works and other materials about Welty. Marrs also indicates Welty materials in other department collections and in other institutions. Also useful is W. U. McDonald Jr. and Robert Alan Shaddy's *A Guide to the Eudora Welty Collection at the Ward M. Canaday Center for Special Collections* (Toledo, OH: University of Toledo Libraries, 1993).

1417.   Thompson, Victor H. **Eudora Welty: A Reference Guide**. Boston: G. K. Hall, 1976. 175p. (Reference Guides in Literature, no. 11). LC 76-1983. ISBN 0-8161-7801-1.

Thompson gives a chronologically arranged, annotated listing of works about Welty published from 1936 through 1975. Coverage includes books, parts of books, journal and newspaper articles and reviews, and dissertations. In addition to subject indexing for broad topics (such as bibliography and biography) as well as others under Welty's name, Thompson also includes fabricated headings that reflect themes and other elements in Welty's works—"The Grotesque," "Obscurantism," and "Social Criticism," among others. Critical coverage is superior to that in Bethany C. Swearingen's *Eudora Welty: A Critical Bibliography, 1936-1958* (Jackson, MS: University Press of Mississippi, 1984), which gives brief descriptive entries for Welty's books, short stories, essays and articles, and other writings but only covers criticism and reviews of Welty in general and on individual works through 1958. See also *Bibliography of American Fiction, 1919-1988*, pp. 529-32, for Thompson's checklist of works by and about Welty. Research on Welty is reviewed by William U. McDonald in *Contemporary Authors: Bibliographical Series: Volume 1: American Novelists*, pp. 383-421; Peggy W. Prenshaw in Duke, Bryer, and Inge's *American Women Writers*, pp. 233-68; and James A. Bryant, Jr., in Flora and Bain's *Fifty Southern Writers After 1900*, pp. 516-25.

Dictionaries, Encyclopedias, and Handbooks

1418.   Pingatore, Diana R. **Reader's Guide to the Short Stories of Eudora Welty**. New York: G. K. Hall, 1996. 421p. (Reference Publication in Literature). LC 95-31368. ISBN 0-8161-7371-0.

"A comprehensive guide to the scholarship associated with the 41 short stories" that appear in *The Collected Stories of Eudora Welty* (New York: Harcourt Brace, 1980) (p. xi), offering information on composition and publication history; discussions of relationships and topical, thematic, and technical connections with other works; commentaries on interpretation and criticism; and lists of cited primary and secondary sources. Indexes of Welty's works and names, titles, and selected subjects.

Journals

1419.   **Eudora Welty Newsletter**. Toledo, OH: Department of English, University of Toledo, 1977-. 2/yr. ISSN 0146-7220.

Issues of about 15 stapled pages feature brief articles that generally focus on textual and editorial studies, bibliography, and other primary materials related to Welty. Very few critical studies have been published, although notes occasionally offer new biographical information. The journal includes an annual "Checklist of Welty Scholarship," presently compiled by Pearl A. McHaney, covering editions and international criticisms as well as reviews of new publications related to Welty. Issues also contain conference and other program notices, calls for papers, and Weltyana. Vol. 20.2 (Summer 1996) offers an index to vols. 11-20 (1987-96). With 21.1 (Winter 1997), the editorial office will be located at Georgia State University. *Eudora Welty Newsletter* is indexed in *AHI*, *MHRA*, and *MLA*.

Glenway Wescott, 1901-1987
Bibliographies
See *Bibliography of American Fiction, 1919-1988*, pp. 533-34, for William H. Rueckert's checklist of works by and about Wescott. Wescott's manuscripts are listed in Robbins' *American Literary Manuscripts*, p. 341.

Arnold Wesker, 1932-
Bibliographies
King's *Twenty Modern British Playwrights*, pp. 241-68, lists works by Wesker and describes works about him.

Alick (John Alexander) West, 1895-1972
Bibliographies
Munton and Young's *Seven Writers of the English Left*, pp. 7-24, chronologically arranges descriptive entries for West's publications, including non-English-language editions, from 1916 through 1978.

Jessamyn West, 1907-1984
Bibliographies
See *Bibliography of American Fiction, 1919-1988*, pp. 534-35, for James W. Hipp's checklist of works by and about West. West's manuscripts are listed in Robbins' *American Literary Manuscripts*, p. 341.

Nathaniel West, 1903-1940
Bibliographies
1420. Vannatta, Dennis P. **Nathaniel West: An Annotated Bibliography of the Scholarship and Works.** New York: Garland, 1976. 165p. (Garland Reference Library in the Humanities, vol. 34). LC 75-24093. ISBN 0-8240-9978-8.

In addition to a brief checklist of West's works, including film scripts, plays, and unpublished writings, Vannatta provides extensive, annotated entries for about 500 works about West, covering books, parts of books, articles, reviews of West's writings and reviews of works about West, and dissertations. Duplicative separate listings arrange these items by topics, such as bibliographic studies, surveys of West scholarship, biography, source studies, influence studies, and the like. Vannatta's coverage of secondary materials complements White's coverage of West's primary materials (entry 1421). See also *Bibliography of American Fiction, 1919-1988*, pp. 535-37, for James R. Kelly's checklist of works by and about West.

1421. White, William. **Nathaniel West: A Comprehensive Bibliography.** Kent, OH: Kent State University Press, 1975. 209p. (The Serif Series: Bibliographies and Checklists, no. 32). LC 74-79149. ISBN 0-87338-157-2.

White offers descriptive entries for West's primary works, including separate listings for books (with facsimiles of title pages), contributions to books, unpublished plays, screenplays, contributions to periodicals, unpublished fiction and other writings, and writings included in anthologies. In addition, White provides listings of biographical and critical materials about West. Appends the texts of otherwise uncollected works by West (poems, reviews, and essays). Ray Lewis White's "Nathaniel West: Additional Reviews of His Work, 1933-57," *Yale University Library Gazette* 51 (1977): 218-32, covers selected materials not cited by his earlier guide. Also for works by West, see *First Printings of American Authors*, vol. 1, p. 411. West's manuscripts are listed in Robbins' *American Literary Manuscripts*, pp. 341-42.

Dame Rebecca West (Cicily Isabel Fairfield Andrews), 1892-1983
Bibliographies

1422.   Packer, Joan Garrett. **Rebecca West: An Annotated Bibliography**. New York: Garland, 1991. 136p. (Garland Reference Library of the Humanities, vol. 1158). LC 91-11183. ISBN 0-8240-5692-2.

Covers works by and about West. The first part presents brief bibliographic information and summary contents for first and subsequent editions and translations of West's works in 192 entries in sections for books, stories and essays, and reviews. Introduction surveys West's critical reception. The second part covers works about West in sections including descriptively annotated entries for three bibliographies, 16 books and dissertations, and 154 chapters, articles, and reviews. Name and title index.

Edward Noyes Westcott, 1846-1898
Bibliographies

For works by Westcott, see *Bibliography of American Literature*, vol. 9, pp. 1-2. See *Bibliography of American Fiction, 1866-1918*, p. 346, for Barbara Bell's checklist of works by and about Westcott.

Edith (Newbold Jones) Wharton, 1862-1937
Bibliographies

1423.   Brenni, Vito J. **Edith Wharton: A Bibliography**. Morgantown, WV: West Virginia University Library, 1966. 99p. LC 66-24417.

Brenni gives brief descriptive entries for Wharton's primary works, including separate publications and collected editions of her novels, short stories, poems, nonfiction, and book reviews. In addition, Brenni identifies about 700 critical and biographical studies about Wharton.

1424.   Garrison, Stephen. **Edith Wharton: A Descriptive Bibliography**. Pittsburgh, PA: University of Pittsburgh Press, 1990. 514p. (Pittsburgh Series in Bibliography). LC 89-25034. ISBN 0-8229-3641-0.

The standard guide to Wharton's works. Full bibliographic descriptions of Wharton's works chronologically arranged in sections for separate publications in English through 1986; collected editions; contributions to books and pamphlets; contributions to magazines and newspapers; and books edited by Wharton. Entries for 52 books give title- and copyright-page facsimiles and descriptions of pagination, collation, typography, paper, contents, and bindings; and notes on publication history, with copy locations. Garrison gives brief information for 251 first periodical appearances, with citations for reprintings. Appends list of selected major works about Wharton (pp. 493-94). Index of titles and names. Also for works by Wharton, see *First Printings of American Authors*, vol. 3, pp. 341-56. Wharton's manuscripts are listed in Robbins' *American Literary Manuscripts*, p. 342. See *Bibliography of American Fiction, 1866-1918*, pp. 347-50, for Alfred Bendixen's checklist of works by and about Wharton. Research on Wharton is reviewed by James W. Tuttleton in Duke, Bryer, and Inge's *American Women Writers*, pp. 71-108.

1425.   Lauer, Kristin O., and Margaret P. Murray. **Edith Wharton: An Annotated Secondary Bibliography**. New York: Garland, 1990. 528p. (Garland Reference Library of the Humanities, vol. 1027). LC 89-37067. ISBN 0-8240-4636-6.

Superseding the coverage of secondary materials for Wharton offered in Marlene Springer's *Edith Wharton and Kate Chopin: A Reference Guide* (entry 253), Lauer and Murray cover Wharton scholarship appearing through 1988, arranging about 1,200 annotated entries in separate listings for bibliographies; biographical studies; studies of literary relationships; general book-length studies and essay collections; contemporary criticism; surveys; general discussions; critical studies and reviews of the novels, short fiction, poetry, nonfiction, collections, translations, and manuscripts (in collections at Yale and Princeton universities); and dissertations. Wharton materials at Princeton are also described in R. W. B. Lewis' *Edith Wharton: A Biography* (New York: Harper & Row, 1976).

Journals

1426.   **Edith Wharton Review**. Brooklyn, NY: Edith Wharton Society, 1984-. 2/yr. OCLC 15498748.

Formerly *Edith Wharton Newsletter* (1984-89) and sponsored by the Edith Wharton Society, issues of *Edith Wharton Review* publish critical and biographical articles, notes, and reviews of new publications about the life and works of Wharton. Typical contributions offer close readings of specific works; studies of Wharton's characters and themes (in particular, most recently, female sexuality); narrative techniques; surveys of literary relations with other writers (such as Goethe, Emily Bronte, Henry James, Willa Cather, Abraham Cahan, Louis Bromfield, T. S. Eliot, and F. Scott Fitzgerald); discussions of biographical documents; essay reviews on Wharton's critical reception (in Italy, Japan, Spain, and elsewhere); and checklists and guides to current scholarship. Clare Colquitt's "Contradictory Possibilities: Wharton Scholarship 1992-1994: A Bibliographic Essay," 12.2 (Fall 1995): 37-44; and Alfred Bendixen's "New Directions in Wharton Criticism: A Bibliographic Essay," 10.2 (Fall 1993): 20-24, are recent bibliographic contributions. Special issues devoted to specific topics include "Edith Wharton and Children," 12.1 (Spring 1995). *Edith Wharton Review* is indexed in *MLA*.

Phillis Wheatley, 1753?-1784
Bibliographies

1427.   Robinson, William H. **Phillis Wheatley: A Bio-Bibliography**. Boston: G. K. Hall, 1981. 166p. (A Reference Publication in Afro-American Studies). LC 81-900. ISBN 0-8161-8318-x.

Following a checklist of Wheatley's primary materials, Robinson chronologically arranges annotated entries for about 600 works about Wheatley published from 1761 through 1979. Coverage includes critical and biographical studies in books; articles in scholarly journals, magazines, and newspapers; and manuscript collections. Annotations are critical and evaluative. The index limits subject access to headings under Wheatley's name. Wheatley's manuscripts are listed in Robbins' *American Literary Manuscripts*, p. 342. Research on Wheatley is reviewed by Jerome Klinkowitz in Inge, Duke, and Bryer's *Black American Writers*, vol. I, pp. 6-15.

Charles Stearns Wheeler, 1816-1843
Bibliographies

Joel Myerson reviews research on Wheeler in Myerson's *The Transcendentalists*, pp. 299-300.

John (Brooks) Wheelwright, 1897-1940
Bibliographies

For works by Wheelwright, see *First Printings of American Authors*, vol. 5, pp. 353-54. Wheelwright's manuscripts are listed in Robbins' *American Literary Manuscripts*, p. 343.

James Abbott McNeill Whistler, 1834-1903

Bibliographies

1428. Getscher, Robert H., and Paul G. Marks. **James McNeill Whistler and John Singer Sargent: Two Annotated Bibliographies.** New York: Garland, 1986. 520p. (Garland Reference Library of the Humanities, vol. 467). LC 83-49311. ISBN 0-8240-9000-4.

Pages [1] through 377 provide a listing of works by and about Whistler in mostly chronologically arranged sections for Whistler's books, pamphlets, and letters; letters in newspapers; original illustrations and designs in publications; catalogs of works (etchings, lithographs, and oils); biographies of Whistler and his family; memoirs of acquaintances; general works; critical studies; chapters and other sections in more general works; articles on Whistler's art (some 423 entries); articles about Whistler and his family; exhibitions; catalogs of Whistleriana and notable auctions; miscellanea, including Walter Greaves; and 10 other bibliographies. Entries for Whistler's books give brief bibliographic details (about pagination and bindings), describe contents, and cite subsequent editions, translations, and reprintings. Generally critical entries for secondary works indicate comprehensiveness and significance. Single cumulative index of names and titles, including museums, galleries, periodicals, and newspapers but not subjects. Also for works by Whistler, see *Bibliography of American Literature*, vol. 9, pp. 3-15; and for a bibliography of works by and about Whistler, see *NCBEL*, III, p. 368. Reviews of Whistler's works in selected periodicals are identified in Wells' *The Literary Index to American Magazines, 1850-1900*, p. 406. Whistler's manuscripts are listed in Robbins' *American Literary Manuscripts*, p. 343.

Frances Miriam Whitcher, 1814-1852

Bibliographies

See *Bibliography of American Fiction Through 1865*, p. 277, for a checklist of works by and about Whitcher. Robbins' *American Literary Manuscripts*, p. 343, lists one manuscript for Whitcher.

E(lwyn) B(rooks) White, 1899-1985

Bibliographies

1429. Anderson, A. J. **E. B. White: A Bibliography**. Metuchen, NJ: Scarecrow Press, 1978. 199p. (The Scarecrow Author Bibliographies, no. 37). LC 78-2783. ISBN 0-8108-1121-9.

Anderson gives an unannotated, chronologically arranged listing of works by and about White published from 1914 through 1977, including brief bibliographic information in separate listings for first printings in English of books and pamphlets; contributed verse, articles, short stories, and other prose works; editorials; theater, film, and book reviews; contributions to books of others (forewords, introductions, and the like); and miscellaneous writings (such as newspaper columns), as well as biographical and critical studies and reviews of White's works. Additional descriptions of White's primary materials are included in Katherine Romans Hall's *E. B. White: A Bibliographic Catalogue of Printed Materials in the Department of Rare Books, Cornell University Library* (New York: Garland, 1979), which describes Cornell University's E. B. White Collection of editions of White's books and pamphlets, contributions to books or edited works, contributions to journals and newspapers, and literary manuscripts. White's manuscripts are also listed in Robbins' *American Literary Manuscripts*, p. 344. Also see *Bibliography of American Fiction, 1919-1988*, pp. 537-39, for Susan F. Beegel's checklist of works by and about White.

Gilbert White, 1720-1793

Bibliographies

For a bibliography of works by and about White, see *NCBEL*, II, p. 1594, by Robert Halsband.

Stewart Edward White, 1873-1946

Bibliographies

For works by White, see *First Printings of American Authors*, vol. 5, pp. 355-62. White's manuscripts are listed in Robbins' *American Literary Manuscripts*, pp. 344-45. See *Bibliography of American Fiction, 1866-1918*, pp. 351-52, for Gwen L. Nagel's checklist of works by and about White.

T(erence) H(anbury) White, 1906-1964

Bibliographies

1430. Gallix, Francois. **T. H. White: An Annotated Bibliography**. New York: Garland, 1986. 148p. (Garland Reference Library of the Humanities, vol. 655). LC 86-18444. ISBN 0-8240-8589-2.

Including a detailed chronology and illustrations of title pages, Gallix's work provides descriptive entries for White's primary materials in separate listings for books, short stories, poems, articles, published correspondence, unpublished works in complete and incomplete manuscripts in the University of Texas' Harry Ransom Humanities Research Center, and radio and television appearances. Entries give extensive details on contents, composition histories, and manuscript sources rather than full bibliographic descriptions. In addition, Gallix lists selectively annotated entries for about 100 works about White in sections for books and theses, parts of books, and articles. Coverage extends through 1986.

William Allen White, 1868-1944

Bibliographies

1431. Johnson, Walter, and Albert Pantle. **A Bibliography of the Published Works of William Allen White**. Topeka, KS: Kansas Historical Quarterly, 1947. 20p. LC 48-19642.

Reprinted from the *Kansas Historical Quarterly* 17.1 (February 1947): 22-41. Very selectively annotated, chronologically arranged checklist of White's "books, [contributions to books], most of the magazine articles, and certain special newspaper features," omitting newspaper editorials and "innumerable short [book] reviews" (p. [1]), published from 1888 to 1944. Offers a sound starting point for more detailed bibliographic work. Also for works by White, see *First Printings of American Authors*, vol. 2, pp. 369-80. White's contributions to and reviews of White's works in selected periodicals are identified in Wells' *The Literary Index to American Magazines, 1850-1900*, p. 407. White's manuscripts are listed in Robbins' *American Literary Manuscripts*, p. 345.

Brand Whitlock, 1869-1934

Bibliographies

1432. Steffens, Eleanor Stratton. **Brand Whitlock: An Essay, a Checklist, and an Annotated Bibliography**. Ph.D. dissertation. Cleveland, OH: Case Western Reserve University, 1972. 294 leaves. OCLC 5802509.

Appends a two-part comprehensive bibliography of works by and about Whitlock. In the first part Steffens chronologically arranges full bibliographic descriptions of Whitlock's published writings in sections for books and pamphlets, contributions to books and pamphlets, short stories and essays, poems, and newspaper interviews. Entries for Whitlock's 20 books give title-page transcriptions, collations, binding descriptions, and notes on publication histories for first and subsequent editions, translations, and reprintings. Coverage excludes Whitlock's newspaper articles written from 1887 to 1893. Also contains brief descriptions of unpublished works, including manuscripts and letters, in American Academy of Arts and Letters and two other collections, with a very detailed register of "over 40,000 items" in the Brand Whitlock Papers in the Library of Congress (pp. 189-230). The second part alphabetically lists annotated entries for approximately 350 works about Whitlock in sections for books, periodicals, dissertations and theses, and selected newspaper articles. Although certainly dated, any new guide to Whitlock should be based on Steffens' original work. Also see *Bibliography of American Fiction, 1866-1918*, pp. 353-54, for Richard W. Oram's checklist of works by and about Whitlock. Whitlock's manuscripts are listed in Robbins' *American Literary Manuscripts*, p. 346.

Sarah Helen (Power) Whitman, 1803-1878
Bibliographies

For works by Whitman, see *Bibliography of American Literature*, vol. 9, pp. 16-27; and *First Printings of American Authors*, vol. 3, pp. 357-58. Contributions by Whitman and criticism and reviews of Whitman's works in selected periodicals are identified in Wells' *The Literary Index to American Magazines, 1815-1865*, p. 163; and *The Literary Index to American Magazines, 1850-1900*, pp. 407-408. Whitman's manuscripts are listed in Robbins' *American Literary Manuscripts*, p. 346.

Walt(er) Whitman, 1819-1892
Bibliographies

1433.   Giantvalley, Scott. **Walt Whitman, 1838-1939: A Reference Guide**. Boston: G. K. Hall, 1981. 465p. (A Reference Guide to Literature). LC 81-6538. ISBN 0-8161-7856-9.

Giantvalley offers comprehensive coverage of English-language books, articles, reviews, and various miscellaneous items about Whitman dating through 1939, providing nearly 5,000 chronologically arranged, annotated entries. Significant items receive extensive descriptions. A detailed author and subject index gives solid access. Giantvalley's listing and Kummings' bibliography covering criticism published from 1940 through 1975 (entry 1434) constitute the major compilations of Whitman scholarship. Annual bibliographies featured in *Walt Whitman Quarterly Review* (entry 1439) identify criticism after 1975. Research on Whitman is reviewed by Roger Asselineau in Woodress' *Eight American Authors*, pp. 225-72; and Jerome Loving in Myerson's *The Transcendentalists*, pp. 375-83. *ALS* annually features a review essay on Whitman scholarship.

1434.   Kummings, Donald G. **Walt Whitman, 1940-1975: A Reference Guide**. Boston: G. K. Hall, 1982. 264p. (A Reference Guide to Literature). LC 82-11845. ISBN 0-8161-7802-x.

Continuing Giantvalley's bibliography (entry 1433), Kummings chronologically arranges descriptively annotated entries for 3,172 books, parts of books, articles, reviews, dissertations in English and non-English languages published from 1940 through 1975. The detailed author and subject index offers excellent access to topics, literary personalities, and bibliographic formats. Kummings' and Giantvalley's guides supersede all other listings of Whitman scholarship, including Gay Wilson Allen's *Twenty-Five Years of Walt Whitman Bibliography, 1918-1942* (Boston: Faxon, 1943); Evie Allison Allen's "A Checklist of Whitman Publications, 1945-1960," in Gay Wilson Allen's *Walt Whitman: Man, Poet, and Legend* (Carbondale, IL: Southern Illinois University Press, 1961), pp. 179-244; and James T. F. Tanner's *Walt Whitman: A Supplementary Bibliography: 1961-1967* (Kent, OH: The Kent State University Press, 1968); as well as Jeanetta Boswell's *Walt Whitman and the Critics: A Checklist of Criticism, 1900-1978* (Metuchen, NJ: Scarecrow Press, 1980).

1435.   Myerson, Joel. **Walt Whitman: A Descriptive Bibliography**. Pittsburgh, PA: University of Pittsburgh Press, 1993. 1,097p. (Pittsburgh Series in Bibliography). LC 92-25927. ISBN 0-8229-3739-5.

An outstanding example of modern descriptive bibliography and now the standard bibliography of Whitman's works, with coverage generally extending through 1991. Myerson gives full bibliographic descriptions in chapters for Whitman's separate publications; collected editions; miscellaneous collections; contributions to books and pamphlets; contributions to magazines and newspapers; proof copies, circulars, and broadsides; prose and poetry reprinted in books (published through 1892); and separately published individual poems and prose. Forty-six entries for first and subsequent editions, printings, and states of Whitman's books include title and copyright facsimiles; descriptions of format, collation, contents, typography, paper, and bindings; notes on publication history; and copy locations. Myerson identifies 3,026 first periodical appearances, with citations for reprintings. Bibliography of selected works about Whitman (pp. 983-89). Index of poems in *Leaves of Grass* and a comprehensive index of titles and names offer excellent access. Also for works by Whitman, see *Bibliography of American Literature*, vol. 9, pp. 28-103. Whitman's manuscripts are listed in Robbins' *American Literary Manuscripts*, pp. 346-47. Myerson's bibliography supersedes Carolyn Wells and Alfred F. Goldsmith's *A Concise Bibliography of the Works of Walt Whitman* (Boston: Houghton Mifflin, 1922), which offered chronologically arranged, incomplete descriptions of separately published works and collections, including Whitman's works; and Gloria A. Francis and Artem Lozynsky's *Whitman at Auction 1899-1972* (Detroit, MI: Gale, 1978), which reprints descriptive listings from 43 auction catalogs, with notes on collections and collectors, including the major collections of Charles E. Feinberg in the Library of Congress, Madeleine Buxton Holmes in the Berg Collection of the New York Public Library, and Richard Maurice Bucke at Duke University. Other useful catalogs of these collections include Ellen Frances Frey's *Catalogue of the Whitman Collection in the Duke University Library Being Part of the Trent Collection Given by Dr. and Mrs. Josiah C. Trent* (Durham, NC: Duke University Library, 1945); and *Walt Whitman: A Catalog Based Upon the Collections of the Library of Congress, with Notes on Whitman Collections and Collectors* (Washington, DC: GPO, 1955).

Dictionaries, Encyclopedias, and Handbooks

1436.   Allen, Gay Wilson. **The New Walt Whitman Handbook**. New York: New York University Press, 1975. 423p. LC 74-21595. ISBN 0-8147-0556-1.

Allen includes a chronology of Whitman's life and career and chapters on biographical scholarship on Whitman, his poetry, social, political, and philosophical ideas, literary techniques, and influence and critical reception. Listings of selected primary and secondary materials conclude the volume. Additional introductory information on themes and other topics related to Whitman is included in Allen's *A Reader's Guide to Walt Whitman* (New York: Farrar, Straus & Giroux, 1970). Not a reference companion, Ezra Greenspan's *The Cambridge Companion to Walt Whitman* (Cambridge: Cambridge University Press, 1995) is a collection of 11 original, critical essays and interpretive readings of Whitman's poetry and performance, politics, women's responses, and other topics.

Indexes and Concordances

1437.   Eby, Edwin H. **A Concordance of Walt Whitman's Leaves of Grass and Selected Prose Writings**. Seattle, WA: University of Washington Press, 1949-55. 964p. LC 50-9002.

This concordance gives volume, page, and line references to the Camden edition of *Leaves of Grass*, published by Whitman in 1876. Also available in a reprinted edition (New York: Greenwood Press, 1969).

Journals

1438.   **The Mickle Street Review.** Camden, NJ: Walt Whitman Association, 1979-90. 2/yr. ISSN 0194-1313.

Sponsored by the Walt Whitman Association, *The Mickle Street Review* featured critical and biographical articles and reviews of new publications about the life and works of Whitman and the Whitman tradition. A significant number of contributions focused on sexual and political themes and symbols in Whitman's works, such as "Strategies of Sex in Whitman's Poetry" and "Whitman and the Founding Fathers." Other articles assessed Whitman's contemporary reception and critical recognition around the world. Specific features also discussed Whitman in the former Soviet Union and China. Special issues on specific topics included "Walt Whitman and the Visual Arts," 12 (1990), containing articles on Whitman and painting, sculpture, and architecture. *The Mickle Street Review* was indexed in *AHI* and *MLA*.

1439.   **Walt Whitman Quarterly Review**. Iowa City, IA: The University of Iowa, 1955- . 4/yr. ISSN 0737-0679.

Typical issues of this major scholarly journal, formerly *Walt Whitman Newsletter* (1955-58) and *Walt Whitman Review* (1959-82), include three to five substantial articles and briefer notes, reviews of new publications, a current bibliography, and announcements and other information of value to scholars, particularly regarding newly discovered Whitman materials. Many major features address textual and editorial questions and describe primary materials. Significant critical attention has been given to comparisons of Whitman and other artists, such as Robert Penn Warren, William Saroyan, Thomas Mann, van Gogh, Frank Lloyd Wright, William Carlos Williams, and Bram Stoker, among others. Each issue contains "Whitman: A Current Bibliography," presently compiled by Ed Folsom of the University of Iowa, a comprehensive, very briefly annotated listing of books, articles, dissertations, reviews, and other comments, including references from newspapers. Past issues have published bibliographic contributions, including an addendum to Giantvalley's bibliography (entry 1433) in 4 (Summer 1986): 24-40. *Walt Whitman Quarterly Review* is indexed in *AES, AHI, A&HCI, MHRA,* and *MLA.* Patterson's *Author Newsletters and Journals*, pp. 342-45, describes other previously published journals for Whitman.

Adeline Dutton Train Whitney, 1824-1906
Bibliographies

See *Bibliography of American Fiction Through 1865,* pp. 278-79, for a checklist of works by and about Whitney.

(Edward) Reed Whittemore (II), 1919-
Bibliographies

For works by Whittemore, see *First Printings of American Authors*, vol. 1, pp. 413-14. Whittemore's manuscripts are listed in Robbins' *American Literary Manuscripts*, p. 347.

John Greenleaf Whittier, 1807-1892
Bibliographies

1440.   Currier, Thomas F. **A Bibliography of John Greenleaf Whittier.** Cambridge: Harvard University Press, 1937. 692p. LC 37-5316.

This is the standard (albeit dated) descriptive bibliography of Whittier's primary materials, providing detailed entries for editions and leaflets; poems, prose essays, and tales contributed to books and journals; and newspapers edited by Whittier, with lists of his editorial contributions; and letters. In addition to other listings for selected biographical and critical works, appendixes describe Whittieriana, such as editions for the blind, musical settings, and attributed works. A chronologically arranged list of Whittier's poems and an index of persons, places, institutions, and titles provide access. Reprinted (New York: Russell & Russell) in 1971. Also for works by Whittier, see *Bibliography of American Literature*, vol. 9, pp. 104-280. Whittier's manuscripts are listed in Robbins' *American Literary Manuscripts*, pp. 347-48.

1441. Von Frank, Albert J. **Whittier: A Comprehensive Bibliography**. New York: Garland, 1976. 273p. (Garland Reference Library of the Humanities, vol. 35). LC 75-24094. ISBN 0-8240-9977-x.

Von Frank chronologically lists works by and about Whittier in separate listings for formats and topics, including biographical studies, standard editions, bibliographies and manuscript guides, literary influences and associations, politics, journalism, religion, individual works, and the like. Brief, selective annotations usually merely cite a work's title, although significant studies are reviewed in detail. Reviews of Whittier's works in selected periodicals are identified in Wells' *The Literary Index to American Magazines, 1815-1865*, pp. 163-65; and *The Literary Index to American Magazines, 1850-1900*, pp. 412-15. Research on Whittier is reviewed by Karl Keller in Harbert and Rees' *Fifteen American Authors Before 1900*, pp. 468-500. Boswell's *The Schoolroom Poets* (entry 177) offers 531 entries for Whittier, supplementing Von Frank's coverage.

Journals

1442. **Whittier Newsletter**. Amesbury and Haverhill, MA: Whittier Clubs and Homes, 1966-88. 2/yr. ISSN 0511-8832.

Usually including eight to 16 pages, *Whittier Newsletter*'s most significant contribution was an annual "Whittier Bibliography" that briefly reviewed books, articles, dissertations, media, and research then in progress related to Whittier. In addition, the newsletter published notes and queries on such topics as Whittier's signature, illustrations of Whittier, and the origins of the Barbara Fritchie story, as well as information about the activities of Whittier Clubs and Homes. *Whittier Newsletter* was indexed in the *MLA* through 1976.

Patterson's *Author Newsletters and Journals*, p. 345, describes other previously published journals on Whittier.

Widsith, c. seventh century

Bibliographies

Greenfield and Robinson's *A Bibliography of Publications on Old English Literature to the End of 1972*, pp. 280-85, lists editions, translations, and studies of the Old English *Widsith*, with citations for reviews.

Elie Wiesel, 1928-

Bibliographies

1443. Abramowitz, Molly. **Elie Wiesel: A Bibliography**. Metuchen, NJ: Scarecrow Press, 1974. 206p. (Scarecrow Author Bibliographies, no. 22). LC 74-17166. ISBN 0-8108-0731-9.

This gives brief bibliographic information and descriptions of contents (including notes on translations) for 102 works by Wiesel, covering his books, prefaces and forewords, and contributions to periodicals (stories, legends, memoirs, reviews, addresses, and presentations). In addition, Abramowitz briefly describes 907 works about Wiesel in listings for books; articles; interviews; reviews of Wiesel's works (arranged by works); reviews of works in French, Hebrew, and other languages; dissertations; radio, television, film, and stage notices; and lectures, awards, and news articles. Indexing is limited to personal names.

Kate Douglas Wiggin, 1856-1923
Bibliographies

    For works by Wiggin, see *Bibliography of American Literature*, vol. 9, pp. 281-311. Wiggin's contributions to selected periodicals and reviews of Wiggin's works are identified in Wells' *The Literary Index to American Magazines, 1850-1900*, pp. 415-16. Wiggin's manuscripts are listed in Robbins' *American Literary Manuscripts*, p. 348. See *Bibliography of American Fiction, 1866-1918*, pp. 354-56, for Jennifer Meta Robinson's checklist of works by and about Wiggin.

Richard (Purdy) Wilbur, 1921-
Bibliographies

1444.   Bixler, Frances. **Richard Wilbur: A Reference Guide**. Boston: G. K. Hall, 1991. 266p. (Reference Guide to Literature). LC 91-11042. ISBN 0-8161-7262-5.

    Updating the coverage of works about Wilbur provided in Field's *Richard Wilbur: A Bibliographical Checklist* (entry 1445), Bixler chronologically arranges annotated entries for criticisms of Wilbur from 1935 to 1991. Comprehensive coverage ranges from newspaper notices of Wilbur's activities as a juvenile and entries in biographical dictionaries to substantial critical studies published as books, chapters, articles, dissertations and master's theses, and non-English-language criticisms. The majority of the approximately 700 descriptively annotated entries, however, identify book and performance reviews. An introduction surveys critical responses to Wilbur and indicates major critical and bibliographic studies and works. "Finding List" (pp. 241-42) describes special collections for Wilbur. Includes foreword by Wilbur and brief chronology of his life and career. Detailed topical indexing under Wilbur and primary titles offers good access. Bruce Michelson reviews research on Wilbur in *Contemporary Authors: Bibliographical Series: Volume 2: American Poets*, pp. 335-68.

1445.   Field, John P. **Richard Wilbur: A Bibliographical Checklist**. Kent, OH: Kent State University Press, 1971. 85p. (The Serif Series: Bibliographies and Checklists, no. 16). LC 79-626237. ISBN 0-8733-8035-5.

    Field describes Wilbur's primary works in separate listings for books of poetry; translations, musical lyrics, and compilations; edited works; collaborative edited works; individual poems (with publishing histories); articles; reviews; interviews; manuscripts; and miscellaneous writings (such as diaries, letters, tapes, films, and the like). In addition, Field identifies books, parts of books, articles, and reviews about Wilbur. Describes Wilbur materials in Amherst College's Robert Frost Library, which includes most of Wilbur's papers; and the collection in the Lockwood Memorial Library of the State University of New York at Buffalo, among others (pp. 45-56). According to Bixler (entry 1444), p. 240, John Lancaster and Jack W. C. Hagstrom are presently preparing a new descriptive bibliography for Wilbur. Also for works by Wilbur, see *First Printings of American Authors*, vol. 2, pp. 381-85. Wilbur's manuscripts are listed in Robbins' *American Literary Manuscripts*, p. 349.

Oscar Fingal O'Flahertie Wills Wilde, 1854-1900
Bibliographies

1446.   Mason, Stuart. **Bibliography of Oscar Wilde**. New ed. London: Bertram Rota, 1967. 605p. LC 67-82624.

    The major bibliography of Wilde's primary materials first published in 1914 (London: T. W. Laurie), Mason's work offers extensive bibliographic descriptions of Wilde's writings in separate listings for contributions to periodicals (some 300 entries subarranged by journals), separate editions, collected editions, and selections, in addition to listing secondary works about Wilde. Entries include title-page transcriptions (with illustrations) and extensive physical details and publishing histories. Employing outdated principles of organization and description, the work needs to be updated. Coverage of Wilde's separate publications and contributions to periodicals in Mikolyzk's *Oscar Wilde: An Annotated Bibliography* (entry 1448) partially supplements Mason. Other useful descriptions of Oscar Wilde materials in the William Andrews Clark Library are provided in Robert Ernest Cowan and William Andrews Clark, Jr.'s five-volume *The Library of William Andrews Clark, Jr.: Wilde and Wildeiana* (San Francisco: J. H. Nash, 1922-31); and John Charles Finzi's *Oscar Wilde and His Literary Circle: A Catalogue of Manuscripts and Letters in the William Andrews Clark Memorial Library* (Berkeley, CA: University of California Press, 1957), which lists items acquired from 1929 through 1957. Also for a bibliography of works by and about Wilde, see *NCBEL*, III, pp. 1182-88.

1447.   Mikhail, E. H. **Oscar Wilde: An Annotated Bibliography of Criticism.** Totowa, NJ: Rowman and Littlefield, 1978. 249p. LC 77-26968. ISBN 0-8476-6014-1.

Mikhail offers brief descriptive entries for more than 3,000 items about Wilde published through 1975 in classified sections for bibliographies, reviews of Wilde's books (arranged by works), and criticisms of Wilde in books and periodicals, reviews of stage and film productions of Wilde's works or about Wilde, dissertations, recordings, and satires on Wilde published in *Punch*. Although substantially superseded by secondary coverage in Mikolyzk's *Oscar Wilde: An Annotated Bibliography* (entry 1448), Mikhail's guide remains convenient for its listings for individual works.

1448.   Mikolyzk, Thomas A. **Oscar Wilde: An Annotated Bibliography.** Westport, CT: Greenwood, 1994. 489p. (Bibliographies and Indexes in World Literature, vol. 38). LC 93-14052. ISBN 0-313-27597-1.

Covering works by and about Wilde, Mikolyzk's guide supplements and updates the important primary bibliography of Mason (entry 1446) and largely supersedes the secondary bibliography of Mikhail (entry 1447). Mikolyzk provides annotated entries in separate sections for Wilde's books and separate publications (chronologically arranged by first editions), and contributions to periodicals (mainly alphabetically arranged in groupings for essays, stories, poems, miscellaneous, and specific periodicals). Entries for primary works lack the bibliographic detail of Mason's descriptions but offer supplemental information about publication and production histories as well as identification of subsequent, pirated, and other variant editions and reprints unrecorded by or unknown to Mason. Primary coverage extends through 1989. Other sections alphabetically arrange annotated entries for books fully about Wilde (416 entries), partially about Wilde (1,023 entries), articles about Wilde (1,742 entries), and dissertations (142 unannotated entries). Comprehensive coverage extending from earliest critical responses to the 1990s includes entries for Wilde in yearbooks and reference works; non-English-language criticisms; reviews of Wilde's works and of works about Wilde; and poems, satires, plays, and other literary works alluding to Wilde. Mikolyzk's descriptive annotations are fuller than those provided for criticisms also identified by Mikhail. Mikolyzk does not, however, cover everything included in Mikhail. Also includes a Wilde chronology. Indexes of primary titles, critics, and detailed subjects (such as "Aestheticism," "Bibliographies," names of authors, and Wilde's works). Research on Wilde is reviewed by Ian Fletcher and John Stokes in Finneran's *Anglo-Irish Literature*, pp. 48-137; Wendell V. Harris in DeLaura's *Victorian Prose*, pp. 459-68; Lionel Stevenson in Faverty's *The Victorian Poets*, pp. 383-84; Elizabeth M. Richmond-Garza in Demastes and Kelly's *British Playwrights, 1880-1956*, pp. [409]-23; and Averil Gardner in Schrank and Demastes' *Irish Playwrights, 1880-1995: A Research and Production Sourcebook*, pp. 375-87.

Dictionaries, Encyclopedias, and Handbooks

1449.   Page, Norman. **An Oscar Wilde Chronology.** Boston: G. K. Hall, 1991. 105p. LC 90-27552. ISBN 0-8161-7298-6.

Selective and often superficial record of Wilde's life and career emphasizing Wilde's whereabouts and personal contacts. Supplying brief information on composition, revision, and publication only for "Wilde's more important works" (p. x), Page does not attempt to account for the circumstances for all of his writings. Gives perfunctory data for Wilde's many lecture engagements and tours and very little information on Wilde's reading. Depends heavily on Rupert Hart-Davis' edition of Wilde's letters, *The Letters of Oscar Wilde* (London: Rupert Hart-Davis, 1962), and on *More Letters of Oscar Wilde* (Oxford: Oxford University Press, 1985) and Richard Ellmann's standard biography, *Oscar Wilde* (London: H. Hamilton, 1987). All are cited throughout as sources for fuller information. Appends "The Oscar Wilde Circle," a directory briefly identifying family members, acquaintances, associates, and other individuals whom Wilde admired. Includes bibliographic sources (pp. 99-100). Indexes limited to titles of Wilde's major works and names of persons prohibit tracking Wilde's many activities, such as review writing and traveling. *An Oscar Wilde Chronology* is less useful than other chronologies by Page and others in the G. K. Hall/Macmillan series, under Page's general editorship.

Indexes and Concordances

1450.   Keyes, Ralph. **The Wit & Wisdom of Oscar Wilde: A Treasury of Quotations, Anecdotes, and Repartee**. New York: HarperCollins, 1996. 204p. ISBN 0-06-017367-X.

Topically arranges selected quotations from Wilde's writings, with appended citations to Wilde's works by title abbreviations and pages. "America," "Human Nature," "Pleasure," and "Virtue" are among the topical headings. Includes bibliography of sources (pp. 159-[61]). Thorough index of keywords. Keyes' compilation is generally more useful for research than Karl Beckson's *I Can Resist Everything Except Temptation: And Other Quotations from Oscar Wilde* (New York: Columbia University Press, 1996), an unindexed topical arrangement of excerpts from Wilde's works, with specific page and line references for first and reprinted appearances. Slightly less useful, Gyles Brandreth's *The Oscar Wilde Quotation Book: A Literary Companion* (London: Robert Hale, 1995) is a similarly arranged but unindexed collection citing titles of Wilde's works but not identifying editions or page and line references. Also available is Maria Leach's *The Importance of Being a Wit: The Insults of Oscar Wilde* (New York: Carroll and Graf, 1997), a topically arranged, unindexed listing of about 750 selected quotations from identified works by Wilde, but lacking specific citations and references to source editions.

Journals

1451.   **Wild About Wilde Newsletter**. Mount Airy, MD: Carmel McCaffrey, 1985- . 2/yr. ISSN 1068-9737.

Brief critical features on productions of Wilde's works as well as biographical and source studies. Occasional bibliographic contributions include Patrick M. Horan's "Researching Oscar Wilde," 8-9 (16 October 1990): 3-6. *Wild About Wilde Newsletter* is selectively indexed in *MLA*.

Amos N. Wilder, 1895-1993

Bibliographies

1452.   Beardslee, William A. **The Poetics of Faith: Essays Offered to Amos Niven Wilder**. Missoula, MT: Scholars Press, 1978. 2 vols. (Semeia, vols. 12-13). OCLC 4579977.

Vol. 2, pp. 263-87, contains an "Amos Niven Wilder Bibliography and Vita," giving brief imprint information in chronologically arranged sections for Wilder's works (books and contributions to periodicals, including Biblical and theological articles, poems, and book reviews), reviews of Wilder's works, three audiotape recordings of Wilder's works, two bibliographies, seven miscellaneous works about Wilder, and five works dedicated to Wilder. Coverage extends from 1920 to 1978. Unindexed. Also for works by Wilder, see *First Printings of American Authors*, vol. 3, pp. 359-62. Wilder's manuscripts are listed in Robbins' *American Literary Manuscripts*, p. 349.

Laura Ingalls Wilder, 1867-1957

Bibliographies

1453. Subramanian, Jane M. **Laura Ingalls Wilder: An Annotated Bibliography of Critical, Biographical, and Teaching Studies**. Westport, CT: Greenwood Press, 1997. 115p. (Bibliographies and Indexes in American Literature, no. 24). LC 96-33047. ISBN 0-313-29999-4.

Limited to works about Wilder. Descriptively annotated entries for about 400 books, booklets, dissertations, theses, articles, and book reviews published through mid-1995 alphabetically arranged in sections for critical works on Wilder, biographical works, Wilder and the Ingalls and Wilder families, teaching studies and materials, teaching kits, serial publications (four currently published titles), and book reviews. Source, author, and subject indexes. A significant number of items were not seen by Subramanian. Despite this caveat, Subramanian's coverage of works about Wilder supersedes that in Mary J. Mooney-Getoff's *Laura Ingalls Wilder: A Bibliography for Researchers, Writers, Teachers, Librarians, Students and Those Who Enjoy Reading About Laura*, 2d printing (Southold, NY: Wise Owl Press, 1981), although Mooney-Getoff's guide remains useful for brief bibliographic descriptions for Wilder's writings, with summaries and citations for subsequent appearances (including translations) and notes on primary research needs for Wilder (pp. 15-16). See *Bibliography of American Fiction, 1919-1988*, pp. 540-41, for Ellen M. Millsaps' checklist of works by and about Wilder. Wilder's manuscripts are listed in Robbins' *American Literary Manuscripts*, p. 350.

Thornton (Niven) Wilder, 1897-1975

Bibliographies

1454. Walsh, Claudette. **Thornton Wilder: A Reference Guide, 1926-1990**. New York: G. K. Hall, 1993. 449p. (Reference Guide to Literature). LC 91-13287. ISBN 0-8161-8790-8.

An "attempt to consolidate all literary criticism written in English about the works of Thornton Wilder from 1926 through 1990" (p. xi), Walsh chronologically arranges annotated entries for approximately 2,500 criticisms of Wilder published from 1926 to 1990. A substantial portion of the coverage includes book reviews featured in newspapers. Neutral annotations indicate reprintings and cite other works. Significant studies are described at length. Introduction briefly surveys Wilder's career and critical reception. Includes a Wilder chronology. Separate author and subject indexes offer limited access. The latter provides headings for proper names of persons and places and titles but not for topics. Walsh essentially supersedes coverage of works about Wilder in Goldstone and Anderson's *Thornton Wilder: An Annotated Bibliography of Works by and About Thornton Wilder* (entry 1455) and earlier checklists. See *Bibliography of American Fiction, 1919-1988*, pp. 542-44, for Goldstone's checklist of works by and about Wilder. Christopher J. Wheatley identifies works by and about Wilder in Demastes' *American Playwrights, 1880-1945*, pp. 437-52.

1455. Goldstone, Richard H., and Gary Anderson. **Thornton Wilder: An Annotated Bibliography of Works by and About Thornton Wilder**. New York: AMS, 1982. 104p. (AMS Studies in Modern Literature, no. 7). LC 79-6273. ISBN 0-404-18046-9.

Goldstone and Anderson describe works by and about Wilder published through 1979. Brief descriptive entries (largely summaries of contents) in separate listings cover his books and pamphlets; stories and plays contributed to periodicals; poems; literary criticisms; lectures and addresses; homages (published tributes to other authors); interviews and comments; introductions, prefaces, and forewords; published letters; screenplays; and miscellaneous works, such as librettos, excerpted conversations, and the like. Goldstone and Anderson briefly note the manuscripts of nearly all of Wilder's published novels and plays in the Collection of American Literature in Yale University's Beinecke Library (pp. 1-2). In addition, Goldstone and Anderson list about 500 books, articles and parts of books; reviews (arranged by works); and dissertations about Wilder. Selected secondary works are briefly described. Coverage of Wilder's primary materials largely supersedes that provided in J. M. Edelstein's *A Bibliographical Checklist of the Writings of Thornton Wilder* (New Haven, CT: Yale University Press, 1959), although Edelstein's work remains valuable for title-page descriptions and extensive physical details. Also for works by Wilder, see *First Printings of American Authors*, vol. 3, pp. 363-74. Wilder's manuscripts are listed in Robbins' *American Literary Manuscripts*, p. 350.

Charles W(alter) S(tansby) Williams, 1886-1945
Bibliographies
1456.   Glenn, Lois. **Charles W. S. Williams: A Checklist**. Kent, OH: Kent State University Press, 1975. 128p. (The Serif Series, Bibliographies and Checklists, no. 33). LC 75-17277. ISBN 0-87338-179-3.

Glenn gives brief bibliographic information (with contents) for works by Williams, including books of poetry, novels, plays, criticism, theology, and biographies; poems and stories; articles and letters; reviews; and edited works. In addition, Glenn identifies and selectively describes critical books, articles, parts of books, dissertations, and reviews (arranged by primary works) about Williams. Also for a bibliography of works by and about Williams, see *NCBEL*, IV, pp. 772-74.

Journals
See also *Mythlore* (entry 1371).

Heathcote Williams, 1941-
Bibliographies
King's *Twenty Modern British Playwrights*, pp. 269-71, lists works by Williams and describes works about him.

John A(lfred) Williams, 1925-
Bibliographies
For works by Williams, see *First Printings of American Authors*, vol. 2, pp. 387-88. See *Bibliography of American Fiction, 1919-1988*, pp. 545-46, for Gilbert H. Muller's checklist of works by and about Williams.

Jonathan Williams, 1929-
Bibliographies
1457.   Jaffe, James S. **Jonathan Williams: A Bibliographical Checklist of His Writings, 1950-1988**. Haverford, PA: James S. Jaffe Rare Books, 1989. 55p. ISBN 0-9622236-0-3.

Jaffe gives physical descriptions and brief publishing histories (with illustrations of title pages) for Williams' books, broadsides, postcards, and miscellaneous contributions dating from 1950 through 1988. Williams' manuscripts are listed in Robbins' *American Literary Manuscripts*, p. 351. John E. Bassett surveys works by and about Williams in Bain and Flora's *Contemporary Poets, Dramatists, Essayists, and Novelists of the South*, pp. [523]-34.

Tennessee (Thomas Lanier) Williams, 1911-1983
Bibliographies

1458.   Crandell, George W. **Tennessee Williams: A Descriptive Bibliography**. Pittsburgh, PA: University of Pittsburgh Press, 1995. 673p. (Pittsburgh Series in Bibliography). LC 93-27928. ISBN 0-8229-3769-7.

A much-needed guide—certain to be the standard—to the works of Williams. Chronologically arranges full bibliographic descriptions of Williams' works in sections for separate publications, with a subsection for collected editions; first-appearance contributions to books, pamphlets, and occasional publications; first appearances in magazines and newspapers, excluding interviews and articles quoting Williams; first appearances in magazines and newspapers of interviews and articles with previously unpublished quotes from Williams; Williams' works set to music; blurbs; sound recordings; and translations. Also includes notes on possible publications and other works not elsewhere described. Entries for all printings of Williams' 57 books, broadsides, and pamphlets in English through 1991 give facsimiles of title and copyright pages; collations; paginations; contents; descriptions of typography, paper, binding, and dust jackets; information on selected major performances; and notes on printing and publication histories, with copy locations. Supplies particularly detailed information on variants distinguishing subsequent reprintings of first and later editions. Identifies and locates 395 non-English-language editions of Williams. Comprehensive index of names and titles, with headings for publishers, printers, theaters, and the like.

1459.   Gunn, Drewey Wayne. **Tennessee Williams: A Bibliography**. Metuchen, NJ: Scarecrow Press, 1991. 2d ed. 434p. (Scarecrow Author Bibliographies, no. 89). LC 91-34939. ISBN 0-8108-2495-7.

Superseding Gunn's earlier *Tennessee Williams: A Bibliography* (Metuchen, NJ: Scarecrow Press, 1980) in scope and detail, Gunn's revision unfortunately amounts to an awkwardly arranged bibliographic handbook for both primary and secondary materials for Williams to 1991. Criticism (scholarship and reviews) on specific Williams' plays is grouped within sections for the individual plays that include substantial information about editions and productions. Gunn gives brief bibliographic descriptions of Williams' works in sections for plays and screenplays (subarranged for individual titles, with data for productions, collections, criticism, reports on conferences, and parodies and admonishments); short stories and novels (individual titles, with data for adaptations, collections, and criticism); poems and lyrics (individual titles, collections, criticism, and productions); occasional pieces, autobiography, and letters (individual titles, collections, published letters, and last will and testament); miscellaneous materials (recorded readings, paintings and sketches, and productions based on words or ideas); biographical sources (interviews and biographies, eulogies, other tributes, "Romans and Drames a Clef," productions based on Williams' life); manuscripts; translations and non-English-language productions; and other bibliographies. Entries for plays briefly identify plot and note archival materials; describe composition, production, and publication histories; list first and subsequent publications and versions (acting, anthologized, and the like), with citations for reviews; list scholarship and criticism (unannotated); and identify first and subsequent stage and media productions, with credits and citations for production reviews. Williams' papers in the Harry Ransom Humanities Research Center and manuscripts in collections at other institutions are also identified (pp. 338-63). Includes brief overview of Williams' career, a chronology of his life, and chronological list of his publications with references to entries. Separate indexes for names of actors, directors, and others associated with productions; musicians; and critics, editors, reviewers, and others associated with publications. Although the most comprehensive listing of works by and about Williams, the awkward arrangement, absence of annotations for criticism, and perfunctory indexing make Gunn's guide less than convenient. McCann's guide (entry 1460) remains useful for annotations and accessibility to earlier criticism. Williams' manuscripts are listed in Robbins' *American Literary Manuscripts*, pp. 351-52.

1460. McCann, John S. **The Critical Reputation of Tennessee Williams: A Reference Guide**. Boston: G. K. Hall, 1983. 430p. (A Reference Guide to Literature). 430p. LC 82-15706. ISBN 0-8161-8635-9.

McCann describes writings about Williams published from 1939 through 1981. Emphasis is on domestic reviews of publications and productions, although coverage includes popular and scholarly works, criticisms in non-English languages, dissertations, and book reviews. Annotations are descriptive and neutral. In addition to a solid introduction to Williams scholarship, McCann provides an excellent index. References for primary titles include subheadings for specific productions. Topical headings reference studies of "Christ figures" and Sigmund Freud, among others. Additional coverage of dissertations on Williams is offered in Tetsumaro Hayashi's *Arthur Miller and Tennessee Williams: Research Opportunities and Dissertation Abstracts* (Jefferson, NC: McFarland, 1983). Research on Williams is reviewed by Nancy M. Tischler in Flora and Bain's *Fifty Southern Writers After 1900*, pp. 526-34; and Pearl Amelia McHaney in *Contemporary Authors: Bibliographical Series: Volume 3: American Dramatists*, pp. 385-429.

Journals

1461. **Tennessee Williams Literary Journal**. Metairie, LA: W. Kenneth Holditch, 1989-. Annual. ISSN 1077-453X.

Published in association with the Tennessee Williams/New Orleans Literary Festival, this picks up in the wake of *Tennessee Williams Newsletter* (1979-80) and *Tennessee Williams Review* (1980-83). *Tennessee Williams Literary Journal* features critical articles and reviews of new publications. Contributions have addressed themes in Williams' works, discussed productions, and reviewed Williams' reception in Germany and the former Soviet Union. A bibliographic feature, "A Checklist of Tennessee Williams Scholarship," covering 1988 to 1990 and compiled by Pearl Amelia McHaney, last appeared in 2.1 (Winter 1990-91): 57-63. "Tennessee Williams Calendar" gives reports and information about productions, announcements for forthcoming publications, festivals, productions, conferences, and research in progress. Publication is nearly two years behind schedule. *Tennessee Williams Literary Journal* is indexed in *MLA*.

William Carlos Williams, 1883-1963

Bibliographies

1462. Wagner, Linda W. **William Carlos Williams: A Reference Guide**. Boston: G. K. Hall, 1978. 166p. (A Reference Publication in Literature). LC 77-9056. ISBN 0-8161-7977-8.

Wagner chronologically lists briefly annotated entries for about 1,200 secondary materials, covering books, articles, dissertations, and reviews. Annotations are descriptive. An index of names, with selected topical subheadings under Williams' name, provides access. Supplementing Wagner to 1982, Joseph Brogunier's "An Annotated Bibliography of Works About William Carlos Williams: 1974-1982," in Carroll F. Terrell's *William Carlos Williams: Man and Poet* (Orono, ME: National Poetry Foundation, University of Maine at Orono, 1983), pp. [453]-585, offers detailed descriptions of 231 works about Williams, covering books, articles, and dissertations, with citations to reviews. Research on Williams is reviewed by Wagner in Bryer's *Sixteen Modern American Authors*, pp. 573-85; and its supplement by Wagner-Martin (formerly Wagner) in Bryer's *Sixteen Modern American Authors: Volume 2: A Survey of Research and Criticism Since 1972*, pp. 675-715.

1463.   Wallace, Emily Mitchell. **A Bibliography of William Carlos Williams**. Middletown, CT: Wesleyan University Press, 1968. 354p. LC 68-27541.

The definitive bibliography of Williams' primary materials, Wallace's work gives detailed descriptions for books, pamphlets, and translations by Williams; contributions to books; contributions to periodicals (some 635 entries); miscellaneous writings (such as broadsides, leaflets, greeting cards, and the like); musical settings; recordings and radio scripts and transcripts; dust-jacket blurbs; an article in a medical journal; and translations of Williams' works (arranged by languages). Entries give title-page transcriptions, collations, contents, and publishing histories. Also for works by Williams, see *First Printings of American Authors*, vol. 3, pp. 375-92. Williams' manuscripts are listed in Robbins' *American Literary Manuscripts*, p. 352. Neil Baldwin and Steven L. Meyers' *The Manuscripts and Letters of William Carlos Williams in the Poetry Collection of the Lockwood Memorial Library* (Boston: G. K. Hall, 1978) describes the State University of New York at Buffalo's extensive collection of Williams materials, including manuscripts of poems, creative and critical prose, notebooks, letters, and other materials.

Journals

1464.   **William Carlos Williams Review**. Austin, TX: University of Texas, 1975- 2/yr. ISSN 0196-6286.

Formerly *William Carlos Williams Newsletter*, this journal features substantial scholarly studies as well as brief notes on biographical and critical topics related to Williams and interpretive studies of his works. Special issues have focused on Williams and history, women and feminist criticism, Marianne Moore, and Wallace Stevens (which contained bibliographies of Williams-Stevens correspondence and studies of the Williams-Stevens literary relationship). A double issue in 19.1-2 (Spring-Fall 1993) honors Mary Ellen Solt and Hugh Kenner. Additionally, *William Carlos Williams Review* publishes bibliographic features, such as Zhaoming Qian's "Works from the Library of William Carlos Williams at Fairleigh Dickinson: Addenda to the Descriptive List," 21.1 (Spring 1995): 53-67; and Christopher MacGowan's "William Carlos Williams and Rutherford: The Rutherford Free Public Library Collection," 20.2 (Fall 1994): 52-57. Since 1986 the journal has published a current bibliography of works (including media and research in progress) by and about Williams. *William Carlos Williams Review* is indexed in *AES*, *AHI*, *MHRA*, and *MLA*.

Jack Williamson, 1908-

Bibliographies

1465.   Myers, Robert E. **Jack Williamson: A Primary and Secondary Bibliography**. Boston: G. K. Hall, 1980. 93p. (Masters of Science Fiction and Fantasy). LC 79-18471. ISBN 0-8161-8158-6.

Myers' awkwardly organized guide provides separate chronological lists of Williamson's works by genre, covering fiction books, stories, and selections published from 1928 through 1979 (161 entries); miscellaneous media (scripts, recordings, and the like) from 1933 through 1978; nonfiction from 1928 through 1978 (168 entries); criticisms and reviews; and non-English-language editions. Entries generally describe contents. Appendixes add other materials (unannotated). A complex set of indexes for these formats attempts to pull the listings together.

Calder (Baynard) Willingham, (Jr.), 1922-1995

Bibliographies

For works by Willingham, see *First Printings of American Authors*, vol. 1, pp. 415-16. Willingham's manuscripts are listed in Robbins' *American Literary Manuscripts*, p. 352.

N(athaniel) P(arker) Willis, 1806-1867

Bibliographies

For works by Willis, see *Bibliography of American Literature*, vol. 9, pp. 312-66. Contributions by Willis and criticism and reviews of Willis' works in selected periodicals are identified in Wells' *The Literary Index to American Magazines, 1815-1865*, pp. 165-67; and *The Literary Index to American Magazines, 1850-1900*, pp. 417-18. Willis' manuscripts are listed in Robbins' *American Literary Manuscripts*, pp. 352-53.

Sir Angus Frank Johnstone Wilson, 1913-1991

Bibliographies

1466. Stape, J. H., and Anne N. Thomas. **Angus Wilson: A Bibliography, 1947-1987**. London: Mansell, 1988. 327p. LC 87-31246. ISBN 0-7201-1872-7.

Covers works by and about Wilson. Stape and Thomas supply separate listings for Wilson's books; contributions to books, edited works, and stories in anthologies; contributions to periodicals and newspapers (615 entries); translations of Wilson's works (arranged by languages); interviews; recordings; broadcast talks, radio and television interviews, discussions, and productions; manuscripts, working papers, and letters; miscellaneous works, such as international editions, editions for the blind, misattributed works, and reported speeches; and works announced but not published. Also contains unannotated entries for 191 books, articles, theses, dissertations, 1,271 reviews (arranged by works), and other works about Wilson. The University of Iowa's extensive collection of Wilson's materials is described in Frederick P. W. McDowell and E. Sharon Graves' *The Angus Wilson Manuscripts in the University of Iowa Libraries* (Iowa City, IA: Friends of the University of Iowa Libraries, 1969), as well as in Stape and Thomas' bibliography (pp. 133-43). Stape and Thomas' coverage for works by and about Wilson supersedes that provided in Stanton's *A Bibliography of Modern British Novelists*, pp. 997-1071, 1110-23. Also for a bibliography of works by and about Wilson, see *NCBEL*, IV, pp. 776-77.

Augusta Jane Evans Wilson, 1835-1909

Bibliographies

For works by Wilson, see *Bibliography of American Literature*, vol. 9, pp. 369-72. Wilson's manuscripts are listed in Robbins' *American Literary Manuscripts*, p. 353. See *Bibliography of American Fiction Through 1865*, pp. 280-81, for a checklist of works by and about Wilson. Lynne P. Shackelford surveys works by and about Wilson in Bain and Flora's *Fifty Southern Writers Before 1900*, pp. 530-40.

Colin Henry Wilson, 1931-

Bibliographies

1467. Stanley, Colin. **Work of Colin Wilson: An Annotated Bibliography & Guide**. San Bernardino, CA: Borgo Press, 1989. 312p. (Bibliographies of Modern Authors, no. 1). LC 84-11181. ISBN 0-89370-817-8.

Describing works by and about Wilson, Stanley gives brief bibliographic information, notes on translations and reprintings, summaries of contents, brief critical comments, and references to secondary studies and reviews in separate listings for Wilson's books, short fiction, nonfiction (340 selectively annotated entries), introductions and afterwords, book reviews, recordings, and edited works. In addition, Stanley cites books, articles, interviews, and other works about Wilson. Stanley's guide also details the Shea Collection of Wilson's primary and secondary materials in the University of California at Riverside's Special Collections Department of the Tomas Rivera Library and another important collection in the University of Texas' Harry Ransom Humanities Research Center (pp. 242-43).

Harriet Wilson, 1808-c. 1870

Bibliographies

See *Bibliography of American Fiction Through 1865*, p. 282, for a checklist of works by and about Wilson.

Harry Leon Wilson, 1867-1939

Bibliographies

See *Bibliography of American Fiction, 1866-1918*, p. 357, for David M. Craig's checklist of works by and about Wilson. Wilson's manuscripts are listed in Robbins' *American Literary Manuscripts*, p. 353.

Lanford Wilson, 1937-

Bibliographies

King's *Ten Modern American Playwrights*, pp. 235-43, gives brief bibliographic information for Wilson's primary works and annotated entries for criticism of Wilson, with a classified list of reviews. Martin J. Jacobi reviews research on Wilson in *Contemporary Authors: Bibliographical Series: Volume 3: American Dramatists*, pp. 431-54.

Margaret Wilson, 1882-1973

Bibliographies

For works by Wilson, see *First Printings of American Authors*, vol. 5, pp. 363-64. Wilson's manuscripts are listed in Robbins' *American Literary Manuscripts*, p. 354.

Thomas Wilson, c. 1525-1581

Bibliographies

For a bibliography of works by and about Wilson, see *NCBEL*, I, pp. 1824, 2276, 2308, 2329. Wilson's manuscripts are described in *Index of English Literary Manuscripts*, I, pt. 2:557-59.

Donald Windham, 1920-

Bibliographies

1468.   Kellner, Bruce. **Donald Windham: A Bio-Bibliography**. New York: Greenwood, 1991. 92p. (Bio-Bibliographies in American Literature, no. 2). LC 91-10777. ISBN 0-313-26857-6.

Chronologically arranges entries for works by and about Windham in sections for books and pamphlets, including translations; edited books and contributions to books and pamphlets; contributions to periodicals; ephemera; and biography and criticism, with annotated entries for 132 reviews, interviews, introductions and chapters in books, citations in reference works, and the like, published from 1943 through 1987. Full bibliographic descriptions of primary works, with title-page transcriptions, collations, contents, binding descriptions, and publication histories for first and subsequent editions. Introduction reviews Windham's writings and life; also includes "Footnote from a Would-be Lop-eared Rabbit," by Windham. Index of primary titles and personal names as authors and subjects.

William Winter, 1836-1917

Bibliographies

For works by Winter, see *Bibliography of American Literature*, vol. 9, pp. 373-408. Winter's contributions to selected periodicals and reviews of Winter's works are identified in Wells' *The Literary Index to American Magazines, 1850-1900*, pp. 418-19. Winter's manuscripts are listed in Robbins' *American Literary Manuscripts*, pp. 355-56.

(Arthur) Yvor Winters, 1900-1968

Bibliographies

1469. Powell, Grosvenor. **Yvor Winters: An Annotated Bibliography, 1919-1982.** Metuchen, NJ: Scarecrow Press, 1983. 202p. (Scarecrow Author Bibliographies, no. 66). LC 83-14466. ISBN 0-8108-1653-9.

Powell describes works by and about Winters. Separate listings for primary materials cover separately published books and collections of essays; books of poetry; edited books; essays and review articles; poems; translations of poetry; recorded readings; reviews; and miscellaneous writings, such as brief notes, letters in journals, and other works. Entries give brief bibliographic information, with extended summaries of contents. Coverage of secondary works (selectively and less extensively annotated) includes books and collections of essays, articles, reviews, dissertations, and passing references. Helpful author, title, and subject indexing concludes the volume. Also for works by Winters, see *First Printings of American Authors*, vol. 2, pp. 389-92. Winters' manuscripts are listed in Robbins' *American Literary Manuscripts*, p. 356.

Theodore Winthrop, 1828-1861

Bibliographies

For works by Winthrop, see *Bibliography of American Literature*, vol. 9, pp. 409-12. Winthrop's manuscripts are listed in Robbins' *American Literary Manuscripts*, p. 356. See *Bibliography of American Fiction Through 1865*, pp. 283-84, for a checklist of works by and about Winthrop.

John Wise, 1652-1725

Bibliographies

For works by Wise, see *First Printings of American Authors*, vol. 4, p. 389. Robbins' *American Literary Manuscripts*, p. 357, lists one manuscript for Wise.

Adele Wiseman, 1928-1992

Bibliographies

1470. Panofsky, Ruth. **Adele Wiseman: An Annotated Bibliography.** Toronto: ECW Press, 1992. 130p. LC 92-94014. ISBN 1-550-22103-5.

Describes works by and about Wiseman. Part I provides chronologically arranged listings of Wiseman's books (novels, plays, poetry, children's books, nonfiction, editorial works), excerpts, and manuscripts; contributed short fiction, poems, articles, book reviews, letters, and audiovisual materials; and awards and honors. Entries for books give brief bibliographic data for editions, including reprintings and translations. Entries for manuscripts describe specific holdings in special collections. Part II consists of descriptively annotated entries for some 181 selected reviews listed in sections for Wiseman's individual works, 192 articles in newspapers, interviews, and profiles, and 190 chapters and parts of books, entries in references works, creative works in which Wiseman appears, and other mentions of Wiseman. Indexed by critics.

Owen Wister, 1860-1938

Bibliographies

For works by Wister, see *First Printings of American Authors*, vol. 4, pp. 391-97. Wister's contributions to selected periodicals and reviews of Wister's works are identified in Wells' *The Literary Index to American Magazines, 1850-1900*, p. 420. Wister's manuscripts are listed in Robbins' *American Literary Manuscripts*, pp. 357-58. Also available is the Library of Congress' Manuscript Division's *Owen Wister: A Register of His Papers in the Library of Congress* (Washington, DC: Library of Congress, 1972). See *Bibliography of American Fiction, 1866-1918*, pp. 358-60, for Gary E. Lovan's checklist of works by and about Wister. Neal Lambert surveys works by and about Wister in Erisman and Etulain's *Fifty Western Writers*, pp. 519-31.

George Wither, 1588-1667
Bibliographies
For a bibliography of works by and about Wither, see *NCBEL*, I, pp. 1191-94. Wither's manuscripts are described in *Index of English Literary Manuscripts*, II, pt. 2:637-48.

Sir P(elham) G(renville) Wodehouse, 1881-1975
Bibliographies
1471.   Heineman, James H., and Donald R. Bensen. **P. G. Wodehouse: A Centenary Celebration, 1881-1981**. New York: Pierpont Morgan Library and Oxford University Press, 1981. 197p. LC 81-83357. ISBN 0-1952-0357-7.
Now mainly useful for essays on the composition and publication of Wodehouse's works, this also includes Eileen McIlvaine's "A Bibliography of P. G. Wodehouse" (pp. 91-197), which gives detailed descriptions in separate listings for first English and American editions of novels, collected works, semiautobiographical works, plays, Tauchnitz editions, autograph editions, contributions to anthologies, introductions and prefaces, translations, and stage and screen productions, as well as for books, parts of books, articles, and other works about Wodehouse, such as imitations and parodies. Entries for primary materials present title-page transcriptions (with illustrations), physical descriptions, and publishing histories. Largely superseded by McIlvaine, Sherby, and Heineman's *P. G. Wodehouse: A Comprehensive Bibliography and Checklist* (entry 1472).

1472.   McIlvaine, Eileen, and Louise S. Sherby, and James H. Heineman. **P. G. Wodehouse: A Comprehensive Bibliography and Checklist**. New York: James H. Heineman, Inc., 1990. 489p. ISBN 0-87008-125-X.
Expanding the bibliography in Heineman and Bensen's *P. G. Wodehouse: A Centenary Celebration, 1881-1981* (entry 1471), McIlvaine, Sherby, and Heineman's guide gives full bibliographic descriptions of Wodehouse's works in sections for the novels and semiautobiographical works; "omnibus volumes" (collections and anthologies of short stories and plays); published plays, including adaptations; contributions to periodicals (briefly listing 1,765 articles arranged under the titles of 148 different journals); contributions to anthologies, introductions, and prefaces; translations (arranged by language); and published music. Other sections list works about Wodehouse (with some 283 unannotated entries); the "Dramatic Wodehouse" (stage and film adaptations); named editions (Autograph, Tauchnitz, and other special editions); imitations, parodies, tributes, and other creative works about Wodehouse; manuscripts and archives; and letters and correspondence. Also contains checklists of major private collections and Wodehouse societies, dealers, collectors, libraries with Wodehouse collections, and so forth. Entries for 103 first editions and American issues give title-page transcriptions, collations, physical details of bindings and dust jackets, contents, notes on publication history, and extensive citations for reissues and other subsequent editions. Index of names and titles. Also for a bibliography of works by and about Wodehouse, see *NCBEL*, IV, pp. 778-81. McIlvaine, Sherby, and Heineman's guide gives far more bibliographic data than David A. Jasen's *A Bibliography and Reader's Guide to the First Editions of P. G. Wodehouse* (entry 1474), which is more a dictionary of characters than a bibliography.

Dictionaries, Encyclopedias, and Handbooks
1473.   Garrison, Daniel H. **Daniel Garrison's Who's Who in Wodehouse**. New York: Peter Lang, 1987. 219p. LC 86-27657. ISBN 0-8204-0517-5.
Straight forward guide to Wodehouse's characters. Briefly identifies and locates (with cross-references to first editions of novels and collections) more than

2,100 characters in Wodehouse's writings, of whom, according to Garrison, more than 300—"about one in seven" (p. x)—reappears elsewhere. Appends tables of titles and collections and lists of drones, butlers, and valets.

1474. Jasen, David A. **A Bibliography and Reader's Guide to the First Editions of P. G. Wodehouse**. 2d ed., revised and expanded. London: Greenhill Books, 1986. 306p. LC 73-105397. ISBN 0-9478-9818-2.

Revising his 1970 edition (Hamden, CT: Archon Books), Jasen gives brief bibliographic information for first editions of Wodehouse's 91 novels to 1970 but the work is mainly valuable as a dictionary of characters. Identifies and cross-references fictional persons, places, and things by the pages in which they appear in first editions. Indexes to publishers and their titles, characters, and places and things. *Daniel Garrison's Who's Who in Wodehouse* (entry 1473) expands on Jasen's coverage. Also a straightforward index of persons, places, and things in Wodehouse (covering 91 works) is Geoffrey Jaggard's *Wooster's World: A Companion to the Wooster-Jeeves Cycle of P. G. Wodehouse, LL.D.* (London: Macdonald, 1967). Conflating and updating his previous *Wodehouse at Work to the End* (London: Herbert Jenkins, 1961; revised London: Barrie & Jenkins, 1976) and *A Wodehouse Companion* (London: Elm Tree Books/Hamish Hamilton, 1981), Richard Usborne's *The Penguin Wodehouse Companion* (London: Penguin Books, 1988) gives plot summaries aimed at readers already familiar with Wodehouse.

Indexes and Concordances

1475. Usborne, Richard. **Wodehouse Nuggets**. 1983; reprint New York: Heineman, 1993. 231p. LC 91-138009. ISBN 0-87008-073-3.

Intended more for bed-and-bath reading than for research. Arranges approximately 2,000 brief quotations from Wodehouse's works (without page references) in some 17 rather picturesque categories; such as "Aunts and Uncles," "Golf," and "Insults and Other Hints of Disapproval." Lacks list of sources and index. A more scholarly verbal index is among Wodehouse desiderata.

Larry (Alfred) Woiwode, 1941-

Bibliographies

For works by Woiwode, see *First Printings of American Authors*, vol. 2, p. 393.

Gene Wolfe, 1931-

Bibliographies

See *Bibliography of American Fiction, 1919-1988*, pp. 547-48, for Harold Billings' checklist of works by and about Wolfe. See Donald G. Keller's summary biography, critical assessment of major works, and selected primary and secondary bibliography for Wolfe in McCaffery's *Postmodern Fiction: A Bio-Bibliographical Guide*, pp. 554-58.

Dictionaries, Encyclopedias, and Handbooks

1476. Andre Driussi, Michael. **Lexicon Urthus: A Dictionary for the Urth Cycle**. San Francisco: Sirius Fiction, 1994. 280p. ISBN 0-9642795-9-2.

"A brief Lexicon to Gene Wolfe's *The Book of the New Sun, The Urth of the New Sun*, and *Empires of Foliage and Flower* as well as shorter stories, including glosses on Biblical Allusions, Ships of Sail and Oar, Kabbalistic Notions, Archaic English Words, Diverse Arms and Armor, Extinct and Exotic Animals, Latin Terms military and civic, in addition to Myths and Legends, from China, Greece, Arabia, Oceania, Rome, India, Persia, and South America" (p. [xv]). Entries specifically cross-reference chapters and pages mostly in Wolfe's book-club hardcover editions and other sources (listed on p. xvi and in the "Selected bibliography," pp. 279-80) as well as sources such as the *OED* and standard dictionaries of myths. Wolfe's "Green Man" from *The Claw of the Conciliator*, for example, is related to "the Arthurian 'Green Knight' as well as the American Bigfoot" (p. 118). Includes tables of elements, holidays, saints, the solar system, and time lines, with black-and-white illustrations. Appends selective classified listings of animals, armor, arms, gods and goddesses, hydrography, peoples, settlements, and ships.

Thomas (Clayton) Wolfe, 1900-1938
Bibliographies

1477.   Bassett, John E. **Thomas Wolfe: An Annotated Critical Bibliography**. Lanham, MD: Scarecrow Press, 1996. 432p. (Scarecrow Author Bibliographies, no. 96). LC 96-4420. ISBN 0-8108-3146-5.

Bassett's "reasonably comprehensive listing" (p. [xi]) of English-language criticism and scholarship and selected non-English-language works on Wolfe is "not intended to replace" Phillipson's *Thomas Wolfe: A Reference Guide* (entry 1479). Offers 2,876 selectively annotated entries in awkwardly arranged sections for books (works of more than 100 pages) about Wolfe; reviews and critical articles in sublistings for each of the four novels; reviews in sublistings for each of the collections of short stories, plays, and other writings published before and after 1970; critical studies of short stories, plays, and other writings; general critical, biographical, and bibliographic studies; and other materials, including reviews of books about Wolfe, dissertations, non-English-language criticisms, and other items. Coverage extends to 1994. Typically brief annotations critically assess scholarly contributions, identifying works as superseded as well as indispensable. Introduction summarizes critical responses to Wolfe from earliest reviews to the present. Indexing limited to critics' names.

1478.   Johnston, Carol. **Thomas Wolfe: A Descriptive Bibliography**. Pittsburgh, PA: University of Pittsburgh Press, 1987. 295p. (Pittsburgh Series in Bibliography). LC 86-16192. ISBN 0-8229-3546-5.

The definitive listing of Wolfe's primary works, Johnston's guide supersedes Elmer D. Johnson's *Thomas Wolfe: A Checklist* (Kent, OH: Kent State University Press, 1970). Johnston provides detailed bibliographic descriptions for first American and British editions of separately published works (with illustrations of title pages and dust jackets), including novels, letters, interviews, and plays; posthumously published collections; first appearances in books; contributions to journals and newspapers; privately printed works, including contributions by Wolfe; and writings attributed to Wolfe, including juvenilia. Appends a selective, unannotated list of principal works about Wolfe. Also for works by Wolfe, see *First Printings of American Authors*, vol. 1, pp. 417-20. Wolfe's manuscripts are listed in Robbins' *American Literary Manuscripts*, p. 358.

1479.   Phillipson, John S. **Thomas Wolfe: A Reference Guide**. Boston: G. K. Hall, 1977. 218p. (Reference Guides in Literature). LC 76-43352. ISBN 0-8161-7878-x.

Phillipson's work chronologically arranges annotated entries for about 800 secondary materials published from 1929 through 1976. Coverage includes books, parts of books, and articles, with separately listed, unannotated entries for dissertations and non-English-language criticisms. Annotations are descriptive and unbiased, although significant studies receive extended review. Phillipson briefly notes important collections of Wolfe's primary materials in Harvard University's William B. Wisdom Collection and at other institutions (p. xi). The index of names offers headings for primary works and topics under Wolfe's name (such as "And Jews" and "Death of"). Phillipson updates coverage in "Thomas Wolfe: A Reference Guide Updated," *Resources for American Literary Study* 11 (1981): 37-80; and supersedes coverage of Paschal Reeves' *Thomas Wolfe: The Critical Reception* (New York: David Lewis, 1975). See also *Bibliography of American Fiction, 1919-1988*, pp. 549-52, for Carol Johnston's checklist of works by and about Wolfe. Research on Wolfe is reviewed by C. Hugh Holman in Bryer's *Sixteen Modern American Authors*, pp. 587-624; and the supplement by Richard S. Kennedy in Bryer's *Sixteen Modern American Authors: Volume 2: A Survey of Research and Criticism Since 1972*, pp.

716-55; and by Kennedy in Flora and Bain's *Fifty Southern Writers After 1900*, pp. 535-44.

Dictionaries, Encyclopedias, and Handbooks

1480.　Idol, John Lane, Jr. **A Thomas Wolfe Companion**. Westport, CT: Greenwood Press, 1987. 205p. LC 87-268. ISBN 0-313-23829-4.

　　　　A guide to Wolfe's life, career, writings, and critical reception. Idol summarizes each of Wolfe's works and identifies characters and places (with charts for familial relationships). In addition, Idol notes reference resources for research on Wolfe and lists selected criticisms, updating Phillipson's secondary bibliography (entry 1479).

Journals

1481.　**The Thomas Wolfe Review**. Akron, OH: Thomas Wolfe Society, 1977-. 2/yr. ISSN 0276-5683.

　　　　"Reminiscences, criticism, bibliography, and in general, news of interest to readers and students of Wolfe, professionally, or otherwise" are among the five to eight brief articles and features that regularly appear in issues of this journal, formerly titled *Thomas Wolfe Newsletter*. Critical studies tend to focus on particular works, problems, or questions. Other contributions have discussed Wolfe and Ovid, Melville, Mencken, and T. S. Eliot, among others. A significant number provide biographical information. Issues publish poems in imitation of Wolfe and report on the annual Thomas Wolfe Festival. Several regularly published significant features offer Wolfe scholars and hobbyists a range of information. "Wolfe Trails: News and Notes" relates recent activities of prominent Wolfe scholars, collectors, acquaintances, and associates; some possess scholarly value. "The Wolfe Pack: Bibliography" is an annotated list of recent criticism, covering books, articles, and media and noting forthcoming works. "Wolfe Calls: Questions and Answers" is a veritable notes and queries for Wolfeiana. Finally, "Thomas Wolfe Society News" announces prizes, papers, publications, meetings, call for papers, and the like. *The Thomas Wolfe Review* is indexed by *AHI, A&HCI, MHRA*, and *MLA*.

Maritta Wolff, 1918-

Bibliographies

　　　　For works by Wolff, see *First Printings of American Authors*, vol. 3, pp. 393-94. Wolff's manuscripts are listed in Robbins' *American Literary Manuscripts*, p. 358.

Mary Wollstonecraft, 1759-1797

Bibliographies

1482.　Todd, Janet M. **Mary Wollstonecraft: An Annotated Bibliography**. New York: Garland, 1976. 124p. (Reference Library in the Humanities, vol. 36). LC 75-24095. ISBN 0-8240-9976-1.

　　　　Following an excellent critical introduction to Wollstonecraft's primary and secondary materials and a checklist of her works (with descriptive summaries), Todd chronologically arranges (within sections for the periods 1788 to 1800, 1800 to 1900, and 1900 to 1975) descriptions for more than 700 mostly English-language secondary works (including reviews) about Wollstonecraft. No index whatsoever is included. Also for John Barnard's bibliography of works by and about Wollstonecraft, see *NCBEL*, II, pp. 1254-56.

Journals

　　　　See Patterson's *Author Newsletters and Journals*, p. 348, for previously published journals for Wollstonecraft.

Charles Wood, 1932-

Bibliographies

King's *Twenty Modern British Playwrights*, pp. 273-77, lists works by Wood and describes works about him.

Sarah Sayward Barrell Keating Wood, 1759-1855

Bibliographies

See *Bibliography of American Fiction Through 1865*, pp. 284-85, for a checklist of works by and about Wood.

George Edward Woodberry, 1855-1930

Bibliographies

For works by Woodberry, see *Bibliography of American Literature*, vol. 9, pp. 413-38. Woodberry's contributions to selected periodicals and reviews of Woodberry's works are identified in Wells' *The Literary Index to American Magazines, 1850-1900*, pp. 425-26. Woodberry's manuscripts are listed in Robbins' *American Literary Manuscripts*, p. 359.

Samuel Woodworth, 1785-1842

Bibliographies

For works by Woodworth, see *Bibliography of American Literature*, vol. 9, pp. 439-69. Contributions by Woodworth and criticism and reviews of Woodworth's works in selected periodicals are identified in Wells' *The Literary Index to American Magazines, 1815-1865*, p. 168. Woodworth's manuscripts are listed in Robbins' *American Literary Manuscripts*, p. 359.

Leonard Sidney Woolf, 1880-1969

Bibliographies

1483.   Luedeking, Leila, and Michael Edmonds. **Leonard Woolf: A Bibliography**. Winchester: St. Paul's; Oak Knoll, 1992. 296p. (Winchester Bibliographies of 20th Century Writers). ISBN 1-873040-10-5.

Full bibliographic descriptions of Woolf's works published from 1901 to 1991 chronologically arranged in sections for separately published books and pamphlets, contributions to books, contributions to periodicals, and manuscript collections in the United Kingdom, United States, and Canada, with appendixed descriptions of Woolf's writings for the cooperative movement, Labor Party and Fabian Society, and book reviews. Forty-six entries for first and subsequent editions, issues, printings, and translations of books give title-page transcriptions, format and collation, binding descriptions, and notes on composition and publication history. Includes brief chronology of Woolf's life. Entries for Woolf's 1,566 periodical contributions give brief bibliographic information with summary contents and citations for other appearances. Name, title, and limited subject indexing.

(Adeline) Virginia Woolf, 1882-1941

Bibliographies

1484.   Kirkpatrick, B. J. **A Bibliography of Virginia Woolf**. 3d ed. New York: Oxford University Press, 1980. 268p. (Soho Bibliographies, no. 9). LC 79-42786. ISBN 0-19-818185-x.

First published in 1957 and revised in 1967 (both London: Hart-Davis), Kirkpatrick is the best listing of Woolf's primary works, including full bibliographic descriptions in separate listings for English and American editions and variants of books and pamphlets (with locations of copies), contributions to books and books translated by Woolf, contributions to journals and newspapers, translations of Woolf's works, miscellaneous works (non-English editions, parodies, announced but unpublished works, large-print editions, and the like), published single or collected letters, and manuscript collections. Kirkpatrick's guide (pp.

241-42) describes Woolf's notebooks, manuscripts of published works, diaries, and other materials in the Berg Collection of the New York Public Library, as well as other major collections at King's College, Cambridge (p. 243), which contains the papers of Clive Bell, Vanessa Bell, and Duncan Grant; and the University of Sussex, which holds the Monk's House Papers. Entries include title-page transcriptions and detailed publication histories. Indexing is limited to titles and authors. References in the bibliographic descriptions are not indexed. Woolf manuscripts in the Berg collection are also covered in *The Virginia Woolf Manuscripts: From the Henry W. and Albert A. Berg Collection at the New York Public Library: A Comprehensive, Convenient Source for Studying This Remarkable Woman & Her World* (Woodbridge, CT: Research Publications International, 1993). Woolf materials in the University of Texas' Harry Ransom Humanities Research Center are described in the *Catalogue of the Books from the Library of Leonard and Virginia Woolf* (London: Holleyman and Treacher, 1975).

1485.   Rice, Thomas Jackson. **Virginia Woolf: A Guide to Research**. New York: Garland, 1984. 258p. (Garland Reference Library of the Humanities, vol. 432). LC 83-48264. ISBN 0-8240-9084-5.

Superseding the coverage of Robin Majumdar's *Virginia Woolf: An Annotated Bibliography of Criticism, 1915-1974* (New York: Garland, 1976), Rice provides descriptive and evaluative entries for 1,358 works by and about Woolf published through 1984. Detailed descriptions of contents are provided for Woolf's primary works, including novels, short fiction, essays, autobiographies, diaries, letters, and manuscript transcriptions and scholarly editions. Coverage of secondary materials includes bibliographies, biographies, and criticisms in books, articles, and dissertations, including non-English-language scholarship. Also for a bibliography of works by and about Woolf, see *NCBEL*, IV, pp. 472-81.

Dictionaries, Encyclopedias, and Handbooks

1486.   Bishop, Edward. **A Virginia Woolf Chronology**. Boston: G. K. Hall, 1989. 268p. LC 88-4097. ISBN 0-8161-8982-x.

As in other chronologies in this Macmillan/G. K. Hall series (published in England as the "Macmillan Author Chronologies" series), the chronology's integrity depends on the authority of the sources on which it is based. Bishop employs a wide range of standard autobiographical, biographical, and bibliographic sources to produce an effective research tool. Among those included are Anne Oliver Bell and Andrew McNellie's edition of *Diary of Virginia Woolf* (London: Hogarth Press, 1977-84); Nigel Nicolson and Joanne Trautmann's edition of *The Letters of Virginia Woolf* (London: Hogarth Press, 1975-80); Jeanne Schulkind's edition of *Moments of Being: Unpublished Autobiographical Writings of Virginia Woolf*, 2d ed. (London: Hogarth Press, 1985); Leonard Woolf's *Autobiography* (London: Hogarth Press, 1960-69); Quentin Bell's *Virginia Woolf: A Biography* (London: Hogarth Press, 1972); and B. J. Kirkpatrick's bibliography (entry 1484). Other sources in the Berg Collection of the New York Public Library and in the Monk's House Papers, University of Sussex, are also cited. Entries reference concurrent literary, artistic, social, and political events as well as titles of works published by the Hogarth Press. The result is a chronology that is both authoritative, insightful, and accessible.

1487.   Hussey, Mark. **Virginia Woolf A to Z: A Comprehensive Reference for Students, Teachers, and Common Readers to Her Life, Work, and Critical Reception**. New York: Facts on File, 1995. 452p. LC 94-36500. ISBN 0-8160-3020-0.

A very readable handbook to Woolf's life and works. Lengthy and well-cross-referenced entries for each of the novels and other works outline plots, discuss composition and background, and survey critical responses, with citations to works for further reading. Other entries identify fictional and real persons, places, events, and things in Woolf's works and life. Includes bibliographic references (pp. 397-429) and index. Topical list of entries and comprehensive index provide excellent access.

1488. Steele, Elizabeth. **Virginia Woolf's Literary Sources and Allusions: A Guide to the Essays**. New York: Garland, 1983. 364p. (Garland Reference Library of the Humanities, vol. 397). LC 82-49166. ISBN 0-8240-9169-8.

Steele supplies brief information about Woolf's reading and writing and the sources and allusions appearing in Woolf's reading notes and papers for her more than 500 critical reviews and essays published in 10 collections. Appendixes list the reviews and essays by collection and identify addenda to literary works in Woolf's library, now at Washington State University and in the University of Texas' Harry Ransom Humanities Research Center. This guide is complemented by Steele's *Virginia Woolf's Rediscovered Essays: Sources and Allusions* (New York: Garland, 1987), which identifies sources and allusions in 268 uncollected essays by Woolf published in periodicals and newspapers from 1904 through 1941.

Indexes and Concordances

1489. Haule, James M., and Philip H. Smith, Jr. **A Concordance to the Novels of Virginia Woolf**. New York: Garland, 1991. 3 vols. (Garland Reference Library of the Humanities, vol. 1005). LC 91-12218. ISBN 0-8240-6339-2.

A "union" or combined text concordance to Woolf's nine novels, based on the Harcourt Brace first American editions and impressions (cited below), with cumulative stop-word and frequency appendixes. Haule and Smith previously published the concordances to each of the novels in *Concordances to the Novels of Virginia Woolf* (Ann Arbor, MI: University Microfilms International, 1988), consisting of 85 microfiche. This set includes the concordances to *The Voyage Out* (based on the New York: Harcourt, Brace, 1926 edition) and *Jacob's Room* (based on the New York: Harcourt, Brace, 1923 edition) in vols. 8 and 9 and reprints the concordances of vols. 1 through 7 which were first separately published as:

1489.1. Haule, James M., and Philip H. Smith, Jr. **A Concordance to Between the Acts by Virginia Woolf**. Oxford: Oxford Microform Publications, 1982. 7 microfiche. (Concordances to the Novels of Virginia Woolf, vol. 1). ISBN 0-9047-3581-8.

This concords the text of the first American edition of *Between the Acts* (New York: Harcourt, Brace, 1941).

1489.2. Haule, James M., and Philip H. Smith, Jr. **A Concordance to The Waves by Virginia Woolf**. Oxford: Oxford Microform Publications, 1981. 14 microfiche. (Concordances to the Novels of Virginia Woolf, vol. 2). ISBN 0-9047-3574-5.

Concords the text of the first American edition of *The Waves* (New York: Harcourt, Brace, 1931).

1489.3. Haule, James M., and Philip H. Smith, Jr. **A Concordance to To the Lighthouse by Virginia Woolf**. Oxford: Oxford Microform Publications, 1983. 7 microfiche. (Concordances to the Novels of Virginia Woolf, vol. 3). ISBN 0-9047-3581-8.

Based on the first American edition of *To the Lighthouse* (New York: Harcourt, Brace, 1927).

1489.4. Haule, James M., and Philip H. Smith, Jr. **A Concordance to The Years by Virginia Woolf**. Oxford Microform Publications, 1984. 11 microfiche. (Concordances to the Novels of Virginia Woolf, vol. 4). ISBN 0-0803-3344-3.

This concords the text of the first American edition of *The Years* (New York: Harcourt, Brace, 1937).

1489.5. Haule, James M., and Philip H. Smith, Jr. **A Concordance to Mrs. Dalloway by Virginia Woolf**. London: Oxford Microform Publications, 1984. 7 microfiche. (Concordances to the Novels of Virginia Woolf, vol. 5). ISBN 0-0803-3345-1.
Concords the text of *Mrs. Dalloway* (New York: Harcourt, Brace, 1925).

1489.6. Haule, James M., and Philip H. Smith, Jr. **A Concordance to Orlando by Virginia Woolf**. London: Oxford Microform Publications, 1985. 8 microfiche. (Concordances to the novels of Virginia Woolf, vol. 6). ISBN 0-0803-3534-9
Based on the text of *Orlando: A Biography* (New York: Harcourt, Brace, 1928).

1489.7. Haule, James M., and Philip H. Smith, Jr. **A Concordance to Night and Day by Virginia Woolf**. Oxford: Oxford Microform Publications, 1986. 14 microfiche. (Concordances to the Novels of Virginia Woolf, vol. 7). ISBN 0-0803-3539-X.
Concords the text of *Night and Day* (New York: Harcourt, Brace, 1931).

Journals

1490.   **Virginia Woolf Miscellany**. Rohnert Park, CA: Sonoma State University, 1973- . 2/yr. ISSN 0736-251x.
Sponsored by the Virginia Woolf Society, the slim eight-page issues of the *Virginia Woolf Miscellany* feature a few brief notes on Woolf's primary materials and report on library collections and exhibitions and other topics of biographical interest (descriptions of photographs, records, and the like). Issues regularly contain reviews of new publications, notes on works in progress, calls for papers and conference information, and other news of interest to society members. *Virginia Woolf Miscellany* is indexed in *AES, AHI, A&HCI, MHRA*, and *MLA*.
Patterson's *Author Newsletters and Journals*, pp. 348-50, describes other previously published journals for Woolf.

Cornell Woolrich (George Hopley, William Irish), 1903-1968
Bibliographies
1491.   Nevins, Francis M., Jr. **Cornell Woolrich: First You Dream, Then You Die**. New York: Mysterious Press, 1988. 613p. LC 88-40066. ISBN 0-8929-6297-6.
Nevins appends to this massive biobibliographic survey of Woolrich, "the greatest writer of suspense fiction that ever lived" (p. vii), a listing of works by and about Woolrich, "Cornell Woolrich: A Checklist" (pp. 525-603). Includes sections for published writings, domestic and international film adaptations, radio adaptations, television adaptations, and books and journal and newspaper articles about Woolrich (approximately 70 briefly annotated items). Nevins gives brief bibliographic information for first and subsequent editions and reprintings in chronologically arranged subsections for novels, separately published short novels, collections of short stories, and contributed short fiction (subarranged by publication titles). Entries for media adaptations contain performance and production dates and full credits. Coverage extends to 1987. Index of names and titles cites discussions of specific works in Nevin's survey. Essentially a sale catalog, Enola Stewart's *Cornell Woolrich (William Irish, George Hopley): A Catalogue of First and Variant Editions of His Work, Including Anthology and Magazine Appearances* (Pocono Pines, PA: Gravesend, 1975) contains alphabetically arranged listings for 157 of Woolrich's separate and contributed works that are largely useful for data on bibliographic points and publication histories. Also for works by Woolrich, see *First Printings of American Authors*, vol. 3, pp. 395-400. See *Bibliography of American Fiction, 1919-1988*, pp. 553-54, for Michael J. Pettengell's checklist of works by and about Woolrich.

Constance Fenimore Woolson, 1840-1894

Bibliographies

1492. **A Catalogue of Memorabilia Relating to Constance Fenimore Woolson**. Winter Park, FL: Woolson House, Rollins College, 1938. 41p. OCLC 10339359.

Largely useful for information about Woolson materials at Rollins College. Includes very brief checklists of Woolson's books, manuscripts, letters, and books from her library, as well as fuller descriptions of some 130 items of furniture, pictures, sculptures, glass, silver, and other realia associated with Clare Benedict, Woolson's niece and donor of Rollins College's Woolson House. Also contains Fred Lewis Pattee's "Constance Fenimore Woolson and the South" (pp. 8-16). For fuller details on works by Woolson, see *Bibliography of American Literature*, vol. 9, pp. 470-79. Woolson's contributions to selected periodicals and reviews of Woolson's works are identified in Wells' *The Literary Index to American Magazines, 1850-1900*, pp. 426-27. Woolson's manuscripts are listed in Robbins' *American Literary Manuscripts*, p. 360. See *Bibliography of American Fiction, 1866-1918*, pp. 361-62, for Pamela R. Matthews and Mary Loeffelholz's checklist of works by and about Woolson.

William Wordsworth, 1770-1850

Bibliographies

1493. Bauer, N. S. **William Wordsworth: A Reference Guide to British Criticism, 1793-1899**. Boston: G. K. Hall, 1978. 467p. (A Reference Publication in Literature). LC 77-23883. ISBN 0-8161-7828-3.

Bauer chronologically arranges brief, descriptively annotated entries for about 2,500 criticisms and comments about Wordsworth published from 1793 through 1899. Coverage is comprehensive, including books and articles as well as letters to editors, accounts of speeches, poems, memoirs, anonymous reviews, and the like. An excellent index covers critics, names cited in annotations (such as Horace, Shakespeare, and "Seventeenth century poets"), and primary titles. Subheadings for broad topics ("bibliography," "biography," and "political opinions of," for example) under Wordsworth's name. Providing significant coverage of contemporary responses to Wordsworth's works, Bauer's guide complements James V. Logan's *Wordsworthian Criticism: A Guide to Bibliography* (1947; reprint Columbus, OH: Ohio State University Press, 1961), which covers studies through 1944; Elton Henley and David H. Stam's *Wordsworthian Criticism: 1945-1964*, revised ed. (New York: New York Public Library, 1965); David H. Stam's *Wordsworthian Criticism 1964-1973, Including Additions to Wordsworthian Criticism 1945-1964* (New York: New York Public Library and Readex Books, 1974); and Jones and Kroeber's guide (entry 1495).

1494. Hanley, Keith, and David Barron. **An Annotated Critical Bibliography of William Wordsworth**. London: Prentice-Hall, Harvester Wheatsheaf, 1995. 329p. LC 95-97936. ISBN 0-1335-5348-5.

The starting point for research on Wordsworth, selectively updating Jones and Kroeber's *Wordsworth Scholarship* (entry 1495) by offering evaluative information for texts and studies. Critically annotated, topically arranged guide to the full range of standard editions, reference resources, and scholarship on Wordsworth published from 1798 to 1993. Sections cover first and subsequent early editions; modern standard collected, selected, and separate editions of individual works of poetry, prose, and letters; manuscripts and facsimiles; primary and secondary bibliographies, concordances, handbooks, and other aids to research; biographies and memoirs; and criticism, with some 708 items sublisted for the periods 1798 to 1899 (collections, contemporary comments, and later Victorian criticism) and 1900 to 1993 (collections, full-length studies, and articles and chapters). Hanley and Barron's thorough annotations clearly indicate standard or otherwise important and valuable works. Indexes of Wordsworth's works, subjects and persons, and critics provide excellent access.

1495. Jones, Mark, and Karl Kroeber. **Wordsworth Scholarship and Criticism, 1973-1984: An Annotated Bibliography: With Selected Criticism, 1809-1972.** New York: Garland, 1985. 316p. (Garland Reference Library of the Humanities, vol. 536). LC 84-45384. ISBN 0-8240-8840-9.

This amounts to a guide to essential primary and secondary materials for the study of Wordsworth. Jones and Kroeber describe standard and selected editions of collected and individual works, letters, and journals; reference works, bibliographies, and biographies; major critical studies published through 1972, supplementing all previous secondary bibliographies (see entry 1493); and criticism (arranged by years) from 1973 through 1984. Annotations are critical and helpful, clearly identifying standard works. Excellent indexing entails an index of critics and a subject index offering detailed subheadings under Wordsworth's name and individual works (for "Manuscript studies," "Milton and Wordsworth," and studies of "suffering" in "The Ruined Cottage"). Also for a bibliography of works by and about Wordsworth, see *NCBEL*, III, pp. 182-211. Research on Wordsworth is reviewed by J. C. Maxwell and S. C. Gill in Dyson's *English Poetry*, pp. 167-87; and Karl Kroeber in Frank Jordan's *The English Romantic Poets*, pp. 255-340.

1496. Wise, Thomas J. **A Bibliography of the Writings in Prose and Verse of William Wordsworth.** 1916; reprint Folkestone: Dawsons of Pall Mall, 1971. 268p. LC 72-188874. ISBN 0-7129-0520-0.

Although employing outdated principles of description, Wise gives valuable, full bibliographic descriptions for Wordsworth's primary materials in separate listings for books; contributions to journals and books, including published letters and dedications; collected editions; and "Wordsworthiana" (some 72 works about Wordsworth). Entries give title-page transcriptions (with facsimiles of title pages and excerpts from texts) and physical descriptions. Reprinted edition available (Folkestone: Dawsons, 1971). A comprehensive, modern descriptive bibliography of Wordsworth's primary materials does not exist. The most thorough descriptions of Wordsworth's works are provided in George Harris Healey's *The Cornell Wordsworth Collection: A Catalogue of Books and Manuscripts Presented to the University by Mr. Victor Emanuel Cornell, 1919* (Ithaca, NY: Cornell University Press, 1957). Other useful catalogs of Wordsworth's primary materials include *The Indiana Wordsworth Collection: A Brief Account of the Collection, Together with a Catalogue of the Exhibit Held in the Lilly Library on the Occasion of the Bicentenary of Wordsworth's Birth* (Bloomington, IN: The Lilly Library, 1970); C. H. Patton's *The Amherst Wordsworth Collection* (Amherst, MA: Amherst College, 1936); Wise's *Two Lake Poets: A Catalogue of Printed Books, Manuscripts and Autograph Letters by William Wordsworth and Samuel Taylor Coleridge* (London: Privately printed, 1927), which describes materials in the British Library; John D. Gordon's *William Wordsworth, 1770-1850: An Exhibition* (New York: New York Public Library, 1950), which describes materials in the Berg Collection of the New York Public Library; and W. H. White's *A Description of the Wordsworth and Coleridge Manuscripts in the Possession of Mr. T. Norton Longman* (London: Longmans, 1897), which describes materials now at Yale University. Also of interest for the study of Wordsworth's primary materials is Chester L. Shaver and Alice C. Shaver's *Wordsworth Library: A Catalogue: Including a List of Books Housed by Wordsworth and Coleridge from c.1810 to c.1830* (New York: Garland, 1979), which uses a sale catalog of Wordsworth's books, an unpublished manuscript catalog of the library, and other records to reconstruct Wordsworth's library. Duncan Wu's *Wordsworth's Reading, 1770-1799* (Cambridge: Cambridge University Press, 1993) identifies and dates Wordsworth's known and suggested reading (based on library lending records, books owned by Wordsworth, and allusions to books in Wordsworth's writings) to 1800.

Dictionaries, Encyclopedias, and Handbooks

1497.   Pinion, F. B. **Wordsworth Chronology**. Boston: G. K. Hall, 1988. 255p. LC 87-25208. ISBN 0-8161-8950-1.

Pinion gives day-by-day summaries of events in Wordsworth's life. Principal sources include the six series of *The Letters of William and Dorothy Wordsworth* (New York: Oxford University Press, 1967-82); Ernest de Selincourt's edition of *The Letters of William and Dorothy Wordsworth: The Later Years* (Oxford: Clarendon Press, 1939); and Mark L. Reed's *Wordsworth: A Chronology of the Early Years, 1770-1799* (Cambridge: Harvard University Press, 1967) and *Wordsworth: A Chronology of the Middle Years, 1800-1815* (Cambridge, MA: Harvard University Press, 1975). A very selective dictionary of "Persons of Importance in Wordsworth's Life" (excluding family and close acquaintances) and indexes of names, places, and things and of Wordsworth's works conclude the volume. Better coverage of people associated with Wordsworth is provided in Pinion's *A Wordsworth Companion* (entry 1498).

1498.   Pinion, F. B. **A Wordsworth Companion: Survey and Assessment**. London: Macmillan, 1984. 351p. LC 84-38877. ISBN 0-333-30395-5.

Pinion surveys Wordsworth's life, his literary aesthetics and ideas, his works, and the critical responses to them. In addition, prominent people in his life (such as Coleridge, Dorothy Wordsworth, and Sara Hutchinson) are described in detail. The guide includes maps and illustrations of locations and people. J. R. Tutin's *The Wordsworth Dictionary of Persons and Places, With the Familiar Quotations from His Works (Including Full Index) and a Chronologically-Arranged List of His Best Poems* (Hull: s. n., 1891; reprint New York: Burt Franklin, 1968) offers several dictionaries of topics not covered in modern Wordsworth companions, such as contemporary, historical, mythical, legendary, Biblical, and fictional characters; places in the Lake District and elsewhere in England, Britain, Europe, and the world; birds; and trees, plants, and flowers in Wordsworth's works.

Indexes and Concordances

1499.   Cooper, Lane. **A Concordance to the Poems of William Wordsworth**. London: Smith, Elder, 1911. 1,136p. OCLC 15728600.

Cooper concords the text of Thomas Hutchinson's edition of the *Poetical Works* (1895; London: Oxford University Press, 1904). Also available in a reprinted edition (New York: Russell & Russell, 1965). Patricia McEahern and Thomas Beckwith's *A Complete Concordance to the Lyrical Ballads of Samuel Taylor Coleridge and William Wordsworth: 1798 and 1800 Editions* (New York: Garland, 1987) offers parallel indexes to these texts, with separate indexes to notes and prefaces of the first editions.

Journals

1500.   **Wordsworth Circle**. New York: Wordsworth-Coleridge Association, 1970- . 4/yr. ISSN 0043-8006.

Sponsored by the Wordsworth-Coleridge Association, *Wordsworth Circle* focuses on writers of the English Romantic period, including Wordsworth, Coleridge, Hazlitt, De Quincey, Lamb, Shelley, Landon, Jane Austen, Walter Scott, and Mary Wollstonecraft, among others. Biographical, critical, and textual studies on these writers and aspects of their works predominate. An annual review issue, in autumn, contains reviews of as many as 50 new publications. Special issues report on and publish papers from a wide range of conferences that focus on individual writers and the Romantic movement. Regular reports on conferences are prominent, as well as announcements of new books, reports of research in progress, and other news of interest to specialists. *Wordsworth Circle* is indexed in *AHI, A&HCI, MHRA,* and *MLA.*

Patterson's *Author Newsletters and Journals*, pp. 350-51, describes other previously published journals for Wordsworth.

Sir Henry Wotton, 1568-1639
Bibliographies

For a bibliography of works by and about Wotton, see *NCBEL*, I, pp. 1325-26. Wotton's manuscripts are described in *Index of English Literary Manuscripts*, I, pt. 2:561-87, 635-36.

Herman Wouk, 1915-
Bibliographies

For works by Wouk, see *First Printings of American Authors*, vol. 1, pp. 421-23. Wouk's manuscripts are listed in Robbins' *American Literary Manuscripts*, p. 360. See *Bibliography of American Fiction, 1919-1988*, pp. 555-56, for Mark J. Charney's checklist of works by and about Wouk.

Harold Bell Wright, 1872-1944
Bibliographies

1501.   DeGruson, Gene. **Kansas Authors of Best Sellers: A Bibliography of the Works of Martin and Osa Johnson, Margaret Hill McCarter, Charles M. Sheldon, and Harold Bell Wright**. Pittsburg, KS: Kansas State College of Pittsburg, 1970. 30p. LC 78-630507.

Pages 27 through 30 (with inserted pp. 28a to 28b) give brief bibliographic information for Wright's books, periodical publications, and about 20 works about Wright. Also for works by Wright, see *First Printings of American Authors*, vol. 2, pp. 395-97. Wright's manuscripts are listed in Robbins' *American Literary Manuscripts*, pp. 360-61. See *Bibliography of American Fiction, 1866-1918*, pp. 363-64, for Sally Dee Wade's checklist of works by and about Wright.

James (Arlington) Wright, 1927-1980
Bibliographies

1502.   Roberson, William H. **James Wright: An Annotated Bibliography**. Metuchen, NJ: Scarecrow Press, 1995. 312p. (Scarecrow Author Bibliographies, no. 94). LC 95-1504. ISBN 0-8108-3000-0.

Part 1 contains descriptions of Wright's writings from 1949 through 1993 in chronologically arranged sections for books (in subsections for poetry and prose and translations), prose pieces, poems in periodicals (about 450 entries), translations in periodicals, poems in books, translations in books, sound recordings, video recordings, and book blurbs. Full bibliographic descriptions for first and subsequent editions of Wright's 37 books give title-page transcriptions, collations, contents, and binding information. Part 2 arranges by year approximately 500 works about Wright in sections for books, articles and parts of books, reviews (subarranged by Wright's works), dissertations, poems, dedications, and miscellaneous. Annotations note reprintings and give critical evaluations. Includes a brief Wright chronology. Part 1 is indexed by name and title; part 2 by name, title, and subject. Also for works by Wright, see *First Printings of American Authors*, vol. 1, pp. 425-26.

Indexes and Concordances

1503.   Colvin, Claude R. **A Concordance of the Poetry of James Wright**. S. l.: s. n., 1988. 429p. OCLC 22879770.

An *index verborum*, not a full concordance. Contains separate word indexes to "four volumes of poetry . . . selected because of their availability" (table of contents)— *Collected Poems, Two Citizens, To a Blossoming Pear Tree*, and *This Journey*—with additional indexes (including context lines) to "as" and "like" similes and sensate and cognitive verbs ("feel," "hear," "see," "smell," "taste," "touch," "know," "understand"). Appends word index to 18 prose poems from *The Shape of Light* and a frequency list. Colvin does not specifically identify editions used as copy texts. Entries reference page numbers, not lines.

Richard (Nathaniel) Wright, 1908-1960

Bibliographies

1504. Davis, Charles T., and Michel Fabre. **Richard Wright: A Primary Bibliography**. Boston: G. K. Hall, 1982. 232p. (A Reference Publication in Afro-American Studies). LC 81-13398. ISBN 0-8161-8410-0.

This is a comprehensive, descriptive listing of Wright's primary bibliography. Emphasis is on manuscripts. Chronologically arranged entries in sections (for plays, fiction, nonfiction, and poetry) give brief bibliographic information and detailed descriptions of contents and manuscript sources (with locations) for published works, as well as descriptions of unpublished materials, translations of Wright's works, and writings of others related to Wright's works. Unpublished materials include play, film, and television scripts; letters are excluded. An appendix references translations of Wright's works (arranged by languages). Also for works by Wright, see *First Printings of American Authors*, vol. 1, pp. 427-30. Wright's manuscripts are listed in Robbins' *American Literary Manuscripts*, p. 361. Also useful for "accurate information for the study of intertextuality" (p. ix) in Wright's works, Michel Fabre's *Richard Wright: Books and Writers* (Jackson, MS: University Press of Mississippi, 1990) attempts to identify books owned or read by Wright.

1505. Kinnamon, Keneth. **A Richard Wright Bibliography: Fifty Years of Criticism, 1933-1982**. New York: Greenwood Press, 1988. 983p. (Bibliographies and Indexes in Afro-American and African Studies, no. 19). LC 87-27831. ISBN 0-313-25411-7.

Intending to cover every mention of Wright in print in all languages, Kinnamon chronologically arranges annotated entries for 13,117 works published from 1933 through 1982. Many descriptions are necessarily brief, although significant studies receive thorough review. The comprehensive index (extending some 200 pages) references real and fictional names of persons, places, and things; titles; and selected topics, such as "bibliography," "interviews," and "Communists." See also *Bibliography of American Fiction, 1919-1988*, pp. 556-61, for Kinnamon's checklist of works by and about Wright. Research on Wright is reviewed by John M. Reilly in Inge, Duke, and Bryer's *Black American Writers*, vol. II, pp. 1-46; and Thadious M. Davis in Flora and Bain's *Fifty Southern Writers after 1900*, pp. 545-59.

Wulfstan, d. 1023

Bibliographies

Greenfield and Robinson's *A Bibliography of Publications on Old English Literature to the End of 1972*, pp. 381-83, lists editions, translations, and studies of Wulfstan, with citations for reviews. Also for a bibliography of works by and about Wulfstan, see *NCBEL*, I, pp. 321-24.

Dictionaries, Encyclopedias, and Handbooks

1506. Dodd, Loring Holmes. **A Glossary of Wulfstan's Homilies**. 1908; reprint Hildesheim: Georg Olms, 1968. 244p. (Yale Studies in English, vol. 35). OCLC 38407.

Straightforward Old English vocabulary, with a selective bibliography (pp. [243]-44).

Rudolph Wurlitzer, 1937-

Bibliographies

For works by Wurlitzer, see *First Printings of American Authors*, vol. 2, p. 399.

Sir Thomas Wyatt, 1503-1542

Bibliographies

1507. Jentoft, Clyde W. **Sir Thomas Wyatt and Henry Howard, Earl of Surrey: A Reference Guide**. Boston: G. K. Hall, 1980. 192p. (A Reference Guide to Literature). LC 80-16434. ISBN 0-8161-8176-4.

Jentoft separately lists annotated entries for criticisms of Wyatt, of Surrey, and of both writers. Extending from 1542 through 1975, coverage includes books, parts of books, articles, reviews of secondary works, and dissertations. Non-English-language dissertations and reviews are excluded. Annotations are descriptive, although works of particular significance receive extended review. In addition, Jentoft lists manuscript sources and selected editions of Wyatt's and Surrey's works. An index of names and primary and secondary works includes topical subheadings (for "diction," "imagery," and "satires," for example) under Wyatt's and Surrey's names. For a bibliography of works by and about Wyatt, see *NCBEL*, I, pp. 1020-23. Wyatt's manuscripts are described in *Index of English Literary Manuscripts*, I, pt. 2:589-626, 636.

Indexes and Concordances

1508. Hangen, Eva Catherine. **A Concordance to the Complete Poetical Works of Sir Thomas Wyatt**. Chicago: The University of Chicago Press, 1941. 527p. LC 41-11854.

Concords the text of A. K. Foxwell's *The Poems of Sir Thomas Wyatt* (London: University of London Press, 1914). Gives short titles for each poem and lines for each headword and context line. Includes lists of short titles for the poems and "Wyatt editions and collections" (p. xi). Also available in a reprinted edition (New York: Johnson Reprint, 1969).

William Wycherley, 1641-1715

Bibliographies

1509. McCarthy, B. Eugene. **William Wycherley: A Reference Guide**. Boston: G. K. Hall, 1985. 195p. (A Reference Guide to Literature). LC 84-28963. ISBN 0-8161-8184-5.

McCarthy chronologically arranges briefly annotated entries for all editions of Wycherley's works published from 1669, as well as all writings (including books, articles, dissertations, and reviews of modern productions in all languages) about him through 1982. Contains about 1,000 entries. Annotations are descriptive and nonevaluative. The introduction surveys the stage histories of Wycherley's plays in detail. Indexing for critics, names cited in annotations (Shakespeare, Pope, and the like), and primary titles includes extensive topical subheadings that reference editions, sources, productions, and other aspects of Wycherley's works. For a bibliography of works by and about Wycherley, see *NCBEL*, II, pp. 742-44. Wycherley's manuscripts are described in *Index of English Literary Manuscripts*, II, pt. 2:649-56. Research on Wycherley is reviewed by John Barnard in Wells' *English Drama*, pp. 173-98.

John Wyclif, c. 1330-1384

Bibliographies

Ernest W. Talbert and S. Harrison Thomson offer a comprehensive guide to primary materials for Wyclif and Wyclifite writings with a bibliography of editions and criticism in Severs and Hartung's *A Manual of the Writings in Middle English*, vol. II, pp. 354-80, 517-33. For Henry Hargreaves's bibliography of works by and about Wyclif, see *NCBEL*, I, pp. 491-96. Anne Hudson reviews research on "Wycliffite Prose" in Edwards' *Middle English Prose*, pp. 249-70.

Elinor (Hoyt) Wylie, 1885-1928
Bibliographies

For works by Wylie, see *Bibliography of American Literature*, vol. 9, pp. 480-93. Wylie's manuscripts are listed in Robbins' *American Literary Manuscripts*, p. 361.

Philip Wylie, 1902-1971
Bibliographies

See *Bibliography of American Fiction, 1919-1988*, pp. 561-62, for Margaret Donovan DuPriest's checklist of works by and about Wylie. Wylie's manuscripts are listed in Robbins' *American Literary Manuscripts*, p. 361.

Elizabeth (Lillie) Buffum Chace Wyman, 1847-1929
Bibliographies

See *Bibliography of American Fiction, 1866-1918*, p. 365, for James Nagel's checklist of works by and about Wyman.

Richard Yates, 1926-
Bibliographies

See *Bibliography of American Fiction 1919-1988*, p. 563, for Richard Baughman's checklist of works by and about Yates.

William Butler Yeats, 1865-1939
Bibliographies

1510. Balliet, Conrad A., and Christine Mawhinney. **W. B. Yeats: A Census of the Manuscripts**. New York: Garland, 1990. 520p. (Garland Reference Library of the Humanities, vol. 772). LC 89-17226. ISBN 0-8240-6629-4.

Most valuable for descriptions and locations of Yeats' manuscripts. Balliet and Mawhinney list manuscripts by genres or types, giving sections for books, inscriptions, letters, miscellany (diaries and journals, theatrical materials, lists, quoted passages, etc.), works of other authors including Yeats' materials, plays, poems, unpublished poems, prose, and speeches, with a separate listing of names and addresses of libraries and other owners. Bibliography of manuscript catalogs and other resources (pp. 457-64). Alphabetical and geographical indexes for libraries and other owners. Index of manuscripts references titles and proper names (of authors, recipients of letters, and the like).

1511. Jochum, K. P. S. **W. B. Yeats: A Classified Bibliography of Criticism**. 2d ed., revised and enlarged. Urbana, IL: University of Illinois Press, 1990. 1,176p. LC 90-10981. ISBN 0-2520-1762-5.

A revision of *W. B. Yeats: A Classified Bibliography of Criticism Including Additions to Allan Wade's Bibliography of the Writings of W. B. Yeats and a Section on the Irish Literary and Dramatic Revival* (Urbana, IL: University of Illinois Press, 1978), Jochum's guide remains the best listing of critical materials about Yeats. With the objective of international "completeness" (p. xii), Jochum includes selectively annotated entries for more than 10,000 works by and about Yeats (the 1978 edition covered some 7,900). Generally follows the arrangement of the first edition, supplying sections for bibliographies, concordances, and catalogs; biographical studies; general criticisms; criticisms of poems, plays, and prose; critical and introductory materials in books; reviews of Yeats' works; recordings, films, and musical adaptations; creative works based on Yeats; and works dealing with the Irish literary and dramatic revivals, including works on individual writers. Annotations are generally very brief, although important studies receive thorough review. Entries also give citations for reviews. The list of catalogs (pp. 16-29) provides brief information on manuscripts and special collections. Coverage extends through 1986, with some entries from 1987 and 1988. Elaborate indexes of names, institutions, collections of criticism, primary and secondary titles, subjects, periodicals and series, and chronology offer excellent access. Jochum's work supersedes K. G. W. Cross and R. T. Dunlop's *A Bibliography of Yeats's Criticism, 1887-1965* (New York: Macmillan, 1971) as well as John Stoll's *The Great Deluge: A Yeats Bibliography* (Troy, NY: Whitston, 1971). Also for a bibliography of works by and about Yeats, see *NCBEL*, III, pp. 1915-34.

1512.   Timm, Eitel, and Eric Wredenhagen. **W. B. Yeats: A Century of Criticism.** Columbia, SC: Camden House, 1990. 101p. (Studies in English and American Literature, Linguistics, and Culture, vol. 6). LC 89-22373. ISBN 0-938100-68-8.

First published in 1987, Timm's narrative (translated by Wredenhagen) surveys major contributions in the first 100 years of Yeats' scholarship, neatly complementing Jochum's comprehensive secondary bibliography (entry 1511) as well as Finneran's more concise survey in Finneran's *Anglo-Irish Literature*, pp. 216-314. Approaches Yeats' criticisms chronologically and by genre. Particularly valuable for assessing major non-English-language scholarship. Bibliography of editions and criticism (pp. 76-95). Indexing limited to proper names of subjects (Virgil, Ben Jonson, Poe) and critics. In addition to Finneran's essay in Finneran's *Anglo-Irish Literature*, research on Yeats is reviewed by Jon Stallworthy in Dyson's *English Poetry*, pp. 345-59; and James Fisher in Schrank and Demastes' *Irish Playwrights, 1880-1995: A Research and Production Sourcebook*, pp. 402-18.

1513.   Wade, Allan, and Russell K. Alspach. **A Bibliography of W. B. Yeats.** 3d ed., revised. London: Rupert Hart-Davis, 1968. 514p. LC 70-376371. ISBN 0-246-64138-x.

First published in 1951 and revised in 1958 (both London: Hart-Davis), Alspach's revision of Wade's standard descriptive bibliography of Yeats' primary materials includes detailed entries in separate listings for books, books and periodicals edited by Yeats, books with prefaces and introductions by Yeats, contributions to books, contributions to periodicals, translations of Yeats' works (published as books or included in periodicals), and Japanese publications in English. Appendixes list the publications of the Cuala Press, selected works about Yeats (with brief annotations), and descriptions of broadcasts by and about Yeats dating from 1939 through 1957. Entries include title-page transcriptions, collations, contents, and detailed information on printing and publishing. A comprehensive index of titles and names of persons, publishers, and institutions gives solid access. Balliet and Mawhinney's *W. B. Yeats: A Census of the Manuscripts* (entry 1510) lists Yeats' manuscripts. Also valuable for information on primary materials is R. O. Dougan's *W. B. Yeats Manuscripts and Printed Books in the Library of Trinity College, Dublin, 1956* (Dublin: Lochlainn, 1956). In addition, Edward O'Shea's *A Descriptive Catalog of W. B. Yeats's Library* (New York: Garland, 1985) describes a substantial collection of Yeats' materials in the hands of his daughter, Anne Yeats.

Dictionaries, Encyclopedias, and Handbooks
1514.   Bushrui, S. B., and Tim Prentki. **An International Companion to the Poetry of W. B. Yeats.** Savage, MD: Barnes & Noble Books, 1990. 255p. LC 90-40363. ISBN 0-3892-0905-8.

A slim but useful handbook for concise information on Yeats' life and times, people and places in his works, and his individual and collected poems. Entries for Yeats' poems give first lines, brief publication information, summaries, glosses of difficult words, and critical commentaries on language, themes, images, and the like. Selected bibliography of editions and criticism (pp. 235-38). Indexes of poem titles and first lines; general index with detailed subject headings. Also useful, James P. McGarry and Edward Malins' *Place Names in the Writings of William Butler Yeats* (Gerrards Cross: Colin Smythe, 1976) confines substantial identifications to "places actually mentioned" (p. 9) by Yeats as opposed to places described but unnamed. Illustrated entries give work and page numbers in standard editions of Yeats' works for such places as the Abbey Theatre, Coole Park, and Drumcliff Cross.

1515. Malins, Edward, and John Purkis. **A Preface to Yeats**. 2d ed. London: Longman, 1994. 218p. (Preface Books). LC 93-39017. ISBN 0-582-09093-8.

Purkis revises Malins' useful reference guide to selected major poems by Yeats as well as to Yeats' life and works, first published in 1974 (New York: Scribner's). In general, the new edition preserves verbatim information in Malins' sections on historical and literary background, including the useful chronology of Yeats' life and career; survey essays on Irish history, with references to Yeats' works; descriptions of Yeats' reading; biographical directory of family, friends, and associates; literary gazetteer; and lists of places, symbols and allusions, and Gaelic place names. "Further reading" selections (pp. 202-205) are thoroughly updated to identify new editions and scholarship. Purkis "rewrites entirely" the critical survey sections, "adjusting the focus of the book to the expectations of the new reader of Yeats" (p. viii). In fact, Purkis reprints and evaluates 10 different poems from Malins' first edition. Among Purkis' selections are "Cuchulain's Fight with the Sea," "The Magi," "The Second Coming," and "Sailing to Byzantium." Whereas Malins' discussions emphasized "biographical links," Purkis' systematically present information on publication history, close readings of themes and other features, and critical overviews. Purkis also provides a detailed general index and an index of Yeats' works. Both Malins' 1974 edition and Malins and Purkis' 1994 revision are more detailed than John Unterecker's *A Reader's Guide to W. B. Yeats* (1959; Syracuse, NY: Syracuse University Press, 1996), which surveys themes and criticisms of Yeats' major works.

Indexes and Concordances

1516. Spence, Joseph. **The Sayings of W. B. Yeats**. London: Duckworth, 1993. 64p. LC 94-15423. ISBN 0-7156-2457-1.

Arranges a limited selection of quotations from Yeats' poetry and prose (including letters) under 13 broad topics, including "Love," "Ireland," and "Politics & War." Entries cite work and date but do not reference specific editions. No source bibliography or index.

1517. Domville, Eric. **A Concordance to the Plays of W. B. Yeats**. Ithaca, NY: Cornell University Press, 1972. 2 vols. (Cornell Concordances). LC 71-162547. ISBN 0-8014-0663-3.

Based on *The Variorum Edition of the Plays* (New York: Macmillan, 1966), edited by Russell K. Alspach. Appends index words in order of frequency.

1518. Parrish, Stephen Maxfield. **A Concordance to the Poems of W. B. Yeats**. Ithaca, NY: Cornell University Press, 1963. 967p. (Cornell Concordances). LC 63-11493.

Concords the text of *The Variorum Edition of the Poems of W. B. Yeats* (New York: Macmillan, 1957), edited by Peter Allt and Russell K. Alspach. Includes index words in order of frequency.

Journals

1519. **Yeats: An Annual of Critical and Textual Studies**. Ann Arbor, MI: University of Michigan, 1983-. Annual. ISSN 0742-6224.

Volumes include substantial articles, review essays, reviews, and brief notices (shorter reviews) of the full range of topics related to Yeats. Occasional volumes focus on specific topics, such as "Yeats and the Theatre" 10 (1992). Important bibliographic contributions include Thomas Parkinson's "Fifty Years of Yeats Criticism (in homage to Richard Ellman)," 9 (1991): 107-15; and Conrad A. Balliet and Margaret Kelleher's "A Partial List of W. B. Yeats Manuscripts: The 30,000 Series," 11 (1994 [for 1993]): 3-86. Other regular important bibliographic features include K. P. S. Jochum's annual checklist of Yeats' scholarship, which updates the standard bibliography (entry 1511) and abstracts of recent dissertations on Yeats and his contemporaries, presently compiled by Scott E. Johnson. The series is increasingly out of date, with the most recent volume, vol. 12 for 1994, appearing in 1996. *Yeats* is indexed in *MLA*.

1520. **Yeats Annual**. London: Macmillan, 1982-. Annual. (Macmillan Literary Annuals). ISSN 0278-7687.

Volumes include substantial articles and shorter notes on topics related to Yeats' biography, sources, and texts as well as critical studies of his works. Illustrations and facsimiles accompany featured articles. In early volumes, a significant number of articles described primary materials, manuscripts, and special collections. "Significant Research Collections" has profiled Yeats holdings of Emory University, University of Reading, London University, University of Kansas, and other institutional and private collections. In addition, past volumes regularly included "A Recent Yeats Bibliography": This bibliography, however, does not appear in recent volumes. *Yeats Annual* also publishes reviews of new publications and lists of publications received. *Yeats Annual* is indexed in *MLA*.

1521. **Yeats Eliot Review: A Quarterly Journal of Scholarship, Criticism, and Opinion in Cooperation with the National Poetry Foundation**. Little Rock, AR: Yeats Eliot Review, 1974-. 2/yr. ISSN 0704-5700.

Formerly *T. S. Eliot Newsletter* (1974-75) and *T. S. Eliot Review* (1975-77), issues of *Yeats Eliot Review* typically publish four to seven scholarly critical and interpretive articles on aspects of the lives and works of Yeat and Eliot. A special double issue, 12.3-4 (Winter 1994), included papers from the 1990 international conference on Yeats and Pound sponsored by the National Poetry Foundation. Vol. 16 (1997) is scheduled to be a double issue marking the 75th anniversary of the serial appearance of "The Waste Land." The journal also lists announcements of conferences, new publications, and other events of interest to scholars of modern literature. Past issues have published a few reviews. From 1974 to 1982, the journal continued the bibliographic feature, "Bibliographical Update," that reviewed new publications. *Yeats Eliot Review* is indexed in *AES, AHI, MHRA,* and *MLA*.

Patterson's *Author Newsletters and Journals*, pp. 351-52, describes other previously published journals for Yeats.

Arthur Young, 1741-1820
Bibliographies

For a bibliography of works by and about Young, see *NCBEL*, II, p. 1894.

Edward Young, 1683-1765
Bibliographies

1522. Cordasco, Francesco. **Edward Young: A Handlist of Critical Notices & Studies**. New York: Published for Long Island University Press by Burt Franklin, 1950. 9p. (18th Century Bibliographical Pamphlets, no. 11). LC 51-912.

Selective checklist of 39 general critical and biographical books and articles, with selected references to reviews, including a few items in German and French, published from 1892 to 1950. For Henry Pettit's bibliography of works by and about Young, see *NCBEL*, II, pp. 493-97.

1523. May, James E., and Nora J. Quinlan. **The Henry Pettit Edward Young Collection at the University of Colorado at Boulder Libraries: A Bibliography**. Boulder, CO: University of Colorado at Boulder, 1989. 86p. LC 90-622273.

No full descriptive listing of Young's works exists. Based on what May calls "one of the best collections of works by Edward Young in the world" (p. 3), especially of early editions of *The Complaint; or, Night Thoughts*, May and Quinlan's catalog covers only Young's works to 1900 in sections for manuscripts (three letters by Young to publisher Robert Dodsley and one other), separate editions (197 items), collections (23 items), and "Youngiana" (12 publications before 1800 related to Young or at some time attributed to him). Entries for books give brief bibliographic information (titles, paginations, sizes and formats, shelf numbers, etc.), with additional notes on unique features, such as contents, contemporary bindings, and provenance, that distinguish particular copies, but do not give complete collations. Index of titles.

Journals
    "Recent Articles" in *The Scriblerian and the Kit Cats* (entry 1084) also regularly includes a selection of reviews of studies on Young.

Marguerite Young, 1909-
Bibliographies
    For works by Young, see *First Printings of American Authors*, vol. 2, p. 401. Young's manuscripts are listed in Robbins' *American Literary Manuscripts*, p. 362.

Stark Young, 1881-1963
Bibliographies
    For works by Young, see *First Printings of American Authors*, vol. 3, pp. 401-405. Young's manuscripts are listed in Robbins' *American Literary Manuscripts*, p. 362. See *Bibliography of American Fiction, 1919-1988*, pp. 564-65, for John Pilkington's checklist of works by and about Young. John Pilkington surveys works by and about Young in Flora and Bain's *Fifty Southern Writers After 1900*, pp. 560-71.

Israel Zangwill, 1864-1926
Bibliographies
    For a bibliography of works by and about Zangwill, see *NCBEL*, III, p. 1084.

George Zebrowski, 1945-
Bibliographies
    1524. Elliot, Jeffrey M., and Robert Reginald. **The Work of George Zebrowski: An Annotated Bibliography & Guide**. 2d ed., revised and expanded. San Bernardino, CA: Borgo Press, 1990. 118p. (Bibliographies of Modern Authors, no. 4). LC 89-7093. ISBN 0-8095-0514-2.
    First published in 1986 (San Bernardino, CA: Borgo Press), Elliot and Reginald's guide describes works by and about Zebrowski in sections for books; short fiction; nonfiction; edited works; writings for juveniles; unproduced film scripts and an unpublished short story; a dramatic adaptation of "Heathen God"; honors and awards; public appearances; biographical references (27 entries); and miscellanea, including brief information about the Zebrowski special collections at Temple University. Entries for books give brief bibliographic information, lists of subsequent editions and translations, plot summaries and contents, and citations for criticisms and reviews. Also includes brief biography, chronology of his life and career, a selection of excerpted criticisms, and an afterword by Zebrowski. Index of titles.

Roger Zelazny, 1937-
Bibliographies
    1525. Levack, Daniel J. H. **Amber Dreams: A Roger Zelazny Bibliography**. San Francisco, CA: Underwood-Miller, 1983. ISBN 0-934438-40-4.
    Levack attempts to "cite all the published works of Roger Zelazny through late 1982" (p. [11]). The bulk of the guide contains 251 alphabetically arranged entries in sections for books, edited books, and stories by Zelazny. Entries cumulate data for first and subsequent editions, translations, and contributed works,

identify forms (nonfiction, verse, etc.), give plot summaries and contents, and supply brief bibliographic data that emphasize distinguishing points. Levack provides many facsimiles of title pages and dust jackets. Other sections list magazines containing Zelazny's works, works about Zelazny (25 unannotated entries), two miscellaneous items (a radio program and a game), connected stories and continuing characters, pseudonyms, collaborations, verse and nonfiction works. A final section lists Zelazny's works in chronological order of publication from 1953 to 1982. Also available in a reprinted edition (Westport, CT: Meckler, 1986). Levack's guide is slightly more up to date but less comprehensive than Sanders' bibliography (entry 1526).

1526. Sanders, Joseph L. **Roger Zelazny: A Primary and Secondary Bibliography**. Boston: G. K. Hall, 1980. 154p. (Masters of Science Fiction and Fantasy). LC 80-20253. ISBN 0-8161-8081-4.

Sanders, with Zelazny's assistance, chronologically arranges works by and about Zelazny in separate listings, including brief bibliographic descriptions of Zelazny's fiction, poetry, and nonfiction (with descriptions of contents) published from 1953 through 1979, in addition to selectively annotated entries for about 300 criticisms and comments (mostly reviews) on Zelazny since 1969. Appendixes list Zelazny's awards, non-English-language editions of primary works, and manuscripts and papers in special collections at Syracuse University, which includes the Roger Zelazny Papers (pp. 120-33), and the University of Maryland—Baltimore County (pp. 134-36). Separate indexes for primary titles and for critics and secondary titles provide access. See *Bibliography of American Fiction, 1919-1988*, pp. 566-67, for Carl B. Yoke's checklist of works by and about Zelazny. See also Yoke's summary biography, critical assessment of major works, and selected primary and secondary bibliography for Zelazny in McCaffery's *Postmodern Fiction: A Bio-Bibliographical Guide*, pp. 561-64.

Dictionaries, Encyclopedias, and Handbooks

1527. Krulik, Theodore. **The Complete Amber Sourcebook**. New York: Avonva, 1996. 494p. LC 95-35076. ISBN 0-380-75409-6.

Extensive entries identify characters, places, events, and other elements keyed by page references to Zelazny's Amber novels. Major entry for the city of Amber covers Zelazny's elaborate mythic systems of justice, education, religion, commerce, and the like. Appends correspondence tables of time in Amber and Shadow Earth. Includes bibliographic references (pp. 493-94).

Louis Zukofsky, 1904-1978

Bibliographies

1528. Zukofsky, Celia. **A Bibliography of Louis Zukofsky**. Los Angeles, CA: Black Sparrow Press, 1969. 52p. LC 68-59629.

This gives brief information for a substantial selection of Zukofsky's primary works, including separate lists for books and broadsides dating from 1934 through 1969; contributions to anthologies; contributions to periodicals; miscellaneous writings, including translations of Zukofsky's works, prefaces and introductions, edited works, and the like; and tape recordings of readings. No real index is provided. A chronological list of poetry and prose surviving in manuscripts that cross-references published editions approximates an index. This is not a definitive bibliography of Zukofsky's primary materials. Supplementary information about Zukofsky's separate works is available in Marcella Booth's *A Catalogue of the Louis Zukofsky Manuscript Collection* (Austin, TX: Humanities Research Center, The University of Texas at Austin, 1975), which describes copies of published works as well as the manuscripts of collected and individual poems, criticisms, essays, reviews, novels, short stories, plays, miscellaneous writings (such as scripts of broadcasts, proposed works, readings, and the like), and letters. Zukofsky's manuscripts are also listed in Robbins' *American Literary Manuscripts*,

p. 362. No up-to-date guide to criticism of Zukofsky now exists. *Louis Zukofsky, Man and Poet* (Orono, ME: National Poetry Foundation, 1979, edited and with an introduction by Carroll F. Terrell), includes Terrell's "A Bibliography of Works About Louis Zukofsky with Extended Commentary" (pp. 401-43), with thorough annotated entries for 70 studies of Zukofsky, as well as an updated description of the Zukofsky Papers at the University of Texas at Austin (pp. 393-400), by Booth.

Chronological Appendix

501-600 Sixth Century
d. 570, Gildas

601-700 Seventh Century
Widsith
c.750, *Finnsburh, The Fight at*
fl. 670, Caedmon
673-735, Bede

701-800 Eighth Century
c. early 8th century, *Exodus*
Cynewulf
Beowulf
c. 790-830, *Christ*
c. 8th century, *Genesis A* and *B*

801-900 Ninth Century
Deor
Phoenix
Cynewulf
Judith
Andreas
848-899, Alfred

901-1000 Tenth Century
Deor
before about 940, *Seafarer*
before about 940, *Wanderer*
before late tenth century, *Waldere*
c. 1000, *Maldon, Battle of*
c. 10th century, *Dream of the Rood*
c. 937, *Brunanburh*
c. 955-c. 1010, Aelfric

1001-1100 Eleventh Century
d. 1023, Wulfstan

1101-1200 Twelfth Century
c. 1154, *Anglo-Saxon Chronicle*

1201-1300 Thirteenth Century
Mystery Plays
c. 1225, *King Horn*
c. 1230, *Ancrene Wisse*

1301-1400 Fourteenth Century
Mystery Plays
c. 1330-c. 1386, Langland, William
fl. 1356/7, Mandeville, Sir John
d. 1396, Hilton, Walter

c. 1300-1349, Rolle, Richard
c. 1350-1400, *Cloud of Unknowing*
c. 1373-c. 1439, Kempe, Margery
c. 1375, *Gawain and the Green Knight, Sir*
before 1320, *Isumbras, Sir*
1330?-1408, Gower, John
1330-1384, Wyclif, John
1340?-1402, Trevisa, John
1342-after 1416, Julian of Norwich
1343-1400, Chaucer, Geoffrey
1369?-1426, Hoccleve, Thomas
1370?-1449, Lydgate, John
1394-1437, James I, King of Scotland

1401-1500 Fifteenth Century
Mystery Plays
fl. 1486, Medwall, Henry
d. 1471, Malory, Sir Thomas
c. 1486-1555, Lindsay, Sir David
1422-1491, Caxton, William
1424?-1506?, Henryson, Robert
1456?-1513?, Dunbar, William
1460?-1529, Skelton, John
1475?-1522, Douglas, Gavin
1475?-1552, Barclay, Alexander
1475-1511, Hawes, Stephen
1477?-1535, More, Sir Thomas
1490-1546, Elyot, Sir Thomas
1495-1536, Tyndale, William
1495-1563, Bale, John
1497?-1580?, Heywood, John

1501-1600 Sixteenth Century
Mystery Plays
c. 1503-1552, Leland, John,
c. 1525-1581, Wilson, Thomas
c. 1552-1599, Spenser, Edmund
c. 1578-c. 1632, Webster, John
1503-1542, Wyatt, Sir Thomas
c. 1504-1556, Udall, Nicholas
1515/16-1568, Ascham, Roger
1516-1587, Foxe, John
1517?-1547, Surrey, Henry Howard,
      Earl of
c. 1529-1591, Puttenham, George
c. 1534-1577, Gascoigne, George
1536?-1605?, Golding, Arthur
1536-1608, Sackville, Thomas, 1st Earl
      of Dorset, Baron Buckhurst
1551-1623, Camden, William

1552-1616, Hakluyt, Richard
c. 1553-1625, Florio, John
1554?-1600, Hooker, Richard
1554?-1606, Lyly, John
1554?-1618, Ralegh, Sir Walter
1554-1586, Sidney, Sir Philip
1554-1628, Greville, Fulke, 1st Baron
    Brooke
1555?-1626?, Breton, Nicholas
1555-1626, Andrewes, Lancelot,
1556-1596, Peele, George
1558-1592, Greene, Robert
1558-1594, Kyd, Thomas
1558-1625, Lodge, Thomas
1559?-1634, Chapman, George
1560?-1600, Deloney, Thomas
1560-1633, Munday, Anthony
1561?-1595, Southwell, Saint Robert
1561-1612, Harington, Sir John
1561-1626, Bacon, Francis
1563-1619, Daniel, Samuel
1563-1631, Drayton, Michael
1564-1593, Marlowe, Christopher
1564-1616, Shakespeare, William
1567-1601, Nashe, Thomas
1567-1620, Campion, Thomas
1568-1639, Wotton, Sir Henry
1569-1626, Davies, John
1570?-1632, Dekker, Thomas
1572/3-1637, Jonson, Ben
1572-1631, Donne, John
1574?-1641, Heywood, Thomas
1574-1627, Barnfield, Richard
1574-1656, Hall, Joseph
1575?-1626, Tourneur, Cyril
1577?-1634, Marston, John
1577-1640, Burton, Robert
1578?-1653, Taylor, John
1578-1644, Sandys, George
1579-1625, Fletcher, John
1580-1627, Middleton, Thomas
1580-1631, Smith, Captain John
1582-1635, Corbett, Richard
1582-1648, Herbert, Edward, of
    Cherbury
1582-1650, Fletcher, Phineas
1583-1640, Massinger, Philip
1584-1616, Beaumont, Francis
1584-1652, Cotton, John
1585?-1623, Fletcher, Giles, the Younger
1585?-1626, Rowley, William
1585-1649, Drummond, William, of
    Hawthornden
1586-1647, Hooker, Thomas

1586-after 1639, Ford, John
1588-1667, Wither, George
1588-1679, Hobbes, Thomas
1590?-1645?, Browne, William, of
    Tavistock
1590-1652/3, Brome, Richard
1590-1657, Bradford, William,
1591-1674, Herrick, Robert
1592-1644, Quarles, Francis
1592-1669, King, Henry
1593-1633, Herbert, George
1593-1683, Walton, Izaak
1594/5-1640, Carew, Thomas
1596-1666, Shirley, James
1596-1669, Mather, Richard
1598-1672, Johnson, Edward

1601-1700 Seventeenth Century
d. 1635, Fairfax, Edward
c. 1635-c. 1678, Rowlandson, Mary
1601?-1665, Earle, John
1602-1645, Strode, William
1605-1635, Randolph, Thomas
1605-1649, Shepard, Thomas
1605-1654, Habington, William
1605-1682, Browne, Sir Thomas
1606-1668, D'Avenant, William
1606-1687, Waller, Edmund
1608-1661, Fuller, Thomas
1608-1674, Milton, John
1609-1642, Suckling, Sir John
1609-1674, Clarendon, Edward Hyde,
    1st Earl of
1611-1660, Urquhart, Sir Thomas
1611-1677, Harrington, James
1612/13-1649, Crashaw, Richard
1612-1672, Bradstreet, Anne
1613-1658, Cleveland, John
1613-1667, Taylor, Jeremy
1613-1680, Butler, Samuel
1614-1687, More, Henry
later 1638-1706, Sackville, Charles,
    Lord Buckhurst, 6th Earl of
    Dorset
1615-1669, Denham, John
1615-1691, Baxter, Richard
1616-1704, L'Estrange, Roger
1618-1657/8, Lovelace, Richard
1618-1667, Cowley, Abraham
1620-1706, Evelyn, John
1621-1678, Marvell, Andrew
1621-1695, Vaughan, Henry
1623-1723, Newcastle, Margaret,
    Dutchess of

1627-1691, Boyle, Robert
1628-1688, Bunyan, John
1628-1699, Temple, Sir William
1630-1687, Cotton, Charles
1631-1664, Philips, Katherine
1631-1700, Dryden, John
1633-1695, Halifax, George Savile, 1st
  Marquis of
1633-1703, Pepys, Samuel
1634?-1691, Etherege, George
1637-1674, Traherne, Thomas
1639?-1701, Sedley, Sir Charles
1640?-1689, Behn, Aphra
1641-1715, Wycherley, William
1642?-1692, Shadwell, Thomas
1644-1729, Taylor, Edward
1647-1680, Rochester, John Wilmot, 2nd
  Earl of
1649?-1692, Lee, Nathaniel
1650-1726, Collier, Jeremy
1652-1685, Otway, Thomas
1652-1725, Wise, John
1653-1723, D'Urfey, Thomas
1657-1734, Dennis, John
1660-1731, Defoe, Daniel
1663-1704, Brown, Thomas
1663-1712, King, William
1663-1728, Mather, Cotton
1664-1721, Prior, Matthew
1664-1726, Vanbrugh, Sir John
1665-1724, Gildon, Charles
1666-1727, Knight, Sarah Kemble
1667-1731, Ward, Edward
1667-1735, Arbuthnot, John,
1667-1745, Swift, Jonathan
1669-1723, Centlivre, Susannah
1670-1729, Congreve, William
1670-1733, Mandeville, Bernard de
1671-1713, Shaftesbury, Anthony
  Ashley Cooper, 3rd, Earl of
1671-1757, Cibber, Colley
1672-1719, Addison, Joseph
1672-1729, Steele, Sir Richard
1674-1718, Rowe, Nicholas
1674-1744, Byrd, William, II
1674-1748, Watts, Isaac
1674-1749, Philips, Ambrose
1677?-1707, Farquhar, George
1678-1751, Bolingbroke, Henry St. John,
  1st Viscount
1679-1718, Parnell, Thomas
1683-1765, Young, Edward
1685-1732, Gay, John
1686-1758, Ramsay, Allan

1687?-1743, Carey, Henry
1688-1744, Pope, Alexander
1689-1761, Richardson, Samuel
1689-1762, Montagu, Lady Mary
  Wortley
1693-1739, Lillo, George
1694-1773, Chesterfield, Philip Dormer
  Stanhope, 4th Earl of
1697-1737, Green, Matthew
1699-1757, Dyer, John
1699-1777, Bartram, John

1701-1800 Eighteenth Century
fl. 1769-1772, "Junius"
c. 1762-1824, Rowson, Susanna
1700-1748, Thomson, James
1703-1758, Edwards, Jonathan
1706-1790, Franklin, Benjamin
1707-1754, Fielding, Henry
1707-1788, Byles, Mather
1709-1779, Armstrong, John,
1709-1784, Johnson, Samuel
1709-1789, Cleland, John
1713-1768, Sterne, Laurence
1714-1763, Shenstone, William
1715-1804, Graves, Richard
1716-1771, Gray, Thomas
1717-1779, Garrick, David
1717-1797, Walpole, Horace
1718-1800, Blair, Hugh
1720-1777, Foote, Samuel
1720-1793, White, Gilbert
1720-1804, Lennox, Charlotte
1720-c. 1800, Hammon, Jupiter
1721-1759, Collins, William
1721-1770, Akenside, Mark
1721-1771, Smollett, Tobias George
1722-1771, Smart, Christopher
1722-1800, Warton, Joseph
1723-1791, Price, Richard
1723-1792, Reynolds, Sir Joshua
1727-1805, Murphy, Arthur
1728-1790, Warton, Thomas
1728-1814, Warren, Mercy Otis
1729-1797, Burke, Edmund
1729-1807, Reeve, Clara
1729-1811, Percy, Thomas
1730?-1774, Goldsmith, Oliver
1731-1800, Cowper, William
1731-1806, Banneker, Benjamin
1732-1764, Churchill, Charles
1732-1794, Colman, George, the Elder
1732-1811, Cumberland, Richard

1735-1813, de Crevecouer, Michel-
　　Guillaume St. Jean
1736-1796, MacPherson, James
1737-1794, Gibbon, Edward
1737-1809, Paine, Thomas
1739-1823, Bartram, William
1740-1795, Boswell, James
1741-1820, Young, Arthur
1743-1824, Barbauld, Anna Laetitia
1743-1826, Jefferson, Thomas
1744-1798, Belknap, Jeremy
1744-1803, Hitchcock, Enos
1745-1831, MacKenzie, Henry
1748-1806, Smith, Charlotte
1748-1816, Brackenridge, Hugh Henry
1750-1831, Trumbull, John
1751-1816, Sheridan, Richard Brinsley
1752-1770, Chatterton, Thomas
1752-1783, Bleecker, Ann Eliza
1752-1817, Dwight, Timothy
1752-1827, Tucker, St. George
1752-1832, Freneau, Philip
1752-1840, Burney, Fanny
1753?-1784, Wheatley, Phillis
1754-1812, Barlow, Joel
1754-1828, Imlay, Gilbert
1754-1832, Crabbe, George
1754-1848, Cumberland, George
1756-1836, Godwin, William
1757-1826, Tyler, Royall
1757-1827, Blake, William
1758-1840, Foster, Hannah Webster
1759-1796, Burns, Robert
1759-1797, Wollstonecraft, Mary
1759-1812, Mitchell, Isaac
1759-1844, Beckford, William
1759-1846, Morton, Sarah Wentworth
1759-1855, Wood, Sarah Sayward Bar-
　　rell Keating
1761-1815, Alsop, Richard
1762-1836, Colman, George, the
　　Younger
1762-1837, Tenney, Tabitha Gilman
1763-1835, Cobbett, William
1763-1855, Rogers, Samuel
1764-1823, Radcliffe, Ann
1764-1846, Dwight, Theodore
1765-1793, Brown, William Hill
1765-1850, Bodman, Manoah
1766-1839, Dunlap, William
1768-1812, Dennie, Joseph
1768-1849, Edgeworth, Maria
1769-1854, Royall, Anne Newport
1770-1835, Hogg, James

1770-1850, Wordsworth, William
1771-1798, Smith, Elihu Hubbard
1771-1810, Brown, Charles Brockden
1771-1832, Scott, Sir Walter
1772-1834, Coleridge, Samuel Taylor
1774-1843, Southey, Robert
1775-1817, Austen, Jane
1775-1818, Lewis, M. G.
1775-1826, Allen, Paul,
1775-1834, Lamb, Charles
1775-1854, Davis, John
1775-1861, Tucker, George
1775-1864, Landor, Walter Savage
1777-1844, Campbell, Thomas
1778-1830, Hazlitt, William
1778-1841, Austin, William
1778-1860, Paulding, James Kirke
1779-1843, Allston, Washington,
1779-1843, Key, Francis Scott
1779-1852, Moore, Thomas
1779-1863, Moore, Clement Clarke
1780-1840, Flint, Timothy
1780-1842, Channing, William Ellery
1780-1863, Trollope, Frances
1782-1824, Maturin, Charles Robert
1783-1854, Watterson, George
1783-1859, Irving, Washington
1784-1851, Tucker, Nathaniel Beverley
1784-1858, Barker, James Nelson
1784-1859, Hunt, Leigh
1785?-1830, Walker, David
1785-1842, Woodworth, Samuel
1785-1845, McHenry, James
1785-1851, Audubon, John James
1785-1851, Noah, Mordecai Manuel
1785-1859, De Quincey, Thomas
1785-1866, Peacock, Thomas Love
1787?-1844, Warren, Caroline Matilda
1787-1858, Leslie, Eliza
1787-1879, Dana, Richard Henry, Sr.
1788-1824, Byron, George Gordon, Lord
1788-1863, Elliot, William
1788-1879, Hale, Sarah Josepha
1789-1841, Hillhouse, James Abraham
1789-1851, Cooper, James Fenimore
1789-1867, Sedgwick, Catharine Maria
1790-1867, Halleck, FitzGreene
1790-1870, Longstreet, Augustus
　　Baldwin
1791-1852, Payne, John Howard
1791-1865, Sigourney, Lydia Huntley
1792-1822, Shelley, Percy Bysshe
1792-1844, Stone, William Leete
1792-1848, Marryat, Captain Frederick

1792-1868, Smith, Seba
1793-1860, Goodrich, Samuel Griswold
1793-1864, Clare, John
1793-1864, Sealsfield, Charles
1793-1868, Hall, James
1793-1876, Neal, John
1794-1842, Marsh, James
1794-1845, Brooks, Maria Gowen
1794-1878, Bryant, William Cullen
b. 1794-, Cushing, Eliza L.
1795?-1868?, Davis, Charles Augustus
1795-1820, Drake, Joseph Rodman
1795-1821, Keats, John
1795-1856, Percival, James Gates
1795-1863, Francis, Convers
1795-1868, Thompson, Daniel Pierce
1795-1870, Kennedy, John Pendleton
1795-1881, Carlyle, Thomas
1796-1828, Brainard, John Gardiner
    Calkins
1796-1859, Prescott, William Hickling
1796-1865, Haliburton, Thomas
    Chandler
1796-1876, Bulfinch, Thomas
1797-1851, Shelley, Mary Wollstonecraft
1797-1852, Ware, William
1798-1842, Clarke, McDonald
1798-1855, Hart, Joseph C.
1798-1863, Hall, Baynard Rush
1799-1845, Hood, Thomas
1799-1854, Smith, Richard Penn
1799-1888, Alcott, Bronson

1801-1900 Nineteenth Century
fl. 1840s, Lane, Charles
fl. 1820s-1847?, Ripley, Sophia Dana
c. 1858-1914, Lewis, Alfred Henry
1800-1856, Hentz, Caroline Lee
1800-1859, Macaulay, Thomas
    Babington
1800-1880, Reed, Sampson
1800-1891, Bancroft, George
1801-1864, Kirkland, Caroline Stansbury
1801-1866, Carlyle, Jane Baillie Welsh
1801-1886, Barnes, William
1801-1890, Newman, John Henry
1802-1828, Pinkney, Edward Coote
1802-1839, Praed, Winthrop Macworth
1802-1846, Caruthers, William
    Alexander
1802-1864, Morris, George Pope
1802-1880, Child, Lydia Maria
1802-1880, Ripley, George
1803-1844, Fairfield, Sumner Lincoln

1803-1849, Beddoes, Thomas Lovell
1803-1859, Dawes, Rufus
1803-1873, Bulwer-Lytton, Edward
    George Earle, Lytton, 1st Bar-
    ron Lytton
1803-1876, Brownson, Orestes Augustus
1803-1878, Whitman, Sarah Helen
1803-1881, Borrow, George Henry
1803-1882, Emerson, Ralph Waldo
1803-1889, Calvert, George Henry
1804-1848, Snelling, William Joseph
1804-1864, Hawthorne, Nathaniel
1804-1876, Judah, Samuel B. H.
1804-1877, Briggs, Charles Frederick
1804-1881, Disraeli, Benjamin
1804-1894, Peabody, Elizabeth Palmer
1805-1882, Adams, John Turvill
1805-1882, Ainsworth, William Harrison
1805-1890, Hedge, Frederic Henry
1806-1854, Bird, Robert Montgomery
1806-1861, Browning, Robert
1806-1866, Thomas, Frederick William
1806-1867, Willis, N. P.
1806-1870, Simms, William Gilmore
1806-1873, Mill, John Stuart
1806-1884, Hoffman, Charles Fenno
1807-1847, Neal, Joseph Clay
1807-1858, Herbert, Henry William
1807-1865, Hildreth, Richard
1807-1882, Longfellow, Henry
    Wadsworth
1807-1892, Whittier, John Greenleaf
1807-1898, Fay, Theodore Sedgwick
1808-1841, Clark, Willis Gaylord
1808-1894, Gallagher, William Davis
1808-1895, Smith, Samuel Francis
1808-c. 1870, Wilson, Harriet
1809-1849, Poe, Edgar Allan
1809-1858, Chivers, Thomas Holley
1809-1860, Ingraham, Joseph Holt
1809-1864, Benjamin, Park
1809-1882, Darwin, Charles Robert
1809-1883, FitzGerald, Edward
1809-1885, Arthur, T. S.
1809-1891, Pike, Albert
1809-1892, Tennyson, Alfred
1809-1894, Holmes, Oliver Wendell
1810-1850, Fuller, Margaret
1810-1860, Parker, Theodore
1810-1865, Gaskell, Elizabeth Cleghorn
1810-1866, Jones, John Beauchamp
1810-1884, Channing, William Henry
1810-1888, Clarke, James Freeman
1811-1833, Hallam, Arthur Henry

1811-1850, Osgood, Frances Sargent
1811-1859, Bacon, Delia Salter
1811-1863, Thackeray, William
     Makepeace
1811-1872, Parton, Sara Payson Willis
1811-1895, Mayo, William Starbuck
1811-1896, Stowe, Harriet Beecher
1812-1870, Dickens, Charles
1812-1878, Myers, Peter Hamilton
1812-1882, Thompson, William Tappan
1812-1885, Delany, Martin R.
1812-1888, Lear, Edward
1812-1889, Browning, Elizabeth Barrett
1813-1853, Judd, Sylvester
1813-1871, Tuckerman, Henry Theodore
1813-1880, Sargent, Epes
1813-1880, Very, Jones
1813-1883, Brooks, Charles T.
1813-1892, Cranch, Christopher Pearse
1813-1893, Dwight, John S.
1813-1894, Cooper, Susan Fenimore
1813-1900, Bartol, Cyrus Augustus
1814-1852, Whitcher, Frances Miriam
1814-1869, Harris, George Washington
1814-1873, LeFanu, J. S.
1814-1877, Hosmer, William H. C.
1814-1877, Motley, John Lothrop
1814-1884, Reade, Charles
1814-1890, Shillaber, Benjamin
     Penhallow
1815-1852, Phelps, Elizabeth
1815-1857, Griswold, Rufus Wilmot
1815-1862, Hooper, Johnson Jones
1815-1864, Baldwin, Joseph Glover
1815-1878, Thorpe, T. B.
1815-1882, Dana, Richard Henry, Jr.
1815-1882, Trollope, Anthony
1816?-1884, Brown, William Wells
1816-1843, Wheeler, Charles Stearns
1816-1855, Bronte, Emily
1816-1887, Saxe, John Godfrey
1816-1891, Lowell, Robert Traill Spence
1816-1892, Kimball, Richard Burleigh
1817-1848, Bronte, Anne
1817-1852, Wallace, Horace Binney
1817-1862, Thoreau, Henry David
1817-1878, Lewes, G. H.
1817-1881, Fields, James T.
1817-1889, Mathews, Cornelius
1817-1895, Douglass, Frederick
1818-1848, Bronte, Patrick Branwell
1818-1869, Cozzens, Frederick
     Swartwout
1818-1875, Taliaferro, Harden E.

1818-1879, Weiss, John
1818-1885, Shaw, Henry Wheeler
1818-1901, Channing, William Ellery
1818-1903, Bain, Alexander
1819-1856, Webber, Charles Wilkins
1819-1861, Clough, Arthur Hugh
1819-1875, Kingsley, Charles
1819-1880, Eliott, George
1819-1881, Holland, Josiah Gilbert
1819-1885, Warner, Susan Bogert
1819-1891, Lowell, James Russell
1819-1891, Melville, Herman
1819-1892, Longfellow, Samuel
1819-1892, Parsons, Thomas Williams
1819-1892, Whitman, Walt
1819-1895, Story, William Wetmore
1819-1899, Southworth, E. D. E. N.
1819-1900, Ruskin, John
1819-1902, English, Thomas Dunn
1819-1910, Howe, Julia Ward
1820-1849, Bronte, Charlotte
1820-1871, Cary, Alice
1820-1872, Brownell, Henry Howard
1820-1890, Boucicault, Dion
1820-1894, Newcomb, Charles King
1820-1900, Hale, Lucretia Peabody
1821-1873, Tuckerman, Frederick
     Goddard
1822-1854, Lippard, George
1822-1872, Read, Thomas Buchanan
1822-1882, Johnson, Samuel
1822-1888, Arnold, Matthew
1822-1895, Frothingham, Octavius
     Brooks
1822-1898, Johnston, Richard Malcolm
1822-1905, Bennett, Emerson
1822-1908, Mitchell, Donald Grant
1822-1909, Hale, Edward Everett
1823-1861, Derby, George Horatio
1823-1884, Duganne, Augustine Joseph
     Hickey
1823-1887, Cobb, Sylvanus, Jr.
1823-1890, Boker, George Henry
1823-1893, Parkman, Francis
1823-1896, Patmore, Coventry Kersey
     Dighton
1823-1902, Stoddard, Elizabeth Drew
1823-1911, Higginson, Thomas
     Wentworth
1824-1871, Cary, Phoebe
1824-1889, Allingham, William,
1824-1889, Collins, Wilkie
1824-1892, Curtis, George William
1824-1893, Larcom, Lucy

1824-1903, Leland, Charles Godfrey
1824-1906, Whitney, Adeline Dutton
    Train
1825-1850, Tensas, Madison, M.D.
1825-1873, Chesebro', Caroline
1825-1878, Taylor, Bayard
1825-1894, Ballantyne, R. M.
1825-1895, Huxley, T. H.
1825-1902, Butler, William Allen
1825-1903, Stoddard, Richard Henry
1825-1907, Holmes, Mary Jane
1825-1911, Harper, Frances Ellen
    Watkins
1826-1877, Bagehot, Walter
1826-1897, Hutton, Richard Holt
1826-1903, Byrn, Marcus Lafayette
1826-1903, Smith, Charles Henry
1826-1906, De Forest, John William
1827-1866, Cummins, Maria Susanna
1827-1892, Cooke, Rose Terry
1827-1905, Wallace, Lew
1827-1915, Warner, Anna Bartlett
1827-1916, Trowbridge, J. T.
1828-1861, Winthrop, Theodore
1828-1862, O'Brien, Fitz-James
1828-1867, Timrod, Henry
1828-1882, Rossetti, Dante Gabriel
1828-1883, Bagby, George William
1828-1909, Finley, Martha
1828-1909, Meredith, George
1829-1868, Halpine, Charles Graham
1829-1871, Robertson, T. W.
1829-1879, Dallas, Eneas Sweetland
1829-1900, Warner, Charles Dudley
1829-1914, Mitchell, S. Weir
1830-1885, Jackson, Helen Hunt
1830-1886, Cooke, John Esten
1830-1886, Dickinson, Emily
1830-1886, Hayne, Paul Hamilton
1830-1894, Kirkland, Joseph
1830-1894, Rossetti, Christina Georgina
1830-1922, Terhune, Mary Virginia
1831-1875, Thomson, Mortimer Neal
1831-1891, Lytton, Edward Robert Bul-
    wer, 1st Earl, of Lytton
1831-1894, Austin, Jane Goodwin
1831-1901, Donnelly, Ignatius
1831-1905, Dodge, Mary Mapes
1831-1910, Davis, Rebecca Harding
1831-1917, Sanborn, Franklin Benjamin
1831-1923, Harrison, Frederic
1832-1888, Alcott, Louisa May
1832-1898, Dodgson, Charles Lutwidge
1832-1899, Alger, Horatio, Jr.

1832-1904, Stephen, Sir Leslie
1832-1907, Conway, Moncure Daniel
1832-1911, Allen, Elizabeth Akers,
1833-1888, Locke, David Ross
1833-1896, Dodge, Mary Abigail
1833-1900, Robinson, Rowland Evans
1833-1908, Stedman, Edmund Clarence
1833-1913, Blake, Lillie Devereux
1834-1867, Browne, Charles Farrar
1834-1882, Thomson, James
1834-1896, Morris, William
1834-1902, Stockton, Frank R.
1834-1903, Whistler, James Abbott
    McNeill
1835-1894, Thaxter, Celia
1835-1902, Butler, Samuel
1835-1908, Moulton, Louise Chandler
1835-1909, Wilson, Augusta Jane Evans
1835-1910, Clemens, Samuel Langhorne
1835-1917, Piatt, John James
1835-1921, Spofford, Harriet Prescott
1836-1901, Newell, Robert Henry
1836-1902, Harte, Bret
1836-1907, Aldrich, Thomas Bailey
1836-1911, Gilbert, William Schwenck
1836-1917, Winter, William
1836-1926, Holley, Marietta
1837-1902, Eggleston, Edward
1837-1909, Swinburne, Algernon
    Charles
1837-1920, Howells, William Dean
1837-1921, Burroughs, William S.
1838-1886, Ryan, Abram Joseph
1838-1888, Roe, E. P.
1838-1905, Hay, John
1838-1905, Tourgee, Albion W.
1838-1914, Muir, John
1838-1915, Smith, Francis Hopkinson
1838-1918, Adams, Henry
1838-1923, Morley, John
1839-1894, Pater, Walter Horatio
1839-1910, Landon, Melville De Lancey
1840-1893, Symonds, John Addington
1840-1894, Woolson, Constance
    Fenimore
1840-1921, Dobson, Austin
1840-1928, Hardy, Thomas
1841?-1913, Miller, Joaquin
1841-1887, Sill, Edward Rowland
1841-1898, Pool, Maria Louise
1841-1922, Hudson, W. H.
1842-1881, Langstaff, Launcelot (see
    Paulding, James, Kirke) Lanier,
    Sidney

1842-1893, Bynner, Edwin Lassetter
1842-1901, Fiske, John
1842-1914?, Bierce, Ambrose
1843-1909, Stoddard, Charles Warren
1843-1912, Torrey, Bradford
1843-1916, James, Henry
1843-1920, Harrison, Constance Cary
1844-1889, Hopkins, Gerard Manley
1844-1890, O'Reilly, John Boyle
1844-1901, Thompson, Maurice
1844-1909, Gilder, Richard Watson
1844-1911, Ward, Elizabeth Stuart
　　Phelps
1844-1914, Burdette, Robert Jones
1844-1924, Lothrop, Harriett Mulford
　　Stone
1844-1925, Cable, George Washington
1844-1930, Bridges, Robert
1845-1909, Tabb, John B.
1845-1912, Carleton, Will
1845-1918, Mitchell, John Ames
1845-1921, Pringle, Elizabeth Waties
　　Allston (Patience Pennington)
1845-1933, Saintsbury, George Edward
　　Bateman
1846-1898, Westcott, Edward Noyes
1846-1901, Greenaway, Kate
1846-1935, Green, Anna Katharine
1847-1902, Catherwood, Mary
1847-1904, Fawcett, Edgar
1847-1929, Wyman, Elizabeth Buffum
　　Chace
1847-1930, Hardy, Arthur Sherburne
1847-1938, Foote, Mary Hallock
1848-1887, Jefferies, Richard
1848-1895, Boyesen, Hjalmar Hjorth
1848-1908, Harris, Joel Chandler
1849-1883, MacDowell, Katherine
1849-1887, Lazarus, Emma
1849-1903, Henley, W. E.
1849-1909, Jewett, Sarah Orne
1849-1913, Janvier, Thomas Allibone
1849-1916, Riley, James Whitcomb
1849-1924, Burnett, Frances Hodgson
1849-1925, Allen, James Lane
1849-1928, Gosse, Edmund
1850-1894, Stevenson, Robert Louis
　　Balfour
1850-1895, Field, Eugene
1850-1896, Nye, Bill Edgar (Wilson)
1850-1898, Bellamy, Edward
1850-1904, Hearn, Lafcadio
1850-1922, Murfree, Mary Noailles
1850-1934, French, Alice

1851-1898, Lathrop, George Parsons
1851-1904, Chopin, Kate
1851-1929, Jones, Henry Arthur
1851-1932, King, Grace Elizabeth
1852-1929, Matthews, Brander
1852-1930, Freeman, Mary E. Wilkins
1852-1932, Gregory, Augusta, Lady
1852-1933, Moore, George Augustus
1852-1933, Van Dyke, Henry
1852-1936, Cunninghame Graham,
　　Robert Bontine
1853-1879, Russell, Irwin
1853-1911, Pyle, Howard
1853-1922, Page, Thomas Nelson
1853-1937, Howe, E. W.
1854-1900, Wilde, Oscar Fingal
　　O'Flahertie Wills .
1854-1909, Crawford, Francis Marion
1855-1896, Bunner, H. C.
1855-1919, Adams, Oscar Fay
1855-1921, Saltus, Edgar Evertson
1855-1930, Woodberry, George Edward
1855-1934, Pinero, Sir Arthur Wing
1856-1898, Frederic, Harold
1856-1913, Major, Charles
1856-1915, Washington, Booker T.
1856-1919, Baum, L. Frank
1856-1923, Wiggin, Kate Douglas
1856-1925, Haggard, H. Rider
1856-1935, Lee, Vernon
1856-1950, Shaw, Bernard
fl. 1857-1870, Webb, Frank J.
1857-1903, Gissing, George Robert
1857-1909, Davidson, John
1857-1921, Huneker, James Gibbons
1857-1923, Hough, Emerson
1857-1924, Conrad, Joseph
1857-1929, Fuller, Henry Blake
1857-1945, Deland, Margaret
1857-1948, Atherton, Gertrude
1857-1948, Brown, Alice
1858-1932, Chesnutt, Charles W.
1859-1907, Thompson, Francis
1859-1930, Doyle, Arthur Conan
1859-1930, Hopkins, Pauline
1859-1935, Adams, Andy
1859-1936, Housman, A. E.
1859-1950, Bacheller, Irving
1859-1952, Dewey, John
1860-1916, Sherman, Frank Dempster
1860-1935, Gilman, Charlotte Perkins
1860-1937, Barrie, Sir J. M.
1860-1938, Wister, Owen
1860-1940, Garland, Hamlin

1860-1951, Cahan, Abraham
1861-1905, Harland, Henry
1861-1909, Remington, Frederic
    Sackrider
1861-1920, Guiney, Louise Imogen
1861-1929, Carman, Bliss
1861-1937, Paine, Albert Bigelow
1862-1910, Porter, William Sydney
1862-1919, Fox, John, Jr.
1862-1922, Bangs, John Kendrick
1862-1937, Wharton, Edith
1863-1924, Stratton-Porter, Gene
1863-1945, Rives, Amelie, Princess
    Troubetzkoy
1863-1947, Machen, Arthur Llewelyn
1864-1900, Hovey, Richard
1864-1916, Davis, Richard Harding
1864-1926, Zangwill, Israel
1864-1946, Dixon, Thomas, Jr.
1865-1902, Ford, Paul Leicester
1865-1909, Fitch, Clyde
1865-1914, Cawein, Madison
1865-1933, Chambers, Robert W.
1865-1934, Anstey, F.
1865-1936, Kipling, Rudyard
1865-1939, Yeats, William Butler
1865-1945, Symons, Arthur William
1866-1928, McCutcheon, George Barr
1866-1934, Gray, John Henry
1866-1943, Bianchi, Martha Gilbert
    Dickinson
1866-1944, Ade, George
1866-1946, Wells, H. G.
1866-1947, Nicholson, Meredith
1867-1900, Dowson, Ernest Christopher
1867-1902, Johnson, Lionel Pigot
1867-1911, Phillips, David Graham
1867-1931, Bennett, Arnold
1867-1933, Galsworthy, John
1867-1935, Russell, George William
1867-1936, Dunne, Finley Peter
1867-1939, Rackham, Arthur
1867-1939, Wilson, Harry Leon
1867-1957, Wilder, Laura Ingalls
1868?-1950, Masters, Edgar Lee
1868-1920, Porter, Eleanor Hodgman
1868-1926, Bell, Gertrude Magaret
    Lowthian
1868-1934, Austin, Mary
1868-1938, Herrick, Robert
1868-1938, Lucas, E. V.
1868-1944, White, William Allen
1868-1952, Douglas, Norman
1868-1963, DuBois, W. E. B.

1869-1910, Moody, William Vaughan
1869-1924, Chester, George Randolph
1869-1926, Sterling, George
1869-1934, Rhodes, Eugene Manlove
1869-1934, Whitlock, Brand
1869-1935, Robinson, Edwin Arlington
1869-1946, Tarkington, Booth
1869-1951, Blackwood, Algernon
1869-1968, Dargan, Olive Tilford
1870-1902, Norris, Frank
1870-1936, Johnston, Mary
1870-1942, Rice, Alice Hegan
1870-1944, Lincoln, Joseph C.
1870-1953, Belloc, Hilaire
1871-1900, Crane, Stephen
1871-1909, Synge, John Millington
1871-1938, Johnson, James Weldon
1871-1940, Davies, W. H.
1871-1945, Dreiser, Theodore
1871-1947, Churchill, Winston
1871-1958, Adams, Samuel Hopkins
1871-1962, Hodgson, Ralph Edwin
1872-1898, Beardsley, Aubrey Vincent
1872-1906, Dunbar, Paul Laurence
1872-1930, Griggs, Sutton E.
1872-1939, Grey, Zane
1872-1944, Wright, Harold Bell
1872-1956, Beerbohm, Max
1872-1963, Powys, John Cowper
1872-1966, Craig, Gordon
1873-1904, Carryl, Guy Wetmore
1873-1909, Lodge, George Cabot
1873-1939, Ford, Ford Madox
1873-1945, Glasgow, Ellen
1873-1946, White, Stewart Edward
1873-1947, Cather, Willa
1873-1956, de la Mare, Walter
1873-1957, Richardson, Dorothy Miller
1874-1925, Lowell, Amy
1874-1936, Chesterton, G. K.
1874-1938, Gale, Zona
1874-1946, Stein, Gertrude
1874-1963, Frost, Robert
1874-1965, Burgess, Thornton W.
1874-1965, Maugham, W. Somerset
1875-1935, Dunbar-Nelson, Alice Moore
1875-1940, Buchan, John, 1st Baron
    Tweedsmuir
1875-1950, Burroughs, Edgar Rice
1875-1953, Powys, T. F.
1876-1916, London, Jack
1876-1931, Rolvaag, O. E.
1876-1941, Anderson, Sherwood
1876-1944, Cobb, Irvin S.

1876-1958, Rinehart, Mary Roberts
1877-1947, Anderson, Fredrick Irving
1877-1949, Beach, Rex
1877-1951, Douglas, Lloyd C.
1877-1967, Toklas, Alice B.
1878-1914, Crapsey, Adelaide
1878-1927, Curwood, James Oliver
1878-1937, Marquis, Don
1878-1952, Johnson, Owen
1878-1957, Coppard, A. E.
1878-1957, Dunsany, Edward John
      Moreton Drax Plunkett, 18th
      Baron
1878-1957, Gogarty, Oliver Joseph St.
      John
1878-1967, Masefield, John Edward
1878-1967, Sandburg, Carl
1878-1968, Sinclair, Upton
1879-1944, Gerould, Katharine Fullerton
1879-1955, Stevens, Wallace
1879-1958, Cabell, James Branch
1879-1958, Canfield, Dorothy
1879-1970, Forster, E. M.
1880-1932, Strachey, Giles Lytton
1880-1946, Runyon, Damon
1880-1950, Poole, Ernest
1880-1954, Hergesheimer, Joseph
1880-1956, Mencken, H. L.
1880-1957, Asch, Sholem
1880-1957, Kyne, Peter B.
1880-1961, Peterkin, Julia
1880-1964, O'Casey, Sean
1880-1964, Van Vechten, Carl
1880-1969, Woolf, Leonard Sidney
1881-1938, Abercrombie, Lascelles
1881-1941, Roberts, Elizabeth Madox
1881-1949, Antin, Mary,
1881-1963, Young, Stark
1881-1964, Kelland, Clarence Budington
1881-1965, Stribling, Thomas Sigismund
1881-1966, McFee, William
1881-1972, Colum, Padraic
1881-1973, Neihardt, John G.
1881-1975, Wodehouse, Sir P. G.
1882?-1969, Traven, B.
1882-1937, Drinkwater, John
1882-1940, Gill, Eric
1882-1941, Joyce, James Augustine
      Aloysius
1882-1941, Woolf, Virginia
1882-1948, Glaspell, Susan
1882-1950, Stephens, James
1882-1956, Milne, A. A.
1882-1957, Lewis, Wyndham

1882-1973, Wilson, Margaret
1882-1974, Armstrong, Martin
      Donisthorpe
1883-1916, Lyon, Harris Merton
1883-1956, Mulford, Clarence E.
1883-1963, Williams, William Carlos
1884-1933, Biggers, Earl Derr
1884-1939, Powys, Llewelyn
1884-1951, Micheaux, Oscar
1884-1956, Kelley, Edith Summers
1885-1928, Wylie, Elinor
1885-1930, Lawrence, D. H.
1885-1933, Lardner, Ring W.
1885-1940, Heyward, DuBose
1885-1941, Rourke, Constance
1885-1942, Percy, William Alexander
1885-1951, Lewis, Sinclair
1885-1957, Roberts, Kenneth
1885-1972, Pound, Ezra
1886-1918, Kilmer, Joyce
(1886-1926), Firbank, Ronald
1886-1945, Williams, Charles W. S.
1886-1950, Fletcher, John Gould
1886-1950, Stapledon, Olaf
1886-1961, H. D.
1886-1963, Brooks, Van Wyck
1886-1967, Sassoon, Siegfried Loraine
1886-1970, Steele, Wilbur Daniel
1886-1975, Stout, Rex
1887-1915, Brooke, Rupert Chawner
1887-1947, Nordhoff, Charles Bernard
1887-1951, Hall, James Norman
1887-1959, Muir, Edwin
1887-1962, Jeffers, Robinson
1887-1964, Sitwell, Dame Edith Louisa
1887-1968, Ferber, Edna
1887-1969, Dell, Floyd
1887-1972, Moore, Marianne
1888-1916, Seeger, Alan
1888-1923, Mansfield, Katherine
1888-1928, Newman, Frances
1888-1935, Lawrence, T. E.
1888-1944, Boyd, James
1888-1953, O'Neill, Eugene
1888-1956, Long, Haniel
1888-1957, Cary, Joyce
1888-1957, Parrish, Anne
1888-1959, Anderson, Maxwell
1888-1959, Chandler, Raymond
1888-1965, Eliot, T. S.
1888-1974, Ransom, John Crowe
1888-1981, Loos, Anita
1889-1928, Byrne, Donn
1889-1940, Beer, Thomas

1889-1949, Allen, Hervey
1889-1957, Murry, John Middleton
1889-1970, Gardner, Erle Stanley
1889-1973, Aiken, Conrad
1889-1975, Tunis, John R.
1890?-1979, Rhys, Jean
1890-1937, Lovecraft, H. P.
1890-1948, McKay, Claude
1890-1957, Morley, Christopher
1890-1968, Richter, Conrad
1890-1976, Christie, Dame Agatha
1890-1980, Porter, Katherine Anne
1891-1958, Paul, Elliott Harold
1891-1973, Gunn, Neil Miller
1891-1974, Loeb, Harold
1891-1980, Miller, Henry
1892-1942, James, Will
1892-1944, Bishop, John Peale
1892-1944, Brand, Max
1892-1950, Millar, Kenneth (see Macdonald, Ross) Millay, Edna St.
   Vincent
1892-1960, Suckow, Ruth
1892-1962, Aldington, Richard
1892-1967, Rice, Elmer
1892-1969, Herbst, Josephine
1892-1970, Crosby, Caresse
1892-1973, Buck, Pearl S.
1892-1973, Tolkien, J. R. R.
1892-1977, Cain, James M.
1892-1978, Flanner, Janet
1892-1978, MacDiarmid, Hugh (Christopher Murray Grieve)
1892-1982, Barnes, Djuna
1892-1982, MacLeish, Archibald
1892-1983, West, Dame Rebecca
1893-1918, Owen, Wilfred
1893-1938, Weaver, John V. A.
1893-1954, March, William Edward
1893-1957, Sayers, Dorothy L.
1893-1960, Marquand, J. P.
1893-1963, Scott, Evelyn
1893-1967, Gold, Michael
1893-1967, Parker, Dorothy
1893-1973, Behrman, S. N.
1894-1948, Putnam, Howard Phelps
1894-1948, Taggard, Genevieve
1894-1961, Hammett, Dashiell
1894-1961, Thurber, James
1894-1962, Cummings, E. E.
1894-1963, Huxley, Aldous Leonard
1894-1967, Toomer, Jean
1894-1980, Stewart, Donald Ogden

1894-1981, Green, Paul
1894-1984, Priestley, J. B.
1894-1985, Nathan, Robert
1895-1957, Pinckney, Josephine
1895-1968, Fisher, Vardis
1895-1972, West, Alick
1895-1974, Jones, David Michael
1895-1978, Leavis, F. R.
1895-1980, Stewart, George R.
1895-1981, Gordon, Caroline
1895-1985, Graves, Robert van Ranke
1895-1990, Mumford, Lewis
1895-1993, Wilder, Amos N.
1896-1931, Black, MacKnight
1896-1940, Fitzgerald, F. Scott
1896-1953, Rawlings, Marjorie Kinnan
1896-1956, Bromfield, Louis
1896-1956, McAlmon, Robert
1896-1959, Springs, Elliott White
1896-1966, Sandoz, Mari
1896-1970, Dabbs, James McBride
1896-1970, Dos Passos, John
1896-1974, Blunden, Edmund
1896-1974, Clarke, Austin
1896-1981, Cronin, A. J.
1896-1984, O'Flaherty, Liam
1897-, Gibson, Walter B.
1897-1940, Wheelwright, John
1897-1955, McCoy, Horace
1897-1962, Faulkner, William
1897-1965, Powell, Dawn
1897-1970, Bogan, Louise
1897-1973, Coates, Robert M.
1897-1975, Wilder, Thornton
1898-1929 Crowfield, Christopher (see
   Stowe, Harriet Beecher),
   Crosby, Harry
1898-1963, Lewis, C. S.
1898-1982, Rickword, Edgell
1898-1989, Cowley, Malcolm
1899-, Bates, Ralph
1899-, Lewis, Janet
1899-1932, Crane, Hart
1899-1944, Cobb, Humphrey
1899-1948, Fitzgerald, Zelda
1899-1950, Haycox, Ernest
1899-1951, Adamic, Louis
1899-1961, Hemingway, Ernest
1899-1973, Bowen, Elizabeth
1899-1973, Coward, Noel
1899-1977, Nabokov, Vladimir
1899-1978, Josephson, Matthew
1899-1979, Tate, Allen

1899-1980, Conroy, Jack
1899-1985, White, E. B.
1899-1988, Adams, Leonie

1901-2000 Twentieth Century
1900-1937, Fox, Ralph
1900-1938, Wolfe, Thomas
1900-1949, Mitchell, Margaret
1900-1968, Winters, Yvor
1900-1977, Dahlberg, Edward
1901?-1960, Hurston, Zora Neale
1901-1957, Campbell, Roy
1901-1978, Brace, Gerald Warner
1901-1987, Wescott, Glenway
1901-1991, Guthrie, A. B.
1901-1991, Riding, Laura
1902-1934, Thurman, Wallace
1902-1961, Fearing, Kenneth
1902-1964, Asch, Nathan
1902-1967, Hughes, Langston
1902-1968, Steinbeck, John
1902-1971, Nash, Ogden
1902-1971, Smith, Stevie
1902-1971, Wylie, Philip
1902-1973, Bontemps, Arna (Wendell)
1902-1995, Lytle, Andrew Nelson
1902-1995, Waters, Frank
1903-, Edmonds, Walter D.
1903-, Upward, Edward Falaise
1903-, Voelker, John Donaldson
1903?-1980, Lumpkin, Grace
1903-1940, West, Nathaniel
1903-1946, Cullen, Countee
1903-1950, Orwell, George
1903-1966, Waugh, Evelyn
1903-1968, Jackson, Charles
1903-1968, Woolrich, Cornell
1903-1977, Nin, Anais
1903-1978, Cozzens, James Gould
1903-1987, Caldwell, Erskine
1903-1994, Boyle, Kay
1903-1995, Horgan, Paul
1904-, Eberhart, Richard
1904?-1988, Graham, Sheilah
1904-1962, Holmes, John
1904-1964, Basso, Hamilton
1904-1972, Day-Lewis, Cecil
1904-1972, Smith, Betty
1904-1977, Kantor, MacKinlay
1904-1978, Zukofsky, Louis
1904-1979, Farrell, James T.
1904-1979, Perelman, S. J.
1904-1986, Isherwood, Christopher
1904-1988, Simak, Clifford D.

1904-1991, Geisel, Theodor Seuss
1904-1991, Greene, Graham
1904-1991, Singer, Isaac Bashevis
1905-, Kunitz, Stanley J.
1905-, Powell, Anthony Dymoke
1905-1967, Kavanagh, Patrick
1905-1970, O'Hara, John
1905-1974, Bates, H. E.
1905-1975, Trilling, Lionel
1905-1980, Snow, C. P.
1905-1982, Rand, Ayn
1905-1983, Koestler, Arthur
1905-1984, Hellman, Lillian
1905-1986, Warner, Rex
1905-1989, Warren, Robert Penn
1906-, Brooks, Cleanth
1906?-, Roth, Henry
1906-1963, Odets, Clifford
1906-1964, White, T. H.
1906-1977, Molloy, Robert
1906-1984, Betjeman, John
1906-1984, Empson, William
1906-1989, Beckett, Samuel
1907-, Charteris, Leslie
1907-, Ensley, Evangeline Walton
1907-, Fry, Christopher
1907-1937, Caudwell, Christopher
1907-1963, MacNeice, Louis
1907-1964, Carson, Rachel
1907-1968, Baker, Dorothy
1907-1972, Carter, Hodding
1907-1973, Auden, W. H.
1907-1984, Stuart, Jesse
1907-1984, West, Jessamyn
1907-1988, Heinlein, Robert A.
1907-1991, Schaefer, Jack
1907-1997, Michener, James A.
1908-, Gellhorn, Martha
1908-, Williamson, Jack
1908-1960, Wright, Richard
1908-1963, Roethke, Theodore
1908-1975, Short, Luke
1908-1978, Cantwell, Robert
1908-1981, Saroyan, William
1908-1986, Arnow, Harriette
1908-1988, Hale, Nancy
1909-, Coker, Elizabeth Boatwright
1909-, Fuchs, Daniel
1909-, Olson, Elder
1909-, Spender, Sir Stephen Harold
1909-, Welty, Eudora
1909-, Young, Marguerite
1909-1955, Agee, James
1909-1957, Lowry, Malcolm

1909-1971, Clark, Walter Van Tilburg
1909-1971, Derleth, August
1909-1981, Algren, Nelson
1909-1984, Himes, Chester
1909-1993, Stegner, Wallace
1910-, Bowles, Paul
1910-, Johnson, Josephine
1910-, Leiber, Fritz
1910-, Morris, Wright
1910?-1988, L'Amour, Louis
1910-1968, Scott, Winfield Townley
1910-1970, Olson, Charles
1910-1993, De Vries, Peter
1911-, Bretnor, Reginald
1911-, Calisher, Hortense
1911-, Gilbreth, Frank B., Jr.
1911-, Newhouse, Edward
1911-, Petry, Ann
1911-1968, Peake, Mervyn Laurence
1911-1972, Goodman, Paul
1911-1972, Patchen, Kenneth
1911-1979, Bishop, Elizabeth
1911-1983, Williams, Tennessee
1911-1985, Cunningham, J. V.
1911-1986, Attaway, William
1911-1993, Golding, William
1912-, Boyd, John
1912-, Manfred, Frederick
1912-, Norton, Andre
1912-, Sarton, May
1912-, Van Vogt, A. E.
1912-1965, Motley, Willard
1912-1982, Cheever, John
1912-1989, McCarthy, Mary
1912-1990, Durrell, Lawrence George
1912-1991, Frye, Northrop
1912-1994, Everson, William
1913-, Clark, Eleanor
1913-, Ferrini, Vincent
1913-, Nims, J. F.
1913-, Rocklynne, Ross
1913-, Shapiro, Karl
1913-1966, Schwartz, Delmore
1913-1966, Smith, Cordwainer
1913-1973, Inge, William
1913-1973, Kelly, Walt
1913-1980, Hayden, Robert
1913-1980, Pym, Barbara Mary
    Crampton
1913-1984, Shaw, Irwin
1913-1987, Bester, Alfred
1913-1991, Wilson, Sir Angus Frank
    Johnstone
1914-, Gibson, William

1914-, Gill, Brendan
1914-, Schulberg, Budd
1914-1948, Lockridge, Ross, Jr.
1914-1953, Thomas, Dylan Marlais
1914-1965, Jarrell, Randall
1914-1972, Berryman, John
1914-1986, Malamud, Bernard
1914-1993, Hersey, John
1914-1994, Ellison, Ralph
1914-1997, Burroughs, John
1915-, Bellow, Saul
1915-, Condon, Richard
1915-, Miller, Arthur
1915-, Walker, Margaret Abigail
1915-, Wouk, Herman
1915-1969, Merton, Thomas
1915-1978, Brackett, Leigh
1915-1979, Stafford, Jean
1915-1983, Goyen, William
1915-1983, Macdonald, Ross
1915-1993, Del Rey, Lester
1916-, Foote, Shelby
1916-, Stanford, Ann
1916-, Summers, Hollis
1916-, Vance, Jack
1916-1965, Jackson, Shirley
1916-1985, Ciardi, John
1916-1986, MacDonald, John D.
1916-1987, Killens, John Oliver
1916-1990, Percy, Walker
1917-, Auchincloss, Louis
1917-, Brooks, Gwendolyn
1917-, Clarke, Arthur C.
1917-, Eastlake, William
1917-, Epstein, Seymour
1917-, Metcalf, Paul
1917-, Powers, J. F.
1917-1967, McCullers, Carson
1917-1973, Bowles, Jane
1917-1977, Lowell, Robert
1917-1994, Burgess, Anthony
1917-1994, Taylor, Peter
1918-, Bronk, William
1918-, Elliot, George P.
1918-, L'Engle, Madeleine
1918-, Settle, Mary Lee
1918-, Spark, Dame Muriel Sarah
    Camberg
1918-, Spillane, Mickey
1918-, Wolff, Maritta
1918-1968, O'Connor, Edwin
1918-1985, Sturgeon, Theodore
1919-, Lessing, Doris May Taylor
1919-, Meredith, William

1919-, Murdoch, Dame Iris Jean
1919-, Pohl, Frederik
1919-, Salinger, J. D.
1919-, Simpson, N. F.
1919-, Whittemore, Reed
1919-1980, Grubb, Davis
1919-1988, Duncan, Robert
1920-, Dykeman, Wilma
1920-, Ferlinghetti, Lawrence
1920-, Guest, Barbara
1920-, Nemerov, Howard
1920-, Puzo, Mario
1920-, Windham, Donald
1920-1986, Herbert, Frank
1920-1992, Asimov, Isaac
1920-1994, Bukowski, Charles
1920-1996, Bradbury, Ray
1921-, Brown, George MacKay
1921-, Carruth, Hayden
1921-, Spencer, Elizabeth
1921-, Wilbur, Richard
1921-1975, Blish, James
1921-1977, Jones, James
1922-, Amis, Kingsley
1922-, Baker, Elliott
1922-, Bourjaily, Vance
1922-, Brossard, Chandler
1922-, Davie, Donald Alfred
1922-, Gaddis, William
1922-, Hardy, John Edward
1922-, Harris, Mark
1922-, Paley, Grace
1922-, Vonnegut, Kurt, Jr.
1922-1969, Kerouac, Jack
1922-1971, Philbrick, Charles
1922-1985, Larkin, Philip Arthur
1922-1986, Braine, John Gerard
1922-1987, Moss, Howard
1922-1995, Willingham, Calder
1923-, Dickson, Gordon R.
1923-, Dugan, Alan
1923-, Gordimer, Nadine
1923-, Gregor, Arthur
1923-, Heller, Joseph
1923-, Hoffman, Daniel
1923-, Levertov, Denise
1923-, Mailer, Norman
1923-, Miller, Walter M., Jr.
1923-, Purdy, James
1923-, Simpson, Louis
1923-1964, Behan, Brendan
1923-1968, Stacton, David
1923-1997, Dickey, James
1924-, Alexander, Lloyd

1924-, Berger, Thomas
1924-, Connell, Evan S., Jr.
1924-, Faust, Irvin
1924-, Gass, William H.
1924-, Gold, Herbert
1924-, Humphrey, William
1924-, Uris, Leon
1924-, Villarreal, Jose Antonio
1924-1984, Capote, Truman
1924-1987, Baldwin, James
1924-1995, Bolt, Robert
1925- , Styron, William
1925-, Booth, Philip E.
1925-, Cormier, Robert
1925-, Hawkes, John
1925-, Jones, Madison Percy
1925-, Vidal, Gore
1925-, Williams, John A.
1925-1964, O'Connor, Flannery
1925-1994, Wain, John Barrington
1926- , Shaffer, Anthony
1926-, Ammons, A. R.
1926-, Anderson, Poul
1926-, Bly, Robert
1926-, Buechner, Frederick
1926-, Creeley, Robert
1926-, Donleavy, J. P.
1926-, Fowles, John Robert
1926-, Fox, William Price
1926-, Hunter, Evan
1926-, Knowles, John
1926-, Lee, Harper
1926-, Leonard, Hugh
1926-, Lurie, Alison
1926-, Markfield, Wallace
1926-, McCaffrey, Anne
1926-, Shaffer, Peter Levin
1926-, Snodgrass, W. D.
1926-, Yates, Richard
1926-1962, Wallant, Edward Lewis
1926-1966, O'Hara, Frank
1926-1971, Blackburn, Paul
1926-1988, Holmes, John Clellon
1926-1995, Merrill, James
1926-1997, Ginsberg, Allen
1927-, Ashbery, John
1927-, Carroll, Paul
1927-, Eigner, Larry
1927-, Ely, David
1927-, Grossman, Alfred
1927-, Herlihy, James Leo
1927-, Jellicoe, Ann
1927-, Kahn, Roger
1927-, Kinnell, Galway

1927-, Matthiessen, Peter
1927-, Merwin, W. S.
1927-, Nichols, Peter Richard
1927-, Simon, Neil
1927-, Smith, William Gardner
1927-1980, Wright, James
1928-, Albee, Edward
1928-, Candelaria, Nash
1928-, Ford, Jesse Hill
1928-, Greeley, Andrew M.
1928-, Hazo, Samuel
1928-, Keane, John B.
1928-, Kennedy, William
1928-, Oliver, Chad
1928-, Ozick, Cynthia
1928-, Sendak, Maurice
1928-, Sillitoe, Alan
1928-, Wiesel, Elie
1928-1974, Sexton, Anne
1928-1982, Dick, Philip K.
1928-1984, Mayfield, Julian
1928-1992, Wiseman, Adele
1929-, Dorn, Ed
1929-, Douglas, James
1929-, Exley, Frederick
1929-, Friel, Brien
1929-, Garrett, George
1929-, Gover, Robert
1929-, Grau, Shirley Ann
1929-, Gunn, Thom
1929-, Hinojosa, Rolando
1929-, Kennedy, X. J.
1929-, LeGuin, Ursula K.
1929-, Levin, Ira
1929-, Porter, Peter Neville Frederick
1929-, Sorrentino, Gilbert
1929-, Williams, Jonathan
1929-1967, Beaumont, Charles
1929-1994, Osborne, John James
1930-, Arden, John
1930-, Ballard, J. G.
1930-, Barth, John
1930-, Bradley, Marion Zimmer
1930-, Breslin, Jimmy
1930-, Dawson, Fielding
1930-, Elkin, Stanley
1930-, Friedman, Bruce Jay
1930-, Hughes, Ted
1930-, M., Miguel Mendez
1930-, Oppenheimer, Joel
1930-, Pinter, Harold
1930-, Pollini, Francis
1930-, Sheed, Wilfred
1930-, Snyder, Gary

1930-1965, Hansberry, Lorraine
1931-, Barnes, Peter
1931-, Brodeur, Paul
1931-, Doctorow, E. L.
1931-, Gores, Joe
1931-, Hazzard, Shirley
1931-, Ing, Dean
1931-, Kennedy, Adrienne
1931-, Le Carre, John
1931-, May, Julian
1931-, Morrison, Toni
1931-, Rothenberg, Jerome
1931-, Salas, Floyd
1931-, Wilson, Colin Henry
1931-, Wolfe, Gene
1931-1989, Barthelme, Donald
1932- , Greenberg, Joanne
1932-, Coover, Robert
1932-, Fugard, Athol
1932-, Gelber, Jack
1932-, Naipaul, V. S
1932-, O'Brien, Edna
1932-, Rumaker, Michael
1932-, Terry, Megan
1932-, Updike, John
1932-, Wesker, Arnold
1932-, Wood, Charles
1932?-, Blechman, Burt
1932-1963, Plath, Sylvia
1933-, Gaines, Ernest J.
1933-, McCarthy, Cormac
1933-, McKenna, James
1933-, Portis, Charles
1933-, Price, Reynolds
1933-, Roth, Philip
1933-, Sontag, Susan
1933-, Storey, David Malcolm
fl. 1933-1946, Cain, Paul
1933-1967, Orton, Joe
1933-1982, Gardner, John
1933-1991, Kosinski, Jerzy
1934-, Bond, Edward
1934-, Didion, Joan
1934-, Jones, LeRoi
1934-, Kilroy, Thomas
1934-, Momaday, N. Scott
1934-, Rechy, John
1934-, Sandy, Stephen
1934-, Speicher, John
1935- , Bullins, Ed
1935-, Bowering, George
1935-, Crews, Harry
1935-, Eshleman, Clayton
1935-, Kesey, Ken

1935-, Murphy, Thomas
1935-, Silverberg, Robert
1935-1984, Brautigan, Richard
1935-1984, Rivera, Tomas
1936-, Bryan, C. D. B.
1936-, DeLillo, Don
1936-, Gray, Simon James Holliday
1936-, McMurtry, Larry
1937-, Charyn, Jerome
1937-, Harrison, Tony
1937-, Kelley, William Melvin
1937-, Kopit, Arthur L.
1937-, Larner, Jeremy
1937-, Pynchon, Thomas
1937-, Russ, Joanna
1937-, Stoppard, Tom
1937-, Wakoski, Diane
1937-, Wambaugh, Joseph
1937-, Wilson, Lanford
1937-, Wurlitzer, Rudolph
1937-, Zelazny, Roger
1938-, Blume, Judy
1938-, Neugeboren, Jay
1938-, Oates, Joyce Carol
1938-, Reed, Ishmael
1938-1989, Carver, Raymond
1939-, Atwood, Margaret
1939-, Ayckbourn, Alan
1939-, Beagle, Peter S.

1939-, Drabble, Margaret
1939-, Heaney, Seamus
1939-, Higgins, George V.
1939-, McGuane, Thomas
1940-, Coetzee, J. M.
1940-, Heyen, William
1940-, Rabe, David
1941-, Busch, Frederick
1941-, Tyler, Anne
1941-, Williams, Heathcote
1941-, Woiwode, Larry
1942-, Delany, Samuel R.
1942-, Jong, Erica
1943-, Shepard, Sam
1943-, Tate, James
1943-, Watson, Ian
1944-, Walker, Alice
1945-, Zebrowski, George
1946-, Hampton, Christopher
1947-, King, Stephen
1947-, Mamet, David
1947-, Norman, Marsha
1947-, Rushdie, Salman
1948-, Reginald, Robert
1948-, Sargent, Pamela
1948-, Shange, Ntozake
1950-, Wasserstein, Wendy
1952-, Henley, Beth

Nationality Appendix

American

Adamic, Louis, 1899-1951
Adams, Andy, 1859-1935
Adams, Henry, 1838-1918
Adams, John Turvill, 1805-1882
Adams, Leonie, 1899-1988
Adams, Oscar Fay, 1855-1919
Adams, Samuel Hopkins, 1871-1958
Ade, George, 1866-1944
Agee, James, 1909-1955
Aiken, Conrad, 1889-1973
Albee, Edward, 1928-
Alcott, Bronson, 1799-1888
Alcott, Louisa May, 1832-1888
Aldrich, Thomas Bailey, 1836-1907
Alexander, Lloyd, 1924-
Alger, Horatio, Jr., 1832-1899
Algren, Nelson, 1909-1981
Allen, Elizabeth Akers, 1832-1911
Allen, Hervey, 1889-1949
Allen, James Lane, 1849-1925
Allen, Paul, 1775-1826
Allen's wife, Josiah (see Holley,
    Marietta)
Allston, Washington, 1779-1843
Alsop, Richard, 1761-1815
Ammons, A. R., 1926-
Anderson, Fredrick Irving, 1877-1947
Anderson, Maxwell, 1888-1959
Anderson, Poul, 1926-
Anderson, Sherwood, 1876-1941
Antin, Mary, 1881-1949
Arnow, Harriette, 1908-1986
Arthur, T. S., 1809-1885
Asch, Nathan, 1902-1964
Asch, Sholem, 1880-1957
Ashbery, John, 1927-
Asimov, Isaac, 1920-1992
Atherton, Gertrude, 1857-1948
Attaway, William, 1911-1986
Auchincloss, Louis, 1917-
Auden, W. H., 1907-1973
Audubon, John James, 1785-1851
Austin, Jane Goodwin, 1831-1894
Austin, Mary, 1868-1934
Austin, William, 1778-1841
Bacheller, Irving, 1859-1950
Bacon, Delia Salter, 1811-1859
Bagby, George William, 1828-
    1883

Baker, Dorothy, 1907-1968
Baker, Elliott, 1922-
Baldwin, James, 1924-1987
Baldwin, Joseph Glover, 1815-1864
Bancroft, George, 1800-1891
Bangs, John Kendrick, 1862-1922
Banneker, Benjamin, 1731-1806
Baraka, Imamu Amiri (see Jones, LeRoi)
Barker, James Nelson, 1784-1858
Barlow, Joel, 1754-1812
Barnes, Djuna, 1892-1982
Barth, John, 1930-
Barthelme, Donald, 1931-1989
Bartol, Cyrus Augustus, 1813-1900
Bartram, John, 1699-1777
Bartram, William, 1739-1823
Basso, Hamilton, 1904-1964
Baum, L. Frank, 1856-1919
Beach, Rex, 1877-1949
Beagle, Peter S., 1939-
Beaumont, Charles, 1929-1967
Behrman, S. N., 1893-1973
Belknap, Jeremy, 1744-1798
Bellamy, Edward, 1850-1898
Bellow, Saul, 1915-
Benjamin, Park, 1809-1864
Bennett, Emerson, 1822-1905
Berger, Thomas, 1924-
Berryman, John, 1914-1972
Bester, Alfred, 1913-1987
Bianchi, Martha Gilbert Dickinson,
    1866-1943
Bierce, Ambrose, 1842-1914?
Biggers, Earl Derr, 1884-1933
Billings, Josh (see Shaw, Henry
    Wheeler)
Bird, Robert Montgomery, 1806-1854
Bishop, Elizabeth, 1911-1979
Bishop, John Peale, 1892-1944
Black, MacKnight, 1896-1931
Blackburn, Paul, 1926-1971
Blake, Lillie Devereux, 1833-1913
Blechman, Burt, 1932?-
Bleecker, Ann Eliza, 1752-1783
Blish, James, 1921-1975
Blume, Judy, 1938-
Bly, Robert, 1926-
Bodman, Manoah, 1765-1850
Bogan, Louise, 1897-1970
Boker, George Henry, 1823-1890

Bonner, Sherwood (see MacDowell, Katherine)
Bontemps, Arna (Wendell), 1902-1973
Booth, Philip E., 1925-
Boucicault, Dion, 1820-1890
Bourjaily, Vance, 1922-
Bowles, Jane, 1917-1973
Bowles, Paul, 1910-
Boyd, James, 1888-1944
Boyesen, Hjalmar Hjorth, 1848-1895
Boyle, Kay, 1903-1994
Brace, Gerald Warner, 1901-1978
Brackenridge, Hugh Henry, 1748-1816
Brackett, Leigh, 1915-1978
Bradbury, Ray, 1920-1996
Bradford, William, 1590-1657
Bradley, Marion Zimmer, 1930-
Bradstreet, Anne, c. 1612-1672
Brainard, John Gardiner Calkins, 1796-1828
Brand, Max, 1892-1944
Brautigan, Richard, 1935-1984
Breitmann, Hans (see Leland, Charles Godfrey)
Breslin, Jimmy, 1930-
Bretnor, Reginald, 1911-
Briggs, Charles Frederick, 1804-1877
Brodeur, Paul, 1931-
Bromfield, Louis, 1896-1956
Bronk, William, 1918-
Brooks, Charles T., 1813-1883
Brooks, Cleanth, 1906-
Brooks, Gwendolyn, 1917-
Brooks, Maria Gowen, c. 1794-1845
Brooks, Van Wyck, 1886-1963
Brossard, Chandler, 1922-
Brown, Alice, 1857-1948
Brown, Charles Brockden, 1771-1810
Brown, William Hill, 1765-1793
Brown, William Wells, 1816?-1884
Browne, Charles Farrar, 1834-1867
Brownell, Henry Howard, 1820-1872
Brownson, Orestes Augustus, 1803-1876
Bryan, C. D. B., 1936-
Bryant, William Cullen, 1794-1878
Buck, Pearl S., 1892-1973
Buechner, Frederick, 1926-
Bukowski, Charles, 1920-1994
Bulfinch, Thomas, 1796-1876
Bullins, Ed, 1935
Bunner, H. C., 1855-1896
Burdette, Robert Jones, 1844-1914
Burgess, Thornton W., 1874-1965
Burnett, Frances Hodgson, 1849-1924

Burroughs, Edgar Rice, 1875-1950
Burroughs, John, 1837-1921
Burroughs, William S., 1914-1997
Busch, Frederick, 1941-
Butler, William Allen, 1825-1902
Byles, Mather, 1707-1788
Bynner, Edwin Lassetter, 1842-1893
Byrd, William, II, 1674-1744
Byrn, Marcus Lafayette, 1826-1903
Byrne, Donn, 1889-1928
Cabell, James Branch,1879-1958
Cable, George Washington, 1844-1925
Cahan, Abraham, 1860-1951
Cain, James M., 1892-1977
Cain, Paul, fl. 1933-1946
Caldwell, Erskine, 1903-1987
Calisher, Hortense, 1911-
Calvert, George Henry, 1803-1889
Campbell, William Edward (see March, William Edward)
Candelaria, Nash, 1928-
Canfield, Dorothy, 1879-1958
Cantwell, Robert, 1908-1978
Capote, Truman, 1924-1984
Carleton, Will, 1845-1912
Carroll, Paul, 1927-
Carruth, Hayden, 1921-
Carryl, Guy Wetmore, 1873-1904
Carson, Rachel, 1907-1964
Carter, Hodding, 1907-1972
Caruthers, William Alexander, 1802-1846
Carver, Raymond, 1938-1989
Cary, Alice, 1820-1871
Cary, Phoebe, 1824-1871
Cather, Willa, 1873-1947
Catherwood, Mary, 1847-1902
Cawein, Madison, 1865-1914
Chambers, Robert W., 1865-1933
Chandler, Raymond, 1888-1959
Channing, William Ellery, 1780-1842
Channing, William Ellery, 1818-1901
Channing, William Henry, 1810-1884
Charteris, Leslie, 1907-
Charyn, Jerome, 1937-
Cheever, John, 1912-1982
Chesebro', Caroline, 1825-1873
Chesnutt, Charles W., 1858-1932
Chester, George Randolph, 1869-1924
Chestre, Thomas (see *King Horn*)
Child, Lydia Maria, 1802-1880
Chivers, Thomas Holley, 1809-1858
Chopin, Kate, 1851-1904
Churchill, Winston, 1871-1947

Ciardi, John, 1916-1985
Clark, Eleanor, 1913-
Clark, Walter Van Tilburg, 1909-1971
Clark, Willis Gaylord, 1808-1841
Clarke, James Freeman, 1810-1888
Clarke, McDonald, 1798-1842
Clavers, Mary (see Kirkland, Caroline Stansbury)
Clemens, Samuel Langhorne, 1835-1910
Coates, Robert M., 1897-1973
Cobb, Humphrey, 1899-1944
Cobb, Irvin S., 1876-1944
Cobb, Sylvanus, Jr., 1823-1887
Coker, Elizabeth Boatwright, 1909-
Colum, Padraic, 1881-1972
Condon, Richard, 1915-
Connell, Evan S., Jr., 1924-
Conroy, Jack, 1899-1980
Conway, Moncure Daniel, 1832-1907
Cooke, John Esten, 1830-1886
Cooke, Rose Terry, 1827-1892
Cooper, Frank (see Simms, William Gilmore)
Cooper, James Fenimore, 1789-1851
Cooper, Susan Fenimore, 1813-1894
Coover, Robert, 1932-
Cormier, Robert, 1925-
Cowley, Malcolm, 1898-1989
Cozzens, Frederick Swartwout, 1818-1869
Cozzens, James Gould, 1903-1978
Craddock, Charles Egbert (see Murfree, Mary Noailles)
Cranch, Christopher Pearse, 1813-1892
Crane, Hart, 1899-1932
Crane, Stephen, 1871-1900
Crapsey, Adelaide, 1878-1914
Crawford, Francis Marion, 1854-1909
Creeley, Robert, 1926-
Crews, Harry, 1935-
Crosby, Caresse, 1892-1970
Crosby, Harry, 1898-1929
Crowfield, Christopher (see Stowe, Harriet Beecher)
Cullen, Countee, 1903-1946
Cummings, E. E., 1894-1962
Cummins, Maria Susanna, 1827-1866
Cunningham, J. V., 1911-1985
Curtis, George William, 1824-1892
Curwood, James Oliver, 1878-1927
Cushing, Eliza L., b. 1794-
Dabbs, James McBride, 1896-1970
Dahlberg, Edward, 1900-1977
Dana, Richard Henry, Jr., 1815-1882

Dana, Richard Henry, Sr., 1787-1879
Dargan, Olive Tilford, 1869-1968
Davis, Charles Augustus, 1795?-1868?
Davis, John, 1775-1854
Davis, Rebecca Harding, 1831-1910
Davis, Richard Harding, 1864-1916
Dawes, Rufus, 1803-1859
De Forest, John William, 1826-1906
De Vries, Peter, 1910-1993
Del Rey, Lester, 1915-1993
Deland, Margaret, 1857-1945
Delany, Martin R., 1812-1885
Delany, Samuel R., 1942-
DeLillo, Don, 1936-
Dell, Floyd, 1887-1969
Dennie, Joseph, 1768-1812
Derby, George Horatio, 1823-1861
Derleth, August, 1909-1971
Dewey, John, 1859-1952
Dick, Philip K., 1928-1982
Dickey, James, 1923-1997
Dickinson, Emily, 1830-1886
Dickson, Gordon R., 1923-
Didion, Joan, 1934-
Dixon, Thomas, Jr., 1864-1946
Doctorow, E. L., 1931-
Dodge, Mary Abigail, 1833-1896
Dodge, Mary Mapes, 1831-1905
Donnelly, Ignatius, 1831-1901
Dorn, Ed, 1929-
Dos Passos, John, 1896-1970
Douglas, James, 1929-
Douglas, Lloyd C., 1877-1951
Douglass, Frederick, 1817-1895
Drake, Joseph Rodman, 1795-1820
Dreiser, Theodore, 1871-1945
DuBois, W. E. B., 1868-1963
Dugan, Alan, 1923-
Duganne, Augustine Joseph Hickey, 1823-1884
Dunbar, Paul Laurence, 1872-1906
Dunbar-Nelson, Alice Moore, 1875-1935
Duncan, Robert, 1919-1988
Dunlap, William, 1766-1839
Dunne, Finley Peter, 1867-1936
Dwight, John S., 1813-1893
Dwight, Theodore, 1764-1846
Dwight, Timothy, 1752-1817
Dykeman, Wilma, 1920-
Eastlake, William, 1917-
Eberhart, Richard, 1904-
Edmonds, Walter D., 1903-

Edwards, Jonathan, 1703-1758
Eggleston, Edward, 1837-1902
Eigner, Larry, 1927-
Elkin, Stanley, 1930-
Elliot, George P., 1918-
Elliot, William, 1788-1863
Ellison, Ralph, 1914-1994
Ely, David, 1927-
Emerson, Ralph Waldo, 1803-1882
English, Thomas Dunn, 1819-1902
Ensley, Evangeline Walton, 1907-
Epstein, Seymour, 1917-
Eshleman, Clayton, 1935-
Exley, Frederick, 1929-
Fairfield, Sumner Lincoln, 1803-1844
Farrell, James T., 1904-1979
Faulkner, William, 1897-1962
Faust, Frederick (see Brand, Max)
Faust, Irvin, 1924-
Fawcett, Edgar, 1847-1904
Fay, Theodore Sedgwick, 1807-1898
Fearing, Kenneth, 1902-1961
Feikema, Feike (see Manfred, Frederick)
Ferber, Edna, 1887-1968
Ferlinghetti, Lawrence, 1920-
Fern, Fanny (see Parton, Sara Payson
    Willis)
Ferrini, Vincent, 1913-
Field, Eugene, 1850-1895
Fields, James T., 1817-1881
Finley, Martha,1828-1909
Fisher, Dorothy Canfield (see Canfield,
    Dorothy)
Fisher, Vardis, 1895-1968
Fiske, John, 1842-1901
Fitch, Clyde, 1865-1909
Fitzgerald, F. Scott, 1896-1940
Fitzgerald, Zelda, 1899-1948
Flanner, Janet, 1892-1978
Fletcher, John Gould, 1886-1950
Flint, Timothy, 1780-1840
Foote, Mary Hallock, 1847-1938
Foote, Shelby, 1916-
Ford, Jesse Hill, 1928-
Ford, Paul Leicester, 1865-1902
Forester, Frank (see Herbert, Henry
    William)
Foster, Hannah Webster, 1758-1840
Fox, John, Jr., 1862-1919
Fox, William Price, 1926-
Francis, Convers, 1795-1863
Franklin, Benjamin, 1706-1790
Frederic, Harold, 1856-1898
Freeman, Mary E. Wilkins, 1852-1930

French, Alice, 1850-1934
Freneau, Philip, 1752-1832
Friedman, Bruce Jay, 1930-
Frost, Robert, 1874-1963
Frothingham, Octavius Brooks, 1822-
    1895
Fuchs, Daniel, 1909-
Fuller, Henry Blake, 1857-1929
Fuller, Margaret, 1810-1850
Gaddis, William, 1922-
Gaines, Ernest J., 1933-
Gale, Zona, 1874-1938
Gallagher, William Davis, 1808-1894
Gardner, Erle Stanley, 1889-1970
Gardner, John, 1933-1982
Garland, Hamlin, 1860-1940
Garrett, George, 1929-
Gass, William H., 1924-
Geisel, Theodor Seuss, 1904-1991
Gelber, Jack, 1932-
Gellhorn, Martha, 1908-
Gerould, Katharine Fullerton, 1879-1944
Gibson, Walter B., 1897-
Gibson, William, 1914-
Gilbert, William Schwenck, 1836-1911
Gilbreth, Frank B., Jr., 1911-
Gilder, Richard Watson, 1844-1909
Gill, Brendan, 1914-
Gilman, Charlotte Perkins, 1860-1935
Ginsberg, Allen, 1926-1997
Glasgow, Ellen, 1873-1945
Glaspell, Susan, 1882-1948
Gold, Herbert, 1924-
Gold, Michael, 1893-1967
Goodman, Paul, 1911-1972
Goodrich, Samuel Griswold, 1793-1860
Gordon, Caroline, 1895-1981
Gores, Joe, 1931-
Gover, Robert, 1929-
Goyen, William, 1915-1983
Graham, Sheilah, 1904?-1988
Grau, Shirley Ann, 1929-
Greeley, Andrew M., 1928-
Green, Anna Katharine, 1846-1935
Green, Paul, 1894-1981
Greenberg, Joanne, 1932-
Gregor, Arthur, 1923-
Grey, Zane, 1872-1939
Griggs, Sutton E., 1872-1930
Griswold, Rufus Wilmot, 1815-1857
Grossman, Alfred, 1927-
Grubb, Davis, 1919-1980
Guest, Barbara, 1920-
Guiney, Louise Imogen, 1861-1920

Guthrie, A. B., 1901-1991
H. D., 1886-1961
Hale, Edward Everett, 1822-1909
Hale, Lucretia Peabody, 1820-1900
Hale, Nancy, 1908-1988
Hale, Sarah Josepha, 1788-1879
Hall, Baynard Rush, 1798-1863
Hall, James Norman, 1887-1951
Hall, James, 1793-1868
Halleck, FitzGreene, 1790-1867
Halpine, Charles Graham, 1829-1868
Hammett, Dashiell, 1894-1961
Hammon, Jupiter, c. 1720-c. 1800
Hansberry, Lorraine, 1930-1965
Hardy, Arthur Sherburne, 1847-1930
Hardy, John Edward, 1922-
Harland, Henry, 1861-1905
Harland, Marion (see Terhune, Mary
    Virginia)
Harper, Frances Ellen Watkins, 1825-
    1911
Harris, George Washington, 1814-1869
Harris, Joel Chandler, 1848-1908
Harris, Mark, 1922-
Harrison, Constance Cary, 1843-1920
Hart, Joseph C., 1798-1855
Harte, Bret, 1836-1902
Hawkes, John, 1925-
Hawthorne, Nathaniel, 1804-1864
Hay, John, 1838-1905
Haycox, Ernest, 1899-1950
Hayden, Robert, 1913-1980
Hayne, Paul Hamilton, 1830-1886
Hazo, Samuel, 1928-
Hearn, Lafcadio, 1850-1904
Hedge, Frederic Henry, 1805-1890
Heinlein, Robert A., 1907-1988
Heller, Joseph, 1923-
Hellman, Lillian, 1905-1984
Hemingway, Ernest, 1899-1961
Henley, Beth, 1952-
Henry, O. (see Porter, William Sydney)
Hentz, Caroline Lee, 1800-1856
Herbert, Frank, 1920-1986
Herbert, Henry William, 1807-1858
Herbst, Josephine, 1892-1969
Hergesheimer, Joseph, 1880-1954
Herlihy, James Leo, 1927-
Herrick, Robert, 1868-1938
Hersey, John, 1914-1993
Heyen, William, 1940-
Heyward, DuBose, 1885-1940
Higgins, George V., 1939-

Higginson, Thomas Wentworth, 1823-
    1911
Hildreth, Richard, 1807-1865
Hillhouse, James Abraham, 1789-1841
Himes, Chester, 1909-1984
Hinojosa, Rolando, 1929-
Hitchcock, Enos, 1744-1803
Hoffman, Charles Fenno, 1806-1884
Hoffman, Daniel, 1923-
Holland, Josiah Gilbert, 1819-1881
Holley, Marietta, 1836-1926
Holme, Saxe (see Jackson, Helen Hunt)
Holmes, John Clellon, 1926-1988
Holmes, John, 1904-1962
Holmes, Mary Jane, 1825-1907
Holmes, Oliver Wendell, 1809-1894
Hooker, Thomas, 1586-1647
Hooper, Johnson Jones, 1815-1862
Hopkins, Pauline, 1859-1930
Horgan, Paul, 1903-1995
Hosmer, William H. C., 1814-1877
Hough, Emerson, 1857-1923
Hovey, Richard, 1864-1900
Howe, E. W., 1853-1937
Howe, Julia Ward, 1819-1910
Howells, William Dean, 1837-1920
Hughes, Langston, 1902-1967
Humphrey, William, 1924-
Huneker, James Gibbons, 1857-1921
Hunter, Evan, 1926-
Hurston, Zora Neale, 1901?-1960
Imlay, Gilbert, c. 1754-1828
Ing, Dean, 1931-
Inge, William, 1913-1973
Ingraham, Joseph Holt, 1809-1860
Irving, Washington, 1783-1859
Isherwood, Christopher, 1904-1986
Jackson, Charles, 1903-1968
Jackson, Helen Hunt, 1830-1885
Jackson, Shirley, 1916-1965
James, Henry, 1843-1916
James, Will, 1892-1942
Janvier, Thomas Allibone, 1849-1913
Jarrell, Randall, 1914-1965
Jeffers, Robinson, 1887-1962
Jefferson, Thomas, 1743-1826
Jewett, Sarah Orne, 1849-1909
Johnson, Edward, 1598-1672
Johnson, James Weldon, 1871-1938
Johnson, Josephine, 1910-
Johnson, Owen, 1878-1952
Johnson, Samuel, 1709-1784
Johnson, Samuel, 1822-1882

Johnston, Mary, 1870-1936
Johnston, Richard Malcolm, 1822-1898
Jones, James, 1921-1977
Jones, John Beauchamp, 1810-1866
Jones, LeRoi, 1934-
Jones, Madison Percy, 1925-
Jong, Erica, 1942-
Josephson, Matthew, 1899-1978
Judah, Samuel B. H., 1804-1876
Judd, Sylvester, 1813-1853
Kahn, Roger, 1927-
Kantor, MacKinlay, 1904-1977
Kelland, Clarence Budington, 1881-1964
Kelley, Edith Summers, 1884-1956
Kelley, William Melvin, 1937-
Kelly, Walt, 1913-1973
Kennedy, Adrienne,1931-
Kennedy, John Pendleton, 1795-1870
Kennedy, William, 1928-
Kennedy, X. J., 1929-
Kerouac, Jack, 1922-1969
Kerr, Orpheus C. (see Newell, Robert Henry)
Kesey, Ken, 1935-
Key, Francis Scott, 1779-1843
Killens, John Oliver, 1916-1987
Kilmer, Joyce, 1886-1918
Kimball, Richard Burleigh, 1816-1892
King, Grace Elizabeth, 1851-1932
King, Stephen, 1947-
Kinnell, Galway, 1927-
Kirkland, Caroline Stansbury, 1801-1864
Kirkland, Joseph, 1830-1894
Knight, Sarah Kemble, 1666-1727
Knowles, John, 1926-
Kopit, Arthur L., 1937-
Kosinski, Jerzy, 1933-1991
Kunitz, Stanley J., 1905-
Kyne, Peter B., 1880-1957
L'Amour, Louis, 1910?-1988
L'Engle, Madeleine, 1918-
Landon, Melville De Lancey, 1839-1910
Lane, Charles, fl. 1840s
Langstaff, Launcelot (see Paulding, James Kirke)
Lanier, Sidney, 1842-1881
Larcom, Lucy, 1824-1893
Lardner, Ring W., 1885-1933
Larner, Jeremy, 1937-
Lathrop, George Parsons, 1851-1898
Lazarus, Emma, 1849-1887
Lee, Harper, 1926-

LeGuin, Ursula K., 1929-
Leiber, Fritz, 1910-
Leland, Charles Godfrey, 1824-1903
Leslie, Eliza, 1787-1858
Levin, Ira, 1929-
Lewis, Alfred Henry, c. 1858-1914
Lewis, Janet, 1899-
Lewis, Henry Clay (see Tensas, Madison, M.D.)
Lewis, Sinclair, 1885-1951
Lincoln, Joseph C., 1870-1944
Lippard, George, 1822-1854
Locke, David Ross, 1833-1888
Lockridge, Ross, Jr., 1914-1948
Lodge, George Cabot, 1873-1909
Loeb, Harold, 1891-1974
London, Jack, 1876-1916
Long, Haniel, 1888-1956
Longfellow, Henry Wadsworth, 1807-1882
Longfellow, Samuel, 1819-1892
Longstreet, Augustus Baldwin, 1790-1870
Loos, Anita, 1888-1981
Lothrop, Harriett Mulford Stone, 1844-1924
Lovecraft, H. P., 1890-1937
Lowell, Amy, 1874-1925
Lowell, James Russell, 1819-1891
Lowell, Robert Traill Spence, 1816-1891
Lowell, Robert, 1917-1977
Lumpkin, Grace, 1903?-1980
Lurie, Alison, 1926-
Luska, Sidney (see Harland, Henry)
Lyon, Harris Merton, 1883-1916
Lytle, Andrew Nelson, 1902-1995
MacDonald, John D., 1916-1986
Macdonald, Ross, 1915-1983
MacDowell, Katherine, 1849-1883
MacLeish, Archibald, 1892-1982
Mailer, Norman, 1923-
Major, Charles, 1856-1913
Malamud, Bernard, 1914-1986
Mamet, David, 1947-
Manfred, Frederick, 1912-
March, William Edward, 1893-1954
Markfield, Wallace, 1926-
Marquand, J. P., 1893-1960
Marquis, Don, 1878-1937
Marsh, James, 1794-1842
Marvell, Ik (see Mitchell, Donald Grant)
Masters, Edgar Lee, 1868?-1950
Mather, Cotton, 1663-1728
Mathews, Cornelius, 1817-1889

Matthews, Brander, 1852-1929
Matthiessen, Peter, 1927-
May, Julian, 1931-
Mayfield, Julian, 1928-1984
Mayo, William Starbuck, 1811-1895
McAlmon, Robert, 1896-1956
McCaffrey, Anne, 1926-
McCarthy, Cormac, 1933-
McCarthy, Mary, 1912-1989
McCoy, Horace, 1897-1955
McCullers, Carson, 1917-1967
McCutcheon, George Barr, 1866-1928
McFee, William, 1881-1966
McGuane, Thomas, 1939-
McHenry, James, 1785-1845
McKay, Claude, 1890-1948
McKenna, James, 1933-
McMurtry, Larry, 1936-
Melville, Herman, 1819-1891
Mencken, H. L., 1880-1956
Mendez M., Miguel, 1930-
Meredith, William, 1919-
Merrill, James, 1926-1995
Merton, Thomas, 1915-1969
Merwin, W. S., 1927-
Metcalf, Paul, 1917-
Micheaux, Oscar, 1884-1951
Michener, James A., 1907-1997
Millar, Kenneth (see Macdonald, Ross)
Millay, Edna St. Vincent, 1892-1950
Miller, Arthur, 1915-
Miller, Henry, 1891-1980
Miller, Joaquin, 1841?-1913
Miller, Walter M., Jr., 1923-
Mitchell, Donald Grant, 1822-1908
Mitchell, Isaac, c. 1759-1812
Mitchell, John Ames, 1845-1918
Mitchell, Margaret, 1900-1949
Mitchell, S. Weir, 1829-1914
Molloy, Robert, 1906-1977
Momaday, N. Scott, 1934-
Moody, William Vaughan, 1869-1910
Moore, Clement Clarke, 1779-1863
Moore, Marianne, 1887-1972
Morley, Christopher, 1890-1957
Morris, George Pope, 1802-1864
Morris, Wright, 1910-
Morrison, Toni, 1931-
Morton, Sarah Wentworth, 1759-1846
Moss, Howard, 1922-1987
Motley, John Lothrop, 1814-1877
Motley, Willard, 1912-1965
Moulton, Louise Chandler, 1835-1908
Muir, John, 1838-1914

Mulford, Clarence E., 1883-1956
Mumford, Lewis, 1895-1990
Murfree, Mary Noailles, 1850-1922
Myers, Peter Hamilton, 1812-1878
Nabokov, Vladimir, 1899-1977
Nasby, Petroleum Vesuvius (see Locke,
    David Ross)
Nash, Ogden, 1902-1971
Nathan, Robert, 1894-1985
Neal, John, 1793-1876
Neal, Joseph Clay, 1807-1847
Neihardt, John G., 1881-1973
Nemerov, Howard, 1920-
Neugeboren, Jay, 1938-
Newcomb, Charles King, 1820-1894
Newell, Robert Henry, 1836-1901
Newhouse, Edward, 1911-
Newman, Frances, 1888-1928
Nicholson, Meredith, 1866-1947
Nims, J. F., 1913-
Nin, Anais, 1903-1977
Noah, Mordecai Manuel, 1785-1851
Nordhoff, Charles Bernard, 1887-1947
Norman, Marsha, 1947-
Norris, Frank, 1870-1902
Norton, Andre, 1912-
Nye, Bill Edgar (Wilson), 1850-1896
O'Brien, Fitz-James, c. 1828-1862
O'Cataract, Jehu (see Neal, John)
O'Connor, Edwin, 1918-1968
O'Connor, Flannery, 1925-1964
O'Hara, Frank, 1926-1966
O'Hara, John, 1905-1970
O'Neill, Eugene, 1888-1953
O'Reilly, John Boyle, 1844-1890
O'Reilly, Miles (see Halpine, Charles
    Graham)
Oates, Joyce Carol, 1938-
Odets, Clifford, 1906-1963
Oliver, Chad, 1928-
Olson, Charles, 1910-1970
Olson, Elder, 1909-
Oppenheimer, Joel, 1930-
Osgood, Frances Sargent, 1811-1850
Ozick, Cynthia, 1928-
Page, Thomas Nelson, 1853-1922
Paine, Albert Bigelow, 1861-1937
Paine, Thomas, 1737-1809
Paley, Grace, 1922-
Parker, Dorothy, 1893-1967
Parker, Theodore, 1810-1860
Parkman, Francis, 1823-1893
Parley, Peter (see Goodrich, Samuel
    Griswold)

Parrish, Anne, 1888-1957
Parsons, Thomas Williams, 1819-1892
Parton, Sara Payson Willis, 1811-1872
Patchen, Kenneth, 1911-1972
Paul, Elliott Harold, 1891-1958
Paulding, James Kirke, 1778-1860
Payne, John Howard, 1791-1852
Peabody, Elizabeth Palmer, 1804-1894
Pennington, Patience (see Pringle, Elizabeth Waties Allston)
Percival, James Gates, 1795-1856
Percy, Walker, 1916-1990
Percy, William Alexander, 1885-1942
Perelman, S. J., 1904-1979
Perkins, Eli (see Landon, Melville De Lancey)
Peterkin, Julia, 1880-1961
Petry, Ann, 1911-
Phelps, Elizabeth, 1815-1852
Philbrick, Charles, 1922-1971
Phillips, David Graham, 1867-1911
Piatt, John James, 1835-1917
Pike, Albert, 1809-1891
Pinckney, Josephine, 1895-1957
Pinkney, Edward Coote, 1802-1828
Plath, Sylvia, 1932-1963
Poe, Edgar Allan, 1809-1849
Pohl, Frederik, 1919-
Pollini, Francis, 1930-
Pool, Maria Louise, 1841-1898
Poole, Ernest, 1880-1950
Porter, Eleanor Hodgman, 1868-1920
Porter, Gene Stratton (see Stratton-Porter, Gene)
Porter, Katherine Anne, 1890-1980
Porter, William Sydney, 1862-1910
Portis, Charles, 1933-
Postl, Karl (see Sealsfield, Charles)
Pound, Ezra, 1885-1972
Powell, Dawn, 1897-1965
Powers, J. F., 1917-
Prescott, William Hickling, 1796-1859
Price, Reynolds, 1933-
Pringle, Elizabeth Waties Allston (Patience Pennington), 1845-1921
Purdy, James, 1923-
Putnam, Howard Phelps, 1894-1948
Puzo, Mario, 1920-
Pyle, Howard, 1853-1911
Pynchon, Thomas, 1937-
Rabe, David, 1940-
Rand, Ayn, 1905-1982
Ransom, John Crowe, 1888-1974

Rawlings, Marjorie Kinnan, 1896-1953
Read, Thomas Buchanan, 1822-1872
Rechy, John, 1934-
Reed, Ishmael, 1938-
Reed, Sampson, 1800-1880
Reginald, Robert, 1948-
Remington, Frederic Sackrider, 1861-1909
Rhodes, Eugene Manlove, 1869-1934
Rice, Alice Hegan, 1870-1942
Rice, Elmer, 1892-1967
Richter, Conrad, 1890-1968
Riding, Laura, 1901-1991
Riley, James Whitcomb, 1849-1916
Rinehart, Mary Roberts, 1876-1958
Ripley, George, 1802-1880
Ripley, Sophia Dana, fl. 1820s-1847?
Rivera, Tomas, 1935-1984
Rives, Amelie, Princess Troubetzkoy, 1863-1945
Roberts, Elizabeth Madox, 1881-1941
Roberts, Kenneth, 1885-1957
Robinson, Edwin Arlington, 1869-1935
Robinson, Rowland Evans, 1833-1900
Rocklynne, Ross, 1913-
Roe, E. P., 1838-1888
Roethke, Theodore, 1908-1963
Rolvaag, O. E., 1876-1931
Roth, Henry, 1906?-
Roth, Philip, 1933-
Rothenberg, Jerome, 1931-
Rourke, Constance, 1885-1941
Rowlandson, Mary, c. 1635-c. 1678
Rowson, Susanna, c. 1762-1824
Royall, Anne Newport, 1769-1854
Rumaker, Michael, 1932-
Runyon, Damon, 1880-1946
Russ, Joanna, 1937-
Russell, Irwin, 1853-1879
Ryan, Abram Joseph, 1838-1886
Salas, Floyd, 1931-
Salinger, J. D., 1919-
Saltus, Edgar Evertson, 1855-1921
Sanborn, Franklin Benjamin, 1831-1917
Sandburg, Carl, 1878-1967
Sandoz, Mari, 1896-1966
Sandy, Stephen, 1934-
Sargent, Epes, 1813-1880
Sargent, Pamela, 1948-
Saroyan, William, 1908-1981
Sarton, May, 1912-
Saxe, John Godfrey, 1816-1887
Schaefer, Jack, 1907-1991
Schulberg, Budd, 1914-

Schwartz, Delmore, 1913-1966
Scott, Evelyn, 1893-1963
Scott, Winfield Townley, 1910-1968
Sealsfield, Charles, 1793-1864
Sedgwick, Catharine Maria, 1789-1867
Seeger, Alan, 1888-1916
Sendak, Maurice, 1928-
Settle, Mary Lee, 1918-
Sexton, Anne, 1928-1974
Shange, Ntozake, 1948-
Shapiro, Karl, 1913-
Shaw, Henry Wheeler, 1818-1885
Shaw, Irwin, 1913-1984
Shepard, Sam, 1943-
Shepard, Thomas, 1605-1649
Sherman, Frank Dempster, 1860-1916
Shillaber, Benjamin Penhallow, 1814-
    1890
Short, Luke 1908-1975
Sidney, Edward William (see Tucker,
    Nathaniel Beverley)
Sidney, Margaret (see Lothrop, Harriett
    Mulford Stone)
Sigourney, Lydia Huntley, 1791-1865
Sill, Edward Rowland, 1841-1887
Silverberg, Robert, 1935-
Simak, Clifford D., 1904-1988
Simms, William Gilmore, 1806-1870
Simon, Neil, 1927-
Simpson, Louis, 1923-
Sinclair, Upton, 1878-1968
Singer, Isaac Bashevis, 1904-1991
Smith, Betty, 1904-1972
Smith, Captain John, 1580-1631
Smith, Charles Henry, 1826-1903
Smith, Cordwainer, 1913-1966
Smith, Elihu Hubbard, 1771-1798
Smith, Francis Hopkinson, 1838-1915
Smith, Richard Penn, 1799-1854
Smith, Samuel Francis, 1808-1895
Smith, Seba, 1792-1868
Snelling, William Joseph, 1804-1848
Snodgrass, W. D., 1926-
Snyder, Gary, 1930-
Sontag, Susan, 1933-
Sorrentino, Gilbert, 1929-
Southworth, E. D. E. N., 1819-1899
Speicher, John, 1934-
Spencer, Elizabeth, 1921-
Spillane, Mickey, 1918-
Spofford, Harriet Prescott, 1835-1921
Springs, Elliott White, 1896-1959
Stacton, David, 1923-1968
Stafford, Jean, 1915-1979

Stanford, Ann, 1916-
Stedman, Edmund Clarence, 1833-
    1908
Steele, Wilbur Daniel, 1886-1970
Stegner, Wallace, 1909-1993
Stein, Gertrude, 1874-1946, and Toklas,
    Alice B., 1877-1967
Steinbeck, John, 1902-1968
Sterling, George, 1869-1926
Stevens, Wallace, 1879-1955
Stewart, George R., 1895-1980
Stockton, Frank R., 1834-1902
Stoddard, Charles Warren, 1843-1909
Stoddard, Elizabeth Drew, 1823-1902
Stoddard, Richard Henry, 1825-1903
Stone, William Leete, 1792-1844
Story, William Wetmore, 1819-1895
Stout, Rex, 1886-1975
Stowe, Harriet Beecher, 1811-1896
Stratton-Porter, Gene, 1863-1924
Stribling, Thomas Sigismund, 1881-
    1965
Stuart, Jesse, 1907-1984
Sturgeon, Theodore, 1918-1985
Styron, William, 1925-
Suckow, Ruth, 1892-1960
Summers, Hollis, 1916-
Tabb, John B., 1845-1909
Taggard, Genevieve, 1894-1948
Taliaferro, Harden E., 1818-1875
Tarkington, Booth, 1869-1946
Tate, Allen, 1899-1979
Tate, James, 1943-
Taylor, Bayard, 1825-1878
Taylor, Edward, c. 1644-1729
Taylor, Peter, 1917-1994
Tenney, Tabitha Gilman, 1762-1837
Tensas, Madison, M.D., 1825-1850
Terhune, Mary Virginia, 1830-1922
Terry, Megan, 1932-
Thanet, Octave (see French, Alice)
Thaxter, Celia, 1835-1894
Thayer, Caroline Matilda Warren (see
    Warren, Caroline Matilda)
Thomas, Frederick William, 1806-1866
Thompson, Daniel Pierce, 1795-1868
Thompson, Maurice, 1844-1901
Thompson, William Tappan, 1812-1882
Thomson, Mortimer Neal, 1831-1875
Thoreau, Henry David, 1817-1862
Thorpe, T. B., 1815-1878
Thurber, James, 1894-1961
Thurman, Wallace, 1902-1934
Timrod, Henry, 1828-1867

Titcomb, Tomothy (see Holland, Josiah
    Gilbert)
Toklas, Alice B. (see Stein, Gertrude)
Toomer, Jean, 1894-1967
Torrey, Bradford, 1843-1912
Tourgee, Albion W., 1838-1905
Traven, B., 1882?-1969
Trilling, Lionel, 1905-1975
Troubetzkoy, Princess (see Rives,
    Amelie, Princess Troubetzkoy)
Trowbridge, J. T., 1827-1916
Trumbull, John, 1750-1831
Tucker, George, 1775-1861
Tucker, Nathaniel Beverley, 1784-1851
Tucker, St. George, 1752-1827
Tuckerman, Frederick Goddard, 1821-
    1873
Tuckerman, Henry Theodore, 1813-
    1871
Tunis, John R., 1889-1975
Tyler, Anne, 1941-
Tyler, Royall, 1757-1826
Updike, John, 1932-
Uris, Leon, 1924-
Van Dyke, Henry, 1852-1933
Van Vechten, Carl, 1880-1964
Van Vogt, A. E., 1912-
Vance, Jack, 1916-
Very, Jones, 1813-1880
Vidal, Gore, 1925-
Villarreal, Jose Antonio, 1924-
Voelker, John Donaldson, 1903-
Vonnegut, Kurt, Jr., 1922-
Wakoski, Diane, 1937-
Walker, Alice, 1944-
Walker, David, 1785?-1830
Walker, Margaret Abigail, 1915-
Wallace, Horace Binney, 1817-1852
Wallace, Lew, 1827-1905
Wallant, Edward Lewis, 1926-1962
Wambaugh, Joseph, 1937-
Ward, Artemus (see Browne, Charles
    Farrar)
Ward, Elizabeth Stuart Phelps, 1844-
    1911
Ware, William, 1797-1852
Warner, Anna Bartlett, 1827-1915
Warner, Charles Dudley, 1829-1900
Warner, Susan Bogert, 1819-1885
Warren, Caroline Matilda, 1787?-1844
Warren, Mercy Otis, 1728-1814
Warren, Robert Penn, 1905-1989
Washington, Booker T., 1856-1915
Wasserstein, Wendy, 1950-

Waters, Frank, 1902-1995
Watterson, George, 1783-1854
Weaver, John V. A., 1893-1938
Webb, Frank J., fl. 1857-1870
Webber, Charles Wilkins, 1819-1856
Weiss, John, 1818-1879
Welty, Eudora, 1909-
Wescott, Glenway, 1901-1987
West, Jessamyn, 1907-1984
West, Nathaniel, 1903-1940
Westcott, Edward Noyes, 1846-1898
Wetherell, Elizabeth (see Warner, Susan
    Bogert)
Wharton, Edith, 1862-1937
Wheatley, Phillis, 1753?-1784
Wheeler, Charles Stearns, 1816-1843
Wheelwright, John, 1897-1940
Whistler, James Abbott McNeill, 1834-
    1903
Whitcher, Frances Miriam, 1814-1852
White, E. B., 1899-1985
White, Stewart Edward, 1873-1946
White, William Allen, 1868-1944
Whitlock, Brand, 1869-1934
Whitman, Sarah Helen, 1803-1878
Whitman, Walt, 1819-1892
Whitney, Adeline Dutton Train, 1824-
    1906
Whittemore, Reed, 1919-
Whittier, John Greenleaf, 1807-1892
Wiesel, Elie, 1928-
Wiggin, Kate Douglas, 1856-1923
Wilbur, Richard, 1921-
Wilder, Amos N., 1895-1993
Wilder, Laura Ingalls, 1867-1957
Wilder, Thornton, 1897-1975
Williams, John A., 1925-
Williams, Jonathan, 1929-
Williams, Tennessee, 1911-1983
Williams, William Carlos, 1883-1963
Williamson, Jack, 1908-
Willingham, Calder, 1922-1995
Willis, N. P., 1806-1867
Wilson, Augusta Jane Evans, 1835-1909
Wilson, Harriet, 1808-c. 1870
Wilson, Harry Leon, 1867-1939
Wilson, Lanford, 1937-
Wilson, Margaret, 1882-1973
Windham, Donald, 1920-
Winter, William, 1836-1917
Winters, Yvor, 1900-1968
Winthrop, Theodore, 1828-1861
Wise, John, 1652-1725
Wister, Owen, 1860-1938

Wodehouse, Sir P. G., 1881-1975
Woiwode, Larry, 1941-
Wolfe, Gene, 1931-
Wolfe, Thomas, 1900-1938
Wolff, Maritta, 1918-
Wood, Sarah Sayward Barrell Keating,
    1759-1855
Woodberry, George Edward, 1855-
    1930
Woodworth, Samuel, 1785-1842
Woolrich, Cornell, 1903-1968
Woolson, Constance Fenimore, 1840-
    1894
Wouk, Herman, 1915-
Wright, Harold Bell, 1872-1944
Wright, James, 1927-1980
Wright, Richard, 1908-1960
Wurlitzer, Rudolph, 1937-
Wylie, Elinor, 1885-1928
Wylie, Philip, 1902-1971
Wyman, Elizabeth Buffum Chace, 1847-
    1929
Yates, Richard, 1926-
Young, Marguerite, 1909-
Young, Stark, 1881-1963
Zebrowski, George, 1945-
Zelazny, Roger, 1937-
Zukofsky, Louis, 1904-1978

Australian
Hazzard, Shirley, 1931-
Porter, Peter Neville Frederick, 1929-
Stewart, Donald Ogden, 1894-1980

British
Abercrombie, Lascelles, 1881-1938
Addison, Joseph, 1672-1719
Aelfric, c. 955-c. 1010
Ainsworth, William Harrison, 1805-1882
Akenside, Mark, 1721-1770
Aldington, Richard, 1892-1962
Alfred, 848-899
Amis, Kingsley, 1922-
Andrewes, Lancelot, 1555-1626
Anglo-Saxon Chronicle, c. 1154
Anstey, F., 1865-1934
Arden, John, 1930-
Armstrong, Martin Donisthorpe, 1882-
    1974
Arnold, Matthew, 1822-1888
Ascham, Roger, 1515/16-1568
Austen, Jane, 1775-1817
Ayckbourn, Alan, 1939-
Bacon, Francis, 1561-1626

Bagehot, Walter, 1826-1877
Bale, John, 1495-1563
Ballard, J. G., 1930-
Barbauld, Anna Laetitia, 1743-1824
Barclay, Alexander, 1475?-1552
Barnes, Peter, 1931-
Barnes, William, 1801-1886
Barnfield, Richard, 1574-1627
Bates, H. E., 1905-1974
Bates, Ralph, 1899-
Baxter, Richard, 1615-1691
Beardsley, Aubrey Vincent, 1872-
    1898
Beaumont, Francis, 1584-1616, and
    Fletcher, John, 1579-1625
Beckford, William, 1759-1844
Beddoes, Thomas Lovell, 1803-1849
Bede, 673-735
Beer, Thomas, 1889-1940
Beerbohm, Max, 1872-1956
Behn, Aphra, 1640?-1689
Bell, Gertrude Magaret Lowthian, 1868-
    1926
Belloc, Hilaire, 1870-1953
Bennett, Arnold, 1867-1931
Beowulf, 8th century
Betjeman, John, 1906-1984
Blackwood, Algernon, 1869-1951
Blake, William, 1757-1827
Blunden, Edmund, 1896-1974
Bolingbroke, Henry St. John, 1st
    Viscount, 1678-1751
Bolt, Robert, 1924-1995
Bond, Edward, 1934-
Borrow, George Henry, 1803-1881
Boyle, Robert, 1627-1691
Braine, John Gerard, 1922-1986
Breton, Nicholas, 1555?-1626?
Bridges, Robert, 1844-1930
Brome, Richard, c. 1590-1652/3
Bronte, Anne, 1820-1849, Bronte, Char-
    lotte, 1816-1855, Bronte, Emily,
    1818-1848, and Bronte, Patrick
    Branwell, 1817-1848 (see The
    Brontes)
Brooke, Rupert Chawner, 1887-1915
Brown, Thomas, 1663-1704
Browne, Sir Thomas, 1605-1682
Browne, William, of Tavistock, 1590?-
    1645?
Browning, Elizabeth Barrett, 1806-1861,
    and Browning, Robert, 1812-
    1889

Browning, Robert (see Browning, Elizabeth Barrett)

Brunanburh, c. 937

Bulwer-Lytton, Edward George Earle Lytton, 1st Barron Lytton,1803-1873

Bunyan, John, 1628-1688

Burgess, Anthony, 1917-1994

Burke, Edmund, 1729-1797

Burney, Fanny, 1752-1840

Burton, Robert, 1577-1640

Butler, Samuel, 1613-1680

Butler, Samuel, 1835-1902

Byron, George Gordon, Lord, 1788-1824

Caedmon, fl. 670

Cambridge Platonists (see More, Henry)

Camden, William, 1551-1623

Campbell, Roy, 1901-1957

Campion, Thomas, 1567-1620

Carew, Thomas, 1594/5-1640

Carey, Henry, 1687?-1743

Carroll, Lewis (see Dodgson, Charles Lutwidge)

Caudwell, Christopher, 1907-1937

Cavendish, Margaret, Duchess of Newcastle (see Newcastle, Margaret, Duchess of)

Caxton, William, c. 1422-1491

Centlivre, Susannah, 1669-1723

Chapman, George, 1559?-1634

Chatterton, Thomas, 1752-1770

Chaucer, Geoffrey, c. 1343-1400

Chesterfield, Philip Dormer Stanhope, 4th Earl of, 1694-1773

Chesterton, G. K.,1874-1936

Christie, Dame Agatha,1890-1976

Churchill, Charles, 1732-1764

Cibber, Colley, 1671-1757

Clare, John, 1793-1864

Clarendon, Edward Hyde, 1st Earl of, 1609-1674

Clarke, Arthur C., 1917-

Cleland, John, 1709-1789

Cleveland, John, 1613-1658

Clough, Arthur Hugh, 1819-1861

Cobbett, William, 1763-1835

Coleridge, Samuel Taylor, 1772-1834

Collier, Jeremy, 1650-1726

Collins, Wilkie, 1824-1889

Collins, William, 1721-1759

Colman, George, the Elder, 1732-1794

Colman, George, the Younger, 1762-1836

Congreve, William, 1670-1729

Conrad, Joseph, 1857-1924

Cooper, Anthony Ashley, 3rd Earl of Shaftesbury (see Shaftesbury, Anthony Ashley Cooper)

Coppard, A. E., 1878-1957

Corbett, Richard, 1582-1635

Cotton, Charles, 1630-1687

Cotton, John, 1584-1652

Coward, Noel, 1899-1973

Cowley, Abraham, 1618-1667

Cowper, William, 1731-1800

Crabbe, George, 1754-1832

Craig, Gordon, 1872-1966

Crashaw, Richard, 1612/13-1649

Crevecouer, Michel-Guillaume St. Jean de, 1735-1813

Cumberland, George, 1754-1848

Cumberland, Richard, 1732-1811

Cynewulf, late eighth or ninth century

D'Avenant, William, 1606-1668

D'Urfey, Thomas, 1653-1723

Daniel, Samuel, 1563-1619

Darwin, Charles Robert, 1809-1882

Davidson, John, 1857-1909

Davie, Donald Alfred, 1922-

Davies, John, 1569-1626

Davies, W. H., 1871-1940

de la Mare, Walter, 1873-1956

De Quincey, Thomas, 1785-1859

Defoe, Daniel, 1660-1731

Dekker, Thomas, 1570?-1632

Deloney, Thomas, 1560?-1600

Denham, John, 1615-1669

Dennis, John, 1657-1734

Dickens, Charles, 1812-1870

Disraeli, Benjamin, 1804-1881

Dobson, Austin, 1840-1921

Dodgson, Charles Lutwidge, 1832-1898

Donne, John, 1572-1631

Douglas, Norman, 1868-1952

Dowson, Ernest Christopher, 1867-1900

Drabble, Margaret, 1939-

Drayton, Michael, 1563-1631

Dream of the Rood, c. 10th century

Drinkwater, John, 1882-1937

Dryden, John, 1631-1700

Durrell, Lawrence George, 1912-1990

Dyer, John, 1699-1757

Earle, John, 1601?-1665

Edgeworth, Maria, 1768-1849

Eliot, T. S., 1888-1965

Eliott, George, 1819-1880

Elyot, Sir Thomas, c. 1490-1546

Empson, William, 1906-1984

Dallas, Eneas Sweetland, 1829-1879
Etherege, George, 1634?-1691
Evelyn, John, 1620-1706
Everson, William, 1912-1994
Fairfax, Edward, d. 1635
Fielding, Henry, 1707-1754
Firbank, Ronald (1886-1926)
FitzGerald, Edward, 1809-1883
Fletcher, Giles, the Younger, 1585?-1623
Fletcher, John (see Beaumont, Francis)
Fletcher, Phineas, 1582-1650
Florio, John, c. 1553-1625
Foote, Samuel, 1720-1777
Ford, Ford Madox, 1873-1939
Ford, John, 1586-after 1639
Forster, E. M., 1879-1970
Fowles, John Robert, 1926-
Fox, Ralph, 1900-1937
Foxe, John, 1516-1587
Fry, Christopher, 1907-
Fulgrens and Lucrece (see Medwall,
    Henry)
Fuller, Thomas, 1608-1661
Galsworthy, John, 1867-1933
Garrick, David, 1717-1779
Gascoigne, George, c. 1534-1577
Gaskell, Elizabeth Cleghorn, 1810-1865
Gawain and the Green Knight, Sir, c. 1375
Gay, John, 1685-1732
Gibbon, Edward, 1737-1794
Gildas, d. 570
Gildon, Charles, 1665-1724
Gill, Eric, 1882-1940
Gissing, George Robert, 1857-1903
Godwin, William, 1756-1836
Golding, Arthur, 1536?-1605?
Golding, William, 1911-1993
Gosse, Edmund, 1849-1928
Gower, John, 1330?-1408
Graves, Richard, 1715-1804
Graves, Robert van Ranke, 1895-1985
Gray, John Henry, 1866-1934
Gray, Simon James Holliday, 1936-
Gray, Thomas, 1716-1771
Green, Matthew, 1697-1737
Greenaway, Kate, 1846-1901
Greene, Graham, 1904-1991
Greene, Robert, 1558-1592
Greville, Fulke, 1st Baron Brooke, 1554-
    1628
Gunn, Thom, 1929-
Habington, William, 1605-1654
Haggard, H. Rider, 1856-1925
Hakluyt, Richard, 1552-1616

Halifax, George Savile, 1st Marquis of,
    1633-1695
Hall, Joseph, 1574-1656
Hallam, Arthur Henry, 1811-1833
Hampton, Christopher, 1946-
Hardy, Thomas, 1840-1928
Harington, Sir John, c. 1561-1612
Harrington, James, 1611-1677
Harrison, Frederic, 1831-1923
Harrison, Tony, 1937-
Hawes, Stephen, c. 1475-1511
Hazlitt, William, 1778-1830
Henley, W. E., 1849-1903
Herbert, Edward, of Cherbury, 1582-
    1648
Herbert, George, 1593-1633
Herrick, Robert, 1591-1674
Heywood, John, 1497?-1580?
Heywood, Thomas, 1574?-1641
Hilton, Walter, d. 1396
Hobbes, Thomas, 1588-1679
Hoccleve, Thomas, 1369?-1426
Hodgson, Ralph Edwin, 1871-1962
Hood, Thomas, 1799-1845
Hooker, Richard, 1554?-1600
Hopkins, Gerard Manley, 1844-1889
Housman, A. E., 1859-1936
Howard, Henry, Earl of Surrey (see Sur-
    rey, Henry Howard, Earl of)
Hudson, W. H., 1841-1922
Hughes, Ted, 1930-
Hunt, Leigh, 1784-1859
Hutton, Richard Holt, 1826-1897
Huxley, Aldous Leonard, 1894-1963
Huxley, T. H., 1825-1895
Hyde, Edward, 1st Earl of Clarendon
    (see Clarendon, Edward Hyde,
    1st Earl of)
Jefferies, Richard, 1848-1887
Jellicoe, Ann, 1927-
Johnson, Lionel Pigot, 1867-1902
Jones, David Michael, 1895-1974
Jones, Henry Arthur, 1851-1929
Jonson, Ben, 1572/3-1637
Julian of Norwich, c. 1342-after 1416
Keats, John, 1795-1821
Kempe, Margery, c. 1373-c. 1439
King, Henry, 1592-1669
King, William, 1663-1712
Kingsley, Charles, 1819-1875
Kipling, Rudyard, 1865-1936
Koestler, Arthur, 1905-1983
Kyd, Thomas, 1558-1594

L'Estrange, Roger, 1616-1704
Lamb, Charles, 1775-1834
Landor, Walter Savage, 1775-1864
Langland, William, perhaps c. 1330-
     c. 1386
Larkin, Philip Arthur, 1922-1985
Lawrence, D. H., 1885-1930
Lawrence, T. E., 1888-1935
Le Carre, John, 1931-
Lear, Edward, 1812-1888
Leavis, F. R., 1895-1978
Lee, Nathaniel, 1649?-1692
Lee, Vernon, 1856-1935
Leland, John, c. 1503-1552
Lennox, Charlotte, 1720-1804
Lessing, Doris May Taylor, 1919-
Levertov, Denise, 1923-
Lewes, G. H., 1817-1878
Lewis, C. S., 1898-1963
Lewis, Cecil Day (see Day-Lewis,
     Cecil)
Lewis, M. G., 1775-1818
Lewis, Wyndham, 1882-1957
Lillo, George, 1693-1739
Lodge, Thomas, 1558-1625
Lovelace, Richard, 1618-1657/8
Lowry, Malcolm, 1909-1957
Lucas, E. V., 1868-1938
Lydgate, John, 1370?-1449
Lyly, John, 1554?-1606
Lytton, Edward Earle Lytton Bulwer-
     (see Bulwer-Lytton, Edward
     George Earle Lytton, 1st Barron
     Lytton)
Lytton, Edward Robert Bulwer, 1st Earl
     of Lytton, 1831-1891
Macaulay, Thomas Babington, 1800-
     1859
Machen, Arthur Llewelyn, 1863-1947
MacNeice, Louis, 1907-1963
Malory, Sir Thomas, d. 1471
Mandeville, Bernard de, 1670-1733
Mandeville, Sir John, fl. 1356/7 (wrote
     in French)
Mansfield, Katherine, 1888-1923
Marlowe, Christopher, 1564-1593
Marryat, Captain Frederick, 1792-1848
Marston, John, 1577?-1634
Marvell, Andrew, 1621-1678
Masefield, John Edward, 1878-1967
Massinger, Philip, 1583-1640
Mather, Richard, 1596-1669
Maugham, W. Somerset, 1874-1965
Medwall, Henry, fl. 1486

Meredith, George, 1828-1909
Middleton, Thomas, 1580-1627
Mill, John Stuart, 1806-1873
Milne, A. A., 1882-1956
Milton, John, 1608-1674
Montagu, Lady Mary Wortley, 1689-
     1762
More, Henry, 1614-1687
More, Sir Thomas, 1477?-1535
Morley, John, 1838-1923
Morris, William, 1834-1896
Munday, Anthony, 1560-1633
Murdoch, Dame Iris Jean, 1919-
Murry, John Middleton, 1889-1957
Mystery Plays, thirteenth-sixteenth
     centuries
Nashe, Thomas, 1567-1601
Newcastle, Margaret, Duchess of, 1623-
     1723
Newman, John Henry, 1801-1890
Nichols, Peter Richard, 1927-
"Junius," fl. 1769-1772
Old English Homilies (see Homilies,
     Old English)
Orton, Joe, 1933-1967
Orwell, George, 1903-1950
Osborne, John James, 1929-1994
Otway, Thomas, 1652-1685
Owen, Wilfred, 1893-1918
Pater, Walter Horatio, 1839-1894
Patmore, Coventry Kersey Dighton,
     1823-1896
Peacock, Thomas Love, 1785-1866
Peake, Mervyn Laurence, 1911-1968
Peele, George, 1556-1596
Pepys, Samuel, 1633-1703
Percy, Thomas, 1729-1811
Philips, Ambrose, 1674-1749
Philips, Katherine, 1631-1664
Pinero, Sir Arthur Wing, 1855-1934
Pinter, Harold, 1930-
Pope, Alexander, 1688-1744
Powell, Anthony Dymoke, 1905-
Powys, John Cowper, 1872-1963
Powys, Llewelyn, 1884-1939
Powys, T. F., 1875-1953
Praed, Winthrop Macworth, 1802-
     1839
Priestley, J. B., 1894-1984
Prior, Matthew, 1664-1721
Puttenham, George, c. 1529-1591
Pym, Barbara Mary Crampton, 1913-
     1980

Wain, John Barrington, 1925-1994
Wakefield Master (see Mystery
    Plays)
Waller, Edmund, 1606-1687
Walpole, Horace, 1717-1797
Walton, Izaak, 1593-1683
Ward, Edward, 1667-1731
Warner, Rex, 1905-1986
Warton, Joseph, 1722-1800, and
    Thomas Warton, 1728-1790
Warton, Thomas (see Warton, Joseph)
Watson, Ian, 1943-
Watts, Isaac, 1674-1748
Waugh, Evelyn, 1903-1966
Webster, John, c. 1578-c. 1632
Wells, H. G., 1866-1946
Wesker, Arnold, 1932-
West, Alick, 1895-1972
West, Dame Rebecca, 1892-1983
White, Gilbert, 1720-1793
White, T. H., 1906-1964
Williams, Charles W. S., 1886-1945
Williams, Heathcote, 1941-
Wilmot, John, 2nd Earl of Rochester
    (see Rochester, John Wilmot,
    2nd Earl of)
Wilson, Colin Henry, 1931-
Wilson, Sir Angus Frank Johnstone,
    1913-1991
Wilson, Thomas, c. 1525-1581
Wither, George, 1588-1667
Wollstonecraft, Mary, 1759-1797
Wood, Charles, 1932-
Woolf, Leonard Sidney, 1880-1969
Woolf, Virginia, 1882-1941
Wordsworth, William, 1770-1850
Wotton, Sir Henry, 1568-1639
Wulfstan, d. 1023
Wyatt, Sir Thomas, 1503-1542
Wycherley, William, 1641-1715
Wyclif, John, c. 1330-1384
Young, Arthur, 1741-1820
Young, Edward, 1683-1765
Zangwill, Israel, 1864-1926

Canadian
Atwood, Margaret, 1939-
Bowering, George, 1935-
Carman, Bliss, 1861-1929
Frye, Northrop, 1912-1991
Haliburton, Thomas Chandler, 1796-
    1865
Wiseman, Adele, 1928-1992

Irish
Keane, John B., 1928-
Boyd, John, 1912-
A.E. (see Russell, George William)
Allingham, William, 1824-1889
Beckett, Samuel, 1906-1989
Behan, Brendan, 1923-1964
Bowen, Elizabeth, 1899-1973
Cary, Joyce, 1888-1957
Clarke, Austin, 1896-1974
Dawson, Fielding, 1930-
Day-Lewis, Cecil, 1904-1972
Donleavy, J. P., 1926-
Dunsany, Edward John Moreton Drax
    Plunkett, 18th Baron, 1878-1957
Farquhar, George, 1677?-1707
Friel, Brien, 1929-
Gogarty, Oliver Joseph St. John, 1878-
    1957
Goldsmith, Oliver, 1730?-1774
Gregory, Augusta, Lady, 1852-1932
Heaney, Seamus, 1939-
Joyce, James Augustine Aloysius, 1882-
    1941
Kavanagh, Patrick, 1905-1967
Kilroy, Thomas, 1934-
LeFanu, J. S., 1814-1873
Leonard, Hugh, 1926-
Maturin, Charles Robert, 1782-1824
Moore, George Augustus, 1852-1933
Moore, Thomas, 1779-1852
Murphy, Arthur, 1727-1805
Murphy, Thomas, 1935-
O'Brien, Edna, 1932-
O'Casey, Sean, 1880-1964
O'Flaherty, Liam, 1896-1984
Parnell, Thomas, 1679-1718
Plunkett, Edward John Moreton Drax,
    18th Baron Dunsany (see Dun-
    sany, Edward John Moreton
    Drax Plunkett, 18th Baron)
Russell, George William, 1867-1935
Shaw, Bernard, 1856-1950
Stephens, James, 1882-1950
Swift, Jonathan, 1667-1745
Synge, John Millington, 1871-1909
Wilde, Oscar Fingal O'Flahertie Wills,
    1854-1900
Yeats, William Butler, 1865-1939

Scottish
Arbuthnot, John, 1667-1735
Armstrong, John, 1709-1779
B. V. (see Thomson, James)

Bain, Alexander, 1818-1903
Ballantyne, R. M., 1825-1894
Barrie, Sir J. M., 1860-1937
Blair, Hugh, 1718-1800
Boswell, James, 1740-1795
Brown, George MacKay, 1921-
Buchan, John, 1st Baron Tweedsmuir, 1875-1940
Burns, Robert, 1759-1796
Campbell, Thomas, 1777-1844
Carlyle, Jane Baillie Welsh, 1801-1866
Carlyle, Thomas, 1795-1881
Cronin, A. J., 1896-1981
Cunninghame Graham, Robert Bontine, 1852-1936
Douglas, Gavin, 1475?-1522
Doyle, Arthur Conan, 1859-1930
Drummond, William, of Hawthornden, 1585-1649
Dunbar, William, 1456?-1513?
Graham, Robert Bontine Cunninghame (see Cunninghame Graham, Robert Bontine)
Grieve, Christopher Murray (see MacDiarmid, Hugh)
Gunn, Neil Miller, 1891-1973
Henryson, Robert, 1424?-1506?
Hogg, James, 1770-1835
James I, King of Scotland, 1394-1437

Lindsay, Sir David, c. 1486-1555
MacDiarmid, Hugh (Christopher Murray Grieve), 1892-1978
MacKenzie, Henry, 1745-1831
MacPherson, James, 1736-1796
Muir, Edwin, 1887-1959
Ramsay, Allan, 1686-1758
Scott, Sir Walter, 1771-1832
Smollett, Tobias George, 1721-1771
Spark, Dame Muriel Sarah Camberg, 1918-
Stevenson, Robert Louis Balfour, 1850-1894
Thomson, James, 1700-1748
Thomson, James, 1834-1882
Urquhart, Sir Thomas, 1611-1660

South African
Coetzee, J. M., 1940-
Fugard, Athol, 1932-
Gordimer, Nadine, 1923-

Trinidadian
Naipaul, V. S, 1932-

Welsh
Price, Richard, 1723-1791
Thomas, Dylan Marlais,1914-1953
Vaughan, Henry, 1621-1695

Author/Title Index

The following lists all authors of main entries, all main entries (bold type), and all annotation references (italic type). Numbers refer to entry numbers unless followed by *(p)*, which indicates page number.

A to Z of the Novels and Short Stories of Agatha Christie, An, 255

A&HCI, 120, 272, 375-77, 385, 467, 770, 826, 960, 961, 1079, 1084, 1102, 1202, 1278, 1291, 1439, 1481, 1490, 1500

A. A. Milne: A Critical Bibliography, 951

A. E. Housman: A Bibliography, 690

A. E. Housman: An Annotated Handlist, 690

A. J. Cronin: A Reference Guide, 326

Abbott, Craig S., 967, 968

About the House, 52

Abraham Cowley: A Bibliography, 302

Abramowitz, Molly, 1443

Absalom, Absalom!, 485, 488

Absalom, Absalom!: A Concordance to the Novel, 487.11

Academic Graffiti, 52

Account of Books and Manuscripts of Francis Thompson, An, 1348

Achievement of Marianne Moore, The: A Bibliography, 1907-1957, 967

Achievement of Robert Lowell, 1939-1959, The, 863

Achievement of Robert Lowell, The, 862

Achievement of William Styron, The, 1305

Ackerley, Chris, 868

Adam and His Work: A Bibliography of Sources by and About Paul Goodman (1911-1972), 577

Adam, R. B., 677

Adams, Elsie B., 1210.1

Adams, Laura, 887

Adams, Maurianne, 278

Addenda and Corrigenda, 955.1

Addenda to Lafcadio Hearn: A Catalogue of the Collection at the Howard-Tilton Memorial Library, Tulane University, 640

Addresses and Lectures, 465

Adele Wiseman: An Annotated Bibliography, 1470

Aden, John M., 424

Adler, Betty, 928, 928.1

Adler, Doris Ray, 352

Adventures of Huckleberry Finn, 642

Aelfric: A New Study of His Life and Writings, 7

Aelfric: An Annotated Bibliography, 7

AES, 99, 120, 156, 210, 244, 295, 375, 377, 415, 448, 621, 689, 723, 770, 779, 800, 854, 927, 960, 1026, 1197, 1201, 1202, 1215, 1291, 1362, 1439, 1464, 1490, 1521

African Review, The, 608

Agatha Christie A to Z: The Essential Reference to Her Life and Writings, 255

Agatha Christie Chronology, An, 255

Agatha Christie Companion, The, 255

Agatha Christie Companion, The: The Complete Guide to Agatha Christie's Life and Work, 256

Agatha Christie Who's Who, The, 255

Age of Johnson, 739

Age of Johnson, The: A Scholarly Annual, 739

AHI, 120, 175, 213, 272, 295, 375, 380, 415, 420, 467, 586, 636, 660, 689, 770, 793, 826, 837, 854, 927, 930, 960, 1011, 1084, 1096, 1278, 1360-62, 1409, 1419, 1438, 1439, 1464, 1481, 1490, 1500, 1521

Aho, Gary L., 978

Ahouse, John B., 1233

Alan Sillitoe: A Bibliography, 1228

Albee, 11

Albert, Sydney S., 726

Aldous Huxley, 1894-1963: A Centenary Catalog, 708

Aldous Huxley: A Bibliography, 708

Aldous Huxley: A Bibliography, 1916-1959, 708

Aldous Huxley: An Annotated Bibliography of Criticism, 708

Alexander Pope: A Bibliography, 1080

Alexander Pope: A Life, 1082

Alexander Pope: A List of Critical Studies Published from 1895-1944, 1081

Subject Index

Numbers cited are entry numbers.